The Routledge Handbook of Corpus Linguistics

The Routledge Handbook of Corpus Linguistics provides a timely overview of a dynamic and rapidly growing area with a widely applied methodology. Through the electronic analysis of large bodies of text, corpus linguistics demonstrates and supports linguistic statements and assumptions. In recent years it has seen an ever-widening application in a variety of fields: computational linguistics, discourse analysis, forensic linguistics, pragmatics and translation studies.

Bringing together experts in a number of key areas of development and change, the handbook is structured around six themes which take the reader through building and designing a corpus to using a corpus to study literature and translation.

A comprehensive introduction covers the historical development of the field and its growing influence and application in other areas. Structured around five headings for ease of reference, each contribution includes further reading sections with three to five key texts highlighted and annotated to facilitate further exploration of the topics.

The Routledge Handbook of Corpus Linguistics is the ideal resource for advanced undergraduates and postgraduates.

Anne O'Keeffe is senior lecturer in Applied Linguistics, Department of English Language and Literature, Mary Immaculate College, University of Limerick, Ireland. She is co-author of *Introducing Pragmatics in Use* (Routledge, 2011).

Michael McCarthy is Emeritus Professor of Applied Linguistics at the University of Nottingham, UK, Adjunct Professor of Applied Linguistics at the Pennsylvania State University, USA, and Adjunct Professor of Applied Linguistics at the University of Limerick, Ireland.

Contributors: Annelie Ädel, Svenja Adolphs, Carolina P. Amador-Moreno, Gisle Andersen, Guy Aston, Sarah Atkins, Fiona Barker, Douglas Biber, Ronald Carter, Angela Chambers, Winnie Cheng, Brian Clancy, Susan Conrad, Janet Cotterill, Averil Coxhead, Philip Durrant, Jane Evison, Fiona Farr, Lynne Flowerdew, Gaëtanelle Gilquin, Sylviane Granger, Chris Greaves, Michael Handford, Kevin Harvey, Rebecca Hughes, Susan Hunston, Martha Jones, Marie-Madeleine Kenning, Dawn Knight, Almut Koester, Natalie Kübler, David Lee, Xiaofei Lu, Jeanne McCarten, Michael McCarthy, Dan McIntyre, Rosamund Moon, Mike Nelson, Kieran O'Halloran, Anne O'Keeffe, Randi Reppen, Christoph Rühlemann, Mike Scott, Passapong Sripicharn, Paul Thompson, Scott Thornbury, Elena Tognini Bonelli, Christopher Tribble, Elaine Vaughan, Thuc Anh Vo, Brian Walker, Steve Walsh, Elizabeth Walter, Martin Warren.

Routledge Handbooks in Applied Linguistics

Routledge Handbooks in Applied Linguistics provide comprehensive overviews of the key topics in applied linguistics. All entries for the handbooks are specially commissioned and written by leading scholars in the field. Clear, accessible and carefully edited *Routledge Handbooks in Applied Linguistics* are the ideal resource for both advanced undergraduates and postgraduate students.

The Routledge Handbook of Forensic Linguistics
Edited by Malcolm Coulthard and Alison Johnson

The Routledge Handbook of Corpus Linguistics
Edited by Anne O'Keeffe and Mike McCarthy

The Routledge Handbook of World Englishes
Edited by Andy Kirkpatrick

The Routledge Handbook of Applied Linguistics
Edited by James Simpson

The Routledge Handbook of Discourse Analysis
Edited by James Paul Gee and Michael Handford

The Routledge Handbook of Second Language Acquisition
Edited by Susan Gass and Alison Mackey

The Routledge Handbook of Intercultural Communication
Edited by Jane Jackson

The Routledge Handbook of Language Testing
Edited by Glenn Fulcher and Fred Davidson

The Routledge Handbook of Multilingualism
Edited by Marilyn Marting-Jones, Adrian Blackledge and Angela Creese

The Routledge Handbook of Translation Studies
Edited by Carmen Millán-Varela and Francesca Bartrina

The Routledge Handbook of Corpus Linguistics

Edited by
Anne O'Keeffe and Michael McCarthy

First published 2010
by Routledge

First published in paperback 2012
by Routledge
2 Park Square, Milton Park, Abingdon, Oxon OX14 4RN

Simultaneously published in the USA and Canada
by Routledge
711 Third Avenue, New York, NY 10017

Routledge is an imprint of the Taylor & Francis Group, an informa business

British Library Cataloguing in Publication Data
A catalogue record for this book is available from the British Library

Library of Congress Cataloging in Publication Data
O'Keeffe, Anne.
The Routledge handbook of corpus linguistics / Anne O'Keeffe and Michael McCarthy.
p. cm. -- (Routledge handbooks in applied linguistics)
1. Corpora (Linguistics)--Handbooks, manuals, etc. 2. Discourse analysis--Handbooks, manuals, etc. I. McCarthy, Michael, 1947- II. Title. III. Title: Handbook of corpus linguistics.
P128.C68R68 2012
410.1′88--dc23
2012016346

ISBN: 978-0-415-46489-5 (hbk)
ISBN: 978-0-415-62263-9 (pbk)
ISBN: 978-0-203-85694-9 (ebk)

Typeset in Bembo by
Taylor & Francis Books

Contents

Illustrations

Figures

Tables

Contributors

Annelie Ädel's main research areas are discourse and text analysis, corpus linguistics and English for academic purposes (EAP). She earned her PhD in English Linguistics in 2003 at Göteborg University, Sweden. For five years she was affiliated with universities in the US, first as a visiting scholar at Boston University, then as a postdoctoral fellow at the University of Michigan's English Language Institute (ELI), and then as Director of Applied Corpus Linguistics at the same institute. This last position involved managing and developing the corpus-linguistic projects of the ELI, such as MICASE (the Michigan Corpus of Academic Spoken English) and MICUSP (the Michigan Corpus of Upper-level Student Papers). Currently, Ädel is a research fellow in the Department of English at Stockholm University, Sweden. Her book-length publications include the monograph 'Metadiscourse in L1 and L2 English' (John Benjamins, 2006) and 'Corpora and Discourse: The Challenges of Different Settings', a volume co-edited with Randi Reppen (John Benjamins, 2008).

Svenja Adolphs is Associate Professor in Applied Linguistics at the University of Nottingham, UK. Her research interests are in corpus linguistics and discourse analysis, and she has published widely in these areas. Recent books include *Introducing Electronic Text Analysis* (Routledge, 2006) and *Corpus and Context: Investigating Pragmatic Functions in Spoken Discourse* (John Benjamins, 2008). A particular focus of this work has been on the exploration of linguistic patterns in specific domains of discourse, in particular in the area of health communication. She has been involved in a range of corpus development projects, including the development of a multi-modal corpus of spoken discourse. This resource has led to a number of studies on the relationship between language and gesture, and on the way in which prosodic information might be used to analyse multi-word expressions in spoken interaction. She is working on a project which explores the relationship between language use and measurements of different aspects of context gathered from multiple sensors in a ubiquitous computing environment.

Carolina P. Amador-Moreno is a lecturer in the Department of English at the University of Extremadura, Spain. After completing her PhD, she joined the Department of Languages and Cultural Studies at the University of Limerick, where she taught for three years. Before returning to Extremadura, she was also a lecturer at University College Dublin. Her research interests centre on the English spoken in Ireland and include sociolinguistics, stylistics and pragmatics as well as corpus linguistics. She is a member of the IVACS (Inter-Varietal Applied Corpus Studies) research centre, and an associate member of CALS (Centre for Applied Language Studies), at the University of Limerick. She is the author of *An Introduction to Irish English* (Equinox, 2009), and has also co-edited *The Representation of the Spoken Mode in Fiction* (Edwin Mellen, 2009).

Gisle Andersen is the author of *Pragmatic Markers and Sociolinguistic Variation – A Relevance-theoretic Approach to the Language of Adolescents* (John Benjamins, 2001) and he has co-authored *Trends in Teenage Talk – Corpus Compilation, Analysis and Findings* (with Anna-Brita Stenström and Ingrid Kristine Hasund; John Benjamins, 2002). He has also co-edited *Pragmatic Markers and Propositional Attitude* (with Thorstein Fretheim; John Benjamins, 2000). Andersen has published articles on different topics relating to spoken interaction, with a specific focus on the use of corpora for studies in pragmatics, discourse analysis and sociolinguistics. His work also focuses on written communication, lexicography and terminology, and the influence of English on Norwegian language. Andersen has been deeply involved in various corpus compilation projects, including COLT (The Bergen Corpus of London Teenage Language) and the Norwegian Newspaper Corpus, and he has coordinated and participated in projects within language technology and language resources. He is a participant in various projects funded by the European Commission and the Norwegian Research Council. Andersen is also a board member of the ICAME organisation (International Computer Archive of Modern and Medieval English).

Guy Aston began his academic career in Italy in the 1970s. After studying applied linguistics with Henry Widdowson in Edinburgh and London, and coordinating the PIXI research group on the contrastive pragmatics of interaction, he taught English Language and Computer-Assisted Translation to trainee interpreters and translators at the University of Bologna. Over the last fifteen years, he has worked extensively on the uses of corpora in language and translation teaching and learning, particularly in the contexts of the British National Corpus project, the Teaching and Language Corpora conferences, and the Corpus Use and Learning to Translate (CULT) workshops. His research interests concern the roles of corpora in developing learner fluency in speech and writing.

Sarah Atkins is an ESRC postgraduate research student at the University of Nottingham where she is completing her PhD studies on the language of peer-led health advice groups on the Internet. She has broad research interests in the field of discourse analysis, specialising in particular in the language of healthcare and the sociolinguistics of Internet communication as well as deixis and the semiotics of space in various modes of discourse. She has published on the topics of vague language in healthcare with Kevin Harvey (in Joan Cutting (ed.) *Vague Language Explored*; Palgrave, 2007) and with Ronald Carter on creative language use (in James Paul Gee and Michael Handford (eds) *Routledge Handbook of Discourse Analysis*; Routledge, forthcoming). She has, further, completed research projects on behalf of the University of Nottingham, studying the indexing of gender in workplace talk in the Cambridge and Nottingham Spoken Business English Corpus (CANBEC), and an ESRC research position at the British Library on the framing of the stem cell research debate in the British media.

Fiona Barker joined Cambridge ESOL after gaining a PhD in Language Description and Corpus Linguistics from Cardiff University and teaching in the UK secondary sector. She has published several peer-reviewed articles (in journals such as *Assessing Writing* and *Modern English Teacher*) and several chapters in edited volumes on corpus analysis within Systemic Functional Linguistics and Language Testing and Assessment. She has presented on related topics at an invited plenary, workshops and conferences. At Cambridge ESOL, Fiona develops corpora of learner output and exam materials and works with internal and external researchers on various corpus-informed projects. She is editor of Cambridge ESOL's quarterly publication *Research Notes*, which reports on a wide range of research and validation activities in language assessment. Her research interests include the use of corpora in testing, learner corpus development, comparative analysis of learner speech and writing, and vocabulary range/growth. She is currently developing the range of exams in the Cambridge Learner Corpus and its spoken equivalent and is working with English Profile colleagues to describe the lexis of the Common European Framework of Reference (CEFR) levels, using a corpus-informed approach.

Douglas Biber is Regents' Professor of English (Applied Linguistics) at Northern Arizona University. His research efforts have focused on corpus linguistics, English grammar and register variation (in English and cross-linguistic; synchronic and diachronic). He has written 13 books and monographs, including academic books published with Cambridge University Press (1988, 1995, 1998, 2009), John Benjamins (2006, 2007) and the co-authored *Longman Grammar of Spoken and Written English* (1999).

Ronald Carter is Professor of Modern English Language at Nottingham University. He has written and edited more than fifty books in the fields of language and education, applied linguistics and the teaching of English. Recent books include: *Language and Creativity* (Routledge, 2004), *Cambridge Grammar of English* (with Michael McCarthy; Cambridge University Press, 2006) and *From Corpus to Classroom* (with Anne O'Keeffe and Michael McCarthy; Cambridge University Press, 2007). Professor Carter is a fellow of the Royal Society of Arts, a fellow of the British Academy for Social Sciences and was chair of the British Association for Applied Linguistics (2003–6).

Angela Chambers is Professor of Applied Languages and Director of the Centre for Applied Language Studies in the University of Limerick, Ireland. She completed her BA and PhD at Queen's University Belfast, and worked in the universities of Bordeaux, Ulster and Lille III. She joined the University of Limerick as senior lecturer in French in 1990, and was appointed a professor in 2002. She has co-edited a number of books and published several articles on aspects of language learning, in particular Computer-Assisted Language Learning. Her research focuses on the use of corpus data by language learners. She has created two corpora for use by language learners, of journalistic discourse in French and academic writing in French. In 1998, she was awarded the honour of Chevalier dans l'Ordre des Palmes Académiques, a French government honour awarded for services to the French language and to education.

Winnie Cheng is a Professor, and the Director of Research Centre for Professional Communication in English (RCPCE), in the Department of English, The Hong Kong Polytechnic University. Her research interests include corpus linguistics, discourse intonation, conversation analysis, (critical) discourse analysis, pragmatics, intercultural communication, professional communication, lexical studies, collaborative learning and assessment, and online learning and assessment. She has published widely in the leading applied linguistics, pragmatics, corpus linguistics and higher education journals. Her book *Intercultural Communication* (2003) and co-authored book *A Corpus-driven Study of Discourse Intonation* (2008) are both published by John Benjamins. Together with Martin Warren and Chris Greaves, she has published papers on concgrams. She is the chief editor of the *Asian ESP Journal*.

Brian Clancy teaches in the areas of academic writing and support at Mary Immaculate College, University of Limerick, Ireland. He is currently completing his PhD research, which is a comparative analysis of Southern-Irish family discourse from two distinct socio-cultural groups. He has published articles and book chapters on various aspects of discourse analysis such as politeness strategies in family discourse and the exchange structure in casual conversation. His research interests include discourse in intimate settings, small corpora and language varieties. He is also involved in research projects on academic discourse, both spoken and written, and has published in this area. He is co-author, with Anne O'Keeffe and Svenja Adolphs, of *Introducing Pragmatics in Use* (Routledge, forthcoming 2010).

Susan Conrad is Professor of Applied Linguistics at Portland State University, Portland, Oregon, USA. She has used corpus linguistics techniques to study how English grammar is used in a variety of contexts, from general conversation to engineering documents. Her publications include the *Longman Grammar of Spoken and Written English, Corpus Linguistics: Investigating Language Structure and Use* and *Register, Genre, and Style*, as well as the ESL/EFL student text *Real Grammar: A Corpus-based Approach to English* and other books and articles. Her experiences teaching ESL/EFL grammar and writing classes in southern Africa, South Korea and the US convinced her of the usefulness of corpus techniques even before she became a teacher-trainer and researcher.

Janet Cotterill is a Reader in Language and Communication and Director of Research in Forensic Linguistics at Cardiff University. She is an experienced consultant and expert witness in forensic linguistics and runs a consultancy business. She is the current President of the International Association of Forensic Linguists (IAFL) and member of the Executive Committee. Janet has co-edited *The International Journal of Speech, Language and the Law* (formerly *Forensic Linguistics*) and is a founding member of the International Association of Language and Law as well as co-editor of its accompanying e-journal. With a background in translation/interpreting and TEFL/Applied Linguistics, Janet has worked/lived in the UK, France, Egypt and Japan. She has published eight books to date and more than forty articles/book chapters, and is currently working on two new monographs: one on the language of the courtroom and one on the discourse of multiple sclerosis.

Averil Coxhead is a Senior Lecturer in Applied Linguistics in the School of Linguistics and Applied Language Studies, Victoria University of Wellington. Averil developed and evaluated the Academic Word List (AWL) and is the author of *Essentials of Teaching Academic Vocabulary* (Houghton Mifflin, 2006). She is interested in many aspects of second language lexical studies, including corpus linguistics and EAP, vocabulary use in writing, classroom tasks, vocabulary list development and evaluation, phraseology, and pedagogical approaches to lexis. Her current research projects include vocabulary size measurements, vocabulary teaching and learning in secondary schools, and the collocations and phraseology of the AWL in written texts.

Philip Durrant is currently Visiting Assistant Professor in the Graduate School of Education at Bilkent University, in Ankara, Turkey, where he teaches on the MA programme in Teaching English as a Foreign Language. He has previously taught English as a Foreign Language, English for Academic Purposes, and Applied Linguistics at schools and universities in Turkey and in the UK. Phil studied Philosophy at the University of Sussex and Applied Linguistics at the University of Nottingham, where he completed his PhD on the topic of collocations in second language learning. He also holds a Cambridge Diploma in English language teaching. His main research interests are in corpus linguistics, second language acquisition, English for Academic Purposes, and all aspects of formulaic language. He is particularly interested in how methods and insights from across these areas can be combined to inform the theory and practice of language teaching.

Jane Evison lectures in TESOL in the School of Education at the University of Nottingham. Her teaching interests centre on classroom discourse, pragmatics and grammar, and she has contributed both to the development of the *Cambridge Grammar of English* (Cambridge University Press, 2006) and to recent corpus-based English-language teaching materials. Conversational interaction is at the centre of her research, and she is especially interested in how turns open and close. Her research tends to use a combination of corpus analytical techniques and the kind of fine-grained investigation associated with Conversation Analysis and Exchange Structure Analysis. She has used this dual approach to investigate turn construction in informal social conversation and academic encounters in the CANCODE corpus, and to explore identity creation in a smaller corpus of podcast talk which she is developing.

Fiona Farr is Lecturer in English Language Teaching at the University of Limerick, Ireland, where she is also Assistant Dean, Academic Affairs, Faculty of Arts, Humanities, and Social Sciences. She has been involved in teacher education at undergraduate and postgraduate levels for over ten years, and has supervised many students in their MA research projects. She is also currently involved in supervising a number of PhD students researching areas of language teacher education, spoken discourse and ESOL, all of whom employ corpus-based methodologies. She has published in many edited books and in journals such as *TESOL Quarterly*, *The Journal of English for Academic Purposes* and *Language Awareness*. She is co-manager of the Limerick Corpus of Irish–English (L-CIE), and part of the Inter-Varietal Applied Corpus Studies

(IVACS) research network, which hosts bi-annual conferences in the field of applied corpus-based research. Her professional and research interests include language teacher education, especially teaching practice feedback, spoken language corpora and their applications, discourse analysis and language variety.

Lynne Flowerdew has published numerous articles on different aspects of corpus linguistics. Her other areas of interest include genre analysis, (critical) discourse analysis, systemic-functional linguistics, EAP/ESP materials and syllabus design. She is a member of the editorial board of *TESOL Quarterly*, *English for Specific Purposes*, *The Journal of English for Academic Purposes* and *Text Construction*. Her books include *Corpus-based Analyses of the Problem-solution Pattern* (John Benjamins, 2008).

Gaëtanelle Gilquin is a Research Associate with the Belgian National Fund for Scientific Research (FNRS). She is a member of the Centre for English Corpus Linguistics (Université catholique de Louvain) and the coordinator of the LINDSEI project (Louvain International Database of Spoken English Interlanguage). Her research interests include the use of (native and learner) corpora for the description and teaching of language, as well as the comparison of Learner Englishes and World Englishes. She is also interested in the combination of corpus and experimental data, and more generally in the integration of corpus and cognitive linguistics.

Sylviane Granger is Professor of English Language and Linguistics at the Université catholique de Louvain (Belgium). She is the director of the Centre for English Corpus Linguistics, where research activity is focused on the compilation and exploitation of learner corpora and bilingual corpora. In 1990, she launched the International Corpus of Learner English project, which has grown to contain learner writing by learners of English from nineteen different mother-tongue backgrounds and is the result of collaboration from a large number of universities internationally. She has written numerous articles and (co-)edited several volumes on these topics and gives frequent invited talks, seminars and workshops to stimulate learner corpus research and to promote its application to ELT materials design and development. Her publications include *Learner English on Computer* (Addison Wesley Longman, 1998), *Computer Learner Corpora, Second Language Acquisition and Foreign Language Teaching* (Granger, Hung and Petch-Tyson (eds); Benjamins, 2002), *Lexis in Contrast. Corpus-Based Approaches* (Altenberg and Granger (eds); Benjamins, 2002), *Corpus-Based Approaches to Contrastive Linguistics and Translation Studies* (Granger, Lerot and Petch-Tyson (eds); Rodopi, 2003), *Phraseology: An Interdisciplinary Perspective* (Granger and Meunier (eds); Benjamins, 2008) and *Phraseology in Foreign Language Learning and Teaching* (Meunier and Granger (eds); Benjamins, 2008).

Chris Greaves is a Senior Research Fellow in the Research Centre for Professional Communication based in the English Department at The Hong Kong Polytechnic University. His research interests include corpus linguistics, corpus linguistics software development, discourse intonation and phraseology. He has written and developed a number of corpus linguistics computer programs such as ConcGram (*ConcGram 1.0: A Phraseological Search Engine*) and iConc, which is the software behind another publication (*A Corpus-driven Study of Discourse Intonation*), both published by John Benjamins.

Michael Handford is Associate Professor in English Language at the University of Tokyo, where he teaches courses on intercultural communication, professional communication, discourse analysis and English as an international language. He regularly conducts consultancy work with Japanese companies which are involved in international business, focusing on interpersonal aspects of communication in company to company relationships. He gained his PhD in Applied Linguistics in 2007 from Nottingham University's School of English Studies, where he also taught for four years. For his PhD thesis, he developed and analysed CANBEC (the Cambridge and Nottingham Business English Corpus), a one-million-word corpus of authentic spoken business English. He is the author of *The Language of Business Meetings* (Cambridge University Press, 2010), which combines corpus linguistic and discourse analysis approaches to pinpoint recurrent discursive practices in business meetings, and is co-editor with James Paul Gee of *The Routledge Handbook of Discourse Analysis*. He has also been involved in developing a specialised multi-modal corpus of international communication in the construction industry.

Kevin Harvey is a lecturer in sociolinguistics at the University of Nottingham. His principal research specialities lie in the field of applied sociolinguistics, discourse analysis and corpus linguistics. His work involves interdisciplinary approaches to professional communication, with a special emphasis on health communication and its practical implications for healthcare deliveries.

Rebecca Hughes is Chair of Applied Linguistics at the University of Nottingham, and Director of the Centre for English Language Education (CELE). Her research interests are in spoken language, academic literacy and internationalisation of higher education. She has published widely in applied linguistics including *English in Speech and Writing, Investigating Language and Literature* (Routledge, 1996); *Exploring Grammar in Context* (with Ronald Carter and Michael McCarthy; Cambridge University Press, 2000); *Teaching and Researching Speaking* (Longman, 2000); *TESOL, Applied Linguistics and the Spoken Language: Challenges for Theory and Practice* (editor; Palgrave Macmillan, 2006); *Exploring Grammar in Writing* (Cambridge University Press, 2005). Her work on internationalisation and academic literacy includes articles in the *Guardian* newspaper, and *Higher Education Management and Policy,* and participation in the OECD Institute of Managers in Higher Education (presentations on language policy and international collaboration/equity), UNESCO (invited observer), Centre for Educational Research and Innovation (invited observer), and Universitas21 (lecture series on English language policies and the international market for HE).

Susan Hunston is Professor of English Language at the University of Birmingham, UK. She specialises in corpus linguistics and discourse analysis and teaches on courses in these subjects at undergraduate and postgraduate level. She is author of *Corpora in Applied Linguistics* (Cambridge University Press, 2002), co-author of *Pattern Grammar: A Corpus-driven Approach to the Lexical Grammar of English* (Benjamins, 1999) and co-editor of *Evaluation in Text: Authorial Stance and the Construction of Discourse* (Oxford University Press, 2000) and *System and Corpus: Exploring the Connections* (Equinox, 2005). She has also published numerous articles on the expression of stance or evaluation, especially in academic prose, on the use of corpora to describe the grammar and lexis of English, and on the interface between corpus and discourse studies.

Martha Jones is Head of Teacher Training in EAP at the Centre for English Language Education, University of Nottingham. She directs the Postgraduate Certificate Course in Teaching English for Academic Purposes. She has a Diploma in Advanced Studies in Education, an MA in Language Studies and a PhD in Linguistics, all from Lancaster University. Her research interests are corpus-based analysis of spoken and written discourse and the development and use of multimedia for teaching and teacher training purposes. She has given papers at conferences on corpus analysis of spoken and written discourse, the use of technology in EAP teaching and on the acquisition of academic vocabulary and phrases. She has worked on funded research projects to develop a CD-ROM focusing on the language of academic seminars, a small corpus of spoken discourse and ePortfolio material. She has published chapters in edited publications on the subjects of disciplinary vocabulary in seminars, corpus linguistics, ELT materials development and the use of ePortfolios in teacher education.

Marie-Madeleine Kenning is Senior Lecturer in French and Linguistics at the University of East Anglia, UK. Her research fields include the application of technology to language learning and language teaching, autonomy, materials design, and English-language teaching in Cambodia. Her interest in corpora led to her involvement in the Lingua project which funded the development of the multilingual parallel concordancer *Multiconcord*. Among her publications are one of the first books to appear on computer assisted language teaching – *An Introduction to Computer Assisted Language Teaching* (with M. J. Kenning, Oxford University Press, 1983) – and *ICT and Language Learning: From Print to the Mobile Phone* (Palgrave Macmillan, 2007), an exploration of the interplay of ICT and language learning.

Dawn Knight completed a PhD in Applied Linguistics at the University of Nottingham entitled 'A Multi-modal Corpus Approach to the Analysis of Backchannelling Behaviour' (May 2009). She is currently working as a Research Associate on the ESRC-funded DReSS Project (Understanding New Forms of Digital Record project). This project is part of the National Centre for eSocial Science (NCeSS) Node programme, and has involved staff in the Mixed Reality Lab (MRL) in the School of Computer Science and IT, the School of Psychology and staff from the Centre of Research in Applied Linguistics (CRAL) at the University of Nottingham. In collaboration with members from the project team, she has published a number of articles and delivered a range of papers on the construction and use of multi-modal corpus resources, and how such can assist in our analysis and understanding of the complex relationships between language and gesture in human communication.

Almut Koester is Senior Lecturer in English Language in the School of English, Drama and American and Canadian Studies at the University of Birmingham, where she teaches courses in Discourse Analysis, Genre Analysis, Business English and Applied Linguistics. She has a PhD in Applied Linguistics from the University of Nottingham, for which she investigated naturally occurring workplace conversations using a combination of corpus linguistic and discourse analytic methods. She is author of two books, *The Language of Work* (Routledge, 2004) and *Investigating Workplace Discourse* (Routledge, 2006), and she has written for international journals and contributed to edited volumes. Her research focuses on spoken workplace discourse, and her publications have examined genre, modality, relational language, vague language and idioms. She also has many years of experience as a teacher and teacher trainer in General and Business English in France, Germany, the United States and the United Kingdom. She is interested in the application of research in discourse analysis and corpus research to teaching English, and she has run workshops for teachers and written teaching material.

Natalie Kübler started working as an assistant at the Language and Speech Processing Lab at the University of Neuchâtel (Switzerland), finishing her studies in German, Linguistics and French. In 1990, she came to write her PhD at the University Paris 7 with Maurice Gross, while working part-time with François Grosjean at the University of Neuchâtel on a project aiming at automatically correcting grammatical errors made by French and German speakers in English. In 1995, she became a lecturer at the University Paris 13, where she started working on specialised corpora for teaching English to French speakers. In 1999, she moved to the University Paris 7 and started working on corpus use and learning to translate, after having met Guy Aston at the TaLC and CULT conferences at the end of the 1990s. She was the promoter of the MeLLANGE project between 2004 and 2007, in which a learner translator corpus in several European languages was developed. Since 2005, she has been a full professor, teaching corpus linguistics and machine translation to translators. Her current interests mainly deal with the relationship between corpus linguistics and translation theory, and corpus-based writing aids in English for Specific Purposes for French-speakers.

David Y.W. Lee's primary research interest is in corpus-based language description, ESP/EAP and applied linguistics. He maintains a major resource site for corpus linguists (http://tiny.cc/corpora) that links to corpora, tools, references and related resources. He is currently compiling several research corpora, including CUCASE (City University Corpus of Academic Spoken English), for research on second language speaking and listening; CAWE (Chinese Academic Written English), for research on the dissertation writing of English majors in mainland China; and the Hong Kong component of ICCI (the International Corpus of Cross-linguistic Interlanguage), consisting of children's English language essays. Before taking up his current position in Hong Kong, he taught linguistics, applied linguistics, English communication and cross-cultural communication at universities in the UK, the US, Japan and Thailand, and also worked as a post-doctoral research fellow at the English Language Institute, University of Michigan, as part of the Michigan Corpus of Academic Spoken English (MICASE) project. He recently co-authored a book on BNCweb, a user-friendly web interface to the British National Corpus (*Corpus Linguistics with BNCweb: A Practical Guide* (Peter Lang, 2009).

Xiaofei Lu is Assistant Professor of Applied Linguistics in the Department of Applied Linguistics at the Pennsylvania State University, where he teaches undergraduate and graduate-level courses in applied linguistics, corpus linguistics, statistical analysis, computer-assisted language learning and TESL methods. He received his PhD in Linguistics, with a specialisation in Computational Linguistics, from the Ohio State University in 2006. His current research interests include annotation and analysis of native and learner corpora, use of natural language processing technology in computer-assisted language learning, and first- and second language lexical and grammatical development. He is a member of the editorial board of *The Linguistics Journal* and co-chair of the Special Interest Group in Intelligent Computer-Assisted Language Learning of the Computer Assisted Language Instruction Consortium. His publications can be found in the *International Journal of Corpus Linguistics*, the *LDV-Forum* and the proceedings of various international conferences on computational linguistics.

Jeanne McCarten taught English as a foreign language in Sweden, France, Malaysia and the UK before starting a publishing career with Cambridge University Press. As a publisher, she has many years' experience of commissioning and developing ELT materials, specialising in the areas of grammar and vocabulary. She was also involved in the development of the spoken English sections of the Cambridge International Corpus, including the CANCODE spoken corpus. Currently a freelance ELT materials writer, she is co-author of two corpus-informed projects: the four-level series in North American English, *Touchstone*, and *Grammar for Business,* both published by Cambridge University Press.

Michael McCarthy is Emeritus Professor of Applied Linguistics at the University of Nottingham, UK, Adjunct Professor of Applied Linguistics at the Pennsylvania State University, USA, and Adjunct Professor of Applied Linguistics at the University of Limerick, Ireland. He is author of *Vocabulary* (Oxford University Press, 1990), *Discourse Analysis for Language Teachers* (Cambridge University Press, 1991) *Language as Discourse* (with Ronald Carter; Longman, 1994), *Exploring Spoken English* (with Ronald Carter; Cambridge University Press, 1997), *Vocabulary: Description, Acquisition and Pedagogy* (co-edited with Norbert Schmitt; Cambridge University Press, 1997), *Spoken Language and Applied Linguistics* (Cambridge University Press, 1998), *Issues in Applied Linguistics* (Cambridge University Press, 2001), the *Cambridge Grammar of English* (with Ronald Carter; Cambridge University Press, 2006) and *From Corpus to Classroom* (with Anne O'Keeffe and Ronald Carter; Cambridge University Press, 2007). He is also co-author of a number of titles in the corpus-informed *English Vocabulary in Use* series (with Felicity O'Dell; Cambridge University Press, 1994–). He is co-author of the four-level corpus-informed adult course *Touchstone* (with Jeanne McCarten and Helen Sandiford; Cambridge University Press, 2004–6). He is editor of the Routledge series *Domains of Discourse* (2006–). All told, he is author/co-author/ editor of more than forty books, and author/co-author of more than eighty academic papers. He is co-director (with Ronald Carter) of the CANCODE spoken English corpus project, and the CANBEC spoken business English corpus, both sponsored by Cambridge University Press, at the University of Nottingham. He is a Fellow of the Royal Society of Arts.

Dan McIntyre is Reader in English Language and Linguistics at the University of Huddersfield, UK, where he teaches courses on stylistics, corpus linguistics and the history of English. He is the author of *Point of View in Plays* (John Benjamins, 2006) and *History of English: A Resource Book for Students* (Routledge, 2008), co-editor of *Stylistics and Social Cognition* (Rodopi, 2007) and has published widely on stylistics and related areas of language study. He is co-author of *Stylistics* (Cambridge University Press, 2010) and a co-editor of *Teaching Stylistics* (Palgrave and the English Subject Centre, 2010). Dan is series editor of *Advances in Stylistics* (Continuum), and with Lesley Jeffries is co-editor of the Palgrave series *Perspectives on the English Language*. He holds the post of Treasurer of the international Poetics and Linguistics Association (PALA). He also works on a corpus-based research project investigating discourse presentation in Early Modern English writing.

Rosamund Moon is a senior lecturer in the School of English, Drama, and American and Canadian Studies, University of Birmingham, where she teaches English language and linguistics. Most of her research relates to lexis and phraseology, lexicography, corpus linguistics and figurative language, and she has written over forty papers on these areas. Her publications include the books *Fixed Expressions and Idioms in English: A Corpus-based Approach* (Oxford University Press, 1998), and, co-authored with Murray Knowles, *Introducing Metaphor* (Routledge, 2006). She previously worked as a lexicographer for Oxford University Press and HarperCollins, and was one of the senior editors on the *Collins Cobuild Dictionary of the English Language* (1987: editor in chief, John Sinclair), the pioneering corpus-based dictionary for learners of English.

Mike Nelson has been teaching language for specific purposes in Finland for the last twenty-six years. The need for specific purposes materials and an interest in lexis has been the main driving force behind his research. His Master's dissertation focused on analysing the needs of students and relating them to current materials, whilst his doctorate looked at the lexis used by business people using a corpus-based approach. He has worked in EAP and has used corpora to study the lexical layering in medical anatomy texts. At present, Mike works in the Language Centre at the University of Turku in Finland.

Kieran O'Halloran is Senior Lecturer in Linguistics in the Centre for Language and Communication at the Open University, UK. He is interested in the application of corpus linguistics to discourse analysis – specifically to critical discourse analysis, literary stylistics and argumentation – as well as cognitive issues in critical discourse analysis. He was co-investigator on an Arts and Humanities Research Council (AHRC)-funded project, The Discourse of Reading Groups (2008). Publications include *Critical Discourse Analysis and Language Cognition* (Edinburgh University Press, 2003), *Applying English Grammar: Functional and Corpus Approaches* (with Coffin and Hewings; Hodder Arnold, 2004), *The Art of English: Literary Creativity* (with Goodman; Palgrave Macmillan, 2006), 'Researching Argumentation in Educational Contexts: New Directions, New Methods' (special issue) *International Journal of Research and Method in Education*, 2008, 31(3) (guest edited with Coffin), and *Applied Linguistics Methods: A Reader* (with Coffin and Lillis; Routledge, 2009).

Anne O'Keeffe is Senior Lecturer at Mary Immaculate College, University of Limerick, Ireland. She is author of numerous journal articles and book chapters on corpus linguistics, media discourse and on language teaching. She has published three books, *Investigating Media Discourse* (Routledge, 2006), *From Corpus to Classroom* with Ronald Carter and Michael McCarthy (Cambridge University Press, 2007) and *The Vocabulary Matrix*, with Michael McCarthy and Steve Walsh (Heinle, 2009). She has also guest-edited *Teanga* (the Irish Yearbook of Applied Linguistics), *Language Awareness* and *The International Journal of Corpus Linguistics*.

Randi Reppen is Professor of Applied Linguistics at Northern Arizona University where she teaches in the MA TESL and PhD in Applied Linguistics programmes. Corpus linguistics is her main area of research. Randi is particularly interested in how to use information from corpus research to inform language teaching and material development. She has recently authored *Using Corpora in the Language Classroom* (Cambridge University Press, forthcoming).

Christoph Rühlemann has taught English and German as foreign languages for many years in various educational contexts. He has now started to give lectures at the Ludwig-Maximilians-University, Munich, from which he obtained a PhD in English Linguistics in 2006. He has published on a range of topics related to corpus linguistics and conversational grammar, including *Conversation in Context. A Corpus-driven Approach* published by Continuum in 2007. His research focuses on the intersection of corpus linguistics, sociolinguistics and pragmatics and the applicability of corpus findings to foreign language teaching. He is currently involved in the construction and annotation of a corpus of British conversational narrative, the Narrative Corpus.

Mike Scott's official career has been as a language teacher concentrating on TEFL, and this has taken him to work in Brazil and Mexico, in the 1980s as a specialist in ESP working for the Brazilian National ESP Project, and to a series of countries for research purposes. However, what started as a hobby in the early 1980s has since the mid-1990s become his main research interest: corpus linguistics. He is the author of *MicroConcord* (with Tim Johns; Oxford University Press, 1993) and *WordSmith Tools* (Oxford University Press, various editions starting in 1996). This software suite is now widely used for studying patterns of word and phrase in a whole range of languages. Mike Scott is now working at Aston University in Birmingham.

Passapong Sripicharn is a lecturer in the English Department, Faculty of Liberal Arts, Thammasat University, Bangkok, Thailand. He received his PhD in Applied Linguistics from the University of Birmingham, UK. His initial interest in corpus linguistics was on corpus-based materials and the use of DDL activities with Thai learners of English. At present, his research focus ranges from applications of language corpora in EFL writing and lexicology to the use of English and Thai corpora as resources for English–Thai and Thai–English translation, and more recently to the use of specialised corpora in small-scale terminological projects. He also runs introductory and advanced workshops on corpus linguistics with an emphasis on classroom concordancing for postgraduate students, translators, university lecturers and high school teachers in Thailand.

Paul Thompson is the Director of the Centre for Corpus Research at the University of Birmingham. His research interests are: the applications of corpus linguistics, particularly in education; academic literacy; and the uses of computer technologies in language teaching. With Hilary Nesi, he has developed two major corpora of academic English, the British Academic Spoken English (BASE) corpus and the British Academic Written English (BAWE) corpus. He is currently Secretary of the British Association for Applied Linguistics (BAAL), founding convener of the BAAL Corpus Linguistics Special Interest Group and is a co-editor of *The Journal of English for Academic Purposes*.

Scott Thornbury is Associate Professor of English Language Studies at the New School in New York. Prior to that he taught English and trained teachers in Egypt, UK, Spain and in his native New Zealand. He has written a number of books for teachers on language and methodology, including *Beyond the Sentence: Discourse Analysis for Language Teachers* (Macmillan, 2005) and *Conversation: From Description to Pedagogy* (with Diana Slade; Cambridge University Press, 2006). He is interested in discourse analysis, corpus linguistics and pedagogical grammar. He is series editor for the *Cambridge Handbooks for Teachers*.

Elena Tognini Bonelli holds a Chair in English Language and Linguistics at the University of Siena. She has a PhD from the University of Birmingham, where she spent ten years during the 1990s as a lecturer. She is an Honorary Research Fellow of the University of Birmingham. She is General Editor of the Benjamins Series of Monographs *Studies in Corpus Linguistics*.

Christopher Tribble is a lecturer at King's College, London University, where he runs programmes in English for Academic Purposes and Managing and Evaluating Innovation on the MA in ELT and Applied Linguistics, and introductory and advanced courses in Text and Corpus Analysis on the BA in English Language and Communication. He has published and presented widely on the teaching of writing and on corpus applications in language education (most recently with Mike Scott, *Textual Patterns: Key Words and Corpus Analysis in Language Education*, 2006, in the Benjamins' *Studies in Corpus Linguistics* series) and has been a member of the Teaching and Language Corpora organising committee for the past ten years. Apart from this academic work, Chris Tribble is a consultant and trainer in project management and project and programme evaluation, and a documentary photographer specialising in work with development organisations and in theatre and performance.

Elaine Vaughan is Teaching and Learning Advocate at Mary Immaculate College, University of Limerick, Ireland. She completed her PhD research on community and identity in the workplace talk of English language teachers. Her published work has been based around interdisciplinary analyses of institutional discourse and focuses on linguistic markers of identity in the community of practice, such as in-group language, humour and laughter. Her research interests include applying corpus-based methods to the analysis of pragmatic features of spoken language in different settings, the discourses of teaching as a profession and the functions of humour and laughter in conversation.

Thuc Anh Vo is a research student in the School of English Studies at University of Nottingham. Her PhD thesis seeks to explore in depth the potential for creativity in idioms in relation to their internal semantic structures and cognitive motivation, contexts and co-texts, thereby characterising the inherent degrees of creativity in idioms in discourse. Using corpus data and techniques in combination with other discourse analysis methods, the research is also dedicated to detailed observations and assessments of the 'helpfulness' of corpus linguistics towards idiomatic creativity studies in particular and creativity studies in general. Before her PhD course, she taught applied linguistics and English communication skills at Vietnam National University.

Brian Walker is a research student in the Department of Linguistics and English Language at Lancaster University. His PhD thesis combines stylistic and corpus-based approaches to investigate the characters in Julian Barnes' novel *Talking It Over*. By using a combination of these two different approaches his research explores how stylistics and corpus linguistics can work together in the analysis of literary texts.

Steve Walsh is Senior Lecturer in Applied Linguistics and TESOL and Postgraduate Research Director in the School of Education, Communication and Language Sciences at Newcastle University. He has been involved in English Language Teaching for more than twenty years and has worked in a range of overseas contexts. He has many publications in the areas of classroom discourse, educational linguistics, conversation analysis, second language teacher education and professional discourse and is the editor of the journal *Classroom Discourse*, published by Routledge.

Elizabeth Walter is a lexicographer and writer. During many years working for publishers her projects have included a huge range of dictionaries: monolingual and bilingual, ELT and native speaker, general and specialist, paper and electronic. For many years, she was senior commissioning editor for dictionaries at Cambridge University Press. With her colleague Kate Woodford, she now runs Cambridge Lexicography and Language Services, an editorial company specialising in lexicography and related projects. She has written and lectured widely on lexicography.

Martin Warren is a professor in Applied Linguistics and a member of the Research Centre for Professional Communication based in the English department at the Hong Kong Polytechnic University. His research interests include corpus linguistics, discourse analysis, discourse intonation, intercultural communication, pragmatics and phraseology. His publications include a number of joint papers with Winnie Cheng based on the Hong Kong Corpus of Spoken English and two books published by John Benjamins – *The Features of Naturalness in Conversation* (2006) and *A Corpus-driven Study of Discourse Intonation* (co-authored with Winnie Cheng and Chris Greaves, 2008).

Acknowledgements

Reproduced with kind permission from Cambridge University Press: Chapter 6 two extracts taken from CANBEC © Cambridge University Press, Chapter 19 one extract from CANCODE, © Cambridge University Press, Chapter 12 one extract taken from CANCODE, © Cambridge University Press, Chapter 30 five extracts from Cambridge International Corpus, © Cambridge University Press, Table 19.1 extracts from Cambridge International Corpus, © Cambridge University Press, Figure 30.1 taken from Michael McCarthy, Jeanne McCarten and Helen Sandiford, *Touchstone Student's Book 3* © Cambridge University Press, 2006, Figures 30.2 and 30.3 taken from Michael McCarthy, Jeanne McCarten and Helen Sandiford, *Touchstone Student's Book 1* © Cambridge University Press, 2005. Figure 30.5 taken from Michael McCarthy, Jeanne McCarten and Helen Sandiford, *Touchstone Student's Book 4* © Cambridge University Press, 2007.

R. Simpson, S. Leicher and Y.-H. Chien (2007) for *Figuring Out the Meaning or Function of Spoken Academic English Formulas*, available online at http://lw.lsa.umich.edu/eli/micase/ESL/FormulaicExpression/Function1.htm

Pearson Education and D. Schmitt and N. Schmitt for a collocation taken from *A Focus on Vocabulary: Mastering the Academic Word List* (2005).

Pearson Education for a dictionary entry from *The Longman Dictionary of Contemporary English, Fifth Edition* (2009).

Pearson Education for 'Forensic Analysis of Personal Written Texts: A Case Study', in J. Gibbons (ed.) *Language and the Law* (1994).

Oxford University Press and R. M. Coulthard for an extract from 'Author Identification, Idiolect, and Linguistic Uniqueness', *Applied Linguistics* 25(4): 431–47.

Chapter 25 extracts from Chambers-Le Baron Corpus of Research Articles in French, © Oxford Text Archive, *The Chambers-Rostand Corpus of Journalistic French/Le Corpus Chambers-Rostand de français journalistique*. © Oxford Text Archive, and The Chambers-Rostand Corpus of Journalistic French © Oxford Text Archive.

Chapter 38 extracts from Howard, Paul, *The Curious Incident of the Dog in the Nightdress*. © Dublin: Penguin, 2005, Chapter 39 screen shot from ELAN, (the Eudico

Linguistic Annotator), by courtesy of Max Planck Institute, Netherlands, Chapter 44 extracts from the SACODEYL corpus © 2008, Universidad de Murcia (Spain).

Every effort has been made to contact copyright holders. If any have been inadvertently overlooked the publishers will be pleased to make the necessary arrangements at the first opportunity.

Section I

Introduction

1

Historical perspective

What are corpora and how have they evolved?

Michael McCarthy and Anne O'Keeffe

1. The historical origins

Corpus linguistics nowadays is perhaps most readily associated in the minds of linguists with searching through screen after screen of concordance lines and wordlists generated by computer software, in an attempt to make sense of phenomena in big texts or big collections of smaller texts. This method of exegesis based on detailed searches for words and phrases in multiple contexts across large amounts of text can be traced back to the thirteenth century, when biblical scholars and their teams of minions pored over page after page of the Christian Bible and manually indexed its words, line by line, page by page. Concordancing arose out of a practical need to specify for other biblical scholars, in alphabetical arrangement, the words contained in the Bible, along with citations of where and in what passages they occurred.

The etymology of *concordantia* is the Latin *cum*, meaning 'with', and *cor* meaning 'heart', which ties in with the original ideological underpinning of this painstaking endeavour, namely to underscore the claim that the Bible was a harmonious divine message rather than a series of texts from a multitude of sources. Anthony of Padua (1195–1231) is associated with the first known (anonymous) concordance of the bible, the *Concordantiae Morales*, based on the Vulgate (the fifth-century Latin version of the Bible). A well-documented work around the same time was by Cardinal Hugo of St Caro (also referred to as St Cher), who in 1230, aided by a 500-strong team of Dominican monks at St James' convent in Paris, put together 'a word index' of the Vulgate (Bromiley 1997: 757; see also Tribble this volume). Since then numerous other concordances of the Bible have evolved, including Cruden's 1737 *A Complete Concordance to the Holy Scriptures* and Strong's 1890 *Exhaustive Concordance of the Bible*. Nowadays, computer concordancing programs replicate the work of 500 monks in micro-seconds.

The works of Shakespeare were also the subject of concordancing as a means of assisting scholars, for example Becket's 1787 *A Concordance to Shakespeare*. As Tribble (this volume) illustrates by way of extract from Becket's concordance, the word and its linguistic context and location in the Shakespeare canon is given. For a literary scholar, this provides an immense resource. Though concordances from former times were laboriously compiled by hand, their spirit and intentions live on in the software programs we are now familiar with.

2. What drove the creation of modern corpora?

While the process of concordancing and indexing has its origins in the painstaking work of biblical and literary scholars, the drive to create electronic corpora did not come from these quarters entirely. There was an influence from the work of Jesuit priest Roberto Busa, who created a electronic lemmatised index of the complete works of St Thomas Aquinas, *Index Thomisticus,* beginning in the 1950s and completing it in the late 1970s (see Tognini Bonelli, this volume). At least two other forces are more significant, namely the work of lexicographers and that of pre-Chomskyan structural linguists. In both cases, collecting attested data was essential to their work. Dr Samuel Johnson's first comprehensive dictionary of English, published in 1755, was the result of many years of working with a paper corpus: that is, endless slips of paper logging samples of usage from the period 1560 to 1660. And perhaps the most famous example of the 'corpus on slips of paper' is the more than three million slips attesting word usage that the *Oxford English Dictionary* (*OED*) project had amassed by the 1880s, stored in what nowadays might serve as a garden shed. These millions of bits of paper were, quite literally, pigeon-holed in an attempt to organise them into a meaningful body of text from which the world-famous dictionary could be compiled.

As Leech (1992) points out, it was in the 1950s, in the era of American structuralists such as Harris, Fries and Hill among others, when the notion of collecting real data came into its own. Where the work of the early biblical and literary scholars provides the background modus operandi of word searching and indexing, the structuralists were the forerunners of corpora not only in the sense of data gathering but in terms of the commitment to putting real language data at the core of what linguists study.

It is perhaps worth mentioning too that interest in first language acquisition based on transcribed data goes back a considerable way, with the earliest transcripts in the CHILDES Language Database dating back to the 1960s, even though the project was only formally established in 1984 (see its website, childes.psy.cmu.edu/). We should not forget, either, that literary scholars have for decades supplied useful concordances of the works of major authors. Already by 1979, Howard-Hill saw computer-generated concordances as a 'general-purpose working tool for the study of literature' (Howard-Hill 1979: 30). At least eight concordances of works by Conrad were published between 1979 and 1985, thanks to scholars such as Bender and Higdon, while other concordances for writers such as Gerard Manley Hopkins and T. S. Eliot were published around the same time.

The first computer-generated concordances had appeared in the late 1950s, using punched-card technology for storage (see Parrish 1962 for an early discussion of the issues). At that time, the processing of some 60,000 words took more than twenty-four hours. However, considerable improvements came about in the 1970s. Meanwhile, from as early as 1970, library and information scientists had developed a keen interest in Key Word In Context (KWIC) concordances as a way of replacing catalogue indexing cards and of automating subject analysis (Hines *et al.* 1970), and many well-known bibliographies and citation source works benefited from advances in computer technology. Such work was going on when the concerns of many of the contributors to the present volume were unarticulated and hardly conceived as jobs for the computer. It was the 1980s and 1990s which really saw the arrival of corpora as we know them now as tools for the linguist or applied linguist.

Before it found its way into the linguistic terminology, the term *corpus* had long been in use to refer to a collection or binding together of written works of a similar nature. The *OED* attests its use in this meaning in the eighteenth century, such that scholars might refer to a 'corpus of the Latin poets', or a 'corpus of the law'. The *OED*'s first citation of the word *corpus* in the linguistic literature is dated at 1956, in an article by W. S. Allen in the *Transactions of the Philological Society*, where it is used in the more familiar meaning of 'the body of written or spoken material upon which a linguistic analysis is based' (*OED*: second edition, 2009). McEnery *et al.* (2006) note that the more specific term *corpus linguistics* did not come into common usage until the early 1980s; Aarts and Meijs (1984) is seen as the defining publication as regards coinage of the term.

3. The influence of technology: from mainframe to modem to multi-modality

By the time computers came to be usable by anyone other than a tiny group of specialists, the traditions of (a) trawling through texts to find all examples of a particular piece of language, (b) writing dictionaries based on attested usage, and (c) analysing language based on actual informant data were all well-established. It was the revolution in hardware and software in the 1980s and 1990s which really allowed corpus linguistics as we know it to emerge. For a start, the assumption that any large-scale computing required a huge mainframe computer was to be challenged by the seemingly unstoppable increases in desktop computing power in the 1990s, enabling small teams and individuals to take on quite ambitious corpus projects. The parallel growth of the internet and fast download speeds meant that data and results could be transferred easily from scholar to scholar, while the role of the clumsy text scanners of the early 1980s – some as big as household chest-freezers – could be replaced by instant access to vast quantities of text already in electronic form. In tandem, heavy and cumbersome reel-to-reel tape recorders were replaced by manageable analogue cassette recorders in the 1970s and later by miniature digital recorders and small but high-powered video and DVD recorders, with a consequent positive effect on the ability of scholars to create spoken corpora.

However, the first efforts of linguists to harness computational power to study language as evidenced in large volumes of text were hampered by the limitations of machines. Sinclair, for instance, in his earliest exploratory years of corpus analysis that were to culminate in the ground-breaking COBUILD project, used cumbersome punched-card systems for data-storage, a method which, in its most basic form, could be dated back to the eighteenth century! And many corpus linguists of the 'second generation' of computing will recall the unforgiving nature of early DOS-based proprietary software such as the *Oxford Concordance Program* (OUP 1987) popular in the late 1980s and early 1990s, where the smallest error in writing the required string of commands could result in the hair-tearing frustration of a broken search. Such frustrations seemed to vanish forever with the advent of user-friendly GUI-based software suites such as Scott's *WordSmith Tools* (1996–) and Barlow's *Monoconc* (1996–), which, along with other programs mentioned by the authors in the present volume, have become the natural tools of today's applied linguists, powerful, easy to use and more than up to the tasks that researchers demand of them.

4. Corpus developments: from mega-corpus to mini-corpus and from mono- to multi-modal

Technology has been the major enabling factor in the growth of corpus linguistics but has both shaped and been shaped by it. The ability to store masses of data on relatively small computer drives and servers meant that corpora could be as big as one wanted. In this regard, lexicographers led the way. Their aim has always been to collect the maximum amount of data possible, so as to capture even the rare events in a language. The early COBUILD corpora were measured in tens of millions of running words, other publishing projects soon competed and pushed the game up to hundreds of millions of words and, by the middle of the first decade of the twenty-first century, the Cambridge International Corpus (Cambridge University Press) had topped a billion running words of text. Very soon, researchers began to realise the potential of the entire world-wide web as a corpus, with its trillions of words, a veritable treasure-trove of linguistic phenomena accessible at the click of a mouse (see Lee, this volume, on the potential of the world-wide web as a corpus).

However, precisely because of the ease with which data can be assembled and stored, the reverse of the coin of ever-bigger corpora has also manifested itself. Small, carefully targeted corpora (by which we commonly mean corpora of fewer than a million words of running text) have proved to be a powerful tool for the investigation of special uses of language, where the linguist can 'drill down' into the data in immense detail using a full armoury of software and shed light on particular uses of language. Several of the chapters in this volume report on relatively small corpus projects which have yielded invaluable information for their compilers (see Chapters by Clancy, Evison, Farr, Koester, McIntyre and Walker, Thornbury, Vaughan, among others).

Technology also enabled the creation of multi-modal corpora, in which various communicative modes (e.g. speech, body-language, writing) could all be part of the corpus, all linked by simple technologies such as time-stamping and all accessible at one go. No longer did the spoken corpus linguist have to rely only on the transcript of a speech event; now there was the evidence of a video and audio stream tied to the transcript offering invaluable contextual and para-linguistic and extra-linguistic support to the analysis (see Adolphs and Knight, this volume).

Equally, linguists have had a role in shaping the technology in ways best suited to their needs. Statistical operations such as Mutual Information scores were seen as ways of getting at the elusiveness of collocation, while benchmark statistical comparisons could be harnessed to tease out the significant 'fingerprints' of specialised uses of language (manifest in the Key Word function of Scott's *WordSmith Tools*, for example; see Scott, this volume). Such capabilities are not inherent in the computer's architecture and require the vision of linguists and applied linguists to see the potential for translating various types of counting operations that the computer can carry out into linguistically useful forms of informational output. More recently, Smith *et al.* (2008) have drawn up *desiderata* from the linguist's point of view for the ongoing design of corpus tools which might better reflect linguists' needs for annotation and analysis.

5. The many applications of corpus linguistics

Corpus Linguistics (CL), for many, is an end it itself. That is, it provides a means for the empirical analysis of language and in so doing adds to its definition and description. This process has led to the refinement of our descriptions of lexis, leading to immensely enhanced coverage in dictionaries (as discussed above) and we have seen a proliferation of empirical studies about aspects of grammar (often in fine detail), as well as large-scale corpus-based reference grammars such as Biber *et al.* (1999) and Carter and McCarthy (2006). Increasingly, however, CL is being used in the pursuit of broader research questions: that is, in areas such as language teaching and learning, discourse analysis, literary stylistics, forensic linguistics, pragmatics, speech technology, sociolinguistics and health communication, among others. As this volume testifies, CL has had much to offer other areas by providing a better *means* of doing things. In this sense, CL is a means to an end rather than an end in itself. That is, CL leads to insights beyond the realms of lexis or grammar by applying its techniques to other questions, some more easily answered by computational analysis than others. In areas as diverse as second language acquisition and media studies, CL can be applied as a research tool.

In this volume, we have tried to bring together as diverse as possible a sample of the applications of CL so as to capture the state-of-the-art in terms of its how CL is being applied and might be applied in the future. Crucially for the development and vibrancy of CL, this process of application of CL to other areas has a *wash-back effect* for CL and in particular on how corpora and corpus software are designed, as we asserted above. As mentioned (see also Walter, this volume), the initial application of CL in our profession was in the area of lexicography, and software and corpora were co-designed so that lexicographers could make better dictionaries. Now the application of CL is diverse in the extreme, as are the needs of its users. While a lexicographer is interested in how best to profile a word semantically (see chapters by Walter and Moon, this volume), someone using CL in the study of second language acquisition may be interested in how aspects of language develop over time in one individual or a group of users (see Lu, this volume). These polar needs bring about divergent corpora and software design principles. The result is that there has never been a more fertile period in the discipline of CL. We now briefly survey some of the areas in which corpora have been adopted and audit the challenges and wash-backs that arise from these.

Language teaching and learning

Individuals such as Johns and Tribble have, for many years, championed the use of corpora in language learning in the form of Data-driven Learning (DDL) (see chapters by Tribble, Chambers and Sripicharn, this volume). Bringing corpora or corpus data into the classroom has brought many challenges over the years. By its nature, it turns the traditional order within the classroom upon its head. The corpus becomes the centre of knowledge, the students take on the role of questioner and the teacher is challenged to hand over control and facilitate learning. Chambers and O'Sullivan (2004) have shown the democratising effect of devolving the correction and remediation of student writing through the use of error tagging and follow-up student corpus investigation, for example.

As discussed in Chambers', Sripicharn's and Tribble's chapters in this volume, the teacher has to do a lot of preparation work in building up students' skills of investigation leading to hands-on work with corpora or concordance print outs (see also Allan 2008).

Reading a set of KWIC concordance lines, the key skill in DDL, is not something which can be assumed to be automatic. It demands the reader to abstract meaning through vertical reading of the node(s), and often through both left-to-right and right-to-left reading relative to a node on the concordance, and initially at the level of fragmented text (see chapters by Hunston and Tribble, this volume). It demands new micro-cognitive skills whereby the reader moves from phrase pattern to meaning by way of hypothesising and inference. This is a wash-back effect which has still to be properly addressed in DDL.

Another area of innovation within pedagogical applied linguistics which is directly related to CL is the development of learner corpora: that is, collections of spoken and written learner language. The work of Granger and her associates leads the way in this field (see Gilquin and Granger, this volume). This moves the focus of the corpus from native speaker dominance. It brings the language of the learner into focus and allows, at a classroom level, a body of language which learners can both create and work with. Another step away from the monolithic native speaker corpus model has been the development of corpora of expert users such as the HKSCE (Cheng *et al.* 2005) and the VOICE corpus (Seidlhofer 2004). These developments, along with the work of Granger *et al.*, have challenged the notion of the corpus as a model of Standard English (or other language). The English Profile project (see its website, englishprofile.org), set up to provide empirical underpinning for the descriptions of the various levels of the Common European Framework of Reference (CEFR), also deals in learner data, such that the proficiency levels need not be defined solely in terms of the (usually unattainable) performances of native speakers. The ideological wash-backs of learner corpora have yet to be felt in their full force, but there is no doubt that CL has enabled researchers to ask new questions within new paradigms.

Other areas within pedagogical applied linguistics where we are seeing rapid development in the application and development of corpora include testing and teacher education. For both of these areas, the use of corpora can add to professionalisation in differing ways. The use of corpora in the area of testing, as detailed in Barker (this volume), can shed empirical light on issues of key standards and rating, manifested again in the research of the English Profile project. The project offers a core empirical framework upon which to base and score exams internationally, as well as potentially leading to new benchmarks for the design of teaching materials and curricula. Professionalisation of the area of Language Teacher Education (LTE) through the use of corpora for reflective practice has been championed by Farr, and her chapter in this volume gives numerous insights into how CL can aid practice and professional development. A wash-back implication, in this area of application, is the need to make CL a core part of LTE programmes (see O'Keeffe and Farr 2003; McCarthy 2008).

Though it has been a slow process, more and more language teaching materials are now 'corpus-informed'. Increasingly, publishers are investing more in developing corpora; for example, major publishers such as Cambridge University Press, Oxford University Press, Pearson-Longman, Collins-COBUILD and Macmillan all closely guard multi-million-word corpora and regularly launch new materials which are corpus-informed. The splenetic debates that raged in the pages of applied linguistics journals in the 1990s seem to have quelled to an acceptance that *corpus-informed* is not a bad or dangerous term (see Sinclair 1991a, 1991b; Widdowson 1991, 2000; Aston 1995; Carter and McCarthy 1995; Owen 1996; Prodromou 1996, 1997a, 1997b; Carter 1998; Cook 1998; Seidlhofer 1999; Bernardi 2000). The long-running debates of the 1990s may have had a very positive spin-off for CL in that more applied linguists and especially practising teachers became aware of corpora and wanted to learn more. More and more papers were presented at major conferences on the uses of corpora in language teaching. However, there still exists a gulf between the world of corpus linguistics and the everyday language teacher. As stressed by O'Keeffe *et al.* (2007), more corpus linguists need to engage with applied linguists and language teachers, and vice versa. Much of the purely descriptive research conducted by corpus linguists into language use (that is, as an end in itself) would be of immense value to language teachers and materials designers if more widely disseminated. If CL is to have an optimum impact for language learners, this process of engagement between CL and pedagogical applied linguistics needs to be improved. In this volume, we include the work of many corpus linguists who are also language teachers and materials designers in an attempt to showcase the benefits of the synergy between CL and AL (see chapters by Chambers, Cheng, Conrad, Flowerdew, Hughes, Handford, Jones and Durrant, Thornbury, McCarten, Gilquin and Granger, Sripicharn, Vaughan, Walsh, among others).

Discourse analysis

Analysing discourse is another area where CL has been adopted as a means of looking at language patterns over much larger datasets. Existing models for above-sentence analysis such as Conversation Analysis (CA), Discourse Analysis (DA) and Critical Discourse Analysis (CDA) are all benefiting from the use of CL (see Thornbury, this volume, as well as chapters by Evison, O'Halloran and Walsh). CL can automate many (but certainly not all) of the processes of CA, DA and CDA through the use of wordlists, concordances and key word searches (see Evison, this volume). The process is not one-way however. CL on its own is not the basis for the analysis of discourse. It can provide the means for analysis but researchers invariably draw on theories and applications of either CA, DA or CDA. One example is the use of the CA notion of 'baseline': that is, whereby the turn structure of an interaction, for example a telephone call opening, is compared to the 'canonical' or baseline interaction between 'unmarked' interactants. For example, O'Keeffe (2006) compared the turn sequence of an opening of a call to a radio station with the canonical sequence of a call between people who are neither strangers nor intimately related (see Sacks *et al.* 1974). In the same way, CL uses 'reference corpora' against which results are compared (see Evison, this volume for an example of this).

Literary studies and translation studies

Comparison is also a key concern in the study of literature, poetry and drama. Burrows (2002) has noted that traditional and computational forms of stylistics have much in common in that they both involve the close analysis of texts and benefit from opportunities for comparison (see also Wynne 2005). The application of corpora to the study of literature, poetry and drama is surveyed in chapters by McIntyre and Walker and Amador-Moreno. McIntyre and Walker show the application of *Wmatrix*, a software tool which greatly facilitates the comparison of texts. *Wmatrix*, in this case, is used to compare two volumes of poetry by William Blake as well as the texts of twelve blockbuster movie scripts. A function of the software which is illustrated very well in the chapter is its ability to assign semantic categories to key words in the corpora which are being compared. *Wmatrix* was developed to assign semantic tags by matching the text against a computer dictionary of semantic domains (see Rayson *et al.* 2004 for details of this procedure). This means that both key words and key semantic domains can be compared (see Rayson *et al.* 2004; Rayson 2008). This offers immense scope for the automated study of stylistics (see Wynne 2005). Amador-Moreno (this volume) gives an illustration of the usefulness of CL in the analysis of a whole novel. Because the novel is written in the first person, in Irish English, she is able to draw on a one-million-word corpus of the same variety (the Limerick Corpus of Irish English) as a reference for comparison.

Another area which has driven CL from outside has been that of translation. CL has much to offer this area in terms of aiding automatically the comparison of patterns across languages by comparing source and target texts. The constant need to better the tools of the trade has led to numerous innovations in corpus and software design. The challenge of how to align texts and their translations is discussed and illustrated in chapters by Kübler and Aston, and Kenning (this volume).

Forensic linguistics

Increasingly, linguists are being consulted within the legal sector to authenticate authorship. A number of case scenarios are provided in Cotterill (this volume). The corpus linguist is turned into an expert witness in the courtroom. This brings the challenge of communicating findings to a non-linguist audience. The adaptation of CL to this area is interesting to survey from the perspective of how CL is used or viewed. As Cotterill (this volume) notes, 'forensic linguists tend to refer to [CL] as a tool or a resource since no method of analysis, corpus or otherwise, can guarantee the identification or elimination of authors'. Clearly, CL, for forensic linguists, is a means to a very real end. In terms of wash-back effect, forensic linguists have added to the area of CL through their need to show succinctly and statistically how one or more texts contain features or patterns of typicality which prove beyond reasonable doubt that they were or were not written by the same author. This is referred to in terms such as *uniqueness* and *genuineness* (cf. the seminal work of Coulthard 2004). The power of CL again here is its ability to automatically compare on a grand scale so as to corroborate evidence (or not) of uniqueness or genuineness in a text or texts. Cotterill (this volume) raises the important issue of whether forensic linguists can be called scientific (which ultimately washes back to the question as to whether CL can be called scientific). In the US court system, as Cotterill explains, scientific evidence, to be admissible, has to: (1) have a theory which has been tested; (2) have been subjected to peer review and publication; (3) have a known rate of error; and (4) have a theory which is generally accepted in the scientific community (see Solan and Tiersma 2004 for a detailed discussion).

Pragmatics

Pragmatics is the study of language in use and so CL seems a logical ally to the field. However, much of the work in the area of pragmatics draws on elicited data from role-plays, interviews and Discourse Completion Tasks (DCTs), and early classic pragmatic studies relied on intuited data. The application of CL to this area has been slow and there are good reasons for this. Not least of all, there are relatively few corpora of spoken language (the main site for the study of pragmatics in use) and corpora are not designed with the study of pragmatics in mind. Pragmatic features such as speech acts, politeness, hedges, boosters, vague language, and so on, are not automatically retrievable from a corpus. Rühlemann (this volume) discusses the many challenges for those interested in using a corpus to study pragmatics. Nonetheless, there are a number of insightful pragmatic studies which have used CL very successfully (see Rühlemann, this volume). Schauer and Adolphs (2006) show how CL can work in tandem with existing methods, in their case DCTs.

Many individual pragmatic features have been studied using CL. Pragmatic markers, including deictics, hedges, discourse markers, boosters, markers of shared knowledge (see Carter and McCarthy 2006) have been studied in both spoken and written contexts using corpora. Interestingly, a very fertile area has been the use of corpora to compare pragmatic features across different languages: Aijmer and Simon-Vandenbergen (2006) brings together chapters on pragmatic markers across a number of languages. Lewis (2006) examines adversative relational markers in French and English. Stenström (2006) explores Spanish pragmatic markers *o sea* and *pues* and their English equivalents while Downing (2006) looks at *surely* and its Spanish counterpart and Johansson looks at *well* and its equivalents in Norwegian and German.

Other areas which have amassed a considerable number of CL-based studies include hedging and politeness, vague language, irony, humour, hyperbole (McCarthy and Carter 2004), metaphor (Deignan 2005), deixis and modality, among others. Clearly, the strength corpus linguistics brings to the study of pragmatics is its power to automatically search for and retrieve particular items. Unfortunately this does not extend to all aspects of pragmatics. The wash-back effect from pragmatics has been the push for better capture and tagging of spoken language; in particular, the innovations in the area of multi-modal corpora have sprung from this demand.

Sociolinguistics, media discourse and political discourse

The interest in non-formal features of language provides a natural territory of expansion for CL into sociolinguistics and other areas of language in society such as media discourse and political discourse. Sociolinguistics is quintessentially concerned with language users, and here the question of metadata clearly raises itself in CL. It is not sufficient for a sociolinguist to work with a purely textual transcript; vital information about speakers such as age, gender, educational background, geographical origin, etc., become integral features of the corpus-analytical process (see chapters by Andersen and Clancy, this volume). The wash-back on corpus design is most obviously in the kinds of metadata that must be gathered at the time of data collection, leading to elaborate questionnaire or interview demands on informants and a slew of new ethical considerations about data protection and privacy. These problems apart, there have been a number of successful corpus projects with a sociolinguistic motivation (e.g. the COLT corpus of London teenager language), as well as creative ways of using the existing demographic and morpho-syntactic information in corpora such as the BNC (see Andersen, this volume) and other tagged and heavily annotated resources. Detailed annotation and the ability to access and filter metadata are all-important in sociolinguistic versions of CL, and the wash-back effects on software design and use are already apparent.

The study of media discourse has as its natural (but not exclusive) ally critical discourse analysis (CDA). CDA attempts to expose the ideologies which inform and underlie texts, and media texts are clearly a rich source for critical analysts. Benchmark analyses between media corpora and other, non-media corpora (where terms occurring with statistically significant frequency in particular media texts can be listed) can be used to focus on language choices which may be ideologically motivated. O'Halloran's chapter in this volume provides a discussion and examples, and looks further at the investigation of culturally significant key words using CL techniques. CDA has not been without its critics (see O'Halloran's chapter for a summary); the exploitation of CL and future refinements may make the case for CDA stronger by providing empirical evidence from sources such as corpora of media texts. In the same breath one might include the concerns of researchers into political discourse, where CL studies of language in contexts such as political speeches and parliamentary debates, as well as political news coverage, lead corpus linguists into areas such as key word analysis and comparisons across corpora. Ädel (this volume) provides extensive coverage of the field and its preoccupations.

All in all, CL can be argued to be a healthy, vibrant discipline within the general umbrella of language study. Its origins were non-computational but its explosion and expansion in the fields of descriptive and applied linguistics are due mainly to the information revolution of the late twentieth century, a revolution which continues, and from which CL will undoubtedly continue to benefit. In this handbook we have tried to capture the variety, the fluidity, the momentum and vision of CL as it exists at the time of publication, and to assess its contributions and applications within our several professions which all have language in common. The contributors to this volume are representatives of a large and growing community of academics and professionals who have designed, used, adapted and applied corpora and associated software. Individually, their interests differ greatly; collectively, we hope that a single image, however grainy, will emerge to illustrate this fascinating field.

References

Aarts, J. and Meijs, W. (eds) (1984) *Corpus Linguistics: Recent Developments in the Use of Computer Corpora in English Language Research*. Amsterdam: Rodopi.

Aijmer, K. and Simon-Vandenbergen, A.-M. (eds) (2006) *Pragmatic Markers in Contrast*. Amsterdam: Elsevier.

Allan, R. (2008) 'Can a Graded Reader Corpus Provide "Authentic" Input?' *ELT Journal* 63: 23–32.

Aston, G. (1995) 'Corpora in Language Pedagogy: Matching Theory and Practice', in G. Cook and B. Seidlhofer (eds) *Principle and Practice in Applied Linguistics: Studies in Honour of H. G. Widdowson*. Oxford: Oxford University Press, pp. 257–70.

Bernardi, S. (2000) *Competence, Capacity, Corpus*. Bologna: CLUEB.

Biber, D., Johansson, S., Leech, G., Conrad, S. and Finnegan, E. (1999) *The Longman Grammar of Spoken and Written English*. London: Longman.

Bromiley, G. W. (1997) *The International Standard Bible Encyclopedia: Vol I: A–D*. Grand Rapids, MI: William B. Eerdmans.

Burrows, J. (2002) 'The Englishing of Juvenal: Computational Stylistics and Translated Texts', *Style* 36(4): 677–9.

Carter, R. A. (1998) 'Orders of Reality: CANCODE, Communication and Culture', *ELT Journal* 52: 43–56.

Carter, R. A. and McCarthy, M. J. (1995) 'Grammar and the Spoken Language', *Applied Linguistics* 16 (2): 141–58.

——(2006) *Cambridge Grammar of English*. Cambridge: Cambridge University Press.

Chambers, A. and O'Sullivan, Í. (2004) 'Corpus Consultation and Advanced Learners' Writing Skills in French', *ReCALL* 16(1): 158–72.

Cheng, W., Greaves, C. and Warren, M. (2005) 'The Creation of a Prosodically Transcribed Intercultural Corpus: The Hong Kong Corpus of Spoken English (prosodic)', *ICAME* 29: 47–68.

Cook, G. (1998) 'The Uses of Reality: A Reply to Ronald Carter', *ELT Journal* 52: 57–63.

Coulthard, M. (2004) 'Author Identification, Idiolect, and Linguistic Uniqueness', *Applied Linguistics* 25(4): 431–47.

Deignan, A. (2005) *Metaphor and Corpus Linguistics*. Amsterdam: John Benjamins.

Downing, A. (2006) 'The English Pragmatic Marker *Surely* and its Functional Counterparts in Spanish', in K. Aijmer and A.-M. Simon-Vandenbergen (eds) *Pragmatic Markers in Contrast*. Amsterdam: Elsevier, pp. 39–58.

Hines, T. C., Harris, J. L. and Levy, C. L. (1970) 'An Experimental Concordance Program', *Computers and the Humanities* 4(3): 161–71.

Howard-Hill, T. H. (1979) *British Bibliography and Textual Criticism: A Bibliography*. Oxford: Clarendon Press.

Leech, G. (1992) 'Corpora and theories of linguistic performance', in Svartvik, J. (ed.) *Directions in corpus linguistics: proceedings of Nobel symposium 82*. Berlin and New York: Mouton de Gruyter, pp. 125–148.

Lewis, D. M. (2006) 'Contrastive Analysis of Adversative Relational Markers using Comparable Corpora', in K. Aijmer and A.-M. Simon-Vandenbergen (eds) *Pragmatic Markers in Contrast*. Oxford: Elsevier, pp. 139–53.

McCarthy, M. J. (2008) 'Accessing and Interpreting Corpus Information in the Teacher Education Context', *Language Teaching* 41(4): 563–74.

McCarthy, M. J. and Carter, R. A. (2004) '"There's Millions of Them": Hyperbole in Everyday Conversation', *Journal of Pragmatics* 36(2): 149–84.

McEnery, T., Xiao, R. and Tono, Y. (2006) *Corpus-based Language Studies: An Advanced Resource Book*. London: Routledge.

O'Keeffe, A. (2006) *Investigating Media Discourse*. London: Routledge.

O'Keeffe, A. and Farr, F. (2003) 'Using Language Corpora in Language Teacher Education: Pedagogic, Linguistic and Cultural Insights', *TESOL Quarterly* 37(3): 389–418.

O'Keeffe, A., McCarthy, M. and Carter, R. (2007) *From Corpus to Classroom: Language Use and Language Teaching*. Cambridge: Cambridge University Press.

Owen, C. (1996) 'Do Concordances Need to be Consulted?' *ELT Journal* 50(3): 219–24.

Parrish, S. M. (1962) 'Problems in the Making of Computer Concordances', *Studies in Bibliography* 15: 1–14.

Prodromou, L. (1996) 'Correspondence', *ELT Journal* 50(4): 371–3.

——(1997a) 'Corpora: The Real Thing?' *English Teaching Professional* 5: 2–6.

——(1997b) 'From Corpus to Octopus', *IATEFL Newsletter* 137: 18–21.

Rayson, P. (2008) *Wmatrix: A Web-based Corpus Processing Environment*, Computing Department, Lancaster University; available at http://ucrel.lancs.ac.uk/wmatrix/

Rayson, P., Archer, D., Piao, S. and McEnery, T. (2004) 'The UCREL Semantic Analysis System', in *Proceedings of the Workshop on Beyond Named Entity Recognition Semantic Labelling for NLP Tasks, in association with the 4th International Conference on Language Resources and Evaluation* (LREC 2004), Lisbon: European Language Resources Association, pp. 7–12.

Sacks, H., Schegloff, E. A. and Jefferson, G. (1974) 'A Simplest Systematics for the Organisation of Turn-Taking for Conversation', *Language* 50(4): 696–735.

Schauer, G. A. and Adolphs, S. (2006) 'Expressions of Gratitude in Corpus and DCT Data: Vocabulary, Formulaic Sequences, and Pedagogy', *System* 34(1): 119–34.

Seidlhofer, B. (1999) 'Double Standards: Teacher Education in the Expanding Circle', *World Englishes* 18: 233–45.

——(2004) 'Research Perspectives on Teaching English as a Lingua Franca', *Annual Review of Applied Linguistics* 24: 209–39.

Sinclair, J. (1991a) *Corpus, Concordance and Collocation*. Oxford: Oxford University Press.

——(1991b) 'Shared Knowledge', in J. Alatis (ed.) *Georgetown University Round Table on Languages and Linguistics*. Washington, DC: Georgetown University Press, pp. 489–500.

Smith, N., Hoffmann, S. and Rayson, P. (2008) 'Corpus Tools and Methods, Today and Tomorrow: Incorporating Linguists' Manual Annotations', *Literary and Linguistic Computing* 23(2): 163–180.

Solan, L. and Tiersma, P. (2004) 'Author Identification in American Courts', *Applied Linguistics* 25(4): 448–65.

Stenström, A.-B. (2006) 'The Spanish Discourse Markers *o sea* and *pues* and their English Correspondences', in K. Aijmer and A.-M. Simon-Vandenbergen (eds) *Pragmatic Markers in Contrast*. Amsterdam: Elsevier, pp. 155–72.

Widdowson, H. G. (1991) 'The Description and Prescription of Language', in J. Alatis (ed.) *Georgetown University Round Table on Languages and Linguistics*, Washington, DC: Georgetown University Press, pp. 11–24.

——(2000) 'On the Limitations of Applied Linguistics', *Applied Linguistics* 21(1): 2–25.

Wynne, M. (2005) 'Stylistics: Corpus Approaches', in K. Brown (ed.) *Encyclopaedia of Language and Linguistics*. Oxford: Elsevier, available at http://eprints.ouls.ox.ac.uk/archive/00001003/01/Corpora_and_stylistics.pdf

2
Theoretical overview of the evolution of corpus linguistics

Elena Tognini Bonelli

1. The origins of corpora

The starting point of corpus linguistics can be traced by considering the issue of observable data and how this has been handled in different periods and across different theoretical schools. Of necessity, historical linguistics has always been corpus-based since by far the principal evidence of language change and evolution is found in collections of texts of different periods and locations (Johansson 1995: 22). Indeed modern linguistics owes its impetus to the lively work of the historical linguists of the nineteenth century. It may come as a surprise therefore that in a relatively short space of time it should shift its focus to an approach based on intuition and introspection from that data-based approach. But it is a fact that, in spite of its data-based origins, modern linguistics, after the historical-evolutionist period, shifted away from the observation of data and, starting with Saussure, the object of linguistics was defined as the system, abstract par excellence, and non-identifiable in single tokens.

Under the influence of the positivist and behaviourist trend, post-Bloomfieldian linguistics in the USA became concerned to account for the observable data, and there was little room for abstract speculation. With Chomsky, though, the pendulum swung back towards a refusal of observable data as the basis for linguistic statements. Chomsky's position as to observable data in general and corpus linguistics in particular is made clear in the following quotes:

> Like most facts of interest and importance … information about the speaker-hearer's competence … is neither presented for direct observation nor extractable from data by inductive procedures of any known sort.
>
> (Chomsky 1965: 18)

> Corpus Linguistics does not exist.
>
> (Chomsky, in an interview with Bas Aarts, 2000)

The contrast between this position and the theoretical assumptions of corpus linguistics is obvious: corpus linguistics represents a definite shift towards a linguistics of *parole*; the focus is on 'performance' rather than 'competence'. The linguist aims to describe language use rather than identify linguistic universals. The quantitative element (frequency of occurrence) is considered very significant and, depending on the specific approach, is taken to determine the categories of description.

The idea of a corpus grew in the 1960s, deriving mainly from the tradition of lexicography (Francis 1992). While Dr Johnson, the reference point for English lexicography, used for his examples sentences quoted from great scholars like Hume, Johnson's focus was on *the meaning of the words in use*, and not on the ideas expressed in the sentences. Well-known writers were cited because they were authority figures in a prescriptive tradition. But as well as gathering the words of the great and famous, another tradition of scholarship that grew with modern linguistics was that of the *field linguists*, who spread all over the world reaching ever more remote communities and building up records of the languages – usually spoken – that they found. Their informants were in the main quite ordinary people, their conversations also ordinary.

The modern corpus was mainly based on these prior methods of acquiring data for language study. Nevertheless, the thought of compiling a collection of texts which would provide sound evidence of the state of a language was new. Instead of capturing the great signs of culture, the early corpora had modest aims: to collect a good variety of language in use by fairly ordinary people in order to study better the grammar and vocabulary currently in use. As noted by Biber (this volume), an early example of corpus-based work is found in C. C. Fries' grammars of written and spoken American English (1940 and 1952, respectively). By the end of the 1960s there existed a few small corpora, constructed on diverse principles.

The Survey of English Usage, led by Randolph Quirk from its inauguration in 1959 (see website) was an exception to the trend of the time. The Survey focused on the everyday linguistic interactions, spoken and written, of non-celebrities and accumulated a large database on file cards at University College London (see website). There were, however, no plans to computerise it until many years later.

2. The influence of technology in the development of corpora

It was not the linguistic climate but the technological one that stimulated the development of corpora. The electronic computer was on the horizon, and although the first computers were extremely difficult to work with, their great potential was correctly assessed from an early date. Computational work on texts began with Father Busa's *Index Thomisticus* before 1950 (completed in 1978, see Busa 2000), continuing the scholarly tradition of making concordances to works of high status, but using the clerical potential of the computer. There is now a large library of electronic versions of literary, philosophical and religious texts, and the word *corpus* often stretches to cover some of these collections (see *special* corpora below).

The digitisation of a vast range of documents is of more recent origin. Starting with databases of legal and journalistic documents, the movement has grown in parallel with the access provided by the internet, and the world-wide web in particular.

The first electronic corpus of written language was the Brown Corpus, compiled in the 1960s at Brown University by Nelson Francis and Henry Kučera (Francis and Kučera 1964) and still very much in use (see website). This corpus contains a million words of American English from documents which had been published in the year 1961. Its design (see *sample* corpora below) became the standard for some years, and some thirty years later was repeated in the Frown Corpus (see *diachronic* corpora below).

Advances in technology also enabled the collection of spoken data through the invention of the tape recorder. Portable tape recorders were just coming on the market in the late 1950s, and speech could be played back again and again, and studied as a sound wave. A side-benefit of this activity was that speech events could be transcribed without using shorthand, and the first electronic corpus of spoken language was assembled at the University of Edinburgh in the years 1963–5 on Sinclair's initiative (see Krishnamurthy 2004). It contained 166,000 words of informal conversations in English, recorded and transcribed. So the written and spoken corpora of the early 1960s were prepared over the same period (by Francis and Kučera on the one hand for the written language and by Sinclair on the other for the spoken), but the researchers were not initially aware of each other's work.

The 1970s was a period of consolidation and modest spread to a number of languages and different types of corpus. Development was slow, and this was also mainly because of the state of the available technology. Computers were still calculating machines with small memories, and programming languages were not devised with the manipulation of character strings in mind. Nevertheless, this is the time when corpora in excess of one million words were assembled, and annotated corpora were first considered, and also a spoken corpus in a detailed phonological transcription, the spoken section of the Survey of English Usage (see London–Lund website). All of these advances came from Sweden, and Scandinavian scholars such as Sture Allén, Knut Hofland, Stig Johansson and Jan Svartvik set the shape of mainstream corpus linguistics for a generation; they were not alone, however, and important corpus work was in progress with French, Hebrew and Frisian, among other projects. The first corpus of a special variety of a language was the Jiao Da English for Science and Technology (JDEST) corpus, compiled by Yang Huizhong in Shanghai around the same time (see JDEST corpus website).

Here again the timing was the result of technological advances. The invention of scanners improved access to the printed word enormously, and the growth of computer typesetting pushed the horizon out of sight. As Sinclair was fond of pointing out, by about 1990 linguistics had changed from a subject that was constrained by a scarcity of data to one that was confused by more data than the methodologies could cope with. Some may even claim that it has not yet come to terms with this abundance.

Certain classes of data are still scarce, and this is not likely to change in the very near future. Anything that is not available in electronic and alphanumeric form has still to undergo skilled and expensive processing at the input stage. The sound wave is still not amenable to automatic linguistic interpretation despite some successes in the field of speech recognition. Handwritten material has to be transcribed, and a lot of older printed material resists the best scanners. Meanwhile advances in graphics and the emergence of animated text and mixed media communication have set new descriptive goals for which linguistics was ill-prepared.

The large corpora of today often privilege material from an essentially unlimited source – journalism. This feature maintains the controversies about 'balance' and 'representativeness' which have been important issues since computer typesetting became almost universal. There is a clear risk that some features presented as characteristic of a language are actually characteristic mainly of its journalism. More recently the growth of electronic communication has given rise to several new and equally abundant sources, notably web pages, e-mail and blogging. All of these are uncharted territories whose communicative properties are, at the time of writing, largely unknown.

To conclude this section we could say that, in a rough-and-ready way, the relatively brief progress of electronic corpus building and availability can be seen as falling into three stages, or 'generations' (Tognini Bonelli and Sinclair 2006: 208):

(a) The first twenty years, c. 1960–80; learning how to build and maintain corpora of up to a million words; no material available in electronic form, so everything has to be transliterated on a keyboard.
(b) The second twenty years, 1980–2000; divisible into two decades:
  (i) The eighties, the decade of the scanner, where with even the early scanners a target of twenty million words becomes realistic.
  (ii) The nineties, the First Serendipidity, when text becomes available as the by-product of computer typesetting, allowing another order of magnitude to the target size of corpora.
(c) The new millennium, and the Second Serendipidity, when text that never had existence as hard copy becomes available in unlimited quantities from the internet.

3. A quantitative and a qualitative revolution

The technological advances outlined above are strictly interwoven with the emergence of corpus linguistics as a discipline and the progressive penetration of the computer in corpus linguistics work needs to be considered further. In the first stage the computer was seen simply as a tool: it was used to process, in real time, a quantity of information that could hardly be envisaged a few years ago. This is still the most impressive contribution of corpora to language research. But in changing the dimension of evidence, the computer reached a second stage of penetration into linguistic work: not only was it providing an abundance of new evidence, it was by its nature affecting the methodological frame of enquiry by speeding it up, systematising it, and making it applicable in real time to ever larger amounts of data. So Leech (1992) saw that there was now a distinctive methodology associated with corpus work; while a corpus was little more than a big collection of evidence, one approached it in a different way from the perusal of separate texts. The means of retrieving information were getting more and more sophisticated, and the results required more and more skilled interpretation.

Leech (ibid.) drew a clear distinction between corpus linguistics and such varieties as sociolinguistics and psycholinguistics, which, although manifestly hybrid, were regarded as disciplines in their own right; the corpus advanced the methodology but did not change the categorial map drawn by linguistic theory. For many linguists, that is the limit of the changes brought about by the addition of corpora to the computational toolkit. The computer as a tool was not expected to upturn the theoretical assumptions behind the original enquiries themselves, and so no such effect was expected. It was not even felt necessary to look out for such fundamental changes.

However, we can now show that a further development has taken place in the 1990s, a third stage of penetration. What started as a methodological enhancement but included a quantitative explosion (I am referring here to the quantity of data processed thanks to the aid of the computer) has turned out to be a theoretical and qualitative revolution in that it has offered insights into the language that have shaken the underlying assumptions behind many well-established theoretical positions in the field.

Writing a little after Leech, Halliday foresaw the signs of a qualitative change in the results of the quantitative studies opened up by corpus research. He warned that not only language but semiotic systems in general would be affected by this new proximity of theory and data (Halliday and James 1993: 1–25). This is clearly a stage beyond methodology.

Others expressed similar points of view around this time; one theme concerned the effect of increasing the arithmetic power under the command of the linguist. Clear (1993) pointed out the connection between the use of computational, and consequently algorithmic and statistical, methods on the one hand and the qualitative change in the observations. Not only could language researchers speed up the process of analysis, they could carry out procedures which were just not feasible before computers became available. The difference of scale led to a qualitative difference in the observations. It is strange to imagine that just more data and better counting could trigger philosophical repositionings, but that indeed is what has happened.

Saussure's famous words, '*c'est le point de vue qui crée l'objet*' (it is the viewpoint which creates the object), can be reinterpreted in this turn of events: if the dimensions of the viewpoint change as they did, or the granularity of the research results, the object created is substantially different from before. What we have witnessed in the development of corpus linguistics as a discipline is that our chosen methodological standpoint has progressively determined both the object and the aim of the enquiry. In other words, in this instance, the methodology has ended up defining the domain of the discipline.

Given these premises, we should note a few points. Linguistic data are now available in such large quantities that patterns emerge that could not be seen before. In the debate centred around the issues arising in corpus linguistics there is a lot of talk of 'the web as a corpus' and the explosion of information that affects corpus building. The change in the quality of evidence is now obvious to most scholars and observations about instances of language use affect systematically the statements about the language system in general. The problem for the linguist has shifted from accessing large enough quantities of data to elaborating a reliable methodology to describe and take into account this type of unprecedented evidence. This is what a scholar like Sinclair observed (Sinclair 1991: 1 and ff.) and much of his theoretical work on the definition of units of meaning for language description amply proves this point.

Halliday's point about the converging paths of theory and data raises question marks around some of the most familiar dichotomies of modern linguistics, in particular 'competence' and 'performance'. Although this separation between linguistic theory and linguistic evidence could be seen as a methodological convenience, it certainly cuts right across the descriptive framework which is necessary for deriving linguistic information from corpora. While before corpora came along such buffers were needed because no way could be envisaged of accounting directly for all the evidence, corpus work offers no reason or motivation for selecting some evidence and ignoring the rest. The theoretical statement derived from corpus evidence, especially nowadays when large corpora are at everybody's disposal, has to start from new presuppositions. This point has been discussed in detail in Tognini Bonelli (2001) and was at the basis of the distinction between *corpus-based* and *corpus-driven* linguistics.

4. The theoretical shift from text-linguistics to corpus linguistics

There is another point that is worth noting. Given that a corpus is a collection of texts, the aim of corpus linguistics has rightly been seen as the analysis and description of *language use, as realised in text(s)*. Corpus linguistics started from the same premises as text-linguistics in that texts were assumed to be the main vehicle for the creation of meaning. The question that arose, however was: could *corpus evidence* be evaluated in the same way as a *text* was evaluated? This issue is in no way resolved. Different scholars continue to approach it in different ways and there are still those who advocate that, in order to understand and evaluate corpus data better, the analyst has to have direct and full access to the individual texts at any point in time. Most scholars, however, now accept that, in spite of the initial starting point which corpus and text share, the two approaches are fundamentally and qualitatively different from several points of view (summarised in Table 2.1).

Working within the Firthian framework of a contextual theory of meaning, the text has been seen in a unique communicative context as a single, unified language event mediated between two (sets of) participants. The switch in focus from a text-linguistic perspective to a corpus-linguistics one has brought about a different approach. The corpus is not 'just like a text, only more of it'. It brings together many different texts and therefore cannot be identified with a unique and coherent communicative event; the citations in a corpus – expandable from the Key Word in Context (KWIC) format to include *n* number of words – remain fragments of texts and lose out on the integrity of the text (for a detailed treatment of KWIC searches, see Tribble, this volume). The significant elements in a corpus become the patterns of repetition and patterns of co-selection. In other words, in corpus linguistics it is the frequency of occurrence that takes pride of place.

This difference entails a different 'reading' of a corpus compared to one of a text (Tognini Bonelli 2001): the text is to be read horizontally, from left to right in the case of English and other western languages, paying attention to the boundaries between larger units such as clauses, sentences and paragraphs, possible markers of the macro-structure. A corpus, on the other hand, examined at first in KWIC format with the node word aligned in the centre, is read vertically, scanning for the repeated patterns present in the context of the node.

Furthermore, the text has a function which is realised in a verbal context, but also extends to a situational and a wider cultural context. It is interpreted by looking at the functions it has as a communicative event. The corpus, on the other hand, does not have a unique function, apart from the one of being a sample of the language gathered for linguistic analysis; the parameters for corpus analysis are above all formal.

The type of information one draws from a text is interpreted as meaningful in relation to both verbal and non-verbal actions in the context in which they occur – and the consequences of such actions. The type of information gathered from a corpus is

Table 2.1 A qualitative comparison of a text versus a corpus

A text	*A corpus*
read whole	read fragmented
read horizontally	read vertically
read for content	read for formal patterning
read as a unique event	read for repeated events
read as as individual act of will	read as a sample of social practice
instance of *parole*	gives insights into *langue*
coherent communicative event	not a coherent communicative event

evaluated as meaningful in so far as it can be generalised to the language as a whole, but with no direct connection with a specific instance.

Using a Saussurian terminology one can conclude by saying that text is an instance of *parole* while the patterns shown up by corpus evidence yield insights into *langue*.

The series of contrasts between corpus and text outlined above have the purpose of differentiating two sources of evidence that may appear similar but entail very different analytical steps. A corpus contains text evidence and therefore, given a different methodological framework of analysis, it yields insights into the specific text as well. The corpus, in fact, is in a position to offer the analyst a privileged viewpoint on the evidence, made possible by the new possibility of accessing simultaneously the individual instance, which can be read and expanded on the horizontal axis of the concordance, and the social practice retrievable in the repeated patterns of co-selection on the vertical axis of the concordance. Here, frequency of occurrence is indicative of frequency of use, and this gives a good basis for evaluating the profile of a specific word, structure or expression in relation to a norm. The horizontal axis also portrays, at the local level, the syntagmatic patterning, while the vertical axis yields the paradigmatic availability; this is the choice available to a speaker or a writer at a given point and within a certain language system.

5. Corpus typology

Here we briefly consider some of the most common types of corpora available at the time of writing and their different characteristics. There are now so many corpora for so many purposes that it is impossible to list them, and only a sketchy classification can be attempted (see Lee, this volume, who provides a detailed coverage of corpora available and an alternative typology into which they are organised). The typology offered here was originally proposed in the course of an EU project (see EAGLES website, also Tognini Bonelli and Sinclair 2006).

Sample corpora

Most corpora are 'snapshots' in time, and as such they are samples of a given language at a given moment. They are often referred to as *sample corpora*. The primary aim of a sample corpus is to present the normal linguistic features of a language or variety in approximately the proportions found in general use. The Brown Corpus, the original sample corpus, is still a very clear example of the way in which such a corpus is constructed. It is divided into Informative and Imaginative prose, then into sixteen subcategories of these, and finally into 500 samples each containing approximately 2,000 words. Although sample corpora may have been amassed over a period and deal with texts that cover twenty years or more, their aim is to present a state-of-a-language, with the time dimension frozen. Their main drawback is that they fall out of date rather quickly. *Monitor* corpora and *diachronic* corpora (see below) introduce the time dimension as a design factor in a corpus.

When a sample corpus claims to be a reasonably reliable repository of all the features of a language, it can be called a *reference* corpus. Nowadays it will have to be quite large – 100 million words is the typical size – and it will contain substantial amounts of all the main kinds of language that are found in a society. Language, spoken and written, public and private, informative and fictional, etc., will all be there.

Corpora for comparison

Two or more corpora can be designated *comparable* when they are built on the same design criteria and are of similar size (see chapter by Kenning, this volume, for extensive coverage of comparable corpora). Although the term was first used to designate a variety of multilingual corpora (see below), corpora which were designed to be compared with each other had already been compiled in the monolingual area.

Geographical

The first corpus designed to be comparable was the Lancaster–Oslo–Bergen (LOB) corpus. It was given the same design as the Brown Corpus, but selected from British English, where the Brown Corpus selected from American English. All the texts in both corpora were printed during the year 1961, and LOB was completed in 1978. The availability of this comparable resource led to a landmark publication in corpus linguistics – Hofland and Johansson (1982).

The Survey of English Usage (SEU) developed into a project to build a group of comparable corpora which would also facilitate research into language variety, this time on a global basis – the International Corpus of English (ICE). Launched in 1990, the plan was to explore the world-wide varieties of English by building corpora of local varieties in many regions, using a design based on the Survey's holdings (see Lee, this volume). Each corpus contains only around a million words, but twenty varieties are under investigation, and six of the ICE corpora are now available (for details see ICE website).

Historical

These corpora are designed to be compared along a time dimension – see below.

Topic

Some students of discourse like to collect texts organised by topic – e.g. a number of newspaper reports of the same event. These tend, however, to be very small.

Contrastive

In principle any pair of corpora can be compared and contrasted. But sometimes a corpus is built with the specific purpose of making contrasts within itself and declares at the outset that certain of its major components are expected to contrast sharply. A contrastive corpus is thus a single corpus whose principal components have been chosen to facilitate the study of variety. Whereas sample corpora are mostly designed so that the various differences among varieties blend into a general picture of the patterns of usage, a contrastive corpus is designed to bring out the characteristic patterning of distinguishable varieties. Clearly this is a matter of degree. Just as any two corpora can be contrasted, any corpus with distinguishable components can be examined contrastively. But there are internal differences. Each principal component of a contrastive corpus is designed without reference to the others, so the comparability that is maintained in, say, Brown and LOB, is not found. An example of a contrastive corpus is that compiled by Biber, contrasting four varieties of modern English, which provides the evidence for a substantial grammar (Biber *et al.* 1999).

Special corpora

The term *corpus* has been usually associated with the study of language in and for itself and, as we mentioned above, this was later narrowed to feature the ordinary, everyday language of normal people going about their daily business. Such corpora, it is assumed, will be a repository of evidence about a language or variety in its natural state; repeated patterns of occurrence in such corpora will provide evidence which is independent of the idiolect of one particular informant. If several apparently unconnected people are observed constructing patterns with strong similarities to each other, such patterns are likely to be patterns of *langue*, the shared area of meaning-creation in a speech community.

There are, however, collections of texts which do not provide this kind of evidence, but which are still referred to as types of corpora. The selection method, or the pool of texts from which the selection is made, is not designed to be representative of a language or variety. Many of these are important collections, and to mark both their importance and their difference from 'ordinary language' corpora they are called *special corpora.*

The works of Shakespeare, Goethe or Proust are not reliable exemplars of contemporary English, German or French; they are chosen not for their ordinariness but for their extraordinariness. It is the uniqueness of their language choices, and not the universality of them, that causes them to be collected.

Special corpora have been in use for many years, and the advent of computers offered a powerful platform for study; as noted above, the first project to transfer language text into electronic form concerned the works of St Thomas Aquinas. One of the earliest corpora available to researchers was the Leuven Drama Corpus and Frequency List, made by L. K. Engels and colleagues at the University of Leuven in 1975 (see Goethals *et al.* 1990). This pioneering corpus consisted of sixty-one plays written between 1965 and 1972, written in standard English and in ordinary spelling. It was the same size as Brown, one million words, and part of its rationale was to offer an imitation of spoken dialogue to complement the exclusively written genres of the Brown Corpus.

Corpora along the time dimension

Corpora which include the time dimension as a design feature are not very common, and are of two kinds. *Diachronic* corpora present 'snapshots' at intervals of time, usually spanning at least a generation, while *monitor* corpora are devised so that language change can be plotted as it occurs.

The first diachronic corpus was the Helsinki corpus, which offers exemplars of English texts from c.750 to c.1700 (see website). Since the first sample corpora come from the 1960s, it is now feasible to replicate their design with current texts and make detailed comparisons. There is now the Frown corpus, of similar architecture to its parent Brown but with a time interval of thirty years, so that it records the American printed English of a generation later than the Brown. The design of Frown is thus to make it *comparable*; it and its sister corpus Flob were assembled by Christian Mair at the University of Freiburg (see website), aiming to be updated versions of the Brown and LOB corpora, and encouraging four-way comparisons along the geographical and time dimensions.

These corpora are restricted to printed texts. For the spoken language the diachronic dimension is restricted to the period since the invention of sound recording techniques. At the time of writing, a recently completed venture is the Diachronic Corpus of Present-Day Spoken English (DCPSE), a corpus which presents two spoken corpora dated a generation apart in a format which facilitates comparison. The corpora are the London–Lund Corpus, which is the spoken element of the Survey of English Usage, recorded in the 1960s, and the ICE-GB Corpus, recorded in the 1990s. For details see DCPSE website.

Monitor corpora were originally put forward by Sinclair (1982) (see also Clear 1987) as attempts to keep synchronic corpora up to date. Instead of discarding material that was to be replaced with more recent exemplars, it was more prudent to retain it with a time tag, and thus add a diachronic dimension to the corpus. Because of the rapidly growing size of corpora, it required the uniformity and the substantial dimensions of newspaper publishing to make monitor corpora feasible. After several years of development, they are still in a provisional state because their intrinsic importance is not as yet fully recognised. The first attempt was the Aviator project, which layered an annual ten million words of *The Times* newspaper and devised software that would detect innovations of various kinds (see AVIATOR website).

Bilingual and multilingual corpora

The development of bilingual and multilingual corpora was initially tied to the perceived needs of mechanical translation, the original goal of computational linguistics (Kay 2003, see also chapters by Kübler and Aston, and Kenning, this volume). The Canadian Parliament was both bilingual and technologically aware, and from about 1980 it was possible to obtain the Proceedings in both English and French, in electronic form. The first *parallel* corpus (see website, Canadian Hansard) began to take shape.

This alignment procedure worked reasonably well for a wide range of bureaucratic, administrative and legal documents, and encouraged the building of suitable corpora, for example in the European Union. However, the procedure relied on one particular kind of close translation, where translation equivalence is virtually guaranteed for units as small as the sentence. Other kinds of translation work to less rigid criteria, and offer a 'freer' translation which is claimed to be less dependent on the source text and more faithful to the phraseological conventions of the target language (see Tognini Bonelli and Manca 2002, and chapters by Kübler and Aston, and Kenning, this volume).

Multilingual corpora based on a relationship of translation among the constituent texts are called *parallel* corpora (see Kenning, this volume). One concern for researchers in the 1990s was that translated text might not be a good specimen of the target language in its normal usage, and this led to two developments.

The multilingual comparable corpus

Here the correspondence among participating languages is at the level of design rather than at the level of the choice of actual texts. As far as possible, given cultural differences, the same quantities of the same types of texts would be assembled. Usually all the texts are originals in the language they represent, to avoid any influence of the translation. Translation equivalence at the level of the sentence is thus not possible, but a more complex network can be built up to aid translation (see Sinclair 1996). The comparable corpus has a wide range of applications, and the PAROLE Corpus (see ELDA website) is an instance of its application to all the official languages of the European Union at the time (see Kenning, this volume).

The contrastive corpus

This refers to a corpus consisting of two sub-corpora, one of translated texts and the other of untranslated texts, in the same language. There is no translation relationship between individual texts because this corpus is designed to pursue Baker's hypothesis (Baker 1993: 245) that some linguistic features are characteristic of translated text, regardless of the source language. Such a corpus is therefore classified as *contrastive*. Formerly the general opinion was that where features of translated text differed from text that was independently composed in the same language, they would be explicable with reference to features of the source language (see also e.g. Kenny 1998: 52) for a classification within Translation Studies and chapters by Kübler and Aston, and Kenning, this volume).

Other variations on parallel and comparable corpora include the English–Norwegian Parallel Corpus (a standard reference point around the turn of the millennium which has broadened out into the Oslo Multilingual Corpus) and the Corpus of Translated Finnish (CTF) (a comparable corpus which consists of ten million words altogether, consisting both of translations into Finnish in several genres, and comparable texts originally written in Finnish).

Normativeness

The first corpora were deliberate attempts to record the normal usage of members of a language-using community. There was an implication that most if not all of the authors and speakers would be native speakers, and probably fairly accomplished native speakers, of the language concerned. The Brown Corpus was called a 'standard' corpus, and by being restricted to printed documents it acquired all the features of standardisation that are provided in the printing and publishing process. As corpora became more easily available, their use in providing models for language learners was appreciated; this has been a controversial area but corpora are now widely accepted despite some doubts concerning their reliability as repositories of 'correct' sentences.

One of the first multi-million-word corpora, the Birmingham Collection of English Texts (Sinclair 1987), the precursor of the Bank of English (see website) specifically set out to be normative, aiming at adult native speakers for the originators of the texts and advanced foreign learners as the recipients of the dictionaries, grammars and other publications that were produced from corpus evidence.

Normativeness is not an easy feature to realise in spoken text (see below), but is built into the normal practices of legal and administrative transcription – court reporting, *Hansard* (the official transcript of the UK parliament's proceedings) and the like. These, on the other hand, were among the first electronic representations of spoken language that became available. Normalisation is of course absent from corpora of dialectal material, spoken or written.

The possibility of corpus building has led to reappraisals of standards, targets and models for non-native users of languages and ex-colonial varieties, which had generally low status. Following political independence, there was no reason for the native speaker to reign supreme when corpora could be gathered of high-quality users of established local varieties. See, for example, the recent interest in English as a Lingua Franca (see ELFA website). Reference has already been made to the ICE project (see website), which may play a normative role in the future, though that is not seen as its principal function.

Non-native speaker corpora

Corpora in the context of language learning have found other uses, and one popular one is corpora of learner language. By gathering instances of the usage of learners and comparing these with normative model corpora, the language of learners can be explored in a much more profound way than the previous work on error analysis was able to do. The main work in Europe on learner corpora is at the University of Louvain in Belgium (see CECL website), but there are many other projects in learner corpora around the world (see Nesselhauf 2004; see also Gilquin and Granger, this volume).

Spoken corpora

There are now many different kinds of collections of spoken language, whose electronic representations follow a host of different conventions (see Adolphs and Knight, this volume). One group, called *speech corpora*, are built for the detailed study of individual sounds and phonetic features, and do not need to be continuous texts, nor do they need to be collected in natural situations (see Lee, this volume). Many are recorded in high-tech laboratories in order to maximise the detail on the recorded version. Speech corpora are thus part of the class of *special* corpora (see above), those which for one reason or another are not intended to be representative of the ordinary language in its characteristic use as communication.

Large modern reference corpora usually incorporate some spoken material – typically around 10 per cent – and this is in a simple orthographic transcription so that the query software will retrieve instances of a word or phrase in both spoken and written texts. But there is a growing number of spoken corpora which are adapting to the particular character of spoken language and offering new routes to study (see Lee, this volume).

Throughout the period of access to corpora, and despite the prominence of the written corpus from Brown onwards, there has been a high value placed on the recording of impromptu language, typically conversations involving a few people known to each other. While the more formal kinds of spoken language – lectures, speeches, etc. – seemed reasonably familiar as minor variations of the written norms, there was a novel quality about capturing informal interaction that opened up the study of discourse and made it absolutely clear that the received grammars were not constructed to cope with the meaningful patterns that emerged from the conversations; they were heavily biased in favour of written language of medium formality.

Renewed interest in the structure of the spoken language (Carter and McCarthy 2006; Stenström *et al.* 2002) has given us new and valuable corpora. The MICASE corpus of academic American English is freely available (see website), and the C-ORAL-ROM project has published a set of comparable corpora of spontaneous speech for the principal Romance languages, French, Italian, Portuguese and Spanish, about 1,200,000 words in all (Cresti and Moneglia 2005; see also website). A particularly valuable feature of this product is text-to-speech synchronisation (see Adolphs and Knight, this volume).

The internet accepts any type of any language, and some of the new varieties, such as e-mail, chatrooms and blogging, are mostly informal and subject to no conventions of usage. To some observers they seem to be close in style to ordinary spoken conversation, being a kind of written conversation and conducted often in real time. This has led to optimistic claims that the internet could overcome the technical hitches that prevent researchers accessing large quantities of speech; however, the claim has not yet been validated, and speaking remains probably the most intricate of human activities.

Further reading

Hunston, S. (2002) *Corpora in Applied Linguistics*. Cambridge: Cambridge University Press. (An excellent introduction to the use of corpora in Applied Linguistics with useful chapters on corpus data interpretation, and plenty of examples.)

Sinclair, J. (1991) *Corpus Concordance Collocation*. Oxford: Oxford University Press. (Still the best way into an inductive methodology and corpus-driven linguistics.)

Tognini Bonelli, E. (2001) *Corpus Linguistics at Work*. Amsterdam and Philadelphia, PA: John Benjamins. (Following in the footsteps of the above, looking at theoretical, methodological and applied issues with worked examples from both English and Italian.)

Websites

David Lee's website: http://www.devoted.to/corpora
The Corpora list website: http://gandalf.aksis.uib.no/corpora/

References

Aarts, B. (2001) 'Corpus Linguistics, Chomsky and Fuzzy Tree Fragments', in C. Mair and M. Hundt (eds) *Corpus Linguistics and Linguistic Theory*. Amsterdam: Rodopi, pp. 5–13. (Reprinted in W. Teubert and R. Krishnamurthy (eds) (2007) *Corpus Linguistics: Critical Concepts in Linguistics*, volume 1, London: Routledge, pp. 173–81.)

Baker, M. (1993) 'Corpus Linguistics and Translation Studies', in M. Baker, G. Francis and E. Tognini Bonelli (eds) *Text and Technology. In Honour of John Sinclair*. Amsterdam: John Benjamins, pp. 233–50.

——(ed.) (1998) *Routledge Encyclopedia of Translation Studies*. London and New York, Routledge.

Baker, M., Francis, G. and Tognini Bonelli, E. (1993) *Text and Technology. In Honour of John Sinclair*. Amsterdam: John Benjamins.

Biber, D., Johansson, S., Leech, G., Conrad, S. and Finegan, E. (1999) *The Longman Grammar of Spoken and Written English*. Harlow: Pearson Education.

Busa, R. (2000) 'Half a Century of Literary Computing: Towards a "New" Philology', available at www.uni-tuebingen.de/zdv/tustep/kolloq.html#50

Carter, R. A. and McCarthy, M. J. (2006) *Cambridge Grammar of English: A Comprehensive Guide to Spoken and Written Grammar and Usage*. Cambridge: Cambridge University Press.

Chomsky, N. (1965) *Aspects of the Theory of Syntax*. Cambridge, MA: MIT Press.

Clear, J. (1987) 'Trawling the Language: Monitor Corpora', in M. Snell-Hornby (ed.) *ZURILEX Proceedings*. Tübingen: Francke.

——(1993) 'From Firth Principles – Computational Tools for the Study of Collocation', in M. Baker, G. Francis and E. Tognini Bonelli (eds) *Text and Technology. In Honour of John Sinclair*. Amsterdam: John Benjamins, pp. 271–92.

Cresti, E. and Moneglia, M. (2005) *C-ORAL-ROM. Integrated Reference Corpora for Spoken Romance Languages*. Amsterdam: John Benjamins.

Francis, W. (1992) 'Language Corpora B.C.', in J. Svartvik (ed.) *Trends in Linguistics. Studies and Monographs* 65. Berlin and New York: Mouton de Gruyter, pp. 17–32.

Francis, W. and Kučera, H. (1964) *Manual of Information to Accompany a Standard Corpus of Present-Day Edited American English, for Use with Digital Computers*. Providence, RI: Brown University, Department of Linguistics (revised 1971; revised and amplified 1979).

Fries, C. (1952) *The Structure of English: An Introduction to the Construction of Sentences*. New York: Harcourt-Brace.

Fries, C. and Traver, A. (1940) *English Word Lists. A Study of their Adaptability and Instruction*. Washington DC: American Council of Education.

Goethals, M., Engels, L. K. and Leenders, T. (1990) 'Automated Analysis of the Vocabulary of English Texts and Generation of Practice Materials. From Main Frame to PC, the Way to the Teacher's Electronic Desk', in M. A. K. Halliday, J. Gibbons and H. Nicholas (eds) *Learning, Keeping and Using Language. Selected Papers from the 8th World Congress of Applied Linguistics, Sydney, 16–21 August 1987, Vol. 2*. Amsterdam: Benjamins, pp. 231–68.

Halliday, M. A. K. (1992) 'Language as System and Language as Instance: The Corpus as a Theoretical Construct', in J. Svartvik (ed.) *Directions in Corpus Linguistics: Proceedings of the Nobel Symposium 82*. Berlin and New York: Mouton de Gruyter, pp. 1–25.

Halliday, M. A. K. and James, Z. (1993) 'A Quantitative Study of Polarity and Primary Tense in the English Finite Clause', in J. M. Sinclair, M. Hoey and J. Fox (eds) *Techniques of Description: Spoken and Written Discourse*. London: Routledge.

Hofland, K. and Johansson, S. (1982) *Word Frequencies in British and American English*. London: Longman.

Johansson, S. (1995) '*Mens Sana in Corpore Sano*: On the Role of Corpora in Linguistic Research', *The European English Messenger* IV(2): 19–25.

Kay, M. (2003) 'Introduction', in R. Mitlov (ed.) *The Oxford Handbook of Computational Linguistics*. Oxford: Oxford University Press, pp. xvii–xx.

Kenny, D. (1998) 'Corpora in Translation Studies', in M. Baker (ed.) *Routledge Encyclopedia of Translation Studies*. London and New York, Routledge, pp. 50–3.

Krishnamurthy, R. (ed.) (2004) *English Collocation Studies*. London: Continuum (new edition of J. Sinclair, S. Jones and R. Daley (1970) *English Lexical Studies*).

Leech, G. (1992) 'Corpora and Theories of Linguistic Performance', in J. Svartvik (ed.) *Directions in Corpus Linguistics: Proceedings of the Nobel Symposium 82*. Berlin and New York: Mouton de Gruyter, pp. 125–48.

Nesselhauf, N. (2004) *Collocations in a Learner Corpus*. Amsterdam: John Benjamins.

Saussure, F. de (1922) *Cours de Linguistique Generale*. Paris: Payot.

Sinclair, J. (1982) 'Reflections on Computer Corpora in Linguistic Research', in S. Johansson (ed.) *Computer Corpora in English Language Research*. Bergen: Norwegian Computing Centre for the Humanities, pp. 1–6.

——(ed.) (1987) *Looking Up*. London: HarperCollins.

——(1991) *Corpus, Concordance, Collocation*. Oxford: Oxford University Press.

——(1996) 'Corpus to Corpus: A Study of Translation Equivalence', special issue of *International Journal of Lexicography* 9(3): 179–96.

——(ed.) (2004) *How to Use Corpora for Language Teaching*. Amsterdam: John Benjamins.

Sinclair, J., Payne, J. and Pérez Hernandez, C. (eds) (1996) ' Corpus to Corpus: A Study of Translation Equivalence,' special issue of *International Journal of Lexicography* 9(3): 179–276.

Stenström, A-B., Andersen, G. and Hasund, K. (2002) *Trends in Teenage Talk*. Amsterdam: John Benjamins.

Svartvik, J. (ed.) (1992) *Directions in Corpus Linguistics: Proceedings of the Nobel Symposium 82*. Berlin and New York: Mouton de Gruyter.

Tognini Bonelli, E. (2001) *Corpus Linguistics at Work*. Amsterdam and Philadelphia: John Benjamins.

Tognini Bonelli, E. and Manca, E. (2002) 'Welcoming Children, Pets and Guests: Towards Functional Equivalence in the Languages of "Agriturismo" and "Farmhouse Holidays"', *Textus* XV(2): 317–34.

Tognini Bonelli, E. and Sinclair, J. (2006) 'Corpora', in K. Brown (ed.) *Encyclopedia of Language and Linguistics*, second edition. Amsterdam: Elsevier, pp. 206–19.

Section II

Building and designing a corpus

What are the key considerations?

3

Building a corpus

What are the key considerations?

Randi Reppen

1. Building a corpus: what are the basics?

As can be seen from this volume, a corpus can serve as a useful tool for discovering many aspects of language use that otherwise may go unnoticed. Unlike straightforward grammaticality judgements, when we are asked to reflect on language use, our recall and intuitions about language often are not accurate. Therefore, a corpus is essential when exploring issues or questions related to language use. The wide range of questions related to language use that can be addressed through a corpus is a strength of this approach. Questions that range from the level of words and intonation to how constellations of linguistic features work together in discourse can all be explored through the lens of corpus linguistics. Questions related to aspects of how language use varies by situation, or over time, are also ideal areas to explore through corpus research.

Each year, the number of corpora that are available for researchers to use is increasing. So, before tackling the task of building a corpus, be sure that there is not an existing corpus that meets your needs. Each day, more and more corpora of different languages are becoming available on the web. However, you might be interested in exploring types of language that are not adequately represented by existing corpora. In this case you will need to build a corpus. Depending on the types of research questions being addressed, the task of constructing a corpus can be a reasonably efficient and constrained task, or it can be quite a time-consuming task. Having a clearly articulated question is an essential first step in corpus construction since this will guide the design of the corpus. The corpus must be representative of the language being investigated. If the goal is to describe the language of newspaper editorials, collecting personal letters would not be representative of the language of newspaper editorials. There must be a match between the language being examined and the type of material being collected (Biber 1993). Representativeness is closely linked to size, which is addressed in the next section.

2. What kind of data do I use and how much?

The question of corpus size is a difficult one. There is not a specific number of words that answers this question. Corpus size is certainly not a case of one size fits all (Carter and McCarthy 2001). For explorations that are designed to capture all the senses of a particular word or set of words, as in building a dictionary, then the corpus needs to be large, very large – tens or hundreds of millions of words. However, for most questions that are pursued by corpus researchers, the question of size is resolved by two factors: representativeness (have I collected enough texts (words) to accurately represent the type of language under investigation?) and practicality (time constraints). In some cases it is possible to completely represent the language being studied. For example, it is possible to capture all the works of a particular author, or historical texts from a certain period, or texts from a particular event (e.g. a radio or TV series, political speeches). In these cases, complete representation of the language can be achieved. An example of this is the 604,767-word corpus of nine seasons of the popular television sitcom *Friends* (Quaglio 2008). However, in most cases it is not possible to achieve complete representation, and in these cases corpus size is determined by capturing enough of the language for accurate representation. For example, Vaughan (2008) examined the role of humour in English language teacher faculty meetings at two institutions. Since this was a very specific question, in a very specific context, a relatively small corpus (40,000 words) was adequate to explore the role of humour in these two settings.

Smaller, specialised corpora, such as the examples above, can be very useful for exploring grammatical features, but for studies of rare grammatical features or lexical studies such as compiling a dictionary, millions of words are needed to ensure that all the senses of a word are captured (Biber 1990), thus reinforcing the interrelationship of research question, representativeness, corpus design and size.

3. How do I collect texts?

Once a research question is articulated, corpus construction can begin. The next task is identifying the texts and developing a plan for text collection. In all cases, before collecting texts, it is important to have permission to collect them. When collecting texts from people or institutions, it is essential to get consent from the parties involved. The rules that apply vary by country, institution and setting, so be sure to check before beginning collection. There are texts that are considered public domain. These texts are available for research and permission is not needed. Public domain texts are also available for free, as opposed to copyrighted material, which in addition to requiring permission prior to use may also have fees associated with it. Even when using texts for private research, it is important to respect copyright laws. This includes material that is available online.

When creating a corpus there are certain procedures that are followed, regardless of whether the corpus is representing spoken or written language. Some issues that are best addressed prior to corpus construction include: What constitutes a text? How will the files be named? What information will be included in each file? How will the texts be stored (file format)?

In many cases, what constitutes a text is predetermined. When collecting a corpus of in-class writing, a text could be defined as all the essays written in the class on a particular day, or a text could be each student's essay. The latter is the best option. It is always best to create files at the smallest 'unit', since it is easier to combine files in analysis rather than to have to open a file, split it into two texts, and then resave the files with new names prior to being able to begin any type of analysis. So, even if you are creating a corpus of in-class writing with the goal of comparing across different classes, having the essays stored as individual files rather than as a whole class will allow the most options for analysis. When considering spoken language, the question of what constitutes a text is a bit messier. Is a spoken text the entire conversation, including all the topic shifts that might occur? Or, is a spoken text a portion of a conversation that addresses a particular topic or tells a story? The answers to these questions are, once again, directly shaped by the research questions being explored.

Before saving a text, file naming conventions need to be established. File names that clearly relate to the content of the file allow users to sort and group files into sub-categories or to create sub corpora more easily. Creating file names that include aspects of the texts that are relevant for analysis is helpful. For example, if the research involved building a corpus of *Letters to the Editor* from newspapers that represented two different demographic areas (e.g. urban vs rural) and included questions related to the gender of the letter writer, then this information could be included in the file name. In this case, abbreviating the newspaper name, including the writer's gender and also including the date of publication would result in a file name that is reasonably transparent and also a reasonable length. For example, a letter written by a woman in a city in Arizona printed in October of 2008 could have a file of: azcf108. It is ideal if file names are about seven to eight characters. If additional space is needed a dot (.) followed by three additional characters can be used. File names of this length will not cause problems with analytical tools or software backup tools. Using backup software and keeping copies of the corpus in multiple locations can avoid the anguish of losing the corpus through computer malfunction, fire or theft.

In many cases a *header* is included at the beginning of each corpus file. A header contains information about the file. This might include demographic information about the writer or speaker, or it could include contextual information about the text, such as when and where it was collected and under what conditions. If a header is used, it is important that the format of the header is consistent across all files in the corpus. Since creating a corpus is a huge time investment it is a good idea to include any information in the header that might be relevant in future analysis.

Headers often have some type of formatting that helps to set them apart from the text. The header information might be placed inside angle brackets (< >), or have a marking to indicate the end of the header and the beginning of the text. This formatting can be used to keep information in the header from being included in the analysis of the text, avoiding inflating frequency counts and counting information in the header as part of the text. Below is an example of a header from a conversation file.

Example header:

< File name = spknnov06.mf >
< Setting = two friends chatting at a coffee shop >
< Speaker 1 = Male 22 years old >
< Speaker 2 = Female 33 years old >
< Taped = November 2006 >
< Transcribed = Mary Jones December 2006 >
< Notes: Occasional background traffic noise makes parts unintelligible >

Determining the file format for storing texts may seem inconsequential; however, saving files in a format that is not compatible with the tools that will be used for analysis will result in many extra hours of work. Most corpus analysis tools function well with the file format *plain text.* When scanning written texts, downloading texts from the internet or entering texts (keyboarding), you are always given an option as to how to save the file. From the drop-down '*Save as*' menu, chose the option *plain text.* If the text is already in electronic format and has been saved by a word processing program, use the '*Save as*' option and select *plain text,* or add the file extension (the part after the dot (.) in the file name) *txt.*

Whether creating a corpus of spoken or written texts, there are decisions that are best made during the design phase. Creating a corpus of written texts is an easier task than building a corpus of spoken texts, but both have challenges associated with them. Often written texts are already in electronic format; however, if the texts are not in electronic format, they will need to be entered in electronic form. If the texts represent learner language, novice writing or children's writing, it is important to preserve the non-standard spelling and grammar structures. These may be of keen interest. Decisions about how to treat any art, or non-orthographic markings, will also need to be made. These challenges pale in comparison to the many decisions that need to be made when collecting a spoken corpus.

First of all, a spoken corpus obviously does not exist in written form, but will need to be recorded and then transcribed in order to be analysed using currently available corpus tools. Spoken texts can be collected with either analogue or digital recorders. If many people, across different locations, are involved in collecting spoken texts, analogue recorders might eliminate some potential errors, unless all the participants are trained to use digital recorders. However, the sound quality, ease of storage and the ability to link digital audio files to the transcription may outweigh any advantages of using analogue recordings.

Once the files have been recorded, it is necessary to transcribe the spoken recordings into an electronic format. Unfortunately, current speech recognition software is not able to accurately convert the spoken files into text files, so this is accomplished by individuals listening to the recordings and transcribing, or keying them, into the computer. Transcribing a spoken text into a written format is a very time-consuming and tedious process. Depending on the quality of the recording and the level of detail included in the transcription (marking prosody, marking intonation, timing pauses, etc.), it can take ten to fifteen hours to transcribe an hour of spoken language.

If analogue tapes are used, transcription machines are available that make the process a bit easier. These machines use a foot pedal allowing the transcriber's hands to remain on the keyboard. The foot pedal can be used to pause, rewind and also resume playing the tape. Transcription machines also have settings that allow the rate of speech to be slowed without distorting the sound quality. If digital recorders are used there are several freeware programs that can be used to transcribe sound files (see Thompson, this volume). Foot pedals are also available that can be attached to the computer for use with digital files.

Before beginning to transcribe, there are several decisions that must be made. Some of the more common questions that need to be addressed prior to transcription include: How will reduced forms be transcribed? If the speaker says *wanna* or *gonna* for *want to* or *going to*, will what the speaker actually said be transcribed, or will the complete form be transcribed, or will both forms (double coding) be transcribed (e.g. wanna / want to) allowing maximum flexibility for analysis? Many times it is difficult to hear or understand what was said; this can be because of background noises or the speaker not being near the recording device. What will be transcribed in these instances? The transcriber can make a best guess and indicate that with *(?)* after the guessed word. Or, the transcriber might simply write *unclear* and the number of syllables (e.g. *unclear – two syllables*) after the utterance. Overlapping speech is another challenge in transcribing natural speech events. Speakers often talk at the same time or complete each other's turns. Often listeners will use conversational facilitators or minimal responses (e.g. uh huh, mmm, hum, etc.) to show that they are listening and attentive to what the speaker is saying. These overlaps and insertions are a challenge for transcribers. It is a good idea to standardise the spelling of these conversational facilitators. For example, it might be that *mmm* is always spelled with three *M*s, or that the reduced form of *because* is always represented as *cuz*.

How laughter will be transcribed is another decision. Making these decisions ahead of time will save many hours of anguish as you search files for particular features, only to realise that you need to spend time standardising these forms. Repetitions and pauses are also features of spoken language that require transcribing decisions. Will pauses be timed? Or will the transcription conventions simply guide the transcriber to note short (maybe two to five seconds in length) and long pauses (maybe those longer than six seconds) through the use of … for short pauses and …… for long pauses? Again, this decision will be informed by the research goals of the corpus. Some corpora are carefully transcribed and include prosodic information (Cheng *et al.* 2008). This type of transcription is very time-consuming but allows researchers to capture many of the aspects of spoken language that are typically lost through the transcription process. Creating a prosodically transcribed corpus is often done in two stages: first, just creating a transcription, and then, going back and adding the prosodic markings. In some cases the corpus can be set up to have multiple layers of annotations. These multiple layers of annotation can greatly enhance the types of analysis that can be performed, but they also need to be governed by practical considerations (Cook 1990).

4. How much mark-up do I need?

The term 'mark-up' refers to adding information to a corpus file. Not all corpora contain mark-up; however, certain types of mark-up can facilitate corpus analysis. Mark-up can be divided into two types: document mark-up and annotations. Document mark-up refers to markings much like HTML codes that are used to indicate document features such as paragraphs, fonts, sentences, including sentence numbers, speaker identification, and marking the end of the text. At a basic level the header can be considered a type of mark-up since it provides addition information about the text. The prosodic markings of a spoken corpus, mentioned in the previous section, are a form of mark-up. Annotations cover a wide range of possibilities. The most common form of corpus annotation involves including parts of speech (POS) tags which label each word in a corpus as to its grammatical category (e.g. noun, adjective, adverb, etc.). These tags can be very useful for addressing a number of questions and help to resolve many of the issues related to simply searching on a particular word. Many words are polysemous, yet when a word's part of speech is known much is accomplished to disambiguate and focus search results. For example, a POS tagged corpus makes a search of the modal verb *can* much more efficient by not including instances of *can* as a noun.

By using a template for corpus mark-up, it is possible for corpus texts to have multiple annotations. For example, a text could be viewed as just a plain text or it could also be viewed with the POS tags, or possibly the POS and prosodic annotations. This is a very useful way of marking up a corpus and yet providing the users with access to the versions that meet their needs.

5. Looking to the future

Given the enormous changes in the world of technology over the last five years, it is difficult to imagine the scope of changes that might take place in the area of corpus construction and tools. However, making a wish list for the future is always a delightful task. One of the changes that we will see in the near future is greater availability of spoken corpora. This could be a result of two factors. First, researchers may be more able and willing to share the spoken corpora that they have assembled. Second, hopefully, creating spoken corpora will benefit from technological advances in speech recognition, thus making the task of transcribing spoken language to text files a much more efficient process and more automated task. Perhaps digital sound files will be fed through a conversion program and then the researcher can go through to edit any areas that are problematic. This would be a tremendous boost to spoken language researchers.

The development and use of video and multi-modal corpora is another area that will probably change dramatically in the next decade. Some research is already being done in this area (Carter and Adolphs 2008; Knight and Adolphs 2008; Dahlmann and Adolphs 2009) and given how quickly technology can advance, this seems to be the next area that can provide new levels of corpus building and analysis, allowing us to ask and answer questions that are not even imagined at this point in time.

Further reading

Biber, D., Conrad, S. and Reppen, R. (1998) *Corpus Linguistics: Exploring Language Structure and Use*. Cambridge: Cambridge University Press. (This book provides an overview of corpus linguistics and its many applications, from discovering patterns of language use to researching language change over time. The chapters build from the lexical to the discourse level, each with detailed examples of studies related to the topic being covered in the chapter. The book ends with a series of methodology boxes that provide readers with answers to many of the methodological processes related to using corpora for research.)

McEnery, T, Xiao, R. and Tono, Y. (2006) *Corpus Based Language Studies: An Advanced Resource Book*. London: Routledge. (This book is divided into three parts. Part A is an introduction and overview of corpus linguistics. Part B contains a collection of reprinted articles that provide greater depth for various aspects that are presented in Part A. Finally, Part C is a series of case studies and tasks that are designed to involve the reader.)

O'Keeffe, A., McCarthy, M. J. and Carter, R. (2007) *From Corpus to Classroom: Language Use and Language Teaching*. Cambridge: Cambridge University Press. (The authors have done extensive research on language and patterns of use. This information is the foundation for the practical applications of corpus research that is presented to English language teachers. In addition to English language teachers, language researchers will see this book as a wonderful resource on many aspects of language, especially spoken language.)

Reppen, R. and Simpson, R. (2002). 'Corpus Linguistics', in N. Schmitt (ed.) *An Introduction to Applied Linguistics*. London: Arnold, pp. 92–111. (This chapter presents an overview of corpus linguistics and highlights how the methodology of corpus linguistics can be used to explore many areas of interest in the area of applied linguistics.)

References

Biber, D. (1990) 'Methodological Issues Regarding Corpus-Based Analysis of Linguistic Variation', *Literary and Linguistic Computing* 5(4): 257–69.

——(1993) 'Representativeness in Corpus Design', *Literary and Linguistic Computing* 8(4): 243–57.

Carter, R. and Adolphs, S. (2008) 'Linking the Verbal and Visual: New Directions for Corpus Linguistics', 'Language, People, Numbers', special issue of *Language and Computers* 64: 75–291.

Carter, R. and McCarthy, M. J. (2001) 'Size Isn't Everything: Spoken English, Corpus and the Classroom', *TESOL Quarterly* 35(2): 337–40.

Cheng, W., Greaves, C. and Warren, M. (2008) *A Corpus-driven Study of Discourse Intonation*. Amsterdam: John Benjamins.

Cook, G. (1990) 'Transcribing Infinity: Problems of Context Presentation', *Journal of Pragmatics* 14: 1–24.

Dahlmann, I. and Adolphs, S. (2009) 'Spoken Corpus Analysis: Multi-modal Approaches to Language Description', in P. Baker (ed.) *Contemporary Approaches to Corpus Linguistics*. London: Continuum Press, pp. 125–39.

Knight, D. and Adolphs, S. (2008) 'Multi-Modal Corpus Pragmatics: The Case of Active Listenership', in J. Romeo (ed.) *Corpus and Pragmatics*. Berlin: Mouton de Gruyter, pp. 175–90.

Leech, G. (2005) 'Adding Linguistic Annotation', in M. Wynne (ed.) *Developing Linguistic Corpora: A Guide to Good Practice*. Oxford: Oxbrow Books, pp. 17–29; also at http://ahds.ac.uk/linguistic-corpora/ (retrieved 17 October 2008).

Quaglio, P. (2008) 'Television Dialogue and Natural Conversation: Linguistic Similarities and Differences', in A. Ädel and R. Reppen (eds) *Corpora and Discourse: The Challenges of Different Settings*. Amsterdam: John Benjamins, pp. 189–210.

Vaughan, E. (2008) '"Got a Date or Something?" An Analysis of the Role of Humor and Laughter in the Workplace Meetings of English Language Teachers', in A. Ädel and R. Reppen (eds) *Corpora and Discourse: The Challenges of Different Settings*. Amsterdam: John Benjamins, pp. 95–115.

4
Building a spoken corpus
What are the basics?

Svenja Adolphs and Dawn Knight

1. Overview

Throughout the development of corpus linguistics there has been a noticeable focus on analysing written language, and with written corpora now exceeding the one-billion-word mark, the possibilities for generating new insights into the way in which language is structured and used are both exciting and unprecedented. Spoken corpora, on the other hand, tend to be much smaller in size and thus often unable to offer the same level of recurrence of individual items and phrases when compared to their written counterparts. In addition, the analysis of spoken discourse as recorded in spoken corpora requires specific attention to elements beyond the text, such as intonation, gesture and discourse structure, which cannot easily be explored with the use of the kinds of frequency-based techniques used in the analysis of written corpora.

Nevertheless, spoken corpora provide a unique resource for the exploration of naturally occurring discourse, and the growing interest in the development of spoken corpora is testament to the value they provide to a diverse number of research communities. Following on from the early developments of relatively small spoken corpora in the 1960s, such as the London–Lund Corpus for example, the past two decades have seen major advances in the collection and development of spoken corpora, particularly in the English language, but not exclusively. Some examples of spoken corpora are the Cambridge and Nottingham Corpus of Discourse in English (CANCODE; McCarthy 1998), a five-million-word corpus collected mainly in Britain; the Limerick Corpus of Irish English (LCIE; Farr *et al.* 2004); the Hong Kong Corpus of Spoken English (HKCSE; Cheng and Warren 1999, 2000, 2002); the Michigan Corpus of Academic Spoken English (MICASE; Simpson *et al.* 2000) and the spoken component of the British National Corpus (BNC; see Lee, this volume). In addition, there is a growing interest in the development of spoken corpora of international varieties of English (e.g. the ICE corpora) and other languages, as well as of learner language (e.g. De Cock *et al.* 1998; Bolton *et al.* 2003). These corpora provide researchers with rich samples of spoken language-in-use which form the basis of new and emerging descriptions of naturally occurring discourse.

In recognition of the fact that spoken discourse is multi-modal in nature, a number of spoken corpora that are now being developed align audio and visual data streams with the transcript of a conversation. Examples of these include the Nottingham Multi-Modal Corpus (NMMC: a 250,000-word corpus of videoed single-speaker and dyadic discourse; see Knight *et al.* 2006; Carter and Adolphs 2008); the Augmented Multi-Party Interaction Corpus (AMI: a 100-hour meeting room video corpus; see Ashby *et al.* 2005) and the SCOTS Corpus (a corpus of Scottish texts and speech, comprised of audio files with aligned transcriptions; see Douglas 2003; Anderson and Beavan 2005; Anderson *et al.* 2007; see Thompson, this volume).

Research outputs based on the analysis of spoken corpora are wide-ranging and include, for example, descriptions of lexis and grammar (e.g. Biber *et al.* 1999; Carter and McCarthy 2006), discourse particles (Aijmer 2002), courtroom talk (Cotterill 2004), media discourse (O'Keeffe 2006) and healthcare communication (Adolphs *et al.* 2004; see also Biber, this volume, for further references). This research covers phenomena at utterance level as well as at the level of discourse. A number of studies start with the exploration of concordance outputs and frequency information as a point of entry into the data and carry out subsequent analyses at the level of discourse (e.g. McCarthy 1998), while others start with a discourse analytical approach followed by subsequent analyses of concordance data.

Before a spoken corpus can be subjected to this kind of analysis, the data has to be collected, transcribed and categorised in a way that allows the researcher to address specific research questions. This chapter deals with the basic steps that need to be taken when assembling a spoken corpus for research purposes. We will discuss the different considerations behind corpus design, data collection and associated issues of permission and ethics, transcription and representation of spoken discourse.

2. Corpus design

Issues of corpus design need to be addressed prior to any discussion of the content of the corpus, and the methods used to organise the data. Often, design and construction principles are locally determined (Conrad 2002: 77); however, Sinclair's principles articulated in relation to corpus design can be seen as general guidelines for both spoken and written corpora (for similar prescriptions see Reppen and Simpson 2002: 93; Stuart 2005: 185; Wynne 2005). Sinclair (2005) sets out the following guidelines:

1 The contents of a corpus should be selected without regard for the language they contain, but according to their communicative function in the community in which they arise.
2 Corpus builders should strive to make their corpus as representative as possible of the language from which it is chosen.
3 Only those components of corpora which have been designed to be independently contrastive should be contrasted.
4 Criteria for determining the structure of a corpus should be small in number, clearly separate from each other, and efficient as a group in delineating a corpus that is representative of the language or variety under examination.
5 Any information about a text other than the alphanumeric string of its words and punctuation should be stored separately from the plain text and merged when required in applications.

6 Samples of language for a corpus should wherever possible consist of entire documents or transcriptions of complete speech events, or should get as close to this target as possible. This means that samples will differ substantially in size.
7 The design and composition of a corpus should be documented fully with information about the contents and arguments in justification of the decisions taken.
8 The corpus builder should retain, as target notions, representativeness and balance. While these are not precisely definable and attainable goals, they must be used to guide the design of a corpus and the selection of its components.
9 Any control of subject matter in a corpus should be imposed by the use of external, and not internal, criteria.
10 A corpus should aim for homogeneity in its components while maintaining adequate coverage, and rogue texts should be avoided.

Some of these guidelines can be difficult to uphold because of the nature of language itself; a 'population without limits, and a corpus is necessarily finite at any one point' (Sinclair 2008: 30). The requirement for ensuring representativeness, balance and homogeneity in the design process is thus necessarily idealistic. They are also specific and relative to individual research aims, and thus have to be judged in relation to the different questions that are asked of the data.

With regard to the guidelines above, there are a number of issues that pertain specifically to the construction of spoken corpora. These are best described in relation to the fundamental stages of construction (see also Psathas and Anderson 1990; Leech *et al.* 1995; Lapadat and Lindsay 1999; Thompson 2005; Knight *et al.* 2006):

- Recording
- Transcribing, coding and mark-up
- Management and analysis

These have to be considered at the design stage and are best seen as interacting parts of a research system, with each stage influencing the next. The stage of recording data is determined by the type of analysis that is planned, which in turn determines the granularity and detail of transcription, coding and mark-up. It is therefore important to plan the development of a corpus carefully and to consider all practical and ethical issues that may arise (see Psathas and Anderson 1990 and Thompson 2005 for further discussion on the importance of planning). While the planning phase is an important stage of the design process, the approach that emerges during the process of construction is to be reconsidered and modified throughout.

It is important to note that the process of planning necessarily leads to an informed selection of discourse events that are being recorded, and thus it is impossible to create a 'complete picture' of discourse in corpora (Thompson 2005; also see Ochs 1979; Kendon 1982: 478–9; Cameron 2001: 71). This is true regardless of whether the corpus is of a specialist or of a more 'general' nature.

Given that the process of selection is unavoidable, it is the responsibility of the corpus constructor(s) to limit the potential detrimental effect that the selection may have on the representativeness, homogeneity and balance of the corpus. The use of a checklist or log to chart progress can be helpful, and acts as an invaluable point of reference for discussing anomalies or 'gaps' that may occur in the data, as well as accounting for interesting patterns that may be found in subsequent analyses.

We will now discuss the different stages in the construction of spoken corpora.

Recording

The recording stage is the data collection phase. At this stage it is important that all recordings are both suitable and rich enough in the information required for in-depth linguistic enquiry as well as being of a sufficiently high quality to be used and re-used in a corpus database (Knight and Adolphs 2006). It is therefore advisable to strive to collect data which is as accurate and exhaustive as it can be, capturing as much information from the content and context of the discursive environment as possible (Strassel and Cole 2006: 3). This involves documenting information about the participants, the location and the overall context in which the event takes place, as well as about the type of recording equipment that is being used, and the technical and physical specifications that are being applied to the recording itself. This is because the loss or omission of data cannot be easily rectified at a later date, since real-life communication cannot be authentically rehearsed and replicated.

It is 'impossible to present a set of invariant rules about data collection because choices have to be made in light of the investigators' goals' (Cameron 2001: 29, also see O'Connell and Kowal 1999). The decisions made concerning the recording phase are thus specific to the research aims. Despite this, it is vital to ensure that 'the text collection process for building a corpus … [is] principled' (Reppen and Simpson 2002: 93) in order to achieve those aims.

As regards the equipment used for recording data, there are now a number of high-quality voice recorders available for recording spoken interaction. Most are now digital and recordings can be easily transferred to a PC or other device. Video recordings of spoken interactions are increasingly becoming an important alternative to pure sound recordings, as the resulting data offers further scope for analysis. Video recording equipment is thus starting to offer a useful alternative to sound recorders, and the availability of very small and unintrusive video recording equipment means that this procedure can now be used in a variety of different contexts (see Crabtree *et al.* 2006; Morrison *et al.* 2007; Tennent *et al.* 2008).

As part of the planning process for the recording stage it is essential that decisions are made determining the *design* of the recording process (i.e. what kind of data needs to be recorded and how much), as well as the physical *conditions* under which the recordings take place (i.e. the when and where the recording is to take place and the equipment that is being used).

Since the construction of spoken corpora is very expensive, the issue of cost effectiveness is an important factor when it comes to all stages of construction. Thompson (2005) highlights that there is a need to decide between 'breadth' and 'depth' of what is to be recorded. The cost–benefit consideration assesses the relative advantages between capturing large amounts of data (in terms of time, number of encounters or discourse contexts), the amount of detail added during the transcription and annotation phase, and the nature of analyses that might be generated using the recordings. In terms of the number of hours of recording needed to achieve a particular word count, in previous corpus development projects, such as the CANCODE project for example, one hour of recorded casual conversation accounted for approximately 10,000 words of transcribed data. This is only a very broad estimate as the number of words per hour recording depends on a range of different factors, including among others the discourse context and the rate of speech of the participants.

This discussion leads to the wider question of 'How much data is enough?', a complex and challenging question which requires a number of different perspectives to be considered.

At the heart of this question is the variable under investigation and a key 'factor that affects how many different encounters you may have to record is how frequently the variable you are interested in occurs in talk' (Cameron 2001: 28). Thus, the amount of data we need to record to analyse words or phrases that occur very frequently is less than we would need to study less frequent items. The study of minimal response tokens in discourse, such as *yeah*, *mmhm*, etc., which are very frequent in certain types of interaction, therefore requires less data to be collected than the study of more lexicalised patterns which function as response tokens and which may be less frequent, such as *that's great* or *brilliant*.

3. Metadata

Apart from the process of recording the actual interaction between participants engaging in conversation, it is also important to collect and document further information about the event itself. Metadata, or 'data about data', is the conventional method used to do this. Burnard states that 'without metadata the investigator has nothing but disconnected words of unknowable provenance or authenticity' (2005: 31). Thus, metadata is critical to a corpus to help achieve the standards for *representativeness, balance* and *homogeneity* etc, outlined above (Sinclair 2005).

Burnard (2005) uses 'metadata' as an umbrella term which includes editorial, analytic, descriptive and administrative categories:

- Editorial metadata – providing information about the relationship between corpus components and their original source.
- Analytic metadata – providing information about the way in which corpus components have been interpreted and analysed.
- Descriptive metadata – providing classificatory information derived from internal or external properties of the corpus components.
- Administrative metadata – providing documentary information about the corpus itself, such as its title, its availability, its revision status, etc.

Metadata can be extremely useful when the corpus is shared and re-used by the community, and it also assists in the preservation of electronic texts. Metadata can be kept in a separate database or included as a 'header' at the start of each document (usually encoded through mark-up language). A separate database with this information makes it easier to compare different types of documents and has the distinct advantage that it can be further extended by other users of the same data. The documentation of the design rationale, as well as the various editorial processes that an individual text has been subjected to during the collection and archiving stages, allows other researchers to assess its suitability for their own research purposes, while at the same time enabling a critical evaluation of other studies that have drawn on this particular text to be carried out.

Permission and ethics

Typical practice in addressing ethics on a professional or institutional level suggests that corpus developers should ensure that formal written consent is received from all participants involved, *a priori* to carrying out the recording. Conventionally, this consent stipulates how recordings are to take place and how data is presented, and outlines the research purposes for which it is used (Leech *et al.* 1995; Thompson 2005). While a participant's consent to record may be relatively easy to obtain, and commonly involves a signature on a consent form, it is important to ensure that this consent holds true at every stage of the corpus compilation process.

It is also important to consider *consent to distribute* recorded material. This is distinct from the *consent to record* and should include reference to the way in which recorded data is accessed and by whom, as well as the channel by which it may be distributed. Participants should be informed that once the data is distributed, it can be difficult or impossible to deal with requests for retraction of consent at a later stage. It is therefore important that systems used for distribution and access of data can deal with different levels of consent, and replay the data, accordingly, to different end users.

A further issue when dealing with ethics of recording relates to the notion of anonymity and the process that is applied to the data to ensure that anonymity can be maintained. Traditional approaches to corpus development emphasise the importance of striving for anonymity when developing records of discourse situations, as a means of protecting the identities of those involved in the interaction. To achieve this, the names of participants and third parties are often modified or completely omitted, along with any other details which may make the identity of referents obvious (see Du Bois *et al.* 1992, 1993). The quest for anonymity can also extend to the use of specific words or phrases used, as well as topics of discussion or particular opinions deemed as 'sensitive' or 'in any way compromising to the subject' (Wray *et al.* 1998: 10–11).

Issues of anonymity are more easily addressed when constructing text-based, monomodal corpora. If the data used is already in the public domain and freely available, no alterations to the texts included are usually required. Otherwise, permission needs to be obtained from the relevant authors or publishers of texts (copyright holders), and specific guidelines concerning anonymity can subsequently be discussed and addressed with the authors, and alterations to the data made as necessary. Similar procedures are involved when constructing spoken corpora which are based solely on transcripts of the recorded events. Modifications in relation to names, places and other identifiers can here be made at the transcription stage, or as a next step following initial transcription of data.

Anonymity is more problematic when it comes to audio or video records of conversations in corpora. Audio data is 'raw' as it captures vocalisations of a person, existing as an 'audio fingerprint', which is specific to an individual. This makes it relatively easy to identify participants when audio files are replayed. Alteration of vocal output for the purpose of anonymisation can make it difficult for the recording to be used for further phonetic and prosodic analysis and is thus generally not advisable. A similar problem arises with the use of video data. Although it is possible to shadow, blur or pixellate video data in order to conceal the identity of speakers (see Newton *et al.* 2005 for a method for pixellating video), these measures can be difficult to apply in practice (especially with large datasets). In addition, such measures obscure facial features of the individual, blurring distinctions between gestures and language forms. As a result, datasets may become unusable for certain lines of linguistic enquiry.

Considering the difficulties involved in the anonymisation of audio-visual data, it is important to discuss these issues fully with the participants prior to the recording, and to ensure that participants understand the nature of the recording and the format of distribution and access. And while those who agree for their day-to-day activities to be recorded for research purposes may not be concerned about anonymity, the issue of protecting the identity of third parties remains an ethical challenge with such data, as does the issue of re-using and sharing contextually sensitive data recorded as part of multi-modal corpora.

This situation then raises a challenge that is central to the development of any corpus, namely, how can multi-site, multi-user, multi-source, multi-media datasets protect the rights of study participants as an integral part of the way in which they are constructed and used? Reconciling the desire for the traceability and probity of corpus data with the need for confidentiality and data protection requires serious consideration and should be addressed at the outset of any corpus development project.

4. How do I transcribe spoken data?

One of the biggest challenges in corpus linguistic research is probably the representation of spoken data. There is no doubt that the collection of spoken language is far more laborious than the collection of written samples, but the richness of this type of data can make the extra effort worthwhile. Unscripted, naturally occurring conversations can be particularly interesting for the study of spoken grammar and lexis, and for the analysis of the construction of meaning in interaction (McCarthy 1998; Carter 2004; Halliday 2004). However, the representation of spoken data is a major issue in this context as the recorded conversations have to undergo a transition from the spoken mode to the written before they can be included in a corpus. In transcribing spoken discourse we have to make various choices as to the amount of detail we wish to include in the written record. Since there are so many layers of detail that carry meaning in spoken interaction, this task can easily become a black hole (McCarthy 1998: 13) with a potentially infinite amount of contextual information to record (Cook 1990). The reason for this is that spoken interaction is essentially multi-modal in nature, featuring a careful interplay between textual, prosodic, gestural and environmental elements in the construction of meaning.

In terms of individual research projects it is therefore important to decide exactly on the purpose of the study, to determine what type of transcription is needed. It is advisable to identify the spoken features of interest at the outset, and to tailor the focus of the transcription accordingly. For example, a study of discourse structure might require the transcription to include overlaps but not detailed prosodic information. Transcription is thus 'a theoretical process reflecting theoretical goals and definitions' (Ochs 1979: 44, also see Edwards 1993 and Thompson 2005). It is best viewed as being 'both interpretative and constructive' (Lapadat and Lindsay 1999: 77; also see O'Connell and Kowal 1999: 104 and Cameron 2001).

At the same time there is a need to follow certain guidelines in the transcription in order to make them re-usable by the research community. This, in turn, would allow both the size and quality of corpus data available for linguistic research to be enhanced, without individuals or teams of researchers expending large amounts of time and resources in starting from scratch each time a spoken corpus is required.

There are now a number of different types of transcription conventions available, including those adopted by the Network of European Reference Corpora (NERC), which was used for the spoken component of the COBUILD project (Sinclair 1987). This transcription system contains four layers, ranging from basic orthographic representation to very detailed transcription, including information about prosody. Another set of guidelines for transcribing spoken data has been recommended by the Text Encoding Initiative (TEI) and has been applied, for example, to the British National

Corpus (BNC – see Sperberg-McQueen and Burnard 1994). These guidelines include the representation of structural, contextual, prosodic, temporal and kinesic elements of spoken interactions and provide a useful resource for the transcription of different levels of detail required to meet particular research goals.

The level of detail of transcription reflects the basic needs of the type of research that they are intended to inform. One of the corpora that has been transcribed to a particularly advanced level of detail is the London–Lund corpus (Svartvik 1990). Alongside the standard encoding of textual structure, speaker turns and overlaps, this corpus also includes prosodic information and has remained a valuable resource for a wide range of researchers over the years.

Wray *et al.* (1998) provide a rubric for some of the more universally used notations for orthographic transcription, which mark, for example, who is speaking and where interruptions, overlaps, backchannels and laughter occur in the discourse, as well as some basic distinct pronunciation variations. Basic textual transcription can be extended through the use of phonemic and phonetic transcription. Phonemic transcription is used to represent pronunciation. Phonetic transcription, on the other hand, uses the International Phonetic Alphabet (IPA – refer to Laver 1994; Wray *et al.* 1998; Canepari 2005), and indicates how specific successive sounds are used in a specific stretch of discourse.

The amount of information that can be included within a phonetic transcript is substantial, and as a result, again, it pays to be selective and to concentrate on marking only those features relevant to a specific research question.

Layout of transcript

Once decisions have been taken as to the features which are to be transcribed, and the level of granularity and detail of the information to be included, the next step is to decide on an appropriate layout of the transcription. There are many different possibilities for laying out a transcript but it is important to acknowledge that 'there will always be something of a tension between validity and ease of reading' (Graddol *et al.* 1994: 185).

The most commonly used format is still a linear representation of turns with varying degrees of detail in terms of overlapping speech, prosody and extra-linguistic information. The example in Figure 4.1 is taken from a sub-component of the Nottingham

```
<$2> <$=> Oh well I <\$=> I'm just reading things at the moment and
     just+
<$1> Right.
<$2> +kind of vague+
<$1> So what given that the amount of stuff on metaphor is huge?
<$2> Yeah well I've been looking through some of the stuff on scientific
     metaphors and+
<$1> Uh-huh.
<$2> +er particularly how they're used for educational purposes in+
<$1> Right.
<$2> +explaining concepts erm+
<$1> Yeah.
```

Figure 4.1 An example of transcribed speech, taken from the NMMC.

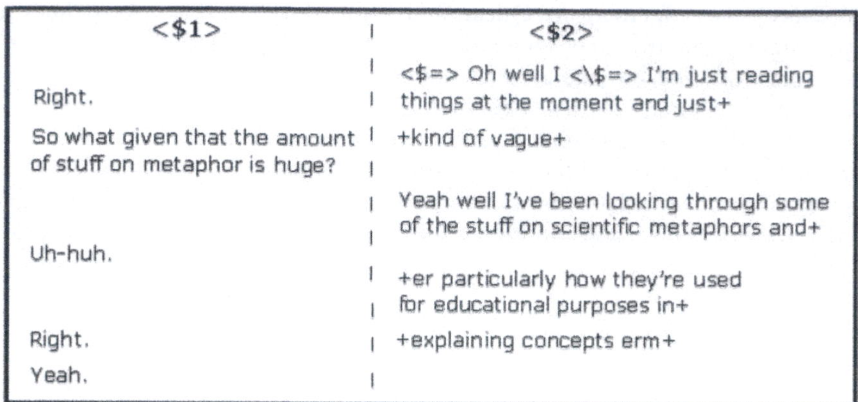

Figure 4.2 A column-based transcript.

Multi-Modal Corpus (NMMC). While this corpus is fully aligned with audio and video streams, the basic transcriptions are formatted as shown.

In Figure 4.1, speakers are denoted by < $1 > and < $2 > tags, false starts are framed by < $ = > and < \$ = >, while interruptions are indicated by the presence of the + tag.

The transcript seen in Figure 4.1 presents the data linearly, ordering the conversation in a temporal way, rather like a conventional drama script. It is relevant to note that, using a linear format of transcription, it is particularly difficult to show speaker overlap, and for this reason some prefer to use different columns and thus separate transcripts according to who is speaking (see Thompson 2005). Therefore, since speech is rarely 'orderly' in the sense that one speaker speaks at a time, linear transcription may be seen as a misrepresentation of discourse structure (Graddol *et al.* 1994: 182). This criticism is particularly resonant if, for example, four or five speakers are present in a conversation and where there is a high level of simultaneous speech.

The use of column transcripts (Figure 4.2) allows for a better representation of overlapping speech, presenting contributions from each speaker on the same line rather than with one positioned after the other (for further discussion on column transcripts see Graddol *et al.* 1994: 183; Thompson 2005).

A final, alternative method of representing speech in a transcript can be seen in Figure 4.3 (based on Dahlmann and Adolphs 2007; see also Dahlmann and Adolphs 2009).

Here the speech is presented as a musical score, with the talk of each speaker arranged on an individual line (or track) on the score. Speech is arranged according to the time at which it occurred. Overlapping contributions are indicated (as with Figure 4.2) as text which is positioned at the same point along the score, the time line, across each individual speaker track. The contributions of multiple speakers can be represented using this method of transcription. This method of transcription is based on a similar principle to that used in transcription and coding software, such as Anvil (Kipp 2001) and DRS (French *et al.* 2006).

Ongoing advancements in the representation and alignment of different data streams have started to provide possibilities for studying spoken discourse in an integrated framework including textual, prosodic and video data. The alignment of the different elements and the software needed to analyse such a multi-modal resource are still in the early stages of development, and at the present time it is probably beyond the scope of

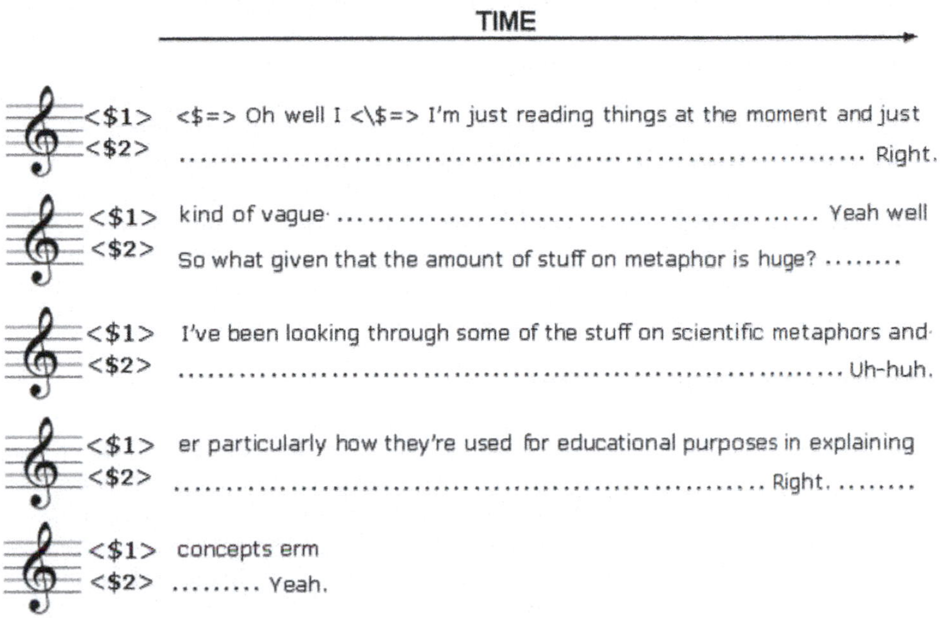

TIME

<$1> <$=> Oh well I <\$=> I'm just reading things at the moment and just
<$2> .... Right.

<$1> kind of vague· .... Yeah well
<$2> So what given that the amount of stuff on metaphor is huge? ....

<$1> I've been looking through some of the stuff on scientific metaphors and·
<$2> .... Uh-huh.

<$1> er particularly how they're used for educational purposes in explaining
<$2> .... Right. ....

<$1> concepts erm
<$2> .... Yeah.

Figure 4.3 Line-aligned transcription in a musical score type format.

the majority of individual corpus projects to develop a searchable resource that includes the kind of dynamic representation that would address the need for a less linear layout of transcription.

Coding spoken data

The coding stage refers to 'the assignment of events to stipulated symbolic categories' (Bird and Liberman 2001: 26). This is the stage where qualitative records of events start to become quantifiable, as specific items that are relevant to the variables under consideration are marked up for future analyses (Scholfield 1995: 46). The coding stage is essentially a development of the transcription stage, providing further detail to the basic systems of annotation and mark-up applied through the use of transcription notation. The coding stage thus operates at a higher level of abstraction compared to the transcription stage, and may include, among others, annotation of grammatical, semantic, pragmatic or discoursal features or categories.

Coding is a key part of the process of annotating language resources. This process is often undertaken with the use of coding software. The majority of corpora include some type of annotation as they allow corpora to be navigated in an automated way.

Early standards for the mark-up of corpora, known as the SGML (Standard Generalised Mark-up Language, which has been succeeded by XML), were developed in the 1980s. SGML was traditionally used for marking up features such as line breaks and paragraph boundaries, typeface and page layout, providing standards for structuring both transcription and annotation. SGML is used in the 100-million-word BNC corpus. With modern advances in technology, and associated advances in the sophistication of corpora and corpora tools, movements towards a redefinition of SGML have been prompted.

Most notably, in the late 1990s, early advances were made for what was termed the CES, *Corpus Encoding Standard*. The CES promised to provide 'encoding conventions for linguistic corpora designed to be optimally suited for use in language engineering and to serve as a widely accepted set of encoding standards for corpus-based work' (Ide 1998: 1). The CES planned to provide a set of coding conventions to cater for all corpora of any size and/or form (i.e. spoken or written corpora), comprising of an XML-based mark-up language (known as XCES). The standardised nature of these conventions aims to allow coded data and related analyses to be re-used and transferred across different corpora. However, the majority of corpora today still use modified versions of the SGML, or adopt their own conventions (mainly based on XML, as used in the BNC).

5. Analysing spoken corpora

There are a number of chapters in this volume which deal with the analysis of spoken corpora, so this issue will not be covered here in any detail. Other chapters in this volume discuss the implications of the unique nature of spoken discourse in terms of its implications for any type of spoken corpus analysis (see, for example, chapters by Evison, Vo and Carter, Rühlemann, this volume). The discourse level frameworks that may be of use for the analysis of spoken corpora are not necessarily compatible with the kind of concordance-based and frequency-driven analysis that is often used in large-scale lexicography studies. One of the key differences between spoken and written corpora is that most spoken discourse is collaborative in nature and as such it is more fluid and marked by emerging and changing orientations of the participants (McCarthy 1998).

Yet it is important to identify external categories for grouping transcripts in a corpus, especially when we are concerned with analysing levels of formality and other functions which need to be judged against the wider context of the encounter. This is often more straightforward when dealing with written texts as many of the genres that tend to form the basis of large written corpora are readily recognised as belonging to a particular category, such as fiction versus non-fiction, letters versus e-mails, etc. The group membership of such texts is more clearly demarcated than is the case with the majority of spoken discourse. The development of suitable frameworks for analysing spoken corpus data is thus particularly complex and further research is needed to explore and evaluate ways in which the analysis of concordance data and discourse phenomena can be fully integrated.

The development of techniques and tools to record, store and analyse naturally occurring interaction in spoken corpora has revolutionised the way in which we describe language and human interaction. Spoken corpora serve as an invaluable resource for the research of a large range of diverse communities and disciplines, including computer scientists, social scientists and researchers in the arts and humanities, policy makers and publishers. In order to be able to share resources across these diverse communities, it is important that spoken corpora are developed in a way that enables re-usability. This can be achieved through the use of guidelines and frameworks for recording, representing and replaying spoken discourse. In this chapter we have outlined some of the issues that surround these three stages of spoken corpus development and analysis. As advances in technology allow us to develop new kinds of spoken corpora, which include audio-visual data-streams, as well as a much richer description of contextual variables, it will become increasingly important to agree on conventions for recording and representing this kind of data, and the associated metadata. Similarly, advances in voice-to-text software may ease the burden of transcription, but will also rely heavily on the ability to follow clearly articulated conventions for coding and transcribing communicative events. Adherence to agreed conventions of this kind, especially when developing new kinds of multi-modal and contextually enhanced spoken corpora, will significantly extend the scope of spoken corpus linguistics in the future.

Further reading

Adolphs, S. (2006) *Introducing Electronic Text Analysis*. London and New York: Routledge. (This book contains chapters on spoken corpus analysis and corpus pragmatics.)

Kress, G. and van Leeuwen, T. (2001) *Multimodal Discourse: The Modes and Media of Contemporary Communication*. London: Arnold. (This text provides an introduction to the notion of the 'multi-modal' in linguistic research.)

McCarthy, M. (1998) *Spoken Language and Applied Linguistics*. Cambridge: Cambridge University Press. (This book covers a wide range of issues relating to the use of spoken corpora in the broad area of Applied Linguistics.)

Wynne, M. (ed.) (2005) *Developing Linguistic Corpora: A Guide to Good Practice*. Oxford: Oxbow Books. (This book provides a general overview of some of the key issues and challenges faced in the construction of corpora; from collection to analysis.)

References

Adolphs, S., Brown, B., Carter, R., Crawford, P. and Sahota, O. (2004) 'Applying Corpus Linguistics in a Health Care Context', *Journal of Applied Linguistics* 1: 9–28.

Aijmer, K. (2002) *English Discourse Particles: Evidence from a Corpus*. Amsterdam: John Benjamins.

Anderson, J., Beavan, D. and Kay, C. (2007) 'SCOTS: Scottish Corpus of Texts and Speech', in J. Beal, K. Corrigan and H. Moisl (eds) *Creating and Digitizing Language Corpora: Volume 1: Synchronic Databases*. Basingstoke: Palgrave Macmillan, pp. 17–34.

Anderson, W. and Beavan, D. (2005) 'Internet Delivery of Time-synchronised Multimedia: The SCOTS Corpus', *Proceedings from the Corpus Linguistics Conference Series* 1(1): 1747–93.

Ashby, S., Bourban, S., Carletta, J., Flynn, M., Guillemot, M., Hain, T., Kadlec, J., Karaiskos, V., Kraaij, W., Kronenthal, M., Lathoud, G., Lincoln, M., Lisowska, A., McCowan, I., Post, W., Reidsma, D. and Wellner, P. (2005) 'The AMI Meeting Corpus', in *Proceedings of Measuring Behavior 2005*. Wageningen, Netherlands, pp. 4–8.

Biber, D., Johansson, S., Leech, G., Conrad, S. and Finegan, E. (1999) *Longman Grammar of Spoken and Written English*. Longman: Pearson.

Bird, S. and Liberman, M. (2001) 'A Formal Framework for Linguistic Annotation', *Speech Communication* 33(1–2): 23–60.

Bolton, K., Nelson, G. and Hung, J. (2003) 'A Corpus-based Study of Connectors in Student Writing: Research from the International Corpus of English in Hong Kong (ICE-HK)', *International Journal of Corpus Linguistics* 7(2): 165–82.

Burnard, L. (2005) 'Developing Linguistic Corpora: Metadata for Corpus Work', in M. Wynne (ed.) *Developing Linguistic Corpora: A Guide to Good Practice*. Oxford: Oxbow Books, pp. 30–46.

Cameron, D. (2001) *Working with Spoken Discourse*. London: Sage.

Canepari, L. (2005) *A Handbook of Phonetics*. Munich: Lincom Europa.

Carter, R. (2004) *Language and Creativity: The Art of Common Talk*. London: Routledge.

Carter, R. and Adolphs, S. (2008) 'Linking the Verbal and Visual: New Directions for Corpus Linguistics'', 'Language, People, Numbers', special issue of *Language and Computers* 64: 275–91.

Carter, R. and McCarthy, M. (2006) *Cambridge Grammar of English: A Comprehensive Guide to Spoken and Written Grammar and Usage*. Cambridge: Cambridge University Press.

Cheng, W. and Warren, M. (1999) 'Facilitating a Description of Intercultural Conversations: The Hong Kong Corpus of Conversational English', *ICAME Journal* 23: 5–20.

——(2000) 'The Hong Kong Corpus of Spoken English: Language Learning through Language Description', in L. Burnard and T. McEnery (eds) *Rethinking Language Pedagogy from a Corpus Perspective: Papers from the Third International Conference on Teaching and Language Corpora*. Frankfurt: Lang, pp. 133–44.

——(2002) '// aa beef ball // a you like //: The Intonation of Declarative-Mood Questions in a Corpus of Hong Kong English', *Teanga* 21: 1515–26.

Conrad, S. (2002) 'Corpus Linguistic Approaches for Discourse Analysis', *Annual Review of Applied Linguistics* 22: 75–95.

Cook, G. (1990) 'Transcribing Infinity: Problems of Context Presentation', *Journal of Pragmatics* 14: 1–24.

Cotterill, J. (2004) 'Collocation, Connotation and Courtroom Semantics: Lawyers Control of Witness Testimony through Lexical Negotiation', *Applied Linguistics* 25: 513–37.

Crabtree, A., Benford, S., Greenhalgh, C., Tennent, P., Chalmers, M. and Brown, B. (2006) 'Supporting Ethnographic Studies of Ubiquitous Computing in the Wild', in *DIS'06: Proceedings of the 6th Conference on Designing Interactive Systems*. New York, USA, pp. 60–9.

Dahlmann, I. and Adolphs, S. (2007) 'Designing Multi-modal Corpora to Support the Study of Spoken Language – A Case Study', poster delivered at the Third Annual International eSocial Science Conference, October 2007, University of Michigan, USA.

——(2009) 'Spoken Corpus Analysis: Multi-modal Approaches to Language Description', in P. Baker (ed.) *Contemporary Approaches to Corpus Linguistics*. London: Continuum Press, pp. 125–39.

De Cock, S., Granger, S., Leech, G. and McEnery, T. (1998) 'An Automated Approach to the Phrasicon of EFL Learners', in S. Granger (ed.) *Learner English on Computer*. London: Longman, pp. 67–79.

Douglas, F. (2003) 'The Scottish Corpus of Texts and Speech: Problems of Corpus Design', *Literary and Linguistic Computing* 18(1): 23–37.

Du Bois, J., Schuetze-Coburn, S., Paolino, D. and Cumming, S. (1992) 'Discourse Transcription', *Santa Barbara Papers in Linguistics*, Vol. 4. Santa Barbara, CA: UC Santa Barbara.

——(1993) 'Outline of Discourse Transcription', in J. A. Edwards and M. D. Lampert (eds) *Talking Data: Transcription and Coding Methods for Language Research*. Hillsdale, NJ: Lawrence Erlbaum, pp. 45–89.

Edwards, J. (1993) 'Principles and Contrasting Systems of Discourse Transcription', in J. Edwards and M. Lampert (eds) *Talking Data: Transcription and Coding in Discourse Research*. Hillsdale, NJ: Lawrence Erlbaum Associates, pp. 3–44.

Farr, F., Murphy, B. and O'Keeffe, A. (2004) 'The Limerick Corpus of Irish English: Design, Description and Application', *Teanga* 21: 5–29.

French, A., Greenhalgh, C., Crabtree, A., Wright, W., Brundell, B., Hampshire, A. and Rodden, T. (2006) 'Software Replay Tools for Time-based Social Science Data', in *Proceedings of the 2nd Annual International e-Social Science Conference*, available at www.ncess.ac.uk/events/conference/2006/papers /abstracts/FrenchSoftwareReplayTools.shtml (accessed 1 February 2009).

Graddol, D., Cheshire, J. and Swann, J. (1994) *Describing Language*. Buckingham: Open University Press.

Halliday, M. A. K. (2004) 'The Spoken Language Corpus: A Foundation for Grammatical Theory', in K. Aijmer and B. Altenberg (eds) *Advances in Corpus Linguistics*. Amsterdam: Rodopi, pp. 11–38.

Ide, N. (1998) 'Corpus Encoding Standard: SGML Guidelines for Encoding Linguistic Corpora', First International Language Resources and Evaluation Conference, Granada, Spain.

Kendon, A. (1982) 'The Organisation of Behaviour in Face-to-face Interaction: Observations on the Development of a Methodology', in K. R. Scherer and P. Ekman (eds) *Handbook of Methods in Nonverbal Behaviour Research*. Cambridge: Cambridge University Press, pp. 440–505.

Kilgarriff, A. (1996) 'Which Words are Particularly Characteristic of a Text? A Survey of Statistical Procedures', in *Proceedings of the AISB Workshop of Language Engineering for Document Analysis and Recognition*. Guildford: Sussex University, pp. 33–40.

Kipp, M. (2001) 'Anvil – A Generic Annotation Tool for Multimodal Dialogue', in P. Dalsgaard, B. Lindberg, H. Benner and Z.-H. Tan (eds) *Proceedings of 7th European Conference on Speech Communication and Technology 2nd INTERSPEECH Event Aalborg, Denmark*. Aalborg: ISCA, pp. 1367–70, available at www.isca-speech.org/archive/eurospeech_2001

Knight, D. and Adolphs, S. (2006) *Text, Talk and Corpus Analysis* [academic online module, restricted access], University of Nottingham, UK.

Knight, D., Bayoumi, S., Mills, S., Crabtree, A., Adolphs, S., Pridmore, T. and Carter, R. A. (2006) 'Beyond the Text: Construction and Analysis of Multi-modal Linguistic Corpora', *Proceedings of the 2nd International Conference on e-Social Science, Manchester, 28–30 June 2006*, available at www.ncess.ac.uk/events/conference/2006/papers/abstracts/KnightBeyondTheText.shtml (accessed 4 January 2009).

Lapadat, J. C. and Lindsay, A. C. (1999) 'Transcription in Research and Practice: From Standardisation of Technique to Interpretative Positioning', *Qualitative Inquiry* 5(1): 64–86.

Laver, J. (1994) *Principles of Phonetics*. Cambridge: Cambridge University Press.

Leech, G., Myers, G. and Thomas, J. (eds) (1995) *Spoken English on Computer: Transcription, Mark-up and Application*. London: Longman.

McCarthy, M. (1998) *Spoken Language and Applied Linguistics*. Cambridge: Cambridge University Press.

Morrison, A., Tennent, P., Williamson, J. and Chalmers, M. (2007) 'Using Location, Bearing and Motion Data to Filter Video and System Logs', in *Proceedings of the Fifth International Conference on Pervasive Computing*. Toronto: Springer, pp. 109–26.

Newton, E. M., Sweeney, L. and Malin, B. (2005) 'Preserving Privacy by De-identifying Face Images', *IEEE Transactions on Knowledge and Data Engineering* 17(2): 232–43.

Ochs, E. (1979) 'Transcription as Theory', in E. Ochs and B. B. Schieffelin (eds) *Developmental Pragmatics*. New York: Academic Press. pp. 43–72.

O'Connell, D.C. and Kowal, S. (1999) 'Transcription and the Issue of Standardisation', *Journal of Psycholinguistic Research* 28(2): 103–20.

O'Keeffe, A. (2006) *Investigating Media Discourse*. London: Routledge.

Psathas, G. and Anderson, T. (1990) 'The "Practices" of Transcription in Conversation Analysis', *Semiotica* 78(1/2): 75–99.

Reppen, R. and Simpson, R. (2002) 'Corpus Linguistics', in N. Schmitt (ed.) *An Introduction to Applied Linguistics*. London: Arnold, pp. 92–111.

Scholfield, P. (1995) *Quantifying Language*. Clevedon: Multilingual Matters.

Simpson, R., Lucka, B. and Ovens, J. (2000) 'Methodological Challenges of Planning a Spoken Corpus with Pedagogic Outcomes', in L. Burnard and T. McEnery (eds) *Rethinking Language Pedagogy from a Corpus Perspective: Papers from the Third International Conference on Teaching and Language Corpora*. Frankfurt: Lang, pp. 43–9.

Sinclair, J. (1987) 'Collocation: A Progress Report', in R. Steele and T. Threadgold (eds) *Language Topics: Essays in Honour of Michael Halliday*. Amsterdam: John Benjamins.

——(2004) *Trust the Text: Language, Corpus and Discourse*. London: Routledge.

——(2005) 'Corpus and Text-basic Principles', in M. Wynne (ed.) *Developing Linguistic Corpora: A Guide to Good Practice*. Oxford: Oxbow Books, pp. 1–16.

——(2008) 'Borrowed Ideas', in A. Gerbig and O. Mason (eds) *Language, People, Numbers – Corpus Linguistics and Society*. Amsterdam: Rodopi BV, pp. 21–42.

Sperberg-McQueen, C. M. and Burnard, L. (1994) *Guidelines for Electronic Text Encoding and Interchange (TEI P3)*. Chicago and Oxford: ACH-ALLC-ACL Text Encoding Initiative.

Strassel, S. and Cole, A. W. (2006) 'Corpus Development and Publication', Proceedings of the Fifth International Conference on Language Resources and Evaluation (LREC) *2006*, available at http://papers.ldc.upenn.edu/LREC2006/CorpusDevelopmentAndPublication.pdf (accessed 4 January 2009).

Stuart, K. (2005) 'New Perspectives on Corpus Linguistics', *RAEL: revista electrónica de lingüística aplicada* 4: 180–91, available at http://dialnet.unirioja.es/servlet/articulo?codigo=1426958 (accessed 4 January 2009).

Svartvik, J. (ed.) (1990) 'The London Corpus of Spoken English: Description and Research', *Lund Studies in English 82*. Lund: Lund University Press.

Tennent, P., Crabtree, A. and Greenhalgh, C. (2008) 'Ethno-goggles: Supporting Field Capture of Qualitative Material', *Proceedings of the 4th International e-Social Science Conference*, 18–20 June, University of Manchester: ESRC NCeSS.

Thompson, P. (2005) 'Spoken Language Corpora', in M. Wynne (ed.) *Developing Linguistic Corpora: A Guide to Good Practice*. Oxford: Oxbow Books, pp. 59–70, available at http://ahds.ac.uk/linguistic-corpora/ (accessed 4 January 2009).

Wray, A., Trott, K. and Bloomer, A. (1998) *Projects in Linguistics: A Practical Guide to Researching Language*. London: Arnold.

Wynne, M. (2005) 'Archiving, Distribution and Preservation', in M. Wynne (ed.) *Developing Linguistic Corpora: A Guide to Good Practice*. Oxford: Oxbow Books, pp. 71–8.

5

Building a written corpus

What are the basics?

Mike Nelson

1. Introduction: what does building a written corpus entail?

It is clear at the outset that there are a huge number of variables involved in building a written corpus that need to be considered before beginning what can be a very daunting task. Some of these issues are related to all corpus creation, and others can be seen to be specific to written corpora. In general terms, the very first question to ask oneself is 'Do I have to do this?' The exponential rise of available electronic corpora over the last twenty years has provided the academic community with an enormous amount of ready-made data that can be accessed easily on-line. Thus the question of 'Why build a new corpus?' must be very seriously considered. If you do decide to continue, then the purpose of the corpus must be very clear – what do you want to achieve by creating the corpus and what will it be used for? Depending on your answer to these questions, there then come crucial decisions to make regarding the size of the corpus, of how it should be balanced, the sampling methods to use, the kinds of texts that should be used, the use of full, or samples of, text and how representativeness could be achieved. Further issues concern whether you want to create a corpus for a specialist purpose or for more general purposes. When you have planned your corpus and the content it will contain, will you stick to this plan rigidly, or will you take texts from where you can readily get them? Finally, there are psychological elements attached to corpus creation: planning, finding, gathering and formatting data over a long period of time can be mentally very taxing and requires a project planner's approach to the task.

There are also further issues that are specific to written corpora. There is a commonly held belief that creating a written corpus is easier than creating a spoken corpus. While this may to some extent be true, there are still many difficulties involved in the creation of a written corpus: for example, in the choosing of texts, gaining access to the texts you require and dealing with the process of turning text into a computer-readable format, followed by storage and analysis. This chapter will attempt to provide assistance and advice on these issues and hopefully provide an insight into the whole process of building a written corpus from inception to completion. In the first part of the chapter the general areas mentioned above will be considered with reference to the literature and also with specific reference to how some well-known written corpora have been designed. The next section deals with the gathering, computerising and organisation of written data, including a brief review of optical character recognition (OCR) software. There is then a mention of storage and analysis of data. In my own research, I have created three different written corpora that each presented different challenges. As the chapter progresses, these corpora are referred to so that the theory behind corpus building can be given a practical application.

2. Planning a written corpus

There is common consensus in the world of corpora that a corpus is 'not simply a collection of texts' (Biber *et al.* 1998: 246). By implication, therefore, a clear and detailed plan needs to be created long before anything else can be done. This notion should also be tempered with the realities of data collection (Kilgariff *et al.* 2006 discuss detailed corpus design and the comparison made between the design document and final corpus composition). Whatever the difficulties, however, the initial planning document is of great importance and the following section will now address the elements that need to be considered when designing a written corpus. The first design element, however, is whether a design is needed at all.

Why create a new written corpus?

Reading the chapter by David Lee in this book will give you an idea of the vast number of corpora available today. His website presents, among other things, an overview of corpora currently available (see also the *CALPER* website of the Pennsylvania State University, USA). Thus, before any decision is made regarding corpus creation, a great deal of thought needs to be given to whether or not an existing corpus would serve the purposes of your research. It may be that a given corpus may have a small section within it that would be suitable, or possibly could be used to supplement a corpus that you may later create. Essentially, you have to ask yourself whether creating a new corpus will bring something new to both your research and the research community. One further factor that must also be taken into consideration is that although many corpora do already exist, access to them may not always be possible, leaving you in the unfortunate position of having to re-invent the wheel. Contact with the creators at an early stage of your work should tell you whether this will be a problem or not.

If you decide to go ahead with creating a written corpus, there must follow several decisions that need to be made in the planning process. All these decisions depend on the purpose to which you will put your corpus. The different types of corpora are discussed elsewhere in this book and so will not be discussed in detail here, but, whatever the purpose of your corpus, one of the first considerations is how big it should be.

How big should the written corpus be?

The question of the size of corpora has been central to recent corpus development, and there has been the overriding belief among many corpus creators that 'biggest is best'. Briefly, the discussion can be seen in terms of creating corpora to be as large as possible, for example for lexicographic projects, as opposed to creating smaller, more specialist corpora, often for pedagogical purposes. Thus, the purpose to which the corpus is ultimately put is a critical factor in deciding its size. If you are reading this book and considering corpus creation, it is probable that a smaller corpus is more likely to be your aim, but some issues of what is considered to be an adequate size for a corpus need to be discussed (see Sinclair 2002 for a succinct summary of this issue, which he refers to as the 'incredible shrinking corpora'.)

While the early corpora of the 1960s were modest in size by the standards of today, there was already a pervasive attitude that bigger corpora would be better. Halliday and Sinclair (1966) proposed the necessity of a corpus of around twenty million words. This was unrealistic at the time, but between the 1960s and 1980s corpora rapidly grew in size, encompassing the 'three generations' of Leech (1991) from several hundred thousand words to several hundred million (British National Corpus [BNC], Bank of English, Cambridge International Corpus [CIC], which stands at one billion words). This view of the need for large corpora was summed up by Sinclair when he said that 'The only guidance I would give is that a corpus should be as large as possible and keep on growing' (1991: 18). Sinclair based this need for large corpora on the fact that words are unevenly distributed in texts and that most words occur only once. Thus 'In order to study the behaviour of words in texts, we need to have available quite a large number of occurrences' (Sinclair 1991: 18). While this view of corpora was the prevailing one, it did not go unchallenged.

A movement then grew in the 1990s that was more concerned with corpus exploitation than corpus exploration (Ma 1993; Tribble 1997, 1998; Flowerdew 1998). This movement saw the value of smaller corpora and stressed their pedagogical purpose over their lexicographical potential. Small corpora, it was held, can be very useful, providing they can offer a 'balanced' and 'representative' picture of a specific area of the language. This recognition of a need for smaller, more specialised corpora increased. Ma (1993) noted that the division of corpora based on size is between corpora that are used for examining 'general' English, and those that are used for examining more specific areas of language use. The usefulness of smaller corpora was seen to be a *pedagogical* usefulness, as opposed to a *general explorative* usefulness – Ma related this utility of smaller corpora to 'groups of learners' (1993: 17). He also listed a number of 'pedagogic' corpora ranging in size from a corpus of philosophy texts at 6,854 words to a corpus of over one million words (Ma 1993: 17). Tribble's use of 'exemplar texts' to exemplify genres, while keeping the overall size of the corpus down to manageable levels, continued this trend and he noted that 'If you are involved in language teaching rather than lexicography, single word lists from small selective corpora can be seriously useful' (Tribble 1997). The further pedagogical usefulness of small corpora was suggested by Howarth (1998) in relation to teaching non-native speakers and de Beaugrande (2001) distinguished between small specialist corpora and what he terms 'learnable' corpora that are built using examples of language that match the fluency levels of specific groups of learners.

To summarise, corpora that have been used for lexicographical purposes – looking at the whole language – have, perhaps by necessity, always been created to be as large as possible. However, the need for smaller corpora – looking at specific areas of the language – has been recognised, especially in relation to teaching and use in the language classroom. Kennedy (1998: 68) noted that researchers should therefore 'bear in mind that the quality of the data they work with is at least as important [as the size]'.

Case study: Determining the size of a corpus

The Business English Corpus (BEC) was created between 1998 and 2000 to represent the language used in business by native speakers (see website for full details.) The corpus has both written and spoken elements, but the principles used to determine size can be applied to written corpora; three main criteria were used: *pragmatic*, *historical* and *pedagogical*. Practical considerations must always play a part in corpus creation and the larger lexicographical corpora such as the BNC and COBUILD that run into hundreds of millions of words were not a feasible option for one lone researcher to undertake. Meyer (2002: 32–3) notes that for the American component of ICE it was calculated that eight hours of work was needed to process a 2,000-word sample of written text. Thus resources must always be weighed against projected corpus size. Once the decision had been made that a smaller corpus was to be created, the figure of one million words was arrived at as a result of the two remaining criteria. The second criterion used was that of historical precedent. The figure of one million seems to be a 'magic' number in terms of older corpora size. Many influential older corpora – what Leech (1991) called the 'first generation' – were around the one-million-word mark or often much smaller in size. Examples of this are the Survey of English Usage (SEU) at University College London at one million words, and the Brown Corpus. There was, therefore, a historical reason for the one-million-word target size of the BEC. In addition to this tradition, smaller, specialist corpora, of which the BEC is one, have often used the one-million-word mark (or smaller) as a target number of running words. Comparative specialist corpora to the BEC would be the Guangzhou Petroleum English Corpus of 411,612 words, the Hong Kong University of Science and Technology (HKUST) Computer Science Corpus at one million words and the Århus Corpus of Contract Law, also at one million words. Fang (1993) in describing the creation of the HKUST corpus, specifically referred to the older generation of corpora, giving their size as one of the reasons for their choice of size. Additionally, he added that 'one million words represent a reasonably large proportion of the finite subset of the language under study' (Fang 1993: 74). As the BEC is not meant as a general English corpus, and in line with the specialist corpora noted above, one million words was deemed a reasonable sample size in order to achieve a representative picture of Business English. The final reason for the one-million-word size of the BEC was pedagogical. Smaller corpora enable easier access to the data found in them. This in turn leads to easier transferral of results to the classroom.

One final point can be mentioned. In some cases, the overall size of a corpus can be secondary to the need for adequate sampling. Thus, a second, written corpus of Business English textbooks that was created for the same project (Nelson 2000) had no predetermined goals for overall size. In this case, the sampling procedures, to be described later in this chapter, set the final number of books to be included at thirty-three, which in turn affected the final size of the corpus, which came to 593,294 running words (Meyer 2002: 33 refers to Biber's 1993 use of statistical procedures to determine corpus size by calculating the frequency of occurrences of linguistic features in a text).

Once the size of the corpus has been considered, the issues of sampling, balance and representativeness are then the next matters to be dealt with.

3. Sampling, balancing and making your written corpus representative

These three issues cannot be seen in isolation: in order to achieve an acceptable level of representativeness, the problems of sample size and balance must also be addressed. However, it should also be remembered that the corpus itself is a sample and needs to be representative of a given aspect or aspects of language so that 'The first step towards achieving this aim is to define the whole of which the corpus is to be a sample'(Renouf 1987: 2).

Defining the sample base

Any corpus creator is faced with a 'chicken and egg' situation. In order to study language, be it general or specific, one must first decide what that language is, what defines it and where it can be found. As a result of this 'chicken and egg' situation, sampling and representativeness are difficult problems. These problems have dogged corpus linguists since the beginning and still do today. Clear (1992) gave three main reasons why sampling can be problematic for the corpus linguist. First, there is the problem noted above, that the population from which the sample is to be drawn is poorly defined. Second, 'there is no obvious unit of language which is to be sampled and which can be used to define the population' (Clear 1992: 21). Finally, considering the size of any aspect of language, the researcher can never be sure that all instances have been accounted for satisfactorily, and Clear on the 'Corpora' bulletin board noted as follows:

> I have a favourite analogy for corpus linguistics: it's like studying the sea. The output of a language like English has much in common with the sea; e.g. – both are very very large ... – and difficult to define precisely, – subject to constant flux, currents, influences, never constant, – part of everyday human and social reality. Our corpus building is analogous to collecting bucketfuls of sea water and carrying them back to the lab. It is not physically possible to take measurements and make observations about all the aspects of the sea we are interested in *in vivo*, so we collect samples to study *in vitro*.
>
> (Clear 1997, personal communication)

More recently, Kilgariff *et al.* noted that 'There are no generally agreed objective criteria that can be applied to this task: at best, corpus designers strive for a reasonable representation of the full repertoire of available text types' (Kilgariff *et al.* 2006: 129). A corpus, virtually by definition, is therefore biased to a greater or lesser extent. Yet despite the difficulties, sampling is still necessary. We need to determine how many samples will be representative, how big the samples should be, and what kind of samples to use (full text or extracts).

How many samples?

The number of samples to be used in a corpus must be determined by the area under study, the linguistic variation that can be found in that area and the final purpose to which the corpus will be put. In influential work done in the 1980s and 1990s, Biber argued that the internal variation found within a given genre should determine how much of that genre should be included in a corpus (Biber 1988). However, Douglas (2003) reporting on work done with the Scottish Corpus of Texts and Speech (SCOTS Project), while stressing the importance of familiarity with the linguistic idiosyncrasies of the language varieties under analysis, noted that it is difficult to know where one variety ends and another begins, making the problem of linguistic variation more thorny. Yet there is help to be found with the problem of the number of samples to use. Meyer

(2002: 42–4) gives a useful summary of sampling techniques used in the social sciences by establishing a 'sampling frame' which is achieved 'by identifying a specific population that one wishes to make generalizations about' (Meyer 2002: 42). This methodical use of pre-selected samples is known as 'probability sampling'.

A good example of this approach was in the creation of the BNC. In order to determine the number of samples used, various sources of information were utilised to gain an overview of the chosen area. In the written section of the corpus the creators first made the distinction between language that is produced (written) and language that is received (read). They then gathered information on written texts from catalogues of books published per annum, best-seller lists, prize-winners, library lending statistics, lists of current magazines and periodicals and periodical circulation figures. These all dealt with published data and the project faced a problem with unpublished data; therefore, in this area intuition had to be used (see the BNC User Manual, available online).

Another approach to sampling that is commonly used, though sometimes frowned upon, is that of 'non-probability' sampling. This means, in its extreme form, essentially just taking samples from where it is possible to get them; it is often termed 'convenience' or 'opportunistic' sampling. This practice has been widespread in corpus creation and has even been used in large and prestigious projects such as the BNC (see Burnard 2001 for an explanation of what went wrong in the design of the BNC). A further common practice is to use a combination of both: to set out a plan for the corpus and then attempt to fulfil it but then adopt a certain flexibility according to what texts can be obtained.

Whatever the approach used to determine the number of samples, the use of common sense, pragmatics and intuition seem to play a role in even the most carefully planned corpus. Further, the purpose of the corpus exerts a keen influence at this stage of design. The number of samples needs to be adjusted according to what is going to be studied: more samples for more general language issues and fewer for more specific. The next stage is then to determine the size and type of sample that is then gathered.

Sample size and make-up

There has long been a debate in the literature regarding optimal sample sizes in corpora. Early corpora used sample sizes of around 2,000 words randomly taken from carefully selected texts. Other writers criticised the small sample size of the early corpora but have suggested that an increase to around 20,000 words would provide a sample of adequate size to be representative of a genre. Oostdijk (1991) and Kennedy (1998) took this line and Oostdijk suggested that 'A sample size of 20,000 words would yield samples that are large enough to be representative of a given variety' (Oostdijk 1991: 50). In larger projects such as the BNC, target sample sizes of 40,000 words have been used. Once again, the size of your samples will depend on what linguistic features you are attempting to elucidate. In the BEC, which was discussed earlier, a minimum sample size of 20,000 words was decided upon for each genre. Yet this in itself can cause problems. There is, as Biber has pointed out, considerable variation within genre, in that for some genres 20,000 words would provide an adequate sample size. For others this would not. A good example of this dilemma was encountered in creating the BEC. For approximately 20,000 words, 114 faxes were collected from different sources. However, in the category of 'business books', 20,000 words would not cover even one book. For this reason, a larger sample size of 50,000 words was used for books, taking five 10,000 word samples from five different books. It is clear from this that for the faxes, all the text in the faxes was used: in the books only an extract was taken. This leads us to the next issue in sample make-up: that of the use of whole text or only extracts.

The choice of whether to use extracts or full texts has a significant impact on the kind of data that can be studied. Studies of discourse have shown us that 'few linguistic features of a text are distributed evenly throughout' (Stubbs 1996: 32) with the result that the use of only a small 'sample' of given text will inevitably miss out a great many features present. This is especially important when studying genre. Studies into genre have noted how certain linguistic features are typical of certain parts of a text and an approach to corpus creation that only takes extracts at random will fail to gain a representative sample in this respect. Thus, as with other aspects of corpus design, the purpose to which the corpus will be put is critical in deciding whether to use whole texts or not. The BNC, with 40,000 word extracts, did not use full text (partially for copyright reasons). They used continuous text within a whole, cutting the sample at a logical point such as at the end of a chapter. This approach is well suited to study of general language. In the BEC written section, which was concerned with the specialist language of business, whole texts were used wherever possible. The corpus was first categorised into language used for writing about business (books, journals, magazines) and then into language used for actually doing business. A breakdown of the written section can be seen in Tables 5.1 and 5.2.

Table 5.1 Writing about business

Part of corpus	*Tokens*	*Contents*
Business books	53,470	5 extracts from different books (approx. 10,000 words each)
Business newspapers	64,291	121 articles
Business journals & magazines	78,846	52 articles
Total	**196,607**	

Table 5.2 Writing to do business

Part of corpus	*Tokens*	*Contents*
Annual reports	34,537	3 annual reports
Bus press releases	21,656	29 business press releases
Business contracts	29,602	13 contracts/agreements
Business faxes	23,105	114 faxes
Business letters	26,793	94 letters
Business reports	62,908	17 reports
Company brochures	23,239	13 company brochures
Emails	28,857	202 e-mails
Job advertisements	22,293	87 job advertisements
Manuals	21,160	5 manuals
Memos	12,542	47 memos
Minutes	34,805	15 sets of minutes
Product brochures	26,175	19 product brochures
Quotations	8,997	21 quotations
Miscellaneous	2,427	Oht, job description and agendas
Total	**379,096**	

Balance and representativeness

The discussions on size and sampling above have necessarily touched on questions of representativeness and balance. When attempting to balance a corpus in order to give a representative view of the language chosen it is necessary to ask the question 'Representative of what?' In reality, there are so many variables that the notion of 'representativeness' can almost be seen as a 'non-concept'. Kennedy notes that 'it is not easy to be confident that a sample of texts can be thoroughly representative of all possible genres or even of a particular genre or subject field or topic' (Kennedy 1998: 62). Any attempt at corpus creation is therefore a compromise between the hoped for and the achievable. Yet we have already seen from work done on the BNC how representativeness and balance can be attempted by carefully stratifying the corpus beforehand. In the written component of the BNC, texts were included according to three selection criteria: domain, time and medium. In this way it was felt first that a 'microcosm' of the language could be presented and second that different types of texts could be compared with each other. However, retrospectively, Burnard (2001) admitted that the availability of electronic texts in some areas led to a skewing of data input to the BNC.

Case study: The Published Materials Corpus

In the corpus designed to represent published Business English materials, the Published Materials Corpus (PMC; Nelson 2000), balance and representativeness were achieved by surveying the popularity of use of books in the general market in order to provide an overview of those books actually in use at the time.

For the purpose of the study, the initial population for the PMC was defined as Business English materials published in the UK between 1986 and 1996. In order to gain a representative sample of this population, the PMC presented different problems from the BEC. A representative sample of Business English materials was needed in order to analyse exactly what the language of Business English teaching materials is. The problem was solved in the following way. In 1997, seven major distributors of EFL materials were contacted by phone and were asked to provide a list of their best-selling Business English titles of 1996. Of these, five of the seven responded. Actual sales figures were not available, but the rank order of popularity was obtained from each bookshop. Once the lists were collected, the books were ranked according to their position of popularity at each bookshop and averaged out over the five, so that an overall ranking of popularity was obtained covering all five bookshops. A total of thirty-eight books were obtained for the final list. The main factor, therefore, behind the content of the PMC was popularity of use of the books – it was considered of prime importance to have a corpus that represented the Business English books that teachers and students actually use. Once the sample had been gained in the manner described above, the books included could be broken down in terms of type of book included, gender of author and those books focusing on one or more of the 'four skills'.

Once specifications had been made as to the content of the corpora, the data had to be actually collected and entered into the computer. This stage represented the most difficult of all in this research and, in all, took just over three years to complete.

4. Gathering, computerising and organising written texts

Perhaps the greatest challenge facing corpus developers is that of obtaining the required texts. Where should one get text from? How do copyright issues affect data gathering and how should the texts be entered, stored, arranged and catalogued once they have been obtained?

At the outset it should be stated that perhaps the best source of texts for corpus usage are other, pre-existing corpora. It was noted earlier in this chapter that careful searching for similar corpora to what you may have in mind is perhaps the best place to start. It is then possible to perhaps collect a certain amount of data yourself and then supplement it with relevant sections of existing corpora. Once this avenue has been explored, it is possible to see that data can be obtained from two basic sources: publicly available texts and privately available sources.

Publicly available data

Publicly available data can be gathered from a variety of sources – newspapers, journals, magazines and a number of sites on the Internet. In a recent study, Ekbal and Bandyopadhyay (2008) describe the creation of their web-based Bengali news corpus. The data were gathered from the web archive of a popular Bengali newspaper by means of a web crawler that was able to automatically retrieve text in HTML format. The files were then cleaned of HTML formatting to leave just that text related to news items. Modern text analysis programs such as *WordSmith* version 5 (Scott 2007) allow automated web searching and download through its webfile downloader function. (An interesting problem occurred with the NCI project in that on downloading text from newswire services, it was found to contain duplicate text: different sources producing the same or very similar text. This had to be manually eliminated.) In all of the instances, the problem of copyright rears its head. Meyer (2002) notes that US copyright law states that while it is acceptable to copy texts for private/research usage, it is not allowed to put that text into electronic format and distribute it as part of a corpus. Further, laws vary from country to country, so the corpus compiler needs to be aware not only of the laws in their own country, but also of the laws in the country from where the text is being taken. One method to avoid problems with copyright is to use texts if appropriate from one of the many open source text archives available on the internet, such as Project Gutenberg. Using Google to search for 'text archives' results in a number of very useful sites (see especially www.copyright.gov/title17/ for a collection of open source text sites).

Private data

'Private' data here refers to data that are not in the public domain. The best advice that can be given here is that, depending on the type of corpus you are creating, you should use any personal contacts you may have, however tentative, to gain access to the documents you require. If one is personally known to the subjects beforehand, the chances of actually getting data are greatly increased. However, even with people one knows already, it is not always easy to persuade them to help. There has to be a degree of polite ruthlessness, as, depending on their position within a given company or institution, it is sometimes easier for them to refuse to help than to assist in the data gathering process. Thus a certain amount of persistence is needed. A further key issue is that of anonymisation of personal data, for example names and place names. In the BEC, text used a standardised format of replacement such, for example, that any person's name became the word 'personname' and any company became the word 'companyname'.

Data entry

Sinclair (1991: 14) identified three main methods of preparing data for entry into a corpus: *adaptation of data in electronic format, scanning* and *keyboarding*.

Adaptation of material already in electronic form

Text already in electronic format is perhaps the easiest to deal with and to obtain. However, there are some problems arising from the fact that many corpus readers need texts to be in .txt format. Therefore, the original texts need to be stripped of all formatting coding, be it related to word processing (bold, italics) or HTML coding. Once again, corpus programs such as *WordSmith* have text conversion components that can help in this matter.

The simplicity of using electronic text can be seen in the creation of the Medical Anatomy Corpus (MAC) (Nelson 2008). After applying for permission, the whole of *Gray's Anatomy* was downloaded by simply copying and pasting into Word and then storing the files as fourteen .txt files. Each file represented one area of the body, e.g. osteology, veins, embryology. The whole process took two hours. *WordSmith* was then used for both lexical analysis and the development of pedagogical materials (Nelson 2009).

Conversion by optical scanning

For this, two essential items of electronic equipment are needed: a good scanner and efficient OCR (Optical Character Recognition) software. Since the 2000 project of the BEC and PMC, advances have been made in scanner software and there is today a wide variety of very good software available. It is possible to find good reviews of this software on the web and, for example, PCMag.com (see website) regularly reviews software, giving a clear overview of what is available. Wikipedia also has a chart comparing OCR programs produced by the leading companies. You can also Google the phrase 'OCR software review' and retrieve free trial versions of different programs. It should be noted that while scanning often gives very good results, if the quality of the original text has degenerated in any way – for example, if it is a photocopy – then accuracy can go down to 40 or 50 per cent. Thus, every text has to be very carefully manually processed to make sure that the computer text matches the original. This obviously is very time-consuming; for example, 373,011 words were scanned into the BEC over a period of eighteen months and each page required multiple corrections. No matter what the standard of the OCR, this element of manual checking cannot be excluded.

Conversion by keyboarding

When all else fails, the only available option is to enter the text by use of keyboarding. This can be seen as the most time-consuming of all methods. This is necessary, for example, when the original text is in such a degraded condition that it will not scan correctly. It must also be used when original documents are in hand-written format as many scanners/ software are not able to work on hand-written text with any degree of accuracy.

Finally, combinations of methods can be used. In the New Corpus for Ireland (NCI), for example, Kilgariff *et al.* (2006) report that a combination of using existing corpora, contacting publishers and newspapers for permission and collecting data from the web was used.

Confidentiality and ethics

When contacting potential sources of texts, it is essential to ensure both that the data you collect is treated according to the laws of copyright and also that you observe the privacy of the authors, if the texts come from the private domain. It is often both sensible or legally required that you draw up a contract on the usage of the data that you receive from respondents. Once all the data have been gathered, the next step is to store them and make them easily available for retrieval.

Data storage and retrieval

Storage and easy retrieval of data is of central importance in the creation of any corpus that will be used by more than one researcher. The BNC used SGML tagging to provide data on, for example, author's name and recording location. In the BEC a database was set up to allow retrieval of data from the 1,102 texts that form the BEC according to the following criteria: (1) file name; (2) URL (where applicable); (3) text topic; (4) text title; (5) text source; (6) text length; (7) text nationality; (8) gender; (9) text type; (10) date of text origin; and (11) corpus sector. In this way it is possible to search for text according a variety of search criteria.

Annotation

The issue of annotation of corpus data will be dealt with in detail elsewhere in this book, but it is worth noting that as a rule at least one version of your corpus should follow the 'clean-text policy' of Sinclair (1991) who proposed that 'The safest policy is to keep the text as it is, unprocessed and clean of other codes' (Sinclair 1991: 21). Sinclair's reasons for this were two-fold: different researchers impose different priorities in corpus data, and a lack of standardisation in analytical measures would create problems for later research of a different nature. Similarly, there is a lack of agreement on basic linguistic features such as words and morphological division. For the BEC, two versions of the corpus were created. First came a 'clean-text' version, where the corpus consists purely of the texts themselves with no annotation at all. A second version of the corpus of the BEC was then created which was Part-of-Speech (POS) tagged using an automatic tagger – *Autasys* (Fang 1998) – which assigned a grammatical tag to each word. The *LOB* tag-set was used for POS assignation.

5. Concluding comments on written corpora

This chapter has attempted to elucidate the issues that are involved when building a written corpus. Despite the fact that written corpora are purportedly easier to create than spoken, largely because of the problems of spoken language transcription, there are still a wide range of issues that need to be addressed at all stages of the process from planning to data gathering and organisation. In building a written corpus, especially if working alone, one has to some extent to balance academic integrity with practical realities, accuracy with expediency and size with efficiency. Of the three corpora I have created, one took two years to build (BEC), one took eighteen months (PMC) and one took an afternoon (Medical Anatomy Corpus of 556,000 words). Thus, although it can initially seem a daunting task, careful choice of target linguistic features can facilitate valid research that is not necessarily overwhelming for the lone researcher.

Further reading

BNC User Manual, available online at www.natcorp.ox.ac.uk/docs/userManual/design.xml.ID=wrides (The best way to learn how to do something is to see how others have done it well, in order not to have to re-invent the wheel. You can just focus on the written section, but also get insight into the creation of spoken elements at the same time if you wish.)

Douglas, F. (2003) 'The Scottish Corpus of Texts and Speech: Problems of Corpus Design', *Literary and Linguistic Computing* 18(1): 23–37. (This article focuses not just on size and balance issues, but on establishing norms for good practice in corpus creation. Again, reading how things have been done in practice can give invaluable insight for one's own work.)

Hundt, M., Nesselhauf, N. and Biewer, C. (eds) (2007) *Corpus Linguistics and the Web*. Amsterdam and New York: Rodopi. (This provides a thorough overview of exploiting the web to create corpora and using the web as a corpus itself.)

References

Biber, D. (1988) *Variation across Speech and Writing*. Cambridge: Cambridge University Press.

Biber, D., Conrad, S. and Reppen, R. (1998) *Corpus Linguistics. Investigating Language Structure and Use*. Cambridge: Cambridge University Press.

Burnard, L. (2001) 'Where Did We Go Wrong? A Retrospective Look at the Design of the BNC', available at http://users.ox.ac.uk/~lou/wip/silfitalk.html (accessed 28 March 2008).

Clear, J. (1992) 'Corpus Sampling', in G. Leitner (ed.) *New Directions in English Language Corpora*. Berlin and New York: Mouton de Gruyter, pp. 21–31.

de Beaugrande, D. (2001) 'Large Corpora, Small Corpora, and the Learning of Language', in M. Ghadessy (ed.) *Small Corpus Studies and ELT. Theory and Practice*. Philadelphia, PA: John Benjamins, pp. 3–28.

Douglas, F. (2003) 'The Scottish Corpus of Texts and Speech: Problems of Corpus Design', *Literary and Linguistic Computing* 18(1): 23–37.

Ekbal, A. and Bandyopadhyay, S. (2008) 'A Web-based Bengali News Corpus for Named Entity Recognition', *Language Resources and Evaluation* 42(2): 173–82.

Fang, A. (1993) 'Building a Corpus of the English of Computer Science', in J. Aarts, P. de Haan and N. Oostdijk (eds) *English Language Corpora: Design, Analysis and Exploitation*. Amsterdam and Atlanta, GA: Rodopi, pp. 73–8.

——(1998) Autasys Version 1. Tagging Program on view at www.phon.ucl.ac.uk/home/alex/home.htm

Flowerdew, L. (1998) 'Corpus Linguistic Techniques Applied to Textlinguistics', *System* 26: 541–52.

Halliday, M. A. K. and Sinclair, J. (1966) 'Lexis as a Linguistic Level', in C. E. Bazell, J. C. Catford, M.A. K. Halliday and R. H. Robins (eds) *In Memory of J. R. Firth*. London: Longman, pp. 148–62.

Howarth, P. (1998) 'Phraseology and Second Language Proficiency', *Applied Linguistics* 19(1): 24–44.

Hundt, M., Nesselhauf, N. and Biewer, C. (eds) (2007) *Corpus Linguistics and the Web*. Amsterdam and New York: Rodopi.

Kennedy, G. (1998) *An Introduction to Corpus Linguistics*. Harlow: Addison Wesley Longman.

Kilgariff, A., Rundell, M. and Uí Dhonnchadha, E. (2006) 'Efficient Corpus Development for Lexicography: Building the New Corpus for Ireland', *Language Resources and Evaluation* 40: 127–52.

Leech, G. (1991) 'The State-of-the-Art in Corpus Linguistics', in K. Aijmer and B. Altenberg (eds) *English Corpus Linguistics, Studies in Honour of Jan Svartvik*. London and New York: Longman, pp. 8–29.

Ma, K. C. (1993) 'Small-corpora Concordancing in ESL Teaching and Learning', *Hong Kong Papers in Linguistics and Language Teaching* 16: 11–30.

Meyer, C. (2002) *English Corpus Linguistics*. Cambridge: Cambridge University Press

Nelson, M. (2000) 'A Corpus-based Study of the Lexis of Business English and Business English Teaching Materials', unpublished thesis. University of Manchester, available at http://users.utu.fi/micnel/thesis.html

——(2008) 'The Medical Anatomy Corpus' (unpublished).

——(2009) *Using Key Words in Corpus-based Teaching and Research in Perspectives on Language Learning in Practice*. University of Turku Language centre 30-years Celebration. Turku: University of Turku.

Oostdijk, N. (1991) *Corpus Linguistics and the Automatic Analysis of English*. Amsterdam and Atlanta, GA: Rodopi.

Renouf, A. (1987) 'Corpus Development', in J. Sinclair (ed.) *Looking Up: An Account of the COBUILD Project in Lexical Computing*. Birmingham: HarperCollins, pp. 1–41.

Scott, M. (2007) *WordSmith Tools 5*. Oxford: Oxford University Press.

Sinclair, J. (1991) *Corpus, Concordance, Collocation*. Oxford: Oxford University Press.

——(2002) 'Introduction', in M. Ghadessy (ed.) *Small Corpus Studies and ELT. Theory and Practice*. Philadelphia, PA: John Benjamins, pp. xvii–xxiii.

Stubbs, M. (1996) *Text and Corpus Analysis*. Oxford: Blackwell.

Svartvik, J. (1992) 'Corpus Linguistics Comes of Age', in J. Svartvik (ed.) *Directions in Corpus Linguistics, Proceedings of Nobel Symposium 82 Stockholm, 4–8 August 1991*. Berlin and New York: Mouton de Gruyter, pp. 7–17.

Tribble, C. (1997) E-mail to Corpora Discussion Group, corpora@huib.no

——(1998) 'Genres, Keywords, Teaching: Towards a Pedagogic Account of the Language of Project Proposals', in L. Burnard (ed.) *Teaching and Language Corpora 98 – Proceedings of the 1998 TALC Conference*. Oxford: Oxford University Press, pp. 188–98.

6
Building small specialised corpora

Almut Koester

1. What's the point of a small corpus?

There are currently two opposing trends in the compilation of corpora. On the one hand, corpora are getting ever larger, with 'mega-corpora', such as the Bank of English and the Cambridge International Corpus having hundreds of millions of words. On the other hand, smaller, more specialised corpora are being compiled, focusing on specific registers and genres (Flowerdew 2002).

But what is the point of a small corpus? Surely, the point of a computer-based corpus is to allow the electronic storage and machine analysis of huge amounts of text which could not be handled manually. According to John Sinclair (2004), the 'father' of Corpus Linguistics, 'small is not beautiful; it is simply a limitation' (p. 189). While he concedes that it may be possible, in some cases, to get valid results from a small corpus, he argues that these results will be limited. In a large corpus, on the other hand, 'underlying regularities have a better chance of showing through the superficial variations' (ibid.: 189). To illustrate this, Sinclair looked for the phrase *fit into place* in a two-million, twenty-million and 200-million-word corpus respectively, and did not find any examples until he searched the largest 200-million-word corpus, and even then he only found half a dozen examples.

This anecdote certainly illustrates the fact that small corpora are not suitable for certain types of analysis, in particular lexis and phraseology; but others have argued that a smaller corpus may be perfectly adequate for some purposes. Lexical items, except for the most common words, are relatively infrequent, and therefore a large corpus is necessary to carry out lexicographical research (see Walter, this volume). However, grammatical items, such as pronouns, prepositions and auxiliary and modal verbs, are very frequent, and can therefore be reliably studied using a relatively small corpus (Carter and McCarthy 1995). There may even be some disadvantages to working with a very large corpus. The sheer volume of data for high-frequency items may become unmanageable and result in analysts having to work with a smaller sub-sample (ibid.: 143). In a small corpus, on the other hand, *all* occurrences, and not just a random sample, of high frequency items can be examined. Furthermore, in working with very large corpora, where the samples examined will come from many vastly different contexts, it is very difficult, if not impossible, to say anything about the original context of use of the utterances (Flowerdew 2004).

This is where smaller, more specialised corpora have a distinct advantage: they allow a much closer link between the corpus and the contexts in which the texts in the corpus were produced. Where very large corpora, through their de-contextualisation, give insights into lexico-grammatical patterns in the language as a whole, smaller specialised corpora give insights into patterns of language use in particular settings. With a small corpus, the corpus compiler is often also the analyst, and therefore usually has a high degree of familiarity with the context. This means that the quantitative findings revealed by corpus analysis can be balanced and complemented with qualitative findings (Flowerdew 2004; O'Keeffe 2007). As we shall see, specialised corpora are also usually carefully targeted and set up to reflect contextual features, such as information about the setting, the participants and the purpose of communication. Therefore, analysis of such corpora can reveal connections between linguistic patterning and contexts of use (O'Keeffe 2007).

This link between the corpus and the contexts of use is particularly relevant in the fields of English for Specific Purposes (ESP) and English for Academic Purposes (EAP), where small specialised corpora have been compiled in recent years to inform pedagogy (Flowerdew 2002, 2004). Tribble (2002) argues that large corpora do not meet the needs of teachers and learners in ESP/EAP, as they provide 'either too much data across too large a spectrum, or too little focused data, to be directly helpful to learners with specific learning purposes' (p. 132). Smaller, more focused corpora, which have been set up for a specific research or pedagogical purpose, are much more likely to yield insights that are directly relevant for teaching and learning for specific purposes (Flowerdew 2002; Tribble 2002).

Furthermore, from a practical point of view, any corpus an individual researcher or practitioner, such as a teacher of ESP or EAP, will be able to construct will necessarily be small, through the limitation of collecting and, for a spoken corpus, transcribing the data. The aim of this chapter is therefore to provide some guidelines for building a small specialised corpus, and to discuss, with concrete examples, what can be learnt from such a corpus.

2. How small and how specialised?

But just how small and how specialised can a corpus be? The answer to this question depends very much on what the corpus will be used for: that is, the purpose of the research. But let's first define what we mean by a 'small' corpus. There are different opinions about what is considered 'large' or 'small' when it comes to corpora. First of all, it depends on whether the corpus is written or spoken; as it takes quite a long time to compile a spoken corpus (see Adolphs and Knight, this volume), spoken corpora tend to be smaller than written ones. According to O'Keeffe *et al.* (2007: 4), any spoken corpus containing over a million words of speech is considered large, whereas with written corpora anything under five million words of text is quite small. But many small corpora, even written ones, are a great deal smaller than that, and Flowerdew (2004: 19) notes that there is general agreement that small corpora contain up to 250,000 words.

As already noted, when analysing high-frequency items, a relatively modest corpus may still yield robust and powerful findings, for example the 52,000 POTTI Corpus of post-observation teacher trainee interaction (Farr and O'Keeffe 2002) and Koester's

(2006) 34,000-word Corpus of American and British Office Talk (ABOT). Cutting (1999, 2000) used only 25,000 words of conversation between students to investigate grammatical items contributing to in-group identity. What is more important than the actual size of the corpus is how well it is designed and that it is 'representative'. There is no ideal size for a corpus; it all depends on what the corpus contains and what is being investigated (Flowerdew 2004). Nevertheless, it is possible to give some general guidelines regarding minimal sample size. These issues will be discussed in Section 3.

As regards the degree of specialisation, a corpus may be more or less specialised, and it may be specialised in different ways, depending, again, on the purpose of the research (see also Hunston 2002: 14). Flowerdew (2004: 21) lists a number of different parameters according to which a corpus can be specialised:

- Specific purpose for compilation, e.g. to investigate a particular grammatical or lexical item.
- Contextualisation: particular setting, participants and communicative purpose.
- Genre, e.g. promotional (grant proposals, sales letters).
- Type of text/discourse, e.g. biology textbooks, casual conversation.
- Subject matter/topic, e.g. economics.
- Variety of English, e.g. Learner English.

While some specialised corpora are compiled to study a particular variety of English, for example the Limerick Corpus of Irish English or the International Corpus of Learner English (ICLE), others focus on particular academic or professional genres, such as the Michigan Corpus of Spoken Academic English (MICASE). Specialised corpora are not necessarily that small: for example, ICLE currently contains three million words of writing from learners with twenty-one different mother tongue backgrounds, while the Cambridge Learner Corpus, part of the Cambridge International Corpus, contains over thirty million words of student writing in examinations.

The degree of specialisation also varies: for example, corpora representing a particular language variety, such as Irish English, are quite general in terms of the genres they comprise. However, such corpora can be set up to include more specialised sub-corpora: for example, the Hong Kong Corpus of Spoken English has four sub-corpora: conversation, business discourse, academic discourse and public discourse (Warren 2004). Many ESP/EAP corpora are very specialised indeed, as they have been compiled for very specific research or pedagogical purposes, for example the 250,000-word Corpus of Environmental Impact Assessment (EIA) consisting of sixty summary reports commissioned by the Hong Kong Environmental Protection Department (Flowerdew 2008). An example of a corpus designed for a specific pedagogical purpose is the Indianapolis Business Learner Corpus (IBLC), which consists of 200 letters of application (Connor *et al.* 1997; Upton and Connor 2001). The letters were written by business communication students from three different countries as part of an international business writing course (see Section 3). Specialised corpora like these are designed to provide insights into the particular genres investigated, such as very specific types of scientific (e.g. environmental impact statements) or academic writing (e.g. letters of application). They will obviously not be useful for predicting language patterns in other registers and genres, or, for example, for teaching English for General Purposes.

While specialised corpora may vary in size, an important point is that such corpora do not need to be as large as more general corpora to yield reliable results. The reason for this is that as specialised corpora are carefully targeted, they are more likely to reliably represent a particular register or genre than general corpora. Even with relatively small amounts of data, 'specialized lexis and structures are likely to occur with more regular patterning and distribution' than in a large, general corpus (O'Keeffe *et al.* 2007: 198).

The next two sections will provide some practical guidelines for building a small specialised corpus, but see also Chapter 3 for general guidelines for corpus design, Chapter 4 for compiling spoken corpora, and Chapter 5 for written corpora.

3. Important considerations in the designing of a small specialised corpus

As with any corpus, the most important consideration in designing a small, specialised corpus is that it should be representative (see Reppen, this volume). Biber (1993: 243) defines representativeness as 'the extent to which a sample includes the full range of variability in a population'. Biber (ibid.) identifies two types of variability: *situational* and *linguistic*. Situational variability refers to the range of registers and genres in the target 'population', i.e. in the text types or speech situation to be included in the corpus. Linguistic variability refers to the range of linguistic distributions found in the population. The samples collected for the corpus should reflect both kinds of criterion, but situational criteria must be used first, as there is no way of establishing that the corpus is linguistically representative without first having established that it is situationally representative.

If a very specific type of genre is being investigated, then it may be quite straightforward to establish situational representativeness, as all the samples collected will accurately represent that genre. However, in most cases, there is some degree of variability even within a given genre, and it is therefore important to ensure that the full range of variability found is included in the corpus. For example, there may be different subgenres, or perhaps the genre is used in different types of organisations, or by different people. If all the samples come from just one organisation, then the corpus will be representative of the genre as used in that organisation, but not of the genre as a whole. Of course, the aim of the research may simply be to study the genre in that particular organisation, but generally the purpose of a corpus is to yield insights, not only into itself but also into typical language use in the genre, register or variety from which it was taken (Tognini Bonelli 2001: 53–4).

There are, of course, practical limitations to sampling, and it will never be possible, particularly for a small corpus, to collect samples from *all* the situations in which a fairly widespread genre is used. What is important is to ensure that the samples are collected from a range of fairly typical situations. For example, data for the ABOT Corpus, which was designed to investigate the most frequently occurring genres in spontaneous face-to-face office interactions, were collected from offices in a range of organisations and business sectors, including higher education, publishing, the paper trade, advertising and retail (Koester 2006). Only those genres which occurred across a range of office settings were selected for inclusion in the corpus, thereby ensuring that the corpus was not biased towards any one particular setting. Good sampling is therefore essential for designing a corpus that is representative. However, we should bear in mind that it is not possible to evaluate 'representativeness' entirely objectively (Tognini Bonelli 2001: 57). We may only discover that a corpus is *not* representative if it turns out that the results are skewed in some way.

Let us return to the notion of linguistic representativeness – ensuring that the range of linguistic distributions found in the target situation are reproduced in the corpus. Biber (1993) states that linguistic representativeness depends first of all on situational representativeness, but also on the number of words per text sample, and number of samples per register or genre included in the corpus. By running a number of statistical tests, Biber discovered that the most common linguistic features (e.g. personal pronouns, contractions, past and present tense and prepositions) are relatively stable in their occurrence across 1,000-word samples. He also looked at how many text samples are needed to adequately represent a register or a genre in a corpus, and found that the linguistic tendencies are quite stable with ten (and to some extent even five) text samples per genre or register (Biber 1990).

Biber's studies indicate that it is not necessary to have millions of words or a huge number of texts in a corpus to get reliable results (at least for high frequency items). But even these relatively modest criteria cannot always be met: for example, having text samples that contain at least 1,000 words. This is especially the case for a spoken corpus, as many spoken interactions (for example, service encounters) are relatively short and do not amount to 1,000 words; and even some written texts, especially in workplace contexts (e.g. e-mail) may be less than 1,000 words. It is more important to collect complete texts or interactions, rather than artificially controlled samples of a certain length, to adequately represent the genre or text type (Flowerdew 2004). One can still try to ensure that any sub-corpus within the corpus (for example, a particular genre or sub-genre) is represented by at least 1,000 words (even if these are spread across different texts or conversations), and that every sub-corpus contains at least five, if possible ten, different samples.

The ABOT Corpus will again be used to illustrate how a small corpus can be designed, as well as to indicate some of the problems and pitfalls. A 'corpus-driven' approach (see chapters by Handford, Cheng and Flowerdew, this volume) was used to establish the genres in the ABOT Corpus: that is, the data were investigated to determine the genres that occurred; the study did not set out to collect a pre-determined set of genres. This meant that it was not possible from the outset to gather a minimum number of exemplars per genre. If specific genres were targeted for inclusion in the corpus, this would of course be possible. Linguistic evidence of speakers' goals (see Koester 2006: Chs 2 and 3) was then used to pick out recurring genres and organise exemplars of these into sub-corpora. Some genres, such as decision-making and procedural discourse (involving instructions), were much more frequent than others, such as reporting, which meant that some sub-corpora contain more generic episodes or 'texts' than others. About half of the sub-corpora contain between seven and eleven text samples, but others contain fewer than five. Clearly for those genres represented by fewer than five exemplars, the results of corpus analysis will be less reliable than for the genres with more text samples. But again, this reflects the reality of the target situation in that certain genres are typically more frequent in office interactions than others.

With genres that are under-represented, the problem of 'local densities' (Moon 1998: 68) arises: certain items may appear to be frequent in a genre simply because they occur frequently in one particular encounter. Such local densities are, however, usually fairly easy to spot – i.e. if most of the examples of a lexical item come from one particular encounter – and this should be taken into account when interpreting the results. To ensure that results from analysing the ABOT Corpus were reliable, comparisons were often made between 'macro-genres' (similar genres grouped together), rather than between individual genres (see Handford, this volume). Most of the comparisons between individual genres were made between decision-making and procedural discourse, which were the most frequently occurring genres and were represented by the largest number of text samples (see Koester 2006: Ch. 5).

These examples of how one small spoken corpus was designed have served to illustrate how the principles of corpus design interact with practical considerations relating to the nature of the data collected, and how limitations regarding sampling can be dealt with. While every effort should be made to make the corpus as representative as possible, optimum representative sampling may not always be possible, particularly when compiling a spoken corpus, because of restrictions in relation to access and obtaining permissions, or simply limitations on the researcher-cum-corpus-compiler's time (particularly as transcription is very time-consuming). Hunston (2002: 26) makes the point that arguments about corpus size are often 'academic', and that corpus users tend to make use of the data that is available to them.

The most important consideration regarding corpus design is that the corpus should be set up in a way that is suitable for the purpose of the research. While many larger corpora were compiled for research into general linguistic phenomena, specialised corpora are often designed to answer specific research questions. For example, the aim of the Indianapolis Business Learner Corpus (IBLC) was 'to study language use, accommodation across cultures, and genre acquisition of native and non-native speaking students in an undergraduate business communication class' (Upton and Connor 2001: 316). The data collected for the corpus consisted of letters of application written by business communication students in institutions in different countries as part of the US–Flemish–Finnish writing project. The project involved students at each university reading and evaluating letters of students from other countries as part of a business simulation (see Connor *et al.* 1997). The corpus thus included data from both native and non-native students, had a cross-cultural element and involved a specific genre (letters of application), and could therefore be said to be well designed to answer the research question.

4. Compiling and transcribing a small specialised spoken corpus

Many of the limitations of a small corpus can be counterbalanced by reference to the context. Indeed, for specialised corpora, gathering contextual data about the setting from which the texts or discourse were collected can be essential, as it is often not possible to make sense of such specialised discourse without some background knowledge. For the 500,000-word sub-corpus of business discourse collected as part of the Hong Kong Corpus of Spoken English (HKCSE), data collection was preceded by a period of observation in the organisation which enabled the research assistant to choose sites for recording that would reflect a cross-section of the organisation's functions (Warren 2004). Warren notes that this period of observation and orientation was found to be essential at a later stage in order to interpret the data.

Although methods of ethnographic observation, note-taking and interview are usually associated with case studies, and not with corpus studies, there is no reason these methods cannot also inform and complement corpus analysis (ibid.: 137). In the case of small specialised corpora, such contextual information is extremely valuable: it is often essential for interpreting the data, and it can be drawn on in qualitatively analysing the corpus results. In addition to field notes and interview data, untranscribed data can provide useful background information. In order to have sufficient useable data for a spoken corpus, much more is usually recorded than is subsequently transcribed, and knowledge of untranscribed recorded data can also inform the analysis in various ways. For example, the data for the ABOT Corpus come from thirty hours of audio-recording, but only a small portion of this was transcribed for the corpus. In some cases, it may be necessary to consult participants in the discourse or other representatives of the organisation in order to aid with transcription or with the corpus compilation. Warren (2004) gives the example of an encounter which the compilers of the business sub-corpus of HKCSE were not able to assign to any of the team's list of genres. After consulting an employee of the organisation, a new genre category was created for the sub-corpus.

Background information is useful not only in interpreting the data, but can also be an integral part of corpus design. Having detailed information about the speakers or writers, the goals of the interactions or texts and the setting in which they were produced as part of the corpus database means that linguistic practices can easily be linked to specific contextual variables. This can be done by having each contributor complete a speaker/writer information sheet (for written texts, this may of course not be possible, for example if they are collected from publicly available sources), and obtaining as much information as possible about the text samples (e.g. through participant observation and interviews with people in the organisation). This information can be included as a header at the top of each text file or transcript and/or stored in a database, which can be drawn on in carrying out the analysis. Speaker information collected for HKCSE includes place of birth, gender, occupation, educational background, time spent living or studying abroad, and mother tongue (Warren 2004). In designing the Cambridge and Nottingham Business English Corpus (CANBEC), a spoken meetings corpus of one million words, Handford (forthcoming) collected information in the following main categories:

1. Relationship between the speakers, e.g. peer, manager–subordinate, colleagues from the same/different departments.
2. Topic, e.g. sales, marketing, production.
3. Purpose of the meeting, e.g. internal/external, reviewing, planning.
4. Speaker information, e.g. age, title, department, level in the company.
5. Company type and size.

In Section 5, we will see how this information was used in the corpus analysis.

Data collected for a spoken corpus will need to be transcribed, and decisions made as to how detailed or 'close' the transcription should be. If the corpus is fairly small, it may be possible to transcribe the recording in more detail than for a large corpus, where there may be so much data to transcribe that time-consuming close transcription is not possible. As with decisions about corpus size and sampling, the level of detail required for the transcription depends on the aim of the project (O'Keeffe *et al.* 2007: 6). For example, there is no need to transcribe prosodic features (intonation), if these features will not be analysed. However, it is worth remembering that the more detailed the transcription is, the more faithfully it represents the original interaction, and the more features are available for later analysis. The transcription conventions used also need to be computer-readable, and as most corpus software requires texts to be stored as plain text files, any codes used should be available in plain text format.

Small spoken corpora are often used to examine interactive features, and for such analysis pauses, overlaps, interruptions and unfinished words or utterances as well as non-linguistic features of interaction, such as laughter, should be indicated. The Limerick Corpus of Irish English is an example of a spoken corpus that is transcribed to show such

Table 6.1 VOICE Transcription Conventions 2.1 from VOICE website

Code	*Example*
Pauses: Every brief pause in speech (up to a good half-second) is marked with a full stop in parentheses	SX-f: because they all give me different (.) different (.) points of view
Other continuation: Whenever a speaker continues, completes or supports another speaker's turn immediately (i.e. without a pause), this is marked by "="	S1: what up till (.) till twelve? S2: **yes=** S1: **=really**. so it's it's quite a lot of time.
Emphasis: If a speaker gives a syllable, word or phrase particular prominence, this is written in capital letters.	S3: toMORrow we have to work on the presentation already
Intonation: Words spoken with rising intonation are followed by a question mark "?"	S1: that's what my next er slide? does
Words spoken with falling intonation are followed by a full stop "."	S7: that's point two. absolutely yes.

interactive features, but does not transcribe prosodic features (see Limerick Corpus of Irish English website, transcription conventions). An even closer transcription would also code for certain features of intonation, showing, for example, any syllables that are emphasised or whether an utterance ends in a rising or falling tone, as is done for the Vienna–Oxford Corpus of International English (VOICE) – see below. The most detailed prosodic transcription that has been carried out for a specialised corpus is probably for the Hong Kong Corpus of Spoken English, which uses Brazil's (1997) discourse intonation system, where the utterances are transcribed as tone units, and prominence, tone and key (pitch) are shown (see Cheng *et al.* 2008).

Table 6.1 shows examples from the transcription conventions used for VOICE, illustrating some of the ways in which a selection of interactive features and prosody can be represented in a corpus.

Some of the transcription conventions used for VOICE reflect specific features of the data, which consist of interactions between lingua franca speakers of English, meaning that none of the speakers have English as their mother tongue. For example, codes were devised to show when speakers switch to their mother tongue or where pronunciation deviates markedly from the standard (see VOICE website). This illustrates the important point that the transcription conventions should capture the most significant and distinctive features of the data and be suitable for the research purposes. With smaller corpora, there may be a tendency to 'one-offness', as the transcription system is usually devised to meet the specific needs of the research project. The same conventions may not be suitable for other projects, and might need to be adapted. More detailed guidelines on transcription can be found in Adolphs and Knight (this volume).

5. What can be learnt from a small specialised corpus?

Having covered the issues involved in designing and compiling a small specialised corpus, in this section we will discuss the advantages of small corpora in terms of what can be learnt from them. As already mentioned at the beginning of this chapter, one of the main advantages of a small specialised corpus is that, unlike with a large corpus, the language is not de-contextualised. On the contrary, there is a very close link between language and context; as O'Keeffe (2007) says, 'the texts behind the numbers are more accessible'.

Flowerdew (2008) points out that there are in fact two ways in which the context is relevant for corpus analysis:

1) The context can inform the corpus-based analysis, for example when the compiler-cum-analyst of a small specialised corpus has access to background information to aid in the interpretation of the data.
2) The linguistic patterns identified through corpus analysis can tell us something about the social and cultural context from which the data were taken.

For both types of contextual links between corpus and context, small specialised corpora have a clear advantage over large corpora. The first type was discussed in Section 4 on corpus compilation; here we will examine the second more closely.

O'Keeffe (2007) specifies the process by which patterns identified in a small, specialised corpus can reveal insights into the context of use. The patterns can first of all be linked to a particular context, because the corpus analysis shows that they are concentrated within that context. We can see that these patterns are localised, as they are traceable to local situational conditions, such as gender, power or discourse goal. As a result, the patterns can be linked to pragmatically specialised uses within that particular context of situation. Thus the 'specificity of representation narrows and concentrates coverage and brings into clear focus signature uses of language in given contexts of use' (ibid.). An example of a 'signature use of language' is given by O'Keeffe *et al.* (2007: 182) from the CANBEC corpus of business interactions. The corpus has many examples of the pattern *going forward*, for example:

- make sure that your forecast *going forward* is actually correct

The use of this phrase, rather than a synonym such as 'in the future', can be seen as marking in-group membership in a business community; and the phrase can therefore be seen as a kind of 'signature' of that community of practice. Such localised uses would not necessarily show up in a larger corpus, where uses will be spread across a much greater range of contexts.

Let us now turn to some specific examples of how factors such as genre, topic or the relationship between the participants can influence local contexts of use. As we saw in Section 4, CANBEC was designed in such a way that information about the topic and purpose of the meetings, and the relationship between the speakers, is retrievable. Quantitative findings, such as frequency counts, can therefore be linked to these different factors. The use of the lexical items *issue* and *problem* in CANBEC provides an interesting illustration of the role such factors can play in influencing local contexts. These words apparently are synonyms and, looking at the corpus as a whole, their use seems very similar: they both have a very high frequency and enter into similar collocational patterns. However, the frequency of these two lexical items varies considerably when one looks at the topics discussed in the meetings and the relationship between the speakers (Handford 2007). *Issue*, for example is more frequent in human resources and marketing meetings, whereas *problem* occurs most in procedural and technical meetings. In terms of speaker relationship, *issue* occurs more in interactions between managers and subordinates, whereas *problem* is used more in peer discussions. Handford gives the following example from a meeting between peers, in which both *issue* and *problem* are used, to illustrate how these two words actually perform slightly different functions:

> Well I-I thi-think that's another **issue**. And the other the and and another **issue** which comes on-onto that is that erm I'm still waiting he s-that cos (1.5 secs) Apparently one of the **problems** with getting some of the information off the computer is the fact that-erm that particular (1 sec) the s-the software is not as powerful as the stuff we've got on the the new computer that he's got. (3 secs) There was an **issue** about getting the stuff off ...
>
> (Handford 2007: 252–3)

Handford (ibid.: 253) notes that while both words have the 'prosody of difficulty', *problem* seems to indicate more of a concrete obstacle, something that should be solved, whereas *issue* is somewhat more nebulous, and perhaps indicates that further discussion is needed. This fits with the nature of the meetings topics in which each of these words is more frequently used: in technical and procedural meetings, one would expect concrete problems to be raised, whereas in human resources and marketing wider discussion 'around' issues might be required. Furthermore, if we consider the interpersonal dimension of these words, *problem* comes across as more categorical, and its use could therefore potentially be face-threatening. This explains its higher frequency in peer meetings, where threats to face are less likely, thanks to the equal relationship between participants. In meetings between unequal participants (managers and subordinates), *issue* may be a useful euphemistic alternative to *problem*, serving to mitigate a potentially face-threatening act.

The use of these two apparent synonyms also varies with the nature of the activity or genre in CANBEC. Comparing their use in external meetings (between two different companies) and internal meetings, both words combined are more than twice as frequent in internal meetings than external meetings. This can be explained by the fact that internal meetings typically focus on decision-making, where *issues* and *problems* are discussed and frequently resolved; whereas in external meetings decisions are often not made, but rather explained, contested or evaluated.

In the ABOT Corpus, a much smaller spoken corpus of workplace interactions (see Section 3), we can also observe the influence of local contexts on the frequency and use of various words and patterns. Both CANBEC and ABOT show that modals of obligation (*have to*, *need to*, *should*) are very frequent in workplace interactions (Koester 2006; Handford forthcoming). However, in both corpora, these modals, as well as their collocational patterns, are differentially distributed according to local contexts, such as genre and speaker relationship. The genres in ABOT are grouped into two 'macro-genres': unidirectional and collaborative. In unidirectional genres one of the speakers clearly plays a dominant role, for example imparting information or giving instructions. In collaborative genres, such as decision-making and planning, participants contribute more or less equally towards accomplishing the goal of the encounter. In the ABOT Corpus, all the modals of obligation are more frequent in collaborative genres than in unidirectional genres, as shown in Table 6.2 (Koester 2006).

Table 6.2 also shows that the difference in frequency is greater the stronger the modal: i.e. *have to* which is the most forceful, occurs nearly twice as frequently, whereas *should*, the least forceful, is only marginally more frequent in collaborative genres.

Table 6.2 Total number of occurrences of modals of obligation in each macro-genre

	Collaborative	*Unidirectional*
have to	46	26
need (to)	32	22
should	24	20

Moreover, collocational patterns of modals and pronoun combinations also vary systematically with genre. Thus in collaborative genres, *we* and *you* are the most frequent pronouns used with the above modals, whereas in unidirectional genres, *I* occurs most frequently in combination with all three modals. In unidirectional genres, *you have to* does not occur at all: there is just one example of *you'll have to* and a few instances of *you don't have to*.

Both the lower frequency of the more forceful modals and the infrequent use of the pronoun *you* in combination with all three modals of obligation can be linked to the feature that all unidirectional genres have in common, namely the fact that one speaker plays a dominant role. Regardless of the actual social or institutional relationship between the speakers, this imbalance in the speakers' roles means more care is taken to avoid face-threatening acts. This results in more indirect and hedged language, as illustrated in the following example, where a speaker makes a request using *I need you to* instead of *you need to*:

- I need you to sign off on this pack too.

(Author's data)

Another reason for the frequency of the first person pronoun *I* is that in procedural discourse/directive or instruction-giving (the most frequent unidirectional genre), the person receiving instructions frequently 'invites' directives by saying *should I*, e.g.:

- What should I do. Just – get the estimate …

(Author's data)

In collaborative genres, on the other hand, participants play a more equal role, and therefore more direct forms, such as *you have to* or *you should* are unproblematic, e.g.:

- You have to make sure you can get access to that.
- You need to update this too.

(Author's data)

Also, most collaborative genres are action-orientated, i.e. people are trying to get things done (decisions, plans, arrangements), which results in the frequent use of modals of obligation with the first person pronoun *we*, e.g.:

- Right. We'll have to go through it.
- We need to get it moving.

(Author's data)

Collocations can also take on specific pragmatic meanings or 'semantic prosodies' (see Flowerdew, this volume) within a specialised genre, and this is something corpus analysis can reveal. Flowerdew (2008) found that the collocation *associated with* was very frequent in a corpus of environmental reports. Not only did it occur 139 times in the 250,000-word corpus, but it was found across all twenty-three companies from which the reports were drawn, indicating that this is a phrase that is typical for the genre, and not a result of 'local prosody' (see Section 3). In 135 of these instances, the phrase seemed to have a negative semantic prosody, for example:

- difficulties *associated with* hydraulic dredging
- Health hazards *associated with* proximity to high tension power lines.

(Flowerdew 2008: 121)

Flowerdew (2008: 121) concludes that this phrase is 'most likely an attenuated form of "caused by"' which is used by scientists to 'avoid claiming a direct causal effect, thereby forestalling any challenges from their peers', and therefore forms part of the discourse practices of the genre of environmental reports. In order to determine whether this finding is generalisable to other types of scientific writing, Flowerdew searched for the phrase *associated with* in the much larger seven-million-word Applied Science domain of the British National Corpus, and found that in 40 per cent of the samples examined the phrase also has a negative semantic prosody. Such comparisons with a larger corpus covering a similar variety or genre as the smaller specialised corpus are very useful in testing the validity of findings from such corpora, and reinforcing the robustness of any generalisations made (see also Flowerdew 2003). By comparing a small corpus against a larger 'benchmark' corpus, 'keywords' can also be identified (e.g. using *WordSmith Tools*; Scott 1999): these are words that are unusually frequent in the small corpus compared to their normal frequency in the language (see Evison, this volume).

This chapter has shown that while small corpora are not suitable for all types of analysis, a small specialised corpus can nevertheless provide valuable insights into specific areas of language use, and can even have certain advantages over large corpora. The main advantage is in the close link that exists between language patterns and contexts of use, as illustrated throughout this chapter from corpus design, through compilation and transcription to corpus analysis and findings. This interplay of language and context in corpus studies can be followed up in other chapters in this volume which deal with special areas of language use. Chapter 19 looks in more detail at what a corpus can tell us about specialist genres, and other chapters focus on specific genres, for example Coxhead examines English for Academic Purposes, Cotterill looks at forensic linguistics, and Atkins and Harvey explore health communication.

Transcription conventions used in data extracts

.	falling intonation at end of tone unit
...	turn continuation
-	sound abruptly cut off, e.g. false start
(1.5 secs)	length of pauses indicated in parentheses

Further reading

Flowerdew, L. (2002) 'Corpus-based Analyses in EAP', in J. Flowerdew (ed.) *Academic Discourse*, Longman: Pearson, pp. 95–114. (This chapter provides a review of corpora compiled in the area of

English for Academic Purposes (EAP), including specific areas such as science and technology, medicine, business and finance.)

——(2004) 'The Argument for Using English Specialized Corpora to Understand Academic and Professional Settings', in U. Connor and T. Upton (eds) *Discourse in the Professions: Perspectives from Corpus Linguistics*. Amsterdam: John Benjamins, pp. 11–33. (This chapter is useful for anyone wanting to build a specialised corpus: as well as presenting a rationale for using specialised corpora, it provides useful guidelines for defining a specialised corpus and for corpus design.)

O'Keeffe, A., McCarthy, M. J. and Carter, R. A. (2007). *From Corpus to Classroom*. Cambridge: Cambridge University Press. (This book provides a very accessible introduction to the most important topics in corpus research. The role of qualitative as well as quantitative analysis is a theme throughout the book, and many chapters address the topic of what can be learned from small specialised corpora, in particular Chapters 8 and 10.)

References

Biber, D. (1990) 'Methodological Issues Regarding Corpus-based Analyses of Linguistic Variation', *Literary and Linguistic Computing* 5(4): 257–69.

——(1993) 'Representativeness in Corpus Design', *Literary and Linguistic Computing* 8(4): 243–57.

Brazil, D. (1997) *The Communicative Role of Intonation in English*. Cambridge: Cambridge University Press.

Carter, R. and McCarthy, M. (1995) 'Grammar and the Spoken Language', *Applied Linguistics* 16(2): 141–58.

Cheng, W., Greaves, C. and Warren, M. (2008). *A Corpus-driven Study of Discourse Intonation*. Amsterdam and Philadelphia, PA: John Benjamins.

Connor, U. and Upton, T. (eds) (2004) *Discourse in the Professions: Perspectives from Corpus Linguistics*. Amsterdam: John Benjamins.

Connor, U., Davis, K., De Rycker, T., Phillips, E. M. and Verckens, J. P. (1997) 'An International Course in International Business Writing: Belgium, Finland, the United States', *Business Communication Quarterly* 60(4): 63–74.

Cutting, J. (1999) 'The Grammar of the In-group Code', *Applied Linguistics* 20(2): 179–202.

——(2000) *Analysing the Language of Discourse Communities*. Oxford: Elsevier Science.

Farr, F. and O'Keeffe, A. (2002) '*Would* as a Hedging Device in an Irish Context: Intra-varietal Comparison of Institutionalised Spoken Interaction', in R. Reppen (ed.) *Using Corpora to Explore Linguistic Variation*. Philadelphia, PA: John Benjamins, pp. 25–48.

Flowerdew, L. (2002) 'Corpus-based Analyses in EAP', in J. Flowerdew (ed.) *Academic Discourse*, London: Pearson, pp. 95–114.

——(2003) 'A Combined Corpus and Systemic–Functional Analysis of the Problem–Solution Pattern in a Student and Professional Corpus of Technical Writing', *TESOL Quarterly* 37(3): 489–511.

——(2004) 'The Argument for Using English Specialized Corpora to Understand Academic and Professional Settings', in U. Connor and T. Upton (eds) *Discourse in the Professions: Perspectives from Corpus Linguistics*. Amsterdam: John Benjamins, pp. 11–33.

——(2008) 'Corpora and Context in Professional Writing', in V. K. Bhatia, J. Flowerdew and R. H. Jones (eds) *Advances in Discourse Studies*. London: Routledge, pp. 115–31.

Handford, M. (2007) 'The Genre of the Business Meeting: A Corpus-based Study', unpublished PhD thesis, University of Nottingham.

——(forthcoming) *The Language of Business Meetings*. Cambridge: Cambridge University Press.

Hunston, S. (2002) *Corpora in Applied Linguistics*. Cambridge: Cambridge University Press.

Koester, A. (2006) *Investigating Workplace Discourse*. London: Routledge.

Limerick Corpus of Irish English Website, University of Limerick, transcription conventions available at www.ul.ie/~lcie/concordance_3.htm (accessed 8 November 2008).

Moon, R. (1998) *Fixed Expressions and Idioms in English: A Corpus-based Approach*. Oxford: Clarendon Press.

O'Keeffe, A. (2007) 'The Pragmatics of Corpus Linguistics', keynote paper presented at the fourth Corpus Linguistics Conference held at the University of Birmingham, Birmingham, July 2007.

O'Keeffe, A., McCarthy, M. J. and Carter, R. A. (2007) *From Corpus to Classroom*. Cambridge: Cambridge University Press.

Scott, M. (1999). *WordSmith Tools*, Version 3 (corpus analytical software suite). Oxford: Oxford University Press.

Sinclair, J. (2004) *Trust the Text: Language, Corpus and Discourse*. London: Routledge.

Tognini Bonelli, E. (2001) *Corpus Linguistics at Work*. Amsterdam: John Benjamins.

Tribble, C. (2002) 'Corpora and Corpus Analysis: New Windows on Academic Writing', in J. Flowerdew (ed.) *Academic Discourse*. London: Longman, pp. 131–49.

Upton, T. A. and Connor, U. (2001) 'Using Computerized Corpus Analysis to Investigate the Textlinguistic Discourse Moves of a Genre', *English for Specific Purposes* 20: 313–29.

VOICE Website, VOICE Transcription Conventions [2.1], available at www.univie.ac.at/voice/voice.php?page=transcription_general_information (accessed 7 November 2008).

Warren, M. (2004) '//↘ so what have YOU been WORKing on REcently//: Compiling a Specialized Corpus of Spoken Business English', in U. Connor and T. Upton (eds) *Discourse in the Professions: Perspectives from Corpus Linguistics*. Amsterdam: John Benjamins, pp. 115–40.

7

Building a corpus to represent a variety of a language

Brian Clancy

1. What is a variety of a language?

In the literature, a *variety* of a language is, to say the least, broadly defined. Crystal (2001: 6–7) maintains that in its most general sense, the notion of a variety includes 'speech and writing, regional and class dialects, occupational genres (such as legal and scientific language), creative linguistic expression (as in literature), and a wide range of other styles of expression.' Similarly, McEnery *et al.* (2006: 90) suggest that varieties of a language are equally expansive, covering, for example, 'the standard language (standardised for the purposes of education and public performance), dialects (geographically defined), sociolects (socially defined), idiolects (unique to individual speakers) and jargons (particular to specific domains)'. This very broad definition of variety is in itself problematic, especially for the corpus builder(s). Nevertheless, according to Crystal (2001: 6–7), 'a variety of language is a system of expression whose use is governed by situational factors … varieties are, in principle, systematic and predictable.' This view is echoed by McEnery *et al.* (2006: 90) who maintain that 'a language variety can be broadly defined as a variant of a language that differs from another variant of the same language systematically and coherently.' Therefore, as Crystal (2001: 7) observes,

> it is possible to say, with some degree of certainty in a given language, how people from a particular region will speak, how lawyers will write, or how television commentators will present a type of sport. Notions such as 'British English', 'Liverpool English', 'legal French' and 'sports commentary' are the result.

Quirk (1995) refers to this profusion of linguistic varieties and the confusion that these cause. He cites the example of the word *English* preceded by a specific adjective or noun to designate a specific variety. This list of varieties of English includes, but is certainly not limited to, *American English*, *legal English*, *BBC English*, *working-class English*, *Chicano English* and *South African English*. He claims that although each is referred to as a variety, they are all formed on 'desperately different taxonomic bases' (p. 22). For example, academic English is a variety that may be used equally by speakers of both American English and British English, and speakers of other languages such as Spanish. This in turn raises the question of whether or not there exists a variety of American Academic English as opposed to one of British Academic English as opposed to Spanish Academic English. One of the reasons for the variety of varieties listed by Quirk (ibid.) is that corpus linguists have a different method of conceptualising language variation from sociolinguists. In terms of corpus linguistics, varieties are generally explored according to *register variation* or *genre variation*. Biber *et al.* (1999: 15) use *register* and *variety* interchangeably, where register is used as a cover term for 'varieties relating to different circumstances and purposes'. These registers are delimited in non-linguistic terms, with respect to situational characteristics such as mode, interactiveness, domain, communicative purpose or topic. This results in varieties being classified in terms of registers such as academic English, legal English, crime fiction, etc. An example of a corpus constructed in this way is the Longman Spoken and Written English Corpus (LSWE, see Biber *et al.* 1999) which consists of forty million words across four core registers: conversation, fiction, news and academic prose. It was built to describe the main grammatical features of English and the actual use of each major feature, thereby allowing the study of how language varies according to the context in which it occurs. The LSWE also samples two national varieties – American English and British English. Biber *et al.* (ibid.) refer to differences within American English and British English as *dialectal* differences, and it is to this distinction that we now turn.

Although the term *register* is also widely used in sociolinguistics to refer to 'varieties according to use' (Hudson 1980: 48), the primary focus of this discipline is on *dialect*, that is 'varieties according to user' (ibid.). McEnery *et al.* (2006) define language variety geographically. They refer to national variants of a language such as American, British or Irish English as language varieties whereas regional variants (the English used in New York, Norwich or Belfast, for example) are referred to as dialects. Biber *et al.* (1999: 17) define dialects as varieties associated with different groups of speakers, 'distinguished primarily by pronunciation, and to a lesser extent by lexical and grammatical differences'. Although pronunciation has received some attention in corpus linguistics (see, for example, Knowles 1990; Cheng *et al.* 2008), sociolinguistics has long been characterised by a study of dialectal variation that concentrates primarily, though by no means exclusively, on pronunciation features (see, for example, Labov 1966, 1972; Trudgill 1974; Milroy 1987; Wolfram and Schilling-Estes 2006). In sociolinguistics, the primary focus is how sociolinguistic variables such as age, gender and social class affect the way that individuals use language. These studies in turn give rise to the varieties such as BBC English, working-class English and Chicano English in Quirk's (1995) list. According to Meyer (2002), the main reason that there are not more corpora used to study sociolinguistic variation is that 'it is tremendously difficult to collect samples of speech, for instance, that are balanced for gender, age and ethnicity' (p. 18). Most corpora, for example the BNC, the Corpus of London Teenage English (COLT), CANCODE or LCIE, do contain information on sociolinguistic variables; however, corpus linguists appear, in the main, to be primarily concerned with what the speakers are doing rather than who they are.

Accordingly, the starting point for the building of a corpus for a variety of a language could usefully be based on a fundamental decision: is the proposed corpus being built to represent a *Variety* of a language, such as American English or British English, or is it representing a *variety* of a language such as legal English or academic English. A *Variety* is defined geographically and is 'user-related' (Quirk 1995: 23), where an individual is in a sense 'tied' to, and identified by, the Variety. Therefore, Irish people speak Irish English, and this includes its corresponding dialects. On the other hand, a *variety* is defined situationally and is 'use-related' (ibid.); therefore, it involves the discourse activity the individual is involved in or the purpose for which he/she is using language. Therefore, a conversation between two academics could feature two language Varieties, say American English and Irish English, but one language variety, academic English. Indeed, many recent corpora constructed to represent a Variety of a language are built using a range of varieties of that language (see, for example, CANCODE or ICE). The decision made to choose between Variety and variety will be largely based on the research questions the corpus is expected to answer. This fundamental choice also has defining repercussions in relation to issues of corpus design such as the construction of the corpus sampling frame, which in turn has implications on corpus size, diversity of texts selected and corpus representativeness.

2. Issues of corpus design for a variety of a language

Building a corpus for either a Variety or a variety of a language involves building something that is representative of a whole; therefore, the design of the corpus is of particular importance to the corpus builders (see Reppen, this volume). Many of the decisions made by the corpus builder(s) in the design stage are based on the proposed uses of the corpus and on the research questions that these entail (see Koester, this volume). However, as McEnery *et al.* (2006: 73) caution, 'corpus building is of necessity a marriage of perfection and pragmatism'. Although the corpus builder(s) should always strive to build the perfectly representative corpus, issues such as corpus size, text diversity and number and length of texts, as outlined in this section, may result in the corpus builder(s) making decisions based on factors that are outside their control.

Issue 1: Address corpus size

In general, the primary issue connected to corpus size is that of resources, and it is here that the corpus builder(s) may have to 'cut their coat according to their cloth'. In the design stage, the corpus builder has to consider the issue of the amount of time it will take to collect, computerise, annotate and, if required, tag and parse the corpus. One of the fundamental decisions that must also be made is whether the corpus will consist of written texts or spoken texts or both. Chafe *et al.* (1991) observe that it takes six person-hours to transcribe one minute of speech for the Santa Barbara Corpus. McCarthy (1998: 12) maintains that it takes, on average twenty hours to transcribe one hour of recorded spoken data, and, 'even then, there will inevitably be inaudible segments and segments undecipherable even to the original speakers'. Estimates for the American component of ICE range from ten hours to transcribe a 2,000-word carefully prepared monologue to twenty hours for a dialogue containing numerous speaker overlaps (Meyer 2002). For this reason, corpora such as CANCODE (exclusively spoken texts) and the BNC (10 per cent spoken text) have required considerable funding both from universities and major publishing houses in Britain. Written texts can also prove problematic when building a corpus, especially when issues of copyright are considered (see Atkins *et al.* 1992: 4; McEnery *et al.* 2006: 77–9).

Biber (1990) maintains that the underlying parameters of linguistic variation can be replicated in a relatively small corpus, if that corpus represents the full range of variation. In contrast, larger corpora are not adequate for overall analyses of textual variation if they fail to represent the range of variation. Biber (1993) examines statistical formulae for determining sample size based on a normal distribution of grammatical features such as nouns in 481 spoken and written texts (taken from Biber 1988: 77–8). He found that, for nouns, a sample of 59.8 × 2,000 word texts (approximately 120,000 words) would be required for representativeness; however, for less common grammatical features such as conditional clauses, a sample of 1,190 × 2,000 texts would be required (approximately 2.4 million words). Meyer (2002) points out that, in general, the lengthier the corpus, the better. Similarly, Biber (1993) claims that the most conservative approach to designing a corpus is to design one that represents the most widely varying feature (in this case, the conditional clause); see also Handford, this volume.

The answer to how big a corpus should be in order to represent a language Variety, or indeed a language variety, is also strongly linked to the purpose of the corpus. For example, the Bank of English is a 450-million-word corpus of 'standard' British English designed for lexicographic purposes and is, therefore, by necessity a 'mega-corpus' (see Walter, this volume). However, in terms of a Variety of language, this corpus makes no attempt to account for regional or social variability in Britain. The BNC has 100 million words and the spoken component is demographically sampled (see Crowdy 1993 for a full outline of the process of demographic sampling undertaken by the BNC). This makes the BNC a useful resource for a wide range of research purposes. In contrast, LCIE is a one-million-word spoken corpus of Irish English designed to describe the lexico-grammatical features of the Variety which, as Section 4 will show, is a task that can be accomplished using a much smaller corpus. In terms of corpus size and corpora constructed to represent a variety of a language, the Michigan Corpus of Spoken Academic English (MICASE), designed to examine the characteristics of contemporary American academic speech, has approximately 1.8 million words. In addition to this, two of the original corpora built to represent a written Variety of a language, the Brown Corpus and the LOB corpus, are one million words each in size.

Therefore, when building the corpus, the corpus builder(s) must carefully consider issues of purpose and resources. A comprehensive examination of the lexicon of a given Variety of a language would require a large corpus such as the BNC and this corpus would also suffice to explore rarer grammatical features. A corpus used to explore a spoken Variety (or variety) is generally smaller, because of the difficulties associated with data collection and transcription. Similarly, a corpus used to account for lexico-grammatical features can be as small as one million words. The primary issue is that the corpus be as representative as possible within the allocated resources. Atkins *et al.* (1992) argue that overambition could turn out to be unsustainable, and this is particularly relevant to building a corpus to represent a Variety of a language. According to them, 'experience teaches us that it is better to aim to record initially an essential set of attributes and values which may be expanded if resources permit' (p. 6). Meyer (2002: 34) echoes this view, suggesting that, ultimately, the size of a corpus might be better determined 'not by focusing too intently on the overall length of the corpus but by focusing more on the internal structure of the corpus'. The internal structure of a corpus refers to matters such as diversity of texts, length of texts and number of texts to include.

Issue 2: Consider the diversity of texts to include

Many corpora representative of a Variety of a language have been, in essence, multipurpose. They can, for example, be used to describe the lexical and grammatical features of the Variety they represent, to study the differences between them and other national Varieties or to study variation within the different registers/genres that comprise the corpus. Therefore, a corpus of this type necessarily requires a wide range of texts. The Brown Corpus' sampling frame was derived from the collection of books and periodicals in the Brown University Library and Providence Athenaeum in 1961. The LOB corpus chose two sampling frames; for books, the publications listed for 1961 in *The British National Bibliographic Cumulated Subject Index, 1960–1964*, and for periodicals and newspapers, those listed in *Willing's Press Guide* (1961) (see Johansson *et al.* 1978). In terms of diversity, the BNC consists of 90 per cent written texts and 10 per cent spoken texts. The written texts were collected under three criteria: *domain*, *time* and *medium*. *Domain* refers to the context-type of the text (the BNC identified nine different context-types: for example, leisure, applied science, world affairs), *time* refers to when the texts were produced (the BNC sampled texts in the period 1960–93) and *medium* refers to the type of text publication (book, journal, newspaper, etc.). One part of the spoken part of the corpus was collected by a process of demographic sampling. Texts were collected from individuals and demographic information such as name, age, occupation, sex and social class was noted. This was further subdivided into region and interaction type (monologue or dialogue). The demographically sampled corpus was complemented by texts collected on context-governed criteria. These texts related to more formal speech contexts such as those encountered in educational or business settings (see Aston and Burnard 1998 for a full description of the design of the BNC).

The ICE corpus, which is composed of 60 per cent spoken texts and 40 per cent written, contains a genre range similar in scope to that of the BNC; however, the genres are much more specifically delineated in ICE than in the BNC (see Nelson 1996; Meyer 2002: 30–8). The written segment of the ICE corpus contains both printed and non-printed (for example, student essays, social letters) material, although the printed material accounts for 75 per cent of the written corpus. From a spoken viewpoint, similar to the BNC, ICE contains 60 per cent dialogic material and 40 per cent monologic; again, these are more thoroughly specified in ICE, with dialogues divided into public and private and monologues into scripted and unscripted. In the ICE corpus, the speakers chosen were adults of eighteen years of age or older who had received a formal education through the medium of English to at least secondary school level (however, this design proved to be flexible in the case of well-known, established political leaders and radio or television broadcasters whose public status made their inclusion appropriate). Information was also recorded about sex, ethnic group, region, occupation and status in occupation and role in relation to other participants (Greenbaum 1991). MICASE also employed context-governed criteria in collecting the data. The corpus contains speech events across the major academic disciplines in a university, for example biological and health sciences, physical sciences and engineering, and humanities and the arts. However, the professional disciplines of law, medicine and dentistry were excluded. Demographic information such as age, gender, academic role and first language were also recorded.

In relation to exclusively spoken corpora that represent a Variety, in their initial corpus design phase the CANCODE team developed a set of spoken text-types to correspond to existing text typologies for the written language. They adopted what McCarthy (1998) terms a 'genre-based' approach where not only is a population of speakers targeted, but the context and environment in which the speech is produced is also taken into consideration. The framework used for CANCODE sought to combine the nature of speaker relationship with goal-types prevalent in everyday, spoken interaction. The nature of the speaker relationship was divided into five broad contexts: *transactional, professional, pedagogical, socialising* and *intimate*. For each of these contexts, three goal-types were identified; *information provision, collaborative task* and *collaborative idea* (see McCarthy 1998: 9–10 for a definition of the terms). Therefore, for example, a university lecture would take place in a pedagogical context with an information provision goal-type, whereas a family cooking together would be an example of an intimate collaborative task. This, according to McCarthy (ibid.: 9) 'offers the possibility of linking their [the data] contextual and social features directly with the lexico-grammatical "nuts and bolts" of their step-by-step creation'.

Issue 3: Address text length and number

In determining how 'long' a text should be in order to warrant inclusion in the corpus, the issue of corpus size must be returned to. Both spoken and written texts range dramatically in size from a few words (for example, a quick note to a friend) to millions of words (for example, a long novel), and therefore a relatively small corpus can be skewed by a relatively long text. This raises the question as to whether whole texts or parts of texts should be included in the corpus. Sinclair (2005) maintains that the best answer to this dilemma is to build a corpus large enough to dilute even the lengthiest text. However, if this is not practical, which it may not be through a range of factors such as resources and permission, then it is necessary to select a portion of the text. Meyer (2002: 40) maintains that 'corpus compilers should strive to include more different kinds of texts in corpora rather than lengthier text samples'. However, in selecting samples to be included in a corpus, attention must also be paid to ensure that text initial, middle and end samples are balanced (McEnery *et al.* 2006). Biber (1990) demonstrates a high level of stability across a range of linguistic features, for example pronouns, contractions, present and past tenses across 1,000-word samples of texts from the Brown and London–Lund corpora. He concludes that given this stability between 1,000-word samples, it seems safe to conclude that the 2,000-word and 5,000-word samples are reliable representatives of their respective text categories for analyses of this type. He also used three ten-text samples from five genres across the LOB and London–Lund corpora – conversations, public speeches, press reportage, academic prose and general fiction – and found that these ten-text sub-samples accurately represent the linguistic characteristics of genre categories, including both the central tendency and range of variation. He concludes that anywhere between eight and eighty texts within a given category is adequate for an analysis of linguistic variation (see also Biber 1993).

Where corpora have been constructed to represent a Variety of a language, for example in the ICE corpus, each text contains approximately 2,000 words with the ending occurring at a suitable discourse break (Greenbaum 1991). In addition to this, the ICE compilers decided that each regional corpus would be one million words; therefore, each one is comprised of 500 texts. They also decided on ten texts (20,000 words) as the minimum for each text category. Texts in the Brown and LOB corpora are also 2,000 words long, and therefore each corpus contains 500 texts. Both text length and number of texts differ across the spoken and written components of the BNC. For example, the demographically sampled part of the spoken corpus consists of 153 texts and approximately 4.2 million words, giving an average text length of approximately 27,500 words. The context-governed portion of the corpus consists of 708 texts and approximately

5.4 million words, giving an average of approximately 7,600 words per text. The CANCODE matrix of speech-genres (see McCarthy 1998: 9–10) yields fifteen cells and the initial target was to gather approximately 65,000 words per cell. Corpora built to represent a variety of a language show a similar diversity in terms of text number and length. For example, MICASE contains a total of 152 speech events ranging in type from lectures to meetings to dissertation defences to service encounters and, therefore, seeks to cover all speech which occurs in an academic setting. These speech events range in length from 19 to 178 minutes and in word count from 2,805 to 30,328 words (see Simpson *et al.* 2007).

3. Assessing the representativeness and balance of a corpus

Leech (1991: 27) maintains that a corpus is representative if 'findings based on its contents can be generalised to a larger hypothetical corpus'. Therefore, in the case of a corpus said to represent a language variety, it is in fact representative if its findings can be generalised to the said language variety (or Variety). Sinclair (2005: 4) outlines six defining steps towards achieving as representative a corpus as possible. The first four of these steps relate to the overall corpus design, such as the construction of the proposed corpus sampling frame, steps that can be dealt with in the pre-corpus building stage:

1 Decide on the structural criteria that you will use to build the corpus, and apply them to create a framework for the principal corpus components.
2 For each component draw up a comprehensive inventory of text types that are found there.
3 Put the text types in a priority order, taking into account all the factors that you think might increase or decrease the importance of a text type.
4 Estimate a target size for each text type, relating together (i) the overall target size for the component, (ii) the number of text types, (iii) the importance of each and (iv) the practicality of gathering quantities of it.
5 As the corpus takes shape, maintain comparison between the actual dimensions of the material and the original plan.
6 (Most important of all) document these steps so that users can have a reference point if they get unexpected results, and that improvements can be made on the basis of experience.

The fifth and sixth steps here are concerned with the *balance* of the corpus, something that is difficult to account for in the planning stages of the corpus but that may be done after a pilot or provisional corpus has been built. A balanced corpus relies heavily on intuition and best estimates (Atkins *et al.* 1992; Sinclair 2005; McEnery *et al.* 2006). This has led Sinclair (2005) to refer to balance as a rather vague notion but important nonetheless. However, in relation to corpora built to represent a language Variety or variety, when assessing the balance of a corpus it is useful to examine other corpora, and it is becoming increasingly popular, 'for good or ill' (McEnery *et al.* 2006: 17), to adopt an existing corpus model and, in doing so, to assume that issues of balance have been addressed. Written corpora like the Brown Corpus and the LOB are generally accepted as balanced written corpora. The BNC, despite the imbalance between the spoken and written components, is generally accepted to be a balanced corpus, the spoken component all the more so given that it was collected using both demographic and context-governed approaches. This corpus design has been used by the American National Corpus, the Korean National Corpus and the Polish National Corpus. ICE could be considered a better example of a balanced corpus given that it is more heavily weighted in favour of spoken texts. However, a sixty–forty split like that in ICE is probably still not sufficient to represent the everyday linguistic experience of most people, who would experience much more speech than writing in their day-to-day lives. The LSWE contains four core registers (or varieties): *conversation*, *newspaper language*, *fiction* and *academic prose*. According to Biber *et al.* (1999: 25), these four were selected on the basis of balance in that they 'include a manageable number of distinctions while covering much of the range of variation in English'. For example, conversation is the register most commonly encountered by native speakers, whereas academic prose is a highly specialised register that native speakers encounter infrequently. Between these two extremes are the popular registers of newspapers and fiction. The corpus was designed to contain 5,000,000 words per register.

CANCODE, whose genre-based design was successfully adapted in the creation of LCIE (see Farr *et al.* 2004), is also considered a balanced corpus; however, this notion of balance was arrived at in a slightly different way from corpora such as the BNC. As already mentioned, the initial target for the CANCODE team was a figure of 65,000 words per cell. It was found that certain data, for example intimate conversation and business meetings, were more difficult to collect than other types because of their sensitive nature. Therefore, some cells were found to be more 'full' than others. The progress from the initial one million words to the final target of five million addressed these imbalances and attempted, where possible, to equally cover all the context types in the corpus. McCarthy (1998: 11) maintains that a fluid corpus design like that of CANCODE is essential as 'in the past, corpora have tended to become fossilised either because the initial design is rigidly and uncompromisingly held to, or because a particular numerical target has been achieved'. This notion of corpus design as fluid or organic in order to maintain balance is echoed in what Biber (1993: 255) calls the 'bottom-line' in corpus design. According to Biber, 'the parameters of a fully representative corpus cannot be determined at the outset. Rather, corpus work proceeds in a cyclical fashion' (ibid.: 255–6). Approaching corpus design in this way allows researchers to explore language change over a period of time, an important aspect of the study of any language Variety. However, in corpus linguistics in general, there exists a relative paucity of diachronic corpora, especially in the area of spoken language (see, however, Cutting 2001 for an example of a spoken diachronic corpus).

Hunston (2002: 30) contends that the real question as regards representativeness is how the balance of a corpus should be taken into account when interpreting data from that corpus. Any corpus that is built to represent a Variety and/or a variety of a language is by its nature a multi-purpose corpus, therefore, the builder(s) cannot predict all the queries that may be made of it. Thus, according to Sinclair (2005), it is necessary to document all decisions made in regard to the criteria decided upon in building the corpus. The analyst can then check this documentation to ensure that the corpus is suitable for the proposed purpose. Hunston (2002), Meyer (2002), Sinclair (2005) and McEnery *et al.* (2006) all maintain that the responsibility for corpus analysis is a shared one. Moreover, as Hunston (2002: 23) notes, 'a statement about evidence in a corpus is a statement about that corpus, not about the language or register of which the corpus is a sample'.

4. What can a corpus tell us about a language Variety? The case of LCIE

LCIE is a one-million-word corpus of naturally occurring spoken Irish English built to allow the description of Irish English as a Variety in itself rather than how it is similar to or different from other Varieties of English such as British English (for a full description of the design of LCIE see Farr *et al.* 2004). Because of the size of the corpus, much of the research done to date using LCIE is not simply quantitative in nature, a feature of much of the analysis relating to the 'mega-corpora', but also features a large degree of qualitative analysis. In addition to this, much of the research centred on the corpus has focused on the realm of pragmatics. This has allowed researchers working with the corpus to provide some very interesting insights into lexico-grammatical representations of socio-cultural norms in Irish society.

One area that has received a lot of attention is the use of hedging as a politeness strategy in Irish English. From a quantitative viewpoint, on a Varietal level, Farr and O'Keeffe (2002) found that the hedges *I would say* and *I'd say* are used more frequently by Irish speakers than by British or American speakers. Indeed, they discovered that Irish speakers are twice as tentative as their American counterparts. They label this initial finding 'restrictive in its insightfulness' (p. 29) because of the fact that geographically constrained frameworks do not further an understanding of how or why hedges are used in face-to-face interaction. In reaction to this, they analyse two varietal sub-corpora from LCIE, a 55,000-word corpus of radio phone-ins and a 52,000-word corpus of post-observation teacher training interaction (POTTI), in order to more thoroughly explore the use of *would* as a hedging device in an Irish institutional setting. In addition to confirming that Irish speakers soften face-threatening acts such as disagreement or giving advice, they also found that speakers would very often downtone when speaking about themselves, even where the propositional content is undisputed (*My hair would be brown* or *I'd be from Clare*, for example). They propose that, in order to fully understand why speakers hedge, it is necessary to consider the Irish socio-cultural context. They maintain that 'in Irish society, directness is very often avoided … "forwardness", which ranges from being direct to being self-promoting, is not valued' (p. 42). Therefore, Irish speakers may feel added pressure to hedge in situations where British or American speakers may think it unnecessary.

This research also points towards another socio-cultural element of Irish English, in that speakers appear to be acutely aware of asymmetrical speech relationships and often the speaker with the most power will seek to facilitate a more symmetric interaction. Hedging is one strategy that Irish people frequently use to overcome this asymmetry. Farr *et al.* (2004) analysed the occurrence of hedging across five contexts in LCIE: family discourse, teaching training feedback, service encounters, female friends chatting and radio phone-ins. They found the lowest instance of hedging occurred in service encounters where 'there is an existing social schema for the interaction within exogenous roles' (pp. 16–17), which simultaneously allows maximum transactional efficiency and minimum threat to face. The next least hedged context was the family, where although the speaker relationships are asymmetric in nature, the context of family discourse acts as a 'meta-hedge' (see Section 5 below). They also demonstrate that hedging is far more frequent in the more formal contexts of radio phone-ins and in teacher training feedback. O'Keeffe (2005) focuses on question forms in radio phone-ins and illustrates that, although many asymmetrical norms of institutional discourse apply to this context, there is widespread downtoning of power at a lexico-grammatical level. In addition to using hedges, the presenter of the radio show employs a variety of features such as first name vocatives, latching and reflexive pronouns, as in *What are you doing with yourself nowadays?*, to create a 'pseudo-intimate' (p. 340) environment between speaker and caller. Similarly, Farr (2005) explores the use of three relational strategies present in her POTTI corpus to demonstrate how cultural features of Irish discourse serve to lessen asymmetrical speech relationships. She claims that small talk, in particular talk about health issues, is a socially typical way of establishing solidarity between speakers in this context. Furthermore, she demonstrates how shared socio-cultural references such as *muinteóir*, the Gaelic word for teacher, are a method of diluting institutional power on the part of the teacher trainer in interaction with the trainee.

Recently, LCIE has also been utilised in the area of *variational pragmatics* (see Schneider and Barron 2005). LCIE was designed as a comparable corpus to CANCODE. This allows researchers working with the corpus to address questions at both a Varietal level (Irish English versus British English) and a varietal level (variation within Irish English itself in different contexts of use). O'Keeffe and Adolphs (2008) analyse two 20,000-word corpora of casual conversation taken from LCIE and CANCODE in order to examine the differences between the use of listener response tokens by British and Irish females around the age of twenty. They found that although the discourse and pragmatic functions of these tokens remain constant across the two datasets, there are marked differences between the form and frequency of the tokens. In relation to form, tokens which have religious reference or are swear words, for example *Jesus*, are more common in Irish English. Farr (2005) has shown that these tokens occur even in the formal context of teacher training. O'Keeffe and Adolphs link the higher occurrence of tokens with religious reference to different socio-cultural norms that exist between the two societies. The higher frequency of these tokens is attributed to the continuing importance of religion in Irish society. They also demonstrate that, in terms of overall frequency, listener response tokens are 59 per cent more frequent in the British English data than in Irish English. The authors raise a number of interesting questions concerning discourse norms in both societies – for example: Are British people better listeners? Do Irish people talk more and respond less? Do Irish people yield turns less and interrupt more? – which will hopefully form the basis of much of the future work on LCIE.

5. What can a corpus tell us about a language variety? The case of Irish family discourse

As already mentioned, modern corpora built to represent a Variety of a language, such as LCIE, are constructed using a range of varieties of the language in question. Therefore, in the same way that LCIE enables researchers to describe a language Variety, smaller sub-corpora of this can also allow for descriptions of situational variation in varieties or registers. Register variation is generally associated with the work of Biber throughout the years (for example, Biber 1988, 1995). Biber *et al.* (1999) developed a matrix of situational characteristics that distinguish one register from another and this is applied to family discourse in Table 7.1. The characteristic *participant roles* (adapted from Ventola 1979) has been added to account for the unique speaker relationships that exist in this context; there exist pre-established speaker roles wherein the speakers are bound in an asymmetrical power relationship in an intimate and informal register.

Table 7.1 The situational characteristics of family discourse

The family
Register • *Mode* – spoken: face-to-face • *Interactive online production* – spontaneous, no advanced planning • *Shared immediate situation* – the family home • *Main communicative purpose/content* – personal communication • *Audience* – private, immediate family members only • *Participant roles* – hierarchic/asymmetrical – parents – children, sibling – sibling Fixed/stable and pre-established speaker relationship – family – father, mother, brothers, sisters • *Dialect domain* – local: base-level dialect (Crystal 2000).

It has previously been noted that researchers working with LCIE have demonstrated that family discourse is markedly less hedged than discourse in other context types such as female friends chatting and radio phone-ins (Farr *et al.* 2004). Building on this work, the present author (Clancy 2005) used a corpus of c.12,500 words of casual conversation recorded in the home/family environment to compare the occurrences of eight hedges prominent in Irish English across two distinct context-types – family discourse and radio phone-ins. It was found that hedges occur more than twice as frequently in radio phone-ins than in family discourse, and this was again attributed to the unique nature of family discourse. For example, some hedges, such as *kind of/sort of*, function to reduce the social distance between speakers and also to indicate the speaker's desire for a relaxed relationship with the addressee (Holmes 1993: 101), something that has to be worked at in contexts such as radio phone-ins in order to create the pseudo-intimacy crucial to the success of the interaction, but that is unnecessary in the family as the speakers perceive social distance as being negligible. Furthermore, it has been shown (Clancy, 2011a) that it appears that all utterances in family discourse are 'meta-hedged' by the context itself, thereby eliminating the need for lexical realisations of the strategy. The present author contends that it may be hypothesised that the more intimate the context-type, the more direct a speaker can be and the less chance there is of participants perceiving an attack to their face. Therefore, it could be proposed that the more intimate the data the less need there is to hedge or soften utterances.

From the perspective of variational pragmatics within Irish society itself, the present author (Clancy 2011b) has employed two datasets representing spoken language collected in the home/family environment, one from a middle-class Irish family and one from a family belonging to the Irish Travelling community, to illustrate how hedging is far more frequent in a settled family than in a Traveller family. This can be attributed to socio-cultural factors such as the primacy of the family in Traveller culture and the differing educational profiles of the two communities. It is argued that hedges such as *I think*, *like*, *you know*, *actually* and *just* represent those that are critical to politeness in 'mainstream' Irish culture. They are the absolute minimum needed for polite interaction among participants in Irish society and ensure a smooth transition from the family community of practice to the wider social world. They are in a sense 'redundant' in the Travelling community, given that they rarely move into the realm of mainstream society.

Further reading

Aston, G. and Burnard, L. (1998) *The BNC Handbook: Exploring the British National Corpus with SARA*. Edinburgh: Edinburgh University Press.

Meyer, C. (2002) *English Corpus Linguistics: An Introduction*. Cambridge: Cambridge University Press. (This book provides an accessible introduction to corpus linguistics in addition to a step-by-step guide to corpus design, construction and analysis. Meyer draws heavily on corpora representing different Varieties of English such as the BNC and ICE in order to illustrate each stage.)

Simpson, R., Lee, D., Leicher, S. and Ädel, A. (2007) *MICASE Manual*. Available at http://lw.lsa.umich.edu/eli/micase/MICASE_MANUAL.pdf (accessed 7 November 2008). (These represent two essential guides for any researcher wishing to construct a corpus that represents either a language Variety (the BNC) or variety (MICASE)).

Schneider, K. and Barron, A. (eds) (2008) *Variational Pragmatics: A Focus on Regional Varieties in Pluricentric Languages*, Amsterdam: John Benjamins. (Not a corpus publication *per se*; however, there are three chapters that illustrate how corpora can be used to examine the nuances that exist between different language Varieties in a variety of contexts. O'Keeffe and Adolphs examine differences between Irish (LCIE) and British (CANCODE) English. Jautz compares British (BNC) and New Zealand (Wellington Corpus of Spoken New Zealand English) English and Plevoets *et al.* explore Netherlandic and Belgian Dutch (*Corpus Gesproken Nederlands*)).

References

Aston, G. and Burnard, L. (1998) *The BNC Handbook: Exploring the British National Corpus with SARA*. Edinburgh: Edinburgh University Press.

Atkins, S., Clear, J. and Ostler, N. (1992) 'Corpus Design Criteria', *Literary and Linguistic Computing* 7(1): 1–16.

Biber, D. (1988) *Variation across Speech and Writing*. Cambridge: Cambridge University Press.

——(1990) 'Methodological Issues Regarding Corpus-based Analyses of Linguistic Variation', *Literary and Linguistic Computing* 5(4): 257–69.

——(1993) 'Representativeness in Corpus Design', *Literary and Linguistic Computing* 8(4): 243–57.

——(1995) *Dimensions of Register Variation*. Cambridge: Cambridge University Press.

Biber, D., Johansson, S., Leech, G., Conrad, S. and Finnegan, E. (1999) *The Longman Grammar of Spoken and Written English*. London: Longman.

Chafe, W., Du Bois, J. and Thompson, S. (1991) 'Towards a New Corpus of American English', in K. Aijmer and B. Altenberg (eds) *English Corpus Linguistics*. London: Longman, pp. 64–82.

Cheng, W., Greaves, C. and Warren, M. (2008) *A Corpus-driven Study of Discourse Intonation*. Amsterdam: John Benjamins.

Clancy, B. (2005) '*You're Fat. You'll Eat Them All*: Politeness Strategies in Family Discourse', in A. Barron and K. Schneider (eds) *The Pragmatics of Irish English*. Berlin: Mouton de Gruyter, pp. 177–99.

——(2011a) '*Do you want to do it yourself like?* Hedging in Irish Traveller and Settled Family Discourse', in: B. Davies, M. Haugh and A. Merrison (eds) *Situated Politeness*. London: Continuum, pp. 129–46.

——(2011b) 'Complementary Perspectives on Hedging Behaviour in Family Discourse: The Analytical Synergy of Corpus Linguistics and Variational Pragmatics', *International Journal of Corpus Linguistics* 16(3): 372–91.

Crowdy, S. (1993) 'Spoken Corpus Design', *Literary and Linguistic Computing* 8(4): 259–65.

Crystal, D. (2000) 'Emerging Englishes', *English Teaching Professional* 14: 3–6.

——(2001) *Language and the Internet*. Cambridge: Cambridge University Press.

Cutting, J. (2001) 'The Speech Acts of the In-group', *Journal of Pragmatics* 33: 1207–33.

Farr, F. (2005) 'Relational Strategies in the Discourse of Professional Performance Review in an Irish Academic Environment: The Case of Language Teacher Education', in A. Barron and K. Schneider (eds) *The Pragmatics of Irish English*. Berlin: Mouton de Gruyter, pp. 203–34.

Farr, F. and O'Keeffe, A. (2002) '*Would* as a Hedging Device in an Irish Context: An Intra-varietal Comparison of Institutionalised Spoken Interaction', in R. Reppen, S. Fitzmaurice and D. Biber (eds) *Using Corpora to Explore Linguistic Variation*. Amsterdam: John Benjamins, pp. 25–48.

Farr, F., Murphy, B. and O'Keeffe, A. (2004) 'The Limerick Corpus of Irish English: Design, Description and Application', *Teanga* 21: 5–29.

Greenbaum, S. (1991) 'The Development of the International Corpus of English', in K. Aijmer and B. Altenberg (eds) *English Corpus Linguistics*. London: Longman, pp. 83–91.

Holmes, J. (1993) '"New Zealand Women are Good to Talk to": An Analysis of Politeness Strategies in Interaction', *Journal of Pragmatics* 20: 91–116.

Hudson, R. (1980) *Sociolinguistics*. Cambridge: Cambridge University Press.

Hunston, S. (2002) *Corpora in Applied Linguistics*. Cambridge: Cambridge University Press.

Johansson, S., Leech, G. and Goodluck, H. (1978) *Manual of Information to Accompany the Lancaster/Oslo-Bergen Corpus of British English, for Use with Digital Computers*. Oslo: Department of English, University of Oslo.

Knowles, G. (1990) 'The Use of Spoken and Written Corpora in the Teaching of Linguistics', *Literary and Linguistic Computing* 5(1): 45–48.

Labov, W. (1966) *The Social Stratification of English in New York City*. Washington, DC: Centre for Applied Linguistics.

——(1972) *Sociolinguistic Patterns*. Philadelphia, PA: University of Pennsylvania Press.

Leech, G. (1991) 'The State of the Art in Corpus Linguistics', in K. Aijmer and B. Altenberg (eds) *English Corpus Linguistics*. London: Longman, pp. 8–30.

McCarthy, M. (1998) *Spoken Language and Applied Linguistics*. Cambridge: Cambridge University Press.

McEnery, T., Xiao, R. and Tono, Y. (2006) *Corpus-based Language Studies: An Advanced Resource Book*. London: Routledge.

Meyer, C. (2002) *English Corpus Linguistics: An Introduction*. Cambridge: Cambridge University Press.

Milroy, L. (1987) *Language and Social Networks*. Oxford: Blackwell.

Nelson, G. (1996) 'The Design of the Corpus', in S. Greenbaum (ed.) *Comparing English Worldwide: The International Corpus of English*. Oxford: Oxford University Press, pp. 27–36.

O'Keeffe, A. (2005) '*You've a Daughter Yourself?* A Corpus-based Look at Question Forms in an Irish Radio Phone-in', in A. Barron and K. Schneider (eds) *The Pragmatics of Irish English*. Berlin: Mouton de Gruyter, pp. 339–66.

O'Keeffe, A. and Adolphs, S. (2008) 'Response Tokens in British and Irish Discourse: Corpus, Context and Variational Pragmatics', in K. Schneider and A. Barron (eds) *Variational Pragmatics: A Focus on Regional Varieties in Pluricentric Languages*. Amsterdam: John Benjamins, pp. 69–98.

Quirk, R. (1995) *Grammatical and Lexical Variance in English*. London: Longman.

Schneider, K. and Barron, A. (2005) 'Variational Pragmatics: Contours of a New Discipline', unpublished paper presented at the 9th International Pragmatics Conference, Riva del Garda, 10–15 July.

Simpson, R., Lee, D., Leicher, S. and Ädel, A. (2007) *MICASE Manual*. Available at http://lw.lsa.umich.edu/eli/micase/MICASE_MANUAL.pdf (accessed 7 November 2008).

Sinclair, J. (2005) 'Corpus and Text – Basic Principles', in M. Wynne (ed.) *Developing Linguistic Corpora: A Guide to Good Practice*. Oxford: Oxbow Books, pp. 1–16; available at http://ahds.ac.uk/linguistic-corpora/ (accessed 28 October 2008).

Trudgill, W. (1974) *The Social Differentiation of English in Norwich*. Cambridge: Cambridge University Press.

Ventola, E. (1979) 'The Structure of Casual Conversation in English', *Journal of Pragmatics* 3: 267–98.

Wolfram, W. and Schilling-Estes, N. (2006) *American English: Dialects and Variation*. Oxford: Blackwell.

8

Building a specialised audio-visual corpus

Paul Thompson

1. What are specialised audio-visual corpora and what are they used for?

Writing a chapter about building audio-visual corpora is a challenge as this is an area of considerable growth in corpus linguistics, computational linguistics, behavioural sciences and language pedagogy, among others, and, by the time this chapter appears, it is likely that technological advances will have moved the field substantially further forward.

In broad terms, an audio-visual corpus is a corpus that consists of orthographic transcripts of spoken language communication events, and the audio and/or video recordings of the original events. Such a corpus is likely to have links in the transcripts, which makes it possible to locate the relevant parts of the audio-visual records. In a basic form the links could consist of indexical information included with the transcripts which would allow the researcher to find the section of the recording manually, but in a more sophisticated form such annotation, included in an electronic document, would allow the user to click on a button or activate a hyperlink within the electronic version of the transcript and automatically open the file in a media player at the exact point. A further, alternative type of audio-visual corpus is one in which existing audio-visual texts, such as films, poster advertisements or online news pages, are annotated for multimodal analysis (see Adolphs and Knight, this volume). Such annotations may be organised on a range of levels, coding features such as voice, music, other sounds, graphically represented words, hand gestures, facial gestures, location, and so on, and these codes can be organised in parallel rows or columns. Baldry and Thibault (2006), for example, present a framework for transcription and analysis of multimodal texts using television advertisements and websites as example texts, and their approach can be applied to collections of multimodal texts.

A specialised audio-visual corpus may therefore contain recordings of sets of spoken language events that are used for analysis of situated language behaviours in specialised settings – such as doctor–patient consultations, child–caregiver interactions or classroom task activities – or it may contain samples of certain categories of multimodal texts. The purpose of constructing an audio-visual corpus is to make it possible to identify relationships between the non-linguistic and linguistic features of human or textual interaction, or to allow access to information that supplements the plain orthographic transcription. In this chapter, the focus is primarily on corpora in which the transcripts are linked to the video or audio recordings, or in which the video data have been made searchable for certain coded features.

Some linguistic investigations are more heavily dependent on audio-visual information than others. An example of the former is the study of sign languages, which are gestural and where the facility to record language performance on video (frontal view of the signer, with facial expression and hand gestures clearly presented) constitutes an excellent alternative to simple orthographic representation, or to a succession of still photographs, each portraying a single gesture. Such a project does, however, also present its own challenges as the video data have to be searchable by some means. If one is to look within a sign language corpus for the representation of 'a large red ball', for example, one has to have either the means to enter the orthographic form 'a large red ball' (which would use non-sign language means to retrieve sign language representations), or some graphic means by which a sign language user could formulate a non-orthographic query capable of locating all examples of this concept within the corpus. The British Sign Language corpus and the corpus of German Sign Language data are two major projects building large-scale audio-visual corpus resources for the sign linguistics community.

There are many purposes for which linked transcript and video data can be used. In language teaching, the presentation of communicative events visually as well as orthographically can help the learner to relate language use to the contexts in which it occurs. An audio-visual corpus can be used in the same way as a multimedia language learning package, except that it also offers the user the opportunity to retrieve multiple examples of a phrase or a grammatical structure and hear/see those examples, one after another. The EU-funded SACODEYL project, for instance, exploits clips of commissioned video recordings of teenagers, from seven different European language groups, speaking about their interests, experiences, friends and families, and the SACODEYL website (see also Chambers, this volume) contains language learning activities which prompt students to watch clips from the videos and search for answers to set questions. At one level, the video provides language learners with good listening practice, with orthographic transcripts provided so that the learner can check his or her understanding, but, on another level, the learner can search the data to locate certain features. The SACODEYL data have been annotated so that one can search by topic, grammatical point and part of speech, among other features, and one can also do concordance searches. When the concordance lines appear, it is then possible to select any one line, click 'Go to section', and open the relevant wider section of the transcript. The learner can then choose to view that section of the video, online.

Another example of the use of an audio-visual corpus is in the investigation of language use in education. The Singapore Corpus of Research in Education (SCoRE) project at the Centre for Research in Pedagogy and Practice, National Institute of Education, Singapore, is collecting recordings of classroom interactions in a variety of subject areas (English, Mandarin, Malay, Tamil, Maths, Science) in different levels of education in Singapore. The corpus interface allows the user to search for words or phrases in the corpus and then choose to view a video clip (if available) or listen to an audio clip. The corpus data have also been annotated on a number of levels: it is consequently possible to search by part of speech, by semantic category or by syntactic, pragmatic or pedagogical features. The recordings have been divided into speaker turns, and for each turn there is a sound file. The user is given the choice for any search to receive the results in turns (in other words, with each word shown within the full turn of the speaker) rather than as KWIC concordances; if this option is chosen, the user is given the text for each turn in which the search items occur and also a link to the audio or video file. In addition to the access to the audio-visual material, the interface also generates statistics on the frequency of occurrence of each feature in each file, both in raw terms and also as a percentage of the entire file.

Constructing an audio-visual corpus involves providing the links between the transcript and the audio or video files. In the previous example, that of the SCoRE, the corpus developers have devoted an enormous amount of time, resources and expertise to preparing the corpus. Recording the data is in itself a major task, but after that the recordings have to be transcribed and speaker turns identified. Audio files for each turn are then created and given unique identifying names. The transcripts are annotated for the various features mentioned above, and the information stored in a searchable database. The interface then has to be built, trialled, revised and extended, exploiting existing technologies. Not every audio-visual corpus will have the same levels of multilayered annotation as the SCoRE but it has to be recognised that working with audio-visual corpora is a demanding enterprise.

An alternative way to work with audio data is to use a popular concordance program such as *WordSmith Tools* (Scott 2008) with a corpus of transcripts and audio recordings (see chapters by Scott and Tribble, this volume). Such a solution might be more appropriate for end-users who are trained in the use of the particular computer program for corpus analysis work and who, on a specific investigation, require access to the audio files for closer analysis. In the case of a study of phraseology in seminar talk, for example, analysts may want to be able to do concordance searches in a corpus of seminar transcripts for a variety of lexical chunks. Within *WordSmith Tools*, provided the corpus has been prepared in advance and the program's tag settings have been configured, the user can click in the Tag column of *WordSmith Tools Concord* to activate the audio player at the right point, and hear the intonational contours of the lexical chunks. To prepare the files, one needs to insert tags into the transcripts that refer to the audio recordings (the default audio file formats supported in *WordSmith Tools* are .mp3 and .wav but other formats can be accommodated). An example of the tagging is as follows, where the first tag is placed at the part of the transcript referred to and it identifies the .mp3 file that is to be played, while the closing tag indicates where the recording ends:

> < soundfile name = ah02e001.mp3 > on a double-sided sheet and once again i haven't put a summary on this one but what i have put < /soundfile >

The Help files for the program offer some guidance in this, but, again, it must be recognised this is a time-consuming task, and there are several complexities involved. The files can be set up in such a way that it is possible to listen to small clips of the audio files, as in the above example, but this requires creating many small files, with a high degree of precision, from the original audio recording. The more fine-grained the detail, the more time-intensive the task, but without fine granularity the corpus may be too limited in its uses. Another point that needs to be taken into account is that annotation of the data in order to make it useable in *WordSmith Tools* would not necessarily make it useable in other applications. In other words, the corpus is then tied into a particular package, when a more useful solution would be to make it useable in a range of programs.

So far we have proposed a number of reasons why a researcher might want to build an audio-visual corpus, and we have identified some of the ways in which a researcher might link audio and video inputs with orthographic transcripts. The purpose of the rest of this chapter is to give an overview of what the process of building an audio-visual corpus entails, from initial conception through project design to data collection, processing and finally the development of tools and interfaces for exploitation. Design criteria and data collection are discussed in Section 2, and transcription and annotation issues are reviewed in Section 3.

There are several tools available for the development of audio-visual corpora which make the job of linking points in the transcript to points in the video and audio files much easier. Some of these tools tie the developer into the proprietary system, while others use systems which have a higher degree of potential for interchangeability. A number of these tools will be discussed in Sections 3 and 4. As suggested in the first paragraph of this chapter, technology is advancing quickly, and it is dangerous to provide too much information on specific tools and platforms, so the discussion below will not attempt to be exhaustive. It is useful at this point to suggest that XML technologies offer flexibility (the 'X' in XML stands for 'extensible') and power, and that with researchers now starting to build better tools and interfaces for handling XML documents, it is probable that XML will become a standard for audio-visual corpora in the future. The final section of this chapter looks towards the future and speculates on what advances may be made in the coming years.

2. Collecting data

Corpus design is discussed in detail elsewhere in this volume (see Reppen, this volume, who discusses key considerations in building a corpus, and Koester, this volume, who deals with specialised corpora). Before collecting data through video recording, it is essential that appropriate ethical procedures are followed. Where the participants can clearly be identified through their physical features (on video), or acoustic features (through audio), they must be asked fairly to provide informed consent, and the researchers need to decide in advance what the data are to be used for, and to ensure that the data will be used only for the purposes stated. In some cases, the data will only be used by the research team and it is therefore easier to preserve anonymity, but if the audio and video recordings are to be made public in any form (such as in conference presentations or on the internet), permissions must be obtained before the data are collected. It is advisable to consult a legal expert in cases where the video recordings are to be put into the public domain. It is also important to consider carefully what possible uses the data may be put to in advance of data collection, as it is difficult to return to all participants after the data collection in order to collect consent retrospectively.

Data for such purposes are most likely to be collected in pre-determined locations, such as a room that has been set up specifically for the purposes of recording. For good audio recording it may be necessary to use more than a single microphone, and one solution for recording group conversations is to record each participant individually. Perez-Parent (2002) collected recordings of pupil–staff interactions in British primary school classrooms, in which each speaker was recorded on a mini-disc recorder with lapel microphone. The recordings were then brought together in a multichannel version, which allowed for much clearer distinction of each speaker's contribution, but Perez-Parent notes that, counter to expectation, the mini-disc recorders functioned at slightly different speeds and therefore the recordings had to be further processed, with some 'stretching' of the files, in order to synchronise them.

Quality video recording in particular requires good lighting and camera work, as well as good equipment. Decisions about the camera angles to take and the lighting required will depend on the purposes of the project. In the Headtalk project conducted at the University of Nottingham, UK (see Adolphs and Knight, this volume), the focus is on the uses of head nodding and hand gestures in conversation. The team has developed techniques for the automatic analysis of the video data, which identifies head and hand movements and tracks the movements. To make the head and hand identifiable, however, it was necessary to ensure that people in the video recordings were seated, with face towards the camera, in a well-lit location and wearing long sleeves, so that it was possible to distinguish each hand clearly from the rest of the arm. One of the elements to be considered in preparing for good data collection, then, may be that of visual detail – what clothes the participants are wearing, what the background is, how well the speakers' features stand out against that background, whether lighting is required to improve the visibility of key features, and so on.

Another example is the AMI (Augmented Multi-party Interaction) Meeting Corpus which consists of 100 hours of meeting recording. The data in the corpus are drawn from video material recorded with a number of cameras in a given smart room, set optimally to capture different shots of participants, and a range of audio captures on several microphones, which have then to be synchronised. The cameras are set to capture each participant's facial and hand gestures (most are seated around the table and can only be seen from the midriff up) and the view provided is a fish-eye lens view, so that more peripheral information can be gathered. For analysis purposes, three or four camera angles can be placed in a row alongside each other on the screen, so that a more comprehensive perspective of the event can be captured. In addition to the individual view camera shots, there are also cameras set to capture the whole room, and output from a slide projector and an electronic whiteboard.

The Computers in the Human Interaction Loop (CHIL) project (Mostefa *et al.* 2007) went further by recording lectures and meetings in five different locations, each of which was a smart room. The main purpose of the project was to support the development and evaluation of multimodal technologies in the analysis of realistic human interaction, and the project added the variation of location as an extra challenge. In each location the minimum specifications for the data collection set-up included at least eighty-eight microphones capturing both close-talking and far-field acoustic data, four fixed cameras (one in each corner of the room), a fixed panoramic camera under the room ceiling and one active pan–tilt–zoom camera. The size of the project is impressive, with huge quantities of data collected and processed. While not immediately replicable, it provides a full and useful range of evaluations of the technologies for data capture and for semi-automatic to automatic analysis of the data.

The quality of data collected for an audio-visual corpus will depend not only on the positioning and number of recording devices but also on the equipment used and the processes by which data are transferred, synchronised, saved and transformed, and also on the skill of those who capture the data. It is not possible to examine these in detail here, but it should be noted that generally speaking it is advisable to capture data at the highest resolution and then to make use of compression technologies at later stages, when smaller file sizes, and faster transfer times, are required, and keep the high resolution recordings as archive material.

3. Preparing transcriptions and annotations

One of the first decisions to be made is that of which transcription and spelling conventions to use. The choice will be determined to a large extent by the nature of the research, and, in cases where a corpus is being developed as a resource to be placed in the public domain, predictions of the range of potential uses for the corpus. For more detailed discussion of the issues, see Reppen and Adolphs and Knight, this volume.

Consistency is a main concern whatever the system chosen. The team that is responsible for making the transcription needs to set up a shared document for specifying the conventions to be used. This document sets out the agreed conventions but is subject to addition and amendment as the team encounters problematic cases of spelling or coding that have to be decided on during the course of transcription. Where the members of the team are working in geographically diverse locations, it is advisable to set up shared documents, using an online document-sharing facility, or to set up a discussion Wiki.

Transcription and coding can be performed concurrently or sequentially; in other words, one approach is to produce an orthographic transcription quickly and then use this as the basis for one or many layers of annotation, while another approach is to make the transcription and insert the time stamps at the same time, and possibly to insert other levels of annotation as well. If working with CLAN, for example, the tool developed for use with the Child Language Data Exchange System (CHILDES) database, one can insert the time stamps directly into the transcripts from within the program. Alternatively, working with *Praat*, the freeware research transcription tool for the synthesis, analysis and manipulation of speech, the transcriber can work from the spectrogram to the orthographic (or other) transcription and link the two at whatever level is required (for example, phoneme, word or utterance).

When working with video data, some transcribers prefer to work with the audio input first as they find the visual mode distracts their attention from the oral, while other transcribers have a preference for a bimodal view of the event, on the basis that paralinguistic, gestural and other features help them to make sense of the audio input.

For the transcriber who is used to the physical audiocassette transcription machine there is a simple program called *Soundscriber*, developed by Eric Breck for the MICASE corpus project. This program plays audio and video files and has a 'walk' facility which plays a chunk of the file (say, four seconds long) three times on a loop and then moves to the next chunk, with a slight overlap built in.

The programs mentioned in the previous paragraphs are primarily for the transcription of audio data. A comprehensive set of links to annotation tools, including transcription tools, can be found on the Linguistic Data Consortium website, where there is a separate page for annotation tools used for the mark-up of gesture. It is to the latter that we now turn, taking two examples of existing tools.

Michael Kipp has developed a video annotation and analysis tool called *Anvil*. This program presents a multiple view, of the video input in one window (or more, if there is more than one video input), the video controls in another window, a description of the gesture codes applied to the present view of the video and, below all this, the transcription within a multilevel representation that is similar to a musical score. As the video moves, the transcription lines move past, too, and at any point in the transcription the researcher can see the multiple levels of annotation applied. This window can also present speech waveforms and the *Praat* intensity diagrams (*Anvil* imports *Praat* files directly). In addition to *Praat* files, *Anvil* can also import Rhetorical Structure Theory (RST) files from the RST program made by O'Donnell (for coding clause relations). *Anvil* is an XML tool and the program produces XML files, which gives the potential for interchangeability.

A commercial program that can used for annotation of behavioural features of video data is the *Observer XT* program which supports the creation of timestamped state and event codes, either in independent layers or in layers related in a hierarchical decomposition. As with *Anvil*, it is possible to open several windows together, to see the video, the timeline, the codes, the speech waveform, in addition to the transcription, and also to export to XML. An additional advantage to the program is that it offers the facility to conduct collaborative coding of the data with members of a team working independently in space and time.

Two toolkits that are Open Source at the time of writing and which create XML files are the *NITE Toolkit*, used on the AMI project (see Carletta *et al.* 2003), and *EXMARaLDA*. The *NITE Toolkit* is a set of libraries and tools for the creation, analysis and browsing of annotated multimodal, text or spoken language corpora, and it can represent both timing and rich linguistic structure. It also contains libraries for developers and a number of end user tools. The *EXMARaLDA* project has developed a set of concepts and tools for the transcription and annotation of spoken language, and for the creation and analysis of spoken language corpora. The tools are Java programs which can be used for editing transcriptions in partitur (musical score) notation, and for merging the transcriptions with their corresponding recordings into corpora and enriching them with metadata (see also Adolphs and Knight, this volume). A demonstration of data that have been marked up using *EXMARaLDA* can be found on its website.

The discussion so far has concentrated on processes and technologies for annotating data without providing an example of what annotation frameworks might be used with multimodal data. Pastra (2008) introduces a framework based on Rhetorical Structure Theory which describes the semantic interplay between verbal and non-verbal communication. The framework, called COSMOROE, has three core relations (equivalence, complementarity and independence) to describe the relationship between verbal and non-verbal content, and for each core relation there are sub-types. This framework, it is claimed, provides a 'language' for investigating cross-channel dialectics, and is clearly developed for a purpose. The framework has been implemented on a corpus of TV travel programmes and the data were annotated using *Anvil*.

The annotation scheme for the AMI corpus (see Section 2 above) describes individual actions and gestures on four 'layers': head gestures, hand gestures (further separated into deictic and non-deictic), leg gestures and trunk gestures. The trunk events, to take an example, are coded as one of the following: shrug, sit_upright, lean_forward, lean_backward, other_trunk, no_trunk, or off_camera. The coding is added using one of the tools in the *NITE Toolkit*, the Event Editor, and it is entered into an XML file that is created purely for trunk gesture information. In other words, each layer of coding is held in a separate file.

4. The interface: assembly and analysis

In programs such as *Anvil* or *Observer XT*, the interface is built into the program. These interfaces require that the user possess a licence for the program and that the program is installed locally. In some projects, however, the aim may be to make the corpus available to the wider research community in a more independent manner, and the most likely medium for this is the world-wide web. This offers a number of challenges, including the following:

- Download speeds
- File formats
- Provision of adequate flexibility.

The corpus builder needs to consider the limitations of access to the internet for potential users of the corpus, particularly the differing speeds of data transfer, and also the frequent congestion of the system. When investigating an audio-visual corpus, the user does not want to wait several minutes for a video to open in the local browser, and preferably the video should open almost immediately. Clearly there is much to be said for creating lighter data, particularly in the size of the video files that are called for when a hyperlink is clicked. A file which is 100 MB in size will take much longer to send and load than a 10 MB file. One solution is to use video streaming, which is a technique for transferring compressed video data to a computer over the internet in a continuous flow so that a user can begin viewing it before the entire file has been received. One factor affecting the choice between streaming and non-streaming video is that of whether the corpus holder wants to prevent the video being held temporarily (at least) on the user's computer – in the case of steaming video, this is prevented, but if the file is downloaded to the user's computer it is possible that the user will save a copy locally.

The second problem is that of the file formats. At the time of writing, there is a variety of video file formats such as *Real Audio* (.ra), *Shockwave* (.swf), *QuickTime* (.mov), *Audio/Video Interleaved* (.avi) and *Windows Media Video* (.wmv). One's choice of video file format will be partly determined by the quality of the picture and by the size of files produced, but it will also be affected by the currency of the player required for playback of the file. In most cases, video player plug-ins can be downloaded for popular internet browsers, but the corpus developer will probably want to choose a media player that is widely used and that is likely to have a long life (with new plug-ins regularly created for newer versions of the browsers).

The Scottish Corpus of Texts and Speech (SCOTS) website contains video data that is accessible through a browser. The transcripts are segmented into tone units and the user is able to click on any given point on the transcript, then select the video view icon from the bottom of the screen and activate the video at that point of the file. The video is activated by a Java script command that communicates with a *QuickTime* plug-in. The video starts playing at that point and then continues until manually stopped. The benefit of this method is that the mark-up of the document is relatively simple: a timestamp is recorded for the beginning point of each segment, and the HTML for the document has an identifier which is linked to that timestamp. It is not necessary to add information about the closing point of each segment (although, technically, it would not be difficult to retrieve that information from the timestamp for the next segment). This is an approach taken on several corpus websites which provide access to audio or video files.

Some researchers, however, may prefer to have only a smaller section played, either because this is seen to be a more economical way to transfer data from one source to another (if the user is going to activate a video at a given point and then play the video straight through, then all of the video file has to be transmitted, potentially), or because the user is interested in working intensively with that section. Approaches that can be taken here are:

- Split the audio file into short chunks, in an arbitrary manner.
- Split the files at selected points, such as at turn boundaries.
- Select parts of a recording on the grounds of a query.

The COLT corpus team at the University of Bergen made the sound files for the corpus available through a web interface (Hofland 2003). The sound files were split into ten-second chunks (this can done automatically using a file-splitting command), and then timestamps were added into the files at the break points. The ten-second files load reasonably quickly and the method of aligning text to sound is efficient, but one drawback is that a ten-second extract does not necessarily have natural boundaries.

The SCoRE (mentioned in Section 1 above) has employed the second method: individual sound files have been created for each of the speaker turns in the original audio files. The interface employs Java script to activate the media player (built around the Adobe Flash player) to play the sound files. Each turn in the transcripts is coded with information about the corresponding sound file, and when a turn is retrieved and displayed in a search results page a hyperlink to the sound file is created. It is this link which retrieves the sound file and opens the media player. Once the media player opens, it then automatically plays the file. The controls to the player allow the user to manipulate the file, with play and pause functionality.

A similar approach but with added sophistication, exemplifying the third option of selecting points of a recording through timestamp information, is taken in the design of the GLOSSA corpus query interface created at the Tekstlab at the University of Oslo and used by two corpus projects: a corpus of the Oslo dialect of Norwegian, and a Scandinavian dialect corpus of five Nordic languages (Norwegian, Swedish, Danish, Icelandic and Faroese). Among many functions available in the interface, we shall choose the playback features (for a screenshot, see Andersen, this volume).

The video picture is displayed in the top right corner through a *QuickTime* plug-in, with controls to the right of the video image which allow the viewer to start and stop the playback. Pressing either button opens up a digital counter and the user can change the start and end points of the clip using these counters. At the bottom are the concordances for the search term, and the small icons at the beginning of each line allow the user to activate either the audio or video playback. On the left side of the video player is the relevant section of the transcript – here showing the selected concordance line and three more before and after (this option was selected using the 'context' menu above the start control). Each line of the transcript has been given a timestamp, in the preparation of the corpus. The context drop-down menu is a powerful feature as it allows the user to expand the context of the utterance in the same way that one can in a KWIC concordance program, by asking to be shown more data both before and after the line, but in this audio-visual corpus the user can access more lines both in the transcript and also in the video.

5. Looking to the future

As suggested earlier, it is difficult to make predictions about the technologies to be used in the future, but there seems to be an increasing adoption of Extensible Markup Language

(XML) solutions in the development of corpora and of tools for querying corpora. Mention has been made of the *NITE Toolkit* used on the AMI project and of *EXMARaLDA*, which use XML for creating the corpus files, and it is likely that more projects will follow suit (although it should also be noted that XML is criticised for its 'bulkiness', and that alternatives exist).

One prediction that can be made with confidence is that data transfer speeds and storage power are going to increase rapidly, and this will change current concepts about the size and potential of such corpora. As such, the Human Speech Project (HSP), based at the Massachusetts Institute of Technology, may be a sign of the future. This project follows the language development of a single child in the first three years. To gather the data, cameras and microphones have been set up in all rooms in the house, and these recording devices are running from morning to evening every day. While the project itself is so specialised that it is unlikely to be replicated, the technologies that have been developed to process the huge quantities of data suggest that automatic processing of visual data is likely to be an area of major development in the creation of AV corpora. Basically, with so much video data to be examined, it is necessary to identify which parts of the data require attention, and so the HSP team have created methods for automatically reading the video data and noticing which cameras are picking up movement. On the basis of this information, the human coders are then able to focus their attention on the video information that is relevant to them. Second, in order to speed up the job of transcribing all the oral interaction, speech recognition tools are used in order to provide a rough initial transcription of the speech, and a human transcriber then listens to the recordings and corrects the transcription as necessary. The possibility of creating speech recognition programs that can accurately translate audio signals into words remains remote (particularly in the case of spontaneous group talk) but there has been substantial progress in improving the quality of output. Developers of audio-visual corpora are likely to contribute to, and benefit from, advances in the semi-automatic processing, transcription and annotation of data.

The HSP team have observed that language use is often connected to location and activity. Certain communicative events tend to be enacted in the kitchen, for example, such as at the time that the parents make coffee. Audio-visual corpora make it possible to search for the relationships between location, activity and language use in ways that are unique and these observations may lead to new developments in linguistic theory. Such work may offer further confirmation for those who have previously shown links between language and physical contexts of use (e.g. Mitchell 1957).

As observed in Section 2 above, one serious constraint on the creation of audio-visual corpora to be placed in the public domain is the need to obtain informed consent from all participants who are recorded, particularly where video information is captured. Projects such as the AMI corpus and the CHIL corpus have therefore worked with participants in controlled environments. At the same time, linguistic and behavioural researchers will need to gather information about language in use in natural settings. A possible solution in coming years may be the use of techniques used in motion tracking and face and gesture analysis (see the Headstart project as part of the Nottingham Multi-Modal Corpus, Adolphs and Knight, this volume) to build models of human physical activity from video input (see, for example, Kipp 2004), and then convert these models into anonymised computer-generated animated figures that behave in the ways that the original subjects did, without compromising their identity.

Other areas in which there is likely to be development are in the retrieval of information, and also in the playback and manipulation of the video data. First, if there are to be more XML corpora, then researchers are going to need more powerful XML-aware corpus query tools. Popular text-concordancing programs may have some limited capacity to work with audio files, but cannot cope with multi-layered annotation in XML. As discussed above, there is a lack of standardisation in video file format, and therefore also in the technologies required for playback. It is possible that in future years there may be a move towards standardisation, but at the same time the likelihood of success in such an endeavour is slim.

Further reading

(2007) 'Multimodal Corpora for Modeling Human Multimodal Behaviour', special issue of *Language Resources and Evaluation*, 41(3–4): 215–429. (This special issue has a wide range of articles on multimodal corpus development, annotation and analysis projects.)

References

Baldry, A. and Thibault, P. (2006) *Multimodal Transcription and Text Analysis*. London: Equinox.

Carletta, J., Evert, S., Heid, U., Kilgour, J., Robertson, J. and Voormann, H. (2003) 'The NITE XML Toolkit: Flexible Annotation for Multi-Modal Language Data', *Behavior Research Methods, Instruments, and Computers* 35(3): 353–63.

Hofland, K. (2003) 'A Web-based Concordance System for Spoken Language Corpora', paper presented at Corpus Linguistics 2003, Lancaster; available at ucrel.lancs.ac.uk/publications/CL2003/papers/hofland_abstract.pdf (accessed 5 June 2009).

Kipp, M. (2004) *Gesture Generation by Imitation – From Human Behavior to Computer Character Animation*. Boca Raton, FL: Dissertation.com

Mitchell, T. F. (1957) 'The Language of Buying and Selling in Cyrenaica: A Situational Statement', *Hespéris* XLIV: 31–71.

Mostefa, D., Moreau, N., Choukri, K., Potamianos, G., Chu, S., Tyagi, A., Casas, J., Turmo, J., Cristoforetti, L., Tobia, F., Pnevmatokakis, A., Mylonakis, V., Talantzis, F., Burger, S., Stiefelhagen, R., Bernadin, K. and Rochet, C. (2007) 'The CHIL Audio-visual Corpus for Lecture and Meeting Analysis Inside Smart Rooms', *Language Resources and Evaluation* 41: 389–407.

Pastra, K. (2008) 'COSMOROE: A Cross-Media Relations Framework for Modelling Multimedia Dialectics', *Multimedia Systems* 14: 299–323.

Perez-Parent, M. (2002) 'Collection, Handling, and Analysis of Classroom Recordings Data: Using the Original Acoustic Signal as the Primary Source of Evidence', *Reading Working Papers in Linguistics* 6: 245–54; available at www.reading.ac.uk/internal/appling/wp6/perezparent.pdf (accessed 5 June 2009).

Scott, M. (2008) *WordSmith Tools version 5*. Liverpool: Lexical Analysis Software.

Section III

Analysing a corpus

What are the basics?

9 What corpora are available?

David Y. W. Lee

1. Corpora, text collections, archives and corpus distribution sites

Given how rapidly new electronic corpora come into existence, a chapter such as this may, on the face of it, seem to run the risk of going out of date quite quickly. However, there is a case to be made for having a general survey of currently available corpora: it will help give newcomers to the field a quick overview of what is available (the corpus universe) as well as an understanding of the differences that can be found between one corpus and another (the different stars and constellations within the universe and their distinguishing characteristics). Many types of corpora for a huge variety of languages have sprung up all over the world (particularly in the last decade, in the case of languages other than English), and the trend looks set to continue apace largely because research within the corpus paradigm has proven so fruitful. The bird's-eye view of currently available corpora in this chapter will provide a launching pad for those seeking out resources for research or pedagogical applications, but it is not intended to be exhaustive. This chapter is restricted to the description of 'ready-made' corpora – i.e. specially organised collections of text that are called corpora by their creators. There are many text-collection or text-library sites such Gutenberg or American Rhetoric where you may download individual books, plays, speeches, interviews, and so forth, to create your own personal corpus. Such electronic text libraries are certainly worth visiting, but are not the focus of this chapter.

2. Accessing and categorising corpora

One of the first problems a newcomer to the field faces is: Where do I go? How do I get access to a ready-made corpus? These are actually two different questions. Where you go to, first of all, is usually a website, where the copyright, user agreement and/or purchase form for the corpus may be downloaded. Many corpora are distributed through one of the international corpus distribution agencies or archive sites, such as the International Computer Archive of Modern and Medieval English (ICAME), the Linguistic Data Consortium (LDC) or the Oxford Text Archive (OTA). ICAME is a repository for many contemporary and historical English language corpora and also distributes many of the major English language corpora that linguists use for research. The LDC, in contrast, is very much multilingual in nature, as well as more 'applied' or 'industrial' in focus, being geared more towards the needs of computational linguists and people in natural language processing. The LDC includes a much wider range of 'data sets', including some that may be only marginally recognised as 'corpora' by some linguists. For example, the LDC has many collections of individual words, isolated numbers or phrases read aloud, as well as human-computer 'conversations', speech recorded in noisy environments, and so forth. Such data are mainly for the purposes of research in speech recognition, speech synthesis or machine translation rather than language description. However, the LDC also holds many specialised corpora of genres such as news reportage, telephone conversations, meetings, parallel translated texts, etc., that linguists would definitely find of interest. The third major distributor, the Oxford Text Archive, also has a multilingual collection (ranging from Latin and ancient Greek to modern languages), although its holdings are mostly of English. If you are confused about where to go because of these different sites, help is at hand: a new initiative called the Open Language Archives Community (OLAC) has a search engine that is a good one-stop shop for getting information on catalogued, major corpora, since its database of resources spans across the different sites.

The second issue mentioned above concerns the accessibility or the actual use of corpora. In an ideal world, all corpora would be easily accessible and freely searchable on-line. In reality, however, the majority of corpora are not accessible with a single click. There are a few notable exceptions, but even in these cases copyright, privacy and distribution issues usually restrict access to no more than a small window of context (a few words to the left and right of the search term you type in). Practically all published texts are the copyright of someone, so it is fair to say that most corpora cannot be free or cannot be fully and publicly accessible. Many corpora (e.g. the British National Corpus) have restrictions because they were collected with private funding, mainly from dictionary publishing houses, or because they contain whole or partial texts that are not copyright-cleared for distribution. Short snippets can, however, usually be accessed without problem, and web interfaces to some copyrighted corpora are on-line and without passwords because the built-in limitations ensure that there is no way to read any text in its entirety. For some classroom activities and research purposes, the limited web-accessible versions may well be sufficient. For deeper and more extensive analyses, however, you will probably need to obtain the actual text files, and will thus need to obtain or purchase a licence.

In view of the fact that the majority of corpora are of the English language, along with corresponding research on corpora, this survey will concentrate on English language resources. However, corpora of other languages are certainly increasing in number variety, and quality; and, in the case of endangered languages, such corpora may, regrettably, even be the last repositories of knowledge about those languages in the future.

This chapter will take a simple approach, first focusing on monolingual English language corpora, categorising them broadly into general, speech, parsed, historical and specialised, and then touching briefly on multimedia corpora and the concept of the web as a corpus. Within each of these categories there are, of course, possibilities for further subdivisions (e.g. spoken versus written), and some categories overlap, but the categories used here are in general use and perhaps the most helpful. The next major section is on 'non-expert corpora', those containing native-speaker developmental language, non-native or learner language, and lingua franca speech. These represent growing areas of interest in corpus-based research. The last major section covers monolingual corpora for languages other than English, as well as multilingual corpora in all their flavours: translation, comparable and parallel corpora.

3. Major English language corpora

'General language' corpora (spoken, written and both)

Much of the research in the early years was based on the first generation of 'standard' corpora – so-called because they set the standard for future corpora and also because they were compiled along roughly the same sampling lines: the Brown Corpus of written American English, the Lancaster Oslo-Bergen (LOB) corpus of written British English, the Wellington Corpus of Written New Zealand English, the Australian Corpus of English (ACE) and the Kolhapur Corpus of Indian English are all approximately one million words in size, and designed to be more or less comparable with each other. They all contain 500 texts, of about 2,000 words each, sampled across a wide variety of written genres. In terms of time period, the texts were from the 1960s in the case of Brown and LOB, the 1970s in the case of the Kolhapur, and the 1980s in the case of ACE and the Wellington corpus. Recently, more contemporary analogues to the Brown and LOB have been compiled, and are similarly named to show the connection: FROWN (Freiburg–Brown Corpus of American English) and FLOB (Freiburg–LOB Corpus of British English) contain texts from the 1990s but in other respects follow the same sampling criteria and text domain proportions as Brown and LOB. In addition, a corpus covering the early 1930s, the period before the LOB sampling frame, has also been compiled, and another one-million-word comparable corpus, the BE06 Corpus, has been compiled to represent the texts of the mid-2000s, as a further update. This multiple copying of the original Brown/LOB design is not because the sampling criteria and genre proportions therein are considered ideal (indeed, they are not). It is rather because the compilers wanted maximal comparability for regional and diachronic research.

Among the many one-million-word corpora in existence are the various national components of the International Corpus of English (ICE). This ambitious and wide-ranging project was launched in 1990 with the aim of collecting material for comparative studies of English worldwide. At the time of writing, eighteen research teams around the world have finished or are currently preparing corpora of their own national or regional variety of English, all following a common corpus design as well as a common scheme for grammatical annotation in order to allow cross-corpus comparisons. While ICE follows the Brown/LOB format of 500 texts of approximately 2,000 words each, it differs in that spoken texts are included (making up 60 per cent of the one-million-word total).

The second generation of corpora are products of the internet age, and are therefore mostly very large. The first mega-corpus that should be mentioned is the Bank of English, which was launched in 1991 covering both spoken and written English, and different regional varieties (British English, 70 per cent; American, 20 per cent; and other varieties of English, 10 per cent). This corpus was a continuation of the COBUILD corpus at the University of Birmingham which had started earlier, in 1980. In the same year that the Bank of English was launched, the ambitious British National Corpus (BNC) project was also initiated, and by 1994 had completed its mission of creating a broad-coverage mega-corpus of 100 million words, of which a tenth was composed of transcribed speech. The BNC has so far proved to be one of the most heavily used and researched corpora, and therefore will be described in some detail. While the Bank of English may be bigger, uptake of the BNC by universities and researchers appears to have been greater, perhaps because it was promoted more actively, but also because it has been more freely accessible to the general public (at the time of writing, there are at least three public web interfaces to the BNC, whereas only a fifty-six-million-word subset of the Bank of English is freely searchable through a web interface that gives very restricted access to the texts). The ten-million-word spoken component of the BNC has both a demographically sampled (mostly 'casual conversation') component and a 'context-governed' (mostly 'task-oriented') component, in the ratio of 6:4. The task-oriented component contains the more formal speech varieties, typically those with one speaker but many listeners, such as broadcast news, radio interviews, formal speeches and lectures. The written component of the BNC (ninety million words) was drawn mainly from published sources, although small amounts of unpublished, miscellaneous texts were also sampled. The huge variety of types of text included in the BNC has made it very valuable for research, and accounts for its continued popularity of use (see Lee 2001 for a detailed breakdown of the genres in the corpus).

The success of the BNC in stimulating linguistic research on British English soon resulted in a push for a North American counterpart, and also inspired numerous national corpora for other languages (see the section on 'Non-English corpora' below). In 1999, the American National Corpus (ANC) consortium was set up, and in 2003 the first component (about ten million words) was released, followed by a second release (about twenty-two million words) a few years later. When completed, the ANC is expected to have a core corpus of at least 100 million words, comparable in variety to the BNC, except that new genres of the internet that were only nascent or nonexistent when the BNC was being compiled, such as personal e-mails, internet chat and web pages, are included in the ANC. Corpus of Contemporary American English (COCA) is a mega-corpus that attempts to capture a snapshot of English as it is used in the United States. Its texts are mostly culled from the web or other electronic sources under a 'fair use' understanding of copyright law, and the corpus is thus not available to download, but can be searched online, with limited concordance contexts given for search results. The corpus contains more than 385 million words at the time of writing, and is equally sampled for the broad genre categories of speech, fiction, popular magazines, newspapers and academic texts. The spoken texts are transcripts from broadcast interviews, talk shows and so forth, however, rather than demographically sampled conversations, so 'informal conversation' is one area that is lacking. COCA is designed to have new data added every six to nine months, and can therefore serve as a record of linguistic changes in American English.

Speech corpora

If you are interested in studying spoken English, then in addition to the spoken English transcripts that form part of 'general language' corpora such as the BNC and ANC, there are some spoken corpora that may meet your needs more precisely, particularly if you are interested in studying the actual speech signal and not just text transcripts. Some researchers use the term 'speech corpus' to refer to such multimedia corpora, to distinguish them from others that are available in transcript form only or that contain poor sound recordings that are unsuitable for phonetic studies. The BNC, for example, does not qualify as a 'speech corpus', as the original sound recordings can currently only be accessed at the National Sound Archive of the British Library, apart from the subset of recordings that are shared with the Bergen Corpus of London Teenage Language (COLT), which is available on CD-ROM.

For general studies of British Received Pronunciation (RP), the Spoken English Corpus (SEC; 53,000 words), consisting mainly of radio broadcasts between 1984 and 1991, is still a good choice in spite of the slightly dated material. This is because the SEC is accompanied by not only orthographic transcripts and sound recordings, but also phonemic and prosodic mark-up, along with part-of-speech tags and grammatical parse trees. The associated Machine Readable Spoken English Corpus (MARSEC) is an updated version of the SEC, containing digitised versions of the original tape recordings, time-aligned with the transcripts. The original prosodic mark-up in the SEC was also converted to ASCII characters for easier processing. The Aix-MARSEC database is a further extension, adding annotations for syllables, stress feet, rhythm units and other phenomena.

Another spoken corpus that is prosodically marked up, but a bit older in provenance (recordings were made in the 1960s and 1970s), is the London–Lund Corpus of Spoken English (LLC). This 500,000-word corpus consists of about 100 texts of 5,000 words each. The highly detailed prosodic and other annotations in the LLC indicate stress, tones, tone units, pauses and other prosodic and paralinguistic phenomena, and are therefore useful for speech researchers.

If you think that the SEC and LLC represent a rather conservative brand of spoken British English, you may now choose from a range of speech corpora that go beyond the standard dialects. For the speech of native speakers from across the British Isles, there is the IViE (Intonational Variation in English) Corpus, containing nine urban varieties of English (read-aloud speech as well as free conversation), and FRED (the Freiburg Corpus of English Dialects), which contains oral history interviews. More specialised dialectal speech corpora include the following: the Newcastle Electronic Corpus of Tyneside English (NECTE), which contains dialect speech from Tyneside in Northeast England; the Limerick corpus of Irish English (L-CIE), which contains speech from all parts of Ireland; and the Scottish Corpus of Texts and Speech (SCOTS), representing speech from across Scotland, including Scots Gaelic.

Mention should be made of CANCODE, the Cambridge and Nottingham Corpus of Discourse in English, which is a five-million-word collection of spoken British English (copyright Cambridge University Press), transcribed from recordings made between 1995 and 2000 across a wide variety of situations: casual conversation, people working together, shopping, finding out information, having discussions, and so forth. The files encode information about the relationships between the speakers: whether they were intimates, casual acquaintances, work colleagues or strangers. This corpus has been the basis of a large number of publications. Unfortunately, CANCODE is currently not accessible to the general public.

For spoken American English, there is the Switchboard Corpus (three million words, 240 hours of speech), which consists of spontaneous telephone conversations, averaging six minutes in length, recorded in the early 1990s using speakers from every major dialect of American English. For better quality and face-to-face speech, there is the Santa Barbara Corpus of Spoken American English (SBCSAE; 249,000 words), which consists of recordings of (non-surreptitious) spontaneous speech across different regions of the

United States and from speakers of all ethnic backgrounds, sex, age, and so forth, though it was not designed to support demographically accurate sociolinguistic studies of accent. SBCSAE includes speech events such as casual conversations, family chats, visits to a veterinarian's office, lectures, sermons, and so forth. The transcripts are time-aligned with the sound recordings, and contain detailed prosodic mark-ups that mirror those of the LLC. Some parts of the Saarbrücken Corpus of Spoken English (SCoSE) contain speech by native speakers of English (stories, jokes and interviews), and the Monroe Corpus contains dialogue recorded in a simulated situation in a laboratory (task-oriented speech). Both have transcripts aligned with sound files and constitute useful additions to the stable of American speech corpora. The publishers Pearson Longman also have a large corpus of American speech as part of their Longman Corpus Network. Finally, special mention should be made of the Michigan Corpus of Academic Spoken English (MICASE), which has sound recordings available, though these are not aligned with the transcripts. MICASE is discussed below in the section on specialised corpora.

Parsed corpora

A brief mention should be made here of several corpora that have been parsed (syntactically analysed at the phrasal or functional level). If you are interested in quantitative studies of grammatical structures that cannot be easily found by searching word strings alone, a parsed corpus allows you to search 'parse trees' or structural syntactic tags. As might be expected, parsed corpora are typically smaller than normal/unparsed corpora because most of them are hand-checked for accuracy. The Lancaster–Leeds Treebank, probably the first syntactically parsed corpus, is a manually analysed small subset (45,000 words) of the LOB Corpus that was used to train the computer programs that were later used to produce the Lancaster Parsed Corpus (LPC), which is a larger analysed subset (about 144,000 words) of LOB. The various Penn Treebank releases (containing news reports, Brown Corpus texts, manuals, radio transcripts, Switchboard Corpus transcripts, etc.) may also be of interest. They employ tags for different types of phrases and clauses that mirror the Lancaster scheme.

Geoff Sampson's SUSANNE Corpus (Surface and Underlying Structural Analyses of Naturalistic English; 130,000 words) is a freely downloadable parsed corpus based on a subset of the Brown corpus of American English that has not only phrasal and clausal tags but also surface function tags for roles such as 'logical subject' and 'agent of passive'. Sampson's LUCY Corpus (165,000 words) contains mostly modern texts from the 1990s: some from the BNC, and some from A-level secondary school exams and university-level coursework and essays. (LUCY also contains children's writing taken from a 1960s project.) The parsing scheme used for LUCY was an adaptation of the SUSANNE scheme, as it had to deal with non-standard structures not found in the more polished writing that machine parsers are trained on (see Sampson 1995).

For parsed speech, there is CHRISTINE (80,500 words), also by Sampson, which is based on a subset of the BNC, the London–Lund Corpus, and the Reading Emotional Speech Corpus. Again, the parse scheme is slightly different, this time adapted to deal with spoken phenomena such as pauses, discourse items and speech repairs.

As noted earlier, ICE-GB, the British component of the International Corpus of English, is fully parsed and manually checked, and is a very good choice if you are looking for a syntactically analysed corpus of both spoken and written English. One advantage it has over the other parsed corpora is that it can be explored interactively using the dedicated tool ICECUP that not only allows sophisticated 'fuzzy' queries to be made through a visual interface, but also provides synchronised audio playback of the text fragments returned by the word or syntactic searches.

Finally, note that many of the corpora of historical varieties of English (see next section) have been parsed. The Penn–Helsinki Parsed Corpus of Middle English version 2 (PPCME2) and the York–Helsinki Parsed Corpus of Old English Poetry, for example, share a common annotation scheme, and can be searched using a Java software tool called *CorpusSearch*. There is also the Parsed Corpus of Early English Correspondence, which covers the period 1410–1681.

Historical corpora

There is a wealth of corpora covering the English of earlier periods, and much empirical research has already been conducted on these corpora to describe and track changes in the language. There are three main collections of historical English that cover a wide span of time and genres: the diachronic part of the Helsinki Corpus of English, ARCHER (A Representative Corpus of Historical English Registers), and COHA (Corpus of Historical American English). The Helsinki Corpus (1.6 million words) covers the period from around 750 to 1700, and thus spans Old English (413,300 words), Middle English (608,600 words) and early modern (British) English (551,000 words). ARCHER is a multi-genre corpus (currently 1.8 million words) covering the early modern English period right up to the present (1650–1990) for both British and American English. It is divided into fifty-year blocks to facilitate comparisons (though not all periods are available for American English). ARCHER is, at the time of writing, undergoing correction, expansion and tagging. The corpus is not publicly available, but the several universities involved in the project are willing to host visits by interested scholars. COHA's aim is to create a 300-million-word corpus of historical American English covering the early 1800s to the present time, and is 'balanced' in each decade for the genres of fiction, popular magazines, newspapers and academic prose.

Other historical corpora focus on a specific historical period, or on a specific genre. The Lampeter Corpus (about one million words) is a collection of non-literary prose tracts covering the 100-year period from 1640 to 1740. For letters and newsletters, there are quite a number of corpora: the Newdigate Newsletters Corpus (one million words), containing manuscript newsletters dated 1674–92; the Corpus of Early English Correspondence (CEEC; 2.7 million words) covering 1417 to 1681; the Corpus of Late Eighteenth-Century Prose (300,000 words) containing letters on practical subjects from the period 1761–90; and the Corpus of late Modern English Prose (100,000 words) consisting of informal private letters by British writers from the period 1861 to 1919. There are also some letters (182,000 words) in ICAMET (Innsbruck Computer Archive of Machine-Readable English Texts), which also contains a Middle English prose component of six million words. For historical newspapers, the Zurich English Newspaper Corpus (ZEN; 1.2 million words) covers the period 1661 to 1791. For obvious reasons, historical corpora are almost all written data. However, for a window into how people used to speak, the Old Bailey Corpus and the Corpus of English Dialogues (CED) offer speech-related genres such as trial proceedings, witness depositions, drama and fictional dialogues.

Finally, for early literary texts, there are now many electronic text libraries from which you can download your own selections: for example, Early English Books On-line (EEBO; mainly 1500s–1600s), Literature Online (LION; mainly 1700s–1800s), and

Bartleby and Project Gutenberg (many periods and genres). Even the *Oxford English Dictionary*'s quotations database may now be searched just like a corpus, to get samples of earlier usages of English words.

Specialised corpora

The category of 'specialised corpora' is where we place corpora that are not 'general' (or 'national') corpora' – those that do not aim to comprehensively represent a language as a whole, but only specialised segments of it (e.g. domains or genres). Specialised corpora are usually smaller in scale than general language corpora precisely because of their narrower focus. This is not a problem, however, as the greater homogeneity among texts in a specialised area confers the advantage of fewer texts being required for the corpus to be representative of that language variety. One important specialised area is that of academic English, and quite a few corpora have been created to serve the needs of practitioners of English for Academic Purposes (EAP). MICASE (the Michigan Corpus of Academic Spoken English; 1.8 million words) is a corpus of spoken English transcribed from about 190 hours of recordings of various speech events in a North American university (Simpson *et al.* 2003). It has spawned various national equivalents, including BASE (the British Academic Spoken English corpus; 1.6 million words), LIBEL CASE (Limerick-Belfast Corpus of Academic Spoken English), and CUCASE (City University Corpus of Academic Spoken English, in Hong Kong). These corpora allow researchers to examine differences across national contexts. For written academic English, in addition to the LOB category J texts ('learned and scientific writings') and the academic component of the BNC (see Lee 2001), the following two purpose-built corpora may be useful: the Chemnitz Corpus of Specialised and Popular Academic English (SPACE), consisting of comparable academic texts taken from scholarly papers (specialised expert-to-expert communication) and derived popular versions (broader journalist-to-layperson communication); and the Reading Academic Text corpus (RAT), consisting of research articles and PhD theses from the fields of Agriculture, Agricultural Botany and Agricultural and Food Economics (with plans for expansion to other disciplines in the future).

An international organisation called the Professional English Research Consortium (PERC) is also, at the time of writing, creating a 100-million-word corpus of professional English, by which is meant journal texts used by professionals in science, engineering, technology, law, medicine, finance and other fields. This PERC Corpus (formerly called 'Corpus of Professional English') will aid research and generate educational applications in the area of ESP/Professional English, feeding into the development of educational resources such as specialised dictionaries, handbooks, language tests and other materials.

For general business English, there is the Wolverhampton Business English Corpus: this is a collection of over ten million words from the general domain of business, taken from twenty-three different websites around the world between 1999 and 2000. There is also a Business Letters Corpus (BLC; one million words) composed of samples of US and UK business letters (mostly model letters from textbooks rather than real-life letters). The BLC is accessible through an on-line concordancer.

Multimedia corpora, multimodal texts

A growing number of corpora are now fully multimedia in the sense of having transcripts that are aligned or synchronised with the original audio or video recordings. This allows researchers and ordinary users of a corpus to go beyond the written word to embrace the audio and visual elements of situated discourse: the use of prosody, gestures, gaze, space, and so forth. We now have audio/video-to-transcript aligned corpora that can be played and viewed through any web browser. At the TalkBank website, the audio/video files of the Santa Barbara Corpus of Spoken American English (SBCSAE) can be easily played, with the transcripts scrolling in sync. A similar multimedia browsing facility is offered with the spoken texts of the multimedia Scottish Corpus of Texts and Speech (SCOTS), a four-million-word written and spoken corpus that captures the languages of Scotland, from Broad Scots to Scottish English. As an example of a pedagogical application of multimedia corpora, ELISA (English Language Interview Corpus as a Second-Language Application) is pioneering: it is a small corpus of interviews with people from different professional careers, and offers a multimedia facility along with exercises and other teaching materials. As Braun (2005) argues, such an integration of text and video is much needed in order to help learners more easily authenticate decontextualised corpus materials, and thus get the most out of them.

This ability to see or hear recordings and follow along with the transcript represents an important and significant advance for both research and pedagogy, and the SACODEYL project (Peréz-Paredes and Alcaraz-Calero 2009) now provides a suite of tools that will assist in the compilation and distribution of time-aligned transcripts (SACODEYL also includes ready-to-use multimedia corpora of European teenager talk). Perhaps the most ambitious example of a multimodal corpus is the Singapore Corpus of Research in Education (SCoRE), which is a multilevel annotated multimedia corpus of spoken and written material collected from primary and secondary schools in Singapore. It contains video- and audio-recorded classroom interactions, along with teaching materials and students' assignments, and is annotated not only for part of speech, but also discourse-level phenomena such as Initiation, Response and Feedback.

The web as a corpus

In the era of the internet, with the innumerable electronic documents that continually grow in number and diversity, many corpus linguists question the need to cling to the old paradigm of corpus research: design a corpus, collect the texts, tag them with bibliographical or source information, format them to conform to an international standard, add linguistic annotations, then release the finished product. Some people now feel that a much simpler way is to intelligently harvest the web for texts that we want, either dynamically ('on the fly', with no way to duplicate the exact same collection of texts later) or statically (texts are trawled from the web, possibly cleaned up in some way, and then compiled into a finished corpus).

The most important question is: can the web be considered a corpus in the first place? Here, Kilgarriff and Greffenstette (2003: 334) offer their point of view:

> [many linguists] mix the question 'What is a corpus?' with 'What is a good corpus (for certain kinds of linguistic study)?', muddying the simple question 'Is corpus *x* good for task *y*?' with the semantic question, 'Is *x* a corpus at all?' ... We define a corpus simply as 'a collection of texts'. If that seems too broad, the one qualification we allow relates to the domains and contexts in which the word is used rather than its denotation: *A corpus is a collection of texts when considered as an object of language or literary study*. The answer to the question 'is the web a corpus?' is yes.

Whether or not you agree with this definition, if you want to concordance the web dynamically, you can use a so-called web concordancer such as WebCorp, WebKWiC, or KWiCFinder. It is also possible to do a more sophisticated search based on syntactic structure by using the Linguist's Search Engine, a tool that makes it possible to retrieve sentences from the web on the basis of a parse tree. If 'live' concordancing is too dynamic and unreplicable, you can concordance a static, ready-made web-culled corpus using Birmingham University's WebCorpLSE, which will query a large collection of web-sourced texts (currently around seventy million words). Another example of a ready-made web-derived corpus is 'ukWaC', a two-billion-word corpus of British English (part-of-speech tagged and lemmatised) taken from web pages in the '.uk' internet domain (Ferraresi *et al.* 2008). This corpus has been analysed and appears to stand up well when compared with traditionally compiled corpora such as the BNC, with differences well accounted for by divergences in time period and subject domains. Similar web-derived corpora exist for other languages such as German and Italian.

4. Developmental, learner and lingua franca corpora

Developmental language corpora

Since the term 'learner' usually connotes 'foreign learner', it is better to use the terms 'non-expert' or 'developmental' to describe the various data contained in the CHILDES database and the Polytechnic of Wales (POW) Corpus, which are collections of native-speaker language produced by children at various developmental stages. Another developmental corpus is LUCY (mentioned earlier), as part of it consists of essays written in the 1960s by nine- to twelve-year-old British children. LUCY has real utility as a suitable reference corpus against which the writing of non-native writers of the same age can be compared.

There are also some corpora containing the output of non-expert teenage and young adult native speakers who are not necessarily as proficient or polished as the published writers that typically dominate native-speaker corpora. One example is the Louvain Corpus of Native English Essays (LOCNESS; 324,000 words), which contains essays (mostly argumentative) written by British and American students, post-secondary to university level. This corpus is often used for direct comparisons with the ICLE Corpus of non-native speaker writing (see next section) because they represent the same genre and topics. In terms of actual disciplinary writing by native-speaker university students (i.e. not argumentative essays written for proficiency or composition classes), there are two main corpora: the British Academic Written English Corpus (BAWE; 6.5 million words) and its American counterpart, the Michigan Corpus of Upper-level Student Papers (MICUSP; two million words). Both corpora include the writing of both native and non-native speakers, but native speakers predominate.

ESL/EFL learner corpora

Two major learner corpus projects that are international in scope are ICLE (International Corpus of Learner English; 3.7 million words so far) for written language and LINDSEI (Louvain International Database of Spoken English Interlanguage; 1.1 million words, at the time of writing) for spoken. ICLE consists of mainly argumentative essays from undergraduate and graduate students of English from twenty-one different language backgrounds, while LINDSEI contains transcripts of two types of speech by speakers from eleven different L1 backgrounds: informal interviews (based on a given topic) and picture-prompted speech (based on a standard set of pictures that illustrate a story). There are two other ongoing projects that are collecting writing samples from university students: LANCAWE (Lancaster Corpus of Academic Written English), based in the UK, and MELD (Montclair Electronic Language Learners' Database; 98,000 words) in the US. They differ from ICLE in that the participants are in an English-immersion environment.

The types of writing contained in the above corpora represent the general linguistic proficiency of university-level learners of English, but in terms of research writing, where the writing is done for the communication of disciplinary content or research rather than for the sake of a language proficiency class or test, there are few existing learner corpora. Two possible sources are BAWE and MICUSP, which, as mentioned earlier, have some non-native speaker contributions, but the genres of text in these corpora are very varied, and not all are research-based. A dedicated corpus of learner research writing is the CAWE corpus (Chinese Academic Written English; 408,000 words, at the time of writing, and growing), consisting of undergraduate dissertations written by English majors in mainland China. These texts represent extended pieces of research writing that may be compared to either native-speaker dissertations or published journal articles in the same field to reveal the extent to which learners are successful in writing 'like the experts'.

While the various learner corpora above represent the writing of advanced or upper-level students, there is much less data on the writing of younger learners of English, especially those who are producing their first essays or paragraphs in a foreign language. The International Corpus of Crosslinguistic Interlanguage (ICCI) aims to fills this gap, and is underway in Austria, Hong Kong, Israel, Poland, Spain and Taiwan. When completed, it will contain the writing of primary school to pre-university learners of English across various proficiency levels and L1 backgrounds. The overall design and essay topics in ICCI will closely mirror the already completed JEFLL Corpus (Japanese EFL Learner Corpus; 700,000 words), which is a collection of compositions written by more than 10,000 Japanese learners of English, mostly from junior to senior high school levels.

There are also some specialised corpora of learner English. For research on business letters, you can conduct on-line searches on the Learner Business Letters Corpus (Learner BLC), which contains over 200,000 words taken from samples of business letters written by Japanese business people (with errors intact). For phonetic research on learner speech, the LeaP Corpus (Learning Prosody in a Foreign Language) provides over twelve hours of speech (read speech, prepared speech, free speech and nonsense words) from 131 different learners of German and English as a foreign language, across thirty-two different native language backgrounds (it also has some recordings of native speakers for comparison).

As mentioned at the start of this chapter, corpora can belong to more than one category. The Hong Kong Corpus of Conversational English (HKCCE; 500,000 words) could conceivably be classified under 'Speech corpora' above, or put together with the various components of 'world Englishes' that are part of the ICE project. However, since the typical focus of research using the HKCCE is on the learner-like features of Hong Kong speakers of English in contexts where they are speaking to (mostly) native speakers of English, the corpus fits better in this section. HKCCE comprises about fifty hours of recordings of conversations, as well as academic, business and public discourses.

Lingua franca corpora

While the so-called New Englishes of the former British colonies are represented in the ICE project, along with a few other World English varieties, few corpora deal specifically with intercultural encounters where English is used as a lingua franca among speakers who do not share an L1 or a similar cultural or national background. Two corpora have filled the gap: the VOICE Corpus (Vienna–Oxford International Corpus of English; one million words; 120 hours) and the ELFA Corpus (English as a Lingua Franca in Academic Settings; one million words, 131 hours). VOICE comprises naturally occurring, non-scripted face-to-face interactions in English between speakers from different first-language backgrounds (e.g. a Korean sales representative negotiating a contract with a German client in Luxembourg). ELFA is a similar, complementary corpus, where the contexts of speech are academic rather than business or general. Perhaps as research into lingua franca English increases, more such corpora will be compiled in the future.

5. Non-English corpora and multilingual corpora

The above corpora have all been about English, and this reflects the imbalance in the field. Nevertheless, numerous non-English corpora have arisen in the past few decades, and some of the major ones will be introduced here. They will be divided into the broad categories of monolingual, parallel and comparable corpora.

Monolingual non-English corpora

The British National Corpus model has inspired and spawned a host of other national corpora based on a similar design, among which we can include the following: CORIS/CODIS (Italian), Czech National Corpus (Česk Národní Korpus), Hungarian National Corpus, Hellenic National Corpus (also known as the ILSP Corpus), German National Corpus, Modern Chinese Language Corpus (MCLC), Polish National Corpus, Russian Reference Corpus (BOKR), Slovak National Corpus and the Korean National Corpus (or Sejong Balanced Corpus). Many of these, being products of the internet age, are mega corpora that exceed the 100-million-word size of the BNC.

For the European languages, there is also the PAROLE (Preparatory Action for Linguistic Resources Organisation for Language Engineering) project that has resulted in a set of common-design corpora and lexicons for fourteen European languages (fifteen, if you include English). About twenty million words have been collected for each of the following languages: Belgian French, Catalan, Danish, Dutch, French, Finnish, German, Greek, Irish, Italian, Norwegian, Portuguese and Swedish. The harmonised standards and specifications used in these resources allow cross-linguistic comparisons to be made.

Not all countries/languages are equal in resources, however: German has one of the largest collections of text, COSMAS, with two billion words; Portuguese has a 180-million-word corpus of newspaper text (CETEMPúblico), a mixed corpus of forty-five million words (Corpus do Português), and several other written and spoken corpora (the Linguateca site has listings); Spanish has the Corpus del Español (100 million words and growing); Dutch has a large ten-million-word spoken corpus (Corpus Gesproken Nederlands) and many large written corpora (search the Institute for Dutch Lexicology, INL, for their listings).

In Asia, the Balanced Corpus of Contemporary Written Japanese (BCCWJ) is a 100-million-word corpus. For Chinese, there now are practically too many corpora to mention, but some of the well-known ones include: Academia Sinica Balanced Corpus (five million words of Taiwanese Mandarin); the Peking University corpora (hundreds of millions of Chinese characters); Modern Chinese Language Corpus (MCLC; 700 million characters); PH corpus (3.7 million characters); and a large fifty-million-word general corpus compiled for the making of a frequency dictionary (Xiao *et al.* 2009). There are also several one-million-word corpora that allow various types of comparison: Lancaster Corpus of Mandarin Chinese (LCMC; texts from 1990s); UCLA Chinese Corpus (UCLACC; texts from the period 2000–5); Lancaster–Los Angeles Spoken Chinese Corpus (LLSCC); ZJU Corpus of Translational Chinese (ZCTC).

Corpora are not restricted to the major languages, however. Some minority-language corpora include the following: the New Corpus for Ireland (NCI; thirty million words of Irish, and twenty-five million words of Irish English); Cronfa Electroneg o Gymraeg (one million words of Welsh); Scottish Corpus of Texts and Speech (SCOTS; target of four million words); Oslo Corpus of Bosnian Texts (1.5 million); and the 'Brown' Corpus of Bulgarian (one million words). Some smaller corpora include those representing fourteen South Asian languages that are in the EMILLE (Enabling Minority Language Engineering) Corpus (ninety-two million words). The data here is mainly written, with only around 2.6 million words of spoken data for Bengali, Gujarati, Hindi, Punjabi and Urdu.

Parallel and comparable multilingual corpora

Johansson (2007: 9–11) gives the following definitions: *translation corpora* contain 'original texts and their translations into one or more other languages'; *comparable corpora* contain 'original texts in two or more languages matched by criteria such as genre, time of publication, etc.', while the term *parallel corpus* is reserved for 'bidirectional translation corpora', a combination of translation corpora and comparable corpora that use the same framework (i.e. comparable originals in at least two languages plus their translations into the other language(s)). Johansson's equation of *parallel* with *bidirectional* is not observed by everyone, and for the purposes of this chapter, the terms and definitions given by Aston (1999) will be used instead, summarised in Table 9.1 (see also chapters by Kenning, and Kübler and Aston, this volume).

Table 9.1 Comparable and parallel multilingual corpora

	Language A			*Language B*
Comparable corpora (multilingual)	Specialised corpus	≈		Specialised corpus of same design
Unidirectional parallel corpora	Specialised corpus	⇒		Translations of texts contained in A
Bidirectional parallel corpora	A1 Specialised corpus	≈		B1 Specialised corpus of same design as A1
	A2 Translations of B1	⇙	⇘	B2 Translations of A1

Source: Adapted from Aston 1999.

In parallel corpora, the two components are aligned on a paragraph-to-paragraph or sentence-to-sentence basis. The English–Norwegian Parallel Corpus (ENPC) and English–Swedish Parallel Corpus (ESPC) are good examples of a parallel bidirectional corpus: each corpus has four related components, allowing for various types of comparison to be carried out. This design is also the basis for the Oslo Multilingual Corpus (OMC), which has German, French and Finnish source texts and translations in various combinations. Other examples of bidirectional parallel corpora are the IJS–ELAN Slovene–English Parallel Corpus and COMPARA (English and Portuguese). Examples of bidirectional parallel corpora for an Asian language would be the BFSU Chinese–English Parallel Corpus (by Beijing Foreign Studies University), and the Babel Chinese–English Parallel Corpus. Some multilingual corpora, however, are only unidirectional. Examples include Kacenka (English to Czech), MULTEXT-East (English to nine different languages) and the HKIEd English–Chinese Parallel Corpus, which has both English- and Chinese-origin texts and their translations, but the source texts do not follow the same sampling frame and are thus not comparable.

This chapter has given a very broad survey of available corpora, and is intended to help readers orient themselves to particular areas of interest. The taxonomy and the categorisation of corpora used here are only one of many possibilities, and many corpora fit under more than category. Nevertheless, it is hoped that the descriptions here have given readers a good sense of the scope of corpora that are available, and helped facilitate research endeavours.

Further reading

Granger, S. (ed.) (1998) *Learner English on Computer*. Essex: Addison Wesley Longman. (Chapter 1 describes the design of the ICLE corpus, while the rest of the book exemplifies the kinds of research and pedagogical application that can come out of learner corpus research.)

Kennedy, G. (1998) *An Introduction to Corpus Linguistics*. London: Longman. (Chapter 2 of this book gives a very good and detailed history of the development of corpora, especially the earlier ones.)

References

Aston, G. (1999) 'Corpus Use and Learning to Translate', *Textus* 12: 289–314.

Biber, D. (1990) 'Methodological Issues Regarding Corpus-based Analyses of Linguistic Variation', *Literary and Linguistic Computing* 5: 257–69.

——(1993) 'Representativeness in Corpus Design', *Literary and Linguistic Computing* 8(4): 243–57.

Braun, S. (2005) 'From Pedagogically Relevant Corpora to Authentic Language Learning Contents', *ReCALL* 17(1): 47–64.

Ferraresi, A., Zanchetta, E., Baroni, M. and Bernardini, S. (2008) 'Introducing and Evaluating ukWaC, a Very Large Web-Derived Corpus of English,' in S. Evert, A. Kilgarriff and S. Sharoff (eds) *Proceedings of the 4th Web as Corpus Workshop (WAC-4) Can We Beat Google?* Marrakech, Morocco, 1 June 2008, available at http://webascorpus.sourceforge.net/

Johansson, S. (2007) *Seeing through Multilingual Corpora: On the Use of Corpora in Contrastive Studies*. Amsterdam: John Benjamins.

Kilgarriff, A. and Greffenstette, G. (2003) 'Introduction' to 'The Web as Corpus', special issue of *Computational Linguistics* 29(3): 333–47.

Lee, D. Y. W. (2001) 'Genres, Registers, Text Types, Domains, and Styles: Clarifying the Concepts and Navigating a Path through the BNC Jungle', *Language Learning and Technology* 5(3): 37–72.

Park, B. (2001) 'Introducing the Korean National Corpus', paper presented at Corpus Research Group, Lancaster University, 19 November (see also http://www.sejong.or.kr/).

Peréz-Paredes, P. and Alcaraz-Calero, J. M. (2009) 'Developing Annotation Solutions for Online Data Driven Learning', *ReCALL* 21(1): 55–75.

Sampson, G. (1995) *English for the Computer: The SUSANNE Corpus and Analytic Scheme*. Oxford: Clarendon Press.

Simpson, R. C., Lee, D. Y. W. and Leicher, S. (2003) *MICASE Manual*. Ann Arbor, MI: English Language Institute, University of Michigan.

Xiao, R., Rayson, P. and McEnery, T. (2009) *A Frequency Dictionary of Mandarin Chinese: Core Vocabulary for Learners*. London: Routledge.

10
What are the basics of analysing a corpus?

Jane Evison

1. Analysing a corpus: the basics

Manipulating corpus data: frequency and concordancing

In themselves, corpora can tell us nothing but because they are collections of electronic texts, they are susceptible to computerised analysis using corpus access software. As Hunston (2002: 3) puts it, 'a corpus does not contain new information about language, but the software offers us a new perspective on the familiar'. In order to gain this new perspective, the first analytical steps generally involve two related processes: the production of frequency lists (either in rank order, or sorted alphabetically) and the generation of concordances (examples of particular items in context; see Tribble, this volume). There is an increasing range of software available to carry out such processes, from established commercial software such as *WordSmith Tools* (Scott 1999), *Monoconc Pro* (2000) and *Word Sketch Engine* (Kilgarriff *et al.* 2004) to freeware downloadable from the internet. These two corpus-handling techniques – generating frequency lists and concordances – are built on the very basic foundation that electronic collections of texts can be searched very rapidly. This means that automatic frequency list generation can quickly produce a complete list of all the items in a corpus, ranging from the most ubiquitous ones, the frequency of which may run into millions in the largest corpora, to those more unusual items which occur just once in a particular corpus. Concordance analysis, also a basic technique, begins with a specific item that the researcher has decided to search for. This search brings onto the screen all the examples of the searched-for item, in context. These two basic operations represent two core corpus-handling techniques, but of course, simply counting items or displaying their occurrences does not actually tell us anything in itself; it is the associated analysis, which may be both quantitative and qualitative, which provides the insights.

Considering the issues

First of all, there is the question of how much data is needed (see Nelson, this volume). In the early years of corpus linguistics, there was certainly a drive towards the analysis of larger and larger corpora, with the unwritten assumption that 'biggest is best' (Kennedy 1998). This can be attributed in part to the excitement engendered by the possibility of collecting a million words of data (a figure that was for some time put forward as being the minimum size for a corpus), and to the specific needs of the dictionary-compilers who were important early users of corpus data (see Walter, this volume). These lexicographers needed large data sets so that they could extract sufficient examples of infrequent words to allow the production of reliable descriptions of their use. However, subsequent analysis of corpora by applied linguists with different interests, such as the investigation of high-frequency grammatical patterns or discourse features, has shown that having very large corpora can mean that too much data is generated if one is searching for very frequent items or interested in carrying out detailed analysis. Solutions to the problem of generating too much data include random sampling and the construction of smaller sub-corpora. This latter approach has proved successful for the analysis of high-frequency grammatical features such as pronouns and verb forms. For example, Biber (1990) demonstrates that just 1,000 words of data are able to produce results that are reliable, and Tribble (1997) argues convincingly that if a register is very specialised, a smaller corpus will be adequate to provide insight into the features of that register. Two examples of this kind of small study are Koester's (2006) investigation of workplace discourse, which uses a corpus of just under 34,000 words and O'Keeffe's (2003) study of radio discourse, based on a sample of 55,000 words of phone-in data.

If one does not wish to study a small quantity of data, it can be useful to randomise searches for particularly frequent items. For example, the corpus software can be asked to display concordances for one occurrence in 50, 100 or 500 (Scott 1999). On the other hand, Sinclair (1999) suggests that, if one is looking for patterns of occurrence, a possible solution is to repeat the process of generating thirty random lines (a number that can be comfortably viewed on the screen at one time) until no new patterns are observed. The results of the analysis of a particular corpus can also be validated against those from other comparable corpora. For example, in their paper on basic spoken vocabulary, McCarthy and Carter (2003) validate the results of the analysis of the Cambridge and Nottingham Corpus of Discourse in English (CANCODE) with a frequency list generated for a five-million-word spoken element of the British National Corpus (the BNC). It is also possible to triangulate corpus findings. For example, in the case of the analysis of spoken language, this can be achieved by observing the kinds of spoken encounters which make up the corpus, or by questioning participants though interview or questionnaire.

The sections which make up the rest of this chapter exemplify the basics of frequency and concordance analysis. Frequency analysis can be done by anyone who has a collection of electronic texts, basic computer skills and the appropriate software. Concordancing is even more accessible, and can be carried out on corpora searchable via the internet as well as on those stored on a personal computer. It is important to point out here that the example analyses that are presented in this chapter are limited to basic techniques involving counting and searching for single items, rather than the kinds of multi-word units referred to in Greaves and Warren (this volume).

2. Exploring word frequency lists

Displaying frequency data

The first basic corpus technique that we will consider is that of frequency analysis. When we generate a frequency list for a particular corpus, the software searches every item in that corpus in order to establish how many tokens there are in total – at the simplest level a token and a word can be considered to be the same thing – and how many different types constitute this total. The software then outputs the final counts as a frequency list, which can be displayed in rank order of frequency or in alphabetical order (or, in the case of *WordSmith Tools*, in reverse word order, useful, for example, if one is interested in the frequency of suffixes or inflexions). In Table 10.1 we can see the beginning of a rank order frequency list for a small corpus of just over 4,000 words of paired discussion tasks. In addition to the rank order (N) and the raw frequency (actual number of occurrences) of each token, we can see the percentage of tokens in the whole corpus that each frequency count represents.

Alphabetical frequency lists can be generated at the same time as rank order ones, but give a different picture of the same frequency distribution. In order to exemplify this, Table 10.2 shows the tokens in positions 265–74 in the alphabetical list for the same small corpus of discussion tasks.

The alphabetical frequency list extract in Table 10.2 raises two important issues in relation to frequency list generation. First, it shows that the corpus software counts tokens, which may or may not be words in the traditional sense. As well as including vocalisations such as *huh* and *hum*, the first two items on the list, most software will count

Table 10.1 Frequency list (rank order)

N	*Token*	*Freq.*	*%*
1	the	203	4.76
2	I	129	3.02
3	a	116	2.72
4	and	109	2.55
5	it	89	2.09
6	to	86	2.02
7	think	81	1.9
8	of	80	1.87
9	you	78	1.83
10	yeah	76	1.78

Source: Data from Evison (2001).

Table 10.2 Frequency list (alphabetical)

N	*Token*	*Freq.*	*%*
265	huh	14	0.33
266	hum	4	0.09
267	hundred	1	0.02
268	hundreds	2	0.05
269	I	129	3.02
270	I'd	5	0.12
271	I'm	6	0.14
272	idea	10	0.23
273	if	15	0.35
274	imagine	1	0.02

Source: Data from Evison (2001).

the contractions *I'll* and *I'd* as single items even though they are traditionally seen as contractions of two separate words. Although corpus linguists tend to consider contractions such as *I'll* and *I'd* as single words, as major corpus-based grammars attest (Biber *et al.* 1999; Carter and McCarthy 2006), more traditional grammars may consider them as two. Second, there is the issue of lemmatisation. The alphabetical frequency list in Table 10.2 shows that when it was generated, the program listed all the different tokens in the corpus under investigation separately, rather than grouping together related forms such as *hundred* and *hundreds,* which instead have separate entries. This is generally the way that basic frequency list generation works. However, some frequency software (e.g. *WordSmith Tools* version 5) can generate frequency lists for lemmas (e.g. one count for the lemma *smile*, which would include *smile(s), smiled* and *smiling*). Nevertheless, the software used for this process is not always sophisticated enough to pick up other similarities such as comparative and superlative forms of adjectives, or to avoid conflating the counts for unrelated words (e.g. the verb *sit* and the unrelated noun *site*). A useful discussion of the limitations of lemmatisation can be found in O'Keeffe *et al.* (2007: 32–3).

Exploiting frequency data

Having established what frequency lists look like, we can now turn our attention to what frequency lists can tell us. Frequency lists can be useful documents for lexicographers (see Walter, this volume) and language syllabus and materials designers (see McCarten, this volume). Their importance is underlined by the range of frequency information that is available. In the case of the BNC, for example, a selection of lists (Leech *et al.* 2001) is supported by updated information on the BNC website. The Compleat Lexical Tutor (available online) utilises the Academic Wordlist (see Coxhead, this volume) and the much older General Service List (West 1953) as the basis of its lexical profiling programs. Such programs rely on the establishment of frequency bands, something that Sinclair (1991) highlights as particularly useful. Research into spoken language such as McCarthy (1998, 1999) and McCarthy and Carter (2003) exploits frequency bands, using the sudden drop-off in frequency which occurs after about 1,800 words in a rank frequency list generated from the CANCODE corpus to argue that a basic spoken vocabulary of English must include these 1,800 items. Further discussion of frequency bands can be found in O'Keeffe *et al.* (2007: 31ff). Finally, frequency lists form the basis of more complex statistical measures such as Mutual Information (MI) scores, *t*-scores and *z*-scores, which express the strength of collocations; in other words the likelihood of items – such as *dark* and *hair* – co-occurring. See chapters by Moon and Greaves and Warren, this volume, for further discussion, as well as McEnery *et al.* (2006).

Comparing frequency lists

It can be useful to compare the rank order of items in two or more corpora by looking at them side by side, as in Table 10.3, which shows the top ten most frequent items in 50,000 words of conversation extracted from the BNC, and the top ten items from a corpus of 54,000 words of podcast talk (TESOL Talk from Nottingham, or TTFN). The TTFN corpus is made up of informal broadcast conversations between two university lecturers and occasional guests about topics relating to the subjects that they are teaching on an MA programme for English Language Teachers.

Table 10.3 Comparison of rank frequency

N	*BNC*	*TTFN*
1	**I**	the
2	**you**	and
3	it	of
4	the	**I**
5	and	a
6	a	to
7	to	that
8	that	**you**
9	yeah	in
10	oh	it

Source: BNC data extracted from the BNC Baby. TTFN data from Evison (2009).

In Table 10.3, we can see that while eight out of the ten items are common to both lists, the first and second person pronouns *I* and *you* occur higher up the list for intimate conversations and lower down that for the more academic conversations. We can understand the relatively high frequency of the interactive pronouns *I* and *you* in casual conversation in terms of the topicality of the participants themselves, and their orientation towards each other (McCarthy 1998; Biber *et al.* 1999). In the frequency list for the academic podcast conversations, however, we find that *I* and *you* have been 'displaced'; the higher positions of *the* and *of*, suggesting that topics are being referred to using noun phrases (e.g. ***the*** *teaching* ***of*** *speaking;* ***the*** *importance* ***of*** *grammar*). Of course, these hypotheses need to be investigated further by more detailed analysis of examples in context.

Normalisation

In order to compare frequency counts across corpora of different sizes, a process of normalisation is required. This process involves extrapolating raw frequencies from the different-sized corpora which are being compared so that they can be expressed by a common factor such as a thousand or a million words. For example, the pronoun *we* occurs 2,142 times in a sub-corpus of meetings extracted from the BNC Sampler corpus, and 2,666 times in another sub-corpus of the BNC Sampler made up of casual conversation. However, because the two corpora are of such different sizes, these raw frequencies mean very little relative to each other. In order to normalise the figure for the meeting sub-corpus, the raw frequency of 2,142 is divided by 148,624 (the total word count of the meeting sub-corpus) and multiplied by 1,000, giving a figure of fourteen occurrences per thousand words. In order to compare this normalised frequency with that of *we* in the sub-corpus of casual conversation, we take the raw frequency of 2,666, divide it by 483,913 (the total word count in the conversational sub-corpus) and multiply by 1,000, which results in a normalised count of six occurrences per thousand words. We can now see that *we* is more than twice as frequent in the sub-corpus of meetings (fourteen occurrences per thousand) than in that of casual conversation (six occurrences per thousand). Its frequency in the meeting sub-corpus is related to both the demands of immediate group reference and the construction of corporate authority and responsibility, issues which McCarthy and Handford (2004) discuss in relation to the use of *we* in business English specifically (see also Handford, this volume).

3. Exploring key-word lists

Keyness

Key words are not necessarily the most frequent words in a corpus, but they are those words which are identified by statistical comparison of a 'target' corpus with another, larger corpus, which is referred to as the 'reference' or 'benchmark' corpus. This identification involves the automatic comparison of word lists using software such as the *WordSmith Tools Keyword* program. A key-word list includes items that are either significantly frequent (positive key words) or infrequent (negative key words), and is a useful starting point for many corpus linguistic analyses (Scott 1999 and this volume; Hunston 2002; Reppen and Simpson 2002; McEnery *et al.* 2006). Although there are several ways of calculating statistical significance available, a test of 'keyness' is especially useful for the analysis of corpus data because, being based on a log-likelihood (LL) test (Dunning 1993), it is not predicated on the assumption that data have a normal distribution (see McEnery *et al.* 2006: 55–6).

Positive key words

Table 10.4 shows the top ten (positive) key words generated when the frequency list for a 75,000-word sub-corpus of sociology and history essays extracted from the British Academic Written English (BAWE) corpus of student writing is compared with a larger, more general corpus made up of five million words of written English (the reference corpus) extracted from the BNC Sampler. The table details both raw frequencies and percentages; where there is no percentage given for the reference corpus, this is because the value is too small to be of use to this comparison. The zero figures in the *p*-value column simply indicate that the results are significant; it is the keyness values in the preceding column which are useful for comparative purposes.

We can see in Table 10.4 that four of the nouns with the highest keyness values (*class*, *society*, *women*, *power*) and the only adjective (*social*) reflect typical sociological or historical topics of the essays in the corpus. At first sight, however, the reason for the high keyness value of *archer* (a person who fires an arrow) is not apparent. This is a case where the analyst is likely to examine the item in context (through a concordance search for *archer*)

Table 10.4 Positive key words in sociology and history texts

N	*Key word*	*Freq.*	*%*	*RC Freq.*	*RC %*	*Keyness*	*P Value*
1	social	372	0.5	229	0.02	1,269.90	0.000
2	p	394	0.53	294	0.03	1,258.83	0.000
3	class	259	0.35	159	0.01	884.6	0.000
4	society	222	0.3	179	0.02	688.54	0.000
5	women	263	0.35	341	0.03	658.91	0.000
6	power	209	0.28	269	0.03	525.51	0.000
7	archer	87	0.12	1		465.55	0.000
8	of	3,408	4.59	33,798	3.15	410.23	0.000
9	ibid	67	0.09	0		366.84	0.000
10	that	1,110	1.5	8,555	0.8	333.6	0.000

Note: RC = Reference Corpus.
Source: Data extracted from BNC Sampler and BAWE Corpus.

Table 10.5 Negative keywords in sociology and history essays

N	*Key word*	*Freq.*	*%*	*RC Freq.*	*RC %*	*Keyness*	*P Value*
615	she	20	0.03	2,485	0.23	–209.44	0.000
616	I	99	0.13	6,218	0.58	–356.58	0.000
617	you	17	0.02	4,044	0.38	–415.28	0.000

Note: RC = Reference Corpus.
Source: Data extracted from BNC Sampler and BAWE Corpus.

in order to find some kind of explanation for its relatively high frequency. In this example, such an examination shows that the key item is in fact *Archer,* a very commonly cited reference in a number of the essays. The statistical significance of the two abbreviations in the essay corpus (*p* and *ibid*) is also related to referencing: the convention of writing *p* for page number, and *ibid* to indicate reference to a previously cited work. The remaining two items in Table 10.4 are the grammatical items *of* and *that.* Both have strong associations with academic writing: the former because it is a constituent in post-modified noun phrases (e.g. *the end **of** the Cold War*) and the latter because of its multi-functionality – not only does *that* function as a subordinator, it also follows reporting verbs, often as part of *it* patterns such as *it is reported* ***that*** (see Biber 2006; O'Keeffe *et al.* 2007).

Negative key words

We can also identify negative key words, or those items which occur significantly less often in the target corpus than in the reference one. Table 10.5 shows the three most significantly infrequent words in the same corpus of sociology and history essays for which we displayed the positive key words.

Here we can see that the three most significantly underrepresented words are pronouns (*you, I, she*) and that their unusually low frequency reflects the impersonal style of academic writing compared with the more personal focus of the reference corpus, which contains a broader range of written genres including many which tend to be more individually oriented, such as works of fiction, letters and journalistic prose. This difference in orientation of the writers in the essay corpus – less focus on individual women and more on women as a group – is nicely exemplified by the contrasting negative value for the third person singular female subject pronoun *she* (-209.44) and the positive keyness value (+658.91) for the more general female plural noun *women*.

4. Exploring concordance lines

Online concordancing

Also known as KWIC (key word in context) analysis, concordance analysis is probably the first basic corpus analytic technique that many people interested in corpus analysis undertake. This is because of the increasing numbers of websites which offer internet users the chance to search their corpora for specific words or phrases. The COBUILD Concordance and Collocations Sampler and the Corpus-based Concordances which make up part of The Compleat Lexical Tutor (available free online) are two examples of online concordancing programs particularly popular with language teachers and learners.

These websites, like many others, allow users to carry out concordance searches of the corpora which they hold, although they do not let them download the corpus files themselves. Corpora such as the BNC, in addition to being purchased, can be freely searched online. In general there are restrictions on how many results are displayed when doing online concordancing, and only random samples may be available. However, multiple searches for the same item can be carried out in order to generate different random samples which can then be accumulated, a procedure which can help validate the results. Some online corpora, such as the Michigan Corpus of Academic Spoken English (MICASE), do not limit the number of hits when concordancing, although if a very frequent item is being searched for, the software does give the option of limiting the numbers of results that are displayed.

Concordancing is a valuable analytical technique because it allows a large number of examples of an item to be brought together in one place, in their original context. It is useful both for hypothesis testing and for hypothesis generation. In the case of the latter, a hypothesis can be generated based on patterns observed in just a small number of lines, and subsequently tested out through further searches. However, as Hunston argues, when using concordancing to test a hypothesis, it is important to consider items which do not appear to support the hypothesis being tested, and, if necessary, review one's hypothesis rather than rejecting the forms themselves (2002: 52ff) (see also Hunston, this volume).

Searching and sorting

A concordance program allows any item (a single word, a wild-card item or a string of words) to be searched for within a corpus, and the results of that search displayed on the screen (see Tribble, this volume). These results are known as concordances or concordance lines. All the occurrences of the target item (or node word) are displayed, vertically centred, on the screen along with a preset number of characters either side (however, see Tribble, this volume, for discussion of a range of different concordance types). For example, if we search – with the wildcard asterisk – for the target item *shop** in a corpus of discussion tasks, all words beginning with these letters will be displayed as in the list below, which contains *shop, shops* and *shopping*.

1 t know about that, erm, the **shopping** mall. I'm not so sure about the
2 Bournemouth has got enough **shopping** centres I suppose ... The people won't go
3 't it really? Cos they like **shopping** more than boys. Yeah. I suppose so ...
4 uppose really ... and time to **shop**, and money to shop. How's it gonna
5 . I'm not so sure about the **shopping** mall myself ... I can't imagine it on
6 n't there? There's loads of **shops** isn't there? Hundreds of things. There's
7 three options we have are a **shopping** centre, a park or entertainment
8 ey don't have really enough **shop**, er big shopping malls in Bournemouth.
9 ppose really ... and time to **shop**, and money to shop. How's it gonna
10 k their cider. Erm, OK ... This **shopping** mall. shopping mall. It will attract,

(Data from Evison 2001)

Concordancing is particularly useful because the lines displayed can be sorted. Although the node item is relatively easy to see in randomly generated concordance lines, if we sort them, regularities of occurrence can be identified more easily. For example, below the same concordance lines for *shop** have been sorted alphabetically first by the centre item and then by the first and second words to the right (usually expressed as centre, R1, R2 in the options offered by the software). Now they have been sorted, we can see any regularities more clearly.

1 ppose really … and time to **shop,** and money to shop. How's it gonna
2 ey don't have really enough **shop,** er big shopping malls in Bournemouth.
3 uppose really … and time to **shop,** and money to shop. How's it gonna
4 three options we have are a **shopping** centre, a park or entertainment
5 Bournemouth has got enough **shopping** centres I suppose … The people won't go
6 t know about that, erm, the **shopping** mall. I'm not so sure about the
7 . I'm not so sure about the **shopping** mall myself … I can't imagine it on
8 k their cider. Erm, OK … This **shopping** mall. shopping mall. It will attract,
9 't it really? Cos they like **shopping** more than boys. Yeah. I suppose so …
10 n't there? There's loads of **shops** isn't there? Hundreds of things. There's

These very simple concordance lines demonstrate the versatility of concordance programs, and show the potential that they have to provide insight into the *typicality* of item use. In particular, concordance analysis can provide evidence of the most frequent meanings, or the most frequent collocates (co-occurring items) such as *shopping centre* or *shopping mall* (see Biber *et al.* 1998; Scott 1999; Tognini Bonelli 2001; Hunston 2002; Reppen and Simpson 2002; McEnery *et al.* 2006). A more detailed discussion of concordancing can also be found in Tribble (this volume), and exemplification of its role in data-driven learning in chapters by Gilquin and Granger, and Sripicharn, this volume.

5. Exploring discourse

Corpora and discourse

While it is true that large-scale analysis of part-of-speech tagged corpora, such as that carried out by Biber and his colleagues (see Biber, this volume), can tell us a great deal about the differences and similarities between different types of discourses (or registers, as Biber prefers to call them; see Biber, this volume), it is also true that the use of basic corpus analysis of untagged corpora (using freeware or relatively inexpensive proprietary software) can yield useful insights into discourse-level features of language (see O'Keeffe *et al.* 2007 for a recent survey of such analysis). For this reason, the final section of this chapter focuses on what basic corpus techniques can tell us about discourse, although more details about the kinds of methodology and data that are required to analyse discourse can be found in Thornbury, this volume. Here we will exemplify how basic corpus techniques can be used to explore the discourse functions of some common items in spoken language, focusing primarily (but not exclusively) on concordancing because this technique does not necessarily require the user to compile or purchase their own corpus; as we observed earlier, internet users can search a range of corpora online (see Lee, this volume).

Exploiting basic corpus techniques

Investigating the discourse functions of particular forms is complicated by the fact that these items often have clause-level, as well as discourse-level, functions. The word *now* is a good example. Although most dictionary entries for *now* highlight its temporal meaning of 'at the present time' (i.e. *now* as a temporal adverb), many users of English will be very well aware of its use as a focusing device (e.g. ***Now***, *what did we do in class yesterday – can anyone remember?*). Researchers such as Swales and Malczewski (2001) have in fact investigated this use of *now* in the MICASE corpus of academic talk, and a quick look at a frequency list generated for that corpus shows us that *now* is in 68th position overall, occurring over 4,000 times and being used at least once in every academic event in the corpus. If we go on to generate concordance lines for *now* in MICASE and sort them three places to the left (L1, L2, L3), we are able to see when *now* is functioning as a temporal adverb and when it has broader discourse-level functions:

1	t, accumulation. <PAUSE DUR = ":05"/>	**now**	let's, we've now covered the t
2	t we know today. <PAUSE DUR = ":05"/>	**now**	you will see something that wi
3	it's an agonist. <PAUSE DUR = ":04"/>	**now**,	let's see there were a couple
4	s. and look how many we've already,	**now**	i don't know if you wanna read
5	e strategy we're kind of engaged in	**now**	is a strategy of making sure p
6	and they're writing what they know.	**now**	do we fault them for writing w
7	e, just give them some stars. okay?	**now**.	let's, let it sit for a while
8	relevance, in revolutionary Paris.	**now**	i don't know whether Schikaned
9	yeah </U> and </U> <U WHO = "S1">	**now**	you see this here, this is a c
10	of, um, anatomy. </U> <U WHO = "S1">	**now**	do you believe that you're gon
11	hat's the (skull) </U> <U WHO = "S1">	**now**	do you notice what happened wi
12	WHO = "S3"> yeah </U> <U WHO = "S1">	**now**,	you're going to be meeting wi
13	"> right. </U> i the state here we	**now**	have a bike helmet law that sa
14	s happened in Minnesota, is that we	**now**	have a huge population of Cana
15	you know it seems to, seems to you	**now**	that you're in this classroom

(Data from the MICASE corpus)

By sorting to the left in this way, we are able to see easily that in only four lines is *now* clause-medial, and acting as a temporal adverb (lines 5, 13–15). In the remaining eleven lines it is clause-initial and has discourse-level functions, signalling a change of focus or topic (see Carter and McCarthy 2006: 112). In three of these cases, we can also see that *now* occurs immediately after a pause (denoted by < PAUSE DUR = " ... "/ >), and in four after a new speaker tag (denoted by < U WHO = "S1" >). If we now right sort these eleven lines (R1, R2, R3), we can see more clearly how *now* functions at a discourse level.

1	and they're writing what they know.	**now**	do we fault them for writing w
2	of, um, anatomy. </U> <U WHO = "S1">	**now**	do you believe that you're gon
3	hat's the (skull) </U> <U WHO = "S1">	**now**	do you notice what happened wi
4	s. and look how many we've already,	**now**	i don't know if you wanna read
5	relevance, in revolutionary Paris.	**now**	i don't know whether Schikaned
6	e, just give them some stars. okay?	**now**.	let's, let it sit for a while
7	it's an agonist. <PAUSE DUR = ":04"/>	**now**,	let's see there were a couple
8	t, accumulation. <PAUSE DUR = ":05"/>	**now**	let's, we've now covered the t
9	yeah </U> and </U> <U WHO = "S1">	**now**	you see this here, this is a c
10	WHO = "S3"> yeah </U> <U WHO = "S1">	**now**,	you're going to be meeting wi
11	t we know today. <PAUSE DUR = ":05"/>	**now**	you will see something that wi

(Data from the MICASE corpus)

With the concordance lines sorted in this way, we can see four patterns associated with *now*. The signalling of question forms shows up more clearly because the occurrences of the auxiliary verb *do* appear underneath each other (lines 1–3). Lines 4 and 5 exemplify the indirect structure *I don't know if/whether* … , while in lines 6–8 we can observe *now* introducing *let*-imperative structures, and in lines 9–11 the use of *now* + *you* which allows the speaker to address the listeners specifically in order to focus their attention. Interestingly, we can see how, in these concordance lines, *now* precedes language such as the personal pronouns *I* and *you*, questions, and *let*-constructions which has been shown to be part of an interactive teaching style (e.g. Morell 2004).

This discussion of the functions of *now* in pedagogic discourse illustrates how we can use concordancing to look more deeply behind initial quantitative results gained from frequency analysis, or begin the research process by searching for examples of a specific word that is of special interest, perhaps because of a hunch or because of previous research (or a mixture of the two). When used in this way, these basic techniques can be understood as part of a corpus-based approach which 'does not go to the extreme of rejecting intuition while attaching importance to empirical data' (McEnery *et al.* 2006: 7).

Combining corpus techniques with other approaches: the case of turn-taking

In addition to using quantitative data analysis, many researchers also explore their data through qualitative analysis (e.g. McCarthy 1998; Carter 2004; O'Keeffe 2006; O'Keeffe *et al.* 2007) and small domain-specific corpora such as those discussed by Koester (this volume) are particularly susceptible to qualitative readings. In fact, there are growing numbers of researchers who suggest that combining automatic corpus analytic techniques with more fine-grained qualitative investigation, such as Conversation Analysis (CA), is a robust methodology for dealing with the intricacies of spoken language in particular (e.g. Tao 2003; O'Keeffe 2006; Walsh and O'Keeffe 2007). In this respect, Walsh and O'Keeffe (ibid.: 123) argue that there can be a 'synergy of CA and corpus approaches', which they suggest can 'offer a greater understanding of … interactional processes'. Such processes include turn-taking, a feature of discourse very strongly associated with CA, but one which is increasingly being investigated using corpus techniques in conjunction with fine-grained analysis. Turn-openings are one position in the discourse which have been exploited in this way (e.g. Tao and McCarthy 2001; McCarthy 2002, 2003; Farr 2003; Tao 2003; Evison 2008).

Because new turns in corpus data are identified by speaker tags such as < U WHO = "S1" > (the tags used in the MICASE corpus and exemplified earlier), it is possible to establish the regularised ways in which turns open by generating concordance lines for all the new speaker tags in a corpus using a wildcard search. In the case of MICASE, we simply need to insert a wildcard (indicated by an asterisk) so the search item becomes < U WHO = "S*" >. By sorting to the right, we are able to see turn-initial regularities, such as the occurrence of *yeah no* as shown below.

1 this, it's just to show you know, <U WHO = "S4"> **yeah no no** i know i'm
2 o-math i didn't mean to there but <U WHO = "S4"> **yeah no no no no no** w
3 ay oh i though you said on Tuesday <U WHO = "S1"> **yeah, no.** okay and yea
4 okay, okay okay? does that help? <U WHO = "S3"> **yeah no** panicking it's
5 it in the economics part? um yeah <U WHO = "S4"> **yeah? no** problem, i was

6 hi, can i pay a fine here? <U WHO = "S52"> **yeah. no** problem. the
7 's what i was kinda looking into. <U WHO = "S1"> **yeah, no** that i mean t
8 then we have one over Z-bar right? <U WHO = "S1"> **yeah no.** then we have
9 maybe it's a new term they have. <U WHO = "S3"> **yeah no** they do call it
10 thanks. yeah. sorry i forgot to <U WHO = "S1"> **yeah no** uh'uh. yeah u

(Data from the MICASE corpus)

Tao (2003) uses this method to investigate American English and Evison (2008) to study British English. Their results are strikingly similar; in both cases the twenty most frequent forms account for 60 per cent of all turn-openings. There are some differences between the two varieties: *yeah*, *mhm* and *right* are more frequent in American English compared with British, and *yes*, *no* and *mm* are more frequent in British English than American (Evison 2008) – these comparative findings confirming those of Tottie's earlier corpus-based study of British and American English (Tottie 1991).

Once concordance analysis has been able to establish patterns of turn-initial items, further detailed analysis can of course be carried out on specific examples that have first been identified. For example, the talk immediately preceding the turn-initial *yeah no* (line 9 in the list above) is shown in Extract 1. Here we can see that three students are working hard to co-create an understanding of their subject, and that they signal strong other-orientation; in fact, each of the three turns opens with a responsive item. It is the importance of acknowledging prior talk that results in the sequence *yeah no*; first S3 acknowledges S2's contribution (*yeah*), before signalling suggesting that it may in fact be incorrect.

Extract 1 [Data from MICASE Transcript ID: SGR175SU123]

S1: okay. so where does it say Q cycle?
S2: oh, in our book it was like later in the_ was it, when they talk about, complex three, how ca-i don't know ma-maybe it's a new term they have.
S3: **yeah no** they do call it the Q, something or other.

By examining the sequence *yeah no* in context, we get a clear sense that the turn-initial position is 'the locus of choice where speakers frequently select items which contribute to the non-transactional stratum of the talk, and where [a] set of "small" items does its work of supporting, converging, bridging and facilitating transitions' (McCarthy 2003: 38). This example shows us how detailed analysis of corpus transcripts can be used in conjunction with basic corpus techniques such as frequency analysis and concordancing to give us greater insight into discourse.

Further reading

Hunston, S. (2002) *Corpora in Applied Linguistics*. Cambridge: Cambridge University Press. (This book contains useful chapters on corpus data interpretation with plenty of examples.)

McEnery, T., Xiao, R. and Tono, Y. (2006) *Corpus-based Language Studies: An Advanced Resource Book*. London: Routledge. (This book provides a useful overview of corpus analytical techniques as well as a set of case studies which exemplify how analysis works in practice.)

O'Keeffe, A., McCarthy, M. and Carter, R. (2007) *From Corpus to Classroom: Language Use and Language Teaching*. Cambridge: Cambridge University Press. (This book summarises recent corpus-based studies which are particularly important to corpus-informed pedagogy.)

Sinclair, J. McH. (1991) *Corpus, Concordance, Collocation.* Oxford: Oxford University Press. (This classic volume by the late John Sinclair exemplifies how basic corpus analytical techniques can reveal much about language and is a vibrant account of the emergence of corpus linguistics.)

References

Biber, D. (1990) 'Methodological issues regarding corpus-based analyses of linguistic variation', *Literary and Linguistic Computing* 5: 257–69.

——(2006) *University Language: A Corpus-based Study of Spoken and Written Registers.* Amsterdam: John Benjamins.

Biber, D., Conrad, S. and Reppen, R. (1998) *Corpus Linguistics: Investigating Language Structure and Use.* Cambridge: Cambridge University Press.

Biber, D., Johansson, S., Leech, G., Conrad, S. and Finegan, E. (1999) *The Longman Grammar of Spoken and Written English.* London: Longman.

Carter, R. A. (2004) *Language and Creativity: The Art of Common Talk.* London: Routledge.

Carter, R. A. and McCarthy, M. J. (2006) *The Cambridge Grammar of English: A Comprehensive Guide to Spoken and Written English Grammar and Usage.* Cambridge: Cambridge University Press.

Dunning, T. (1993) 'Accurate Methods for the Statistics of Surprise and Coincidence', *Computational Linguistics* 19(1): 61–74.

Evison, J. (2001) 'The Language in First Certificate Discussion Tasks: Are the Exponents of Agreement and Disagreement Presented in Exam Preparation Materials the Same as Those Used by Post-First Certificate Level Non-native Speakers and Native Speakers during Discussion?', unpublished MA dissertation, University of Portsmouth.

——(2008) 'Turn-openers in Academic Talk: An Exploration of Discourse Responsibility', unpublished PhD thesis, University of Nottingham.

——(2009) '"It's Goodbye from Me … and It's TTFN from Me": Creating Podcast(er) Identity in Broadcast Academic Conversations', paper given at IVACS Annual Symposium, University of Edinburgh, January.

Farr, F. (2003) 'Engaged Listenership in Spoken Academic Discourse: The Case of Student–Tutor Meetings', *Journal of English for Academic Purposes* 2(1): 67–85.

Kennedy, G. (1998) *An Introduction to Corpus Linguistics.* London: Longman.

Kilgarriff, A., Rychl, P., Smrž, P. and Tugwell, D. (2004) 'The Sketch Engine', in *Proceedings of the Eleventh EURALEX International Congress.* Lorient, France: Universite de Bretagne-Sud, 105–16; available at http://nlp.fi.muni.cz/publications/euralex2004_kilgarriff_pary_smrz_tugwell/ (accessed 6 January 2009).

Koester, A. (2006) *Investigating Workplace Discourse.* London: Routledge

Leech, G., Rayson, P. and Wilson, A. (2001). *Word Frequencies in Written and Spoken English.* Harlow: Pearson Education.

McCarthy, M. J. (1998) *Spoken Language and Applied Linguistics.* Cambridge: Cambridge University Press.

——(1999) 'What Constitutes a Basic Vocabulary for Spoken Communication?' *Studies in English Language and Literature* 1: 233–49; available at www.cambridge.org/elt/touchstone/images/pdf/What%20constitutes%20a%20basic%20vocabulary.pdf (accessed 20 October 2008).

——(2002) 'Good Listenership Made Plain: British and American Non-minimal Response Tokens in Everyday Conversation', in R. Reppen, S. Fitzmaurice and D. Biber (eds) *Using Corpora to Explore Linguistics Variation.* Amsterdam: John Benjamins, pp. 49–71.

——(2003) 'Talking Back: "Small" Interactional Response Tokens in Everyday Conversation', in J. Coupland (ed.) 'Small Talk', special issue of *Research on Language in Social Interaction* 36(1): 33–6.

McCarthy, M. J. and Carter, R. A. (2003) 'What Constitutes a Basic Spoken Vocabulary?' *Cambridge ESOL Research Notes* 13: 5–7; available at www.cambridgeesol.org (accessed 16 October 2006).

McCarthy, M. J. and Handford, M. (2004) '"Invisible to Us": A Preliminary Corpus-based Study of Spoken Business English', in U. Connor and T. Upton (eds) *Discourse in the Professions: Perspectives from Corpus Linguistics.* Amsterdam: John Benjamins, pp. 167–201.

Monoconc Pro Concordance Software, Version 2 (2000) Houston, TX: Athelstan.

Morell, T. (2004) 'Interactive Lecture Discourse for University EFL Students', *English for Specific Purposes* 23(3): 325–38.

O'Keeffe, A. (2003) 'Strangers on the Line: A Corpus-based Lexico-grammatical Analysis of Radio Phone-in', unpublished PhD thesis, University of Limerick.

——(2006) *Investigating Media Discourse*. London: Routledge.

O'Keeffe, A., McCarthy, M. J. and Carter, R. A. (2007) *From Corpus to Classroom: Language Use and Language Teaching*. Cambridge: Cambridge University Press.

Reppen, R. and Simpson, R. (2002) 'Corpus Linguistics', in N. Schmitt (ed.) *An Introduction to Applied Linguistics*. London: Arnold, pp. 92–111.

Scott, M. (1999) *WordSmith Tools*. Oxford: Oxford University Press.

Sinclair, J. M. (1999) 'A Way with Common Words', in H. Hasselgård and S. Oksefjell (eds) *Out of Corpora: Studies in Honor of Stig Johansson*. Amsterdam: Rodopi, pp. 157–79.

Swales, J. M. and Malczewski, B. (2001) 'Discourse Management and New Episode flags in MICASE', in R. C. Simpson and J. M. Swales (eds) *Corpus Linguistics in North America: Selections from the 1999 Symposium*. Michigan: University of Michigan, pp. 45–164.

Tao, H. (2003) 'Turn Initiators in Spoken English: A Corpus-based Approach to Interaction and Grammar', in P. Leistyna and C. F. Meyer (eds) *Corpus Analysis: Language Structure and Language Use*. Amsterdam: Rodopi, pp. 187–207.

Tao, H. and McCarthy, M. (2001) 'Understanding Non-restrictive Which-clauses in Spoken English, Which is Not an Easy Thing', *Language Sciences* 23: 651–77.

Tognini Bonelli, E. (2001) *Corpus Linguistics at Work*. Amsterdam and Philadelphia, PA: John Benjamins.

Tottie, G. (1991) 'Conversational Style in British and American English: The Case of Backchannels', in K. Aijmer and B. Altenberg (eds) *English Corpus Linguistics*. London: Longman, pp. 254–71.

Tribble, C. (1997) 'Improvising Corpora for ELT: Quick and Dirty Ways of Developing Corpora for Language Teaching', in B. Lewandowska-Tomaszczyk and J. Melia (eds) *Proceedings of the First International Conference on Practical Applications in Language Corpora*. Łodz: Łodz University Press, pp. 106–17; available at www.ctribble.co.uk (accessed 16 March 2004).

Walsh, S. and O'Keeffe, A. (2007) 'Applying CA to a Modes Analysis of Higher Education Spoken Academic Discourse', in H. Bowles and P. Seedhouse (eds) *Conversation Analysis and Language for Specific Purposes*. Bern: Peter Lang, pp. 100–39.

West, M. P. (1953) *A General Service List of English Words*. London: Longman.

11
What can corpus software do?

Mike Scott

1. General constraints

It is important to put the computer in its proper place. Just as in the early days of the motor-car some people ran risks we would not think of running now, so in the beginnings of computing there were misapprehensions such as the estimation that very few computers would ever be needed (Cohen 1998), in an age when computers were air-conditioned, weighed tons and were chiefly used by the superpowers for computing ballistic equations. Nowadays there are not likely to be people who view the computer as a semi-magic being, as there were twenty or thirty years ago when the personal computer was a novelty and there was much excitement about artificial intelligence and the 5th Generation. Most of us experience computers every day and that experience is more likely to be frustrating or routine than rewarding. In order to get the best from Corpus Linguistics, though, it is important to know something more about what computers are good at, what they are bad at, and why.

Things computers do really well

Computers don't get tired. As long as they are fed and watered with sufficient electricity and internet connectivity, they go on with routine tasks night and day, even updating their own calendars as daylight-saving comes in, all automatically and with rather little attention. As a matter of fact, most of the time the computer chips are not actually doing anything at all, however. Like Marvin, the android in the science-fantasy story *The Hitch-Hiker's Guide to the Galaxy* (Adams 1978), they spend by far the majority of their clock cycles simply watching and waiting, or in the jargon, *polling*. That is, polling the keyboard to see whether a key has been pressed, polling the inputs to detect incoming e-mails, etc. In Marvin's fictional case the result is boredom and frustration, but in reality computers are quite unable to get bored or frustrated – those are qualities of their users.

Computers can multi-task. Strictly speaking, most of them don't actually do all the operations I shall describe simultaneously, but to the user it appears that they do, because the main computer processing unit (CPU) 'attention' is shared out so that it seems that the computer can multi-task. The computer, at the same time as it is polling the keyboard, is also displaying results on the screen, calculating more results and, perhaps in another tab or another window, running numerous other operations. If an e-mail arrives, it may play a sound to show that it has recognised the arrival, probably checked the message for spam and possibly deleted it if so. (In that case why did it sound the bell, I wonder? The arrival of spam is not something I want to have my shoulder tapped for!)

The word *computer* comes from the fact that it can carry out routine numerical computations such as adding up numbers, rapidly, tirelessly, always getting the exact same answer. It is also true but less well known that it may actually get the wrong answer. According to Wolfram MathWorld:

> A notorious example is the fate of the Ariane rocket launched on June 4, 1996 … In the 37th second of flight, the inertial reference system attempted to convert a 64-bit floating-point number to a 16-bit number, but instead triggered an overflow error which was interpreted by the guidance system as flight data, causing the rocket to veer off course and be destroyed.
>
> (http://mathworld.wolfram.com/RoundoffError.html, accessed 2008)

The technical parts in that quote refer to how the computer stores its data, in 16-bit, 32-bit or 64-bit chunks. For our purposes in the present chapter, we do not need to concern ourselves with single bits, but it is important to understand that a number or a letter in an alphabet will need to be represented somehow and stored in the machine's memory chips or on a disk or pen-drive, etc., and to understand why, if the storage is not managed properly, an error may occur.

Imagine you want to display a pre-arranged cryptic message to a confederate, that you are being held under house arrest and unable to communicate normally. The only way of sending a message is to cover or obscure one of the panes of a window with a book or a cushion. Suppose further that your window has two panes. Covering the right-hand pane means 'carry on, the hidden supplies have still not been found' whereas the left pane means 'flee abroad, all our supplies have been discovered'. The message has only two possible options and there are only two panes to use for these messages. What if there were a need to communicate more messages, though? Our crude window-pane system could possibly be made to carry a little more information because it would be possible to use the absence of anything covering either pane to mean a third message such as 'we still don't know whether the supplies have been detected', but obviously enough, the method of covering up window-panes will be quite limited as a means of communication and it is unlikely that we could ever express a much larger range of different messages using this system. We might bring in time itself, by establishing a convention that each pane was covered or not covered for a long or a short time, or use a convention of part-covering panes, but still the system is very limited. The point is that for any messaging system, a set of choices must exist (number of panes, covered versus uncovered, etc.) and a system with inherently few choices built into it cannot express many alternative different messages. Meaning implies choice.

In the 64-bit floating point reference given above, what happened is that a floating point number (i.e. involving decimals such as 3.1412456321) was originally stored successfully in an area of computer memory but then copied out into another area of its memory only one quarter the size, into which it didn't really fit, and when that happened it was interpreted as if it had a quite different meaning, as if someone accidentally sat by the left window pane and caused a major panic.

Analogously, the personal computer of the 1980s and 1990s could easily fit a symbol from the English alphabet like *J* or *K* into a small space in its memory, simply because the range of alternatives envisaged was small: all the alphabet from *A* to *Z* and again from *a* to *z*, plus a few punctuation symbols and numbers. The people designing the systems themselves mostly spoke and wrote English, a language that uses a tiny alphabet. The total number of symbols in routine use in those computers was fewer than 300. What about people who wrote in Spanish or German? These needed a few more symbols, such as *ñ* and *Ñ* and *ü* and *Ü* (or else they just didn't bother because without the accents the text was still usually perfectly readable). Fitting those into the *character-set* was not difficult, but fitting Japanese, Hindi, Chinese or Korean symbols in too was really a difficulty. To take account of the many thousands of extra character shapes used in such languages required a bigger storage area than that which was OK for a mere 2–300. Technically, these alternatives fitted into a system which reserved one *byte* for each character, while the many thousands of alternatives of Chinese characters require a system using two or more bytes for each. Just as the complex Ariane rocket number was misinterpreted when it was read into a simpler system, the Chinese character 龍, if stored in a single byte system, would get misperceived as either *ù* or *Ä*. Why those particular characters, you may ask – they don't look a bit like 龍. One way of representing these characters is by the numerical code that has been allocated in the storage system, and for most purposes we use decimal numbers for that. Character 龍 is 63940. In other words, in the Unicode (of which more anon) convention, that particular character is number 63,940 in a set which starts off with characters like *A* and *B*. In computer science a different way of representing the same number, hex, represents the same number as 'F9C4'. If we take that number in byte-sized chunks, we get F9 and C4. Yes, you've guessed it, F9 is the character *ù* and C4 is *Ä*. Reading something intended to be F9C4 as F9 or C4 alone is definitely a mistake. It probably would not crash a rocket, though it might set off a serious dispute if it involved speakers of oriental languages!

Other tasks computers are good at are storing numbers, strings (text), or records (data structures) on disk, reading them and changing them. They don't usually lose them, muddle them up or get them corrupted, at least they do so much less than humans would if asked to retrieve and replace information from file stores very many times.

Computers can sort data into alphabetical or numerical order quickly and reliably; they can straightforwardly display, in fairly accurate colours, text or numbers on a screen or via a printer on paper, if the symbols belong to a standard character set. They can scan an image as a vast array of tiny dots, rather like a digital camera.

Computers remember when something was done. Without your doing anything, your documents get stored with a record of when they were last written to: day, month, year, hour, minute, second – even to the 100th of second. Computers may remember more than you expect: your .docs also almost certainly contain hidden information about who owned the software being used, what has been deleted, printers available and so on. (To see what is in a .doc, just open it using a program such as Microsoft's *Notepad*; it can be quite a shock to see what is in there.)

Computers are also good at storing links between pieces of information: the information can thus be organised in a database, where ideally every piece of data is typed in once only, and every single time the data is needed it is extracted from the database. For example, in a university, the publications, teaching and administrative duties and achievements of staff could each be stored in one place only and the data retried via linkages to generate a portfolio for staff promotion, a report for the national research assessment system, applications for research awards, staff web-pages, etc. Computers are so good at these linkages, in fact, that the terms *hypertext*, *web* and *networking* have come about with the world of personal computers.

Finally, computers are quite robust in normal use. The parts that most often give trouble are keyboards, disk drives and printers – the bits with moving parts – but by and large the hardware is not likely to break down.

Things computers cannot do at all

Computers do not notice what they are doing at all. Ask them to perform a task 200 times and they will not assume the next request will again be for that same task, or helpfully do it without being asked. This is a tremendous strength. Many human errors come from our noticing patterns of repetition: 'she asked me to pass the salt again' leading to 'she fancies me', or 'they always ring the fire-alarm in the second week of term' to 'carry on, class, we can ignore it'.

Could software for computers be designed so that it would notice what it is doing? Well, it would be easy to do that at a simple level; for example, I have programmed into *WordSmith Tools* (Scott 2009) routines which offer advice when appropriate (such as when it would be best to sort one's data) but which also offer a 'don't tell me again' box – if the user ticks this box the reminder will not be offered next time. The software in a very simple sense learns what that user wants. Perhaps a better example would be if the software kept a log of every operation which each user performed, adding to a database each time, so that as time went by it had increasingly better records of what that user did, much as the supermarket software keeps a log (if you pay by card) of your detailed purchases. It would then be easy for the corpus software to offer a message such as 'shall I select the same set of text files again and get ready for concordancing straight away?' once a pattern had become sufficiently established. It would be as if the supermarket recognised you entering the door and immediately prepared a half-full shopping trolley with your favourite regular items already in there. In other words, it is possible for a programmer to imagine a system for *pseudo-noticing*, giving the appearance of noticing. This is not at all the same as an animal such as a mouse noticing, for example, that there's a smell of cheese and moving towards it, chiefly because it is the programmer who has anticipated certain possible options and events in advance, not the computer, whereas the mouse does its own noticing of varied changes in its environment.

Computers cannot prefer one answer to another, as a mouse could, or complain. Nor could they know what any data *means*. To them, 'to be or not to be' is just a string of bytes, eighteen bytes long (not thirteen as each space also takes up room), or eighteen pairs of bytes in length if written using Unicode, the system which makes Chinese much easier to represent. It is just a string of bytes, not a meaningful question about a quandary as well as a reference to a Shakespeare play. Nor can a computer know what the user *meant*. If s/he leans over the computer and a sleeve accidentally presses a key, there's no way the computer can guess that this was involuntary.

Things computers can do, with difficulty

Comparing strings

Computers can compare 'hell' with 'hello', easily spotting that *hell* is shorter and that *hello* contains *hell* within it, but would not be able to see that 'The hell of war' is similar to

'The hellishness of war' unless previously programmed to treat *hell* and *hellishness* as synonyms. Programming a computer to treat two forms as synonymous is hard. To determine that, say, *start* and *begin* are synonymous is liable to generate **the car won't begin*, or to seriously misread Barry *et al.*'s 2007 article 'START (Screening Tool to Alert Doctors to the Right Treatment) – An Evidence-based Screening Tool to Detect Prescribing Omissions in Elderly Patients'. *May* is sometimes an auxiliary, sometimes a female name, sometimes a month, sometimes a flower – and programming software to decide which is not at all easy. You might like to try the armchair exercise of deciding how you might go about it.

Recognising a pattern

Pattern-recognition is a very tricky exercise. Computers are very good at shuffling data around, re-ordering it, extracting sought strings as in a concordancer. In so doing, they very often present the user with some sort of configuration which to a human looks patterned. But the computer itself will not easily find a pattern. For example, a sequence of *o*s and hyphens makes a pattern:

o-o-o-o-o-o-o-o-o-o-o-o-o-o-o-o-o-o-o-o-o-o-o-o-o-o-o-o-o-o-

and to a human a sequence of four symbols with a hyphen between is a roughly similar but less attractive-looking (because less symmetrical) pattern:

hyug-hyug-hyug-hyug-hyug-hyug-hyug-hyug-hyug-hyug-hyug-hyug-

but for computer software to see the similarity it has to recognise a *rule*, roughly of the type:

repeat a certain number of times (more than two and less than infinity)
a sequence of at least one single and optionally up to roughly seven or eight differing characters
followed by a hyphen or similar (where similar means in the following set such as [dot, slash, comma etc])

A device which trades on this poor computer pattern recognition is the *captcha* (Completely Automated Turing Test To Tell Computers and Humans Apart), a visual device designed to be easy for a human but hard for software to read, so as to be sure any response received came from a human and not from software (see Figure 11.1).

Unfortunately, in practice captchas can be hard for humans too! Recognising a scanned text in terms of its component letters is a similar problem. Optical Character Recognition (OCR) exists but is not yet 100 per cent reliable; it is more reliable in

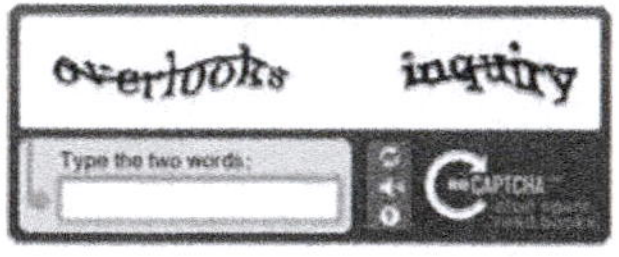

Figure 11.1 Captcha (www.captcha.net).

English than in, say, French or Greek, as most work has been done on it in relation to English. Accordingly, there is not only the time for the scanner to look at the text (roughly the same time as a photocopier takes) but also OCR time and then a process of correcting mistakes in the text, probably with the help of a spell-checker. If you want text for corpus purposes, it is generally much better to spend time finding it already in electronic form than scanning it!

Learning

Computers, unlike babies, get switched off. They might store a lot of information in memory when switched on, but do not remember it unless they have been programmed to, as in spam detection, which attempts to identify and recognise certain words and phrases and use a growing stored list of them to check mail against. For Artificial Intelligence, they need some means of getting access to databases of information, procedures for sifting through it, and a means of storing inferences.

Graphics and speech

Animation, as in cartoons, video and speech reproduction or playback, is not too difficult, but does take up a lot of a PC's memory. Speech recognition, on the other hand, is still very much in its infancy and limited to a few hundred words.

Giving useful feedback on what is happening inside it

In 2002 Sinclair discussed the human–machine interface in terms of discourse analysis, showing how very rigid and limited it was. This is still very true: programming a computer to do a useful job and at the same time inform the user as to how it is progressing, what has been done and what remains to be done is still extremely difficult. Error messages are well known to be cryptic and get very widely ignored. Logging systems do exist but remain arcane for the majority of users. The hourglass and progress bar are in general use but the information they provide is very limited. It is as if the PC got tired and could not do two things at once, which as we have seen is not at all the case.

Things computers are sometimes expected or believed to be able to do

Sinclair (2001) talks disparagingly of 'tomorrow's Information Paradise', and 'the hype of New Age communications' and it isn't rare to see the sort of headline shown in Figure 11.2.

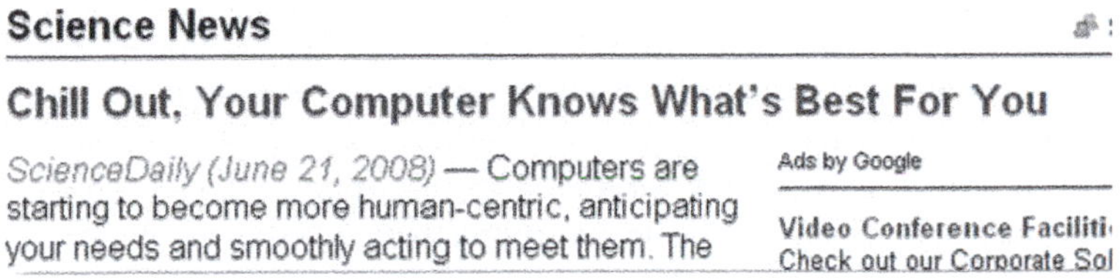

Science News

Chill Out, Your Computer Knows What's Best For You

ScienceDaily (June 21, 2008) — Computers are starting to become more human-centric, anticipating your needs and smoothly acting to meet them. The

Figure 11.2 Information Paradise?

In the *ScienceDaily* case above, the story concerned attempts to process data about where customers move about in stores and from that build up software that can aid in identifying suspicious behaviour, and in similar kinds of research such as face recognition software. Probably the cause of the optimistic headline was when the story moved on to a project to get software running a house to be able to predict its occupants' needs, presumably controlling heating and lighting as the occupants moved from room to room and suchlike. This is not a case where computers know best; it is merely a case of getting sensors to react when fairly simple rules apply (nobody in the room? turn the lights off!).

Let us examine a more corpus-related example and indeed with a much less hyped title: 'Predicting Human Brain Activity Associated with the Meanings of Nouns'. Mitchell *et al.* (2008) have programmed computers to predict human brain scans after subjects heard ordinary concrete nouns belonging to familiar categories such as *celery* (food) and *airplane* (vehicles), by processing large corpora (one trillion tokens) and determining their collocational configurations. That is, their computers generated pseudo brain scan images on the basis of word patterns after being trained with (a) lots of word data which might, for example, find that items like *airplane* and *helicopter* share similar lexical environments, and (b) genuine brain scans generated with magnetic resonance imaging equipment after subjects had been prompted with relevant words. This is an impressive feat, though it must be noted that the degree of matching the computer obtained was not at all high, even if it was statistically much greater than chance, and that one person's brain scan itself after hearing a word like *celery* or *airplane* is in any case not very like another's. Essentially the impressive feature of all these projects is the imagination and persistence of the programmers. To process an enormous corpus attempting to build up contextual profiles of certain nouns is quite impressive if this database can subsequently be used to generate predictions. In this case the predictions are concerned with the images generated by brain scans, but what matters in principle is that a complex database can be made to generate patterns and these patterns can then be matched up, sometimes, with others in the real world. A database of movements in a store might thus identify suspicious loitering. There is no magic. The computers which do so well at chess do it by using algorithms clever programmers have designed to take advantage of the things discussed above – that in a flash a computer can be made to evaluate millions of board positions.

2. Sorting out your data

Re-formatting and re-organising to match up better with what computers can manage

Because computers have no intelligence, we need to prepare our corpora carefully in advance so that the texts contain nothing unexpected and are in the right format for use. We have already seen that there is an issue of whether the underlying text format assumes that each written character is to be stored using one byte or more than one. What if some characters take up one byte but others take up two, three, four or more, though? In widespread current use, there is a format called UTF-8 which stores many characters as single bytes but some others as more than 1.

Figure 11.3 shows a tiny text prepared using Microsoft *Word 2007*, and then saved as Plain Text (.txt) using the standard defaults offered, then re-opened in MS *Notepad*.

Figure 11.3 Plain text with curly quotes.

If you look carefully you will see that the quotation marks and the apostrophe are not symmetrical and that they are slightly curved. In the format which *Word* considers standard plain text, the underlying character codes are as shown in Figure 11.4 where the opening double-quote is coded 93 and the closing double-quote 94, 92 being used for the apostrophe.

If we now re-save the same text in a format called UTF-8 (Figure 11.5), and again open up the text file in *WordSmith's* File Viewer (Figure 11.6), what we find is that although the letters expressing wonderful are straightforward, one byte per character, there is now a 'signature' (EF-BB-BF) telling the computer that the whole file is in UTF-8 and then the curly double-quote at the beginning needs three byte-codes (E2–80–9C) and the double-quotes at the end similarly have E2–80–9D. The apostrophe has now grown to an E2-80–99 sequence.

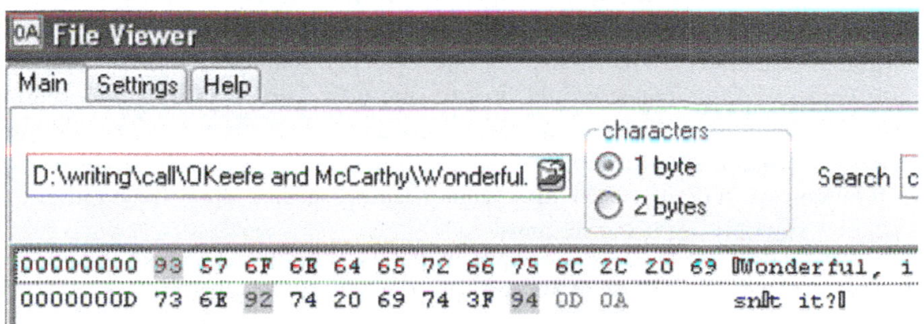

Figure 11.4 Plain text with different quote characters.

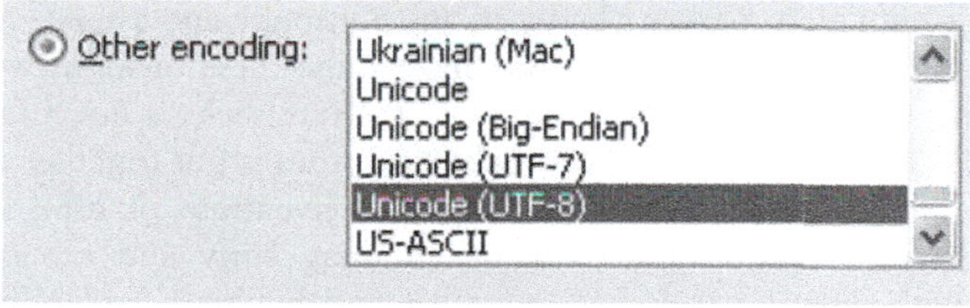

Other encoding:
Ukrainian (Mac)
Unicode
Unicode (Big-Endian)
Unicode (UTF-7)
Unicode (UTF-8)
US-ASCII

Figure 11.5 Saving as UTF-8 in *Word 2007*.

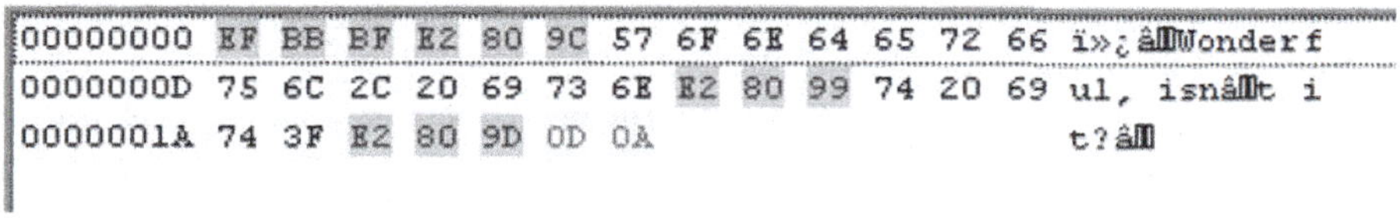

```
00000000 EF BB BF E2 80 9C 57 6F 6E 64 65 72 66 ï»¿â Wonderf
0000000D 75 6C 2C 20 69 73 6E E2 80 99 74 20 69 ul, isnâ t i
0000001A 74 3F E2 80 9D 0D 0A                   t?â
```

Figure 11.6 Plain UTF-8 text with some multi-byte characters.

This sort of low-level fact is normally kept hidden from users of the computer, of course. However, the fact that a rather weird system is in use can end up unexpectedly affecting corpus linguistic findings. I call the system weird, because everything would be so much more straightforward if it were possible to assume that a text file of 1,000 bytes contained exactly 1,000 characters, and that the 500th character was to be found by leaping forward 500 places from the start. In the case of the text above, the second character of the text, a W (represented by code 57), is in fact to be found after a three-byte signature and another three-byte character, at the seventh byte in the text stream.

The need for this strange kludge came about because on the one hand many users like to see curly quotes (even if sometimes the word processor curves them the wrong way!), and on the other hand disk and other memory space were for years at a premium, so operating systems and software didn't want to waste bytes unnecessarily. It is 'cheaper' to use one byte for most characters and then three for odd ones like curly quotes or m-dashes, rather than to use two bytes for every single character. And that way English text was stored economically (even if Japanese took up more bytes, and Cherokee or Hindi could not be represented at all …).

However, in the year 2008 and for some years prior to that, disk space and computer memory have been relatively cheap. At the time of writing it is possible in the UK to buy a 500 GB drive for a price equivalent to about seventeen large hamburgers. That is only the burgers, no chips or soft drinks to go with them. A 500 GB drive would hold a lot of text, which would take more than seventeen mealtimes to read: Charles Dickens' novel, *Bleak House*, the 800 pages of which when printed weigh a lot more than a big hamburger, is just under 2MB in size (at one byte per character) and that means more than 500 copies of *Bleak House* would fit into one GB. The 500 GB drive could therefore store 500 times 500 copies – you would not have shelf space for 250,000 copies of *Bleak House*, I suspect. A similar picture obtains for the computer's internal memory, its RAM. The cost of 2GB of RAM (best-selling laptops in late 2008 have either 2GB or 4GB) is approximately eight hamburgers.

Now that we are well into the new millennium, it would not be problematic to use a double-byte system; indeed, gradually, the world's computer services and operating systems have mostly moved that way. New documents are beginning to be routinely stored that way, too. There are several implications here. One is that it is quite likely that without the user thinking much about it, a coding difference can easily come between a left- and a right-quotation mark, or between an apostrophe and a single quotation mark. When corpus software comes to process them, because these forms as we have seen are encoded differently, there is a danger that what the user seeks is not found because of a trivial mismatch. This will typically occur when a corpus is put together containing texts formatted by different people following different conventions or using different word-processing software. There will be some texts using curly and others using straight quotes, some with differing n-dashes, m-dashes and hyphens, and others which have them all the same as each other.

Another implication is that corpus software may end up showing oddities. If software which does not handle UTF-8 is asked to process it, as is the case with the now obsolete *WordSmith 3.0*, anomalies may appear (Figure 11.7).

The 'word' *Â* is *WordSmith 3.0*'s capitalisation of *â*, which is character E2, and as we have seen above E2 is one of the components of a three-byte character. That is not the only anomaly – the 9C visible to the left of the 57 for the *W* of Wonderful has come out in the default font as Œ.

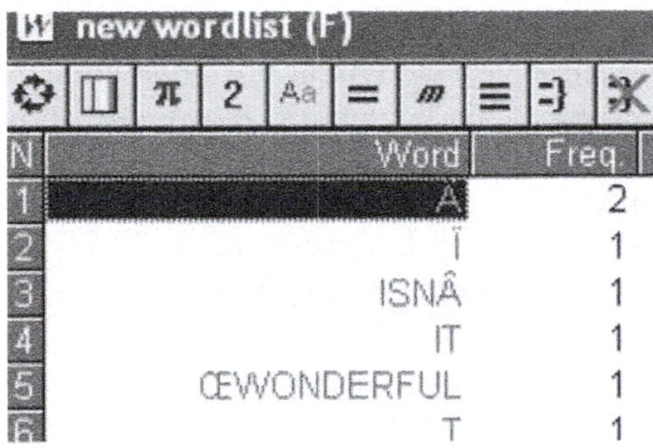

Figure 11.7 UTF-8-inspired oddities in WS3 word list.

And a further implication is that corpus software has to be flexible to recognise and handle these various formats. *WordSmith 3.0*, which ceased development at the end of the last millennium, did not recognise or handle two-byte text at all, and as we have seen makes mistakes with some characters in UTF-8. As time goes by, it is very likely that these problems will fade away; old legacy texts will either be dropped completely or else converted to more modern standards, and the world will be one of Unicode.

But what exactly is Unicode? After all, MS *Word 2007*'s options for saving plain text visibly include four different Unicodes! Well, UTF-7 and UTF-8 are basically one-byte systems. UTF-7 is a one-byte-per-character system which won't handle any accented characters like *é* at all. What MS *Word 2007* calls 'Unicode' is in fact a system of two bytes per character, and 'Unicode (Big-Endian)' is the same but with the two bytes reversed. (This is like the tradition of first name, surname: the French and some other cultures in many contexts prefer the order DUPONT, Charles, while for many similar contexts the English prefer the first name to come first, as in Charles DUPONT. Big-Endian would represent the character 龍 [F9C4] with the F9 and C4 in reverse order as C4F9). Whether 'Unicode' or 'Unicode (Big-Endian)', *Word* will generally use two bytes for each character.

The Unicode Consortium, which controls these things and which is endorsed and supported by all the major software companies, announces at its site

Unicode provides a unique number for every character,
no matter what the platform,
no matter what the program,
no matter what the language.

(Unicode's slogan taken from
http://www.unicode.org/standard/WhatIsUnicode.html)

In other words, Unicode allows for the possibility of encoding any character for use in any language. A character is, roughly speaking, what we think of as a letter, although *A* is usually considered a different character from *a*. The actual shape as displayed will depend on the font which will represent it using the *glyph* designed for that font. For example *A* and **A** are different glyphs representing the same character.

Shapes are also needed, naturally, for all sorts of symbols that do not represent alphabetic or equivalent characters, such as dashes of varying lengths, copyright symbols, mathematical symbols for equations, and so forth. Many of these took up valuable space in the character sets of the 1960s to 1990s, elbowing out the Portuguese *ã*, for example.

Now in the discussion above, I distinguished between single-byte and double-byte systems, and implied that a double-byte system was good enough for MS *Word 2007*. In fact, even a double-byte system has limitations. As we saw above, a single-byte system can cope with a couple of hundred choices (256 to be precise), so how many can a double-byte system represent? The answer is 65,536 (from hex 0 to hex FFFF). Now with 65,000 character shapes a lot of languages can be handled, but it is also clear that 65,000 will not be enough for all the world's languages and scripts, living and dead – Chinese alone could require as many as 47,000. Accordingly, the Unicode consortium also allows for character encoding using up to four bytes per character. Using four bytes would allow for up to four billion different characters to be encoded.

In practice, we still live with the kludge described above. Even using a two-byte system, in some cases three or four pairs of bytes may be needed to represent specific characters (Unicode Technical Reports 17) and some combinations of characters are much more complex to handle than the description here can cover, as in cases analogous to Œ where two characters affect each other in some sort of special partnership.

However, I suspect that in a few more years we will have moved to a more rational simple system where all characters are stored using four-byte characters and there are no longer any limits to the character or other shapes that can be shown, and where it is certain that the thousandth character can immediately be found by leaping in exactly 4,000 bytes into a text file, in true random access.

You might wonder why I keep mentioning 'leaping into a text file' a given distance. In routine word-processing, e-mailing, etc., nobody ever does this. In corpus processing software, however, quite often one needs to open up a text file and start reading from a given spot, e.g. when showing the user the wider context of a concordance line.

The Unicode endeavour covers an enormous number of languages and their scripts. The Unicode CLDR Charts Languages and Scripts chart (2008) lists over 500 languages which are represented in varying scripts using Unicode. The consortium is still attempting to add more to the encoding. At the time of writing, the following scripts, whether ancient or modern, were still not perfectly represented: Meetei Mayek (Meitei Mayek, Manipuri, Kanglei), Miao (Pollard), Moso (Naxi), Mandaic, Mayan, Meroitic (Kush), Modi – and that is only the ones starting with the letter M. See the Unicode website for the current listing.

The problem is that text is all around us, but in slightly divergent formats. To the human reader these slight divergences pass unnoticed, but to software they can cause confusion and error. Analogously, when preparing a corpus of Shakespeare plays, the edition I was using abbreviated the character names before each speech so that the *to be or not to be* soliloquy originated in 'Ham.' To the human this is not a problem, which is why text editions used such abbreviations, but to the computer there would not be an easy linkage to *Hamlet* because computers are incapable of guessing. From all this, then, it follows that the user will need either to accept some slight 'noise' in the analysis, because of format inconsistencies, or else to try to put the basic corpus into a shape which will be handled appropriately by our corpus software. In practice, it is likely that some slight noise will always be present. The very existence of some of *WordSmith Tools*' utilities, such as its Text Converter and File Viewer, has arisen from the need to remove inconsistencies. The File Viewer was accordingly designed to look deep into the innards of a text file so as to see exactly how it is encoded; the Text Converter (www.lexically.net/downloads/version5/HTML/?convert_text_file_format.htm) was designed to be able to convert to Windows, for example, from formats used in Unix or Macintosh systems, which differ slightly from those used in Windows chiefly in regard to paragraph and line end formats producing plain Unicode text, in order to standardise a mixed corpus, or to re-structure the files using a more intuitive folder system, particularly necessary for the BNC with its uninformative filenames.

3. Concordances

Once the corpus has been put together and cleaned up, one is in a position to generate concordances. Tribble (this volume) explains and illustrates concordances themselves in depth, so here only a few basic observations on how a concordance is generated will be made (see also Evison, this volume).

There are two basic methods: the 'on the fly' system and an index-based one. If working 'on the fly', the concordancer reads each text file in order and searches for the desired string(s) in the long stream of bytes which it has just read in. If it finds the desired string, it then checks to see whether any other contextual requirements are met, such as whether the string is bounded appropriately to left and right, for example by a space or a tab or a punctuation symbol. It may also search the environment for another string that the user has specified must be present in the environment. If these tests are passed, some part of the context will be stored in the computer's memory or in a disk file, along with information about the filename, the place within the file where the hit was found, and so on. A set of such pieces of information is stored for each successful 'hit'.

Alternatively, the entire corpus is first processed to build up an index which gives a set of pointers. This processing usually involves tokenising where each word of the source text is represented by a number, and a sizeable database is created which 'knows' (i.e. holds pointers to) all the instances of all the words. Then when the search starts, the database is asked for all instances of the word being sought, and additional requirements such as context words can be put to the database too. Once the request has been met, again the program builds up a set of structured pieces of information about the context, the filename, the exact location of each word in the context, and so forth.

With such a set of records, it is then possible to sort the output in a desired way, and present it to the user using appropriate colours. The KWIC (key word in context) context is usually, though not always, presented so that the search-word or phrase appears centred both horizontally and vertically in the output, and often with a colour or typeface marking to help it stand out visually.

4. Word lists

Word lists are usually created 'on the fly' as described above. A 'current word' variable is first allocated in the computer's memory and set to be empty. Then, as the stream of bytes is processed, every time a character is encountered that is alphanumeric, it's added to that 'current word'. If on the other hand the character turns out to be non-alphanumeric, such as a comma or a tab or a space, the program assumes that an end-of-word may have been reached. It may have to check this in certain cases such as the apostrophe in *mother's*, where a setting may allow for that character not to count as an end-of-word character. To do so, it might have to be able to handle not only straight apostrophes but also curly ones, as we have seen. Whenever the program determines that the end of the 'current word' has been reached, it stores that word much as, when concordancing, it clears the 'current word' ready for new data, and proceeds in the stream of bytes.

As the word gets stored, a search process will be needed, to find out whether that same word token has already been encountered. If it has, then a frequency counter will need to be incremented. It may be that the program will also check whether that word-type has already been found in the text file which is currently being handled, and if necessary increment a counter recording how many times it occurs in each text.

At some point the set of words stored needs to be sorted and displayed, possibly alphabetically and by frequency order, and maybe with some accompanying statistical information such as type-token or standardised (Scott 2008) type-token ratios, which report on how the different word-forms (types) relate to the numbers of running words (tokens) in the text or corpus.

Word lists by themselves are often best seen as a first approach to a corpus. It is by processing the words and looking at the most frequent of them that one can get a rough idea of the kinds of topics being explored, the wealth of vocabulary being used – as well as any formatting anomalies as shown above! It may be possible to select word(s) in a word list and have the corpus software generate a concordance of that/those words in the very same text files.

Finally, it may be possible to get software to show word lists of n-grams where pairs or triples of words are shown in their text clusters or bundles (Biber and Conrad 1999), by identifying any repeated consecutive sequences of words of the length desired (see Greaves and Warren, this volume).

Figure 11.8 shows a word list based on three-word clusters in Shakespeare plays. It is clear that *I pray you* is not only a frequent n-gram but it is also widespread since it occurs in thirty-four (out of thirty-seven) plays.

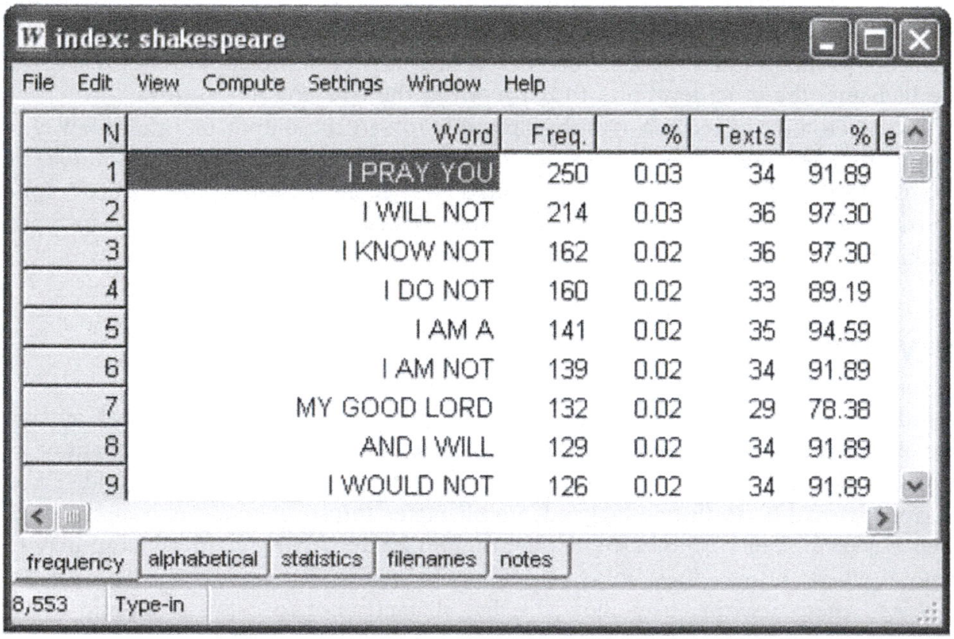

index: shakespeare

File Edit View Compute Settings Window Help

N	Word	Freq.	%	Texts	%
1	I PRAY YOU	250	0.03	34	91.89
2	I WILL NOT	214	0.03	36	97.30
3	I KNOW NOT	162	0.02	36	97.30
4	I DO NOT	160	0.02	33	89.19
5	I AM A	141	0.02	35	94.59
6	I AM NOT	139	0.02	34	91.89
7	MY GOOD LORD	132	0.02	29	78.38
8	AND I WILL	129	0.02	34	91.89
9	I WOULD NOT	126	0.02	34	91.89

frequency | alphabetical | statistics | filenames | notes

8,553 Type-in

Figure 11.8 Three-word-cluster word list.

5. Key word lists

A key word, as identified in *WordSmith Tools*, is a word (or word cluster) which is found to occur with unusual frequency in a given text or set of texts. As such it may be found to occur much more frequently than would otherwise be expected or much less frequently (a negative key word). In order to know what is expected, a reference of some sort must be used. In *WordSmith*'s implementation, key word lists use as their starting points word lists created as described above. One word list is first made of the text or set of texts which one is interested in studying, and another one is then made of some suitable reference corpus. This may be a superset of the text-type including the one(s) being studied, such as when one uses a word list based on the *Daily Mirror*'s news texts 2004–7 as a reference when studying one specific *Daily Mirror* text. Or it might be a general-purpose corpus like the British National Corpus (BNC) used as a reference corpus when one is studying the specific *Daily Mirror* text.

When the specific word list and the reference corpus word list are ready, the key word software simply goes through the specific word list and checks each word (or cluster) in it with the corresponding word or cluster in the reference corpus word list. In most cases these comparisons do not reveal much difference in percentage frequency. For example, THE may be roughly equally frequent as a percentage of a given *Daily Mirror* text as it is of a large set of *Daily Mirror* texts, say around 5 per cent in both cases. Similarly, it is likely that I PRAY YOU is about equally frequent in *Othello*, say, or *As You Like It* as it is in all the Shakespeare plays where, as we see above, its frequency is 0.03 per cent of the running words of the plays. Some of the strings, though, will be found to be unusually high or low. *Unusually* is determined using statistical procedures, generally Dunning's (1993) Log Likelihood procedure. As with the concordancing and word listing procedures described above, once an item has been found to meet the criterion, the program will store it; eventually it will sort the stored forms, e.g. in alphabetical order or keyness order, and display them.

The screenshot in Figure 11.9 shows the key word clusters of the play *Hamlet*, compared with the clusters of all the Shakespeare plays (including *Hamlet*) as identified in the word list above.

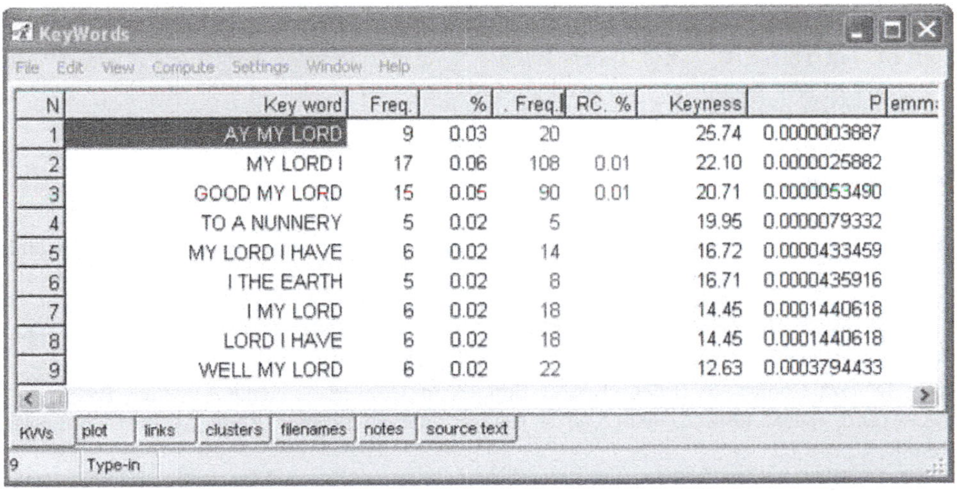

KeyWords

File Edit View Compute Settings Window Help

N	Key word	Freq.	%	. Freq.	RC. %	Keyness	P	Lemm
1	AY MY LORD	9	0.03	20		25.74	0.0000003887	
2	MY LORD I	17	0.06	108	0.01	22.10	0.0000025882	
3	GOOD MY LORD	15	0.05	90	0.01	20.71	0.0000053490	
4	TO A NUNNERY	5	0.02	5		19.95	0.0000079332	
5	MY LORD I HAVE	6	0.02	14		16.72	0.0000433459	
6	I THE EARTH	5	0.02	8		16.71	0.0000435916	
7	I MY LORD	6	0.02	18		14.45	0.0001440618	
8	LORD I HAVE	6	0.02	18		14.45	0.0001440618	
9	WELL MY LORD	6	0.02	22		12.63	0.0003794433	

KWs plot links clusters filenames notes source text

9 Type-in

Figure 11.9 KW clusters in *Hamlet*.

GOOD MY LORD | 20.71 | 14
TO A NUNNERY | 19.95 | 5

Figure 11.10 KW plot of clusters in *Hamlet*.

Most of them include 'my Lord', a speech formality which suggests that relationships or argumentation may be especially important here. The cluster GOOD MY LORD occurs with a frequency of 0.05 per cent of the running words in the play, which contrasts with the 0.01 per cent overall in the Shakespeare plays as a whole, and this is why the algorithm has found it to be key. AY MY LORD, on the other hand, though it is slightly *less* frequent, is found to be more striking in its frequency in *Hamlet*; its frequency in the whole set of plays is below 0.01 and hence not shown.

A plot of the locations of some of these clusters (Figure 11.10) is akin to a map of the play, with the left edge of the plot representing the beginning and the right edge the end of the pay. TO A NUNNERY is quite sharply located in one specific burst in Act III Scene 1, while GOOD MY LORD is more globally located.

The most appropriate interpretation of these key words or key word clusters is as pointers; they suggest some statistical anomaly which itself merits further research. There is probably a pattern underlying some of the clustered strings in *Hamlet* but as yet we are not close enough to it. It is definitely necessary to concordance these clusters, for example, to find out who keeps addressing whom as 'my lord'.

The researcher's aim is really to find such patterns, but as we have seen here, to do that effectively it is often necessary to look 'under the hood' to see how corpus software does some of its work, and to see how texts it may process are structured and formatted.

Further reading

Hunston, S. (2002) *Corpora in Applied Linguistics*. Cambridge: Cambridge University Press. (This provides a solid introduction to many aspects of Corpus Linguistics.)

Scott, M. (2008) 'Developing *WordSmith*', in M. Scott, P. Pérez-Paredes and P. Sánchez-Hernández (eds) 'Monograph: Software-aided Analysis of Language', special issue of *International Journal of English Studies* 8(1): 153–72. (This paper discusses principles of software development.)

Scott, M. and Tribble, C. (2006) *Textual Patterns: Keyword and Corpus Analysis in Language Education*. Amsterdam: John Benjamins. (This develops many of the above ideas in book form.)

References

Adams, D. (1978) *The Hitch-Hiker's Guide to the Galaxy*. BBC 4 radio programme (book published 1979, London: Pan Books).

Barry, P. J., Gallagher, P., Ryan, C. and O'Mahony, D. (2007) 'START (Screening Tool to Alert Doctors to the Right Treatment) – An Evidence-based Screening Tool to Detect Prescribing Omissions in Elderly Patients', *Age and Ageing* 36(6): 632–8.

Biber, D. and Conrad, S. (1999) 'Lexical Bundles in Conversation and Academic Prose', in H. Hasselgard and S. Oksefjell (eds) *Out of Corpora: Studies in Honor of Stig Johansson*. Amsterdam: Rodopi, pp. 181–9.

Cohen, B. (1998) 'Howard Aiken on the Number of Computers Needed for the Nation', *IEEE Annals of the History of Computing* 20(3): 27–32.

Dunning, T. (1993) 'Accurate Methods for the Statistics of Surprise and Coincidence', *Computational Linguistics* 19(1): 61–74.

Mitchell, T. M., Shinkareva, S. V., Carlson, A., Chang, K.-M., Malave, V. L., Mason, R. A., Just, M. A. (2008) 'Predicting Human Brain Activity Associated with the Meanings of Nouns', *Science* 320(5880): 1191–5.

Scott, M. (2008) *WordSmith Tools* online help, available at www.lexically.net/downloads/version5/HTML/?type_token_ratio_proc.htm

——(2009) *WordSmith Tools*. Liverpool: Lexical Analysis Software Ltd.

Sinclair, J. (2001) 'The Deification of Information', in M. Scott and G. Thompson (eds) *Patterns of Text: In Honour of Michael Hoey*. Amsterdam: John Benjamins, pp. 287–314.

Unicode Technical Reports 17, available at www.unicode.org/reports/tr17/ (accessed October 2008).

Unicode CLDR Charts Languages and Scripts, 25 July 2008. available at www.unicode.org/cldr/data/charts/supplemental/languages_and_scripts.html (accessed October 2008).

Wolfram MathWorld, available at http://mathworld.wolfram.com/RoundoffError.html (accessed 10 Oct 2008).

12
How can a corpus be used to explore patterns?

Susan Hunston

1. What is a pattern?

A pattern is essentially repetition. A symbol may occur once only:

⌘

but when it occurs twice or more it becomes a minimal pattern:

⌘⌘⌘

A combination of two symbols, such as ⌘ and –, may form a sequence that when repeated comprises a more noticeable pattern:

⌘⌘⌘ – ⌘⌘⌘ – ⌘⌘⌘ – ⌘⌘⌘ – ⌘⌘⌘
⌘⌘⌘ – ⌘⌘⌘ – ⌘⌘⌘ – ⌘⌘⌘ – ⌘⌘⌘
⌘⌘⌘ – ⌘⌘⌘ – ⌘⌘⌘ – ⌘⌘⌘ – ⌘⌘⌘

In language, pattern is observed when words, sounds, rhythms or structures are repeated. These are often observed in poems and nursery rhymes, such as this one quoted by Carter (2004: 1):

> Hickory, dickory, dock
> The mouse ran up the clock.

There is considerable repetition even in these two lines: the same sounds and rhythm in *hickory* and *dickory*; the same end sounds in *dock* and *clock*; the same combination of weakly and strongly stressed syllables in *the mouse* and *ran up* and *the clock*. Carter goes on to note that creative repetition is more common than might be imagined in ordinary speech. What has been more frequently observed is that prepared oratory, such as in politicians' speeches, also tends to contain repetition (see for example Tannen 1989: 175). Here are some examples from a speech delivered by (at the time of writing) US presidential candidate Barack Obama:

> I've gone to some of the best schools in America and lived in one of the world's poorest nations.

Repetition of the superlative and its co-text: *some of the best schools in America*; *one of the world's poorest nations.*

> The church contains in full the kindness and cruelty, the fierce intelligence and the shocking ignorance, the struggles and successes, the love and yes, the bitterness and bias that make up the black experience in America.

Repetition of binomial opposites: *the kindness and cruelty; the intelligence and the ignorance; the struggles and successes; the love and the bitterness.*

The speech also contains a lengthy section in which a series of sentences begin with *This time we want to talk about*:

> This time we want to talk about the crumbling schools ...
> This time we want to talk about how the lines in the Emergency Room ...
> This time we want to talk about the shuttered mills ...
> This time we want to talk about the fact that the real problem ...
> This time we want to talk about the men and women of every color and creed ...
> We want to talk about how to bring them home from a war ...

In each of the examples above, it may be supposed that the pattern has been consciously designed. Words are chosen (or invented) in nursery rhymes to fit the sound and rhythm of the surrounding words. The writers of political speeches select the parallel words and structures for rhetorical effect.

It is apparent, however, that repetition, and therefore patterning, occurs in language without anyone having planned it. As an introduction to this chapter we will consider a few examples of this from the 450-million-word Bank of English corpus (owned jointly by the University of Birmingham and HarperCollins publishers; all examples in this chapter unless otherwise indicated come from this corpus).

The first example is the phrase *the black experience*, taken from Obama's speech quote above. If we search for *the* followed by *experience* we find that one set of words occurring frequently between those two refers to groups of people: *American*, *black*, *human*, *undergraduate*, *customer* and *British*. Replacing *the* by *a* or *an* gives very different results: in this case the word preceding *experience* usually expresses an affective response to the experience: *great*, *new*, *wonderful*, *bad*, *traumatic* and *pleasant*, for example. In short, there is a repeated phrase *the black experience*, but there is also a more frequently repeated pattern: '*the* + group of people + *experience*'.

The second example also comes from the speech above: *one of the best schools in America*. This represents a very common use of superlative adjectives (such as *best*) in English. Taking a random 1,000 instances of *best* followed by a noun, the word that occurs most frequently before it is *the*. The most frequent word before *the best* is *of*, and the most frequent word before *of the best* is *one*. In other words, '*one of the best* + noun' is a relatively frequent phrase. What is more, the most frequent single word following the noun is *in*, introducing prepositional phrases such as *in the country*, *in Europe*, *in the world*. If the exercise is repeated with adjectives occurring with *most*, the results are the same. The sequence '*one of the most* + adjective + noun + *in* + time or place' occurs relatively frequently, and is one of the most typical environments in which the superlative occurs.

The final example interprets 'pattern' slightly differently, as a co-occurrence of a language form and a particular context. Conrad and Biber (2000: 63) note that stance adverbials of all kinds are more frequent in conversation than in either academic or newspaper prose. To a large extent, this difference is accounted for by the much greater number of epistemic adverbials in conversation, including items such as *of course, probably, actually, really* and *sort of* which are very much more frequent in conversation than in the written contexts. Such differences emerge also when the mode is the same. O'Keeffe *et al.* (2007: 208) notice considerable differences in word frequency between corpora of spoken conversation, business English and academic English. For example, although pronouns are frequently used in each of the corpora, *we* is significantly more frequent in the business corpus than in the other two.

2. Why are patterns difficult to spot?

This section will consider why individual language users and researchers may find it difficult to identify patterns. I will suggest three reasons, each of which approaches the problem from a slightly different perspective.

The first reason: repetition in naturally occurring conversation is transient, fleeting; it may have no perceptible effect, or its effects may not be ascribed to the repetition itself. In other words, it is not noticed. Carter (2004: 2) quotes an example from a corpus of spoken English where the following interaction takes place:

A: Yes, he must have a bob or two.
B: Whatever he does he makes money out of it, just like that.
C: Bob's your uncle.

As Carter points out, the word *bob* is used twice, once by speaker A in the phrase *a bob or two* ('quite a lot of money') and once by speaker C in the phrase *Bob's your uncle* ('it happens without effort'); in addition, speaker B repeats the idea in speaker A's utterance without repeating the actual words. Carter notes that it is difficult to say why speaker C says what he/she does, and whether the repetition is conscious or unconscious, and what effect it has on the other speakers. It is only very recently that examples such as this in ordinary conversation have been identified and commented upon. Carter's point is that repetitions of this kind are creative rather than conventional and that they deserve the same kind of attention as creativity in literature or art.

The second reason: speakers of a language have relatively untuned intuitions about frequency, and about frequency of co-occurrence in particular. This is a point made by Sinclair (1991: 39) as an argument in favour of using a corpus as a source of evidence about collocations and other kinds of patterning.

Intuitions often come into play when a user of a language encounters something that sounds unusual. Here is an example from a student for whom English is a second language. She writes: 'Three verbs were found frequent in both corpora.' This use of the passive *were found* followed by the adjective *frequent* strikes me as odd: intuitively I would re-write this as 'Three verbs were found *to be* frequent in both corpora' with the explanation that 'find something + adjective' is used when the adjective is an evaluative one (*strange*, *interesting* or *exciting*, for example) but not when the adjective does not indicate subjective judgement. A corpus search corroborates this to a certain extent. Examples of FIND followed by *them* and an adjective suggest that adjectives such as *interesting*, *attractive*, *difficult*, *useful* and *boring* are particularly frequent in this environment. On the other hand, searching for 'FIND + *them* + *to be* + adjective' shows both 'objective' and 'subjective' adjectives, with examples such as *she looked inside all of them one by one, but found them to be clean* as well as *he explored it and found that to be nonsense*. It turns out, however, that when the verb FIND is used in the passive, and followed by an adjective, a small range of subjective adjectives such as *helpful* and *useful* do occur, but much more frequent are the adjectives *guilty* and *innocent*, as well as *alive*, *unconscious*, *safe* and *naked*. When the adjective is subjective (*useful*) the subject of the clause indicates an inanimate object; when the adjective is objective (*alive*) the subject of the clause indicates a human being. My intuition that *be found frequent* is an unusual usage is correct, but the reasoning I used intuitively to explain this turns out to be totally incorrect.

The third reason: patterning involves the repetition of 'things', but those 'things' may be of many different kinds. Two or more words may frequently co-occur, as in *was found guilty*, but we may also regard adjectives such as *dead*, *alive*, *unconscious* and the phrase *in a coma* as belonging to a single category, so that *was found dead/ alive/ unconscious/ in a coma* would represent a single pattern. Similarly, a sequence of individual words such as *it is ironic that* may be considered representative of a more general pattern which begins with *it*, ends with a that-clause (with or without *that*), and contains a link verb that might be BE but could just as well be SEEM or LOOK and an adjective that indicates an evaluation of a situation. Examples of this pattern, illustrating the degree of variation possible, would include:

It is not surprising that …
It seems very peculiar that …
It is absolutely right that …
It looks very unlikely that …
It's obvious he doesn't want …

Observing pattern in this set of examples involves perceiving a similarity between items that have no surface similarity. A more extreme example is illustrated by the following concordance lines:

I'm male I can learn how women react to women's texts, as opposed to
platform. And I wonder how did you react to that as Republicans? Do you have
them it's just a question of how they react to it. < p > Some teams suffer with
went to a cattery to check how he'd react to my cat.' Beverley thinks the
and I couldn't predict how he would react to my presence. < p > Cain, it's cold
But it's not clear how Ankara would react to a request because any such move
knows us knows exactly how we would react to the of thing our manager was
then watched how they behaved and reacted to her. A video of each child was
and first asked her how people were reacting to the suspension, given the
test the waters to see how the press reacts to an idea of some sort of militar

These lines were obtained by a search for REACT + *to* preceded by the word *how*. The lines might be said to have more in common than the search terms, however. Looking at the items preceding *how*, we might identify a general sense of 'finding out' and 'knowing' or 'not knowing': *I can learn how, I wonder how, it just a question of how, to check how, I couldn't predict how, it's not clear how, knows exactly how, watched how, asked her how* and *to see how*. A sub-set of these, identified by the presence of *would*, indicates a hypothetical situation. 'Seeing' a pattern such as this one is not as simple a matter as, for example, recognising the frequency of *to* following REACT. The pattern is realised by a very diverse set of items, and is difficult to discover automatically, that is, without a human observer. For the same reason it is more difficult to quantify. We might also feel that whereas *react to* might be said to indicate a particular sense of REACT (as opposed to *react on* as in *lichens react on rocks*), the items preceding *how ... react to* occur simply because this is the kind of thing people often need to say about reactions (they are unpredictable). There is no question of '(in)correct English' here. Furthermore, the identification of the 'finding out + how someone reacts to something' pattern is very much open to debate – many people might deny that this pattern exists at all.

3. Concordances and how to read them

The identification of pattern in a corpus implies a connection between theory, method and technique. It implies a theory of meaning in language that stresses that meaning is discovered in language situated in context, not in words in isolation (Sinclair 2004; Teubert 2005). Such a theory both requires and is borne out by a methodology that prioritises the search for repetition and co-occurrence. The technique often used to carry out such a search is the 'key word in context' (KWIC), or the concordance line.

Examples of concordance lines have been given in other chapters in this volume (see in particular chapters by Scott, Greaves and Warren). Essentially they consist of a node word or phrase with a small amount of context (measured in characters) to the left and the right. In most concordancing programs the amount of context can be increased on demand; showing a line longer than can be accommodated on a standard screen or page without wrapping allows more context to be observed but reduces the visual impact of any repetition. Most programs, too, allow the concordance lines to be manipulated in ways that make repetition visually salient. These techniques range from being able to sort lines so that the word(s) before or after the node occur in alphabetical order to using colour to identify word class (see Scott, this volume).

To illustrate this, here is an example of twenty-five randomly selected concordance lines with the word *view* as the search word and the node.

the success of their treatment. This view of clients as experts on matters
s numbers, most elephant specialists view culling and the ivory trade as two
from any abstract ethical point of view - Judeo-Christian, whatever - from any
on. < p > I have to take as positive a view as possible and I would like to
in Capital and Class (1986). 10 This view was expounded by RIIA prominents
lays the foundation of a broader view. It connects the idea of democracy
time and stood looking at a fantastic view across the mountains whilst I waited
< p > Others take a more sympathetic view. Bishop Skinner offer special
Black himself did not have a clear view of the age at which a child could
things that they didn't need. But the view that design is dead portrays the
medieval scholars. Yet this was the view that all major Christian theologians
got stuck in the 1960s, with a world view in which collectivism was compulsory

eventually takes place. However, the view from the Moroccan side of the wall
efforts. And I think there's a shared view here that we would hope the
historians by and large take a dim view of my grandfather's role and
dome - is never obscured from view by new developments. < p > Regina
unions represent a radical left-wing view to students and many have embarked
for all time. < p > Hidden from view in the Staffordshire Moorlands,
you get them together for a long view back. Stack up the fact that he's
which reflected a market-frame view of the state's responsibility to
differently, for instance, do women view rock? Who do they think are its
from the applicant. It took the view that the risk of his association
the proceedings had reinforced his view in the report that Mr Irving has
biological and chemical weapons. This view was then supported by a senior
texts but always from a point of view. If you look at his project closely

Sorting these lines alphabetically to the left of *view* focuses our attention on prepositions occurring before *view* and in particular the phrases *hidden/ obscured from view* and *point of view*:

dome - is never obscured from view by new developments. < p > Regina
for all time. < p > Hidden from view in the Staffordshire Moorlands,
from any abstract ethical point of view - Judeo-Christian, whatever - from any
texts but always from a point of view. If you look at his project closely

It also brings together, and so makes noticeable, those lines where *view* is preceded by *the* or *this*. *The view* focuses attention on the phrase *the view that* and incidentally suggests that *the view that* may be used frequently (in three of the four instances cited here) in a contrastive statement (*But the view that* ... *Yet this was the view that* ...), though more evidence would be needed to be sure of this:

things that they didn't need. But the view that design is dead portrays the
medieval scholars. Yet this was the view that all major Christian theologians
eventually takes place. However, the view from the Moroccan side of the wall
from the applicant. It took the view that the risk of his association

Finally, the frequency of *This view* ... suggests that *view* is often used to refer back and to summarise a segment of the preceding discourse ('encapsulation' in Sinclair's 2004 terminology):

the success of their treatment. This view of clients as experts on matters
in Capital and Class (1986). 10 This view was expounded by RIIA prominents
biological and chemical weapons. This view was then supported by a senior

Sorting the lines to the right additionally draws attention to phrases where *view* is followed by *of* and is preceded by an adjective:

the success of their treatment. This view of clients as experts on matters
Black himself did not have a clear view of the age at which a child could
historians by and large take a dim view of my grandfather's role and
which reflected a market-frame view of the state's responsibility to

Marking word class in addition separates those instances where *view* is a verb from the majority where it is a noun:

```
s numbers, most elephant specialists view culling and the ivory trade as two
 differently, for instance, do women view rock? Who do they think are its
```

Expanding the concordance lines allows ambiguities to be resolved. For example, expanding the lines where *view* is followed by *that* shows that there are two distinct patterns – *view* + appositive clause and *view* + relative clause:

Appositive clause

```
But the view that design is dead portrays the same lack of perspective for which
the 1980s themselves are so famous.
```

Relative clause

```
Yet this was the view that all major Christian theologians insisted on - and
many still do today.
```

What should be obvious, however, is that the concordancing programs only find and organise the data. Interpretation is a human activity. We now consider what skills are needed to find pattern in concordance lines.

The first skilled activity is formulating the search that will produce the concordance lines (see chapters by Tribble, Evison, Scott, Chambers, Sripicharn, Walter). Too general a search leads to too much 'noise'; too specific a search leads to important information being overlooked. For example, searching for *it is surprising that* will yield plenty of concordance lines (176 in the Bank of English, for example). However, performing the same search but allowing for an additional word between *is* and *surprising* yields many more lines (almost ten times as many). The concordance lines then show that only about 10 per cent are of the form *it is surprising that*; a further 20 per cent are *it is hardly surprising that*, 65 per cent are *it is not surprising that*, and there are additional less frequent occurrences of *it is scarcely surprising that* and *it is perhaps/therefore/somewhat surprising that.*

Once concordance lines are obtained, they must be interpreted. As noted above, observing pattern involves identifying similarity and forming notional categories. It also involves ignoring distractors, that is, separating what might be important from what is unlikely to be so. (Note, though, that it is impossible to be precise about what is and is not patterned – what is overlooked by one observer might be noticed by another.) These points will be illustrated with a small set of concordance lines obtained by searching for the lemma REACT. The result of this search gives examples of all wordforms in the lemma: *react, reacted, reacting, reacts.* Twenty random lines have been selected and then sorted so that the words following the node word (REACT) are in alphabetical order.

```
1       could not believe the way Vieira reacted after he was dismissed. The
2    at all. When asked today how they'd react if the White House sent them a ne
3     step, which will enable viewers to react immediately to what they have see
4         two-thirds of the radical pairs reacting (in a field of typically only
```

```
5        any more, I don't know how he would react. Is there any point in making
6       growth because stock markets could react.' Mr Visco said stock markets in
7              police officer at Selhurst Park reacted similarly to the Cantona inciden
8             mail, in New York, Adrian Clark reacted to Simon Hoggart's discussion of
9      market has come, and how people will react to it. The best seats and places
10     strength of a substance and the body reacts to fight off any diseases which
11            from the air and induce them to react to form harmless gases. Last
12                 is the poster!' Herzen was reacting to a swelling trade in images. T
13          efforts you may find the magician reacting too early or late. Also bear in
14       conference was to see how he would react when asked questions by journalis
15    protect. How is management likely to react when a group threat-ens to quit?
16          twenty-year-old son felt free to react with such ferocity indicates that
17    eposition sulfur and nitrogen oxides react with atmospheric water vapor to
18     above such common tasks, refusing to react with the molecular masses. < p > Bu
19              Commentators and crowd alike reacted with astonishment when Lara
20          during the investigation. They reacted with anger and said: The findin
```

Which of these lines might be grouped together to illustrate the 'same pattern'? Looking only at what follows the node word, we might observe the following:

- a full stop (lines 5 and 6);
- the word *to* (lines 8, 9, 10, 11, 12);
- the word *when* (lines 14 and 15);
- the word *with* (lines 16, 17, 18, 19, 20).

Looking at the same evidence but in a more linguistically informed way we might express this somewhat differently:

- a subordinating conjunction (*after* in line 1, *if* in line 2 and *when* in lines 14 and 15), noting that in each case the subordinate clause indicates an event that is the stimulus of the reaction
- a preposition (*to* in lines 8, 9 and 12, *with* in lines 16–20);
- an adverb (lines 3 and 7), noting that in each case the adverb is followed by the preposition *to*;
- a to-infinitive clause (lines 10 and 11), noting that the clause indicates a reason for the reaction.

A further observation might be that *react with* in lines 17 and 18 works differently from *react / reacted with* in lines 16, 19 and 20. The question that might prompt line 17 or 18 is something like 'what does the object / substance (not) react with?' whereas the question prompting the other lines is something like 'how did the person / people react?' Putting all this together suggests that a maximum of eight different patterns might be identified in these lines:

1. REACT followed by a subordinate clause indicating stimulus:

```
1        could not believe the way Vieira reacted after he was dismissed. The
2     at all. When asked today how they'd react if the White House sent them a ne
```

14 conference was to see how he would react when asked questions by journalis
15 protect. How is management likely to react when a group threat-ens to quit?

2. REACT followed by the preposition *to*:

8 mail, in New York, Adrian Clark reacted to Simon Hoggart's discussion of
9 market has come, and how people will react to it. The best seats and places
12 is the poster!' Herzen was reacting to a swelling trade in images. T

3. REACT followed by an adverb and then by the preposition *to*:

3 step, which will enable viewers to react immediately to what they have see
7 police officer at Selhurst Park reacted similarly to the Cantona inciden

4. REACT followed by a to-infinitive clause indicating consequence:

10 strength of a substance and the body reacts to fight off any diseases which
11 from the air and induce them to react to form harmless gases. Last

5. REACT followed by the preposition *with* answering the question 'how?'

16 twenty-year-old son felt free to react with such ferocity indicates that
19 Commentators and crowd alike reacted with astonishment when Lara
20 during the investigation. They reacted with anger and said: The findin

6. REACT followed by the preposition with answering the question 'what?'

17 eposition sulfur and nitrogen oxides react with atmospheric water vapor to
18 above such common tasks, refusing to react with the molecular masses. < p > Bu

7. REACT followed by a full stop:

5 any more, I don't know how he would react. Is there any point in making
6 growth because stock markets could react.' Mr Visco said stock markets in

8. Other lines:

4 two-thirds of the radical pairs reacting (in a field of typically only
13 efforts you may find the magician reacting too early or late. Also bear in

Some observers might wish to amalgamate some of these groups. For example, it might be argued that group 3 is simply a variant of group 2 – that the presence or absence of the adverb does not affect the pattern of 'REACT + *to* + noun group'. It is possible too to join group 6 with groups 2 and 3 because in each case the prepositional phrase is obligatory. Others might argue that groups 1, 4 and 7 should be conflated because in each case REACT is the end of a clause. Still others would want to add group 5 to those because, it could be argued, in those lines the prepositional phrase beginning with *with* adds only peripheral information. Discounting the 'other lines' (group 8), this would yield only two groups:

(A) REACT coming at the possible end of a clause:

```
1        could not believe the way Vieira reacted after he was dismissed. The
2     at all. When asked today how they'd react if the White House sent them a ne
5      any more, I don't know how he would react. Is there any point in making
6     growth because stock markets could react.' Mr Visco said stock markets in
10   strength of a substance and the body reacts to fight off any diseases which
11         from the air and induce them to react to form harmless gases. Last
14      conference was to see how he would react when asked questions by journalis
15   protect. How is management likely to react when a group threat-ens to quit?
16       twenty-year-old son felt free to react with such ferocity indicates that
19           Commentators and crowd alike reacted with astonishment when Lara
20          during the investigation. They reacted with anger and said: The findin
```

(B) REACT followed by the preposition *to* or *with* as a necessary part of the clause:

```
3     step, which will enable viewers to react immediately to what they have see
7          police officer at Selhurst Park reacted similarly to the Cantona inciden
8         mail, in New York, Adrian Clark reacted to Simon Hoggart's discussion of
9    market has come, and how people will react to it. The best seats and places
12               is the poster!' Herzen was reacting to a swelling trade in images. T
17   eposition sulfur and nitrogen oxides react with atmospheric water vapor to
18   above such common tasks, refusing to react with the molecular masses. < p > Bu
```

There are of course intermediate positions – it is possible to make three or four groups here as well as eight or two. The point is that no one grouping is absolutely right or wrong; all the groupings use formal information (that is, information based on the form of words) but also linguistic interpretation (distinguishing between the preposition *to* and the *to*-infinitive, for example, or between the two uses of *with*). A smaller number of groups tends to give a limited amount of information – the division into groups A and B, for example, tells us very little except that REACT may occur with *to* and *with* or may not. On the other hand, division in many groups runs the danger of masking genuine similarities – placing the lines with adverbs into a different group from those without tends to hide the importance of the link between REACT and *to*.

In addition, of course, quite different groups can be made if different aspects of the concordance lines are brought into account. For example, all the lines in which the subject of REACT is non-intentional (not a thinking human being or animal) can be grouped together, giving a set comprising these lines (in line 18 the subject is *Gold*):

```
4         two-thirds of the radical pairs reacting (in a field of typically only
6     growth because stock markets could react.' Mr Visco said stock markets in
10   strength of a substance and the body reacts to fight off any diseases which
11         from the air and induce them to react to form harmless gases. Last
18   above such common tasks, refusing to react with the molecular masses. < p > Bu
```

It is noticeable that this set includes all the lines from the original where REACT is followed by a to-infinitive clause and the only line where it is followed by *with* giving essential information.

To summarise: observing pattern in concordance lines essentially involves grouping those lines together. In most examples, several alternative groupings could be proposed, each highlighting different kinds of information. There is no objectively correct grouping, although some will be more useful for particular purposes than others. Although the presence of individual words may provide help in grouping, usually a wider context and more interpretation is needed to form groups (that is, to identify patterns) that might be thought to be appropriate.

4. Short cuts and how to find them

There seems to be a limit to the amount of data a human observer can usefully process using concordance lines. (It is partly for this reason that some people advocate limiting the size of a corpus, so that no search will produce more concordance lines than can reasonably be studied.) Most concordancing programs will allow a limited number of lines to be selected from a larger set; in effect every 'nth' line is displayed, giving a random sample (see Evison, this volume). If the corpus is large, and/or if the word is one that occurs frequently, however, a sample that can reasonably be dealt with may be too small in relative terms to reliably demonstrate patterns. For example, in the 450-million-word Bank of English there are 705,866 instances of the noun *time*. Looking at all those concordance lines would be a daunting task. If 100 lines are selected, some patterns start to be revealed, such as *the first time* (four occurrences), *at the same time* (four occurrences), *at the time* (five), *at the time of* (three), *it is time to* (three), *by the time* (four) and so on. Some patterns which occur in this sample only once, however, include: *by this time* (one), *for a time* (one), *it's just a matter of time* (one), *it wasn't the first time that* (one). By contrast, the phrase '*it* + BE + negative + *the first time* + clause' (as in *it wasn't the first time that*) occurs in the whole Bank of English 564 times. In short, obtaining a manageable sample of concordance lines for a very frequent word can make it difficult to observe patterns reliably. An alternative method of finding patterns needs to be found, or rather, an alternative way of focusing searches so that a smaller number of lines with a smaller range of patterns is identified.

Fortunately, because the starting point for identifying patterns is linguistic form, the collocates of a given word can be used to narrow down the search. Many concordancers allow two-or-three-word phrases (n-grams) containing a given word to be identified. For example, the most frequently occurring three-word phrases including the word *time* are:

the first time
at the time
the same time
a long time
by the time
all the time
at a time
the time of
a time when
of the time

Each of these can then be the starting point for further, more manageable, searches. For example, *a time when* occurs in longer frequent phrases such as *at a time when, there was a time when, to a time when, there will come a time when*. Random concordance lines based on the phrase *to a time when* show further patterning:

< p > If Brett wants to go back to a time when you could get the shit kicked
a common impulse to 'hark back to a time when Christmas was simpler, more
day United States, going back to a time when the southwestern states were a
gratification of having children to a time when they would have a better shot
many of which speak directly to a time when things were fragile and
belongs to an earlier era – to a time when current-account imbalances, not
victory will provide a flashback to a time when the US was at the height of its
Dream' address, looking forward to a time when racial prejudice no longer
and we hope and look forward to a time when this technique, along with
it is possible to see forward to a time when ARM will prosper. < p > Indeed,
set back the opening 30 minutes to a time when generally sufficient liquidity
injections. He immediately went to a time when he was only about five years

From these lines it appears that the word *to* links to phrases indicating a figurative movement in time, either backwards (*go back to, hark back to, provide a flashback to, set something back to*) or forwards (*look forward to, see forward to*). The clause beginning with *when* indicates a situation contrasting with the present one: *Christmas was simpler; racial prejudice no longer existed; they would have a better shot at supporting them*. The contrast is often an evaluative one, that is, things in the past or future are either better (*Christmas was simpler, more authentic*) or worse (*things were fragile and uncertain*) than the present. From a simple three-word phrase, therefore, we have established a much longer pattern that might be represented as 'reference to past or future time + *to a time when* + evaluatively contrasting situation'.

Using collocation gradually to refine a search for pattern does not depend solely on the identification of n-grams. A technique of 'accumulative collocation' (Bang 2009) can be used to perform recursive searches that gradually refine what is observed. This was demonstrated above in the discussion of *some of the best schools in America*. The example given below partially replicates one given in Hunston (2008) and starts with the word-form *distinguishing*. The most frequent adjacent-word collocate of *distinguishing* is *between*, so the string *distinguishing between* is then taken as the starting point for a further search. The most frequent adjacent collocate of *distinguishing between* is *of*. Taking *of distinguishing between* as the node, the words which most frequently precede this string are: *way, capable, importance, difficulty, means, incapable, task, point, method* and *ways*. These might be divided into three sets: (1) *way, means, method, ways, task*; (2) *capable, difficulty, incapable*; (3) *importance, point*. What is important here, in terms of method, is that none of these words, individually, is very frequent. For example, the string *ways of distinguishing between* occurs only twice in the Bank of English, so techniques that identify frequent n-grams are unlikely to find it. This point will be taken up again in the next section.

Before going any further, we might note that other prepositions also occur frequently before *distinguishing between*. These are: *in, by* and *for*. Repeating the exercise above for each of these expands the three sets, as shown in Table 12.1.

Each set can then be taken as the starting point for further searches.

Table 12.1 Collocates of 'distinguish between' divided according to meaning

'method'	*'able/unable'*	*'importance'*
Way/s of	Capable of	Importance of
Means of	Difficulty of	Point of
Method of	Incapable of	Important for
Task of	Difficulty/ies in	
Done by	Problems in	
Achieved by		
Basis for		
Method for		

5. A note on frequency

This chapter has made some assumptions about the notion of 'frequency'; some of these will now be made explicit.

Statements about frequency are always relative (although figures can be attached to them). For example, describing a word as 'frequent' means that it is frequent compared with other words. In a corpus of spoken British English (one of the spoken components of the Bank of English), for instance, the word *time* occurs just under 1,670 times per million words, whereas the word *circumstance* occurs only twice per million words. It is reasonable to say, therefore, that *time* is frequent in this corpus and that *circumstance* is less frequent. Programs such as the Keywords function in *WordSmith Tools* (Scott 1999) identify significant differences in the frequency of a given word in two corpora; the usefulness of this is discussed in Scott (this volume).

Frequency of co-occurrence is also relative. Much of the discussion in the previous section relied on a calculation of the words that co-occurred most frequently with a node word. There are statistical computations that measure the significance of co-occurrence (this is explained in Scott, this volume), but in this chapter 'raw frequency' of co-occurrence is all that has been used. Raw frequency may be an absolute concept (for example, in the spoken corpus mentioned above *at the time* occurs over 100 times per million words), but the concept of accumulated collocation assumes that a sequence or phrase can be identified as patterned not because it occurs frequently as such but because each element in the phrase co-occurs relatively frequently with the cumulative other elements. For example, although *way of distinguishing between* is relatively infrequent (occurring only 0.1 times per million in the Bank of English corpus), as a phrase it can be built up by taking *distinguishing* as the node and then progressively identifying the most frequent adjacent collocate (*distinguishing between,* then *of distinguishing between*, then *way of distinguishing between*).

It has further been assumed that the elements that are identified as frequent may not have a formal similarity. To illustrate this I shall take a sample sentence which uses the verb REACT that was discussed in some detail above:

```
It is somewhat ironic how people in general react to the circumstances in their lives.
```

(http://ezinearticles.com/?expert=Kenia_Morales (accessed 11 August 2008))

In all probability this sentence is unique. It certainly occurs only once in a search of the world-wide web. On the other hand, the sentence does 'feel' familiar, because it is composed of elements that are highly predictable because they are part of the patterning of English. Not all this patterning relies on repeated words, however. For example, although *it is somewhat ironic* occurs less than 0.1 times per million in the Bank of English, *it* followed by some form of *be* or *seem* followed optionally by an adverb and finally by *ironic* occurs nearly three times per million words, accounting for 28 per cent of the total instances of *ironic*. Similarly, a sequence *it* followed by some form of *be* followed by an adjective followed by *how* occurs about four times per million words, and the same sequence with any one of *what, where, when, why, who, if* or *how* as the final item occurs almost fourteen times per million words. It might be argued, then, that what is perceived as 'pattern' is not *it is somewhat ironic how* but '*it* + link verb + *ironic*' and '*it* + link verb + adjective + wh-word'.

It was noted above that REACT *to* frequently follows expressions of 'not knowing' or of 'finding out'. This is not the case in the sample sentence, however. To discover whether REACT *to* frequently follows the '*it* + adjective' pattern we can ask whether specifying a sequence of 'adjective + how + someone reacts to something' reveals an alternative pattern into which the sample sentence would fit. A search for this sequence gives these concordance lines:

```
rock. It's amazing how ordinary folk react to a fiddle in the safety of a
nd it will be critical how consumers react to the new tax system.'
an never be certain how someone will react to something which may have been
PLO. It is not clear how Israel will react to the advisory council. Israel TV
It is less clear how consumers will react to the growing financial turmoil.
It's not clear how Moscow will react to this latest move. The position
But it's not clear how Ankara would react to a request because any such move
It isn't clear how Americans would react to the new IRA proposals because
of erm It's interesting how people react to something like this. Okay. < M01 >
< p > It was unclear how Cigar would react to a wet and sticky racing surface
for his reply, yet unsure how she'd react to it. May we know how she died,
```

The dominant pattern here is indeed an anticipatory *it* and an evaluative adjective. This might be further subdivided into cases where the adjective indicates lack of clarity (*never certain, not clear*) and the reaction is hypothetical (*will/would react*) – these examples have something in common with the 'not knowing' examples given above – and a smaller set where the adjective indicates other kinds of evaluation (*amazing, critical* and *interesting*) and the reaction is actual.

In short, the sample sentence exemplifies both pattern and non-pattern. At quite an abstract level, the sequence 'evaluation of reaction + reaction + stimulus to reaction' recurs, though it is less frequent than other sequences such as 'not knowing/finding out + hypothetical reaction + stimulus'. In grammatical terms, the sequence '*it is* adjective *how*' occurs relatively frequently before REACT. In more specific lexical terms, that sequence with the adjective *ironic* is relatively infrequent, though by no means unknown. At every stage of this investigation varying concepts of what constitutes frequency have been used.

Further reading

Hunston, S. and Francis, G. (1999) *Pattern Grammar: A Corpus-driven Approach to the Lexical Grammar of English*. Amsterdam: John Benjamins. (This book takes a rather more restricted view of 'pattern' than the one discussed in this chapter, but it goes into quite a lot of detail about the relationship between pattern and meaning.)

Partington, A. (1998) *Patterns and Meanings: Using Corpora for English Language Research and Teaching*. Amsterdam: John Benjamins. (This book is rich in examples of lexical patterning and how concepts such as this might be applied.)

Sinclair, J. (2004) *Trust the Text*. London: Routledge. (This book sets the concept of pattern within a more general theory of language.)

Stubbs, M. (2001) *Words and Phrases: Corpus Studies of Lexical Semantics*. New York: Blackwell. (Along with Sinclair 2004, see above, this develops a theory of language based on patterns.)

Tognini Bonelli, E. (2001) *Corpus Linguistics at Work*. Amsterdam: John Benjamins. (Another book with a lot of examples in both English and Italian.)

References

Bang, M. (2009) 'The Representation of Foreign Countries in the US Press', unpublished PhD thesis, University of Birmingham.

Carter, R. A. (2004) *Language and Creativity: The Art of Common Talk*. London: Routledge.

Conrad, S. and Biber, D. (2000) 'Adverbial Marking of Stance in Speech and Writing', in S. Hunston and G. Thompson (eds) *Evaluation in Text: Authorial Stance and the Construction of Discourse*. Oxford: Oxford University Press, pp. 57–73.

Hunston, S. (2008) 'Starting with the Small Words: Patterns, Lexis and Semantic Sequences', *International Journal of Corpus Linguistics* 13: 271–95.

Obama, B. (2008) http://my.barackobama.com/page/content/hisownwords (accessed 7 September 2008).

O'Keeffe, A., McCarthy, M. J. and Carter, R. A. (2007) *From Corpus to Classroom: Language Use and Language Teaching*. Cambridge: Cambridge University Press.

Scott, M. (1999) *WordSmith Tools version 3*. Oxford: Oxford University Press.

Sinclair, J. (1991) *Corpus Concordance Collocation*. Oxford: Oxford University Press.

——(2004) *Trust the Text*. London: Routledge.

Tannen, D. (1989) *Talking Voices: Repetition, Dialogue, and Imagery in Conversational Discourse*. Cambridge: Cambridge University Press.

Teubert, W. (2005) 'My Version of Corpus Linguistics', *International Journal of Corpus Linguistics* 10: 1–13.

13

What are concordances and how are they used?

Christopher Tribble

1. What is a concordance?

It's likely that anyone who has even a passing interest in the use of corpora in language studies and language teaching will have come across the term *concordance*. It's equally likely that many of these people will have seen a printout for a concordance such as the one in Figure 13.1.

In this example the search word (*cat*) is presented at the centre of a fixed context of words or characters – a format commonly known by the acronym KWIC (Key Word In Context), and there are many commercial, free or on-line products available to assist those who wish to look at language in use in this way (Barlow 2002; Anthony 2007; Scott 2008; and see Lee, this volume). However, it is important to remember that a KWIC concordance is only one way of looking at corpus data, and that the definition of a concordance offered by Sinclair (1991) is one that we should continue to bear in mind:

> A *concordance* is a collection of the occurrences of a word-form, each in its own textual environment. In its simplest form it is an index. Each word-form is indexed and a reference is given to the place of occurrence in a text.
>
> (Sinclair 1991: 32)

2. Concordances before the computer age

Sinclair's definition is important because it reminds us that, originally, a concordance was a manually prepared list of the word-forms found in a text or set of texts along with references to their precise locations (by book, verse, line, etc.). We stress *word-form* here because with most corpora and corpus tools it would require two searches to find the singular and plural form of e.g. *cat* and *cats*. More of this later.

The first recorded concordance in the Western tradition was based on the work of Cardinal Hugo of St Caro (also referred to as St Cher), who, 'with the help of hundreds of Dominican monks at St James convent in Paris, compiled a word index of the

Vulgate in the year 1230' (Bromiley 1997: 757). Given the huge human effort involved in such a project, it is not surprising that in the pre-computer age, these were only developed for a few culturally valued texts (e.g. Cruden's 1737 *A Complete Concordance to the Holy Scriptures*, Strong's 1890 *Exhaustive Concordance of the Bible*, or Becket's 1787 *A Concordance to Shakespeare*). These books provided scholars with two kinds of resource. The first was an exhaustive account of where words were used in a closed set of texts (in Strong 1890, the 8,674 Hebrew root words in the Old Testament and the 5,624 Greek root words in the New Testament). The second, (e.g. Becket 1787) was

1	ht, I should think!' (Dinah was the	**cat**	.) 'I hope they'll remember her
2	And yet I wish I could show you our	**cat**	Dinah: I think you'd take a fa
3	to talk about her pet: 'Dinah's our	**cat**	. And she's such a capital one
4	n here, and I'm sure she's the best	**cat**	in the world! Oh, my dear Dina
5	sneeze, were the cook, and a large	**cat**	which was sitting on the heart
6	s for her to speak first, 'why your	**cat**	grins like that?' 'It's a Ches
7	grins like that?' 'It's a Cheshire	**cat**	,' said the Duchess, 'and that'
8	tle startled by seeing the Cheshire	**Cat**	sitting on a bough of a tree a
9	ough of a tree a few yards off. The	**Cat**	only grinned when it saw Alice
10	where you want to get to,' said the	**Cat**	. 'I don't much care where – ' s

Figure 13.1 KWIC concordance
Source: Lewis Carroll *Alice in Wonderland* http://www.gutenberg.org/files/11/11.txt, accessed 15 August 2008.

WORD

What ſaid he? How looked he? Wherein went he?
What makes he here? Did he aſk for me? Where remains he?
How parted he with thee? And when ſhalt thou ſee him again?
Anſwer me in one word.

As you like it, A. 3, S. 2.

– Hear me, Hubert! drive theſe men away,
And I will ſit as quiet as a lamb;
I will not air, nor wince, nor ſpeak a word,
Nor look upon the iron angerly :
Thruſt but theſe men away, and I'll forgive you.

King John, A. 4, S.

– Theſe haughty words of hers
Have batter'd me like roaring cannon-ſhot,
And made me almoſt yield upon my knees.

Henry VI. P. 1, A. 3, S.

Gregory, o' my word, we'll not carry coals.

Romeo and Juliet, A. 1, S

Figure 13.2 WORD in Becket's concordance.

designed as a source of insight and illumination for a wider readership, the author claiming that:

> the Editor has endeavoured to exhibit the most striking sentiments of the 'great poet of nature', cleared of all impurities, of all 'eye-offending' dross. He has broken and disjointed several of the speeches, but this must not be urged against as a fault: – The nature of the work demanded it; and as the reader is referred to the act and scene of every play, in which the more beautiful of such speeches are to be found, and as there are likewise innumerable compilations in which they are given entire, there is consequently the less occasion for apology.
>
> (Becket 1787: vi)

In Becket's concordance, an example of the word is given, along with its linguistic context and location in the Shakespeare canon (Play, Act, Scene) as in the example for *WORD* given in Figure 13.2.

In computer assisted linguistic analysis, concordances continue to be, at heart, indexes of instances, but they can be generated for a range of new purposes and across a range of ever-expanding texts and text types. A printed concordance of a Greek root word in Strong (1890) would have assisted scholars concerned with biblical exegesis by giving a comprehensive account of how often and where this word was used across the King James Authorised Version of the New Testament. Indeed, this tradition continued until the 1980s with printed concordances of Henry James (e.g. Bender 1987), Joseph Conrad (e.g. Bender 1979) and T. S. Eliot (Dawson 1995).

Useful as these concordances have been, a computer can now be used to create an equivalent to the Strong concordance in the blink of an eye, and it can also support a much wider range of analytic purposes and does not suffer from the limitations of its paper counterpart. In the following sections we will be reviewing the different ways in which computerised concordances can be generated, and how they can be used to present and analyse language data.

3. Computer generated concordances: approaches, tools and resources

As we have seen, before the days of digitised texts and modern computers, concordances were made by dedicated individuals or teams, working often over long periods of time. Team members would read the text, identify words that mattered to the analysis and painstakingly build up tables which allowed one to record where each instance of that word was found. Whether lines, verses, chapters, books, scenes, acts or other units were used would depend on the text type being worked with. At the simplest level, a paper-based concordance for *rabbit* (underlined in Figure 13.3, in an extract from Lewis Carroll's *Alice in Wonderland*) could take two main forms.

Assuming a text such as the example above, where chapter, page and line numbering are known, a concordance in the Strong 1890 tradition might give us an entry for *rabbit* such as in Table 13.1.

Each time the word *rabbit* appeared in a page, the tally would be increased and a cumulative log would be kept of the chapter, page and line reference so that a cumulative total and list of locations could be compiled at the end of the research process.

A concordance in the Becket 1787 tradition might look more like:

> … when suddenly a White Rabbit with pink eyes ran close by her. (Chapter 1, p.1, l.9)
>
> Alice started to her feet, for it flashed across her mind that she had never before seen a rabbit with either a waistcoat-pocket, or a watch to take out of it … (Chapter 1, p.1, l.18)

… the editor having decided that these two uses of *rabbit* were more interesting than other instances in the text.

This paper and pencil approach to concordance-making has not entirely disappeared, having its parallels in projects like the *Oxford English Dictionary*'s 'Reading Programme'. This is still the basis for many of the millions of quotations on which examples in the dictionary are based (see 'The Reading Programme' on the *OED* website), but it has been largely superseded by computer concordances of electronically readable texts.

ALICE'S ADVENTURES IN WONDERLAND

CHAPTER I. Down the **Rabbit**-Hole

1. Alice was beginning to get very tired of sitting by her sister on the
2. bank, and of having nothing to do: once or twice she had peeped into the
3. book her sister was reading, but it had no pictures or conversations in
4. it, 'and what is the use of a book,' thought Alice 'without pictures or
5. conversation?'

6. So she was considering in her own mind (as well as she could, for the
7. hot day made her feel very sleepy and stupid), whether the pleasure
8. of making a daisy-chain would be worth the trouble of getting up and
9. picking the daisies, when suddenly a White **Rabbit** with pink eyes ran
close by her.

10. There was nothing so VERY remarkable in that; nor did Alice think it so
11. VERY much out of the way to hear the **Rabbit** say to itself, 'Oh dear!
12. Oh dear! I shall be late!' (when she thought it over afterwards, it
13. occurred to her that she ought to have wondered at this, but at the time
14. it all seemed quite natural); but when the **Rabbit** actually TOOK A WATCH
15. OUT OF ITS WAISTCOAT-POCKET, and looked at it, and then hurried on,
16. Alice started to her feet, for it flashed across her mind that she had
17. never before seen a **rabbit** with either a waistcoat-pocket, or a watch
18. to take out of it, and burning with curiosity, she ran across the field
19. after it, and fortunately was just in time to see it pop down a large
20. **rabbit**-hole under the hedge.

Figure 13.3 Sentence concordance – *Alice in Wonderland*
Source: Project Gutenberg Edition (http://www.gutenberg.org/files/11/11.txt accessed 13 August 2008).

Table 13.1 Basic index

count	*word*	*chapter*	*page*	*line*
1	rabbit	1	1	9
2				12
3				15
4				18

Table 13.2 One-word context concordance

the	cat	sat
the	mat	
sat	on	the
cat	sat	on
	the	cat
on	the	mat

Simple concordances

In contemporary computer-assisted analyses of texts, we expect to be able to access all the information we found in a paper concordance (i.e. frequency of occurrences and exact location in the text), along with a great deal more information. Using a modern concordancer such as *WordSmith Tools version 5* (Scott 2008), it is possible to look at a word-form in a number of ways, each of which has its value for the researcher.

As a way of demonstrating the principle which underlies a concordance, Sinclair (1991: 33) gives an example of a concordance of a complete short text, '*The cat sat on the mat*.' Here, each word is treated as a node word-form (i.e. the string of characters which the computer has been instructed to search for in the corpus). These notes have then been sorted in alphabetic order (rather than being presented in text sequence) and a one-word-form context at either side has been provided (Table 13.2).

Although such full text concordances continue to be a possibility, it would be unusual to use this approach for larger texts or text collections. A more common format is one in which a single *node* or search term (this can be a word-form or phrase) is looked for in all its contexts across a text. Given in Figure 13.4 is a KWIC concordance for the word-form *rabbit* in *Alice in Wonderland* by Lewis Carroll. In the current display, the first ten occurrences of the word-form are presented in text sequence at the centre of a context of seventy characters (spaces and punctuation are counted as characters).

In the next example the same concordance is shown, but this time with the additional information of the position at which the word-string occurs in the text (word number / sentence number / file name) (Figure 13.5).

It should be remembered that the KWIC format is not the only way of displaying concordance data, and that it is not always the best. The concordance extract in Figure 13.6 gives an alternative view of the data in which complete sentences are shown and the node word is underlined.

```
ALICE'S ADVENTURES IN WONDERLAND

N       Concordance
1         wis Carroll CHAPTER I. Down the Rabbit-Hole Alice was beginning
2       the daisies, when suddenly a White Rabbit with pink eyes ran close by
3       RY much out of the way to hear the Rabbit say to itself, 'Oh dear! Oh
4       eemed quite natural); but when the Rabbit actually TOOK A WATCH OUT O
5         that she had never before seen a rabbit with either a waistcoat-pock
6        n time to see it pop down a large rabbit-hole under the hedge. In
7          d she was to get out again. The rabbit-hole went straight on like a
8        other long passage, and the White Rabbit was still in sight, hurrying
9        en she turned the corner, but the Rabbit was no longer to be seen: sh
10       what was coming. It was the White Rabbit returning, splendidly dresse
```

Figure 13.4 KWIC concordance for *rabbit*.

N	Concordance	Word #	Sent. #	File
1	I should think!' (Dinah was the cat.) 'I hope they'll remember	796	36	c_alicew.txt
2	yet I wish I could show you our cat Dinah: I think you'd take a	3,861	179	c_alicew.txt
3	about her pet: 'Dinah's our cat. And she's such a capital one	5,782	301	c_alicew.txt
4	and I'm sure she's the best cat in the world! Oh, my dear	5,921	312	c_alicew.txt
5	were the cook, and a large cat which was sitting on the	11,540	646	c_alicew.txt
6	her to speak first, 'why your cat grins like that?' 'It's a Ch	11,581	647	c_alicew.txt
7	ns like that?' 'It's a Cheshire cat,' said the Duchess, 'and	11,588	648	c_alicew.txt
8	startled by seeing the Cheshire Cat sitting on a bough of a tree	12,644	699	c_alicew.txt
9	of a tree a few yards off. The Cat only grinned when it saw	12,657	700	c_alicew.txt
10	you want to get to,' said the Cat. 'I don't much care where--'	12,755	705	c_alicew.txt

Figure 13.5 KWIC concordance + provenance data.

```
1    (Dinah was the cat.)
2    And yet I wish I could show you our cat Dinah.
3    Alice replied eagerly, for she was always ready to talk about her pet:
     'Dinah's our cat.
4    'Nobody seems to like her, down here, and I'm sure she's the best cat in the
     world!
5    The only things in the kitchen that did not sneeze, were the cook, and a
     large cat which was sitting on the hearth and grinning from ear to ear. '
6    'Please would you tell me,' said Alice, a little timidly, for she was not
     quite sure whether it was good manners for her to speak first, 'why your cat
     grins like that?' '
7    'It's a Cheshire cat,' said the Duchess, 'and that's why.
8    And she began thinking of other children she knew, who might do very well as
     pigs, and was just saying to herself, 'if one only knew the right way to
     change them--' when she was a little startled by seeing the Cheshire Cat
     sitting on a bough of a tree a few yards off.
9    The Cat only grinned when it saw Alice.
10   'That depends a good deal on where you want to get to,' said the Cat. '
```

Figure 13.6 Sentence concordance.

There are advantages and disadvantages to this kind of display as we shall see (see Sripicharn, this volume), but in the early stages of introducing concordancing to learners and other students of language it is sometimes the case that a sentence view of concordance data can be more useful than the KWIC display as it presents fewer reading challenges to newcomers to corpus analysis.

Word-forms and lemmas

The first concordance examples we looked at in this chapter were for single word-forms. While such searches can be very revealing, there are times when a researcher needs to move beyond individual word-forms. Thus, in many studies, it will be important to investigate a *lemma* rather than a simple word-form. Sinclair defines *lemma* as follows:

> A lemma is what we normally mean by a 'word'. Many words in English have several actual word-forms – so that, for example, the verb *to give* has the forms *give, gives, given, gave, giving,* and *to give*. In other languages, the range of forms can be ten or more, and even hundreds. So 'the word *give*' can mean either (i) the four letters **g**, **i**, **v**, **e**, or (ii) the six forms listed above.

> In linguistics and lexicography we have to keep these meanings separate; otherwise it would not be possible to understand a sentence like '*Give* occurs 50 times in this text'. For this reason, the composite set of word-forms is called the lemma.
>
> (Sinclair 1991: 173)

In other contexts, researchers may need to search for particular phrases (fixed combinations of word-forms) which have importance for them or even for non-contiguous patterns where the node is separated from a list of required context words by a set span of word-forms or characters. Modern concordancing software offers resources which make both of these tasks relatively straightforward. With an unmarked-up corpus (i.e. one that does not contain part-of-speech tags, lemma information or other codes) two strategies can be used. The first requires the user to enter a list of the word-forms which constitute the lemma of a stem: e.g. cat/cats or smile/smiles/smiling/smiled. Figure 13.7 shows what a concordance for cat/cats in *Alice in Wonderland* will look like.

An alternative approach to typing all the word-forms you wish to find is to use the *wild-card* facility (*regular expression* in UNIX environments) which different concordancing programs offer. A *wild-card* is a symbol which can be used to stand for one or many alpha-numeric characters. In a *Windows* operating system environment wild-cards might include examples such as shown in Table 13.3.

There is no point in giving an exhaustive list of such symbols here as wild-card symbols can and do change from one program or operating system to another. Finding out what wild-card searches are available to you is one of the first things you need to do when working with a new concordancing program. Once you have learned what wild-cards are available in the software you are using, the next thing to remember is that wild-card searches will usually produce a mix of wanted and unwanted results, especially in an unmarked-up corpus. Thus the search string *cat** will give you *cat* and *cats*, but it also produces *catch*. Similarly, although a search using **ing* will generate concordances for all the present participles, it will also find word-forms such as *sing* or *nothing* which will have to be edited out.

Phrases

Concordancing software does not restrict you to searching for individual word-forms. It is also possible to look for closed and open phrase patterns, using a mix of full word-forms and wild-cards to create search algorithms that most closely meet your needs. Thus, in a corpus of business correspondence (for example, look up Mike Nelson's Business English Lexis Site) a search for *thank you for* will produce results like those in Figure 13.8, while a search for *do not * to* will produce Figure 13.9.

```
N
1     ht, I should think!' (Dinah was the cat.) 'I hope they'll remember her
2     very like a mouse, you know. But do cats eat bats, I wonder?' And here
3     rself, in a dreamy sort of way, 'Do cats eat bats? Do cats eat bats?'
4      sort of way, 'Do cats eat bats? Do cats eat bats?' and sometimes, 'Do
5      bats?' and sometimes, 'Do bats eat cats?' for, you see, as she couldn
6     gs. 'I quite forgot you didn't like cats.' 'Not like cats!' cried the
7     ot you didn't like cats.' 'Not like cats!' cried the Mouse, in a shril
8     , passionate voice. 'Would YOU like cats if you were me?' 'Well, perha
9     And yet I wish I could show you our cat Dinah: I think you'd take a fa
10    inah: I think you'd take a fancy to cats if you could only see her. Sh
```

Figure 13.7 Concordance sample for *cat/cats* in *Alice in Wonderland*.

Table 13.3 *Windows* wild-cards

Wild-card	*Search*	*Result*
★ any character at the end of a word (including punctuation)	cat★	I'm afraid, but you might **catch** a bat, and that's a mouse, you know. But do **cats** eat bats, I wonder? a dreamy sort of way, 'Do **cats** eat bats? Do cats e ay, 'Do cats eat bats? Do **cats** eat bats?' and some d sometimes, 'Do bats eat **cats?**' for, you see, as
★ any character at the beginning of a word (including punctuation)	★ing	the Rabbit-Hole Alice was **beginning** to get very tired ning to get very tired of **sitting** by her sister on the ister on the bank, and of **having** nothing to do: once o n the bank, and of having **nothing** to do: once or twice o the book her sister was **reading**, but it had no pictu
★ any whole word	have ★ to	poky little house, and **have next to** no toys to e! I do wonder what CAN **have happened to** me! When an–but then–always to **have lessons to** learn! Oh eshire Cat: now I shall **have somebody to** talk to. what you had been would **have appeared to** them to
? any single character	Engl?	. The further off from **England** the nearer is to and yet it was certainly **English.** 'I don't quite c remedies–' 'Speak **English**!' said the Eaglet oon submitted to by the **English**, who wanted leade ps it doesn't understand **English**,' thought Alice;

1 land Dear Mr Personname I write to **thank you for** your services over t
2 ll be your sole point of contact. I **thank you for** your greatly valued
3 ess Southern Ireland Dear Firstname **Thank you for** attending our meetin
4 ss Southern Ireland Dear Firstname **Thank you for** arranging and chairi
5 or opening the new TG Dublin depot. **Thank you for** all of your efforts
6 ies. May I take this opportunity to **thank you for** your interest in our
7 00 60 3 716 0953 Dear Mr Personname **Thank you for** your letter addresse
8 ease do not hesitate to contact me. **Thank you for** your assistance. You
9 00 91 591 31120S Dear Mr Personname **Thank you for** your letter regardin
10 rly on the outside of the envelope. **Thank you for** your co-operation in

Figure 13.8 Phrase search.

1 mpanyaddress Tick here if you **do not want to** receive any further
2 g will show that great negotiators **do not need to** use any tricks but y
3 mpanyaddress Tick here if you **do not want to** receive any further
4 u have any further queries, please **do not hesitate to** contact me.
5 ou require more information please **do not hesitate to** contact either m
6 ve any queries on the above please **do not hesitate to** contact me. Th
7 re any further information, please **do not hesitate to** contact me on my
8 re any further information, please **do not hesitate to** contact me on my
9 database searches further, please **do not hesitate to** contact me on 01
10 f you need any further information **do not hesitate to** contact me on ..

Figure 13.9 Wild-card phrase search.

```
1   k he's got in the office today and if he hasn't got enough to worry ab
2    offered to act as Promoter for us if we could donate enough to provid
3   he full employment level of output if prices are high enough to make t
4   o say constitutes a legal warning. If you are foolish enough to close
5   nt is the price for higher returns if you are lucky enough to make it
6               chievement to sink in. If I am lucky enough to be chosen i
7               chievement to sink in. If I am lucky enough to be chosen i
8   a time are homeless in Gloucester. If they're not lucky enough to find
9   ls of post Thatcher Britain. Here, if you are lucky enough to own an o
10   million miles from feeling. Adam, if you'd be good enough to finish w
```

Figure 13.10 Wild-card multiword phrase search.

In a larger corpus, it begins to be possible to search for quite extended patterns and obtain a surprisingly large number of results. Thus a search in the BNC for *if * * * enough to* produces 156 results. (NB in the example in Figure 13.10 the contracted word-form *hasn't* counts as a one word. This is a feature common to most concordancing programs.)

And this brings us to our next section. How do you manage the data once you start to get more than you can conveniently see on your screen?

4. Working with corpus data

Sorting

The first way of dealing with a surfeit of results is to take advantage of the fact that your concordance is electronic. You can sort the output so that like is grouped with like. There are at least three ways of re-sorting concordance data: by the node word itself, by the left context of the node and by the right context. Of course, sorting can be done in ascending or descending order. If further information is available, the data can also be sorted by text, by tag or by any other available category. The three examples for the search string *look** below demonstrate the potential for this approach. A search for *look** in *Through the Looking Glass* produces 155 results. This is not a huge amount of data, but it is still more than you can take in without some further processing. As Figure 13.11 shows, sorting the node word first reveals which form of *look** occurs most frequently (*looking*, with seventy-one occurrences) and which form is least frequent (in this instance *looks*, which only occurs once).

Sorting by the left context shows us the typical subjects for *look** as verb, as in Figure 13.12, while sorting by the right context can show typical collocating adverbs, prepositions, complements, etc. (Figure 13.13).

```
145   the crown, NOW!' the Unicorn said, looking slyly up at the crown, whi
146  t she had never seen such a strange-looking soldier in all her life. H
147  candles all grew up to the ceiling, looking something like a bed of ru
148  y bit of the worsted while I wasn't looking! 'That's three faults, Kit
149  se, would you tell me--' she began, looking timidly at the Red Queen.
150   use talking about it,' Alice said, looking up at the house and preten
151  about 'em,' the Sheep said, without looking up from her knitting: 'I d
152  nt to buy?' the Sheep said at last, looking up for a moment from her k
153  no!' 'What volcano?' said the King, looking up anxiously into the fire
154  sonable child,' said Humpty Dumpty, looking very much pleased. 'I mean
155  corn rise to their feet, with angry looks at being interrupted in thei
```

Figure 13.11 *Look** (by the node word).

```
3        hard at Alice as he said do. Alice looked at the jury-box, and saw th
4       n, what makes them so shiny?' Alice looked down at them, and considere
5       d into hers began to tremble. Alice looked up, and there stood the Que
6        sound of many footsteps, and Alice looked round, eager to see the Que
7        said in an encouraging tone. Alice looked all round the table, but th
8       ' The baby grunted again, and Alice looked very anxiously into its fac
9       terpillar The Caterpillar and Alice looked at each other for some time
10      question certainly was, what? Alice looked all round her at the flower
```

Figure 13.12 Left sort.

```
1        d pretended not to see it: but it looked a LITTLE ashamed of itself,
2        d it round for him. 'I thought it looked a little queer. As I was say
3            to carve a joint before. 'You look a little shy; let me introduce
4       on't understand,' the Knight said, looking a little vexed. 'That's wh
5          an't get at me!' Then she began looking about, and noticed that wha
6       caught the shawl as she spoke, and looked about for the owner: in ano
7       What AM I to do?' exclaimed Alice, looking about in great perplexity,
8          ' 'Don't tease so,' said Alice, looking about in vain to see where
9          away at full speed. Alice stood looking after it, almost ready to c
10      n wool. Alice rubbed her eyes, and looked again. She couldn't make out
```

Figure 13.13 Right sort.

Depending on the software you are working with, sorts can also extend beyond the immediate context of the node, with sorts at one, two, three or more words to the right or left of the node being possible.

Sampling

If you are still overloaded with data from a concordance search, there are three main ways of reducing the amount of information the program throws at you. One approach is to reduce the amount of data that you are working with. For example, a search for *into* in the BNC will produce 157,925 concordance lines. This is probably too much information for your needs! Biber (1990) has, however, shown that for investigations of word-classes such as prepositions, a corpus of 1,000,000 words can be more than sufficient to make useful linguistic generalisations. So one answer to our problem is to turn to a smaller corpus – in this case the four-million-word BNC Baby Corpus (*The BNC Baby* 2005). This produces a (slightly) more manageable 5,982 results.

If this is still more than you need, but you want to make sure that you are selecting from across a representative sample of the language, an alternative strategy to adopt is to make a randomised selection from the data. If your software permits, you can randomise your selection by a set number. A search with a limit of one in twenty instances across the BNC Baby Corpus produces 300 results, a much easier quantity of data to work with, and one which allows one to begin to select instances that have pedagogic or other kinds of relevance, or which can be used in the first stages of hypothesis development (Figure 13.14).

Restricted searches

If sorting and sampling don't bring the results down to manageable levels – or if you are spending too much time weeding out examples that are not relevant to the research that you are doing – then you need to start to refine the searches that you are making. Even

```
1       emed as if the world was to divide into three main trading blocks: the
2       tart of something which could grow into a very significant development
3           Spycatcher saga as a book goes into print, giving the inside story
4       uite nice for me to be able to pop into town and get a bit of meat or
5        to, she says she would have to go into a home. Elaine went .
6                Those involved in research into the drug and with the women ta
7       leading Pandava brother is enticed into a dice game he knows he will l
8       t apart. Tear bits off it. Turn it into the sort of jangled pile of me
9       ke me, like us, who are dissolving into the whirling water too.
10      eration of Jumbo trams, which went into service in 1979, was one that
```

Figure 13.14 Concordance lines of *into* from BNC Baby Corpus.

with an untagged corpus, there are many ways of producing more useful results by making use of the features that most modern concordancing programs provide.

Clearly, with a part-of-speech (POS) tagged corpus such as the British National Corpus, it is possible to specify the word classes that will be included in a search (Aston and Burnard 1998). Thus, rather than looking for, say, *rabbit* (2,571 results), it would be possible to look for it as verb only (thirty-nine results). However, if you have a reasonable knowledge of a structure of the language in question, and a small degree of cunning, it is possible to develop simple algorithms which will greatly improve the searches that you make.

For example, in academic discourse, the ways in which extended noun phrases are post-modified is an important component in the construction of meaning in impersonal, fact-oriented written texts (Biber 2006). Assuming you have access to a corpus of experimental science research journal articles which have not been part-of-speech tagged, how do you go about collecting examples of, say, extended noun phrases in grammatical subject or sentence theme position for research or teaching purposes (see Halliday 1994 for an extended discussion of theme and rheme)?

If you have access to a concordancer which uses asterisk (*) as a whole- or part-word wild-card, it is possible to make the following search algorithm:

> Search for "the * of" in the context of "*." up to four words to the right
> [i.e. search for any word preceded by a definite article and followed by the preposition *of* in the context of a preceding full-stop up to four word-forms to the right of the node]

This produces results such as those in Figure 13.15 (shown in sentence concordance format with extended theme in bold and node underlined).

Similarly, should you wish to refine the search so as to find nouns that are both pre- and post-modified, the search algorithm:

> *Search for* 'the * * of' *in the context of* '*.' *up to four words to the left*
> [i.e. search for any two word-forms that are preceded by a definite article and followed by the particle *of* in the context of a preceding full-stop up to four word-forms to the left of the node]

... will produce results as in Figure 13.16.

Further refinements of this simple algorithm can be devised, making it possible to identify, quantify and describe other kinds of noun post-modification (present- or past-participle, relative clause and other prepositional phrases) and, of course, it is then

1 **To determine the significance of these banding patterns following the MEE analysis of samples of pools of individuals we** compared individual worms with the pools using the rational and allozyme interpretation as detailed by Andrews and Chilton (1999).
2 **The usefulness of the application of MEE to provide answers to parasite systematics** has been reviewed by Andrews and Chilton (1999).
3 **To date, the roles of genetic variation of O. viverrini on this observed variability in infection, transmission and associated disease** are not known.
5 **The specificity of this PCR, in addition to its sensitivity (50 pg),** demonstrates its usefulness in Leishmania typing.

Figure 13.15 'the * of'—data source Acta Tropica (http://www.sciencedirect.com/science/journal/0001706X accessed 19 August 2008).

1 **The last repeat of the cpb cluster** was named cpbE for L. infantum and cpbF for L. donovani.
2 **The species profiles of the An. dirus and An. minimus complexes in north-east India** are largely unknown and need investigation for improved understanding.
3 **The trypanosome stock** can play a role (Maudlin and Welburn, 1994) as well as numerous extrinsic factors.
4 **The theoretical digest of the 648 bp Ade2 amplicon** gave 35425638 bp and 610 38 bp fragments for the resistant and sensitive strains, respectively.
5 **The expected sizes of the three PCR products** were 616 bp (Ade1 amplicon), 648 bp (Ade2 amplicon) and 518 bp (Ade3 amplicon) for the first, the second and the third respectively.

Figure 13.16 'the * * of'.

possible to devise other searches to identify other lexico-grammatical or discourse features. Being able to develop such algorithms has long been part of the skill set of the corpus analyst. In earlier days when programs such as *Oxford Concordancing Programme* were the state-of-the-art tools of the trade, you could spend a long time making sure that the syntax of command lines was right – the computer was completely unforgiving if a single character was out of place. Life is a little easier these days, but there is still a need to be able to think through this kind of extended query.

Reading concordances

Once you have a page (or more than one pages) of concordance data in front of you, how do you read them? Sinclair (2003: xvi–xvii) proposes a seven-stage procedure for working with concordance data, and this offers an excellent starting point for carrying out a careful and comprehensive account of the data that you have found through a concordance search. We summarise the procedure below (and strongly recommend that anyone with an interest in this area returns to the much more extensive discussion and activities in the original).

Given a context where a researcher or teacher wished to investigate citation practices in the Academic Writing section of the BNC Baby Corpus, how might you use Sinclair's procedure? The following search algorithm will produce a useful set of concordances.

> Find all instances of '(19★★) NOT in the context of '★.' 5 word-forms to the right [i.e. search for all dates included in round brackets that are NOT at the ends of

sentences and which are therefore more likely to be associated with sentence integral citation forms]

(See Thompson and Tribble 2001)

Step 1 Initiate

This is a process of looking for patterns to the right or left of the node which have some kind of prominence, and which may be worth focusing on in order to assess their possible salience to the analysis in question (Figure 13.17).

At the *initiate* stage in an analysis of this data you may first notice that there is a major pattern of ***SURNAME*** + *(DATE)*.

Step 2 Interpret

Sinclair comments for this stage:

> Look at the repeated words, and try to form a hypothesis that may link them or most of them. For example, they may be from the same word class, or they may have similar meanings.
>
> (Sinclair 2003: xvi)

In the present context, an initial working hypothesis could be:

> In academic writing, a pattern *SURNAME* + *(DATE)* is used to represent published work to which a reference is being made. Neither first name nor initials are used.

1	r people and relationships. **Maslow**	(1966)	and Hudson (1966 and 1968) s
2	e data. Similarly, **Openshaw et al.**	(1986)	report that the data in the
3	assified by **Flowerdew and Openshaw**	(1987)	and several examples are giv
4	cheme devised by **Ellis and Schmidt**	(1977)	, singularities in maximal, f
5	to recall that **Elementary Matrices**	(1938)	was printed nine times in U.
6	o shapes social reality. As **Davies**	(1981)	has pointed out, speech is t
7	ersities). **Montefiore and Ishiguro**	(1979)	point out: The universities
8	except for those noted by **Fillmore**	(1971)	, notably come and go, which
9	ation estimation because as **Tobler**	(1979)	points out, there is a dange
10	obation Service. Indeed, as **Bochel**	(1976)	has shown, the establishment
11	s originally postulated by **Erikson**	(1965)	and then developed by Marcia
12	exact solution of Khan and **Penrose**	(1971)	described in Chapter 3, ther
13	on has been considered by **Szekeres**	(1972)	, who found that, for collidi
14	his work was generalized by **Sbytov**	(1976)	to plane gravitational waves
15	s-areal interpolation methods. **Lam**	(1983)	suggests that there are two
16	by **Chandrasekhar and Xanthopoulos**	(1986c)	, and in the aligned case by
17	telligent interpolation. **Flowerdew**	(1988)	developed a theoretically so
18	ounterexample proposed by **Stoyanov**	(1979)	has proved to be incorrect a
19	s type, given by Bell and **Szekeres**	(1974)	, the singularity on the hype
20	central question noted by **Levinson**	(1983)	is whether the study of deix

Figure 13.17 Citation concordance.

Base pattern
SURNAME (DATE)

Step 3 Consolidate

In this stage you look further away from the node to assess if there are additional patterns or other variations in the pattern. In this instance you may notice that certain kinds of verb are associated with Pattern A (these are underlined in Figure 13.17). Your conclusion could be:

(a) A small set of verbs is associated with this pattern. These verbs either precede or follow the initial surname + date node, and produce two distinct new patterns:

Pattern A VERB + by + SURNAME + (DATE)
Pattern C SURNAME + (DATE) + VERB

(b) It also appears that there is a difference between those verbs which precede the node and those which follow it, and it may also be the case that these verbs can be classified evaluatively. This could lead to further research questions, e.g. to what extent does the verb choice indicate whether the writer approves or does not approve of the cited source? To what extent does the verb choice indicate the relative authority or certainty of the cited source? These verb forms are listed in Table 13.4.

Step 4 Report

Here Sinclair comments:

> When you have exhausted the patterns you can observe, and have revised your hypothesis so that it is as flexible as it needs to be and as strong as it can be, write it out so that you have an explicit, testable version for the future.
>
> (Sinclair 2003: xvii)

In the present case, a possible hypothesis is as shown in Table 13.5.

Table 13.4 Verb forms

Preceding	*Following*
classified (by)	report
devised (by)	pointed out
noted (by)	pointed out
postulated (by)	has shown
considered (by)	described
generalised (by)	suggests
proposed (by)	
given (by)	
noted (by)	

Table 13.5 Hypothesis 1

Hypothesis #1

In certain contexts a researcher may wish to incorporate or comment on the opinions, conclusions, etc., of authorities during the development of their own arguments. This can be done through the use of two main patterns:

Pattern A SURNAME (DATE) + VERB
Pattern B VERB + by + SURNAME (DATE)

Verbs associated with pattern A include: *describe / point out / show / report / suggest*
Verbs associated with pattern B include: *classify / consider / devise / generalize / give / note / postulate / propose*

Step 5 Recycle

This stage involves a further rigorous consideration of the extended contexts in which the node is found. This could lead to the discovery that evaluation or other comment on the authority cited may be shown through additional structures (Table 13.6).

This produces two further patterns:

Pattern C ADVERBIAL [*] + SURNAME + (DATE)
Pattern D VERB + by + SURNAME + (DATE) + VERB + TO INFINITIVE + EVALUATIVE ADJECTIVE

Step 6 Result

These observations can be recorded as a focus for further study and will be incorporated into a fuller report which contains a second working hypothesis, as in Table 13.7.

Table 13.6 Extended patterns

2	e data. **Similarly,** Openshaw et al. (1986)	report that the data in the
10	obation Service. **Indeed,** as Bochel (1976)	has shown, the establishment
18	ounterexample proposed by Stoyanov (1979)	**has proved to be incorrect** a

Table 13.7 Hypotheses 1 + 2

Hypothesis 1

In certain contexts a researcher may wish to incorporate or comment on the opinions, conclusions, etc., of authorities during the development of their own arguments. This can be done through the use of two main patterns:

Pattern A SURNAME (DATE) + VERB
Pattern B VERB + by + SURNAME (DATE)

Verbs associated with pattern A include: *describe / point out / show / report / suggest*
Verbs associated with pattern B include: *classify / consider / devise / generalize / give / note / postulate / propose*

Hypothesis 2

Further qualifying information can be added to Patterns A and B in two ways:

Pattern A (q) ADVERBIAL [+ optional additional word form] + SURNAME (DATE) + VERB
Pattern B (q) VERB + by + SURNAME + (DATE) + VERB + TO INFINITIVE + EVALUATIVE ADJECTIVE

Step 7 Repeat

The seventh stage in this process (but not the final stage!) is to repeat the process with more data. This enables the researcher to test, and then extend, refine or revise the hypothesis in order to render it as robust and useful as possible for your particular purposes.

5. Why concordances are not enough

In this chapter we have seen how concordances have developed since their first use several hundreds of years ago, how the results of searches through electronic corpora can be displayed, and how concordances can be read in order to find answers to questions about how language is used – in general and in particular. We have also discussed some of the strategies you can use to reduce the amount of data that can come churning out of the system if you work with very large corpora. Herein lies one of the limitations of the concordance and the reason why it has been necessary to develop new approaches to corpus investigation which make it possible to identify how lexical items collocate and how they are differentially distributed within and across texts and text collections.

We started this chapter by describing a concordance as the result of many years of labour of a small army of monks. Within the last few years, we have moved to a new situation in which, if researchers have access to the simplest of computing resources or to the internet, it is possible for them to produce enough concordance lines to occupy another army of monks. In later chapters in this book, we will see how new tools have been developed to carry out these new tasks.

Further reading

O'Keeffe, A, McCarthy, M. and Carter, R. (2007) *From Corpus to Classroom: Language Use and Language Teaching*. Cambridge: Cambridge University Press. (Although it ranges widely beyond the topic of concordances, this book gives language teachers an extensive insight into the potential of corpus data in language description and language teaching, with a particularly strong emphasis on the use of spoken language data.)

Sinclair, J. M. (2003) *Reading Concordances*. Harlow: Pearson Longman. (This unique book offers a systematic and authoritative account of how to go about the process of reading concordances. It is accessible to those with little or no background in linguistics, but also highly relevant to teachers and students who wish to become more proficient at reading concordances.)

Thurston, J. and Candlin, C. N. (1997) *Exploring Academic English: A Workbook for Student Essay Writing*. Sydney: NCELTR. (A practical demonstration of how a one-million-word corpus of academic texts can be used as the basis for practical teaching materials to support students who wish to develop academic writing skills.)

Tribble, C. and Jones, G. (1997) *Concordances in the Classroom: A Resource Book for Teachers*. Houston, TX: Athelstan. (This is a reprint of Tribble and Jones 1990. It continues to be one of the few resources which gives practical demonstrations of how to turn concordance output into practical teaching materials. Aimed at the teacher with access to small amounts of data, it shows the reader how to design simple concordance searches and format the results for on-screen or paper-based language teaching purposes.)

References

Anthony, L. (2007) *AntConc 3.2.1w*. Waseda: Waseda University.

Aston, G. and Burnard, L. (1998) *The BNC Handbook: Exploring the British National Corpus with SARA*. Edinburgh: Edinburgh University Press.

Barlow, M. (2002) *Monoconc Pro version 2*. Houston, TX: Athelstan.

Becket, A. (1787) *A Concordance to Shakespeare; Suited to All the Editions*. London: Robinson.

Bender, T. K. (1979) *A Concordance to Conrad's* The Secret Agent. New York: Garland.

——(1987) *A Concordance to Henry James's* Daisy Miller. New York: Garland.

Biber, D. (1990) 'Methodological Issues Regarding Corpus Based Analyses of Linguistic Variation', *Literary and Linguistic Computing* 5(4): 257–69.

——(2006) *University Language: A Corpus-based Study of Spoken and Written Registers*. Amsterdam and Philadelphia, PA: John Benjamins.

The BNC Baby, version 2. (2005). Distributed by Oxford University Computing Services on behalf of the BNC Consortium, available at www.natcorp.ox.ac.uk/

Bromiley, G. W. (1997) *The International Standard Bible Encyclopedia: Vol I: A–D*. Grand Rapids, MI: William B. Eerdmans.

Cruden, A. (1738) *A Complete Concordance to the Holy Scriptures*. London: Midwinter.

Dawson, J. (1995) *Concordance to the Complete Poems and Plays*. London: Faber & Faber.

Halliday, M. A. K. (1968) 'Notes on Transitivity and Theme in English III', *Journal of Linguistics* 4(2): 179–215.

——(1994) *An Introduction to Functional Grammar*, second edition. London: Edward Arnold.

O'Keeffe, A, McCarthy, M. and Carter, R. (2007) *From Corpus to Classroom: Language Use and Language Teaching*. Cambridge: Cambridge University Press.

Scott, M. (2008) *WordSmith Tools version* 5. Liverpool: Lexical Analysis Software.

Sinclair, J. M. (1991) *Corpus, Concordance and Collocation*. Oxford: Oxford University Press.

——(2003) *Reading Concordances*. Harlow: Pearson Longman.

Strong, J. (1890) *Strong's Exhaustive Concordance of the Bible*. Abingdon: Abingdon Press.

Thompson, P. and Tribble, C. (2001) 'Looking at Citations: Using Corpora in English for Academic Purposes', *Language Learning and Technology* 5(3): 91–105.

Thurston, J. and Candlin, C. N. (1997) *Exploring Academic English: A Workbook for Student Essay Writing*. Sydney: NCELTR.

Tribble, C. and Jones, G. (1990) *Concordances in the Classroom*. Harlow: Longman.

——(1997) *Concordances in the Classroom: A Resource Book for Teachers*. Houston, TX: Athelstan.

14

What can corpus software reveal about language development?

Xiaofei Lu

1. What is language development?

Language development refers to the process in which the language faculty develops in a human being. First language development is concerned with how children acquire the capability of their native language, while second language development is concerned with how children and adults acquire the capability of a second language.

Theories of first language development generally need to address at least the following three questions: what children bring to the language learning task, what mechanisms drive language acquisition, and what types of input support the language-learning system (Pence and Justice 2008). Psychologists have taken drastically different approaches to answering these questions, among which the rationalist, empiricist and pragmatist paradigms have been the most influential (Russell 2004). The rationalist approach, inspired by Chomskyan linguistics, takes the view that the language faculty does not depend on external sources for its content, but is internal to each individual. For rationalists, children are born with innate formal knowledge of a universal grammar, and they bring this domain-specific knowledge to the task of acquiring the I-language (i.e. the internal and individual language) of their native tongue. Language input is used to discover the parameters their native language uses to satisfy the universal grammar. The empiricist approach, upheld by connectionists, believes that the content of the language faculty is not innate, but is derived from perceptual experience. For empiricists, children employ domain-general mechanisms of associative learning to acquire the rules and representations of their native language through experience with sufficient speech input. The pragmatist or socio-cognitivist approach advocates that children recruit their socio-cognitive capacity to actively construct their language faculty. Within this paradigm, language is viewed as a socio-cultural action, and the language development process is viewed as involving children constructing a series of models or working theories of their mother tongue from the evidence that is available to them.

Theories of second language development generally seek to explain a different set of questions, including the nature of second language knowledge, the nature of interlanguage, the contributions of knowledge of the first language, the contributions of the linguistic environment, and the role of instruction (Ortega 2007). Nine contemporary theories of second language development are presented in VanPatten and Williams (2007), some of which are rooted in theories of child language development. These theories take different stances with respect to the various aspects of second language development. For example, concerning the nature of second language knowledge, the Chomskyan universal grammar theory, which is committed to nativism, argues that second language learners cannot obtain knowledge of ungrammaticality and ambiguity from linguistic input, but possess pre-existing knowledge of the grammar that constrains their learning task (White 2007). Contrastively, the skill acquisition theory, which is committed to conscious processing, claims that development happens from initial representation of knowledge through proceduralisation of knowledge to eventual automatisation of knowledge (DeKeyser 2007). Still different is the Vygotskian socio-cultural theory, which views human cognition as a social faculty and posits that second language development 'takes place through participation in cultural, linguistic, and historically formed settings' (Lantolf and Thorne 2007: 201) and through interaction within social and material environments.

2. How do we measure language development?

In addition to the theoretical question of how language development takes place, another important and more practical question that is of interest to teachers, researchers, parents and/or clinicians is what stage of language development a particular child or second language learner is in, or, in other words, how much a child or second language learner knows about the language system and its use at a particular point. Measurement of language development is especially important for children suffering any delay or disorder in their language development. There are a number of different ways to answer this question, including naturalistic observation; production, comprehension, and judgment tasks; formal testing; and language sample analysis, among others. In this section, we focus on how language development can be measured through analysing spoken or written language samples produced by a child or second language learner.

A number of measures of language development have been proposed and explored in the child language development literature. Some measures are based on verbal output, e.g. mean length of utterance (MLU) (Brown 1973) and number of different words (NDWs), while others are based on structural analysis, e.g. Developmental Sentence Scoring (DSS) (Lee 1974), and Index of Production Syntax (IPSyn) (Scarborough 1990). Both DSS and IPSyn were developed to evaluate children's grammatical development, although they work in different ways. The DSS metric assigns a score to each sentence. It considers eight different types of grammatical forms, including indefinite pronouns, personal pronouns, main verbs, secondary or embedded verbs, conjunctions, negatives and two types of questions. Variants of the same type of grammatical form are scored differently based on the order in which children develop the ability to use them. The score of a sentence is the sum of the points for each type plus one point if the sentence is fully grammatical. The average DSS of a speaker can be computed using a representative language sample. The IPSyn metric does not apply to individual sentences, but examines the number of times fifty-six target grammatical structures are used in a sample produced by a speaker. These include various types of noun phrases, verb phrases, questions and some specific sentence structures. Each occurrence of any of the target grammatical structures in the language sample receives one point. However, a maximum of two occurrences of each structure are counted, and the maximum score a language sample can receive is 112.

In the second language development literature, a number of developmental index studies have attempted to identify objective measures of fluency, accuracy and complexity of production that can be used to index the learner's level of development or overall proficiency in the target language. This is generally achieved by assessing the development of second language learners at known proficiency levels in the target language using various measures. Developmental measures identified in such a way allow teachers and researchers to evaluate and describe the learner's developmental level in a more precise way. In addition, they can also be used to examine the effect of a particular pedagogical treatment on language use. Wolfe-Quintero *et al.* (1998) provided a comprehensive review of the measures explored in thirty-nine second and foreign language writing studies and recommended several measures that were consistently linear and significantly related to programme or school levels as the best measures of development or error. These include three measures of fluency, i.e. mean length of T-unit, where a T-unit is a main clause plus any subordinate clauses (Hunt 1965), mean length of clause, and mean length of error-free T-unit; two measures of accuracy, i.e. error-free T-units per T-unit, and errors per T-unit; two measures of grammatical complexity, i.e. clauses per T-unit, and dependent clauses per clause; and two measures of lexical complexity, i.e. total number of word types divided by the square root of two times of total number of word tokens, and total number of sophisticated word types divided by total number of word types.

3. How can we use a corpus to find out more about first language development?

In this section, we discuss several ways in which a corpus of child language development data may be used to find out more about first language development. Some of these will be illustrated using the following corpora and corpus analysis software: the Child Language Data Exchange System (CHILDES) database, the Computerized Language Analysis (CLAN) program (MacWhinney 2000), and Computerized Profiling (Long *et al.* 2008). We briefly introduce each of these first.

The CHILDES database contains transcripts and media data collected from conversations between young children of different ages and their parents, playmates and caretakers. These data are contributed by researchers from many different countries, following the same data collection and transcription standards. Each file in the database contains a transcript of a conversation and includes a header that encodes information about the target child or children (e.g. age, native language, whether the child is normal in terms of language development, etc.), other participants, the location and situation of the conversation, the activities that are going on during the conversation, and the researchers and coders collecting and transcribing the data. The conversation is transcribed in a one-utterance-per-line format, with the producer of each utterance clearly marked in a prefix. Each utterance is followed by another line that consists of a morphological analysis of the utterance. Any physical actions accompanying the utterance are also provided in a separate line. The CLAN program is a collection of computational tools designed to automatically analyse data transcribed in the CHILDES format. Some of the automatic analyses that the program can run on one or more files in the CHILDES database include word frequency, type/token ratio, a measure of vocabulary diversity called D (Durán *et al.* 2004), mean length of turn, mean length of utterance, DSS score, among others.

Computerized Profiling is a set of programs designed to analyse both written language samples and phonetically transcribed spoken language samples. Linguistic analysis at a range of different levels can be performed, including simple corpus statistics, semantics, grammar, phonology, pragmatics and narratives. For example, at the grammar level, the following four procedures can be run: IPSyn, DSS, Black English Sentence Scoring (BESS) (Nelson 1998), which is an adaptation of DSS for use with speakers of African American Vernacular English, and the Language Assessment, Remediation, and Screening Procedure (LARSP) (Crystal *et al.* 1989), a system for profiling the syntactic and discourse development of children that is related to both age and stage.

First of all, a corpus can be used to describe the characteristics of language produced by children in different age groups or different stages of development. Children may exhibit a considerable amount of variability in terms of language development. However, it is useful to understand the average capability as well as the range of capabilities exhibited by children within the same age group. Researchers generally agree that there are certain milestones in child language development, or approximate ages at which specific language capabilities usually emerge or mature. For example, at approximately twelve months of age, words start to emerge; at approximately twenty-four months of age, children possess more than fifty vocabulary items and begin to spontaneously join these items into self-created two-word phrases; and at approximately thirty months of age, children produce utterances with at least two words, and many with three or even five words (Lenneberg 1967). A large corpus consisting of language samples produced by children of different age groups can be used to complement or confirm naturalistic observation for establishing or revisiting such milestones. The CHILDES database constitutes a good example of such a corpus. Given a set of data that consists of transcripts of conversations involving target children in a particular age group, e.g. eighteen months, it is fairly straightforward to use CLAN to find out the average as well as the range of vocabulary size, mean length of turn, mean length of utterance, lexical diversity, DSS score, etc., exhibited by all the children in the group.

Second, a corpus can be used to investigate the sequence or order in which children acquire different aspects of the grammar of their native language as well as to track the development of individual children over time. This type of investigation necessitates a corpus of longitudinal data, i.e. data collected from the same child or group of children over an extended period of time, e.g. one to five years. One example of this type of research is Ramer (1976), who conducted a longitudinal study to investigate the developmental sequence of syntactic acquisition in seven children. Specifically, she aimed to find out whether there is 'a universal sequence of emergence of grammatical relations leading up to the production of S + V + O constructions' (p. 144). She analysed her corpus data using a hypothesised simplicity–complexity dimension based on the number of grammatical relations produced and their expansions. She reported that the sequence of acquisition specified in the hypothesised dimension was observed in the data from all seven children.

Third, a corpus can be used to assess the validity and adequacy of the various metrics proposed for measuring child language development. This is an important enterprise as such measures are often used for evaluating the level of language development of children with developmental delays or disorders. One of the ways to approach this problem is closely related to the descriptive and longitudinal research discussed above. Since these measures were proposed to measure language development, many of them were based on observation of child language acquisition. Given a particular measure, it is sensible to evaluate whether it reflects the development sequence or significantly differentiates the developmental levels of children in different age groups. A second way to approach this problem is to examine whether a proposed measure significantly differentiates between the developmental levels of children with and without developmental disorders within the same age group. A good example of this line of research is Hewitt *et al.* (2005). They compared scores of kindergarten children with a mean age of six years with and without specific language impairment (SLI) on three commonly used measures, i.e. MLU in morphemes, IPSyn, and NDWs. They found that children with SLI showed significantly lower mean scores for all of the three measures, except for some subtests of the IPSyn. In relation to this line of research, a corpus can also be used to provide normative information for valid and adequate measures. To improve the feasibility of applying these measures in practical situations and to enable researchers and clinicians to make sense of the analytical results using these measures, it is necessary to have normative information for different age groups for benchmarking purposes. The CHILDES database could again be used for providing such normative information.

Finally, a corpus can also be used to gain in-depth understanding of language development disorders. Through comprehensive contrastive analyses, it is possible to qualitatively and quantitatively describe the developmental differences between children with and without language disorders, e.g. in terms of vocabulary size and range of syntactic structures. In addition, longitudinal data can also be used to investigate the effect of a particular therapeutic intervention. Early interventions play a critical role in optimising the developmental trajectory of children with language disorders during the best window of opportunity (Pence and Justice 2008). By analysing language samples produced before and after a particular intervention, it is possible to evaluate whether targeted changes have systematically occurred in a statistically significant way.

4. How can we use a corpus to find out more about second language development?

In this section, we discuss a number of ways that a corpus of learner language can be used to find out more about second language development. The International Corpus of Learner English (ICLE) (Granger *et al.* 2009) constitutes an excellent example of such a corpus. The ICLE corpus consists of sixteen subcorpora, each of which contains 200,000 words of academic essays, mostly argumentative, by intermediate to advanced learners of English, mostly university students, representing a different mother tongue background. The texts across the subcorpora are similar in terms of mode (written), genre (academic essay), field (general) and length (500 to 1,000 words). The following learner variables are recorded: age, learning context, proficiency level, gender, mother tongue, region, knowledge of other foreign languages and L2 exposure. As is discussed below, many of these variables may affect the learner's L2 development.

Various corpus processing tools can be used to analyse learner corpora in the different ways to be discussed below. The Graphic Online Language Diagnostic (GOLD) system that is being developed at the Center for Advanced Language Proficiency Education and Research (CALPER) at the Pennsylvania State University is especially designed for tracking learner development as it is happening. The system allows the users to compile, upload and update their own learner corpora, to share corpora with each other, and to analyse any subset of data defined by the value or values of one or more variables (e.g. the learner's gender, native language, programme level, standardised test score, L2 exposure, etc.) within one corpus or across multiple corpora. Users who are experienced with XML may compile a corpus by creating their own XML file following the required format, and those who are not may use the guided XML creation interface in the system. Users may choose to make their own corpora accessible to themselves only, but they may also give selected or all other users the right to view or modify their corpora. The system is able to perform detailed frequency analysis, lexical analysis and concordance and collocation analysis. Provided that detailed metadata information, i.e. information about the students and the language samples, is encoded in the corpora, the system allows one to easily compare different subsets of data from one or more corpora in various different ways. For example, one may compare data from the same learner or group of learners over time to track their language development, or one may compare data from different groups of learners exposed to different instruction to examine the effect of instruction on the learner's development. This functionality makes GOLD an especially useful interface for analysing learner corpora in second language development research.

The first way a corpus can be used to reveal second language development is as a database for describing the characteristics of the interlanguage of learners at known proficiency levels. To this end, it is necessary to have a learner corpus that encodes information about the learner's proficiency level. Proficiency level can be conceptualised in a number of different ways, e.g. classroom grades, holistic ratings, programme levels, school levels and standardised test scores, among others (Wolfe-Quintero *et al.* 1998). One may choose to focus on a particular aspect of the interlanguage, for example the degree to which informal, colloquial patterns or styles are used in formal, written language. One may also attempt to provide a comprehensive description of the lexico-grammatical system of the interlanguage.

This type of descriptive study can benefit both from error analysis and from contrastive analysis of learner data and native speaker data. To conduct an error analysis, it is necessary to first design an error annotation scheme, which should be consistently followed in identifying and annotating errors in learner text. A good example of an error annotation scheme can be found in Granger (2003), which assigns each error first to one of the following nine major domains: form, morphology, grammar, lexis, syntax, register, style, punctuation and typo, and then to a specific category within the domain. For example, the syntax domain consists of the following four categories: word order, word missing, word redundant and cohesion. Each domain and category is labelled by a unique tag, e.g. < X > for the syntax domain and < ORD > for the word order category. An error-annotated learner corpus enables one to easily identify the common errors that learners at a given proficiency level tend to make.

A contrastive study of learner data and native speaker data helps us to look at the characteristics of the interlanguage from a different perspective, in particular, how it converges to or deviates from native speaker usage. For example, one may assess whether learners tend to overuse or underuse certain words, phrases, collocations, grammatical constructions, speech acts, etc., relative to native speakers (Granger 1998). It is important, however, to ensure that the learner data and the native speaker data are of comparable nature in terms of mode, genre and field, etc. One excellent resource for this type of contrastive study is the Michigan Corpus of Academic Spoken English (MICASE). This corpus is a collection of transcripts of academic speech events recorded at the University of Michigan. The online interface allows one to search these transcripts and specify desired speaker attributes and transcript attributes. Speaker attributes include academic position or role of the speaker (e.g. junior undergraduate, senior undergraduate, etc.), native speaker status (e.g. non-native speaker, native speaker of American English, native speaker of British English, etc.) and first language. Transcript attributes include speech event type (e.g. advising session, dissertation defence, etc.), academic division (e.g. humanities and arts, social sciences and education, etc.), academic discipline (e.g. American culture, business administration, etc.), participant level (e.g. junior undergraduates, senior graduate students, etc.), and interactivity rating (e.g. highly interactive, highly monologic, etc.). The structure of the corpus and the functions of the online search interface make it possible for one to conduct a contrastive analysis of comparable non-native and native speaker data.

Second, a corpus can be employed in developmental sequence studies to examine the order in which morphosyntactic structures of the target language are acquired. This generally necessitates the analysis of learner errors and performance using longitudinal data. For example, studies of the order of morpheme acquisition or the stages involved in the development of certain grammatical structures, e.g. relative clause or negation, may examine the frequency and accuracy at which learners use different morphemes or different realisations of the target grammatical structure at different time points during the developmental process.

Third, a corpus may be used in developmental index studies to identify objective measures of accuracy, fluency and complexity that can be used to index levels of second language development or the learner's overall language proficiency. As summarised in Wolfe-Quintero *et al.* (1998), a number of cross-sectional studies have investigated the differences in syntactic complexity of second language writing between different proficiency levels. However, there is substantial variability among these studies in terms of choice and definition of measures, writing task used, sample size, corpus length, timing condition, etc. This variability makes it challenging to compare the results reported in different studies. To eliminate such inconsistency and variability, it is desirable to evaluate the full set of measures that have been in use in developmental index studies using one large corpus of learner data. Lu (2011) constitutes an effort in this direction. A computational tool was designed to automatically compute the syntactic complexity of college-level ESL writing samples using fourteen different measures, including, e.g. mean length of clause, number of complex T-units per T-unit, number of complex nominals per T-unit, etc. This tool was then used to analyse large-scale ESL data from the Written English Corpus of Chinese Learners (WECCL) (Wen *et al.* 2005). The corpus is a collection of over 3,000 essays written by English majors in nine different colleges in China. Each essay in the corpus is annotated with a header that includes the following information: mode (written or spoken), genre (argumentation, narration or exposition), school level (first, second, third or fourth year in college), year of admission (2000, 2001, 2002 or 2003), timing condition (timed with a forty-minute limit or untimed), institution (a two- to four-letter code), and length (number of words in the essay). Students in the same school level within the same institution wrote on the same topics, but topics varied from institution to institution. Given the information that is available in the corpus, proficiency level is conceptualised using school level. Through the analysis, this study provided useful insights on how different syntactic complexity measures perform as indices of college-level ESL writers' language development, how they relate to each other, and how their performances are affected by external factors.

Fourth, a corpus can also be used to examine the contributions of knowledge of the first language as well as the effect of L1 transfer. One the one hand, knowledge of the first language may prove helpful in learning certain aspects of the L2, and learners with different L1 background may show strengths in learning different aspects of the L2. On the other hand, the intrusion of L1 may result in difficulty in acquiring certain lexico-grammatical aspects of the L2 and prevalence of certain forms or grammatical patterns that deviate from the target language in the interlanguage. Consequently, the interlanguages of learners at the same proficiency level but with different L1 background may demonstrate some significantly different characteristics. A contrastive study of such interlanguages may provide evidence of L1 influence, either positive or negative, on learner output. The ICLE corpus constitutes an excellent source of data for this type of research, as students with diverse L1 background are represented. A contrastive study of a learner's L1 and interlanguage will provide further evidence on the L1 influence.

Finally, a corpus may be used to examine the role of instruction or the effect of a particular pedagogical intervention on language development. For example, by examining corpus data of different groups of learners at the same school level or programme level that are exposed to different types of instruction method, material or linguistic environment, we may better understand whether differences in instruction result in differences in L2 development. In addition, by comparing the learner's production prior to and after a period of targeted pedagogical intervention, we may assess whether the intervention is effective in helping the learner acquire particular aspects of the L2.

5. Looking to the future

As a field, corpus-based language development research will benefit tremendously from the following future developments. First, language samples produced by children and second language learners often contain many errors and as such present a challenge to natural language processing (NLP) technology, especially when it comes to measures that involve syntactic, semantic and discourse analysis. Therefore, continued enhancement of existing NLP technology and development of robust new NLP technology will facilitate more accurate and reliable automatic analysis of language samples using more diversified measures. A second avenue for future development in the field lies in the systematic collection and sharing of large-scale child and second language development data that encodes richer information about the children or learners producing the data. For child language development research, large-scale longitudinal data and data of children with language disorders are particularly valuable. For second language development research, systematical annotation of the learner's proficiency level using as many conceptualisations as possible will prove especially useful to second language development researchers. These include school levels, programme levels, standardised test scores, holistic ratings, classroom grades, etc. Large-scale data with richer information will make it easier to draw more reliable conclusions for many of the types of research discussed above. Finally, analysis of second language development data will benefit from the development of consistent and standardised error annotation standards as well as improved automatic error detection techniques. Second language development researchers have often devised their own annotation schemes for error analysis, which makes comparison and sharing of research results problematic. The field in general will benefit from a more consistent annotation scheme. There has also been an increasing stream of research in automatic error detection and correction (Heift and Schulze 2003). The maturity of such techniques will facilitate automatic error analysis of large-scale second language development data and enable researchers to gain more reliable insights into second language use.

Disclaimer

The contents of this publication were developed under a grant from the US Department of Education (CFDA 84.229, P229A020010) to the Center for Advanced Language Proficiency Education and Research at the Pennsylvania State University. However, the contents do not necessarily represent the policy of the Department of Education, and one should not assume endorsement by the Federal Government.

Further reading

Granger, S., Dagneaux, E., Meunier, F. and Paquot, M. (2009) *International Corpus of Learner English. Version 2.* Louvain-la-Neuve: Presses Universitaires de Louvain. (This describes the design and structure of the International Corpus of Learner English and discusses how it may be used and analysed in corpus-based second language research.)

MacWhinney, B. (2000) *The CHILDES Project: Tools for Analyzing Talk*, third edition. Mahwah, NJ: Lawrence Erlbaum Associates. (This provides hands-on instruction on how to transcribe naturalistic child language development data following the CHILDES format and automatically analyse such data using CLAN. Readers are introduced to a set of computational tools designed to improve the readability of transcripts, to automate the data analysis process, and to facilitate the sharing of transcribed data.)

Pence, L. K. and Justice, L. M. (2008) *Language Development from Theory to Practice.* Upper Saddle River, NJ: Pearson. (This provides an extremely accessible introduction to the theory and practice of child language development. The material presented in the book is also highly relevant to clinical, educational and research settings.)

VanPatten, B. and Williams, J. (eds) (2007) *Theories in Second Language Acquisition: An Introduction.* Mahwah, NJ: Lawrence Erlbaum Associates. (This is a collection of papers that present a comprehensive introduction to early and contemporary theories in second language acquisition. It provides an excellent overview of each of these compelling theories.)

References

Brown, R. (1973) *A First Language.* Cambridge, MA: Harvard University Press.

Crystal, D., Fletcher, P. and Garman, M. (1989) *Grammatical Analysis of Language Disability*, second edition. London: Cole & Whurr.

DeKeyser, R. (2007) 'Skill Acquisition Theory', in B. VanPatten and J. Williams (eds) *Theories in Second Language Acquisition: An Introduction.* Mahwah, NJ: Lawrence Erlbaum Associates, pp. 97–114.

Durán, P., Malvern, D., Richards, B. and Chipere, N. (2004) 'Developmental Trends in Lexical Diversity', *Applied Linguistics* 25(2): 220–42.

Granger, S. (ed.) (1998) *Learner English on Computer.* Austin, TX: Addison Wesley Longman.

——(2003) 'Error-tagged Learner Corpora and CALL: A Promising Synergy', *CALICO Journal* 20(3): 465–80.

Granger, S., Dagneaux, E., Meunier, F. and Paquot, M. (2009) *International Corpus of Learner English. Version 2.* Louvain-la-Neuve: Presses Universitaires de Louvain.

Heift, T. and Schulze, M. (2003) 'Error Diagnosis and Error Correction', *CALICO Journal* 20(3): 433–46.

Hewitt, L. E., Scheffner, H. C., Yont, K. M. and Tomblin, J. B. (2005) 'Language Sampling for Kindergarten Children with and without SLI: Mean Length of Utterance, IPSYN, and NDW', *Journal of Communication Disorders* 38(3): 197–213.

Hunt, K. W. (1965) *Grammatical Structures Written at Three Grade Levels* (Research Report No. 3). Champaign, IL: National Council of Teachers of English.

Lantolf, J. P. and Thorne, S. L. (2007) 'Sociocultural Theory and Second Language Learning', in B. VanPatten and J. Williams (eds) *Theories in Second Language Acquisition: An Introduction*. Mahwah, NJ: Lawrence Erlbaum Associates, pp. 201–24.

Lee, L. (1974) *Developmental Sentence Analysis*. Evanston, IL: Northwestern University Press.

Lenneberg, E. H. (1967) *Biological Foundations of Language*. New York: John Wiley.

Long, S. H., Fey, M. E. and Channell, R. W. (2008) *Computerized Profiling (Version 9.7.0)*. Cleveland, OH: Case Western Reserve University.

Lu, X. (2011) 'A Corpus-based Evaluation of Syntactic Complexity Measures as Indices of College-level ESL Writers' Language Proficiency', *TESOL Quarterly* 45(1): 36–42.

MacWhinney, B. (2000) *The CHILDES Project: Tools for Analyzing Talk*, third edition. Mahwah, NJ: Lawrence Erlbaum Associates.

Nelson, N. W. (1998) *Childhood Language Disorders in Context: Infancy Through Adolescence*, second edition. Boston, MA: Allyn & Bacon.

Ortega, L. (2007) 'Second Language Learning Explained? SLA across Nine Contemporary Theories', in B. VanPatten and J. Williams (eds) *Theories in Second Language Acquisition: An Introduction*. Mahwah, NJ: Lawrence Erlbaum Associates, pp. 225–50.

Pence, L. K. and Justice, L. M. (2008) *Language Development from Theory to Practice*. Upper Saddle River, NJ: Pearson.

Ramer, A. L. H. (1976) 'The Development of Syntactic Complexity', *Journal of Psycholinguistic Research* 6(2): 145–61.

Russell, J. (2004) *What is Language Development? Rationalist, Empiricist, and Pragmatist Approaches to the Acquisition of Syntax*. Oxford: Oxford University Press.

Scarborough, H. S. (1990) 'Index of Productive Syntax', *Applied Psycholinguistics* 11(1): 1–22.

VanPatten, B. and Williams, J. (eds) (2007) *Theories in Second Language Acquisition: An Introduction*. Mahwah, NJ: Lawrence Erlbaum Associates.

Wen, Q., Wang, L. and Liang, M. (2005) *Spoken and Written English Corpus of Chinese Learners*. Beijing: Foreign Language Teaching and Research Press.

White, L. (2007) 'Linguistic Theory, Universal Grammar, and Second Language Acquisition', in B. VanPatten and J. Williams (eds) *Theories in Second Language Acquisition: An Introduction*. Mahwah, NJ: Lawrence Erlbaum Associates, pp. 37–56.

Wolfe-Quintero, K., Inagaki, S. and Kim, H.-Y. (1998) *Second Language Development in Writing: Measures of Fluency, Accuracy, and Complexity* (Technical Report No. 17). Honolulu, HI: University of Hawai'i, Second Language Teaching and Curriculum Center.

Section IV

Using a corpus for language research

What can a corpus tell us about language?

15

What can a corpus tell us about lexis?

Rosamund Moon

1. Lexis and the lexicon

For corpus linguists, it is difficult to see how anyone can learn much about lexis *without* using a corpus, or could fail to learn something from each new corpus search. Lexis can be researched simply through exploring individual lexical items and their behaviour, or by using corpus data to examine the lexicon as a whole or to test lexical theory. This chapter gives an introductory overview of some key aspects of English lexis, all of which can be straightforwardly investigated with corpora. Data is drawn from the 450-million-word Bank of English corpus (BoE), created by COBUILD at the University of Birmingham (71 per cent British English, 21 per cent North American, 8 per cent Australian; 86 per cent written, 14 per cent transcribed spoken data).

The general lexicon

What do corpora tell us about the English lexicon? This kind of information is best obtained from a large reference corpus (ideally, at least fifty million words), since smaller and specialist corpora are likely to show skewings, with too few examples of rarer words. However, the obvious question – how many words are there in English? – is unanswerable, even with very large corpora. All corpora do is reveal which words are used in their constituent texts and how frequent they are.

A more useful question is how many words comprise the main vocabulary of a language, its central lexicon. Here word frequency lists provide a starting point, demonstrating that a comparatively small set of words accounts for a large proportion of text. Table 15.1 shows the cumulative proportions of BoE comprised by the *N* most frequent lemmas (base forms and inflections), and their approximate frequencies per million words of corpus text. Beyond this is a long tail of infrequent items, including hapaxes (words occurring once), of which many in BoE are names, numbers or errors.

Unsurprisingly, most very high frequency items are grammatical words: BoE's top ten lemmas are *the*, *be*, *of*, *and*, *a*, *in*, *to* (infinitive particle), *have*, *to* (preposition) and *it*. It is usually the lexical words, though, which seem more interesting: BoE's top 100 includes the noun lemmas *year*, *time*, *person/people*, *day*, *man*, *way*, verbs *say*, *go*, *make*, *get*, *take*,

Table 15.1 Distribution of lemmas in BoE

Number of items	*Percent age of BoE*	*Approximate rate of occurrence*
top 10	23.5	8,000+ occurrences per million
top 100	44.9	1,000+ per million
top 1,000	68.5	100+ per million
top 10,000	88.9	5+ per million
top 25,000	92.5	1+ per million
top 100,000	94.5	1+ per 20 million

know, see, come, think, give and adjectives *new, good*. These are all fairly general words, many associated with semi-grammatical functions – for example, deictic uses of *year(s)*, causative and phrasal uses of *make*:

```
rule rather than the exception. Last year 44 per cent of secretaries placed by
a mere flight of fancy just a few years ago, but not any more.
government collapsed earlier this year. As an aside, the White House
turn negative. < p > Over the past five years Central London has seen the UK's
Hadjout. < o > Beside her slept her two-year-old daughter, Belle, the child's
```

```
athletics. Few athletes, if any, have made a greater contribution to the
details of all staff which will be made available to a range of companies
make ILT membership worthless, and making entry so hard and time-consuming
than curiosity. Her husband's motives made no difference to the legal act which
who are able to participate in trials make up only 5 per cent of the total.
```

This kind of data is replicated in other reference corpora, though exact rank orderings of words and rates of occurrence vary according to corpus composition and lemmatisation policies. The effect of composition is evident when we consider distribution: even high frequency words may have quite different frequencies in different types of text. See Hunston (2002: 3ff) for discussion of word frequency; also O'Keeffe *et al.* (2007: 31ff) with respect to applied linguistics. Leech *et al.* (2001) list frequencies in the British National Corpus; Biber *et al.* (1999) distributions of words within grammatical categories across discourse types.

Lemmatised frequencies are useful, but equally important are the relative frequencies of individual inflections and what these suggest about usage. While it is unsurprising that in BoE *peas* is twice as frequent as *pea*, it seems more surprising that *fact* is eight times as frequent as *facts*, though corpus data quickly shows why *fact* is so common:

```
cannot be made to grow elsewhere; in fact Devonshire gardens, full as they are
probably fewer would even care. The fact is, we meet so many new people all
any drug. The judge said: The mere fact that a customer picks up a bottle of
a hiding. There was no denying the fact that players of the calibre of Brian
and the insecurities, that are, in fact, the complex characteristics of
```

See Sinclair (1991: 37–79); Stubbs (2001: 27ff); Hunston (2002: 60–62) for discussion of forms, frequency and usage.

Word formation

General corpora also provide information about derivation and compounding, helping establish which potential words are actually institutionalised. In BoE, for example, principal derivatives from the high-frequency root *colour/color* include *colourful, colourless, discolour, colourant, colourist, colourise, colouration, uncoloured*…; also *colourable, colourism, colouristic, recolour*, etc. Formations such as *colo(u)rous, miscolour* are morphologically possible, but not found. Similarly with words formed with specific morphemes, for example the prefix *hyper-*: among the most frequent in BoE are *hypertension, hyperactive, hyperinflation, hypermarket, hypertext, hyperventilate, hypersensitive*. However, rare or hapax items often reveal more about creative processes of word formation, with hyphenated forms especially interesting: thus marginal items such as *hyper-accurate, hyper-addictive, hyper-animated, hyper-assertive, hyper-babbling, hyper-blues*…may suggest patterns or motivations for coinage. As for compounding, corpora show which formations recur and have specific meanings: for example, BoE has *watercolour, colourway, colour-blind, colour-fast, colour-washed, colour-coded, hair colour* (dye), adjectivals *full-colour, two/four-colour* (of printing), and so on.

2. Phraseology and phrases

It is much more interesting, of course, to look at words in their corpus contexts than in isolation. Here the interdependence of words becomes most obvious, showing how the phraseological patternings of words are critically important in relation to meaning as well as usage. A consistent finding in corpus studies has been the extent to which words occur as parts of phraseologies, whether collocational, structural, or both: for discussion, see Sinclair (1987; 2004: 24–48); Stubbs (2001: 80ff); O'Keeffe *et al.* (2007: 14–15, 59ff, 100ff). Phraseology is also covered in other chapters in this handbook (see chapters by Greaves and Warren and by Hunston), but it is too important with respect to lexis not to discuss here too.

Collocation and patterning

What can we learn about a word from looking at its collocates, the words with which it co-occurs? We might expect these to be least interesting in the case of items with specific meanings, for example a natural-kind entity like *aphid*:

be found on the roots. Lettuce root aphid can overwinter on lettuce roots,
by spraying under the leaves with the aphid-specific Rapid insecticide. < p > < c >
are produced by this insect. This aphid pest attacks many plants in the
livefood one can supply, since aphids, caterpillars and the like will
The larvae of this tiny insect eats aphids, thus reducing the number that can
insects like red spider, thrips and aphids. At Brisbane Botanic Gardens, Mt

(Here and elsewhere, concordances are randomised BoE samples.) Co-texts show something about the semantics of *aphid*: even without knowing what aphids are, we deduce that they are insects or insect-like, small, parasitic on plants, and preyed on by other insects. This is reinforced in listings of *aphid*'s significant collocates: *control, spider, insects, species, mealybugs, plants, thrips, pests, caterpillars, larvae, attack* …

For many words, collocational and syntagmatic patterns are more noticeable, as even a few lines for the less concrete noun *refuge* show:

```
   mythologised home and family as a refuge from a threatening world of change
    referred to the YMCA library as a refuge for many half-homeless wanderers
    Our consciences had been our last refuge. Their sanctity was destroyed.' < p >
  relief prior to reaching a place of refuge. In many cases religious persecution
Park. < p > Losure: The river provides refuge for migrating ducks, geese and
       for him to leave Boston to seek refuge in England, Anne and he were forced
   of two policewomen who had sought refuge in a nearby doorway. Part of the car
       and he had regressed and taken refuge in amnesia as a defense against the
  more than 200 militiamen have taken refuge in a local monastery and sent the
            after more Cubans had taken refuge in the Spanish Embassy during the
```

Phraseological patterns include *seek/take refuge, refuge in/for/from, last refuge, place of refuge*; the first line contains a recurrent collocation with *world*, with *world* representing a difficult, frightening or uncongenial situation.

Corpus data for verbs demonstrates recurrent or mandatory grammatical structures, typical subject and object realisations, and so on. Verbs of motion are typically followed by adverbials or prepositional phrases of direction or manner, even when metaphorical:

```
      against the blood-red sky; a man walking along the curving road; lights
   order. They left the others. As they walked, at first in silence, Serena tried
      remaining and isn't considering walking away before or after that deal
protect identities. Why would a mother walk out and leave her children in the
       in the world. The first person to walk to both the North Pole and the
figure with an aristocratic demeanour, walked with the help of a cane. His
```

With other verbs, grammatical structure and kinds of collocate seem more restricted. For example, *comply* is typically preceded by something indicating coercion, necessity, willingness, etc. (*incentive, must, force, fail(ure), hesitate*), and/or is followed by *with*, itself typically followed by a noun phrase indicating a constraint (*agreement, decision, law, obligation* …). The specific meaning of *comply* is inseparable from such a pattern:

```
       which is a powerful incentive to comply. Ms Coward might have mentioned the
     recited. President Milosevic must comply in full with the agreements he made
   assault weapons and ammunition. To comply, owners must either remove them
           as external strictures, to be complied with or rebelled against but not
surprising that Franco hesitated to comply with this condition until dwindling
1998 be increased by $246 million to comply with the decision by the New Jersey
        that would force signatories to comply with nuclear safety standards. The
        that de Klerk has also failed to comply with UN resolutions demanding the
     or changed their name. Failure to comply with the new law is punishable by a
                 bout, unless and until he complies with his obligation to fight
```

See Sinclair (1987), Partington (1996: 15–28 and passim) and Hunston (2002: 39ff, 68ff and passim) for discussion of collocation and patterning: see also chapters by Evison, Hunston, Tribble, Greaves and Warren, this volume.

Fixed expressions and idioms

In many cases, recurrent collocates, especially when syntagmatically fixed, represent some kind of multi-word lexical item. In the following, *of course*, *on course* (*to/for*) and *stay the course* have holistic meanings:

```
         today,' Woods said. This golf course is not easy. Birdies are hard to
        him to drop out of his medical course < /h > < b > By JOJO MOYES < /b > < p >
   swamped by that silly role. And of course often she had to play it while I
      who would have guessed? But, of course, it makes sense.' Then I saw the
 of between 80 and 85%. That does, of course, leave a fairly sizeable margin of
       < p > He doesn't stand a chance of course and neither did Ronald Reagan,
         in some future century? And of course, if we wish to explore our
       < /h > < p > Steffi Graf is still on course to retain her title at the women's
         fixed and invariant during the course of therapy. I cannot even predict
  varieties a year, very few stay the course, despite the fact they are good,'
```

In fact, BoE evidence for *course* is dominated by phrasal uses, particularly *of course*. Similarly, much of the corpus evidence for high-frequency verbs such as *take* and *get* consists of occurrences in phrasal verbs and other fixed expressions, while an important feature of data for nouns such as *hand*, *head* and *heart* is the way in which they are used metonymically and metaphorically, including in idioms.

It is difficult to generalise about multi-word items since the range is wide and behaviour varies greatly. Some individual phrasal verbs and compound nouns are themselves very frequent, as are fixed expressions like *of course*, *as well (as)*, *for example*, *in particular*, *take place*, *take part*, *sort of* … , all with important grammatical or discourse functions. However, corpus studies of idioms, proverbs and other such items suggest that most are infrequent, tending to occur mainly in journalism and fiction. A number of claims have been made in the literature about the essential ambiguity of idioms, or their frozenness and syntactic defectiveness; these claims can be correlated with corpus data. Do literal counterparts to idioms actually occur? (only rarely). Are passivisable idioms actually used in the passive? (in BoE *bury the hatchet* is passive in about 5 per cent of instances, *spill the beans* in fewer than 1 per cent).While many idioms are indeed lexically frozen, many others are unstable. Thus corpus searches need to be flexible and recursive to find all idiom occurrences, including creative exploitations and interruptions: for example, *keep something under one's hat* and … *under one's cap/turban/bonnet*; or *upset the proverbial/political/establishment applecart*. Proverbs too are often shortened or varied: BoE has evidence for canonical *what's sauce for the goose is sauce for the gander*, truncated *what's sauce for the goose*, variants *what is good for the goose (is good for the gander)*, and manipulations (*liberal goose/conservative gander*, etc.). The discourse contributions of such expressions, their evaluations and cohesiveness, become apparent from their corpus contexts:

> I seem to recall that it was Ashdown who … almost upset the whole Alliance apple-cart. He did so by overturning the leadership on a major question of defence policy. Sauce for the Czech goose should not mean arsenic for the Slovak gander.

See Moon (1998) for a corpus-based overview of English fixed expressions and idioms; McCarthy 1998: 129–49; Moon 1998: 260–64, 300–5; and O'Keeffe *et al.* 2007: 80–99) for discussion of idioms in interaction.

3. Meaning

Context and meaning

By forcing us to consider words in context, corpus concordances make us aware of how far the meanings of words are derived from context – even raising the question of whether words have independent meanings at all. This interdependence of meaning and context is clearest in the case of semantically depleted words, such as much-discussed *take*:

court. < subh > Boasts < /subh > It would take a huge investment of police time and
that Whitbread crews are willing to take boats into treacherous waters and
so that I know that I've the time to take erm antibiotics and i+ erm not wait
< p > It would seem that Nine is taking its rival very seriously indeed.
in our work, what will it mean that I take off certain Jewish holy days but
send 2300 more men to the Balkans to take part in a future peacekeeping force.
< p > mcilroy said: David practises taking penalty kicks for half-an-hour
the early 1960s an economic miracle took place in West Germany under the '
would foment a revolution. Well, it took us a long time, but we finally
which was lucky. After two hours they took us to our hotel and made us collect

Trying to abstract an essential meaning seems pointless: each use needs a different explanation of meaning or paraphrase. There are some fixed expressions (*take part, take place, take something seriously*); others are simply recurrent usages, and a proper sample would provide many more. What *is* the commonality of meaning, the meaning of 'take-ness'? Another case is the noun *heed*:

their own vendettas with little heed to a common tactical plan. Air cover
and male chauvinism to give much heed to claims that the equal rights
all-American halls of fame to pay any heed to what the Olympic Museum has done
also starting to run. Anna paid no heed but kept on going, in seconds
the only contributor to pay serious heed to the four directions, so crucial
Edwina Currie should have taken heed. It was Mr Winterton who said, the
with millions of women taking heed of such advice. Reading the book I
card but after he failed to take heed of the warning, they were forced to
Businesses might need to take heed of pressure groups if the latter
pursuing its rational ends without heed of the wider consequences. Darwin

We might feel that *heed* means 'attention, notice', but corpus evidence shows that it normally occurs in a restricted range of structures, including the curiously synonymous *pay/give/take heed*. If its usage is so restricted, how versatile can its meaning really be? *Can* meaning be separated from phraseology? We can pursue this point with the adjective *heinous*, which a dictionary might gloss as 'odious, wicked':

apparently sensible people consider heinous. < p > A concept of obscenity
university student. This was a most heinous crime, savage and brutal in
by the rope were guilty of such heinous crimes. Many innocents had already
blacks. < p > While offering their own heinous schemes for raising Americans #

```
Certain crimes, it said, were so heinous that the normal immunities granted
that their behaviour is criminal. Heinous. Unjust. Unfair. Inequitable.' Her
```

Heinous indicates unacceptability, but part of its meaning is supplied through collocation with *crime* and related words. While *take* and *heinous* represent very different kinds of word in terms of meaning, a corpus perspective suggests that both reflect the way in which meaning is a construction of context, not intrinsic to the word. It might be objected that there are plenty of other words in the lexicon which are semantically full, have specific denotations and are not collocationally restricted: words like *new*, *walk*, *year* or *aphid*, *peas*, *hypertension*. Any number of words could be substituted in the following concordances, changing meanings, but still maintaining syntactic and collocational well-formedness:

```
The larvae of this tiny insect eats aphids, thus reducing the number that can
medication they had received for hypertension. The fish oil supplement used
publishers are convinced that the new book is guaranteed to be a best-seller
and spices, then add the tomatoes and peas. Simmer until cooked - about 15-20
against the blood-red sky; a man walking along the curving road; lights
turn negative. < p > Over the past five years Central London has seen the UK's
```

What can corpora tell us about the meanings of such words? One response is that corpora show us typical contexts in which we encounter a word – even if we first acquire them through ostension (*walking*, *peas*, *aphids*) – and that part of our knowledge of a word relates to its associations with other words: cf. Firth's comment 'One of the meanings of *night* is its collocability with *dark*, and of *dark*, of course, collocation with *night*' (1957: 196).

Polysemy

Another aspect of word meaning to explore is polysemy: how many different senses or uses words have, and how these are distinguished in context. Collocates discriminate by indicating topic and semantic field, with different senses often associated with different phraseological patterns and structures. The noun *race* is relatively straightforward:

```
The reigning champ has won 2,641 races - three behind Arthur Stephenson.
years to promote racial equality. Are race relations getting worse? Have your
< p > Mr. ERROT: Every religion, every race, every profession, every age group
colored by the signifiers of gender, race, class, and culture that obtain and
nuclear war in which the entire human race was wiped out except for the
the title to be decided in the last race was probably the best thing as it
the personalities in the presidential race: the current president, Joaquin
with victory in the Five Valleys road race at Port Talbot, South Wales, on
overall lead in the Paris-Nice stage race yesterday, despite an attack on his
be $41 better off by not going to the races each Saturday and going to the
```

The primary sense distinction between 'competitive activity' and 'ethnic grouping' is clear, reinforced by words such as *champ*, *won*, *title*, *victory* on the one hand, *relations*, *religion*, *gender*, *human* on the other. Since *race* derives from two distinct roots, it is homonymic rather than polysemous; a more synchronic view, consistent with corpus approaches, is to see this in terms of a major semantic discontinuity and lack of collocational overlap.

See also has multiple senses, with a primary distinction between vision and comprehension. In context, these are distinguished through the nature of what is seen – physical objects (bodies, trees, a horse, text) or entertainment, and ideas (contrast, one's status, situations):

the rest of the family. < M01 > Yes. I see. And where did you settle in Britain
had lunch at Grill & C. then went to see Billy Liar with Albert Finney being
authority in her behaviors (that is, saw herself as having no real' power)
12 The contrast can be clearly seen in the worlds of employers and class
gauging local opinion. I don't see it as a national forum,' he says.
because it is now clear for all to see that he leads two Conservative
described what he saw. ANATOL LIEVEN: I saw the bodies of four Lithuanian
She glanced out of the window and saw long, thin trees standing in lines
supernatural powers - such as seeing through solid objects - by
onto the same chip as the microarrays (see Water gets weird', *New Scientist*,

Adjective senses can be distinguished through types of noun collocate, the entity being described. For *colourful*, we might group together physical objects and places (cloth, gardens); people and their lives, sometimes with an implication of notoriety; and then more abstract things (lively descriptions, mixes of culture):

The centre of Harare is at its most colourful at this time of year: the avenues
made of transparent plastic with colourful balls inside. The base has
how to manage a football team. The colourful businessman, a close pal of Serb
back legs chained and covered in colourful cloth full of pattern and finery,
just fade away. < p > Mr Norris's colourful description of what a Clarke
although the settings are colourful enough. The mix of images and
his address by noting Fairfax's colourful history, saying this had included
show of Ericas make the garden so colourful. I have therefore arranged that
the imagination wandering. < p > The colourful mix of cultures adds a further
speculation and finance. The colourful yet elusive baron, aged 72 this

One analyst might say that these senses are substantially the same, a core idea with contextualised metaphorical applications. Another might find further nuances of meaning. There are arguments for and against fine-grainedness of sense distinction: what corpus data contributes is a way of having the argument in the first place. With *take*, an extreme example of a polysemous word, we have already seen that its meanings are tied up with phraseology. It would be impossible to investigate this robustly without a corpus. See Sinclair (2004: 24–48, 131–48) for discussion of meaning, ambiguity and phraseology; see Hunston (2002: 38–66) for further examples and analysis.

Metaphor, connotation and ideology

Figurative senses such as *see* 'understand' and *colourful* 'lively' are institutionalised: corpora also contain large quantities of more creatively figurative language, but it is not always easy to locate. Systematic studies of metaphor or metonymy may start by searching for a specific item, such as a set of verbs of vision/cognition, or a metaphor-rich word like *heart*. The following sample omits literal uses, and includes fixed expressions (*break one's heart, change of heart, take heart*) and more generalised allusion to the heart as source of emotions:

```
To see a little kid just breaks your heart. < p > I tell them how brave their
welcomed Mr Trimble's change of heart', as did Sinn Fein and the
in the group, though Ireland can take heart from their efforts in frustrating
But it was a sight to gladden the hearts of supporters of the English bid.
the highest standard comes from the heart, not a textbook. 7 Innovate or die.
states in his introduction # at the heart of this book's analysis is the
fit as he was when he captured the hearts of all Australians along with his
form of resistance - in the mind, the heart. Outwardly, she would try to comply
Bobb and her record label is a real heart warmer. Her first single, Dreams,
blood was even more overpowering. My heart was beating so fast it felt like
```

The last line is arguably literal, but such uses typically also imply psychological states (*one's hands shake, one's stomach churns* ...).

Connotational meaning seems to depend on intuition and suggestion, but are there traces in corpus data? If we follow Firthian principles of meaning by collocation, then collocates may well provide answers. For example, a word such as *claret* denotes a kind of red wine while connoting a certain lifestyle:

```
Bosses said they now sell more claret and champagne than cheap plonk. The
is renowned predominantly for claret and Sauternes, it also produces
Sainsbury's. Classic medium-ranking claret from the finest recent Bordeaux
in port and Stilton after duck and claret is not the wisest behaviour for a
waiting for me alongside a glass of claret. Sorry,' I said to Jack. I'll now
advising Mr Chairman on what claret to buy in for his cellar. Claret?
```

Its collocates include *bottle, glass, drink*; general adjectives such as *good, old, classic*; wine-related items *burgundy, bordeaux, champagne, port, cru, decanter*; *vintage, fruity, fine, full-bodied*; foods *duck, stilton*. As a set, they seem to point to that intuited claret lifestyle. See Stubbs (1996: 85–6, 106ff) for discussion of connotation and further examples.

The recurrent lexicogrammatical patterning of words such as *refuge, comply, storm* also helps us explore connotation in relation to semantic prosodies (Louw 1993; Stubbs 2001: 198ff and passim; Hunston 2002: 141ff, whose term is 'discourse prosody'). We can start by identifying canonical semantic structures:

(*take*) *refuge from* + UNDESIRABLE SITUATION + *in* + SAFE PLACE
someone (+ MODAL) + *complies with* + OFFICIAL INSTRUCTION

The interesting cases are those which deviate from these patterns, belittling, criticising or creating irony by subverting the canonical evaluation or downtoning a semantic feature:

```
presented by some contributors as a refuge from academic life where there is
and he had regressed and taken refuge in amnesia as a defense against the
to see the outside world, forced to comply with the whims of researchers. Yet
```

Following on from connotation, prosodies and collocation is the use of corpus data to explore ideologically significant items. We might look, for example, at gender issues through *he/she* (cf. discussion of gendered pairings in Section 4) or ethnicity through *race*; or else look at 'keywords' in Raymond Williams' terms (1983). One of Williams' words is *bourgeois*; corpus examples point to something of what it now suggests:

```
novels is a caricature. Not all bourgeois consumers of print read novels;
  between them did much to define bourgeois manhood in the nineteenth
      increasing prosperity, and bourgeois satisfaction, if not complacency.
capitalist economic order and of bourgeois society. Although their recipes
descended, and definitely not nice, bourgeois, unsoulful Ealing), and images of
  of this study reflects the ideas of bourgeois Western culture, in which the
```

This is reinforced in its collocates (*society*, *culture*, *family/families*, *life*, *values*; *revolution*, *ideology*, *democracy*, *liberalism*, *hegemony*, *class*), which in turn suggest discursive associations to be examined. Stubbs (1996: 157–95; 2001: 145–93) has extended discussion of culturally loaded items and keywords; Krishnamurthy (1996) looks at *racial, tribal and ethnic*; Baker (2006) provides many further case studies: see also O'Halloran (this volume).

4. Sets and synonyms

Lexical sets

Words fall into lexical sets, fitting into semantic fields, though these are not always easily identified from corpus data. However, where a corpus/subcorpus is limited to a particular field, especially if technical, we can learn something about the lexis with which that field is discussed. For example, in the BoE subcorpus of business-focused texts, almost 40 per cent of its top 100 words are lexical and topic-specific (*fund(s)*, *shares*, *securities*, *investment*, *company*, *market*, *business*, *income*, *value*, *sales* …). Similarly, collocate listings for words may reveal co-hyponyms: those for *aphid* include a range of insects and other small creatures, often sharing a semantic feature 'parasitic' (*ants*, *blackfly*, *greenfly*, *caterpillars*, *lacewings*, *mealybugs*, *moths*, *slugs*, *snails*, *spiders*, *thrips*, *weevils* …). Another approach to exploring sets is through phraseological frames, looking at what kinds of word occur within a particular slot. For example, the noun slot in the phraseology (QUANTIFIER) + NOUN + *ago* is realised by not just the obvious set of time words (*years*, *months*, *weeks*, *days*, *seasons* …) but also items considered as periods of time (*generations*, *games*, *moons*, *vintages*, *albums* …). Cf. the way that *comply with* (see above) is typically followed by collocates which indicate a constraint: another kind of semantic set.

Synonyms

It is often said that English has no perfect synonyms: that is, words which can be used interchangeably in any context. Corpora make it possible to test this by examining collocation, phraseological structure, genre, variety and frequency. *Asylum* seems to occupy a similar semantic space, 'place of safety', to *refuge* (roughly twice as frequent: see Section 2, 'Collocation and patterning', for concordances):

```
of course, extended to every case. Asylum was never carried to the point of
black economy by illegally employing asylum seekers. < p > There, not too
be reviewed sympathetically'. If asylum is refused to this group, the white
However, although the numbers of asylum seekers coming to the UK had risen
caused by the growing number of asylum-seekers in Calais. Among the
the writer who sought political asylum in Paris earlier this week. Dr
A CHINESE doctor seeking political asylum in the United States said that he
last March after being refused asylum in Italy and France. < subh > Choice
and she has married since seeking asylum. In the meantime she is happy to
of visitor's refusals under the Asylum and Immigration Appeals Act (1993)
```

But even a few lines show differences: *seek** seems to collocate with both, but *take** only with *refuge*; *asylum* is more politicised. Another pairing is *colourless* and *drab*:

```
Mulcahy and starring a rather colourless Alec Baldwin in the title role of
Then the cast seems a trifle colourless. And finally the script does lie
silicate. X-ray analysis of the colourless crystals reveals five oxygen
and Hermann-Otto Solms, a colourless economist. All these hopefuls
on the outside with something colourless? It can be exasperating.' As a
all bleached glare and a strangely colorless ocean. Air temperature is forty-
You've been very kind,' but this colourless understatement made me despair of
to gas can't it? And if the gas is colourless, you could say it disappears, but

scratch. The downtown I remember - drab, Calvinistic, with white men in dark
His eyes roamed anxiously around the drab conference room, and he forced his
for exotic ingredients during the drab days of rationing - you were lucky
housewives in the study led a pretty drab existence. On the average, we found
he walks past it along the rather drab green corridor. But after enjoying
drive home the message of a typically drab memo, chart or graph. Color can
cutting a swathe through the grey, drab ordinariness of contemporary music
a gash of brilliant colour in our drab surroundings, was our school. There,
```

Drab, roughly twice as common as *colourless*, here refers to appearances, experiences and situations; *colourless* means 'lacking pigment, colour' or is applied metaphorically to uninteresting performances and people. While *drab/colourless* (and *dull/dreary/lacklustre*) are only partial synonyms, there are many more problematic pairs like *wide/broad* or *begin/start* where corpora can similarly help disentangle their different usages. See Partington (1996: 29–47) and Stubbs (2001: 35ff, 102ff) for discussion of examples.

Antonyms and opposites

Conventional antonyms can also be explored with corpus data, in particular to establish whether they share ranges of reference and phraseological patterns. Are, for example, morphological counterparts such as *acceptable/unacceptable*, *important/unimportant* and *colourful/colourless* also counterparts in usage? What about *happy* with its two antonyms, *unhappy* and *sad*? A third choice, *not happy*, may need to be considered too:

```
< p > Jones said: He probably wasn't happy because he wasn't in the squad and
make the home happy,' yet she is not happy playing that role. < p > Arlie
```

```
getting on with my life. They weren't happy that I hadn't returned to school. I
      Crossin after he said he was not happy with the environmental impact
      Force. Many of these men are not happy working alongside the American
```

Of other types of oppositeness, one of the most obvious to investigate is gendered pairings, such as *man/woman, boy/girl, husband/wife*, where collocation often shows up gender stereotyping. For example, looking in the BoE books subcorpora at the pattern ADJECTIVE + *husband/wife*, it appears that collocationally a husband is *abusive, unfaithful, wayward, hardworking, drunken*, a wife *good, perfect, battered, pregnant, beautiful*. . .: there are interesting implications ideologically. For studies, see those by Pearce of *man/woman* (2008), Sigley and Holmes of *boy/girl* (2002), Baker of *bachelor/spinster* (2006: 95ff).

5. Lexis in spoken language

This final section looks briefly at lexis in the most distinctive of all discourse subtypes, spoken interaction, here drawing on BoE's twenty-million-word subcorpus of British conversation and local radio broadcasts. One significant feature is its lexicon: smaller and more homogenised, with fewer types, just under 47,000 non-hapaxes. Correspondingly, its top 100 and 1,000 types comprise a larger proportion of the corpus, or to put it another way, are used proportionately more. Lexical items in its top 100 include *mean, sort, thing, want*, all more common than in written English; also discourse markers and phatics *yeah, yes, right, well, okay, er, erm, mm, oh*. Many are strongly patterned phraseologically, all have important pragmatic functions. See McCarthy and Carter (1997) for an overview of spoken lexis; O'Keeffe *et al.* (2007: passim) for extended discussion.

Phraseology

The following, extracted from BoE, shows some of the features of spoken lexis:

> **AA** ... and good shoes ... and ... and buy the things to me that are erm practical they need ... th that ... that something that might need to be in use constantly every day and therefore has to be you know a good thing. Erm and not to buy it on silly frivol you know ... d+ ... don't spend your money on silly frivolities and
> **BB** Mm
> **AA** the things that you don't need. I mean it's okay to do that providing that you've already taken care of all the other needs.

Features include hesitations, repetitions and relexicalisations; the chunked nature of the language is also clear. Among more lexical words, *know* and *mean* occur in phraseologies with discourse functions; others have fairly general meanings (*good, thing/things, need/needs*) or occur in common collocations or phrases (*in use, every day, spend money, take care*). Only *shoes, buy, practical, constantly, silly, frivolities* have fuller meanings or seem more independent.

Predictably, if we compare data drawn from written and spoken subcorpora for a word like *know*, we find phraseological differences. From British broadsheet journalism:

```
   the story first.' But she must have known, as a scandal-peddler herself, how
< /date > It was the stare of a man who knew he was going to get his way. We'd
```

```
cover their tracks these days. I know his wife by sight, though not to
food because, though we think we know how to cook, we do not know how to
33 sites have been identified. Nobody knows how many people were killed in the
as previous Celtic players have been known to do, will now come ready salted.
moor. This painting will become known to the rest of the group as Mike's
not the end of the world', and we knew we really were in trouble. I have
```

and from the spoken subcorpus, where 94 per cent of occurrences are as the base form *know*:

```
models saying well we don't really know < ZGY > < M02 > Yeah. < ZF1 > And < ZF0 >
know. They don't talk actually you know < tc text = laughs > < tc text = pause >
< ZF1 > I do + erm I < ZF0 > I don't know how you would whether you would say
They know the basics of a bike you know how to balance them < M0X > Yeah.
we were < ZF0 > we were chasing you know maybe fighting the Belgians or the
system installed < ZG1 > now < ZG0 > You know one of the things we were talking
say it's a virus 'cos they don't know what else it is. < F03 > Yeah. < F01 >
Yeah that's what you were asking me I knew you had something to get back to er
```

Even in terms of collocates, there can be marked distinctions between speech and writing. If we take a structure such as ADVERB + *happy* to explore the ranges of sub-modifiers used, and compare realisations in BoE generally with those in the spoken subcorpus, there are interesting contrasts. Items such as *very*, *quite*, *perfectly*, *really*, *reasonably* are found in both subcorpora; in BoE overall, further significant collocates include *blissfully*, *deliriously*, *ecstatically*, *fantastically*, *gloriously*, *idyllically*, *infectiously*, *insanely*, *irrationally*, *radiantly*, *serenely*, *supremely*, *unspeakably*, *wonderfully*, etc. But the only such item to occur significantly in the spoken subcorpus is *deliriously*, suggesting a simpler vocabulary, characteristic of the spoken lexicon.

Meaning and usage

Perhaps the most important and complex aspect of lexis in spoken language is the way in which words and phraseologies fulfil pragmatic functions: meaning effectively has to be explored in terms of function, as in the case of *know*. While *I know*, *I don't know*, *you know* are not semantically opaque, they contribute interactionally, indicating hesitation and uncertainty, appealing to shared knowledge or understanding, pre-empting contradiction. With *thing*, corpus data shows its functions as a proform or vagueness marker, or, in the formula *the* NOUN *is*, prefacing a reason, point or new information:

```
< M01 > something some development thing that will indicate they've er < ZG1 >
and FX think October would be a good thing you know because FX said it sets
d finished with it. But the only good thing about it was that erm it was < ZF1 >
lectures say it is the most important thing in the whole lecture course I think
and the customer and that sort of thing. < F0X > Right. < M0X > How you're
< ZF1 > the o+ < ZF0 > the only thing I would say < tc text = pause > that
and the line-to-line movement of the thing. Erm there's a much more er basic
it's a very good question. I mean the thing is if you were to kill er the
f+ on the er < F01 > Er thermostat thing? < F03 > Yeah. < F01 > Fan. < F0X > Mm.
bit older and what's been the worse thing about getting a little bit older? I
```

For words and phrases like these, corpora provide a means for exploring usage, co-textual patterning and positioning, and so on. Less directly, concordances of such words may suggest other items or phenomena to explore: patterns of repetition and relexicalisation, particular phraseologies, and other narrative devices, as in:

in those days < ZF1 > it < ZF0 > it was very very hard er for the family like
< F01 > Mm. < M01 > They were really very very hot on quality. < F01 > Mm. Mm.
Yes. < F02 > But her he's very nice very very nice and I like him very much.
words. < M0X > Thirty million a year is very very roughly a hundred thousand a
and suited well for what she does very very well which is pantomime. Erm
out in practice they saw it as a good thing and I'm sure that's < ZF1 > will
I think it's going to be a good thing for Birmingham. It's going to be a
that. And I think that's er a good thing. It sort of challenges them and
on the estate as well which is a good thing. Erm so t+ so < ZF1 > th < ZF0 > there
Is he a fool is he wise is it a good thing? And if you want to talk about

Discourse pragmatics can only be studied properly with full transcripts and intonational data, yet there is still much to learn about the spoken lexicon from corpora. It is also salutary to remember that assertions made about lexis in homogenised general corpora provide only part of the truth: there may be extraordinary dissimilarities within corpora, alongside the extraordinary similarities of lexical and phraseological patterning, and patterns of conventionalised usage.

Further reading

Biber, D., Johansson, S., Leech, G., Conrad, S. and Finegan, E. (1999) *Longman Grammar of Spoken and Written English*. Harlow: Longman. (This provides useful data about the different kinds of word and phraseological structure associated with four discourse types – conversation, fiction, journalism and academic writing.)

Sinclair, J. (1966) 'Beginning the Study of Lexis', in C. E. Bazell, J. C. Catford, M. A. K. Halliday and R. H. Robins (eds) *In Memory of J. R. Firth*, London: Longman, pp. 410–30. (An early corpus linguistics text, this sets an agenda for corpus studies of lexis, and, significantly, predicts the extensiveness of phraseological patterning and the inseparability of phraseology and meaning.)

——(1987) 'Collocation: A Progress Report', in R. Steele and T. Threadgold (eds) *Language Topics: Essays in Honour of Michael Halliday*, II. Amsterdam: John Benjamins, pp. 319–31. (Reprinted in Sinclair 1991, pp. 109–21) (An important counterpart to Sinclair 1966, this draws on extensive corpus research into lexis, introducing the Idiom Principle, alongside the Open Choice Principle, to explain the role of collocation in determining lexical choice.)

Stubbs, M. (2001) *Words and Phrases: Corpus Studies of Lexical Semantics*. Oxford: Blackwell. (This includes a stimulating array of corpus studies of words and phrases, along with discussions of the relevant linguistic issues.)

References

Baker, P. (2006) *Using Corpora in Discourse Analysis*. London: Continuum.

Biber, D., Johansson, S., Leech, G., Conrad, S. and Finegan, E. (1999) *Longman Grammar of Spoken and Written English*. Harlow: Longman.

Firth, J. R. (1957) *Papers in Linguistics 1934–1951*. London: Oxford University Press.

Hunston, S. (2002) *Corpora in Applied Linguistics*. Cambridge: Cambridge University Press.

Krishnamurthy, R. (1996) 'Ethnic, Racial and Tribal: The Language of Racism?' in C. Caldas-Coulthard and M. Coulthard (eds) *Texts and Practices: Readings in Critical Discourse Analysis*. London: Routledge, pp. 129–49.

Leech, G., Rayson, P. and Wilson, A. (2001) *Word Frequencies in Written and Spoken English*. Harlow: Longman.

Louw, W. (1993) 'Irony in the Text or Insincerity in the Writer? – the Diagnostic Potential of Semantic Prosodies', in M. Baker, G. Francis and E. Tognini Bonelli (eds) *Text and Technology: in Honour of John Sinclair*. Amsterdam: John Benjamins, pp. 157–76.

McCarthy, M. J. (1998) *Spoken Language and Applied Linguistics*. Cambridge: Cambridge University Press.

McCarthy, M. J., and Carter, R. A. (1997) 'Written and Spoken Vocabulary', in N. Schmitt and M. J. McCarthy (eds) *Vocabulary: Description, Acquisition and Pedagogy*. Cambridge: Cambridge University Press, pp. 20–39.

Moon, R. (1998) *Fixed Expressions and Idioms in English: A Corpus-based Approach*. Oxford: Oxford University Press.

O'Keeffe, A., McCarthy, M. J. and Carter, R. A. (2007) *From Corpus to Classroom: Language Use and Language Teaching*. Cambridge: Cambridge University Press.

Partington, A. (1996) *Patterns and Meanings*. Amsterdam: John Benjamins.

Pearce, M. (2008) 'Investigating the Collocational Behaviour of MAN and WOMAN in the BNC using Sketch Engine', *Corpora* 3(1): 1–29.

Sigley, R. and Holmes, J. (2002) 'Looking at *Girls* in Corpora of English', *Journal of English Linguistics* 30 (2): 138–57.

Sinclair, J. (1966) 'Beginning the Study of Lexis', in C. E. Bazell, J. C. Catford, M. A. K. Halliday, and R. H. Robins (eds) *In Memory of J. R. Firth*, London: Longman, pp. 410–30.

——(1987) 'Collocation: a Progress Report', in R. Steele and T. Threadgold (eds) *Language Topics: Essays in Honour of Michael Halliday*, II. Amsterdam: John Benjamins, pp. 319–31. Reprinted in J. Sinclair, *Corpus, Concordance, Collocation*. Oxford: Oxford University Press, pp. 109–21.

——(1991) *Corpus, Concordance, Collocation*. Oxford: Oxford University Press.

——(2004) *Trust the Text*. London: Routledge.

Stubbs, M. (1996) *Text and Corpus Analysis*. Oxford: Blackwell.

——(2001) *Words and Phrases: Corpus Studies of Lexical Semantics*. Oxford: Blackwell.

Williams, R. (1983) *Keywords: A Vocabulary of Language and Society* (revised edition). London: Flamingo.

16

What can a corpus tell us about multi-word units?

Chris Greaves and Martin Warren

1. Background

The idea that we best know the meaning of a word, not by examining it in isolation, but by the company that it keeps, is usually ascribed to Firth (1957) who describes the ways in which meanings are often created by the associations of words rather than by individual words. Firth terms these associations 'meaning by "collocations"' to which, he argues, it is possible 'to apply the test of "collocability"' (1957: 194). He provides examples of meaning by collocation such as 'one of the meanings of *ass* is its habitual collocation with an immediately preceding *you silly*, and with other phrases of address or of personal reference' (1957: 195). Similarly, he states that 'one of the meanings of *night* is its collocability with *dark*, and of *dark*, of course, collocation with *night*' (1957: 196). The test of collocability refers to the notion that words are collocates when they are found to be associated with sufficient frequency to exclude the possibility that they are chance co-occurrences. This has been taken one step further and, based on abundant corpus evidence, corpus linguists have concluded that words often have a preference for what they combine with. For example, O'Keeffe *et al.* (2007: 59–60) point out that the verbs *go* and *turn* both combine with *grey*, *brown* and *white*, but they do not always both combine with other words. For example, one can say 'people go mad, insane, bald or blind', but not 'people turn mad, insane, bald or blind' (2007: 59–60). The latter are instances of words which do not collocate and these are investigated by Renouf and Banerjee (2007). They describe such cases as being the opposite of collocation, which they term 'lexical repulsion' (2007: 417): that is, the tendency for words not to be associated. In this chapter, we are concerned with word associations, although it should be noted that studying why words do not associate can also offer insights into register, style and semantics (Renouf and Banerjee 2007: 439).

For the first computer-mediated corpus-driven study 'to test the assumption that collocation was an important part of the patterning of meaning' (Sinclair *et al.* 2004: xvii), we need to go back to the 1960s. A research team, led by John McH. Sinclair, compiled a spoken corpus of 135,000 words in order to study English collocation (Sinclair *et al.* 1970). The final report (see Sinclair *et al.* 1970, reprinted in 2004) and Sinclair's later work contain three fundamental findings which have far-reaching consequences for corpus linguistics in general, and research into multi-word units of meaning in particular. First, the primacy of lexis over grammar in terms of meaning creation – 'on the whole grammar is not involved in the creation of meaning, but rather concerned with the management of meaning' (Sinclair *et al.* 2004: xxv). Second, that meaning is created through the co-selection of words. Third, that, by virtue of the way in which meaning is created, language is phraseological in nature which is embodied in his famous 'idiom principle' (Sinclair 1987). It is not overstating Sinclair's role in corpus linguistics to say that he has placed the study of multi-word units of meaning at the centre of corpus linguistics through his emphasis on language study ultimately being the study of meaning creation.

What is a multi-word unit?

Despite the fact that the importance of collocation was established in the 1960s (Halliday 1966; Sinclair 1966; Sinclair *et al.* 1970), it is only relatively recently that the study of multi-word units has become more widespread. These studies have begun to explore the extent of phraseology, or to analyse the inner workings of the phraseological tendency, in the English language. For example there have been studies of extended units of meaning, pattern grammar, phraseology, n-grams (sometimes, termed lexical bundles, lexical phrases, clusters and chunks), skipgrams (these include a limited number of intervening words), phrase-frames and phrasal constructions (see, for example, Sinclair 1987, 1996, 2004a, 2005, 2007a, 2007b; Stubbs 1995, 2001, 2005; Partington 1998; Biber *et al.* 1999; Hunston and Francis 2000; Tognini Bonelli 2001; Hunston 2002; Biber *et al.* 2004; Hoey 2005; Teubert 2005; Wilks 2005; Carter and McCarthy 2006; Fletcher 2006; Nesi and Basturkmen 2006; Scott and Tribble 2006; O'Keeffe *et al.* 2007; Cheng and Warren 2008; Meunier and Granger 2008). Here we do not focus on pattern grammar (see Hunston, this volume) because it is not concerned with the meanings of a particular unit of meaning but rather with 'words which share pattern features, but which may differ in other respects in their phraseologies' (Hunston and Francis 2000: 247–8). An example of pattern grammar is '*N as to wh,* where a noun is followed by *as to* and a clause beginning with a wh-clause' and which is shared by a number of nouns (Hunston and Francis 2000: 148). It is important to bear in mind that it has been established by pattern grammarians (see, for example Sinclair 1991; Hunston and Francis 2000) that 'it is not patterns and words that are selected, but phrases, or phraseologies, that have both a single form and meaning' (Hunston and Francis 2000: 21).

Most of the studies of multi-word units have focused on n-grams. N-grams, which have attracted a variety of labels such as 'lexical bundles', 'chunks' and 'clusters', are frequently occurring contiguous words that constitute a phrase or a pattern of use (e.g. *you know, in the, there was a, one of the*). Typically, n-grams are grouped together based on the number of words they contain, with the result that two-word n-grams may be referred to as bi-grams, three-word as tri-grams and so on. Determining the cut-off for including n-grams in frequency lists varies, but a common cut-off is twenty per million (see for example, Biber *et al.* 1999; Scott and Tribble 2006) with others setting it lower, for example, 'at least 20 in the five-million word corpus' (O'Keeffe *et al.* 2007: 64). This decision is partly driven by the size of the corpus being examined, especially when researchers want to analyse larger n-grams. Interestingly, the frequency of n-grams decreases dramatically relative to their size so that while Carter and McCarthy (2006: 503) find 45,015 two-word n-grams in their five-million-word corpus, they find only thirty-one six-word n-grams with twenty instances or more. This observation has important implications because the undoubted prevalence of phraseology in the language does not mean that language use is not unique or creative.

This point has been made very convincingly by Coulthard in his role as a forensic linguist appearing as an expert witness in court cases around the world (see, for example, Coulthard and Johnson 2007). Coulthard (2004) demonstrates that the occurrence of two instances of a nine-word n-gram, *I asked her if I could carry her bags*, in two separate disputed texts, one a statement and the other an interview record, is so improbable as to cast serious doubt on their reliability as evidence in a court case (Coulthard and Johnson 2007: 196–8). Coulthard (2004) bases his findings on a Google search conducted in 2002 in which he found 2,170,000 instances of the two-word n-gram *I asked*, 86,000 instances of the four-word n-gram *I asked if I*, four instances of the seven-word n-gram *I asked her if I could carry*, and no instances of the full nine-word n-gram (2007: 197). Importantly, Coulthard and Johnson draw the conclusion that 'we can assert that even a sequence as short as ten running words has a very high chance of being a unique occurrence' (2007: 198). This intriguing finding both confirms the phraseological tendency in language (Sinclair 1987) as well as its uniqueness and creativity, a fact that should not be lost sight of when we study multi-word units.

Most studies of multi-word units in the form of n-grams adopt an inclusive approach to phraseology and keep all recurring contiguous groupings of words in their lists of data as long as they meet the threshold frequency level, if any (see, for example, Biber *et al.* 1999; Cortes 2002; Carter and McCarthy 2006). Some, however, have a less inclusive view, exemplified by Simpson (2004) who ignores 'strings that are incomplete or span two syntactic units' (2004: 43). Thus *and in fact*, *in terms of* and *you know what I mean* are included in her study of formulaic language in academic speech, while *and in fact you*, *in terms of the* and *you know what I* are excluded (2004: 42–3).

Placing restrictions on the size of the n-grams examined is another decision often made by researchers. It is quite common for researchers to focus on larger n-grams in their studies and various arguments are put forward for ignoring the far more numerous two-word and three-word n-grams. For example, for Cortes (2004) two-word n-grams do not even qualify as what she terms 'lexical bundles'. She argues that

> even though lexical bundles are frequent combinations of three or more words, the present study investigated the use of four-word lexical bundles because many four-word bundles hold three-word bundles in their structures, as in *as a result of*, which contains *as a result*.
>
> (Cortes 2004: 401)

In fact, of course, all four-word n-grams contain within them two three-word n-grams and three two-word n-grams. Cortes (2004) continues that four-word n-grams are more frequent than five-word n-grams and so they afford a wider variety of structures and functions to analyse. Similarly, Hyland (2008: 8) states that he decided 'to focus on 4-word bundles because they are far more common than 5-word strings and offer a clearer range of structures and functions than 3-word bundles'. Such a selective approach to the study of n-grams is not without its critics and Sinclair (2001), for example, is critical of those who ignore two-word n-grams, which easily outnumber all the rest of the n-grams in a corpus combined, simply for reasons of convenience. He states that by not examining the largest group, researchers avoid the fundamental issue of 'whether a grammar based on the general assumption that each word brings along its own meaning independently of the others is ultimately relevant to the nature of language text' (2001: 353) and, in effect, they misrepresent the prevalence of n-grams. Other researchers (see, for example, Carter and McCarthy 2006; Scott and Tribble 2006; and O'Keeffe *et al.* 2007) do include all n-grams, irrespective of size, in their studies and such an approach is important for a fuller understanding of the importance of these multi-word units in the language.

2. Why study multi-word units of meaning?

The study of multi-word units of meaning has led to many new and interesting findings which in turn have pedagogical implications. Some of these findings with regard to n-grams are described and discussed below.

Once the n-grams have been identified, researchers have classified them in terms of their structural patterns, functions and register/genre specificity. In a study of four corpora, each representing a different register (conversation, fiction, news and academic prose), Biber *et al.* (1999: 996–7) identify the most frequent n-grams (they use the term 'lexical bundles') in their data. They classify them based on the structural patterns they encompass – for example, personal pronoun plus lexical verb phrase (plus complement clause), pronoun/noun phrase (plus auxiliary) plus copula *be* (plus), noun phrase with post modifier fragment, and so on – along with the grammatical category of the final word in the n-gram (verb, pronoun, other function words, noun, etc.) (1999: 996–7). Carter and McCarthy (2006: 503–4) also focus on the structure of the n-grams (termed 'clusters') in their corpus and most frequently find prepositions plus articles, subject plus verb, subject plus verb with complement items, and noun phrases plus *of*.

Studies of n-grams have sought to determine their functions. Carter and McCarthy (2006: 505 a–f) examine the functions which n-grams perform, and the list includes: relations of time and space, other prepositional relations, interpersonal functions, vague language, linking functions, and turn-taking. Biber *et al.* (1999) also categorise n-grams based on their discourse functions. They arrive at four main categories: referential bundles, text organisers, stance bundles and interactional bundles. The first two are more frequently found in academic discourse while the others are more widespread in conversation. Referential bundles include time, place and text markers, such as *at the beginning of, the end of the, or at the same time*, whereas text organisers express, for example, contrast (e.g. *on the other hand*), inference (e.g. *as a result of*) or focus (e.g. *it is important to*). Stance bundles convey attitudes towards some proposition, such as *I don't know why* and *are more likely to*, and interactional bundles signal, for example, politeness, or are used in reported speech, as in *thank you very much* and *and I said to him.*

Firth does not apply his notion of meaning by collocations to a corpus in the modern-day sense, but he does observe that the value of 'the study of the usual collocations of a particular literary form or genre or of a particular author makes possible a clearly defined and precisely stated contribution to what I have termed the spectrum of descriptive linguistics' (Firth 1957: 195). He conducts what must be the earliest diachronic genre-based study of collocation. In his study, Firth examines the use of collocation in a collection of eighteenth- and early nineteenth-century letters in order to determine which collocations remain current and which 'seem glaringly obsolete' (ibid.: 204). He finds a number of collocates no longer in use, for example, *disordered* and *cold* (as in the illness) in *I have been disordered by a cold*, and others which are still collocates today, for example, *criminally* and *neglected* in *you are not to think of yourself forgotten, or criminally neglected*' (1957: 204–5). This interest in register and genre specific usage of multi-word units has been the focus of a number of studies in recent years (see, for example, Biber *et al.* 1999; Cortes 2002; Carter and McCarthy 2006; Nesi and Basturkmen 2006; Scott and Tribble 2006; O'Keeffe *et al.* 2007; Forchini and Murphy 2008; Hyland 2008).

Biber *et al.* (1999, 2004), Carter and McCarthy (2006) and Hyland (2008), for example, have all found that the analysis of the n-grams in a register or genre affords an important means of differentiation. Thus the functions performed by n-grams identified by Carter and McCarthy (2006), and described above, differentiate spoken and written language. For example, the use of n-grams to express time and place relations, often by means of prepositional phrases, is more commonplace in written discourse (2006: 505a). They give the examples of *I'll see you in the morning, she sat on the edge of the bed* and *in the middle of the night.* Another function, more often associated with written discourse, is the use of n-grams such as *of a/the, to the* and *with a/the*, which writers use when describing possession, agency, purpose, goal and direction (2006: 505b). One more function more frequently found in written discourse is that of linking, especially in written language that is complex in structure, which is exemplified by n-grams such as *at the same time, in the first place* and *as a result of* (2006: 505e). Spoken discourse also has its distinctive functions typified by specific n-grams and Carter and McCarthy (2006: 505c) find that the use of n-grams to reflect interpersonal meanings is one such function. Examples of these n-grams are *you know, I don't know, I know what you mean* and *I think.* Being vague is also more frequently found in spoken discourse (2006: 505d), whether it is because the speaker cannot be specific or the context does not require specificity. Again, Carter and McCarthy (2006: 505d) identify frequently occurring n-grams which express vagueness and these include *kind of, sort of thing, (or) something like that, (and) all the rest of it* and *this, that and the other.*

Academic genres have attracted a disproportionate amount of interest compared with other genres (see, for example, Cortes 2002, 2004; Biber *et al.* 2004; Charles 2006; Nesi and Basturkmen 2006; Hyland 2008). These studies have all served to demonstrate how a detailed examination of n-grams can reveal genre-specific features in language use. It is now well known that academic language contains distinctive high-frequency n-grams which characterise the conventions of academic spoken and written discourses, as well enabling us to better appreciate differences between the various disciplines. Examples of n-grams typical of academic language include: *for example, the importance of* and *in the case of* (Carter and McCarthy 2006: 505g).

Scott and Tribble (2006: 132) argue that clusters provide insights into the phraseology used in different contexts and they examine the top forty three- and four-word n-grams in the whole of the British National Corpus (BNC), and three sub-corpora within the BNC (i.e. conversations, academic writing and literary studies periodical articles). The top ten n-grams for the whole of the BNC and the sub-corpora (2006: 139–40) show that while the top four three-word n-grams are the same for the whole of the BNC and the conversations (*a lot of, be able to, I don't know* and *it was a*), the top four in academic writing, and literary studies periodical articles are different, although these two sub-corpora have a number of overlapping n-grams in the top ten (*as well as, in terms of, it is a, it is not* and *one of the*).

Scott and Tribble find that certain structures occur with differing frequencies across the four corpora and they investigate one particular structure – noun phrase with *of*-phrase fragment – as in *one of the*. They demonstrate how the most frequent right collocates of this n-gram comprise an important set of terms in academic discourse (2006: 141). Examples (the rankings are given in brackets) of these genre-specific n-grams are *one of the most* (1), *one of the main* (2), *one of the major* (3), *one of the first* (4), *and one of the reasons* (7), *one of the parties* (8), *one of the earliest* (10) and *one of the problems* (11). With the exception of *one of the most*, all of these n-grams are more frequently found in academic discourse.

While studies of n-grams make up the majority of the studies of multi-word units, another form of multi-word unit is the idiom, although the borderline between n-grams and idioms is not without ambiguity. O'Keeffe *et al.* (2007: 82–3) suggest useful methodologies for extracting idioms from a corpus given that idioms cannot be automatically identified by corpus linguistics software. They point out that certain words are 'idiom-prone' (2007: 83) because they are 'basic cognitive metaphors' and give the examples of parts of the body, money, and light and colour. They illustrate one method by first searching for *face* in CANCODE and then studying the 520 concordance lines which revealed fifteen different idioms: for example, *let's face it*, *on the face of it*, *face to face* and *keep a straight face* (2007: 83). The second method is to first sample texts from the corpus in order to study them qualitatively to identify idioms. The idioms found are then searched for in the corpus as whole. This method has led to the identification of many idioms in CANCODE and the five most frequently occurring are *fair enough*, *at the end of the day*, *there you go*, *make sense* and *turn round and say* (2007: 85). Also, idioms, like n-grams, can be described in terms of their functions and register- and genre-specificity (McCarthy 1998).

3. From n-grams to phraseological variation

The criticism from Sinclair (2001: 351–2) that the practice of only examining longer n-grams of three words or more neglects by far the largest group, i.e. two-word n-grams which, based on their prevalence, merit the most attention, has already been mentioned. However, Sinclair's (2001) criticism of n-gram studies does not end there. He raises other issues which question the extent to which the concentration on examining n-grams has led to other forms of multi-word units being overlooked. He points out that the 'classification of the bundles is by the number of words in a string, there is no recognition of variability of exponent or of position or of discontinuity' (2001: 353). He also criticises attempts to relate n-grams to 'the nearest complete grammatical structure' because 'reconciliation with established grammatical units is doomed to fail' (2001: 353). His reason for this prediction is that 'a grammar must remain aware of lexis, and that the patterns of lexis cannot be reconciled with those of a traditional grammar' (2001: 353).

It should be noted that at least some of the limitations of concentrating on the study of n-grams have not gone unnoticed by some engaged in such studies. Nesi and Basturkmen (2006), for example, point out that the identification of n-grams 'does not permit the identification of discontinuous frames (for example, *not only … but also …*)' (ibid.: 285). Similarly, Biber *et al.* (2004: 401–2) state that one of their research goals 'is to extend the methods used to identify lexical bundles to allow for variations on a pattern'. However, they point out that the problem with undertaking this more comprehensive kind of study is in 'trying to identify the full range of lexical bundles across a large corpus of texts'.

Sinclair's criticisms raise fundamental issues about what he terms the phraseological tendency in language (1987), and he proposes his own model for identifying and describing 'extended unit of meanings', or 'lexical items' (1996 and 1998). Sinclair later expresses a preference for the term 'meaning shift unit' rather than 'lexical item' (Sinclair 2007a; Sinclair and Tognini Bonelli, in press). The lexical item is taken to 'realize an element of meaning which is the function of the item in its cotext and context' (Sinclair 2004b: 121) and is 'characteristically phrasal, although it can be realized in a single word' (2004b: 122). It is made up of five categories of co-selection, namely the core, semantic prosody, semantic preference, collocation and colligation. The core and the semantic prosody are obligatory, while collocation, colligation and semantic preference are optional. The core is 'invariable, and constitutes the evidence of the occurrence of the item as a whole' (Sinclair 2004b: 141): that is, the word(s) is always present. Semantic prosody is the overall functional meaning of a lexical item and provides information about 'how the rest of the item is to be interpreted functionally' (2004b: 34). Collocation and colligation are related to the co-occurrences of words and grammatical choices with the core, respectively (2004b: 141). The semantic preference of a lexical item is 'the restriction of regular co-occurrence to items which share a semantic feature, e.g. about sport or suffering' (ibid.: 142). These co-selections are also described in terms of the process by which they are selected. It is the selection of semantic prosody by the speaker that then leads to the selection of the core and the other co-selections of a lexical item.

Clearly, Sinclair's lexical item encompasses much more than we might find in lists of n-grams, but how do we find these co-selections in a corpus? This question links back to the problem raised by Biber *et al.* (2004) in looking for variations in their n-grams. Cheng *et al.* (2006) have developed the means to fully automatically retrieve the co-selections which comprise lexical items from a corpus. The corpus linguistics software is ConcGram (Greaves 2009) and the products of its searches are concgrams (Cheng *et al.* 2006, 2009). These researchers argue that it is important to be able to identify lexical items without relying on single-word frequency lists, lists of n-grams or some form of user-nominated search. The reasons for this are that single-word frequencies are not a reliable guide to frequent phraseologies in a corpus, and n-grams miss instances of multi-word units that have constituency (AB, A★B, A★★B, etc.) and/or positional (AB, BA, B★A, etc.) variation (Cheng *et al.* 2006). While there are programs available which find skipgrams (Wilks 2005) and phrase-frames (Fletcher 2006), which both capture a limited amount of constituency variation, they still miss many instances of both constituency and positional variation (Cheng *et al.* 2006). ConcGram identifies all of the co-occurrences of two or more words irrespective of constituency and/or positional variation fully automatically with no prior search parameters entered and so it supports corpus-driven research (Tognini Bonelli 2001).

Cheng *et al.* (2009) distinguish between 'co-occurring' words (i.e. concgrams) and 'associated' words (i.e. phraseology) because, while ConcGram identifies all of the co-occurrences of words in a wide span, not all of these instances are necessarily meaningfully associated. In order to illustrate the difference between a typical concordance display and a concgram concordance, a sample of the two-word concgram 'expenditure/reduce' is given in Figure 16.1. All of the examples of concgrams are from a five-million-word sample of the British National Corpus (three million written and two million spoken).

The concordance lines in Figure 16.1 illustrate the benefits of uncovering the full range of phraseological variation as the search for this particular concgram found thirty-eight instances, but only four of the thirty-eight are n-grams. Another interesting point is

2-word concgram: reduc / expenditure

1	one of two things to put matters right. (i) **Reduce expenditure** on imported foreign goods, **reduce**
2	that the 112-year-old ABA had failed to try to **reduce expenditure** or increase income sufficiently.
3	groups in society. The Arias government did not **reduce** public **expenditure**, especially on social
4	state. Various strategies have been adopted to **reduce** the level of **expenditure**. These will be examined
5	has also used the policy of privatization to **reduce** the size of public **expenditure** (Treasury 1982).
6	instigated a range of policies which sought to **reduce** further the overall level of **expenditure**.
7	find that they are compelled to use **expenditure-reducing** fiscal and monetary policies in the attempt
8	However in five, six, its net **expenditure** would **reduce** to erm, two hundred and twelve thousand pounds.
9	planned levels of **expenditure** can be painlessly **reduced**. The definition of public **expenditure** is by
10	limit to which **expenditure** of this kind can be **reduced**. It is therefore to the second alternative -

Figure 16.1 Sample concordance lines for 'expenditure/reduce'.

that while there are forty-two instances of 'expenditure/increase' in this corpus, there is only one instance of 'decrease/expenditure', and so while *reduce* and *expenditure* are collocates, *expenditure* and *decrease* are an example of lexical repulsion (Renouf and Banerjee 2007). By not simply focusing on the node, concgram concordance lines highlight all of the co-occurring words, which shifts the reader's focus of attention away from the node to all of the words in the concgram.

Studies of concgrams suggest that they help in the identification of three kinds of multi-word units (Warren 2009). These are collocational frameworks (Renouf and Sinclair 1991), meaning shift units (also termed 'lexical items'; Sinclair 1996, 1998) and organisational frameworks.

It is well known that so-called 'grammatical' or 'function' words top single-word frequency lists and it is therefore no surprise that these words also top concgram frequency lists. Renouf and Sinclair (1991) call the co-selections of these words 'collocational frameworks' and, even though they are such common multi-word units, they are rarely studied. Initial studies of concgrams to find collocational frameworks (Greaves and Warren 2008; Li and Warren 2008) show that the five most frequent are *the … of*, *a/an … of*, *the … of the*, *the … in* and *the … to* (Li and Warren 2008). A sample of one of the most frequent collocational frameworks is in Figure 16.2.

The widespread use of collocational frameworks suggests that they deserve greater attention from researchers, teachers and learners. As long ago as 1988, Sinclair and Renouf (1988) argued that they should be included in a lexical syllabus, but to date they remain overlooked. Newer grammars based on corpus evidence list and describe n-grams (see, for example, Biber *et al.* 1999; Carter and McCarthy 2006). For example, Carter and McCarthy (2006: 503–5) list four-word n-grams in written texts including: *the end of the*, *the side of the*, *the edge of the*, *the middle of the*, *the back of the*, *the top of the* and *the bottom of the*. If collocational frameworks are to be included in future grammars, these n-grams might in future be preceded by a description of their three-word collocational framework, *the … of the*.

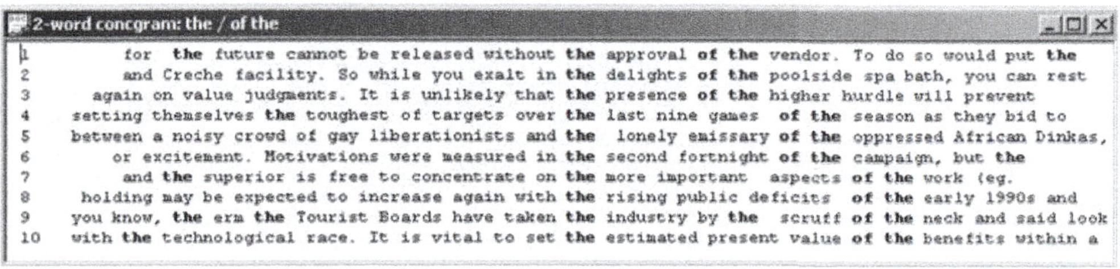

2-word concgram: the / of the

1	for **the** future cannot be released without **the** approval **of the** vendor. To do so would put **the**
2	and Creche facility. So while you exalt in **the** delights **of the** poolside spa bath, you can rest
3	again on value judgments. It is unlikely that **the** presence **of the** higher hurdle will prevent
4	setting themselves **the** toughest of targets over **the** last nine games **of the** season as they bid to
5	between a noisy crowd of gay liberationists and **the** lonely emissary **of the** oppressed African Dinkas,
6	or excitement. Motivations were measured in **the** second fortnight **of the** campaign, but **the**
7	and **the** superior is free to concentrate on **the** more important aspects **of the** work (eg.
8	holding may be expected to increase again with **the** rising public deficits **of the** early 1990s and
9	you know, **the** erm **the** Tourist Boards have taken **the** industry by **the** scruff **of the** neck and said look
10	with **the** technological race. It is vital to set **the** estimated present value **of the** benefits within a

Figure 16.2 Sample concordance lines for the collocational framework *the … of the*.

The idea behind searching for concgrams was to be able to identify and describe meaning shift units (Sinclair 2007a). These multi-word units are important for a fuller description of phraseology and Cheng *et al.* (2009) outline a procedure for analysing concgrams which can help to identify meaning shift units. They analyse the two-word concgram ‘play/role’ and a sample of the concordance lines is in Figure 16.3.

In their study (Cheng *et al.* 2009), all of the concordance lines of ‘play/role’ are studied and all the concgram configurations and their frequencies are described. The canonical form is identified and its meaning described. In Figure 16.3, the canonical form is exemplified in lines 1–3 which is the most frequent configuration. The canonical form is then used as a benchmark for all of the other concgram configurations, and the result is a ranking of the concgram configurations based on the extent of their adherence to the canonical form. At the end of this process, a meaning shift unit is identified and described with all of its potential variations which together comprise a ‘paraphrasable family with a canonical form and different patterns of co-selection’ (Cheng *et al.* 2009).

There is a type of multi-word unit which can exhibit extreme constituency variation. Hunston (2002: 75) briefly describes such multi-word units and provisionally labels them ‘clause collocations’. They are the product of the tendency for particular types of clause to co-occur in discourses. She provides an example, *I wonder ... because*, where *I wonder* and *because* link clauses in the discourse (ibid.: 75). Hunston points out that such collocations are difficult to find because the *I wonder* clause can contain any number of words (ibid.: 75). Based on the distinction between organisation-oriented elements and message-oriented elements used in linear unit grammar (Sinclair and Mauranen 2006), Greaves and Warren (2008) term these multi-word units ‘organisational frameworks’ to denote the ways in which organisational elements in the discourse, such as conjunctions, connectives and discourse particles, can be co-selected. Searches for concgrams uncover organisational frameworks because they retrieve co-occurring words across a wide span. Sample concordance lines of the organisational framework *I think ... because* are given in Figure 16.4.

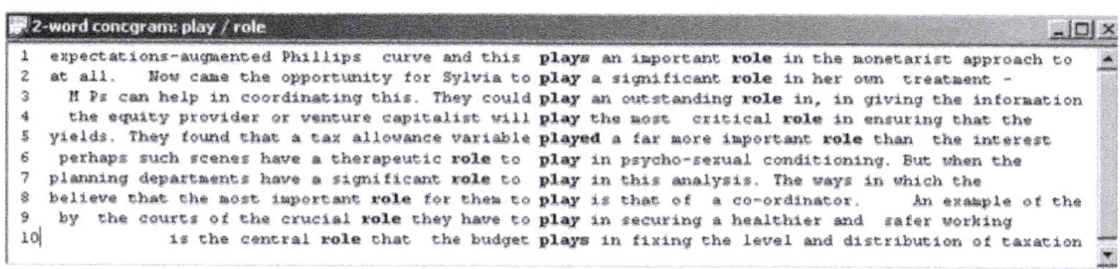
2-word concgram: play / role

1 expectations-augmented Phillips curve and this **plays** an important **role** in the monetarist approach to
2 at all. Now came the opportunity for Sylvia to **play** a significant **role** in her own treatment -
3 M Ps can help in coordinating this. They could **play** an outstanding **role** in, in giving the information
4 the equity provider or venture capitalist will **play** the most critical **role** in ensuring that the
5 yields. They found that a tax allowance variable **played** a far more important **role** than the interest
6 perhaps such scenes have a therapeutic **role** to **play** in psycho-sexual conditioning. But when the
7 planning departments have a significant **role** to **play** in this analysis. The ways in which the
8 believe that the most important **role** for them to **play** is that of a co-ordinator. An example of the
9 by the courts of the crucial **role** they have to **play** in securing a healthier and safer working
10 is the central **role** that the budget **plays** in fixing the level and distribution of taxation

Figure 16.3 Sample concordance lines for the meaning shift unit ‘play/role’.

2-word concgram: because / I think

1 be better **I think** if we had ours in the back **because** the, the telephone thing comes in from the back
2 Away . **I think** Bryony likes erm Smarties **because** she's always sucking the juice out of beans.
3 lawyer, but **I think** that a lot of people say no **because** of the media pres , presentation, you only hear
4 off oh **I think** Peter was at erm play school **because** they go to play school two afternoon's a week
5 off **I think** it was probably the other day **because** erm the wa the ducks were swimming on the road
6 Oh **I think** it'd be nice to have a video, **because** like, when Rebecca gets older erm cos I
7 daughter **I think** she must have been getting on **because** around the time she told me that she was
8 printers, **I think** that you suggest are left on **because** you never know when it'll be [unclear] to. Er,
9 really **I think** that this hasn't been looked at **because** its male dominated Its not necessary the
10 nd **I think** it's fair enough to read that, **because** a sighted person would go in and pick it up

Figure 16.4 Sample concordance lines for the organisational framework *I think ... because*.

Some instances of organisational frameworks are well known, and are sometimes listed in grammars as 'correlative conjunctions', for example, *either … or*, *not only … but also* and *both … and*. There are others, however, such as *I think … because* and Hunston's *I wonder … because*, which are not so familiar, and possibly others which are currently unknown, which deserve more attention.

There has been considerable interest in keywords and the notion of keyness (see Scott, in this volume) in corpus linguistics (see, for example, Scott and Tribble 2006). Given that multi-word units are so pervasive in language, concgrams can be used to extend the notion of keyness beyond individual words to include the full range of multi-word units. They are a starting point for quantifying the extent of phraseology in a text or corpus and determining the phraseological profile of the language contained within it. There is plenty of evidence to suggest that n-grams, including those made up entirely of grammatical words, can be genre-sensitive, which has been described earlier, and there is evidence that this is also the case for concgrams. Early studies using concgrams to examine the aboutness of texts and corpora (see Tognini Bonelli 2006; Greaves and Warren 2007; Cheng 2008, 2009; Milizia and Spinzi 2008; O'Donnell *et al.* 2008) suggest that these multi-word units offer a more comprehensive phraseological profile of texts and corpora. Word associations which are specific to a text or corpus are termed 'aboutgrams' (Sinclair, personal communication; Sinclair and Tognini Bonelli, in press).

4. What has corpus research into multi-word units told us about phraseology that we did not know before?

As observed by Stubbs (2005), although many of the studies of n-grams, phrasal constructions and extended lexical units involve research within quite different methodological traditions, they have arrived at similar conclusions about 'how to model *units of meaning*' (2005: 8). We now know much more about the key role played by multi-word units in the English language and this has resulted in a reappraisal of the status of lexis.

Biber *et al.* (1999: 995) find that 45 per cent of the words in their conversation corpus occur in recurrent n-grams of two or more words. They set the cut-off at twenty per million to arrive at this percentage. Altenberg (1998) puts the percentage as high as 80 per cent by including all n-grams that occur more than once. Whatever the percentage, these findings provide conclusive evidence for the 'phraseological tendency' (Sinclair 1987) in language. However, it needs to be borne in mind that both these figures exclude multi-word units with constituency and or positional variation, and we are now only just beginning to realise that only looking at n-grams leaves much of the phraseological variation in English undiscovered. If phraseological variation is added to the percentage of n-grams in a corpus, the figure would be closer to 100 per cent.

The findings from studies of multi-word units have impacted lexicography along with the writing of English language grammars, and English language textbooks generally. The reason why many of the findings have fed into the fields of English for Academic Purposes and English for Specific Purposes is that studies have also been conducted which compare the use of multi-word units by expert and novice writers and speakers. For example, Cortes (2004) makes the point that the use of multi-word units, in the forms of collocations and fixed expressions associated with particular registers and genres, are a marker of proficient language use in that particular register or genre. Similarly, in his study of four-word n-grams, Hyland (2008: 5) states that these multi-word units are 'familiar to writers and readers who regularly participate in a particular discourse, their very "naturalness" signalling competent participation in a given community'. He finds that the opposite is often true of novice members of the community and the absence of discipline-specific n-grams might signal a lack of fluency. This means that learners need to acquire an 'appropriate disciplinary-sensitive repertoire' of n-grams (Hyland and Tse 2007).

Another indication that our understanding of language has been enhanced by research into multi-word units is the notion of 'lexical priming' put forward by Hoey (2005) as a new theory of language which builds on the five categories of co-selection (Sinclair 1996, 1998, 2004a) and argues that patterns of co-selection require that speakers, writers, hearers and readers are primed for appropriate co-selections.

> A word is acquired by encounters with it in speech and writing. A word becomes cumulatively loaded with the contexts and co-texts in which they are encountered. Our knowledge of a word includes the fact that it co-occurs with certain other words in certain kinds of context. The same process applies to word sequences built out of these words; these too become loaded with the contexts and co-texts in which they occur.
>
> (Hoey 2005: 8)

In support of the notion of lexical priming, Hoey puts forward ten priming hypotheses (2005: 13). Every word is primed to occur with particular other words, semantic sets, pragmatic functions and grammatical positions. Words which are either co-hyponyms or synonyms differ with respect to their collocations, semantic associations and colligations, as do the senses of words which are polysemous. Words are primed for use in one or more grammatical roles and to participate in, or avoid, particular types of cohesive relation in a discourse. Every word is primed to occur in particular semantic relations in the discourse and to occur in, or avoid, certain positions within the discourse. These hypotheses are a result of Hoey's extensive study of lexical cohesion and he concludes that naturalness depends on speakers and writers conforming to the primings of the words that they use (2005: 2–5).

5. Implications and future research

Findings from the study of multi-word units have implications for the learning and teaching of applied linguistics, language studies, English for Academic Purposes and English for Specific Purposes. It is clear that multi-word units have a role to play in data-driven learning (DDL) activities (Johns 1991), and should further advance the learning and teaching of phraseology.

Sinclair's claim that 'a grammar must remain aware of lexis, and that the patterns of lexis cannot be reconciled with those of a traditional grammar' (2001: 353) predicts a break with traditional grammar and this prediction is made elsewhere by Sinclair and is summed up in the following quote:

> By far the majority of text is made of the occurrence of common words in common patterns, or in slight variants of those common patterns. Most everyday words do not have an independent meaning, or meanings, but are components of a

rich repertoire of multi-word patterns that make up a text. This is totally obscured by the procedures of conventional grammar.

Sinclair (1991: 108)

The inadequacies of conventional grammar have been addressed, at least in part, by Sinclair and Mauranen's (2006) linear unit grammar which 'avoids hierarchies, and concentrates on the combinatorial patterns of text'. Sinclair (2007b) also advocates local grammars as a better way of handling phraseological variation. Both local grammars and linear unit grammar have yet to be widely applied in studies of multi-word units, but Hunston and Sinclair (2000), for example, demonstrate the applicability of a local grammar to the concept of evaluation, and these grammars have considerable potential in furthering our descriptions and understanding of multi-word units.

Another of Sinclair's yet-to-be-realised ambitions is the compilation of a dictionary which fully captures the phraseology of language. 'A dictionary containing all the lexical items of a language, each one in its canonical form with a list of possible variations, would be the ultimate dictionary' (Sinclair in Sinclair *et al.* 2004: xxiv). As our knowledge of phraseology grows with the study of multi-word units, such a dictionary becomes ever more feasible.

Sinclair (2001: 357) states that for him any corpus 'signals like a flashing neon sign "Think again"' and it is Sinclair's notion of the idiom principle (1987) and his work on units of meaning which have led all of us to think again about whether meaning is in individual words or whether the source of meaning in language is through the co-selections made by speakers and writers. All of the corpus evidence confirms Sinclair's fundamental point that it is not the word that is a unit of meaning, but the co-selection of words which comprise a unit of meaning (2001: xxi). The future exploration of multi-word units in corpus linguistics promises to tell us much more about how meaning is created.

Acknowledgements

We gratefully acknowledge the support we received from Professor John McHardy Sinclair who was a member of the concgram team and worked with us on concgrams from the outset. His brilliant ideas led directly to many of ConcGram's functions and helped enormously in our analyses of concgrams. Another member of the team is Elena Tognini Bonelli whose research into aboutness has helped in further developing the applications of concgramming. Winnie Cheng, of course, is also in the team and her input has been invaluable.

The work described in this chapter was substantially supported by a grant from the Research Grants Council of the Hong Kong Special Administrative Region (Project No. PolyU 5459/08H, B-Q11N)

Further reading

Cheng, W., Greaves, C., Sinclair, J. and Warren, M. (2009) 'Uncovering the Extent of the Phraseological Tendency: Towards a Systematic Analysis of Concgrams', *Applied Linguistics* 30(2): 236–52. (This paper explains how to analyse the phraseological variation to be found in *concgram* outputs.)

Granger, S. and Meunier, F. (eds) (2008) *Phraseology: An Interdisciplinary Perspective*. Amsterdam: John Benjamins. (This is a wide-ranging collection of papers by leading researchers in the field.)

O'Keeffe, A., McCarthy, M. J. and Carter, R. A. (2007) *From Corpus to Classroom: Language Use and Language Teaching*. Cambridge: Cambridge University Press. (This book has a number of chapters which explore the forms and function of multi-word units.)

Sinclair, J. (2004) *Trust the Text*. London: Routledge. (Chapters 2 and 8 provide a good account of Sinclair's notion that a lexical item is comprised of up to five co-selections.)

Stubbs, M. (2009) 'The Search for Units of Meaning: Sinclair on Empirical Semantics', *Applied Linguistics* 30(1): 115–37. (This is a good overview of current 'Sinclairian' corpus linguistics research in phraseology with a thought-provoking discussion on its implications.)

References

Altenberg, B. (1998) 'On the Phraseology of Spoken English: The Evidence of Recurrent Word Combinations', in A. P. Cowie (ed.) *Phraseology: Theory Analysis and Applications*. Oxford: Oxford University Press, pp. 101–22.

Biber, D., Johansson, S., Leech, G., Conrad, S. and Finegan, E. (1999) *The Longman Grammar of Spoken and Written English*. Harlow, England: Pearson Education.

Biber, D., Conrad, S. and Cortes, V. (2004) 'If You Look at … : Lexical Bundles in University Teaching and Textbooks', *Applied Linguistics* 25(3): 371–405.

Carter, R. A. and McCarthy, M. J. (2006) *Cambridge Grammar of English*. Cambridge: Cambridge University Press.

Charles, M. (2006) 'Phraseological Patterns in Reporting Clauses Used in Citation: A Corpus-Based Study of Theses in Two Disciplines', *English for Specific Purposes* 25(3): 310–31.

Cheng, W. (2008) 'Concgramming: A Corpus-driven Approach to Learning the Phraseology of Discipline-specific Texts', *CORELL: Computer Resources for Language Learning* 1(1): 22–35.

——(2009) '*Income/Interest/Net*: Using Internal Criteria to Determine the Aboutness of a Text in Business and Financial Services English', in K. Aijmer (ed.) *Corpora and Language Teaching*. Amsterdam/ Philadelphia: John Benjamins, pp. 157–77.

Cheng, W. and Warren, M. (2008) '// -> ONE country two SYStems //: The Discourse Intonation Patterns of Word Associations', in A. Ädel and R. Reppen (eds) *Corpora and Discourse: The Challenges of Different Settings*. Amsterdam: John Benjamins, pp. 135–53.

Cheng, W., Greaves, C. and Warren, M. (2006) 'From n-gram to skipgram to concgram,' *International Journal of Corpus Linguistics* 11(4): 411–33.

Cheng, W., Greaves, C., Sinclair, J. and Warren, M. (2009) 'Uncovering the Extent of the Phraseological Tendency: Towards a Systematic Analysis of Concgrams', *Applied Linguistics* 30(2): 236–52.

Cortes, V. (2002) 'Lexical Bundles in Freshman Composition', in D. Biber, S. Fitzmaurice and R. Reppen (eds) *Using Corpora to Explore Linguistic Variation*. Philadelphia, PA: John Benjamins, pp. 131–45.

——(2004) 'Lexical Bundles in Published and Student Disciplinary Writing: Examples from History and Biology', *English for Specific Purposes* 23(4): 397–423.

Coulthard, M. (2004) 'Author Identification, Idiolect, and Linguistic Uniqueness', *Applied Linguistics* 25 (4): 431–47.

Coulthard, M. and Johnson, A. (2007) *An Introduction to Forensic Linguistics: Language in Evidence*. London: Routledge.

Firth, J. R. (1957) *Papers in Linguistics 1934–1951*. London: Oxford University Press.

Fletcher, W. H. (2006) 'Phrases in English', home page, at http://pie.usna.edu/ (accessed 15 February 2006).

Forchini, P. and Murphy, A. (2008) 'N-Grams in Comparable Specialized Corpora: Perspectives on Phraseology, Translation, and Pedagogy'. *International Journal of Corpus Linguistics* 13(3): 351–67.

Greaves, C. (2009) *ConcGram 1.0: A Phraseological Search Engine*. Amsterdam: John Benjamins.

Greaves, C. and Warren, M. (2007) 'Concgramming: A Computer-Driven Approach to Learning the Phraseology of English', *ReCALL Journal* 17(3): 287–306.

——(2008) 'Beyond Clusters: A New Look at Word Associations', IVACS 4, 4th International Conference: Applying Corpus Linguistics, University of Limerick, Ireland, 13–14 June.

Halliday, M. A. K. (1966). 'Lexis as a Linguistic Level', in C. E. Bazell, J. C. Catford, M. A. K. Halliday and R. H. Robins (eds) *In Memory of J. R. Firth*. London: Longmans.

Hoey, M. (2005) *Lexical Priming: A New Theory of Words and Language*. London: Routledge.

Hunston, S. (2002) *Corpora in Applied Linguistics*. Cambridge: Cambridge University Press.

Hunston, S. and Francis, G. (2000) *Pattern Grammar: A Corpus-driven Approach to the Lexical Grammar of English*. Amsterdam: John Benjamins.

Hunston, S. and Sinclair, J. (2000) 'A Local Grammar of Evaluation', in S. Hunston and G. Thompson (eds) *Evaluation In Text: Authorial Stance and the Construction of Discourse*. Oxford: Oxford University Press, pp. 75–100.

Hyland, K. (2008) 'As Can Be Seen: Lexical Bundles and Disciplinary Variation', *English for Specific Purposes* 27(1): 4–21.

Hyland, K. and Tse, P. (2007) 'Is There an "Academic Vocabulary"?' *TESOL Quarterly*, 41(2): 235–53.

Johns, T. (1991) 'Should You Be Persuaded: Two Samples of Data-driven Learning Materials', in T. Johns and P. King (eds) *Classroom Concordancing*. Birmingham: English Language Research, Birmingham University, pp. 1–16.

Li, Y. and Warren, M. (2008) '*in. … of*: What Are Collocational Frameworks and Should We Be Teaching Them?' 4th International Conference on Teaching English at Tertiary Level. Zhejiang, China, 11–12 October.

McCarthy, M. J. (1998) *Spoken Language and Applied Linguistics*. Cambridge: Cambridge University Press.

Meunier, F. and Granger, S. (eds) (2008) *Phraseology in Foreign Language Learning and Teaching*. Amsterdam: John Benjamins, pp. 223–43.

Milizia, D. and Spinzi, C. (2008) 'The "Terroridiom" Principle Between Spoken and Written Discourse', *International Journal of Corpus Linguistics* 13(3): 322–50.

Nesi, H. and Basturkmen, H. (2006) 'Lexical Bundles and Signalling in Academic Lectures', in J. Flowerdew and M. Mahlberg (eds) 'Lexical Cohesion and Corpus Linguistics', special issue of *International Journal of Corpus Linguistics* 11(3): 283–304.

O'Donnell, M. B., Scott, M. and Mahlberg, M. (2008) 'Exploring Text-initial Concgrams in a Newspaper Corpus', 7th International Conference of the American Association of Corpus Linguistics, Brigham Young University, Provo, Utah, USA, 12–15 March.

O'Keeffe, A., McCarthy, M. J. and Carter, R. A. (2007) *From Corpus to Classroom: Language Use and Language Teaching*. Cambridge: Cambridge University Press.

Partington, A. (1998) *Patterns and Meanings*. Amsterdam: John Benjamins.

Renouf, A. and Banerjee, J. (2007) 'Lexical Repulsion Between Sense-related Pairs', *International Journal of Corpus Linguistics* 12(3): 415–44.

Renouf, A. and Sinclair, J. (1991) 'Collocational Frameworks in English', in K. Ajimer and B. Altenberg (eds) *English Corpus Linguistics*. Cambridge: Cambridge University Press, pp. 128–43.

Scott, M. and Tribble, C. (2006) *Textual Patterns: Key Words and Corpus Analysis in Language Education*. Amsterdam: John Benjamins.

Simpson, R. C. (2004) 'Stylistic Features of Academic Speech: The Role of Formulaic Expressions', in U. Connor and T. Upton (eds) *Discourse in the Professions: Perspectives from Corpus Linguistics*. Amsterdam: John Benjamins, pp. 37–64.

Sinclair, J. (1966) 'Beginning the Study of Lexis,' in C. E. Bazell, J. C. Catford, M. A. K. Halliday and R. H. Robins (eds) *In Memory of J. R. Firth*. London: Longmans.

——(1987) 'Collocation: A Progress Report', in R. Steele and T. Threadgold (eds) *Language Topics: Essays in Honour of Michael Halliday*. Amsterdam: John Benjamins, pp. 319–31.

——(1991) *Corpus, Concordance, Collocation*. Oxford: Oxford University Press.

——(1996) 'The Search for Units of Meaning', *Textus* 9(1): 75–106.

——(1998) 'The Lexical Item', in. E. Weigand (ed.) *Contrastive Lexical Semantics*. Amsterdam: John Benjamins, pp. 1–24.

——(2001) 'Review of *The Longman Grammar of Spoken and Written English*', *International Journal of Corpus Linguistics* 6(2): 339–59.
——(2004a) *Trust the Text*. London: Routledge.
——(2004b) 'Meaning in the Framework of Corpus Linguistics', *Lexicographica* 20: 20–32.
——(2005) 'Document Relativity' (manuscript), Tuscan Word Centre, Italy.
——(2006) 'Aboutness 2' (manuscript), Tuscan Word Centre, Italy.
——(2007a) 'Collocation Reviewed' (manuscript), Tuscan Word Centre, Italy.
——(2007b) 'Defining the Definiendom – New' (manuscript), Tuscan Word Centre, Italy.
Sinclair, J. and Mauranen, A. (2006) *Linear Unit Grammar*. Amsterdam: John Benjamins.
Sinclair, J. and Renouf, A. (1988) 'A Lexical Syllabus for Language Learning', in R. A. Carter and M. J. McCarthy (eds) *Vocabulary and Language Teaching*. London: Longman, pp. 140–60.
Sinclair, J. and Tognini Bonelli, E. (in press) *Essential Corpus Linguistics*. London: Routledge.
Sinclair, J., Jones, S. and Daley, R. (1970) 'English Lexical Studies,' report to the Office of Scientific and Technical Information.
——(2004) *English Collocation Studies: The OSTI Report*. London: Continuum.
Stubbs, M. (1995) 'Collocations and Cultural Connotations of Common Words', *Linguistics and Education* 7(3): 379–90.
——(2001) *Words and Phrases: Corpus Studies of Lexical Semantics*. Oxford: Blackwell.
——(2005) 'The Most Natural Thing in the World: Quantitative Data on Multi-word Sequences in English', paper presented at Phraseology 2005, Louvain-la-Neuve, Belgium, 13–15 October.
Teubert, W. (ed). (2005) *Corpus Linguistics-Critical Concepts in Linguistics*. London: Routledge.
Tognini Bonelli, E. (2001) *Corpus Linguistics at Work*. Amsterdam: John Benjamins.
——(2006) 'The Corpus as an Onion: The CÆT Corpus Siena (a Corpus of Academic Economics Texts)', International Seminar: Special and Varied Corpora, Tuscan Word Centre, Certosa di Pontignano, Tuscany, Italy, October.
Warren, M. (2009) 'Why Concgram?' in Chris Greaves (ed.) *ConcGram 1.0: A Phraseological Search Engine*. Amsterdam: John Benjamins, pp. 1–11.
Wilks, Y. (2005) 'REVEAL: The Notion of Anomalous Texts in a Very Large Corpus', Tuscan Word Centre International Workshop. Certosa di Pontignano, Tuscany, Italy, 1–3 July.

17

What can a corpus tell us about grammar?

Susan Conrad

1. Understanding grammar through patterns and contexts: moving from correct/incorrect to likely/unlikely

In traditional descriptions of grammar and in most linguistic theories, grammar is presented from a dichotomous perspective. Sample sentences are considered either grammatical or ungrammatical, acceptable or unacceptable, accurate or inaccurate (e.g. see discussions in Cook 1994). From this perspective, to describe the grammar of a language, all a researcher needs is a native speaker because any native speaker can judge grammaticality. To teach a language, teachers focus only on the rules for making grammatical sentences, and proficiency for second language speakers equates with accuracy.

This dichotomous view works well for certain grammatical features. For example, it is grammatically incorrect to have zero article before a singular count noun in English: **I saw Ø cow*. Aside from a few exceptions such as in the locative prepositional phrases *at home* or *in hospital*, this rule is absolute. However, any reflective language user will realise that many other grammatical choices cannot be made on the basis of correct/incorrect. For example, in the previous sentence the *that* could have been omitted: … *will realise many other grammatical choices* … Both versions are equally grammatical.

Of course, for decades, work in sociolinguistics and from a functional perspective has emphasised language choices for different contexts. In language classes, students may have been taught a few variants for politeness (e.g. in English using *could you* … for requests instead of *can you* …), but descriptions of grammar remained focused on accuracy. In a 1998 address to the international TESOL convention, Larsen-Freeman sought to 'challenge the common misperception that grammar has to do solely with formal accuracy', arguing instead for a 'grammar of choice' (Larsen-Freeman 2002). Being able to describe the typical choices that language users make, however, requires doing large-scale empirical analyses. The analyses must be empirical – rather than introspective – since language users often are not consciously aware of their most typical choices. The analyses must cover numerous data in order to tell which language choices are widespread, which occur predictably although under rare circumstances, and which are more idiosyncratic.

The great contribution of corpus linguistics to grammar is that it increases researchers' ability to systematically study the variation in a large collection of texts – produced by far more speakers and writers, and covering a far greater number of words, than could be analysed by hand. Corpus linguistic techniques allow us to determine common and uncommon choices and to see the patterns that reveal what is typical or untypical in particular contexts. These 'patterns' show the correspondence between the use of a grammatical feature and some other factor in the discourse or situational context (e.g. another grammatical feature, a social relationship, the mode of communication, etc.). Corpus linguistics therefore allows us to focus on the patterns that characterise how a large number of people use the language, rather than basing generalisations on a small set of data or anecdotal evidence, or focusing on the accurate/inaccurate dichotomy. As O'Keeffe *et al.* (2007) explain, corpus analyses lead us to describing grammar not just in structural terms, but in probabilistic terms – describing the typical social and discourse circumstances associated with the use of particular grammatical features.

This chapter reviews some major aspects of this new paradigm for describing grammar. The first section reviews the types of grammatical patterns typically covered in corpus studies. The chapter then discusses the investigation of numerous contextual factors simultaneously, the development of descriptions of the grammar of speech, and the most commonly discussed problem that arises in this new paradigm – the role of acceptability judgements. Throughout, points are exemplified with descriptions of English. The contributions of corpus linguistics are equally applicable to the grammar of any language; however, corpus-based descriptions of English far outnumber any other language. Furthermore, although numerous studies are mentioned, it is no coincidence that the chapter repeatedly cites two recent reference grammars of English, the *Longman Grammar of Spoken and Written English* (Biber *et al.* 1999) and the *Cambridge Grammar of English* (Carter and McCarthy 2006). These comprehensive grammars make extensive use of corpus analyses to describe English structure and use, and are currently the single clearest manifestations of corpus linguistics' impact on the study of grammar.

As a first step, before further discussing the contribution of corpus linguistics to grammar, a brief review of some methodological principles for corpus linguistic investigations of grammar is in order.

Methodological principles in corpus-based grammar analysis

Any analysis of 'typical' or 'probable' choices depends on frequency analysis. The very mention of a choice being 'typical' or 'unusual' implies that, under given circumstances, it happens more or less often than other choices. For reliable frequency analysis, a corpus does not necessarily have to be immense, but it must be designed to be as representative as possible (see the chapters in Section I of this volume) and as fine-grained as needed to describe the circumstances associated with the variable choices. For example, McCarthy and Carter (2001) explain the need for fine-grained distinctions in spoken corpora to describe when ellipsis is and is not common. They find ellipsis to be rare in narratives, while it is common in many other genres of talk. Any corpus that did not include numerous conversational genres or any analysis which neglected to differentiate among them would fail to discover this pattern.

Frequency counts are not sufficient for describing grammar, however. Instead, they point to interesting phenomena that deserve further investigation and interpretation. As Biber *et al.* (2004) explain,

> we do not regard frequency data as explanatory. In fact we would argue for the opposite: frequency data identifies patterns that must be explained. The usefulness of frequency data (and corpus analysis generally) is that it identifies patterns of use that otherwise often go unnoticed by researchers.
>
> (p. 176)

In corpus-based grammar studies, interpretations of frequency analyses come from a variety of sources. They can be based on cognitive principles such as the principle of 'end weight' (heavy, long constituents are harder to process than short constituents and so are placed at the ends of clauses); on aspects of linguistic theory, such as principles defined in Systemic Functional Linguistics; on the historical development of the language; or on reasonable explanations of the functions or discourse effect of a particular linguistic choice. Interpretation always includes human judgements of the impact of the language choices and speakers/writers' (usually subconscious) motivations in making these choices. Thus, a corpus linguistics perspective on grammar has not made human judgements superfluous; it has actually expanded the judgements and interpretations that are made.

2. Types of grammatical patterns

This section describes and exemplifies the four types of patterns that are most common in corpus-based grammar analyses. Grammatical choices are associated with (1) vocabulary, (2) grammatical co-text, (3) discourse-level factors, and (4) the context of the situation.

Grammar–vocabulary associations (lexico-grammar)

Associations between grammar and vocabulary are often called 'lexico-grammar.' The connection between words and grammar was extensively studied in the Collins COBUILD project (e.g. see Sinclair 1991). Although designed initially as a lexicography project, it became clear that grammar and lexis were not as distinct as traditionally presented, and the project also resulted in a number of books presenting 'pattern grammar' – explanations of grammatical structures integrated with the specific lexical items most commonly used in them (see Hunston and Francis 1999; Hunston, this volume). Although few publications now discuss grammar in its lexical patterns as extensively, lexico-grammatical relationships have been a common contribution of corpus studies.

One type of lexico-grammatical relationship concerns the lexical items that tend to occur with a particular grammatical structure. This type of pattern can be illustrated with verbs that are most common with *that*-clause objects, e.g. *I guess* ***I should go*** or *The results suggest* ***that there is no effect*** … A large number of verbs are possible with this structure. However, beyond looking at what is *possible*, corpus-based grammar references present findings for the verbs that are actually most commonly used (Biber *et al.* 1999: 668–70; Carter and McCarthy 2006: 511). The reference grammars explain that the common verbs are related to expressing speech and thought. For example, Biber *et al.* (1999) find that *think, say* and *know* are by far the most common verbs with *that*-clauses in both British and American conversation (with the addition of *guess* in American English conversation). They also find that the structure is less common overall with any verb in academic prose, but *suggest* and *show* are most common. Rather than reporting thoughts and feelings, the verb + *that*-clause structures in academic prose are used to report previous research, often with non-human entities acting as the subject, for example:

> **Reports suggest** that in many subject areas, textbooks and materials are not available.

Thus, the frequency analyses reveal the lexico-grammatical patterns – that is, which verbs occur most commonly with *that*-clauses – and the interpretation for the frequency is that the most important function of this structure is to report thoughts, feelings, and in the case of academic prose, previous research.

Another type of lexico-grammatical relationship concerns the specific words that occur as a realisation of a grammatical function. A simple illustration is verb tense. Traditionally, a grammatical description would explain the form of tenses – e.g. that simple present tense in English is uninflected except in third person singular when *-s* is added, that past tense is formed with *-ed* for regular verbs, etc. In these traditional descriptions, there is no empirical investigation of the verbs that are most common in these tenses. In contrast, a modern corpus-based reference grammar can provide that information. For example, Table 17.1 displays the list of verbs that occur 80 per cent of the time in present tense, contrasted with those that occur 80 per cent of the time in past tense, as analysed in the Longman Spoken and Written English Corpus, a corpus of over forty million words representing conversation, fiction, newspapers, academic prose as well as some planned speech and general prose (see Biber *et al.* 1999: 25).

The verbs most strongly associated with present tense convey mental, emotional and logical states. Many of these are used in short, common expressions in conversations expressing the speaker's mental or emotional state, for example:

> It doesn't **matter**.
> Never **mind**.
> I **suppose**.

Others, however, are used to describe the states of others or to make logical interpretations, as in these examples from newspaper texts:

> The yield on the notes is slightly higher because of the 'short' first coupon date which **means** that investors will get their interest payment quicker.
> Some experts **doubt** videotex will develop a following among the general public.

The verbs most strongly associated with past tense, on the other hand, convey events or activities, especially body movements and speech:

Table 17.1 Lexico-grammatical associations of verbs and tenses

Tense	*Verbs occurring over 80 per cent of the time in the tense*
present	*bet, doubt, know, matter, mean, mind, reckon, suppose, thank*
past	*exclaim, eye, glance, grin, nod, pause, remark, reply, shrug, sigh, smile, whisper*

Source: summarised from Biber *et al.* 1999: 459.

He **shrugged** and **smiled** distractedly …
… Paul **glanced** at him and **grinned**.

Not surprisingly, such descriptions are especially common for describing characters and actions in fiction writing.

The associations between a grammatical structure and lexical items can also be analysed in terms of the semantic characteristics of the lexical items, leading to what has been called an analysis of 'semantic prosody' – the fact that certain structures tend to be associated with certain types of meaning, such as positive or negative circumstances (Sinclair 1991). For example, O'Keeffe *et al.* (2007: 106–14) provide an extended corpus-based analysis of *get*-passives (e.g. *he got arrested*). They show that the *get*-passive is usually used to express unfortunate incidences, manifest in the lexico-grammatical association of verbs such as *killed*, *sued*, *beaten*, *arrested*, *burgled*, *intimidated*, *criticised* and numerous others. None of these verbs is common individually, but as a group they form the most common type of verb. O'Keeffe *et al.* further point out, however, that the adverse nature of the *get*-passive is not only a matter of a simple lexico-grammatical pattern with verbs of a certain semantic category. Verbs that are not inherently negative can nonetheless convey adverse conditions when used with negation or in a discourse context that makes the adverse conditions clear.

O'Keeffe *et al.* (2007) also discuss the type of subjects usually found with *get*-passives (often human subjects – the people to whom the unfortunate incident happened) and the lack of adverbials in these clauses. The authors thus move into discussion of another type of pattern, the grammatical co-text.

Grammatical co-text

In addition to describing lexical items that are associated with a grammatical structure, corpus studies also investigate associations with other grammatical structures – that is, the extent to which a particular grammatical feature tends to occur with specific other grammatical features.

Grammatical descriptions in traditional textbooks sometimes make claims about the grammatical co-text of features, and corpus studies can provide empirical testing of these claims. One interesting example is provided by Frazier (2003), who investigated *would*-clauses of hypothetical or counterfactual conditionals. Concerned about the way that ESL grammars virtually always present the *would* clause as adjacent to an *if*-clause, he examined the extent to which this was true in a combination of spoken and written corpora totalling slightly over a million words.

Interestingly, Frazier (2003) found that almost 80 per cent of the hypothetical/counterfactual *would*-clauses were not adjacent to an *if*-clause. Some of these clauses were part of continuing discourse that had been framed with an *if*-clause at a lengthy distance from the *would*-clause (thus connecting the grammatical structure to a larger discourse context, a factor discussed in the next section). The other clauses fell into several other categories of use, including those that were used with a tentative degree of commitment – e.g. in expressions such as 'this would seem to indicate … ' – or with emphatic negative statements – e.g. 'a man would never do that' (Frazier 2003: 454–5). The largest category of *would*-clauses without *if*-clauses were those that had implied, covert conditionals. It further turned out that these clauses tended to occur with certain other grammatical features. For example, the co-occurring grammatical features include infinitives and gerunds, as in these examples from Frazier (2003: 456–7):

> If there is nothing evil in these things, if they get their moral complexion only from our feeling about them, why shouldn't they be greeted with a cheer? **To greet** them with repulsion **would** turn what before was neutral into something bad.
>
> **Letting** the administration take details off their hands **would** give them more time to inform themselves about education as a whole.

Frazier's systematic corpus analysis thus highlights two aspects of grammatical co-text for hypothetical/counter-factual *would*-clauses: the traditional claim that they usually occur with *if*-clauses is not true, but they do often occur with infinitives and gerunds (among other features described in the study).

Looking at grammatical co-occurrence patterns can also help to explain when rare constructions occur. For example, subject position *that*-clauses, as illustrated here, are very rare:

> **That there are no meteorites of any other age, regardless of when they fell to Earth,** suggests strongly that all meteorites originated in other bodies of the solar system that formed at the same time that the Earth did.
>
> (Biber *et al.* 1999: 677)

Considering constructions both with *that*- and *the fact that*-, subject position clauses occur about twenty to forty times per million words in academic prose and newspapers, and almost never occur in conversation, while *that*-clauses in other positions occur over 2,000–7,000 times per million words in the different registers (Biber *et al.* 1999: 674–6). These subject position clauses are obviously harder for listeners or readers to process, since they have a long constituent before the main verb. It is perhaps not surprising, then, that the subject position clauses tend to occur when the predicate of the sentence has another heavy, complex structure – a complicated noun phrase or prepositional phrase, or a complement clause, as in the above example. In addition, these clauses tend to be used in particular discourse contexts, a topic further discussed in the next section.

Discourse-level factors

Because many people's introduction to corpus linguistics is with simple concordance searches, they sometimes believe that corpus linguistics has little to offer discourse-level study. However, this clearly is not the case (see further Conrad 2002; Thornbury, this volume).

Many of the examples in the previous sections have noted associations that were found by analysing text at the discourse level, rather than considering only discrete lexical or grammatical features. Determining the semantic prosody of *get*-passives, for instance, required considering discourse context. Another perspective is added by further analysis of subject-position *that*-clauses, which shows that they are associated with information structuring in the discourse. That is, when *that*-clauses are in subject position, they tend to restate information that has already been mentioned or implied in the previous discourse. The subject clauses thus provide an anaphoric link. Fuller context for the example in the last section illustrates this pattern:

> One of the triumphs of radioactive dating emerged only gradually as more and more workers dated meteorites. It became surprisingly apparent that all meteorites

> are of the same age, somewhere in the vicinity of 4.5 billion years old … **That there are no meteorites of any other age, regardless of when they fell to Earth**, suggests strongly that all meteorites originated in other bodies of the solar system that formed at the same time that the Earth did.

Analysis of discourse-level factors affecting grammar often requires interpreting meaning, organisation, and information structure in texts, as in the example above. Such analysis is part of the more qualitative, interpretive side of a corpus study, focusing on how a grammatical structure is used in context. However, it is also possible to design a corpus-based study that uses computer-assisted techniques to track a grammatical feature's occurrence throughout texts in order to describe its use on a discourse-level. These studies generally require writing specialised computer programs, rather than using commercially available software. Burges (1996) describes such a study, using computational analysis to track how writers refer to their audience (e.g. *I*, *you*, *faculty*) in memos that are written to groups of superiors, inferiors or those of equal hierarchical standing in institutions. She finds that the choices that writers make between nouns and pronouns and their level of prominence (in theme or rheme position) constructs and manipulates the writers' authority as the memo progresses. A similar technique is exemplified in Biber *et al.* (1998: Ch. 5). They map the choice of verb tense and voice throughout science research articles, finding that areas of numerous shifts – i.e. when occurrences of verbs alternate between active and passive voice, or between past and present – correspond to transition zones that are of particular rhetorical interest.

Overall, few studies have used this approach of mapping the use of a grammatical feature through a text. Nevertheless, the technique has great potential for increasing our understanding of grammatical features on a discourse level. From this perspective, the description of noun and pronoun selection, or of verb tense and voice, becomes far more a matter of rhetorical function and authorial power than typically found in traditional grammatical descriptions.

Context of the situation

A number of factors in the context of the situation may be associated with the choice of a particular grammatical feature. Sociolinguistic studies have long considered how language use is affected by audience, purpose, participant roles, formality of the situation, and numerous other social and regional characteristics, and corpus-based techniques can be applied in these areas (see Andersen, this volume). Thus far in studies of grammar, the most common perspective on variation has concerned registers (also called genres) – varieties associated with a particular situation of use and communicative purpose, and often identified within a culture by a specific name, such as academic prose, text messaging, conversation or newspaper writing.

Making comparisons across registers as part of a description of a grammatical feature has already been exemplified in a number of examples above. For instance, the discussion of verb + *that*-clause objects explained that the frequency of the structure and the most common lexico-grammatical associations differed between conversation and academic prose, with conversation using the structure to report thoughts and feelings, and academic prose using it to report research findings. Throughout the *Longman Grammar of Spoken and Written English* (Biber *et al.* 1999) grammatical features are described with reference to their frequency and use in conversation, fiction writing, newspaper writing and academic prose. The *Cambridge Grammar of English* (Carter and McCarthy 2006) makes numerous comparisons between the use of features in speech and writing.

Other studies compare registers in more restricted domains. Grammatical features used in particular academic settings have received considerable attention. Numerous studies have used the Michigan Corpus of Academic Spoken English to analyse grammatical features in typical settings in an American university – e.g. Fortanet (2004) describes details of the pronoun *we* in lectures, and Louwerse *et al.* (2008) discuss the use of conditionals. Biber (2006: Ch. 4) compares numerous grammatical features across ten spoken and written registers from four American universities in the Spoken and Written Academic Language corpus.

Whether focused on restricted or general settings, studies that make comparisons across registers all demonstrate that it is usually misleading to characterise the frequency and use of a grammatical feature in only one way. Rather, accurate grammatical descriptions require describing differences across registers (see further Biber, this volume; Conrad 2000).

Traditional sociolinguistic variables such as social class, ethnic group and age have been less studied in corpus-based grammar research. As Meyer (2002) explains, this is partly because of the difficulty of compiling a large spoken corpus that is representative of these different variables. Corpus-based studies of social variables have generally been large-scale regional comparisons such as British and American English differences (e.g. in various comparisons throughout Biber *et al.* 1999; Carter and McCarthy 2006: Appendix), or differences in varieties of world Englishes (Nelson 2006; Kachru 2008). The Bergen Corpus of London Teenage Language (a sub-corpus built from the British National Corpus) has made it possible to study some specific grammatical features of British teenager talk such as aspects of reported speech, some non-standard grammatical features, and the use of intensifiers (Stenström *et al.* 2002).

In the future, it is likely that new corpus projects will facilitate more study of the sociolinguistic variation of grammatical features (e.g. see Kretzschmar *et al.* 2006). However, as Kachru (2008) points out, roles and relationships are negotiated throughout a social interaction, and thus far, corpus techniques have not often been applied to studying these interpersonal dynamics. Specially written software programs could aid in the analysis of the interactions in a corpus that had social relationships thoroughly documented, and could add to our understanding of the most typical uses of specific grammatical features in the course of interactions. However, few researchers currently undertake the combination of computational analysis and intensive conversational analysis that would be required.

3. Investigating multiple features/conditions simultaneously

From the previous sections it is probably already apparent that it is often difficult to focus on only one type of pattern when explaining grammatical choices. There is often more than one contextual factor corresponding to the use of a particular feature. Without computer assistance for the analysis, it is often unfeasible to consider these multiple factors in a large number of texts simultaneously. Another contribution of corpus linguistics has been to describe more about the multiple factors that simultaneously have an impact on grammatical choices.

For example, consider the case of omitting the optional *that* in a *that*-complement clause – e.g. *I think Ø I'll go*. Virtually any grammatical description includes the fact that the *that* is optional. Some textbooks for ESL students explain that it is especially common to delete it in speech (e.g. Azar 2002: 248). More detailed corpus analysis shows that the omission of *that* is actually associated with a number of factors (Biber *et al.* 1999: 681), as shown in Figure 17.1. One factor is a lexico-grammatical association: *that* is omitted more often when the verb in the main clause is *say* or *think* rather than any other verb. Two factors concern the grammatical co-text: (1) *that* is omitted more often when the main clause and complement clause have co-referential subjects (rather than subjects that refer to different entities), and (2) *that* is omitted more often when the *that*-clause has a personal pronoun subject rather than a full noun phrase. Another factor concerns the situational context, specifically the register: *that* is omitted more often in conversation than in newspaper writing generally, but the lexico-grammatical and grammatical co-text factors have a stronger effect in newspapers. That is, the choice of verb and subject types corresponds to a greater difference in percentage of *that* omission in newspapers than in conversation. In sum, corpus analysis shows that the choice of omitting or retaining *that* is much more complex than noted in traditional descriptions, but there are nonetheless identifiable patterns in the choice.

Two other approaches are also used for analysing multiple influences on grammatical choices. One is to consider a functional system within a language and describe factors that influence the grammatical features that are used to realise the system. For example, studies have included investigations of how metadiscourse is realised differently in different registers (e.g. Mauranen 2003a, 2003b) and how stance is conveyed grammatically across registers (Biber *et al.* 1999: Ch. 12; Biber 2004). The other approach is to study the grammar of a variety. In this approach the focus shifts from describing grammar to describing the variety, covering as many grammatical and lexical features as possible. This approach is covered by Biber (this volume).

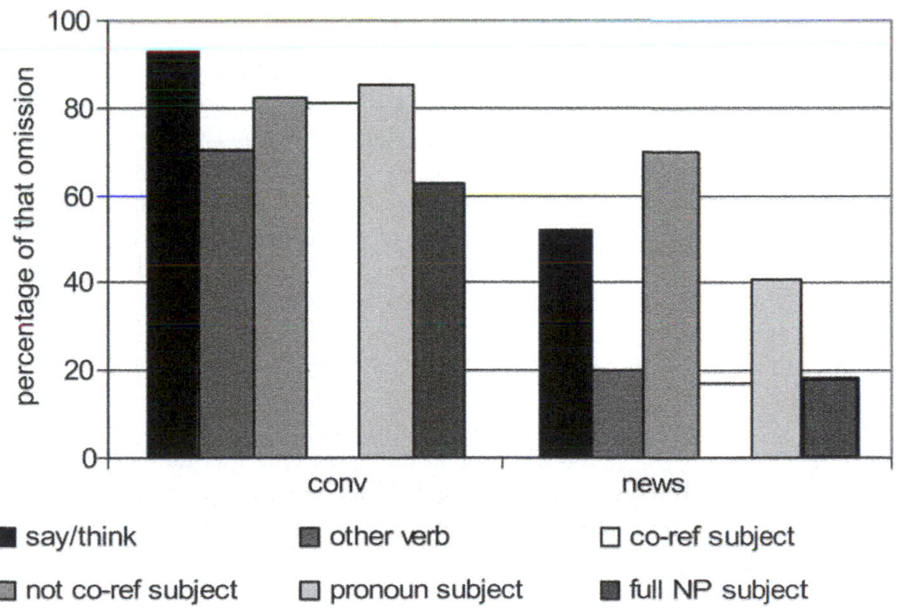

Figure 17.1 Conditions associated with omission of *that* in *that*-clauses.

4. The grammar of speech

The above sections have all made mention of grammatical features in spoken discourse. Before corpus studies became popular, grammatical descriptions virtually always were based on written language (McCarthy and Carter 1995; Hughes and McCarthy 1998). Unplanned spoken language was neglected or, at best, considered aberrant, with its 'incomplete' clauses, messy repairs and non-standard forms. In contrast, corpus analyses have emphasised the fact that many features of speech directly reflect the demands of face-to-face interactions. Spoken grammar has become studied as a legitimate grammar, not a lacking form of written grammar.

One factor often noted for grammatical choices in conversation concerns the need to minimise imposition and be indirect. For example, Conrad (1999) discusses the common choice of *though* rather than *however* as a contrastive connector in conversation. Placed at the end of the clause and conveying a sense of concession more than contrast, the use of *though* is a less direct way to disagree than *however* is. A typical example in a conversation is as follows:

[Watching a football game, discussing a penalty call]
A: Oh, that's outrageous.
B: Well, he did put his foot out **though**.

Speaker B clearly disagrees with A's contention that the call is 'outrageous', but the use of *though* (along with the discourse marker *well*) downplays the disagreement. The desire to convey indirectness can also result in the use of verb tenses or aspects not normally found in writing. For example, McCarthy and Carter (2002: 58) describe the use of present progressive with verbs of desire, as when a customer tells a travel agent that she and her husband *are wanting* to take a trip. The use of present progressive makes the desire sound more tentative, and the request for help less imposing. Other features affecting the grammatical forms that are typical of face-to-face interactions include the shared context (and in many cases shared background knowledge), the expression of emotions and evaluations, and the constraints of real-time production and processing (see further the summary of factors and features in Biber *et al.* 1999: Ch. 14; and Carter and McCarthy 2006: 163–75).

Traditionally, the grammar of conversation has been thought to be simple when compared to writing. A further contribution of corpus studies, however, has been to show that there is grammatical complexity in conversation – but complexity of a particular sort. While expository writing tends to have complex noun phrases, conversation has more complexity at a clausal level. Even with limited time for planning ahead, speakers can produce highly embedded clauses, as in this speaker's explanation of trying to find his cat:

[The trouble is [[if you're the only one in the house] [he follows you] [and you're looking for him] [so you can't find him.]]] [I thought [I wonder [where the hell he's gone]]] [I mean he was immediately behind me.]]

(Biber *et al.* 1999: 1068)

Although such utterances could be documented before the use of corpus techniques, it was only with the publication of corpus-based grammatical studies that the complexities of conversational grammar gained prominence. Corpus investigations of grammar also provide frequency information as evidence that certain complex structures are more common in conversation than writing. For example, *that*-clauses as complements of verbs and adjectives are over three times more common in conversation than academic prose (Biber *et al.* 1999: 675).

5. New challenges for judging acceptability

As the examples above have illustrated, corpus linguistics has given us the tools to describe the most typical grammatical choices that speakers and writer make. Even for structures that are relatively rarely used – such as subject position *that*-clauses – we can identify the specific conditions under which they are most typically used. However, describing grammatical choices in a more probabilistic way makes judgements about acceptability far more complex than they used to be. Further complicating these judgements is the fact that variation in grammatical choices exists not only through lexical, grammatical, discourse and situational context, as described in this chapter, but also for stylistic reasons (see Biber and Conrad, 2009). Speakers and writers are also creative with language (see Vo and Carter this volume). Given this complexity, if a rare choice is attested in a corpus, how are we to determine whether it is just a rare choice or an error? Does a certain level of frequency imply acceptability – and if so, how would that level be determined? Interestingly, this issue of the relationship between corpus data and acceptability judgements is of most concern to two groups whose concerns often do not overlap: linguistic theorists and teachers.

Much linguistic theory is focused on describing what people know when they know the grammar of a language, and disagreement exists as to whether the empirical analysis of corpora has a role to play in determining that knowledge. Newmeyer (2003) views grammar and usage as distinct. He argues that 'knowledge of grammatical structure is only one of many systems that underlie usage' (p. 692). Since those 'many systems' are at play on any language produced in a real context, the only way to clearly investigate a person's knowledge of grammatical structure is through intuition. In this view, corpus linguistics can shed light on usage, but not on grammaticality. Meyer and Tao (2005) counter, however, that intuition can only provide insight into one person's individual grammar and thus analyses of corpora are important because they allow researchers to investigate what large numbers of people consider acceptable. Sampson (2007) argues that basing scientific inquiry on subjective knowledge and intuition is an outdated practice, and thus corpus analysis – a form of empirical investigation – deserves a larger role in building linguistic theory.

For theorists, this argument about the relationship between what is acceptable in grammatical form and what speakers and writers use in real texts (and therefore how great a contribution corpus linguistics can make to linguistic theory) is not likely to be resolved any time soon. At this stage in the development of corpus linguistics, the contribution it will make to linguistic theory is an open question. In fact, in the early years of corpus linguistics, few studies applied themselves to issues of linguistic theory. However, a noteworthy development is the international peer-reviewed journal *Corpus Linguistics and Linguistic Theory*, which started publication in 2005.

For most teachers and students, the relationship between what is found in a corpus and what is grammatically acceptable is a much more immediate and practical issue than for linguistic theorists. As corpus techniques were gaining popularity for teaching grammar in the mid-1990s, Owen (1996) raised this issue in a now well-known paper that used the sentence 'Many more experimental studies require to be done' to demonstrate the difficulties with consulting a corpus for enhancing prescription (p. 222). He explained that most native speakers are likely to find the structure unacceptable, but an ESL student looking at the British National Corpus would find some similar sentences – e.g. explanations describing that 'fruit trees require to be pruned' – and the student would likely believe that *require* + a passive *to*-infinitive clause is acceptable. Hunston (2002: 177) explains that the apparent conflict is resolved by considering the semantics of the lexico-grammatical association. Specifically, in the corpus, almost all the verbs occurring in the infinitive clause express a specific meaning, and the subjects are clearly the recipients of an action (e.g. *trees are changed by the pruning*). In Owen's example, in contrast, the verb *do* has a very general meaning and the subject, *many more experimental studies*, is not actually acted upon (i.e. *do a study* does not mean that a specific action was done to a study but rather is a way to express the process of conducting research).

This analysis addresses the problem of the corpus appearing to have many occurrences of a structure most native speakers find unacceptable; in fact, when the lexico-grammatical associations are further examined, it does not. However, such an analysis requires quite sophisticated linguistic explanations and can be time-consuming – and so does not address the pedagogical problem of reconciling corpus data and grammaticality judgements. Rather, virtually all corpus researchers who address teaching issues agree that teachers' intuition and prescriptive grammar rules have a role when students need judgements about acceptability. As Hunston puts it, 'Distinguishing between what is said and what is accepted as standard may need the assistance of a teacher or a grammar book' (Hunston 2002: 177; see further discussion of grammar teaching in Hughes, this volume).

The real contribution of corpus linguistics to grammar has not been to help make judgements about acceptability easier. Rather, it has been to complicate judgements of acceptability to make them reflect reality more accurately. As research in sociolinguistics has shown for many decades, acceptability varies with context. One clear sign of corpus linguistics' impact on the field of grammar can be seen in the way that recent corpus-based grammar books of English handle standards and acceptability. Biber *et al.* (1999) have six and a half pages devoted to discussion of standard English, non-standard English and variation in them. Carter and McCarthy (2006: 5) cover four descriptions of acceptability that consider register and regional factors (in addition to an 'unacceptable in all contexts' category). Clearly, work in corpus linguistics is moving the field beyond the dichotomous view of grammatical structures as acceptable versus unacceptable and accurate versus inaccurate.

In a chapter of this size, a number of important areas are inevitably neglected. For the methods of corpus-based grammar studies, much more could be said especially about the role of statistics (see e.g. Oakes 1998) and the usefulness of grammatically annotated corpora (see chapters by Reppen and Lee, this volume). Among the topic areas that deserve far more coverage is the development of grammar over time, including both historical studies (e.g. Fitzmaurice 2003; Leech and Smith 2006) and studies of emergent forms (e.g. Barbieri's 2005 study of new quotative forms such as *be like*, *be all* and *go*). Corpus studies are also beginning to make considerable contributions to our understanding of the grammar of specific varieties of English in the world (e.g. see de Klerk 2006 on Xhosa English) and to English used as a lingua franca (e.g. Seidlhofer 2001; Mollin 2006). In addition, corpus studies have addressed grammar in many languages other than English (e.g. see the collections edited by Johansson and Oksefjell 1998; Wilson *et al.* 2006). Despite its inability to do justice to all related topics, however, the chapter has sought to show that corpus linguistics has already had a profound effect on our understanding of grammar and is likely to continue to do so in the future.

Further reading

Biber, D., Johansson, S., Leech, G., Conrad, S. and Finegan, E. (1999) *Longman Grammar of Spoken and Written English.* Harlow, England: Pearson Education. (This covers frequency information, lexico-grammar patterns and comparisons of use in conversation, fiction writing, newspaper writing and academic prose for all major structures in English, as well as including chapters on fixed phrases, stance and conversation.)

Carter, R. and McCarthy, M. (2006) *Cambridge Grammar of English.* Cambridge: Cambridge University Press. (This emphasises more general spoken versus written language, but also includes many similar lexico-grammatical analyses, and covers some more functional categories of language – e.g. describing typical grammatical realisations of speech acts – and typical ESL difficulties.)

References

Azar, B. (2002) *Understanding and Using English Grammar*, third edition. White Plains, NY: Longman.

Barbieri, F. (2005) 'Quotative Use in American English: A Corpus-based, Cross-register Comparison', *Journal of English Linguistic* 33(3): 222–56.

Biber, D. (2004) 'Historical Patterns for the Grammatical Marking of Stance: A Cross-register Comparison', *Journal of Historical Pragmatics* 5(1): 107–35.

——(2006) *University Language: A Corpus-based Study of Spoken and Written Registers.* Amsterdam: John Benjamins.

Biber, D. and Conrad, S. (2009) *Register Genre Style.* Cambridge: Cambridge University Press.

Biber, D., Conrad, S. and Reppen, R. (1998) *Corpus Linguistics: Investigating Language Structure and Use.* Cambridge: Cambridge University Press.

Biber, D., Johansson, S., Leech, G., Conrad, S. and Finegan, E. (1999) *Longman Grammar of Spoken and Written English.* Harlow, England: Pearson Education.

Biber, D., Conrad, S. and Cortes, V. (2004) '"Take a Look At … ": Lexical Bundles in University Teaching and Textbooks', *Applied Linguistics* 25(3): 401–35.

Burges, J. (1996) 'Hierarchical Influences on Language Use in Memos', unpublished dissertation, Northern Arizona University.

Carter, R. and McCarthy, M. (2006) *Cambridge Grammar of English.* Cambridge: Cambridge University Press.

Conrad, S. (1999) 'The Importance of Corpus-based Research for Language Teachers', *System* 27 (1): 1–18.

——(2000) 'Will Corpus Linguistics Revolutionize Grammar Teaching in the 21st Century?' *TESOL Quarterly* 34(3): 548–60.

——(2002) 'Corpus Linguistic Approaches for Discourse Analysis', *Annual Review of Applied Linguistics* 22 (*Discourse and Dialog*): 75–95.

Cook, V. (1994) 'Universal Grammar and the Learning and Teaching of Second Languages', in T. Odlin (ed.), *Perspectives on Pedagogical Grammar.* Cambridge: Cambridge University Press, pp. 25–48.

de Klerk, V. (2006) *Corpus Linguistics and World Englishes: An Analysis of Xhosa English.* London: Continuum.

Fitzmaurice, S. (2003) 'The Grammar of Stance in Early Eighteenth-century English Epistolary Language', in P. Leistyna and C. Meyer (eds) *Corpus Analysis: Language Structure and Language Use.* Amsterdam: Rodopi, pp. 107–32.

Fortanet, I. (2004) 'The Use of "We" in University Lectures: Reference and Function', *English for Specific Purposes* 23(1): 45–66.

Frazier, S. (2003) 'A Corpus Analysis of *Would*-clauses Without Adjacent *If*-clauses', *TESOL Quarterly* 37(3): 443–66.

Hughes, R. and McCarthy, M. (1998) 'From Sentence to Grammar: Discourse Grammar and English Language Teaching', *TESOL Quarterly* 32(2): 263–87.

Hunston, S. (2002) *Corpora in Applied Linguistics*. Cambridge: Cambridge University Press.

Hunston, S. and Francis, G. (1999) *Pattern Grammar: A Corpus-driven Approach to the Lexical Grammar of English*. Amsterdam: John Benjamins.

Johansson, J. and Oksefjell, S. (eds) (1998) *Corpora and Cross-linguistic Research: Theory, Method and Case Studies*. Amsterdam: Rodopi.

Kachru, Y. (2008) 'Language Variation and Corpus Linguistics', *World Englishes* 27(1): 1–8.

Kretzschmar, W., Anderson, J., Beal, J., Corrigan, K., Opas-Hänninen, L. and Plichta, B. (2006) 'Collaboration on Corpora for Regional and Social Analysis', *Journal of English Linguistics* 34(3): 172–205.

Larsen-Freeman, D. (2002) 'The Grammar of Choice', in E. Hinkel and S. Fotos (eds) *New Perspectives on Grammar Teaching in Second Language Classrooms*. Mahwah, NJ: Erlbaum, pp. 103–18.

Leech, G. and Smith, N. (2006) 'Recent Grammatical Change in Written English 1961–92', in A. Renouf and A. Kehoe (eds) *The Changing Face of Corpus Linguistics*. Amsterdam: Rodopi, pp. 185–204.

Louwerse, M., Crossley, S. and Jeuniauxa, P. (2008) 'What If? Conditionals in Educational Registers', *Linguistics and Education* 19(1): 56–69.

McCarthy, M. and Carter, R. (1995) 'Spoken Grammar: What Is It and How Do We Teach It?' *ELT Journal* 49(3): 207–18.

——(2001) 'Size Isn't Everything: Spoken English, Corpus, and the Classroom', *TESOL Quarterly* 35(2): 337–40.

——(2002) 'Ten Criteria for a Spoken Grammar', in E. Hinkel and S. Fotos (eds) *New Perspectives on Grammar Teaching in Second Language Classrooms*. Mahwah, NJ: Lawrence Erlbaum, pp. 51–75.

Mauranen, A. (2003a), '"But Here's a Flawed Argument": Socialisation into and through Metadiscourse', in P. Leistyna and C. Meyer (eds) *Corpus Analysis: Language Structure and Language Use*. New York: Rodopi, pp. 19–34.

——(2003b) '"A Good Question". Expressing Evaluation in Academic Speech', in G. Cortese and P. Riley (eds) *Domain-Specific English: Textual Practices across Communities and Classrooms*. New York: Peter Lang, pp. 115–40.

Meyer, C. (2002) *English Corpus Linguistics: An Introduction*. Cambridge: Cambridge University Press.

Meyer, C. and Tao, H. (2005) 'Response to Newmeyer's "Grammar Is Grammar and Usage is Usage"', *Language* 81(1): 226–8.

Mollin, S. (2006) 'English as a Lingua Franca: A New Variety in the New Expanding Circle?' *Nordic Journal of English Studies* 5(2): 41–57.

Nelson, G. (2006) 'The Core and Periphery of World English: A Corpus-based Exploration', *World Englishes* 25(1): 115–29.

Newmeyer, F. (2003) 'Grammar is Grammar and Usage is Usage', *Language* 79(4): 682–707.

Oakes, M. (1998) *Statistics for Corpus Linguistics*. Edinburgh: University of Edinburgh.

O'Keeffe, A., McCarthy, M. and Carter, R. (2007) *From Corpus to Classroom*. Cambridge: Cambridge University Press.

Owen, C. (1996) 'Does a Corpus Require to Be Consulted?' *ELT Journal* 50(3): 219–24.

Sampson, G. (2007) 'Grammar without Grammaticality', *Corpus Linguistics and Linguistic Theory* 3(1): 1–32.

Seidlhofer, B. (2001) 'Closing a Conceptual Gap: The Case for a Description of English as a Lingua Franca', *International Journal of Applied Linguistics* 11(1): 133–58.

Sinclair, J. (1991) *Corpus, Concordance, Collocation*. Oxford: Oxford University Press.

Stenström, A.-B., Andersen, G. and Hasund, I. (2002) *Trends in Teenage Talk: Corpus Compilation, Analysis and Findings*. Amsterdam: John Benjamins.

Wilson, A., Archer, D. and Rayson, P. (eds) (2006) *Corpus Linguistics around the World*. Amsterdam: Rodopi.

18

What can a corpus tell us about registers and genres?

Douglas Biber

1. The register perspective and the genre perspective

Text category is the most important organising principle of most modern corpora. Even the earliest electronic corpora, such as the Brown, LOB and London–Lund corpora, are organised in terms of text categories. For example, the Brown and LOB corpora are structured to represent text categories like press reportage, press editorials, biographies and essays, academic prose, general fiction, etc. The London–Lund Corpus was structured in terms of text categories like face-to-face conversations, telephone conversations, broadcasts, spontaneous speeches and planned speeches.

The centrality of text category for corpus design continues up to the present day, although the categories are often more narrowly specified than in early corpora. For example, MICASE, a large corpus of university spoken English, includes specific text categories like lectures, labs and dissertation defences (Simpson-Vlach and Leicher 2006). Similarly, CANCODE, a large corpus of conversational English, includes specific text varieties relating to different situations (e.g. workplace, academic and everyday conversation) and speaker relationships (e.g. intimate, socialising, professional; see McCarthy 1998 for details).

Given the centrality of text category in corpus design and construction, it should come as no surprise that many corpus-based studies include analysis of linguistic differences across categories. These studies often use the cover terms *register* and *genre* to refer to the text categories distinguished in corpora. Building on earlier research by Halliday, Ferguson and others, Biber and Conrad (2009) distinguish between genre and register as two approaches or perspectives for the analysis of text varieties (cf. Biber *et al.* 2007). In the *genre* perspective, the focus is on the linguistic characteristics that are used to structure complete texts. These are conventional linguistic characteristics that usually occur only once in a text. For this reason, genre studies must be based on analysis of complete texts from the variety. These language features are conventionally associated with the genre: they conform to the culturally expected way of constructing texts belonging to the variety. For example, scientific research articles conventionally begin with an abstract, followed by the main body of the text, which is usually structured as four main sections – Introduction, Methods, Results, Discussion – which is in turn followed by the references.

In contrast, the *register* perspective focuses on the pervasive linguistic characteristics of representative text excerpts from the variety. The register perspective characterises the typical linguistic features of text varieties, and connects those features functionally to the situational context of the variety. Because the focus is on words and grammatical features that are frequent and pervasive, the analysis can be based on a sample of text excerpts rather than complete texts. For example, from a register perspective, we can discover that business letters have a higher use of first and second person pronouns than expository registers, like newspaper reportage or scientific research articles. Similarly, there are numerous linguistic features that occur more commonly in scientific research articles than in most other text varieties, such as nominalisations, attributive adjectives, prepositional phrases, etc. These features occur frequently in the target text variety because they are well-suited functionally to the communicative purposes and situational context of the variety.

For several reasons, most corpus-based studies of text varieties have taken a register perspective rather than a genre perspective. First, corpora have traditionally been much better designed for the analysis of register than genre. That is, corpora have often been composed of text excerpts rather than complete texts, making it possible to identify the linguistic features that are used pervasively throughout texts (register features), but not possible to identify conventional features that are used at a particular place in a complete text (the genre perspective). Similarly, software tools like concordancers have been designed for the analysis of pervasive and frequent linguistic characteristics (register features) rather than features that occur only once or twice in a text (genre features). In fact, corpus-based descriptions are usually focused on frequency analyses of lexico-grammatical features: what words or grammatical structures are common, how much more frequent are some features than others, etc. These are register characteristics rather than genre characteristics. In contrast, the genre perspective typically describes the rhetorical organisation of texts, with no consideration of frequency. Such descriptions require detailed analysis of individual texts, rather than exploring linguistic patterns across a large sample of text extracts. In recent years, special-purpose corpora have been developed for such analyses.

2. Corpus studies of linguistic variation that use register as a predictor: when the focus is on a particular linguistic feature

Studies focused on the description of a particular linguistic feature can be divided into two major types. First, several studies focus on the linguistic variants associated with a feature, using register differences as one factor to account for the patterns of linguistic variation. However, there are an even larger number of studies that have focused on the use of a particular linguistic feature in a single register; in this case, the goals of the study are to describe both the discourse functions of the linguistic feature and the target register itself. Studies of both types can be further subdivided according to the linguistic level of the target feature (e.g. vocabulary, grammatical class, dependent clause type, etc.). In addition, both types of study include descriptions of synchronic patterns of use as well as descriptions of historical patterns of variation.

Well before it was fashionable to claim that a study was 'corpus-based', descriptive studies of grammatical features were often based on empirical analyses of a text collection: the equivalent of a non-computerised corpus. An especially noteworthy example of this type is the work of C. C. Fries, who wrote two corpus-based grammars of American English. The first, published in 1940, had a focus on usage and social variation, based on a corpus of letters written to the government. The second is essentially a grammar of conversation: it was published in 1952, based on a 250,000-word corpus of telephone conversations. It includes authentic examples taken from the corpus, and discussion of grammatical features that are especially characteristic of conversation (e.g. the words *well*, *oh*, *now* and *why* when they initiate a 'response utterance unit'; Fries 1952: 101–2).

Functional linguists like Prince and Thompson continued this descriptive tradition, arguing that (non-computerised) collections of natural texts could be studied to identify systematic differences in the functional use of linguistic variants. For example, Prince (1978) compares the discourse functions of Wh-clefts and *it*-clefts in spoken and written texts. Thompson has been especially interested in the study of grammatical variation in conversation; for example, Thompson and Mulac (1991) analysed factors influencing the retention versus omission of the complementiser *that* in conversation, while Fox and Thompson (1990) studied variation in the realisation of relative clauses in conversation.

More recently, studies in this research tradition have adopted the tools and techniques available from computer-based corpus linguistics, with its greater emphasis on the representativeness of the text collection, and its computational tools for investigating distributional patterns across registers and across discourse contexts in large text collections. The textbook treatments by Kennedy (1998), Biber *et al.* (1998) and McEnery *et al.* (2006) provide good introductions to the methods used for these studies as well as surveys of previous research.

Corpus-based studies of linguistic features using register as a predictor have investigated linguistic variation from all grammatical levels, from simple part-of-speech categories to variation in the realisation of syntactic phrase and clause types. These studies have shown that descriptions of grammatical variation and use are not valid for the language as a whole. Rather, characteristics of the textual environment interact with register differences, so that strong patterns of use in one register often represent only weak patterns in other registers. The *Longman Grammar of Spoken and Written English* (Biber *et al.* 1999) and *Cambridge Grammar of English* (Carter and McCarthy 2006) are comprehensive reference works with this goal, applying corpus-based analyses to show how any grammatical feature can be described for structural characteristics as well as patterns of use across spoken and written registers.

As noted above, many corpus-based studies use register differences as a predictor of linguistic variation, while others study linguistic features in the context of a single register. Thus, for example, Tottie (1991) is a book-length discussion of the linguistic factors associated with the choice between synthetic and analytic negation, as in:

> He could find *no* words to express his pain.
> versus
> He could*n't* find any words to express his pain.

Among other factors, Tottie shows that synthetic negation is strongly preferred in written rather than spoken registers, while analytic negation is more commonly used in spoken registers. In contrast, Hyland (1998) focuses on the single register of scientific research articles, describing variation in the use of hedges within that register.

As noted above, these studies have documented the use of lexico-grammatical features at all linguistic levels. Several studies analyse a single part-of-speech category, documenting the patterns of variation and use in particular registers. Studies taking the perspective of register variation include Barbieri (2005) on quotative verbs and Römer (2005a) on progressive verbs.

Several other studies describe linguistic variation within the context of a single spoken register, such as conversation. Quaglio and Biber (2006) survey the distinctive grammatical characteristics of conversation identified through corpus research, while other studies provide detailed descriptions of a particular feature in conversation. For example, McCarthy (2002) describes non-minimal response tokens; Aijmer (2002) provides a book-length description of discourse particles; Carter and McCarthy (2006) describe the discourse functions of the *get*-passive; Tao and McCarthy (2001) focus on non-restrictive *which*-clauses; Norrick (2008) describes the discourse functions of interjections in conversational narratives. Other studies of a single spoken register have focused on academic speech in university settings, based on analysis of the MICASE Corpus. For example, Fortanet (2004) focuses on the pronoun *we* in university lectures; Lindemann and Mauranen (2001) describe the use of *just* in academic speech; and Swales (2001) provides a detailed description of the discourse functions served by *point* and *thing* in university academic speech.

A much larger number of studies have described linguistic variation within the context of a particular written register, most often a type of academic writing. Many of these have focused on the kinds of verbs used in research writing (e.g. Thomas and Hawes 1994), or the referring expressions in research articles (e.g. Hyland 2001 on the use of self-mentions, and Kuo 1999 on the role relationships expressed by personal pronouns). Other studies deal with simple grammatical structures, but again most often within the context of academic writing. For example, Hyland (2002a) and Swales *et al.* (1998) describe variation in the use of imperatives and the expression of directives, while Hyland (2002b) and Marley (2002) focus on the use of questions in written registers.

The study of linguistic variation related to the expression of stance and modality has been especially popular in corpus-based research. Several of these studies compare the ways in which stance is expressed in spoken versus written registers. Biber and Finegan (1988) and Conrad and Biber (2000) focus on adverbial markers of stance in speech and writing, while Biber and Finegan (1989b) and Biber *et al.* (1999: Ch. 12) survey variation in the use of numerous grammatical stance devices (including modal verbs, stance adverbials and stance complement clause constructions), again contrasting the patterns of use in spoken versus written registers. Biber (2006a) and Keck and Biber (2004) take a similar approach but applied to university spoken and written registers.

Many other studies focus exclusively on the expression of stance and modality in written registers (usually academic writing). These include Vilha's (1999) study of modality in medical research writing, the studies of stance by Charles (2003, 2006, 2007) on academic writing from different disciplines, and several studies that focus on hedging in academic writing (e.g. Salager 1994; Hyland 1996, 1998; Grabe and Kaplan 1997). Related studies have been carried out under the rubric of 'evaluation', again usually focusing on academic writing (e.g. Hunston and Thompson 2000; Stotesbury 2003; Tucker 2003; Hyland and Tse 2005; Römer 2005b; cf. Bednarek's 2006 study of evaluation in newspaper language). Fewer studies have described the linguistic devices used to express stance and evaluation in spoken registers; some of these have focused on conversation (e.g. McCarthy and Carter 1997, 2004; Tao 2007), while others have focused on academic spoken registers (e.g. Mauranen 2003, 2004; Mauranen and Bondi 2003; Swales and Burke 2003).

A second especially productive area of research has been the corpus-based (and corpus-driven) investigation of formulaic language in spoken and written registers. Although the study of lexical collocation is one of the best-known contributions of corpus research (see, e.g., Sinclair 1991; Partington 1998), such research has usually disregarded register differences. (Two interesting exceptions are Gledhill 2000 and Marco 2000, which both describe the functions of collocations in academic research writing.) In contrast, corpus studies of longer formulaic expressions are normally carried out in the context of a particular register, or for the purposes of describing patterns of register variation. For example, Simpson (2004) and Simpson and Mendis (2003) describe the function of idioms in academic spoken registers.

Many other studies have taken a corpus-driven approach to this research domain, identifying the sequences of words that are most common in different spoken and written registers (rather than starting with a set of formulaic expressions identified *a priori* based on their perceptual salience). These common word sequences, often referred to as 'lexical bundles', are usually not idiomatic and not complete structures, but they are important building blocks of discourse. Corpus studies have shown, however, that the types and functions of lexical bundles are very different among spoken and written registers. Thus, for example, Altenberg (1998) focuses on spoken English, while Biber *et al.* (1999: Ch. 13) compare conversation and academic writing. Applying that framework, several studies have considered the types and functions of lexical bundles in additional registers: university classroom teaching and textbooks (Biber *et al.* 2004; Nesi and Basturkmen 2006), university student writing (Cortes 2004), university institutional and advising registers (Biber and Barbieri 2007), political debate (Partington and Morley 2004).

Dependent clauses and more complex syntactic structures have also been the focus of numerous corpus-based studies that consider register differences. Several studies contrast the patterns of use in spoken and written registers: Collins (1991) on cleft constructions, de Haan (1989) on nominal postmodifiers, Geisler (1995) on relative infinitives, Johansson (1995) on relative pronoun choice, Biber (1999) on complement clause constructions. Other studies have focused on the use of a syntactic construction in a particular register, like the study of conditionals in medical discourse (Ferguson 2001) or the study of extraposed constructions in university student writing (Hewings and Hewings 2002).

All of the kinds of studies surveyed in the preceding paragraphs can be approached from a historical perspective rather than a synchronic perspective, and numerous studies have taken that approach. For example, many of the papers in the edited volumes by Nevalainen and Kahlas-Tarkka (1997) and Kytö *et al.* (2006) incorporate register comparisons, to describe historical change for linguistic features like existential clauses, adverbial clauses and relative clauses. Biber and Clark (2002) contrast the kinds of noun modifiers common in academic versus popular written registers. Several historical studies of stance and modality have included analysis of register differences, such as Kytö (1991) on modal verbs in written and speech-based registers, Culpeper and Kytö (1999) on hedges in Early Modern English dialogues, Salager-Meyer and Defives (1998) on hedges in academic writing over the last two centuries, Fitzmaurice (2002b) on stance and politeness in early eighteenth-century letters, and Biber (2004) on historical change in the use of stance and modal features across a range of speech-based and written registers. A few studies have focused on recent (twentieth-century) historical change; for example, Hundt and Mair (1999) contrast the rapid grammatical change observed in 'agile' registers (like newspaper writing) with the much slower pace of change observed in 'up-tight' registers like academic prose. Leech *et al.* (forthcoming) track historical change in the twentieth century, using the register categories distinguished in the Brown/LOB family of corpora.

3. Corpus studies of register variation: when the focus is on describing registers

The studies surveyed in the preceding section focus on a particular linguistic feature, using register to describe the use of that feature. In the present section, the analytical perspective is reversed: these studies focus on the overall description of a register, considering a suite of linguistic features that are characteristic of the register.

Many studies of this type describe spoken registers, including conversation (e.g. Carter and McCarthy 1997, 2004; Quaglio and Biber 2006; Biber 2008; Biber and Conrad 2009: Ch. 4), service encounters (e.g. McCarthy 2000), call centre interactions (Friginal 2008, 2009), spoken business English (McCarthy and Handford 2004), television dialogue (Rey 2001; Quaglio 2009), spoken media discourse (O'Keeffe 2006) and spoken university registers like classroom teaching, office hours and teacher-mentoring sessions (e.g. Biber *et al.* 2002; Csomay 2005; Biber 2006b; Reppen and Vásquez 2007).

However, written registers have received considerably more attention than spoken registers. Academic prose has been the best described written register (see, e.g., Conrad 1996, 2001; McKenna 1997; Connor and Mauranen 1999; Connor and Upton 2004; Freddi 2005; Tognini Bonelli and Camiciotti 2005; Biber 2006b; Biber *et al.* 2007). But many other written registers have also been described using corpus-based analysis, including personal letters (e.g. Precht 1998; Fitzmaurice 2002a; Connor and Upton 2003), written advertisements (e.g. Bruthiaux 1994, 1996, 2005), newspaper discourse (e.g. Jucker 1992; Herring 2003; Bednarek 2006) and fiction (e.g. Semino and Short 2004; Thompson and Sealey 2007; Mahlberg, forthcoming). Electronic registers that have emerged over the past few decades, from e-mail communication to weblogs and texting, have been an especially interesting and productive area of research (see, e.g., Gains 1999; Danet and Herring 2003; Herring and Paolillo 2006; Morrow 2006; Hundt *et al.* 2007; Biber and Conrad 2009: Ch. 7).

4. Multi-dimensional studies of register variation

Most of the studies listed above have the primary goal of describing a single register. However, corpus analysis can also be used to describe the overall patterns of variation among a set of spoken and/or written registers. Perhaps the best-known approach used for descriptions of this type is Multi-Dimensional (MD) analysis: a corpus-driven methodological approach that identifies the frequent linguistic co-occurrence patterns in a language, relying on inductive empirical/quantitative analysis (see, e.g., Biber 1988, 1995; Biber and Conrad 2009: Ch. 8). Frequency plays a central role in the analysis, since each dimension represents a constellation of linguistic features that frequently co-occur in texts. These 'dimensions' of variation can be regarded as linguistic constructs not previously recognised by linguistic theory. Thus, MD analysis is a corpus-driven (as opposed to corpus-based) methodology, in that the linguistic constructs – the 'dimensions' – emerge from analysis of linguistic co-occurrence patterns in the corpus.

MD studies of register variation have been used to describe the patterns of register variation in many different discourse domains, including general spoken and written registers (Biber 1988), spoken and written university registers (Biber *et al.* 2002; Biber 2006a), American English (AmE) versus British English (BrE) written registers (Biber 1987), AmE versus BrE conversational registers (Helt 2001), conversational text types (Biber 2008), biology versus history student and academic writing (Conrad 1996, 2001), elementary school spoken and written registers (Reppen 2001), direct mail letters (Connor and Upton 2003), non-profit grant proposals (Connor and Upton 2004) and author styles (Biber and Finegan 1994; Connor-Linton 2001). MD analyses have also been coupled with more detailed discourse analyses, to study variation among moves within biochemistry research articles (Kanoksilapatham 2005, 2007) and variation among discourse units in biology research articles (Biber and Jones 2005; Biber *et al.* 2007).

Corpus-driven MD studies of English registers have uncovered both surprising similarities and notable differences in the underlying dimensions of variation. Two parameters seem to be fundamentally important, regardless of the discourse domain: a dimension associated with informational focus versus (inter)personal focus, and a dimension associated with narrative discourse. At the same time, these MD studies have uncovered dimensions particular to the communicative functions and priorities of each different domain of use.

Finally, corpus analysis has been especially important for historical descriptions of registers (see Biber and Conrad 2009: Ch. 6). Multi-dimensional analysis has been used to document historical patterns of register variation (e.g. Atkinson 1992, 1996, 1999; Biber and Finegan 1989a; Biber 2001). However, there have been an even larger number of studies that provide a detailed description of a single historical register. A few MD studies have focused on a specific register, such as the study of historical change in fictional dialogue by Biber and Burges (2000) or the study of recent changes in television dialogue (Rey 2001). But most of these studies provide detailed descriptions of the linguistic characteristics of a historical register. Several of these studies analyse spoken registers from earlier historical periods (e.g. Culpeper and Kytö 2000, forthcoming; Kryk-Kastovsky 2000, 2006; Kytö and Walker 2003; Kahlas-Tarkka and Rissanen 2007). The large majority, though, focus on written historical registers, such as letters (Fitzmaurice 2002a; Nevala 2004), medical recipes and herbals (Taavitsainen 2001; Mäkinen 2002) and medical and scientific writing (e.g. Taavitsainen and Pahta 2000, 2004).

5. Corpus-based genre studies

Finally, there have been numerous corpus-based descriptions of a genre, documenting the moves or rhetorical structure of texts of a particular type. Most of these have focused on specific kinds of research writing, such as particular sections from research articles (e.g. abstracts, introductions or discussion sections; see Holmes 1997; Samraj 2002, 2005; Kanoksilapatham 2005, 2007; Ozturk 2007); PhD dissertations from various disciplines (Bunton 2002, 2005; Hyland 2004; Kwan 2006); grant proposals (Connor 2000), conference proposals (Halleck and Connor 2006), professional letters and application statements (Dos Santos 2002; Flowerdew and Dudley-Evans 2002; Henry and Roseberry 2001; Upton and Connor 2001; Upton 2002; Flowerdew and Wan 2006; Ding 2007). Biber *et al.* (2007) provide a book-length exploration of the ways in which corpus analysis can be used to explore the internal discourse structure of texts from particular genres, synthesising the goals and methods of detailed discourse analysis with large-scale quantitative corpus analysis.

Further reading

Biber, D. (2006) *University Language: A Corpus-Based Study of Spoken and Written Registers.* Amsterdam: John Benjamins. (A corpus-based description of registers like classroom teaching, office hours, study groups, textbooks and course syllabi.)

Biber, D. and Conrad, S. (2009) *Register, Genre, and Style.* Cambridge: Cambridge University Press. (This is a textbook introduction to register, genre and style, with a focus on methods of analysis and example descriptions.)

Friginal, E. (2009) *The Language of Outsourced Call Centers.* Amsterdam: John Benjamins. (This is an in-depth corpus-based study of call centre interactions between agents and customers.)

Quaglio, P. (2009) *Television Dialogue: The Sitcom* Friends *versus Natural Conversation.* Amsterdam: John Benjamins. (An in-depth corpus-based comparison of television dialogue to natural face-to-face conversation.)

References

Aijmer, K. (2002) *English Discourse Particles.* Amsterdam: John Benjamins.

Altenberg, B. (1998) 'On the Phraseology of Spoken English: The Evidence of Recurrent Word-combinations', in A. Cowie (ed.) *Phraseology: Theory, Analysis and Applications.* Oxford: Oxford University Press, pp. 101–22.

Atkinson, D. (1992) 'The Evolution of Medical Research Writing from 1735 to 1985: The Case of the Edinburgh Medical Journal', *Applied Linguistics* 13: 337–74.

——(1996) 'The Philosophical Transactions of the Royal Society of London, 1675–1975: A Socio-historical Discourse Analysis', *Language in Society* 25: 333–71.

——(1999) *Scientific Discourse in Sociohistorical Context: The Philosophical Transactions of the Royal Society of London, 1675–1975.* Hillsdale, NJ: Lawrence Erlbaum Associates.

Barbieri, F. (2005) 'Quotative Use in American English: A Corpus-based, Cross-register Comparison', *Journal of English Linguistics* 33(3): 222–56.

Bednarek, M. (2006) *Evaluation in Media Discourse. Analysis of a Newspaper Corpus.* London: Continuum.

Biber, D. (1987) 'A Textual Comparison of British and American Writing', *American Speech* 62: 99–119.

——(1988) *Variation across Speech and Writing.* Cambridge: Cambridge University Press.

——(1995) *Dimensions of Register Variation: A Cross-linguistic Comparison.* Cambridge: Cambridge University Press.

——(1999) 'A Register Perspective on Grammar and Discourse: Variability in the Form and Use of English Complement Clauses', *Discourse Studies* 1: 131–50.

——(2001) 'Dimensions of Variation among Eighteenth-century Speech-based and Written Registers', in S. Conrad and D. Biber (eds) *Variation in English: Multidimensional Studies.* Harlow: Longman, pp. 200–14.

——(2004) 'Historical Patterns for the Grammatical Marking of Stance: A Cross-register Comparison', *Journal of Historical Pragmatics* 5: 107–35.

——(2006a) 'Stance in Spoken and Written University Registers', *Journal of English for Academic Purposes* 5: 97–116.

——(2006b) *University Language: A Corpus-based Study of Spoken and Written Registers.* Amsterdam: John Benjamins.

——(2008) 'Corpus-based Analyses of Discourse: Dimensions of Variation in Conversation', in V. Bhatia, J. Flowerdew and R. Jones (eds) *Advances in Discourse Studies.* London: Routledge, pp. 100–14.

Biber, D. and Barbieri, F. (2007) 'Lexical Bundles in University Spoken and Written Registers', *English for Specific Purposes* 26: 263–86.

Biber, D. and Burges, J. (2000) 'Historical Change in the Language Use of Women and Men: Gender Differences in Dramatic Dialogue', *Journal of English Linguistics* 28: 21–37.

Biber, D. and Clark, V. (2002) 'Historical Shifts in Modification Patterns with Complex Noun Phrase Structures: How Long Can You Go Without a Verb?' in T. Fanego, M. J. López-Couso and J. Pérez-Guerra (eds) *English Historical Syntax and Morphology*. Amsterdam: John Benjamins, pp. 43–66.

Biber, D. and Conrad, S. (2009) *Register, Genre, Style*. Cambridge: Cambridge University Press.

Biber, D. and Finegan, E. (1988) 'Adverbial Stance Types in English', *Discourse Processes* 11: 1–34.

——(1989a) 'Drift and the Evolution of English Style: A History of Three Genres', *Language* 65: 487–517.

——(1989b) 'Styles of Stance in English: Lexical and Grammatical Marking of Evidentiality and Affect', *Text* 9: 93–124.

——(1994) 'Multi-dimensional Analyses of Authors' Styles: Some Case Studies from the Eighteenth Century', in D. Ross and D. Brink (eds) *Research in Humanities Computing 3*. Oxford: Oxford University Press, pp. 3–17.

Biber, D. and Jones, J. K. (2005) 'Merging Corpus Linguistic and Discourse Analytic Research Goals: Discourse Units in Biology Research Articles', *Corpus Linguistics and Linguistic Theory* 1: 151–82.

Biber, D., Conrad, S. and Reppen, R. (1998) *Corpus Linguistics: Investigating Language Structure and Use*. Cambridge: Cambridge University Press.

Biber, D., Johansson, S., Leech, G. Conrad, S. and Finegan, E. (1999) *The Longman Grammar of Spoken and Written English*. London: Longman.

Biber, D., Conrad, S., Reppen, R., Byrd, P. and Helt, M. (2002) 'Speaking and Writing in the University: A Multi-dimensional Comparison', *TESOL Quarterly* 36: 9–48.

Biber, D., Conrad, S. and Cortes, V. (2004) '*If You Look at …* : Lexical Bundles in University Teaching and Textbooks', *Applied Linguistics* 25: 371–405.

Biber, D., Connor, U. and Upton, T. A. (eds) (2007) *Discourse on the Move: Using Corpus Analysis to Describe Discourse Structure*. Amsterdam: John Benjamins.

Bruthiaux, P. (1994) 'Me Tarzan, You Jane: Linguistic Simplification in "Personal Ads" Register', in D. Biber and E. Finegan (eds) *Sociolinguistics Perspectives on Register*. Oxford: Oxford University Press, pp. 136–54.

——(1996) *The Discourse of Classified Advertising: Exploring the Nature of Linguistic Simplicity*. Oxford: Oxford University Press.

——(2005) 'In a Nutshell: Persuasion in the Spatially Constrained Language of Advertising', in H. Halmari and T. Virtanen (eds) *Persuasion across Genres: A Linguistic Approach*. Amsterdam: John Benjamins, pp. 135–52.

Bunton, D. (2002) 'Generic Moves in PhD Thesis Introductions', in J. Flowerdew (ed.) *Academic Discourse*. London: Longman, pp. 57–75.

——(2005) 'The Structure of PhD Conclusion Chapters', *Journal of English for Academic Purposes* 4: 207–24.

Carter, R. and McCarthy, M. (1997) *Exploring Spoken English*. Cambridge: Cambridge University Press.

——(1999) 'The English Get-passive in Spoken Discourse: Description and Implications for an Interpersonal Grammar', *English Language and Linguistics 3*(1): 41–58.

——(2004) 'Talking Creating: Interactional Language, Creativity and Context', *Applied Linguistics* 25 (1): 62–88.

——(2006) *Cambridge Grammar of English*. Cambridge: Cambridge University Press.

Charles, M. (2003) '"This Mystery … ': A Corpus-based Study of the Use of Nouns to Construct Stance in Theses from Two Contrasting Disciplines', *Journal of English for Academic Purposes* 2: 313–26.

——(2006) 'The Construction of Stance in Reporting Clauses: A Cross-disciplinary Study of Theses', *Applied Linguistics* 27(3): 492–518.

——(2007) 'Argument or Evidence? Disciplinary Variation in the Use of the Noun T*hat* Pattern', *English for Specific Purposes* 26: 203–18.

Collins, P. (1991) *Cleft and Pseudo-cleft Constructions in English*. London: Routledge.

Connor, U. (2000) 'Variation in Rhetorical Moves in Grant Proposals of US Humanists and Scientists', *Text* 20: 1–28.

Connor, U. and Mauranen, A. (1999) 'Linguistic Analysis of Grant Proposals: European Union Research Grants', *English for Specific Purposes* 18(1): 47–62.

Connor, U. and Upton, T. A. (2003) 'Linguistic Dimensions of Direct Mail Letters', in C. Meyer and P. Leistyna (eds) *Corpus Analysis: Language Structure and Language Use*. Amsterdam: Rodopi, pp. 71–86.

——(2004) 'The Genre of Grant Proposals: A Corpus Linguistic Analysis', in U. Connor and T. A. Upton (eds) *Discourse in the Professions: Perspectives from Corpus Linguistics*. Amsterdam: John Benjamins, pp. 235–56.

Connor-Linton, J. (2001) 'Authors Style and World-view: A Comparison of Texts about Nuclear Arms Policy', in S. Conrad and D. Biber (eds) *Variation in English: Multidimensional Studies*. Harlow: Longman, pp. 84–93.

Conrad, S. (1996) 'Investigating Academic Texts with Corpus-based Techniques: An Example from Biology', *Linguistics and Education* 8: 299–326.

——(2001) 'Variation among Disciplinary Texts: A Comparison of Textbooks and Journal Articles in Biology and History', in S. Conrad and D. Biber (eds) *Variation in English: Multidimensional Studies*. Harlow: Longman, pp. 94–107.

Conrad, S. and Biber, D. (2000) 'Adverbial Marking of Stance in Speech and Writing', in S. Hunston and G. Thompson (eds) *Evaluation in Text: Authorial Stance and the Construction of Discourse*. Oxford: Oxford University Press, pp. 56–73.

——(eds) (2001) *Variation in English: Multi-dimensional Studies*. London: Longman.

Cortes, V. (2004) 'Lexical Bundles in Published and Student Disciplinary Writing: Examples from History and Biology', *English for Specific Purposes* 23: 397–423.

Csomay, E. (2005) 'Linguistic Variation within University Classroom Talk: A Corpus-based Perspective', *Linguistics and Education* 15: 243–74.

Culpeper, J. and Kytö, M. (1999) 'Modifying Pragmatic Force: Hedges in Early Modern English Dialogues', in A. H. Jucker, G. Fritz and F. Lebsanft (eds) *Historical Dialogue Analysis (Pragmatics and Beyond New Series 66)*. Amsterdam and Philadelphia, PA: John Benjamins, pp. 293–312.

——(2000) 'Data in Historical Pragmatics: Spoken Interaction (re)Cast as Writing', *Journal of Historical Pragmatics* 1(2): 175–99.

——(forthcoming) *Early Modern English Dialogues: Spoken Interaction as Writing*. Cambridge: Cambridge University Press.

Danet, B. and Herring, S. C. (eds) (2003) 'The Multilingual Internet: Language, Culture, and Communication in Instant Messaging, Email and Chat', special issue of *Journal of Computer Mediated Communication* 9(1).

de Haan, P. (1989) *Postmodifying Clauses in the English Noun Phrase: A Corpus-based Study*. Amsterdam: Rodopi.

Ding, H. (2007) 'Genre Analysis of Personal Statements: Analysis of Moves in Application Essays to Medical and Dental Schools', *English for Specific Purposes* 26: 368–92.

Dos Santos, V. B. M. P. (2002) 'Genre Analysis of Business Letters of Negotiation', *English for Specific Purposes* 21: 167–99.

Ferguson, G. (2001) 'If You Pop Over There: A Corpus-based Study of Conditionals in Medical Discourse', *English for Specific Purposes* 20: 61–82.

Fitzmaurice, S. M. (2002a) *The Familiar Letter in Early Modern English*. Amsterdam and Philadelphia, PA: John Benjamins.

——(2002b) 'Politeness and Modal Meaning in the Construction of Humiliative Discourse in an Early Eighteenth-century Network of Patron–Client Relationships', *English Language and Linguistics* 6: 239–66.

Flowerdew, J. and Dudley-Evans, T. (2002) 'Genre Analysis of Editorial Letters to International Journal Contributors', *Applied Linguistics* 23(4): 463–89.

Flowerdew, J. and Wan, A. (2006) 'Genre Analysis of Tax Computation Letters: How and Why Tax Accountants Write the Way They Do', *English for Specific Purposes* 25: 133–53.

Fortanet, I. (2004) 'The Use of "We" in University Lectures: Reference and Function', *English for Specific Purposes* 23: 45–66.

Fox, B. A. and Thompson, S. A. (1990) 'A Discourse Explanation of the Grammar of Relative Clauses in English Conversation', *Language* 66: 297–316.

Freddi, M. (2005) 'Arguing Linguistics: Corpus Investigation of One Functional Variety of Academic Discourse', *Journal of English for Academic Purposes* 4: 5–26.

Fries, C. C. (1940) *American English Grammar*. New York: NCTE.

——(1952) *The Structure of English*. London: Longman.

Friginal, E. (2008) 'Linguistic Variation in the Discourse of Outsourced Call Centers', *Discourse Studies* 10: 715–36.

——(2009) *The Language of Outsourced Call Centers*. Amsterdam: John Benjamins.

Gains, J. (1999) 'Electronic Mail – A New Style of Communication or Just a New Medium? An Investigation into the Text Features of Email', *English for Specific Purposes* 18(1): 81–101.

Geisler, C. (1995) *Relative Infinitives in English*. Uppsala: Uppsala University.

Gledhill, C. (2000) 'The Discourse Function of Collocation in Research Article Introductions', *English for Specific Purposes* 19: 115–35.

Grabe, W. and Kaplan, R. (1997) 'On the Writing of Science and the Science of Writing: Hedging in Science Text and Elsewhere', in R. Markkanen and H. Schroder (eds) *Hedging and Discourse: Approaches to the Analysis of a Pragmatic Phenomenon in Academic Texts*. Berlin: Walter De Gruyter, pp. 151–67.

Halleck, G. B. and Connor, U. M. (2006) 'Rhetorical Moves in TESOL Conference Proposals', *Journal of English for Academic Purposes* 5: 70–86.

Helt, M. E. (2001) 'A Multi-dimensional Comparison of British and American Spoken English', in S. Conrad and D. Biber (eds) *Variation in English: Multidimensional Studies*. Harlow: Longman, pp. 157–70.

Henry, A. and Roseberry, R. L. (2001) 'A Narrow-angled Corpus Analysis of Moves and Strategies of the Genre: "Letter of Application"', *English for Specific Purposes* 20: 153–67.

Herring, S. C. (ed.) (2003) 'Media and Language Change', special issue of *Journal of Historical Pragmatics* 4(1).

Herring, S. C. and Paolillo, J. C. (2006) 'Gender and Genre Variation in Weblogs', *Journal of Sociolinguistics* 10(4): 439–59.

Hewings, M. and Hewings, A. (2002) '"It is Interesting to Note That … ": A Comparative Study of Anticipatory "It" in Student and Published Writing', *English for Specific Purposes* 21: 367–83.

Holmes, R. (1997) 'Genre Analysis, and the Social Sciences: An Investigation of the Structure of Research Article Discussion Sections in Three Disciplines', *English for Specific Purposes* 16(4): 321–37.

Hundt, M. and Mair, C. (1999) '"Agile" and "Uptight" Genres: The Corpus-based Approach to Language Change in Progress', *International Journal of Corpus Linguistics* 4: 221–42.

Hundt, M., Nesselhauf, N. and Biewer, C. (eds) (2007) *Corpus Linguistics and the Web*. Amsterdam: Rodopi.

Hunston, S. and Thompson, G. (eds) (2000) *Evaluation in Text: Authorial Stance and the Construction of Discourse*. New York: Oxford University Press.

Hyland, K. (1996) 'Writing without Conviction? Hedging in Science Research Articles', *Applied Linguistics* 17(4): 433–54.

——(1998) *Hedging in Scientific Research Articles*. Amsterdam: John Benjamins.

——(2001) 'Humble Servants of the Discipline? Self-mention in Research Articles', *English for Specific Purposes* 20: 207–26.

——(2002a) 'Directives: Argument and Engagement in Academic Writing', *Applied Linguistics* 23(2): 215–39.

——(2002b) 'What Do they Mean? Questions in Academic Writing', *Text* 22(4): 529–57.

——(2004) 'Graduates' Gratitude: The Generic Structure of Dissertation Acknowledgements', *English for Specific Purposes* 23: 303–24.

Hyland, K. and Tse, P. (2005) 'Hooking the Reader: A Corpus Study of Evaluative *That* in Abstracts', *English for Specific Purposes* 24: 123–39.

Johansson, C. (1995) *The Relativizers Whose and Of Which in Present-day English: Description and Theory*. Uppsala: Uppsala University.

Jucker, A. H. (1992) *Social Stylistics: Syntactic Variation in British Newspapers*. Berlin: Mouton.

Kahlas-Tarkka, L. and Rissanen, M. (2007) 'The Sullen and the Talkative: Discourse Strategies in the Salem Examinations', *Journal of Historical Pragmatics* 8(1): 1–24.

Kanoksilapatham, B. (2005) 'Rhetorical Structure of Biochemistry Research Articles', *English for Specific Purposes* 24: 269–92.

——(2007) 'Rhetorical Moves in Biochemistry Research Articles', in D. Biber, U. Connor and T. A. Upton (eds) *Discourse on the Move: Using Corpus Analysis to Describe Discourse Structure*. Amsterdam: John Benjamins, pp. 73–120.

Keck, C. M. and Biber, D. (2004) 'Modal Use in Spoken and Written University Registers: A Corpus-based Study', in R. Facchinetti and F. Palmer (eds) *English Modality in Perspective: Genre Analysis and Contrastive Studies*. Frankfurt am Main: Peter Lang, pp. 3–25.

Kennedy, G. (1998) *An Introduction to Corpus Linguistics*. London: Longman.

Kryk-Kastovsky, B. (2000) 'Representations of Orality in Early Modern English Trial Records', *Journal of Historical Pragmatics* 1(2): 201–30.

——(2006) 'Impoliteness in Early Modern English Courtroom Discourse', *Journal of Historical Pragmatics* 7(2): 213–43.

Kuo, C.-H. (1999) 'The Use of Personal Pronouns: Role Relationships in Scientific Journal Articles', *English for Specific Purposes* 18(2): 121–38.

Kwan, B. S. C. (2006) 'The Schematic Structure of Literature Reviews in Doctoral Theses of Applied Linguistics', *English for Specific Purposes* 25: 30–55.

Kytö, M. (1991) *Variation and Diachrony, with Early American English in Focus*. Frankfurt: Peter Lang.

Kytö, M. and Walker, T. (2003) 'The Linguistic Study of Early Modern English Speech-related Texts: How "Bad" Can "Bad" Data Be?' *Journal of English Linguistics* 31(3): 221–48.

Kytö, M., Rydén, M. and Smitterberg, E. (eds) (2006) *Nineteenth-century English: Stability and Change*. Cambridge: Cambridge University Press.

Leech, G. N., Hundt, M., Mair, C. and Smith, N. (forthcoming) *Contemporary Change in English: A Grammatical Study*. Cambridge: Cambridge University Press.

Lindemann, S. and Mauranen, A. (2001) '"It's Just Really Messy": The Occurrence and Function of *Just* in a Corpus of Academic Speech', *English for Specific Purposes* 20: 459–75.

McCarthy, M. J. (1998) *Spoken Language and Applied Linguistics*. Cambridge: Cambridge University Press.

——(2000) 'Captive Audiences: The Discourse of Close Contact Service Encounters', in J. Coupland (ed.) *Small Talk*. London: Longman, pp. 84–109.

——(2002) 'Good Listenership Made Plain: British and American Non-minimal Response Tokens in Everyday Conversation', in R. Reppen, S. M. Fitzmaurice and D. Biber (eds) *Using Corpora to Explore Linguistic Variation*. Amsterdam: John Benjamins, pp. 49–71.

McCarthy, M. and Carter, R. (1997) 'Grammar, Tails, and Affect: Constructing Affective Choices in Discourse', *Text* 17: 405–29.

——(2004) '"There's Millions of Them": Hyperbole in Everyday Conversation', *Journal of Pragmatics* 36: 149–84.

McCarthy, M. and Handford, M. (2004) 'Invisible to Us: A Preliminary Corpus-based Study of Spoken Business English', in U. Connor and T. Upton (eds) *Discourse in the Professions: Perspectives from Corpus Linguistics*. Amsterdam: John Benjamins, pp. 167–201.

McEnery, A., Xiao, R. and Tono, Y. (2006) *Corpus-based Language Studies*. London: Routledge.

McKenna, B. (1997) 'How Engineers Write: An Empirical Study of Engineering Report Writing', *Applied Linguistics* 18(2): 189–211.

Mahlberg, M. (forthcoming) *Corpus Stylistics and Dickens's Fiction*. London: Routledge.

Mäkinen, M. (2002) 'On Interaction in Herbals from Middle English to Early Modern English', *Journal of Historical Pragmatics* 3(2): 229–51.

Marco, M. J. L. (2000) 'Collocational Frameworks in Medical Research Papers: A Genre-based Study', *English for Specific Purposes* 19: 63–86.

Marley, C. (2002) 'Popping the Question: Questions and Modality in Written Dating Advertisements', *Discourse Studies* 4(1): 75–98.

Mauranen, A. (2003) '"A Good Question". Expressing Evaluation in Academic Speech', in G. Cortese and P. Riley (eds) *Domain-Specific English: Textual Practices across Communities and Classrooms*. New York: Peter Lang, pp. 115–40.

——(2004) '"They're a Little Bit Different": Variation in Hedging in Academic Speech', in K. Aijmer and A.-B. Stenström (eds) *Discourse Patterns in Spoken and Written Corpora*. Amsterdam: John Benjamins, pp. 173–97.

Mauranen, A. and Bondi, M. (2003) 'Evaluative Language Use in Academic Discourse', *Journal of English for Academic Purposes* 2: 269–71.

Morrow, P. R. (2006) 'Telling about Problems and Giving Advice in an Internet Discussion Forum: Some Discourse Features', *Discourse Studies* 8(4): 531–48.

Nesi, H. and Basturkmen, H. (2006) 'Lexical Bundles and Discourse Signaling in Academic Lectures', *International Journal of Corpus Linguistics* 11: 283–304.

Nevala, M. (2004) 'Accessing Politeness Axes: Forms of Address and Terms of Reference in Early English Correspondence', *Journal of Pragmatics* 36(12): 2125–60.

Nevalainen, T. and Kahlas-Tarkka, L. (eds) (1997) *To Explain the Present*. Helsinki: Societé Neophilologique.

Norrick, N. R. (2008) 'Using Large Corpora of Conversation to Investigate Narrative: The Case of Interjections in Conversational Storytelling Performance', *International Journal of Corpus Linguistics* 13: 438–64.

O'Keeffe, A. (2006) *Investigating Media Discourse*. London: Routledge.

Ozturk, I. (2007) 'The Textual Organization of Research Article Introductions in Applied Linguistics: Variability in a Single Discipline', *English for Specific Purposes* 26: 25–38.

Partington, A. (1998) *Patterns and Meanings*. Amsterdam: John Benjamins.

Partington, A. and Morley, J. (2004) 'From Frequency to Ideology: Investigating Word and Cluster/Bundle Frequency in Political Debate', in B. Lewandowska-Tomaszczyk (ed.) *Practical Applications in Language and Computers – PALC 2003*. Frankfurt am Main: Peter Lang, pp. 179–92.

Precht, K. (1998) 'A Cross-cultural Comparison of Letters of Recommendation', *English for Specific Purposes* 17(3): 241–65.

Prince, E. F. (1978) 'A Comparison of *Wh*-clefts and *It*-clefts in Discourse', *Language* 54: 883–906.

Quaglio, P. (2009) *Television Dialogue: The Sitcom* Friends *versus Natural Conversation*. Amsterdam: John Benjamins.

Quaglio, P. and Biber, D. (2006) 'The Grammar of Conversation', in B. Aarts and A. McMahon (eds) *The Handbook of English Linguistics*. Oxford: Blackwell, pp. 692–723.

Reppen, R. (2001) 'Register Variation in Student and Adult Speech and Writing', in S. Conrad and D. Biber (eds) *Variation in English: Multidimensional Studies*. Harlow: Longman, pp. 187–99.

Reppen, R. and Vásquez, C. (2007) 'Using Corpus Linguistics to Investigate the Language of Teacher Training', in J. Walinski, K. Kredens and S. Gozdz-Roszkowski (eds) *Corpora and ICT in Language Studies*. Frankfurt: Peter Lang, pp. 13–29.

Rey, J. M. (2001) 'Historical Shifts in the Language of Women and Men: Gender Differences in Dramatic Dialogue', in S. Conrad and D. Biber (eds) *Variation in English: Multidimensional Studies*. Harlow: Longman, pp. 138–56.

Römer, U. (2005a) *Progressives, Patterns, Pedagogy*. Amsterdam: John Benjamins.

——(2005b) '"This Seems Counterintuitive, Though … ": Negative Evaluation in Linguistic Book Reviews by Male and Female Authors', in E. Tognini Bonelli and G. Del Lungo Camiciotti, *Strategies in Academic Discourse*. Amsterdam/Philadelphia: John Benjamins, pp. 97–116.

Salager, F. (1994) 'Hedges and Textual Communicative Function in Medical English Written Discourse', *English for Specific Purposes* 13(2): 149–70.

Salager-Meyer, F. and Defives, G. (1998) 'From the Gentleman's Courtesy to the Scientist's Caution: A Diachronic Study of Hedges in Academic Writing (1810–1995)', in I. Fortanet, D. Posteguillo, J. C. Palmer and J. F. Coll (eds) *Genre Studies in English for Academic Purposes*. Castello de la Plana: Publicacions de la Universitat Jaume I, pp. 133–72.

Samraj, B. (2002) 'Introductions in Research Articles: Variations across Disciplines', *English for Specific Purposes* 21: 1–17.

——(2005) 'An Exploration of a Genre Set: Research Article Abstracts and Introductions in Two Disciplines', *English for Specific Purposes* 24: 141–56.

Semino, E. and Short, M. (2004) *Corpus Stylistics: Speech, Writing and Thought Presentation in a Corpus of English Writing*. London: Routledge.

Simpson, R. (2004) 'Stylistic Features of Spoken Academic Discourse: The Role of Formulaic Expressions', in U. Connor and T. A. Upton (eds) *Discourse in the Professions: Perspectives from Corpus Linguistics*. Amsterdam: John Benjamins, pp. 37–64.

Simpson, R. and Mendis, D. (2003) 'A Corpus-based Study of Idioms in Academic Speech', *TESOL Quarterly* 37: 419–41.

Simpson-Vlach, Rita C. and Leicher, S. (2006) *The MICASE Handbook: A Resource For Users of the Michigan Corpus of Academic Spoken English*. Ann Arbor, MI: University of Michigan Press.

Sinclair, J. (1991) *Corpus, Concordance, Collocation*. Oxford: Oxford University Press.

Stotesbury, H. (2003) 'Evaluation in Research Article Abstracts in the Narrative and Hard Sciences', *Journal of English for Academic Purposes* 2: 327–41.

Swales, J. M. (2001) 'Metatalk in American Academic Talk: The Cases of *Point* and *Thing*', *Journal of English Linguistics* 29: 34–54.

Swales, J. M. and Burke, A. (2003) '"It's Really Fascinating Work": Differences in Evaluative Adjectives across Academic Registers', in P. Leistyna and C. F. Meyer (eds) *Corpus Analysis: Language Structure and Language Use*. New York: Rodopi, pp. 1–18.

Swales, J. M, Ahmad, U.K., Chang, Y.-Y., Chavez, D., Dressen, D. F. and Seymour, R. (1998) 'Consider This: The Role of Imperatives in Scholarly Writing', *Applied Linguistics* 19(1): 97–121.

Taavitsainen, I. (2001) 'Middle English Recipes: Genre Characteristics, Text Type Features and Underlying Traditions of Writing', *Journal of Historical Pragmatics* 2(1): 85–113.

Taavitsainen, I. and Pahta, P. (2000) 'Conventions of Professional Writing: The Medical Case Report in a Historical Perspective', *Journal of English Linguistics* 28(1): 60–76.

——(eds) (2004) *Medical and Scientific Writing in Late Medieval English*. Cambridge: Cambridge University Press.

Tao, H. (2007) 'A Corpus-based Investigation of *Absolutely* and Related Phenomena in Spoken American English', *Journal of English Linguistics* 35(1): 5–29.

Tao, H. and McCarthy, M. (2001) 'Understanding Non-restrictive *Which*-clauses in Spoken English, Which is Not an Easy Thing', *Language Sciences* 23: 651–77.

Thomas, S. and Hawes, T. P. (1994) 'Reporting Verbs in Medical Journal Articles', *English for Specific Purposes* 13(2): 129–48.

Thompson, P. and Sealey, A. (2007) 'Through Children's Eyes? Corpus Evidence of the Features of Children's Literature', *International Journal of Corpus Linguistics* 12(1): 1–23.

Thompson, S. A. and Mulac, A. (1991) 'The Discourse Conditions for the Use of the Complementizer *That* in Conversational English', *Journal of Pragmatics* 15: 237–51.

Tognini Bonelli, E. and Camiciotti, G. Del Lungo (2005) *Strategies in Academic Discourse*. Amsterdam and Philadelphia, PA: John Benjamins.

Tottie, G. (1991) *Negation in English Speech and Writing: A Study in Variation*. San Diego: Academic Press.

Tucker, P. (2003) 'Evaluation in the Art-historical Research Article', *Journal of English for Academic Purposes* 2: 291–312.

Upton, T. A. (2002) 'Understanding Direct Mail Letters as a Genre', *International Journal of Corpus Linguistics* 7(1): 65–85.

Upton, T. A. and Connor, U. (2001) 'Using Computerized Corpus-analysis to Investigate the Textlinguistic Discourse Moves of a Genre', *English for Specific Purposes* 20: 313–29.

Vilha, M. (1999) *Medical Writing: Modality in Focus*. Amsterdam: Rodopi.

19

What can a corpus tell us about specialist genres?

Michael Handford

1. Corpora, specialised corpora and mega-corpora

Corpus and the study of genres: an introduction

While corpus linguistics is undoubtedly one of the modern success stories in applied linguistics, evidenced in part by the creation of this handbook, the value of corpora is not universally accepted (Flowerdew 2004). Many of the criticisms within applied linguistics are concerned with the following three areas:

- Corpus data are decontextualised data (Widdowson 1998, 2000).
- Corpora require a bottom-up approach (Swales 2002).
- Corpora are quantitative, number-crunching tools (see Baker 2006: 8).

A further issue is that of size, which in corpus linguistics impacts notions of representativeness. A widely held assumption in corpus linguistics, and a reason for some linguists, such as discourse analysts, being put off by corpora (Baker 2006), is that researchers need to collect considerable quantities of data because:

- The bigger the corpora the better (Sinclair 1991; Stubbs 1996).

Through exploring a selection of studies that combine corpus and genre approaches, this chapter will critically deal with all of these arguments. In so doing, we will be looking at how two of the most powerful approaches in discourse studies today (Bhatia *et al.* 2008: 3) which are 'charting new courses' in discourse analysis, can be fruitfully combined. This combination of genre analysis and corpus linguistics occurs through the development and analysis of what will be referred to as corpora of specialised genres (CSGs). Such corpora are created to research various aspects of language such as gender comparisons in spoken conversations, changes over time in region-based communication, or styles of writing in academic journal articles (see Hunston 2002: 14). In this chapter we will look at CSGs involving written academic, spoken business and service-encounter discourse.

This complementary combination of corpus and genre is a logical and desirable development in discourse analysis: corpora have much to say about language, but they can be lacking in contextual interpretability; genres are intrinsically contextual entities, but their linguistic features may be under-exposed. The combination is possible because, as Lee reminds us, 'Most discourse analysts would probably concur with the corpus-based view of language: after all, what is discourse but actual, situationally embedded, used and re-used language?' (Lee 2008: 88).

This chapter therefore has relevance to two of the most important and recurring problems in social science in general (Giddens 1984) and in the analysis of language in particular (Gee 2005): how can we relate the specific instance (such as the text, the discourse move or the lexicogrammatical item) to the wider social context within which it occurs and which it reflexively recreates, and how can quantitative and qualitative approaches be effectively combined?

Specialist corpora and mega-corpora

According to Flowerdew (2002: 96), two recent developments in the field of corpus linguistics have been:

1. the increase in the number of 'mega-corpora';
2. the creation of smaller, genre-based corpora.

'Mega-corpora' are large general corpora, comprising millions or hundred of millions of words, such as the BNC or the Bank of English. At the time of writing, the Cambridge International Corpus (CIC) is one of the world's biggest corpora, weighing in at over one billion words.

Many of the criticisms levelled against corpus linguistics have been aimed at such large, general corpora (Flowerdew 2004): if you are dealing with such an enormous amount of text, then indeed you cannot say much about context, and probably the only way into the data is through a bottom-up, automated, quantitative approach. Some have even argued that the point of corpora is to provide decontextualised data (Hunston 2002: 110). While such very large corpora have borne paradigm-shaking fruit in the fields of lexis and grammar, most notable in the works of Sinclair both theoretically (e.g. 1991) and also practically (the revolutionary Cobuild dictionary), general corpora do not tend to be suitable for studying specialised language (Biber 1988; Flowerdew 2004; Lee 2008).

There are several reasons why smaller corpora are more suited for studying specialist genres. As Lee (ibid.) states, the sampling of most mega-corpora is not based on genre, and while classifying a mega-corpus post hoc is possible, it is hardly ideal (see Lee 2001 for an ad hoc classification of the BNC corpus). Furthermore, because of the way mega-corpora are designed, accessing the individual sub-corpora is not always possible; access can also be blocked because of the confidentiality of the data itself (Flowerdew 2004). There is also a widespread tendency for mega-corpora to be comprised of far more written than spoken data, although this emphasis on writing is arguably more to do with practical and financial as opposed to ideological issues than would traditionally have been the case. Moreover, there are no multimodal mega-corpora to date (Lee 2001). A further problem with such general corpora is that they do not always contain complete texts, but may be limited to 2,000 word excerpts (see Nelson, this volume). Given that one of the possible defining features of a genre is that it specifies conditions for beginning and ending texts (Couture 1986: 86), not having the endings (or other sections) of longer texts would be something of a concern. It also means studying the extent to which items are primed to occur according to their position in the overall discourse (Hoey 2005) is not possible.

We will discuss the methodological advantages of smaller corpora over general corpora below; before that, we shall look at what is meant by 'specialist genres', the related term 'specialised corpora' and their rationale.

Specialist genres

In a way, the expression 'specialist genres' is somewhat tautological, as all genres could be seen as inherently specialised. Whether we are thinking about business letters, funeral speeches, PhD thesis abstracts or even conversations between friends, it is possible to pinpoint certain aspects of the genre which distinguish it from other communicative events and therefore make it a 'specialist' genre. Looking at one of the most invoked definitions of genre should help us understand this:

> genre comprises a class of communicative events, the members of which share some set of communicative purposes. These purposes are recognised by the expert members of the parent discourse community, and thereby constitute the rationale for the genre. This rationale shapes the schematic structure of the discourse and influences and constrains choice of content and style.
>
> (Swales 1990: 58)

There are several words and phrases here that indicate the inherently 'specialist' nature of genre: *class, expert members, parent discourse community, rationale, the schematic structure* and perhaps most importantly *constrains*. As any parent of young children would testify, even 'having a chat' within a specific culture takes years to master. The child needs to develop tacit knowledge of various constraints and possibilities, such as knowing suitable topics and their relevant vocabulary, when they can/cannot be discussed (for example at the dinner table) and with whom (the neighbours, teachers, friends), appropriate turn-taking, listening skills and behaviour, and various paralinguistic features like touching and volume.

Nevertheless, some genres are certainly more specialist than others in that they are employed by highly trained, expert members of particular communities (Swales 1990; Bazerman 1994; Wenger 1998; Scollon and Scollon 2001) with very specific goals in mind and are achieved through highly constrained and specialised communicative behaviours, linguistic and otherwise.

The rationale for a genre approach

Genre itself is a highly contested notion, sometimes contrasted and sometimes used synonymously with other related terms such as *register, style* and *text* (Biber 1988; Martin 1992; Stubbs 1996; see Lee 2001 for an extended discussion). Under the umbrella term 'genre analysis', there are three broad branches (Hyon 1996): genre as goal-driven communicative event associated with discourse communities (Swales 1990, 2004); genre as rhetorical and social action (Bazerman 1994), associated with the New Rhetoric School; and genre as a staged, social process (Martin 1992), associated with Australian systemic functional linguistics (SFL).

These approaches differ in terms of the emphasis given to predictability and dynamism of the genre's formal features, or the importance given to the wider social context. Despite the differences, the three branches all prioritise conventions, and in so doing provide a justification for conducting genre analysis. As Bhatia (2004: 23) states:

> Genre essentially refers to language use in a conventionalised communicative setting in order to give expression to a specific set of communicative goals of a disciplinary or social institution, which give rise to stable structural forms by imposing constrains (sic) on the use of lexicogrammatical as well as discoursal resources.

This quote highlights the related concepts of constraint and convention and, crucially for corpus linguists, how such concepts find regular, recurrent realisation in lexico-grammatical and discoursal form. Studying genre can show us how to link the words speakers and writers use to the social practices they follow, recreate and sometimes challenge, such as maintaining manager/subordinate relationships in the workplace (Handford, forthcoming).

2. What are the methodological advantages of specialised corpora in analysing genres?

In the beginning of this chapter I listed four issues that have been seen as problematic in corpus linguistics: size, context, quantitative analysis and a bottom-up approach. This section shows how a specialised genre approach, as opposed to one utilising general corpora, can practically address these concerns.

One key methodological issue for anyone either compiling or analysing a corpus is that of size: how big should the corpus be? The issue of size is important for obvious practical and financial reasons, but also because it affects the representativeness of the corpus in question (see chapters by Adolphs and Knight, Nelson and Reppen, this volume). One clear advantage that CSGs have over general corpora is that they can be markedly smaller and still validly claim to be representative to some degree (Tognini Bonelli 2001; Tribble 2002). Although guaranteeing or even evaluating representativeness may not be objective (Tognini Bonelli 2001: 57), it seems plausible that the more specialised the genre, the smaller the corpus can be (Lee 2008).

In terms of actual size, a specialised corpus can be defined as large (O'Keeffe *et al.* 2007) if it contains a million words such as CANBEC, the Cambridge and Nottingham Business English Corpus, a one-million-word corpus of authentic spoken business English, or CANCODE, the Cambridge and Nottingham Corpus of Discourse English, which contains five million words of authentic everyday speech; however, some such specialised spoken corpora that have produced powerful and wide-ranging findings are made up of fewer than 60,000 words (for example Koester's (2006) corpus of American and British Office Talk, ABOT). As noted above, spoken corpora are usually much smaller than written corpora, but it should also be remembered that transcripts of spoken corpora usually contain far more than just words, for example paralinguistic and even functional information (e.g. interrupting codes). Perhaps the comparison in terms of word count is erroneous: if the comparison is made on contextual information, many spoken corpora are far more detailed.

A further point concerning the issue of accurately describing the genre is made by Hyland (2006: 58). He argues that language corpora have enabled genre analysts, for example those involved in language education, to demonstrate that the observed principles and regularities they highlight are representative of the genre in question. The corpus can provide 'an evidence-based approach to language teaching' (ibid.). Such an approach is needed because human intuition is not a reliable guide to the linguistic patterns a genre involves.

Hyland's position presupposes that the corpus we are using has sufficient relevant contextual information to allow plausible interpretation of the item in question. Yet it is the role of context that has given rise to perhaps the most serious criticisms against corpus linguistics (Hunston 2002). Widdowson argues that corpus data is not authentic language, given that the text is separated from its original context (Widdowson 1998, 2000): it is at best a decontextualised sample and should therefore be used with great care in, for example, language-learning settings. While Widdowson's point may carry some weight when looking at the larger general corpora discussed earlier, CSGs provide a powerful riposte to this challenge because they can, in principle, allow for not only description, but also interpretation and explanation of the data (see Candlin and Hyland 1999: 1–17). Methodologically, genre corpora are of particular value because the analyst is 'probably also the compiler and does have familiarity with the wider socio-cultural dimension in which the discourse was created' (Flowerdew 2004: 16). The possibility to look at a particular linguistic feature across a collection of instances of the relevant genre, and use text-external understanding to interpret the data which contains that feature, is revolutionising not only corpus linguistics and genre analysis, but also the interdisciplinary field of discourse analysis (Lee 2008).

The perception that corpora are number-crunching quantitative tools that necessitate a bottom-up approach has, nevertheless, led to a methodological and indeed theoretical aversion on the part of many social scientists (see Baker 2006: 1–10). The size and composition of many CSGs, however, means that they do lend themselves to qualitative-based analyses (Flowerdew 2004). In one such approach, the user inserts tags which demonstrate the specific move structures across a collection of texts, a necessarily manual procedure which can therefore only be conducted with smaller corpora (Flowerdew 1998). Other studies which employ qualitative analyses will be discussed below. Also, recent research by Swales (Swales and Lee 2006), on the pedagogical applications and implications of using comparative corpora with language learners, shows that Swales now agrees corpora can, in fact, be interpreted with top-down approaches more typically associated with genre analysis (Lee 2008).

After all, a CSG is merely a collection of contextually linked, machine-readable texts which allows for a multi-methods analysis: whether we approach the texts individually or as a whole, manually or automatically, is not dictated by the data itself, but by the research question we want to answer. In the following sections we will explore various studies that exemplify such an approach.

3. What can a corpus tell us about academic genres?

There have been numerous corpus studies of academic language, and although these tend largely to be of written texts (Flowerdew 2002), there have also been some outstanding studies of spoken discourse. The Michigan University MICASE corpus should be noted, both because of the research emanating from it (e.g. Simpson 2004; Swales 2004) and also because it is a free, publicly accessible corpus of over 1,800,000 words which permits straightforward analysis of various spoken texts recorded on the university campus. These include lectures, dissertation defences and meetings, but also service encounters (a web search of MICASE will bring you to the home page). The British companion corpus is the BASE corpus is also freely accessible online. This corpus has video as opposed to transcribed data. The written equivalent, the British Academic Written English (BAWE), is also freely available online. Another excellent site is the Purdue University 'Owl' writing laboratory website. Further work on spoken academic genres, as well as other speech genres, has been conducted on Nottingham's CANCODE corpus (O'Keeffe *et al.* 2007: Ch. 10) and on an academic subset of it (Evison 2008), and Csomay (2005) has explored variation in differing genres using corpora.

A comprehensive survey of the extensive literature on written and written/spoken genres is beyond the scope of this chapter, but some of the most important studies are Biber 1988; Swales 1990, 2004; Biber *et al.* 1998; Flowerdew 2002; Hyland 2003; Connor and Upton 2004. Research has been conducted on comparing different academic disciplines (Flowerdew 1998; Hyland 2000; Ghadessy *et al.* 2001). Another approach is the analysis of particular features such as vague language (Cutting 2007) and hedges (Hyland and Milton 1997) in academic genres.

The study we will look at, by Tribble (2002), is of an invited short academic journal report written by a respected researcher who discusses recent developments in his field. The text is taken from the RAT corpus (Reading Academic Text Corpus, of Reading University). There are three basic steps in Tribble's study: choose a text which is an 'expert performance' (Bazerman 1994: 131) of the relevant genre; compile contextual information about the creation of the text; and conduct linguistic analyses which can be integrated with the context.

Tribble's study has been chosen because he explicitly integrates many of the themes we have discussed so far, most importantly specialised (written academic) corpus data and genre analysis. He also combines the three branches of genre analysis (Flowerdew 2008) outlined above, allowing for a thorough contextual integration with the corpus data (thereby addressing one of the most recurrent criticisms of corpus linguistics). The study is also interesting because it develops useful pedagogical practice based on the findings, which is not always the case with corpus studies (Swales and Lee 2006: 57).

In terms of traditional corpus linguistic approaches (e.g. Sinclair 1991), Tribble's analysis is somewhat unusual in the extent to which the text-external context is emphasised (see Table 19.1); furthermore, the analysis is primarily concerned with a single text. Nevertheless, he does employ recognisable corpus techniques such as frequency and concordance searches, and accesses a larger reference corpora (the one-million-word BNC sampler) to conduct keyword searches (Scott 1996). Keywords (ibid.) are statistically significant items in a corpus or text, and can provide an empirically valid impression of the typifying language of the genre (see Scott, this volume).

The first seven headings and associated questions provide an explanation of the social/cultural dimensions of the text in question. For example, under the second point, *social context*, Tribble (2002: 134) states: 'The article was written for publication in a specialist academic journal. In writing such a short piece, the author faces special constraints in terms of content and extent, but also has to meet normal academic standards of warrant and referencing.' Such insights are important because they help us, and Tribble's students, understand the context in which the text is produced, and the constraints under

Table 19.1 Tribble's analytical framework

Contextual analysis	
1. name	What is the name of the genre of which this text is an exemplar?
2. social context	In what social setting is this kind of text typically produced? What constraints and obligations does this setting impose on writers and readers?
3 communicative purpose	What is the communicative purpose of this text?
4. roles	What roles may be required of writers and readers in this genre?
5. cultural values	What shared cultural values may be required of writers and readers in this genre?
6. text context	What knowledge of other texts may be required of writers and readers in this genre?
7. formal text features	What shared knowledge of formal text features (conventions) is required to write effectively in this genre?
Linguistic analysis	
8. lexico-grammatical features	What lexico-grammatical features of the text are statistically prominent and stylistically salient?
9. text relations/textual patterning	Can textual patterns be identified in the text? What is the reason for such textual patterning?
10. text structure	How is the text organised as a series of units of meaning? What is the reason for this organisation?

Source: Tribble (2002: 133).

which the writer is working. On a practical pedagogical level, such understanding can then be transferred to academic writing requirements the students may have.

The second part of Tribble's analytical framework deals with three aspects of linguistic analysis: lexicogrammatical features, text relations/textual patterning, and text structure. The first step is to conduct a keyword search of the article, showing that words such as *membrane*, *enzyme* and *ethylene* are statistically significant in comparison to the reference corpus. According to Tribble, this type of information is essential for those who wish to participate in the target discourse community, because keywords pinpoint the requisite content knowledge of the text (2002: 137), as well as the collocational and colligational patterns which feature these genre-specific terms. Keywords can also clarify which interpersonal features are typical in a genre (Handford, forthcoming).

The next step in the analysis is to do basic frequency counts across the text and the reference corpora, and run left and right concordances of the most frequent words. Interestingly, Tribble argues that this allows for deeper insights into the 'stylistically salient' lexicogrammatical features of the text in question than either keyword searches or a single frequency list can produce.

The keyword and frequency analyses have also thrown up aspects of the next level of linguistic analysis, textual patterning. One such pattern was that *that* clauses are employed in the reporting of claims, as in this sentence. Textual patterns are important because they contribute to the text's particular identity and are evidence of 'the constraints which the writer has had to respond to in order to ensure that the text is an allowable contribution to a specialist genre' (Tribble 2002: 142). In this instance, the constraints include the requirement for claims to be made in academic research, and for them to be communicated in a particular stylistic fashion, often through referencing others, e.g. 'Y *found* **that** … '

The final stage of Tribble's linguistic analysis looks at text structure, specifically the moves that organise the text's information. He finds that the text follows the Situation–Problem–Response–Evaluation discourse model (Hoey 1983) in terms of the overall relational patterns, but also in terms of the paragraphing of the text. Such understanding of a text's moves is of considerable value to novice learners, and according to Swales and Lee (2006) is the first step in acquiring genre-awareness. For a fuller exploration of how texts can be linguistically explored using concordances see Tribble, this volume.

Flowerdew (2008) has argued that Tribble's (2002) approach is suitable for analysts who are 'unfamiliar with the institutionalized practices of the genre', perhaps because it first involves a thoroughgoing analysis of the contextual features. She states that Tribble's position 'is to see the role of context as very much informing corpus-based analyses' (2008: 115), and by implication the importance of collecting and digesting sufficient relevant information about the communicative context and the author's purpose *before* we analyse the language.

A possible criticism of this approach, given that it is 'corpus-based' (Flowerdew 2008) and not 'corpus-driven' (Tognini Bonelli 2001: 65) is that the relationship between the corpus data and the context might be 'vague' and 'difficult to validate' (ibid.). In a corpus-driven approach, the methodology is 'observation leads to hypothesis leads to generalisation leads to unification in theoretical statement' (ibid.: 85). But we should remember that the corpus-driven approach has been developed in alliance with large corpora. CSGs, in contrast, are contextually driven corpora.

4. What does a corpus tell us about professional genres?

As with academic discourse, most of the research on professional genres has explored written texts, for example Bhatia (1993, 2004), Berkenkotter and Huckin (1995), Bargiela-Chiappini and Nickerson (1999), as well as collections which include academic as well as professional studies such as Christie and Martin (1997), Candlin and Hyland (1999) and Connor and Upton (2004). Furthermore, it is only the Connor and Upton collection that explicitly applies corpus linguistics. Research into spoken professional genres is a challenging proposition, not least because of the difficulty in obtaining permission to record authentic data. Nevertheless, work on CSGs of professional discourse includes McCarthy and Handford (2004), Koester (2004, 2006), Adolphs *et al.* (2007) and Handford (forthcoming), Atkins and Harvey (this volume).

A relevant question is, 'What counts as a corpus, professional or otherwise?' Some very important studies of spoken professional discourse have been referred to as 'corpus-based', such as Bargiela-Chiappini and Harris's (1997) study of business meetings, or the outstanding, multidimensional Language in the Workplace (LWP) project headed by Janet Holmes in New Zealand, accessible through the Victoria University website. Studies such as these have been highly influential, not least in the area of spoken genres, and yet the data does not seem to be fully transcribed, as there are no quantitative findings from either study (although see Vine 2004 for work on modal verbs). It is debatable whether such studies are indeed corpus-based, because the data itself does not appear to be in machine-readable form. Therefore, in this chapter, only machine-readable datasets will be considered as corpora and analysed as such.

Another important question is 'What do we mean by professional?' The term has received various definitions (e.g. McCarthy 1998; Sarangi and Roberts 1999), but here it is defined as intra-organisational or interorganisational communication between people whose professional identities are salient. In answer to the question of why genres are important in professional communication, it is because professionals achieve their goals and develop professional solidarity through genres (Bhatia 2004: 21).

The analysis of speech creates some different challenges from that of writing. Whereas written texts are much more clear-cut and are usually the finished product when we see them, speech is far fuzzier – it unfolds as a process, and it may not be clear where it's going, where it begins and where it ends, and whether the audience differs from the participants. But for all of this, there is the argument that speech is more important systemically, more layered semantically, and more interesting analytically, than writing (Halliday 1985/1994). This is because spoken language 'responds continually to the small but subtle changes in its environment, both verbal and non-verbal … The context of spoken language is in a constant state of flux, and the language has to be equally mobile and alert' (Halliday 1985/1994: xxiii–xxiv). It is partly for these reasons that two of the three studies explored in this chapter look at spoken as opposed to written discourse.

In this section we will be looking at Koester's work on spoken workplace communication (Koester 2004, 2006). Koester's ABOT (American and British Office Talk) corpus is taken from thirty hours of recordings from various workplaces in the US and UK, although the actual amount of transcribed and contextualised data is 34,000 words. Her work is a demonstration of the depth of analysis possible with a small but carefully selected and painstakingly studied dataset.

Koester is concerned with accounting for the stability and variation evident in spoken genres, and argues that a Swalesian approach, which prioritises communicative purpose, is well suited to do this. She also draws insights and applies tools from systemic function linguistics (SFL) in particular, but argues communicative purpose should be the defining feature of a genre. She distinguishes between transactional and non-transactional (or 'relational') workplace discourse, and then categorises such discourse into separate genres, such as decision-making and office gossip, respectively (see Figure 19.1).

In contrast with Tribble (2002), the first methodological step for Koester is to identify the discourse goals by looking at the evidence of the data, and as such is more in line with corpus-driven (Tognini Bonelli 2001) approaches. By applying ethnographic methods from communicative goals studies and interactional sociolinguistics, the genre classification is gleaned from the discourse frames of the participants, as opposed to those of the analyst.

TRANSACTIONAL DISCOURSE

unidirectional	*Discursive roles of the participants*	*collaborative*
Genres briefing service encounters procedural and directive discourse requesting action/permission/goods reporting		Genres making arrangements decision-making discussing and evaluating

NON-TRANSACTIONAL DISCOURSE

Genres

Office gossip

Small talk

Figure 19.1 Summary of Koester's (2006) generic framework.

In accordance with a Hallidayan perspective, Koester quantitatively and qualitatively explores interpersonal meanings in both transactional and relational goal-oriented discourse; the interpersonal language features she analyses include modal verbs, idioms, vague language, hedges and intensifiers. The point is to understand the relationship between such features and the workplace genres. For example, in decision-making (a transactional genre), speakers tend to use particular modal verbs (an interpersonal language feature), such as *have to* much more frequently than other modals (e.g. *should*), and such differences can be explained by considering interpersonal issues like the perceived degree of obligation of the action and the relationship between the speakers. Also, modal verbs (like idioms) in general occur more frequently in collaborative genres like decision-making than in unidirectional or non-transactional discourse (see Figure 19.1).

In addition to specific language items, Koester also discussed the structural patterns in genres. For instance, she pinpoints the same 'problem–solution' pattern (Hoey 1983) that was found in Tribble's analysis above, in decision-making episodes, arguing that such episodes usually begin with the speakers identifying some problem. She gives the following example from an American food cooperative, where the bookkeeper needs to read a handwritten item from a staff list:

Extract 1

1.	Ann	Anyone wanna decipher some handwriting?
2.	Greta	I will. I will.
…		
11.	Greta	It looks like S-H. O-W-Y, showy
12.	Ann	Mhm.
13.	Ann	or *soury* … soury.
14.	Greta	(sou : r I think that's a G)

(Koester 2006: 37)

Eventually, after over thirty turns, they decide the word is 'sherry'. The first turn signals a problem through the word *decipher*, i.e. a word Ann cannot read. It is also worth noting that this turn contains the interpersonal modal verb *wanna*, and the request is worded grammatically as a question, a choice which can also be interpreted interpersonally. Ann could instead have worded the request, 'Somebody decipher this now please,' as the transactional goal is the same, but the interpersonal force would be very different and highly inappropriate in this context. By thus pinpointing typical language features in genres and speculating on other ways of representing the message, such features can cast light on how speakers are communicatively constrained by their communities, roles and goals.

5. What can a corpus tell us about non-institutional genres?

Some discourse is clearly non-institutional, as demonstrated by research into CSGs of everyday communication by Carter and McCarthy on the CANCODE corpus (McCarthy 1998; O'Keeffe *et al.* 2007), as well as that of Eggins and Slade (1997) who employ a systemic functional linguistics (SFL) approach to the analysis of gossip and other relational genres. Nevertheless, the boundary between institutional and non-institutional discourse is necessarily fuzzy. Given the participation of interlocutors whose professional identity is not salient, we could say there are also transactional genres that are not strictly institutional (i.e. neither wholly professional nor academic). CANCODE data, for example, has five contextual categories: intimate, socialising, pedagogical, professional and transactional (see McCarthy 1998). Examples include communication in the media between professionals and members of the public, such as O'Keeffe (2006), and studies of service encounters.

This section is based around McCarthy's (2000) chapter on the genre of close contact service encounters, in this case a hairdressing encounter, which appears in Coupland's edited collection *Small Talk* (Coupland 2000). The data is from the transactional section of the CANCODE corpus, and although McCarthy does not conduct keyword or concordance searches, he does provide quantitative comparisons of the amount of transactional and interpersonal language, which are discussed below. Nevertheless, the analysis of the text is largely qualitative, demonstrating how a corpus of whole texts and discourse analytical techniques can be integrated.

Service encounters are essentially transactional genres, but they often contain a lot of interpersonal discourse. For example, 92.5 per cent of the communication that takes place in the above encounter is interpersonal (McCarthy 2000) as it does not directly relate to the task at hand (in this case, the transaction of cutting hair) but instead is relational in nature. This is an important finding because it shows that in an apparently transactional genre like a hairdressing encounter, the vast majority of the language can be non-transactional. Such a finding has implications for the degree of rigidity we can reasonably apply in describing the discourse of a genre, and means that goals-driven descriptions of genre need to account for the interpersonal as well as transactional (Coupland 2000). It also raises the issue of constraint: such interpersonal communication may be expected by those concerned within this context, and an encounter that comprised purely transactional language could be perceived as inappropriate and uncomfortable.

McCarthy breaks the encounter down into eight stages, from the client being invited to 'come through', to her paying the bill and leaving. In terms of whether the stages are primarily transactional or interpersonal, McCarthy argues that they are all transactional, but contain varying degrees of interpersonal talk. This is particularly evident in Extract 2 from the second stage of the encounter, the initial discussion of how the client's hair will be cut.

Extract 2

1. <Server> Are you alright?
2. <Client> I'm fine thanks and you?
3. <Server> I'm fine thanks you yes {<Client> {Laughs}} are we cutting it as normal or 4 anything different or?
5. <Client> Erm any suggestions or {laughs}?
6. <Server> I always ask you that {laughs}.

(McCarthy 2000: 93)

In this extract, the cutter refers to the fact that the client has had her hair cut on numerous occasions by this cutter (lines 3–6). The encounter also begins with phatic greetings. Other stages, while clearly fulfilling a transactional goal, also contain a high degree of interpersonal, positively evaluative language, for example *Oh that's lovely* …

better … smashing. Such language is statistically more significant in CANCODE than in the business-discourse corpus CANBEC (Handford, forthcoming).

In terms of how speakers achieve their interpersonal goals through their use of language, it is evident in the above extract and throughout the encounter that both the client and the servers make considerable efforts to create a positive and friendly atmosphere. Apart from the aspects noted in the previous paragraph, in this extract we also see an interesting choice of pronouns (*are we cutting it as normal*) which creates a communal tone, even though, strictly speaking, the client is not involved in the act of cutting. There is a high degree of laughter, and when the cutter does make a suggestion it is hedged (*I mean you could … sort of have a … like a sort of …*). Such hedging ensures that the suggestions do not appear too forceful, thereby addressing the negative face needs of the client and allowing her the option to disagree with the suggestions without threatening the positive face needs of the cutter (Brown and Levinson 1987).

Furthermore, it should also be remembered that the stages are all primarily transactional: the other 90 per cent of the encounter is made up of language that is wholly interpersonal. Such findings show how important the maintenance and development of the relationship is in such regular service encounters. For the client, we can infer that the hair-cutting ability and price are not the only factors in choosing a hairdresser: having a comfortable relationship with the cutter is important. Conversely, for the cutter, it seems that the efforts spent on developing the relationship will help ensure the customer returns. Such findings add weight to the argument that interpersonal language can be employed to fulfil transactional goals (Iacobucci 1990; Handford, forthcoming).

On a more abstract level, this linguistic behaviour arguably shows how the participants in this interaction are very much 'conforming to type': the client and servers, through drawing on their previous relevant experiences, both assume and recreate the social roles and relationships associated with the constraints of this social context. In so doing, they ratify the social practices that characterise this genre (such as 'having your hair done' in a provincial British women's hairdressers). As such, we could say that such a genre approach highlights the dependence of texts (the language that is produced) on social context, and allows the analyst to make powerful inferences about what is allowed and what is controlled (that is, permitted and not permitted) in terms of the discourse features. For example, while it is possible that the speakers might baldly interrupt each other, doing so would probably be seen as highly inappropriate in this context (but not in other contexts, such as a cross-examination in a British court). Therefore we can say that the text is dependent very much on the social context in which it is embedded and to which it contributes.

This chapter has provided a flavour of the combination of genre and corpus approaches, and shown how CSGs can answer many of the criticisms levelled at corpus linguistics. Areas including the role and importance of context, fruitful combinations of quantitative and qualitative techniques, and the types of top-down and bottom-up approaches to the data have been discussed. In so doing, we have seen that corpora are not only large, decontextualised collections of words necessitating bottom-up, statistical approaches, but can be employed to explore nebulous issues in applied linguistics and discourse analysis. For instance, we have also seen how primarily transactional genres feature interpersonal language, and how goals and practices are evidenced in the data.

The underlying theme of this chapter is that it is the social actions the participants (both expert and apprentice) perform in relation to the particular conventions and constraints which best explains what happens in genres, that is why speakers and writers do what they do. Well-designed and compiled CSGs can thus allow the analyst to uncover empirical evidence of the goals and practices that manifest themselves in the typical and therefore normative patterns in the discourse. By applying the compatible range of methods outlined here that corpus and genre approaches provide, we can attempt to see 'the whole of the elephant' (Bhatia 2004: xv).

In terms of what the future holds, it seems plausible that research may increasingly attempt to combine such qualitative and quantitative, genre and corpus approaches, but with increased emphasis on the insights that close linguistic analysis can offer on wider social practices and discourses (Gee 2005). One possible observation of much CSG-based research is that it could still go further in interpreting and explaining the contexts in which the texts occur. Fairclough's (2000) keyword-based study of political language is one example of how such insights can be produced. Furthermore, according to Bhatia, a tendency in genre analysis can be towards oversimplification (2004), but basing descriptions on appropriately sampled, carefully analysed CSGs should enable the researcher to avoid questionable idealisations. One relatively unexplored area is that of corpora of professional discourse.

Through the processes of intertextuality and interdiscursivity (Bhatia 2004) there are new genres forming all the time, which have yet to be adequately described and interpreted. These include teleconferencing, videoconferencing, as well as internet-based genres like blogs and other cybergenres relating to eParticipation. Also, while each of the three texts examined here have been analysed in isolation, the reality is that they each form part of an ongoing genre network (Swales 2004). CSGs can therefore provide fecund datasets for these research fields.

Further reading

Baker, P. (2006) *Using Corpora in Discourse Analysis*. London: Continuum. (This is a very accessible introduction to the themes and issues surrounding this powerful combination of corpora and discourse analysis. Baker does not shy away from tackling some of the thornier issues like ideology and data, and he discusses in detail how corpus techniques like keyness and concordances relate to discourse analysis.)

Flowerdew, L. (2005) 'An Integration of Corpus-based and Genre-based Approaches to Text Analysis in EAP/ESP: Countering Criticisms against Corpus-based Methodologies', *English for Specific Purposes* 24: 321–32. (This paper explores several of the criticisms levelled against corpus linguistics, and discusses how a genre approach to corpus linguistics can practically address these concerns. Flowerdew draws on the Swalesian and New Rhetoric approaches to genre.)

Upton, T. and Connor U. (2001) 'Using Computerized Corpus Analysis to Investigate the Textlinguistic Discourse Moves of a Genre', *English for Specific Purposes* 20: 313–29. (This paper shows how a corpus can shed light on both the lexicogrammatical features and moves within the genre of application letters among three different nationalities, and how politeness can be operationalised.)

References

Adolphs, S., Atkins, S. and Harvey, K. (2007) 'Caught between Professional Requirements and Interpersonal Needs: Vague Language in Health Care Contexts', in J. Cutting (ed.) *Vague Language Explored*. Basingstoke: Palgrave Macmillan, pp. 62–78.

Baker, P. (2006) *Using Corpora in Discourse Analysis*. London: Continuum.

Bargiela-Chiappini, F. and Harris, S. (1997) *Managing Language: The Discourse of Corporate Meetings*. Amsterdam: John Benjamins.

Bargiela-Chiappini, F. and Nickerson, C. (eds) (1999) *Writing Business: Genres, Media and Discourses*. Harlow: Longman.

Bazerman, C. (1994) 'Systems of Genres and the Enhancement of Social Intentions', in A. Freedman and P. Medway (eds) *Genre and New Rhetoric*. London: Taylor & Francis, pp. 79–101.

Berkenkotter, C. and Huckin, T. (1995) 'Rethinking Genre from a Sociocognitive Perspective', *Written Communication* 10: 475–509.

Bhatia, V. (1993) *Analysing Genre: Language Use in Professional Settings*. Harlow: Longman.

——(2004) *Worlds of Written Discourse*. London: Continuum.

Bhatia, V., Flowerdew, J. and Jones, R. (eds) (2008) *Advances in Discourse Studies*. London: Routledge.

Biber, D. (1988) *Variation across Speech and Writing*. Cambridge: Cambridge University Press.

Biber, D., Conrad, S. and Reppen, R. (1998) *Corpus Linguistics: Investigating Language Structure and Use*. Cambridge: Cambridge University Press.

Brown, P. and Levinson, S. (1987) *Politeness: Some Universals in Language Usage*. London: Cambridge University Press.

Candlin, C. and Hyland, K. (eds) (1999) *Writing: Texts, Processes and Practices*. London: Longman.

Christie, F. and Martin, J. (eds) (1997) *Genres and Institutions*. London: Continuum.

Collins Cobuild Learners' Dictionary (1987) Glasgow: Collins.

Connor, U. and Upton, T. (eds) (2004) *Discourse in the Professions: Perspectives from Corpus Linguistics*. Amsterdam: John Benjamins.

Coupland, J. (ed.) (2000) *Small Talk*. Harlow: Pearson Education.

Couture, B. (1986) *Functional Approaches to Writing: Research Perspectives*. Norwood: Ablex.

Csomay, E. (2005) 'Linguistic Variation within Classroom Talk: A Corpus-based Perspective', *Linguistics and Education* 15(3): 243–74.

Cutting, J. (ed.) (2007) *Vague Language Explored*. Basingstoke: Palgrave Macmillan.

Eggins, S. and Slade, D. (1997) *Analysing Casual Conversation*. London: Cassell.

Evison, J. (2008) 'Turn-openers in Academic Talk: An Exploration of Discourse Responsibility', unpublished PhD thesis, University of Nottingham.

Fairclough, N. (2000) *New Labour, New Language?* London: Routledge.

Flowerdew, J. (ed.) (2002) *Academic Discourse*. Harlow: Longman.

Flowerdew, L. (1998) 'Concordancing on an Expert and Learner Corpus for ESP', *CALL Journal* 8(3): 3–7.

——(2002) 'Corpus-based Analyses in EAP', in J. Flowerdew (ed.) *Academic Discourse*. Harlow: Longman, pp. 95–114.

——(2004) 'The Argument for Using English Specialized Corpora to Understand Academic and Professional Settings', in U. Connor and T. Upton (eds) *Discourse in the Professions: Perspectives from Corpus Linguistics*. Amsterdam: John Benjamins, pp. 11–36.

——(2008) 'Corpora and Context in Professional Writing', in V. Bhatia, J. Flowerdew and H. Jones (eds) *Advances in Discourse Studies*. London: Routledge, pp. 115–27.

Gee, J. P. (2005) *An Introduction to Discourse Analysis*. London: Routledge.

Ghadessy, M., Henry, A. and Roseberry, R. (eds) (2001) *Small Corpus Studies and ELT: Theory and Practice*. Amsterdam: John Benjamins.

Giddens, A. (1984) *The Construction of Society: Outline of a Theory of Structuration*. Cambridge: Cambridge University Press.

Halliday, M. (1985/1994) *An Introduction to Functional Grammar*. London: Edward Arnold.

Handford, M. (forthcoming) *The Language of Business Meetings*. Cambridge: Cambridge University Press.

Hoey, M. (1983) *On the Surface of Discourse*. London: George Allen & Unwin.

——(2005) *Lexical Priming*. London: Routledge.

Holmes, J. and Stubbe, M. (2003) *Power and Politeness in the Workplace*. London: Longman.

Hunston, S. (2002) *Corpora in Applied Linguistics*. Cambridge: Cambridge University Press.

Hyland, K. (2000) *Disciplinary Discourses: Social Interactions in Academic Writing*. Harlow: Longman.

——(2003) *Second Language Writing*. Cambridge: Cambridge University Press.

——(2006) *English for Academic Purposes*. London: Routledge.

Hyland, K. and Milton, J. (1997) 'Qualification and Certainty in L1 and L2 Students' Writing', *Journal of Second Language Writing* 6(2): 183–206.

Hyon, S. (1996) 'Genre in Three Traditions: Implications for ESL', *TESOL Quarterly* 30: 693–722.

Iacobucci, C. (1990) 'Accounts, Formulations and Goal Attainment Strategies in Service Encounters', in K. Tracy and N. Coupland (eds) *Multiple Goals in Discourse*. Clevedon, Avon: Multilingual Matters, pp. 85–99.

Koester, A. (2004) 'Relational Sequences in Workplace Genres', *Journal of Pragmatics* 36: 1405–28.

——(2006) *Investigating Workplace Discourse*. Routledge: London.

Lee, D. (2001) 'Genres, Registers, Text Types, Domains, and Styles: Clarifying the Concepts and Navigating a Path through the BNC Jungle', *Language Learning and Technology* 5: 37–72.

——(2008) 'Corpora and Discourse Analysis: New Ways of Doing Old Things', in V. Bhatia, J. Flowerdew and H. Jones (eds) *Advances in Discourse Studies*. London: Routledge, pp. 86–99.

McCarthy, M. J. (1998) *Spoken Language and Applied Linguistics*. Cambridge: Cambridge University Press.

——(2000) 'Mutually Captive Audiences: Small Talk and the Genre of the Close-contact Service Encounters', in J. Coupland (ed.) *Small Talk*. Harlow: Pearson Education, pp. 84–109.

McCarthy, M. J. and Handford, M. (2004) '"Invisible to Us": A Preliminary Corpus-based Study of Spoken Business English', in U. Connor and T. Upton (eds) *Discourse in the Professions: Perspectives from Corpus Linguistics*. Amsterdam: John Benjamins, pp. 167–201.

Martin, J. (1992) *English Text: System and Structure*. Amsterdam: John Benjamins.

——(1997) 'Analysing Genre: Functional Parameters', in F. Christie and J. Martin (eds) *Genre and Institutions: Social Processes in the Workplace and School*. London: Continuum, pp. 3–39.

O'Keeffe, A. (2006) *Investigating Media Discourse*. London: Routledge.

O'Keeffe, A., McCarthy, M. J. and Carter, R. A. (2007) *From Corpus to Classroom: Language Use and Language Teaching*. Cambridge: Cambridge University Press.

Sarangi, S. and Roberts, C. (eds) (1999) *Talk, Work and Institutional Order*. Berlin: Mouton de Gruyter.

Scollon, R. and Scollon, S. W. (2001) *Intercultural Communication: A Discourse Approach*. 2nd edn. Oxford: Blackwell.

Scott, M. (1996) *WordSmith Tools*. Oxford: Oxford University Press.

Simpson, R. (2004) 'Stylistic Features of Spoken Academic Discourse: The Role of Formulaic Expressions', in U. Connor and T. Upton (eds) *Discourse in the Professions: Perspectives from Corpus Linguistics*. Amsterdam: John Benjamins, pp. 37–64.

Sinclair, J. (1991) *Corpus, Concordance, Collocation*. Oxford: Oxford University Press.

Stubbs, M. (1996) *Text and Corpus Analysis*. London: Blackwell.

Swales, J. (1990) *Genre Analysis*. Cambridge: Cambridge University Press.

——(2002) 'Integrated and Fragmented Worlds: EAP Materials and Corpus Linguistics', in J. Flowerdew (ed.) *Academic Discourse*. Harlow: Longman, pp. 150–64.

——(2004) *Research Genres: Explorations and Applications*. New York: Cambridge University Press.

Swales, J. and Lee, D. (2006) 'A Corpus-based EAP Course for NNS Doctoral Students: Moving from Available Specialized Corpora to Self-compiled Corpora', *English for Specific Purposes* 25: 56–75.

Tognini Bonelli, E. (2001) *Corpus Linguistics at Work*. Amsterdam: John Benjamins.

Tribble, C. (2002) 'Corpora and Corpus Analysis: New Windows on Academic Writing', in J. Flowerdew (ed.) *Academic Discourse*. Harlow: Longman, pp. 131–49.

Vine, B. (2004) 'Modal Verbs in New Zealand English Directives', *Nordic Journal of English Studies* 3(3): 205–20.

Wenger, E. (1998) *Communities of Practice: Learning, Meaning and Identity*. Cambridge: Cambridge University Press.

Widdowson, H. (1998) 'Context, Community and Authentic Language', *TESOL Quarterly* 32(4): 705–16.

——(2000) 'On the Limitations of Linguistics Applied', *Applied Linguistics* 21: 3–25.

20
What can a corpus tell us about discourse?

Scott Thornbury

1. What is discourse?

The term *discourse* is both slippery and baggy: slippery because it eludes neat definition, and baggy because it embraces a wide range of linguistic and social phenomena. In this chapter the term will be limited to two basic senses – the formal sense: *discourse as connected text* (or *discourse*[1], for convenience) and the functional one: *discourse as language in use* (or *discourse*[2]). These two senses are well captured in the following definition:

> A piece of discourse is an instance of spoken or written language that has describable internal relationships of form and meaning … that relate coherently to an external communicative function or purpose and a given audience/interlocutor. Furthermore, the external function or purpose can only be properly determined if one takes into account the context and participants … in which the piece of discourse occurs.
>
> (Celce-Murcia and Olshtain 2000: 4)

The reference to the context and the participants can, of course, include not just the immediate *context of situation* but the larger social and cultural context as well. As Schiffrin (1994) puts it: 'To understand the language of discourse … we need to understand the world in which it resides' (1994: 419). Accordingly, I will invoke a third sense of the term discourse: *discourse as social practice* (Fairclough 1989), where the focus is 'not so much on how meanings are linguistically realized in texts, as on how they are socially constructed' (Widdowson 2007: xv). I will revisit this third sense of discourse (=*discourse*[3]) later in the chapter.

But the main focus of this chapter will be less on what corpus analysis can tell us about discourse as language in use (i.e. language in *context*), and more on what it can tell us about 'the describable internal relationships' of texts (i.e. language and its *co-text*). This is partly because the relationship between language and context is dealt with elsewhere in this volume (in particular chapters by Biber, on register, and Rühlemann, on pragmatics), and partly because – as we shall see in Section 3 – corpus linguistics is more comfortable handling *co-text* than it is *context*.

What, then, is subsumed under 'the describable internal relationships' of texts? For convenience, we can distinguish between two broad areas:

- *cohesion* across sentences and utterances, using grammatical and lexical devices, such as conjuncts, referring expressions and lexical repetition (Halliday and Hasan 1976);
- the *organisation* and *management* of discourse (both spoken and written), including the distribution of given and new information, topic management, the use of discourse markers, turn-taking, exchanges, scripts, rhetorical structures and macro-structures, such as narratives (Brown and Yule 1983; Coulthard 1985; McCarthy 1991).

2. What can a corpus tell us about discourse?

For reasons that will be discussed in Section 3, discourse analysts have been slower off the mark than, say, lexicographers or grammarians, in responding to the opportunities offered by corpora and the tools to investigate them with. Of course, few if any contemporary discourse studies are *not* informed by the analysis of collections of texts. But, as Partington (2004) notes, 'simply employing a corpus in one's research does not necessarily make it a study in Corpus Linguistics' (2004: 12). To qualify as such, analysts would need to use quantitative methods with the aim of producing findings that are both descriptive and explanatory.

The descriptive findings are generated by searching for particular discourse features in a corpus – typically a collection of texts of a specific register, but possibly a single extended text, such as a textbook or a novel – using computational means. Explaining the frequency, significance and use of these features generally involves reference to context, either the immediate co-textual environment, or to other texts or other corpora of texts. For, as Stubbs (2001a) reminds us, 'in corpus work, context means two rather different things: not only co-text (a short span of a few words within one single text), but also inter-text (repeated occurrences, often a very large number, of similar patterns across different, independent texts)' (2001a: 57). Thus, the analyst may compare and contrast an individual text, or a sub-corpus of texts of a specific type, with texts of another type, or with a larger and more general reference corpus. An example of this approach is Stubbs' own (1994) comparison of two school textbooks, using the Lancaster Oslo/Bergen corpus as a benchmark.

What, then, do corpora permit us to generalise about discourse, and, specifically, about the describable internal relationships in texts? Put another way, what is *quantifiable* about discourse?

In the same way that corpus-derived frequency information has revolutionised language description at the level of lexis and grammar, so too has the study of discourse hugely benefited from the kinds of quantitative data that corpora yield. Thus, researchers, such as Altenberg (1990), Stenström (1994) and Aijmer (1996), using the London–Lund Corpus of Spoken English, identified and quantified characteristic features of spoken interaction, including interactional signals, discourse markers and hedging devices. Gardner (1998) and O'Keeffe *et al.* (2007) have used spoken corpora to classify different kinds of response tokens. Biber *et al.* (1999), drawing on the British National Corpus, extend their description of English grammar to include a treatment of conversational structure, including the use of discourse markers and ellipsis, and thereby set out to 'explore the interface between grammar and discourse analysis, lexis, and pragmatics' (1999: 45).

In a similar spirit, the *Cambridge Grammar of English* (Carter and McCarthy 2006) includes a section called 'Grammar Across Turns and Sentences', in which 'the emphasis is on the grammar of texts and the part played by grammar in achieving textual coherence' (2006: 243). In this way, corpus studies have been instrumental in dissolving the rigid distinctions between grammar and discourse. 'Grammar becomes discourse when conventional sentence-based units of description fail to account for the facts' (McCarthy 1998: 82). Corpus analysis uncovers the facts.

Generalising from these facts, from a discourse perspective, typically involves identifying the micro-features of specific text types and from these extrapolating textual macro-features. For example, the distribution of tense, aspect and modality verb forms in academic papers, and the way that such forms correlate to specific textual functions, has been the subject of a number of studies (Crookes 1986; Swales and Najjar 1987; Swales 1990; Flowerdew 2002). Likewise, researchers have used small corpora to investigate the generic features of such registers as sports commentary (Ghadessy 1988), economics texts (Bondi 1999) and computer conferencing (Yates 1996). But, because the focus of such studies is mainly on the way that texts instantiate the contextual variables of specific discourse communities, these are more properly dealt with as *register* studies (see Biber, this volume).

Using corpus tools to identify what makes individual texts cohesive, on the other hand, or to track their internal organisation through the use of discourse markers, is more problematic. Corpus tools cannot easily detect cohesive ties, such as pronominal reference, unless they have been tagged as such. And even so, it is another matter to identify what a device is cohesive *with*. However, innovative procedures are being developed to overcome these problems. Biber *et al.* (1998) describe the use of 'an interactive text analysis program' that functions like a spellchecker: it searches tagged text corpora for targeted features, such as noun phrases, 'while retaining human decision-making for those difficult analyses that involve meaning distinctions' (1998: 113). Using this tool, the researchers were able to code and compare the characteristics of anaphoric referring expressions in different registers.

The identification of discourse markers (Schiffrin 1987) presents similar challenges. One approach is to search the corpus for pre-selected items. Pulcini and Furiassi (2004), for example, investigate the choice and distribution of discourse markers in a corpus of teacher–student interviews by starting with an inventory of such markers and then searching the corpus for occurrences. A more inductive approach involves specifying, not the items to be searched for, but the contexts in which to look. Tao (2003), for example, investigates turn-taking mechanisms by searching a corpus of transcribed conversation for the word or words immediately following the speaker-tag. By this means he is able to show that a relatively small repertoire of turn-initiators – such as *and, yeah, well, right* – are put to extensive use, for both cohesive and pragmatic purposes.

Biber, Conrad and Cortes (2004) search corpora of two different registers – classroom teaching and textbooks – for frequently occurring word sequences ('lexical bundles') and find that many, such as *going to talk about* and *has to do with the*, have a discourse organising function. Their relative frequency in classroom teaching leads the researchers to conclude that 'these lexical bundles serve as discourse framing devices: they provide a kind of frame expressing stance, discourse organization, or referential status, associated with a slot for the expression of new information relative to that frame' (2004: 400). Again, such a conclusion depends not on frequency data alone, but on the use of concordance data in order both to infer the functional categories of these bundles, and to explain their relative frequency in different registers.

More amenable to corpus analysis are features of lexical cohesion (Halliday and Hasan 1976) including *reiteration* (the direct and indirect repetition of words, the use of synonyms, near synonyms and general terms) and *collocation*. With regard to collocation, corpus tools can, of course, easily identify words in a corpus that co-occur (and co-occur with more than chance frequency): this is one of their more robust functions. But they are limited to a relatively short co-textual span: typically from one to five words either side of the node. They are less sensitive to co-occurrences over larger stretches of text, even in adjacent sentences. (Some corpus tools, such as *Sketch Engine*, developed by Adam Kilgarriff, Lexical Computing Ltd, do however allow collocation searches over much wider spans, and developments in semantic tagging may soon allow researchers to capture more extensive meaning networks encoded in the lexis; see Walter, this volume, for an illustration of a *Sketch Engine* search.)

Corpus tools are better suited to identifying and tallying instances of reiteration, both direct and indirect, in a text. Frequency lists, after all, are simply a record of a text's – or a corpus of texts' – lexical repetitions. From the point of view of topical cohesion, a list of the words that are *key* in the texts may be more revealing than a simple frequency list. *Keyness* is defined as 'a quality words may have in a given text or set of texts, suggesting that they are important, [that] they reflect what the text is really about' (Scott and Tribble 2006: 73). Keyword analysis allows the analyst to explore 'not just how sentences are structured but how whole sections of text flow and move' (2006: 7).

Stubbs (2001a) shows how this textual 'flow' is achieved through the recurrence not just of individual words or their derivatives but of 'lexico-semantic units', including collocations and other formulaic lexical combinations, thereby creating 'a relatively unexplored mechanism of text cohesion' (2001a: 120). Similarly, Hoey (2005), building on his previous studies (e.g. 1991) of how chains of related lexis form *textual collocations* that ripple through whole texts and thereby create coherence, uses corpus data to identify which words frequently occur in such chains, and are thus *primed* for textual cohesion. Of particular relevance to discourse analysis is his claim that 'every lexical item (or combination of lexical items) is capable of being primed (positively or negatively) to occur at the beginning or end of an independently recognised "chunk" of text' (2005: 129), an effect that he terms *textual colligation*.

Hoey stresses that such primings are genre-specific. This point is demonstrated in a study of business communication (Scott and Tribble 2006) where a single keyword (*hope*) was found to correlate with the same discourse moves and to occur in similar textual environments across a number of texts in a small corpus of business correspondence. The researchers conclude that 'a combination of KW [keyword] analysis and discourse analysis offers teachers and students a powerful way of coming to an understanding of how language is used in professional settings' (2006: 109).

To similar ends Biber, Csomay *et al.* (2004) use a more elaborated approach in order to identify what they call Vocabulary-Based Discourse Units (VBDUs), 'based on the assumption that different discourse units tend to use different sets of words, reflecting shifts in topic and purpose' (2004: 24). Using a computer program that progressively scans sequences of text for evidence of lexical repetition, VBDUs were identified in a variety of genres. These units were then subjected to closer scrutiny, in order to identify any distinctive linguistic properties, and to map these on to their situational, social and cognitive functions. Using cluster analysis, seven VBDU types were identified, such as *extreme oral narrative* and *literate + content-focused*, with a view to 'studying how sequences of DU-types work together in different registers, supporting different major rhetorical patterns' (2004: 38).

Flowerdew (2003) also combines genre analysis and corpus linguistics – specifically, a keyword analysis – in order to investigate the problem-solution pattern in two corpora of technical academic writing, one by professionals and the other by students. Her particular focus is on the language of *appraisal* (Martin and Rose 2003). Stubbs (2007) approaches the same goal – of mapping specific semantic units on to the discourse structure of particular text-types – from the perspective of phraseology. His claim is that 'many frequent phrasal constructions have textual functions of evaluation and information management' (2007: 182), and goes on to argue that 'studies of phraseology must combine corpus analysis (which phrasal constructions are frequent in the corpus?) and textual analysis (how do these constructions organize individual texts?)' (2007: 182).

The above studies are concerned mainly with using corpus tools to identify and describe the internal relationships in texts (what, earlier, we termed *discourse*[1]). Corpus-based studies that focus on *discourse as language in use* (or *discourse*[2]) and which 'take[.] into account the context and participants … in which the piece of discourse occurs' (Celce-Murcia and Olshtain 2000: 4) require the kind of contextual data that few large corpora provide (see the next section). Nevertheless, studies combining corpus data and other research tools, such as discourse completion tests (DCTs), provide insights into how the corpus data are realised in specific contexts and between specific participants (see, for example, Schauer and Adolphs 2006). Small corpora, gathered in restricted contexts, allow closer tracking of contextual factors. McCarthy (2000), for example, used two contextually coded extracts from the much larger CANCODE spoken corpus to investigate small talk at the hairdressers' and during driving lessons. Kuiper and Flindall (2000) gathered a small corpus of exchanges at supermarket checkouts in order both to describe and to explain the structure of these exchanges. Studies like these, that combine the thick contextual descriptions of ethnography with the quantifiable linguistic data of a corpus, offer useful methodological models for investigating discourse in action.

What is notable about all these studies is the way that they combine corpus-based procedures with research methods from other disciplines, such as genre analysis, phraseology, pragmatics and ethnography. Research into the third level of discourse, *discourse-as-social-practice*, is similarly eclectic in its methods. Stubbs (1996), for example, situates his corpus research firmly within the critical discourse analysis paradigm. In one study (1996), he uses quantitative methods to analyse patterns of transitivity in two school textbooks, in order to reveal their ideological biases. Elsewhere, however, he leans more in the direction of stylistics: in Stubbs (2005), using corpus tools again, he peels back the thematic sub-text of Joseph Conrad's *Heart of Darkness*. The value that a corpus-based methodology brings to these studies is that it 'helps to ensure that analysts do not merely pick evidence to fit their preconceptions' (Stubbs 1996: 154). This does not mean, though, that *discourse*[3]-analysis is purely objective. As Teubert (2007) makes clear: 'The generation of relevant concordances and the statistical analysis of this data is never more than a first step. What the evidence means is a matter of interpretation. Without interpretation any study in corpus linguistics would be incomplete' (2007: 124–5). Teubert's own study (2000) of the language of British Euroscepticism, as expressed on websites opposed to the European Union, is a case in point. So, too, is the study by Koteyko *et al.* (2008) on media and government discourses about the 'superbug' (a particularly virulent micro-organism found in hospitals), where the value of using concordance programs to search corpora was that 'this allowed us to validate qualitative "hunches" using quantitative data' (2008: 239). Likewise, a study by Baker (2006), again using concordance data, of how newspaper texts construe refugees, leads him to conclude that

> the patterns of language which are found (or overlooked) [in a corpus] may be subject to the researcher's own ideological stance. And the way that they are interpreted may also be filtered through the researcher's subject position. This is true of many other, if not all, forms of discourse analysis. However, the corpus-based approach at least helps to counter some of this bias, by providing quantitative evidence of patterns that may be more difficult to ignore.
>
> (Baker 2006: 92)

3. What are the limitations of using a corpus in the study of discourse and how might we overcome them?

If discourse analysts have been slow to embrace the opportunities offered by corpus linguistics, this is in part due to the perception that corpora consist mainly of de-contextualised text fragments, assembled from a fairly random range of sources – an inevitable consequence of their original, primarily lexicographical, purpose. Discourse analysis, on the other hand, requires whole texts, often of the same type, as its database. And the bias, in many early corpora, towards written texts meant they were of little practical use to researchers of spoken language.

Now, however, specialised corpora of specific registers, including spoken language, have proliferated, and most corpora of general English, including many that are freely available online, are tagged for text-type and register. Most also allow access to more of each text than simply concordances of individual words. Nevertheless, analysts still lack tools that will perform many of the kinds of operations that are traditionally done manually. As Biber *et al.* (1998) point out, many features of connected text – such as the distribution of given versus new information, or the identification of pronoun referents and of other cohesive devices – cannot be detected automatically.

But there is a more fundamental problem facing the discourse analyst. While corpus tools allow researchers to track, tally and plot the surface features of discourse – such as its linking devices, discourse markers and instances of lexical repetition – these remain simply that: surface features. They do not necessarily correlate with, or explain, the underlying semantic relations between parts of a text, including those which account for the text's coherence and its generic structure. This is a limitation of the study of cohesion in general, and one that Halliday and Hasan (1976) were well aware of:

> Cohesion expresses the continuity that exists between one part of the text and another. It is important to stress that continuity is not the whole of texture. The organization of each segment of a discourse in terms of its information structure, thematic patterns and the like is also part of its texture ... no less important than the continuity of one segment to another.
>
> (Halliday and Hasan 1976: 299)

Where such features leave lexical traces (as, for example, in the form of lexical chains), a corpus-based analysis is warranted (as Hoey 1991 and Biber, Csomay *et al.* 2004 have demonstrated), but such an analysis can only complement and not replace a more interpretative approach. In the end, discourse is more than words. As Baker (2006) warns, 'at present, a great deal of corpus-based discourse analysis is still focused at the lexical level. The challenge to future researchers is to find way to make grammar- and semantic-based analysis of corpora a more feasible option' (2006: 174).

Even were such means available, they would be of little practical use in the absence of detailed information about *context*. The lack of thick data relating to the contextual conditions of text production and interpretation continues to handicap the application of corpus analysis tools to the analysis of discourse. As Baker (2006) observes:

> Questions involving production such as who authored a text, under what circumstances, for what motives and for whom, in addition to questions surrounding the interpretation of a text: who bought, read, accessed, used the text, what were their responses, etc. can not be simply answered by traditional corpus-based techniques.
>
> (Baker 2006: 18)

Baker's concerns reflect Widdowson's (2004) well-rehearsed complaint that 'corpus analysis does not … account for context' (2004: 124), and that corpus linguists 'cannot … directly infer contextual factors from co-textual ones, and use textual data as conclusive evidence of discourse' (2004: 126). While this argument is hotly contested (see, for example, Stubbs 2001b), the use of smaller, more localised corpora (as was mentioned in the last section), where contextual information is rigorously specified, is an attempt to deal with the problem of lack of context.

In the end, quantitative data alone are not going to answer all – or even, any – of the questions that analysts bring to the study of discourse. As we have seen, a combination of computation and interpretation, in mutually informing cycles of investigation, and drawing on a variety of related disciplines – offers the most promising way forward. The next section demonstrates how this can work in practice.

4. How does a corpus-based approach work in practice?

It is now time to demonstrate how the application of corpus linguistics to discourse analysis might work in practice, with a view not only to validating the procedures involved, but to confronting some of the problems outlined in the previous section. The approach is essentially a bottom-up and inductive one: starting with frequency lists and word searches, the analyst identifies regularities in a corpus of texts of the same provenance and register, with a particular focus on those features that offer evidence of the internal relationships of the text-type in question. Studying these data, the researcher then constructs a provisional schematic for the overall structure of the text-type, which can then be checked against individual instances, and refined if necessary. Using the resulting description, and taking into account the contextual and cultural factors in which the texts are produced and interpreted, the researcher is then in a position to speculate as to how the formal features of the texts encode their communicative and social functions.

With these ends in mind, a small corpus (10,000 words) of teenage written narratives, hereafter referred to as the Cringe Text Corpus, was compiled, using an online teenage magazine as the source. The corpus consists of 143 short narratives of this type:

> One day I was walking in the park, and I saw a major babe and wanted to impress him. I started running in the sand volleyball courts and ran straight into the net! I fell flat on my back and started crying. He started laughing at me and it was terrible!

With the aim of identifying the internal relationships, including the generic discourse structure of the texts that comprise this corpus, *WordSmith Tools* (Scott 2008) was used, first to compile a list of the most frequent words in the corpus, and then to search these for linkers, specifically coordinating and subordinating conjunctions, and linking adjuncts. Because the linkers in the corpus were not tagged as such, a concordance program was then used in order to eliminate instances of linkage at the phrase level, such as *my best friend and I*, or polysemes, such as *I was so embarrassed*; *I ate too much*). Table 20.1 shows the linkers that occurred at least four times or more in the Cringe Text Corpus, including the number of instances in which the linker occurred at the beginning of a sentence.

The items in Table 20.1 are all single lexemes: a more thorough search, using a concordancer, was needed in order to identify combinations of linkers, such as *and then* (n = 6), as well as phrasal and clausal adjuncts, such as *all of a/the sudden* (n = 10) or combinations with *worse,* such as *even worse* and *to make matters* worse (n = 7). A word search also established that the following linkers (taken from lists in the *COBUILD English Grammar*; Sinclair 1990) do *not* occur in the Cringe Text Corpus: *furthermore, moreover, however, yet, nevertheless, therefore, hence, thus, consequently, secondly* or *thirdly*. (On the other hand, all these items did appear at least once in a corpus of academic journal abstracts.) The prominence of so many coordinating conjunctions, especially *and*, in the Cringe Text Corpus, suggests a markedly paratactic syntax (where sequenced clauses have equal status), in contrast to the more hypotactic style of the academic abstracts (where subordinate clauses are frequent). With regard to position in the sentence, only one linking adjunct (*then*) showed a slight preference for the sentence-initial slot.

As well as showing an item's position in a sentence, corpus tools can also display, graphically, where individual items occur in relation to the whole text. This is done through the use of a *dispersion plot*. Figure 20.1, for example, shows the distribution of all the instances of *sudden** (i.e. *suddenly, all of a sudden*) in the corpus, where the position of

Table 20.1 Linkers with a frequency of ≥ 4 in the Cringe Text Corpus

N	*Word*	*Freq.*	*%*	*Sentence initial*	*Texts (n = 143)*
1	and	366	3.37	1	136
2	so	73	0.67	6	63
3	but	53	0.49	4	45
4	then	26	0.25	15	25
5	finally	10	0.09	3	9
6	later	6	0.06	2	6
7	suddenly	6	0.06	1	6
8	though	4	0.04	0	4
9	too	4	0.04	0	4

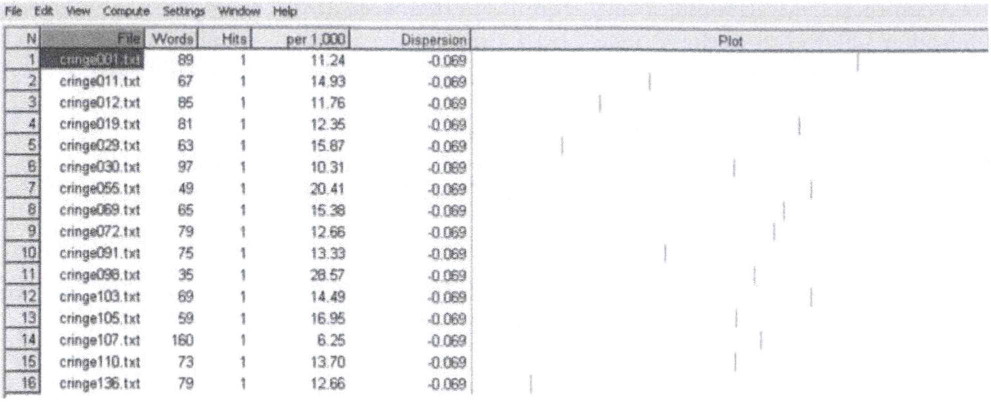

File Edit View Compute Settings Window Help

N	File	Words	Hits	per 1,000	Dispersion	Plot
1	cringe001.txt	89	1	11.24	-0.069	
2	cringe011.txt	67	1	14.93	-0.069	
3	cringe012.txt	85	1	11.76	-0.069	
4	cringe019.txt	81	1	12.35	-0.069	
5	cringe029.txt	63	1	15.87	-0.069	
6	cringe030.txt	97	1	10.31	-0.069	
7	cringe055.txt	49	1	20.41	-0.069	
8	cringe069.txt	65	1	15.38	-0.069	
9	cringe072.txt	79	1	12.66	-0.069	
10	cringe091.txt	75	1	13.33	-0.069	
11	cringe098.txt	35	1	28.57	-0.069	
12	cringe103.txt	69	1	14.49	-0.069	
13	cringe105.txt	59	1	16.95	-0.069	
14	cringe107.txt	160	1	6.25	-0.069	
15	cringe110.txt	73	1	13.70	-0.069	
16	cringe136.txt	79	1	12.66	-0.069	

Figure 20.1 Dispersion plot for *sudden** in the Cringe Text Corpus.

the item in each of the sixteen texts in which it occurs is visually represented by a short vertical line in the column headed *Plot.*

Since the plot has been standardised so that each text file appears to be of the same length, it is possible to compare the point of occurrence of the search item across multiple texts. It is evident, for example, that the majority of instances of *sudden** (ten out of sixteen) occur at, or just after, the midway point in the texts. Such information provides a clue as to the discourse structure of the texts in this particular corpus – the fuller implications of which will be explored shortly.

We have already noted that, without a great deal of manual tagging, the cohesive properties of referring expressions, such as pronouns and demonstrative determiners, are not easily tracked using corpus tools. However, a search of the occurrences of *this* in the Cringe Text Corpus did identify a usage that was sufficiently frequent to qualify as a potential generic feature. Of the twenty-seven instances of *this* in the corpus, twenty are non-referring. That is to say, the noun phrases that they premodify are first mentions in the text. For example:

```
I was flirting with this guy online
One day I told this girl which guy I had a crush on,
and there was this really hot guy taking our money
I wore this skirt that was long and flared out.
```

Of these twenty occurrences, eight follow the pattern '*this [really/totally][hot/cute]* + male' as in *this really hot guy.* Of the remaining seven examples of *this* + NP in the corpus, five form part of the cluster *to this day,* leaving only two that have anaphoric reference. We can conclude that, on this evidence, and to use Hoey's (2005) terminology, *this* is not *primed* for endophoric reference (either anaphoric or cataphoric) in this kind of text.

So far we have been looking at instances of grammatical cohesion – principally conjunction and demonstrative reference. Now we turn our attention to lexical cohesion. As a preliminary stage, a keyword analysis (again using *WordSmith Tools*) was performed, in order to identify words that were unusually frequent in the entire corpus (for detailed coverage of keywords, see Scott, this volume). The top thirty keywords in the Cringe

Text Corpus, excluding function words, as measured against the BNC (world edition, 2001) are displayed in Table 20.2.

These thirty words alone are a strong indicator as to the thematic content of the narratives that comprise the Cringe Text Corpus. The fact that many are semantically related, either because they belong to the same lexical set (*school*, *locker*; *walked*, *ran*) or to the same word family (*friend*, *friends*, *friend's*; *walking*, *walked*), or because they are synonyms (*mortified*, *embarrassed*; *boyfriend*, *crush* (in this context, an informal term for *boyfriend*); *fell*, *tripped*) or because they are collocates (*cute* + *guy*; *fell* + *butt*), is an indicator that the texts that constitute the corpus have what Hasan (1989) terms *texture*: 'The texture of a text is manifested by certain kinds of semantic relations between its individual messages' (1989: 71). The semantic relations are typically instantiated in the form of cohesive *chains*, of which Hasan describes two types. An *identity chain* is a set of items that are co-referential: every member of the set refers to the same person or event. Hasan notes that, in short narratives, identity chains typically run the length of the whole text. In the Cringe Text Corpus narratives, identity chains are mostly realised in the form of the first-person narrator: the pronouns *I* and *my* are the first and third most frequent words in the corpus, together comprising over 11 per cent of all word tokens, and occurring in all but one of the 143 texts.

The items in a *similarity chain*, on the other hand, 'belong to the same general field of meaning, referring to (related/similar) actions, events, and objects and their attributes' (Hasan 1989: 85). A possible similarity chain in the Cringe Text Corpus might be *tripped – fell – butt*. It would need a more fine-grained search to confirm whether this is, in fact, the case. So, while a list of keywords is not in itself a semantic network, it provides the raw data out of which such a network might be constructed.

A short (typically two to six) chain of words that are related simply because they commonly co-occur is called a *cluster* (Scott 1997), also known as *lexical bundles* (Biber *et al.* 1999) or *n-grams* (Fletcher 2003/8) (see Greaves and Warren, this volume). A cluster analysis complements a keyword search, especially at their points of intersection, as it identifies typical contexts in which certain keywords recur. Thus, the four-word clusters that appear five times or more in the Cringe Text Corpus suggest that certain patterns

Table 20.2 Key content words in the Cringe Text Corpus

N	*Word*	*Freq.*	*Keyness*	*No. of texts (n = 143)*	*N*	*Word*	*Freq.*	*Keyness*	*No. of texts (n = 143)*
1	crush	71	872.39	49	16	embarrassed	18	136.06	18
2	mom	25	290.07	16	17	guys	17	131.19	12
3	mortified	20	270.29	20	18	boyfriend	16	127.76	12
4	friends	53	269.29	43	19	locker	12	122.34	9
5	friend	52	255.95	38	20	fell	27	120.50	26
6	laughing	30	223.73	24	21	butt	13	120.41	12
7	guy	30	203.24	23	22	everyone	28	118.93	27
8	really	63	202.28	49	23	cute	12	117.72	12
9	day	66	188.80	54	24	talking	26	102.59	21
10	bathroom	23	161.85	16	25	went	41	100.82	33
11	started	38	158.42	31	26	tripped	10	96.04	9
12	school	49	157.35	39	27	saw	31	94.02	29
13	walking	27	145.37	23	28	ran	19	79.98	19
14	friend's	17	142.99	13	29	walked	19	78.09	18
15	hot	29	142.09	25	30	brother	18	76.72	13

Note: the keyness is calculated according to log likelihood.

(and themes) recur regularly enough to be generic, and that they are talked about in the same way: the writers experience embarrassment when unexpected events, including falls, occur and which are witnessed by their boyfriend (*crush*). (See Table 20.3.)

We have already seen that a dispersion plot suggests that the pattern *all of a sudden* frequently occurs midway in the texts that make up the corpus. Using the same tool, the distribution of *embarrassed* (both a keyword and the nucleus of two of the most frequent four-word clusters) is shown in Figure 20.2.

In other words, the vast majority of the occurrences of *embarrassed* occur at the very tail end of the text. By the same token, the majority (over 60 per cent) of occurrences of the phrase *one day* occur at the beginning of the text.

Working in this fashion – that is, plotting the distribution of keywords and high frequency clusters – the researcher starts to build up a composite picture of the generic structure of the text-type that makes up the corpus. Without detailing each step in the

Table 20.3 Four-word clusters with a frequency of ≥ 5 in the Cringe Text Corpus

N	*Four-word cluster*	*Freq.*
1	I was so embarrassed!'	12
2	in front of my	8
3	all of a sudden	7
4	was so embarrassed!' I	6
5	in the middle of	6
6	front of my crush!	5
7	to go to the	5
8	friend and I were	5
9	right in front of	5
10	I had to go	5
11	was at school and	5
12	had to go to	5
13	the rest of the	5
14	'I was at school	5
15	fell flat on my	5

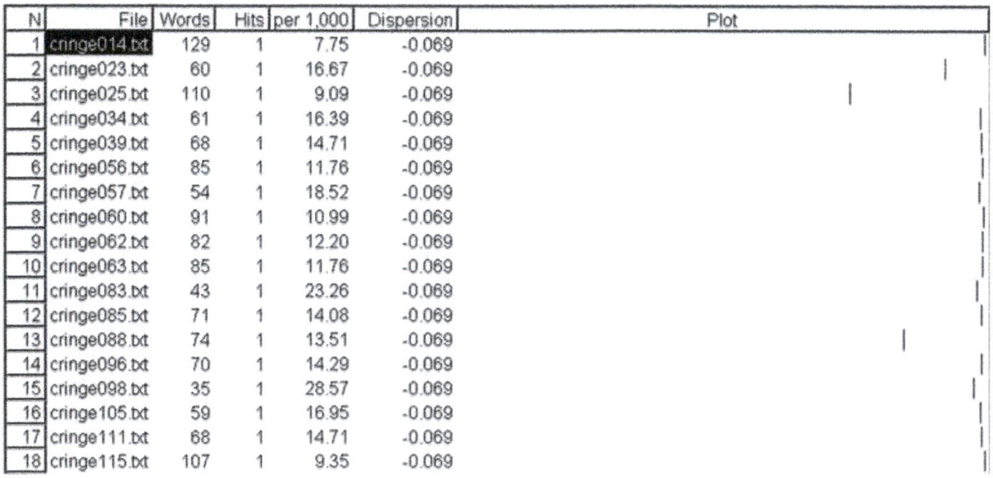

N	File	Words	Hits	per 1,000	Dispersion	Plot
1	cringe014.txt	129	1	7.75	-0.069	
2	cringe023.txt	60	1	16.67	-0.069	
3	cringe025.txt	110	1	9.09	-0.069	
4	cringe034.txt	61	1	16.39	-0.069	
5	cringe039.txt	68	1	14.71	-0.069	
6	cringe056.txt	85	1	11.76	-0.069	
7	cringe057.txt	54	1	18.52	-0.069	
8	cringe060.txt	91	1	10.99	-0.069	
9	cringe062.txt	82	1	12.20	-0.069	
10	cringe063.txt	85	1	11.76	-0.069	
11	cringe083.txt	43	1	23.26	-0.069	
12	cringe085.txt	71	1	14.08	-0.069	
13	cringe088.txt	74	1	13.51	-0.069	
14	cringe096.txt	70	1	14.29	-0.069	
15	cringe098.txt	35	1	28.57	-0.069	
16	cringe105.txt	59	1	16.95	-0.069	
17	cringe111.txt	68	1	14.71	-0.069	
18	cringe115.txt	107	1	9.35	-0.069	

Figure 20.2 Dispersion plot for *embarassed* in the Cringe Texts Corpus

process, Table 20.4 displays some of the most frequent patterns, in the order in which they most commonly occurred, in the Cringe Text Corpus.

Cross-checking with the individual texts in the corpus, it is clear that they follow a narrative structure that shares characteristics with the structure described by Labov and Waletzky (1967), i.e.

abstract – orientation – complication – evaluation – resolution – coda.

The abstract takes the form of a short title (not included in the corpus) such as *Dinner party disaster*. The orientation, which briefly mentions the circumstantial details against which the narrative action unfolds, frequently situates the event in the indefinite past (*one day* or *once*) and introduces a *hot* (or *cute*) *guy*, *older boy*, *senior*, etc., flagged as a key protagonist on first mention by the use of the determiner *this*. The complication is often signalled by a sentence beginning *all of a sudden/suddenly*. In seven of the texts further complications are introduced by the formulae *to make matters worse* or *even worse*. Finally, the evaluation includes derivations of *embarrass* or its synonyms.

Apart from the lack of a coda (which is in any case a minor, if not optional, element in narrative structures) the most significant difference between the teenage narratives and the Labov and Waletzky model is, in the former, the complete absence of a resolution. This finding is substantiated by the absence of any discourse markers, such as *fortunately*, *mercifully*, *happily*, etc., that might signal a resolution.

This raises the question: to what ends and in what contexts would narrators choose to purposefully tell stories at their own expense, leaving themselves in a state of unmitigated humiliation? Why introduce a complication and not resolve it? This in turn raises issues of age and gender: the stories were all written (allegedly) by teenage girls. Gender-based studies of language, such as Tannen 1994; Holmes 1995; and Coates 1996 and 2003, attest to the fact that the stories that women tell one another are often about personal misfortunes, their purpose being to elicit feelings of mutual empathy and to affirm their joint femininity. This is the 'point' of these narratives – and this is why they differ from the stories that men typically tell each other. As Coates (2003) notes: 'Self-disclosure is largely absent from men's narratives, but is a significant feature of the stories told by women to their friends' (2003: 118). And she adds, 'One of the rewards speakers get from self-disclosing is that fellow-speakers are likely to self-disclose in return. Reciprocal self-disclosure makes speakers feel supported by others, since the mirroring behaviour involved in reciprocal self-disclosure communicates understanding and empathy' (2003: 120). In short, story-telling is the way that women – and teenage girls – perform their gender.

A more critical analysis (e.g. Fairclough 1989; Lee 1992) might argue that such discursive practices maintain and reproduce asymmetrical power relations in society, and

Table 20.4 Frequency of some key phrases in the Cringe Text Corpus (n = 143)

N	*Pattern*	*Freq.*
1	one day/once	34
2	… this [really/totally] [hot/cute] [*male*]	10
3	all of a sudden/suddenly …	16
4	I was so embarrassed./ … it was so embarrassing.	25

that the teenage girls' magazines are complicit in a process of discursively positioning their readership as the helpless and disempowered objects of male derision. Again, a corpus search provides evidence of the 'objectification' of the protagonist: the pattern *laugh* at me*, for example, produces eleven instances, e.g. 'Everyone was staring and laughing at me.'

Writing of a related genre – first-person sex narratives in women's magazines – Caldas-Coulthard (1996) concludes,

> Sex narratives as cultural texts and discourses are responsible for maintaining a state of affairs which feminism has fought hard to change: inadequate and insecure women who, to have a voice, have to tell of their secret affairs even though they feel guilty.
>
> (1996: 269)

The same might be said about their daughters' 'cringe stories'.

At this point, we have moved from a discussion of text-level discourse analysis (*discourse*[1]) into discourse-in-context (*discourse*[2]), and, ultimately, discourse as social practice (*discourse*[3]). Corpus analysis has identified surface-level features of the discourse(s) that inform the interpretative work at each stage. The procedure that has been outlined has attempted to show how a bottom-up approach, using a variety of corpus tools, can peel back successive layers of textual meaning. Of course, the same conclusions could just as well have been reached by a close reading of the actual texts, and without recourse to corpus tools at all. Nevertheless, the statistical data that a corpus approach delivers can serve to corroborate the findings of a more impressionistic approach, to confirm – or disconfirm – hunches, and to suggest new directions for further interrogation of the texts themselves. Schiffrin (1987), in arguing the case for the complementarity of quantitative and qualitative approaches in discourse studies, notes that 'quantitative analyses … depend on a great deal of qualitative description prior to counting (in order to empirically ground ones' categories) as well as *after* counting (statistical tendencies have to be interpreted as to what they reveal about causal relations)' (1987: 66). This cyclical alternation between counting and interpreting accurately characterises the application of corpus analysis to discourse.

5. What kind of data do you need to study discourse?

It goes without saying that discourse analysis requires texts – whole written texts, and, if not whole conversations, at least reasonably long stretches of (transcribed) talk. Since most discourse analysis focuses on textual features of specific text-types, a corpus that serves the needs of discourse analysis should consist of sufficient examples of these to provide generalisable data. But this does not mean it has to be enormous. For a start, 'in a collection of texts of similar type, the interactional processes and the contexts they take place in remain reasonably constant' (Partington 2004: 13). Consequently, 'specialised lexis and structures are likely to occur with more regular patterning and distribution, even with relatively small amounts of data' (O'Keeffe *et al.* 2007: 198).

The Cringe Text Corpus (see the previous section) is an example of the kind of corpus that targets a specific text-type and register. Another specific, small corpus that was relatively easily assembled, using texts available on the internet, is a 24,000-word corpus of abstracts from an academic journal. This consists of 139 texts, averaging 174 words each. It probably took about two hours to compile, cutting and pasting from the journal's website. (Obviously, publication of such a corpus, or of extracts from it, would require permission from the publishers.) A corpus this size is sufficient to provide information that can be reliably generalised for descriptive and pedagogical purposes.

For more rigorous research, some form of tagging – whether grammatical, semantic or phonological – is virtually obligatory. But, as Baker (2006) points out, tagging need not be exhaustive: 'Corpus builders need to think about what sort of research questions they intend to ask of their corpus, and then decide whether or not particular forms of tagging will be required' (2006: 42). If the focus, for example, is anaphoric reference, then only the referring expressions in the corpus, and their referents, need be tagged.

The advantage of a small, homogeneous corpus, such as one of journal abstracts, is that the context (of situation) can be precisely specified. As was noted in Section 3, if the study of discourse-as-language-in-context (*discourse*[2]) is the aim, context information is essential. This is equally true for investigations into discourse-as-social-practice (*discourse*[3]). As Mahlberg (2007) notes, in introducing her study of the local textual functions of the collocation *sustainable development:*

> The way in which an analysis of corpus data can be related to social situations depends on the information that is available on the origins and contexts of the texts. If the texts in a corpus are selected according to transparent criteria and information on their contexts is stored together with the texts, corpora can provide useful insights into meanings that are relevant to a society and indicative of the ways in which society creates itself.
>
> (Mahlberg 2007: 196)

In the future, the kinds of data that may be of increasing usefulness are those that support developments in the study of the emergent and ecological properties of language (Hopper 1998; Fill and Mühlhäusler 2001; Kramsch 2002; van Lier 2004), and especially the way that these properties are realised in discourse, both synchronically and diachronically. Developments in the application of complex systems theory to language acquisition and use (Ellis and Larsen-Freeman 2006; Larsen-Freeman and Cameron 2008) suggest we are experiencing the felicitous conjunction of two disciplines – corpus linguistics and psycholinguistics – that have, until now, tended to operate in parallel. After all, both are concerned with frequency effects (frequency of occurrence and frequency of exposure, respectively) and with the importance of usage (usage as data, and usage as performance). The happy alignment of the two fields is already influencing research: Ellis *et al.* (2008) report findings that show 'that formulaic expressions can be identified statistically from corpora of usage, and that native speakers and advanced ESL learners have become sensitive from their usage histories to these expressions so that they process them preferentially' (2008: 389), see also Lu (this volume). It is a short – but exciting – step from studying the processing of formulaic expressions preferentially to studying the processing of whole texts preferentially. Corpus evidence matched against data concerning the mental processing of texts may help reveal how patterns of text correlate with the way mental schemata evolve during comprehension and interaction. Likewise, research may show how the frequency of occurrence of particular discourses, and of variations in their texture, both influence and are influenced by the performance of these discourses – by individuals and across whole socio-cultural groups. As Larsen-Freeman and Cameron

(2008) point out, 'Conventional styles and registers of written text, such as "the small or classified ad" or "the academic essay", are emergent stabilities in the trajectory of social group written discourse. Genres are themselves dynamic and continue changing through use' (2008: 190). Corpus linguistics is well placed to track such changes.

Interdisciplinary collaboration coupled with technological advances in computation herald exciting developments in the field of *corpus discourse analysis*, and vindicate Hoey's (2005) claim

> that corpora are not just important for the study of the minutiae of language – they are central to a proper understanding of discourses as a whole, and that in turn means that there is no aspect of the teaching and learning of a language that can afford to ignore what corpus investigation can reveal.
>
> (Hoey 2005: 150)

Further reading

Baker, P. (2006) *Using Corpora in Discourse Analysis*. London: Continuum. (A practical introduction to applying corpus-based methodologies, such as collocations, concordances and dispersion plots, to the investigation of a range of different text types.)

Hoey, M., Mahlberg, M., Stubbs., M. and Teubert, W. (2007) *Text, Discourse and Corpora*. London: Continuum. (A collection of case studies, interleaved with insightful theoretical argument, that demonstrate the potential of corpus analysis to reveal aspects of textuality that might not otherwise be apparent.)

Partington, A., Morley, J. and Haarman, L. (eds) (2004) *Corpora and Discourse*. Bern: Peter Lang. (A collection of research papers that target a range of discourse areas, using corpus-based procedures, including discourse organisation, signposting and critical discourse.)

Scott, M. and Tribble, C. (2006) *Textual Patterns*. Amsterdam: John Benjamins. (A well-exemplified handbook on how to use corpus analysis tools (such as wordlists and keywords) in investigating the discourse features of a range of different registers.)

References

Aijmer, K. (1996) *Conversational Routines in English. Convention and Creativity*. London and New York: Longman.

Altenberg, B. (1990) 'Spoken English and the Dictionary', in J. Svartvik (ed.) *The London–Lund Corpus of Spoken English: Description and Research* (*Lund Studies in English 82*). Lund: Lund University Press, pp. 193–211.

Baker, P. (2006) *Using Corpora in Discourse Analysis*. London: Continuum.

Biber, D., Conrad, S. and Reppen, R. (1998) *Corpus Linguistics: Investigating Language Structure and Use*. Cambridge: Cambridge University Press.

Biber, D., Johansson, S., Leech, G., Conrad, S. and Finegan, E. (1999) *Longman Grammar of Spoken and Written English*. Harlow: Longman.

Biber, D., Conrad, S. and Cortes, V. (2004) '"*If you look at* …": Lexical Bundles in University Teaching and Textbooks', *Applied Linguistics* 25(3): 371–405.

Biber, D., Csomay, E., Jones, J. K. and Keck, C. (2004) 'Vocabulary-based Discourse Units in University Registers', in A. Partington, J. Morley and L. Haarman (eds) *Corpora and Discourse*. Bern: Peter Lang, pp. 23–40.

Bondi, M. (1999) *English across Genres: Language Variation in the Discourse of Economics*. Modena: Edizioni Il Fiorino.

Brown, G. and Yule, G. (1983) *Discourse Analysis*. Cambridge: Cambridge University Press.

Caldas-Coulthard, C. R. (1996) '"Women Who Pay for Sex. And Enjoy It": Transgression versus Morality in Women's Magazines', in C. R. Caldas-Coulthard and M. Coulthard (eds) *Texts and Practices: Readings in Critical Discourse Analysis*. London/New York: Routledge, pp. 250–70.

Carter, R. and McCarthy, M. (2006) *Cambridge Grammar of English*. Cambridge: Cambridge University Press.

Celce-Murcia, M. and Olshtain, E. (2000) *Discourse and Context in Language Teaching: A Guide for Language Teachers*. Cambridge: Cambridge University Press.

Coates, J. (1996) *Women Talk: Conversation between Women Friends*. Oxford: Blackwell.

——(2003) *Men Talk: Stories in the Making of Masculinities*. Oxford: Blackwell.

Coulthard, M. (1985) *An Introduction to Discourse Analysis*, new edition. London and New York: Longman.

Crookes, G. (1986) 'Towards A Validated Analysis of Scientific Text Structure', *Applied Linguistics* 7(1): 57–70.

Ellis, N. and Larsen-Freeman, D. (2006) 'Language Emergence: Implications for Applied Linguistics – Introduction to the Special Issue', *Applied Linguistics* 27(4): 558–89.

Ellis, N., Simpson-Vlach, R. and Maynard, C. (2008) 'Formulaic Language in Native and Second-Language Speakers: Psycholinguistics, Corpus Linguistics, and TESOL', *TESOL Quarterly* 42(3): 375–96.

Fairclough, N. (1989) *Language and Power*. London: Longman.

Fill, A. and Mühlhäusler, P. (eds) (2001) *The Ecolinguistics Reader: Language, Ecology and Environment*. London/New York: Continuum.

Fletcher, W. (2003/8) 'Phrases in English (PIE)', at www.usna.edu/LangStudy/PIE/ (accessed 7 January 2008).

Flowerdew, L. (2002) 'Corpus-based Analyses in EAP', in J. Flowerdew (ed.) *Academic Discourse*. London: Longman, pp. 95–114.

——(2003) 'A Combined Corpus and Systemic-functional Analysis of the Problem-Solution Pattern in a Student and Professional Corpus of Technical Writing', *TESOL Quarterly* 37(3): 489–512.

Gardner, R. (1998) 'Between Speaking and Listening: The Vocalisation of Understandings', *Applied Linguistics* 19: 204–24.

Ghadessy, M. (1988) 'The Language of Written Sports Commentary: Soccer – A Description', in M. Ghadessy (ed.) *Registers of Written English: Situational Factors and Linguistic Features*. London and New York: Pinter, pp. 17–51.

Halliday, M. A. K. and Hasan, R. (1976) *Cohesion in English*. London: Longman.

Hasan, R. (1989) 'The Texture of a Text', in M. A. K. Halliday and R. Hasan, *Language, Context, and Text: Aspects of Language in a Social-semiotic Perspective*, second edition. Oxford: Oxford University Press, pp. 70–96.

Hoey, M. (1991) *Patterns of Lexis in Text*. Oxford: Oxford University Press.

——(2005) *Lexical Priming: A New Theory of Words and Language*. London and New York: Routledge.

Hoey, M., Mahlberg, M., Stubbs., M. and Teubert, W. (2007) *Text, Discourse and Corpora*. London and New York: Continuum.

Holmes, J. (1995) *Women, Men and Politeness*. London: Longman.

Hopper, P. (1998) 'Emergent Grammar', in M. Tomasello (ed.) *The New Psychology of Language: Cognitive and Functional Approaches to Language Structure*. Mahwah, NJ: Lawrence Erlbaum, pp. 155–76.

Koteyko, N., Nerlich, B., Crawford, P. and Wright, N. (2008) '"Not Rocket Science" or "No Silver Bullet"? Media and Government Discourses about MRSA and Cleanliness', *Applied Linguistics* 29(2): 223–43.

Kramsch, C. (ed.) (2002) *Language Acquisition and Language Socialization: Ecological Perspectives*. London and New York: Continuum.

Kuiper, K. and Flindall, M. (2000) 'Social Rituals, Formulaic Speech and Small Talk at the Supermarket Checkout', in J. Coupland (ed.) *Small Talk*. Harlow: Pearson Education, pp. 183–208.

Labov, W. and Waletzky, J. (1967) 'Narrative Analysis: Oral Versions of Personal Experience', in J. Helm (ed.) *Essays in the Verbal and Visual Arts*. Seattle, WA: University of Washington Press, pp. 12–44.

Larsen-Freeman, D. and Cameron, L. (2008) *Complex Systems and Applied Linguistics*. Oxford: Oxford University Press.

Lee, D. (1992) *Competing Discourses: Perspective and Ideology in Language*. London/New York: Longman.

Mahlberg, M. (2007) 'Lexical Items in Discourse: Identifying Local Textual Functions of *sustainable development*', in M. Hoey, M. Mahlberg, M. Stubbs and W. Teubert, *Text, Discourse and Corpora*, London: Continuum, pp. 191–218.

Martin, J. R. and Rose, D. (2003) *Working with Discourse. Meaning beyond the Clause*. London: Continuum.

McCarthy, M. J. (1991) *Discourse Analysis for Language Teachers*. Cambridge: Cambridge University Press.

——(1998) *Spoken Language and Applied Linguistics*. Cambridge: Cambridge University Press.

——(2000) 'Mutually Captive Audiences: Small Talk and the Genre of Close-Contact Service Encounters', in J. Coupland (ed.) *Small Talk*. Harlow: Pearson Education, pp. 84–109.

O'Keeffe, A., McCarthy, M. J. and Carter, R. A. (2007) *From Corpus to Classroom: Language Use and Language Teaching*. Cambridge: Cambridge University Press.

Partington, A. (2004) 'Corpora and Discourse, a Most Congruous Beast', in A. Partington, J. Morley and L. Haarman (eds) *Corpora and Discourse*. Bern: Peter Lang, pp. 11–20.

Pulcini, V. and Furiassi, C. (2004) 'Spoken Interaction and Discourse Markers in a Corpus of Learner English', in A. Partington, J. Morley and L. Haarman (eds) *Corpora and Discourse*. Bern: Peter Lang, pp. 107–24.

Schauer, G. and Adolphs, S. (2006) 'Expressions of Gratitude in Corpus and DCT Data: Vocabulary, Formulaic Sequences and Pedagogy', *System* 34: 119–34.

Schiffrin, D. (1987) *Discourse Markers*. Cambridge: Cambridge University Press.

——(1994) *Approaches to Discourse*. Oxford: Blackwell.

Scott, M. (1997) *WordSmith Tools Manual*. Oxford: Oxford University Press.

——(2008) *WordSmith Tools* version 5. Liverpool: Lexical Analysis Software.

Scott, M. and Tribble, C. (2006) *Textual Patterns*. Amsterdam: John Benjamins.

Sinclair, J. (ed.) (1990) *Collins COBUILD English Grammar*. London: Collins.

Stenström, A.-B. (1994) *An Introduction to Spoken Interaction*. London: Longman.

Stubbs, M. (1994) 'Grammar, Text, and Ideology: Computer-Assisted Methods in the Linguistics of Representation', *Applied Linguistics* 15(2): 201–23.

——(1996) *Text and Corpus Analysis*. Oxford: Blackwell.

——(2001a) *Words and Phrases: Corpus Studies in Lexical Semantics*. Oxford: Blackwell.

——(2001b) 'Text, Corpora, and Problems of Interpretation: A Response to Widdowson', *Applied Linguistics* 22(2): 149–72.

——(2005) 'Conrad in the Computer: Examples of Quantitative Stylistic Methods', *Language and Literature* 14(1): 5–24.

——(2007) 'Quantitative Data on Multi-word Sequences in English: The Case of the Word *world*', in M. Hoey, M. Mahlberg, M. Stubbs and W. Teubert (eds) *Text, Discourse and Corpora*. London: Continuum, pp. 163–90.

Swales, J. M. (1990) *Genre Analysis: English in Academic and Research Settings*. Cambridge: Cambridge University Press.

Swales, J. M. and Najjar, H. (1987) 'The Writing of Research Article Introductions', *Written Communication* 4: 175–92.

Tannen, D. (1994) *Gender and Discourse*. New York: Oxford University Press.

Tao, H. (2003) 'Turn Initiators in Spoken English: A Corpus Based Approach to Interaction and Grammar', in P. Leistyna and C. Meier (eds) *Corpus Analysis: Language Structure and Language Use*. Amsterdam: Rodopi, pp. 187–207.

Teubert, W. (2000) 'A Province of a Federal Superstate, Ruled by an Unelected Bureaucracy: Keywords of the Eurosceptic Discourse in Britain', in A. Musolff, C. Good, P. Points and R. Wittlinger (eds) *Attitudes Towards Europe: Language in the Unification Process*. Aldershot: Ashgate, pp. 45–86.

——(2007) '*Natural* and *Human Rights, Work* and *Property* in the Discourse of Catholic Social Doctrine', in M. Hoey, M. Mahlberg, M. Stubbs and W. Teubert, *Text, Discourse and Corpora*. London: Continuum, pp. 89–126.

van Lier, L. (2004) *The Ecology and Semiotics of Language Learning: A Sociocultural Perspective*. Dordrecht: Kluwer.

Widdowson, H. G. (2004) *Text, Context, Pretext: Critical Issues in Discourse Analysis*. Oxford: Blackwell.

——(2007) *Discourse Analysis*. Oxford: Oxford University Press.

Yates, S. J. (1996) 'Oral and Written Linguistic Aspects of Computer Conferencing: A Corpus Based Study', in S. Herring (ed.) *Computer-Mediated Communication: Linguistic, Social and Cross-Cultural Perspectives*. Amsterdam: John Benjamins, pp. 30–46.

21
What can a corpus tell us about pragmatics?

Christoph Rühlemann

1. What is pragmatics?

Pragmatics is a relatively young discipline. While its beginnings reach back as far as the early twentieth century, it has established itself as a subfield of linguistics since the 1970s. Pragmatics is distinguished from semantics. The question underlying semantics is, 'What does *X* mean?' The question underlying pragmatics is, 'What does a speaker mean by *X*?' Hence, pragmatics deals with speaker meaning rather than sentence meaning. Key to determining speaker meaning is the context, in its multiple manifestations, in which an utterance is being made: it can contain important cues to help the recipient *infer* what is being meant. Meaning, in other words, is not in the text nor in the context from which inferences are drawn. The role of text and context is merely as *evidence* of meaning, which is itself 'invisible' (Yule 1996: 3).

The following examples are intended as initial illustrations of a few pragmatic phenomena. Unless otherwise indicated, all examples in this chapter are taken from the British National Corpus. More pragmatic phenomena will be dealt with in later sections. Consider (1) as an instance of what Levinson (1983: 54) refers to as 'the most obvious way in which the relationship between language and context is reflected', namely deixis. Here, what point in time is meant by the temporal deictic *in four weeks* can only by understood by the recipient with reference to the time when the utterance was being made:

(1) But er we'll see you **in four weeks**. See how you're doing.

Further, (2) highlights another type of inferential processes involved in determining speaker meaning:

(2) **Cheerful** day, isn't it?

(Roy 1981: 411)

Understood at the semantic level, (2) expresses the speaker's reaction to certain (usually sunny and warm) weather conditions. However, if (2) is said on a day that is overcast and rainy, such an interpretation would be inappropriate. The extra-linguistic context suggests an interpretation of the utterance as irony: that is, as a way of speaking that 'allows us to say the opposite of what we mean – and get away with it' (Roy 1981: 407).

Another type of speaker meaning, which demands even more complex inferential processes, is 'conversational implicature' (Grice 1975). This notion builds on the assumption that talk is conducted according to the 'cooperative principle' (CP) and that speakers, in order to cooperate, observe a set of four 'maxims': the maxims of Quantity (informativeness), Quality (truthfulness), Relation (relevance) and Manner (clarity). Where talk fails to conform to the maxims at the surface level, hearers, following the cooperative principle, will assume that the talk conforms to the maxims at some deeper level – the level of 'implicature'. Example (3), an extract from a 'double-blind' review of a manuscript submitted for publication, is a case in point.

(3) Why the reference to [author X] here? The [phenomenon in question] has been discussed in numerous previous work [sic], and most recently by [author Y], a recognised expert on [phenomenon in question].

(author's data)

The anonymous reviewer questions the usefulness of referring to author X on the grounds that author Y is a recognised expert in the field. On the face of it, this 'reason' is irrelevant to the question whether or not author X should be made reference to, for author X might be a recognised expert in the field as well. That is, the reviewer 'flouts' the maxim of relation, according to which communication should be relevant. In order to uphold the CP and make sense of the comment, the reader needs to infer what is implicated: that the reference to author X should not be made on the grounds that X is *not* what author Y is – a recognised expert in the field.

Conversational implicature is a prime example of how speakers can mean more than they say. It is in this 'more' that pragmatics is particularly interested: In this sense, pragmatics is 'the art of the analysis of the unsaid' (Mey 1991: 245).

2. How does a corpus restrict the study of pragmatics?

If we take pragmatics as the study of meaning of text in context, it becomes clear that the relationship between pragmatics and corpus linguistics is not unproblematic. The reason is simple: corpora record text, not meaning, and they record context only crudely. This is explained in the following.

Corpora are records of very large amounts of naturally occurring text, written and spoken. Normally, particularly in written corpora, the textual record is reliable: all words contained in the source texts are retained in the corpus text files. Many non-textual features, however, such as font size and type, line breaks, integration with photographs, drawings, etc., which serve as visual context for the text, may not be coded. Thus, in written corpora, while the textual record is good, the record of contextual features is, to an extent, impoverished. Spoken corpora, conversely, are impoverished not only contextually but also textually. Spoken corpora are based on transcriptions made from audio recordings. Since tape recorders cannot filter out non-speech noises, thus selectively 'listening' to speech – as humans can – many, and often large, stretches of corpus transcripts may be inaudible or unintelligible, thus tearing the co-textual web apart and preventing the analyst (but not necessarily the participants in the conversation) from understanding what is going on. Spoken corpora also provide information about the contexts in which the spoken texts were produced. However, some of the types of contextual information they provide are merely basic; for example, we get to know who (sex, age, class, etc.) was talking to whom when. Other types of context are recorded only abstractly: we get to know in what kinds of setting the talk occurred, or what type of interaction it was; another type of context, which is considered so crucial that in most large corpora the data are categorised according to it, is 'type of situation', or register, such as academic writing, fiction and conversation. That is, as corpus linguists trying to analyse meaning, we are in a much less privileged situation than the communicative partners that produced the text: not only are we not the intended recipients but merely a kind of eavesdropper cut off from the wealth of background knowledge ratified participants share – nor do we have access to the participants themselves, which would allow us to 'negotiate meaning' by requesting elaboration, clarification etc. Moreover, we are cut off from the almost infinite wealth of situational, nonverbal and social context that conversationalists in their specific contexts of situation are connected to. Take nonverbal context, for example. Most recent corpora are not prosodically annotated: that is, despite the undeniable communicative value of prosody, the way that words are contextualised by the way that they are vocalised cannot be studied. Neither are the large corpora currently in use kinesically annotated: that is, the way that speech is contextualised by the way that speakers use facial expressions, gestures, physical distance, body posture, etc., cannot be studied either (for a description of very recent work towards multi-modal corpora see Section 5 and Adolphs and Knight, this volume). In sum, as corpus linguists interested in pragmatics, we have textual evidence that is better in written corpora than in spoken corpora, and only basic or abstract contextual evidence to study speaker meaning. Because corpora are, hence, relatively decontextualised while pragmatic phenomena essentially depend on context, corpora have long been seen by some researchers as unfit for use in pragmatic research.

Indeed, some pragmatic aspects inevitably escape corpus linguistic analysis. This is because in POS-tagged corpora, most search types require a lexical 'hook' in order to retrieve relevant examples from the corpus and enable quantitative analyses (cf. Adolphs 2008: 9; see also Reppen, this volume). This requirement means that, in a corpus, only those phenomena can be studied fully whose lexical form(s) and pragmatic function(s) display a straightforward one-to-one relationship. This relationship is found, for example, in the word *please*, which typically functions as a politeness marker (cf. Wichmann 2004). It is already weaker in the phrase *I don't know*, which is frequently but not always used to mitigate disagreement (Diani 2004). Where there is a complete form–function mismatch, as in cases of conversational implicature, a quantitative corpus study will be useless: what listeners take to be implicated in an utterance cannot be retrieved exhaustively from a corpus; it can only, with varying degrees of confidence, be inferred *post hoc*.

What a corpus *can* do even in those cases where the form–function mismatch of a phenomenon prevents exhaustive searches, is provide the analyst with illustrative examples that are not only attested and, in this sense, authentic but also embedded in their co-texts, thus giving *some* evidence of the context in which they were used. Such corpus illustrations can usefully complement, or even replace, the invented and often *completely* decontextualised examples that have formed the basis of much pragmatic enquiry.

Another approach to studying pragmatics corpus-linguistically is to use pragmatically annotated corpora. For example, a small subcorpus of the Michigan Corpus of Academic Spoken English (MICASE) is tagged for some speech acts (cf. Maynard and Leicher 2007) and in the Corpus of Verbal Response Mode (VRM) Annotated Utterances, all utterances are coded twice: once for their literal meaning and once for their pragmatic meaning, using a principled taxonomy of speech acts (cf. Stiles 1992). However, the number of such pragmatically annotated corpora is still small and they are coded for selected aspects of pragmatic interest only.

Given these limitations, it may be surprising that corpus analyses of pragmatic phenomena have grown into a large body of literature and produced a wealth of new insights.

The following three sections present corpus pragmatic studies selectively; only a few key studies in key pragmatic fields can be presented. Notably *not* included are studies into important areas such as vagueness (e.g. O'Keeffe 2004), the 'textual pragmatics' of conversational grammar (e.g. Biber *et al.* 1999) and conversational deixis (e.g. Rühlemann 2007).

3. Evaluation: the case of semantic prosody

Since pragmatics deals with speaker rather than sentence meaning, the phenomena that come under the heading of 'evaluation' are undoubtedly at the very heart of the discipline. Evaluation is understood here in the sense that Thompson and Hunston (2000: 4) use it, namely as a cover term for two types of opinions: opinions of likelihood (in Biber and Finegan 1989 referred to as epistemic stance) and opinions of goodness (what Biber and Finegan refer to as affective stance).

Corpus linguistic explorations into evaluation phenomena are numerous. The focus in this section will be on one type of evaluation that, many corpus linguists claim, can only be revealed using corpus linguistic methods: semantic prosody.

One of the most genuinely corpus-linguistic strengths is the analysis of what Sinclair (1991) refers to as the 'idiom principle': that is, broadly, how language patterns at the level of phraseology. A very large body of literature has been accumulated pointing to 'idiom' phenomena such as collocation, collostruction, colligation, and so forth, as important building blocks of phraseological patterning. Another, crucial, phraseological phenomenon is 'semantic prosody', a term first used in Louw (1993: 157), where it is defined as 'an aura of meaning with which a form is imbued by its collocates.' Semantic prosodies probably best illustrate Channell's (2000) claim that some pragmatic phenomena can only be revealed in studies of large corpora. This is because semantic prosodies are normally hidden not only from introspection but also from observation of a small number of examples. Moreover, and crucially in the present context, semantic prosodies carry evaluative meaning and are thus 'on the pragmatic side of the pragmatics/semantics continuum' (Sinclair 2004: 34).

To illustrate, consider the meaning of the phrasal verb *SET in*. Normally, most people would probably agree with the information given in the *Concise Oxford Dictionary* (ninth edition):

> **set in** 1 (of weather, a condition, etc.) begin (and seem likely to continue), become established, 2 insert (esp. a sleeve in a garment).
>
> (*Concise Oxford Dictionary* 1995: 1267)

where sense 1 of *set in* is taken as synonymous with 'begin' and 'become established'. However, inspection of concordance lines shows that this information is insufficient:

(4)
a sort of *bunker mentality* quickly **set in**.
before *severe frosts* **set in**.
since *boredom* can easily **set in** and have a disruptive influence.
'stagflation' **set in** apace, as

If we compare the four concordance lines it becomes instantly evident that the things that set in (the subjects in italics in (4)) invariably refer to unpleasant states of affairs (Sinclair 1991: 74). Inspection of more concordance lines suggests that this patterning is consistent. Therefore, the 'aura of meaning' with which *SET in* is imbued by its collocates – to use Louw's definition again – is a negative evaluation.

While, in principle, any semantic prosody has evaluative potential, this potential may be exploited more fully in cases where speakers/writers deliberately inject a form which clashes with the prosody's consistent series of collocates (Louw 2000). For example, the phrasal verb *BREAK out* overwhelmingly collocates with nouns that share 'physical violence' meanings (by far the most frequent collocate in the BNC is 'war'). However, this collocational 'rule' can be broken: for example, in the BNC, there are six occurrences of *BREAK out* following the noun *peace*. Inspection of concordance lines suggests that covert evaluation is the driving force behind these uses. Consider (5) (from *The Economist*, 1991):

(5) Where will the dollar head when *peace* **breaks out**?

In (5), the prospect of 'peace' (at the time of the Gulf war) is taken as a threat to the dollar, which has risen before the war but, it is suggested, might fall when the war is over. That peace may have bad consequences for the dollar is not made explicit. Rather, the starkly negative 'aura of meaning' which typically surrounds *BREAK out* is covertly projected onto peace.

In sum, prosodies are a useful resource for the diagnosis of covert speaker stance. Moreover, as Louw argues, there is the same well-calculated collocational deviance in instances of irony (Louw 1993, 2000). The prospect, then, is that semantic prosodies may help to computationally uncover irony, a pragmatic phenomenon that has so far escaped systematic empirical study. Moreover, semantic prosodies may assist in the study of persuasion: 'Propaganda, advertising and promotional copy will now be gradable against the semantic prosodies of the whole language' (Louw 1993: 173). Exploiting the diagnostic potential of semantic prosodies for these kinds of speaker meaning has only just begun and more insights may be expected from this promising avenue of research.

4. What pragmatic phenomena have been studied using general corpora?

This section reviews pragmatic corpus research carried out on the basis of POS-tagged corpora. The studies reviewed are concerned with phenomena relating to three areas: conversational organisation, discourse marking and speech act expressions.

Conversational organisation: the case of turn-taking

There is broad consensus among linguists that conversation is the prototypical kind of language usage. Naturally, therefore, conversation has been at the heart of pragmatic research. Most central has been the study of conversational organisation, particularly in research in the tradition of Conversation Analysis (CA). This research has shown conversation to be a highly structured social activity. One of the key concerns in CA has been to elucidate the system of turn-taking in conversation. In CA, turn-taking is seen as rule-governed. Among the rules postulated are: 'one party speaks at a time', 'speaker change recurs' and 'no gap/no overlap'. The first rule, 'one party speaks at a time', means that 'any speaker gets, with the turn, exclusive rights to talk to the first possible completion of an initial instance of a unit-type' (Sacks *et al.* 1974: 706). The second rule, 'speaker change recurs', is made possible because turns are bounded by 'transition-relevance places' (TRP) at which other speakers may seize the 'floor'. 'No gap/no overlap', finally, refers to the fact that occurrences of long stretches of conversation in which no speaker is speaking are very rare and that occurrences of simultaneous speech by two or more speakers are 'common but brief' (Sacks *et al.* 1974: 706). A further crucial observation in CA concerns the ways that turns are allocated. Two techniques are distinguished: a current speaker may select a next speaker or parties may self-select in starting to talk (Sacks *et al.* 1974: 701).

Although, methodologically, CA is a decidedly empirical research tradition, the use of corpora has helped advance the study of these aspects of turn-taking considerably. Here we shall consider three studies. They concern overlap, backchannels and turn initiators.

CA researchers have taken care to emphasise that overlap, though not the 'rule', is still common. Just how common overlap is, remained largely unclear. Levinson (1983: 296) notes that 'less (and often considerably less) than 5 per cent of the speech stream is delivered in overlap' but it is unclear on what empirical basis this statement is made. Corpus analyses demonstrate that overlap is indeed very frequent in conversation. Moreover, corpus research has been able to exploit corpus annotations of overlap as a resource to investigate other turn-taking phenomena such as backchannels (see below).

To establish the frequency of overlap in conversation, Rühlemann (2007) queried the conversational subcorpus of the BNC. An example of overlap in the BNC is (6) (turns are numbered, overlaps are aligned and in curly brackets):

(6) 1 PS1D1 > : {How's}
2 PS000 > : {So}
3 PS1D1 > : married life?
4 PS000 > : Smashing!
5 PS1D1 > : Good!
6 PS000 > : {Yeah.}
7 PS1CX> : {Good!}
8 PS000 > : it is.
9 PS1CX> : Oh that's {good!}
10 PS000 > : {Yeah.} I wished I'd have met when I was [laughing] fifteen!

It can be seen that, in this small excerpt alone, there are three instances of overlapping speech (turn pairs 1/2, 6/7 and 9/10). Further, (6) neatly illustrates that overlaps are overwhelmingly brief – in (6), they invariably involve one word per speaker only – and that they tend to affect turn beginnings and endings.

Occurrences of overlap in the BNC are coded by means of so-called pointer (<PTR>) elements. Rühlemann (2007: 38ff) found that, in a total of 526,112 turns recorded in the conversational subcorpus, 178,320 turns contained at least one <PTR> element marking the beginning and one <PTR> element marking the end of overlapping speech. This indicates that two-party overlap occurs in roughly a third of all turns. This frequency suggests that overlap cannot be seen as a violation of the rule of no gap/no overlap but that it is co-constitutive of conversational turn-taking.

Example (6) illustrates yet another crucial phenomenon of turn-taking: the use of backchannels, a term which refers to essentially non-turn claiming talk: that is, small response tokens such as *mhm* or *yeah* which accompany and support a current speaker's turn rather than constituting a turn in themselves. Indeed, backchannels present us with the paradoxical 'idea of listeners speaking while speakers talk' (Wong and Peters 2007: 480). Accordingly, the most basic function of backchannels is as continuers: that is, as tokens of listenership; additionally, they may index varying degrees of affective involvement (O'Keeffe and Adolphs 2008).

Given their ancillary role as non-turn claiming talk it will not be surprising that backchannels, as the name suggests, commonly occur in the 'back channel' and, thus, in overlap. The co-occurrence of backchannels and overlap has been recently investigated by Wong and Peters (2007). Aiming, *inter alia*, to examine and compare the inventory of backchannels used in Australian and New Zealand English, they use telephone conversations recorded in two ICE corpora – ICE-AUS and ICE-NZ – both of which are annotated for overlapping speech.

Wong and Peters' findings suggest that the most common type of backchannels are single-word backchannels such as *mm*, *yeah* and *right*, accounting in the Australian data for more than three-quarters and in the New Zealand data for nearly two-thirds of all backchannels. The most frequent backchannel clusters were, in Australian English, *oh right*, *oh no* and *oh yeah*, and, in New Zealand English, *oh yeah*, *oh right* and *mm mm*.

Further, Wong and Peters decided to examine what they refer to as 'backchannel anchors': that is, 'the initial, monosyllabic units in backchannel clusters' (Wong and Peters 2007: 497) on the grounds that 'as listeners produce both single and clustered backchannels, some common element must indicate that they are not attempts to steal the turn' (ibid.). By far the most frequent backchannel anchor, in either varieties, was *oh*.

A corpus study concerned with turn allocation through self-selection is Tao (2003). This study examined spoken data from two corpora: the Switchboard corpus, which is a collection of telephone conversations from all regions of the United States, and the Cambridge University Press/Cornell University Corpus, a North-American English corpus consisting of mostly informal face-to-face conversations. The overriding aim of the study was to investigate 'the grammar of turn beginnings' (Tao 2003: 187) by focusing on what Tao refers to as 'turn initiators': that is, 'the very first form with which a speaker starts a new turn in conversation' (Tao 2003: 189).

To illustrate, consider (7):

(7) PS01V > : *When* did he have his operation?
PS01U > : *Monday* morning
PS01V > : *Oh* yeah
PS01U > : *Joe* said he went through night, he said I sat and come home in morning
PS01V > : *Mm*

PS01U > : *so* he come home Wednesday morning
PS01V > : *Oh*

All italicised items in the extract would be considered, according to Tao's very broad definition, turn initiators. Note that under this definition, backchannel forms – *Oh yeah*, *Mm* and *Oh* in the excerpt – count as turn initiators too, although, as noted above, backchannels are often regarded as *listener* talk rather than *speaker* turns.

The four most frequent items that, in Tao's study, were found to 'show some degree of exclusivity as turn initiators' include, in descending order, *mhm*, *uh-huh*, *oh* and *yeah*.

An important finding in this study is that the overwhelming majority of the turn initiators identified were '"syntactically" independent lexical forms or vocalizations which can be used without co-occurrence of any other forms' (Tao 2003: 190). Tao proceeds to suggest that, unlike, for example, Chinese where turn endings are marked with special discourse particles, 'English may belong to the kind of language that chooses turn beginnings as the site for grammaticizing turn transition signals' (Tao 2003: 195). The finding that the turn-initial slot is typically filled with syntactically independent forms is significant in terms of turn allocation: it suggests that, in English, it is typically by means of short free forms that speakers self-select. This observation does not appear to have been made in non-corpus research; it became possible only through analysis of large amounts of corpus data.

Discourse markers

Discourse markers are words or phrases that meta-lingually flag how discourse *relates* to other discourse, as a continuation, elaboration, digression, transition, qualification, quotation or other. That is, they can be seen as a kind of 'processing instruction' and greatly contribute to discourse coherence (Schiffrin 1987). Consider (8). Speakers are discussing the price a club had to pay for a football player:

(8) PS0HM > : How much did he cost? ...
PS0HN > : Three hundred and fifty.
PS0HM > : Three hundred and fifty. No it wasn't, it was three hundred. It was two
PS0HN > : Yes it was. Three hundred and fifty.
PS0HM > : Oh **anyway**, it was still pretty good wasn't it?

In (8), the speakers have different opinions on how much money the player cost the club. Seeing that no agreement can be reached by discussing concrete numbers, speaker PS0HM decides to seek agreement via the more abstract assessment *it was still pretty good wasn't it?* This transition is flagged as such by *anyway*.

Another, extremely versatile, discourse marker is *like*. Beside its grammatical functions – for example, as a verb, noun, preposition, etc. – it can also act in a broad range of discourse functions (e.g. Andersen 2001). Examples (9) and (10) illustrate two of them: in (9), *like* functions as an approximator, indicating that the numerical information is approximate rather than precise; in (10), *like* introduces direct discourse presentation ('quoted speech'):

(9) I mean I've been in two shops now there's fifty pound difference **like**, you know
(10) Yeah that's what I, why, that's what I said to Susanna and she was **like** don't be ridiculous!

Because discourse markers are relatively fixed lexically and thus retrievable from a corpus, corpus linguistic research into discourse markers has been extremely productive and is likely to yield more insights into how speakers attend to the task of marking discourse to facilitate listener comprehension.

Speech act expressions

Speech act theory deals with utterances as performing actions. Utterances are seen as integrating three kinds of acts: a locutionary act (performing the act *of* saying something), an illocutionary act (performing an act *in* saying something) and a perlocutionary act (performing an act *by* saying something). For example, in performing the locutionary act of saying *sorry I didn't get back to you sooner*, a speaker, at least under normal circumstances, performs the illocutionary act of conveying his/her feeling of regret at not having got back sooner, thereby performing the perlocutionary act of prompting the addressee to forgive him/her. For speech acts to achieve their purpose a number of 'felicity conditions' must hold; 'preparatory conditions', for example, relate to whether a person performing a speech act has the authority to do so (for example, not everyone has the institutional power to declare the Olympic Games open). The one category that speech act theory is centrally concerned with is illocution: what is done in saying something. Several categories of speech acts have been proposed. For example, speech acts can be 'representatives' (which commit the speaker to the truth of a proposition, as in conclusions), 'directives' (by which the speaker aims to get the hearer to do something, as in orders), 'commissives' (which commit the speaker to some future kind of action, as in promises), 'expressives' (which express a psychological state, as in apologies), and 'declarations' (which effect immediate changes in the institutional state of affairs, as in christening and marrying) (cf. Levinson 1983: 240).

Further, speech acts can be indirect. Indirect speech acts are 'cases in which one illocutionary act is performed indirectly by way of performing another' (Searle 1975: 60). It is particular with regard to the theory and discussion of indirect speech acts that corpus linguistic research has made valuable contributions. Indeed, corpus analyses have shown that some of the notions developed in this area may have to be re-evaluated. This section will highlight one such study, namely Adolphs (2008), which is based on the CANCODE. Adolphs' aim is to 'establish functional profiles of a number of speech act expressions which are based on the distributional and collocational patterns in use' (2008: 10). The focus is on 'speech act expressions' introducing suggestions; the expressions investigated include, among others, *why don't you*.

Why don't you can be used both in direct and indirect speech acts: when used to introduce a genuine question, a direct speech act is performed; when used to make a suggestion, a question form is used to 'put forward a proposal for consideration' by the addressee (in Searle's above-mentioned taxonomy of speech acts suggestions would thus count as 'directives'):

(11) PS52K > : I don't believe that.
PS52C > : **Why don't you** believe it? It's a survey
(12) PS1C1 > : but I've got nobody to go with!
PS1JA > : Oh! **Why don't you** come with us?

The majority of uses of *why don't you*, Adolphs observes, perform a suggestion. A much debated question in pragmatics is how listeners resolve the ambiguity between, in the case of *why don't you*, question and suggestion or, in the case of the stock example *Can you pass the salt?* used in much linguistic literature, between question and request. It is often assumed that the adequate interpretation of indirect speech acts requires a complex chain of inferences by which a recipient first decodes the literal force – in this case, that a question has been posed to him/her about his/her *ability* to pass the salt – then realises that something is 'up' with this question: for example, that it is not in accordance with the Cooperative Principle because it fails to be relevant in the context of sitting at table having dinner; and only then infers that the question is not to be taken literally but rather indirectly, as a request by the speaker to be passed the salt. Corpus evidence, by contrast, suggests a view of speech act expressions which emphasises the role less of inferences but more of collocational patterning.

Adolphs elaborates a functional profile of *why don't you*, consisting of its collocations, the discourse factors bearing upon its use and its contextual distribution. She observes that suggestion *why don't you,* henceforth S-WDY, is often preceded by a form of SAY which introduces reported speech. S-WDY is hence often used as part of a *reported speech act*, as in (13):

(13) oh I think it's because I was *saying* **why don't you** come up like this week

No such association with speech presentation is reported for question *why don't you*, henceforth Q-WDY.

As to right-hand collocates, at N+1 (that is, in the 'slot' immediately after *why don't you*) S-WDY is regularly followed by a group of transitive verbs such as *ask*, *get*, *tell* and *use*. The set of verbs that Q-WDY collocates with is distinctly different: they include *like*, *want* and *have to*. Another key collocate is also found at N+1: the marker *just* which, in association with S-WDY, serves to down-tone the imposition implied in suggestions (remember that suggestions are a type of 'directives'). Consider:

(14) Why **don't you just** sit down somewhere?

Third, at N+2, S-WDY is regularly followed by a third-person pronoun such as *him*, *it*, *them*, etc. In terms of factors found in the larger discourse, S-WDY and Q-WDY are distinguished by the type of response they typically trigger: while the responses to S-WDY 'range from minimal acknowledgment tokens to agreement, or evaluations of the suggestion' (Adolphs 2008: 62), Q-WDY require a 'more detailed answer' (ibid.). Finally, Adolphs found that S-WDY was most frequent in the 'intimate' speaker relationship category: that is, it occurs most frequently in interactions between people whose social closeness is maximal (partners, family, very close friends). In this context type, speakers are most 'off guard' and the imposition implied in S-WDY as a directive is felt as less threatening.

Thus, we see that the uses of Q-WDY and S-WDY are, indeed, 'idiomatic' in the sense that a large number of distinctly different co-textual and contextual factors bear upon their use and it appears plausible to assume that these 'idiom' factors are salient enough for communicative partners to disambiguate the two speech acts.

This is not to say that all indirect speech acts were idioms and did not require inferential processes for their interpretation. What Adolphs' case study shows is merely that some 'indirect' speech acts may be less indirect than rather idiomatic, and it is as yet by no means clear whether the share of such idiomatic speech acts in all possible types of speech act is large or small. No doubt, it is still early days for corpus linguistic research into speech acts. However, the beginnings are promising and the prospects are that corpora can make important contributions to speech act theory.

5. Looking to the future

Current corpora facilitate fascinating observations of how words are actually used. However, as noted in Section 2, they fail to represent communication beyond the word. A particular challenge for current research is therefore to integrate corpus linguistic methods and theories of multi-modal linguistic research (Carter and Adolphs 2008: 276).

Multi-modal and cross-modal communication

In speech, 'communication processes are multi-modal in nature' (Carter and Adolphs 2008: 275): any verbal choice is integrated within a wealth of nonverbal choices. This semiotic integration would not justify much pragmatic interest if the nonverbal choices were no more than accompaniments or adornments that did not contribute to speaker meaning. Broad agreement, however, suggests that they do. Well-established in linguistics is the communicative value of prosodic choices (see, for example, Brazil 1985). Maybe less well-recognised is the communicative value of kinesic choices. Pioneering work in this field has been done by Birdwhistell (1970) who formulates a theory of kinesics in analogy to morphology and by Arndt and Janney (1987) who propose an integrated model of the 'interplay' of verbal, prosodic and kinesic choices. Crucially, Arndt and Janney (1987: 364) view prosodic and kinesic choices in speech as 'micro-contexts' in whose light verbal choices are interpreted. Because nonverbal choices can be made, to an extent, independently from verbal choices, the micro-context they provide can not only complement but also counteract verbal meaning. For example, what is an offer of assistance (*Should I help you?*) when spoken with falling-rising intonation can be an expression of indifference when uttered with only a falling tone. Further, face-to-face communication is also *cross-modal* in the sense that 'signals in one mode can to a certain extent be substituted for or replaced by signals in other modes' (Arndt and Janney 1987: 393). This observation is crucial to communication on the interpersonal level. For cross-modal strategies allow participants to 'negotiate a kind of buffer zone in which the expression of threatening or uncomfortable emotive information is possible without necessarily having serious interpersonal consequences' (Arndt and Janney 1991: 543). For example, a criticism such as *You're late*, which may be perceived as a threat to a partner's interpersonal face – that is, his/her need for acceptance – can be mitigated by combining the reprimand with a full gaze and a smile to signal acceptance (Arndt and Janney 1987: 379).

Multi-modal corpora

At present, corpora targeted at aspects of multi-modal communication are small in both size and number. Central to them is the aim to explore how meaning is made through 'multi-modal patterns': that is, patterns of interaction between verbal and nonverbal choices (Carter and Adolphs 2008: 281).

Work towards this goal faces major challenges. Given that nonverbal meaning seems to make up a very large chunk of overall meaning – Birdwhistell (1970: 157–8) estimates that 'probably no more than 30 to 35 per cent of the social meaning of a conversation or an interaction is carried by the words' – it will not be surprising that the nonverbal semiotic systems may be as highly differentiated as the verbal system. For example, Rimé and Schiaratura (1991: 248) present a taxonomy of speech-related hand gestures which includes six broad variables: speech markers, ideographs, iconic gestures, pantomimic gestures, deictic gestures and symbolic gestures. Ekman and O'Sullivan (1991: 176) discuss evidence for the cross-cultural recognition of at least six emotions expressed via facial actions: happiness, anger, fear, sadness, surprise and disgust. Variables of prosody include rhythm, volume, tempo, voice quality and intonation with its manifold subvariables (e.g. Wennerstrom 2001). Obviously, developing a coding scheme to corpus-linguistically capture such a wealth of individual variables is a daunting task. It becomes even more daunting considering that the variables *interact* rather than act independently from one another. Therefore, an important desideratum is the development of 'tools that provide an *integrated* approach to the representation of the data' (Carter and Adolphs 2008: 283; emphasis in original). Another complicating factor is that verbal and nonverbal choices are hard to align since 'within any sequence a substantial number of utterances and gestures made by speaker and hearer overlap' (Carter and Adolphs 2008: 284). That is, unlike speaking turns which are taken 'orderly' in the sense that normally 'one speaker speaks at a time', nonverbal 'turns' are much less restricted: while a speaker is speaking (and acting nonverbally) the listener(s) may produce, in response to the speaker's unfolding utterance, nonverbal signals and actions themselves.

Given these challenges, it is small wonder that current multi-modal corpus analyses are decidedly selective, focusing on narrow multi-modal phenomena rather than trying to study multi-modal patterning in its (at present overwhelming) complexity. One such work in progress is Baldry and Thibault (2006) who take a systemic-functional approach to analyse gaze in a corpus of TV car advertisements. Another work in progress is Carter and Adolphs' (2008) 'Headtalk' project. This project, which is based on a small corpus of several hours of video-taped MA and PhD supervision sessions at Nottingham University, is intended to explore the patterning of multi-modal backchannels, focusing specifically on head nods as a type of nonverbal backchannel in co-occurrence with verbal backchannels (see Adolphs and Knight, this volume).

To conclude, multi-modal corpus linguistics 'is very much in its infancy' (Baldry and Thibault 2006: 181). However, since this strand of research offers intriguing prospects for a deeper understanding and better description of how speakers mean more than they say, the construction, annotation and exploitation of multi-modal corpora may in future become a major site of corpus pragmatic research.

Further reading

Adolphs, S. (2008) *Corpus and Context. Investigating Pragmatic Functions in Spoken Discourse*. Amsterdam and Philadelphia, PA: John Benjamins. (This path-breaking study makes important contributions to the theory of speech acts.)

Grice, H. P. (1975) 'Logic and Conversation', in P. Cole and J. L. Morgan (eds) *Syntax and Semantics III*. New York: Academic Press, pp. 43–58. (This paper is maybe one of the most fundamental of all works in pragmatics.)

Louw, B. (1993) 'Irony in the Text or Insincerity in the Writer? The Diagnostic Potential of Semantic Prosodies', in M. Baker, G. Francis and E. Tognini Bonelli (eds) *Text and Technology*. Amsterdam and

Philadelphia: John Benjamins, pp. 157–92. (Although maybe not the first work on semantic prosody, this paper was the first to address the potential of semantic prosodies for the diagnosis of covert evaluation.)

Rühlemann, C. (2007) *Conversation in Context. A Corpus-driven Approach.* London: Continuum. (This study takes a principled approach to studying conversational grammar within a 'textual pragmatics': that is, within a situation-functional framework in which the forms distinctive of conversational language are seen as adapted to constraints set by the conversational situation type; the book also contains large sections on deixis in conversation.)

Sacks, H., Schegloff, E. A. and Jefferson, G. (1974) 'A Simplest Systematics for the Organisation of Turn-taking for Conversation', *Language* 50(4): 696–735. (This work is most widely cited in studies on turn-taking.)

References

Andersen, G. (2001) *Pragmatic Markers and Sociolinguistic Variation. A Relevance-theoretic Approach to the Language of Adolescents.* Amsterdam and Philadelphia, PA: John Benjamins.

Arndt, H. and Janney, R. W. (1987) *InterGrammar. Towards an Integrative Model of Verbal, Prosodic and Kinesic Choices in Speech.* Berlin and New York: Mouton de Gruyter.

——(1991) 'Verbal, Prosodic, and Kinesic Emotive Contrasts in Speech', *Journal of Pragmatics* 15: 521–49.

Baldry, A. and Thibault, P. (2006) 'Multimodal Corpus Linguistics', in G. Thompson and S. Hunston (eds) *System and Corpus: Exploring Connections.* London and Oakville: Equinox, pp. 164–83.

Biber, D. and Finegan, E. (1989) 'Styles of Stance in English: Lexical and Grammatical Marking of Evidentiality and Affect', *Text* 9(1): 93–124.

Biber, D., Johansson, S., Leech, G., Conrad, S. and Finegan, E. (1999) *Longman Grammar of Spoken and Written English.* Harlow: Pearson Education.

Birdwhistell, R. L. (1970) *Kinesics and Context: Essays on Body Motion Communication.* Philadelphia, PA: University of Pennsylvania Press.

Brazil, D. (1985) *The Communicative Value of Intonation in English.* Birmingham: English Language Research, University of Birmingham.

Carter, R. and Adolphs, S. (2008) 'Linking the Verbal and the Visual: New Directions for Corpus Linguistics'. *Language and Computers* 64: 275–91.

Channell, J. (2000) 'Corpus-Based Analysis of Evaluative Lexis', in S. Hunston and G. Thompson (eds) *Evaluation in Text: Authorial Stance and the Construction of Discourse.* Oxford: Oxford University Press, pp. 38–55.

Concise Oxford Dictionary (1995) Ninth edition. Oxford: Clarendon Press.

Diani, G. (2004) 'The Discourse Functions of *I don't know* in English Conversation', in K. Aijmer and A.-B. Stenström (eds) *Discourse Patterns in Spoken and Written Corpora.* Amsterdam and Philadelphia, PA: John Benjamins, pp. 157–71.

Ekman, P. and O'Sullivan, M. (1991) 'Facial Expression: Methods, Means, and Moues', in R. S. Feldman and B. Rimé (eds) *Fundamentals of Nonverbal Behaviour.* Cambridge and New York: Cambridge University Press, pp. 163–99.

Levinson, S. C. (1983) *Pragmatics.* Cambridge: Cambridge University Press.

Louw, B. (2000) 'Contextual Prosodic Theory: Bringing Semantic Prosodies to Life', in C. Heffer and H. Sauntson (eds) *Words in Context,* Discourse Analysis Monograph (CD-ROM). Birmingham: University of Birmingham.

Malinowski, B. (1923) 'The Problem of Meaning in Primitive Languages', in C. K. Ogden and I. A. Richards (eds) *The Meaning of Meaning.* London: Routledge, pp. 296–336.

Maynard, C. and Leicher, S. (2007) 'Pragmatic Annotation of an Academic Spoken Corpus for Pedagogical Purposes', in E. Fitzpatrick (ed.) *Corpus Linguistics beyond the Word. Corpus Research from Phrase to Discourse.* Amsterdam: Rodopi, pp. 107–15.

Mey, J. L. (1991) 'Pragmatic Gardens and their Magic', *Poetics* 20: 233–45.

O'Keeffe, A. (2004) '"Like the Wise Virgin and All that Jazz": Using a Corpus to Examine Vague Categorisation and Shared Knowledge', in U. Connor and T. A. Upton (eds) *Applied Corpus Linguistics. A Multidimensional Perspective*. Amsterdam/New York: Rodopi, pp. 1–20.

O'Keeffe, A. and Adolphs, S. (2008) 'Response Tokens in British and Irish Discourse: Corpus, Context and Variational Pragmatics', in K. P. Schneider and A. Barron (eds) *Variational Pragmatics*. Amsterdam: John Benjamins, pp. 69–98.

Rimé, B. and Schiaratura, L. (1991) 'Gesture and Speech', in R. S. Feldman and B. Rimé, *Fundamentals of Nonverbal Behaviour*. Cambridge and New York: Cambridge University Press, pp. 239–81.

Roy, A. M. (1981) 'The Function of Irony in Discourse', *Text* 1(4): 407–23.

Schiffrin, D. (1987) *Discourse Markers*. Cambridge: Cambridge University Press.

Searle, J. R. (1975) 'Indirect Speech Acts', in P. Cole and J. L. Morgan (eds) *Syntax and Semantics III*. New York: Academic Press, pp. 59–82.

Sinclair, J. (1991) *Corpus, Concordance, Collocation*. Oxford: Oxford University Press.

——(2004) *Trust the Text*. London/New York: Routledge.

Stiles, W. B. (1992) *Describing Talk. A Taxonomy of Verbal Response Modes*. Newbury Park, CA: Sage Publications.

Tao, H. (2003) 'Turn Initiators in Spoken English: A Corpus-based Approach to Interaction and Grammar', in C. Meyer and P. Leistyna (eds) *Corpus Analysis: Language Structure and Language Use*. Amsterdam: Rodopi, pp. 187–207.

Thompson, G. and Hunston, S. (2000) 'Evaluation: An Introduction', in S. Hunston and G. Thompson (eds) *Evaluation in Text: Authorial Stance and the Construction of Discourse*. Oxford: Oxford University Press, pp. 1–27.

Wennerstrom, A. (2001) *The Music of Everyday Speech. Prosody and Discourse Analysis*. Oxford: Oxford University Press.

Wichmann, A. (2004) 'The Intonation of Please-requests: A Corpus-based Study', *Journal of Pragmatics* 36: 1521–49.

Wong, D. and Peters, P. (2007) 'A Study of Backchannels in Regional Varieties of English, Using Corpus Mark-up as Means of Identification', *International Journal of Corpus Linguistics* 12(4): 479–509.

Yule, G. (1996) *Pragmatics*. Oxford: Oxford University Press.

22
What can a corpus tell us about creativity?

Thuc Anh Vo and Ronald Carter

1. Concept of 'creativity' in linguistics

The history of creativity study cannot be described as long, time-wise. Indeed, its first official appearance as an academic subject was in the 1920s (Pope 2005: 19) and it has been actively pursued only since the latter half of the twentieth century. However, achievement-wise, the field is not devoid of valuable findings. During these past fifty years or so, research into creativity within both psychological, socio-cultural and linguistic paradigms has been significantly fruitful, offering an ever-growing understanding of the phenomenon.

The study of creativity in linguistics can be seen as having started, albeit indirectly, with studies of 'literariness' in poetry and literature in the early twentieth century, considering that creativity is a companion that is 'not easily separated from the nature of literariness in language' (Carter 2004: 81). Early inherency models of literariness posit a distinction between 'literary', 'poetic' language and 'ordinary language' whereby the *differentia specifica* of poetic language in relation to ordinary language is believed to be identifiable in formal characteristics of the verbal sign itself, (e.g. metre, formulas), hence the theories of 'defamiliarisation' (Shklovsky 1989 [1917]) or 'deviation' (Jakobson 1960). In other words, literary language essentially shows formal departures from 'normal' rules or patterns of language.

Social influences are seen to have brought 'a cultural politics to literary studies' (Rice and Waugh 1989: 4), forming a body of post-structural works that moved away from the speaker and the text while bringing the reader and social ideology to the fore. For instance, taking the role of the addressee into account, the 'reader response theory' claims 'it is possible to determine [a work's] artistic nature by the nature and degree of its effect on a given audience' (Jauss 1970). An attempt to marry up deviation theory and reader-oriented schema theory was found in 'discourse deviation' theory by Cook (1994:182), who maintains that literary texts typically carry out the function of challenging/altering existing schemata in the reader, which is possible via deviation at the linguistic-structural level.

Further developments in pragmatic approaches to creativity are built on the foundation of Austin's (1962) and Searle's (1969) Speech Act Theory in interaction with reader-response theory. Ohmann (1971) calls literary speech acts 'quasi-speech acts' because, he points out, they do not exist outside literary contexts. The criterion for literary discourse is therefore argued by Ohmann to be 'a discourse whose sentences lack the illocutionary forces that would normally attach to them' (Ohmann 1971: 14). Pratt (1977), however, argues that non-literary categories such as hypothesis, pretence, fantasy, joking, etc., can also display this characteristic, effectively refuting Ohmann's arguments. Pratt herself tries to analyse literary language in terms of its violation and flouting of Austin's and Searle's felicity conditions and Grice's (1975) conversational maxims.

Increasingly, it has been noticed that many of the criteria set out exclusively for literary language can be applied to ordinary language as well. Creativity/literariness is not exclusive to literary texts; it also exists outside of the literature realm. The poetic/ordinary language distinction, therefore, is brought into question and is acknowledged to be unhelpful (Carter 2004). Indeed, 'creative' aspects of language are referred to in Chomsky's (1965) model as the language user's ability to generate an infinite number of sentences from a finite set of rules. Chomsky's 'invisible' creativity, therefore, stands in stark contrast with the more 'visible' and highly valued literary creativity.

Interest in creativity in everyday, non-literary texts grows stronger in the latter half of the twentieth century and the beginning of the twenty-first century, particularly since the birth of electronic corpora. Findings from corpus creativity studies have further validated earlier suggestions: that is, many of the criteria set out exclusively for literary language are found to be applicable to ordinary language as well. It is argued that creativity is neither trivial, all-inclusive (as in Chomsky's theory) nor literature-exclusive (as in earlier models of literary language); creativity is inherent in everyday speech but is still special in certain ways. As Carter and McCarthy (2004) put it, creativity is 'not simply a capacity of special people but a special capacity of all people' (p. 83). Carter (2004) proposes a theory of creativity in all common talk with two components, including *pattern-reforming*, i.e. creativity by displacement of fixedness, reforming and reshaping patterns of language, and *pattern-forming*, i.e. creativity via conformity to language rules rather than breaking them, creating convergence, symmetry and greater mutuality between interlocutors.

In summary, theories of creativity are far from exhaustive and even further from being unanimous. Due to creativity's complicated nature and intertwining relationships with various surrounding entities, researchers often wonder 'if we'll ever reach a consensus about creativity' (Sawyer 2006: 20). Fortunately, as Jakobson (1960) remarks, in scholarly discussions 'disagreement generally proves to be more productive than agreement' (p. 350). This inconclusiveness and diversity should, therefore, be seen as presenting opportunities instead of problems. More research in the field is expected if the big picture is to be completed.

2. Corpora and creativity – contradiction or continuity?

Defined as 'a large and principled collection of natural texts' (Biber *et al.* 1998: 12), 'to *represent*, as far as possible, a language or language variety as a source of data for linguistic research' (Sinclair 2004 – emphasis added), a corpus is characterised by its truthful representation of naturally occurring discourse as it is produced in everyday life activities. It entails a generally accepted fact that at the heart of corpus research lie patterns of language and recurrences of linguistic items. Hoey (2005) admits:

> corpus linguists … have typically seen their goal as the uncovering of recurrent patterns in the language … with probability of co-occurrence … with fluency in language rather than creativity.
>
> (Hoey 2005: 152)

This bias towards patterns in corpus linguistics can be attributed to the popular belief that uniqueness 'cannot be observed with certainty in a corpus, because uniqueness in a corpus does not entail uniqueness in a language' (Sinclair 2004). Since creativity is essentially characterised by 'newness' and 'unexpectedness' or, in other words, 'uniqueness', it appears on the surface that corpora and creativity stand in contradiction to each other and cannot work together.

However, if we look deeper into the developments of creativity studies in the last five decades or so, the relationship between creativity and corpora begins to reveal itself more fully. First of all, it is important to bear in mind that not all aspects of creativity involve newness or uniqueness. Repetitions or figures of speech, for instance, are established phenomena in language and can be analysed using corpus data and techniques. Other aspects, which are indeed characterised by newness and uniqueness, such as new word formations or novel idiomatic exploitations, can only acquire their statuses of being new and creative if a comparative background can be established for newness and creativity to be measured against:

> individual texts can be explained only against a background of what is normal and expected in general language use, and this is precisely the comparative information that quantitative corpus data can provide. *An understanding of the background of the usual and everyday – what happens millions of times – is necessary in order to understand the unique.*
>
> (Stubbs 2005: 5, emphasis added)

Although some researchers might choose to use intuition or the existing set of prescriptive rules of English as their baselines against which new constructions are compared and analysed, others prefer to use the evidence of language norms generated by large corpora analyses. The advantages of this latter approach stem from the fact that many creative uses of language do not necessarily violate any rules of English – they are perfectly grammatical in every sense. The creative nature of such uses might reside in an aspect (e.g. semantic priming, semantic prosody, collocation or colligation) that is generally neither available in grammar books nor assessable by intuitions, particularly of non-native speakers, but can only be detected via concordances and/or other corpus analyses. That is not to mention the fact that the English language is changing rapidly in parallel with social changes. Such items as *netizen* (citizen of the internet community) or *TTFN* (ta-ta for now, meaning 'goodbye') probably will not appear immediately in any dictionary or English grammar book, but a corpus of electronic communication messages will already be updated with these new terms. Corpora, if carefully compiled (or properly chosen) will be far more representative of the norms of contemporary English than any existing set of prescriptive rules, providing much more accurate backgrounds for analyses of creativity/uniqueness.

It is also important to remember that corpora are invaluable sources of data for our quest into linguistic creativity in spoken genres, an achievement that would otherwise be impossible due to the lack of material. Spoken language, which is an unplanned, unscripted activity during which speakers create 'a lot of the performance on the fly'

(Sawyer 2006: 16), is ephemeral in nature; there would have been no product that remains for analysis afterwards had it not been for modern recording technology. Indeed, the linguistic community has continuously been recording spoken language in different contexts and genres, compiling both general reference and specialist spoken corpora with the hope that they will help shed more light on this under-exploited part of discourse. Multimodal corpora with video recordings of language events are also underway and offer more insights into non-verbal communication (see Thompson, this volume).

Admittedly, corpora do not have all the answers to creativity. Socio-cultural or cognitive information about creativity cannot usually be directly elicited from corpora or by corpus techniques. Hence, such aspects as the functions of creative language, its effects on the reader/listener, or the cognitive processes involved in the production and comprehension of creative language, need relevant experiments, possibly inter-disciplinary research designs, to be effectively resolved. Corpora and corpus analyses to date confine themselves to being large electronic databases which offer invaluable statistical information about co-occurrences, trends, tendencies, frequency and distributions with accompanying software to allow a large number of searches and analyses to be carried out faster than any other manual method. However, the speed and the level of sophistication with which corpus annotation is evolving today mean that more layers of social and cultural information are being added, which will arguably bridge the gaps in corpus linguistic creativity studies in the near future.

3. What can corpora reveal about creativity in discourse?

Since the emergence of electronic corpora, pieces of the puzzle of creativity have continuously been added to the big picture. A review of prominent developments in corpus-based and corpus-driven creativity studies will be discussed in this section, illustrating the kinds of information corpora have been able to provide us with about creativity.

Creativity through departure from patterns

While searching their corpora for patterns, many linguists notice a common trend in which some alterations to 'prepatterns' are made, hence the term 'pattern-reforming' creativity suggested by Carter (2004). This category of creativity is essentially seen as the result of the 'flouting of expectations of conventional regularities in language but depends on an intimate familiarity with those conventions' (Prodromou 2007: 17). Aspects of this type of creativity, including the coinage of new words and novel expressions, creative collocations, creative idiomaticity and punning, have gradually been unravelled using information offered by corpora of different types.

Novel word formation

'Real creativity', as Lamb (1998: 205) contends, is when we 'invent new lexemes for new or old concepts; when we build a new concept, especially one that integrates ideas in our conceptual systems that have not been previously connected'. What he highlights (i.e. novel lexical formations) are indeed phenomena easily identified in texts due to their 'newness,' and innovativeness, diachronically speaking.

Searching a corpus of English electronic communications (SMS, e-magazine or web pages), Rua (2007) identifies the prominent trends in e-communication as full off creative lexical manipulations executed via blending, compounding or affixation. Rua, however, emphasises that instances of word formations with new meanings created (e.g. the word *friennaissance* for 'friendship' + 'renaissance' from the TV show *Friends*) are not frequent. In many cases, creative forms are produced for convenience of communication via letter reduction, clipping, initialising, phonetic respelling or using number and letter homophones. (See also Munat 2007 for similar analyses but with data from her corpus of children's literature and science fiction narratives.) The following text message illustrates 'reduction techniques' quite clearly:

> Extract 1
>
> Happy new yr 2 u. Yeh I had a gd nyte ... R we out 2moro nyte then? If so wat sort of time, was thinkin id get bus wime mum at about 7:20, will be in town 4about 7:45 x
>
> [Meaning: Happy new year to you. Yeah I had a good night ... Are we out tomorrow night then? If so what sort of time, was thinking I'd get bus with my mum at about 7:20, will be in town for about 7:45]

With similar interest in creative lexical formations, Renouf (2007), however, places the emphasis on the relationship between these creative forms and the historical contexts, thereby suggesting possible links between social events and developments in linguistic creativity. She draws primarily from a large newspaper corpus of over 700 million words, and examines lexical creativity in a diachronic manner between 1989 and 2005. The study makes use of various filters as well as regular concordancing and word-processing software to detect novel words, word formations and productive inflections. It was found that creative formations are fertile in the corpus. Significant collocates of target words and frequency charts are used to illustrate 'low frequency' and the 'peak' period as well as the popular trends in word combinations over different periods of time. Political and social events during these periods are examined to find underlying influences on these terms and their collocations.

Creative collocations

Linguistic creativity on the basis of the violation of semantic prosodies has been one of the prominent topics of interest among linguists. The concept of 'semantic prosody', first used by Louw (1993), is to some extent comparable with Hoey's concept of *lexical priming,* i.e. the process whereby:

> a word ... becomes cumulatively loaded with the contexts and co-texts in which it is encountered, and our knowledge of it includes the fact that it co-occurs with certain other words in certain kinds of context
>
> (Hoey 2005: 8)

This priming effect, however, as Hoey emphasises, is a matter of weighting, not a matter of requirement. As a result, creativity is still possible through resistance to rules of priming by selective overriding of the primings (see also Hoey 2007). For example, the habitual collocates of *break out,* as found in the British National Corpus (BNC) of more than 100 million words, include unpleasant things and events, a tendency called 'bad, unpleasant or negative' semantic prosodies (Louw 1993: 160; Stubbs 1995: 246). Such co-occurrences dictate that any 'pleasant' collocates of this phrasal verb are to be considered departures from recurrent patterns (Sinclair 1991). As a result, when *freedom* (a desirable state of affairs) is coupled with *break out* as in '*freedom was breaking out everywhere*' (BNC), the sentence is considered creative, unusual and intended to emphasise and draw attention to the statement. Looking further into this type of creativity, Hori (2004) identifies eight categories of creative collocations in the Dickens corpus (a 4.5-million-word corpus of Charles Dickens' work searchable online), including metaphorical, transferred, oxymoronic, disparate, unconventional, modified idiomatic, parodied and relexicalised. More importantly, the coinage of these unusual, unfamiliar collocations shows an important aspect of the author's literary creativity (Hori 2004: 113).

Creative idiomaticity

Creative idiomatic expressions, as a subcategory of creative collocation, have, with the availability of corpora, grown substantially into a separate area of research. Fixed expressions such as proverbs, sayings and idioms, contrary to the traditional views as being fixed, have been found to allow variability to different extents. Fernando (1996), consulting the Birmingham Collection of English Texts and her own corpus of newspaper articles, literary, academic and personal correspondence and conversations, identifies four ways idioms can be manipulated, namely replacement/substitution, additions, permutations (i.e. rearrangements/conversion) and deletions. The following variants of the idiom *open a can of worms* found in BNC are perfect examples of these four categories:

> **Substitution**: *advertising? Ah, well now that's a different erm barrel of worms isn't it really?*
> **Addition**: *would open up an entire can of constitutional worms that the monarch could do without*
> **Deletion**: *a can of worms or a heap of possibilities*
> **Rearrangement**: *in total ignorance of the can of worms she was about to open*

Partington (1998) notices a special type of idiomatic creativity in which the fixed expressions are not formally altered but ambiguity is still possible through 'the process of replacing or coupling an idiomatic sense with a concrete one' (Partington 1998: 134). The process is called 'demetaphorisation', as illustrated in this extract from a conversation between two friends where *kicking* can be understood both metaphorically (meaning 'well') and literally:

Extract 2

A: *Are you alright Simon?*
B: *Yeah, you know, still alive and kicking. Just trying to decide whose ass to kick next*

Similarly, Moon (1998), with the help of the Oxford Hector Pilot Corpus and the Bank of English Corpus, also comes up with a classification of idiomatic creativity that more or less includes the same categories as Fernando's and Partington's. In addition to the valuable evidence she found of one-off creative language uses (which she calls 'exploitations'),

Moon also discovers a vast number of systematic variations that certain idioms can have due to their inherent open nature, i.e. including open slots or having the same 'schemas'.

The important message conveyed is that there is 'massive evidence of the instability of the forms of fixed expressions and idioms' (Moon 1998: 309) as revealed by different corpus studies. Moon, as a result, argues for more corpus studies to classify and correlate the different kinds of lexical and syntactic variations of idioms. So significant and ubiquitous is idiomatic creativity that it is suggested that it be incorporated into classroom activities to raise students' awareness and appreciation of this phenomenon. For example, Stewart (2005) suggests using a list of creative newspaper headlines which contain aspects of idiomaticity or culture-specific references not readily accessible to non-native speakers. Students are then required to use the BNC to work out the wordplay based on any departure from usual patterns shown in concordances. (See also Cook 2000; O'Keeffe *et al.* 2007.)

Punning

While the preceding discussions focus on the formal, structural and semantic play of words and phrases, this subsection focuses on the phonetic and phonological pole. Puns through rhyme and assonance such as *I say these are magic, they leave no stern untoned* (from the TV show *How To Look Good Naked*) or *No turn unstoned for pens that are mightier than the sword* (headline from the *Yorkshire Post* 11 June 2007) are found to constitute an important category of creative manipulations of fixed expressions and idioms. Studying a corpus of cartoon language from the work of Australian cartoonist Cathy Wilcox, Kuiper (2007) identifies two types of 'phonological deformation', including exchanges (in which the 'exchange source' is the original phrase) and addition/substitution.

Admittedly, studies of the creative manipulations of form, structure and meaning have prevailed in the literature over creative sounds and rhythms, partly due to the fact that corpora of spoken language have been less available and more difficult to compile. However, with the rapid development of spoken corpora it is expected that creativity at the phonetic and phonological levels will catch up with its formal and semantic counterparts (for more on available spoken corpora, see Lee, this volume).

Creativity through patterning

Repetition and prepatterning as characteristics of the poetics of talk are observed by Tannen (1989) to be as pervasive in casual conversations as in public speeches or poetry/drama discourse with the prevailing functions of creating meaning, coherence in discourse and interpersonal involvement in the linguistic events. The uses of repetitions, paraphrases and echoes (or shadows) to draw attention and serve special purposes in conversations as such are indeed considered another aspect of linguistic creativity. They are essentially different from the type of purposeless 'negative repetition' as a result of limited linguistic competency that Tannen (1989: 53) mentions. Carter (2004) calls this type of creativity *pattern-forming creativity*, which is found to be ubiquitous in the five-million-word Cambridge and Nottingham Corpus of Discourse in English (CANCODE). Pattern-forming creativity is underscored as an important aspect of spoken discourse in comparison to written discourse, precisely because of the interactional nature of conversations in which interlocutors co-produce the messages and because of the need to create convergence while taking part in conversations as well (Carter 2004: 111).

Repetition and patterns, as a result, are not an impediment to creativity; they should be seen as 'a limitless resource for individual creativity and interpersonal involvement' (Tannen 1989: 97).

Corpora and creativity, as we can see, are not so contradictory after all. It can be seen that corpora and corpus techniques have proven useful in both literary studies (prose style, authorial styles, stylistics teaching) and literariness in non-literary everyday discourse as well (see chapters by Amador-Moreno and McIntyre and Walker, this volume). It is believed that corpora are a significant way forward for creativity studies.

4. Spoken and written creativity

Despite the strong interest in creativity in spoken discourse since the latter half of the twentieth century, research into creativity in written discourse, e.g. poems, prose, printed advertisements, book titles, newspaper articles and columns, graffiti and the like, have admittedly advanced much further (Carter 2004). The unsettling nature of spoken language, the unavailability of necessary equipment and the labour-intensity of the whole process of recording and transcribing data have delayed studies in spoken discourse in general (McCarthy 1998) and spoken creativity in particular. The lack of research into spoken creativity inevitably makes it difficult to draw any concrete conclusion about the similarities and differences between them. To make matters worse, there has not been much comparative research into spoken and written creativity either. Existing literature on the subject consists of a large number of studies whose data are a mixture of written and spoken, literary and non-literary genres treated as part of a common linguistic heritage without any discrimination (e.g. Tannen 1989; Fernando 1996; Moon 1998). A small number of studies, although separating data in writing and speech, do not provide comparative analyses, which do not guarantee the findings being exclusive to either mode. Claims about the similarities and/or differences between written or spoken creativity, therefore, can only be tentative and urgently require further investigations.

By and large, it is generally acknowledged that creativity is more likely to be found in one mode than the other (Partington 1998: 122). To be specific, many spoken genres such as daily conversations, it is argued, trail in the creativity department in comparison to written genres because of the practical limitations of both the online processing time to interpret novel collocations and the cognitive effort required to produce them. Such written genres as poetry, humorous writings, advertising, newspaper headlines are often found to be particularly rich in language play. Some authors, however, argue for the ubiquity of creativity in common talk (Tannen 1989; Cook 2000). It has been observed that not only the frequencies but also the manifestations of creativity in speech and writing show significant overlaps as well. Indeed, a lot of the features traditionally considered written literature specific (new word formations, figures of speech, creative collocations and idiomaticity, etc.) are frequently encountered in spoken genres. The boundary between literary creativity and everyday spoken creativity is thus very blurred, and it is suggested that it is best conceived as a gradation instead of an absolute division (Carter 2004: 81). Carter also maintains that contextual elements such as nature of transaction and relationship between speakers have the greatest impact on the degree of creativity. Conversations of an informal and intimate nature, for instance, are more prone to creativity, while more formal transactional exchanges are less so. In other words, the degree of creativity in different texts varies according to contextual aspects of discourse instead of mode of communication and should be viewed as such.

Data used in creativity studies in speech and writing can range from small, self-collected and self-annotated, specialised corpora to large commercial general reference corpora, depending on the purposes and scale of each study rather than on the mode of discourse. However, through the limited availability of large commercial spoken corpora, the majority of studies into spoken creativity have shown a tendency to consult small, self-collected corpora, whereas those exploring written creativity have had a wider range of choices and have taken more advantage of various large corpora of millions of written words. In terms of methodology, creativity studies in both speech and writing do not differ significantly, following one of the two main approaches, i.e. corpus-based or corpus-driven. In the former approach, i.e. *corpus-based* investigations, corpora are used as sources of empirical data (linguistic, socio-cultural, textual) against which intuitions about creativity are tested or preliminary findings from smaller data sets are validated. In the latter, i.e. *corpus-driven* research, corpora themselves are the data from which creative language uses are uncovered. At the time of writing, the identification and systematic extraction of instances of linguistic creativity in both spoken and written corpora has proved to be the can of worms in the corpus linguistics–creativity nexus. As Carter (2004) admits, purely quantitative methods of retrieving creative language are not yet available as a result of the limitations of software development. Essentially, the lexical and syntax-based search functions available in corpus software and packages to date help us find only the exact phrases/words we want to search, not their creative variants. Most searches for variants are therefore qualitative in such a manner that 'the corpus is "read" like a transcribed, living soap opera' (Carter 2004: 150) or chanced upon as a matter of good fortune (Moon 1998: 51). Others try to overcome this by carrying out repeated searches of a combination of key words, cross-examination of concordances of each individual content word, or searches of syntactic frames using wildcards (Cignoni and Coffey 1998; Francis 1993; Philip 2000). However, the large number of searches to be carried out and the hit-or-miss nature of these searches render the whole process laborious, time-consuming and not always sufficiently reliable.

5. What else is needed of a corpus to facilitate creativity studies?

One of the biggest problems with identifying variants of fixed expressions and idioms in corpora is that we often do not even know what we are looking for. Based on findings so far made available about the nature of creative language and its relationships with surrounding contexts and co-texts, some suggestions are made in this section in the hope that the extraction of linguistic creativity from corpora will be less painstaking, more straightforward and more productive.

Humour, creativity and corpora

First of all, humour, wordplay and creativity are found to be closely related, to the extent that wit and humour are the most frequent functions of creativity in spoken language (Chiaro 1992; Carter 2004). As a result, during the process of tagging a corpus, it is important that laughter (in a spoken corpus) or humour (in a written corpus) is carefully coded in a systematic manner to facilitate searches for creative language. For example, using *WordSmith Tools* (Scott 2004) to concordance 'laughs' in a small corpus of four tourist commentaries recorded on four different London tour buses, twenty-six concordances were retrieved. A sample is presented in Figure 22.1.

N	Concordance
1	that there is a London burger market ((background laughs)) (1) now (0.2) ahead
2	this the Viagra memorial monument ((background laughs)) (5) and coming up i

Figure 22.1 Two lines from a concordance search of laughs.

The phrases *London burger market* and *Viagra memorial monument* are instances of creative collocations due to their unusual combination (neither one of these can be found in the BNC of 100 million words) and humorous effects. Admittedly, in many cases a creative language use is not readily spotted within the span of concordances around 'laughs', but if we go to the source to consider the extended co-texts, creative language can be found:

Extract 3

George III, Mad King George we call him … They thought he was mad because they found him in his garden, dressed in his night shirt at five o'clock in the mor-eve-morning *talking to a tree*. That's no reason to call a man mad. After all, we have a prime minister who keeps *talking to a bush* and nobody seems to think he's crazy < laughs >

Extract 4

Mick Jagger came here but he was confused, he didn't want *LSE* at all. Turned out he wanted an *LSD*. So he left here and went off to join the Rolling Stones < laughs >

In the first extract, there is a pun played by hyponyms (*tree–bush*) and homonyms *bush–Bush* (plantation vs proper name, US president) in the political context of UK former Prime Minister Tony Blair's conversations with US former President Bush. Similarly, the pun in the second extract is based on the phonological similarity between LSE (the initials for London School of Economics) and LSD (Lysergic Acid Diethylamide, a hallucinogenic drug) in the context of rock-singer Mick Jagger's alleged association with this substance at the time.

As we illustrate here in brief, careful tagging of humour in corpora will provide useful pointers to creativity in texts as demonstrated.

Semantic annotation and creative idiomaticity

Various studies in corpus linguistics, supported by other research in the field of cognitive semantics, suggest that the fixedness of idioms is actually conceptual instead of lexical (Moon 1998; Langacker 1987). For example, alongside the canonical form *eat humble pie,* the following variants were found in the BNC among the concordances for the phrase *humble pie*:

were swallowing large slices of humble pie after the reformed
for ever now began to chew humble pie and were drawn to
Yes, I tasted the sourness of humble pie </p><p> 'So do you
He found the taste of humble pie just a little too much to stomach

Although the actual word *eat* is replaced in these examples, the concept is still there, albeit with additional connotation colours to each substitute *swallow*, *chew*, *taste* or *taste the sourness of*, *to stomach*. It is suggested that, first of all, corpora need to be semantically annotated and tagged into semantic categories on the basis of their senses being related to each other at some level, including synonyms, antonyms, hypernyms and hyponyms (the same principles are used in the electronic lexical database WordNet, see Fellbaum 1998). In effect, such a task (i.e. semantic annotation of texts) has been made possible by such a corpus tool as UCREL Semantic Analysis System (USAS) (now more commonly known as *WMatrix*), developed at Lancaster University. The software offers automatic semantic annotation of English texts whereby each content word in the text is assigned a value within twenty-one primary semantic fields, which are then further subdivided into 232 categories (see Wilson and Thomas 1997; Rayson 2008). F1 for example is the category of FOOD. The level of sophistication of these categories might still need further evaluation, but the principles can be applied to any corpus so that each word can be tagged with semantic information as well as grammatical.

The second, and important, step therefore is to develop more sophisticated corpus tools/software which allow all members of selected semantic categories to be included in the query. In the case of *swallow/chew/taste/stomach humble pie* above, for instance, if all the synonyms of 'eat' could be considered and incorporated into the concordances, the probability of identifying creative variants of the idiom would significantly increase while easing the laborious process of performing repeated individual searches for each entry.

Punning and corpora

Instead of semantic grouping, we need a phonological annotation program to cater to such puns as:

Gossip girls live to diss and tell (advertisement for the E4 show *Gossip Girls*)

Hollywood veteran kiss and sell (headline in the *Observer*, 31 August 2008)

By the same principles as semantic annotation, with these puns there is a need for phonologically related items such as *diss*, *sell* to be included in the search results of the phrase *kiss and tell*. For such a search function to be at all possible, corpora first of all need to be annotated with phonemic information, so that homophones, rhymes, assonance, alliteration, consonance, etc., could be grouped into a coherent system. For instance, such words as ***day***, ***pain***, ***whey***, ***rein*** will be grouped together under [e⊠] sound, and so on, using the IPA for English as the tagset. In effect, automatic phonemic annotation of words has been attempted using different grapheme-to-phoneme conversion techniques (see Bosch and Daelemans 1993; Divay and Vitale 1997; Auran *et al.* 2004). As a result, the task of tagging corpora with phonemic information is feasible. The task that actually requires attention is the construction of a search engine which allows all members of a category of similar phonemic quality to be included in the result list, e.g. in the case of *kiss/diss and tell/sell*, assonance.

Creative structures and corpora

The available lexical and syntax-based search functions in commercial corpora will not allow for such an inversion and insertion as in *fairly thin ice on which to skate one's credibility* (BNC) to be identified if the search string were entered as *be skating on thin ice.* A suggestion springs to mind, as all the key words are still present albeit in a different order than in the original, that it would be very helpful if the corpus search engine were amended to allow flexible structures built on key words (without word adjacency) to be retrievable. If this function could then be incorporated into the search engine with other functions (semantic and phonemic relatedness), the researcher would be equipped with better tools to extract creative language from corpora.

In summary, corpora have played a huge part in creativity studies and have undeniably pushed the field forward. Different aspects of creativity have been unravelled using corpus data and analyses, strengthening our understanding of the subject matter. That creative language in the form of everyday metaphors, puns, riddles or verbal duelling, and the like, is ubiquitous in everyday conversations has led many authors to argue that creativity and literariness are not exclusive to literature. Comparative analyses, however, are needed to illuminate the written–spoken creativity relationship. Adjustments and additions to current corpus annotation systems and software are proposed to help increase the probability of finding creative language in corpora while reducing the time and effort put into the task. However, the suggestions are far from exhaustive; there will still be creative uses of language that escape even the most tightly woven net thanks to the limitless capacity for creativity of the human brain. Rather, the suggestions are part of a bigger picture, offering alternative approaches to certain areas of creativity and giving some directions for further research in the fascinating and fast-growing field of corpus creativity studies.

Further reading

Carter, R. A. (2004) *Language and Creativity – The Art of Common Talk.* London: Routledge. (This book provides a detailed description of creativity in spoken language with plenty of examples from CANCODE and presents a proposal for a new theory of everyday spoken creativity.)

Garside, R., Leech, G. and McEnery, T. (1997) (eds) *Corpus Annotation: Linguistic Information from Computer Text Corpora Corpus Annotation.* London: Longman. (This book gives a picture of the area of corpus annotation at different levels (semantics, syntactics, etc.) and different techniques and software developments and applications.)

Munat, J. (2007) (ed.) *Lexical Creativity, Texts and Contexts.* Amsterdam and Philadelphia, PA: John Benjamins. (This volume includes a wide range of subtopics within the field of lexical creativity using corpora of different types and sizes.)

Swann, J., Pope, R. and Carter, R. (2011) *Creativity in Language and Literature: The State of the Art.* Basingstoke: Palgrave. (An edited collection containing contributions from creative practitioners and academic researchers working across different disciplines and covering a range of texts and practices such as poetry, hip hop, film, storytelling and web-chat.)

References

Auran, C., Bouzon, C. and Hirst, D. (2004) 'The Aix-MARSEC Project: An Evolutive Database of Spoken British English', in B. Bel and I. Marlien (eds) *Proceedings of the Second International Conference on Speech Prosody.* Nara, Japan, pp. 561–64.

Austin, J. L. (1962) *How to Do Things with Words*. Oxford: Oxford University Press.

Biber, D., Conrad, S. and Reppen, R. (1998) *Corpus Linguistics: Investigating Language Structure and Use (Cambridge Approaches to Linguistics)*. Cambridge: Cambridge University Press.

Bosch, A. V. D. and Daelemans, W. (1993) 'Data-oriented Methods for Grapheme-to-Phoneme Conversion', *Proceedings of the 6th Conference of the EACL*, pp. 45–53.

Carter, R. A. (2004) *Language and Creativity – The Art of Common Talk*. London: Routledge.

Carter, R. A. and McCarthy, M. J. (2004) 'Creating, Interacting: Creative Language, Dialogue and Social Context', *Applied Linguistics* 25: 162–88.

Chiaro, D. (1992) *The Language of Jokes: Analysing Verbal Play*. London: Routledge.

Chomsky, N. (1965) *Aspects of the Theory of Syntax*. Cambridge, MA: MIT Press.

Cignoni, L. and Coffey, S. (1998) 'A Corpus-based Study of Italian Idiomatic Phrases: From Citation Forms to "Real-life" Occurrences', *Euralex '98 Proceedings*, pp. 291–300.

Cook, G. (1994) *Discourse and Literature: The Interplay of Form and Mind*. Oxford: Oxford University Press.

——(2000) *Language Play, Language Learning*. Oxford: Oxford University Press.

Divay, M. and Vitale, A. J. (1997) 'Algorithms for Grapheme-phoneme Translation for English and French: Applications for Database Searches and Speech Synthesis', *Computational Linguistics* 23(4): 495–523.

Fellbaum, C. (ed.) (1998) *WordNet: An Electronic Lexical Database*. Cambridge, MA: MIT Press.

Fernando, C. (1996) *Idioms and Idiomaticity*. Oxford: Oxford University Press.

Francis, G. (1993) 'A Corpus-driven Approach to Grammar – Principles, Methods and Examples,' in M. Baker, G. Francis and E. Tognini Bonelli (eds) *Text and Technology: In Honour of John Sinclair*. Amsterdam: John Benjamins, pp. 137–54.

Grice, H. P. (1975) 'Logic and Conversation,' in P. Cole and J. Morgan (eds) *Syntax and Semantics*, Volume 3. New York: Academic Press, pp. 41–58.

Hoey, M. (2005) *Lexical Priming: A New Theory of Words and Language*. London: Routledge.

——(2007) 'Lexical Priming and Literary Creativity,' in M. Hoey, M. Mahlberg, M. Stubbs and W. Teubert, *Text, Discourse and Corpora – Theory and Analysis*. London: Continuum, pp. 7–29.

Hohenhaus, P. (2007) 'How to Do (Even More) Things with Nonce Words (Other Than Naming),' in J. Munat (ed.) *Lexical Creativity, Texts and Contexts*. Amsterdam and Philadelphia, PA: John Benjamins, pp. 15–38

Hori, M. (2004) *Investigating Dickens' Style – A Collocational Analysis*. London: Palgrave Macmillan.

Jakobson, R. (1960) 'Closing Statement: Linguistics and Poetics', in T. Sebeok (ed.) *Style in Language*. Cambridge, MA: MIT Press, pp. 350–77.

Jauss, H.-R. (1970) 'Literary History as a Challenge to Literary Theory', trans. Elizabeth Benzinger, *New Literary History* 2: 7–37.

Kuiper, K. (2007) 'Cathy Wilcox Meets the Phrasal Lexicon: Creative Deformation of Phrasal Lexical Items for Humorous Effects,' in J. Munat (ed.) *Lexical Creativity, Texts and Contexts*. Amsterdam and Philadelphia, PA: John Benjamins, pp. 93–114.

Lamb, S. M. (1998) *Pathways of the Brain: The Neurocognitive Basis of Language* (*Current Issues in Linguistic Theory* 170). Amsterdam: John Benjamins.

Langacker, G. (1987) *Foundation of Cognitive Grammar*, Vol 1. Stanford, CA: Stanford University Press.

Langlotz, A. (2006) *Idiomatic Creativity: A Cognitive-linguistic Model of Idiom-representation and Idiom-variation in English*. Philadelphia, PA: John Benjamins.

Louw, B. (1993) 'Irony in the Text or Insincerity in the Writer? The Diagnostic Potential of Semantic Prosodies', in M. Baker, G. Francis and E. Tognini Bonelli (eds) *Text and Technology. In Honour of John Sinclair*. Philadelphia, PA and Amsterdam: John Benjamins, pp. 152–76.

McCarthy, M. (1998) *Spoken Language and Applied Linguistics*. Cambridge: Cambridge University Press.

Moon, R. (1996) 'Data, Description, and Idioms in Corpus Lexicography', *Euralex '96 Proceedings*, pp. 245–56.

——(1998) *Fixed Expressions and Idioms in English – A Corpus-Based Approach*. New York: Oxford University Press.

Munat, J. (2007) 'Lexical Creativity as a Marker of Style in Science Fiction and Children Literature', in J. Munat (ed.) *Lexical Creativity, Texts and Contexts*. Amsterdam and Philadelphia, PA: John Benjamins, pp. 163–87.

Ohmann, R. (1971) 'Speech Acts and the Definition of Literature', *Philosophy and Rhetoric* 4: 1–19.

O'Keeffe, A., McCarthy, M. J. and Carter, R. A. (2007) *From Corpus to Classroom: Language Use and Language Teaching*. Cambridge: Cambridge University Press.

Partington, A. (1998) *Patterns and Meanings*. Philadelphia, PA: John Benjamins.

Philip, G. (2000) 'An Idiomatic Theme and Variations', in C. Heffer and H. Sauntson (eds) *Words in Context: A Tribute to John Sinclair on His Retirement* (*ELR Monograph* 18). Birmingham: University of Birmingham, pp. 221–33.

Pope, R. (2005) *Creativity: Theory, History, Practice*. London: Routledge.

Pratt, M. L. (1977) *Toward a Speech Act Theory of Literary Discourse*. Bloomington, IN: Indiana University Press.

Prodromou, L. (2007) 'Bumping into Creative Idiomaticity', *English Today* 89(3): 14–25.

Rayson, P. (2008) 'From key words to key semantic domains', *International Journal of Corpus Linguistics* 13(4): 519–49.

Renouf, A. (2007) 'Tracing Lexical Productivity and Creativity in the British Media: "The Chavs and the Chav-Nots"', in J. Munat (ed.) *Lexical Creativity, Texts and Contexts*. Amsterdam and Philadelphia, PA: John Benjamins, pp. 61–90.

Rice, P. and Waugh, P. (eds) (1989) *Modern Literary Theory: A Reader*. New York: Routledge.

Rua, L. (2007) 'Keeping up with the Times: Lexical Creativity in Electronic Communication', in J. Munat (ed.) *Lexical Creativity, Texts and Contexts*. Amsterdam and Philadelphia, PA: John Benjamins, pp. 137–62.

Sawyer, R. K. (2006) *Explaining Creativity: The Science of Human Innovation*. New York: Oxford University Press.

Scott, M. (2004) *WordSmith Tools Version 4*. Oxford: Oxford University Press.

Searle, J. R. (1969) *Speech Acts. An Essay in the Philosophy of Language*. Cambridge: Cambridge University Press.

Shklovsky, V. (1989 [1917]) 'Art as Technique', reprinted in P. Rice and P. Waugh (eds) *Modern Literary Theory: A Reader*. New York: Routledge.

Sinclair, J. M. (1991) *Corpus, Concordance, Collocation*. Oxford: Oxford University Press.

——(2004) 'Developing Linguistic Corpora: A Guide to Good Practice Corpus and Text – Basic Principles', *Tuscan Word Centre*, available at http://ahds.ac.uk/creating/guides/linguistic-corpora/chapter1.htm (accessed 17 July 2007).

Stewart, D. (2005) 'Hidden Culture: Using the British National Corpus with Language Learners to Investigate Collocational Behaviour, Wordplay and Culture-Specific References', in G. Barnbrook, P. Danielsson and M. Mahlberg (eds) *Meaningful Texts: The Extraction of Semantic Information from Monolingual and Multilingual Corpora*. London: Continuum, pp. 83–95.

Stubbs, M. (1995) 'Corpus Evidence for Norms of Lexical Collocation', in G. Cook and B. Seidlhofer (eds) *Principle and Practice in Applied Linguistics: Studies in Honour of H G Widdowson*. Oxford: Oxford University Press, pp. 243–56.

——(2005) 'Conrad in the Computer: Examples of Quantitative Stylistic Methods', *Language and Literature* 14(1): 5–24.

Tannen, D. (1989) *Talking Voices: Repetition, Dialogue, and Imagery in Conversational Discourse*. New York: Cambridge University Press.

Wilson, A. and Thomas, J. (1997) 'Semantic Annotation', in R. Garside, G. Leech and T. McEnery (eds) *Corpus Annotation: Linguistic Information from Computer Text Corpora*. London: Longman, pp. 53–65.

Section V

Using a corpus for language pedagogy and methodology

23

What can a corpus tell us about language teaching?

Winnie Cheng

1. Corpora and language learning

Corpus-based language teaching is advocated by Sinclair (2004) as representing a new revolution in language teaching. Corpora, corpus-analytic tools and corpus evidence have been increasingly used in English language teaching and learning for the last two decades (see, for example, Sinclair 1987, 1991, 2004). Applications derived from corpus investigation are found in a number of different areas, for example lexicography, translation, stylistics, grammar, gender studies, forensic linguistics, computational linguistics and, equally importantly, in language teaching (Tognini Bonelli 2001).

Fligelstone (1993) describes three aims of corpus-based linguistics in teaching: teaching about (the principles and theory behind the use of corpora), teaching to exploit (the practical, methodological aspects of corpus-based work), and exploiting to teach (using corpora to derive or drive teaching materials). Renouf (1997) adds a fourth aim which is teaching to establish resources; and this then involves the learners in data collection, corpus design and corpus compilation (Lee and Swales 2006: 70). In a similar vein, Leech (1997) describes three relations between corpora and teaching: teach about corpora, exploit corpora to teach, and teach to exploit corpora. In recent years, increasingly, the focus on corpora and teaching has shifted to corpora and learning. The selection of papers at the 5th Teaching and Language Corpora (TaLC) conference in 2002, for example, is organised into three sections: corpora by learners, corpora for learners, and corpora with learners (Aston *et al.* 2004). In fact, research into learner corpora, that is corpora comprised of texts spoken or written by novices rather than experts, brings about 'exciting pedagogical perspectives in a wide range of areas of English language teaching (ELT) pedagogy: materials design, syllabus design, language testing, and classroom methodology' (Granger 2003: 542).

> The advances in the direct access to corpora by language teachers and learners have created the need to research into a number of pedagogic issues, including 'the types of corpora to be consulted, large or small, general or domain-specific, tagged or untagged'; the kinds of learning strategies to benefit from direct corpus consultation; and the means by which direct access to corpora can be integrated into the language learning context.
>
> (Chambers 2005: 111)

Language corpora provide systematic access to naturally occurring language, and corpus-linguistic methods support exploratory and discovery learning (Bernardini 2004), which encourages autonomous learning and teaching (Braun 2005). Many empirical studies in corpus linguistics have contributed to the understanding of the value and benefits language corpora can bring to language pedagogy, particularly with respect to whether corpora can capture reality, and whether corpora can provide valid models for learners (Gavioli and Aston 2001). Even if corpora are too small to capture the full range of linguistic experience, they are useful to test claims based purely on intuition, and to motivate the decisions for teaching particular linguistic features (Gavioli and Aston 2001). Even if a corpus rarely reflects 'typical' usage in every aspect (Sinclair and Kirby 1990), and hence does not provide valid models for learners, corpus data are a useful means to engage learners in the interpretive process to create models of their own (Leech 1986). The subjective interpretation of corpus data is best seen in the light of Widdowson's (1978) distinction between 'genuineness' and 'authenticity'; and his claim that learners are often unable to authenticate genuine texts as they do not belong to the community for which the texts are created, and so they are unqualified to participate in the discourse process and interpretation (Widdowson 1998). An alternative way for learners to authenticate discourse is for them to adopt the role of a discourse observer, who views the interaction critically and analytically to understand interactional strategies (Aston 1988). Indeed, learners can alternate between the roles of discourse observer and discourse participant, and the latter role allows learners to test interactional strategies (Aston 1988; Gavioli and Aston 2001).

The view that language learners can be simultaneously active learners and language researchers accessing corpus data directly is advocated in Johns' (1991) 'data-driven learning' or DDL (see also chapters by Chambers, Gilquin and Granger, and Sripicharn, this volume):

> What distinguishes the DDL approach is the attempt to cut out the middleman as much as possible and give direct access to the data so that the learner can take part in building his or her own profiles of meanings and uses. The assumption that underlines this approach is that effective language learning is itself a form of linguistic research, and that the concordance printout offers a unique resource for the stimulation of inductive learning strategies – in particular, the strategies of perceiving similarities and differences and of hypothesis formation and testing.
>
> (Johns 1991: 30)

DDL has been found to be a useful language learning methodology, and there is evidence that learners can indeed benefit from being both language learners and language researchers (see, for example, Kennedy and Miceli 2001; Cheng *et al.* 2003; Chambers and O'Sullivan 2004; Lee and Swales 2006).

The relative importance of implicit knowledge and explicit knowledge in language learning is often discussed (Kennedy 2003) and is particularly relevant to DDL-related activities. Implicit knowledge, which is especially acquired from meaning-focused interaction, is learning without awareness, whereas learning explicit knowledge through explicit instruction is learning with awareness. This explicit instruction can speed up implicit learning processes when supported with 'language items, patterns, and rules' (p. 482). The use of language corpora as a resource in language teaching and learning has been shown to contribute to the acquisition of both implicit and explicit knowledge.

While some studies recommend the use of small corpora tailored to the learners' needs (Aston 1997; Roe 2000), Johns (1997) recommends mediation by the teacher through the preparation of corpus-based materials as a first stage, or as Widdowson (2003) puts it, the use of a 'pedagogic mediation of corpora'. Indeed, corpora are no longer used solely by teachers and material writers, and are increasingly used by learners as resources both inside and outside the classroom to 'problematize language, to explore texts, and to authenticate discourse independently and collectively, adding to the reality of the corpus the reality of their own experience of it' (Gavioli and Aston 2001: 244). Language corpora act as tools in the hands of learners 'to observe and participate in real discourse for themselves' (p. 238). As Gavioli and Aston state: 'the question is not whether corpora represent reality but rather, whether their use can create conditions that will enable learners to engage in real discourse, authenticating it on their terms' (p. 240). For example, St John (2001) describes the great benefits in the case of a student of German who was asked to find satisfactory answers to unknown vocabulary and formulate appropriate grammar rules for himself using a parallel corpus and concordance software as the only tools in an unsupervised environment. The conclusion echoes Johns' (1991: 2) notion of DDL, as teachers 'simply provide the evidence needed to answer the learner's questions, and rely on the learner's intelligence to find answers'.

In another study of students' behaviour when using a corpus, and their perceptions of the strengths and weaknesses of corpora as a second language writing tool, Yoon and Hirvela (2004) find that the students generally perceived the corpus approach to be beneficial for the development of L2 writing skills and increased their confidence in L2 writing. In addition, they highlight the importance of adjusting and staging corpus input to meet the specific level of the learners' proficiency (Allan 2009), and emphasise the need for clear guiding principles to enable learners to work within as they are learning the new approach to acquiring lexical and grammatical input. Yoon and Hirvela (2004) also warn against making the assumption that more advanced students embrace corpora readily and that they learn effectively working on their own. They suggest that teachers establish students' learning preferences in this regard, and that teachers should be prudent in their evaluation of learners' needs and the application of corpus-based activities to ensure more effective learning and teaching.

2. Corpus-driven form and function

Based on observations of corpus linguistics in the 1980s, Sinclair (1991) expounds the theory of 'units of meaning' which states that 'in all cases so far examined, each meaning can be associated with a distinct formal patterning … There is ultimately no distinction between form and meaning' (Sinclair 1991: 496). The meaning of language is primarily expressed by linguistic units called 'the lexical item' (Sinclair 1996), which is a unit in the lexical structure to be selected independently and which then selects lexical or grammatical patterns for its expression. Many corpus studies have examined the lexical item and their forms of co-selection. Cheng (2006), for instance, examined the extended meanings of lexical cohesion in a corpus of SARS (Severe Acute Respiratory Syndrome) spoken discourse. She finds that the item 'SARS' does not display any strong collocates; it collocates with 'epidemic' in 15.7 per cent of its occurrences and 'outbreak' in 7.8 per cent of its occurrences. Regarding colligation, 'SARS' is preceded by the definite article (23.5 per cent of occurrences) or a preposition (29.4 per cent). The semantic preference is typically (76.5 per cent) to do with the impact of SARS on Hong Kong and those directly affected by it, with words and phrases such as 'turmoil', 'damage', 'disease', 'crisis', 'infected area', 'patient', 'epidemic', 'outbreak' and 'morbidity'. In certain word co-selections, the semantic preference of 'the impact of SARS' fuses with the semantic prosody of a negative sense of 'embattled/besieged'. However, in the post-SARS texts, a different semantic prosody is observed through the speakers' choice of such phrases and grammatical constructions as 'successfully brought (SARS epidemic) under control', 'positive outcome from the (SARS situation)' and 'in spite of the (turmoil that SARS has caused)' which can be characterised as 'positive assessment' in 21.6 per cent of instances.

Kennedy (2003) examines the collocations of the twenty-four adverbs of degree in the 100-million-word BNC to show how English is structured, and to demonstrate the nature, extent and importance of collocation in language learning. He finds that each modifier collocates 'most strongly with particular words having particular grammatical and semantic characteristics' (p. 467). For instance, when boosters such as 'very', 'really' and 'terribly' occur before 'useful' and 'interesting', they appear to be synonymous and interchangeable, but this does not apply to other boosters such as 'clearly' and 'badly' (p. 467). In addition, some amplifiers are not found to collocate with particular adjectives, for example, '*completely easier, fully classical, badly dead* and *heavily unique*' (p. 474).

In Osborne's (2004) study which exploits learner and native-speaker corpora to provide material for language awareness exercises, what are termed the 'top-down' and 'bottom-up' approaches are employed. The top-down approach refers to 'drawing data from a native-speaker corpus to provide evidence of target usage to increase learners' awareness of the language', and the bottom-up approach refers to 'drawing data from a learner corpus and using the learners' own productions as a starting point for error correction and gradual enrichment' (Osborne 2004: 251). Osborne's study identifies a few features used by non-native French speakers of English in lexical overuse and grammatical anomalies. For example, compared to native speakers, non-native speakers are found to overuse the lexical word 'interesting' by a factor of four in writing, and have three characteristic uses which are almost never found in native-speaker writing; namely '*it is interesting to notice* (or *note*), used with intensifiers (*very, particularly more*, etc. *interesting*), and coordinated adjectives (*relevant and interesting*, etc.)' (p. 254). With regard to grammatical anomalies, the use of the present perfect tense, non-count nouns and connectors are examined. Non-native speakers are found to use the present perfect tense with a similar frequency to native speakers, but they have over-interpreted the function of the tense, and so use it in inappropriate contexts. The major errors in the use of non-count nouns by French-speaking learners of English are the anomalous countable uses of 'informations' and 'a(an) information'. The use of connectors by non-native speakers, particularly 'In fact', 'As a matter of fact' and 'Anyway', is found to be 20–30 per cent higher. All of these findings have pedagogical implications and can be usefully described and discussed by learners and teachers.

3. Corpus evidence as teaching materials

In the past twenty years, empirical analyses of corpora have contributed to the description of the actual patterns of language use in English (Biber and Reppen 2002). Braun (2005) describes both indirect and direct uses of corpora. Regarding indirect use, corpus-based analyses of English have indirectly influenced syllabus design, the methods and materials for language teaching and learning, test design, feedback and evaluation references, and the contents of reference works and grammars. In direct ways, large and small language corpora can be exploited by learners themselves in different ways. A corpus is now perceived as a primary contributor of teaching and learning resources as 'empirical analyses of representative corpora provide a much more solid foundation for descriptions of language use' (Biber 2001: 101) through 'its potential to make explicit the more common patterns of language use' (Tao 2001: 116). Corpus-based descriptions of language provide realistic, rich, illustrative and up-to-date data as a resource for the creation of interesting teaching materials (Braun 2005).

New accounts of the English language which challenge traditional views have been provided by corpus linguists, for example, the large academic grammars at the turn of the millennium. One example is the *Longman Grammar of Spoken and Written English (LGSWE)* (Biber *et al.* 1999) which incorporates the latest achievements of linguistics and offers statistical data on the use of English in both its written and its spoken form, and describes grammatical features for both structural characteristics and discourse patterns of use. Another major reference grammar is the *Cambridge Grammar of English* (Carter and McCarthy 2006) which has English as it is spoken today as its starting point with the necessary reference to English as it is written today.

Biber and Reppen (2002) examine actual language use based on empirical studies and develop ESL–EFL materials for grammar instruction. They contrast the presentation of information in six ESL grammar textbooks, and consider three aspects of materials development for grammar instruction; namely 'the grammatical features to be included, the order of grammatical topics, and the vocabulary used to illustrate these topics' (p. 199). They focus on noun premodifiers when considering which grammatical features to include or exclude, progressive and simple present tense when considering the order of grammatical topics, and the verbs used in the discussion of present progressive and simple present tense when considering specific words to include when illustrating a grammatical feature (p. 201). Biber and Reppen (2002) highlight sharp discrepancies between the information found in grammar materials and the real-life language use that learners encounter. Based on their findings, they argue that 'frequency should play a key role in the development of materials and in the choices that teachers make in language classrooms' (pp. 206–7). They suggest using the frequency studies and register differences described in the *LGSWE* (Biber *et al.* 1999) to facilitate the learning process and so to better integrate pedagogy and research.

Nonetheless, while resources are available and plenty of relevant applied corpus linguistics research exists, there is still a need for more resources of the kind developed by Sinclair (2003). The textbook by Sinclair provides a very thorough treatment of how to interrogate a corpus in an efficient and effective manner. Sinclair tackles the problems faced by newcomers to corpus-driven language study and learning, such as handling large amounts of data and systematically interpreting the evidence in the concordance lines. He proposes a seven-step procedure (2003: xvi–xvii) which he then puts into practice across a range of corpus-driven activities, each of which exemplifies a particular theme (e.g. 'meaning distinction', 'co-selection', 'grammar and lexis' and 'semantic prosody') by means of close analysis of a word/phrase.

Sinclair (2003) describes seven procedural steps to analyse concordance lines, namely initiate, interpret, consolidate, report, recycle, result and repeat. These steps are useful to both researchers and language learners alike. The book convincingly makes the case that concordance lines can be analysed using the above approach to reveal new evidence about language use. The same case is increasingly addressed through other textbooks (see, for example, O'Keeffe *et al.* 2007) which cover aspects such as corpus building, corpus linguistic techniques and the many insights into language use which corpus linguistics is in a unique position to provide.

Research into the grammatical and pragmatic characteristics of spoken English has found that the ability to do inexplicitness, among others such as indirectness and vagueness, is a key component in the repertoire of all competent discoursers, particularly in conversations (Cheng and Warren 1999, 2003). Examination of the Cambridge and Nottingham Corpus of Discourse in English (CANCODE) conducted by McCarthy and Carter (2004) and elsewhere (McCarthy and Carter 1994, 1995) has found that 'ellipsis is a category of grammar that varies markedly according to context, allowing speakers considerable choices in the expression of interpersonal meanings' (McCarthy and Carter 2004: 337). They advise that when selecting a particular structure from a corpus to teach, teachers should consider not only quantitative analysis, i.e. the frequency of occurrence, but also qualitative analysis of the structure in the corpus.

Based on corpus findings relating to amplifier-adjective collocates, Kennedy (2003: 283–4) suggests that the most frequently occurring collocates, e.g. *very good, really good* should be explicitly taught as units of language in order for learners to internalise them, and that less frequent collocates, e.g. 'completely clear', 'highly skilled' or 'clearly visible', are best left for implicit learning.

Braun (2005) describes the construction of the ELISA corpus which serves as pedagogic mediation between corpus materials and the corpus users. The ELISA corpus is a collection of fifteen video recordings of interviews with English native speakers from the US, Britain, Australia and Ireland who are professionals in banking, local politics, tourism, the media, agriculture, environmental technology, and so on. The materials in the ELISA corpus are said to 'support culture-embedded language learning', and fulfil the criteria for communicatively relevant contents as learning a language is 'often done to acquire professional, vocational or somewhat "technical" language' (Braun 2005: 56) and needs to appeal to learners from different backgrounds. The corpus is analysed 'thematically, linguistically and functionally' (p. 56) to generate enrichment materials, namely audiovisual materials, information and explanation, tasks and exercises, and study aids and didactic hints (pp. 57–8). As a result of the potential multidimensional access to the materials, 'different user perspectives, interests and profiles' can be accounted for (p. 61).

In Languages for Specific Purposes (LSP) teaching and learning, the use of specialised corpora for linguistic evidence, input and insights has been gaining in importance (Hewings 2005). Compared to using a general language corpus, a specialised corpus tends to have a greater concentration of vocabulary (Sinclair 2005) and can be particularly useful for those learning and teaching languages in LSP contexts. Bowker and Pearson (2002), for example, discuss how small specialised corpora that contain texts of a particular genre can be extremely useful for language teachers and learners, including identifying specialised terms and detecting collocations in the specialised target language for glossary compilation, term extraction and writing.

Corpus data have helped researchers to identify patterning that differs from traditional models of the English language. Recent studies comparing English presented in ELT textbooks and English used in natural communicative situations outside of the classroom have, however, found that textbook accounts of language use are often decontextualised and lack an empirical basis (Römer 2005; Cheng and Warren 2005). For example, in their studies of the speech acts of disagreement, and giving an opinion, Cheng and

Warren (2005, 2006) conclude that English textbook writers need to incorporate a wider range of and more accurate forms into their materials in order to better reflect the realities of actual language use. Another example is provided by Römer (2006) who examines the use of English conditionals (i.e. if-clauses) in the BNC and compares them with the norms presented in EFL teaching materials in Germany. She finds mismatches between English in use and English in the textbook. She argues that this misrepresentation of English conditionals, coupled with inconsistencies across individual textbooks, then compounds the difficulties encountered by German learners of English.

Osborne's (2004) study which identifies discrepancies between native and non-native choices in lexis, grammar and rhetoric has applications in teaching. A number of exercises have been designed, based on the corpus data, which aim to develop 'critical linguistic distance, and to increase overall sensitivity to the characteristics of native and non-native writing' (p. 260). Other exercises include comparisons, lexical enrichment, collocations, concordance tasks, completion exercises and proof-reading/revision activities. All of these aim to raise learners' awareness of aspects of the target language which are in need of attention.

While corpora of learner language use are a relatively new phenomenon (see, for example, Granger 2003), they all have very clear pedagogical aims (see also Gilquin and Granger, this volume). The International Corpus of Learner English (ICLE) (Granger 1998), for example, is a two-million-word corpus of written essays by students of English representing approximately twenty different first languages. The corpus has been error-coded which enables users to identify patterns of errors as well as the relative over- or under-use of certain forms and items. This corpus has a spoken equivalent, the Louvain International Database of Spoken English Interlanguage (LINDSEI), which can provide similar useful information about learners' spoken language. Such corpora, of course, have been specifically designed to be an invaluable resource for learners and teachers of the English language and can be replicated for other languages. They enable teachers and learners to identify and prioritise very specific and general patterns of use which may need to be addressed.

The very successful *Touchstone* series (see, for example, McCarthy *et al.* 2005) is another example of teaching materials based on corpus evidence and demonstrates how everything from syllabi to textbook examples can be informed entirely by corpus data (see also McCarten, this volume). In another study which explores how to better exploit corpus linguistics in the classroom, O'Keeffe *et al.* (2007: 246–8) outline ways to facilitate synergy between corpus linguistics and language teaching. They make the important point that the links need to be in both directions and that for corpus linguistics to best inform language teaching, 'teachers need to inform corpus linguistics' (p. 246). For this to happen, language teachers need to engage with corpus linguistics as an integral part of their professional training and development. They argue that more of the research questions in corpus linguistics need to be language teacher-driven because they 'arise out of practice' and they are the best 'mediators between corpus findings and practice' (p. 246). They point out the lack of research into feedback on the use of corpora in language teaching which could usefully inform future corpus linguistics research (p. 247). All this takes time, and they remind us that just as teachers and learners have embraced dictionaries and grammars based on corpus evidence, so they can become comfortable with using corpora themselves in their teaching. They propose some improvements to help with this last point: wider availability of corpora and corpus tools online, and a greater diversity of corpora, especially more non-English corpora, more spoken corpora, more non-native user corpora, and more specialised corpora (p. 247). In line with others, they advocate the need to move away from native versus non-native distinctions and argue for corpora which reflect the discourse of 'expert users' (p. 248).

Another development advocated by O'Keeffe *et al.* (2007) is the compilation of multimedia corpora which currently is rarely undertaken. The most notable exception to this observation is the multi-modal corpus currently being compiled by Professor Gu Yueguo of the Chinese Academy of Social Sciences and Beijing Foreign Studies University. This corpus is based on video data and requires eight layers of analysis (e.g. orthographic, phonetic, prosodic, speech act, discourse function and various forms of non-verbal communication), and promises to provide the most complete resource to date for the study of face-to-face communication with huge implications for language teaching (Gu 2008; see also chapters by Adolphs and Knight, and Thompson, this volume).

4. Tasks for language learning

Studies have mainly reported on '*what* can be done in language learning' but 'relatively little on *how* learners actually go about investigations' (Kennedy and Miceli 2001: 77). For those who adopt 'exploration learning', 'discovery learning' (Bernardini 2004), 'data-driven learning' or DDL (Johns 1991; Tribble and Jones 1997; Turnbull and Burston 1998), concordance-based activities, for example, are designed to familiarise learners with various types of investigations and to stimulate the development of appropriate learning strategies through practice. These language learning approaches concur with the contemporary task-based language learning approach (Willis and Willis 2007) which emphasises the development of tasks and activities to engage learners in using the language. These are adopted to exploit the pedagogic context by focusing on both the authenticity of the source text and 'its authenticity by the learner, which arises out of the involvement of the learner with the material, via the task' (Mishan 2004: 219). In other words, the process by which learners 'authenticate' the corpus data as they engage in a 'data-driven learning-cum-research exercise' is both motivational and effective (Lee and Swales 2006: 71).

Kennedy and Miceli (2001: 82), for instance, design activities that engage learners in a four-step approach to corpus investigation: (1) formulate the question, (2) devise a search strategy, (3) observe the examples and select relevant ones, and (4) draw conclusions. Adopting a similar approach, Gavioli and Aston (2001) describe tasks which involve the learner in playing the roles of both the discourse observer and discourse participant. The learner interacts critically with both corpus and dictionary data, identifies patterns, and adapts the patterns in the revision of the essay in which s/he is the discourse participant. In so doing, the learner constructs a model from the data which s/he can authenticate in her/his own discourse. In a similar attempt to train language learners to become language researchers, Cheng *et al.* (2003) report that over 80 per cent of their undergraduate students found the corpus-driven and data-driven projects useful. In Chambers and O'Sullivan's (2004) study, eight MA students of French write a short text, then receive training in corpus consultation skills, and finally try to improve the text by consulting a corpus containing similar texts with the help of concordancing software. The findings show that the learners make changes in (in descending order of frequency) 'grammatical errors (gender and agreement, prepositions, verb forms/mood, negation and syntax); misspellings, accents and hyphens; lexico-grammatical patterning (native language interference, choice of verb and inappropriate vocabulary); and capitalisation' (p. 158). The tools to interrogate corpora, particularly the interactive concordancer, constitute potential learning resources, as they can be used by both the teacher and the learner to investigate lexical, grammatical, semantic and pragmatic features (Zanettin 1994; Sinclair 1996, 2004; St John 2001).

Another study (Kaltenbock and Mehlmauer-Larcher 2005) describes language learning tasks that enable learners to authenticate corpus data. The tasks involve learners as observers and discourse participants respectively. As observers, learners explore and analyse texts to identify patterns of language use and then, as discourse participants, they read corpus texts and carry out tasks which involve exchanges with other learners who read the same text or a similar one (Kaltenbock and Mehlmauer-Larcher 2005: 79). Other tasks adopting such an approach include learners working in groups on deducing the meanings of phrasal verbs based on one lexical word, e.g. '*get on, get off, get by, get through*', or idioms and idiomatic use, e.g. '"on the one hand", "give a big hand to", "out of hand" and "to hand"' (Mishan 2004: 224).

Recent studies using the search engine *ConcGram* (Greaves 2009; Cheng 2007; Greaves and Warren 2007) have highlighted the importance of introducing phraseology in EFL curricula, and how corpus tools may be implemented in CALL environments to help students gain knowledge of phraseological items. In their study of verb-particle combinations (VPCs), Campoy-Cubillo and Silvestre López (2008) analyse the relational unit 'out' as the origin of several *ConcGram* searches to describe its prototypical and derived phraseological uses in a corpus of spoken academic English (MICASE). Campoy and Silvestre describe tasks for learners to conduct similar *ConcGram* searches. For instance, the constituency configuration lists on *ConcGram* help in analysing internal patterns and presenting VPC complementation in the classroom arranged by order of importance in the texts analysed; working on a specific pattern 'V + it + out' that is meaningful in the two-word *ConcGram* search and working from the most literal to the most idiomatic combinations; and designing activities that focus on the uses of the particle, e.g. general (VPCs and Particle) and specific (specific contribution of particle, 'verb' vs. 'verb + out').

Greaves and Warren (2007) outline replicable language learning activities that raise learners' awareness of the prevalence and importance of phraseology, and help to develop in learners the computational and analytical skills needed to conduct an initial study of the phraselogical profile of a text. The specifics of the activities are detailed below.

- Learners work with two texts: Policy Addresses given by the Chief Executive of Hong Kong in October 2006 and October 2005.
- Compile a list of the ten most frequent words in each text.
- Compile a list of the twenty most frequent phrases in each text.
- Monitor and record the frequency with which the most frequent words and phrases found in 2005 Policy Address occur in the 2006 Policy Address and vice versa.
- Discuss the findings from the two texts.
- Throughout the analysis of the two policy addresses, the differing lengths of the two Policy Addresses are noted, and so direct comparison of frequencies need to take this into account.

5. Bridging corpus linguistics and language teaching

Despite the fact that corpus linguistics and DDL have a relatively long history in the field, with many of the publications deriving from the COBUILD project specifically aimed at learners appearing in the late 1980s and 1990s, as Römer (2006) notes, corpus linguistics and its applications have yet to become mainstream in language teacher education programmes or in language teaching. She cites a study by Breyer (2005) who found that corpus linguistics and corpus applications in language learning and teaching receive little attention in teaching training programmes in Germany. Römer (2006: 122) concludes that there is 'strong resistance towards corpora from students, teachers and materials writers'.

In Hong Kong, similar observations have been made by Cheng and Warren (2007) who find mismatches between naturally occurring English and the English that is taught to learners as a model, pointing out the urgency for an improvement in learning and teaching materials in terms of language forms and functions introduced to language learners. They suggest that writers of instructional materials should draw on the findings of corpus researchers, in the form of research papers, dictionaries, reference grammars and other resources, when they write and revise materials, tasks and activities. There is still a serious disconnect between abundant corpus evidence on the one hand and the standard traditional language descriptions to be found in most language textbooks still widely used around the world.

Further evidence for Römer (2006) and Cheng and Warren's (2007) conclusions regarding the current status of corpus linguistics and the use of corpora in language teaching is provided by a corpora-list subscriber who in April 2008 posted a question to other list members to ask why there were fewer DDL resources available than one might think, and requested information on any published or online materials that adopt a DDL approach. A number of colleagues responded to the question, and their responses were summarised by the sender of the enquiry message. The responses included the following comments.

- Concordances are too difficult for learners. After twenty years, DDL remains a tiny minority interest.
- Individual teachers use DDL in class to meet specific needs, but do not publish their work or record it in any permanent form because it is not easy to get resources into a web format.
- People might not want to publish resources that they see as imperfect in some way.
- DDL is inaccessible to many teachers for lack of know-how or resources.
- DDL is inaccessible to many learners, as it presupposes an introspective, reflective approach to study, using new and relatively difficult technology, by learners and teachers who may not be highly motivated.

A response by Adam Kilgarriff to the comment that concordances are too difficult for learners is to select corpus sentences according to readability, and the beta version of his *Sketch Engine* has an option to sort concordances 'best first', from a learner's point of view (Kilgarriff *et al.* 2004). Work is also underway so that corpora can be used in language learning to only show users sentences which learners are likely to be able to read and understand.

In another response from colleagues responsible for MICASE (the online version of the Michigan Corpus of Academic Spoken English), it is stated that there are a number of MICASE-derived teaching materials accessible through their project website on some common topics (and problem areas) in EAP and ESL teaching (e.g. hedging or say–talk–tell). There are also two interactive MICASE-based lessons for self-study: one on spoken academic English formulas and one on clarifying and confirming. In addition, there is the MICASE Kibbitzer page that covers a number of language problems that students (and teachers) can examine further such as 'Less and fewer' and 'End up'.

In Hong Kong, corpus linguistics in language learning has been advocated, and the development of corpus-based learning has gone one step further than those proposed by Römer (2006). The Research Centre of Professional Communication in English (RCPCE) at the Hong Kong Polytechnic University has worked very closely with professional associations such as the Hong Kong Institute for Certified Public Accountants (HKICPA) and the Hong Kong Institution of Engineers (HKIE) to compile specialised corpora (publicly online) based on the spoken and written discourse of those professions. These professional associations have served as consultants to give advice as to the texts and discourses that are representative of their respective professions. Under the auspices of the RCPCE, a series of seminars have been held jointly with these professional bodies for their members to promote the use of corpora as an invaluable resource to enhance professional communication. The findings of corpus-based studies should be explored with respect to the practical implications for curriculum design, materials writing and learning and teaching not only for general English, ESP and LSP, but also for informing professional communicative practices.

Acknowledgement

The work described in this paper was substantially supported by a grant from the Research Grants Council of the Hong Kong Special Administrative Region (Project No. PolyU 5459/08H, B-Q11N).

Further reading

Hunston, S. (2002) *Corpora in Applied Linguistics*. Cambridge: Cambridge University Press. (This book contains useful chapters on corpus data interpretation with plenty of examples.)

O'Keeffe, A. M., McCarthy, M. J. and Carter, R. A. (2007) *From Corpus to Classroom*. Cambridge: Cambridge University Press. (This book provides theoretical points and a large number of practical tasks for learners and teachers.)

Sinclair, J. McH. (2003) *Reading Concordances*. London: Longman. (This book contains eighteen tasks of various types of corpus interrogation arranged at four levels of task complexity, with a large number of theoretical input presented mainly in the keys to the tasks.)

References

Allan, R. (2009) 'Can a Graded Reader Corpus Provide "Authentic" Input?' *ELT Journal* 63: 23–32.

Aston, G. (1988) *Learning Comity: An Approach to the Description and Pedagogy of Interactional Speech*. Bologna: Cooperativa Libraria Universitaria Editrice.

——(1997) 'Small and Large Corpora in Language Learning', in B. Lewandowska-Tomaszczyk and J. P. Melia (eds) *Practical Applications in Language Corpora*. Lodz, Poland: Lodz University Press, pp. 51–62.

Aston, G., Bernardini, S. and Stewart, D. (eds) (2004) *Corpora and Language Learners*. Amsterdam and Philadelphia, PA: John Benjamins.

Bernardini, S. (2004) 'Corpora in the Classroom: An Overview and Some Reflections on Future Developments', in J. Sinclair (ed.) *How to Use Corpora in Language Teaching*. Amsterdam and Philadelphia, PA: John Benjamins, pp. 15–36.

Biber, D. (2001) 'Using Corpus-based Methods to Investigate Grammar and Use: Some Case Studies on the Use of Verbs in English', in R. Simpson and J. Swales (eds) *Corpus Linguistics in North America*. Michigan: University of Michigan Press, pp. 101–15.

Biber, D. and Reppen, R. (2002) 'What Does Frequency Have to Do with Grammar Teaching?' *Studies in Second Language Acquisition* 24: 199–208.

Biber, D., Johansson, S., Leech, G., Conrad, S. and Finegan, E. (1999) *Longman Grammar of Spoken and Written English*. Harlow: Longman.

Bowker, L. and Pearson, J. (2002) *Working with Specialized Language: A Practical Guide to Using Corpora*. London: Routledge.

Braun, S. (2005) 'From Pedagogically Relevant Corpora to Authentic Language Learning Contents', *ReCALL* 17(1): 47–64.

Breyer, Y. (2005) 'Love's Labour's Lost: The Troublesome Relationship between Corpus Linguistics Research and Its Application in EFL Teacher Training in Germany', paper presented at Corpus Linguistics 2005, University of Birmingham, UK, July.

Campoy-Cubillo, M. C. and Silvestre López, A. J. (2008) 'Congraming "Out" in a Spoken Academic Corpus', paper presented in Department of English, the Hong Kong Polytechnic University, 12 December.

Carter, R. and McCarthy, M. (2001) 'Size Isn't Everything: Spoken English, Corpus, and the Classroom', *TESOL Quarterly* 35: 337–40.

——(2006) *Cambridge Grammar of English: A Comprehensive Guide: Spoken and Written English: Grammar and Usage*. Cambridge: Cambridge University Press.

Chambers, A. (2005) 'Integrating Corpus Consultation in Language Studies', *Language Learning and Technology* 9(2): 111–25.

Chambers, A. and O'Sullivan, I. (2004) 'Corpus Consultation and Advanced Learners' Writing Skills in French', *ReCALL* 16(1): 158–72.

Cheng, W. (2006) 'Describing the Extended Meanings of Lexical Cohesion in a Corpus of SARS Spoken Discourse', in J. Flowerdew and M. Mahlberg (eds) 'Corpus Linguistics and Lexical Cohesion', Special Issue of *International Journal of Corpus Linguistics* 11(3): 325–44.

——(2007) 'Concgramming: A Corpus-driven Approach to Learning the Phraseology of Discipline-specific Texts', *CORELL: Computer Resources for Language Learning* 1: 22–35.

Cheng, W. and Warren, M. (1999) 'Inexplicitness: What Is It and Should We Be Teaching It?', *Applied Linguistics* 20(3): 293–315.

——(2003) 'Indirectness, Inexplicitness and Vagueness Made Clearer', *Pragmatics* 13(3/4): 381–400.

——(2005) '// → well I have a *DIF*ferent // ↘ *THIN*king you know //: A Corpus-driven Study of Disagreement in Hong Kong Business Discourse', in M. Gotti and F. Bargiela (eds) *Asian Business Discourse(s)*. Frankfurt am main: Peter Lang, pp. 241–70.

——(2006) '"I would say be very careful of … ": Opine Markers in an Intercultural Business Corpus of Spoken English', in J. Bamford and M. Bondi (eds) *Managing Interaction in Professional Discourse. Intercultural and Interdiscoursal Perspectives*. Rome: Officina Edizioni, pp. 46–58.

——(2007) 'Checking Understandings in an Intercultural Corpus of Spoken English', in A. O'Keeffe and S. Walsh (eds) 'Corpus-based Studies of Language Awareness', Special Issue of *Language Awareness* 16(3): 190–207.

Cheng, W., Warren, M. and Xu, X. (2003) 'The Language Learner as Language Researcher: Corpus Linguistics on the Timetable', *System* 31(2): 173–86.

Cheng, W., Greaves, C. and Warren, M. (2006) 'From N-gram to Skipgram to Concgram', *International Journal of Corpus Linguistics* 11(4): 411–33.

Fligelstone, S. (1993) 'Some Reflections on the Question of Teaching, from a Corpus Linguistics Perspective', *ICAME Journal* 17: 97–110.

Gavioli, L. and Aston, G. (2001) 'Enriching Reality: Language Corpora in Language Pedagogy', *ELT Journal* 55(3): 238–46.

Granger, S. (ed.) (1998) *Learner English on Computer*. Austin, TX: Addison Wesley Longman.
——(2003) 'The International Corpus of Learner English: A New Resource for Foreign Language Learning and Teaching and Second Language Acquisition Research', *TESOL Quarterly* 37(3): 538–46.
Greaves, C. (2009) *ConcGram 1.0*. Amsterdam: Benjamins.
Greaves, C. and Warren, M. (2007) 'Concgramming: A Computer-driven Approach to Learning the Phraseology of English', *ReCALL Journal* 17(3): 287–306.
Gu, Y. G. (2008) 'Come to Grips with Video Data: Introducing Techniques in Agent-oriented Modeling and Video Data-mining', plenary paper presented at Partnerships in Action: Research, Practice and Training Inaugural Conference of the Asia-Pacific Rim LSP and Professional Communication Association, City University of Hong Kong and the Hong Kong Polytechnic University, 8–10 December.
Hewings, M. (2005) *Advanced Grammar in Use*, second edition. Cambridge: Cambridge University Press.
Johns, T. (1991) 'From Printout to Handout: Grammar and Vocabulary Teaching in the Context of Data-driven Learning', *English Language Research Journal* 4: 27–45.
——(1997) 'Contexts: The Background, Development, and Trialling of a Concordance-based CALL Program', in A. Wichmann, S. Fligelstone, T. McEnery and G. Knowles (eds) *Teaching and Language Corpora*. London: Longman, pp. 100–15.
Kaltenbock, G. and Mehlmauer-Larcher, B. (2005) 'Computer Corpora and the Language Classroom: The Language Classroom: On the Potential and Limitations of Computer Corpora in Language Teaching', *ReCALL* 17(1): 65–84.
Kennedy, C. and Miceli, T. (2001) 'An Evaluation of Intermediate Students' Approaches To Corpus Investigation', *Language Learning and Technology* 5(3): 77–90.
Kennedy, G. (2003) 'Amplifier Collocations in the British National Corpus: Implications for English Language Teaching', *TESOL Quarterly* 37(3): 467–87.
Kilgarriff, A., Rychly, P., Smrz, P. and Tugwell, D. (2004) 'The Sketch Engine', *Proc. Euralex* (Lorient, France, July): 105–16.
Lee, D. and Swales, J. (2006) 'A Corpus-based EAP Course for NNS Doctoral Students: Moving from Available Specialized Corpora to Self-compiled Corpora', *English for Specific Purposes* 25: 56–75.
Leech, G. (1986) 'Automatic Grammatical Analysis and Its Educational Applications', in G. Leech and C. Candlin (eds) *Computers in English Language Teaching and Research*. London: Longman, pp. 205–14.
——(1997) 'Teaching and Language Corpora: A Convergence', in A. Wichmann, S. Fligelstone, A. M. McEnery and G. Knowles (eds) *Teaching and Language Corpora*. London: Addison Wesley Longman, pp. 1–23.
McCarthy, M. and Carter, R. (1994) *Language as Discourse: Perspectives for Language Teaching*. London: Longman.
——(1995) 'Spoken Grammar: What Is It and How Do We Teach It?' *ELT Journal* 49: 207–18.
——(2004) 'Size Isn't Everything: Spoken English, Corpus, and the Classroom', *TESOL Quarterly* 35 (2): 337–40.
McCarthy, M., McCarten, J. and Sandiford, H. (2005) *Touchstone Student's Book 2a with Audio CD/CD-Rom*. Cambridge: Cambridge University Press.
Mishan, F. (2004) 'Authenticating Corpora for Language Learning: A Problem and Its Resolution', *ELT Journal* 58(3): 219–27.
O'Keeffe, A., McCarthy, M. J. and Carter, R. A. (2007) *From Corpus to Classroom*. Cambridge: Cambridge University Press.
Osborne, J. (2004) 'Top-down and Bottom-up Approaches to Corpora in Language Teaching', in U. Connor and T. A. Upton (eds) *Applied Corpus Linguistics. A Multidimensional Perspective*. London: Rodopi, pp. 251–65.
Policy Address (2006/7) www.policyaddress.gov.hk/06-07/eng/pdf/speech.pdf
Renouf, A. (1997) 'Teaching Corpus Linguistics to Teachers of English', in A. Wichmann, S. Fligelstone, T. McEnery and G. Knowles (eds) *Teaching and Language Corpora*. London: Longman, pp. 255–66.
Roe, P. (2000) 'The ASTCOVEA German Grammar in conText Project', in B. Dodd (ed.) *Working with German Corpora*. Birmingham: University of Birmingham Press, pp. 199–216.

Römer, U. (2005) *Progressives, Patterns, Pedagogy: A Corpus-driven Approach to English Progressive Forms, Functions, Contexts, and Didactics*. Amsterdam: John Benjamins.

——(2006) 'Pedagogical Applications of Corpora: Some Reflections on the Current Scope and a Wish List for Future Developments', *Zeitschrift für Anglistik und Amerikanistik* 54(2): 121–34.

Sinclair, J. McH. (1987) 'The Nature of the Evidence', in J. McH. Sinclair (ed.) *Looking Up: An Account of the COBUILD Project in Lexical Computing*. London: Collins, pp. 150–9.

——(1991) *Corpus, Concordance, Collocation*. Oxford: Oxford University Press.

——(1996) 'The Search for Units of Meaning', *Textus* 9(1): 75–106.

——(2003) *Reading Concordances*. London: Longman.

——(2004) 'Introduction', in J. M. Sinclair (ed.) *How to Use Corpora in Language Teaching*. Amsterdam and Philadelphia: John Benjamins, pp. 1–13.

——(2005) 'Corpus and Text. Basic Principles', in Martin Wynne (ed.) *Developing Linguistic Corpora: A Guide to Good Practice*. Oxford: Oxbow Books, pp. 1–16.

Sinclair, J. McH. and Kirby, D. M. (1990) 'Progress in English Computational Lexicography', *World Englishes* 9: 21–36.

Sinclair, J. McH. and Mauranen, A. (2006) *Linear Unit Grammar*. Amsterdam: John Benjamins.

St John, E. (2001) 'A Case for Using a Parallel Corpus and Concordance for Beginners of a Foreign Language', *Language Learning and Technology* 5(3): 185–203.

Tao, H. (2001) 'Discovering the Usual with Corpora: The Case of *remember*', in R. Simpson and J. Swales (eds) *Corpus Linguistics in North America: Selections from the 1999 Symposium*. Ann Arbor, MI: University of Michigan Press, pp. 116–44.

Teubert, W. (2005) 'Evaluation and Its Discontents', in E. Tognini Bonelli and G. Del Lungo Camiciotti (eds) *Strategies in Academic Discourse*. Amsterdam: John Benjamins, pp. 185–204.

Tognini Bonelli, E. (2001) *Corpus Linguistics at Work*. Amsterdam: John Benjamins.

Tribble, C. and Jones, G. (1997) *Concordances in the Classroom: Using Corpora in Language Education*. Houston, TX: Athelstan.

Turnbull, J. and Burston, J. (1998) 'Towards Independent Concordance Work for Students: Lessons from a Case Study', *ON-CALL* 12(2): 10–21.

Widdowson, H. G. (1978) *Teaching Language as Communication*. Oxford: Oxford University Press.

——(1991) 'Context, Community and Authentic Language', *TESOL Quarterly* 32(4): 705–15.

——(1998) 'EIL: Squaring the Circles. A Reply', *World Englishes* 17(3): 397–401.

——(2003) *Defining Issues in English Language Teaching*. Oxford: Oxford University Press.

Willis, D. and Willis, J. (2007) *Doing Task-based Teaching*. Oxford: Oxford University Press.

Yoon, H. and Hirvela, A. (2004) 'ESL Student Attitudes toward Corpus Use in L2 Writing', *Journal of Second Language Writing* 13: 257–83.

Zanettin, F. (1994) 'Parallel Words: Designing a Bilingual Database for Translation Activities', in A. Wilson and T. McEnery (eds) *Corpora in Language Education and Research: A Selection of Papers from TALC94 (Technical Papers)* 4. Lancaster, UK: UCREL, pp. 99–111.

24

What features of spoken and written corpora can be exploited in creating language teaching materials and syllabuses?

Steve Walsh

1. Integrating corpus-based approaches in a syllabus

Corpus-based approaches have clearly benefited language learning and teaching in both formal (class-based) and informal or naturalistic learning environments. Few can dispute the enormous developments which have occurred in EFL dictionaries as a result of corpora (see Walter, this volume). While similar developments are now occurring in the fields of morpho-syntax and semantics, the same rate of progress has not yet been seen in the integration of corpus-based approaches in syllabuses. In terms of language teaching methodology, corpus-based approaches have resulted in a more student-centred approach to learning and teaching and enabled learners to become researchers of their own developing interlanguage (see below). One of the main names associated with a problem-based approach to learning is Tim Johns, whose work on data-driven learning (DDL) has revolutionised the ways in which corpus-based approaches are integrated with more traditional methodologies (see, for example, Johns 1994; see also the chapters by Chambers and Sripicharn, this volume).

Learner corpora – that is, collections of students' spoken or written work – are, arguably, one of the most useful ways to help learners understand their own problems and develop new insights into their interlanguage system (see Gilquin and Granger, this volume). The data to which they are exposed is likely to be both more relevant and more appropriate to their needs. In terms of the selection and use of teaching materials, learner corpora allow teachers to really tailor materials to the group of students they are working with. Not only does this ensure that materials are perceived as being relevant by learners, but language acquisition is more likely to occur since the materials are at the appropriate level (cf. Krashen 1983). Using learner corpora can greatly facilitate form-focused instruction (see, for example, Schmidt 1990), considered to be one of the most effective ways of ensuring that second language acquisition occurs.

Other types of commercially available corpora are also helpful in ensuring that the language which is being used in classrooms is authentic. A number of studies have compared textbook materials with spoken and written corpora and identified notable differences in what appears in the published materials and what occurs in 'real life' (see, for example, Biber *et al.* 1994; Gilmore 2004). This has led some writers to base teaching materials on corpora, although, at the time of writing, this is not happening on any wide scale in mainstream EFL course books, with the notable exception of *Touchstone* (McCarthy *et al.* 2005; see also McCarten, this volume).

It is uncontroversial to say that, at the time of writing, the following common features of everyday spoken interaction are often missing from invented textbook dialogues:

- There are few response tokens: speakers do not generally acknowledge each other's contributions.
- There are few if any repetitions, false starts or hesitations.
- The language used is often overwhelmingly transactional; there is often scant attention to the relationship between the speakers.
- There are often very few signs that the dialogue is presented as a 'collaborative enterprise', where both speakers (or several) are working together to achieve a common goal.

In naturally occurring conversation, speakers construct meaning together:

- Fixed expressions like *Is that so? I know what you mean, right*, etc. help to keep the conversation open and 'flowing'.
- Requests for clarification (*How did that happen? Who was it you were talking to?* etc.) are important so that both the speaker and listener arrive at the same understanding.
- Confirmation checks (*So you didn't see it happen? That was yesterday, was it?* etc.) also help to ensure both parties have the same understanding. Confirmation checks are clearly important in second language learning, both as a classroom-internal strategy and for interaction outside of class.
- Response tokens (*yeah, OK, sure, great, fine,* etc.) confirm good listenership and indicate that both parties are engaged in the dialogue (see McCarthy 2002).

In the remainder of this chapter, we will focus on the ways in which evidence from corpora, wedded to corpus-based approaches, might be used to help teach the cornerstone skills of speaking/listening and reading/writing. Finally, we will take a closer look at some of the applications of learner corpora.

2. Using corpus-based materials to teach speaking and listening

Features of spoken language

Learners experience all kinds of difficulty when speaking and listening in English. These include things like initiating discussions and taking part in multi-participant conversations, dealing with listening and speaking at the same time, taking responsibility for deciding who speaks and when, opening, closing and changing topics of conversation, negotiating meaning, expressing personal feelings and using common language chunks appropriately. A corpus can be used to help learners understand and overcome many of these problems.

When we look at examples of spoken language in a corpus, we can immediately see how speakers create patterns and structures which characterise spoken English. The following two extracts have a number of features which can be found in virtually all instances of communication where two or more people are involved.

A: And if we don't use them all up, they can be used, can be used elsewhere, anywhere.
B: Yeah elsewhere, okay.
A: That's right.
B: I'll go for that. It won't be, it won't be wasted.
A: No, okay, well I'll sort that out with Kath then.

(BNC)

Our first observation is that expressions such as *okay* and *that's right* are used to follow up on the other speaker's turn. So, instead of thinking of dialogues as being two-part (A/B, A/B) what we see here is, in fact, three parts (A/B/A, A/B/A). These *three-part exchanges* (see Sinclair and Coulthard 1975; Sinclair and Brazil 1982) are the basic building block or organising function of everyday spoken language. Each exchange consists of:

I	Initiation	A: And if we don't use them all up, they can be used, can be used elsewhere, anywhere.
R	Response	B: Yeah elsewhere, okay.
F	Feedback/follow-up	A: That's right.

Three-part exchanges are often referred to as *IRF exchanges* (Sinclair and Coulthard 1975). The IRF pattern is extremely common in any spoken corpus of everyday interaction. Understanding IRF patterns is useful when we consider the first two learner problems we listed at the start of this chapter: initiating and taking part in discussions freely and dealing with listening and speaking at the same time. A second observation when we look at typical everyday exchanges is that usually only one person is speaking at any one time. Taking turns in a conversation is a precise activity and there are relatively few overlaps or interruptions. A spoken corpus can help us gain a closer understanding of the mechanics of turn-taking and help us to evaluate things like how turns are opened, closed and passed, which words appear in turn initial or turn final place, and so on (Tao 2003). Most of the time, a speaker will have an expectation as to what the next person will say. Turns are context dependent and context renewing (Heritage 1997). That is, one turn is both dependent on a previous one and establishes a context for what might follow.

Corpus-derived evidence of exchange- and turn-construction can be used as the basis of teaching input and items for the syllabus for what McCarthy (2002) refers to as 'good listenership': that is to say, the way listeners acknowledge incoming talk, respond to it appropriately and thereby show understanding. In this way, the traditional listening skill can be integrated with the speaking skill in tasks which demand particular responses which mirror common types found in corpora. Examples of these may be found in the speaking conversation strategy syllabus in McCarthy *et al.* (2005).

Spoken corpora and oral fluency

Traditionally, spoken fluency is measured (Fillmore 1979; Lennon 1990) by considering features such as:

- Coherence: is the contribution relevant and does it 'make sense'?
- Hesitancy: are pauses and hesitations too frequent?
- Long turns: does the speaker produce longer stretches of talk?
- Flexibility: does the speaker use vocabulary in a flexible and varied way?
- Automaticity: including the ability to retrieve and use a repertoire of chunks or fixed formulae.

However, when we look at a corpus, we find that native speakers also hesitate a lot, are not always coherent, frequently use shorter turns, and may use a fairly narrow range of vocabulary. Having said this, expert users do succeed in communicating with apparent ease so that listeners understand their intended meaning. Oral fluency is as much about helping listeners and attending to meaning as it is about producing coherent language forms in monologue. If we want learners to become more fluent, we have to consider listening and speaking together, and not as separate skills. When people speak fluently, they use a range of interactional strategies to help their listener follow their intended meaning (for example, by using appropriate questioning strategies). Meanings do not just happen. Both speakers and listeners work hard to ensure that they are each understood. A spoken corpus can help us to understand the interactional aspect of fluent speech and increase learners' interactional competence.

Language chunks

Another feature of spoken language that a corpus can help us to understand is a category of vocabulary often referred to as fixed and semi-fixed expressions, or variously termed chunks, clusters, lexical bundles and multi-word units (see Greaves and Warren, this volume). Fluent speakers are able to recognise and use a wide repertoire of fixed expressions. Learning to recognise and use language chunks can help learners to become more fluent. In fact, it is almost impossible to think of spoken fluency without having at our disposal hundreds of ready-made chunks; we cannot possibly create each sentence from scratch every time we speak. A corpus can show us how speakers repeat the same chunks over and over, and frequency lists of the most common chunks can be generated with relative ease with proprietary software. Such chunks, when viewed as lexical items, can be incorporated directly into the vocabulary syllabus and can be graded either according to frequency or according to degree of complexity of pragmatic specialisation. McCarthy and Carter (2004) looked at the discourse functions associated with the most frequently used chunks in CANCODE, a five-million-word corpus of spoken discourse, and found that they preformed core spoken language functions such as vagueness (*things like that*) and discourse marking (*I mean, you know*), as well as more advanced strategic acts such as face protection and politeness (*do you think, I don't know if …*) (see also Greaves and Warren, this volume; McCarten, this volume). O'Keeffe *et al.* (2007) offer a discussion of practical teaching concerns for the incorporation of chunks into syllabuses and materials.

One of the main lessons of examining a spoken corpus is that all speakers are listeners and that 'flow' or fluency is a jointly engineered outcome. Pedagogic intervention to foster such natural communicative interaction can take place at the level of both syllabus and classroom materials.

3. Using corpus-based materials to teach reading and writing

Using corpus-based texts to develop reading skills

Learners are commonly held to face a number of problems when reading (see, for example, Nuttall 1996; Ur 1996). These include:

- trying to understand every word;
- not being able to read quickly enough;
- 'getting lost' in a text;
- finding lexical density too high;
- not knowing the cultural content;
- being unfamiliar with the topic;
- having no interest in the topic of the text.

One of the main advantages of a corpus is that teachers have a large resource from which to select texts to use with a group of learners (see Allan 2009 for an example of this). By using a corpus, teachers can select texts according to things like their potential to maximise exposure to a target form, their level or content, all of which choices can be assisted by corpus-analytical software. Text difficulty can be investigated using web-based resources for the lexical profiling of texts – for example, at the time of writing, the excellent and easy-to-use web-based tools provided by Tom Cobb, where lexical difficulty levels of reading texts are generated by comparing any text input by the user against large corpora such as the BNC. Alternatively, measures such as type-token ratios for texts in a corpus can offer useful guidelines in selecting suitable reading material. A corpus-based approach to reading and writing gives teachers much more control over the types of text used. By controlling text types, there is a much greater possibility of minimising some of the difficulties listed above and of maximising the learning potential of the materials. For example, with students at lower levels, we might use (or create) a corpus of graded readers to ensure that the material is manageable for learners (Allan 2009).

There are basically two types of 'homemade' corpus which can be used to help students improve their reading and writing (Aston 1996):

- sets of texts which have been written (Allan 2009), or read by learners in the course of a programme of study (see, for example, Willis 1998); a corpus of learner writing is an especially powerful tool for helping learners to understand and overcome the difficulties they encounter when writing in English (see Seidlhofer 2002);
- collections of one particular text type which contain specific linguistic features, such as specialised vocabulary, recurring grammatical structures, a particular rhetorical structure (see, for example, Varantola 2000).

Both types have a number of advantages:

- They promote a focus on form, whereby learners are given opportunities to identify (or notice, Schmidt 1990) and practise particular linguistic features. In terms of using corpora in teaching, this corresponds to data-driven learning (Johns 1991).

- They allow the use of authentic texts which are taken from and used in contexts that are relevant to learners. Students are more likely to become more proficient readers and writers if they have some interest in or familiarity with the texts being used.

A corpus of reading texts can help enormously with learners' vocabulary development. One approach, known as R-Read (Read Extended and Authentic Documents, Cobb 1997), makes use of web-based helper resources which offer the reader linguistic support in relation to meanings of words, parts of speech, etc. (see Cobb 2007 for one example based on Jack London's *Call of the Wild*).

4. Using texts to develop writing skills

By scrutinising even a small corpus of student academic writing, it is possible to detect common problems, which might include things such as:

- an under- or over-use of discourse markers (see De Cock 2000): *first*, *in addition*, *however*, etc.
- a lack of attention to *cohesion* and *coherence*;
- not using an adequate range of vocabulary (detectable through type-token ratio counts, for example);
- improper use of academic conventions, such as citing, referencing, etc.;
- not paying attention to the audience.

Each of the extracts below is taken from the first 100 words of each dissertation in the Learner Dissertation Writing Corpus (Walsh 2007). They tell us a great deal about these students' writing and could be used to raise awareness about good practice in academic writing. For example, learner awareness might be encouraged by asking questions such as:

1. Which is the best opening sentence and why?
2. Can you identify the topic sentence in each extract?
3. Should the first-person pronoun 'I' be used? Why/why not?
4. How does each writer signpost (using words like *first*, *next*, etc.) for the reader?
5. Comment on the length of sentences in each extract. Are any too long or too short? What changes would you make?
6. Rewrite one extract so that it can be read more easily.

> In this study, I would like to focus on an understanding of student–student interaction in a language classroom. There are many key components in a language classroom, such as textbooks, teaching materials, teachers, and students. The learning environment, learners' age and their reasons for learning are all influencing factors on the way they learn. I will describe their functions in the following sections.

> This dissertation aims to discuss the influences of multi-media teaching materials on second language acquisition (SLA) in a comparative study. The learners are international students in a language classroom. The description and survey will focus on two parts, the first part is language learning materials and the second one is computer-assisted language learning (CALL).

A second type of learner writing corpus entails learners constructing their own, individual corpus taken from, for example, work that they have already submitted. Another alternative is for students to seek out texts that are relevant to their specialised language needs and to create a corpus based on texts from this area: for example, medical students might build a corpus of medical papers. The advantage of this approach is that learners and teachers can adopt a more individualised approach to writing, quickly identifying and addressing common problems.

There are a number of other features of academic writing which might be investigated using a learner writing corpus.

Signposting and linking

One of the most important features of good writing is the way the writer signposts and links the arguments for the reader. One of the most commonly used adverbial linking words is *therefore*. It is frequently over-used, or used where another linking device would be better. In the corpus extract below, for example, there are problems in the ways in which *therefore* is used, both syntactically (its position in a sentence) and semantically (the way it communicates meaning).

> **Therefore**, it is suggested that more research is needed to find out the effects of lexical CALL on learning of vocabulary and comprehension. The research had to communicate with the participants **therefore** beforehand. The language learners **therefore** would not obtain more opportunities to negotiate for meaning and repair the breakdown in communication. Although audio recordings were made of what the conversations were, some aspects of non-verbal conversations could not be recorded and **therefore** they could not be analysed as collected data.
>
> (Walsh 2007)

In this extract, we can see that not only is *therefore* over-used (if normalised, its use here would be about 100 times more frequent than its occurrence in the academic segment of the BNC), but it is used in a way which makes the linkages it suggests rather unclear.

Reporting verbs

Another aspect of academic writing which students often find difficult to cope with is the use of reporting verbs in citations and quotations. We use many different verbs for reporting the work of others, each with a very specific meaning. For example, verbs like *suggested*, *indicated*, *claimed* allow a writer to adopt a particular position or stance while still making valid claims. Reporting verbs also allow writers to hedge, or to be less assertive or confident about the claims they are making.

By going to Tim Johns' web homepage we can learn something about reporting verbs. For example, one study, based on a corpus of around 430,000 words from the scientific journal *Nature*, found that the following are the most common reporting verbs in academic texts (see also McCarthy and O'Dell 2008: 72):

indicate show suggest find demonstrate

When we look at *show* in the learner corpus of academic writing, it is obvious that it is indeed used widely, as indicated in this extract, all taken from one chapter of one student's writing:

> Donato's (1994) findings **show** that learners are able to develop their own L2 knowledge as well as 'extend the linguistic development of their peers' during the process of scaffolding.
>
> The findings of Anton's (1999, p315) study **show** that 'the functions of scaffolded assistance are achieved'.
>
> One example is **shown** in Mattos' (2000) research, which states that learners play different roles when working together on a given task, as a provider and receiver.

Insights like these enable learners to ask questions and address problems in their own writing such as:

- Am I over-using *show* in this chapter?
- What alternatives can I find (for example: *indicate*, *confirm*, *demonstrate*)?
- How is my intended meaning changed if I replace *show* with *suggest*?

Proof-reading and error correction

If learners are to become effective writers, it is important that they acquire good proof-reading skills and are able to correct their own errors. A corpus is very helpful to the development of both sets of skills.

A useful place to look at error correction is the University of Toronto website. Here, learners can find out about the most commonly occurring errors in academic writing, with examples taken from small corpora of student writing. By comparing the most common errors with their own writing, students can learn to avoid many of the pitfalls found in non-native speaker writing.

In a longitudinal study in which learners focused on their own data, Chambers and O'Sullivan (2004) stress the importance of 'corpus consultation' as a means of improving writing. They found that most students in the study were able to make significant improvements to accuracy, especially in grammar and vocabulary. Their work underscores the importance of allowing students access to their own data as a means of increasing autonomy and maximising authenticity.

Cohesive devices

Effective writers make appropriate but not excessive use of cohesive devices (words like *moreover*, *in addition*, *on the other hand*). Similarly, good readers use cohesive devices to quickly find their way through a text.

Tankó (2004) conducted a study in which he found that Hungarian writers used more adverbial connectors but from a narrower range than native speaker writers. For example, connectors like *therefore* (see also above) were used almost twice as frequently by non-native as by native speakers. Tankó also found that the most common types of adverbials used by his students were those which listed (e.g. *firstly*, *next*, *finally*) as a means of structuring an essay. Clearly this use of connectors is over-simplistic and fails to provide adequate coherence in many texts.

Findings like these are useful for a number of reasons:

- They help instructors decide which are the most frequently occurring connectors for the purposes of syllabus grading.
- They indicate that, contrary to expectations, native writers of English use more 'simple' connectors (*so*, *yet*, *that is*) than 'complex' ones (such as *furthermore*, *moreover*, etc.).

Tankó (2004: 164) contends that 'a corpus-based data-driven approach to the teaching of adverbial connectors should be adopted'. By using this approach, Tankó found that his Hungarian students' use of adverbial connectors improved.

5. Exploiting learner corpora

Why use a learner corpus?

In the previous sections of this chapter, we have seen how relatively small samples of student data (essays, reports, recorded role plays, tests, and so on) can be used to produce a learner corpus. In this section, we'll look in more detail at ways of exploiting learner corpora.

Investigating errors

By analysing the language learners produce and making comparisons with what native speakers produce, we can start to interpret errors and offer plausible explanations. Take the following example:

I don't know whether he is going.

I didn't know that he went.
I did'nt know whether he will go.
I don't know does he goes.
I don't know he go or don't go
I don't know he goes or not.
I don't know he will go or not.
I don't know him where to go.
I don't know if he go there.
I don't know if he go.
I don't know if he goes.

(Hiroshima English Learners' Corpus)

Here, we can see that the correct model sentence (*I don't know whether he is going*) has been reproduced by learners with a range of errors. Learner corpora offer us the opportunity to compare learner language with native speaker language and explain why errors occur. Using real data like this has the advantage that it is based on what learners actually produce rather than invented examples. This may be seen as a very effective way of raising learner language awareness.

An early example of a learner corpus was the Louvain-based International Corpus of Learner English (ICLE; Granger 1994). This corpus consists of a collection of written texts (totalling approximately two million words) produced by advanced learners of English from countries such as France, Germany, Spain, Poland, Russia, Japan and China. The ICLE can offer interesting insights into the errors learners produce in terms of lexis, grammar and discourse.

For example, in Table 24.1, we can classify errors in relation to a 'standard' native speaker (NS) utterance like the one given: *She is Mike's sister.*

Once we have classified errors in this way, we can look at their frequency of occurrence and consider the extent to which the errors affect intelligibility. By using a spoken learner corpus, we can gain access to non-native speaker talk and consider how errors might impact on the interaction taking place. For example, the Michigan Corpus of Academic Spoken English (MICASE, available free on the MICASE website) permits users to download examples of NNS talk.

The next extract, taken from MICASE, involves a Japanese student giving a presentation. This data could be used to identify errors (here noted in bold). It could also be used to help the student improve the presentation by making it more transparent to listeners, adding in signpost words, and so on.

> Okay, so, I'm sorry my voice doesn't sound as good **as it should be** but **the** last week I had a crew from Japan who **videotape** various **part** of the on- and off-campus about the child care resource in Ann Arbor. This is something I **report** last year based on a request from the government in Japan. The child care issue I went through as a parent but, **it's not my expertise** and **try** to resign, but I couldn't so **at the end** I did and thought that was it. You know they gave me **a small funding** but I did it and I thought that's the end for good and then they came back this year and said this was really good, we found your report fascinating so we'd like to create **the** video.

Another use of the same extract would be to have students rewrite it, but in a different genre: for example, as the introduction to a report, or a news item reporting the events.

In this chapter, we have considered how corpus-based insights might be incorporated into a syllabus and used to underpin teaching materials. While we are not suggesting that corpora should replace existing materials and syllabuses, we are proposing that they are an extremely useful means of helping learners by extending and consolidating more traditional approaches to teaching and learning. Specifically, in this chapter we have seen how spoken and written corpora have much to offer in terms of helping learners improve their interactional competence and language awareness. The main advantages of corpus-based approaches are that materials can be tailored to both the level and the needs

Table 24.1 She is Mike's sister

Learner error	*Description of the error*
See is Mike sister	Phonological: / si:/ instead of / i:/
Are she mikes sister?	Question form, not a statement
She is a Mike's sister	Article choice
She is Mikes sister	Use of the possessive

Source: Hiroshima English Learners' Corpus.

of particular groups of students, and that students can be more actively involved in the learning process and can develop skills which will help them in their own interlanguage development.

Further reading

Allan, R. (2009) 'Can a Graded Reader Corpus Provide "Authentic" Input?' *ELT Journal* 63(1): 23–32. (Useful article on ways of exploiting a reading corpus by using authentic texts to help students acquire essential reading skills.)

Granger, S. (2002) 'A Bird's Eye View of Learner Corpus Research', in S. Granger, J. Hung and Stephanie Petch-Tyson (eds) *Computer Learner Corpora, Second Language Acquisition and Foreign Language Teaching*. Amsterdam: John Benjamin. (Offers some useful insights into the use of learner corpora for language teaching and learning.)

O'Keeffe, A., McCarthy, M. J. and Carter, R. A. (2007) *From Corpus to Classroom*. Cambridge: Cambridge University Press. (Gives an excellent introduction to the use of corpora in the teaching of all four skills.)

References

Allan, R. (2009) 'Can a Graded Reader Corpus Provide "Authentic" Input?' *ELT Journal* 63(1): 23–32.

Aston, G. (1996) 'The British National Corpus as a Language Learner Resource', in S. Botley, J. Glass, T. McEnery and A. Watson (eds) *Proceedings of Teaching and Language Corpora*. Lancaster: University Centre for Computer Corpus Research on Language, pp. 178–91.

Biber, D., Conrad, S. and Reppen, R. (1994) 'Corpus-based Approaches to Issues in Applied Linguistics', *Applied Linguistics* 15(2): 169–89.

Chambers, A. and O'Sullivan, I. (2004) 'Corpus Consultation and Advanced Learners' Writing Skills in French', *ReCALL* 16(1): 158–72.

Cobb, T. (1997) 'Is There Any Measurable Learning from Hands-on Concordancing?' *System* 25(3): 301–15.

——(2007) 'Computing the Vocabulary Demands of L2 Reading', *Language Learning and Technology* 11(3): 38–63.

De Cock, S. (2000) 'Repetitive Phrasal Chunkiness and Advanced EFL Speech and Writing', in C. Mair and M. Hundt (eds) *Corpus Linguistics and Linguistic Theory. Papers from ICAME 20 1999*. Amsterdam: Rodopi, pp. 51–68.

Fillmore, C. J. (1979) 'On Fluency', in C. J. Fillmore, D. Kempler and W. Wang (eds) *Individual Differences in Language Ability and Language Behavior*. New York: Academic Press, pp. 85–101.

Gilmore, A. (2004) 'A Comparison of Textbook and Authentic Interactions', *ELT Journal* 58(4): 363–74.

Granger, S. (1994) 'The Learner Corpus: A Revolution in Applied Linguistics', *English Today* 39 (10/3): 25–9.

Heritage, J. (1997) 'Conversational Analysis and Institutional Talk: Analysing Data', in D. Silverman (ed.) *Qualitative Research: Theory, Method and Practice*. London: Sage, pp. 223–45.

Johns, T. (1991) 'Should You Be Persuaded?: Two Samples of Data-Driven Learning Materials', *English Language Research Journal* 4: 1–16.

——(1994) 'Data-driven Learning: An Update', *TELL&CALL* 2: 4–10.

Krashen, S. (1983) *The Input Hypothesis*. London: Longman.

Lennon, P. (1990) 'Investigating Fluency in EFL: A Quantitative Approach', *Language Learning* 40 (3): 387–417.

McCarthy, M. J. (2002) 'Good Listenership Made Plain: British and American Non-minimal Response Tokens in Everyday Conversation', in R. Reppen, S. Fitzmaurice and D. Biber (eds) *Using Corpora to Explore Linguistic Variation*. Amsterdam: John Benjamins, pp. 49–71.

McCarthy, M. J. and Carter, R. A. (2004) 'This, That and the Other. Multi-word Clusters in Spoken English as Visible Patterns of Interaction', *Teanga* 21: 30–52.

McCarthy, M. J. and O'Dell, F. (2008) *Academic Vocabulary in Use*. Cambridge: Cambridge University Press.

McCarthy, M. J., McCarten, J. and Sandiford, H. (2005) *Touchstone*. Cambridge: Cambridge University Press.

Nuttall, C. (1996) *Teaching Reading Skills in a Foreign Language*. London: Macmillan.

O'Keeffe, A., McCarthy, M. J. and Carter, R. A. (2007) *From Corpus to Classroom: Language Use and Language Teaching*. Cambridge: Cambridge University Press.

Schmidt, R. W. (1990) 'The Role of Consciousness in Second Language Learning', *Applied Linguistics* 11(2): 129–58.

Seidlhofer, B. (2002) 'Pedagogy and Local Learner Corpora: Working with Learning-driven Data', in S. Granger, J. Hung and S. Petch-Tyson (eds) *Computer Learner Corpora, Second Language Acquisition and Foreign Language Teaching*. Amsterdam: John Benjamins, pp. 213–34.

Sinclair, J. and Brazil, D. (1982) *Teacher Talk*. Oxford: Oxford University Press.

Sinclair, J. and Coulthard, M. (1975) *Towards an Analysis of Discourse*. Oxford: Oxford University Press.

Tankó, G. (2004) 'The Use of Adverbial Connectors in Hungarian University Students' Argumentative Essays', in J. Sinclair (ed.) *How to Use Corpora in Language Teaching*. Amsterdam: John Benjamins, pp. 157–81.

Tao, H. (2003) 'Turn Initiators in Spoken English: A Corpus-based Approach to Interaction and Grammar', in P. Leistyna and C. Meier (eds) *Corpus Analysis: Language Structure and Language Use*. Amsterdam: Rodopi, pp. 187–207.

Ur, P. (1996) *A Course in Language Teaching: Practice and Theory*. Cambridge: Cambridge University Press.

Varantola, K. (2000) 'Translators, Dictionaries and Text Corpora', in S. Bernardini and F. Zanettin (eds) *I Corpora nella Didattica della Traduzione*. Bologna: CLUEB, pp. 117–33.

Walsh, S. (2007) 'Learner Dissertation Writing Corpus', unpublished.

Willis, J. (1998) 'Concordances in the Classroom without a Computer: Assembling and Exploiting Concordances of Common Words', in B. Tomlinson (ed.) *Materials Development in Language Teaching*. Cambridge: Cambridge University Press, pp. 44–66.

25

What is data-driven learning?

Angela Chambers

1. The context of data-driven learning

As the developments described in the previous chapters have shown, the analysis of large collections of naturally occurring discourse, both written and spoken, came to play a central role in linguistic research in the twentieth century. The application of this research in language learning and teaching, however, was a slow process, which has been referred to by metaphors such as percolation (McEnery and Wilson 1997: 5) or trickle down (Leech 1997: 2). The fact that developments did take place is easy to explain when one considers the context of research and practice both in language learning and teaching and in applied linguistics. First, the communicative approach emphasised the use of authentic texts, although for several decades accompanying exercises tended to be based on invented examples, and such examples can still be found. Second, research by McCarthy (1998: 18) and others revealed that the language of course books continued to differ significantly from actual language use, particularly in relation to the spoken language. The production of corpus-based dictionaries and grammars as well as course books now gives learners access to actual language use, but it is nonetheless important to note that a data-driven learning (DDL) approach implies a level of active participation in the learning process which such resources cannot provide in the same way as learner (and teacher) interaction with the corpus itself.

DDL takes the developments listed above a step further, in that it not only uses corpus data in the preparation of language-learning materials, but gives learners access to more substantial amounts of corpus data than can be found in a dictionary, grammar or course book, either indirectly by allowing them to learn about language use by studying concordances prepared in advance by the teacher, or directly by allowing them access to corpora and concordancing software to carry out their own searches. The increasing availability of computers from the 1980s onwards and also of concordancers, either commercially or freely via the web, has made it possible for teachers to have access to – and even create – corpora, and for learners to study the patterns of language use in a corpus, mostly through observing concordances, and work out for themselves how a word or a phrase is used. This process of inductive learning, in which the learner plays an active part in the learning process, is the essence of DDL. It also corresponds closely to current thinking in educational research in general, and in language-learning pedagogy in particular, providing a way 'for students to take more active, reflective and autonomous roles in their learning' (Hyland 2002: 120). As researchers/teachers with an interest in the use of corpus data with language learners experimented with different ways of using the data with their learners, and with using different types of corpus (for example large reference corpora or small genre-specific corpora, monolingual or parallel corpora), a substantial body of research publications appeared reporting on the success of this new approach and the obstacles which the learners noted in their explorations of the corpus data.

This chapter will first provide a brief overview of the history of DDL from the late 1960s to the present, including information on the types of corpora used with learners, the successes and the problems reported by researchers on its use in areas such as the learning of vocabulary, grammar and Languages for Specific Purposes. In addition to an account of the research carried out by those interested in using corpus data with learners, the views of those less convinced of its merits will be noted. This will be followed by an investigation of the type of data which can be obtained from written and spoken corpora in a DDL approach. Only easily available corpora will be included. The relationship between DDL and second language acquisition theory will then be explored, asking questions such as: Are concordances comprehensible input? Does DDL facilitate the application of the idiom principle (Sinclair 1991: 110) in language learning? How important is frequency? Finally the changes in language pedagogy which a DDL approach implies will be discussed, including the changing roles of teacher and learner, native speaker intuition and the non-native speaker teacher's role, and variation and non-standard language. In a brief look to the future the potential for a wider adoption of a data-driven learning approach will be assessed.

2. A brief history of data-driven learning

The first publications disseminating information internationally on developments in the use of corpus data with language learners appeared in the 1980s, notably those by Tim Johns (1986, 1988, 1991), who coined the term DDL. Johns initially used the concordancing software *MicroConcord* as a tool for learners to use, although he also recognised its usefulness for the teacher and linguistic researcher (1986: 158). He introduced concordancing in his work teaching English for Specific Purposes to non-native speakers of English, and also situated it in the context of similar developments by a number of researchers, citing experimentation by his then colleague in Birmingham, Antoinette Renouf, and Ahmad, Corbett and Rogers (1985) in Surrey (Johns 1986: 159). McEnery and Wilson (1997: 12) situate the first attested use of concordances in language teaching as early as 1969, by Peter Roe in Aston University, Birmingham. It was not until the late 1980s and the early 1990s, however, that it was brought to public attention in the discourse community of researchers in applied linguistics by the work of Johns and also of Tribble and Jones (1990). Johns used the simile of the language learner as researcher (1986: 160) and the Sherlock Holmes metaphor (1997: 101) to highlight the more active role of the learner in this approach, and described the computer and the concordancer as a research tool for both learner and teacher (1986: 151). His learners considered working with a concordance printout to be a much more effective way of studying the use of common prepositions, finding that an exercise such as underlining the headword colligating with the preposition *on* ('depending on', 'on demand') was more helpful than a gap-filling exercise involving filling in the prepositions (1986: 160). The concordancer also served as a research tool for Johns himself in his role as teacher (1986: 159).

> It is important that teachers themselves should have experience in using concordance output if they expect their students to make use of it. In my own case, examining output has often proved chastening: for example a concordance of 'if' showed how often in scientific and technical texts it is followed by the bare adjective or past participle e.g. 'if available', 'if known' – a usage I found I had neglected in my materials on conditional constructions in English.

As we shall see, this early experimentation by Johns and others was to develop into a substantial research area from the 1990s onwards, although the researchers involved still recognise that the adoption of this new approach to language learning tends to be restricted to a limited number of researchers and enthusiasts (see, for example, Conrad 2000: 556).

Johns and others, notably Joseph Rézeau, developed websites which provided a bibliography of articles on this emerging area and examples of exercises. From 1990 onwards more sophisticated concordancers, such as *WordSmith Tools* (Scott 2004) and *MonoConc* (Barlow 2000) became available commercially at a relatively modest cost, and more recently free web-based concordancers, such as *AntConc*, have also become available. In addition to these concordancers, which allow users to load and consult the corpus of their choice, huge corpora may be consulted online. The Cobuild Concordance and Collocations Sampler, for example, allows the user to insert a search word and have instant access to forty examples of its use. Similarly, the British National Corpus provides fifty occurrences. Thus a teacher or learner wanting examples of the phrasal verb *end up* could quickly have access to the following examples from Cobuild.

> If you drink with other people who regularly buy rounds for each other, it's easy to **end up** drinking more than you want.
>
> if you forget to spray it with simazine every March you **end up** with a lot of extra weeding.
>
> It's true you do get stared at in clubs, but you know, I am fat, I do live in the real world, and I don't want to **end up** some kind of fat separatist.
>
> was a very tough little man, a very hard little man who knew what he wanted, where he was going and where he was going to **end up**.
>
> As a result, the child may **end up** in a distress-provoking, or even physically dangerous, situation.
>
> Many politicians **end up** simply hating the press.
>
> We're gonna **end up** living in a broom cupboard.
>
> the kids **end up** you know homeless and uneducated at sixteen.
>
> Tony Galluci visited Italy for the first time and almost **ended up** in the army.
>
> Those who have tried to be honest have **ended up** at the bottom of the ladder.

This has the benefit of providing teachers with examples of actual language use to support their teaching, although the easy access to the full text which a concordancer such as *WordSmith Tools* (Scott 2004) or *MonoConc* (Barlow 2000) provides is not possible here. The Business Letter Corpus (Someya 1999) also has the advantage of giving a teacher or learner access to concordance data with no training whatsoever, although here again, access to the full text is not available for copyright reasons. While the above examples involve only English, multilingual resources are also available which allow corpus consultation without the training necessary to use the commercially and freely available concordancers. The *Lextutor* website provides easy access to a variety of corpora in French and English, while the SACODEYL project allows the user to consult interviews with teenagers in a variety of European languages (see Thompson, this volume).

While these easily available and, more important, easy to use resources may well have the greatest potential for popularising the use of corpus data by language learners and teachers, the substantial number of publications reporting on the use of corpora by learners tend to concentrate on the use of commercial concordancers by either the teacher or the learners themselves, using either large corpora such as the British National Corpus (Bernardini 2000) or small corpora created specifically to meet the learners' needs. These corpora were used to investigate a variety of aspects of language learning, particularly the acquisition of vocabulary, grammar and specialised language use. Stevens (1991), for example, created a small corpus based on the physics textbook of his students to investigate whether concordance-based exercises were better than gap-fill exercises for learning vocabulary, and concluded that they were. The small corpus of 180,000 words created by O'Sullivan (O'Sullivan and Chambers 2006: 53) included texts on the history of the French language recommended to the students. Their results revealed the strengths of the small specialised corpus, in that learners could often find multiple relevant examples. Small corpora also have their limits, however, in that they may contain no or very few occurrences of certain items. While Cobb (1997: 304) used a corpus of just 10,000 words assembled from his students' reading materials to investigate the use of corpus data for vocabulary learning, Gaskell and Cobb (2004: 316), who investigated the use of concordances to correct writing errors, concluded that a corpus of more than one million words would be more likely to produce a substantial number of occurrences of the words and expressions which the learners wished to study. In addition, these small corpora created specifically to meet learners' needs, what Willis (1998: 46) calls pedagogic corpora, are often not publicly available.

The results of these and other empirical studies were largely positive. The quantitative studies (Stevens 1991; Cobb 1997; Gaskell and Cobb 2004; Yoon and Hirvela 2004) strongly suggest that learners benefit from corpus consultation in learning vocabulary and grammar, and in improving writing skills. A much larger number of qualitative studies support this view, with the additional benefit of giving the learners themselves a voice in the debate. The learners appreciated having access to a large number of genuine examples of the aspect of language use which they were studying (Cheng *et al.* 2003: 181; Yoon and Hirvela 2004: 275; Chambers 2005: 117). They also enjoyed the exploratory nature of the activity, what Johns had in mind in the well-known phrase 'Every learner a Sherlock Holmes' (Johns 1997: 101). As one learner commented on the activity of direct corpus consultation: 'I discovered that achieving results from my concordance was a highly motivating and enriching experience. I've never encountered such an experience from a textbook' (Chambers 2005: 120).

Negative reactions to corpus consultation by learners come from two sources. First, in the empirical studies even the learners whose reactions were generally very positive found the activity of analysing the corpus data time-consuming, laborious and tedious (Cheng *et al.* 2003: 182–3; Yoon and Hirvela 2004: 274; Chambers 2005: 120). Possible solutions to this include integrating the consultation of corpus data with the study of individual texts, giving learners access to simple resources such as the *Cobuild Concordance and Collocations Sampler* or the SACODEYL corpora, or using concordances prepared in advance by the teacher. One could envisage a gradual process over several years, where learners are first introduced to concordance printouts prepared by the teacher so that they become familiar with learning inductively from concordances, moving on to consultation of easy-to-use online resources, and then finally to independent corpus consultation analysing data from the corpus of their choice.

The second source of negative reactions involves the issue of context. For Widdowson (2000: 7), corpora contain 'decontextualised language'. Charles (2007: 298) comments, however, that it is arguable that a corpus contains more context than much classroom material which consists of extracts, as the learner consulting a corpus of complete texts has access to the full text corresponding to each concordance line. In other publications reporting on the use of corpora with learners, the authors also underline that teachers preparing materials using concordances should ensure that the context is meaningful, that it contains 'somewhere in it some clue, however small, to assist students in placing the target word in that context' (Stevens 1991: 51). In the following occurrences of 'I am/ I'm afraid' in the Business Letter Corpus, for example, it is clear that the expression is used to apologise or to turn down a request, and also to fulfil other roles, such as threatening (legal action).

> Enclosed are some photos, which **I am afraid** did not come out very well.
> much as I would like to help, **I'm afraid** I could not consider it.
> **I am afraid** I will be unable to attend your party.
> **I'm afraid** I'm not the appropriate person for you
> **I am afraid** my correspondence has fallen behind.
> **I am afraid** that we cannot help you, unfortunately
> **I am afraid** we cannot agree to your request.
> Under the circumstances, **I'm afraid** we can't bear the cost of any repairs.
> party is on the extravagant side, **I'm afraid** we have to limit tickets to staff only.
> **I'm afraid** we will be forced to take legal action
> Unfortunately, however, **I'm afraid** we'll have to postpone it.

Like Stevens, Willis (1998: 46) recommends creating what she terms a pedagogic corpus to meet the specific needs of students (see also Braun 2005). These small genre-specific corpora help to minimise the problems learners could encounter when faced with large numbers of occurrences from a variety of genres. At the same time other researchers (Bernardini 2000; Cheng *et al.* 2003) prefer to give their – usually advanced – students access to the large corpora originally created for the purpose of linguistic research. At present all these trends coexist, with large and small corpora increasingly available to learners and teachers, and an increasing number of researchers experimenting with ways to make DDL a reality for the majority of language learners.

3. DDL and actual language use

In this section we shall see how small, easily and freely available written and spoken corpora can provide data which can be used by the teacher or learner in a DDL approach. As written corpora can be created more easily than their spoken counterparts, it is not surprising that they are more readily available. While the concordances quoted earlier in this chapter can be retrieved from the corpus websites with no training, the lack of access to the full context is clearly a limitation. Using a concordancer such as *WordSmith Tools* (Scott 2004) or *MonoConc* (Barlow 2000), a teacher or learner can consult a number of freely available corpora. The examples below are taken from the Chambers–Le Baron Corpus of Research Articles in French (Chambers and Le Baron 2007), a pedagogic corpus of approximately one million words created to be of use to learners when writing essays in French, and available via the Oxford Text Archive. The corpus contains 159 articles taken from twenty journals. The articles, published between 1998 and 2006, belong to one of ten categories: media/culture, literature, linguistics and language learning, social anthropology, law, economics, sociology and social sciences, philosophy, history and communication.

The use of the first person plural in research articles in French has given rise to a substantial amount of phraseology related to the metalanguage of the article, the language used by the author to signal to the reader how the article is organised. The equivalent phrases for 'as we have seen' and 'as we shall see', for example, include a redundant definite article and may refer to the article in spatial rather than temporal terms: 'plus haut' and 'plus loin' rather than 'earlier' and 'later'. I had corrected learner errors by writing in the phrases 'comme nous l'avons vu plus haut', and 'comme nous le verrons plus loin'. I discovered from studying the seventy-four occurrences of 'comme nous' in the corpus, however, that there is a much wider variety of phrases than this, with only fifteen occurrences of the verb 'to see', and verbs such as 'underline', 'indicate', 'mention', 'observe', 'show', 'note' and 'remind' commonly occurring.

Comme nous l'avons souligné précédemment
comme nous l'avons déjà souligné auparavant.
comme nous venons de le décrire.
Comme nous l'avons indiqué plus haut,
Comme nous l'avons déjà indiqué,
Comme nous l'avons mentionné plus haut
Premièrement, **comme nous** l'avons constaté dans le cadre de nos recherches sur l'IRC,
comme nous avons pu le constater à plusieurs reprises lors de l'analyse
D'autre part, **comme nous** l'observerons en seconde partie de cet article,
Comme nous allons tenter de le montrer dans la suite de ce texte,
comme nous le montrerons dans les pages qui suivent.
Comme nous l'avons expliqué dans le paragraphe précédent,
comme nous l'avons exposé dans notre préambule méthodologique
comme nous l'avons rappelé,
Comme nous en avons fait état plus haut,
comme nous allons maintenant le noter,

Alongside 'voir' one also finds verbs such as 'souligner' (five occurrences), 'constater' (three occurrences), 'tenté de le montrer' (three occurrences), and many others. A variety of adverbial expressions is used as well as 'plus haut' and 'plus loin'. In addition, inversion of the subject and verb is sometimes used in these phrases.

Comme nous l'a suggéré un rapporteur anonyme.
Comme nous l'apprend son dossier de faillite,

Comme nous le dit cet interviewé, 'la communauté ne nous appartient pas'.
comme nous l'a précédemment montré la scène de leur premier face à face
comme nous le laisse entendre la section Religion de sa Phénoménologie

Like Tim Johns in the references to the use of 'if' above, I found the consultation of the corpus a useful way of getting immediate information on the practices of a substantial number of native speakers, prompting me to include in my teaching features which I had hitherto neglected.

In addition to formulaic phrases such as these, using the first person plural pronoun 'nous' as a search word can provide information on other aspects of the metalanguage of native speaker authors of research articles. Verbs used to describe the plan of an essay, for example, are easy to identify by searches for different expressions for first, second, then, etc., such as 'premièrement', deuxièmement', 'ensuite', 'dans un premier/deuxième temps', etc. Many other common expressions can also be discovered by examining the occurrences of the first person plural. The verb 'permettre', to permit, for example, is commonly used in academic writing in French, with twenty-three occurrences of 'permett*'. Examples are listed below.

Les statistiques dont nous disposons ne nous **permettent** pas de distinguer explicitement
Ce questionnement nous **permettra** de mettre à jour le degré de compatibilité
L'analyse de ces traces nous **permettra** de répondre à notre interrogation initiale, à savoir :
Cela nous **permettra** de mesurer combien la culture politique corse est étrangère à
L'examen des caractéristiques de la domiciliation nous **permettra** de réfléchir, en creux, aux limites de son usage

Thus, while a detailed study of the first person plural in this corpus would be well beyond the scope of this chapter, it is clear that even a small corpus of one million words can provide a rich source of attested examples in support of learner writing. Data such as this can be exploited in a number of ways in a data-driven learning approach, ranging from concordances prepared by the teacher from which learners inductively learn how native speakers use the language in specific contexts, to direct consultation by learners to find solutions to problems which they encounter.

Although freely available spoken corpora are less common than their written counterparts, they are slowly becoming more accessible. A number of recent projects have created spoken pedagogic corpora which learners and teachers can easily access via the web. SACODEYL, for example, focuses on teen talk, including video-recorded interviews and transcripts of approximately ten minutes with twenty to twenty-five teenagers in each of the following languages: English, French, German, Italian, Lithuanian, Romanian and Spanish. The interview transcripts are available as online corpora (hosted by the University of Murcia). According to the SACODEYL website at the time of writing, they are 'pedagogically annotated and enriched for language learning and teaching purposes' (SACODEYL website, 2009). The interviews cover the following topics: personal information, home and family, present and past living routines, hobbies and interests, holidays, school and education, job experiences, plans for the future, open discussion topics. The SACODEYL site illustrates how the problem of decontextualised concordances can relatively easily be overcome. The concordance can simply serve to produce supplementary examples and to check if an aspect of language use which is evident in one speaker is used by the others as well. In the French sub-corpus component of SACODEYL, for example, one of the speakers, Margaux, uses 'sinon' repeatedly, not necessarily in the sense of 'otherwise', but simply to link the items in a list. A concordance of the sixty occurrences of 'sinon' reveals that it is commonly used in two ways. In the concordance lines below, 'sinon', sometimes preceded by 'or', indicates that what precede and follow the conjunction are alternatives.

> ce serait des études de droit comme mon père. Ou **sinon**, devenir ingénieur dans le domaine scientifique,
> quand je décide quelque chose, j'aime bien y parvenir **sinon**, c'est la catastrophe.
> cinéma ou on va au bowling aussi. Ça dépend. Ou **sinon**, on fait des fêtes chez l'un ou chez l'autre

In the first example the pupil intends either to study law or to become an engineer, mutually exclusive alternatives. Similarly in the second concordance line the pupil likes to succeed or 'c'est la catastrophe'. In the third example a pastime can either be cinema, bowling or a party at someone's house. In the examples below, 'and' is sometimes used rather than 'or' before 'sinon' to list various pastimes.

> deux heures et demie d'anglais par semaine et **sinon**, je fais aussi une option facultative LV3 italien
> j'aime beaucoup de films différents, et **sinon**, j'aime aussi j'aime aussi dessiner
> Mais aussi, je fais du badminton au lycée le lundi **sinon**, j 'aime beaucoup lire
> Au lycée, je fais du badminton. Et **sinon**, je pratique la guitare depuis dix ans.

Interestingly, the third of the first set of examples (cinema, bowling or party) is similar in content to the three examples in the second set. The concordance reveals that these uses of 'sinon' are common among the teenagers, thus making it possible for learners at secondary level who do not have regular interaction with native speakers to encounter multiple examples of the everyday language use of their counterparts in the target language. With its combination of videos, transcripts and concordances, SACODEYL provides a rich learning environment for teenagers, integrating the concordances with more traditional language-learning resources such as text and video.

4. DDL and second language acquisition theory

As empirical studies have revealed generally positive reactions by learners to the consultation of concordances, the question arises as to how this new approach relates to theories of Second Language Acquisition. It could be said to constitute a form of comprehensible input (Krashen 1988), particularly when the content of the corpus is carefully chosen to be familiar to the learners (Allan 2009). It does, however, differ from Krashen's scenario in one important way. The simplified language or caretaker talk which Krashen describes as helpful to the learner (1988: 136) is absent here. Although the content may be familiar, the language in a native speaker monolingual corpus consists of attested examples of actual language use. The multiple contexts do, however, enable the learner to observe patterns. Thus, in the concordance lines with 'end up' listed above, the learner can observe that this phrasal verb is followed by the -ing form of the verb ('end up hating', 'end up living'), by a preposition ('end up in the army'), by an adjective ('end up homeless and uneducated'), or by a noun ('end up some kind of fat separatist'). It cannot be guaranteed, of course, that a learner looking at that concordance will learn all these uses. As no one advocates data-driven learning as the main component in an approach to language learning, but rather as an enhancement of text-based work, the learner may be using the concordance to check if one particular use is correct, and the concordance could confirm that and reinforce the learning process. By providing a rich variety of examples, it might also help the learner to notice – in the sense in which Schmidt (1990) uses the term – the other uses.

The emphasis on grammatical structures in the above example, while justified, does not fully convey the essential characteristics of data-driven learning. While traditional language-learning resources and methods, and even research, tend to separate the learning of grammar and lexis, in DDL they are seen as fully integrated. Distinguishing between the open-choice principle, according to which the language user has freedom to slot different parts of speech together to form utterances, and the 'idiom principle', Sinclair (1991: 110) defines the latter as follows: 'The principle of idiom is that a user has available to him or her a large number of semi-preconstructed phrases that constitute single choices, even though they might appear to be analysable into segments.'

For proponents of this approach to language, concordances facilitate the application of the idiom principle in language learning, giving teachers and learners easy access to large numbers of attested examples of use so that the patterns can become clear and the learners can creatively integrate them in their own language use (see Hunston, this volume). We have seen how these patterns can be illustrated not only in the highly formulaic context of academic writing, but also in casual teenage conversation. Giving learners access to multiple examples of common patterns could help to overcome what Debrock *et al.* (1999: 46) call '*le manque de naturel* [the lack of naturalness]' in learner language. If generally applied in a way that was easily accessible to the learner and teacher, access to multiple examples from appropriate corpus data could thus have a profound effect on language learning and teaching.

The concept of semantic prosody (Louw 1993: 157) takes this patterning a step further, showing how certain forms can be imbued with 'a consistent aura of meaning' by their collocates. Xiao and McEnery (2006: 106) provide a useful table of semantic prosodies which have been observed by various researchers, showing how 'happen', 'cause', 'end up', 'a recipe for', and 'signs of' have negative connotations. They also (p. 106) point out that

> Semantic prosodies are typically negative, with relatively few of them bearing an affectively positive meaning. However, a speaker/writer can also violate a semantic prosody condition to achieve some effect in the hearer – for example irony, insincerity, or humour can be explained by identifying violations of semantic prosody (Louw 1993: 173).
>
> (Xiao and McEnery 2006: 106)

In French, for example, the verb *se jouer* normally has connotations of major events with genuinely or potentially disastrous connotations. In the following concordance lines from a million-word corpus of journalistic writing in French (Chambers and Rostand 2005), the potentially negative connotations are clear. (The corpus contains fifty-four occurrences of this pronomial verb, of which sixteen are literal: eleven referring to sporting events and five to theatrical performances. The remaining thirty-eight are used in the figurative sense as discussed here.)

> les chaises renversées, les traces de sang sur les murs disent le drame qui **s'est joué** ici, où trois kamikaze ont opéré. 'J'ai entendu deux explosions
>
> Dans le box des accusés, celui-ci est tendu. Il sait que son sort **se joue** peut-être dans cette audience.
>
> est devenue politique, au point que l'on peut supposer que tout, en réalité, va **se jouer**, maintenant, entre l'Elysée et la Maison Blanche.
>
> avec Clemenceau et de Gaulle, parmi ces grands irréguliers dont la destinée **s'est jouée** sur un moment crucial où leur singularité l'a emporté
>
> 'Notre avenir **se jouera** demain matin, au tribunal de commerce de Béthunes.

This strong semantic prosody is, however, violated in the reference to 'L'acteur principal du petit drame qui s'est joué à l'arrivée, au télésiège', which describes the journalist's critical reaction to the minor drama of the cancellation of a skiing competition. Consulting a concordance is thus a useful way for a learner at advanced level to discover not only instances of semantic prosody but also the contexts in which it can be violated, thus providing examples of language creativity (see chapter on creativity by Vo and Carter, this volume).

The examples of semantic prosody illustrate another aspect of second language acquisition theory which is of particular relevance to the use of corpora, namely the importance of frequency. The term is used in different ways by corpus linguists and by those researching the language-learning process. For the corpus linguist, frequency refers to the fact that by analysing a corpus one can discover what words, expressions and collocations occur very frequently, information which is important both for researchers in linguistics and also for language-learning professionals so that they can ensure that they are emphasising the most frequently occurring aspects of language use in their classes, course books or grammars, or at the very least not omitting them. In the language-learning context, frequency refers rather to the number of times a learner has to encounter an aspect of language use to be aware of it – what Schmidt (1990) terms 'noticing' – and to be able to use it. Data-driven learning brings these two uses of the term together, by allowing the learners to have access to corpora so that they can discover frequent patterns and, perhaps more importantly, observe a large variety of examples of their use. These examples could include evidence of semantic prosody as well as a small number of violations of that prosody. Thus data-driven learning, while encouraging learners to take an active part in their learning, is also contributing to a revival of interest in frequency, not the mindless repetition of behaviourism, but rather what Ellis (2002: 177) calls 'mindful repetition in an engaging communicative context by motivated learners'.

5. DDL: changing language pedagogy

We have already seen how the role of the learner is more active in DDL, analysing a concordance prepared by the teacher, or consulting a corpus directly to find an answer to a specific problem or to study the language use of a particular group of native speakers, such as teenagers or academic writers. The role of the teacher also changes fundamentally, as s/he is no longer the sole source of knowledge about the target language, but rather a facilitator of the learning process, helping the learners to interpret the data, and giving them advice on how best to search the corpus and analyse their search results. Kennedy and Miceli (2001: 82) propose a four-stage search strategy for learners:

1. Formulate the question.
2. Devise a search strategy.
3. Observe the examples and select relevant ones.
4. Draw conclusions.

As they analyse the results of their students' exploration of a corpus, they develop a series of tips to help the learners to get the most benefit from the data (for more on strategies for preparing learners to use corpora, see the chapter by Sripicharn, this volume). This new learning environment thus demands new skills from teachers, including knowledge about what corpora are available, corpus consultation and analysis skills, and the capacity to decide how best to present the data to the learners, either as pre-prepared concordances or as a resource to be directly explored by the learners. In addition, teachers and learners now engage in a new way of 'reading' a text – not just left to right, but from the centre outwards, and vertically up and down, something which the majority of them will not have done before. In an environment where web literacy is the norm, however, the innovative aspect of this practice may be less of a challenge, particularly for the learners.

In addition to the challenge of acquiring these new skills, consulting corpus data changes the relationship between the teacher and the target language. When faced with examples of variation in a corpus, a teacher is encouraged – or even obliged – to adopt a descriptive rather than a prescriptive approach to target language use. After studying the 236 occurrences of *majorité* in the Chambers–Rostand Corpus of Journalistic French in relation to singular and plural verb forms, one is forced to rethink one's practice of correcting students' use of the plural. Examples from the corpus are given below.

> D'ailleurs Jacques Chirac lui-même l'a dit : ' Je sais que la grande **majorité** des Corses veulent rester français. [plural]
>
> Par contre, une écrasante **majorité** (93%) craint une nouvelle catastrophe sur nos côtes. [singular]
>
> 'Comme je vous l'ai dit, l'écrasante **majorité** des étudiants est favorable au système LMD (licence-mastère-doctorat). [singular]
>
> Pas plus d'un Français sur cinq répond 'oui'. En revanche, une très forte **majorité** (63%) pensent qu'il vaudrait mieux, pour atteindre cet objectif [plural]

It is nonetheless tempting at times to edit a pre-prepared concordance, not with a desire to be prescriptive but to avoid confusing the learners, particularly when looking for examples of an aspect of language use which is problematic for them. A more difficult challenge for teachers is presented by the presence of taboo language in corpora of spontaneous conversation, such as the Corpus of London Teenagers or the Limerick Corpus of Irish English (Farr *et al.* 2004). The teacher wishing to include corpus data thus faces a number of challenges, particularly as the integration of corpora in language learning is not yet included in the majority of language teacher education courses (McCarthy 2008).

A number of researchers in corpora and language learning (Conrad 2000: 556; Farr 2008: 40) recommend such a development as the way to overcome the barrier which currently exists to the addition of corpora to the resources commonly available to learners, the grammar, dictionary and course book. In addition, Chambers and Wynne (2008) suggest a framework for the development of web-based resources for higher education, inspired by Fligelstone's scenario, in which a teacher can advise a learner to 'go to any of the labs, hit the icon which says "corpus" and follow the instructions on the screen' (Fligelstone 1993: 101). This scenario, however, is still a long way from being realised, although the slow development described by Leech (1997:2) as 'trickle down', and by McEnery and Wilson (1997: 5) as 'percolation' is still continuing. In addition to the inclusion of corpus consultation skills in language teacher education courses, the increasing number of corpus resources which are easily available and require no training other than basic web skills may well contribute to the realisation of Fligelstone's vision. A final question arises as to whether the web itself, using a conventional search engine or *WebCorp*, can replace the corpus, using electronic literacy skills already mastered by the vast majority of learners (see Lee, this volume). Rundell (2000) notes on the positive side that no corpus will ever be as up-to-date as the web, but also warns that the web is 'not a corpus at all according to any standard definitions', but rather 'a huge ragbag of digital text whose content and balance are largely unknown'. In the current situation, where it does not seem likely that the majority of language teachers will have easy access to the corpora they need and the skills to make use of them in the immediate or near future, it is difficult to predict the future role of the web as a corpus or rather, taking account of Rundell's comment, as a source of data for language learning and teaching. If the availability of corpora becomes well known to teachers and learners, this may no longer be an issue, as corpus data will be easily available to them, providing them with attested examples of language use in relevant registers.

Further reading

Sinclair, J. McH. (2004) (ed.) *How to Use Corpora in Language Teaching*. Amsterdam and Philadelphia, PA: John Benjamins. (This book contains useful chapters on a variety of ways in which corpora can be used, with a good combination of pedagogy and practice.)

Wichmann, A., Fligelstone, S., McEnery, T. and Knowles, G. (eds) (1997) *Teaching and Language Corpora*. London; New York: Longman. (Although it is not a recent publication, this edited volume from one of the series of conferences on Teaching and Language Corpora provides a wealth of information on aspects of the integration of corpus data in language learning.)

References

Ahmad, K., Corbett, G. and Rogers, M. (1985) 'Using Computers with Advanced Language Learners: An Example', *The Language Teacher* 9(3): 4–7.

Allan, R. (2009) 'Can a Graded Reader Corpus Provide "Authentic" Input?' *ELT Journal* 63(1): 23–32.

Barlow, M. (2000) *MonoConc Pro*. Houston, TX: Athelstan.

Bernardini, S. (2000) 'Systematising Serendipity: Proposals for Concordancing Large Corpora with Language Learners', in L. Burnard and T. McEnery (eds) *Rethinking Language Pedagogy from a Corpus Perspective*. Frankfurt: Peter Lang, pp. 225–34.

Braun, S. (2005) 'From Pedagogically Relevant Corpora to Authentic Language Learning Contents', *ReCALL* 17(1): 47–64.

Chambers, A. (2005) 'Integrating Corpus Consultation in Language Studies', *Language Learning and Technology* 9(2): 111–25.

Chambers, A. and Le Baron, F. (eds) (2007) *The Chambers–Le Baron Corpus of Research Articles in French/ Le Corpus Chambers–Le Baron d'articles de recherche en français*. Oxford: Oxford Text Archive, available at http://ota.ahds.ac.uk/headers/2527.xml (accessed 2 June 2009).

Chambers, A. and Rostand, S. (eds) (2005) *The Chambers–Rostand Corpus of Journalistic French/Le Corpus Chambers–Rostand de français journalistique*. Oxford, University of Oxford: Oxford Text Archive, available at http://ota.ahds.ac.uk/headers/2491.xml (accessed 2 June 2009).

Chambers, A. and Wynne, M. (2008) 'Sharing Corpus Resources in Language Learning', in F. Zhang and B. Barber (eds) *Handbook of Research on Computer-Enhanced Language Acquisition and Learning*. Hershey, PA: IGI Global, pp. 438–51.

Charles, M. (2007) 'Reconciling Top-down and Bottom-up Approaches to Graduate Writing: Using a Corpus to Teach Rhetorical Functions', *Journal of English for Academic Purposes* 6(4): 289–302.

Cheng, W., Warren, M. and Xun-feng, X. (2003) 'The Language Learner as Language Researcher: Putting Corpus Linguistics on the Timetable', *System* 31(2): 173–86.

Cobb, T. (1997) 'Is There Any Measurable Learning from Hands-on Concordancing?' *System* 25(3): 301–15.

Conrad, S. (2000) 'Will Corpus Linguistics Revolutionize Grammar Teaching in the Twenty-first Century?' *TESOL Quarterly* 34(3): 548–60.

Debrock, M., Flament-Boistrancourt, D. and Gevaert, R. (1999) 'Le manque de "naturel" des interactions verbales du non-francophone en français. Analyses de quelques aspects à partir du corpus LANCOM', *Faits de Langue* 13 (*Oral-Ecrit: Formes et théories*): 46–56.

Ellis, N. (2002) 'Frequency Effects in Language Processing. A Review with Implications for Theories of Implicit and Explicit Language Acquisition', *Studies in Second Language Acquisition* 24: 143–88.

Farr, F. (2008) 'Evaluating the Use of Corpus-based Instruction in a Language Teacher Education Context: Perspectives from the Users', *Language Awareness* 17(1): 25–43.

Farr, F., Murphy, B. and O'Keeffe, A. (2004) 'The Limerick Corpus of Irish English: Design, Description and Application', *Teanga* 21: 5–29.

Fligelstone, S. (1993) 'Some Reflections on the Question of Teaching, from a Corpus Linguistics Perspective', *ICAME* 17: 97–109.

Gaskell, D. and Cobb, T. (2004) 'Can Learners Use Concordance Feedback for Writing Errors?' *System* 32(3): 301–19.

Hyland, K. (2002) *Teaching and Researching Writing*. London: Pearson Education.

Johns, T. (1986) 'Micro-Concord: A Language Learner's Research Tool', *System* 14(2): 151–62.

——(1988) 'Whence and Whither Classroom Concordancing', in T. Bongaerts, P. De Haan, S. Lobbe and H. Wekker (eds) *Computer Applications in Language Learning*. Dordrecht: Foris, pp. 9–27.

——(1991) 'Should You Be Persuaded: Two Examples of Data-driven Learning', in T. Johns and P. King (eds) *Classroom Concordancing, ELR Journal 4*. Birmingham: Centre for English Language Studies, University of Birmingham, pp. 1–16.

——(1997) 'Contexts: The Background, Development, and Trialling of a Concordance-based CALL Program', in A. Wichmann, S. Fligelstone, T. McEnery and G. Knowles (eds) *Teaching and Language Corpora*. London: Longman, pp. 100–15.

Kennedy, C. and Miceli, T. (2001) 'An Evaluation of Intermediate Students' Approaches to Corpus Investigation', *Language Learning and Technology* 5(3): 77–90.

Krashen, S. (1988) *Second Language Acquisition and Second Language Learning*. London: Prentice-Hall.

Leech, G. (1997) 'Teaching and Language Corpora: A Convergence', in A. Wichmann, S. Fligelstone, T. McEnery and G. Knowles (eds) *Teaching and Language Corpora*. London: Longman, pp. 1–23.

Louw, B. (1993) 'Irony in the Text or Insincerity in the Writer? The Diagnostic Potential of Semantic Prosodies', in M. Baker, G. Francis and E. Tognini Bonelli (eds) *Text and Technology: In Honour of John Sinclair*. Amsterdam: John Benjamins, pp. 157–76.

McCarthy, M. (1998) *Spoken Language and Applied Linguistics*. Cambridge: Cambridge University Press.
——(2008) 'Accessing and Interpreting Corpus Information in the Teacher Education Context', *Language Teaching* 41(4): 563–74.
McEnery, T. and Wilson, A. (1997) 'Teaching and Language Corpora', *ReCALL* 9(1): 5–14.
O'Sullivan, Í. and Chambers, A. (2006) 'Learners' Writing Skills in French: Corpus Consultation and Learner Evaluation', *Journal of Second Language Writing* 15: 49–68.
Rundell, M. (2000) 'The Biggest Corpus of All', *Humanising Language Teaching* 2(3), at http://www.hltmag.co.uk/may00/idea.htm (accessed 31 May 2009).
SACODEYL website, at www.um.es/sacodeyl/ (accessed 31 May 2009).
Schmidt, R. (1990) 'The Role of Consciousness in Second Language Learning', *Applied Linguistics* 11 (2): 129–58.
Scott, M. (2004) *WordSmith Tools Version 4.0*. Oxford: Oxford University Press.
Sinclair, J. (1991) *Corpus, Concordance, Collocation*. London: Longman.
Someya, Y. (1999) 'A Corpus-based Study of Lexical and Grammatical Features of Written Business English', MA thesis, University of Tokyo.
Stevens, V. (1991) 'Concordance-based Vocabulary Exercises: A Viable Alternative to Gap-fillers', in T. Johns and P. King (eds) *Classroom Concordancing: English Language Research Journal 4*. Birmingham: Centre for English Language Studies, University of Birmingham, pp. 47–63.
Tribble, C. and Jones, G. (1990) *Concordances in the Classroom: A Resource Book for Teachers*. Harlow: Longman.
Wichmann, A., Fligelstone, S., McEnery, T. and Knowles, G. (eds) (1997) *Teaching and Language Corpora*. London; New York: Longman,
Widdowson, H. G. (2000) 'On the Limitations of Linguistics Applied', *Applied Linguistics* 21(1): 3–25.
Willis, J. (1998) 'Concordances in the Classroom without a Computer: Assembling and Exploiting Concordances of Common Words', in B. Tomlinson (ed.) *Materials Development in Language Teaching*. Cambridge: Cambridge University Press, pp. 44–66.
Xiao, R. and McEnery, T. (2006) 'Collocation, Semantic Prosody and Near Synonymy: A Cross-linguistic Perspective', *Applied Linguistics* 27(1): 103–29.
Yoon, H. and Hirvela, A. (2004) 'ESL Student Attitudes Towards Corpus Use in L2 Writing', *Journal of Second Language Writing* 13: 257–83.

26

How can data-driven learning be used in language teaching?

Gaëtanelle Gilquin and Sylviane Granger

1. The pedagogical functions of DDL

Data-driven learning (DDL) consists in using the tools and techniques of corpus linguistics for pedagogical purposes. This type of approach presents several advantages. The first obvious one is that it brings authenticity into the classroom. Not only do corpora make it possible to expose learners to authentic language, but they can actually present them with a large number of authentic instances of a particular linguistic item. This 'condensed exposure' (Gabrielatos 2005: 10) can, among others, contribute to vocabulary expansion or heightened awareness of language patterns.

Second, DDL has an important corrective function. Learners, by comparing their own writing with data produced by (native) expert writers or by consulting a learner corpus where errors have been annotated (see Section 2 on error-tagged learner corpora), can find the help they need to correct their own interlanguage features (misuse, overuse, underuse) and thus improve their writing. As pointed out by Nesselhauf (2004: 140), this is 'particularly useful for points which have already been covered in the classroom, possibly even repeatedly, but which the learners nevertheless still get wrong': that is, for so-called fossilised errors.

The DDL approach also has the advantage of including an element of discovery which arguably makes learning more motivating and more fun. In the DDL literature, learners are described, alternatively, as travellers (Bernardini 2001: 227), researchers (Johns 1997: 101) or detectives with Johns' (1997: 101) slogan 'Every student a Sherlock Holmes'. By means of various activities (see Section 3), learners are encouraged to observe corpus data, make hypotheses and formulate rules in order to gain insights into language (inductive approach) or check the validity of rules from their grammars or textbooks (deductive approach). They thus become more involved, more active and, ultimately, more autonomous in the learning process. The learner is 'empowered' (Mair 2002), which has the effect of boosting his/her confidence and self-esteem.

More generally, learners can acquire (or at least refine) a number of crucial learning skills through the use of DDL. O'Sullivan (2007: 277) lists the following: 'predicting, observing, noticing, thinking, reasoning, analysing, interpreting, reflecting, exploring, making inferences (inductively or deductively), focusing, guessing, comparing, differentiating, theorising, hypothesising, and verifying'. These skills can be used to explore language, but since they are general cognitive skills, they may also be transferred to other fields of study.

2. Data-driven learning materials

In order to adopt a DDL methodology, two main resources are needed: a corpus and a tool to exploit the corpus (concordancing software). The choice of the corpus is crucial for, as rightly emphasised by Whistle (1999: 78), '[t]he value and usefulness of the concordance will be largely determined by the corpus'. It would probably not be wrong to say that any type of corpus may be used in DDL, and indeed, the literature on DDL mentions quite a large range of corpora: written, spoken or multimodal, monolingual or bilingual, general or specialised, native or non-native, tagged or untagged, etc. As can be expected, however, particular corpora are best suited for certain purposes. Consider the example of bilingual corpora. Such corpora may be used for two main purposes. They may help translation trainees, by 'drawing [their] attention to (un)typical solutions for typical problems found by *mature*, expert translators' (Bernardini 2004: 20; see also the chapters by Kenning and Kübler and Aston, this volume). They may also be used, with students who share the same mother tongue, to establish equivalences between the mother tongue and the target language, and especially, as Johns (2002: 114) puts it, to 'wean … students from the myth of one-to-one correspondence between first and second language'.

Whatever the type of corpus chosen, one important issue is that of its authenticity. Of course, in a way, corpora are always authentic in the sense that they contain naturally occurring language data. However, scholars like Widdowson (2000), making a distinction between text production and text reception, argue that corpora may lack authenticity at the receptive end, even though they were initially authentic. Thus, learners may find it hard to relate to texts that were produced in a different culture, within a context that is not necessarily familiar to them. The texts are therefore likely to 'remain an "anonymous mass" to the learners' (Braun 2006: 26). In fact, Sripicharn (2004) demonstrates that, while native speakers are able to contextualise concordance lines (by identifying the setting of the concordances and the text type from which they are extracted), learners usually fail to show such ability. Several solutions have been proposed in the literature to solve this problem and help learners 'authenticate' (Widdowson 2003: 66) the materials they are working with, for example involving learners in the creation of the corpus (Aston 2002), or using a corpus of recent news items (Chambers 2005: 120) or a small specialised corpus drawn from the 'genres which have relevance to the needs and interests of the learners' (Tribble 1997: 2).

Two types of corpora that appear particularly helpful for the process of authentication are the 'pedagogic corpus' (Willis 2003: 163) and the 'local learner corpus' (Seidlhofer 2002). The former consists of the texts used in the classroom to support teaching (texts from the learners' coursebooks, plus any additional texts that the teacher may have brought into the classroom). Although such a corpus may partly consist of concocted texts (in cases where some of the texts used in class were invented), these texts have already been processed for meaning by the learners, and are therefore better contextualised and more directly relevant to them (Granger, 2011). Alternatively, a corpus may also be created that comprises transcriptions of the lectures attended by the students, as experimented by Flowerdew (1993) in an English for Specific Purposes course – although building such a pedagogic corpus will naturally be more time-consuming.

The second type of corpus that seems promising in terms of authenticity is the local learner corpus. Learner corpora, which include data produced by non-native speakers of the language, have remained relatively discreet on the DDL scene up to now (Nesselhauf 2004: 140). Yet learner corpora can be extremely useful for form-focused instruction (see, e.g., Granger and Tribble 1998; Seidlhofer 2000) because they present students with typical interlanguage features, especially when the data were produced by learners from the same mother tongue background as the students. Local learner corpora even go one step further, as they contain data produced by the very same students who will be using the corpus. They are thus 'both participants in and analysts of their own language use' (Seidlhofer 2002: 213), and the interlanguage features represented in the corpus are the features of their own interlanguage. This also means that the teacher can provide 'tailor-made feedback' (Mukherjee 2006: 19) to the learners, either as a group or individually.

Another important issue when it comes to the choice of a corpus is annotation. Corpora can be used as raw text, i.e. with no annotation of any kind, or they can be tagged with additional information such as part-of-speech (POS-tagging), syntactic structure (parsing) or, in the case of learner corpora, errors (error-tagging). Raw corpora offer numerous possibilities for the exploration of language by learners. However, they also have their limitations. For example, a raw corpus may involve a lot of editing (by the teacher or learner) to get rid of unwanted concordance lines, whereas a POS-tagged or parsed corpus may help refine the search query (for example, selecting *to* as a preposition and not as an infinitive marker) and thus reduce the amount of necessary editing. As for error-tagging, it makes it much easier to notice interlanguage features and often comes with possible corrections. It should, however, be borne in mind that the annotation of tagged corpora may sometimes be problematic (mistagging, inconsistencies) and that it always reflects a certain theoretical perspective that may not be shared by the teacher. Moreover, as Gabel (2001: 284) suggests, tagging is not easy to implement within a school context – at least when, as is often the case, the teacher creates his/her own corpus rather than using a ready-made corpus.

Corpora are of little help if they are not combined with a tool to exploit them. Breyer (2006: 173) rightly remarks that the role of the concordancing software 'has hitherto been somewhat overlooked in the discussion about the application of a corpus technology in language pedagogy'. Yet, like the corpus, it is of crucial importance for the ultimate success of DDL. Higgins (1991) makes a distinction between 'research' concordancers and 'classroom' concordancers. While such a distinction is not clear-cut, since research concordancers can be used in the classroom and vice versa (as Higgins himself notes), it is still true that in order to be used in the classroom, a concordancer should ideally possess a number of characteristics. Stevens (1995: 2) gives the following list: the concordancer should be fast and responsive, it should load quickly and allow interruption at any point (with the option to work with the data already loaded at that point), it should be possible to look for more than one word at the same time and for strings of words, to use Boolean operators (AND, OR, NOT, etc.) and wild cards (to indicate any unspecified characters), and to sort the output instantaneously. To this wish list, we would like to add the possibility of easily creating exercises from the concordances. This is the case, for example, of Multiconcord (King and Woolls 1996), which allows the user to produce several types of cloze tests, or WordSmith Tools (Scott

2004), which has an option for blanking out the search-words in concordances. Last but not least, a classroom concordancer should be user-friendly. While this is an important feature for any concordancer, this is even more essential in the case of a concordancer intended for learners, who have to 'get to grips with new material (the corpora), new technology (the software) and a new approach (DDL) all at once' (Boulton 2008a: 38). After having dealt with the corpora and the software, we now turn to the DDL approach proper, and show how corpora can be used in language teaching.

3. The operationalisation of data-driven learning

The range of activities that are possible in DDL is wide and, as Breyer (2006: 162) puts it, 'limited only by the imagination of the user'. Space prevents the reviewing of all these possibilities, but in this section, we give a broad overview of the way DDL may be operationalised and show how the choice of presentation and activity depends on the learning context (e.g. one-to-one consultation vs classroom activity), the level of the learners (language proficiency and familiarity with DDL) and the object of study (e.g. vocabulary or discourse). Note that we will not deal with cases where the results of corpus analysis are used to 'inform teaching decisions' or 'prepare teaching materials' (Johns 1988: 20), although this is sometimes also referred to as DDL. Here, we will only consider cases where the learner directly interacts with the corpus.

It is probably fair to say that most DDL activities involve concordances of some sort. Concordances, however, may be presented in various ways. The concordance lines may be truncated (so-called KWIC – Key-Word-In-Context – view) or take the shape of a complete sentence; the whole concordance may be provided to the learner or just a selection of it; the concordance lines may be edited or presented in their original form; and they may be shown on screen or printed on a handout. Each presentation has its pros and cons. The KWIC view may be confusing, especially for beginners. Johns (1986: 157) observes that learners' first reaction is often to complain about the 'unfinished sentences'. However, the KWIC view, with all the occurrences of the search-word aligned under one another, makes patterns more visible than the sentence view, and Boulton (2009a) actually reports an experiment with lower-intermediate learners where KWICs provided better results than full sentence contexts. The next question is whether the concordancer output should be used as is or whether it should be manipulated in some way. Manipulation may involve the selection of a subset of the concordance, often with the aim of reducing the data to manageable quantities. Several criteria have been proposed in the literature to perform this selection, including readability (the most difficult concordance lines are discarded, cf. Kuo *et al.* 2001), frequency (only the concordance lines illustrating the most frequent uses are kept, cf. Levy 1990: 180) and usefulness (only those concordance lines that are judged useful are kept, cf. Tribble 1997: 4). However, Gabrielatos (2005: 18) rightly points out that '[t]his manipulation should be carried out with the understanding that the adapted samples are not good guides to the frequency of a language item'. Random selection, as opposed to principled selection, may help avoid this bias and maintain some semblance of fidelity to the data (cf. Johns 2002: 110). Manipulation may also consist of editing the concordances, and in particular, simplifying them (cf. Gabrielatos 2005: 18). Boulton (2009b: 89) is not in favour of such a practice, as this, according to him, undermines the 'authenticity' advantage of DDL and does not prepare learners 'for the realities of the authentic language we are presumably preparing them for'. Yet, Nesselhauf's (2004) discussion of a concordance of the verb *suggest* in the LOCNESS corpus (a corpus of argumentative essays by British and American students) and the German subcorpus of the International Corpus of Learner English is a good example of why manipulation is sometimes necessary in DDL (especially with beginners):

> As the lines are now, they could be confusing for learners in many respects: there is at least one typographical error (*suggested than* instead of *that* in LOCNESS); one of the occurrences of *to* after *suggest* does not constitute wrong complementation (*could suggest to her two colleagues*); and, as *suggest + ing* only occurs in the learner but not in the native speaker corpus, learners might even come to the conclusion that this construction is not possible in English.
>
> (Nesselhauf 2004: 143–4)

Finally, concordances may be presented on screen or on a handout (what Gabrielatos 2005: 13 describes as the hard vs soft version of DDL). The choice of the mode of presentation depends on the availability or not of the necessary hardware and software (see Section 5), but it is also a function of learners' level. Thus, Boulton (2008a: 38) suggests that 'DDL in early stages can eliminate the computer from the equation by using prepared materials on paper' (see also Whistle 1999: 78). An interesting alternative, suggested by Charles (2007), is to let the students work on a computer in class and to then provide them with a printout of the concordances for further study at home, or simply as a record of what has been done in class.

DDL activities may be located along a cline ranging from teacher-led to learner-led (Mukherjee 2006: 12; see also Gabrielatos 2005: 11). At the teacher-led end, we find relatively controlled tasks such as cloze tests and fill-in exercises. At the learner-led end, we find what Bernardini (2004: 22) calls 'discovery learning', which consists in 'brows[ing] large and varied text collections in open-ended, exploratory ways'. As we move from one end of the cline to the other, learners have more and more freedom and bear more and more responsibility for their own instruction, deciding, for example, what they are going to investigate and how they want to go about it. This explains why there should ideally be a gradual shift from one end to the other, and why teacher-led activities tend to be better suited to beginners, whereas discovery learning is often claimed to be most appropriate for 'very advanced learners who are filling in gaps in their knowledge rather than laying down the foundations' (Hunston 2002: 171). In between totally teacher-led DDL and totally learner-led DDL, there is a whole range of activities, with various types of 'filters' exercised by the teacher (Gavioli 2005: 30). By way of illustration, here are a few activities that one could propose to students. Learners could be shown a concordance sorted alphabetically and encouraged to notice the repetition of certain lexical chunks, or asked to group the patterns in a meaningful way. They could also be given a series of blanked-out concordances illustrating different contexts of a word and be required to find the missing word. Alternatively, the concordances could come from a bilingual corpus, so that learners can use the translations to help them find the missing word more easily. The potential of DDL for editing one's own work has already been mentioned, and many studies in the literature show how students can use corpora to revise their work, either by correcting problems underlined by the teacher or by deciding themselves what they want to check with the help of the concordancer (Kennedy and Miceli 2001: 81). One use that in our opinion tends to be neglected in the DDL literature is the use of the concordancer as a 'sleeping resource' (Johns 1988:

22), to help learners when the need arises. In the same way as it has become natural to have a dictionary in most language classrooms and to consult it in case of doubt, we would like, one day, to see every classroom equipped with a computer, and students using it to query a corpus in order to answer a question that has suddenly arisen during the lesson.

In what precedes, we have mainly dealt with activities involving concordances. While this is probably the main component of DDL (and in fact, according to some strict definitions, its only component, cf. Johns and King 1991: iii), other possibilities exist. Thus, frequency lists, which list all the words of the corpus in descending order of frequency, may prove to be a valuable resource as well. Aston (2001) suggests using them in (literary) text-analysis, as a means of learning more about the subject of the text and its meaning. It is also possible to compare two frequency lists built on the basis of different corpora. The comparison could involve two varieties of English (e.g. British vs American English) or two genres or text types (e.g. fiction vs journalese, speech vs writing), with the aim of making learners more sensitive to language variation. Learners could also compare a frequency list representing learner production (ideally, their own production) and one representing expert production, which would make them aware of the words that tend to be underused or overused by learners. The words from the frequency lists can then be used as starting points for concordance analysis. Most concordancers nowadays also make it possible to automatically extract collocates and word clusters. These, like frequency lists, may serve as a good starting point for the further analysis of language – in this case, language in its phraseological dimension (cf. Cheng 2007). Another way to exploit corpora in the classroom is to read entire portions of the corpus. This is what Charles (2007: 295) recommends for the study of rhetorical functions: a particular search item is used as 'a probe to locate the part of a text in which a given rhetorical function may occur', and the context is then expanded to the whole paragraph or the whole text to see how the function is expressed.

The choice of presentation and activity depends on a number of factors, among them the learning context, the level of the learners and the object of study. Thus, actual use of the corpus ('hard' version of DDL) and focus on the learner's individual needs may be easier in the context of a one-to-one consultation (such as described by Johns 2002: 111ff) than in the context of a classroom activity – and virtually impossible to implement if a sufficient number of computers is not available in the classroom. An activity meant to be carried out as part of a homework assignment or in distance education (Collins 2000) may have to contain more explicit instructions and 'signposts' than one which takes place in class, with the teacher as a guide and the fellow students as 'travel companions'. The learner's level (in terms of both language proficiency and familiarity with DDL) has already been shown to be important when deciding on a particular presentation of the data and a specific activity. This probably explains why scholars do not seem to agree on the level of the learners for whom DDL is appropriate. Depending on the methods they have in mind, DDL may be suitable for a given audience or not. In fact, it has been argued that DDL is possible with all learners (even beginners), but that (1) the method has to be adapted to the learners' level (Hadley 2002) and (2) results may vary, with beginners 'draw[ing] relatively low-level conclusions about the structuring of the language' and more advanced learners 'mak[ing] more subtle high-level inferences' on the basis of one and the same concordance (Johns 1986: 159). Another aspect that should be taken into account when choosing a way of approaching DDL is the object of study. Many authors claim that DDL is most effective 'on the 'collocational border' between syntax and lexis' (Johns 2002: 109; see also Levy 1990 or O'Sullivan and Chambers 2006). However, it works with other topics too (for example, some aspects of discourse or grammar), although, here again, some adaptation may be required.

A final note is that, despite the attraction of some methods (as noted above, the concordance is particularly popular among DDL specialists) and some linguistic phenomena (Kennedy and Miceli 2001: 83, for example, refer to the 'lure of prepositions'), a key word in DDL is variety. Not only does variety make it possible to prevent tediousness among learners (a problem often highlighted in the literature, cf. Chambers 2007: 12), but it also caters to learners' different preferences and learning styles. Similarly, since it is precisely one of the goals of DDL to develop a more autonomous learning style, the teacher should avoid conformity as far as possible and agree to let the students approach corpora in the way they feel most comfortable with (Hunston 2002: 193).

4. Assessing the effectiveness of data-driven learning

One important question to ask regarding DDL is whether it works and actually facilitates language learning. It must be admitted that, at this stage, very little is known about the effectiveness of DDL, and it is a recurrent theme in the DDL literature that more empirical studies are needed to validate this approach (see, among many others, Bernardini 2001: 247; Hadley 2002: 120 or Mukherjee 2006: 21). Often, the claims about the effectiveness of DDL are more of an act of faith, sometimes relying on subjective observation or informal testing, but usually engaging in pure speculation. Three types of evaluation can be carried out (Boulton 2008b: 41): evaluation of the attitudes (what do participants think about DDL?), practices (how well are the learners doing with DDL?) and efficiency (can learners gain benefit from DDL?). While attitudes and practices are important, the criterion that, ultimately, should be decisive in determining whether DDL is worth doing or not is efficiency. Learners may enjoy DDL and be good at it, but if they do not learn anything from it there is no point in adding this to a curriculum that is already overloaded. Despite the crucial importance of this criterion, Boulton (2008b: 42) observes that very few studies seek to quantitatively assess the efficiency of DDL, and that in most of the studies that do, no control group is involved, which seriously calls into question the validity of these studies.

As regards attitudes, a survey of the literature reveals extremely mixed results. While Ilse (1991: 107) points out that learners found the approach 'fascinating', Whistle (1999: 77) notes that it was 'fairly unpopular with a majority of students'. Some authors report both positive and negative attitudes among the same learners. Kennedy and Miceli's (2001: 80) students, for example, found DDL helpful and confidence-boosting, but sometimes also discouraging, time-consuming and frustrating. The same mixed results appear when considering learners' capacities to do DDL (cf. Kennedy and Miceli 2001, Hadley 2002 and Sripicharn, this volume). As for efficiency, which we consider crucial for the future of DDL, most studies report some gain from DDL, though usually not very substantial (see e.g. Cobb 1997). As Boulton (2009b) rightly points out, however, DDL may have little impact on the knowledge of the question at hand, but have longer-term effects on the development of more general skills.

While these results may not be as outstanding as one may have wished or hoped for on the basis of some of the claims found in the literature, there are encouraging signs that DDL may deserve a place in the language classroom. Yet one must recognise, along with

Barbieri and Eckhardt (2007: 320) and several other scholars, that '[d]espite the wealth of existing publications on classroom concordancing … the impact of concordancing and DDL in LT [language teaching] has been relatively inconspicuous'. This is because the implementation of DDL in the classroom poses a number of practical problems, which may discourage teachers from adopting this methodology, despite its numerous theoretical advantages. The major problems and limitations of DDL are examined in the next section.

5. The problems and limitations of data-driven learning

We will consider four aspects of DDL that may be problematic: the logistics, the teacher's point of view, the learner's point of view and the content of DDL. Logistics is often cited as one of the biggest problems of DDL. If learners are to actually use corpora in the classroom, they need computers (ideally one per student, but at least one for every two or three students), but also corpora and text retrieval software. All this costs a lot of money, which schools and universities are not always able to afford – or are not ready to invest without a clear guarantee that this will be profitable (cf. Hadley 2002: 110). It is true that some resources are freely available: certain concordancers and corpora, or data that can be compiled into a corpus (data from the web, essays produced by one's students, etc.). However, it should be borne in mind that these resources may have more limited functionalities than expensive tools and that, for some data, copyright clearance might be necessary. The soft version of DDL requires slightly less technological equipment. Sometimes it is possible to get hold of ready-made DDL worksheets, but such resources are very rare, especially on the publishing market (Thurstun and Candlin 1997 and Tribble and Jones 1997 are two exceptions). Most of the time, therefore, the teacher will have to create his/her own materials, which still implies access to a computer (but just one), a corpus and a concordancer. Creating one's own materials, however, takes time. Time, precisely, is another obstacle to the implementation of DDL. Not only is it time-consuming for the teacher to prepare the teaching materials, but it is also time-consuming to train students to deal with corpora and, perhaps more importantly, to complete a DDL task (Díez Bedmar 2006 describes an activity that took an hour and a half for just one word). And according to some, the results 'might not repay the time taken' (Willis, cited in Hunston 2002: 178).

If we consider the teacher's point of view, one reason for not doing DDL might simply be that the teacher does not know enough about corpora and the possibility of using corpora in the classroom. There would therefore be a need for 'in-service teacher training programmes' (Mukherjee 2006: 10). As Mauranen (2004: 100) points out, '[b]efore learners can be introduced to good corpus skills, their teachers need to possess them in the first place'. But it could also be that the teacher is familiar with corpora and DDL but prefers, for some reason, not to adopt such a methodology with his/her students. Logistic reasons may account for this choice (see above), or scepticism about the efficiency of DDL (see Section 4), but as pointed out by Boulton (2009b: 99), it might be that these practical objections are actually 'camouflage for more profound theoretical concerns about the nature of learning, and more especially of teachers' and learners' roles'. Although, as noted above, DDL activities may be situated along a continuum from teacher-led to learner-led, it is nonetheless true that teachers have a less central role in DDL than in traditional teaching. They tend to have relatively little control over what happens during the lesson, which may be 'incompatible with the "minimum risk" scenario which can be found in many teaching cultures' (Boulton 2009b: 93). In addition, since the computer becomes the main source of knowledge, this may be experienced as a 'loss of expertise' by the teacher (Hunston 2002: 171). DDL, therefore, requires that teachers take risks, and agree to 'let go' and let the student take pride of place in the classroom.

For learners too, DDL may sometimes appear rather off-putting. Working with corpora is not straightforward and necessitates quite some training to acquire the basic skills – what Mukherjee (2002: 179) calls 'corpus literacy' (see also Sripicharn, this volume on the importance of preparing learners for using language corpora). Whistle (1999: 77) reports the case of some students who 'failed to see anything' and 'failed to formulate any clear rules'. Students may have 'difficulty devising effective search strategies' (O'Sullivan and Chambers 2006: 60) because of faulty spelling, for example, or simply because of the complexity of the processes involved (see Sun 2003: 607–8 for a good example of ineffective search strategy), and they may draw wrong inferences on the basis of the evidence (cf. Sripicharn 2004). It must also be stressed that DDL (and, in particular, the inductive learning strategies that it often entails) may be suitable for certain learners only, depending on their learning style.

The final aspect that may explain some of the reluctance to apply DDL has to do with its content. We have already mentioned the problem of authentication (or lack thereof) of the corpus data. In addition, the output of the search query may contain too much or too little data, or no data at all – which, for learners, poses the question of the distinction between 'does not exist' and 'is not represented in the corpus' (cf. Kennedy and Miceli 2001: 86). It may include too much 'noise', i.e. irrelevant hits, or it may be too difficult for learners to understand because of insufficient knowledge of the target language (Koosha and Jafarpour 2006: 206). It could also be that the corpus shows more details than the student is expected to learn or contains language which the teacher does not want the students to imitate, for example non-standard forms, swear words or literary phrases (see also Aston 1999; Kübler and Aston, this volume on the possible unreliability of translations in bilingual corpora). Another problem is that the DDL approach may not be effective for all aspects of language, with some questions more 'concordance-ready' than others (Johns 1988: 25). Someya (2000), for example, explains that errors in prepositions are more easily dealt with by means of concordances than errors in articles. More generally, Gabrielatos (2005: 21) warns against the dangers of 'corpus worship' and 'frequency worship', thus suggesting that corpora and DDL are no panacea and that other tools besides corpora and other factors besides frequency have to be considered for teaching to be successful.

All this does not mean that DDL should be abandoned altogether. It is a promising technique which, as noted earlier, brings learners into contact with (potentially) authentic language, motivates them by introducing an element of discovery, develops important cognitive skills and, more generally, provides benefits which go well beyond the knowledge of the item under study. However, the above list of problems should encourage us to think more deeply about the best ways of implementing DDL and, in particular, about the importance of adapting DDL to the specific learning situation in which it takes place (learners' levels, object of study, availability of equipment, etc.). Equally important is the necessity of going through a phase of validation – as one would do for any new teaching method – to test the efficiency of DDL. As long as such validation has not been carried out, it might be better to start off with a modest introduction and to leave more radical incorporation of DDL into the curriculum for later, when its efficiency has been proved and when students have got used to it.

Further reading

Boulton, A. (2009) 'Data-driven Learning: Reasonable Fears and Rational Reassurance', *Indian Journal of Applied Linguistics* 35(1): 81–106. (This paper deals with the main obstacles to the implementation of DDL and provides some possible solutions.)

Cobb, T. (1997) 'Is There Any Measurable Learning from Hands-on Concordancing?' *System* 25(3): 301–15. (This is one of the few empirical studies that seek to test the efficiency of DDL.)

Granger, S. and Tribble, C. (1998) 'Learner Corpus Data in the Foreign Language Classroom: Form-Focused Instruction and Data-Driven Learning', in S. Granger (ed.) *Learner English on Computer*. London: Longman, pp. 199–209. (This paper demonstrates the relevance of learner corpora to DDL.)

Johns, T. (1988) 'Whence and Whither Classroom Concordancing?' in T. Bongaerts, P. de Haan, S. Lobbe and H. Wekker (eds) *Computer Applications in Language Learning*. Dordrecht: Foris, pp. 9–33. (This is a good overview of the main uses of concordancing in the classroom.)

Sun, Y.-C. (2003) 'Learning Process, Strategies and Web-Based Concordancers: A Case Study', *British Journal of Educational Technology* 34(5): 601–13. (This paper gives a good example of how learners can go wrong in drawing inferences on the basis of corpus data.)

References

Aston, G. (1999) 'Corpus Use and Learning to Translate', *Textus* 12: 289–314.

——(2001) 'Learning with Corpora: An Overview', in G. Aston (ed.) *Learning with Corpora*. Houston, TX: Athelstan, pp. 7–45.

——(2002) 'The Learner as Corpus Designer', in B. Kettemann and G. Marko (eds) *Teaching and Learning by Doing Corpus Analysis*. Amsterdam: Rodopi, pp. 9–25.

Barbieri, F. and Eckhardt, S. E. B. (2007) 'Applying Corpus-based Findings to Form-focused Instruction: The Case of Reported Speech', *Language Teaching Research* 11(3): 319–46.

Bernardini, S. (2001) '"Spoilt for Choice": A Learner Explores General Language Corpora', in G. Aston (ed.) *Learning with Corpora*. Houston: Athelstan, pp. 220–49.

——(2004) 'Corpora in the Classroom. An Overview and Some Reflections on Future Developments', in J. Sinclair (ed.) *How to Use Corpora in Language Teaching*. Amsterdam: John Benjamins, pp. 15–36.

Boulton, A. (2008a) 'DDL: Reaching the Parts Other Teaching Can't Reach?' in A. Frankenberg-Garcia, T. Rkibi, M. R. Cruz, R. Carvalho, C. Direito and D. Santos-Rosa (eds) *Proceedings of the 8th Teaching and Language Corpora Conference*. Lisbon: Associação de Estudos e de Investigação Cientifica do ISLA-Lisboa, pp. 38–44.

——(2008b) 'Esprit de corpus: promouvoir l'exploitation de corpus en apprentissage des langues', *Texte et Corpus* 3: 37–46.

——(2009a) 'Testing the Limits of Data-driven Learning: Language Proficiency and Training', *ReCALL* 21(1): 37–54.

——(2009b) 'Data-driven Learning: Reasonable Fears and Rational Reassurance', *Indian Journal of Applied Linguistics* 35(1): 81–106.

Braun, S. (2006) 'ELISA: A Pedagogically Enriched Corpus for Language Learning Purposes,' in S. Braun, K. Kohn and J. Mukherjee (eds) *Corpus Technology and Language Pedagogy*. Frankfurt am Main: Peter Lang, pp. 25–47.

Breyer, Y. (2006) '*My Concordancer*: Tailor-made Software for Language Teachers and Learners', in S. Braun, K. Kohn and J. Mukherjee (eds) *Corpus Technology and Language Pedagogy*. Frankfurt am Main: Peter Lang, pp. 157–76.

Chambers, A. (2005) 'Integrating Corpus Consultation in Language Studies', *Language Learning and Technology* 9(2): 111–25.

——(2007) 'Popularising Corpus Consultation by Language Learners and Teachers', in E. Hidalgo, L. Quereda and J. Santana (eds) *Corpora in the Foreign Language Classroom*. Amsterdam: Rodopi, pp. 3–16.

Charles, M. (2007) 'Reconciling Top-down and Bottom-up Approaches to Graduate Writing: Using a Corpus to Teach Rhetorical Functions', *Journal of English for Academic Purposes* 6: 289–302.

Cheng, W. (2007) 'Concgramming: A Corpus-driven Approach to Learning the Phraseology of Discipline-specific Texts', *CORELL: Computer Resources for Language Learning* 1: 22–35.

Cobb, T. (1997) 'Is There Any Measurable Learning from Hands-on Concordancing?' *System* 25(3): 301–15.

Collins, H. (2000) 'Materials Design and Language Corpora: A Report in the Context of Distance Education', in L. Burnard and T. McEnery (eds) *Rethinking Language Pedagogy from a Corpus Perspective*. Frankfurt: Peter Lang, pp. 51–63.

Díez Bedmar, M. B. (2006) 'Making Friends with DDL: Helping Students Enrich Their Vocabulary', *Humanising Language Teaching* 8(3), available at www.hltmag.co.uk/may06/mart02.htm

Flowerdew, J. (1993) 'Concordancing as a Tool in Course Design', *System* 21(2): 231–43.

Gabel, S. (2001) 'Over-indulgence and Under-representation in Interlanguage: Reflections on the Utilization of Concordancers in Self-Directed Foreign Language Learning', *Computer Assisted Language Learning* 14(3–4): 269–88.

Gabrielatos, C. (2005) 'Corpora and Language Teaching: Just a Fling or Wedding Bells?' *TESL-EJ* 8(4): 1–35; available at www.tesl-ej.org/ej32/a1.html

Gavioli, L. (2005) *Exploring Corpora for ESP Learning*. Amsterdam: John Benjamins.

Granger, S. (2011) 'From Phraseology to Pedagogy: Challenges and Prospects', in T. Herbst, S. Faulhaber and P. Uhrig (eds) *The Phraseological View of Language: A Tribute to John Sinclair*. Berlin: Walter de Gruyter, pp. 123–46.

Granger, S. and Tribble, C. (1998) 'Learner Corpus Data in the Foreign Language Classroom: Form-focused Instruction and Data-driven Learning', in S. Granger (ed.) *Learner English on Computer*. London: Longman, pp. 199–209.

Hadley, G. (2002) 'An Introduction to Data-driven Learning', *RELC Journal* 33(2): 99–124.

Higgins, J. (1991) 'Which Concordancer? A Comparative Review of MS-DOS Software', *System* 19(1–2): 91–100.

Hunston, S. (2002) *Corpora in Applied Linguistics*. Cambridge: Cambridge University Press.

Ilse, W.-R. (1991) 'Concordancing in Vocational Training', in T. Johns and P. King (eds) 'Classroom Concordancing', special issue of *ELR Journal* 4: 103–13.

Johns, T. (1986) 'Micro-Concord: A Language Learner's Research Tool', *System* 14(2): 151–62.

——(1988) 'Whence and Whither Classroom Concordancing?' in T. Bongaerts, P. de Haan, S. Lobbe and H. Wekker (eds) *Computer Applications in Language Learning*. Dordrecht: Foris, pp. 9–33.

——(1997) 'Contexts: The Background, Development and Trialling of a Concordance-based CALL Program', in A. Wichmann, S. Fligelstone, T. McEnery and G. Knowles (eds) *Teaching and Language Corpora*. London: Longman, pp. 100–15.

——(2002) 'Data-driven Learning: The Perpetual Challenge', in B. Kettemann and G. Marko (eds) *Teaching and Learning by Doing Corpus Analysis*. Amsterdam: Rodopi, pp. 107–17.

Johns, T. and King, P. (eds) (1991) 'Classroom Concordancing', special issue of *ELR Journal* 4.

Kennedy, C. and Miceli, T. (2001) 'An Evaluation of Intermediate Students' Approaches to Corpus Investigation', *Language Learning and Technology* 5(3): 77–90.

King, P. and Woolls, D. (1996) 'Creating and Using a Multilingual Parallel Concordancer', *Translation and Meaning* 4: 459–66.

Koosha, M. and Jafarpour, A. A. (2006) 'Data-driven Learning and Teaching Collocation of Prepositions: The Case of Iranian EFL Adult Learners', *Asian EFL Journal* 8(4): 192–209.

Kuo, C.-H., Wible, D., Wang, C.-C. and Chien, F. (2001) 'The Design of a Lexical Difficulty Filter for Language Learning on the Internet', in *Proceedings of the IEEE International Conference on Advanced Learning Techniques (ICALT'01), Madison, WI, 6–8 August 2001*, pp. 53–4; available at www2.computer.org/portal/web/csdl/abs/proceedings/icalt/2001/1013/00/10130053abs.htm

Levy, M. (1990) 'Concordances and their Integration into a Word-processing Environment for Language Learners', *System* 18(2): 177–88.

Mair, C. (2002) 'Empowering Non-native speakers: The Hidden Surplus Value of Corpora in Continental English Departments', in B. Kettemann and G. Marko (eds) *Teaching and Learning by Doing Corpus Analysis*. Amsterdam: Rodopi, pp. 119–30.

Mauranen, A. (2004) 'Spoken Corpus for an Ordinary Learner', in J. Sinclair (ed.) *How to Use Corpora in Language Teaching*. Amsterdam: John Benjamins, pp. 89–105.

Mukherjee, J. (2002) *Korpuslinguistik und Englischunterricht: Eine Einführung*. Frankfurt am Main: Peter Lang.

——(2006) 'Corpus Linguistics and Language Pedagogy: The State of the Art – and Beyond', in S. Braun, K. Kohn and J. Mukherjee (eds) *Corpus Technology and Language Pedagogy*. Frankfurt am Main: Peter Lang, pp. 5–24.

Nesselhauf, N. (2004) 'Learner Corpora and their Potential for Language Teaching', in J. Sinclair (ed.) *How to Use Corpora in Language Teaching*. Amsterdam: John Benjamins, pp. 125–52.

O'Sullivan, Í. (2007) 'Enhancing a Process-Oriented Approach to Literacy and Language Learning: The Role of Corpus Consultation Literacy', *ReCALL* 19(3): 269–86.

O'Sullivan, Í. and Chambers, A. (2006) 'Learners' Writing Skills in French: Corpus Consultation and Learner Evaluation', *Journal of Second Language Writing* 15: 49–68.

Scott, M. (2004) *WordSmith Tools version 4*. Oxford: Oxford University Press.

Seidlhofer, B. (2000) 'Operationalizing Intertextuality: Using Learner Corpora for Learning', in L. Burnard and T. McEnery (eds) *Rethinking Language Pedagogy from a Corpus Perspective*. Frankfurt: Peter Lang, pp. 207–23.

——(2002) 'Pedagogy and Local Learner Corpora: Working with Learning-Driven Data', in S. Granger, J. Hung and S. Petch-Tyson (eds) *Computer Learner Corpora, Second Language Acquisition and Foreign Language Teaching*. Amsterdam: John Benjamins, pp. 213–34.

Someya, Y. (2000) 'Online Business Letter Corpus KWIC Concordancer and an Experiment in Data-driven Learning/Writing', paper presented at the 3rd Association for Business Communication International Conference, Kyoto, 9 August.

Sripicharn, P. (2004) 'Examining Native Speakers' and Learners' Investigation of the Same Concordance Data and its Implications for Classroom Concordancing with ELF Learners', in G. Aston, S. Bernardini and D. Stewart (eds) *Corpora and Language Learners*. Amsterdam: John Benjamins, pp. 233–45.

Stevens, V. (1995) 'Concordancing with Language Learners: Why? When? What?' *CAELL Journal* 6(2): 2–10; available at www.vancestevens.com/papers/archive/concordance1996.htm

Sun, Y.-C. (2003) 'Learning Process, Strategies and Web-based Concordancers: A Case Study', *British Journal of Educational Technology* 34(5): 601–13.

Thurstun, J. and Candlin, C. (1997) *Exploring Academic English: A Workbook for Student Essay Writing*. Sydney: CELTR.

Tribble, C. (1997) 'Improvising Corpora for ELT: Quick-and-dirty Ways of Developing Corpora for Language Teaching', paper presented at the first international conference Practical Applications in Language Corpora, University of Lodz, Poland; available at www.ctribble.co.uk/text/Palc.htm

Tribble, C. and Jones, G. (1997) *Concordances in the Classroom: A Resource Book for Teachers*, second edition. Houston: Athelstan.

Whistle, J. (1999) 'Concordancing with Students Using an "Off-the-Web" Corpus', *ReCall* 11(2): 74–80.

Widdowson, H. G. (2000) 'On the Limitations of Linguistics Applied', *Applied Linguistics* 21(1): 3–25.

——(2003) *Defining Issues in English Language Teaching*. Oxford: Oxford University Press.

Willis, D. (2003) *Rules, Patterns and Words. Grammar and Lexis in English Language Teaching*. Cambridge: Cambridge University Press.

27

How can we prepare learners for using language corpora?

Passapong Sripicharn

1. Getting started: finding out what students know and providing general information

Students may have different backgrounds concerning language corpora or different levels of familiarity with corpus-based materials or activities. It is, therefore, important to survey students' basic knowledge of corpora and to avoid a classroom scenario where the teacher wastes the class time introducing corpora and concordancing tools to fairly experienced corpus users.

A wide range of survey techniques can be used to elicit information about learners' backgrounds. The teacher may begin a lesson with a class discussion asking the students to report what they know about language corpora and their experience of using them. Apart from an oral discussion, a written survey in the form of questionnaires, checklists or quizzes can be administered to give the teacher some ideas about learners' prior knowledge of corpus-related issues. Survey questions may include items aiming at checking general understanding of language corpora such as types of corpora, basic functions of corpus analysis tools, and basic terminology. Questions concerning experiences of using such tools or experiences of working on corpus-informed materials and corpus-based tasks can also be part of the questionnaires. In addition, the survey may be conducted to survey learners' attitudes towards the corpus-based approach. A combination of survey formats can be used such as scales, ranks or checklists. To sum up, a survey may be outlined as follows:

Part I: General information about corpora
Part II: Tests on basic corpus terminology
Part III: Corpora and corpus information tools
Part IV: Experiences with corpus-based material
Part V: Attitudes towards corpus-based activities/Problems of using language corpora.

To check the reliability of the survey information, the teacher can give quizzes or tests about language corpora to find out whether students really know what they report in a survey. General questions can be asked, for example, 'What is a corpus?' 'How can a corpus be built?' 'What is a concordancer or concordancing software?' 'What are basic functions of such computer programs?' The students can also be asked to do corpus-based exercises or browse a corpus on a computer, so the teacher can observe the learners' corpus skills and evaluate their familiarity with corpora.

If the survey results or observations of students' work with corpus materials show that the students do not have sufficient background, some general information about language corpora should be provided such as the nature of corpus data, different types of corpora, basic functions of concordancing tools, the unique characteristics of concordance lines, a brief review of the literature on corpus linguistics, and strengths and limitations of language corpora for the purpose of language analysis.

An introduction to language corpora can be given through formal instruction such as an introductory lesson or lecture by either the teacher or a guest lecturer who is an expert or researcher in corpus linguistics. Exercises aimed at giving general information about language corpora can be implemented in an introductory lesson, such as a matching exercise where learners match types of corpora with their definitions. Alternatively, an interactive lesson can be introduced in which students have some hands-on experience with language corpora in a computer lab, such as following an online introductory lesson on corpora, cutting and pasting texts to create a mini-corpus of their own, or doing a simple search or query. More learner-centred approaches can be adopted such as discussion or presentation in which students are asked to do research on general concepts of language corpora, or web-based activities where students are given links to websites which give information or useful links about corpora and their applications and share the information with their peers.

If class time is limited, learners can be asked to find general information about language corpora on their own from introductory books on corpus linguistics or classroom concordancing such as Tribble and Jones (1990); Kennedy (1998); McEnery and Wilson (2001); Meyer and Ebrary (2002); Hunston (2002); Sinclair (2003); Teubert and Cermakova (2007); or books on corpus terminology such as Baker *et al.* (2006).

2. Identifying task objectives and types of corpora

Learner as researcher/discovery learning

Some learners use language corpora to uncover language patterns and use. Corpus-based tasks are particularly useful when learners take the role of researcher or language detective in which their findings or generalisations are driven by corpus data, the approach known as data-driven learning (DDL) (Johns 1991) or Discovery Learning (DL) (Bernardini 2000, 2004), where learners act as travellers exploring a corpus to find possible answers to their linguistic queries. For this purpose, learners should base their conclusions on a fairly large, general corpus to avoid the trap of over-generalisation. They should also be trained to query the data, which will be discussed in some detail in Section 4.

Learners using a corpus for hypothesis testing

Learners may form hypotheses regarding meaning or use of particular words or phrases, and consult a corpus to confirm or reject such hypotheses. For example, they may intuitively form an assumption that, when signalling cause and effect, the phrase 'owing to' seems to correlate with negative situations, whereas the phrase 'thanks to' draws either neutral or positive collocates. Concordance data from the Bank of English corpus can confirm this hypothesis, as 'owing to' collocates strongly with negative words such as 'injury', 'bad weather', 'inability', while 'thanks to' is often followed by words with positive connotation such as 'recent research', 'the latest technology', 'its relationship with' or 'a massive police presence'. Concordance data can be also used to reject hypotheses or provide negative evidence to challenge some prescriptive grammatical rules. For instance, most EFL teachers prescribe that 'ever' will never be used in the perfect aspect in an affirmative sentence (e.g. *I have ever been to Hong Kong'). But learners who look for instances of 'have/has ever' in the BNC corpus will find a number of examples where 'ever' is used with superlative adjectives in a statement such as 'This is the most beautiful place I have ever been' or 'It was the worst performance we have ever given'. Again, learners need a lot of corpus data and some interpretation training to provide evidence or counter-evidence to come up with decent confirmation or rejection of their original assumptions.

Learners using a corpus for error correction

Some learners may want to use a corpus for self-correction of their language output. In a study on learners' self-correction based on corpus data, Watson Todd (2001) asked his students to choose two misused content words for self-correction, consulting data from a web-based concordance such as 'alltheweb' or 'webcorp'. In another study (O'Sullivan and Chambers 2006), the students used corpus data to revise their first-draft writings in a number of areas of grammatical and lexical errors. (See Chambers, this volume, on the use of corpora in the teaching of writing.) Students can browse a general corpus to induce rules or patterns in the revision process. Alternatively, they can exploit a learner corpus, which consists of texts written by learners, to compare and contrast their own writings with texts retrieved from native speaker corpora, which can help them correct language mistakes in their writing tasks. (See various papers about the applications of a learner corpus in Granger 1998; Granger *et al.* 2002; Barbieri 2004; Davies 2004; Nesselhauf 2004; and Zwier 2005).

Learner using a corpus for contrastive studies and translation

Students can study language corpora to explore similarities or differences in terms of word use and pattern across languages (see various papers in Granger *et al.* 2003). Corpora can be particularly useful when comparisons are made between words of similar form from different languages which appear to carry the same meaning but may differ in terms of collocation and connotation such as 'correct' (English) and 'corretto' (Italian) (Partington 1998). Corpora can also be used as resources for translation and translators (Baker 1993). If task objectives are concerned with contrastive studies and translation, learners should be exposed to a wider range of corpora such as monolingual corpora of languages under investigation as well as comparable and parallel corpora (for more on parallel and comparable corpora, see chapters by Kenning and Kübler and Aston, this volume).

Learners using the corpus learn about genre

Learners may learn about different text types such as narrative, academic essays, newspaper articles and so on. In a macro analysis, corpora made up of texts in a particular genre can reveal words, phrases or patterns typical to that text type such as is shown in work by Biber *et al.* (2002), Biber and Ebrary (2006) and Flowerdew (2002). In a micro analysis, collections of extracts from different parts or moves of a text type can help students learn about distinctive lexico-grammatical patterns which characterise a particular move such as reporting clauses in academic citations (Charles 2006) or language features in different stretches of lecture introductions (Lee 2009). To carry out genre analysis tasks, learners can make use of available specialised corpora, but they also need to learn how to compile their own corpora composed of specialised texts to address their specific queries.

Learners using the corpus to generate targets for self-study in specialised areas

Learners can do other tasks on specialised corpora such as generating a word list based on texts under examination, as done in large-scale research such as that of Coxhead and Nation (2001) and Vongpumivitcha *et al.* (2009). In doing so, the students can come up with a small glossary or terminology, or simply create a word list which reflects their needs, and at a later stage methodically learn these words. If the students decide to do tasks of this nature, they should be guided all through the process of compiling their own corpus with an emphasis on criteria for choosing texts such as corpus size, number of texts, text type and authorship (for more details on working with specialised corpora, see Bowker and Pearson 2002; Paulussen 2003; Gavioli 2005; Fuentes 2008).

3. Preparing corpus data

Preparing learners to use available corpus data

Learners may have different access to corpus data. Some students are equipped with subscribed corpora such as the BNC corpus. Others are advised to use freely available corpus resources such as web concordancing. Once the target corpora are identified, learners should study them in detail to make the most of the data. A good starting point is to ask general questions about the composition or characteristics of the corpus under examination such as 'Is it a corpus of written or spoken texts?' 'Is it a general or specialised corpus?' 'Is the corpus tagged or untagged?' 'How many text files make up the corpus?' 'Where are the texts taken from?' 'What are the texts mainly about?' Questions can be asked about the overall lexical information of a corpus such as the types and tokens of words in a corpus or frequency information (e.g. the most frequent words or more specifically the most frequent nouns, verbs or adjectives.)

Next, learners should study the content and composition of the corpus. Commercial corpora usually come with detailed instructions for users which include descriptions on corpus sources and content, so students can choose a corpus, or corpora, that meets their needs the most. Other sources such as online corpora may have fairly limited information about the available corpora, so the students should learn to get more information by themselves. For example, when browsing online corpora, students should take a tour of the web page by scrolling down the list of provided corpora. Some corpus titles contain clues to the characteristics of the corpus e.g. 'BNC Written' (= a corpus of written texts). If the titles do not clearly suggest the data content, learners may put a search word to get some concordance lines and try to identify the content of the corpus based on the context of the data (e.g. clues suggesting that the data are transcriptions of spoken English or texts taken from literary works such as poems or novels).

Preparing learners to build their own corpora

If the tasks demand that students build their own corpora, particularly corpora of specialised texts, students should first of all be informed about criteria for the compilation. (See Bowker and Pearson (2002: 45–52) for a checklist for building your own corpus.) Students should also be aware of some technical issues such as saving texts as a plain text file (with the extension .txt), using file names that give useful information about the data sources, or organising corpus files and folders. Learners should also pay attention to practical issues involving the feasibility of the compilation, source of information, copyrights and permission. As far as legal and ethical issues are concerned, students should be asked to consider whether they can legally download the texts from the target sources or not. A sample letter asking for permission to collect and store texts electronically for corpus analysis is given in Bowker and Pearson (2002: 60).

To give learners some practice, learners may collect texts on any topic they like. Clear instructions should be given at each state of the corpus building. For example, if students are interested in sports such as football, they can be asked to compile a small corpus of football news. The data can be subsequently used for different purposes such as practice in data processing when learners start using concordancing tools, or data for small-scale research on specialised vocabulary, or data for terminology work (e.g. a glossary of football terminology). When doing their own corpus projects, students should begin with a small project aimed at building a monolingual corpus of about 5,000–10,000 words. The texts should be primarily taken from internet or electronic sources so that the students can quickly cut texts from the original sources and paste them into a text file. More experienced compilers can then use a wider variety of sources which include non-electronic materials that are converted into text files in a scanning process.

Preparing learners to deal with a large amount of corpus data

Inexperienced corpus users can be overwhelmed by a large amount of data, whether they use existing or self-compiled corpora. More problems can be expected when the tasks involve unguided browsing of a large corpus. Teachers or trainers may use a scaffolding technique to help students become familiar with the data, starting with handouts with short tasks using clear examples for the corpus data. The following is a set of teacher-selected concordance lines and questions designed to raise awareness of collocation and patterns that can be observed.

```
          of filth on Ted Hughes, stand a chance against the inner life of an ex-
       this season, Haslam has taken his chance and become a regular in the side.
    till the tears came. When Alec got a chance, he put in a word. Mum, Dad said I
            Taylor said. It will be the only chance I'll ever have to be compared with
          In a sense, this is their last chance. If both sides can resolve the
    skills and would therefore stand no chance if either one of these two Tawnies
       betting, in effect, that his best chance is to wait for the management-pilot
       has the imagination to seize this chance is an open question. So it was
```

```
          them what amounts to an outside chance of victory. Whoever wins, to have
         away. All you have to do to have a chance of scooping two briefs is simply
         And that is why he knows his best chance of getting people on side is by
              Belt this year. And to get the chance of appearing on a bill with Naz is
          age of five he had a much greater chance of delinquency than if he was in
          sir. I'm afraid there is little chance of justice. You will go back to
   also decided that the bid had little chance of being revived and marked
          on the pressure. mcmenemy had a chance right in front of goal but failed
                restricted, there is a real chance that the society could go bust.
     one pill each day. Since there is a chance the pill may not work properly in
           Prospective buyers will have a chance to bid for treasures not seen on
     wreaths. The bugler was not given a chance to sound Reveille, which
             that game, but I never had the chance to meet Derek until I came up for
     worried that he would never get the chance to star for his country again. So
           on his jury address as the best chance to save his clients skin. The
```

(Bank of English Corpus)

Questions:

1 What is the search word or the word under examination?
2 What are the adjectives used before 'chance'? What are the other types of words used before 'chance'?
3 What preposition is most frequently used after 'chance'? What are the other types of words used after 'chance'?
4 What are the extended patterns or expressions of 'chance' (e.g. 'have little chance of doing something'?

This presentation of concordance lines on paper can be followed by more complex tasks such as searches on specific items which have been worked through on the handout task. For instance, in the 'chance' task shown above, students can be assigned to browse a large corpus to follow up the searches, narrowing the searches down to the pattern 'have/had + chance', or to retrieve concordance lines for other words such as 'opportunity' or 'occasion' for subsequent analysis on the differences between the three words.

As learners may find the data too overwhelming in such browsing, they should know how to limit the data to make the data manageable, such as specifying the number of concordance lines to be displayed or choosing data only from a specific corpus or sub-corpora. Another way to make the data manageable is to start working with small homogeneous corpora which are made up of short texts of the same type such as 'Lonely Heart' ads (Gavioli 2001). In such a small corpus, learners are more likely to find a small amount of concordance lines for a search word, and the instances generated tend to show recurring patterns which are visible for an analysis.

Preparing learners to query the data

Formulation of questions or queries is an integral part of each learner's preparation to process corpus data. Questions may arise from what students produce, such as errors or wrong use of words or patterns identified by the teacher (Watson Todd 2001). In a more learner-centred approach, such as data-driven learning (DDL) (Johns 1991) or serendipity learning (Bernardini 2000), learners may be encouraged to formulate questions on their own. However, it should be pointed out to the students that some types of questions are more suitable for corpus analysis than others. Specifically, it should be made clear to the students that a corpus is at its best when users look for information about phraseology or pattern of a word or a phrase, or any questions which involve the observation of word or phrase in context.

Examples of areas of investigation and sample questions which can be given to students to facilitate their query formulation are shown in Table 27.1.

4. Getting to know corpus analysis tools

Giving an introduction and technical support

Teachers should be aware that levels of learner computer literacy may vary, so it is important to give a proper introduction and the clearest possible instructions on how to operate corpus analysis tools. Basic technical preparation includes teaching learners how to install and run concordancing tools from a computer, and how to upload corpora to be ready for analysis by the tools.

In a pre-lesson task, the students may be assigned to read articles or textbooks which give explanations about the functions and examples of data output generated by each function: for example, see the introductory section of O'Keeffe *et al.* (2007: 8–14). They may be also required to study manuals of the software that they will be using, which usually explain in some detail how those functions are used. To help learners digest such technical information, the teacher should design a workshop where learners work on computers and do some tasks to develop corpus techniques.

Getting to know a concordancer

For general language analysis, perhaps the most useful function is concordancing, which basically searches the selected corpus files and displays examples of words or phrases with contexts on the screen. As a quick practice, the students can be asked to type in any word or phrase they want and see how many concordance lines they get. This seems to be a more enjoyable experience than being forced to search a word given by the teacher.

Table 27.1 Areas of corpus investigation and sample questions

Areas of investigation	*Sample questions*
Grammatical questions	• Is 'advice' a count or non-count noun? • What is the noun suffix of 'employ'?
Collocation/phraseological questions	• What are common adjectives used in front of 'argument? • What words can we use to describe our body parts (e.g. 'hair', 'nose', 'eyes')?
Connotation/semantic prosody	• What are the differences between 'childish' and 'childlike'? • What are the differences between 'utterly', 'bitterly' and 'absolutely'?
Synonyms/near synonyms	• What are the differences between words in the following pairs: trip–journey; hide–conceal; attempt–try; talk–converse?
Literal/metaphorical use	• What are metaphorical uses of words literally used to describe nature such as 'flood', 'sea', 'light', 'dark'?

In later tasks, guided instruction can be given to focus learners on the examination of particular words in the selected corpora.

When learners start generating concordance lines, it is time to raise their awareness of the characteristics or distinctive features of concordance lines, particularly those presented in the Key-Word-in-Context (KWIC) format. The teacher can present concordance samples and ask learners to comment on the format of the lines, or ask them to compare concordance lines with full-sentence examples taken from other sources such as a dictionary. The teacher should also draw learners' attention to the advantages of presenting data in such a format as well as limitations about what a concordance can tell concordance readers and what it cannot. (See detailed descriptions of basic concordancing functions in the chapter by Tribble in this volume.) For example, the following points should be raised in an introduction to the concordancing function:

- Concordance lines cannot be generated if learners do not specify a target corpus. Learners may ask the program to generate concordance lines from all the target corpora or choose from particular sub-corpora.
- Concordance lines cannot be produced unless learners key in the correct form of query (e.g. some tools allow only simple 'single item' search, others offer complex searches such as multi-word or wildcard searches).
- The number of generated lines can be specified. If not, most tools will display all the hits found in the target corpora. The amount of data can be limited in other ways, such as choosing lines randomly from each sub-corpus.
- Most concordancing software presents KWIC concordance lines, but some tools also have other display options, such as a full-sentence format.
- The data can be saved and edited. Some tools have a straightforward 'save' button and the saved concordance lines will be stored as plain text, which can be edited and printed out using standard word processing software. It should be noted that some editing may be needed so that the search words are neatly presented in the middle of the page as seen on the screen (e.g. using size 8 or 9 of the Courier New font, or setting a wider margin on either side of the page).

Learners also need to learn how to sort immediate left and right contexts of the search word in alphabetical order so that repeated context words are put together to create visual patterns on either side of the search item. Generally, learners should be asked to do both left and right sorting to make patterns of the search word more salient (and some tools allow sorting in both positions to be done at the same time). However, learners should be aware that sorting on either side may reveal different kinds of pattern. For example, if learners are investigating a noun, left sorting would make it easy to notice common adjectives or determiners that precede the search noun, whereas sorting the immediate right context would reveal typical post-nominal patterns such as prepositional phrases or noun clauses.

Getting to know different types of query

It can be seen that generating concordance lines may not require a great deal of training. Where learners may need some practice is in how to form a 'query' or, to put it simply, how to type a word or string of words in the 'search box' to get the sorts of examples they want in order to address their research questions. Students should study the query system or search options available in the software. Standard programs should at least be able to allow single-word searches, while more advanced programs have a wide range of search options, such as searching phrases or strings of words. 'Wildcard' searches (usually adopting the * symbol, e.g. 'financ*') will look for instances of words beginning with the search form/root and include all the possible suffixes or inflections such as 'finance', 'financing', 'finances', 'financial') (see the chapter by Tribble for more on concordance search options).

Some software also has an 'associated word' option which gives only concordance lines where the search word and the specified associated word appear next to or close to each other. For example, a search for 'chance' with the associated word 'have or has' will show concordance lines with patterns such as 'have a good chance', 'have little chance' or 'have no chance'. Learners should be trained to select search options which meet their research questions as illustrated in a sample task below.

Directions: The underlined words or phrases in each of the following statements contain errors or inappropriate use. Get some concordance lines and use the information you get to suggest a revised version for each statement. The query for each search word has been given.

Original version	*Possible Search words*	*Revised version*
If you have any questions, you can contact with any staff at the office.	'contact'	
My roommate always makes me feeling better when I am sad.	'makes me' Or 'made me'	
I was disappoint the results.	'disappoint*'	
We have a very chance to pass the exam.	have (associated word = chance)	

Getting to know other tools

Learners will find other tools such as frequency lists useful when they want to examine a corpus (in most cases a self-compiled corpus) in great detail. For example, making a frequency list would provide basic information about lemmatisation such as the total number of word types and tokens as well as type-token ratios. A list of lexical items created from a corpus can be used by learners to meet their specific needs, such as helping learners to prioritise their vocabulary learning, or to identify key words in a specialised corpus.

It should be pointed out to learners that they can manipulate frequency list to meet different task objectives. For instance, sorting in alphabetical order is more efficient if the task aims at creating a list of all lexical items, while sorting in rank order would be a preferable tool when the task involves extracting term candidates for constructing a glossary of technical terms. Some tools offer the function of reverse word sorting, which can be particularly useful if the students want to study suffixes or inflections. Learners can also use the keyness function to compare a word list under study with other lists. Keyword lists can make specialised vocabulary stand out and help with the study of lexical patterns across genres, as the lists often discard frequent words or grammatical items which seem to appear in all text types.

5. Interpreting corpus results

A number of studies have reported successful DDL activities in which learners use small or large corpora to find answers to their own queries and come up with interesting or even surprising information from the corpus, such as Bernardini (2000), Sripicharn (2004) and various papers in Aston (2001) and Aston *et al.* (2004). However, some research on classroom concordancing has suggested that learners working with a corpus seem to have problems of interpreting corpus results such as over-generalisation of rather limited data (Sripicharn 2003), lack of strategies to draw appropriate conclusions from a corpus (Kennedy and Miceli 2001) or problems of interpreting word lists and concordances (Braun 2007). Therefore, it is important to give new corpus users some training to improve their corpus analytical skills, particularly in the areas discussed below.

Training learners to read and interpret concordance lines

To begin with, learners' attention should be drawn to the characteristics of concordance lines (for example, by introducing some references such as Tribble and Jones 1990; Willis 1998; Sinclair 2003). A table such as Table 27.2, summing up a list of dos and don'ts when reading the concordance output, can be given to the students.

Then, learners' attention should be drawn to the sorts of information that can be noticed in concordance lines. For new corpus users, concordance lines can be pre-selected to make some language features more clearly noticeable. However, it should be noted that such pre-selection of corpus data is used for training purposes only, as random

Table 27.2 A summary of dos and don'ts when reading and interpreting concordance lines

Dos	*Don'ts*
☑ Be aware that a KWIC concordance line was cut and pasted according to a distance to the left and right of the search word. So it may or may not be a complete sentence.	☒ Don't try to find the beginning and the end of a sentence in a KWIC concordance line.
☑ Be aware that the lines were taken from different texts or different positions of the same text. Each line has its own context.	☒ Don't read the lines continuously as if they were taken from a paragraph of the same text.
☑ Pay no great attention to the overall context, e.g. what topic is being discussed or who did what to whom. Only look at some context clues that would help you guess meaning (and sometimes connotation) of the search word.	☒ Don't try to make complete sense of the lines. Don't think that it is a must to understand the context, e.g. where the lines are taken from, what topic is being discussed, what story is going on.
☑ Focus your attention on the search word and its collocates or patterns.	☒ Don't try to read and understand every single word in a line.
☑ Notice immediate left or right contexts of the search word first. But also look for extended patterns as well.	☒ Don't look only at immediate contexts to the left or right of the search word.
☑ Interpret the lines with caution because the data may be too limited to make strong generalisations.	☒ Don't base conclusions completely on the lines that you are observing.

presentation of concordance lines is likely to produce more 'messy' lines which are not relevant to the points under study and may present some exceptions to the rules or observations being generalised. Concordance data can be accompanied by questions or consciousness-raising techniques such as circling or underlining context clues to raise awareness of the points to be observed. More advanced users can put in search words and obtain concordance lines by themselves. To make the observation more meaningful, excerpts from students' tasks or mistakes made by learners can serve as a task 'prompt' or form a basis of a corpus analysis.

Observation and interpretation of concordance lines may begin with the basics, for instance noticing grammatical collocates and other grammatical features, such as the verb 'be' used before an adjective, or a typical preposition that follows a noun or an adjective. At a next level, students should learn how to notice lexical collocates such as V + N or ADJ + N. They can begin their observation by circling or underlining the nouns or adjectives that appear next to either side of the search word. Further interpretation should also be encouraged, such as drawing generalisations about semantic relations of the typical collocates under examination. For example, students may pay attention to common noun collocates of the verb 'conduct' or nouns in strong collocation with the adjective 'hazardous', and then explore the similarity in meaning of the nouns based on provided sets of concordance lines. (See Partington 1998 and Hunston 2002: Ch. 3 for examples of corpus-based analysis on various linguistic features.)

So far, most practices are based on the observation of a set of concordance lines taken from a general corpus. A more advanced training in corpus investigation and interpretation should also deal with noticing data from different corpora such as general versus specific corpora, or written versus spoken corpora. The differences can be highlighted by asking learners to examine the same word that may be used differently or have different meanings when appearing in different types of corpus.

Finally, students should also be trained to read and interpret a wider context of concordance data, particularly when words or phrases are to be examined at a discourse level or when pragmatic meaning is the focus of investigation. For example, Hunston (2002: 58) suggests that a large context of concordance lines for 'I must admit' is needed to deduce subtle meaning and pragmatic function of the phrase, which is often used to signal remarks that can be offensive to either the hearer or a third party. (Also see Partington 1998: Ch. 6 for an investigation of a wider context of concordance data to study cohesion in text.)

Training learners to interpret quantitative results

While most corpus-based activities involve qualitative interpretation of corpus data such as deducing language use and patterns from concordance output, quantitative interpretation of corpus data is also useful, particularly for corpus-based terminology or corpus-based contrastive or interlanguage studies (e.g. comparing frequencies of words in a native speaker corpus and learner corpus to study under- or over-use; see various papers in Granger *et al.* 2002). Therefore, learners should be trained to make sense of the numeral outputs a concordancing tool can generate, such as word frequency, word cluster analysis and keyness values. (See Hunston 2002: Ch. 4 for guidelines for interpreting quantitative corpus data.)

It should be noted that learners may need to make both quantitative and qualitative interpretations when they explore a corpus. Numeral information such as frequency or keyness gives an overview or general descriptive information about the corpus under investigation, while qualitative analysis such as reading concordance lines gives details about word use, meaning and patterns. Decisions can be based on the objectives of the corpus task. For example, terminological work may rely more on numeral and statistical data for choosing term candidates, whereas lexical or pragmatic analysis of words or phrases can be better done qualitatively.

Caution in data interpretation

Finally, it is important to discuss with students some precautions they should take when they interpret corpus data. For example, it should be pointed out to the students that concordance lines cannot tell the reader what is right and wrong. They are simply instances of a search item. (An error-tagged corpus may give such information but usually tagged concordance lines are not so user friendly and students need some training to read and interpret them.)

Learners should be warned about the trap of over-generalisation by making too strong conclusions when they work only on limited data. They also need to consider all the variables that may affect the interpretation. For instance, when comparing frequencies of two or more corpora, results concerning over- or under-use, or statistics, should be interpreted with caution because the compared corpora may not be entirely comparable. So the conclusions should be tentative in nature, and learners should be advised to use hedging words or phrases such as 'seem to', 'is likely to', 'is typically or commonly or frequently used' when they report their interpretation to show that they have made cautious interpretations of the corpus evidence. Training is also needed in recognising skewed data, particularly when the observed data come from a small corpus or from one batch of files where patterns found may be specific to that particular set of data.

Further reading

Aston, G. (2001) *Learning with Corpora*. Houston, TX: Athelstan. (This book suggests rationales for using corpora with learners with an emphasis on how to train learners to explore corpus data autonomously.)

Aston, G., Bernardini, S. and Stewart, D. (2004) *Corpora and Language Learners*. Amsterdam: John Benjamins. (This book discusses a wide range of pedagogical applications of language corpora, and gives a number of examples of activities designed to help learners examine and interpret corpus data.)

Hunston, S. (2002) *Corpora in Applied Linguistics*. Cambridge: Cambridge University Press. (This book gives a clear, easy-to-read introduction to language corpora and concordancing tools, and also contains useful chapters on corpus data interpretation with plenty of examples.)

References

Aston, G. (2001) *Learning with Corpora*. Houston, TX: Athelstan.

Aston, G., Bernardini, S. and Stewart, D. (2004) *Corpora and Language Learners*. Amsterdam: John Benjamins.

Baker, M. (1993) 'Corpus Linguistics and Translation Studies – Implications and Applications', in M. Baker, G. Francis, J. Sinclair and E. Tognini Bonelli (eds) *Text and Technology: In Honour of John Sinclair*. Amsterdam: John Benjamins, pp. 233–52.

Baker, P., Hardie, A. and McEnery, T. (2006) *A Glossary of Corpus Linguistics*. Edinburgh: Edinburgh University Press.

Barbieri, F. (2004) 'Computer Learner Corpora, Second Language Acquisition and Foreign Language Teaching', *Tesol Quarterly* 38(4): 751–3.

Bernardini, S. (2000) *Competence, Capacity, Corpora: A Study in Corpus-aided Language Learning*. Bologna: Cooperativa Libraria Universitaria Editrice Bologna.

——(2004) 'Corpora in the Classroom: An Overview and Some Reflections on Future Developments', in J. M. Sinclair (ed.) *How to Use Corpora in Language Teaching*. Amsterdam: John Benjamins, pp. 15–38.

Biber, D. and Ebrary, I. (2006) *University Language: A Corpus-based Study of Spoken and Written Registers*. Amsterdam: John Benjamins.

Biber, D., Fitzmaurice, S. M. and Reppen, R. (2002) *Using Corpora to Explore Linguistic Variation*. Amsterdam: John Benjamins.

Bowker, L. and Pearson, J. (2002) *Working with Specialized Language: A Practical Guide to Using Corpora*. London: Routledge.

Braun, S. (2007) 'Integrating Corpus Work into Secondary Education: From Data-driven Learning to Needs-driven Corpora', *ReCALL* 19(3): 307–28.

Charles, M. (2006) 'Phraseological Patterns in Reporting Clauses Used in Citation: A Corpus-based Study of Theses in Two Disciplines', *English for Specific Purposes* 25: 310–31.

Coxhead, A. and Nation, P. (2001) 'The Specialized Vocabulary of English for Academic Purposes', in J. Flowerdew and M. Peacock (eds) *Research Perspectives on English for Academic Purposes*. Cambridge: Cambridge University Press, pp. 252–67.

Davies, M. (2004) 'Computer Learner Corpora, Second Language Acquisition, and Foreign Language Teaching', *Modern Language Journal* 88(3): 469–70.

Flowerdew, J. (2002) *Academic Discourse*. London: Longman.

Fuentes, A. C. (2008) 'Corpus Linguistics and Specialized Discourse: Different Points of View', *Discourse Studies* 10(6): 813–15.

Gavioli, L. (2001) 'The Learner as Researcher: Introducing Corpus Concordancing in the Classroom', in G. Aston (ed.) *Learning with Corpora*. Forlí: CLUEB, pp. 108–37.

——(2005) *Exploring Corpora for ESP Learning*. Amsterdam: John Benjamins.

Granger, S. (1998) *Learner English on Computer*. London: Longman.

Granger, S., Hung, J. and Petch-Tyson, S. (2002) *Computer Learner Corpora, Second Language Acquisition and Foreign Language Teaching*. Amsterdam: John Benjamins.

Granger, S., Lerot, J. and Petch-Tyson, S. (2003) *Corpus-based Approaches to Contrastive Linguistics and Translation Studies*. Amsterdam: Rodopi.

Hunston, S. (2002) *Corpora in Applied Linguistics*. Cambridge: Cambridge University Press.

Johns, T. F. (1991) 'Should You Be Persuaded: Two Examples of Data-driven Learning', in T. F. Johns and P. King (eds) *ELR Journal Vol. 4: Classroom Concordancing*. Birmingham: CELS, University of Birmingham, pp. 1–16.

Kennedy, C. and Miceli, T. (2001) 'An Evaluation of Intermediate Students' Approaches to Corpus Investigation', *Language Learning and Technology* 5: 77–90.

Kennedy, G. D. (1998) *An Introduction to Corpus Linguistics*. London; New York: Longman.

Lee, J. J. (2009) 'Size Matters: An Exploratory Comparison of Small- and Large-class University Lecture Introductions', *English for Specific Purposes* 28: 42–57.

McEnery, T. and Wilson, A. (2001) *Corpus Linguistics: An Introduction*. Edinburgh: Edinburgh University Press.

Meyer, C. F. and Ebrary, I. (2002) *English Corpus Linguistics: An Introduction*. Cambridge: Cambridge University Press.

Nesselhauf, N. (2004) 'Learner Corpora and their Potential for Language Teaching', in J. M. Sinclair (ed.) *How to Use Corpora in Language Teaching*. Amsterdam: John Benjamins, pp. 125–52.

O'Keeffe, A., McCarthy, M. J. and Carter, R. A. (2007) *From Corpus to Classroom: Language Use and Language Teaching*. Cambridge: Cambridge University Press.

O'Sullivan, Í. and Chambers, A. (2006) 'Learners' Writing Skills in French: Corpus Consultation and Learner Evaluation', *Journal of Second Language Writing* 15(1): 49–68.

Partington, A. (1998) *Patterns and Meanings: Using Corpora for English Language Research and Teaching*. Amsterdam: John Benjamins.

Paulussen, H. (2003) 'Working with Specialized Language: A Practical Guide to Using Corpora', *Applied Linguistics* 24(4): 553–6.

Sinclair, J. (2003) *Reading Concordances: An Introduction*. London: Pearson/Longman.

Sripicharn, P. (2003) 'Evaluating Classroom Concordancing: The Use of Concordance-based Materials by a Group of Thai Students', *Thammasat Review* 8(1): 203–36.

——(2004) 'Examining Native Speakers' and Learners' Investigation of the Same Concordance Data and its Implications for Classroom Concordancing with EFL Learners', in G. Aston, S. Bernardini and D. Stewart (eds) *Corpora and Language Learners*. Amsterdam: John Benjamins, pp. 233–44.

Teubert, W. and Cermakova, A. (2007) *Corpus Linguistics: A Short Introduction*. London: Continuum.

Tribble, C. and Jones, G. (1990) *Concordances in the Classroom: A Resource Book for Teachers*. London: Longman.

Vongpumivitcha, V., Huanga, J. and Chang, V. (2009) 'Frequency Analysis of the Words in the Academic Word List (AWL) and Non-AWL Content Words in Applied Linguistics Research Papers', *English for Specific Purposes* 28: 33–41.

Watson Todd, R. (2001) 'Induction from Self-selected Concordances and Self-correction', *System* 29: 91–102.

Willis, J. (1998) 'Concordances in the Classroom without a Computer: Assembling and Exploiting Concordances of Common Words', in B. Tomlinson (ed.) *Materials Development in Language Teaching*. Cambridge: Cambridge University Press, pp. 44–66.

Zwier, L. J. (2005) 'Computer Learner Corpora, Second Language Acquisition, and Foreign Language Teaching', *Studies in Second Language Acquisition* 27(1): 10.

Section VI

Designing corpus-based materials for the language classroom

28

What can a corpus tell us about vocabulary teaching materials?

Martha Jones and Philip Durrant

1. What vocabulary is important for my learner?

Language teachers have long used lists of important vocabulary as a guide to course design and materials preparation, and corpus data have always played a major part in developing these lists. As early as the 1890s, Kaeding supervised a manual frequency count of an eleven-million-word corpus to identify important words for the training of stenographers, and similar counts were used by language teachers from at least the early twentieth century onwards (Howatt and Widdowson 2004: 288–92). The argument for prioritising vocabulary learning on the basis of frequency information is based on the principle that the more frequent a word is, the more important it is to learn. Proponents of a frequency-based approach point to the fact that a relatively small number of very common items accounts for the large majority of language we typically encounter. Nation (2001: 11), for example, reports that the 2,000-word families of West's (1953) *General Service List* account for around 80 per cent of naturally occurring text in general English. This suggests that a focus on high-frequency items will pay substantial dividends for novice learners since knowing these words will enable them understand much of what they encounter (Nation and Waring 1997: 9).

The development of computerised corpus analysis has made the job of compiling word-frequency statistics far easier than it once was, and has given impetus to a new wave of pedagogically oriented research (e.g. Nation and Waring 1997; Biber *et al.* 1999; Coxhead 2000). Importantly, the widespread availability of corpora and the ease of carrying out automated word counts seems also to offer individual teachers the possibility of creating vocabulary lists tailored to their learners' own needs. However, it is important to bear in mind that corpus software is not yet able to construct pedagogically useful word lists without substantial human guidance. Teachers wishing to create such lists will need to make a number of important methodological decisions, and to make these decisions well will need to understand the issues surrounding them.

The first set of decisions that need to be made concerns the choice or construction of a suitable corpus. With the large number of corpora available today, and the relative ease of constructing a corpus tailor-made for a given project, it should be possible to ensure a good match between the corpus and the target language. However, it remains essential that this be based on careful needs analysis. Section 3 of the present chapter describes the issues involved in corpus design in more detail.

A second, and less well-researched, decision is that of defining what sorts of items are to be counted as 'words' (Gardner 2008). The teacher will need to decide, for example, whether morphologically related forms (e.g. *run* and *running*) should be listed as two separate words or treated as a single item; in other words, whether they should be 'lemmatised'. Similar decisions must be made for the different senses of polysemous words (e.g. *run* (a race) and *run* (a company)). A list which conflates a range of forms, meanings and phrases under the heading of a single abstract 'word' will achieve excellent economy of description. However, such economy can be bought only with the loss of potentially important information. Clearly, some forms, senses and collocations of a high-frequency headword like *run* are more important to learn than others, and many are probably less important than lower-frequency words. Unless separate frequency counts are given, however, a list will give no grounds for prioritising such learning.

Some researchers have justified the use of abstract word groups on the grounds that once one form of a word is learned, learning the related forms requires little extra effort (Nation 2001: 8), and that abstract semantic representations can be given to cover a range of polysemous senses (Schmitt 2000: 147–8). However, others have noted that the learning of morphologically related items may not be as automatic as has sometimes been thought (Gardner 2008: 249–50; Schmitt and Zimmerman 2002), and it is not clear that abstract meaning representations will give learners the information they need to use words effectively. It also seems likely that learners will need to have multi-word expressions brought explicitly to their attention (Coxhead 2008; see also chapters by Greaves and Warren and Coxhead, this volume).

Any decision on this issue must, in the ultimate analysis, depend on what the list will be used for. If a list is intended primarily as an inventory of important vocabulary for comprehension, for example, then many distinctions between forms and senses may be considered less important, since related forms and meanings may be deducible by learners in context. However, if the intention is to specify items over which learners should have accurate active control, a more fine-grained approach may be needed. Another important factor is the time allowed for carrying out the research: automated corpus analysis tools are not yet able adequately to distinguish between different senses of words, and the accuracy of the quantitative means of identifying collocations on which automatic processing depends remains open to debate (see the next section). Extensive manual analysis would be required in order to provide a listing which takes such variations into account.

A further consideration that needs to be borne in mind by word-list compilers is that frequency is not the only factor which might make a word worthy of attention. In compiling the well-known *General Service List*, West and his colleagues considered a number of criteria other than frequency: less frequent words were included if they could be used to convey a range of important concepts; words were excluded if a synonym was available; words needed to be stylistically neutral; and 'intensive emotional' words (i.e. items 'whose only function is to be the equivalent of underlining, or an exclamation mark') were not included (West 1953: ix–x). Other factors which have been suggested as criteria include the likely difficulty of a word for the learners in question (Ghadessy 1979) and the subjective 'familiarity' and psychological 'availability' of words (i.e. how readily they come to a native speaker's mind), factors which are suggested to identify words which carry important semantic content (Richards 1974). Teachers may also need to consider which words belong together as natural 'sets'. O'Keeffe *et al.* (2007: 40), for example, point out that there are wide differences in the frequencies of the names of different days of the week, with Friday, Saturday and Sunday being the most common, and Tuesday and Wednesday far less frequent. As these authors remark, however, there are few who would propound teaching only the most frequent of these names as basic vocabulary and leaving the others for later. In short, a careful consideration of a range of factors other than frequency is likely to improve the value of any pedagogical list.

2. Vocabulary materials and formulaic language

One of the central insights to come from corpus linguistics in the last thirty years is the extent to which competent language users draw not only on a lexicon of individual words, but also on a range of lexicalised phrasal units which have come to be known as 'formulaic sequences' (Wray 2002; Schmitt 2004). Exactly what should count as a formulaic sequence remains disputed, but a list might include:

- collocations and colligations: *hard luck*, *tectonic plates*, *black coffee*, *by the way*;
- pragmatically specialised expressions: *Happy Birthday*, *Pleased to meet you*, *Come in*;
- idioms: *the last straw*, *fall on your sword*, *part and parcel*;
- lexicalised sentence stems: *what's* X *doing* Y (as in *what's this fly doing in my soup*), X BE *sorry to keep* TENSE *you waiting* (as in *Mr Jones is sorry to have kept you waiting*).

What these items have in common is that they appear to be, in Wray's words, 'prefabricated: that is, stored and retrieved whole from memory at the time of use, rather than being subject to generation or analysis by the language grammar' (Wray 2002: 9).

Defined in this way, such sequences are arguably part of the vocabulary of the language which learners need to acquire, and a number of writers have emphasised the importance for learners of getting to grips with items of this sort (e.g. O'Keeffe *et al.* 2007: Ch. 3; Coxhead 2008). Constructing utterances from formulae, rather than stringing together individual words according to the rules of grammar, is held both to be cognitively efficient (Ellis 2003) and to give the speaker a better chance of hitting on the natural, idiomatic way of expressing themselves (Kjellmer 1990; Hoey 2005). For these reasons, a good knowledge of formulae is generally thought to be important for achieving both fluency (Pawley and Syder 1983; Raupach 1984; Towell *et al.* 1996; Kuiper 2004; Wood 2006) and nativelike production (Pawley and Syder 1983; Kjellmer 1990). More controversially, some researchers have claimed that the acquisition of grammar is based on a process of abstracting away from an inventory of initially rote-learned formulas (Nattinger and DeCarrico 1992: 114–16; Lewis 1993: 95–8), though this idea is hotly disputed (Wray 2000).

If we accept that formulae are an important aspect of vocabulary learning, then our vocabulary materials need to be adapted or extended to include them. However, this raises two difficult problems. First, we need to determine which word strings are formulaic. Second, we need to decide which of the many formulae known to native speakers learners most need to learn.

Wray (2002: Ch. 2) describes four prominent methods for identifying formulae: intuition (formulae are those sequences which the analyst, or their informant(s), recognises as formulaic); frequency (formulae are those sequences which occur with a certain frequency in a corpus); structure (formulae are those sequences which are anomalous in that they do not follow the usual rules of the language); and phonology (formulae are sequences which are phonologically coherent). All of these identification criteria are problematic, however, because all of them are indirect. The definition of formulae as items which are retrieved from memory depends, as Wray notes, on an 'internal and notional characteristic' – retrieval from memory – which is not directly observable (2002: 19). Each approach therefore can only give us clues about, rather than confirmation of, formulaicity.

Within corpus linguistics, the primary identification criterion has been frequency of occurrence. The logic of this approach is two-fold: on the one hand, common phrases are held to be common as a result of their being stored in language users' mental inventories and so frequently retrieved from memory in preference over less conventional expressions; on the other hand, phrases which are common in the language a speaker hears are more likely to become 'entrenched' in their lexicon. The frequency approach has the advantage over other methods of relative objectivity, and of allowing large amounts of text to be easily processed; it also bypasses the possible problems of subjectivity and inconsistency to which human analysts may be prone (Wray 2002: 25). However, it also has a number of important shortcomings.

First, there is the problem of corpus representativeness and variation between speakers: all speakers have a different history of exposure to the language, and a corpus cannot give a perfect reflection of any of them. The fact that a particular phrase is common in a particular corpus does not, therefore, guarantee that it will have been common in the experience of any particular speaker. This problem is compounded by the fact that formulae are often closely associated with particular contexts. Second, the relationship between frequency and formulaicity cannot be a straightforward one because it is known that many archetypally formulaic expressions (especially, for example, idioms) are relatively infrequent, while many word sequences which we would not want to call formulae (especially combinations of high-frequency words which come about by chance or grammatical concord, e.g. *and in the*) can be very frequent (see Greaves and Warren, this volume, who look at this kind of sequence in the context of multi-word units). Relatedly, many writers have questioned the basic assumption that frequent word sequences are frequent because they are stored in the mind. Corpus linguists need to be wary here of the fallacy of 'introjection' (Lamb 2000) – the naive ascription of all patterns of language directly to real features of the human mind. It may be that a sequence is frequent because of some psychological factor, but it is also possible that it is frequent simply because of 'the nature of the world around us': '[t]hings which appear physically together', 'concepts in the same philosophical area', and 'organising features such as contrasts or series' (Sinclair 1987: 320).

Furthermore, the job of the vocabulary materials developer does not end once formulae have been identified. They also need to determine which of the 'hundreds of thousands' of such items estimated to exist in the average native lexicon (Pawley and Syder 1983: 210) learners most need to know. An obvious corpus-based solution would again be to select the most frequent formulae. This would be a natural extension of a frequency-based approach to identification. However, it would also be open to the pedagogical objections discussed in the previous section against using frequency to determine the contents of word lists.

It will be clear to the reader that methods in this important area are still very much in their infancy, and developments are ongoing. To date, perhaps the most sophisticated attempt to come to terms with the problem of estimating formulaicity (i.e. mental storage) from frequency, and of matching both with pedagogical usefulness, has been that of Ellis *et al.* (2008), who combined frequency-based and psycholinguistic methods with a survey of teacher intuitions to construct a listing of useful phrases for students of English for Academic Purposes. If we are to produce principled listings of conventional formulae, much more work along these lines will be needed.

3. What type of corpus is suitable for academic vocabulary learning?

As mentioned in Section 1, a corpus should include the target language students will be exposed to as part of their studies. A number of corpora focusing on English for Academic Purposes have recently been developed in an attempt to meet the needs of international students studying in higher education. For an overview of recently compiled EAP corpora, see chapters by Coxhead and Lee, this volume and Krishnamurthy and Kosem (2007).

Academic written English has long been the focus of corpora compilers and researchers, as EAP students need to learn the appropriate language to read academic texts efficiently and write clearly, accurately and appropriately according to conventions established by the members of academic communities in specific disciplines. The British Academic Written English Corpus (BAWE) (Nesi *et al.* 2005), which has recently been made available to researchers, consists of 6.5 million words of proficient student writing covering four levels of study on undergraduate and taught postgraduate programmes and four broad disciplinary areas (arts and humanities, social sciences, life sciences and physical sciences). This corpus will undoubtedly prove to be valuable to researchers but it is not clear whether EAP practitioners who wish to use some of the data for the development of teaching materials will be able to have access to this material. Another example of an EAP corpus of academic written English which will be made available is the Michigan Corpus of Upper-Level Student Papers (MICUSP). Other smaller EAP corpora, some of which include PhD theses, have been compiled by individuals, but the data are not always readily available.

The Academic Word List (AWL) (Coxhead 2000; Coxhead and Byrd 2007), based on a corpus consisting of approximately 3.5 million words and covering a wide range of academic texts from a variety of subject areas in four faculty areas (arts, commerce, law and science) is now widely used by researchers, materials writers (e.g. McCarthy and O'Dell 2008), EAP practitioners and students. It is considered to be a good example of language-in-use focused on academic writing and the main aim of its compilation was to provide words deemed to be core academic vocabulary worth learning. However, this view is challenged by Hyland and Tse (2007), who found that occurrence and behaviour of individual lexical items varied across disciplines in terms of range, frequency, collocation and meaning, which led to the conclusion that the AWL is not as general as it is claimed to be.

As mentioned in Section 1, careful needs analysis is at the centre of the construction of a corpus which represents the target language. McEnery and Wilson (1996) note that sampling and representativeness are crucial in the compilation of a corpus which is representative of the type of language to be examined, as tendencies of that variety of language together with their proportions can be illustrated accurately. It is important to define a *sampling frame*: that is, the entire population of texts from which samples can be taken. Nesi *et al.* (2005: 2) provide information on possible sampling methods such as random sampling (every subset of the same size has an equal chance of being selected), stratified sampling (population first divided into strata and then random sampling used), cluster sampling (population divided into subgroups and only some of those subgroups are chosen), quota sampling (population is cross-classified along various dimensions deemed important and quotas are established for each of the subgroups), opportunistic sampling (taking whatever members of the population are easy to get hold of) and purposive sampling (an expert in a relevant field chooses cases on the basis of a judgement as to how well they exemplify a particular population).

Corpus size is another important aspect of corpus compilation to consider. While a small corpus (e.g. a corpus of less than a million words) may be sufficient to portray grammatical features for learners to explore, a larger corpus (e.g. one of tens of millions of words) is needed in order to generate frequency lists of words and phrases considered to be representative of the type of language under examination, especially when it comes to 'occurrences of salient but infrequent items so that relevant patterns of use can be observed' (O'Keeffe *et al.* 2007: 55).

In Section 5 we describe the compilation of a corpus of science and engineering research articles, discuss issues related to approaches used for designing vocabulary teaching materials, and provide samples of teaching materials based on this corpus.

4. What vocabulary input do my teaching materials provide?

A number of studies based on comparisons of linguistic features portrayed in academic writing textbooks and corpus-based research into language actually used in expert and student writing have identified a lack of fit between the two. Harwood (2005: 150), for example, notes that 'textbooks are found to understate the enormous disciplinary variation in style and language which corpora reveal' and goes on to add that 'a lack of specificity can mislead and distort' (ibid.: 155).

Another example of the discrepancy between recommendations given in textbooks as regards language use and evidence from corpus-based research of real language usage is the study conducted by Paltridge (2002). He compared the advice on organisation and structure of theses and dissertations and the structure of master's and doctoral theses, as evidenced in a corpus. He found that while published handbooks did cover some aspects of the research *process*, they did not provide information on the content of individual chapters or the range of thesis types that his corpus study revealed.

In Section 1 we suggested that in order to produce pedagogically useful word lists, considerable human guidance is necessary. Ideally, the selection of raw data on which to base teaching materials should be conducted by an EAP teacher with experience in the analysis and exploitation of language corpora although perhaps only a few EAP teachers may have been trained to do so. Evidence of how materials developers give serious consideration to theoretical and pedagogical aspects of materials design and development, whether the materials are produced for local, international, commercial or non-commercial consumption can be found in Harwood (forthcoming).

In the absence of corpus data on which to base materials development or an appropriate textbook, a number of teachers resort to the creation of in-house materials which will involve the adaptation of authentic texts or texts found in textbooks. As Samuda (2005: 235) notes, 'teachers engage in re-design, tweaking, adjusting and adapting materials to suit particular needs'. A number of in-house materials are produced in EAP units for the teaching of academic reading and writing. These materials are often piloted, revised, updated and improved. There is evidence that shows that evaluation methods which involve feedback from different parties are important if materials are to meet the specific needs of students (Stoller *et al.* 2006). Table 28.1 shows a list of keywords – i.e. words whose frequency is unusually high in comparison with some norm (Scott 1999) – generated by *WordSmith Tools 5.0* (Scott 2008). It is based on a comparison of a small corpus of sample in-house EAP materials used for the teaching of academic reading and writing and a reference corpus consisting of the non-academic parts of the British National Corpus. The purpose of this comparison was to ascertain to what extent academic vocabulary and discipline-specific vocabulary is included in this sample of in-house materials.

After a search in the Academic Word List (Coxhead 2000), it was found that only *academic* and *project* from the list in Table 28.1 were academic words. However, further down the frequency keyword list, we have others such as *sources*, *section*, *sections* and *research*, in sublist 1; *conclusion*, in sublist 2; *task* and *technology*, in sublist 3, and *topic* and *extract*, in sublist 7, to name a few. As regards discipline-specific vocabulary, only a few words, such as *genetic*, *obesity*, *collocations* and *thermal* could be considered to be more specialised.

This comparison can lead us to conclude that in-house EAP materials may be suitable for the teaching of academic vocabulary but if the aim is to learn discipline-specific words or phrases, perhaps materials based on a specialised corpus would be required.

Table 28.1 List of the fifty most frequent keywords in a corpus of sample in-house EAP materials

	Word	*Freq.*		*Word*	*Freq.*
1	of	1164	26	fast	105
2	in	953	27	these	101
3	is	613	28	academic	98
4	you	565	29	used	97
5	are	381	30	other	95
6	your	332	31	sentences	86
7	this	272	32	how	86
8	or	227	33	read	83
9	which	212	34	also	80
10	what	208	35	project	78
11	an	184	36	make	78
12	about	155	37	need	75
13	do	153	38	may	75
14	can	152	39	write	74
15	words	141	40	using	74
16	will	140	41	following	69
17	use	132	42	look	66
18	has	132	43	most	65
19	some	128	44	countries	64
20	food	126	45	own	62
21	information	123	46	work	61
22	text	121	47	tourism	60
23	writing	119	48	different	60
24	more	118	49	check	59
25	language	117	50	word	59

5. What approaches should be used for designing teaching materials?

While more and more EAP units are developing in-house materials for the teaching of academic writing, these do not often focus on disciplinary variation. This section describes a corpus of science and engineering journal articles, compiled by the authors, and possible corpus-based approaches to the teaching of vocabulary and formulaic sequences by using word lists and concordance lines as well as awareness-raising tasks based on this corpus.

Academic journal articles which PhD students are likely to draw upon as part of their research can be a useful resource for the teaching of academic vocabulary, and the data are often freely available in electronic form in university libraries. A corpus aimed at first-year PhD science and engineering students at the University of Nottingham was compiled with a view to creating word lists and concordances on which to base vocabulary teaching materials. The corpus consists of 11,624,741 words (accessed on-line) and covers a wide range of disciplines in the faculties of science and engineering. Table 28.2 includes a sample list of keywords generated by using *WordSmith Tools 5.0* (Scott 2008) and based on the comparison of the science and engineering corpus and the same reference corpus described in Section 4. The words on this list were found to be key in all disciplines in our science and engineering corpus.

As mentioned in Section 1, frequency is only one of the criteria used for the selection of particular lexical items to be taught. Other important factors to consider are range of

Table 28.2 List of the most frequent keywords in the science and engineering corpus

	Word	*Freq.*		*Word*	*Freq.*
1	these	25220	26	higher	8648
2	between	22875	27	rate	8437
3	model	22500	28	models	8382
4	also	21547	29	thus	8259
5	used	20662	30	process	8244
6	using	20610	31	conditions	8057
7	data	19223	32	respectively	7845
8	each	16845	33	structure	7698
9	results	16620	34	following	7612
10	different	14645	35	similar	7561
11	both	14230	36	significant	7251
12	study	13723	37	cell	7170
13	however	12895	38	therefore	7036
14	based	11966	39	sample	6896
15	shown	11514	40	size	6893
16	effect	11067	41	parameters	6825
17	values	11064	42	type	6704
18	analysis	11029	43	compared	6613
19	function	10393	44	phase	6602
20	table	10309	45	samples	6386
21	observed	10117	46	lower	6236
22	method	9573	47	total	6186
23	obtained	9420	48	distribution	6086
24	effects	9356	49	shows	5956
25	value	9099	50	response	5936

word meanings, familiarity, availability and level of difficulty. The list of keywords was subsequently examined by one of the present authors in order to select a list of fifty words using her intuition regarding what words would be likely to be useful for thesis writing. Table 28.3 shows this list.

Once a list of keywords has been selected, the next stage in materials development involves the production of concordance lines for students to examine as well as awareness-raising tasks which include clear instructions as to how the data should be analysed and questions which will guide the students' exploratory data analysis. Advocates of data-driven learning (DDL) or inductive approaches to the learning of grammar and vocabulary have made use of concordance texts to develop teaching materials which facilitate the learner's discovery of patterns based on evidence from authentic texts and foster a sense of autonomy, as the learner does not depend on the teacher to work out rules of usage (Tribble 1990; Tribble and Jones 1990; Johns 1991a, 1991b).

More recent studies have described the use of concordances to develop EAP/ESP teaching materials. Thurstun and Candlin (1998) used concordances in combination with a variety of problem-solving activities for independent study of academic vocabulary. They claim that this type of material provides exposure to multiple examples of the same vocabulary item in context and raises awareness of collocational relationships. Nation (2001) also stresses the importance of multiple encounters with new words in order for students to be able to *use* these words in writing. Despite criticisms of the use of corpus-based material in the classroom (Cook 1998; Widdowson 2000), several studies conducted on the teaching of academic writing comment on the value of concordances as a first step to uncover linguistic features which would otherwise be difficult to identify (Hyland 1998, 2003; Thompson and Tribble 2001; Hoon and Hirvela 2004).

Table 28.3 List of fifty words selected from the science and engineering corpus for further examination

1	analysis	26	evaluate
2	applied	27	experimental
3	average	28	factors
4	axis	29	frequency
5	based	30	higher
6	behaviour	31	identified
7	characteristics	32	indicate
8	coefficient	33	investigate
9	compare	34	methods
10	complex	35	observation
11	conclusions	36	occur
12	conditions	37	positive
13	consequently	38	presented
14	considered	39	procedure
15	correlation	40	represents
16	curve	41	response
17	data	42	results
18	decrease	43	sample
19	demonstrate	44	shown
20	determine	45	significant
21	deviation	46	statistical
22	differences	47	study
23	distribution	48	types
24	effect	49	values
25	estimate	50	variable

In the light of the usefulness of concordances discussed so far, we now need to examine the list of 50 keywords shown in Table 28.3. This list was scrutinised in greater detail with the aim of extracting a few words to be included in concordances for our PhD students to examine guided by awareness-raising tasks. The words selected were: *average, behaviour, consequently, higher, positive, presented, response, shown* and *study*.

These nine words could not be considered to be discipline-specific, which may not seem coherent with the arguments for the compilation of discipline-specific lists of academic vocabulary included in Section 3. However, this selection was pedagogically driven on the basis of the following criteria:

a. Frequency (frequently used words in corpus data across disciplines).
b. Words which were frequent *both* in corpus data across disciplines *and* in a sample text our PhD students had previously been asked to read to identify academic vocabulary.
c. Words frequently used
   either: in all three of the following sources: corpus data across disciplines; the sample text given to students to read; and in the Academic Word List (Coxhead 2000);
   or: in two of these.

The students had no previous experience using concordances, so it was hoped that the choice of familiar words would make the first encounter with this type of learning material less alien or threatening.

Figure 28.1 includes sample concordances of *average* which are accompanied by a sample awareness-raising task given to students.

Sample task based on concordances of average

The following questions will help you *notice* patterns either in the left or right context, i.e. to the left or the right of the *Key Word in Context (KWIC)*. Spend some time analysing the concordances of this word and answer the following questions:

1. The word 'average' can be used as a noun or as an adjective. Look at the right context. Which seems to be more frequently used in this body of data?
2. Look at the right context. Find examples of the following uses:
   a. result obtained when adding two or more numbers together and dividing the total by the no. of numbers that were added together;
   b. a number or size that varies but is approximately the same;
   c. typical or normal person or thing;
   d. normal amount or quality for a particular group of things or people;
   e. neither very good nor very bad.
3. Look at the left context. When used as a noun, 'average' is preceded by an article, either definite 'the' or indefinite 'a / an'. Which article is more common in this set of data?
4. Look at the left context. Sometimes 'average' is part of a prepositional phrase. Which prepositional phrases can you find in the concordances?
5. In what section(s) of a journal article do you think you are more likely to find the word 'average'?

If students are able to handle tasks such as this one successfully, future tasks can be made progressively more challenging by asking students to identify formulaic sequences used in their disciplines.

A number of recent studies on academic writing have revealed considerable use of phraseology in discipline-specific texts. In his corpus-based study of engineering textbooks, Ward (2007) notes that there is a strong link between collocation and technicality. His analysis focused on collocations including discipline-specific nouns. He claims that what students need to know about items on a frequency list is their collocational behaviour and that centrality of collocation to specialisation is better shown in data from words common in more than one sub-discipline. Two possible approaches to the

N	Concordance		
1	has about 70% decoding time improvement ratio in	**average**	.
2	surface area of 200 m2/g [22]. AEROSIL® OX 50 has an	**average**	primary particle diameter of 40 nm and a specific
3	observed; each sample was analysed in duplicate, and the	**average**	value is given. Changes in the molecular size
4	with theoretical predictions. The isostress model (or Reuss	**average**	) assumes that the matrix and filler are stressed
5	99.8%, true density = 2.2 g/cm3). AEROSIL® 200 has an	**average**	primary particle diameter of 12 nm and a specific
6	ranges from 100 nm to 1 µm, which is smaller than the	**average**	size 8 µm of nanoparticles received. Further work
7	compared with those of untreated samples (Table 2). The	**average**	MOE for treated samples is almost double that of
8	on the particle surface. Fumed silica particles with	**average**	primary particle diameters of 12 and 40 nm were
9	was seen that the behavior can be reasonably predicted by	**average**	parameters. The tow fraction in the E-glass and
10	will be investigated in the future. Fig. 13 shows the	**average**	tensile shear lap joint strength of the IAF joints
11	and Fig. 9). The virgin 40 wt% fibre composites showed an	**average**	flexural strength and flexural modulus of 57 and
12	(Fig. 1 and Fig. 2). The virgin composites showed an	**average**	TS of 41 MPa and YM of 4553 MPa which reduced
13	density with increased reprocessing. The change in	**average**	fibre length can be correlated with the number of
14	the fact that reprocessing incurred some fibre damage. The	**average**	fibre length was found to decrease from 2.36 mm for
15	by Tasman Pulp & Paper Co. Ltd., New Zealand. The	**average**	fibre length was 2.36 mm and the fibre diameter was
16	and 1.67 N tension forces of the IA fiber. Fig. 15 shows the	**average**	tensile shear strength of IAF joints varying the
17	of the IAF joints compared with non-IAF joints. The	**average**	joint strengths are 5.47 MPa for non-IAF joints and
18	[36] is defined as (30) where ? is the tow radius, Xf is the	**average**	fiber tension strength, L is the tow length, typically
19	least three composite specimens were tested to obtain the	**average**	load-displacement curve at each impact velocity.
20	HF receiving CRT over a modest follow-up period. On	**average**	, increase in creatinine level by 0.1 mg/dL was
21	difference in the effect of LV pacing only, which is, on	**average**	, much better in patients with sinus rhythm
22	(a numerical value assigned to each pixel which is the	**average**	of all the attenuation values contained within the
23	a questionnaire that included general characteristics. The	**average**	blood pressure was taken by a physician using
24	AV node ablation was performed shortly after implant.	**Average**	QRS duration for all patients during right ventricular
25	0.5 ms (N = 5 due to a late exit block in one canine). The	**average**	procedure duration for His lead placement was 40 ±
26	inferior and distal site of right ventricular pacing than the	**average**	site of LV breakthrough for nonpaced QRS
27	rate of left ventricular pressure rise (LV dP/dtmax). The	**average**	LV dP/dt max for all pacing modalities at
28	catheters both quickly reached the targeted tissue. The	**average**	procedure duration for His lead placement was 40 ±
29	The resolution of the spectra is 8 cm-1 and the	**average**	scanning times are 8. The instrument was
30	these assembly seams as this parameter depends on the	**average**	fibre undulation [3]. In contrast, the more
31	the grafted organic components by the nanoclays. As the	**average**	aggregate size of the received nanoclay in powder
32	physical properties of the nanoclays used in this work. The	**average**	aggregate size in the clay powder is 8 µm, and
33	for the thicker polyester yarn. However, the overall	**average**	undulation of the reinforcement fibres appears low
34	allowed to plan in smaller batch sizes; work centres will on	**average**	use half a day to respond to down stream demand;
35	ball rate. By excluding these five weeks (W30 to W34), the	**average**	defect rates were all below 0.5 per cent that means
36	came under Kanban control (Figure 10). This is not the	**average**	lead-time per product as not every product goes
37	to inventory and lead-time reduction. For instance, the	**average**	lead time of all the work centres has been reduced
38	by the following empirical equation: (4) where lN is the	**average**	fibre length at any reprocessed composites, l0 is
39	membrane. The symbol , represents the local volume	**average**	of a quantity associated with the fluid. The
40	parameter and permeability were modeled as functions of	**average**	pore and fiber diameters and porosity (Table 3, Eqs.
41	and Vafai [30] and is adopted here. Using Eq. (34), the	**average**	permeability is found to be Ktotal = 6.22 × 10-18
42	associated with the fluid. The parameters Pf and are the	**average**	pressure inside the fluid and a unit vector oriented
43	a metallic wire. The correlations are functions of porosity,	**average**	pore diameter, and tortuosity (Table 3, Eqs. (6) and
44	report 76 RL practices (0.9 practices per company on	**average**	), six of which have been identified as different (Table
45	companies report 25 SP practices (0.30 per company on	**average**	), two of which have been identified as different
46	df, can be measured using a microscope, and the	**average**	pore diameter, dp, can be estimated by counting
47	volume of the sample and the density of the metal. The	**average**	fiber diameter, df, can be measured using a
48	to the presence of a mass diffusion. The local as well as	**average**	skin-friction, Nusselt number and Sherwood number
49	experimental heat transfer coefficients very well, with an	**average**	mean absolute percentage error of 9%. This error is
50	the present heat transfer calculations indicate that the	**average**	Nusselt number over the inclined and horizontal

Figure 28.1 Concordances of *average* from a corpus of scientific and engineering research articles.

teaching of collocation are recommended in his study. The first is raising students' awareness of the existence and frequency of collocations and the second is teaching the process of reading collocations as chunks.

Gledhill (2000) investigated phraseology found in introductions from a corpus of cancer research articles and argues for the design of a specialised corpus of the research article and a computer corpus-based methodology to describe the phraseology of the research article genre. His study centred specifically on collocations of grammatical words and their role in terms of textual function and recommends a combined approach to genre and corpus analysis. Corpus analysis can reveal recurrent patterns while the genre approach provides the opportunity to observe the series of choices in different sections of the academic research article. Gledhill's study (ibid.: 130) revealed that in some instances collocation involved terminology, thus reflecting the recurrent semantics of the specialist domain, and in other instances collocation revealed the dominant discourse strategies in the research article. At the end of the study, Gledhill concludes that phraseology is part of the defining characteristics of the discourse community.

Other discipline-specific studies have focused on the use of lexical bundles or semantic associations. Cortes (2004) compared the use of lexical bundles in published and student disciplinary writing using a corpus of history and biology research articles and students' papers in the undergraduate lower and upper divisions and graduate level at Northern Arizona University. The study suggests that explicit teaching of lexical bundles is necessary in order to enable students to notice them first and then use them actively in their writing. Nelson (2006) identified the semantic associations of words by using a corpus of spoken and written Business English and demonstrated how words in the Business English environment interact with each other on a semantic level. His study shows that words have semantic prosodies which are unique to business, separate from the prosodies they generate in the general English environment.

Drawing on the literature relevant to vocabulary acquisition, corpus-based studies and the design and development of teaching materials, this chapter has described how a carefully compiled corpus of discipline-specific research articles could be exploited to design EAP vocabulary teaching materials in order to meet the needs of PhD students in their first year of their programmes. It is likely that frequent exposure to this type of material will enable students to recognise and use key vocabulary in their disciplines.

Further reading

Biber, D. (1993) 'Representativeness in Corpus Design', *Literary and Linguistic Computing* 8: 243–57. (Biber's work is an excellent introduction to issues in corpus design and compilation.)

Harwood, N. (ed.) (forthcoming) *Materials in ELT: Theory and Practice*. Cambridge: Cambridge University Press. (Harwood's edited book is an up-to-date collection of studies focusing on materials design and development.)

Nation, P. and Waring, R. (1997) 'Vocabulary Size, Text Coverage and Word Lists', in N. Schmitt and M. McCarthy (eds) *Vocabulary: Description, Acquisition and Pedagogy*. Cambridge: Cambridge University Press, pp. 6–19. (Nation and Waring's work offers an excellent introduction to issues surrounding word-list compilation and use.)

Wray, A. (2002) *Formulaic Language and the Lexicon*. Cambridge: Cambridge University Press. (Wray's work has become a standard introductory text to formulaic language, including reviews of the literature on most aspects of the phenomenon.)

References

Biber, D., Johansson, S., Leech, G., Conrad S. and Finegan, E. (1999) *Longman Grammar of Spoken and Written English*. Harlow: Longman.

Cook, G. (1998) 'The Uses of Reality: A Reply to Ronald Carter', *ELT Journal* 52: 57–64.

Cortes, V. (2004) 'Lexical Bundles in Published and Student Disciplinary Writing: Examples from History and Biology', *English for Specific Purposes* 23: 397–423.

Coxhead, A. (2000) 'A New Academic Wordlist', *TESOL Quarterly* 34: 213–38.

——(2008) 'Phraseology and English for Academic Purposes', in F. Meunier and S. Granger (eds) *Phraseology in Language Learning and Teaching*. Amsterdam: John Benjamins, pp. 149–61.

Coxhead, A. and Byrd, P. (2007) 'Preparing Writing Teachers to Teach the Vocabulary and Grammar of Academic Prose', *Journal of Second Language Writing* 16: 129–47.

Ellis, N. C. (2003) 'Constructions, Chunking, and Connectionism: The Emergence of Second Language Structure', in C. J. Doughty and M. H. Long (eds) *The Handbook of Second Language Acquisition*. Oxford: Blackwell, pp. 63–103.

Ellis, N. C., Simpson-Vlach, R. and Maynard, C. (2008) 'Formulaic Language in Native and Second-language Speakers: Psycholinguistics, Corpus Linguistics, and TESOL', *TESOL Quarterly* 41: 375–96.

Gardner, D. (2008) 'Validating the Construct of *word* in Applied Corpus-based Vocabulary Research: A Critical Survey', *Applied Linguistics* 28: 241–65.

Ghadessy, M. (1979) 'Frequency Counts, Word Lists and Materials Preparation', *English Teaching Forum* 17: 24–7.

Gledhill, C. (2000) 'The Discourse Function of Collocation in Research Article Introductions', *English for Specific Purposes* 19: 115–35.

Harwood, N. (2005) 'What Do We Want EAP Teaching Materials for?', *Journal of English for Academic Purposes* 4: 149–61.

——(forthcoming) (ed.) *Materials in ELT: Theory and Practice*. Cambridge: Cambridge University Press.

Hoey, M. (2005) *Lexical Priming: A New Theory of Words and Language*. London: Routledge.

Hoon, H. and Hirvela, A. (2004) 'ESL Attitudes Toward Corpus Use in L2 Writing', *Journal of Second Language Writing* 13: 257–83.

Howatt, A. P. R. and Widdowson, H. G. (2004) *A History of English Language Teaching*. Oxford: Oxford University Press.

Hyland, K. (1998) *Hedging in Scientific Research Articles*. Amsterdam: John Benjamins.

——(2003) *Second Language Writing*. Cambridge: Cambridge University Press.

Hyland, K. and Tse, P. (2007) 'Is there an "Academic Vocabulary?"', *TESOL Quarterly* 41(2): 235–53.

Johns, T. (1991a) 'Should You Be Persuaded', *ELR Journal* 4: 1–16.

——(1991b) 'From Printout to Handout', *ELR Journal* 4: 27–46.

Kjellmer, G. (1990) 'A Mint of Phrases', in K. Aijmer and B. Altenberg (eds) *English Corpus Linguistics: Studies in Honour of Jan Svartvik*. London: Longman, pp. 111–27.

Krishnamurthy, R. and Kosem, I. (2007) 'Issues in Creating a Corpus for EAP Pedagogy and Research', *Journal of English for Academic Purposes* 6: 356–73.

Kuiper, K. (2004) 'Formulaic Performance in Conventionalised Varieties of Speech', in N. Schmitt (ed.) *Formulaic Sequences: Acquisition, Processing and Use*. Amsterdam: John Benjamins, pp. 37–54.

Lamb, S. (2000) 'Bidirectional Processing in Language and Related Cognitive Systems', in M. Barlow and S. Kemmer (eds) *Usage Based Models of Language*. Stanford, CA: CSLI Publications, pp. 87–119.

Lewis, M. (1993) *The Lexical Approach: The State of ELT and a Way Forward*. London: Thomson Heinle.

McCarthy, M. J. and O'Dell, F. (2008) *Academic Vocabulary in Use*. Cambridge: Cambridge University Press.

McEnery, T. and Wilson, A. (1996) *Corpus Linguistics*. Edinburgh: Edinburgh University Press.

Nation, P. (2001) *Learning Vocabulary in Another Language*. Cambridge: Cambridge University Press.

Nation, P. and Waring, R. (1997) 'Vocabulary Size, Text Coverage and Word Lists', in N. Schmitt and M. McCarthy (eds) *Vocabulary: Description, Acquisition and Pedagogy*. Cambridge: Cambridge University Press, pp. 6–19.

Nattinger, J. R. and DeCarrico, J. S. (1992) *Lexical Phrases and Language Teaching*. Oxford: Oxford University Press.

Nelson, M. (2006) 'Semantic Associations in Business English: A Corpus-based Analysis', *English for Specific Purposes* 25: 217–34.

Nesi, H., Gardner, S., Forsyth, R., Hindle, D., Wickens, P., Ebeling, S., Leedham, M., Thompson, P. and Heuboeck, A. (2005) 'Towards the Compilation of a Corpus of Assessed Student Writing: An Account of Work in Progress', paper presented at Corpus Linguistics, University of Birmingham, published in the *Proceedings from the Corpus Linguistics Conference Series*, 1, available at www.corpus.bham.ac.uk/PCLC

O'Keeffe, A., McCarthy, M. J. and Carter, R. A. (2007) *From Corpus to Classroom: Language Use and Language Teaching*. Cambridge: Cambridge University Press.

Paltridge, B. (2002) 'Thesis and Dissertation Writing: An Examination of Published Advice and Actual Practice', *English for Specific Purposes* 21: 125–43.

Pawley, A. and Syder, F. H. (1983) 'Two Puzzles for Linguistic Theory: Nativelike Selection and Nativelike Fluency', in J. C. Richards and R. W. Schmidt (eds) *Language and Communication*. New York: Longman, pp. 191–226.

Raupach, M. (1984) 'Formulae in Second Language Speech Production', in H. W. Dechert, D. Mohle and M. Raupach (eds) *Second Language Productions*. Tubingen: Gunter Narr, pp. 114–37.

Richards, J. C. (1974) 'Word Lists: Problems and Prospects', *RELC Journal* 5: 69–84.

Samuda, V. (2005) 'Expertise in Pedagogic Task Design', in K. Johnson (ed.) *Expertise in Second Language Learning and Teaching*. Basingstoke: Palgrave Macmillan, pp. 230–54.

Schmitt, N. (2000) *Vocabulary in Language Teaching*. Cambridge: Cambridge University Press.

——(ed.) (2004) *Formulaic Sequences: Acquisition, Processing and Use*. Amsterdam: John Benjamins.

Schmitt, N. and Zimmerman, C. B. (2002) 'Derivative Word Forms: What Do Learners Know?' *TESOL Quarterly* 36: 145–71.

Scott, M. (1999) *WordSmith Tools Users Help File*. Oxford: Oxford University Press.

——(2008) *WordSmith Tools 5.0*. Oxford: Oxford University Press.

Sinclair, J. M. (1987) 'Collocation: A Progress Report', in R. Steele and T. Threadgold (eds) *Language Topics: Essays in Honour of Michael Halliday*. Amsterdam: John Benjamins, pp. 319–31.

Stoller, F. L., Horn, B., Grabe, W. and Robinson, M. S. (2006) 'Evaluative Review in Materials Development', *Journal of English for Academic Purposes* 5: 174–92.

Thompson, P. and Tribble, C. (2001) 'Looking at Citations: Using Corpora in English for Academic Purposes', *Language Learning and Technology* 5: 91–105.

Thurstun, J. and Candlin, C. N. (1998) 'Concordancing and the Teaching of the Vocabulary of Academic English', *English for Specific Purposes* 17: 267–80.

Towell, R., Hawkins, R. and Bazergui, N. (1996) 'The Development of Fluency in Advanced Learners of French', *Applied Linguistics* 17: 84–119.

Tribble, C. (1990) 'Concordancing and an EAP Writing Programme', *CAELL Journal* 1(2): 10–15.

Tribble, C. and Jones, G. (1990) *Concordances in the Classroom*. London: Longman.

Ward, J. (2007) 'Collocation and Technicality in EAP Engineering', *Journal of English for Academic Purposes* 6: 18–35.

West, M. (1953) *A General Service List of English Words*. London: Longman.

Widdowson, H. (2000) 'On the Limitations of Linguistics Applied', *Applied Linguistics* 21: 3–25.

Wood, D. (2006) 'Uses and Functions of Formulaic Sequences in Second Language Speech: An Exploration of the Foundations of Fluency', *Canadian Modern Language Review* 63: 13–33.

Wray, A. (2000) 'Formulaic Sequences in Second Language Teaching: Principle and Practice', *Applied Linguistics* 21: 463–89.

——(2002) *Formulaic Language and the Lexicon*. Cambridge: Cambridge University Press.

29

What a corpus tells us about grammar teaching materials

Rebecca Hughes

1. Grammar, corpora and language description frameworks: what roles do corpus studies play in wider debates in applied linguistics that surround grammar?

The teaching materials that support grammar development in the L2 classroom have a complex status in relation to theories of language and of language learning. Grammar teaching materials, unlike skills development materials (i.e. those created for reading, writing, speaking, listening), tend to be strongly intertwined with the wider debates about views of language theory, varieties of language and, especially, questions of standards, accuracy and correctness. Everyone who works with grammar has a strong opinion about it as it feeds into issues that are at the very heart of language theory, language analysis and attitudes to how best to teach a language.

Instances of the fundamental issues that surround grammar teaching are the well-known 'prescriptive' versus 'descriptive' debate (whether to approach grammar in terms of what people should, versus what they do, say), or the more theoretical 'performance' versus 'competence' division (language in the world versus underlying, innate, system), or the question of whether your grammar is 'data-driven' versus 'data-informed'. The last dichotomy is especially relevant in corpus and computational linguistics as it links to the relatively new dimension in language theory that is provided when large quantities of readily accessible examples of language become available. The question here is whether you derive the model of your grammar from the instances in your corpus (which would be regarded as data-driven) or, in contrast, begin with assumptions about your grammar and find additional facts about these from the data in the corpus (data-informed). In this chapter the term 'data-based' is used as the more general term which incorporates either of these approaches and the distinction between the assumptions underpinning the approach are then made as necessary.

Data-driven commercial teaching materials for grammar are extremely rare, despite nearly thirty years of detailed research findings about various aspects of grammar from corpora (see chapters by Conrad, Gilquin and Granger, and Tribble, this volume). Data-informed materials are becoming more widely discussed and accepted in principle at the time of writing; however, the most popular student grammar materials in the world remain Raymond Murphy's *English Grammar in Use* (this was first published in 1988 and is based on decontextualised examples and gap-fill exercises; Murphy 2004), while for the teacher the mainstay of the reference grammar shelf is still Michael Swan's *Practical English Usage* (which, although the most recent editions pay some attention to corpus data and users' comments, remains largely based on isolated examples and the intuition of the author as to correctness; Swan 2005). The slowness of commercial English Language Teaching (ELT) publishers and the teaching community to adopt corpus insights more enthusiastically is due to the powerful influence of traditional pedagogic grammars promoted by titles such as these and also to other broader factors such as the tendency for a lack of communication between the teacher training community in applied linguistics and the research community.

There are clear links between issues of theoretical orientation to grammar and the practical choices made by the professionals involved in teaching grammar. It flows from this that the materials and methodology used in the classroom will also be affected by the opinion, often strongly held, that any professional teacher has about these debates. Whether you see grammar as a static system of rules beyond the influence of an individual or as a dynamic set of choices in context taken by such an individual will probably be closely linked to the type of teacher you are, and to other significant beliefs and values you have in your teaching. The former – a more systematic and rule-governed approach – will lend itself to the unfashionable (in the 'Western' applied linguistics tradition, at least) but still hugely influential notion of a point in grammar being amenable to techniques such as multiple-choice or close testing, to decontextualised sentence-based examples, and to a straightforward right–wrong answer in the key at the back of the book. The latter, grammar-in-context approach, will appeal more to a classroom approach where the orientation is towards exploration, task-based learning and valuing of a student's autonomous development and creativity. These factors of stance to grammatical theories and teaching approaches in turn affect the nature and choice of materials and how they are written, viewed and used. In effect, because a corpus holds up a mirror to a language and appears to reflect a compelling reality which is, at times, in tension with long-held models of language, these broader debates also constrain and shape the influences of corpus findings on grammar teaching.

2. Corpora and grammar teaching: benefits of using and types of use

One of the major benefits of the corpus-based approach to grammar teaching materials is that it can highlight the differences between assumptions about language structure in the abstract and what is found in real-world use. These differences can be of two kinds. First, the corpus-based approach can provide evidence for the frequency and contexts of well-known structures that do not alter the grammatical 'map' fundamentally. The 1990s and early 2000s were a rich time for these kinds of findings as researchers found themselves able to access very large corpora easily and routinely from their desktop PCs through advances in technology and through the growth in number and size of available corpora. Many of the findings had clear relevance to standard grammar teaching or the table of contents of a pedagogic grammar, and investigated grammar topics that any well-trained teacher would be interested in, for example prepositions (Mindt and Weber 1989), noun phrases (Taylor *et al.* 1989), relative clauses (de Haan 1987), adverbials (Quirk 1984), to name but a few topics, and, in each case, only a single example of many findings. This same technological ease allowed researchers to observe patterns in language in the data-*driven* ways defined above. These often ground-breaking observations took two major directions. The first, which is most relevant to the grammar teaching classroom, is the production of major new reference grammars of English based on corpus data: Quirk *et al.* (1985), Biber *et al.* (1999) and Carter and McCarthy (2006).

Within the varying approaches to corpus-based grammar analysis (from the 1960s with the hand-edited collections on reel-to-reel tapes of the Survey of English to the present day) two clear camps emerged in relation to grammatical insights/knowledge and conclusions that can be reached via very large sets of examples of a given language: those who held strongly to the view that intuitions and pre-decided categories for the grammar were to be retained and those who felt equally strongly that the reverse was the case. It may be the fact that corpus linguists have spent so much time debating methods and frameworks for analysis that has led to a lack of a convincing 'story' about corpus-informed pedagogic grammars, and hence slow uptake by the publishing world and the pedagogic profession. Some bridging work is needed between conclusions couched thus:

> Our results demonstrate quite clearly that a feature based unification grammar employing a recursive and 'deeper' style of analysis captures the relevant generalisations more efficiently than the analysis and implicit formalism employed by Sampson.
>
> (Taylor *et al.* 1989: 63)

and the wider applied linguistics world. The latter will always be more interested in the results they can apply than debates about which analytical method is preferable. A clear and balanced summary of some of these arguments can be found in Baldwin *et al.* (2005) and a useful reminder that linguistic input (i.e. the type of corpus material) and grammatical insights are inevitably linked can be found in Roland *et al.* (2007).

Within the school of thought that based insights primarily on the data and the analyses that were enabled by technological advances in data storage, combined with sophisticated computer programs to analyse very large quantities of data, a significant thread is that of computational linguistics and related approaches or sub-fields such as natural language processing (NLP), automatic grammar parsing, and stochastic or probabilistic frameworks. Like the work touched on above into familiar grammatical topics, these often strongly data-driven approaches have had little impact on pedagogic grammars despite having been incorporated into other applied fields as varied as automatic translation, speech recognition and human–computer interaction. This is discussed further in the section below on future directions in grammar teaching and related materials.

Published classroom materials based on corpora

Despite the fact that corpus linguistics has been carried out since the 1960s and has had a growing impact on our understanding of language, there are very few commercially available grammar textbooks/coursebooks for ELT based on corpus data. The gap between 'authentic' language and, gradually, evidence-based corpus insights and teaching materials has been regularly discussed by applied linguists over the last thirty years or more (Breen 1985; Scotton and Bernsten 1988; Nostrand 1989; O'Connor Di Vito 1991; Glisan and Drescher 1993; Gilmore 2004; Anderson 2007). There would appear to have been plenty of time for the insights of corpus linguistics to filter through to published materials. The textbooks produced by Cambridge University Press from around 2000 from the Cambridge and Nottingham Corpus of Discourse in English (CANCODE) were notable exceptions (McCarthy and O'Dell 1997; Carter *et al.* 2000; Hughes 2005; McCarthy *et al.* 2004; see also McCarten, this volume). But, as Barbieri and Eckhardt (2007) argue, there is still generally a disconnect between the specific findings of corpus studies and the grammar classroom. They provide a useful overview of the debate, and also present their own research into reported speech as found in corpora and in teaching materials. They conclude with a plea for a better linkage between Second Language Acquisition theory and the insights from corpus studies, and provide some ideas as to how this could happen for the speech reporting structures they have investigated.

This final point reminds us of the issue which opened this chapter: that corpus approaches have always had a tense relationship with other powerful trends in linguistics. The question of 'grammaticality' remains a fundamental one, despite the retreat in the field from prescriptive pedagogic grammars. 'Grammaticality' spans the lay person's interest in correctness and the issue for the corpus linguist of what counts as 'noise' in a corpus (as opposed to a string on which to base a statement about frequency of a particular item). The huge popularity of little books to help with correct day-to-day grammar (an internet search for 'bestselling grammars' will almost always fetch a title such as Wines and Taggart (2008) rather than a more worthy, current research and data-informed title) points to a keen interest in the population at large about this. The status of what counts as a grammatical string is also still an issue for the linguistic theorist and those seeking practical applications in other fields such as human–computer interaction. The influential PENN-Treebank, for instance, provides the basis for much computational linguistics work to allow analysis via automatic parsing and other developments. In order for this to function, the basic data is a very large corpus of hand-edited and correctly tagged (e.g. what part of speech and function) samples. Baldwin *et al.* (2005) discuss the need for judgements about grammaticality to inform the expansion of what to include in our description of the language. A key moot point that remains in corpus linguistics and grammar – both theories and applications – is deciding the cut-off point between 'data-driven' insights and native speaker judgements. It is perhaps unsurprising therefore that hard-nosed commercial interests such as the large ELT publishing houses remain to be convinced that what teachers and students want is a radical re-think of the grammar syllabus along corpus-informed lines.

The issue of what teachers and students want, and will use, is a key one in any discussion of grammar materials and Conrad (this volume) looks at some of the possible limitations of corpus approaches from this perspective. The following section, however, completes our look at the benefits of using corpus-based approaches by considering the uses often made by individual teachers outside the realm of published materials.

Teacher-led developments and corpora in the grammar classroom

A major potential benefit for the grammar classroom and related materials that corpus-based approaches bring is the way that they lend themselves to what have become fashionable approaches to the role of the teacher and learner in the ELT classroom. In particular, corpus-based grammars lend themselves well to more autonomous learning and to inductive approaches that encourage the student to see patterns in the language evidence for themselves and test out their own hypotheses about structures and use. At its best this questioning, investigative approach puts the 'learner as researcher' in charge of finding some of their own answers to grammar points from large samples of data provided by a corpus and can also allow individual students to follow up questions that they are particularly motivated to find out about (see Gilquin and Granger, this volume).

These approaches come broadly under the umbrella of 'classroom and teacher-led' developments in corpus-based grammar teaching material and they are not necessarily connected either to the research base in academe or to published materials. Often the individual teacher who becomes interested in moving beyond intuitions and traditional approaches is a particular type of personality and has an unusual combination of skills and inclinations. He or she is often an IT-literate teacher comfortable with using new technology in front of a class, is often a keen champion of ITC in the language teaching classroom, and enjoys the challenging exploratory nature of students and teacher finding answers together. Like the teacher who enjoys teaching pronunciation and thrives on the technical aspects of teaching this, the grammar teacher who uses corpora has often been the exception rather than the norm in the ELT community. Although classroom-based activities that use the internet to access concordancing tools and corpora for student-directed investigations of grammar are becoming more mainstream they have yet to be fully incorporated into teacher training programmes for ELT (see McCarthy 2008). There are a number of reasons why this is the case (the next section dealing with some of the limitations for corpus-based grammar approaches may provide explanation for some of these) but the principles of modern language teaching can clearly be supported via connecting classrooms and corpora more effectively.

- Corpus-based grammar materials and approaches to teaching grammar that are based on corpora can be adapted to suit several very different approaches and individual learning styles. For the analytical individual, whether teacher or student, corpora provide tangible quantitative data on which to test out ideas about language or from which to develop materials for the grammar classroom.
- At a more practical level and whatever their approach, corpora can provide teachers with an immense variety of samples of language which can be adapted for any form of teacher-developed materials.
- Corpus-based grammar materials lend themselves to task-based and communicative activities particularly well as they are readily adaptable to group and project work and autonomous learning contexts. The language learner can be encouraged to develop their own questions about grammatical points and investigate the answers for themselves via corpus examples.
- The teacher facing mixed ability groups will also find corpus-based grammar materials beneficial. With some preparation the same task framework can be used for groups with the same instructions but applied to different language points.

While this is the ideal – exploratory, autonomous and creative learning about language forms through the availability of large amounts of data in the classroom combined with a range of approaches that can be tailored to different kinds of learner – there are a number of issues that surround corpora and grammar teaching which should be considered. Section 3 looks in more detail at the issues surrounding the use of corpora in this area.

To sum up, the major benefits of a corpus-based approach to grammar teaching are:

- that it has clearer relevance and validity in terms of 'real-world' examples than traditional pedagogic grammar-based approaches,

- that it links to authentic language in context and makes this available for teachers and students alike,
- that it promotes learner autonomy and can be tailored to different learning styles and teaching methodologies,
- that it can help promote a more exploratory and inductive approach to teaching grammar,
- that it can help promote a view of language based on choices in context rather than rules in isolation.

Nonetheless, as suggested above, it is clear that corpus-based grammar materials have been slow to reach the ELT classroom worldwide and approaches based on corpora are still not by any means mainstream in the teaching community. The next section looks at the reasons underlying this and the potential limitations of the corpus-based approach to grammar teaching.

3. Constraints and limiting factors

The previous sections have dealt with the role of corpora in grammar teaching in general and some of the outcomes and benefits that have flowed from corpus linguistics in this area over the last forty years or so. It has also been suggested that there is something of a gap between insights from corpora and mainstream classroom teaching in the field of ELT and that this has existed for some time with no real indication of closing. This section considers some of the reasons why this is the case. These can be categorised into issues surrounding the language (syllabus and target level), learners' and teachers' expectations, and access to/uptake of digital media.

Syllabus and target level

Findings about words and structures from a corpus tend to be embedded in their original context. This is one of the great advantages of the method. A student or teacher can use a publicly available concordancer on an online corpus and within a few seconds move from a search on an item or phrase to seeing it highlighted in its original discourse context. This facility, however, is also deeply at odds with the standard approaches of a form-focused grammatical syllabus. Without a consensus as to how to incorporate corpus findings into manageable classroom-friendly topics or units that progress in a coherent way for the learner, the onus is on the teacher to manage the introduction of items to the learner. While the typical table of contents of a traditional intermediate grammar textbook will move through, say, rank-order topics from words and word classes, to phrase structure, to simple and complex sentences, and run through the tense system from 'simple present' to 'talking about the future: *will* versus *be going to*', the data from a corpus presents something of a headache for the teacher. Corpus examples do not fit neatly into a given target 'level'. To use any authentic materials is to accept this, but the nature of a corpus and typical ways for students to interact with it magnify this issue. The rich context in which even lexically oriented grammar points such as '*will* versus *be going to*' occur means that the corpus approach does not lend itself to an atomistic presentation of language beyond, that is, the initial 'search'. It therefore requires particularly deft and confident classroom management. Very often this can lead to a decision simply to label the corpus-based approach as something that is only appropriate for advanced learners.

Ownership of the language and teacher confidence

The issue of confident classroom management brings me to the second area which needs to be considered when evaluating the corpus-based approach to grammar teaching. In the majority of ELT classrooms worldwide it is not only the students who are not native speakers: it is also the teacher. While the teacher who has English as a strong second language may be confident when using traditional published teaching materials, the meaning and use of structures thrown up in context – which would often not be understood by a native speaker teacher when the example is seen in a concordance line, or the original longer sample of discourse – can be particularly off-putting and challenging. Unless the teacher has taken the professional decision to embrace the idea of learning with his/her learners to a very high level, the handling of 'raw' language samples that corpus approaches imply will be disconcerting for both teacher and learner, potentially.

Second, there is the issue of the students' needs and their expectations. It is now a commonplace to say that more speakers of English worldwide are brought up in non-Anglophone environments, acquire their English without visiting such places, and rarely if ever meet native speakers. The issue, therefore, of the relevance in the minds of students of even very large corpora of texts and speech by native speakers becomes questionable, particularly when introduced by a teacher who may also find their cultural distance from the examples quite far. Corpus studies are beginning to address this – Leitner (1992), for instance, looks at the questions around an international corpus and also has chapters on Caribbean and Indian Englishes – but not in ways that will translate quickly into the classroom where, indeed, diverse grammars of diverse Englishes create another layer of complexity for the existing teacher–learner dynamic.

In a sense, these issues are a variant on the questions discussed above about the cut-off point between being led to a conclusion by the corpus data as opposed to bringing preconceptions to it. In using a corpus you will inevitably be presented with examples of language that are confusing or opaque in meaning, and where often hard to explain but significant differences between the same search item will be thrown up. For all these reasons the main purpose and limitations of working with a corpus in the grammar classroom need to be thought through by the institution in which teaching takes place, the individual teacher needs to be allowed to air views on what they are confident they can teach, and something of all this needs to be articulated to the student in advance of adopting a corpus approach in any ELT environment.

Digital divide and classroom realities worldwide

The final area which needs to be considered is the type of classroom in which the greater part of English language teaching takes place. Small classes of highly motivated and autonomous learners working through an exploratory task-based approach are the ideal for corpus-based grammar teaching. The reality of most classrooms is quite far from this, with large class sizes and tightly constrained, examination-focused syllabuses being the norm. To say to the hard-pressed language teacher in China, Africa or South America that there is a valuable resource available to them in terms of grammar teaching means very little if the context in which they work cannot incorporate these 'riches'.

In addition to class size and syllabus constraints, the simple practicalities of accessing digital resources should not be underestimated. Many parts of rural Africa lack basic infrastructure to provide electricity, let alone access to the internet. In China the number of PCs per 1,000 in the population stands around forty compared to over 700 in the US, with similar disparities for internet use (Britannica 2008).

Caution is therefore needed in the research and teacher training community in the assumptions about what can be achieved in terms of adoption of a corpus-based approach. There is always a danger that a model of language that is distant from users, promotes a 'Western' hegemony and in many cases is simply practically inaccessible, will be held to be the basis of English teaching. The abstract and decontextualised nature of traditional pedagogic grammars, interestingly, side-steps many of these issues.

4. State of the debate and future developments that may affect grammar teaching based on corpus findings

With a few notable exceptions commercial publishers have been loathe to take on the challenge of investing in textbooks developed from corpus-based insights. The reasons for this have been discussed in other parts of this chapter, and at the time of writing there is no indication that this is seen as the next 'big thing' on the horizon for corpus-based grammar teaching. The impact of corpora and, more recently, the immense amounts of data available on the worldwide web, have yet to be fully incorporated into general applied linguistics and, specifically, into teacher training, more (in number) standard reference grammars and commercially available teaching materials. At the time of writing, in the first decade of the twenty-first century, it is hard to predict what directions the teaching of grammar and corpora will take, but until there is more consensus around the shape that a grammar syllabus informed by corpus findings would take, in detail, it is unlikely that published materials, in the traditional sense, will take a lead in this field.

New directions in the classroom are more likely to be teacher- and technology-led than dependent on the publishing world. A primary driver in this will be the growth of a community of teachers and students who are confident members of the online world. Those born after 1978 are, it is has been suggested, 'digital natives' (Prensky (2005) claims the invention of the term) and have markedly different interactions with the internet and other technological advances than those born before ('Digital Immigrants' and never as fully 'at home' with the technology as their younger counterparts). They expect answers to be found online, quickly and via innovative, often collaborative, means. Institutions such as the British Council and also commercial language schools are already tapping into this phenomenon by providing free access to a wide range of online language learning resources, some of which link to corpora and help with independent grammar learning online. A visit to their sites can often provide a range of interesting, freely accessible materials and discussion boards. This chapter presented the idea of the individual enthusiastic teacher as the champion of corpus materials in the classroom. Setting aside the issues of discrepancies in the geographical/national access to technology mentioned before, we may see the next generation of ELT students becoming independent users of the resources available to them to help them in their individual path to language learning.

Rather than seeing a growing number of very large separate corpora, we may also see networks of corpora under the developments that have been labelled as Web 2.0.

Institutions are already sharing data (look up 'European Language Resources Association' in a browser to be directed to an interesting example) and indeed the worldwide web may itself become, in effect, a massive meta-corpus for individual students and teachers to investigate language use: 'The World Wide Web can be viewed as a naturally occurring resource that embodies the rich and dynamic nature of language, a data repository of unparalleled size and diversity' (Resnik and Elkiss 2004).

The Linguists' Search Engine is example of a site which may become more common in future – to find this look up 'Linguists Search Engine' in a browser. This allows syntactic and semantically informed searches across multiple web-pages. Similarly, the interface hosted by the Adam Mickiewicz University (look up 'Turbo Lingo' in a browser to be directed to this) allows any URL to be pasted into an online interface and data such as word frequency, concordance and sentence length to be generated immediately. In this world it is not only data to answer individual grammar questions that can be found by individuals: their own choice of texts becomes the corpus material on which the answers are based.

The growth in multi-modal corpora will also lead to the ability to look at grammar in the context of para-linguistic features such as gaze and gesture (see Adolphs and Knight, this volume). These kinds of development would also permit a finer-grained description of spoken grammar in context and with full prosodic elements, and would have the potential to link to insights about grammar, interaction and prosody in more detail. While developments such as these will not overcome the basic issues of what grammar model is presented, and whose language is being analysed or whose standards are regarded as acceptable, they are all of a kind which learners brought up with technology embedded in their lives will be very much at ease using. Their effects, alongside much wider social, technological and cultural changes, may mean that some of these issues simply become less relevant to the language learner who is brought up to expect rapid, engaging, personalised input and to be an active and critical user of digital information. This is not to say that more traditional media will cease to be bastions of views of language that depend on authority: rather, the history of corpora and language teaching has always tended to keep some distance between these and provided a more direct link between the learners' own interests/questions and the available data.

5. Summary of issues

This chapter began by noting that grammar teaching is closely linked to wider issues in applied linguistics and that there is a tendency for those using corpus-based materials to become part of these debates – grammar teaching and corpus linguistics are both areas in applied linguistics that generate strong feelings. People are rarely neutral on either topic.

One of the reasons for this is that corpora can reveal the limitations of current grammar models and materials. A range of benefits to using corpus-based insights in the grammar classroom was introduced, including, for instance, the fact that they lend themselves readily to the design of more task-based, tailored and inductive materials.

Corpus-based insights have generally had greater potential for written than spoken mode. Traditionally, there has been the difficulty of capturing spoken data and analysing it effectively. But this may change soon with advances in multi-media corpora and new technologies to tag and analyse digital files, including video.

Nevertheless, there is always a tendency to return to static, text-based, analysis, and corpora remain easier for written mode than spoken in terms of direct application in materials and classroom grammar.

Teachers need to bear in mind what a corpus can easily tell them about grammar and what it cannot, and to make this clear to the learner. For example, a simple search will tell you very easily the relative frequency of occurrence of two words with similar meaning or form, but not why they were used nor a great deal of semantic and pragmatic information.

The very long time-lag between descriptive grammar based on corpora and materials that teachers will use readily was highlighted. There was a suggestion that at its best the corpus-based approach to grammar teaching is one that side-steps traditional print media altogether and allows the autonomous exploration of data by learners. The chapter also noted the 'digital divide' that is a reality in terms of access in many parts of the globe, and called for some reflection on the potential for a disproportionate influence of those who have the advantage of teaching and researching in contexts where small classes and access to digital media are the norm.

At the other end of the spectrum, in terms of potential new developments, this chapter concluded that along with many aspects of education the ELT grammar classroom will need to adapt to the needs and expectations of a generation of students (and teachers) who are as at ease in the online community as offline and for whom instant answers, personalised pathways to information, and multi-media input are the norm.

Further reading

Aijmer, K. (2009) *Corpora and Language Teaching*. Amsterdam: John Benjamins. (This is an issues-led collection with several chapters relating to grammar teaching.)

Conrad, S. (2000) 'Will Corpus Linguistics Revolutionize Grammar Teaching in the 21st Century?' *TESOL Quarterly* 34(3): 548–60. (This provides a balanced and insightful overview of the interface between corpora and grammar teaching by a leading scholar in the field of corpus linguistics.)

Meunier, F. (2002) 'The Pedagogical Value of Native and Learner Corpora in EFL Grammar Teaching', in S. Granger, J. Hung and S. Petch-Tyson (eds) *Computer Learner Corpora, Second Language Acquisition and Foreign Language Teaching*. Amsterdam: John Benjamins. 119–41. (This provides a thorough look at both the issue of these contrasting corpora and how they might be incorporated into the classroom. A particular focus is on grammar.)

Mukherjee, J. (2006) 'Corpus Linguistics and English Reference Grammars', in A. Renouf and A. Kehoe. *The Changing Face of Corpus Linguistics*. Amsterdam: Rodopi. 337–54 (This is a stimulating 'position paper' from a conference collection. Provides an in-depth analysis of three major grammar reference books. The collection as a whole also contains chapters on the web as corpus.)

References

Anderson, B. (2007) 'Pedagogical Rules and their Relationship to Frequency in the Input: Observational and Empirical Data from L2 French', *Applied Linguistics* 28(2): 286–308.

Baldwin, T., Beavers, J., Bender, E. M., Flickinger, D., Kim, A. and Oepen, S. (2005) 'Beauty and the Beast: What Running a Broad-coverage Precision Grammar over the BNC Taught Us about the Grammar – and the Corpus', in S. Kepser and M. Reis (eds) *Linguistic Evidence: Empirical, Theoretical and Computational Perspectives (Studies in Generative Grammar)*. Berlin: Walter de Gruyter, pp. 49–70.

Barbieri, F. and Eckhardt, S. E. B. (2007) 'Applying Corpus-Based Findings to Form-focused Instruction: The Case of Reported Speech', *Language Teaching Research* 11(3): 319–46.

Biber, D., Johansson, S., Leech, G., Conrad, S. and Finegan, E. (1999) *Longman Grammar of Spoken and Written English*. London: Longman.

Biber, D. and Reppen, R. (2002) 'What Does Frequency Have to Do with Grammar Teaching?' *Studies in Second Language Acquisition* 24: 199–208.

Breen, M. (1985) 'Authenticity in the Language Classroom', *Applied Linguistics* 6(1): 60–70.

Britannica (2008) *Encyclopaedia Britannica Book of the Year*. Chicago, IL: Encyclopaedia Britannica.

Carter, R. A. and McCarthy, M. J. (2006) *Cambridge Grammar of English*. Cambridge: Cambridge University Press.

Carter, R. A., Hughes, R. and McCarthy, M. J. (2000) *Exploring Grammar in Context*. Cambridge: Cambridge University Press.

Conrad, S. (1999) 'The Importance of Corpus-based Research for Language Teachers', *System* 27: 1–18.

——(2000) 'Will Corpus Linguistics Revolutionize Grammar Teaching in the 21st Century?' *TESOL Quarterly* 34(3): 548–60.

de Haan, P. (1987) 'Relative Clauses in Indefinite Noun Phrases', *English Studies* 68: 171–90.

Gilmore, A. (2004) 'A Comparison of Textbook and Authentic Interactions', *ELT Journal* 58(4): 363–71.

Glisan, E. W. and Drescher, V. (1993) 'Textbook Grammar: Does it Reflect Native Speaker Speech?' *The Modern Language Journal* 77(1): 23–33.

Hughes, R. (2005) *Exploring Grammar in Writing*. Cambridge: Cambridge University Press.

Hughes, R. and McCarthy, M. J. (1998) 'From Sentence to Discourse: Discourse Grammar and English Language Teaching', *TESOL Quarterly*, 32(2): 263–87.

Hunston, S. and Francis, G. (2000) *Pattern Grammar: A Corpus-driven Approach to the Lexical Grammar of English*. Amsterdam: John Benjamins.

Johns, T. (1994) 'From Printout to Handout: Grammar and Vocabulary Teaching in the Context of Data-driven Learning', in T. Odlin (ed.) *Perspectives on Pedagogical Grammar*. Cambridge: Cambridge University Press, pp. 293–313.

Kennedy, G. (1991) 'Between and Through: The Company They Keep and the Functions They Serve', in K. Aijmer and B. Altenberg (eds) *English Corpus Linguistics*. London: Longman, pp. 95–110.

Kreyer, R. (2000) 'The Use of Relative Pronouns in Restrictive Adnominal Relative Clauses in EFL Textbooks and in COLT: A Corpus-based Study,' *Neusprachliche Mitteilungen aus Wissenschaft und Praxi* 53(2): 101–8.

Leitner, G. (ed.) (1992) *New Directions in English Language Corpora. Methodology, Results, Software Developments*. Berlin: Mouton de Gruyter.

McCarthy, M. J. (2008) 'Accessing and Interpreting Corpus Information in the Teacher Education Context', *Language Teaching* 41(4): 563–74.

McCarthy, M. J., and Carter, R. A. (1995) 'Spoken Grammar: What Is It and How Can We Teach It?' *ELT Journal* 49: 207–18.

McCarthy, M. J. and O'Dell, F. (1997) *English Vocabulary in Use*. Cambridge: Cambridge University Press.

McCarthy, M. J., McCarten, J. and Sandiford, H. (2004) *Touchstone, Student's Book 1*. Cambridge: Cambridge University Press.

Mindt, D. (2002) 'What is a Grammatical Rule?' in L. E. Breivik and A. Hasselgren (eds) *From the COLT's Mouth … and Others: Language Corpora Studies in Honour of Anna-Brita Stenstrom*. Amsterdam: Rodopi, pp. 197–212.

Mindt, D. and Weber, C. (1989) 'Prepositions in American and British English', *World Englishes* 8(2): 229–38.

Murphy, R. (2004) *English Grammar in Use*, third edition. Cambridge: Cambridge University Press. (First published 1988.)

Nostrand, H. L. (1989) 'Authentic Texts and Cultural Authenticity: An Editorial', *Modern Language Journal* 3(1): 49–52.

O'Connor Di Vito, N. (1991) 'Incorporating Native Speakers Norms in Second Language Materials', *Applied Linguistics* 12(4): 383–95.

Prensky, M. (2005) 'Learning in the Digital Age', *Educational Leadership* 63(4): 8–13; available at www.ascd.org/authors/ed_lead/el200512_prensky.html (accessed 1 January 2009).

Quirk, R. (1984) 'Recent Work on Adverbial Realisation and Position', in J. Aarts and W. Meijs (eds) *Corpus Linguistics II. New Studies in the Analysis and Exploitation of Computer Corpora*. Amsterdam: Rodopi, pp. 185–92.

Quirk, R., Greenbaum, S., Leech, G. and Svartvik, J. (1985) *A Comprehensive Grammar of English*. London: Longman.

Resnik, P. and Elkiss, A. (2004) *The Linguist's Search Engine: Getting Started Guide*, available at http://lse.umiacs.umd.edu:8080/guide/lse_guide_techreport.html (accessed 4 January 2009).

Roland, D., Dick, F. and Elman, J. L. (2007) 'Frequency of Basic English Grammatical Structures: A Corpus Analysis', *Journal of Memory and Language* 57: 348–79.

Scotton, C. M. and Bernsten, J. (1988) 'Natural Conversations as a Model for Textbook Dialogue', *Applied Linguistics* 9(4): 372–84.

Sinclair, J. (1991) *Corpus, Concordance, Collocation*. Oxford: Oxford University Press.

Swan, M. (2005) *Practical English Usage*, third edition. Oxford: Oxford University Press.

Taylor, L., Grover, C. and Briscoe, E. J. (1989) 'The Syntactic Regularity Of English Noun Phrases', in *Proceedings of the Fourth Annual Meeting of the European Chapter of the Association for Computational Linguistics*. Manchester: University of Manchester Institute of Science and Technology, pp. 256–63.

Wines, J. and Taggart, C. (2008) *My Grammar and I (or Should That Be 'Me'?): Old-School Ways to Sharpen Your English*. London: Michael O'Mara Books.

30
Corpus-informed course book design

Jeanne McCarten

1. Introduction

A course book is a carefully sequenced, graded set of teaching materials whose aim is to improve the language knowledge and performance of its users, taking them from one level to another. It is a hugely complex, lengthy and expensive undertaking for both writer and publisher in terms of investment in time, research and production. As such, there is great pressure on all concerned for it to be successful to return that investment. Therefore it must tread a fine balance between offering something new – 'unique selling points' – while remaining user-friendly, familiar and even 'safe'. Typically, course books present and practise grammar, vocabulary, language functions, pronunciation and 'the four skills': reading, writing, listening and speaking, packaged together in thematic units. General course materials usually aim to give equal weight to the various language areas, so their multi-stranded syllabi provide an integrated course balancing accuracy and fluency. Course books may teach 'general' language or more specialised types such as business or academic language, or examination preparation. Corpora have informed English dictionaries and grammar reference books since the publication of the *Collins COBUILD English Language Dictionary* in 1987 and the *Collins COBUILD English Grammar* in 1990. Curiously, with the exception of *The COBUILD English Course* (Willis and Willis 1987–8), course books have generally been slow to exploit corpora as a resource, and several researchers including Biber *et al.* (1998), Tognini Bonelli (2001), Gilmore (2004), Cheng and Warren (2007) and Cullen and Kuo (2007) have pointed to disparities between language descriptions and models in course books and actual language use as evidenced in a corpus.

2. What kind of corpus is needed to write a course book?

Corpora come in different shapes and sizes so it makes sense to use corpora whose content is broadly similar in nature to the language variety, functions and contexts that the end users of the material aspire to learn. In choosing a corpus the following considerations may be useful.

Variety

In the case of English Language Teaching (ELT), most internationally marketed course books fall into two main categories of 'American English' and 'British English' in that the formal language presentations tend to be in one or other main variety. Course-book writers therefore need access to a corpus of the chosen variety to ensure that their syllabus and language models accurately reflect usage in the corpus. A corpus is useful in adapting a course book from one variety to another, a common practice in some international publishing houses. While some differences between North American and British English are well known (e.g. *elevator* vs *lift* and *gotten* vs *got*), a corpus can reveal more subtle differences in frequency and use between the two varieties. For example, the question form *have you got … ?* is over twenty-five times more frequent in spoken British English than in North American English, which favours *do you have … ?*, and so merits an earlier inclusion in an elementary British English course book than it might in a North American one.

Genre

Some course books are described as 'general', 'four skills' courses and others are more specialised, such as business or academic courses. Again, it makes sense for the writer to use a corpus that contains the type of language that is the target for the learner. Corpora of different genres will give different results in terms of their most frequent items of vocabulary, grammar or patterns of use. So if the course book aims to teach conversation skills, a corpus of written texts from newspapers and novels will not give the writer much information about the interactive language of conversation. Equally, a spoken corpus is unlikely to help the writer of an academic writing course identify the common vocabulary and structures which learners need to master. For example, the word *nice* is in the top fifteen words in conversation, and is therefore a useful word to include in a general or conversation course. In contrast, in academic written English *nice* is rare, occurring mainly in quotations of speech from literature or interviews, so may be less useful. Some words may have a similar frequency in conversation and academic written English, but have different meanings or uses. In academic English *see* is mostly used to refer the reader to other books and articles, as in *see Bloggs 2007*. In conversation, *see* has various uses, including leave-taking (*see you later*), showing understanding (*I see*), and in *you see*, to impart what the speaker feels is new information for the listener (*You see, he travels first class*). See Carter and McCarthy (2006: 109b).

Age

Many English corpora such as the British National Corpus (BNC), or the American National Corpus (ANC) contain mostly adult speakers and writers. If the trend towards corpus-informed materials continues, it is hoped that writers of materials for younger learners will be able to draw on corpora of young people's language, in order to present age-appropriate models. A comparison of the Bergen Corpus of London Teenager Language (COLT) (see Andersen and Stenström 1996) with the Cambridge and Nottingham Corpus of Discourse in English (CANCODE) (see McCarthy 1998) reveals that certain stance markers (*to be honest, in fact, I suppose*) and discourse markers, especially the more idiomatic types (*on the other hand, at the end of the day*) occur with greater frequency in the adult corpus. Such comparisons can identify features of language use which are typical and appropriate to a target age group.

Learner and non-native-speaker data

Major publishers, examination bodies, research groups and individual researchers collect corpora of learner data. Such corpora, especially those which have errors coded and classified, contain invaluable information about the language used (or not used) by learners, and common mistakes made. Well-designed corpora can be searched by level or first language background, enabling the writer to find, for example, the most common errors made by lower-intermediate Italian learners, which can be useful for courses aimed at specific markets.

In the case of English, a major debate is the status of the native speaker. Some, including Cook (1999), Widdowson (2000), Seidlhofer (2004, 2005), Jenkins (2006), question whether learners should be judged against the models and norms extracted from native-speaker corpora, and advocate instead those of English as a Lingua Franca (ELF), or World Englishes (Kirkpatrick 2007). They argue that realistic models for learners are to be found in non-native-speaker corpora, such as the Vienna–Oxford International Corpus of English (VOICE) at the University of Vienna (Seidlhofer 2004). Prodromou (2003) proposes the notion of the 'successful user of English' as a focus, rather than the narrowly defined native speaker. Others argue that learners may prefer to approximate native-speaker norms without losing what Timmis (2005) calls their 'cultural integrity' (see also Carter and McCarthy 1996; Timmis 2002).

One important use of learner data is the English Profile project. This aims to establish empirically validated reference-level descriptions for English for the six levels of the Common European Framework of Reference for Languages (CEFR). It is based on the Cambridge Learner Corpus of Cambridge ESOL written examination scripts and spoken learner data gathered internationally from classrooms and other settings. This is set to inform course materials for many years.

Size of corpus

McCarthy and Carter (2001) assert that 'size isn't everything', arguing that small, carefully constructed corpora can yield fruitful research results. For the course-book writer, however, the bigger the corpus the better, not just for linguistic reasons (e.g. frequency of lexical and grammatical items) but also for coverage of a wide range of topics and situations. A typical four-level course-book series might address between fifty and eighty topics and in a larger corpus there is a greater likelihood of finding more topics discussed.

3. What areas of the course book can a corpus inform?

A corpus can assist a course-book writer in several ways, including constructing a graded lexico-grammatical syllabus and finding appropriate texts and realistic settings for the presentation and practice of target language.

Information about the language syllabus

First and foremost a corpus provides information about different aspects of the language, which is normally the basis of the syllabus (see Walsh, this volume). Tognini Bonelli (2001) advocates the 'corpus-driven' approach, where the corpus provides the basis of the description of language usage without recourse to previously held beliefs, above the 'corpus-based' approach, where the corpus provides examples for pre-existing rules. As successful course books generally fit within an established body of knowledge in terms of language description, the course-book writer may be more inclined to the latter (see Gavioli and Aston 2001). McCarthy (1998) advocates a third approach, 'corpus-informed', which borrows from both approaches and is suggested as an alternative possibility.

Vocabulary syllabus

Corpus software can easily generate lists of the most frequent words (whether lemmatised or as individual word-forms) in a given corpus. These enable the writer to establish the common core vocabulary that learners are likely to need as a priority as opposed to a more advanced vocabulary, which can be taught later (see O'Keeffe *et al.* 2007: Ch. 2). Frequency lists which 'band' vocabulary into the most frequent 1,000 words, 2,000 words, etc., can be the basis for organising vocabulary for different levels of a course book. The syllabus of *The Cobuild English Course* (Willis and Willis 1987–8) with its lexical approach was determined by word frequency. The most frequent 700 words with their common patterns were taught in Level 1, the next 800 in Level 2, and so on (see Willis 1990). Frequency also helps the writer to prioritise which members of large lexical sets – for example colours, foods, clothes – to teach first, or see which of two or three synonyms is more frequent (e.g. *sofa* or *couch*; *eat breakfast* or *have breakfast*) and identify the most frequent collocates of delexical verbs such as *make* and *do*. For writers of more specialist courses such as English for Academic Purposes courses, the Academic Wordlist created by Averil Coxhead (Coxhead 2000) from a corpus of 3,500,000 academic texts provides an invaluable resource of lists of 570 word families (excluding the top 2,000 most frequent words in English) from which to devise a vocabulary syllabus (see Coxhead, this volume). Similarly, the Cambridge Learner Corpus of written scripts from Cambridge ESOL examinations provides writers of examination courses with information about typical errors made by candidates in those examinations, around which a syllabus area can be built. See Capel and Sharp (2008) as an example.

While frequency is a useful guide, it may not always be the only criterion in building a syllabus. Members of some vocabulary sets, such as colours, have different frequencies (*red* being six times more frequent than *orange* in spoken North American English), so may occur in different frequency 'bands'. Days of the week provide the best example of why strict banding might not be the only criterion, as only four of the seven occur in the top 1,000 words in conversation, and yet it seems common sense to teach the seven days together. Many corpora are collected in native-speaker environments: homes, work places, social gatherings and service encounters; they contain the everyday interactions of native speakers in their own professional and social settings. Non-native speakers may operate in different settings, interacting either as visitor or host either in their own or a different language environment. Their communication needs are not necessarily always the same as native speakers interacting with native speakers. Furthermore, few corpora include data from classrooms, which have their own specialist vocabulary that would not occur as frequently in general corpora: for example, classroom objects (*board, highlighter pen*), processes and instructions (*underline, fill in the gaps*) and linguistic metalanguage (*noun, verb,* etc.). Finally, some of the most frequent words in a native-speaker corpus may present a major learning challenge to elementary learners because of their associated patterns. For example, *supposed* and *already* are both in the first 500 words in conversation, but in order to use these, learners may need to learn grammatical structures or meanings which are not usually taught or which are difficult to explain at early elementary level. So the writer has to make judgements about which items from the computer-generated lists to include and in what order, balancing what is frequent with what is useful and what is easily taught and learned.

Grammar syllabus

In general, corpus software has not been able to automatically generate lists of the most common grammatical structures in the same way that it can list the most frequent vocabulary. To get a sense of grammatical frequency, one can manually count structures in corpus samples. Not surprisingly, perhaps, conversation contains a high proportion of simple present and past, a lower frequency of continuous verb forms, and complex verb phrases consisting of modal verbs with perfect aspect are less frequent still. Biber *et al.* (1999) is an invaluable resource of such genre-specific grammatical information. Manual counting is also required, for example, to classify the meanings of common modal verbs like *can* and *must*, and again this research can inform the writer's choice of which meaning(s) to present first.

As with vocabulary, frequency may not be the only criterion for deciding what items to teach and in what order. There is a strong expectation in some parts of the English-teaching world of the order in which grammatical structures should be taught. For example, many teachers believe the present continuous forms should be taught before the simple past form, even though the present continuous is far less frequent in a general spoken corpus. This may be because it builds on the present of *be* – traditionally the first grammatical structure taught – or because it is useful in class in describing pictures and actions, as part of vocabulary building. A course book which adheres to linguistic principles but ignores teacher expectation may not succeed.

Lexico-grammatical patterns

Having established a core lexical and grammatical inventory, the writer can then look to a corpus for more information about usage. Basic corpus software such as concordancing applications can clearly reveal information about not just vocabulary patterns, such as collocations, but also patterns that grammar and vocabulary form together. One example is verb complementation, which is often tested at intermediate levels, especially of verbs such as *mind*, *suggest* and *recommend*. What the corpus shows is a far less complex use of these verbs than is suggested by the amount of testing they receive. For example, with the verb *mind* in requests and permission-seeking speech acts with *do you* and *would you*, four basic patterns seem possible:

Requests

1 Do you mind + … ing: e.g. *Do you mind helping me for a second?*
2 Would you mind + … ing: e.g. *Would you mind helping me for a second?*

Asking for permission

3 Do you mind + if: e.g. *Do you mind if I leave early today?*
4 Would you mind + if: e.g. *Would you mind if I leave (or left) early today?*

(In addition there is the possibility of adding an object, e.g. *Would you mind* ***me*** *asking you something?* and the use of a possessive: *Would you mind* ***my asking*** *you something?*)

However, in a corpus of North American English conversation only two patterns emerge as overwhelmingly more frequent than any others, as shown in the concordance lines below, which are a representative selection from the corpus.

	Would you mind taking that day?
	Would you mind?
bus driver said	'**Would you mind** taking the seat by the window because he
	Would you mind seeing if Nick wants cake Joel?
	Would you mind ...
	Would you mind talking to us just for a minute?
	Would you mind?
	Would you mind?
the person says	'**Would you mind** signing this form?'
And I was like	'**Would you mind** driving us to Norris?'
	Would you mind me asking what kind of dog is this?
	Would you mind answering a couple of questions real qui
	Do you mind if I grab this?
	Do you mind if I go get a drink first?
She's like	'**Do you mind**?'
	Do you mind if I put some makeup on real quick?
	Do you mind?
	Do you mind if I uh take the um apple juice in the car
	Do you mind if I take these pretzels?
	Do you mind?
	Do you mind if I take a picture of your chocolates?
	Do you mind us taping it?
	'**Do you mind** if there's like white?
	Do you mind if I put the thing on there?

(Cambridge International Corpus, North American English Conversation)

Do you mind is mostly used in the expression *Do you mind* ***if I*** ... to ask permission to do something and *Would you mind* is mostly used as *Would you mind* + ... ***ing*** to ask other people to do something. In some cases the phrases are used with no complement. The more complex patterns with an object (*Would you mind* ***me*** *asking* ... and *Do you mind* ***us*** *taping* ...) are also much less frequent. This kind of information can help the writer determine what is core common usage and what is more advanced. Similarly, in British English the structure *suggest* + object + base form as in *I suggest you read that article* accounts for only about 5 per cent of uses of the word *suggest* in both spoken and written English, yet this structure has often been tested in English examinations as if it were frequent. The course-book writer may occasionally, therefore, have to 'ignore' what the corpus reveals in order to cover what is in the testing syllabus.

Discourse management

As well as providing lists of single words and sets of collocations, corpus software can also generate lists of items that contain more than one word, normally between two- and seven-word items, variously called 'multi-word units', 'clusters', 'chunks', 'lexical phrases' or 'lexical bundles' (see Greaves and Warren, this volume; Nattinger and DeCarrico 1992; Biber *et al.* 1999; O'Keeffe *et al.* 2007). Some of the items on these lists are 'fragments' or sequences of words that do not have a meaning as expressions in their own right, such as *in the*, *and I* and *of the*. These are frames for extended structures, for example ***in the*** *beginning,* etc. (see Greaves and Warren, this volume). However, there are a large number of items which are expressions with their own intrinsic meaning, as in Table 30.1.

Many of these items are much more frequent than the everyday, basic single words that are normally taught at an elementary level. Chunks such as *I mean, I don't know* and *or something* are more frequent than the single words *six, black* and *woman*, which are undeniably part of a general elementary course syllabus. With such frequency, these multi-word items are worthy of inclusion in the syllabus whether as vocabulary or as part of conversation skills (see O'Keeffe *et al.* 2007).

Such multi-word items can be classified into broad functional categories. For example, in the small selection of items from conversation above there are vague category markers (*and all that, or something like that, and things like that*) and hedging and stance expressions (*a little bit, I guess, as a matter of fact)*, which are characteristic of casual conversation. Many of the four-word chunks in conversation include the phrase *I don't know* (+ *if, what, how*, etc.) which often functions as an 'involving phrase', to acknowledge that the listener may have experience or knowledge of a topic before the speaker gives information or an opinion, as in *I don't know if you've seen that movie, been to that city*, etc. (see Carter and McCarthy 2006: Sections 109 and 505c). O'Keeffe *et al.* (2007) refer to such language as 'relational' as opposed to 'transactional' as it is concerned with establishing and managing relationships with interlocutors. Together with single-word discourse markers (*well, anyway, so, now*) this vocabulary may be said to constitute a vocabulary *of* conversation, i.e. a vocabulary which characterises conversation, as distinct from more general vocabulary found *in* conversation (McCarten 2007). In McCarthy *et al.* (2005a, 2005b, 2006a, 2006b) this relational language and associated discourse management strategies are classified into four broad macro functions, which form the basis of a conversation management syllabus. These are:

- managing your own talk – discourse markers, which enable speakers to manage their own turns in a conversation (*I mean, the thing is, on the other hand*);
- taking account of the listener – such as the vague category markers and involving phrases above, hedging and stance expressions (*just a little bit, kind of, to be honest with you, from my point of view*);

Table 30.1 Expressions from frequency lists in the Cambridge International Corpus, North American Conversation

No. of words in phrase	*Examples*
two	*you know, I mean, I guess, or something*
three	*a little bit, and all that*
four	*or something like that, and things like that, I don't know if*
five	*you know what I mean, as a matter of fact*
six	*it was nice talking to you; and all that kind of stuff*
seven+ words	*a lot of it has to do (with) ...*

- 'listenership' (see McCarthy 2002) – response tokens and expressions to acknowledge the contribution of another speaker (*that's great, I know what you mean*);
- managing the conversation as a whole (*speaking of, going back to*; *well anyway* to end a conversation).

While writing shares some of the relational language of conversation, including more formal vague language (*and so on*, etc.) and discourse marking (*in conclusion, on the other hand*), chunks in writing are more frequently associated with orienting the reader in space and time (*at the end of the, for the first time*) and expressing connections *(in terms of, as a result of)* (see O'Keeffe *et al.* 2007). These chunks perform important strategies and thus merit inclusion in academic writing courses alongside the items on the Academic Word List.

Contexts of use

Close reading of a corpus can also confirm the frequency of structures in certain contexts. One example is the use of the past tense – especially of the verbs *have, need* and *want* – as a way of asking questions indirectly, as in the examples below:

Example 1 (At a US department store perfumery counter)
Clerk: So **did you want** to purchase anything or you just wanted to try 'em?
Customer: We we **wanted** to try.
How much are those?
(Cambridge International Corpus, North American English Conversation)

Example 2 (At a large informal dinner party)
Speaker 1: Can I have a fork? I'm just gonna keep asking you for things until I get everything I need.
Speaker 2: What **did you want?**
Speaker 1: A fork please.
Anything else up there look good?
(Cambridge International Corpus, North American English Conversation)

Another example is the use of the present tense in spoken narratives about the past to highlight events, people or things (Schiffrin 1981). This is common in informal narratives, as in the example below where the speaker switches from the past tense to the present once the context is set:

Example 3 (Informal narrative to a friend)
I was sitting out in the yard and my sister made me eat a mud pie. You know?
Here she **is** eighteen months older than me and **I'm sitting** out in the yard and she she **has** all these mud pies
(Cambridge International Corpus, North American English Conversation)

By observing such uses, the writer can decide whether to augment the traditional grammar syllabus with these 'relational' uses of grammar. The decision may be influenced by space and time factors, teacher or publisher expectation and acceptance and, as noted earlier, the testing syllabus.

Models for presentation and practice

By observing in a corpus how people choose their language according to the situation they are in and the people they are with, the course-book writer can select appropriate, realistic and typical contexts in which to present and practise grammatical structures or vocabulary. An example from grammar is the use of *must* in conversation, which is used overwhelmingly to express speculation rather than obligation and is often found in responses and reactions to what the speaker hears or sees.

Example 4 (Woman talking about business travel to a stranger)
Speaker 1: They put me up in hotels and things.
Speaker 2: Oh that's nice. That's always fun.
Speaker 1: It's not too bad.
Speaker 2: Yeah. It **must be** tough though. Moving back and forth a lot.
(Cambridge International Corpus, North American English conversation)

This can be practised in exercises such as the one in Figure 30.1.

B Think of a response to each sentence using *That must be* or *You must be* plus an adjective from the box. Then practice with a partner.

1. I've been taking dance lessons. ***"That must be fun."***
2. The elevator's not working, so I have to walk up to the tenth floor.
3. I just won a scholarship to go to college.
4. I often get up and study at 5:00 in the morning.
5. I'm going skydiving next week.
6. We're reading a book on ethics in my philosophy class.
7. I'm going out on a blind date tonight.

annoying	hard
bored	interesting
boring	motivated
excited	nervous
exciting	pleased
fascinating	proud
fun	scary
happy	tired

Figure 30.1 Extract from *Touchstone Student Book 3*
Source: McCarthy, McCarten and Sandiford, 2006a: 112.

Similarly, listenership activities can be included alongside listening comprehension activities using simple and familiar exercise formats. In the activity in Figure 30.2, Part A

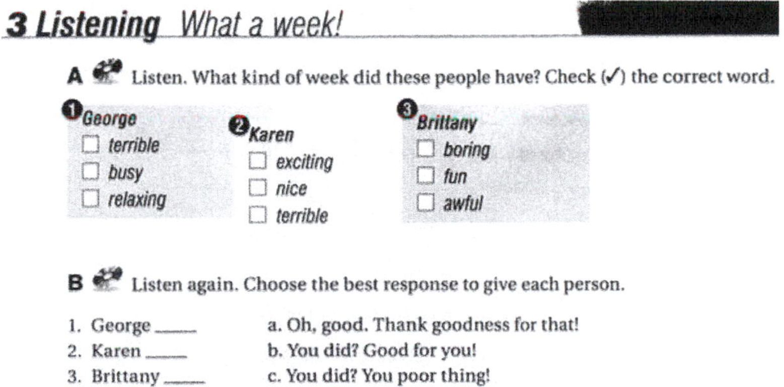
3 Listening *What a week!*

A Listen. What kind of week did these people have? Check (✓) the correct word.

1 *George*
☐ *terrible*
☐ *busy*
☐ *relaxing*

2 *Karen*
☐ *exciting*
☐ *nice*
☐ *terrible*

3 *Brittany*
☐ *boring*
☐ *fun*
☐ *awful*

B Listen again. Choose the best response to give each person.

1. George ____ a. Oh, good. Thank goodness for that!
2. Karen ____ b. You did? Good for you!
3. Brittany ____ c. You did? You poor thing!

Figure 30.2 Extract from *Touchstone Student Book 1*
Source: McCarthy, McCarten and Sandiford, 2005a: 103.

is a more traditional listening comprehension question, in which students listen for a main idea (what kind of week the speaker has had). Part B develops the listenership skill and asks students to choose an appropriate response for each speaker. This can be developed by asking students for further ideas for responses.

4. How can corpus data be used in a course book?

Information about the language

Corpora and the software to analyse them are unfamiliar to many course-book users and are perhaps seen as for specialists. Course books have generally borrowed little from the explicit use of corpus data seen in data-driven learning (DDL) (see chapters by Gilquin and Granger, Chambers and Sripicharn, this volume). However, information derived from corpus research can be used 'invisibly' in materials. The writer can include the most frequent structures, vocabulary, collocations and patterns in a course book without telling users where they came from or why they are included. However, it can be useful to let teachers and learners know more about the language presented. Information about frequency can provide a justification and motivation for learning something and help users see the value of learning high-frequency expressions such as *I mean*, *I guess*, etc. McCarthy *et al.* (2005a, 2005b, 2006a, 2006b) provide 'corpus factoids' about frequency and use such as the ones in Figure 30.3 and 30.4.

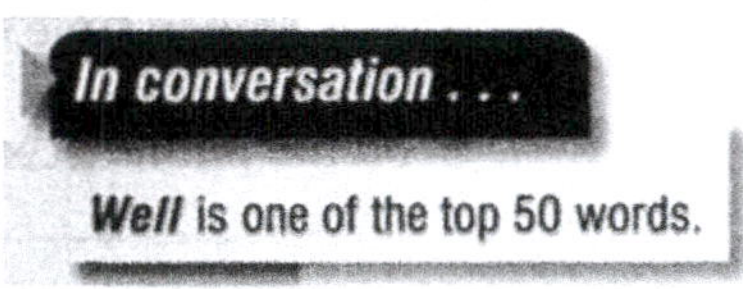

In conversation . . .
Well is one of the top 50 words.

Figure 30.3 Extract from *Touchstone Student Book 1*
Source: McCarthy, McCarten and Sandiford, 2005a: 39.

In conversation . . .

Must means "have to" in 10% of its uses. In this meaning, it is often used in expressions like ***I must admit*** and ***I must say***.

90% of the uses of ***must*** are for speculation:
Things must be hard for couples who marry young.

Figure 30.4 Extract from *Touchstone Student Book 4*
Source: McCarthy, McCarten and Sandiford, 2006b: 45.

Using corpus texts for presentation

Authentic written texts, i.e. texts from real-world sources such as newspapers, advertising and novels, have long been used in course materials, more so than spoken texts, which are often invented. A corpus of real conversations can provide excellent raw material for course-book presentations. However, unedited corpus conversations can be problematic for several reasons.

- They can be of limited interest to others (teaching material has to engage students' interest above all) and have little real-world 'content' to build on in follow-up activities. Few contain the humour that some teachers and learners enjoy.
- It may be difficult for an outside reader to understand the context and purpose of the conversation (see Mishan 2004).
- Conversations may contain references to people, places and things that are only known to the original speakers and may have no discernible start or end.
- They may contain taboo words or topics which are unsuitable for teaching materials.
- Some speakers are not very 'fluent' and their speech contains a lot of repetition and rephrasing, hesitation, false starts and digression. Conversations with these features can be difficult to read – they were not meant to be read, after all – or listen to.
- People often speak at the same time, which is difficult to hear on audio recordings and reproduce in print, especially in multi-party conversations.
- Real conversations may include vocabulary and structures that distract from the main teaching goal, being too advanced or arcane or requiring lengthy explanation.
- Some teachers may feel 'unprepared' to teach features of spoken grammar which are not in the popular training literature or practice resources.
- Dialectal and informal usage may be considered incorrect by some teachers (e.g. non-standard verb forms such as *would have went*, *less* + plural count noun, etc.) Some teachers also disapprove of spoken discourse markers and relational language such as *you know*, *like*, *well* and *I mean*, and hesitation markers *um*, *uh*. In an informal survey of seventy ESL teachers from different sectors in Illinois, USA, McCarthy and McCarten (2002) found teachers more disapproving of these phrases than the grammatically debatable usage of *there's* + plural noun.
- Normally obligatory words are often 'omitted' in speaking (ellipsis), especially when there is a lot of shared context. For example, one colleague might say to another *You having lunch?* or *Having lunch?* or simply *Lunch?* instead of *Are you having lunch?* Some teachers may find it problematic to use such models without a finite verb, subject or auxiliary verb, especially when it appears the grammar 'rules' are broken.
- Real conversations rarely contain the number or variety of examples of a target structure, such as first, second and third persons, singular and plural, affirmative and negative forms.
- Conversations are often too long to reproduce on the page. Elementary course materials often have publisher-imposed limits of fifty–sixty words per presentation.
- Conversations where one speaker has much more to say than the other can be difficult to practise in pairs.

These are many ways in which real conversations differ from those in traditional course books (see Gilmore 2004), but it is possible to replicate natural-sounding conversations by applying some general principles:

- Keep turns generally short, unless someone is telling a story. Even then, back-channelling and non-minimal responses can be included for the listener (McCarthy 2002, 2003).
- Ensure that speakers interact, for example by reacting to the previous speaker, before adding a new contribution to the conversation (see Tao 2003).
- Conversation is usually not very lexically dense and information is not so tightly packed as is often the case in course-book conversations, so ensure a balance of transactional and relational language with an appropriate lexical density (Ure 1971; Stubbs 1986).
- Build in some repetition, rephrasing, fragmented sentences and features of real speech, in ways that do not interfere with comprehension.
- Adhere to politeness norms, in the sense described by Brown and Levinson (1987). Course books occasionally contain discussions where speakers are unrealistically confrontational and face-threatening to each other. While there may be cultural issues to consider here – and course books should not impose English-speakers' cultural norms – it is worth noting that native speakers of English are more likely to prefer indirect strategies in discussion, for example, *I disagree with* ***that*** rather than *I disagree with* ***you***. See also Tao (2007). This is not to deny learners 'the right to be impolite' (Mugford 2008), which is a separate question.

One issue in representing conversation in course books is punctuation of, for example, pauses, incomplete words, ellipsis and false starts. More problematic is that there is no accepted orthographic form for common articulations of some structures (e.g. *wouldn't've* for *wouldn't have; what****'s*** *he do* for *what* ***does*** *he do?*). Also transcription conventions for common features of conversation, such as overlapping or latched turns, are not widely known. Here simplifications may have to be made.

Exploiting authentic spoken data in course material for listening comprehension is well established. Swan and Walter (1984, 1990) were among the first to include what they called '"untidy" natural language' as listening practice. As interest in teaching the spoken language grows, materials will no doubt focus more explicitly on features of conversation management and develop a classroom-friendly metalanguage and methodologies for doing so. Concepts such as 'hedging', 'sentence frames', 'reciprocation' and 'pre-closing' can be translated into more transparent terms for the classroom, for example, 'softening what you say', 'introducing what you say', 'keeping the conversation going' and 'ending the conversation'. As some of these concepts are still new in materials, it is important to find ways to present and practise these features using non-threatening and familiar exercise types. Teaching such features may best be done with techniques that ask learners to 'notice' (see Schmidt 1990), find examples of a feature which has been exemplified or find ways in which speakers perform particular functions.

5. The future of corpus-informed course books

A more corpus-informed future?

It is hoped that more course materials will be corpus-informed and that writers will have greater access to corpora, or else to published output such as frequency lists based on major corpora (Leech *et al.* 2001) and corpus research findings. Specialised corpora such as the language of business (see McCarthy and Handford 2004), tourism and other vocational settings will no doubt inform materials aimed at students of these types of language.

Improved voice-to-text software for transcription will make the collecting of larger spoken corpora easier and cheaper. Developments in analytical software, such as refined automatic tagging and parsing of corpora and more sensitive collocational tools, should enable researchers to gain greater depth of language knowledge to pass on to learners in materials. Areas for further research will include the frequency and distribution of grammar structures or vocabulary in different text types and extended lexico-grammatical patterns.

Print versus electronic delivery

Until recently, courses have been delivered primarily in printed book form for use in classrooms by groups of students with a teacher. With the increasing sophistication of computer software, faster internet speeds and e-books, it is likely that more educational content will be delivered on the internet in virtual learning environments which users can access individually in addition to, or independently of, the classroom. Course *materials* will therefore need to adapt to online learning environments, in more flexible learning packages delivered electronically as well as in book form. The electronic medium can offer teachers and learners easier access to corpora so DDL approaches may enter more mainstream materials. As concordancing software becomes more user-friendly and its aims more transparent to a wider audience, it is possible to envisage concordancers being part of blended learning packages, possibly as complementary to dictionary or grammar reference material. Corpora can be specially compiled to reflect the course content and aims, or can even be graded to help lower-level students access the material, as proposed by Allan (2009).

Multi-modal corpora are now being developed (see Ackerley and Coccetta 2007; Adolphs and Carter 2007; Knight and Adolphs 2007; Carter and Adolphs 2008) in which audio and video are captured alongside the transcribed text. From a research point of view, this should enhance language description, adding information about prosodic features, gesture or body language to our knowledge of grammar, vocabulary and pragmatics. For learners and teachers, multi-modal corpora may be a more user-friendly tool for classroom use.

In summary, there is bright future for corpus-informed course materials. Bringing into the classroom the language of the world outside gives learners greater opportunities to increase their understanding of natural language and the choice to use it. And this is surely the ultimate aim of all of us who are engaged in language teaching.

Further reading

Carter, R. and Adolphs, S. (2008) 'Linking the Verbal and Visual: New Directions for Corpus Linguistics', *Language and Computers* 64: 275–91. (A fascinating look into the future of multi-modal corpus research methodology and findings.)

Cullen, R. and Kuo, I.-C. (2007) 'Spoken Grammar and ELT Course Materials: A Missing Link?' *TESOL Quarterly* 41(2): 361–86. (An interesting analysis of how spoken grammar is represented in course books.)

Gilmore, A. (2004) 'A Comparison of Textbook and Authentic Interactions', *ELT Journal* 58(4): 363–71. (A good overview of differences between real conversations and those in course books.)

O'Keeffe, A., McCarthy, M. J., and Carter, R. A. (2007) *From Corpus to Classroom*. Cambridge: Cambridge University Press. (An excellent introduction to corpus research and its practical pedagogical applications.)

References

Ackerley, K. and Coccetta, F. (2007) 'Enriching Language Learning through a Multimedia Corpus', *ReCALL* 19: 351–70.

Adolphs, S. and Carter, R. (2007) 'Beyond the Word: New Challenges in Analysing Corpora of Spoken English', *European Journal of English Studies* 11(2): 133–46.

Allan, R. (2009) 'Can a graded reader corpus provide "authentic" input?', *ELT Journal* 63(1): 23–32.

Andersen, G. and Stenström, A.-B. (1996) 'COLT: A Progress Report', *ICAME Journal* 20: 133–6.

Biber, D., Conrad, S. and Reppen, R. (1998) *Corpus Linguistics: Investigating Language Structure and Use*. Cambridge: Cambridge University Press.

Biber, D., Johannson, S., Leech, G., Conrad, S. and Finnegan, E. (1999) *Longman Grammar of Spoken and Written English*. London: Longman.

Brown, P. and Levinson, S. (1987) *Politeness: Some Universals in Language Usage*. Cambridge: Cambridge University Press.

Capel, A. and Sharp, W. (2008) *Objective First Certificate, Student's Book*, second edition. Cambridge: Cambridge University Press.

Carter, R. and Adolphs, S. (2008) 'Linking the Verbal and Visual: New Directions for Corpus Linguistics', *Language and Computers* 64: 275–91.

Carter, R. and McCarthy, M. J. (1996) 'Correspondence', *ELT Journal*, 50: 369–71.

——(2006) *Cambridge Grammar of English*. Cambridge: Cambridge University Press

Cheng, W. and Warren, M. (2007) 'Checking Understandings: Comparing Textbooks and a Corpus of Spoken English in Hong Kong', *Language Awareness* 16(3): 190–207.

COBUILD (1987) *Collins COBUILD English Language Dictionary*. London: Collins.

——(1990) *Collins COBUILD English Grammar*. London: Collins.

Cook, V. (1999) 'Going Beyond the Native Speaker in Language Teaching', *TESOL Quarterly* 33(2): 185–209.

Coxhead, A. (2000) 'A New Academic Word List', *TESOL Quarterly* 34(2): 213–38. The Academic Wordlist can be found online at http://language.massey.ac.nz/staff/awl/ (accessed August 2008).

Cullen, R. and Kuo, I.-C. (2007) 'Spoken Grammar and ELT Course Materials: A Missing Link?' *TESOL Quarterly* 41(2): 361–86.

English Profile, www.englishprofile.org/

Gavioli, L. and Aston, G. (2001) 'Enriching Reality: Language Corpora in Language Pedagogy', *ELT Journal* 55(3): 238–46.

Gilmore, A. (2004) 'A Comparison of Textbook and Authentic Interactions', *ELT Journal* 58(4): 363–71.

Jenkins, J. (2006) 'Current Perspectives on Teaching World Englishes and English as a Lingua Franca', *Tesol Quarterly* 40(1): 157–81.

Kirkpatrick, A. (2007) *World Englishes*. Cambridge: Cambridge University Press.

Knight, D. and Adolphs, S. (2007) 'Multi-modal Corpus Pragmatics: The Case of Active Listenership', www.mrl.nott.ac.uk/~axc/DReSS_Outputs/Corpus_&_Pragmatics_2007.pdf (accessed August 2008).

Leech, G., Rayson, P. and Wilson, A. (2001) *Word Frequencies in Written and Spoken English: Based on the British National Corpus*. Harlow: Longman.

McCarten, J. (2007) *Teaching Vocabulary – Lessons from the Corpus, Lessons for the Classroom*. New York: Cambridge University Press Marketing Department.

McCarthy, M. J. (1998) *Spoken Language and Applied Linguistics*. Cambridge: Cambridge University Press.

——(2002) 'Good Listenership Made Plain: British and American Non-minimal Response Tokens in Everyday Conversation', in R. Reppen, S. Fitzmaurice and D. Biber (eds) *Using Corpora to Explore Linguistic Variation*. Amsterdam: John Benjamins, pp. 49–71.

——(2003) 'Talking Back: "Small" Interactional Response Tokens in Everyday Conversation', in J. Coupland (ed.) 'Small Talk', special issue of *Research on Language and Social Interaction* 36(1): 33–63.

McCarthy, M. J. and Carter, R. (2001) 'Size Isn't Everything: Spoken English, Corpus, and the Classroom', *TESOL Quarterly* 35(2): 337–40.

McCarthy, M. J. and Handford, M. (2004) '"Invisible to Us": A Preliminary Corpus-based Study of Spoken Business English', in U. Connor and T. Upton (eds) *Discourse in the Professions. Perspectives from Corpus Linguistics*. Amsterdam: John Benjamins, pp. 167–201.

McCarthy, M. J. and McCarten, J. (2002) Unpublished study of seventy Illinois teachers' reactions to conversation extracts in classroom materials.

McCarthy, M. J., McCarten, J. and Sandiford, H. (2005a) *Touchstone Student's Book 1*. Cambridge: Cambridge University Press.

——(2005b) *Touchstone Student's Book 2*. Cambridge: Cambridge University Press.

——(2006a) *Touchstone Student's Book 3*. Cambridge: Cambridge University Press.

——(2006b) *Touchstone Student's Book 4*. Cambridge: Cambridge University Press.

Mishan, F. (2004) 'Authenticating Corpora for Language Learning: A Problem and its Resolution', *ELT Journal* 58(3): 219–27.

Mugford, G. (2008) 'How Rude! Teaching Impoliteness in the Second-language Classroom', *ELT Journal* 62(4): 375–84.

Nattinger, J. and DeCarrico, J. (1992) *Lexical Phrases and Language Teaching*. Oxford: Oxford University Press.

O'Keeffe, A., McCarthy, M. J. and Carter, R. A. (2007) *From Corpus to Classroom: Language Use and Language Teaching*. Cambridge: Cambridge University Press.

Prodromou, L. (2003) 'In Search of the Successful User of English', *Modern English Teacher* 12(2): 5–14.

Schiffrin, D. (1981) 'Tense Variation in Narrative', *Language* 57(1): 45–62.

Schmidt, R. (1990) 'The Role of Consciousness in Second Language Learning', *Applied Linguistics* 11: 129–58.

Seidlhofer, B. (2004) 'Research Perspectives on Teaching English as a Lingua Franca', *Annual Review of Applied Linguistics* 24: 209–39, Cambridge: Cambridge University Press.

——(2005) 'English as a Lingua Franca', *ELT Journal* 59(4): 339–41.

Sinclair, J. (ed.) (1987) *COBUILD English Language Dictionary*. Glasgow: Collins.

Stubbs, M. (1986) 'Lexical Density: A Computational Technique and Some Findings', in R. M. Coulthard (ed.) *Talking About Text*. Birmingham: English Language Research, pp. 27–42.

Swan, M. and Walter, C. (1984) *The Cambridge English Course Teacher's Book 1*. Cambridge: Cambridge University Press.

——(1990) *The New Cambridge English Course Teacher's Book 1*. Cambridge: Cambridge University Press.

Tao, H. (2003) 'Turn Initiators in Spoken English: A Corpus-based Approach to Interaction and Grammar', in P. Leistyna and C. F. Meyer (eds) *Language and Computers, Corpus Analysis: Language Structure and Language Use*. Amsterdam: Rodopi, pp. 187–207.

——(2007) 'A Corpus-based Investigation of Absolutely and Related Phenomena in Spoken American English', *Journal of English Linguistics* 35(1): 5–29.

Timmis, I. (2002) 'Native-speaker Norms and International English: A Classroom View', *ELT Journal* 56(3): 240–9.

——(2005) 'Towards a Framework for Teaching Spoken Grammar', *ELT Journal* 59 (2): 117–25.

Tognini Bonelli, E. (2001) *Corpus Linguistics at Work*. Amsterdam: John Benjamins.

Ure, J. (1971) 'Lexical Density and Register Differentiation', in G. E. Perren and J. L. M. Trim (eds) *Applications of Linguistics: Selected Papers of the Second International Congress of Applied Linguistics, Cambridge, 1969*. Cambridge: Cambridge University Press, pp. 443–52.

Widdowson, H. G. (2000) 'On the Limitations of Linguistics Applied', *Applied Linguistics* 21(1): 3–25.

Willis, D. (1990) *The Lexical Syllabus, A New Approach to Language Teaching*. Glasgow: Collins.

Willis, D. and Willis, J. (1987–8) *The Cobuild English Course*. Glasgow: Collins.

31
Using corpora to write dictionaries

Elizabeth Walter

1. Why do lexicographers use corpora?

Lexicography is a discipline characterised by an unusual degree of overlap between the commercial and the academic. Collaboration between linguists and dictionary publishing houses has made possible the creation of huge, state-of-the-art corpora and highly sophisticated tools of analysis which have transformed lexicography and had a huge influence on linguistics as a whole.

Any lexicographer working with the English language today must owe a huge debt to that evangelist of corpus lexicography, John Sinclair. While the *American Heritage Dictionary* of 1969 was the first to make use of corpus information, Sinclair and his team at Birmingham University, UK (in collaboration with Collins publishers), went far further in marrying the theory of large-scale corpus analysis with almost every aspect of the practice of lexicography in their groundbreaking *COBUILD* (Collins Birmingham University International Language Database) dictionary of 1987.

At the time, their work was highly controversial. Not surprisingly, publishers balked at the idea that building costly large corpora was necessary to the business of writing dictionaries, and some traditional lexicographers were unwilling to concede that their own intuition might not be adequate to describe the language in general. Twenty years later, however, the debate has been decisively won: lexicographers in all the major publishing houses have access to large corpora of both written and spoken (transcribed) texts, and their methods have spread into other areas of publishing, most notably that of grammars and language teaching materials (see chapters by Hughes and McCarten, this volume).

Corpora or native speaker intuition?

Before the advent of computerised corpora, most lexicographers used a system of citations, or 'reading and marking', where evidence of usages was found in texts and recorded in some way, often stored on index cards. This kind of evidence is still used today, because for some types of information it can usefully complement corpus evidence (see Section 3).

However, as Sinclair points out, 'Especially in lexicography, there is a marked contrast between the data collected by computer and that collected by human readers exercising their judgment on what should or should not be selected for inclusion in a dictionary' (Sinclair 1991: 4). When Boris Becker crashed out of the Wimbledon tennis championship in 1987, the UK tabloid newspaper *The Sun* said he had been spending too much time 'bonking' (a mild, informal term for having sexual intercourse). Challenged on this, Becker replied that he did not know what was meant, as the word was not in his dictionary. Since it had been in wide use for some time by then, one can only assume that lexicographers had made some sort of judgement that this was not a 'real' word and did not merit dictionary status.

Corpus lexicography does not allow of this sort of personal prejudice, nor does it allow the lexicographer simply to ignore tricky usages. Each corpus line must either be accounted for or discarded for a valid reason. It is much more difficult to ignore a meaning that is in front of you in black and white than one which comes into your head, but which you can easily persuade yourself is actually an aberration.

Using corpora forces the lexicographer to become much more objective. Without a corpus, it is easy and tempting (often through no wish to deceive but rather a conviction that one is simply presenting the truth) to come up with evidence that supports a preconceived notion. Example sentences, for instance, will be invented to support the definition that is written (see Section 3). With a corpus, the process is entirely reversed: we must start with the evidence and match the description to it.

Corpora, therefore, help us to analyse language with objectivity, help us to identify senses of words and their relative frequency, and give us the evidence we need to support what we say about language in our dictionaries.

How big does a corpus for lexicographers need to be?

When it comes to corpus size, the general consensus seems to be that big is beautiful, and the increasing availability of text in electronic form has made the collection of huge amounts of data much more viable. Oxford and Cambridge University Presses, for instance, now both boast corpora of over a billion words. To see what this means in practical terms, it is useful to look at some examples. Table 31.1 shows frequency per ten million words (rounded to the nearest whole number) according to the Cambridge International Corpus.

Table 31.1 shows that even in a corpus of one million words, 'effort' is likely to occur around 148 times. However, 'effortless' – a word which would strike most native speakers as not at all obscure – would occur only once or twice. If this sample is representative, even in a twenty-million-word corpus, it may only occur around twenty-six times, which is probably not enough to give reliable information on features such as its typical collocation patterns.

Table 31.1 Word frequency data

Word	*Frequency per ten million words*
effort (includes plural, efforts)	1,484
effortless	13
efficient	184
effusive	6
effusion	3

What should be in the corpus?

Of course, quantity of data is not the only important characteristic. With the internet, it is possible now to gather almost unlimited amounts of text, but without some sort of monitoring and selection of content there is the danger that a very distorted picture of the language could emerge (see Biber 1993; Crowdy 1993; McEnery and Wilson 1996; Biber *et al.* 1998; McCarthy 1998; and chapters by Reppen, Nelson, Koester and Adolphs and Knight, this volume).

It is usual, therefore, when building a corpus, to aim at some notion of a 'representative' sample of the language. Debate rages as to what is meant by 'representative' and, indeed, whether such a notion has any academic or practical validity at all (see McEnery *et al.* 2006). In practice, corpus builders in dictionary publishing houses try to aim for a wide range of genres. It is likely that a template of genres would be drawn up and target numbers for each genre collected.

There are four fundamental divisions of genre for lexicographic corpora:

1. **Written or spoken data?** Written data most usually comprises texts that are available electronically, such as newspapers and novels, though other text may be scanned or re-keyed if particular required genres are not available. Spoken data consists of transcripts of speech ranging from general conversation to TV shows. The third edition of the *Longman Dictionary of Contemporary English* was the first to highlight the use of spoken corpora, giving small graphs comparing the frequencies of some words and phrases in written and spoken data.
2. **Regional language variety?** For English, the corpus builder must decide which varieties (e.g. British, US, Australian, Indian) to include, and in what proportions. Many other languages would have similar considerations where they are spoken in various countries or regions of the world.
3. **Synchronic versus diachronic data?** Synchronic data is contemporary or recent material, used for general, contemporary dictionaries. Diachronic data covers historical data, and may include words and usages that are now considered archaic or have fallen out of use altogether. There is a third form of corpus used by some publishers and researchers, which is known as a 'monitor corpus'. A monitor corpus aims to track language change by constantly adding new material and comparing it to a stable 'reference corpus'.
4. **Native speaker or non-native speaker language?** Several publishers, especially those which produce learner dictionaries, have corpora of texts produced by non-native speakers. This data comes most typically from exam scripts or student course work, and is transcribed electronically (see Section 4).

Within those major divisions, an almost infinite number of sub-genres is possible, and their choice will be determined partly by the type of dictionaries being produced and partly by practical considerations of the time and cost involved in their collection. Some examples of these sub-genres might be: broadsheet newspapers, tabloid newspapers, classic novels, modern novels, emails, personal letters, transcripts of service encounters (business-to-customer contact, for instance interactions in shops), transcripts of business meetings, text on product packaging, text messages, transcripts of radio or TV shows.

For lexicographers, the content of the corpus they use will depend on the type of dictionary they are writing. For a general dictionary such as one for learners of English, they will use general sources such as newspapers, novels and general conversations. More specialised lexicography requires more specialised sources. Most corpora will be structured in such a way that it is possible to pull out sub-corpora chosen from a range of criteria, such as subject type, language variety, source genre, age of speaker, etc. Alternatively, special subject corpora may be built, and used either independently from the main, general corpus, or be added to it. For example, when working on a business dictionary, lexicographers might choose to use a corpus built entirely from business-related texts.

One type of corpus that has been used in bilingual lexicography is that of the 'multilingual aligned corpus', otherwise known as the 'parallel corpus'. This may either be a corpus of translated texts, such as the proceedings of the Canadian parliament in French and English, or collections of texts in different languages that attempt to replicate the same distribution of text types. The advantage of the former type is the exact correspondence of texts, but in the latter, the language is more natural because it does not contain translation (see chapters by Kenning, and Kübler and Aston, this volume). The use of such corpora for lexicography has been primarily for technical lexicons, while work on translation studies and contrastive linguistics feeds into general bilingual dictionaries more indirectly (see Hallebeek 2000).

2. Corpus analysis tools for lexicography

In order to make use of the corpus data available to lexicographers, sophisticated analysis tools have been developed. This sort of software is often referred to as a 'corpus query system' (CQS).

The simplest tools are concordancing packages (see the following sub-section for a discussion of concordancing), and there are several of these commercially available (see Tribble, this volume). However, most dictionary publishers will either use tools developed in-house, or buy in a package from an outside supplier. This is because lexicographers want not simply concordances, but much more detailed ways of analysing the enormous amounts of corpus data at their disposal. A package which is currently used by several dictionary publishers is the *Sketch Engine*, developed by Adam Kilgarriff and his company Lexical Computing Ltd (see Kilgarriff *et al.* 2004). This is a web-based system which can use corpora in any language provided it has an appropriate level of linguistic mark-up, and some of its features are discussed in Section 3.

Any corpus query system relies on extensive processing of the data. The corpus will be 'part-of-speech tagged', meaning that every word in the corpus is assigned a part of speech. This is done using computerised systems, and with varying degrees of accuracy (see Section 5). It is also of great benefit if some sort of parsing can be accomplished, to show the relationship of words in context to one another.

Concordancing

In the early days of corpus lexicography, it was common for lexicographers to be presented with a ream of computer printout containing KWIC (keyword in context) concordance lines for the stretch of words they were working on. Although this was a great advance in the provision of evidence for lexicographers, and did enable them to spot senses and patterns that had previously been unrecorded, the sheer mass of unanalysed data was overwhelming for any reasonably common word. If there are several thousand lines for a single search word, a pattern that crops up only once every couple of hundred lines may be statistically significant, but beyond the capabilities of human brain power to calculate.

Once lexicographers were able to have concordance lines on their own computer screens, tools were developed to allow some manipulation of the data. The most simple, yet for lexicographers extremely useful, example is left and right sorting, where the concordance lines are presented alphabetically according to the word to the right or the left of the search word. This sorting serves to highlight common collocations, such as 'strenuous efforts' and 'make … efforts' in Table 31.2.

Common syntactic and grammatical patterns are also shown, such as the use of the infinitive in the right-sorted lines in Table 31.3.

Other tools for lexicographers

There are many other requirements of corpus analysis tools, of which some of the most important are:

- **Lemmatisation**. This means matching any form of a word, with all its inflections, to a base form, usually the form that would be found as a dictionary headword. Thus, a corpus search on 'find' can return data for the forms 'find', 'finds', 'finding' and 'found'. Some tools also allow the user to *exclude* a particular inflection if it is not wanted. As well as going straight to an amalgamated search of all the inflections of a word, it can often be useful to a lexicographer to note the distribution of the inflections. For instance, when looking at the verb 'flood', we note that the form 'flooded' is by far the most common. (Figures from the Cambridge International Corpus show the following frequencies per ten million: 'flood', twenty-six; 'flooded', seventy; 'flooding', twenty-six; 'floods', seven.) This is because the verb is so often used in passive forms, a fact which is useful to record, particularly in a dictionary for learners of English. A related issue, and one on which it is extremely useful for the lexicographer to have corpus guidance, is that of when an inflection takes on a life of its own, for instance when a form with *-ing* or *-ed* (e.g. 'worrying', 'boiled') achieves adjective status. Sinclair (1991: 8) goes so far as to say: 'There is a good case for arguing that each distinct form is potentially

Table 31.2 Left-sorted BNC concordance lines

Brown has made strenuous	**efforts**	to shed his normally lugubrious
Highland has made strenuous	**efforts**	, through cross-shareholdings and
These groups have made strenuous	**efforts**	to get it right – to get the sound
as possible, I have made strenuous	**efforts**	to trace Mr Mint. These efforts

Table 31.3 Right-sorted BNC concordance lines

keen that we make every	**effort**	to achieve maximum attendance
most of us putting in considerable	**effort**	to achieve as much as possible
independence and willpower in an	**effort**	to achieve control over the mother
certain amount of both skill and	**effort**	to achieve decent result

a unique lexical unit, and that forms should only be conflated into lemmas when their environments show a certain amount and type of similarity.'

- **Part-of-speech tagging**. Where a form has more than one part of speech (e.g. 'hand' verb or 'hand' noun), lexicographers will usually want to select one of them. The lemmatisation must work for different parts of speech too: for instance, the lexicographer will want 'houses' the plural noun separately from 'houses' the present tense, third person singular verb.
- **Case sensitivity**. In some cases, lexicographers may want to exclude capitalised forms of a word, or indeed search only for capitalised forms, so as to distinguish between 'Labour' (the UK political party) and 'labour' (work), or between 'Polish' (from Poland) and 'polish' (substance for cleaning furniture).
- **Random selection of lines**. The smaller the corpus, the more it can be distorted by a single unusual text, and similarly, the smaller the section of corpus looked at, the more likely the same thing is to occur. Some corpus systems get round this by making a randomised search for a number of lines (typically something like 1,000) the default search. Others have this facility as an option. It is always important to be aware of the source of a citation, especially when it appears to show something unusual, and to check that multiple instances of the same thing are not simply repeated uses in the same text.
- **Multi-word unit searches**. A good corpus query system will allow searches on multi-word units, though the limitations of automatic parsing may make searching for items containing very common de-lexicalised words difficult in some systems, for instance the particles in phrasal verbs (see Greaves and Warren, this volume).
- **Expanding context**. The default context for viewing a citation line is usually the width of a computer screen. Sometimes this is not enough to understand the context of the citation, so it is useful to be able to expand the citation as much as necessary.
- **Excluding occurrences of fewer than a certain number of instances**. This is a useful, practical refinement for lexicographers. Especially when working on a new dictionary, where decisions on inclusion are to be made, a lexicographer may want to ask the corpus to list all words in an alphabetical stretch which have a minimum number of occurrences in a certain number of words (ten million is a useful benchmark).
- **Filtering**. Within the corpus, texts may be coded by a number of features, such as age/sex of speaker/writer, date of text, genre of text, name of source. The lexicographer may wish to filter text on any of these features. For instance, when using a learner corpus (see Section 4), it would be common to filter on the level of the student or on their native language.

3. Using a corpus to create dictionary text

Semantic division

The early period of corpus use was a salutary one for lexicographers when it became clear how many senses of words in existing dictionaries were not attested.

Of course, the number of senses of any particular word which are covered in a dictionary, and the degree to which senses are split, depends on the target audience of the dictionary. A comparison of any two dictionaries of similar length and target audience quickly makes it apparent that sense division is not an exact science, and the lexicographer's own views come into the decisions. It is sometimes said that there are two types of semanticist, the 'splitters' and the 'lumpers', the former feeling that even fine shades of meaning denote separate senses, with the latter more inclined to identify fewer core senses and to see minor deviations from them as resonating from that core meaning rather than constituting a separate sense.

To give a practical example, Table 31.4 shows KWIC concordance lines for the word 'production', taken from the Cambridge International Corpus. These lines are in the order that they appeared from the random selection of lines by the CQS.

If we look at the entry for 'production' in the *Oxford Advanced Learner's Dictionary*, seventh edition (OALD), we can see that lines 1, 2 and 7 correspond to their sense 1: 'the process of growing or making food, goods, or materials'. Line 8 is covered by sense 2: 'the quantity of goods that is produced', and line 4 by sense 4: 'a film, a play or a broadcast that is prepared for the public; the act of preparing a film, play, etc.'

This leaves lines 3 and 5. The only remaining sense in OALD is sense 3: 'the act or process of making sth naturally'. A 'lumper' might argue that lines 3 and 5 belong here, since the sound of a voice is produced 'naturally'. A 'splitter' on the other hand would probably argue that there is will and effort involved in the production of words and the production of a particular tone. The OALD sense gives as its example: 'drugs to stimulate the production of hormones', implying that the sense covers processes which happen without volition, and thus does not adequately describe lines 3 and 5, both of which sound entirely plausible to a native speaker ear.

The availability of plentiful corpus lines is likely to encourage splitters, as it is easy to find uses which are not unambiguously covered in existing dictionaries. The lexicographer then has to make a judgement about the validity of those lines, considering for instance whether the style and quality of the surrounding text make it a reliable source of evidence, and also whether this usage is attested elsewhere in the corpus.

Use of corpora has particularly changed the treatment of very polysemous words (words with many different meanings, such as 'get', 'far' or 'set'). These words often have the added complication that their meaning may be rather delexical. Indeed, we now see in many dictionaries a different style of definition evolving to deal with some of these senses, often following formulae such as 'used to express … ', or 'used when you … '. These meanings are often not the ones which first come to mind. However, even with corpus evidence, it is still an enormous challenge to distil the senses of a very polysemous word into a coherent set of senses for a dictionary. The lines in Table 31.5, taken from the BNC, illustrate the complexity of such a word. Even in these few lines, it is extremely difficult to say where separate senses are being illustrated.

Table 31.4 Concordance lines for 'production'

1	on all aspects of wine	**production**	and appreciation, as well as the
2	by a jaded sub-editor late on	**production**	night after an incautious trip to the
3	intensively to improve the	**production**	of the words she had produced up
4	was 17, we put on a school	**production**	called Dracula Spectacular and
5	is not deaf to beauty of tone	**production**	as some have been so foolish as to
6	of the world that increased	**production**	is still an important object; in
7	movie distribution because	**production**	is far cheaper than today's
8	output will show that factory	**production**	declined for the fourth month in a

Table 31.5 Concordance lines for 'have'

to only 3% by 1989. This change	**has**	big implications for health planners
in other cases people don't even	**have**	homes to lose. Men and women
although volunteers continue to	**have**	a vitally important role to play
guarantee that people with HIV	**have**	the best choices and continue to
on family life. ACET already	**has**	experience in caring for children
local government financing both	**having**	their effects. However, we are

Collocation

Collocation is the co-occurrence of words with a frequency that is much higher than it would be by chance. For example, we talk about 'heavy traffic' or say that we 'commit a crime'. All good dictionaries for learners of English (and many dictionaries for learners of other languages) contain information on collocation, because it is a key aspect of fluent English, and often quite idiomatic and difficult to predict. The tools used today for identifying collocation build on the work of Church and Hanks, who began looking at the possibilities of statistical analysis of the co-occurrences of words and patterns in large corpora in the 1980s (see Church and Hanks 1990). They recognised that computer power could be used to spot significant patterns that the human brain could not.

In Section 2, we saw how right- and left-sorting can help to show up common collocations. However, in cases where the collocating word is not adjacent to the headword, they would not be highlighted in this way. Each of the following lines, for instance, illustrates the collocation 'reach' with 'compromise':

> I thought we would never be able to reach a compromise.
> Eventually a compromise was reached.
> We are hoping to be able to reach some sort of compromise.

The CQS needs to be able to spot these combinations wherever they occur. Church and Hanks (1990) devised systems that looked not only at words that occur adjacently, but at the co-occurrence of words in the same chunk of text – in practice usually a sentence – irrespective of their position in that text. They referred to this pattern of co-occurrence as 'Mutual Information', and began to produce statistical information on collocation that had not been previously available.

As well as simple frequency of co-occurrence, a system based on Mutual Information will look at the frequency of both the words involved. In basic terms, the less frequent the words, the less likely it would be that they would co-occur by chance, and therefore the more significant their co-occurrence is deemed to be. It will also probably look at the stability of the position of the collocating word in relation to the headword. In general, the more fixed the position (for instance if the collocate occurs two places before the headword in 90 per cent of occurrences), the stronger the collocation. All these factors are used to provide a list of the most significant collocations.

A more recent development of this sort of information is the *Word Sketch*, the product of Kilgarriff's *Sketch Engine* (see Kilgarriff *et al.* 2004). Where this system differs from previous methods is in combining an analysis of both grammatical and collocational behaviour. A traditional corpus frequency list would make no distinction between the grammatical relationships between collocate and search word (or 'node word'). So, for instance, a list for the search word 'compromise' might include the items 'accept', 'reach', 'between', 'deal', 'solution'. There would be nothing to explain the grammatical or syntactic relationship between them and the node word.

A *Word Sketch* groups collocates according to their grammatical relation to the search word. Figure 31.1 shows a *Word Sketch* for the word 'compromise'. The lists are divided into groups which show features such as verb use when 'compromise' is the object of the sentence (the long list on the left), adjectives that modify 'compromise', words that 'compromise' itself modifies, and groups of words that are used with particular prepositions ('for', 'of', 'to', etc.) before 'compromise'.

Word Sketches can be used by lexicographers for comparing near synonyms, by looking at which patterns and combinations the items have in common and which are more typical of, or even unique to, one word rather than the other. *Word Sketches* were first used for the *Macmillan English Dictionary* (Rundell 2002), but are now being used more widely, and for languages other than English.

Identifying neologisms and new senses

Section 1 mentions the use of monitor corpora, which compare new material with a stable corpus. Without such a corpus, the basic method of searching for neologisms (new words) would be simply to look at all words occurring a certain number of times per ten million within a particular alphabetical stretch and comparing them to an existing wordlist. New senses of existing words (for example the computing uses of 'wallpaper', 'attachment' or 'thread') should be identified by the analysis of corpus lines.

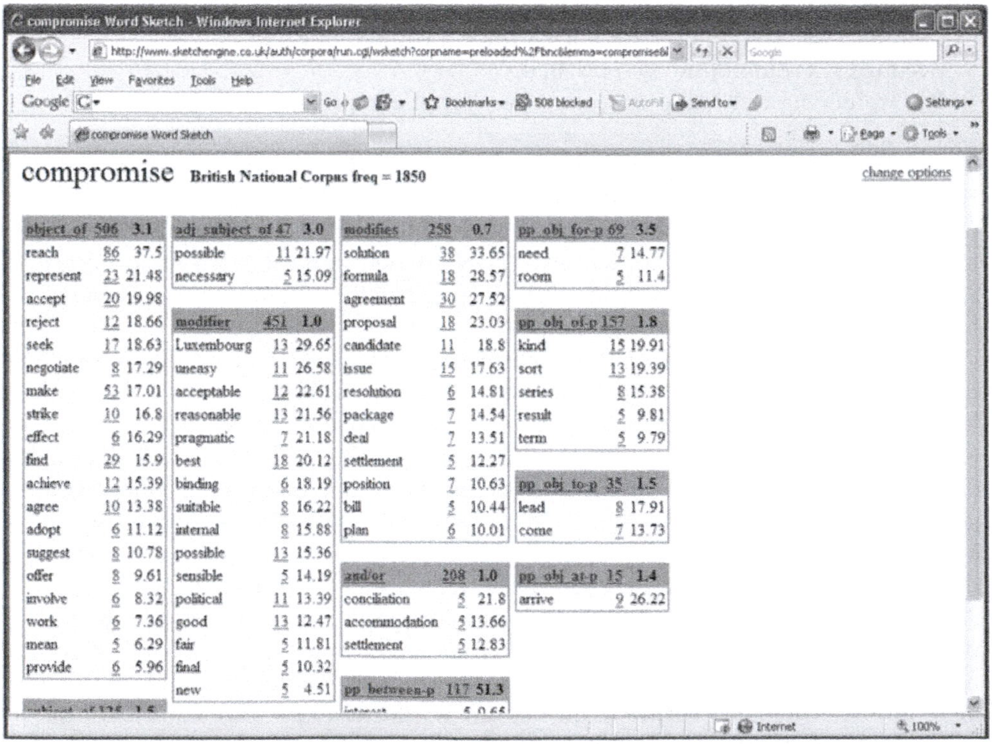

compromise Word Sketch - Windows Internet Explorer
compromise British National Corpus freq = 1850
change options
object_of 506 3.1
reach 86 37.5
represent 23 21.48
accept 20 19.98
reject 12 18.66
seek 17 18.63
negotiate 8 17.29
make 53 17.01
strike 10 16.8
effect 6 16.29
find 29 15.9
achieve 12 15.39
agree 10 13.38
adopt 6 11.12
suggest 8 10.78
offer 8 9.61
involve 6 8.32
work 6 7.36
mean 5 6.29
provide 6 5.96
adj_subject_of 47 3.0
possible 11 21.97
necessary 5 15.09
modifier 451 1.0
Luxembourg 13 29.65
uneasy 11 26.58
acceptable 12 22.61
reasonable 13 21.56
pragmatic 7 21.18
best 18 20.12
binding 6 18.19
suitable 8 16.22
internal 8 15.88
possible 13 15.36
sensible 5 14.19
political 11 13.39
good 13 12.47
fair 5 11.81
final 5 10.32
new 5 4.51
modifies 258 0.7
solution 38 33.65
formula 18 28.57
agreement 30 27.52
proposal 18 23.03
candidate 11 18.8
issue 15 17.63
resolution 6 14.81
package 7 14.54
deal 7 13.51
settlement 5 12.27
position 7 10.63
bill 5 10.44
plan 6 10.01
and/or 208 1.0
conciliation 5 21.8
accommodation 5 13.66
settlement 5 12.83
pp_between-p 117 51.3
pp_obj_for-p 69 3.5
need 7 14.77
room 5 11.4
pp_obj_of-p 157 1.8
kind 15 19.91
sort 13 19.39
series 8 15.38
result 5 9.81
term 5 9.79
pp_obj_to-p 35 1.5
lead 8 17.91
come 7 13.73
pp_obj_at-p 15 1.4
arrive 9 26.22

Figure 31.1 *Word Sketch* for 'compromise'.

However, a corpus is not always the best way to spot neologisms for the simple mathematical reason that an item which has only recently entered the language will not occur as often as one that has been in the language for many years. For this reason, most dictionary publishers still use a manual system of trawling for neologisms in a range of sources, either using their own staff or subscribing to a new words collection service such as the Camlex New Words Service. Some publishers, most notably Oxford University Press, also draw on contributions from the public.

Differences between language genres

Information about the source of corpus material will be recorded, so that it is always possible to know information such as title, genre and date of each citation. Thus we can look, for example, at whether a sense of a word is more common in British or US English, and if we search by date, we can see if that distribution has changed, for instance if a US word has become more widely used in Britain. Similarly, we can see if a particular word is more commonly used in written or spoken language.

The Cambridge International Corpus tools provide a summary of this information before getting to the corpus lines themselves, so it is possible from that point either to get to all the lines for the word in question, or refine the search, for example to British, spoken sources. For the word 'sidewalk', for instance, we find the information in Table 31.6.

We can see that it is, unsurprisingly, more common in US English, and that although it is used relatively often in British written sources (perhaps because of having US authors or writing about the US), it is never used in spoken British English.

The *Sketch Engine* enables the lexicographer to compare uses between different genres. For instance, a comparison of the word 'wicked' shows that in written texts it modifies words such as 'stepmother', 'fairy' and 'witch', and it is only in spoken contexts that we see the much more modern, positive sense of 'very good'.

Grammar and syntax

Identifying common grammatical and syntactic patterns is a key part of the lexicographer's job, and an aspect which has become much more refined as the result of corpus evidence, particularly for those working on dictionaries for learners, where such information is an essential part of what the dictionary entry must offer. Using corpora for studying grammar is covered in depth in chapters by Conrad and Hughes (this volume), but we have seen in Section 3 how the *Sketch Engine* shows the main grammatical and syntactical patterns in which a word occurs, and also in Section 2 how concordances can highlight common patterns, such as the idiom 'barking up the wrong tree' occurring almost exclusively in continuous forms.

Table 31.6 Distribution of 'sidewalk' in the Cambridge International Corpus across four corpora

Word	*All (per 10m words)*	*US spoken*	*US written*	*British spoken*	*British written*
sidewalk	40.4	39.5	88.2	0.0	7.1

Example sentences

Using the corpus as a source of dictionary examples is still a rather controversial topic. John Sinclair was unequivocal in his position that only genuine corpus examples should be used, arguing that segments of language depend on the rest of the text around them, so it is artificial to construct a sentence in isolation.

It is easy to see the logic in his exasperated insistence that: 'It is an absurd notion that invented examples can actually represent the language better than real ones' (Sinclair 1991: 5). His answer to the complaints of lexicographers about the difficulty of finding suitable examples to take verbatim is that larger corpora are needed. As he says, 'One does not study all of botany by making artificial flowers' (Sinclair 1991: 6).

However, it cannot be denied that even with the large corpora available to us today, finding suitable examples can be quite a challenge, particularly when writing dictionaries for learners, where clarity is essential. Common problems of corpus lines include excessive length, culturally specific items and difficult surrounding vocabulary that distracts from understanding the word in question. Given that the lexicographer is likely to be looking not merely for plausible examples, but for ones which illustrate particular features of collocation and grammar, the temptation to creativity can be great indeed.

In her paper on the subject, Liz Potter, in general an advocate of the corpus-only approach, concedes: 'Invented examples demonstrate the linguistic points the lexicographer wishes to convey, without any distraction or added difficulty such as may be introduced by using examples taken directly from real texts' (Potter 1998: 358). She suggests that for dictionaries aimed at lower-level (pre-intermediate) students, a case can be made for simple, invented examples that reinforce the most important features of a word.

Frequency

Most modern dictionaries tend to order senses by frequency, or at least claim to do so, although in fact, as John Sinclair has pointed out (Sinclair 1991: 36), the first meaning that comes to mind, and often the one that appears first in a dictionary, is frequently not the most common usage of a word. The corpus can help us to take a more objective approach to frequency, though at the time of writing there is no system available that will make automatic semantic distinctions, so the lexicographer has to do the necessary analysis of corpus lines.

It may be relatively simple to look at a single word and determine the order of frequency of its senses, but many modern dictionaries, particularly those aimed at learners of a language, attempt to provide relative frequency between headwords. For instance, many dictionaries have some sort of system for marking what they say are the *x* thousand most common words. Some show more than one level of frequency. It is interesting to note that most dictionaries that show frequency in this way do so only at headword level. To provide relative frequency for senses requires extensive coding of large numbers of corpus lines to give a frequency figure that can be measured per million or ten million, and thus compared with others. To date, only the *Cambridge Advanced Learner's Dictionary* has attempted to do this. A major problem of this endeavour is that the frequency of a meaning will depend on what the lexicographer deems that meaning to be. If you are a 'lumper' and identify two meanings of a word, the frequency of both those meanings will be higher than if you are a 'splitter' and have identified three senses for that word.

Another general problem of identifying frequency is that although the corpus gives us more reliable frequency information than introspection, it is clearly dependent on the make-up of its content. It is very easy for a corpus to become unbalanced through a preponderance of newspaper texts which are cheap and easy to collect and store, so that alone may exaggerate the importance of particular words such as sports terminology or words used in the reporting of court cases.

4. Using learner corpora for lexicography

Learner corpora consist of language produced by learners of a language (see Gilquin and Granger, this volume). Typically, they would include transcriptions of written work or examinations, and will often be coded according to the type of error the learners make. Learner corpora are used by lexicographers working on learners' dictionaries or bilingual dictionaries.

Identifying common errors

Concordancing learner corpus lines can enable lexicographers to spot errors that learners make with particular words. Uncoded learner data is of value in this respect, but error-coded data offers a much more focused and statistically valid analysis. Learner texts may be coded for many different sorts of errors. Such coding will be inserted by experienced teachers or examiners working to a highly prescribed system.

Using such codes, it is possible to look at the words which most frequently attract a particular kind of error. For instance, you could see which words were most commonly misspelled, or which uncountable nouns were most commonly used in an incorrect plural form.

It is also possible to group individual lexical items according to the error that learners make with them. Having this information enables the lexicographer to include information in a dictionary entry to help a learner avoid that mistake, for instance by highlighting a grammar code, adding an example sentence, or even adding a specific note or panel to deal with a particular issue. Learner error notes are a common feature of learners' dictionaries.

The other great advantage of error coding is that it usually includes the addition of a 'corrected' version. This is a great help in finding items, since it is much easier, for instance, to search on a correct spelling than to identify several incorrect spellings of a word.

Work on the use of learner corpora in dictionaries is sometimes carried out by publishers' own teams and sometimes in collaboration with academic institutions, such as the work of Macmillan Dictionaries and the Université catholique de Louvain, Belgium, who developed the International Corpus of Learner English (see Granger 1993, 1994, 1996, 1998; Granger *et al.* 2002; Rundell and Granger 2007).

Learner profiles

A learner corpus can also enable the lexicographer to look at specific types of learner. For instance, we can filter the corpus by level of proficiency, which enables us to tailor information so that it is appropriate for the target user of the dictionary.

As well as looking at *how* learners are using words, we can look at *which* words they use. That enables us, if appropriate for a particular dictionary, to give more usage information (e.g. grammar, collocation) in entries for words which learners are likely to try to use productively, as opposed to those they will consult for comprehension. Currently, the English Profile Project (see project website) is using learner corpus data to try to link lexical and grammatical use to Common European Framework levels, a project which will surely feed into dictionaries in future.

Another very useful feature is the ability to sort according to the native language of the learner. Obviously, this is of particular use when working on a dictionary aimed at a particular native speaker group, but it can also help with decisions on when to add a usage note in a general learners' dictionary – the greater the number of native languages on a particular error, the more reason to include a note.

Comparisons with native speaker use

It can be interesting to compare native speaker and learner language. We can see, for instance, that words which are extremely common in native speaker texts are likely to be proportionally even more common in learner texts, because learners will know fewer more interesting synonyms than native speakers. This can give us guidance on where to include thesaurus-type information in our dictionaries.

5. Current limitations and future developments

Corpus make-up

Some types of corpus material are much easier to gather than others and it is a common weakness of lexicographic corpora to have an over-reliance on newspaper text. Particularly for spoken corpora and learner corpora, where texts need to be transcribed, the costs of building corpora large enough to be of value are daunting, and there are challenging issues of copyright and 'anonymising' spoken data to be faced.

One new area of corpus creation which is being worked on at present is that of using the internet in a more sophisticated way to gather data. For example, the BootCaT method (see Baroni and Bernadini 2004) uses a process of selecting 'seed terms', sending queries with the seed terms to Google and collecting the pages that the Google hits point to. This is then a first-pass specialist corpus. The vocabulary in this corpus can be compared with a reference corpus and terms can be automatically extracted. The process can also be iterated with the new terms as seeds to give a 'purer' specialist corpus. The corpus size can be increased simply by sending more queries to the search engine. A service of this kind is available online from *WebBootCaT* (see Baroni *et al.* 2006).

Spoken corpora

Although spoken corpora have led to many insights into the grammar of discourse and the vocabulary of everyday spoken language (see McCarthy and Carter 1997), their value to lexicographers working primarily at the level of a lexical unit is more doubtful. Most people are shocked when they first see transcription of speech. We can hardly believe that we speak in such an incoherent way, stammering, repeating words, changing the subject in the middle of a sentence, interrupting one another or simply petering out. This sort of language is very difficult to analyse, and almost never suitable to be used directly as a dictionary example.

It could be argued that the transcription process itself robs speech of an important layer of meaning. Features such as intonation, speed and tone of voice can be crucial in distinguishing meaning, as can the context of an utterance, which, unlike in most written text, may not be explicitly stated at all. As Rosamund Moon has pointed out: 'The range of conversational implicatures in such formulae as *if you like* or *XX would like* can scarcely be described in a linguistic monograph, let alone within the constrained space and vocabulary of explication in a dictionary' (Moon 1998: 353).

It would of course be very useful to dictionary editors working on pronunciation to have spoken corpus examples in an audio form, but such systems are not yet available.

Corpus query systems

Most lexicographers would probably say that the biggest limitation is still inaccuracy of part-of-speech tagging and the difficulty of parsing. It can be frustrating to search for noun senses of 'side' and discover that a large percentage are actually verb senses, and such problems can make it difficult to make objective statements about frequency. These problems are exacerbated in spoken data, where language conforms less to 'normal' rules of grammar and is therefore even more difficult to analyse automatically.

A related problem is that quite apart from the difficulty in distinguishing different parts of speech, there is the issue of agreeing what those parts of speech *should* be. If the lexicographer decides that 'divorced' is an adjective, but the CQS calls it a past participle of the verb 'divorce', the analysis will not be the one the lexicographer wants.

The tool that would revolutionise the lexicographer's life is one which could distinguish senses, and of course this is the goal of computational linguists working in all manner of academic and commercial areas. Although many avenues such as looking at context, collocation and syntax are being pursued, we are still a long way from having a tool that would be useful for dictionary writers.

In Section 3, the difficulty of finding suitable corpus chunks to be used verbatim in dictionary examples was discussed. Lexical Computing Ltd is currently working on developing a tool that would automatically select corpus lines which conform to certain criteria likely to make them potential candidates as examples.

The role of the lexicographer

One of the biggest problems for a lexicographer can be to decide how to use the resources at their disposal most effectively within time constraints which are probably unimaginable to the academic linguist. Many of the CQS features discussed in this chapter have helped a great deal, but good lexicographers still need to have an excellent feel for the language in order to be able to use them accurately.

Very often, when presented with summarised information, it is necessary to drill down deeper into the corpus to understand fully what is happening in the language. For instance, a collocation search on the word 'run' will highlight the word 'short'. The lexicographer needs the instinct either to guess or to know to check that this is because of the idiom 'in the short run' or the collocation 'run short (of something)', rather than just a literal combination, as in 'I went for a short run.' Similarly, they should be able to spot the likelihood of query results being influenced by a particular text in the corpus, leading to information that would be atypical outside a very limited context. For instance, a word may have a common technical collocation in a financial context, which is over-represented in the corpus because of a newspaper bias, but which would not be appropriate for a general dictionary, and the lexicographer must be alert to these possible distortions.

Thankfully, even in this age of computational sophistication, the role of the lexicographer is far from redundant. Many dictionary publishers sell data to computational linguists, and there is a nice circularity in the fact that it is at least in part the nuggets of linguistic knowledge that lexicographers mine from the corpus which will lead to the development of even better corpus tools in the future.

Further reading

Atkins, B. T. S. and Rundell, M. (2008) *The Oxford Guide to Practical Lexicography*. Oxford: Oxford University Press. (This is a very hands-on guide to dictionary writing and includes detailed discussion of the use of corpus evidence.)

Rundell, M. (2008) 'The Corpus Revolution Revisited', *English Today* 24(1): 23–7. (This paper is an update of the 1992 paper, 'The Corpus Revolution', by Rundell and Stock. It provides an interesting diachronic reflection on how the role of corpora has developed and evolved in that period.)

Sinclair, J. (1987). *Looking Up: An Account of the COBUILD Project in Lexical Computing*. London: Collins. (This details the groundbreaking COBUILD project.)

References

Baroni, M. and Bernardini, S. (2004) BootCaT: Bootstrapping Corpora and Terms from the Web', in *Proceedings of LREC 2004*, Lisbon: ELDA, pp. 1313–16.

Baroni, M., Kilgarriff, A., Pomikálek, J. and Rychl, P.(2006) 'WebBootCaT: Instant Domain-specific Corpora to Support Human Translators', in *Proceedings of EAMT 2006*, Oslo, pp. 247–52.

Biber, D. (1993) 'Representativeness in Corpus Design', *Literary and Linguistic Computing* 8(4): 243–57.

Biber, D., Conrad, S. and Reppen, R. (1998) *Corpus Linguistics Investigating Language Structure and Use*. Cambridge: Cambridge University Press.

Camlex New Words Service, www.camlex.co.uk

Church, K. W. and Hanks, P. (1990) 'Word Association Norms, Mutual Information, and Lexicography', *Computational Linguistics* 16(1):22–9.

Crowdy, S. (1993) 'Spoken Corpus Design', *Literary and Linguistic Computing* 8: 259–65.

English Profile Project, www.englishprofile.org

Granger, S. (1993) 'The International Corpus of Learner English', in J. Aarts, P. de Haan and N. Oostdijk (eds) *English Language Corpora: Design, Analysis and Exploitation*. Amsterdam: Rodopi, pp. 57–69.

——(1994) 'The Learner Corpus: A Revolution in Applied Linguistics', *English Today* 39: 25–9.

——(1996) 'Learner English Around the World', in S. Greenbaum (ed.) *Comparing English World-wide*. Oxford: Clarendon Press, pp. 13–24.

——(1998) 'The Computerized Learner Corpus: A Versatile New Source of Data for SLA Research', in S. Granger (ed.) *Learner English on Computer*. London: Longman, pp. 3–18.

Granger, S., Hung, J. and Petch-Tyson, S. (eds) (2002) *Computer Learner Corpora, Second Language Acquisition and Foreign Language Teaching*. Amsterdam: John Benjamins.

Hallebeek, J. (2000) 'English Parallel Corpora and Applications', *Cuadernos de Filologia Inglesa,* 9(1): 111–23.

Kilgarriff, A., Rychly, P., Smrz, P. and Tugwell, D. (2004) 'The Sketch Engine', *Proc. Euralex*, Lorient, France, July, pp. 105–16.

McCarthy, M. J. (1998) *Spoken Language and Applied Linguistics.* Cambridge: Cambridge University Press.

McCarthy, M. J. and Carter, R. A. (1997) 'Written and Spoken Vocabulary', in N. Schmitt and M. J. McCarthy (eds) *Vocabulary: Description, Acquisition, Pedagogy.* Cambridge: Cambridge University Press, pp. 20–39.

McEnery, T. and Wilson, A. (1996) *Corpus Linguistics.* Edinburgh: Edinburgh University Press.

McEnery, T., Xiao, R. and Tono, Y. (2006) *Corpus-based Language Studies.* London: Routledge.

Moon, R. (1998) 'On Using Spoken Data in Corpus Lexicography', in T. Fontenelle, P. Hiligsmann, A. Michiel, A. Moulin and S. Theissen (eds) *Euralex '98 Proceedings.* Liège: University of Liège, pp. 347–55.

Potter, E. (1998) 'Setting a Good Example: What Kind of Examples Best Serve the Users of Learners Dictionaries?', in T. Fontenelle, P. Hiligsmann, A. Michiel, A. Moulin and S. Theissen (eds) *Euralex '98 Proceedings.* Liège: University of Liège, pp. 357–62.

Rundell, M. (ed.) (2002) *Macmillan English Dictionary.* London: Macmillan.

Rundell, M. and Granger, S (2007) 'From Corpora to Confidence', *English Teaching Professional* 50: 15–18.

Sinclair, J. (1991) *Corpus, Concordance, Collocation.* Oxford: Oxford University Press.

32
Using corpora for writing instruction

Lynne Flowerdew

1. Introduction: an overview

In a 1997 article examining the link between language corpora and teaching, Leech remarks on the 'trickle-down' effect from corpus research to teaching, which only really took off in the early 1990s. The main instigator of the exploitation of corpora in language teaching, specifically on the application to writing, was Johns, whose seminal work in the field of data-driven learning (DDL) is reported in Johns (1984, 1986). Another landmark publication in the field is the volume by Tribble and Jones (1990), which also acted as a catalyst for the pedagogic application of corpora. Since then, as Leech (1997: 2) humorously observes: 'The original "trickle down" from research to teaching is now becoming a torrent'! The purpose of this chapter is to review the veritable cascade of corpus applications to various aspects of writing over the past couple of decades. But first a brief overview of the utility of corpora for enhancing different features of writing is in order.

The multiple lines of concordance output can reveal grammatical features, such as the different use of tenses with *for* and *since* in time expressions. Likewise, concordance data can shed light on vocabulary items, e.g. the most common senses of a word or its meaning. However, aside from individual grammatical or lexical features, the main utility of corpora in writing is in their uniqueness of showing what can loosely be termed as phraseological patterning, involving collocations, colligations and semantic preferences and prosodies. Biber *et al.* (1999: 990) have underscored the importance of lexical bundles, 'sequences of words that commonly go together in natural discourse' in academic writing. Corpora are ideally suited to helping learners master such patterning in writing classes, as these phraseological features tend not to be easily accessible in either dictionaries or grammars.

This focus on the usage patterns of words, and variations thereof has been accompanied by greater attention with regard to their occurrences in specific genres. This has led to more initiatives to build small specialised corpora; see Aston (1997, 2001) for a discussion on the advantages of using small corpora, and Flowerdew (2004) for an overview of such corpora. Moreover, Hyland (2006) has noted that such corpora are ideally suited for genre-based writing instruction as they reveal the prototypical and frequently occurring phraseologies of specific genres. Also Hyland (2003) has made the point that corpus-oriented genre-based instruction should not only aim to increase students' explicit awareness of the linguistic conventions of specialist texts, but also elucidate the interrelationship between rhetorical purpose and lexico-grammatical choices.

The following sections review the increasingly important role that corpora are now playing in writing instruction, especially corpora of a specialist nature. Corpora have principally been used in two main ways to inform writing instruction, either through a *corpus-based* approach where worksheet materials (e.g. gap-filling exercises) are derived from concordance output, or through a *corpus-driven* approach, commonly referred to as data-driven learning (DDL), which requires the student to interact directly with the corpus. It should be pointed out. though. that in reality many writing instruction programmes utilise a combination of these two approaches, although as will be seen the corpus-driven approach is far more prevalent. Moreover, corpora have been exploited at different stages of the writing process from initial drafting through to the final proofreading and editing stages.

In the following sections corpus-based and corpus-driven approaches to informing and designing writing materials are discussed in relation to English for General Academic Purposes (EGAP) and English for Specific Academic Purposes (ESAP) instruction (see Flowerdew 2002 for specific examples of such corpora).

2. Exploiting corpora for EGAP writing instruction

The corpus-based approach in EGAP

One advantage of having students work with worksheet output of concordance data is that it is a valuable means of providing them with 'corpus competence', thereby gently familiarising them with corpus methodologies such as the inductive approach, interpretation of frequency data, etc. (Boulton 2010). Another advantage is that it allows teachers to sift through what may be a vast number of concordance lines to reduce and select data on the basis of utility value. These main advantages are inherent in the corpus-based materials for EGAP writing instruction discussed below.

It is surprising that since the publication of Thurstun and Candlin's (1998a) textbook *Exploring Academic English: A Workbook for Student Essay Writing*, based on the one-million-word MicroConcord Corpus of Academic Texts, there do not seem to have been any other similar initiatives, quite possibly owing to the fact that producing such corpus-based writing activities is a time-consuming task. In this workbook the lexico-grammar is introduced according to its specific rhetorical function, e.g. referring to the literature, reporting the research of others. Within each broad function, each key word (e.g. *claim*, *identify*) is examined within the following chain of activities:

- LOOK at concordances for the key term and words surrounding it, thinking of meaning.
- FAMILIARISE yourself with the patterns of language surrounding the key term by referring to the concordances as you complete the tasks.
- PRACTISE key terms without referring to the concordances.
- CREATE your own piece of writing using the terms studied to fulfil a particular function of academic writing.

(Thurstun and Candlin 1998b: 272)

Such a suite of activities based on a clear progression from controlled to more open-ended writing activities would seem to be inculcating in students the kind of 'corpus competence' after Kreyer (2008).

The corpus-driven approach in EGAP

In contrast to the dearth of corpus-based instructional writing material for EGAP, there are more reports in the literature on the use of corpora in data-driven learning. Two of the pedagogic applications, in common with those reported in Thurstun and Candlin (1998a), concern the use of citations in EAP. Thompson and Tribble (2001) devised DDL class activities for postgraduate students in which they conducted their own analyses of citation practices in small corpora, to develop genre awareness. A key feature of these activities is that they are based on investigations comparing the use of integral and non-integral citations in both doctoral theses and novice student writing (non-integral citations are those that are placed outside the sentence, usually in brackets, and integral citations are those that play an explicit grammatical role within the sentence). For the corpus exercises Thompson and Tribble use a carefully graded procedure, moving from teacher input on a range of citation forms to applications of citations to students' own writing, as outlined below:

Stage 1: Learners are introduced to a range of citation forms appropriate to their level of study.
Stage 2: Learners investigate actual practice in relevant texts, reporting back on the range, form and purpose of the citations they identify.
Stage 3: Learners investigate the practices of their peers in writing assignments.
Stage 4: Learners review their own writing and revise in the light of these investigations.
(Thompson and Tribble 2001: 101)

Thompson and Tribble used Lee's (2001) BNC index to make a micro-corpus of twenty-two extracts from one academic journal – *Language and Literature* – with the assumption that the texts would be of relevance for postgraduate humanities students. The extract in Table 32.1 is from a worksheet for Stage 2, in which students were required to identify different types of citation practices in actual text.

While Thompson and Tribble's postgraduate students may have been able to cope with the level of text difficulty and the metalanguage required for identifying the different types of citations, such sub-corpora would not lend themselves easily to exploitation by lower-level students.

In addition to the choice of corpus to promote writing instruction, a related issue to consider is the choice of concordancing software. These are the main concerns of Bloch (2008, 2009) in his corpus-driven activities for teaching the use of reporting verbs in

Table 32.1 Citation worksheet

Example	*Citation category*
ext-world to their cognitive universe (based on their previous familiarity with the patterns typical of the genre.) Eikmeyer (1989), in a paper from a conference on coherence, points out that reader interpretation depends on the depth of understanding.	Integral verb Controlling

Source: adapted from Thompson and Tribble 2001: 102.

academic writing. Bloch makes the important point that it is necessary to control for the types of language and text that the teacher wants to focus on. To this end, he assembled two types of corpora: an 'analogue' and an 'exemplar' corpus. The 'analogue' corpus consisted of texts similar to the writing task of a critical review, since no articles directly related to the writing assignment were available. The 'exemplar' corpus comprised research reports directly related to the writing task at hand (see Tribble 2002 for more details on the application of these types of corpora). He also designed a program with a user-friendly interface that presented users with only a limited number of hits for each query and a limited number of criteria for querying the database, namely, integral/non-integral; indicative/informative; writer/author; attitude towards claim; strength of claim.

While the corpus materials designed by Thurstun and Candlin (1998a), Thompson and Tribble (2001) and Bloch (2008) focus on individual rhetorical functions, Charles' (2007: 296) EAP materials target the combinatorial function of *defending your work against criticism*, a two-part pattern: 'anticipated criticism → defence and its realisation using signals of apparent concession, contrast and justification'. Another feature of Charles' materials is that she approaches these functions by first using a top-down approach, providing students with a suite of worksheet activities to sensitise them to the extended discourse properties of this rhetorical function. She then supplements these with a more bottom-up-level approach by having students search the corpus to identify typical lexico-grammatical patterns realising these functions, as exemplified in Table 32.2.

In an interesting departure from the usual 'accommodationist' perspective on EAP writing in which students are often encouraged to adhere uncritically to conventionalised forms of expression, Starfield (2004: 139) uses concordancing as 'a strategic engagement with technology' as a means of 'further exploration of issues of power and identity in academic writing'. Starfield devised both worksheet and online concordancing activities as a consciousness-raising activity to foster awareness as to how writers position themselves with regard to the research of others with a view to creating a niche for their own work, and how they structure their own argument at the level of textual metadiscourse. She reported that students experienced a sense of empowerment when they realised they had readily available access to the language resources of authoritative English to expropriate these for their own means. A similar phenomenon has been noted by Lee and Swales (2006) in their students' reaction to the use of corpora as they realised they did not always need access to native speakers to check up on certain language issues.

The following section discusses how corpora of an ESAP nature have been utilised in informing and preparing writing materials concentrating on specialised genres.

Table 32.2 Anticipated criticism and writer's defence

Extract	*Anticipated criticism*
A	Although the results of the experiment are not conclusive,
B	There is nothing **essential in these categories**, and they may **not appear tenable** to other scholars.
C	**While I acknowledge that** in some cases the distinction between institutions and groups may seem rather arbitrary,
D	Unfortunately, specimen preparation is especially laborious for the completed device structure, which meant that further progress …

Source: from Charles 2007: 296.

3. Exploiting corpora for ESAP writing instruction

The corpus-based approach in ESAP

It has been pointed out in the previous section that there is a paucity of materials for corpus-based writing instruction in EGAP, and the same is true for corpus-based writing materials in ESAP. Reasons for this, as exemplified below, may well be that such materials require students to compare either non-technical with sub-technical language or student with professional writing. Some intervention and manipulation of the concordance output by the tutor would seem to be necessary in such cases to avoid overwhelming the student with too numerous or irrelevant examples.

In the realm of engineering, sub-technical vocabulary (i.e. those items such as *current*, *solution*, *tension* which have one sense in general English, but are used in a different sense in technical English) has been found to be problematic for students (Mudraya 2006). In her corpus-based materials, on the basis of findings from a two-million-word Student Engineering English Corpus made up of engineering textbooks, Mudraya proposes a set of queries based around *solution* on the grounds that this word occurs, in its general sense, both as a high-frequency word family and as a frequent sub-technical item. Students are presented with concordance output of carefully selected examples of *solution* and in one exercise are asked to identify, for example, the following: those adjectives used with *solution* (1) in the general sense and (2) in the technical (chemical) sense, and then asked to underline those adjectives that can be used with both senses of *solution*. This type of phraseologically oriented task would serve to highlight collocational sensitivities and may also uncover examples of 'universal' and 'local' semantic prosodies. Tribble (2000) argues that such features play an important role in the teaching of written genres, proposing that there may be a 'universal' semantic prosody for a word in relation to general English, but a 'local' semantic prosody in a specific context or genre.

Other corpus-based materials are those by Hewings and Hewings (2002) and Hewings (2002) on the use of metadiscoursal anticipatory *it* in business writing. An interesting feature of these materials is that they incorporate the findings of both expert texts, i.e. published journal articles from the field of Business Studies, and the findings of student writing, i.e. MBA dissertations written by non-native speakers. Students are asked to compare and discuss the differences of *it seems* … in concordance lines selected from the two corpora, as shown in Table 32.3.

Other examples of business-related, corpus-based writing materials are those by Nelson based on his research of a Business English Corpus of around one million words, made up of both written (56 per cent) and spoken (44 per cent) genres (Nelson 2006). For the written genres of business contracts and minutes of business meetings, Nelson has

Table 32.3 Concordance task for *it seems* … in published articles and student dissertations (Hewings 2002)

Published articles	*Student dissertations*
* It seems clear that as insider holding proportions increase; capitalisation ratios decrease.	* It seems that different studies have shown different results.
* It seems likely that the eighties and nineties will be known as decades of large scale disaggregation.	* It seems that the practice of employing local staff by multinationals is increasing.
* It seems quite probable that consumers would not recognise such relatively small degrees of difference.	* It seems that some individual training courses are below their full capacity.

devised gap-filling and matching function with phrase tasks, targeting key lexis (a web search of business English lexis will bring you to the homepage).

The corpus-driven approach in ESAP

In common with corpus-driven instruction for EGAP, that for ESAP very often combines initial pen-and-paper awareness-raising activities with follow-up direct consultation of the corpus by students. One key methodological feature of these activities is that the majority approach the corpus consultation from a genre-based perspective (Weber 2001; Bhatia *et al.* 2004; Noguchi 2004). See Handford, this volume, for the role of corpus linguistics in analysing specialist genres.

Bhatia *et al.* (2004) propose various move-specific concordancing activities for one genre of legal English, the problem-question genre written by students within academic settings. They note that deductive reasoning plays a major role in this highly specialised genre. One of their major foci, therefore, is to have students examine various types of non-lexical epistemic and pragmatic/discoursal hedges for the role they play in deductive reasoning. This activity thus exemplifies a type of 'local grammar', which 'attempts to describe the resources for only one set of meanings in a language rather than for the language as a whole' (Hunston 2002: 90). Bhatia *et al.* also propose a task-based activity comprising three steps (Awareness; Contextualising; Application) for familiarising students with both the form and function all the various hedges take in different parts of the legal problem answer. In Stage 3: Application, Bhatia *et al.* (2004: 224) suggest having students writing alternative arguments and outcomes.

Another advocate of a concordance- and genre-based approach to academic essay writing in the legal field, specifically formal legal essays written by undergraduates, is Weber (2001). First, Weber's students were inducted into the genre of legal essays by reading through whole essays taken from the University of London LLB Examinations written by native speakers, and identifying some of the prototypical rhetorical features, e.g. identifying and/or delimiting the legal principle involved in the case. They were then asked to identify any lexical expressions which seemed to correlate with the genre features. This was followed up by consulting the corpus of the legal essays to verify and pinpoint regularities in lexico-grammatical expressions. Swales (2002) has contrasted the 'fragmented' world of corpus linguistics with its tendency to adopt a somewhat bottom-up, atomistic approach to text with the more 'integrated' world of ESP material design with its focus on top-down analysis of macro-level features. Weber's tasks, and those by Charles described in the previous section, seem to be achieving a 'symbiosis' between these two approaches, as called for by Partington (1998).

Similar to those tasks proposed by Bhatia *et al.* (2004), Weber also approaches the lexico-grammar from the perspective of a 'local grammar'. For example, items such as *assume, consider, regard and issue*, in various constructions, were all found to act as signals in an opening-type move, delimiting the case under consideration before the principle involved in it was defined, as exemplified by the extract in Table 32.4.

In an interesting departure from the normal type of ESP work, Weber's students were also exposed to corpora of different, non-legal genres in order to sensitise them to the highly specific use and patterning of certain lexical items, such as *held* and *submit*, in legal texts.

However, as legal discourse is such an intricate discourse area, corpus-based methodologies may not completely align themselves with legal writing tasks. For example, Bhatia *et al.* (2004: 224) have underscored the complexity of legal discourse, pointing out that a

Table 32.4 Concordance lines for 'delimiting the case under consideration' (adapted from Weber 2001: 17)

received Brian's letter.	Assuming	the offer does remain open, Brian's Thursda
proceeding on the latter	assumption	In order to discuss the law related to
to discuss. I now have to	consider	whether B's message, left on the answerphone
third party. Bata v. Bata.	Considering	first the story about The BCDs, can the ba
With	regard to	contracts *ex facie* illegal it is necessary to
second part of the story.	Regarding	the potential claim of Evangeline, it is subm
consented to it. The key	issue	here is what caused the injury; was it Geoffrey's
At	issue	here is whether Neil will have a cause of action

number of academic and professional genres in law appear to be 'dynamically embedded in one another'. In view of this, they caution that one has to go beyond the immediate textual concordance lines and look at discursive and institutional concerns and constraints to fully interpret and by extension become a skilled writer of these highly specialised genres. Hafner and Candlin (2007), in their report on the use of legal corpora by university students, also note a tension between professional discourse practices which encourage students to focus on models, and the phraseological approach associated with corpus-driven learning. However, they see this as a tension to be exploited, arguing that 'continuing lifelong learners still need to be able to focus and reflect on the functional lexical phrases that constitute the essence of the texture of the documents they are composing' (p. 312).

Turning to another ESP area, that of psychology, Bianchi and Pazzaglia (2007) adopted a genre perspective in a cycle of activities for helping Italian students write psychology research articles in English. Acknowledging the continuing debate on English as an International Language, they state that their 500,000-word corpus drawn from the areas of language acquisition and developmental psychology 'should be representative of the language of the psychology community, which includes authors from different nationalities using English as a *lingua franca*' (p. 265). An innovative feature of this writing instruction cycle is that students were asked to subdivide their choice of written article into moves and annotate it themselves using a functional and meta-communicative coding system devised by the authors. This was followed by data-driven guided writing tasks, which focused on the lexico-grammatical patterning of key words related to the concept of research and verb tense usage in different moves.

Although in the past few years there has been a steady stream of articles reporting on the manifold applications of corpora to EAP and ESP writing materials at the individual or institutional level, DDL aimed at writing instruction cannot be considered to have percolated through to the language teaching community at large. This situation can be accounted for, by and large, by the three following issues: the user-friendliness of corpora and tools for classroom use; strategy training for both students and teachers; and evaluation on the effectiveness of corpora for improving writing performance. These three considerations are discussed in the following section.

4. Issues in the application of corpora to writing instruction

Corpora and tools

Kosem (2008), in a recent survey on corpus tools for language teaching and learning, notes that one possible reason for the lack of uptake of DDL by the teaching community is not the methodology but the medium. Some tools try to meet the needs of both researchers and teachers, which makes them over-complicated. This issue has also been flagged by Römer (2006) and Granger and Meunier (2008: 251), who have indicated that one future challenge lies in 'creating ready-made and user-friendly interfaces to enable learners and teachers to access multiword units from a variety of genres and text types'. However, very recent endeavours are underway in this area and user-friendly tools, specifically to enhance academic writing skills, are described in Milton (2004), Krishnamurthy and Kosem (2007) and Kaszubski (2011). Another key feature of these tools is that they are accompanied by corpora compiled in-house to meet the needs of specific learners.

A related issue concerns the sometimes inappropriate nature of ready-made corpora for language learners, which could be another reason for the lack of uptake. As Osborne (2004: 252) comments, 'Unless corpus examples are filtered in some way ... many of the contexts are likely to be linguistically and culturally bewildering for the language learner'. In this respect, Chujo *et al.* (2007) note that according to their readability index most of their English–Japanese corpora were rated at the advanced level, and what is needed, therefore, are available e-texts at beginner level. Once again, this is an area where progress is being made. Wible *et al.* (2002) describe a lexical filter which sorts examples according to a flexible threshold of lexical difficulty. A similar function is available in *SketchEngine*, which has an option to sort concordances 'best first' from a learner's point of view (Kilgariff, message posted on Corpus Linguistics discussion list, 16 April 2008).

Strategy training for learners and teachers

Another impediment to the adoption of DDL by classroom practitioners may well be the fact that the writing teachers themselves lack confidence in using the technology or don't possess a pedagogic grounding in exploiting corpora. Interestingly, and somewhat surprisingly, there are very few accounts in the literature which touch on the question of learner training. One writing programme which has integrated strategy training into writing work is reported in Kennedy and Miceli (2002). These practitioners built a corpus of contemporary written Italian to aid students with personal writing on everyday topics. Initially, the teacher gave directions for corpus investigations through a series of leading questions. This was followed up, after a few sessions, with the students encouraged to use the corpus on their own while revising their own work, the teacher acting as facilitator. See also O'Sullivan and Chambers (2006) for an account of how strategy training has been integrated into a writing course to help students improve their writing skills in French.

A detailed overview with examples of exercises for inducting advanced-level students into the skills needed for exploitation of corpus tools and data is given in Lee and Swales (2006). Students were introduced to the 'corpus way' of investigating language through, for example, using context to disambiguate near-synonyms and 'gaining sensitivity to norms and distributional patterns in language (semantic prosody; genre analysis)' (p. 62). One of these induction sessions is given below.

> Wk 6: Corpus, usage patterns and subtle nuances
>
> Guessing/scrutinizing the meanings of words by studying concordances (e.g. *cabal*; *continually* v. *continuously*). Looking at similar lexical items (e.g., *for instance* v. *for example*; *effective* v. *efficient*; *expect* v. *anticipate*; *somewhat* v. *fairly*). Participant-generated examples of puzzling pairs, such as *totally* v. *in total*, *seek* v. *search*.
>
> (Lee and Swales 2006: 66)

In view of the paucity of such induction-type exercises for acculturating students into the 'corpus way' of looking at language from a phraseological perspective, it seems that more such activities should be made available in the literature for different levels of learners.

Likewise, effective induction tasks for teachers, in both pre- and in-service training, also need to be devised for the successful adoption of DDL (Mukherjee 2004; O'Keeffe and Farr 2003). However, as pointed out by O'Keeffe *et al.* (2007), there exists a considerable gap between corpus theory and teacher practice, which has only recently begun to be bridged. See Frankenberg-Garcia (2010) for specific consciousness-raising induction tasks for teacher training, and Coxhead and Byrd (2007) on the specific lexico-grammar features that teacher educators can introduce via computer means in teacher development courses specifically aimed at teachers of academic writing.

A third reason writing teachers may not have integrated DDL into the curriculum is that, to date, there is very little empirical evidence to show the efficacy of corpus methodology on writing performance, as discussed below.

Evaluation of corpora in writing performance

There is no doubt that corpus consultation has potential for enhancing L2 writing at different stages, but to what extent is still to be ascertained. Although some very insightful studies have been conducted on learners' evaluation of corpora (Yoon and Hirvela 2004; Curado Fuentes 2002; Yoon 2008), much more empirical research needs to be carried out on the influence of corpus methodologies on learners' writing *performance*.

In this area the few studies of note are Boulton's (2009) tests on linking adverbials, and Cresswell's (2007) study on the use of connectors in experimental and control writing groups, which showed DDL in the context of the communicative teaching of writing skills to be moderately effective. Three studies which focus on students' writing improvement in the revision stages of writing after being given feedback on errors are those by Watson-Todd (2001), Gaskell and Cobb (2004) and O'Sullivan and Chambers (2006). Watson-Todd's implementation is innovative in that it requires students to build their own concordances of lexical items from internet sources, inducing valid patterns for self-correction. However, interestingly, an exploratory study by Jones and Haywood (2004) found that although students' awareness of formulaic sequences increased through corpus-based tasks, they did not do so well in transferring these phrases to their own writing. Thus the experimental results to date suggest that corpus consultation seems to be most effective for the revising process.

Having reviewed three issues which present potential impediments to the application of corpora to writing, in the following section other considerations for future expansion and extension for the use of corpora in writing are discussed.

5. Future pathways: expansion and extension

Expansion of corpora: into other varieties

A glaring omission in the previous sections is that very little has been done to address writing instruction in other languages. More projects such as those reported in Chambers and O'Sullivan (2004) and O'Sullivan and Chambers (2006) on writing in French, and in Kennedy and Miceli (2002) on writing in Italian, would certainly provide a welcome expansion to the field.

Also, only a few of the corpus/based writing tasks reviewed, such as those by Hewings (2002) and Thompson and Tribble (2001), make use of learner corpora. Corpus linguists, most notably Granger (2004a, 2004b), Gilquin *et al.* (2007) and Nesselhauf (2004), have persuasively argued for the findings from learner corpora to be used to inform EAP writing materials. One experimental classroom project where learner corpora are being integrated in the instruction cycle is reported in Mukherjee and Rohrbach (2006), who advocate individualising writing by having students build mini-corpora of their own writing, and localising the database.

Another consideration is for native language interference to be taken into account as this is also a source of error (Granger 2004a; O'Sullivan and Chambers 2006). A course for teaching technical writing which makes reference to the L1 is described in Foucou and Kübler (2000: 67), who point out that the use of the passive presents difficulties for French speakers as this construction is used less frequently in French than in English (e.g. '*On donne* ci-dessous des conventions pour ces options' would be translated as: 'Below, conventions *are given* for these options'). They deal with such phraseologies using corpora compiled from the web, which then begs the question as to why there are so few accounts of using the web for preparing writing materials.

Moving to the area of critical pedagogies, it was noted that Starfield's students reported a sense of empowerment through accessing corpus data to glean the phraseologies used in authoritative writing. One can also argue from a different angle, as van Rij-Heyligers (2007: 105) does, that this kind of corpus approach 'may contain the hidden message that the native speaker knows best, hence representing elements of linguistic imperialism'. For this reason, van Rij-Heyligers makes a case for using the web for building corpora of academic English for writing instruction, as this source would treat EAP as a lingua franca and convey the sense that academic genres are dynamic entities continually being shaped and negotiated by participants, rather than as prescriptive and fixed artefacts. It could well be the case that the increasing focus on English as a lingua franca will entail more corpus building from the web reflecting this changing nature of English.

Another area for future expansion of corpora in writing is for students to work with tagged corpora of some kind, one possibility being corpora coded for genre features such as moves and steps. From the perspective of Systemic Functional Linguistics, in which choices are made from the lexico-grammar for meaning-making, Ragan (2001) describes a programme in which students worked with learner corpora tagged for features such as different types of process verbs (i.e. material; relational; existential).

Not only is there room for writing instruction to pay attention to other varieties of corpora, but scope also exists for writing instruction to escape the confines of the classroom and extend to other milieus.

Extension of corpora: out of the classroom

Chambers (2007: 13) notes that the next important step in the use of corpora is 'out of the classroom'. It is pertinent to note that to date there have been very few accounts or research on the use of corpora for self-access purposes in writing, one exception being the corpus tools and programmes reported in Milton (1997, 2004). Gavioli and Aston (2001: 244) propose ways (e.g. pre-editing corpus data, grading corpora) 'to progressively develop learners' autonomy so that they become able to select and interact with appropriate data independently'. Flowerdew (2008) reports on a writing programme which systematically moves from teacher-directed convergent tasks to more divergent ones, where students take on a more autonomous role. The detailed suite of tasks undertaken during an induction period outlined in Lee and Swales (2006) would be good preparation to set students on a more autonomous writing path. But what is needed to realise autonomous use of corpus data is training not only of learners but of teachers in teacher education programmes (Mukherjee 2004).

It is to be noted that corpora of professional workplace writing have overwhelmingly been used in the academy for professionals-in-training purposes. It seems that corpora have yet to infiltrate the workplace for writing instruction. There are initiatives underway to compile a 100-million-word Corpus of Professional English in science, engineering, technology and other fields (a search of 'Corpus of Professional English' will bring you to the homepage). It is hoped that endeavours such as this will provide relevant corpora for use not only by professionals-in-training, but also for working professionals in the scheme of lifelong learning.

To conclude, this chapter has revealed the many innovative ways in which corpora have been used to produce materials and corpus-driven learning has been integrated into the different stages of writing programmes. However, this 'torrent' (to use Leech's word) has only burst into applications by individuals or institutions. The applications of corpora to writing are at a watershed at present. Such initiatives are still to be adopted at a more national level or be implemented outside the classroom for autonomous learning, also including professional lifelong learning. However, recent innovations in corpora and tools, and the introduction of strategy training for learners and teachers, hold promise of a trickle-down effect.

Further reading

Aimer, K. (ed.) (2009) *Corpora and Language Learning*. Amsterdam: John Benjamins. (Several of the papers in this volume deal with some of the issues discussed in this chapter, such as learner and teacher training for implementing corpus methodologies.)

Gavioli, L. (2005) *Exploring Corpora for ESP Learning*. Amsterdam: John Benjamins. (This volume provides very useful information on all aspects of using corpora in ESP situations.)

Mukherjee, J. (2006) 'Corpus Linguistics and Language Pedagogy: The State of the Art – and Beyond', in S. Braun, K. Kohn and J. Mukherjee (eds) *Corpus Technology and Language Pedagogy*. Frankfurt am Main: Peter Lang, pp. 5–24. (This article gives a very informative introductory overview of pedagogic applications in writing.)

References

Aston, G. (1997) 'Small and Large Corpora in Language Learning', in B. Lewandowska-Tomaszczyk and J. Melia (eds) *Practical Applications in Language Corpora*. Łodz: Łodz University Press, pp. 51–62.

——(2001) 'Learning with Corpora: An Overview', in G. Aston (ed.) *Learning with Corpora*. Houston, TX: Athelstan, pp. 7–45

Bhatia, V. K., Langton, N. and Lung, J. (2004) 'Legal Discourse: Opportunities and Threats for Corpus Linguistics', in U. Connor and T. Upton (eds) *Discourse in the Professions*. Amsterdam: John Benjamins, pp. 203–31.

Bianchi, F. and Pazzaglia, R. (2007) 'Student Writing of Research Articles in a Foreign Language: Metacognition and Corpora', in R. Facchinetti (ed.) *Corpus Linguistics 25 Years On*. Amsterdam: Rodopi, pp. 259–87

Biber, D., Johannson, S., Leech, G., Conrad, S. and Finnegan, E. (1999) *Longman Grammar of Spoken and Written English*. Harlow: Pearson Education.

Bloch, J. (2008) *Technologies in the Second Language Composition Classroom*. Ann Arbor, MI: University of Michigan Press.

——(2009) 'The Design of an Online Concordancing Program for Teaching about Reporting Verbs', *Language Learning and Technology* 13(1): 59–78.

Boulton, A. (2010) 'Data-driven Learning: Teaching the Computer Out of the Equation', *Language Learning* 60(3).

—— (2009) 'Testing the Limits of Data-driven Learning: Language Proficiency and Training', *ReCALL* 21(1): 37–54.

Chambers, A. (2007) 'Popularising Corpus Consultation by Language Learners and Teachers', in E. Hidalgo, L. Quereda and J. Santana (eds) *Corpora in the Foreign Language Classroom*. Amsterdam: Rodopi, pp. 3–16.

Chambers, A. and O'Sullivan, I. (2004) 'Corpus Consultation and Advanced Learners' Writing Skills', *ReCALL* 16(1): 158–72.

Charles, M. (2007) 'Reconciling Top-down and Bottom-up Approaches to Graduate Writing: Using a Corpus to Teach Rhetorical Functions', *Journal of English for Academic Purposes* 6(4): 289–302.

Chujo, K., Utiyama, M. and Nishigaki, C. (2007) 'Towards Building a Usable Corpus Collection for the ELT Classroom', in E. Hidalgo, L. Quereda and J. Santana (eds) *Corpora in the Foreign Language Classroom*. Amsterdam: Rodopi, pp. 47–69.

Coxhead, A. and Byrd, P. (2007) 'Preparing Writing Teachers to Teach the Vocabulary and Grammar of Academic Prose', *Journal of Second Language Writing* 16(3): 129–47.

Cresswell, A. (2007) 'Getting to "Know" Connectors? Evaluating Data-driven Learning in a Writing Skills Course', in E. Hidalgo, L. Quereda and J. Santana (eds) *Corpora in the Foreign Language Classroom*. Amsterdam: Rodopi, pp. 267–87.

Curado Fuentes, A. (2002) 'Exploitation and Assessment of a Business English Corpus through Language Learning Tasks', *ICAME Journal* 26: 5–32.

Flowerdew, L. (2002) 'Corpus-based Analyses in EAP', in J. Flowerdew (ed.) *Academic Discourse*. London: Longman, pp. 95–114.

——(2004) 'The Argument for Using English Specialized Corpora to Understand Academic and Professional Language', in U. Connor and T. Upton (eds) *Discourse in the Professions: Perspectives from Corpus Linguistics*. Amsterdam: John Benjamins, pp. 11–33.

——(2008) 'Corpus Linguistics for Academic Literacies Mediated through Discussion Activities', in D. Belcher and A. Hirvela (eds) *The Oral–Literate Connection: Perspectives on L2 Speaking, Writing and Other Media Interactions*. Ann Arbor, MI: University of Michigan Press, pp. 268–87.

Foucou, P.-Y., and Kübler, N. (2000) 'A Web-based Environment for Teaching Technical English', in L. Burnard and T. McEnery (eds) *Rethinking Language Pedagogy from a Corpus Perspective*. Frankfurt am Main: Peter Lang, pp. 65–71.

Frankenberg-Garcia, A. (2010) 'Raising Teachers' Awareness of Corpora'. *Language Teaching*, doi:10.1017/S0261444810000480, published online by Cambridge University Press.

Gaskell, D. and Cobb, T. (2004) 'Can Learners Use Concordance Feedback for Writing Errors'? *System* 32: 301–19.

Gavioli, L. and Aston, G. (2001) 'Enriching Reality: Language Corpora in Language Pedagogy', *ELT Journal* 55(3): 238–46.

Gilquin, G., Granger, S. and Paquot, M. (2007) 'Learner Corpora: The Missing Link in EAP Pedagogy', *Journal of English for Academic Purposes* 6(4): 319–35.

Granger, S. (2004a) 'Computer Learner Corpus Research; Current Status and Future Prospects', in U. Connor and T. Upton (eds) *Discourse in the Professions: Perspectives from Corpus Linguistics*. Amsterdam: John Benjamins, pp. 123–45.

——(2004b) 'Practical Applications of Learner Corpora', in B. Lewandowska-Tomaszczyk (ed.) *Practical Applications in Language and Computers (PALC) 2003*. Łodz: Łodz University Press, pp. 291–301.

Granger, S. and Meunier, F. (2008) 'Phraseology in Language Learning and teaching: Where To From Here?' in F. Meunier and S. Granger (eds) *Phraseology in Foreign Language Learning and Teaching*. Amsterdam: John Benjamins, pp. 247–51.

Hafner, C. and Candlin, C. (2007) 'Corpus Tools as an Affordance to Learning in Professional Legal Education', *Journal of English for Academic Purposes* 6(4): 303–18.

Hewings, M. (2002) 'Using Computer-based Corpora in Teaching', paper presented at the TESOL Conference, Utah, March.

Hewings, M. and Hewings, A. (2002) '"It Is Interesting to Note That ... ": A Comparative Study of Anticipatory "It" in Student and Published Writing', *English for Specific Purposes* 21(4): 367–83.

Hunston, S. (2002) *Corpora in Applied Linguistics*. Cambridge: Cambridge University Press.

Hyland, K. (2003) *Second Language Writing*. Cambridge: Cambridge University Press.

——(2006) *English for Academic Purposes: An Advanced Resource Book*. London and New York: Routledge.

Johns, T. (1984) 'From Printout to Handout: Grammar and Vocabulary Teaching in the Context of Data-driven Learning', in T. Odlin (ed.) *Perspectives on Pedagogical Grammar*. Cambridge: Cambridge University Press, pp. 293–313.

——(1986) 'Micro-Concord: A Language Learner's Research Tool', *System* 14(2): 151–62.

Jones, M. and Haywood, S. (2004) 'Facilitating the Acquisition of Formulaic Sequences: An Exploratory Study in an EAP Context', in N. Schmitt (ed.) *Formulaic Sequences*. Amsterdam: John Benjamins, pp. 269–91.

Kaszubski, P. (2011) 'A guided collaboration tool for online concordancing with EPA learners'. in A. Frankenberg-Garcia, L. Flowerdew and G. Aston (eds) *New Trends in Corpora and Language Learning*. London: Continuum.

Kennedy, C. and Miceli, T. (2002) 'The *CWIC* Project: Developing and Using a Corpus for Intermediate Italian Students', in B. Kettemann and G. Marko (eds) *Teaching and Learning by Doing Corpus Analysis*. Amsterdam: Rodopi. pp. 183–92.

Kosem, I. (2008) 'User-friendly Corpus Tools for Language Teaching and Learning', in A. Frankenberg-Garcia, T. Rkibi, M. Braga da Cruz, R. Carvalho, C. Direito and D. Santos-Rosa (eds) *Proceedings of the 8th Teaching and Language Corpora Conference*. Lisbon: ISLA.

Kreyer, R. (2008) 'Corpora in the Classroom and Beyond: Aspects of Corpus Competence', paper presented at the Fourth International Inter-Varietal Applied Corpus Studies (IVACS) Conference, 13 June, University of Limerick, Ireland.

Krishnamurthy, R. and Kosem, I. (2007) 'Issues in Creating a Corpus for EAP Pedagogy and Research', *Journal of English for Academic Purposes* 6(4): 356–73.

Lee, D. (2001) 'Genres, Registers, Text Types, Domains, and Styles: Clarifying the Concepts and Navigating a Path through the BNC Jungle', *Language Learning and Technology* 5(3): 37–72.

Lee, D. and Swales, J. (2006) 'A Corpus-based EAP Course for NNS Doctoral Students: Moving from Available Specialized Corpora to Self-compiled Corpora', *English for Specific Purposes* 25(1): 56–75.

Leech, G. (1997) 'Teaching and Language Corpora: A Convergence', in A. Wichmann, S. Fligelstone, T. McEnery and G. Knowles (eds) *Teaching and Language Corpora*. London: Longman, pp. 1–23.

Milton, J. (1997) 'Providing Computerized Self-access Opportunities for the Development of Writing Skills', in P. Benson and P. Voller (eds) *Autonomy and Independence in Language Learning*. Harlow: Longman, pp. 204–14.

——(2004) 'From Parrots to Puppet Masters: Fostering Creative and Authentic Language Use with Online Tools', in B. Homberg, M. Shelley and C. White (eds) *Distance Education and Languages: Evolution and Change*. Clevedon: Multilingual Matters, pp. 242–57.

Mudraya, O. (2006) 'Engineering English: A Lexical Frequency Instructional Model', *English for Specific Purposes* 25(2): 235–56.

Mukherjee, J. (2004) 'Bridging the Gap between Applied Corpus Linguistics and the Reality of English Language Teaching in Germany', in U. Connor and T. Upton (eds) *Applied Corpus Linguistics: A Multi-dimensional Perspective*. Amsterdam: Rodopi, pp. 239–50.

Mukherjee, J. and Rohrbach, J. (2006) 'Rethinking Applied Corpus Linguistics from a Language–Pedagogical Perspective: New Departures in Learner Corpus Research', in B. Kettemann and G. Marko (eds) *Planing, Gluing and Painting Corpora: Inside the Applied Corpus Linguist's Workshop*. Frankfurt am Main: Peter Lang, pp. 205–31.

Nelson, M. (2006) 'Semantic Associations in Business English: A Corpus-based Analysis', *English for Specific Purposes* 25(2): 217–34.

Nesselhauf, N. (2004) 'Learner Corpora and their Potential for Language Teaching', in J. Sinclair (ed.) *How to Use Corpora in Language Teaching*. Amsterdam: John Benjamins. pp. 125–52.

Noguchi, J. (2004) 'A Genre-analysis and Mini-corpora Approach to Support Professional Writing by Nonnative English Speakers', *English Corpus Studies* 11: 101–10.

O'Keeffe, A. and Farr, F. (2003) 'Using Language Corpora in Initial Teacher Training: Pedagogic Issues and Practical Application', *TESOL Quarterly* 37(3): 389–418.

O'Keeffe, A., McCarthy, M. J. and Carter, R. A. (2007) *From Corpus to Classroom: Language Use and Language Teaching*. Cambridge: Cambridge University Press.

Osborne, J. (2004) 'Top-down and Bottom-up Approaches to Corpora in Language Teaching', in U. Connor and T. Upton (eds) *Applied Corpus Linguistics: A Multi-Dimensional Perspective*. Amsterdam: Rodopi, pp. 251–65.

O'Sullivan, I. and Chambers, A. (2006) 'Learners' Writing Skills in French: Corpus Consultation and Learner Evaluation', *Journal of Second Language Writing* 15(1): 49–68.

Partington, A. (1998) *Patterns and Meanings*. Amsterdam: John Benjamins.

Ragan, P. (2001) 'Classroom Use of a Systemic Functional Small Learner Corpus', in M. Ghadessy, A. Henry and R. L. Roseberry (eds), *Small Corpus Studies and ELT*. Amsterdam: John Benjamins, pp. 207–36.

Römer, U. (2006) 'Pedagogical Applications of Corpora: Some Reflections on the Current Scope and a Wish List for Future Developments', *Zeitschrift Anglistik und Americanstik* 54(2): 121–34.

SketchEngine, http://www.sketchengine.co.uk/ (accessed 8 October 2008).

Starfield, S. (2004) 'Why Does This Feel Empowering? Thesis Writing, Concordancing and the "Corporatising University"', in B. Norton and K. Toohey (eds) *Critical Pedagogies and Language Learning*. Cambridge: Cambridge University Press, pp. 138–57.

Swales, J. (2002) 'Integrated and Fragmented Worlds: EAP Materials and Corpus Linguistics', in J. Flowerdew (ed.) *Academic Discourse*. London: Longman, pp. 150–64.

Thompson, P. and Tribble, C. (2001) 'Looking at Citations: Using Corpora in English for Academic Purposes', *Language Learning and Technology* 5(3): 91–105.

Thurstun, J. and Candlin, C. (1998a) *Exploring Academic English: A Workbook for Student Essay Writing*. Macquarie University: NCELTR.

——(1998b) 'Concordancing and the Teaching of Vocabulary of Academic English', *English for Specific Purposes* 17(3): 267–80.

Tribble, C. (2000) 'Genres, Keywords, Teaching: Towards a Pedagogic Account of the Language of Project Proposals', in L. Burnard and T. McEnery (eds) *Rethinking Language Pedagogy from a Corpus Perspective*. Frankfurt am Main: Peter Lang, pp. 75–90.

——(2002) 'Corpora and Corpus Analysis: New Windows on Academic Writing', in J. Flowerdew (ed.) *Academic Discourse*. London: Longman, pp. 131–49.

Tribble, C. and Jones, G. (1990) *Concordances in the Classroom*. London: Longman.

van Rij-Heyligers, J. (2007) 'To Weep Perilously or W.EAP critically: The Case for a Corpus-based Critical EAP', in E. Hidalgo, L. Quereda and J. Santana (eds) *Corpora in the Foreign Language Classroom*. Amsterdam: Rodopi, pp. 105–18.

Watson-Todd, R. (2001) 'Induction from Self-selected Concordances and Self-correction', *System* 29 (1): 91–102.

Weber, J.-J. (2001) 'A Concordance- and Genre-informed Approach to ESP Essay Writing', *ELT Journal* 55(1): 14–20.

Wible, D., Kuo, C.-H., Chien, F.-Y., Liu, A. and Wang, C. C. (2002) 'Towards Automating a Personalized Concordancer for Data-driven Learning: A Lexical Difficulty Filter for Language Learners', in B. Kettemann and G. Marko (eds) *Teaching and Learning by Doing Corpus Analysis*. Amsterdam: Rodopi, pp. 147–54.

Yoon, H. (2008) 'More than a Linguistic Reference: The Influence of Corpus Technology on L2 Academic Writing', *Language Learning and Technology* 12(2): 31–48.

Yoon, H. and Hirvela, A. (2004) 'ESL Student Attitudes toward Corpus Use in L2 Writing', *Journal of Second Language Writing* 13(4): 257–83.

33

What can corpora tell us about English for Academic Purposes?

Averil Coxhead

1. What can corpora reveal about aspects of academic language in use?

In his book, *Better: A Surgeon's Notes on Performance*, Atul Gawande urges professionals to 'count something'. He reasons, 'If you count something you find interesting, you will learn something interesting' (Gawande 2007: 255). Corpus linguistics has contributed a great deal to English for Academic Purposes (EAP) precisely because researchers, teachers and students now have access to computer-based tools that enable them to systematically 'count something' in the language they encounter in their academic studies. Counting draws attention to features of the language that might otherwise have been ignored. It also addresses two problems for teachers and learners. The first is that intuition has played a major role in deciding what to teach and what to include in EAP materials. The second is knowing what language is problematic for EAP learners. This chapter on EAP and corpora addresses five questions: what can corpora reveal about aspects of academic language in use; how can corpora influence EAP pedagogy; how can corpora be used in EAP materials; what can a corpus tell us about EAP learner language; and what might the future be for corpora in EAP?

EAP is about teaching and learning English for students who speak English as an additional language and who are studying or preparing to study at undergraduate or postgraduate level. It is important to find out more about academic language in use because, as Gilquin *et al.* (2007: 321) point out, 'The distinctive, highly routinised nature of EAP proves undeniably problematic for many (especially novice) native writers, but it poses an even greater challenge to non-native writers.'

Corpus linguistics research has brought to light interesting and at times puzzling data on academic language in use. Gilquin *et al.* (2007: 320) summarise the contribution of corpus-based studies to EAP by saying they have provided 'Detailed descriptions of its distinctive linguistic features, and more specifically its highly specific phraseology, and careful analyses of linguistic variability across academic genres and disciplines'. It is important to remember several key points about academic language that EAP students study and EAP teachers teach. First of all, it is not just written, but it is also spoken. Second, it is not just produced in published form by academics in books and journals, but it is also produced by native and non-native students in the form of essays, reports, theses, as well as PowerPoint and tools such as WebCT, and more. Third, even though there are more and more EAP-focused corpus-based investigations, we still have a great deal more to count, analyse and learn about academic language in use.

The number and size of EAP corpora have boomed somewhat since the early 1990s (see Thompson 2006 or Krishnamurthy and Kosem 2007 for lists of existing EAP corpora; Flowerdew 2002 and McEnery *et al.* 2006 for their survey of corpus resources). Some EAP corpora are publicly available, such as the Michigan Corpus of Spoken American English (MICASE; Simpson *et al.* 2000), the British Academic Spoken English corpus (BASE) and the British Written Academic corpus (BAWE) by Nesi and Thomson. Some corpora contain both written and spoken English, such as the TOEFL 2000 Spoken and Written Academic Language Corpus (T2K-SWAL) (Biber *et al.* 2001), while others focus on learner language such as the International Corpus of Learner English (see the work by Granger and her colleagues at the Catholic University of Louvain, Belgium). Mauranen (2003) reports on a spoken corpus of English as a Lingua Franca and various studies such as Thompson (2006) and Hyland (2008) examine both learner and native speaker written academic output.

Deciding what to put into an academic corpus, in what proportion and why are not easy decisions. The T2K-SWAL corpus, for example, contains a wide range of academic written materials, including textbooks, university brochures and catalogues, whereas other corpora focus on one kind of output such as PhD or Master's theses. Size is an issue in corpus development also and corpus-based EAP studies have been based on small corpora (see Flowerdew 2001) through to reasonably large corpora such as the twenty-five-million-word Hong Kong University of Science and Technology corpus of secondary and university essays (cited in Krishnamurthy and Kosem 2007: 360).

Vocabulary has been a major area of corpus-based research into academic language. Word frequency lists that would have taken many researchers many hours and years to compile in the past can now be generated using programmes such as WordSmith Tools (Scott 2006) and by teachers or learners working online using websites such as the brilliant Compleat Lexical Tutor by Tom Cobb. See O'Keeffe *et al.* (2007: 200–3) for a very accessible description of frequency in written academic English. Word lists have been developed such as the Academic Word List (AWL, Coxhead 2000; see also an investigation of the AWL in medical English in Chen and Ge 2007), a Business word list, (see Nelson n.d.; Konstantakis 2007), and a pilot Science-specific EAP word list (Coxhead and Hirsh 2007). Work on how words behave differently across academic disciplines (Hyland and Tse 2007) reveals further aspects of academic language that are useful for a variety of teachers and learners in an EAP context. Early studies of 'technical' or 'semi-technical' language pointed out that words such as *cost* take on specific meaning in Economics that they do not have in general English (Sutarsyah *et al.* 1994). More corpus-based work on the common collocations and phrases of the AWL words is underway (Coxhead and Byrd forthcoming).

Analyses of textbooks have become more common in the EAP literature. Gabrielatos (2005) states that textbook corpora allow us to examine language that our students are exposed to in their studies and can lead to more pedagogically sound materials (see McCarten, this volume). Comparative studies of textbooks and university classrooms (Biber *et al.* 2001, 2004; Conrad 2004; Reppen 2004) have shown consistently how textbooks could be enhanced by the application of corpus findings. Conrad (2004), for example, provides a powerful example of how the word *though* is used in ESL textbooks and in corpora. Conrad also demonstrates how corpora allow us to investigate multiple features of academic language by comparing an ESL textbook practice lecture with five lectures from the T2K-SWAL. Her analysis showed that the face-to-face lectures contained more interaction than the ESL textbook lecture, which in turn was more information-based. Conrad goes on to recommend that teachers and materials designers might consider integrating examples of face-to-face lectures.

The majority of EAP corpus-based studies have targeted university- or tertiary-level adult learners. A recent study by Jennifer Greene (personal communication, 18 February 2008) looks at the vocabulary of textbooks used in middle schools (sixth–eighth grade; ages eleven–fourteen) in the USA to find out more about the vocabulary these learners encounter in context. Greene compiled an eighteen-million-word corpus of English, Health, Maths, Science and Social Sciences/History textbooks.

Researchers have also looked at multi-word units in academic texts. These units have been called (among other names) formulaic sequences or lexical bundles. Examples of multi-word units are *in relation to* and *on the other hand* (see Biber *et al.* 1999, especially Chapter 13 on lexical bundles in speaking and writing; and O'Keefe *et al.*'s 2007 book for more on lexical chunks). Bundles have been found to be very important for EAP learners. Biber *et al.* (2004) analyse lexical bundles in university classroom teaching and textbooks and find that classroom teaching contains more lexical bundles than conversation, textbooks and academic prose. The authors present a taxonomy of bundles, including stance expressions such as *well I don't know*, discourse organisers such as *if you look at*, and referential expressions such as *one of the most*. Scott and Tribble (2006) examine 'clusters' in a corpus of postgraduate learner writing and articles from the BNC, while Hyland (2008) looks at variation in lexical bundles across disciplines by examining four-word bundles in Biology, Electrical Engineering, Applied Linguistics and Business Studies in three corpora; research articles, PhD theses and MA/MSc theses. Hyland finds substantial variation between and among the three disciplines. The topic of idioms in academic contexts is covered well in O'Keeffe *et al.* (2007: 90–4). See also Simpson and Mendis (2003).

Studies into corpora do not necessarily involve just analysing words in spoken and written texts. Ellis *et al.* (2008) have created an Academic Formulas List by investigating a wide range of corpora including the MICASE corpus mentioned above, finding formulae that fit their selection principles, and asking EAP teachers to discuss the 'teachability' of these formulae in classrooms. The MICASE corpus has been the basis of many interesting investigations. The MICASE website is well worth browsing to search the corpus, use in EAP classrooms, and gain benefit from a substantial amount of research and teaching effort. Another example of using a combination of quantitative and qualitative research methodologies comes from Aktas and Cortes (2008) and their study of 'shell nouns' in published and ESL student writing.

Special aspects of academic writing have also been explored by various researchers. One example is the Thompson and Tribble (2001) investigation into the use of academic citations in doctoral theses in Agricultural Botany and Agricultural Economics. The authors then investigated citations in EAP student writing and noted differences between disciplines and genres (see also Hyland 1999, 2002 for more on academic citations). Thompson and Tribble go on to show how EAP textbooks do not contain explanations or instances that reflect how academic citations are used in different disciplines within the university and suggest ways in which corpora can be used to fill that gap. Hunston (2002) provides an interesting overview of interpersonal meaning in academic texts and as well as EAP and corpora.

2. How can corpora influence EAP pedagogy?

Some clear benefits to using corpora in EAP have been noted, particularly in the area of second language writing. Yoon and Hirvela (2004) find the learners in their study of the use of corpora and concordancing in their L2 writing classrooms responded positively and felt that they had developed confidence in their own writing. Yoon (2008) reports on a study of six L2 writers using corpora in an academic context and finds benefits such as participants using a corpus to look up lexical and grammatical items that were problematic, raised awareness of lexico-grammatical and language, as well as increased confidence and independence as writers.

Tribble (2002: 147) discusses how EAP students might draw on three types of corpora to support their development as academic writers. He suggests 'exemplar' corpora that are specifically related to the kind of writing the learner aspires to; 'analogue' corpora that are similar to that kind of writing; and 'reference' corpora for genre analysis.

Learners and teachers do not have to be limited to using existing corpora. Doctoral students in a study by Lee and Swales (2006) began working with specialised and general corpora to become familiar with the basic concepts and technology and then compiled corpora of their own writing and of 'expert writing' within their field. These personalised corpora focused on the particular discipline interests of students such as pharmacology and educational technology. A learner's own corpus can be used to compare learner language and 'expert' language and 'learners can gain knowledge of how they can vary their own vocabulary or lexico-grammatical structures, with the concordanced examples providing exemplars' (Lee and Swales 2006: 68). Having learners compile their own corpora for investigation has the potential to help EAP teachers in particular, as often EAP classes contain a wide variety of first languages studying EAP to prepare for study in many different academic disciplines (Hunter and Coxhead 2007; Coxhead 2008).

Lexical bundles found in corpus studies have found their way into EAP classrooms. Jones and Haywood (2004) explore learning and teaching formulaic phrases found in common between four EAP course books of academic writing, selected on frequency through a corpus search and sorted according to Biber *et al.*'s (1999) grammatical categorisations of lexical bundles. Despite many efforts in the classroom, the study finds that while the students' awareness of formulaic sequences had risen, learning and using the phrases in writing did not go well. According to Jones and Haywood, students seemed not to commit the target bundles to memory well, or appeared to focus on already known or salient bundles (2004: 289). Coxhead (2008) points out some difficulties or barriers for teachers and learners in teaching and learning phrases for EAP. One of these barriers was highlighted by a second language learner who commented that it was hard enough to learn one word at a time, let alone two.

In a Swedish study of 'hands on' use of corpora into a university-level English grammar course, Vannestål and Lindquist (2007) report,

> When it comes to grammar, most students are so used to reading about rules before they see examples that it can take a lot of time and practice for them to understand how they should think when faced with a concordance list of authentic examples, from which they are supposed to extract rules of language usage.
>
> (Vannestål and Lindquist 2007: 344)

Weaker students, in particular, struggled with the corpus work and the researchers and participants conclude that perhaps corpus work might be more suited to writing development and vocabulary than inductive grammar.

The shell noun study mentioned above by Aktas and Cortes (2008) provides useful insights for ESL pedagogy in both academic writing and reading classes. The researchers found that while the ESL writers used shell nouns in their writing, the nouns did not appear in the same lexico-grammatical patterns in both corpora, nor were they used for the same cohesive purposes in the academic written texts. Insights from studies into learner and native speaker corpora have a great deal to offer both pedagogically and in the design of materials (Meunier 2002).

Corpus linguistics has also contributed to the development and sustainability of learner independence (Barlow 2000; Bernardini 2004; Nesselhauf 2004; Starfield 2004; Gabrielatos 2005; Yoon 2008). Lee and Swales (2006: 71) write that corpus-based language instruction is 'decentring' and empowering in that the learners themselves can take control of their learning through discovering language use for themselves and referring to texts written by different writers (L1 and L2). The learners became independent of native speakers as reference points for language problems and some reported corpora consultation was superior to reference or grammar books in terms of access and exemplification in related contexts and texts that could be explored across disciplines and from different speakers. Barlow points to the benefits of language students becoming language explorers with corpora when he writes,

> One role that the language student can usefully play is that of language researcher (or co-researcher); and like other researchers, the student requires a suitable research environment (tools and data) to facilitate the acquisition of knowledge about a language. By using a corpus and a text analysis program rather than a dictionary, thesaurus, or grammar, the student can learn a language using a rich and adaptable research environment in which the data are selected examples of language use, embedded in their linguistic context.
>
> (Barlow 2000: 106)

Starfield (2004: 154) recounts the experiences of second language PhD students using concordancing as a way for them to begin 'strategically engaging with the resources of authoritative English'. Concordancing led to 'growth and development' in the writing of the postgraduates as well as a growing student empowerment.

Corpora have also been consulted to answer questions teachers in Hong Kong have about language in use (Tsui 2004) with positive results.

Vannestål and Lindquist (2007) comment that working with corpora can be appreciated by some students and not by others. They also find working with corpora to be time-heavy in implementation and that developing independent competent student corpus use can take a great deal of time. It is clear using a corpus needs careful integration with existing curricula and guidance. Studies such as Lee and Swales (2006) and Yoon (2008) allow time for students to become familiar with the tools. Yoon (2008: 45) suggests that one implication of corpus use as an integrated part of an EAP curriculum is that a pedagogy is required that recognises that the acquisition of words and phrases can take longer than traditional or conventional classes tend to allow.

A challenge for EAP and corpus linguistics is to incorporate findings into pedagogy and materials to ensure that all four strands of the language curriculum are involved (see

Nation 2007 for a discussion of the four strands). The four strands comprise three meaning-focused strands where communication of meaning is the main focus. These strands are: meaning-focused input, meaning-focused output and fluency. The fourth strand is language-focus. Nation (2007: 9) posits that these four strands should be given equal amounts of time. Concordances and such like clearly fit within the language-focused strand. Swales (2002) provides examples and personal reflections on how EAP materials and corpus linguistics can integrate several strands. Potentially more such work is being produced in many EAP classrooms, but not many examples of an integrated, four-strand programme of learning appear to exist. For more on L2 teaching and corpus linguistics, see Conrad (2005).

3. How can corpora be used in EAP materials?

Concordances have been a major face of corpus linguistics in EAP materials, beginning with Tribble and Jones (1990) and their *Concordances in the Classroom*, then on to Thurston and Candlin's (1997) presentation of rhetorical functions of frequently used words in academic writing through concordancing. Tim Johns (2000) and his data-driven learning (DDL) concept use kibitzer pages (which Johns defines as 'looking over the shoulder of experts') to provide opportunities for EAP students to notice features of the target language in their own text and compare them with revised versions. The idea of kibitzers has since been taken up by researchers working on MICASE (see MICASE website) where learners and teachers can investigate corpus data and discussion around aspects of academic language. Such activities can help raise awareness of kinds and features of words and phrases to focus on. MICASE also provides some examples of self-study exercises that can be integrated into an EAP programme to raise awareness of language use in spoken academic contexts and to introduce corpus-based exercises to learners. The set of example materials below asks learners to consider examples of *turns out* in sample sentences from the MICASE corpus and match them to some possible functions of *turns out*.

It *turns out* that the average is the same.
It *turns out* that the S values are not very reliable.
That *turns out* to be quite a lot of money.
If your p-value *turns out* to be so small that you'd reject

- announcing a result in mathematical or statistical computations
- introducing the end or next segment of a story
- used when negating, contrasting, or qualifying – but also emphasizing – an important point

(Simpson *et al.* 2007)

Textbooks for EAP developed from corpora studies are steadily becoming available. McCarthy and O'Dell's (2008) *Academic Vocabulary in Use* was prepared by identifying academic vocabulary in the Cambridge International Corpus of written and spoken English and the CANCODE corpus, as well as checking the Cambridge Learner Corpus for common learner errors. The book introduces concepts such as noun phrases in academic texts, and give us as an instance 'widespread long term-damage' (McCarthy and O'Dell 2008: 10). A notable feature of this book is that the first nine units of work are based on concepts of academic vocabulary that learners need to understand, such as exploring what is special about academic vocabulary while presenting target words in context and providing opportunities for practice.

Schmitt and Schmitt's (2005) book, *Focus on Vocabulary: Mastering the Academic Word List*, uses the New Longman Corpus to compile collocation exercises that illustrate how words are used in context. In the example below, adapted from the book, we can see a matching activity that requires learners to notice the position of the word in relation to its collocate (the symbol ~ indicates the position of the target word before the collocation).

COLLOCATION

Match each target word in the box with the group of words that regularly occur with it. If the (~) symbol appears before a word in a list, the target word comes before the word in the list. In all other cases, the target word comes after the word in the list.

brief	chart	implement	monitor
channel	component	integrity	option
1. ______	2. ______	3. ______	4. ______
~ money	~ history	~ progress	~ policy
~ resources	~ mention	~ performance	~ recommendations
~ funds	~ sojourn	~ compliance	~ strategy
~ energy	~ introduction	~ standards	~ reforms

(Schmitt and Schmitt 2005: 196)

Teachers might like to actually complete exercises like this themselves so they can become aware of what knowledge of aspects of words needs attention and can think about follow-up activities in the classroom that could be used to further explore these words and their collocates (see Coxhead 2006 for examples of direct learning activities) and incorporate more of Nation's four strands.

Online sources have become a major source of materials for EAP as we have already seen above, including such sites as the AWL Highlighter by Sandra Haywood at Nottingham University. This website allows teachers and students to input their own texts, or ones supplied by Haywood, and highlight the AWL words up to Sublist 10 in the texts or make gapfills or fill-in-the-blanks activities. See Horst *et al.* (2005) on an interactive online database and its capacity to expand vocabulary.

Coxhead and Byrd (2007) provide some examples of both computer-based and non-computer-based techniques for investigating lexico-grammatical patterns in use in EAP. These examples can be used for developing materials for language classrooms and for the preparation of teachers to teach these features of academic writing. An example of the kind of data from corpus linguistics that can be explored in EAP materials in Coxhead and Byrd is the word *required*, which appears in Sublist 1 of the AWL. *Required* tends to be used most often in academic writing in its passive form, as in 'Every company is *required* to make a statement in writing' (cited in Coxhead and Byrd 2007: 2), and rarely in the simple past tense. EAP teachers and learners could investigate words such as *required* using the Compleat Lexical Tutor concordancer online (Cobb n.d.), search for instances of the word in spoken and written corpora and use this data to draw conclusions about how such words are used in academic contexts. The Compleat Lexical Tutor website also has examples of highlighting particular grammatical patterns from corpora that require learners to decide whether the grammatical patterns in a sentence are correct or incorrect. Exercises and tools for making gap fills (or fill-in-the-blanks) based on the AWL are on Haywood's (n.d.) website called Academic Vocabulary.

Another enormously useful contribution of corpora has been innovations in dictionary making (see Walter, this volume). The ground-breaking Collins COBUILD series (Sinclair 2003 [1987]), working with the Bank of English, pioneered this area of continuing development, with the fourth edition published in 2003. The *Longman Exams Dictionary* (Mayor 2006) includes examples from reports and essays written in academic contexts. These learner dictionaries have also taken up the concept of defining words for second language learners using a common vocabulary of 2,000 words, drawn from corpus research.

Learner corpora have contributed significantly to dictionary making (Granger 2002; Nesselhauf 2004). A recent example is the inclusion of findings and insights from work by researchers such as Gilquin *et al.* (2007) in the second edition of the *Macmillan Dictionary for Advanced Learners* (Rundell 2007). Other examples are the *Longman Dictionary of Contemporary English* (LDOCE), where learner corpora were consulted to provide advice on how not to use a word in context and the *Longman Language Activator*, where common learner errors were drawn from the Longman Learner Corpus. An online search of the LDOCE of *according to* produced the following dictionary entry. Note the advice in the section marked with an exclamation mark (!):

> according to S2 W1
> 1 as shown by something or stated by someone:
> - *According to the police, his attackers beat him with a blunt instrument.*
> - *There is now widespread support for these proposals, according to a recent public opinion poll.*
>
> ! Do not say 'according to me' or 'according to my opinion/point of view'. Say **in my opinion** *In my opinion his first book is much better.*
>
> (LODCE Online n.d., www.ldoceonline.com/dictionary/according-to)

4. What can a corpus tell us about EAP learner language?

We have already seen throughout this chapter that learner corpora have had a major impact on EAP, particularly in dictionary making and research into academic writing in context. Granger and her colleagues in Belgium and other researchers have moved corpus studies for EAP into completely new realms of possibilities through their compilations and analyses of learner corpora. Granger makes a strong case for the importance of learner corpora when she writes,

> Native corpora provide valuable information on the frequency and use of words, phrases and structures but give no indication whatsoever of the difficulty they present for learners in general or for a specific category of learners. They will therefore always be of limited value and may even lead to ill-judged pedagogical decisions unless they are complemented with the equally rich and pedagogically more relevant type of data provided by learner corpora.
>
> (Granger 2002: 21–2)

Granger provides two key uses of learner corpora in classrooms. First, form-focused instruction whereby learners are encouraged to notice the gap between their output and native output: fossilised learners in particular may benefit from this sort of instruction. The second use of learner corpora is data-driven learning, which we have already touched on above (see Gilquin and Granger, this volume). For an overview of learner corpora, see Granger (2002: 3–36) and Flowerdew (2002).

Learner corpora studies have already shown some particularly useful insights into differences between first and second language writers in EAP. Gilquin *et al.* (2007) relate an important finding for EAP learners and teachers, which is that learner language appears to indicate that some of its characteristics are limited to one population of L2 speakers, whereas others appear to be shared with many different L2 speaker populations. Learner corpora have the capacity to compare L2 with L1 as well as L2s with other L2s (Gilquin *et al.* 2007) and learner corpora research has brought to light some interesting findings on the use, misuse and, at times, overuse of particular lexical items. Flowerdew (2001) reviews early work on learner corpora and explores the use of small learner corpora findings on collocations, pragmatic appropriateness and discourse features in the preparation of materials for EAP. She suggests ways in which these findings can be integrated with native corpora. For more on the evidence of learner corpora, see for example Granger *et al.* (2002) and Hunston (2002). For more on learner corpora in materials design and pedagogy see Flowerdew (2001); Granger *et al.* (2002); Nesselhauf (2004).

5. What might the future be for corpora in EAP?

An exciting development in future would be to see more research into language in use in the secondary context to support learning and teaching of younger learners in their school-based studies and in preparation for further studies. Resources such as easily accessible online and paper materials, better dictionaries and school materials based on information concerning what these learners need to learn are very much in need (Pat Byrd, personal communication, 29 October 2008). A more co-ordinated research-, pedagogy- and materials-based agenda for EAP at undergraduate and postgraduate level that incorporates both learner and native corpora internationally is also important.

Developing and exploiting multi-media corpora (Ackerley and Coccetta 2007; Baldry 2008) for EAP may be an avenue for the future. A multi-media corpus can help overcome two difficulties with spoken corpora. The first is that spoken text becomes a written text, and the second is that the visual information which is present with speaking such as gestures and facial expressions is not available with written spoken corpora (Ackerley and Coccetta 2007). Multi-media concordancing allows for analysis of learner and native language in its real context (see Adolphs and Knight, this volume), as well as the inclusion of visual information such as tables, charts, maps, and so on, that are often presented in lectures and textbooks. Ackerley and Coccetta (2007) describe tagging of the corpus for language functions which can be searched through phrases such as 'spelling out a word/expression' and 'expressing dislike'. Multi-media corpora might be able to reflect the complexities of oral presentations in a university context where the speaker is using a visual tool such as PowerPoint and a whiteboard and full picture of such a teaching and learning space. They might also help researchers find out more about learners' interaction and learning from multi-media in their studies (Hunter and Coxhead 2007).

Another potential avenue for the future is parallel corpora for EAP that can be used to examine aspects of language. Some parallel corpora for general purposes already exist, such the ones described in the study of the use of the reflexive in English and in French in Barlow (2000) (see also Kenning in this volume). In the future, perhaps multi-lingual corpora might be developed that can further inform EAP corpus linguistics research. Such corpora may provide insights into how different languages express similar academic concepts in different ways and how frequency of use and collocational restrictions might affect lexical choices, as well as how different subject areas might employ a word differently. Nesselhauf (2004) writes of international corpora where the output of first language speakers of different first languages, and ESL and EFL speakers of the same L1, could be compared to find out more about instructed and natural language acquisition. Gilquin *et al.* (2007) call for textbooks that use learner corpora to inform learners of typical language learner errors such as overuse or misuse of lexical items.

This chapter has looked at some of the ways in which corpora have been developed to inform EAP teachers and learners. This research has not only counted things, as Gawande (2007) encourages professionals to do, but it has broken new ground in corpus linguistics in methodology and analysis. Gradually we have seen that the learner is now at the centre of corpus linguistics for EAP. There is much work yet to be done, particularly in pedagogy and materials design, but this work will be done, and more.

Further reading

Chambers, A. (ed.) (2007) 'Integrating Corpora in Language Learning and Teaching', *ReCALL* 19(3): 249–376. (This special issue contains articles on more general language learning including topics such as computer-based learning of English phraseology and grammar, as well as using a multi-media corpus.)

Sinclair, J. (2004) *How to Use Corpora in Language Teaching*. Amsterdam: John Benjamins. (This excellent, practical book is part of the *Studies in Corpus Linguistics* series, edited by E. Tognini Bonelli.)

Teubert, W. and Krishnamurthy, R. (eds) (2007) *Corpus Linguistics: Critical Concepts in Linguistics*. London: Routledge. (This six-volume set contains a wide range of major articles in corpus linguistics.)

Thomson, P. (2006) 'Assessing the Contribution of Corpora to EAP Practice', in Z. Kantaridou, I. Papadopoulou and I. Mahili (eds) *Motivation in Learning Language for Specific and Academic Purposes*. Macedonia, University of Macedonia [CD Rom], no specific page numbers given, available online. (This article takes an overview of corpora use in EAP including discussion on trends and issues in EAP-related corpora as well as the application of corpus-based findings and methodologies to classroom teaching and its limited uptake in the classroom thus far.)

——(ed.) (2007) 'Corpus-based EAP Pedagogy,' *Journal of English for Academic Purposes* 6(4): 285–374. (This special issue provides an excellent range of articles specifically related to EAP pedagogy and corpus linguistics.)

References

Ackerley, K. and Coccetta, F. (2007) 'Enriching Language Learning through a Multimedia Corpus', *ReCall* 19(3): 351–70.

Aktas, R. and Cortes, V. (2008) 'Shell Nouns as Cohesive Devices in Published and ESL Student Writing', *Journal of English for Academic Purposes* 7: 3–14.

Baldry, A. (2008) 'What are Concordances for? Getting Multimodal Concordances to Perform Neat Tricks in the University Teaching and Testing Cycle', in A. Baldry, M. Pavesi, C. Taylor Torsello and C. Taylor (eds) *From Didactas to Ecolingua: An Ongoing Research Project on Translation*. Trieste: Edizioni Università di Trieste, pp. 35–50; available at http://hdl.handle.net/10077/2847 (accessed 26 March 2009).

Barlow, M. (2000) 'Parallel Texts in Language Teaching', in S. Botley, A. McEnery and A. Wilson (eds) *Multilingual Corpora in Teaching and Research*. Amsterdam: Rodopi, pp. 106–15.

Bernardini, S. (2004) 'Corpora in the Classroom: An Overview and Some Reflections on Future Developments', in J. Sinclair (ed.) *How to Use Corpora in Language Teaching*. Amsterdam: John Benjamins, pp. 15–38,

Biber, D. (2006) *University Language: A Corpus-based Study of Spoken and Written Registers*. Amsterdam: John Benjamins.

Biber, D., Finegan, E., Johansson, S., Conrad, S. and Leech, G. (1999) *Longman Grammar of Spoken and Written English*. London: Longman.

Biber, D., Reppen, R., Clark, V. and Walter, J. (2001) 'Representing Spoken Language in University Settings: The Design and Construction of the Spoken Component of the T2K-SWAL Corpus', in R. Simpson and J. Swales (eds) *Corpus Linguistics in North America*. Ann Arbor, MI: Michigan University Press, pp. 48–57.

Biber, D., Conrad, S. and Cortes, V. (2004) 'If You Look At … : Lexical Bundles in University Teaching and Textbooks', *Applied Linguistics* 25: 371–405.

Chen, Q. and Ge, G. (2007) 'A Corpus-based Lexical Study on Frequency and Distribution of Coxhead's AWL Word Families in Medical Research Articles (RAs)', *English for Specific Purposes* 26: 502–14.

Cobb, T. (n.d.) *The Compleat Lexical Tutor*. Montreal: University of Montreal; available at www.lextutor.ca/ (accessed 26 March 2009).

Conrad, S. (2004) 'Corpus Linguistics, Language Variation, and Language Teaching', in J. Sinclair (ed.) *How to Use Corpora in Language Teaching*. Amsterdam: John Benjamins, pp. 67–85.

——(2005) 'Corpus Linguistics and L2 Teaching', in E. Hinkel (ed.) *Handbook of Research in Second Language Teaching and Learning*. Mahwah, NJ: Lawrence Erlbaum, pp. 393–95.

Coxhead, A. (2000) 'A New Academic Word List', *TESOL Quarterly* 34(2): 213–38.

——(2006) *Essentials of Teaching Academic Vocabulary*. Boston, MA: Houghton Mifflin.

——(2008) 'Phraseology and English for Academic Purposes: Challenges and opportunities', in F. Meunier and S. Granger (eds) *Phraseology in Foreign Language Learning and Teaching*. Amsterdam: John Benjamins, pp. 149–62.

Coxhead, A. and Byrd, P. (2007) 'Preparing Writing Teachers to Teach the Vocabulary and Grammar of Academic Prose', *Journal of Second Language Writing* 16, 129–47.

——(forthcoming) *The Common Collocations and Recurrent Phrases of the Academic Word List*. Ann Arbor, MI: University of Michigan Press.

Coxhead, A. and Hirsh, D. (2007) 'A Pilot Science Word List for EAP', *Revue Française de Linguistique Appliquée* XII(2): 65–78.

Ellis, N., Simpson-Vlach, R. and Maynard, C. (2008) 'Formulaic Language in Native and Second Language Speakers: Psycholinguistics, Corpus Linguistics, and TESOL', *TESOL Quarterly* 42(3): 375–96.

Flowerdew, L. (2001) 'The Exploitation of Small Learner Corpora in EAP Materials Design', in M. Ghadessy, A. Henry and R. Roseberry (eds) *Small Corpus Studies and ELT*. Amsterdam: John Benjamins, pp. 363–79.

——(2002) 'Corpus-based Analyses in EAP', in J. Flowerdew (ed.) *Academic Discourse*. London: Longman, pp. 95–114.

Gabrielatos, C. (2005) 'Corpora and Language Teaching: Just a Fling or Wedding Bells?' *TESL-EJ* 8(4): A-1; available at http://tesl-ej.org/ej32/a1.html (accessed 26 March 2009).

Gawande, A. (2007) *Better: A Surgeon's Notes on Performance*. New York: Metropolitan.

Gilquin, G., Granger, S. and Paquot, M. (2007) 'Learner Corpora: The Missing Link in EAP Pedagogy', *Journal of English for Academic Purposes* 6: 319–35.

Granger, S. (2002) 'A Bird's-eye View of Learner Corpora Research', in S. Granger, J. Hung and S. Petch-Tyson (eds) *Computer Learner Corpora, Second Language Acquisition and Foreign Language Teaching*. Amsterdam: John Benjamins, pp. 3–36.

Granger, S., Hung, J. and Petch-Tyson, S. (2002) *Computer Learner Corpora, Second Language Acquisition and Foreign Language Teaching*. Amsterdam: John Benjamins.

Horst, M., Cobb, T. and Nicolae, I. (2005) 'Expanding Academic Vocabulary with an Interactive On-line Database', *Language Learning and Technology* 9: 90–110.

Hunston, S. (2002) *Corpora in Applied Linguistics*. Cambridge: Cambridge University Press.

Hunter, J. and Coxhead, A. (2007) 'New Technologies in University Lectures and Tutorials: Opportunities and Challenges for EAP Programmes', *TESOLANZ Journal* 15: 30–41.

Hyland, K. (1999) 'Academic Attribution: Citation and the Construction of Disciplinary Knowledge', *Applied Linguistics* 20(3): 341–67.

——(2002) 'Activity and Evaluation: Reporting Practices in Academic Writing', in J. Flowerdew (ed.) *Academic Discourse*. London: Longman, pp. 115–30.

——(2008) 'As Can Be Seen: Lexical Bundles and Disciplinary Variation', *English for Specific Purposes* 27: 4–21.

Hyland, K. and Tse, P. (2007) 'Is There an "Academic Vocabulary"?' *TESOL Quarterly* 41(2): 235–53.

Johns, T. (2000) *Tim John's EAP Page*, at www.eisu2.bham.ac.uk/johnstf/timeap3.htm (accessed 26 March 2009).

Jones, M. and Haywood, S. (2004) 'Facilitating the Acquisition of Formulaic Sequences: An Exploratory Study in an EAP Context', in N. Schmitt (ed.) *Formulaic Sequences*. Amsterdam: John Benjamins, pp. 269–91.

Konstantakis, N. (2007) 'Creating a Business Word List for Teaching Business English', *Elia* 7: 79–102.

Krishnamurthy, R. and Kosem, I. (2007) 'Issues in Creating a Corpus for EAP Pedagogy and Research', *Journal of English for Academic Purposes* 6: 356–73.

Lee, D. and Swales, J. (2006) 'A Corpus-based EAP Course for NNS Doctoral Students: Moving from Available Specialized Corpora to Self-Compiled Corpora', *English for Specific Purposes* 25: 56–75.

Longman Dictionary of Contemporary English (2003) Harlow: Pearson Longman.

McCarthy, M. and O'Dell, F. (2008) *Academic Vocabulary in Use*. Cambridge: Cambridge University Press.

McEnery, T., Xiao, R. and Tono, Y. (2006) *Corpus-based Language Studies: An Advanced Resource Book*. London: Routledge.

Mauranen, A. (2003) 'The Corpus of English as Lingua France in Academic Settings', *TESOL Quarterly* 37(3): 217–31.

Mayor, M. (2006) *Longman Exams Dictionary*. London: Longman.

Meunier, F. (2002) 'The Pedagogical Value of Native and Learner Corpora in EFL Grammar Teaching', in S. Granger, J. Hung and S. Petch-Tyson (eds) *Computer Learner Corpora, Second Language Acquisition and Foreign Language Teaching*. Amsterdam: John Benjamins, pp. 119–41.

Nation, I. S. P. (2007) 'The Four Strands', *Innovation in Language Learning and Teaching* 1(1): 2–13.

Nelson, M. (n.d.) *Mike Nelson's Business English Lexis Site*, available at http://users.utu.fi/micnel/business_english_lexis_site.htm (accessed 25 March 2009).

Nesselhauf, N. (2004) 'Learner Corpora and their Potential for Language Teaching' in J. Sinclair (ed.) *How to Use Corpora in Language Teaching*. Amsterdam: John Benjamins, pp. 125–52.

O'Keeffe, A., McCarthy, M. J. and Carter, R. A. (2007) *From Corpus to Classroom: Language Use and Language Teaching*. Cambridge: Cambridge University Press.

Reppen, R. (2004) 'Academic Language: An Exploration of University Classroom and Textbook Language', in U. Connor and T. Upton (eds) *Discourse in the Professions: Perspectives from Corpus Linguistics*. Amsterdam: John Benjamins, pp. 65–86.

Rundell, M. (2007) *Macmillan Dictionary for Advanced Learners*, second edition. Oxford: Macmillan Education.

Schmitt, D. and Schmitt, N. (2005) *Focus on Vocabulary: Mastering the Academic Word List*. White Plains, NY: Pearson.

Scott, M. (2006) *WordSmith Tools 4*. Oxford: Oxford University Press.

Scott, M. and Tribble, C. (2006) *Textual Patterns: Key Words and Corpus Analysis in Language Education*. Amsterdam: John Benjamins.

Simpson, R. and Mendis, P. (2003) *Idioms Exercise Sets I and II*. Ann Arbor, MI: University of Michigan English Language Institute; available at http://lw.lsa.umich.edu/eli/micase/index.htm (accessed 26 March 2009).

Simpson, R., Briggs, S., Ovens, J. and Swales, J. (2000) *The Michigan Corpus of Academic Spoken English*. Ann Arbor, MI: The Regents of the University of Michigan.

Simpson, R., Leicher, S. and Chien, Y.-H. (2007) *Figuring Out the Meaning or Function of Spoken Academic English Formulas (A)*; available at http://lw.lsa.umich.edu/eli/micase/ESL/FormulaicExpression/Function1.htm (accessed 26 March 2009).

Sinclair, J. (ed.) (2003 [1987]) *Collins COBUILD Advanced Dictionary*, fourth edition. Collins: London.

Starfield, S. (2004) '"Why Does This Feel Empowering?" Thesis Writing, Concordancing, and the Corporatizing University', in B. Norton and K. Toohey (eds) *Critical Pedagogies and Language Learning*. Cambridge: Cambridge University Press, pp. 138–56.

Sutarsyah, C., Nation, I. S. P. and Kennedy, G. (1994) 'How Useful is EAP Vocabulary for ESP? A Corpus-based Case Study', *RELC Journal* 25(2): 34–50.

Swales, J. (2002) 'Integrated and Fragmented Worlds: EAP Materials and Corpus Linguistics', in J. Flowerdew (ed.) *Academic Discourse*. Harlow, Essex: Pearson, pp. 150–64.

Thompson, P. (2006) 'Assessing the Contribution of Corpora to EAP Practice', in Z. Kantaridou, I. Papadopoulou and I. Mahili (eds) *Motivation in Learning Language for Specific and Academic Purposes*. Macedonia: University of Macedonia [CD Rom], no specific page numbers given.

Thompson, P. and Tribble, C. (2001) 'Looking at Citations: Using Corpora in English for Academic Purposes', *Language Learning and Technology* 5(3): 91–105.

Thurston, J. and Candlin, C. (1997) *Exploring Academic English: A Workbook for Student Essay Writing*. Sydney: National Centre for English Language Teaching and Research.

Tribble, C. (2002) 'Corpora and corpus analysis: new windows on academic writing,' in J. Flowerdew (ed) *Academic Discourse*. Harlow, Essex: Pearson, pp. 131–49.

Tribble, C. and Jones, G. (1990) *Concordances in the Classroom*. London: Longman.

Tsui, A. (2004) 'What Teachers have always Wanted to Know and how Corpora Can Help', in J. Sinclair (ed.) *How to Use Corpora in Language Teaching*. Amsterdam: John Benjamins, pp. 39–61.

Vannestål, M. and Lindquist, H. (2007) 'Learning English Grammar with a Corpus: Experimenting with Concordancing in a University Grammar Course', *ReCALL* 19(3): 329–50.

West, M. (1953) *A General Service List of English Words*. London: Longman, Green.

Yoon, H. (2008) 'More than a Linguistic Reference: The Influence of Corpus Technology on L2 Academic Writing', *Language Learning and Technology* 12(2): 31–48.

Yoon, H. and Hirvela, A. (2004) 'ESL Student Attitudes toward Corpus Use in L2 Writing', *Journal of Second Language Writing* 13(4): 257–83.

34

How can teachers use a corpus for their own research?

Elaine Vaughan

1. Using a corpus for your own research: being professionally curious

Practising language teachers engage in corpus research and other types of research for a variety of reasons. The general stimuli and specific motivators for their research may lie in challenges and/or opportunities in the immediate teaching and learning environment, may be based on personal or academic interests, may be stimulated by interaction with colleagues or may be in response to research findings which have been released into the public domain. However, a unifying feature of such research, and one which is crucial to the profession of teaching as a whole, is professional curiosity. This chapter is specifically aimed at practitioners who are interested in conducting their own professional or pedagogical research and would like to explore the possibilities of using a corpus in this regard. Some samples of the directions that corpus research in language teaching have taken are presented before we turn our attention particularly to the language of the wider professional context, specifically the language used by teachers. This is the site of a small but growing number of corpus-based studies, proof, if any were needed, that corpus methods can co-exist harmoniously with any number of paradigms of linguistic research (see, for example, Carter and McCarthy 2002 or Walsh and O'Keeffe 2007). An example of a corpus-based study into the interaction of English language teachers in meetings is presented at the end of the chapter as just one example of research inspired by professional curiosity and how a corpus can inform this type of work. The participation of practitioners and trainee teachers in their own corpus-based research is frequently advocated (e.g. O'Keeffe and Farr 2003; Tsui 2004; Römer 2006, 2009; O'Keeffe *et al.* 2007; McCarthy 2008; Breyer 2009) though this has not necessarily translated into the global provision of corpus analysis modules in teacher education and training programmes (see Farr, this volume; McCarthy 2008; Granath 2009). O'Keeffe *et al.* (2007: 246) further underline the need for reciprocity in the relationship between language researchers and language teachers, and they go as far as to claim that for the future 'research questions need to be driven by teachers, and indeed a more critical response to the findings of corpus linguistics needs to come from teachers'. As not all teacher education programmes offer training in corpus analysis, one of the decisive factors in making this happen will lie in the willingness of practising teachers to 'get their teeth into a corpus', to borrow Aston's (2002) evocative phrase.

A major benefit of corpus-based based research for language teachers lies in its potential as a teacher development tool. Waters (2005) references the common distinctions made between teacher training, teacher education and teacher development. He uses teacher education as a superordinate term, but it is interesting in terms of our question and discussion here to look at what is generally understood to be contained in these distinctions. Teacher training concerns itself, for example, with practical, classroom-based skills, teacher education has been seen as concerned with research and background knowledge, while teacher development has a focus on raising awareness of practices and fostering reflection and change (ibid.: 211). Waters summarises the focus of these three interconnected aspects of 'teacher education' as *doing* (teacher training), *knowing* (teacher education) and *being* (teacher development). While the first two tend to be a mediated experience for teachers, the latter is different in that it is most often self-directed. Dörnyei (2007: 17) suggests that research excellence requires a number of essential characteristics in the researcher: genuine curiosity, common sense, good ideas and a blend of discipline, reliability (in the sense of thoroughness and systematicity displayed by the researcher him- or herself as opposed to the methodological concept) and social responsibility. Refreshingly, he also points out that research does not have to be the preserve of the elite few; the same argument applies to corpus-based research for language teachers. Corpus-based research can be applied as a means of investigating the *doing*, *knowing* and *being* of teaching and learning; what the practitioner-researcher needs is genuine, professional curiosity, a sense of how corpora are built and work and what sort of questions they have the potential to provide whole or partial answers for. We start with the kinds of issues that practitioner-researchers may have in consulting and using corpora in general and building their own corpus in particular. Then we look at the types of questions about language teaching that corpora have been used to pose and answer before taking the less travelled route of looking at the insights that a corpus-based analysis can generate about the profession of language teaching itself.

2. Issues in using and building corpora

If, first of all, we ask what a corpus is, this will provide a shortcut to some of the issues you will face in using a corpus for your own research. Tognini Bonelli (2001: 53) surveys definitions of what a corpus is and highlights that although the definitions she presents diverge, they agree in their basic assertion that a corpus is a collection of language text, 'though not necessarily texts' (ibid.) (see also Tognini Bonelli, this volume). Aarts (1991: 45) suggests the criterion of 'running' text, Sinclair (1991: 171) integrates the idea of the text being 'naturally occurring', while Francis (1982, 1992) introduces the term 'representative'. Crystal defines a corpus as 'a representative sample of language, compiled for the purpose of linguistic analysis' (Crystal 1997: 414), and Biber *et al.* (1998: 4) characterise a corpus as 'a large and principled collection of natural texts'. Tognini Bonelli provides her own, inclusive definition:

> A corpus is a computerised collection of authentic texts, amenable to automatic or semi-automatic processing or analysis. The texts are selected according to specific criteria in order to capture the regularities of a language, a language variety or sub-language.
> (Tognini Bonelli 2001: 55)

All corpora are collections of texts, but one could equally argue that the Web is a 'collection of texts', though clearly it is not a corpus in the conventional sense (see Lee, this volume for a further discussion on the Web as a corpus). So, what makes a corpus different? Sinclair (2001) provides an interesting answer for this, which is incredibly useful to bear in mind if you decide to create your own corpus. A collection of texts becomes a *corpus* when we treat it as such: the texts are gathered according to some kind of external (cf. Clear 1992) criteria (teacher–student interaction or soap opera discourse, say) and we expect 'an investigation into the patterns of the language used will be fruitful and linguistically illuminating' (Sinclair 2001: xi). The crucial idea here is 'patterns': rather than evaluating a text (which of course can be spoken or written) as an object from beginning to end, we are considering its parts – not the sum of its parts, but the parts themselves. Using corpus software, we can search for patterns in the language of the texts and find how these are similar or different to patterns of language use in other corpora and contexts. Corpus-based analysis can be used in tandem with complementary discourse analytic methods, thus exploiting to the full the corpus contents.

The issue of how large a corpus should be, or even how small a corpus *can* be, has been a bone of contention. There does not appear to be an upper limit on corpora: the British National Corpus (BNC) contains 100 million words, the American National Corpus (ANC) (currently twenty-two million words) when complete will also have 100 million words and the COBUILD Bank of English stands at a massive 450 million words. The Cambridge International Corpus (CIC) is even more of a behemoth at over one billion words. These corpora represent a mixture of spoken and written texts, though not necessarily in equal proportions: for example, the BNC consists of 90 per cent written text and only 10 per cent spoken text. Representativeness within a corpus, 'or the extent to which a sample includes the full range of variability in a population' (Biber 1993: 243), is probably the more salient issue. Language data have proven resistant to standard approaches to statistical sampling (Clear 1992: 21) and sampling frames. However, Biber proposes strata and sampling frames for representative corpus design based on *register*, or situationally defined text categories such as 'fiction', 'news article', etc., and linguistically defined text types, such as various written or spoken modes. With regard to sample size, his previous research on 1,000-word samples from the London–Lund and Lancaster/Oslo/Bergen corpus concluded that these relatively small samples yielded similar functional and grammatical findings (Biber 1990). The register approach taken by Biber *et al.* (1999), for example, has meant that, among other things, it is possible to compare and contrast how language is used in different contexts.

In terms of consulting an existing corpus, there are a number of issues for the novice corpus researcher (see chapters by Tribble and Evison, this volume). One that is not always emphasised across a literature that, on the whole, assumes its audience is the university-based language teacher/pre-service trainee, is access to resources such as computer labs and corpus software. While these are a pre-requisite for *hands-on* activities with language learners, the lack of these types of facilities in your teaching environment does not preclude engagement with corpus-based research and pedagogical activity. There is much that can be done with access to a personal computer, the internet and a printer. As Conrad (1999) has pointed out, without any computer facilities at all, the findings of corpus-based studies can still be (and have still been) of use to language teachers; for the purpose of this chapter, we will assume that the minimum of PC, internet access and printer is available to the reader. Practical concerns aside, there are a number of essential skills practitioners new to using corpora need to develop. Frankenberg-Garcia (2010) summarises these and suggests that teachers need to know the following:

1 What corpora are available;
2 How to formulate a corpus query;
3 How to interpret the results of this query.

First, teachers need to know what corpora are freely and commercially available (see Lee, this volume); more importantly, it is essential to develop an awareness of what these available corpora can and cannot offer. Being able to critically evaluate what is available and make an informed choice in relation to whether an existing corpus is appropriate for the investigation of a research question, or whether a new, more specialised, corpus is required is the first step for the budding teacher-researcher (see Reppen, this volume). For example, the Michigan Corpus of Academic Spoken English (MICASE) is an excellent resource if you wish to investigate the kind of language it will be necessary to teach your students so that they will be able to operate in the (North American) academic domain, but it will not provide much information about how friends interact with one another in casual conversation. Second, once an appropriate corpus resource has been chosen or created, it is necessary to be able to adequately frame corpus queries, or ask relevant questions. For the teacher embarking on corpus-based research, this is possibly less of a difficulty as the likelihood is that you have already isolated a particular genre of discourse or particular language feature that you want to investigate. Again, it is worth emphasising that choosing an appropriate corpus is crucial – if you want to analyse occurrences of the item *it*, for example, a very large corpus may contain far more information than it is feasible to analyse and a smaller corpus size may be more than adequate (cf. Biber 1990). Finally, once these queries have yielded results, the teacher-researcher needs to be able to interpret these results and take into account considerations such as corpus size and composition and their impact on the type of data that is generated. In other words, an ability to interpret what corpus data 'means', what variables are impacting on the corpus results being returned and what follow-up queries may be required in order to explore them are skills, or as Mukharjee (2002: 179) puts it, 'corpus literacy', that teachers need to cultivate. Given these complexities, online professional development courses for practising teachers such as *An Introduction to Corpora in English Language Teaching* (McCarthy *et al.* 2007) are invaluable. This course provides modules on how to use corpora to investigate and teach grammar and vocabulary and the implications of the corpus evidence in skills-based teaching. Evison (this volume) gives a thorough introduction to how to 'get your teeth into' a corpus from exploring word frequencies to exploring discourse, and in the further reading section at the end of this chapter, other texts that give accessible and practical introductions are recommended.

3. Building your own corpus

In terms of building and using a corpus for your own research, there are some points to consider which benefit from further discussion (for a more extensive coverage, see Reppen, this volume). Broadly, these are:

- Access and consent
- Recording and transcribing spoken data/compiling and storing written data
- Your position in the research.

Practising teachers have a significant advantage when it comes to investigating the language of language teaching, as their position in teaching institutions means that the data required is within immediate proximity. Once you have identified the language you require, the next step is securing consent to record/collect and use that data. This means that you will need to approach your students or your colleagues and ask their permission to record (in the case of spoken data) or compile (in the case of written data) language material that 'belongs' to them. Most learners and colleagues are very cooperative if you are upfront about why you want to research a particular sphere of language use and what you will do with it. This is even more the case if the results of your analysis are going to address a practical problem or highlight good practices. Always obtain consent in written form and do so at the beginning of the research. The consent form should assure the learners or colleagues who cooperate in the research that you will anonymise the data and treat it ethically. It should also make clear what the data may be used for: it is best to cover all the possibilities in this regard as it may not always be possible to predict the research paths you will be taken along as you collect the data. For example, you may end up publishing your research, using extracts in conference presentations or other professional meetings, creating/contributing to a larger project, etc. A thorough consent form will cover all these possibilities. Make sure that your corpus design is replicable and that you keep as much contextual information about it as possible. The first of these considerations is crucial. As a rule of thumb, once you have finalised your corpus design, another researcher should be able to add to your corpus, or build a companion corpus, by adhering to your design principles. More importantly, you will be able to maintain and add to your corpus so that it becomes an organic entity.

If your corpus is to contain spoken texts, then you will need to have recording equipment and a means of transcribing and storing the audio files (see Adolphs and Knight, this volume). Sound quality is essential for spoken data collection, and the more speakers that will be present, the more important this is. As long as the quality of the recording it allows is good, any recording device can be used. However, a digital recorder is the better investment as it is possible to download free transcription software (two examples are *Express Scribe* and *SoundScriber*) which allows you, among other things, to control the playback of your audio recordings using 'hot' keys on the keyboard and slow down the playback (a very valuable aid to accurate transcription). Transcription is a slow process; McCarthy (2008: 571) estimates that one hour of talk can take twelve to fifteen hours to transcribe. Despite its labour-intensive nature, the transcription of spoken data is an excellent skill to hone. One of the benefits of collecting and transcribing spoken data yourself is that your familiarity with the texts that your corpus contains grows exponentially. In addition, as you transcribe, you may identify particular language features which will be interesting to look into in greater detail when you do your preliminary analyses. Whether or not the same is true with written texts depends on your sources. If you are using material from the internet, your job may be to gather on principle rather than physically input the data (while observing copyright restrictions). If, however, you are creating a corpus of, for example, student essays or other written work, you will more than likely be typing these using a word processing programme and thus gaining the same sort of familiarity and insight mentioned above in relation to spoken data transcription. Many books and studies that deal with transcribed data provide transcription conventions that you could potentially use and modify (see, for example, Eggins and Slade 1997: 1–5; O'Keeffe *et al.* 2007: 6).

Two final points should be made on the collection of spoken corpora which are implicated in the third of the issues outlined above, the position of the researcher. When teachers create their own spoken corpora, they are more often than not among the participants in the interaction they are recording; for example, a corpus of students performing interactive classroom tasks may include the instructions given by the class teacher, who is also the corpus compiler. Being involved in an authentic situation as a participant and as an analyst can be extraordinarily positive, but it is also important to acknowledge, and be conscious of, the potential biases that this dual role may bring. In setting out to record authentic, spoken interaction, an oft-mentioned Catch-22-like situation occurs: we inevitably introduce a degree of artificiality into a previously authentic situation, which is physically present as the microphone. The impact that recording has can be mitigated in the early stages of your study by making sure that your learners and/ or colleagues are clear about why you are collecting the data and that they are confident you will treat it ethically (e.g. by anonymising it). A short time into recording, most participants forget that the microphone is there and so the 'microphone effect' is also mitigated in this way. It is also good practice to ensure that the participants have access to the corpus, or at least the transcribed texts, particularly if you are dealing with data that is sensitive in some way.

4. What can be done with corpora inside and outside the classroom?

The only possible answer to the question 'how can teachers use a corpus for their own research?' is, unfortunately, 'it depends on the question', so rather than second-guessing the multitude of questions one could potentially ask, an admittedly highly selective view of the types of questions language teachers have been asking and the kind of uses corpora have been put to can be presented. We can ask instead how corpora have been deployed in the *doing*, *knowing* and *being* of language teaching. Despite a frosty initial reception, corpora have become 'part of the pedagogical landscape' according to Sinclair (2004: 2). Johansson (2009: 40) suggests that the primary areas of relevance to the 'pedagogical landscape', which corpora have permeated to a greater or lesser degree, are in the production of dictionaries, grammars, textbooks and teaching materials as well as syllabus design, classroom activities, testing and basic research. Some areas, such as compiling dictionaries (e.g. the *Collins COBUILD Dictionary*) or the production of grammar reference books (e.g. Biber *et al.* 1999; Mindt 2000; Carter and McCarthy 2006), are more firmly established, while others, particularly the use of corpora in the classroom, as products of teacher choice and discretion are less widespread. Mindt (1996) and Römer (2004a, 2004b, 2005) have identified a mismatch between corpus evidence based on authentic language use and the content of English language textbooks. A notable exception in these terms is the entirely corpus-informed textbook series *Touchstone* (McCarthy *et al.* 2005a, 2005b; see also McCarten, this volume).

In terms of testing and assessment, Taylor and Barker (2008) review the contribution of corpora from the early 1990s on (see also Barker, this volume). Cambridge ESOL, for example, has used information from the BNC and COBUILD corpus as well as the purpose-built Cambridge Learner Corpus to revise the examinations it administers, among other things. In the USA, the TOEFL 2000 Spoken and Written Academic Language Corpus (T2K-SWAL) has been used to identify patterns of language use in these spoken and written academic contexts and whether the listening and reading components of the TOEFL examination reflected these uses (see Biber *et al.* 2004). Learner corpora are also used in the interrogating the theoretical bases of foreign language teaching. Nesselhauf (2004) and Granger (2009) provide extensive overviews of the potential of learner corpora for the fields of language teaching and second language acquisition research (see chapters by also Gilquin and Granger and Xiaofei Lu, this volume).

Over the last decade or so, the number of studies addressing themselves to the use of corpora in language teaching within and beyond the classroom has proliferated. The studies themselves could usefully be divided into those which deal with data-driven learning (Johns 1986, 1991) involving the direct or mediated use of corpora in the classroom, and studies that use corpora to interrogate the content, theoretical bases and practices of language teaching. In terms of using corpora as resources for language learners, Aston (2002) reports on using the BNC with advanced learners of English as a reference tool when learners come across unfamiliar vocabulary items, such as *blunder* or *hamfisted*, using concordance lines to deduce how and when such items are used, and the contexts where they tend to be used. Bernardini (2001) provides an insightful view of the learner experience of using large corpora for autonomous language learning. Gavioli (2001) discusses how to equip language learners with the skills they need to develop in order to actually benefit from using corpora to learn about language. She also gives examples of the type of graded corpus-based activities she has created using lonely hearts columns, which are very interesting (see also chapters by Gilquin and Granger, Sripicharn, Tribble, this volume). McCarthy (2002) uses five-million-word samples of spoken and written language (from the Cambridge and Nottingham Corpus of Discourse in English and the Cambridge International Corpus) to address the question of what an advanced-level vocabulary for English language students might contain and Coxhead (2002) uses an English academic corpus of over 3.5 million words to develop an academic wordlist in response to the needs of learners preparing for academic study (see Coxhead, this volume). That is not to say that large corpora like these are a prerequisite for corpus-based studies. Tribble (2001) uses a 'micro-corpus' of approximately 14,000 words to explore how a particular writing genre is organised and uses this information to develop the linguistic resources that learners will need to exploit in order to write successfully in this genre (see also Tribble, this volume). The genre represented in the corpus is university promotional material for MA programmes in Applied Linguistics and was compiled using the web search engine *Alta Vista*. From the point of view of how teachers can use corpora as a resource to develop their own language awareness, Tsui (2004, 2005) discusses *TeleNex*, a Hong Kong-based website which provides advice for teachers from language specialists and their peers on queries regarding a range of grammatical and lexical issues, such as discrepancies between prescriptive grammars and authentic usage and queries regarding explaining the usage of synonymous items such as *tall* and *high* to their students. The final aspect of how teachers have been using corpora to carry out research mentioned above, the investigation of language teaching practices and professional research is one that is ripe for expansion: namely, the investigation of teachers' professional language, particularly that which occurs outside the classroom.

The aspects of teacher language that have been prioritised in the existing (not exclusively corpus-based) research is centred, on the whole, on understanding teacher language in connection to how classrooms work and how the profession considers its practices within them reflexively. In terms of teacher language within the classroom in the L2 context, Walsh (2006) reviews and summarises its major features as follows:

- teachers control patterns of communication in the classroom;
- the classroom is dominated by question and answer routines;
- 'repair' or correction of learner errors is a prerogative of the teacher;
- teachers typically modify their speech to accommodate learners.

Walsh posits a framework (Self-Evaluation of Teacher Talk, or SETT) to aid teachers in their description of language used in the L2 classroom context and as a conduit for understanding the complex interactional processes that occur within it (ibid.: 62–92; and see Further Reading) and this provides a useful framework for teachers considering using a corpus to research their linguistic practices within the classroom.

Findings from the field of language teacher education (LTE) are uniquely illuminating in terms of the professional concerns of language teachers. Farr (2005a) analyses trainer–trainee interaction in LTE in terms of the types of interventions used in teaching practice feedback and this focus on the discourse of teacher training is obviously an interesting dimension in language teaching research as it provides us with a very important locale of teacher language (see also Farr, this volume). In fact, what we are seeing in the unique interaction highlighted in studies such as Farr (2003, 2005a, 2005b) and work by Reppen and Vásquez (2007) and Vásquez and Reppen (2007) is trainee teachers captured in the process of *becoming* teachers. The studies referred to here focus on a specific language event in the life of the trainee, feedback meetings on trainees' observed classes, an event which is inherently face-threatening (Reppen and Vásquez 2007: 16) and necessitates deft interpersonal and linguistic negotiation. Vásquez and Reppen's (2007) report on collecting a corpus of post-observation meetings is especially interesting as it illustrates how corpus-based studies can inform and, in the case of this study, transform practices. In their workplace, on an intensive English programme on which their MA in TESL student teachers gain practical ESL teaching experience, the reflective rather than evaluative model of post-observation feedback is favoured. With this in mind, the supervisors/mentors approached the feedback meeting as a discursive space for trainees to reflect on their teaching practices (ibid.: 159). However, corpus-based analyses of participation patterns indicated that, in practice, the supervisors/mentors did more of the talking than the trainees. This insight led to a change in practices for the supervisors/mentors involved: by increasing the number of questions they asked the trainees, they were able to turn the floor over to the trainees more effectively and give them the tools to use the discursive space for reflection.

5. What can a corpus tell us about the profession of language teaching?

The case of C-MELT

This small Corpus of Meetings of English Language Teachers (C-MELT) consists of six meetings in two language teaching institutions, in two different countries, México and Ireland. In all approximately 3.5 hours of interaction was recorded (c. 40,000 words). Its defining characteristic is as the situated language and practices of two local communities

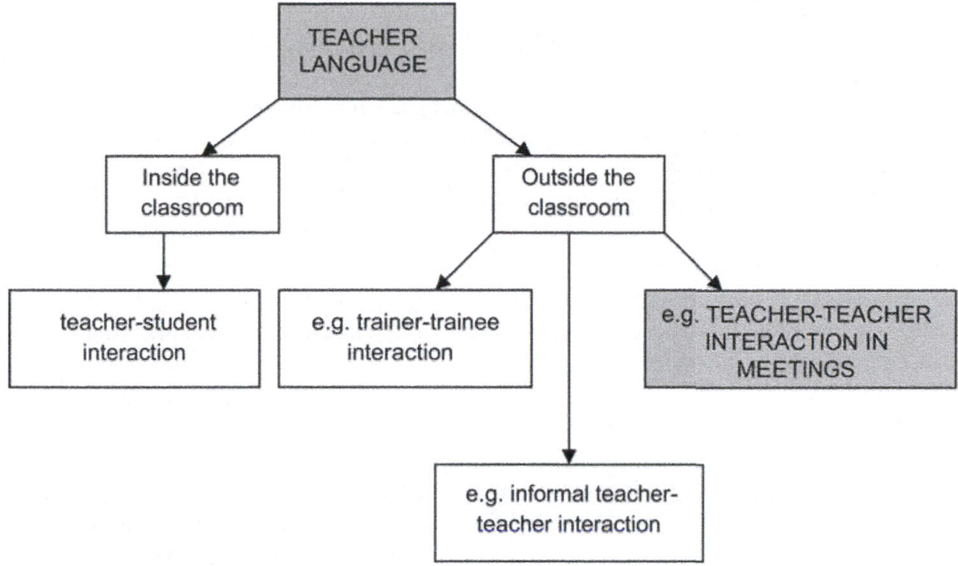

Figure 34.1 Dimensions of teacher language.

of teachers who form part of a (hypothesised) larger, global community. Its underlying purpose was to put teachers in the frame, the rationale being that practices outside the classroom are at least as interesting and just as deserving of research attention as those that occur within it. At the meetings that make up C-MELT, teachers talk about the day-to-day business of teaching: placing students according to ability, examinations/assessment, student attendance and motivation, administrative issues, workplace frustrations, etc. Placing C-MELT in the larger teacher language context, if we look at the range of interaction that teachers engage in, it is possible to divide them into interaction that occurs *inside* and *outside* the classroom (see Figure 34.1 above for some dimensions of teacher language that focus on the face-to-face spoken mode) or characterise them in terms of whether they occur in the professional *frontstage* (classroom) or *backstage* (outside the classroom) (Goffman 1971). Most research on teacher language is conducted with an eye to the classroom, but this research is about what happens unrehearsed in the staffroom when the 'gloves are off'.

Quantitative analyses using the wordlist and concord functions of *WordSmith Tools* (Scott 1999) were carried out and the results were viewed through the prism of the community of practice (after Lave and Wenger 1991; Wenger 1998). It was possible then to isolate and analyse in turn a range of linguistic markers of community and explore them in depth. The wordlist function made it possible to explore aspects of the teachers' shared linguistic and professional repertoire (see Vaughan 2007: 179). Particular shorthand for talking about student ability and negotiating the practice of placing students became evident; Extract 1 below is an example of teachers placing students (taken from a meeting in an Irish language school) and shows how this practice is negotiated.

Extract 1: Student placement meeting

1 **Siobhán:** **He's not strong.**
2 **Sally:** Now **he's he's weak in it you know**.

3 **Siobhán:** Hm.
4 **Sally:** **The others would be all stronger than him.**
5 **Niall:** Ali? I had him on Friday.
6 **Sally:** Yeah did **how did you find him he'd be weak now in that class.**
7 **Niall:** Yeah I would then I'd suggest maybe.
8 **Aoife:** **Switch**.
9 **Niall:** **Swapping** the two of them.

One of the most interesting features of the terms that have become part of the community's shared repertoire is the fact that the language itself is neither highly esoteric in form, nor complex in basic linguistic meaning, but rather encodes highly detailed and entailed professional knowledge.

Information such as laughter, sighing or any other marked extralinguistic behaviour was included in the transcription and the wordlist revealed an unexpected frequency in *laughs*, *laughing* and *laughter*. Humour turned out to be a highly salient, multifunctional, marker of community (Vaughan 2008). It is used to invoke shared knowledge, create and maintain solidarity, resist authority in a socially sanctioned way and downtone potentially face-threatening acts. When the teachers wish to vent frustrations, resist institutional strictures or criticise (or mock) students, the humorous frame provides a way of doing so that will not contravene the professional code. Extract 2 below is a quite typical example of how the teachers in C-MELT use humour.

Extract 2: Student placement meeting
[Note: *ye* is the Irish English form for *you* plural]
1 **Ciarán:** So anyone to go down?
2 **Michaela:** No but it would cheer us up a lot if you could tell us when Juan is leaving.
<$E> laughter </$E>
3 **Siobhán:** That's exactly what I wanted to know.
4 **Ciarán:** **<$E> laughing </$E>** I'll check that out for ye.
5 **Siobhán:** Please do **<$E> laughs </$E>**.
6 **Michaela:** It would make it worth the time.
7 **Siobhán:** Oh he's unbearable. He's unbearable.

These are just two aspects of community that corpus-based analysis prompted and revealed. Many types of practices, communicative or otherwise, make up the work of language teachers. It would be interesting to see further research of naturally occurring language, for example, from blogs or informal conversation, which pertain to the backstage practices of being a teacher. This would, to some extent, extend the purview of language teaching beyond the classroom, and provide some life and colour for the picture of the liminal spaces in the language teaching professionals' life. These are the places where the professional mask that is presented to students is put to one side and a new one, used to do the hidden work of teaching, assumed; the backstage spaces where professional successes and failures are discussed, critiqued and laughed about and bonds of community and professional identity forged. More corpus-based research that pushes the boundaries of what linguistic genres are taken to represent the profession of English language teaching would be most welcome and could be a fruitful starting point for practising teachers who want to use a corpus for their own research.

Further reading

Aijmer, K. (ed.) (2009) *Corpora and Language Teaching*. Amsterdam: John Benjamins. (The papers in this volume are all geared towards the practical issues involved in using corpora in the classroom and for pedagogical research. It looks at new types of corpora, corpora and second language acquisition and direct and indirect approaches in integrating corpus research into the language classroom.)

O'Keeffe, A., McCarthy, M. J. and Carter, R. (2007) *From Corpus to Classroom: Language Use and Language Teaching*. Cambridge: Cambridge University Press. (This book provides a practical introduction to the discipline of corpus linguistics and its relationship to language teaching using numerous examples of the types of linguistic information a corpus can provide. It also contains extensive overviews of previous studies and illustrates corpus insights from a variety of linguistic genres. With regard to the potential of corpus research in relation to teacher language, Chapter 11, 'Exploring Teacher Corpora', is of particular interest.)

Sinclair, J. M. (2004) *How to Use Corpora in Language Teaching*. Amsterdam: John Benjamins. (This collection of papers is divided into sections which investigate how teachers can use corpora in the classroom, as a source of information about how language works – including answering tricky student questions – as a resource, for research and processing and programming resources available for working with corpora.)

Walsh, S. (2006) *Investigating Classroom Discourse*. London: Routledge. (This provides an extensive overview of the history and dimensions of classroom language research and thus a solid grounding in the literature of a particularly dense field of study. In addition, it outlines an extremely useful and user-friendly framework within which to analyse teacher talk in the classroom, Self-Evaluation of Teacher Talk (SETT), which has valuable application to corpus-based research into classroom discourse.)

References

Aarts, J. (1991) 'Intuition-based and Observation-based Grammars', in K. Aijmer and B. Altenberg (eds) *English Corpus Linguistics. Studies in Honour of Jan Svartvik*. London: Longman, pp. 44–62.

Aston, G. (2002) 'Getting One's Teeth into a Corpus', in M. Tan (ed.) *Corpus Studies in the Language Classroom*. Bangkok: IELE Press, pp. 131–43.

Bernardini, S. (2001) '"Spoilt for Choice": A Learner Explores General Language Corpora', in G. Aston (ed.) *Learning with Corpora*. Houston, TX: Athelstan, pp. 220–49.

Biber, D. (1990) 'Methodological Issues Regarding Corpus-based Analyses of Linguistic Variation', *Literary and Linguistic Computing* 5(4): 257–69.

——(1993) 'Representativeness in Corpus Design', *Literary and Linguistic Computing* 8(4): 243–57.

Biber, D., Conrad, S. and Reppen, R. (1998) *Corpus Linguistics: Investigating Language Structure and Use*. Cambridge: Cambridge University Press.

Biber, D., Johansson, S., Leech, G., Conrad, S. and Finegan, E. (1999) *Longman Grammar of Spoken and Written English*. Harlow: Pearson.

Biber, D., Conrad, S., Reppen, R., Byrd, P., Helt, M., Clark, V., Cortes, V., Csomay, E. and Urzua, A. (2004) 'Representing Language Use in the University: Analysis of the TOEFL 2000 Spoken and Written Academic Language Corpus' (Report Number: RM-04-03, Supplemental Report Number: TOEFL-MS-25), Princeton, NJ: Educational Testing Service; available at www.ets.org/Media/Research/pdf/RM-04-03.pdf

Breyer, Y. (2009) 'Learning and Teaching with Corpora: Reflections by Student Teachers', *Computer Assisted Language Learning* 22(2): 153–72.

Carter, R. and McCarthy, M. J. (2002) 'From Conversation to Corpus: A Dual Analysis of a Broadcast Political Interview', in A. Sanchez-Macarro (ed.) *Windows on the World: Media Discourse in English*. Valencia: University of Valencia Press, pp. 15–39.

——(2006) *Cambridge Grammar of English*. Cambridge: Cambridge University Press.

Clear, J. (1992) 'Corpus Sampling', in G. Leitner (ed.) *New Directions in English Language Corpus Methodology*. Berlin: Mouton de Gruyter, pp. 21–31.

Conrad, S. M. (1999) 'The Importance of Corpus-based Research for Language Teachers', *System* 27 (1): 1–18.

Coxhead, A. (2002) 'The Academic Word List: A Corpus-based Word List for Academic Purposes', in B. Kettemann and G. Marko (eds) *Teaching and Learning by Doing Corpus Analysis*. Amsterdam: Rodopi, pp. 73–89.

Crystal, D. (1997) *The Cambridge Encyclopedia of Language*. Cambridge: Cambridge University Press.

Dörnyei, Z. (2007) *Research Methods in Applied Linguistics*. Oxford: Oxford University Press.

Eggins, S. and Slade, D. (1997) *Analysing Casual Conversation*. London: Cassell.

Farr, F. (2003) 'Engaged Listenership in Spoken Academic Discourse', *Journal of English for Academic Purposes* 2(1): 67–85.

——(2005a) 'Reflecting on Reflections: The Spoken Word as a Professional Development Tool in Language Teacher Education', in R. Hughes (ed.) *Spoken English, Applied Linguistics and TESOL: Challenges for Theory and Practice*. Hampshire: Palgrave Macmillan, pp. 182–215.

——(2005b) 'Relational Strategies in the Discourse of Professional Performance Review in an Irish Academic Environment: The Case of Language Teacher Education', in K. P. Schneider and A. Barron (eds) *Variational Pragmatics: The Case of English in Ireland*. Berlin: Mouton de Gruyter, pp. 203–34.

Francis, W. N. (1982) 'Problems of Assembling and Computerising Large Corpora', in S. Johansson (ed.) *Computer Corpora in English Language Research*. Bergen: Norwegian Computing Centre for the Humanities, pp. 7–24.

——(1992) 'Language Corpora B.C.', in J. Svartvik (ed.) *Directions in Corpus Linguistics. Proceedings of Nobel Symposium 82, Stockholm 4–8 August 1991*. Berlin: Mouton de Gruyter, pp. 17–32.

Frankenberg-Garcia, A. (2010) 'Raising Teachers' Awareness to Corpora', in N. Kübler (ed.) *Corpora, Language, Teaching and Resources: From Theory to Practice*. Frankfurt: Peter Lang.

Gavioli, L. (2001) 'The Learner as Researcher: Introducing Corpus Concordancing in the Classroom', in G. Aston (ed.) *Learning with Corpora*. Houston, TX: Athelstan, pp. 108–37.

Goffman, E. (1971) *The Presentation of Self in Everyday Life*. Harmondsworth: Penguin.

Granath, S. (2009) 'Who Benefits from Learning How to Use Corpora?' in K. Aijmer (ed.) *Corpora and Language Teaching*. Amsterdam: John Benjamins, pp. 47–65.

Granger, S. (2009) 'The Contribution of Learner Corpora to Second Language Acquisition and Foreign Language Teaching', in K. Aijmer (ed.) *Corpora and Language Teaching*. Amsterdam: John Benjamins, pp. 13–32.

Johansson, S. (2009) 'Some Thoughts on Corpora and Second Language Acquisition', in K. Aijmer (ed.) *Corpora and Language Teaching*. Amsterdam: John Benjamins, pp. 33–44.

Johns, T. (1986) 'Microconcord: A Language Learner's Research Tool', *System* 14(2): 151–62.

——(1991) 'Should You Be Persuaded – Two Samples of Data-driven Learning Materials', in T. Johns and P. King (eds) *Classroom Concordancing* (*English Language Research* 4). Birmingham: University of Birmingham, pp. 1–16.

Lave, J. and Wenger, E. (1991) *Situated Learning: Legitimate Peripheral Participation*. Cambridge: Cambridge University Press.

McCarthy, M. J. (2002) 'What is an Advanced-level Vocabulary?' in M. Tan (ed.) *Corpus Studies in the Language Classroom*. Bangkok: IELE Press, pp. 15–29.

——(2008) 'Accessing and Interpreting Corpus Information in the Teacher Education Context', *Language Teaching* 41(4): 563–74.

McCarthy, M. J., McCarten, J. and Sandiford, H. (2005a) *Touchstone. Student's Book 1*. Cambridge: Cambridge University Press.

——(2005b) *Touchstone. Student's Book 2*. Cambridge: Cambridge University Press.

McCarthy, M. J., O'Keeffe, A. and Walsh, S. (2007) *An Introduction to Corpora in English Language Teaching. ELT Advantage: Online Courses for Teachers*. Boston, MA: Heinle Cengage, available at http://eltadvantage.ed2go.com/eltadvantage/index.html

Mindt, D. (1996) 'English Corpus Linguistics and the Foreign Language Teaching Syllabus', in J. Thomas and M. Short (eds) *Using Corpora for Language Research*. London: Longman, pp. 232–47.

——(2000) *An Empirical Grammar of the English Verb System*. Berlin: Cornelsen.

Mukharjee, J. (2002) *Korpuslinguistik und Englischunterricht: Eine Einführung* (*Sprache im Kontext* series 14). Frankfurt: Peter Lang.

Nesselhauf, N. (2004) 'Learner Corpora and their Potential for Language Teaching', in J. M. Sinclair (ed.) *How to Use Corpora in Language Teaching*. Amsterdam: John Benjamins, pp. 125–52.

O'Keeffe, A. and Farr, F. (2003) 'Using Language Corpora in Initial Teacher Education: Pedagogic Issues and Practical Applications', *TESOL Quarterly* 37(3): 389–418.

O'Keeffe, A., McCarthy, M. J. and Carter, R. (2007) *From Corpus to Classroom: Language Use and Language Teaching*. Cambridge: Cambridge University Press.

Reppen, R. and Vásquez, C. (2007) 'Using Corpus Linguistics to Investigate the Language of Teacher Training', in J. Waliński, K. Kredens and S. Goźdź-Roszkowski (eds) *Corpora and ICT in Language Studies, PALC 2005*. Frankfurt am Main: Peter Lang, pp. 13–29.

Römer, U. (2004a) 'Comparing Real and Ideal Language Learner Input: The Use of an EFL Textbook Corpus in Corpus Linguistics and Language Teaching', in G. Aston, S. Bernardini and D. Stewart (eds) *Corpora and Language Learners*. Amsterdam: John Benjamins, pp. 151–68.

——(2004b) 'A Corpus-driven Approach to Modal Auxiliaries and their Didactics', in J. M. Sinclair (ed.) *How to Use Corpora in Language Teaching*. Amsterdam: John Benjamins, pp. 185–99.

——(2005) *Progressives, Patterns, Pedagogy: A Corpus-Driven Approach to English Progressive Forms, Functions, Contexts and Dialectics*. Amsterdam: John Benjamins.

——(2006) 'Pedagogical Applications of Corpora: Some Reflections on the Current Scope and a Wish for Future Developments', *Zeitschrift für Anglistik und Amerikanistik* 54(2): 121–34.

——(2009) 'Corpus Research and Practice', in K. Aijmer (ed.) *Corpora and Language Teaching*. Amsterdam: John Benjamins, pp. 83–98.

Scott, M. (1999) *WordSmith Tools Version 3*. Oxford: Oxford University Press.

Sinclair, J. M. (1991) *Corpus, Concordance, Collocation*. Oxford: Oxford University Press.

——(2001) 'Preface', to M. Ghadessy, A. Henry and R. L. Roseberry (eds) *Small Corpus Studies and ELT*. Amsterdam: John Benjamins, pp. vii–xv.

——(2004) 'Introduction', in J. M. Sinclair (ed.) *How to Use Corpora in Language Teaching*. Amsterdam: John Benjamins, pp. 1–10.

Taylor, L. and Barker, F. (2008) 'Using Corpora for Language Assessment', in E. Shohamy and N. H. Hornberger (eds) *Encyclopedia of Language and Education*, second edition; available at www.springerlink.com/content/x1434l3131507322/fulltext.pdf

Tognini Bonelli, E. (2001) *Corpus Linguistics at Work*. Amsterdam: John Benjamins.

Tribble, C. (2001) 'Small Corpora and Teaching Writing: Towards a Corpus-informed Pedagogy of Writing', in M. Ghadessy, A. Henry and R. L. Roseberry (eds) *Small Corpus Studies and ELT*. Amsterdam: John Benjamins, pp. 381–408.

Tsui, A. B. M. (2004) 'What Teachers Have Always Wanted to Know – and How Corpora Can Help Them', in J. M. Sinclair (ed.) *How to Use Corpora in Language Teaching*. Amsterdam: John Benjamins, pp. 39–61.

——(2005) 'ESL Teachers' Questions and Corpus Evidence', *International Journal of Corpus Linguistics* 10 (3): 335–56.

Vásquez, C. and Reppen, R. (2007) 'Transforming Practice: Changing Patterns of Interaction in Post-observation Meetings', *Language Awareness* 16(3): 153–72.

Vaughan, E. (2007) '"I Think We Should Just Accept Our Horrible Lowly Status": Analysing Teacher–Teacher Talk in the Context of Community of Practice', *Language Awareness* 16(3): 173–89.

——(2008) '"Got a Date or Something?" An Analysis of the Role of Humour and Laughter in the Workplace', in A. Ädel and R. Reppen (eds) *Corpora and Discourse*. Amsterdam: John Benjamins, pp. 95–115.

Walsh, S. and O'Keeffe, A. (2007) 'Applying CA to a Modes Analysis of Higher Education Spoken Academic Discourse', in H. Bowles and P. Seedhouse (eds) *Conversation Analysis and Language for Specific Purposes*. Berlin: Peter Lang, pp. 101–39.

Waters, A. (2005) 'Expertise in Teacher Education: Helping Teachers to Learn', in K. Johnson (ed.) *Expertise in Second Language Learning and Teaching*. Basingstoke: Palgrave Macmillan, pp. 210–29.

Wenger, E. (1998) *Communities of Practice: Learning, Meaning, and Identity*. Cambridge: Cambridge University Press.

Section VII

Using corpora to study literature and translation

35

What are parallel and comparable corpora and how can we use them?

Marie-Madeleine Kenning

1. What are parallel and comparable corpora?

Parallel and comparable corpora are collections of electronic texts that are closely related to each other, albeit in different ways. The prototypical parallel corpus consists of a set of texts in language A and their translations in language B (e.g. the works of Dickens and their translations into French). In other words, the relationship lies in shared meaning. By contrast, what links the collections of texts in comparable corpora is that they have been put together according to the same type of criteria (texts of a certain size, on a set topic, from a given period, etc.). The sets themselves, however, remain independent. Newspaper articles, election speeches, job adverts, birth announcements, all of which obey textual conventions that vary across cultures, exemplify the kinds of item of interest to compilers of comparable corpora.

Several points should be stressed from the outset. First, corpus terminology has taken time to settle down so that some earlier articles use the term 'parallel' for what is now called 'comparable', and 'aligned' instead of today's 'parallel'. Even now there remain variations in terminology, with authors prioritising different dimensions in their taxonomies, or adopting more or less liberal classification schemes. As well as parallel and comparable corpora, one finds references to bilingual, multilingual, aligned, comparative and concurrent corpora, the latter representing a subcategory of comparable, i.e. newspaper corpora collected over the same time span in different newspapers (e.g. newspaper reports on the Olympics).

Second, the key difference between parallel and comparable corpora as understood here, and by many scholars, is not that the former comprise translated texts whereas the latter do not, as not all comparable corpora consist exclusively of naturally occurring language. Rather, what distinguishes parallel from comparable corpora is that parallel corpora imply a common source text. This common source may be part of the corpus, or it may lie outside the corpus, as with a parallel corpus where the text pairs consist only of French and German translations of the same Dickens works. Other possibilities include translations in more than one language, and multiple translations of the same text into one particular target language (resulting in a monolingual parallel corpus if the source text is not included).

An important feature for bilingual and multilingual parallel corpora is translation direction. A distinction is made between unidirectional corpora (a set of texts in language A and their translations in language B) and bi-directional corpora (a set of texts in language A and their translations in language B, alongside a set of texts in language B and their translations in language A). The same kind of distinction applies to multilingual parallel corpora, which offer a range of direction possibilities.

As indicated above, the fundamental characteristic of comparable corpora is the existence of a common sampling frame with respect to text size, time span, text types, author characteristics (e.g. gender, age, nationality), etc. As with parallel corpora, there are a number of subtypes, not only in terms of the range of languages involved, but also of the kinds of text assembled. Comparable corpora may, for instance, bring together texts originating from different geographical areas, or drawn from diverse social varieties. They may consist of the same text type across certain historical periods, of translated texts, or of texts produced by learners.

It is worth pointing out that, if collected using similar criteria, the source texts of bi/multi-directional parallel corpora constitute comparable corpora. There is a sense, therefore, in which very large corpora that include texts from a wide variety of genres, and/or regional varieties, or pairs of corpora assembled according to similar criteria, such as the Brown Corpus of Standard American English, the Lancaster–Oslo Bergen corpus, and the Kolhapur Corpus (Indian English), can be regarded as making up comparable corpora. The term, however, tends to be reserved for specialised corpora consisting of particular types of text.

2. Existing corpora and corpus compilation

Existing corpora

Despite a great deal of activity in the area of corpus construction, due in part to the availability of funding from multinational institutions and governments of multilingual countries, there remains a shortage of parallel and comparable corpora. Existing parallel corpora span relatively few genres (mainly fiction, parliamentary proceedings, technical manuals), as well as a limited set of languages. Unless produced by multinational companies or institutions, or consisting of biblical texts, corpora of data in more than one language tend to be bilingual rather than multilingual, with major discrepancies in the availability of particular language pairs. It is possible to get some idea of the kind of ready-made parallel corpora available for research from the catalogue of the Linguistic Data Consortium, hosted by the University of Pennsylvania. Entries include the very popular European Corpus Initiative multilingual corpus, which contains texts in twenty-seven (mostly European) languages; Hansard French/English, a collection of parallel texts in English and Canadian French, drawn from official records of the proceedings of the Canadian Parliament; Arabic English parallel news, Arabic news stories and their English translations; and the Hong Kong Laws parallel text (Chinese, English). Other well-known corpora include the CRATER project (Spanish, French and English), the English–Norwegian parallel corpus, INTERSECT (English, French and German), COMPARA (Portuguese, English), and JRC–Acquis, a Multilingual Parallel Corpus of EU legislative texts covering over twenty European languages.

In the absence of suitable corpora, it will be necessary for one to be built. This is almost certain to be the case for comparable corpora. Off-the-shelf, publicly or commercially available comparable corpora are scarce, and may not serve the objectives of a new type of user. What is appropriate as a design criterion for one study may not be so for another, so that a factor important to a different study may be left uncontrolled or, conversely, the representativeness of the corpus may be affected by the inclusion of a criterion irrelevant to the new study. This underlines the crucial importance of adequate documentation.

Well-known comparable corpora include the International Corpus of English (ICE), made up of individual regional corpora built to a common design; the English Comparable Corpus, consisting of the Translational English Corpus, a collection of translations from a range of source languages, and a collection of spontaneously produced English texts of a similar type and date; and the International Corpus of Learner English, which comprises texts written by advanced learners of English as a foreign language from diverse mother tongue backgrounds.

Corpus compilation: some key issues

The compilation of parallel and comparable corpora follows the same three-step approach (design, text collection, preparation) commonly adopted by compilers of other types of corpora. It involves formulating a set of criteria and requirements about the texts to be collected, finding suitable texts and then preparing them to a lesser or greater degree (scanning, tagging, etc.), depending on their current state and the type of investigation to be conducted. While many of the issues encountered are familiar ones (e.g. questions around availability, quality, representativeness), the relative significance of such issues and the way in which they present themselves vary with the type of corpus, as do the specificities of the compilation process (e.g. relevance of particular search strategies). What follows is therefore a selective treatment prioritising issues peculiar to parallel and/ or comparable corpora. This section looks at the first two steps (design and text collection). The third, more variable step, preparation, is considered in the next section, together with exploitation tools.

Corpus design

As in any corpus building, the compiler's objectives are crucial and, along with the type of corpus, will influence how design issues are dealt with. In the case of parallel corpora, the availability of translated texts is bound to be a constraining factor. Even so, many selection criteria still have to be settled: should different genres be included, should the corpus contain pairs of texts from different periods, how much variety should there be in terms of authors, translators, and so on?

Similar decisions attend the building of comparable corpora, even if locating source materials is less of a problem, owing to the plentiful opportunities for collecting potentially suitable texts offered by the world-wide web. Interestingly, the issue of quality takes on a different complexion in comparable corpora from the one it assumes in parallel corpora. Whereas in the latter case, the focus is likely to be on translation quality, with comparable corpora, quality tends to be linked to authenticity, representativeness, and the need to check the credentials of authors and sources, especially in texts drawn from the world-wide web.

A fundamental issue in the case of comparable corpora is the vagueness of the construct of comparability. As Maia (2003: 34) points out: '[T]o a certain degree, comparability is in the eye of the beholder', a conundrum left unresolved by the common interpretation of comparability as matching communicative function in the community. Taking newspaper corpora as an example, one finds a huge number of possible variations in terms of types and degrees of similarity: the type of newspaper, its standing, the genres to be selected and their function – letters to the editors, for instance, do not have the same function in all cultures – not to mention factors such as number and size of articles, and subject domain. How many aspects are taken into account, what is given priority, and what is taken to be comparable ultimately reflects the purpose for which the corpus is being put together, and some of the decisions cannot but involve an element of subjectivity.

Text collection

With parallel corpora, the difficulties faced in compiling monolingual corpora in certain domains and languages due to disparities in text production find themselves compounded by uneven translation flows, with 'central' and 'peripheral' languages. As revealed by the Unesco Index Translationum, an international bibliographical database of translated books in all disciplines published in over 130 countries since 1979, there are striking imbalances and asymmetries in the involvement of individual languages in book translation. While English, with 984,872 works, comes well ahead of any other language in the list of the top fifty original languages, French, the language at number two, has only 183,469 works, and number fifty, Armenian, 1,034. This gives some idea of the problems encountered by those interested in less widely used languages. Interestingly, English does not come top of the list of top target languages but fourth, after German, Spanish and French.

Whatever type of corpus is being constructed, it is essential to investigate who owns the copyright, bearing in mind that there may be two copyrights in the case of translated work, one protecting the original author and the other the translator.

3. Preparing and analysing parallel and comparable corpora

Corpus preparation

As with other types of corpora, the third step in the construction of a parallel or comparable corpus involves decisions regarding mark-up and annotation. As elsewhere, the desirability of, for example, part-of-speech tagging will depend on the research question to be addressed. However, the presence of two or more sets of texts brings in additional issues, since it may entail the use of language specific annotation schemes, which may be more or less available, accurate or compatible, given the absence of a universal set of categories and differences in analytic approaches.

A distinctive aspect of the preparation of parallel corpora is the need to line up texts so that equivalent segments in the two (or more) languages can be compared. Because translators do not always translate one sentence by one sentence and do not always keep to the order of the source text, identifying corresponding segments is not a straightforward matter. For this reason, it is common practice to align texts automatically at paragraph or sentence level, using alignment software, and then to inspect the output to correct any misalignment manually. There are a range of tools available for this purpose, such as Danielsson and Ridings' 'vanilla' aligner (Danielsson and Ridings 1997), the

Microsoft bilingual sentence aligner (see website), and the modules forming part of translation memory suites such as *SDL Trados WinAlign* (see website). It should be mentioned that while alignment often constitutes a separate stage, it can also be carried out 'on the fly' during searches, as happens with the *Multiconcord* parallel concordancer (see website).

Corpus analysis

Apart from requiring coordinated searches and cross-language comparisons, the analysis of comparable corpora is similar to that of monolingual corpora and can be carried out using the same software. Packages such as Scott's (2008) *WordSmith Tools*, for instance, can handle a range of languages. This makes it possible to run the software on each part of the corpus in turn, although there may be cases (e.g. different scripts) in which some functionalities are not available or appropriate. The various facilities offered by the packages can be used to produce quantitative data for direct comparisons (e.g. type/token information, statistics on sentence length); they can assist with the identification and subsequent comparison of important items (frequency and key word lists); above all, they serve to generate concordances of perceived equivalents that can be used to compare their meaning and behaviour.

Unlike comparable corpora, parallel corpora require a special type of corpus analysis software known as a parallel concordancer. A parallel concordancer trawls through all the parts of a parallel corpus, retrieving not only all the occurrences of the search item in context, but also the sentences that contain the corresponding segments in the other language/languages. The output may be displayed with the source and target interleaved, or may appear in columns or in blocks. Since parallel corpora are normally only aligned at sentence level, it is up to the user to identify the actual equivalent, although some concordancers provide utilities designed to help with this (e.g. Barlow's (2002) *ParaConc*'s 'Hot Words' which retrieves words that occur with a higher than usual frequency in the translated concordance lines). Sort and search facilities mirror, but do not always match, those of monolingual concordancers. The example below shows an extract from an English–French concordance of the lemma *gagner* generated with *Multiconcord*:

> L'exemple anglais suscitait dès le milieu du XIXe siècle une émulation qui gagna toute l'Europe.
> The English example gave rise in the middle of the nineteenth century to an emulation which spread over all of Europe.
>
> L'usage a gagné les ports océaniques, puis ceux du Nord.
> Its use reached the ocean ports, then those of the North.
>
> Cependant, la cause du libre-échange n'était pas gagnée.
> However, the cause of free exchange was not won.
>
> de là, pour gagner la Baltique, le choix s'offrait entre deux passages
> from there to reach the Baltic there was a choice of two routes
>
> Notre essai de synthèse a tout à y gagner.
> Our work of synthesis has everything to gain there.

4. What are parallel and comparable corpora used for?

Parallel and comparable corpora are of interest to many language-related disciplines, from contrastive linguistics and translation studies, to computational linguistics and its various applications, translator training and language teaching. As outlined by Granger (2003a), in recent years, their common reliance on parallel and comparable corpora as major sources of primary data that are exploited through the use of similar methodologies has brought contrastive linguistics and translation studies closer together, although the two fields continue to differ in their objectives. While contrastive linguistics aims to identify similarities and divergences between languages, translation scholars are concerned with the translation process and its products.

Contrastive linguistics

Parallel multilingual corpora are widely regarded as having played a major role, albeit a controversial one, in the revival of contrastive linguistics in the 1990s. The vast quantity of empirical evidence that parallel corpora provide is invaluable for contrastive linguistics. Although the original text and the translation process are bound to exert some influence on the target text, thereby introducing a degree of distortion that affects the reliability of the findings, the ability to draw on a wide variety of texts translated by a range of translators provides a useful means of testing hypotheses and confirming (or disproving) contrastive statements based on intuitions and a small number of examples. This is particularly true of bi-directional corpora, which can be used to study the frequency with which two items or categories are translated into each other, or 'mutual correspondence', with 100 per cent (full correspondence) representing the very unlikely scenario in which item X in language A is always translated by item Y in language B, and item Y in language B is always translated by item X in language A (Altenberg 1999: 254).

Applying this approach to the study of adverbial connectors in English and Swedish, Altenberg first discusses correspondences between different semantic types of conjunct (resultive, contrastive, explanatory, etc.) before examining individual conjuncts (e.g. *however* and *emellertid*). This leads to the conclusion that 'a study of mutual correspondences between categories and items in source texts and translations does not only reveal language-specific properties of the categories compared, but provides fruitful insights into the larger systems of which these categories are a part' (Altenberg 1999: 266).

One asset of bilingual parallel corpora is that translations make it possible to see what happens:

- when one language does not make a distinction which is made in the other language
- when languages divide up semantic fields differently.

(Aijmer 1998: 278)

They can be used for comparisons at different levels of language, from lexis to syntax to discourse. Examples include Ebeling's (1998) study of the behaviour of presentative English *there-* constructions and the equivalent Norwegian *det-* constructions, Viberg's (1998) analysis of *run* and *put* and their translations in Swedish, work on markers of epistemic modality by several scholars (e.g. Aijmer 1998; Simon-Vandenbergen 1998), Goethals' (2007) investigation of asymmetries between Spanish and Dutch in the use of demonstrative determiners and pronouns, and Santos' (2004 and 2008) work on the meanings associated with tense and aspect in English and Portuguese.

By facilitating the mapping of correspondences between languages, parallel corpora can not only shed light on the commonalities and differences between language pairs, but also improve the accuracy of descriptions of individual languages. One area to which they can make a unique contribution is in the exploration of system gaps. For example, Kenning (1999) shows how a parallel English–French corpus can be used strategically to examine the interaction between French personal pronouns and the animate/inanimate distinction. The focus of the study is whether stressed pronouns (e.g. *lui)* can have inanimate antecedents, a question usually ignored by French grammars. The main procedure (arrived at heuristically from comparing the difficulty of translating '*I left without it*' as opposed to '*I left without him')* involves searching the English data for strings consisting of a preposition plus *it*, followed by analysis of the bilingual output.

As well as clarifying issues pertaining to individual languages or pairs of languages, parallel corpora can provide evidence on the extent to which a certain feature is shared by different languages, thereby contributing to language typology and the study of universals. Their use in more theory-oriented studies is illustrated by Dyvik's investigation of the translational properties of three Norwegian lexemes in the English–Norwegian Parallel Corpus, which, the author argues, produces results of interest to the development of linguistic semantics when 'seen as *imposing constraints on the set of possible semantic models for the languages'* (Dyvik 1998: 86 – italics in the original).

The impact of the translation process is, however, a significant drawback: 'Working with translations means working with distorted mirror images of the source language in the medium of the target language, when the objective is to analyse and describe the language in its own right, not just as a target language' (Teubert 1996: 247). For this reason, while parallel corpora can serve as starting points, they need to be supplemented.

Comparable corpora that consist of similar original texts in two or more languages (e.g. war reports) have the advantage over parallel corpora of containing only naturally occurring, un-mediated language. Being easier to assemble through the greater availability of source materials, they can be larger, which tends to make for greater reliability. On the other hand, the exploitation of comparable corpora relies more heavily on the ability of the researcher to map units of meaning across languages and identify cross-linguistic similarities. In the absence of parallel corpora, this has to be done without the benefit of the indirect evidence provided by the collective expertise of professional translators, as enshrined in their translations. How to establish and evaluate comparability across languages is discussed by Tognini Bonelli (2001), who proposes a three-step methodology: (1) analysis of the patterning of the L1 item, followed by identification of the meaning/function of each pattern; (2) identification of a *prima facie* L2 equivalent for each meaning/function (using one's experience, reference works and/or parallel corpora where available); (3) analysis of the formal realisations of each meaning/function in L2.

Areas for which comparable corpora can be useful include cognates and false friends, discourse analysis, and textual and cultural conventions, especially where there is significant divergence between languages. Where they include learner data, comparable corpora can be used for contrastive interlanguage analysis, either by comparing learner data with native speaker data or through comparisons of different kinds of learner data (Granger 2003b).

Translation studies

As is the case with contrastive linguistics, the significance of parallel and comparable corpora for translation studies lies in the amount of data they provide access to. Parallel and comparable corpora are used by practitioners as sources of ideas and information in order to resolve translation problems, and by translation scholars for translation research. They have also become a key resource in many contemporary training courses.

The usefulness of parallel corpora to practitioners is self-evident: parallel corpora enable translators to look up how a particular translation issue has been dealt with by others and draw inspiration from this. But comparable corpora too can serve as translation aids: bilingual comparable corpora can help translators to gain a better understanding of the source text and its terminology, to identify and evaluate potential target language equivalents, and to develop appropriate target language phraseology. These advantages are especially beneficial to translators working with language pairs lacking parallel corpora and/or involved in fast developing fields, where terminology is likely to be in constant evolution.

In addition to being useful to practitioners as sources of ideas for resolving translation problems, parallel corpora offer unprecedented opportunities for translation research. Unlike contrastive linguists, translation scholars do not regard the special features of translated text as problematical, but rather make them an object of study. Not only can parallel and comparable corpora be used to examine the influence of source texts on the patterning of target texts, i.e. translationese (deviant information structures and discourse conventions in terms of sentence length, complexity, etc.); they also lend themselves to the study of the features that distinguish translated language from non-translated language. Thus, in a pilot study on idiomaticity based on evidence from the Translational English Corpus (TEC) and a comparable subset of the British National Corpus (BNC), Baker (2007) found translated English to contain a lower incidence of idioms, together with a clear preference for the literal meanings of idiomatic expressions. Thus, only two of the thirteen occurrences of *off the hook* in TEC were idiomatic, against twenty idiomatic and fifteen literal uses in BNC.

Following Baker's (1993 and 1995) pioneering work, much attention has been paid to the distinctive features of translated text as a textual system, that is to say patterns characteristic of translated language that are independent from the source language and result from constraints inherent in the translation process. An abundant literature has grown around four possible universal features posited by Baker (1996: 176–7):

- simplification (of the language or message, e.g. breaking up of long sentences);
- explicitation (spelling things out, e.g. filling out elliptical units, explaining cultural references);
- normalisation (conforming, to the point of exaggerating them, to patterns and practices typical of the target language);
- levelling out (gravitating around the centre of any continuum).

Over the years, the search for universals has produced findings related to an increasing number of genres, and has broadened to take account of context variables such as differences in audience and purpose. Nevertheless, it remains mostly based on translations of literary works, and, importantly, continues to be a source of controversy (Malmkjær 2008; Mauranen 2008). Findings providing support to the hypothesised universals (simplification in the case of Laviosa's (e.g. 2002) work on lexis, normalisation in May's

(1997) investigation of punctuation, (syntactic) explicitation in the case of Olohan and Baker's (2000) analysis of the (higher) incidence of optional *that* after *say* and *tell*, and Goethals' (2007) article on demonstratives in Spanish and Dutch) are often balanced by results which reveal tendencies that are less clear-cut, or go in the opposite direction (e.g. Puurtinen's (2004) study of clause connectives).

In addition to lending themselves to the study of translationese and the tendencies of translated text, parallel and comparable corpora can be used to investigate the style of individual translators (Baker 2000), or to gain insights into the strategies used by translators in relation to a specific issue, for instance the use of cognates (Vintar and Hansen-Schirra 2005), or how translators ensure linguistic and cultural mediation (e.g. addition or omission of geographical information, like the location of a particular institution). Their usefulness and versatility have earned them a place in translator training, where courses in specialised translation typically provide an overview of existing corpora for the students' languages, introduce students to techniques for analysing concordance output, and engage them in corpus compilation, for instance building a small DIY corpus from the web. There have been many accounts of their use in such a context, from Zanettin's (1998) case study of how a comparable corpus can be exploited by students to check translation hypotheses, to learn about terminology and concept, or to highlight differences in ways of referring to personalities or in the lexis to introduce direct speech, to López-Rodríguez and Tercedor-Sánchez' (2008) description of materials and activities specifically designed to enhance learner autonomy. They also have a place in textbooks (Bowker and Pearson 2002; McEnery *et al.* 2006) and in books on corpora in translator education (Zanettin *et al.* 2003).

Language learning

Pedagogical applications of parallel and comparable corpora are not confined to translator training or translation teaching. As with single monolingual corpora, there are various ways in which parallel and comparable corpora can be used, both offline and online, to support and enhance language learning and teaching.

Like other corpora, they can inform syllabus design by contributing to the identification of features to be taught; they can be exploited to develop materials and activities designed to teach or raise awareness of these features, whether deductively or inductively; finally, they can act as a stimulus and a resource for autonomous language learning. What sets them apart is the ready availability of multiple or contrastive evidence that can be harnessed to highlight cross-linguistic similarities and differences, as well as to support learner processing of target language data. Generally speaking, parallel corpora lend themselves to applications at a range of levels, whereas comparable corpora are more relevant to advanced learners.

Using English–French data, Barlow (2000) sketches out how parallel corpora might be used in the classroom to sensitise students to the way in which different languages encode equivalent meanings. Among the examples given is the use of output from searches on reflexive forms to show students that English reflexives are not necessarily translated with a reflexive in French, and that some forms, such as *speaking for myself*, do not appear to have a close equivalent. Another illustration involves a concordance of *head* to highlight that *head* corresponds not only to *tête*, but also to *chef*, *directeur*, etc. As Barlow acknowledges, this kind of correspondence is contained in dictionaries, but not to the same extent, and without the rich contextualisation afforded by corpora.

It hardly needs stating that the use made of data will vary with learning objectives and the students' level. From this point of view, bilingual parallel corpora represent a flexible resource, leaving the teacher free to decide what to give learners access to, and at what point. One possibility, but there are many others, is the production of various types of C-test and cloze test, such as those offered by *Multiconcord*, a concordancer developed specifically for pedagogical purposes. Essentially, the provision of a translation is a way of scaffolding learning, of bringing within the analytic capabilities of learners what might be too difficult or too time-consuming for them to recall or discover unaided. For example, while it is possible to infer from a small selection of occurrences of French *toujours pas* and *pas toujours* in context, together with their translations, that the former means *still not/not yet* whereas the latter means *not always*, to work this out without a translation represents a much greater challenge. Furthermore, access to a translation (which may be full or partial, automatically displayed or available on demand) enables learners to process occurrences containing vocabulary or strings that they do not know. It opens up autonomous data-driven learning, making it a more realistic proposition. This is attested by the experience of the student quoted by Kenning (2000: 255), who, while exploring the uses of the French subjunctive, employing *soit* and *soient* as search strings 'discovered a very frequent use of *soit* (*soit … soit* meaning *either … or* and *que 'a' soit 'x' ou 'y'* meaning *whether 'a' is 'x' or 'y'*) which [she] had not been aware of'.

Machine translation

Among the other applications of parallel and comparable corpora, which include their use in lexicography, knowledge engineering, terminology extraction and the building of terminology databases and bilingual reference tools, pride of place must be given to machine translation (MT), where, since around 1990, parallel corpora have played a pivotal role in a (partial) paradigm shift from rule-based approaches to statistical and example-based approaches to MT. Essentially, statistical MT (SMT) involves computing the probability that a TL string is the translation of an SL string, based on the frequency of the co-occurrence of these strings in the corpus, whereas example-based MT (EBMT) involves searching for similar phrases in previous translations and extracting the TL fragments corresponding to the SL fragments. That is to say, '[b]oth methods make substantial use of large bilingual corpora, but where SMT is based exclusively on statistical correlations, EBMT applies both statistical techniques and linguistics based methods similar to those of earlier RBMT approaches' (Hutchins 2007). In either case, parallel corpora represent a key source of sets of examples with which to develop, train and test systems in order to improve their performance (Skadina 2005). Data mining now extends to comparable corpora, again using methods that exploit frequency correlations of words in different languages to discover mappings between words in different languages (Tao and Zhai 2005).

5. Parallel and comparable corpora as complementary resources

Growing awareness of the respective advantages and shortcomings of different types of corpora has led to the development of a widespread consensus that parallel and comparable corpora should be viewed as complementary, and that much is to be gained from using several types of corpus in conjunction. For instance, Bernardini and Zanettin

(2004) argue that when searching for translation universals, it is necessary to assess both the status of a corpus of translations against a comparable corpus of originals in the target language, and the status of the source texts against a comparable corpus of originals in the source language. Thus, a type/token ratio that is lower than that of a corpus of comparable texts in the target language can only be regarded as evidence of simplification if there is a smaller difference between the type/token ratio of the source texts and that of a control corpus in the source language. The use of two control corpora is also advocated by Munday (1998), in this case in relation to the study of translation shifts, and there are many cases, including some of the studies cited above, in which researchers move from one type of corpus to another to verify and/or expand their findings, the actual permutations and combinations, like the choice of corpus, varying with the research question.

One of the clearest and most detailed demonstrations of how exploiting several corpora leads to a fuller and more accurate account of the phenomena under investigation is offered by McEnery *et al.*'s (2006: 321–43) exploration of the effect of translation, domain and text type on aspect marking in Chinese. The study draws on three corpora:

- an English–Chinese parallel health corpus;
- a comparable corpus of texts collected from official websites for public health in China;
- a Chinese newspaper corpus containing a mix of domains and text types.

In the first stage of the analysis, the parallel corpus is used to examine how aspectual meanings in English (e.g. the progressive) are translated into Chinese. Next, the authors use the Chinese health corpus to test the hypothesis that the low frequency of aspect markers revealed by the analysis is a consequence of the translation process. This is indeed supported by the data. In the third stage, the newspaper corpus is brought in to study how the distribution of aspect markers varies across domains. It is found that the health corpus contains a much lower frequency of aspect markers than the newspaper corpus, a fact attributed to the expository nature of public health texts. Lastly, internal comparisons within the health corpus and the English part of the parallel corpus serve to highlight significant differences in aspect marker distribution between narrative and expository writing.

In the implementation outlined in Laviosa (2007), the number of corpora is reduced to two, the point of departure is a comparable, not a parallel corpus, and there are three procedural steps instead of four. The focus of the study is the use of anglicisms in Italian business texts. The two corpora are an English–Italian comparable corpus consisting of collections of business texts and a unidirectional parallel corpus of English articles from *The Economist* and the *Financial Times* with their Italian translations. Laviosa begins by identifying the anglicisms contained in the Italian part of the comparable corpus with the WordList facility in *WordSmith Tools*. This is followed by the production of comparable concordances using the Concord facility on both parts of the comparable corpus. The last step involves retrieving parallel concordances for each anglicism from the parallel corpus with *ParaConc*. The article ends with a report on some preliminary findings on the lemma *business*, which is found to be translated with *business* only if it refers to a particular activity, translators showing a preference for native terms or paraphrases.

Another study exploiting the complementarity of comparable and parallel analyses is Kenny (2005). Kenny's work, which builds on Olohan and Baker (2000) and centres on *say*, differs from the previous two studies in adopting a methodology that starts from translated texts. Kenny begins by identifying and analysing instances of *say* in reporting structures translated from German in which optional *that* is possible. This shows *that* and *zero*-connective to be roughly equally probable, in line with Olohan and Baker's (2000) findings. Kenny then examines how many of the instances of *that* can be linked to the use of *daß* in the source texts, before finally turning her attention to the source texts corresponding to *zero*-connective. The data reveal a tendency for patterns of omission of *that* to reflect patterns of omission of *daß*, whereas where *that* is used, only half of the cases have a corresponding *daß*.

In all cases a more complete picture gradually emerges, testifying to the advantages of approaching corpus data from different angles.

Further reading

Bowker, L. and Pearson, J. (2002) *Working with Specialized Language: A Practical Guide to Using Corpora.* London: Routledge. (A useful source of practical advice on using corpora with a chapter on parallel corpora.)

McEnery, T., Ziao, R. and Tono, Y. (2006) *Corpus-based Language Studies: An Advanced Resource Book.* London: Routledge. (This comprehensive introduction to corpus linguistics includes the case study summarised above, which is worth reading in full.)

Maia, B. (2003) 'What are Comparable Corpora?' in *Proceedings of Pre-conference Workshop Multilingual Corpora: Linguistic Requirements and Technical Perspectives, Corpus Linguistics 2003.* Lancaster: Lancaster University, pp. 27–34. (A short but excellent overview of the construction of comparable corpora and their uses.)

References

Aijmer, K. (1998) 'Epistemic Predicates in Contrast', in S. Johansson and S. Oksefjell (eds) *Corpora and Cross-linguistic Research: Theory, Method and Case Studies.* Amsterdam: Rodopi, pp. 277–95.

Altenberg, B. (1999) 'Adverbial Connectors in English and Swedish: Semantic and Lexical Correspondences', in H. Hasselgård and S. Oksefjell (eds) *Out of Corpora: Studies in Honour of Stig Johansson.* Amsterdam: Rodopi, pp. 249–68.

Baker, M. (1993) 'Corpus Linguistics and Translation Studies: Implications and Applications', in M. Baker, G. Francis and E. Tognini Bonelli (eds) *Text and Technology: In Honour of John Sinclair.* Amsterdam: John Benjamins, pp. 233–50.

——(1995) 'Corpora in Translation Studies: An Overview and Suggestions for Future Research', *Target* 7(2): 223–43.

——(1996) 'Corpus-based Translation Studies: The Challenges that Lie Ahead', in H. Somers (ed.) *Terminology, LSP and Translation: Studies in Language Engineering in Honour of Juan C. Sager.* Amsterdam: John Benjamins, pp. 175–86.

——(2000) 'Towards a Methodology for Investigating the Style of a Literary Translator', *Target* 12(2): 241–66.

——(2007) 'Patterns of Idiomaticity in Translated vs Non-translated Text', *Belgian Journal of Linguistics* 21(1): 11–21.

Barlow, M. (2000) 'Parallel Texts in Language Teaching', in S. P. Botley, A. M. McEnery and A. Wilson (eds) *Multilingual Corpora in Teaching and Research.* Amsterdam: Rodopi, pp. 106–15.

——(2002) 'ParaConc: Concordance Software for Multilingual Parallel Corpora', in *Language Resources for Translation Work and Research*, pp. 20–4; available at www.mt-archive.info/LREC-2002-Barlow.pdf

Bernardini, S. and Zanettin, F. (2004) 'When is a Universal not a Universal? Some Limits of Current Corpus-based Methodologies for the Investigation of Translation Universals', in A. Mauranen and P. Kujamäki (eds) *Translation Universals: Do They Exist?* Amsterdam: John Benjamins, pp. 51–62.

Bowker, L. and Pearson, J. (2002) *Working with Specialized Language: A Practical Guide to Using Corpora.* London: Routledge.

Danielsson, P. and Ridings, D. (1997) 'Practical Presentation of a "Vanilla Aligner"', in *Proceedings of the TELRI Workshop on Alignment and Exploitation of Texts*, Ljubljana, available at http://nl.ijs.si/telri/Vanilla/doc/ljubljana/

Dyvik, H. (1998) 'A Translational Basis for Semantics', in S. Johansson and S. Oksefjell (eds) *Corpora and Cross-linguistic Research: Theory, Method and Case Studies.* Amsterdam: Rodopi, pp. 51–86.

Ebeling, J. (1998) 'Contrastive Linguistics, Translation, and Parallel Corpora', *Meta* 43(4): 602–15.

Goethals, P. (2007) 'Corpus-driven Hypothesis Generation in Translation Studies, Contrastive Linguistics and Text Linguistics: A Case Study of Demonstratives in Spanish and Dutch Parallel Texts', *Belgian Journal of Linguistics* 21: 87–103.

Granger, S. (2003a) 'The Corpus Approach: A Common Way Forward for Contrastive Linguistics and Translation Studies', in S. Granger, J. Lerot and S. Petch-Tyson (eds) *Corpus-based Approaches to Contrastive Linguistics and Translation Studies.* Amsterdam: Rodopi, pp. 17–29.

——(2003b) 'The International Corpus of Learner English: A New Resource for Foreign Language Learning and Teaching and Second Language Acquisition Research', *TESOL Quarterly* 37: 538–46.

Hutchins, J. (2007) 'Machine Translation in Europe and North America: A Brief Account of Current Status and Future Prospects', available at www.hutchinsweb.me.uk/JAPIO-2007.pdf

Kenning, M.-M. (1999) 'Parallel Concordancing and French Personal Pronouns', *Languages in Contrast* 1(1): 1–21.

——(2000) 'Corpus Informed Syllabus Development: Parallel Concordances and Pedagogical Grammars', in T. Lewis and A. Rouxeville (eds) *Technology and the Advanced Language Learner.* London: AFLS/CILT, pp. 240–58.

Kenny, D. (2005) 'Parallel Corpora and Translation Studies: Old Questions, New Perspectives?' in G. Barnbrook, P. Danielsson and M. Mahlberg (eds) *Meaningful Texts: The Extraction of Semantic Information from Monolingual and Multilingual Corpora.* London: Continuum, pp. 154–65.

Laviosa, S. (2002) *Corpus-based Translation Studies: Theory, Findings, Applications.* Amsterdam: Rodopi.

——(2007) 'Studying Anglicisms with Comparable and Parallel Corpora', *Belgian Journal of Linguistics* 21: 123–36.

López-Rodríguez, C. I. and Tercedor-Sánchez, M. I. (2008) 'Corpora and Students' Autonomy in Scientific and Technical Translation Training', *JosTRans* (9), available at www.jostrans.org/issue09/art_lopez_tercedor.php

McEnery, T., Ziao, R. and Tono, Y. (2006) *Corpus-based Language Studies: An Advanced Resource Book.* London: Routledge.

Maia, B. (2003) 'What are Comparable Corpora?' in *Proceedings of Pre-conference Workshop Multilingual Corpora: Linguistic Requirements and Technical Perspectives, Corpus Linguistics 2003.* Lancaster: Lancaster University, pp. 27–34.

Malmkjær, K. (2008) 'Norms and Nature in Translation Studies', in G. Anderman and M. Rogers (eds) *Incorporating Corpora: The Linguist and the Translator.* Clevedon: Multilingual Matters, pp. 49–59.

Mauranen, A. (2008) 'Universal Tendencies in Translation', in G. Anderman and M. Rogers (eds) *Incorporating Corpora: The Linguist and the Translator.* Clevedon: Multilingual Matters, pp. 32–48.

May, R. (1997) 'Sensible Elocution: How Translation Works in and upon Punctuation', *The Translator* 3(1): 1–20.

Microsoft Bilingual Sentence Aligner, http://research.microsoft.com/research/downloads/Details/aafd5dcf-4dcc-49b2–8a22-f7055113e656/Details.aspx

Multiconcord: The Lingua Multilingual Parallel Concordancer for Windows, http://artsweb.bham.ac.uk/pking/multiconc/l_text.htm

Munday, J. (1998) 'A Computer-assisted Approach to the Analysis of Translation Shifts', *Meta* 43(4): 542–56.

Olohan, M. and Baker, M. (2000) 'Reporting *that* in Translated English: Evidence for Subconscious Processes of Explicitation?' *Across Languages and Cultures* 1(2): 141–58.

Puurtinen, T. (2004) 'Explicitation of Clausal Relations: A Corpus-based Analysis of Clause Connectives in Translated and Non-translated Finnish Children's Literature', in A. Mauranen and P. Kujamäki (eds) *Translation Universals: Do They Exist?* Amsterdam: John Benjamins, pp. 165–76.

Santos, D. (2004) *Translation-based Corpus Studies: Contrasting Portuguese and English Tense and Aspect Systems*. Amsterdam: Rodopi.

——(2008) 'Perfect Mismatches: "result" in English and Portuguese', in G. Anderman and M. Rogers (eds) *Incorporating Corpora: The Linguist and the Translator*. Clevedon: Multilingual Matters, pp. 217–42.

Scott, M. (2008). *WordSmith Tools*, at www.lexically.net/downloads/version5/HTML/?type_token_ratio_proc.htm

SDL Trados WinAlign, at www.translationzone.com/en/products/sdltrados2007/applications/

Simon-Vandenbergen, A.-M. (1998) '*I think* and its Dutch Equivalents in Parliamentary Debates', in S. Johansson and S. Oksefjell (eds) *Corpora and Cross-linguistic Research: Theory, Method and Case Studies*. Amsterdam: Rodopi, pp. 297–317.

Skadina, I. (2005) 'Studies of English–Latvian Legal Texts for Machine Translation', in G. Barnbrook, P. Danielsson and M. Mahlberg (eds) *Meaningful Texts: The Extraction of Semantic Information from Monolingual and Multilingual Corpora*. London: Continuum, pp. 188–95.

Tao, T. and Zhai, C. X. (2005) 'Mining Comparable Bilingual Text Corpora for Cross-language Information Integration', in *Proceedings of the Eleventh ACM SIGKDD International Conference on Knowledge Discovery in Data Mining*. Chicago: SIGKDD, pp. 691–6.

Teubert, W. (1996) 'Comparable or Parallel Corpora?' *International Journal of Lexicography* 9(3): 238–64.

Tognini Bonelli, E. (2001) *Corpus Linguistics at Work*. Amsterdam: John Benjamins.

Viberg, Å. (1998) 'Contrasts in Polysemy and Differentiation: *running* and *putting* in English and Swedish', in S. Johansson and S. Oksefjell (eds) *Corpora and Cross-linguistic Research: Theory, Method and Case Studies*. Amsterdam: Rodopi, pp. 343–76.

Vintar, Š. and Hansen-Schirra, S. (2005) 'Cognates: Free Rides, False Friends or Stylistic Devices? A Corpus-based Comparative Study', in G. Barnbrook, P. Danielsson and M. Mahlberg (eds): *Meaningful Texts: The Extraction of Semantic Information from Monolingual and Multilingual Corpora*. London: Continuum, pp. 208–21.

Zanettin, F. (1998) 'Bilingual Comparable Corpora and the Training of Translators', *Meta* 43(4): 616–30.

Zanettin, F., Bernardini, S. and Stewart, D. (eds) (2003) *Corpora in Translator Education*. Manchester: St Jerome.

36

Using corpora in translation

Natalie Kübler and Guy Aston

1. Translating: purposes and processes

While recent years have seen considerable corpus-based research in the field of translation studies, aiming to identify the peculiar characteristics of translated texts *qua* products (Baker 1999; Olohan 2004; Mauranen 2007), much less has been done to study translating *qua* process, and to examine the potential roles of corpora in that process – and, in consequence, in the teaching and learning of translation skills. In this chapter we examine applications of corpora in the practice and pedagogy of translation. Our concern here is with *pragmatic translation*, where '"pragmatic" denotes the reader's or readership's reception of the translation' (Newmark 1988: 133) focusing on the perlocutionary effect of the translation in the target language culture (Hickey 1998). The way a text is translated will depend on the reader to whom the translation is addressed: the translator must take into account that reader's knowledge and expectations, which may be very different from those of the target reader of the source text. Here we illustrate how corpora can provide translators with ways of identifying such differences, and of formulating and testing hypotheses as to appropriate translation strategies. Corpora are not a universal panacea for the translator; but insofar as translators may spend over half their time looking for information of various kinds (Varantola 2000: 123), they can often provide a significant resource.

We view the translation process as involving three phases – while recognising that in practice these are intertwined rather than strictly consecutive.

a. *Documentation.* The translator skims through the source text and collects documents and tools which they consider relevant (similar texts, specialised dictionaries, terminology databases, translation memories, etc.). Where the domain is unfamiliar, the translator may spend a significant amount of time simply reading about the topic. In this phase, corpora of documents from that domain can provide readily consultable collections of reading materials, and a basis for acquiring conceptual and terminological knowledge. (The source text itself can be treated as a mini-corpus, and analysed computationally to identify features for which appropriate reference tools will be needed.)

b. *Drafting.* The translator identifies specific problems in interpreting the source text and producing the translated one. They formulate and evaluate possible interpretations of the source text and possible translations, selecting those judged most appropriate. Corpora can assist in all these processes: as Varantola notes (2000: 118), 'Translators need equivalents and other dictionary information, but they also need reassurance when checking their hunches or when they find equivalents they are not familiar with.' Corpora can provide such reassurances.
c. *Revision.* The translator and/or revisor evaluates the draft translation, checking its readability, comprehensibility, coherence, grammaticality, terminological consistency, etc. Again, corpora can reassure in these respects. (The target text itself can be treated as a mini-corpus, and analysed to identify features which may be out-of-place.)

In what follows we illustrate ways in which corpora – either existing, or constructed *ad hoc* – can aid the translator in these three phases. Thereby we hope also to illustrate their relevance to translator training – both as reference tools to be created and consulted, and as means to enhance learner understanding and awareness of the translation process itself. We assume the reader is familiar with standard corpus query functions, such as concordancing, word and n-gram listing and collocate extraction (see chapters by Scott, Tribble, Evison, Greaves and Warren, this volume). Results shown in this chapter were generated using *XAIRA* (Dodd 2007), *AntConc* (Anthony 2007), *ParaConc* (Barlow 2004), and *WordSmith Tools* (Scott 2008).

2. How do corpora fit in?

In principle, corpora are hardly a novelty for translators. There is a long tradition of using 'parallel texts' as documentation – collections of texts similar in domain and/or genre to the source and/or target text (Williams 1996). Before the advent of electronic texts and software to search and analyse them, a use of 'parallel texts' required the translator to first locate them, and then to read them extensively to extract potentially relevant information of various kinds – typically terminology to construct glossaries. Today, queriable corpora make extensive reading less necessary – though compiling and browsing a corpus of 'parallel texts' can still be useful for the translator to familiarise him- or herself with the domain(s) and genre(s) involved (see Section 3).

Drafting the target text requires understanding the source text, and assessing strategies to bring about the desired effect on the target reader. Not only language problems are at stake. The translator needs to have a good knowledge of the source text culture, and of the extent to which this knowledge is likely to be shared by the target reader – bearing in mind that the translator's own knowledge cannot serve as a model. For an educated reader of Italian – and, one hopes, a translator from Italian – a mention of the provincial town of Salò will immediately bring to mind the republic set up after Italy's surrender in the Second World War. For an educated English reader, this association may well have to be spelt out in the target text. A large general corpus of English can show whether this is likely to be necessary: the 100-million-word British National Corpus (BNC-XML 2007) contains only four mentions of the town, and one of these feels the need to explain the association:

Hitler had Mussolini rescued from Rome and installed as head of the Republic of Salò, a small, relatively insignificant town on the western shores of Lake Garda, but it was a temporary measure.

(ANB 226)

Corpora often provide explanations of names and terms which may be unfamiliar to the target reader (or indeed to the translator themselves) – and also, in this case, a ready-made chunk which might be incorporated into the target text with little modification.

Other resources may of course provide such information – dictionaries and encyclopedias, internet search engines, or even friendly experts and discussion lists. But corpora, because they can provide data which is not pre-digested but comes in the shape of samples of actual text, allow translators to acquire and apply skills which are after all central to their trade – ones of text interpretation and evaluation.

This is particularly true for specialised translations, where the translator may need to get acquainted with not only the terms and concepts of the domain, but also the rhetorical conventions of the genre. Consumer advice leaflets in Italian generally opt for an impersonal style *(This should not be done)*, whereas English ones tend to address the reader directly *(Do not do this)*. Italian leaflets also tend to support advice by reference to institutional frameworks. The two texts which follow come from web pages of the Inland Revenue services of the two countries – a nightmare to pragmatically translate (but foreigners also pay taxes):

How to pay Self Assessment

This guide offers a reminder of Self Assessment payment deadlines and explains all of the available payment options.

HM Revenue & Customs (HMRC) recommends that you make your Self Assessment payments electronically. Paying electronically:

- is safe and secure
- gives you better control over your money
- provides certainty about when your payment will reach HMRC
- avoids postal delays
- may lower your bank charges
- lets you pay at a time convenient to you if you use Internet or telephone banking

Now the Italian text – in machine translation, with obvious lexicogrammatical errors corrected:

Practical guide to the payment of taxes

To pay taxes, contributions and duties, all taxpayers, with or without VAT numbers, must use the form 'F24' with the exception of central Administrations of the State and public bodies subject to the 'single treasury system'.

The model is defined as 'unified' in that it allows the taxpayer to effect payment of the sums due in a single operation, compensating payment with any tax credits (on compensation, see chapter 4).

The F24 form is available from banks, collection agencies and post offices, but can also be downloaded from the Internet site of the Revenue Agency.

Comparing corpora of such texts is clearly useful to distinguishing reader expectations in the two cultures, even if this may pose the pragmatic translator as many problems as it solves.

3. What corpus?

Monolingual corpora

General reference corpora

General reference corpora such as BNC-XML (2007) are designed to provide information about the language as a whole, showing how it is generally used in speech and writing of various kinds. Let us consider some of the problems to be faced in drafting a translation of the following sentence into English – assuming English is the translator's second language, as is often the case (Campbell 1998; Stewart 2001).

> Tony's Inn infatti offre le stesse comodità di una camera d'albergo, ma vissute in un ambiente più raccolto e domestico.

This comes from an Italian web page advertising a bed-and-breakfast establishment. Google's machine translation reads:

> Tony's Inn in fact offers the same comforts of a hotel room, but lived in a collected and domestic atmosphere more.

The source text talks about *comodità* … *vissute* (*comforts* … *lived*). Let us first hypothesise that *comforts* is an appropriate translation of *comodità*. This is supported by a search with *XAIRA* in the BNC, which finds 213 occurrences of *comforts* as a plural noun, including several from similar contexts:

1 The hotel combines Tyrolean hospitality with all modern *comforts* in a luxurious setting with a high standard of service. (AMD 1352)
2 The same deal in the swanky Old Istanbul Ramada Hotel with all *comforts* and casino is £326. (ED3 1667)
3 Originally a 17th century patrician house, this is a lovely unpretentious hotel with the *comforts* and atmosphere of a private home. (ECF 4319)

But can you *live comforts*? A collocation query lists the most frequent verb lemmas in the seven words preceding and following the noun *comforts*: BE (95), HAVE (33), ENJOY (16), PROVIDE (11), DO (11), WANT (8), COMBINE (6), OFFER (6), LIVE (6), MAY (6), MAKE (5), GET (5), CAN (5). A specific collocation query for LIVE shows the following concordance lines:

1 Six residents are currently *living* there and enjoying the *comforts* of a very homely atmosphere. (A67 145)
2 I'm afraid we don't have too many *comforts* or luxuries here. We *live* only on the ground floor, of course. (APR 1863)

3 In any case, Charles Henstock cared little for creature *comforts*, and had *lived* there for several years, alone, in appalling conditions of cold and discomfort. (ASE 289)
4 The island abounds in pleasing scenes, and a season may be well spent there by those who desire to *live* near city *comforts*. (B1N 125)
5 Now we are en route to Auxerre and the *comforts* of an English family *living* in France. (CN4 727)
6 She had her *comforts*. She *lived* in luxury. (H9C 1128)

Alas, in none of these is *comforts* the object of LIVE, underlining the importance of looking at actual instances before jumping to conclusions. But looking at these instances suggests an alternative hypothesis, ENJOY (line 1) – one supported by the position of ENJOY in the collocate list. The instances with ENJOY + *comforts* include:

1 Six residents are currently living there and *enjoying* the *comforts* of a very homely atmosphere. (A67 145)
2 Many illustrious visitors, including such notables as Wagner, Oscar Wilde, Garbo and Bogart have *enjoyed* the style and *comforts* of this hotel. (ECF 749)
3 *Enjoy* all modern *comforts* in an historic parador. (C8B 2394)
4 Guests at the Pineta share the landscaped gardens and benefit equally from the excellent service and *comforts enjoyed* by those staying in the main building. (ECF 3332)

This thus seems an appropriate translation hypothesis. And what about *un ambiente più raccolto e domestico* (*a collected and domestic atmosphere more*)? Line 1 in the last concordance suggests the phrase *homely atmosphere*, and looking at other instances of this string, we also find a suggestion for the translation of *raccolto*, namely *intimate*:

1 A delightful Grade 2 listed building of architectural and historical interest with a wealth of oak and elm panelled walls, beamed ceilings and large open fireplaces creating an *intimate* and *homely atmosphere*. (BP6 573)
2 This *intimate* family hotel offers a warm welcome to a *homely atmosphere* and the management prides itself on offering a choice of good local cooking in its dining-room. (ECF 2434)

This leaves little doubt as to the appropriacy of the collocation *intimate* + *atmosphere*, of which further instances appear in similar texts. These also suggest that *intimate* should precede *homely*, our other modifier of *atmosphere*:

1 This is an impressive hotel with an *intimate* and peaceful *atmosphere*. (ECF 3647)
2 This is a property still small and smiling enough to be called a 'home' rather than a hotel, with an *intimate* and friendly *atmosphere*. (ECF 5213)
3 There are just eight bedrooms and two suites so an *intimate*, friendly *atmosphere* prevails. (ECF 5341)
4 *Intimate atmosphere*, excellent menu and friendly service. (ECS 2041)

There is, however, a remaining uncertainty which a sharp-eyed translator will have spotted. Many of these lines come from the same text (ECF) – *Citalia Italy Complete*, a tourist handbook. Are we simply endorsing the idiosyncratic uses of a particular publication? The translator must decide whether this source is linguistically authoritative, and/or whether there are enough other instances to corroborate these uses. Our final choice for this translation would be *an intimate and homely atmosphere* – a phraseology in fact found in another text (BP6).

With this example, we hope to have illustrated how a corpus can provide a means not only of testing particular translation hypotheses, but also of formulating further hypotheses as a result of cotextual encounters. But let us now switch our direction of translation to consider an English source text. A corpus can cast light on aspects of the source text of which the translator may not otherwise be aware, particularly if their knowledge of the source text language is limited. An example is connotation. Aston (1999) discusses the opening sentence of Bruce Chatwin's novel *Utz* (1989: 7):

> An hour before dawn on March 7th 1974, Kaspar Joachim Utz died of a second and long-expected stroke, in his apartment at No. 5 Siroká Street, overlooking the Old Jewish Cemetery in Prague.

A BNC search for collocates of the lemma OVERLOOK shows that the places overlooked (in the literal sense) are mountains, rivers, oceans, ports, squares and gardens – views which generally have pleasant connotations. To use Louw's terms (1993), *overlook* appears to have a positive semantic prosody. In the rare instances where the place overlooked is clearly unpleasant, such use appears to be marked, aiming at a particularly creative effect, such as irony:

> The difficulty is that some people actually like Aviemore. Not only do they tolerate the fast-food shops serving up nutriment that top breeders wouldn't recommend for Fido, they go as far as purchasing two expensive weeks in a gruesome timeshare apartment, and sit smoking all day on a balcony overlooking the A9.
>
> (AS3 1368)

The corpus here suggests two alternative interpretations of the source text. Either Utz's view is to be seen as pleasant, and the Old Jewish Cemetery is a nice place, or else the writer is being ironic, and the view – acting presumably as a reminder of mortality – is rather less pleasant. This being the very first sentence of a literary text, one might argue that it is deliberately designed to leave the reader uncertain as to its interpretation, and that the translator should seek out a formulation which has similar ambiguity to achieve the same effect. Stewart (2009) proposes pedagogic activities to enhance the translator's awareness of semantic prosodies, showing how comparison with a source language corpus can be key to the formulation of appropriate translation hypotheses.

A methodological point to emerge from these examples is the role of collocation in the translator's use of corpora. Our analysis of OVERLOOK was based on its collocates, which enabled identification of its semantic prosody. Our selection of ENJOY + *comforts* derived from observing the collocates of the latter. Even where the translator has no hypothesis as to a possible translation, it may be sufficient to examine the collocates of a nearby item for which a confident hypothesis is available. Possible solutions to many of the translator's lexical problems can be found hidden in the corpus cotext, as Sharoff (2004) demonstrates – though of course they must be tested prior to adoption.

Specialised corpora

As Sinclair pointed out (1991: 24), we should not expect a general reference corpus like the BNC to adequately document specialised genres and domains. For this we need more specialised corpora, containing reasonably 'parallel' texts to that being translated, as more likely to document the conventions of the genre and the concepts and terms of the domain. As we have seen in the examples above, relevant discoveries can often occur while the user is searching for something else, and this is even more probable with specialised corpora. Unlike general corpora, they can also be used in the documentation phase to familiarise the translator with the domain and clarify terminology (Maia 2003). For example, many terms and their definitions and explanations can be located via explicit markers (Pearson 1998: 119). Here is a definition from a specialised corpus in vulcanology, located by searching for *defined as*:

> The third are eruptions confined within paterae (a patera is *defined as* an irregular crater, or a complex one with scalloped edges).

In scientific writing in French, the expression *on dira* has a similar function of introducing definitions or near-definitions. In a corpus on the birth of mountains we find, *inter alia*:

1 Définition de la déformation. *On dira* qu'un corps est déformé s'il y a eu variation de la forme, des dimensions
2 Si la dimension de l'objet augmente, *on dira* alors qu'il y a eu dilatation positive de l'objet
3 *On dira* qu'une déformation sera homogène, si les conditions énoncées ci-dessous
4 Pour tous les autres cas, *on dira* que la déformation sera hétérogène.
5 ne resteront pas perpendiculaires dans l'état déformé. *On dira* alors que la déformation est rotationnelle.
6 de longueurs d'onde différentes *on dira* que les plis sont disharmoniques.

All these lines define or explain terms in this domain.

Specialised corpora do not grow on trees. They have to be compiled, and those who compile them are often reluctant to share what they perceive to be valuable objects. They also have to be appropriate for the task. Establishing the domain and genre of the text to be translated are the first steps a translator needs to take in the documentation phase, asking what the text is trying to do, what it is about, and who it is it aimed at. Is it a didactic text, in which definitions and explanations are provided? Is it a research article, where there will be fewer definitions and explanations, since the author will take it for granted that the reader is already familiar with the subject? A research article may require much research on terminology, while a divulgative text may require more work on cultural allusions and connotations. To translate the former, a specialised corpus will be near-essential, while for the latter a general corpus may be more appropriate. And if a specialised corpus is desirable but not available, how to create one?

Constructing specialised corpora

Creating a corpus involves putting together a collection of relevant documents. Ideally these should already be in electronic form, and this usually means locating and downloading them, converting them to a format which query software can handle, and cleaning them of unnecessary parts such as tables and images, HTML links and formatting instructions (see chapters by Koester, Nelson and Reppen, this volume). You may also want to add markup indicating the source, category and structure of each document, and perhaps categorise each word – decisions which will depend on the resources available. Last and not least, there are copyright issues – is it all legal?

In assessing documents for inclusion in a corpus, we first need to consider their domain and genre, and the extent to which these 'parallel' those of the source/target text. We also need to consider the extent to which they can be considered authoritative (clearly, it could be unwise to treat texts written by non-experts, or by non-native authors, as reliable sources of terminology, explanations or cultural conventions). The source of a document will often provide indications in these respects: a research project's website, for example, is likely to contain material produced by expert authors, a blog or chat less likely to. A third criterion is the intended reader, and their presumed expertise in the field (Bowker and Pearson 2002). Divulgative and/or didactic texts, written by experts (or pseudo-experts) for non-experts, are more likely to contain definitions and explanations (Wikipedia is a notorious example) – potentially useful documentation for the translator, who may well also be a non-expert. This entails, essentially, categorising corpus texts as either 'parallel' or 'explanatory', and 'authoritative' or 'debatably authoritative', so that searches can be performed on different subcorpora as required.

Locating and downloading appropriate documents using internet search engines can be a painful process. WebBootCaT (Baroni *et al.* 2006) allows the user to automatically retrieve and clean large numbers of documents using a series of strings as 'seeds', where the user can gradually refine these to increase precision, and also restrict searches to certain types of sites. But how big does a specialised corpus need to be? Corpas Pastor and Seghiri (2009: 86–92) candidate a software procedure which progressively analyses type/token ratio, indicating when this ceases to decline significantly by addition of further documents.

Reference corpora like the BNC are heavily marked up with information about each document – its source, its categorisation, its structure (sections, headings, paragraphs, notes, sentences, etc.), the part-of-speech and root form of each word, and indeed about its markup, following international guidelines on text encoding (TEI Consortium 2007). The lone translator is unlikely to have the time, resources or expertise to mark up each document in detail. But where a corpus is being constructed as a shared resource for lengthy use, this effort may be worthwhile for the greater search precision and potential for interchange it permits.

And is it all legal? It is generally considered fair practice to retrieve available texts from the web for personal non-commercial use. But it is not considered fair practice to reproduce or modify those texts, making them available to others from a different source or in different forms (Wilkinson 2006). A double-bind: without permission, one can only construct a corpus for personal use, but without wider use it may not be worth the effort to construct it. Without permission, there is no way a translation teacher can construct a corpus to use with learners. If permission is sought, it may not be granted, or else understandably charged for, and limitations may be posed upon the amount of text (Frankenberg-Garcia and Santos 2003). Unless, of course, your corpus consists only of documents of your (or your customer's) own. Or unless your corpus is a virtual one, consisting simply of a set of categorised URLs to which queries are addressed over the internet – a possible direction for the future (see 5 below).

Multilingual corpora

Given that translators are concerned with (at least) two languages, there are advantages in having access to corpora containing similar documents in two – or several – languages. Here we illustrate uses of some of the main types available, limiting ourselves to a bilingual context (see also Kenning, this volume).

Comparable corpora

In the documentation phase, comparable specialised corpora, constructed using analogous criteria for both languages, provide the translator a means to familiarise him- or herself with the domain and genre in both source and target languages, providing ways of identifying intercultural differences and similarities. One typical use is that of identifying equivalent terms. For a small comparable corpus on electric motors in English and Italian, the lists that follow (generated with *AntConc*) show the most frequent words and two- to three-word n-grams in each component (excluding function words):

English	*Italian*
motor	motore
motors	motori
power	elettrici
rotor	corrente
dc	velocità
electric	essere
torque	albero
speed	coppia
brake	tensione
current	tipo
phase	serie
voltage	trifase
field	rotore
winding	alimentazione
series	freno

English	*Italian*
DC motor	motori elettrici
electric motor	albero di uscita
magnetic field	motore elettrico
three phase	corrente continua
electric motors	velocità di rotazione
DC motors	corrente alternata
power supply	giri min
single phase	campo magnetico
frame size	Motori elettrici
induction motor	protezione IP

(Longer) lists could be useful to a translator needing to produce an Italian version of an English electric motor manual, or vice versa. Some equivalents can be seen in the n-gram lists: *electric motor/motore elettrico*; *magnetic field/campo magnetico*; others can be deduced from extending comparisons to the wordlists: *three phase/trifase*. If no equivalent is immediately locatable, collocation methods can be used. For instance, over 10 per cent of the 722 occurrences of *torque* occur with *speed* as a collocate. If we know that the Italian for the latter is *velocità*, a glance at the most frequent lexical collocates of *velocità* in the Italian corpus leads to *coppia* as an equivalent.

It can, however, be difficult to build strictly comparable corpora for specialised domains. Given the dominance of English, analogous scientific writing in other languages may be hard to find. Things may seem easier for technical documents, but we all know how manuals for imported goods contain errors. Comparable corpora always raise issues of just how comparable and authoritative they are.

Parallel corpora

Parallel corpora (not to be confused with 'parallel texts') ideally consist of texts in one language and translations of those same texts in another language. Every translator's dream is a resource which instantly provides reliable candidate translations, and this is what a parallel corpus ideally offers. Figure 36.1 shows a concordance for the English *lax attitude(s),* where the bottom half of the window lists the equivalents in the French part of the corpus. These highlight the preference for *laxisme* (notwithstanding the availability of *attitude laxiste*), with the possible alternatives *laisser-aller* and *lâcher la bride*:

... y of the last 40 years. This has led to lax attitudes towards criminality which have been acc ...
... brought any honour upon itself with its lax attitude to Slovenia over property taken from It ...
... It should not be afraid to confront the lax attitude of some major ports or major shipowners ...
... strong enough. Thanks to the Council 's lax attitude, the 1992 revision of the directive on ...
... ving been proven to be harmful, and the lax attitude, even complicity, of Member States and ...
... n crime since its creation in 1957. The lax attitude to crime which is often fashionable in ...
... hilst striving hard not to give in to a lax attitude, which would have a detrimental effect ...
... of power to the Commission encourages a lax attitude, while any maintenance of Member State ...
... auses of this evil, one of which is the lax attitude of most European nations towards pornog ...
... rt is likely to produce. By favouring a lax attitude towards immigration, in the name of the ...
... ccurs to the present situation. <P> The lax attitude of the Member States not only has a neg ...
... 20 %. <P> This is an indictment of the lax attitude in this country to the enforcement of w ...
... sked in interviews why they have such a lax attitude to the disease, reply, â€which life sh ...
... force the Commission to snap out of its lax attitude to nitrates. It is terrible that, seven ...

... des 40 dernières années qui a provoqué un laisser-aller criminel, avalisé par des gouvernements béats, r
... les autres. <P> Je ne crois pas que le laxisme adopté par l' Italie à l' égard de ...
... qu' elle ne craigne pas d' affronter le laxisme de certains grands ports ou d' importants armateur
... est pas allée assez loin en raison du laxisme du Conseil. Il faut le souligner: le Conseil ...
. nocivité de ces dernières était démontrée et le laxisme, pour ne pas dire la complicité, des États ...
... la criminalité depuis sa création en 1957. Le laxisme pénal qui est souvent à la mode dans ...
... en se gardant bien de céder à un laxisme qui nous entraînerait vers le bas. Ceci passe ...
ansfert de pouvoir vers la Commission accroît le laxisme, tout maintien de pouvoir auprès des États encour
... de ces maux qu' est, entre autres, le laxisme vis-à-vis de la pornographie dans lequel se compla
ète la résolution Oostlander. Car, en favorisant le laxisme vis-à-vis de l' immigration, au nom de la ...
que la situation actuelle change. <P> L' attitude laxiste des États membres n' est pas seulement négative
charges à 20 % du chiffre actuel. <P> L' attitude laxiste en matière d' application des lois sur les ...
dans des interviews pourquoi ils ont une attitude laxiste vis-à-vis de la maladie, répondent «pour quelle vie
... encourage la commission à ne pas lâcher la bride plus longtemps pour les nitrates. Il est scandaleux .

Figure 36.1 Parallel concordance (English–French) for *lax attitude(s)* (*ParaConc*).

Given the difficulty of obtaining permission to use both a text and its translation, publicly available parallel corpora are few, most being based on multilingual official documents. This concordance comes from a corpus of European Parliament proceedings (*OPUS*, see Tiedemann 2009, offers downloadable parallel corpora for European languages from the European Parliament, the European Medicines Agency, Open Office and Open Subtitles. An online query interface is also available online). The original language is unspecified, so the parallel segments may in fact both be translations from a third language. One available parallel corpus where the relationship between text pairs is stated is COMPARA (English and Portuguese: Frankenberg-Garcia and Santos 2003), allowing searching of original texts or translations. COMPARA is also one of the few parallel corpora to allow online querying of copyright material.

One option open to the professional translator (and even more so to the translation agency) is to construct their own parallel corpora, using source and target texts of previous translation jobs. This requires the *alignment* of each text pair, indicating which segment in one text corresponds to which segment in the other, generally on a sentence-by-sentence basis, using programmes such as *Winalign* or *WordSmith Tools* (Chung-Ling 2006; Scott 2008). Unless, that is, a translation memory system was used for the translation, in which case source and target texts may have been saved in an aligned format. Translation memories can themselves be considered parallel corpora, but since they contain pairs of segments rather than pairs of texts, and only one translation per segment, they offer less contextual information, and none on frequency or alternatives.

Parallel corpora lead one to reflect on alternative ways of translating a source text. Their limit is that the user exploits previous translations as a basis for new ones, and hence risks producing 'translationese' rather than conforming to the conventions of original texts in the target language (Williams 2007): in COMPARA, *already* is used twice as often in translations from Portuguese as it is in original English texts (Frankenberg-Garcia 2004: 225). But there are also clear arguments in favour, particularly in training contexts:

> They [translators] have to gauge how much of the material in a source text is directly transferable to the target language, how much of it needs to be adapted or localized in some way, whether any of it can, or indeed should, be omitted. The answers to questions of this nature cannot be found in comparable corpora because these issues never arise in a monolingual text-producing environment. They only arise because of the constraints of a text composed in another language. The answers must therefore be sought in parallel corpora.
>
> (Pearson 2003: 17)

Multiple translation corpora

Pearson's observations also hold for multiple translation corpora. These are parallel corpora which include several translations of the same texts, so a search can find all the corresponding strings in source texts and all the various translations of each. This allows comparison of different translations of the same thing in the same context (Malmkjær 2003). But since multiple translations of the same text are rare, most such corpora use learner translations, particularly lending themselves to error analysis (Castagnoli *et al.* 2009) – again making them of particular value in training contexts.

4. Corpora in translator training

The use of corpora in translator training has to be viewed from several perspectives. Most simply, it can be viewed as providing the skills necessary to use corpora in the professional environment, with simulations of real tasks in the various phases of the translation process. More broadly, it can be seen as a means of raising critical awareness of this process, with wider educational goals (Zanettin *et al.* 2003; Bernardini and Castagnoli 2008). Thus constructing and using comparable corpora may develop awareness of cross-cultural similarities and differences; parallel corpora may develop awareness of strategic alternatives and the role of context. It can also provide opportunities to improve linguistic and world knowledge, to acquire new concepts and new uses (not least through incidental discoveries), along lines discussed in work on teaching and language corpora (Aston 2001; O'Keeffe *et al.* 2007). And it can be an opportunity to develop awareness of the technical issues involved in computer-assisted translation, such as the representativeness and reliability of corpora, standards of encoding and markup, query techniques, procedures of alignment and of term extraction, etc. Such awareness will be essential for the future translator to keep abreast of new technological developments. Last but not least, it may motivate, increasing engagement with the process of translation and with learning how to translate.

5. Future prospects

To the professional translator, time is undoubtedly money. Corpus construction and corpus use are time-consuming, and while survey data indicates a general interest on the part of translators (Bernardini and Castagnoli 2008), in order for corpora to become a standard resource it is essential to find ways of speeding these up.

Corpus construction from the internet can, it has been shown, be largely automated (Baroni *et al.* 2006). However the interfaces offered by the major search engines do not facilitate this, and there are obvious copyright implications attached to any process which involves automatic downloading (rather than consultation) of documents. Improved document categorisation may, however, allow web concordancers to generate concordances and perform other linguistic analyses from 'virtual corpora', by consulting and analysing documents of specified domains, genres and authoritativeness, and simply passing the search results, rather than the documents, to the user (at the time of writing web concordancing services include Birmingham City University's *WebCorp*, see Renouf *et al.* 2007; and *Web Concordancer*, see Fletcher 2007; see Lee, this volume). One day, similar categorisations may even allow generation of parallel concordances from document pairs of a specified type which the search software recognises as being equivalents in different languages (Resnik and Smith 2003), using automatic alignment procedures.

Another area for future development concerns the integration of corpus tools into the translator's workbench. Today's widely used translation memory systems offer few chances of accessing and querying corpora other than previously inserted source text-translation pairs. Compatible interfacing of external corpora with other tools is essential if these are to be perceived by the professional translator as a help rather than an obstacle, with single-click transfer of a source text string to a corpus query, and of selected query output to the draft translation. To this end, more research on the way translators actually use corpora is needed (Santos and Frankenberg-Garcia 2007).

Increasingly, human translators will compete with machine translation, which is itself increasingly corpus-based (Somers 2003). Many of the processes described in this chapter may be incorporated into machine translation packages, thereby reducing the human workload. Currently, machine translation only yields high-quality results with repetitive and/or simplified texts, but performance can be significantly improved with appropriate lexicons (whose construction from corpus data is therefore an appropriate translator concern: Kübler 2002), and by adequate revision of the output – where corpora (as our examples using machine-translated extracts have hopefully shown) can again play an important role.

We can also hope for more research on the productiveness of corpora as translation aids. If corpus use makes for better translation than other tools (Bowker and Barlow 2008), does the quality improvement justify the effort, and at what point does the payoff start to tail off? Are corpus construction and consultation best placed in different hands (Kübler 2003)? How big – and how specialised – does a specialised corpus have to be to provide solutions to a reasonable proportion of a translator's problems (Corpas Pastor and Seghiri 2009)? Are the roles of general and specialised corpora complementary ones (Sharoff 2004; Philip 2009)?

Finally, we can hope for more research on corpora in translator training. What, for example, are suitable corpus-based tasks in a task-based translation pedagogy (Monzó Nebot 2008; Rodriguez Inéz 2009)? And how can the widely documented potential of corpora for autonomous language learning best be interpreted to foster the autonomous acquisition of translation skills (López-Rodríguez and Tercedor-Sánchez 2008)?

Further reading

Beeby, A., Rodriguez Inés, P. and Sánchez-Gijón, P. (eds) (2009) *Corpus Use and Translating*. Amsterdam: John Benjamins. (Selected papers from the third Corpus Use and Learning to Translate conference.)

Bowker, L. and Pearson, J. (2002) *Working with Specialised Language: A Guide to Using Corpora*. London: Routledge. (A practical introduction to compiling and using specialised corpora, with exercises.)

Rogers, M. and Anderman, G. (eds) (2007) *Incorporating Corpora: The Linguist and the Translator*. Clevedon: Multilingual Matters. (A collection of recent papers on corpora in translation studies by some of the major figures in the field.)

Zanettin, F., Bernardini, S. and Stewart, D. (eds) (2003) *Corpora in Translator Education*. Manchester: St Jerome. (Selected papers from the second Corpus Use and Learning to Translate conference.)

References

Anthony, L. (2007) *AntConc 3.2.1*, at www.antlab.sci.waseda.ac.jp/software.html

Aston, G. (1999) 'Corpus Use and Learning to Translate', *Textus* 12: 289–313.

——(2001) 'Learning with Corpora: An Overview', in G. Aston (ed.) *Learning with Corpora*. Houston, TX: Athelstan.

Baker, M. (1999) 'The Role of Corpora in Investigating the Linguistic Behaviour of Translators', *International Journal of Corpus Linguistics* 4: 281–98.

Barlow, M. (2004) *ParaConc*, www.paraconc.com/ (accessed 12 July 2009).

Baroni, M., Kilgarriff, A., Pomikálek, J. and Rychl, P. (2006) 'WebBootCaT: Instant Domain-specific Corpora to Support Human Translators', *Proceedings of EAMT 2006*, available at www.muni.cz/research/publications/638048/ (accessed 12 July 2009).

Beeby, A., Rodriguez Inés, P. and Sánchez-Gijón, P. (eds) (2009) *Corpus Use and Translating*. Amsterdam: John Benjamins.

Bernardini, S. and Castagnoli, S. (2008) 'Corpora for Translator Education and Translation Practice', in E. Yuste Rodrigo (ed.) *Topics in Language Resources for Translation and Localisation*. Amsterdam: John Benjamins.

Bernardini, S. and Zanettin, F. (eds) (2000) *I corpora nella didattica della traduzione/Corpus Use and Learning to Translate*. Bologna: Cooperativa Libraria Universitaria Editrice.

BNC-XML (2007) *The British National Corpus: XML Edition*. Oxford: Oxford University Computing Services.

Bowker, L. and Barlow, M. (2008) 'A comparative evaluation of bilingual concordancers and translation memory systems', in E. Yuste Rodrigo (ed.) *Topics in Language Resources for Translation and Localisation*. Amsterdam: Benjamins.

Bowker, L. and Pearson, J. (2002) *Working with Specialised Language: A Guide to Using Corpora*. London: Routledge.

Campbell, S. (1998) *Translation into the Second Language*. London: Longman.

Castagnoli, S., Ciobanu, D., Kunz, K., Volanschi, A. and Kübler, N. (2009) 'Designing a Learner Translator Corpus for Training Purposes', in N. Kübler (ed.) *Corpora, Language, Teaching, and Resources: From Theory to Practice*. Bern: Peter Lang.

Chatwin, B. (1989) *Utz*. London: Pan.

Chung-Ling, S. (2006) 'Using Trados's WinAlign Tool to Teach the Translation Equivalence Concept', *Translation Journal* 10(2); available at www.accurapid.com/journal/36edu1.htm (accessed 12 July 2009).

Corpas Pastor, G. and Seghiri, M. (2009) 'Virtual Corpora as Documentation Resources: Translating Travel Insurance Documents (English–Spanish)', in A. Beeby, P. Rodriguez Inés and P. Sánchez-Gijón (eds) (2009) *Corpus Use and Translating*. Amsterdam: John Benjamins.

Dodd, A. (2007) *Xaira 1.24*, at http://www.oucs.ox.ac.uk/rts/xaira/Download/ (accessed 12 July 2009).

Fletcher, W. H. (2007), 'Concordancing the Web: Promise and Problems, Tools and Techniques', in M. Hundt, N. Nesselhauf and C. Biewer (eds) *Corpus Linguistics and the Web*. Amsterdam: Rodopi.

Frankenberg-Garcia, A. (2004) 'Lost in Parallel Concordances', in G. Aston, S. Bernardini and D. Stewart (eds) *Corpora and Language Learners*. Amsterdam: Benjamins.

Frankenberg-Garcia, A. and Santos, D. (2003) 'Introducing COMPARA, the Portuguese–English Parallel Translation Corpus', in F. Zanettin, S. Bernardini and D. Stewart (eds) *Corpora in Translator Education*. Manchester: St Jerome.

Hickey, L. (1998) 'Perlocutionary Equivalence: Marking, Exegesis and Recontextualisation', in L. Hickey (ed.) *The Pragmatics of Translation*. Clevedon: Multilingual Matters.

Kübler, N. (2002) 'Creating a Term Base to Customize an MT System: Reusability of Resources and Tools from the Translator's Point of View', in E. Yuste (ed.) *Proceedings of the Language Resources for Translation Work and Research Workshop of the LREC Conference*, 28 May 2002, Las Palmas de Gran Canarias: ELRA.

——(2003) 'Corpora and LSP Translation', in F. Zanettin, S. Bernardini and D. Stewart (eds) *Corpora in Translator Education*. Manchester: St Jerome.

López-Rodríguez, C. and Tercedor-Sánchez, M. (2008) 'Corpora and Students' Autonomy in Scientific and Technical Translation Training', *Journal of Specialised Translation*, 9, available at www.jostrans.org/issue09/art_lopez_tercedor.pdf (accessed 14 July 2009).

Louw, W. (1993) 'Irony in the text or insincerity in the writer? The diagnostic potential of semantic prosodies', in M. Baker, G. Francis and E. Tognini-Bonelli (eds) *Text and Technology: In Honour of John Sinclair*. Amsterdam: Benjamins.

Maia, B. (2003) 'Training Translators in Terminology and Information Retrieval Using Comparable and Parallel Corpora', in F. Zanettin, S. Bernardini and D. Stewart (eds) *Corpora in Translator Education*. Manchester: St Jerome.

Malmkjær, K. (2003) 'On a Pseudo-subversive Use of Corpora in Translator Training', in F. Zanettin, S. Bernardini and D. Stewart (eds) *Corpora in Translator Education*. Manchester: St Jerome.

Mauranen, A. (2007) 'Universal Tendencies in Translation', in M. Rogers and G. Anderman (eds) *Incorporating Corpora: The Linguist and the Translator*. Clevedon: Multilingual Matters.

Monzó Nebot, E. (2008) 'Corpus-based Activities in Legal Translator Training', *The Interpreter and Translator Trainer* 2: 221–52.

Newmark, P. (1988) 'Pragmatic Translation and Literalism', *TTR: traduction, terminologie, rédaction* 1/2: 133–45.

O'Keeffe, A., McCarthy, M. J. and Carter, R. A. (2007) *From Corpus to Classroom: Language Use and Language Teaching*. Cambridge: Cambridge University Press.

Olohan, M. (2004) *Introducing Corpora in Translation Studies*. London: Routledge.

Pearson, J. (1998) *Terms in Context*. Amsterdam: John Benjamins.

——(2003) 'Using Parallel Texts in the Translator Training Environment', in F. Zanettin, S. Bernardini and D. Stewart (eds) *Corpora in Translator Education*. Manchester: St Jerome.

Philip, G. (2009) 'Arriving at Equivalence: Making a Case for Comparable General Reference Corpora in Translation Studies', in A. Beeby, P. Rodriguez Inés and P. Sanchez-Gijon (eds) *Corpus Use and Translating*. Amsterdam: John Benjamins.

Renouf, A., Kehoe, A. and Banerjee, J. (2007) 'WebCorp: An Integrated System for Web Text Search', in C. Nesselhauf, M. Hundt and C. Biewer (eds) *Corpus Linguistics and the Web*. Amsterdam: Rodopi.

Resnik, P. and Smith, N. (2003) 'The Web as a Parallel Corpus', *Computational Linguistics* 29: 349–80.

Rodriguez Inéz, P. (2009) 'Evaluating the Process and Not Just the Product when Using Corpora in Translator Education', in A. Beeby, P. Rodriguez Inés and P. Sanchez-Gijon (eds) *Corpus Use and Translating*. Amsterdam: John Benjamins.

Santos, D. and Frankenberg-Garcia, A. (2007) 'The Corpus, its Users and their Needs: A User-oriented Evaluation of COMPARA', *International Journal of Corpus Linguistics* 12: 335–74.

Scott, M. (2008) *WordSmith Tools 5.0*. Liverpool: Lexical Analysis Software.

Sharoff, S. (2004) 'Harnessing the Lawless: Using Comparable Corpora to Find Translation Equivalents', *Journal of Applied Linguistics* 1: 333–50.

Sinclair, J. (1991) *Corpus, Concordance, Collocation*. Oxford: Oxford University Press.

Somers, H. (2003) 'Machine Translation: Latest Developments', in R. Mitkov (ed.) *Oxford Handbook of Computational Linguistics*. Oxford: Oxford University Press.

Stewart, D. (2001) 'Poor Relations and Black Sheep in Translation Studies', *Target* 12: 205–28.

——(2009) 'Safeguarding the Lexicogrammatical Environment: Translating Semantic Prosody', in A. Beeby, P. Rodriguez Inés and P. Sanchez-Gijon (eds) *Corpus Use and Translating*. Amsterdam: John Benjamins.

TEI Consortium (eds) (2007) *Guidelines for Electronic Text Encoding and Interchange*, available at www.tei-c.org/Guidelines/ (accessed 12 July 2009).

Tiedemann, J. (2009) 'News from OPUS – A Collection of Multilingual Parallel Corpora with Tools and Interfaces', in N. Nicolov, K. Bontcheva, G. Angelova and R. Mitkov (eds) *Recent Advances in Natural Language Processing, Vol. V*. Amsterdam: John Benjamins.

Varantola, K. (2000) 'Translators, Dictionaries and Text Corpora', in S. Bernardini and F. Zanettin (eds) *I corpora nella didattica della traduzione/Corpus Use and Learning to Translate*. Bologna: Cooperativa Libraria Universitaria Editrice.

Wilkinson, M. (2006) 'Legal Aspects of Compiling Corpora to be Used as Translation Resources', *Translation Journal* 10(2), available at www.accurapid.com/journal/36corpus.htm (accessed 12 July 2009).

Williams, I. (1996) 'A Translator's Reference Needs: Dictionaries or Parallel Texts', *Target* 8: 277–99.

——(2007) 'A Corpus-based Study of the Verb *observar* in English–Spanish Translations of Biomedical Research Articles', *Target* 19: 85–103.

Zanettin, F., Bernardini, S. and Stewart, D. (eds) (2003) *Corpora in Translator Education*. Manchester: St Jerome.

37

How can corpora be used to explore the language of poetry and drama?

Dan McIntyre and Brian Walker

1. Poetry, drama and corpora

Recently, methods from corpus linguistics have increasingly been applied in the analysis of literary texts (see, for example, Semino and Short 2004; Mahlberg 2007; O'Halloran 2007). In this chapter we outline some techniques for using corpora to study poetry and drama and demonstrate the value of using a corpus linguistic methodology in stylistic analysis. To demonstrate how corpus linguistic techniques might be applied in the analysis of poetry and drama, we analyse two specially constructed corpora. The first contains the poems from William Blake's *Songs of Innocence and of Experience* and the second is composed of approximately 200,000 words of Hollywood blockbuster film-scripts. We use these to answer a series of research questions, in order to show how corpora can shed light on particular stylistic issues.

2. Background to *Songs of Innocence and of Experience*

William Blake published his first collection of poems in 1783, with *Songs of Innocence* (SoI) following six years later in 1789. *Songs of Experience* (SoE) appeared in 1794, and although 'advertised … as a separate companion volume' (Bottrall 1970: 13) was soon bound together with *Songs of Innocence* and both collections were issued in one volume with the combined title of *Songs of Innocence and of Experience* (hereafter referred to as *Songs*). While the reputation of *Songs* was slow to develop, they have become widely admired and the subject of much critical attention. Bowra, for example, claims that 'the Songs deserve special attention if only because they constitute one of the most remarkable collections of lyrical poems written in English' (Bowra 1970: 136).

3. A corpus-based case study of *Songs of Innocence and of Experience*

SoE and SoI are said to complement each other and are very much intended to be read as a whole (Bowra 1970). According to Bowra, the primary theme of *Songs* is contrast.

Our main research question, then, centres on how these two collections are different. We will explore the lexical and semantic differences that manifest themselves in *Songs*. We compare the words and semantic domains in SoI with the words and semantic domains in SoE, and vice versa. We also consider whether generalisations made by previous analysts are supported by corpus-based generalisations.

We used the software *Wmatrix* (Rayson 2008) to carry out the computer-based analysis of *Songs*, utilising its automatic semantic annotation system. *Wmatrix* assigns semantic tags by matching the text against a computer dictionary of semantic domains developed for use with the software (see Rayson *et al.* 2004 for details of this procedure). The source text used for this study was obtained from Project Gutenberg (see website) and contains forty-seven poems. Two electronic versions of *Songs* were created in plain text files (unformatted .txt), so that we had one file containing SoI and the other containing SoE. The texts we used were checked and amended using facsimiles of Blake's original plates (available online). The amended .txt versions of SoI and SoE were uploaded onto *Wmatrix* and compared with each other at the word level, to produce a list of key words, and at the semantic level, to produce a list of key semantic domains.

The notion of key or keyness here refers to items with an unusually high or an unusually low frequency in a source text or corpus when compared, using a statistical test, to a reference corpus. *Wmatrix* uses the Log Likelihood (hereafter LL) statistical calculation to evaluate differences in frequencies, and the higher the LL value the more key or statistically significant an item is or the higher the likelihood that the unusually high or low occurrence of an item is not due to chance. Keyness, however, is not an indication of whether the occurrence of an item is interpretively significant (for more on keyness, see Scott, this volume). This is up to the analyst to establish by exploring in more detail each key item. Note that in our study of Blake we have only considered key items that (a) occur *more* in our source corpus than in the reference corpus, and (b) that have an LL critical value of 10.63 or more, which indicates 99.9 per cent confidence of significance.

By comparing SoI and SoE against each other, we can see that there are very few key words and key domains with a LL of 10.63 or over. We could say that this is our first result, that lexically and semantically the texts are actually quite similar. There could be an argument, however, that the limited number of key items is connected to the small size of the texts we are comparing: SoI contains 2,433 words; and SoE 2,919 words. But we can show that this is perhaps not entirely the case by comparing *Songs* with a similarly sized but very different text in terms of genre, theme, style and period. For example, comparing SoI with a twenty-first-century academic journal article produces around thirty-nine key words and thirty key domains. So we can see from this that while the two collections of songs are, as Blake states on the title page of *Songs*, 'Shewing the Two Contrary States of the Human Soul', they are doing so using similar language, lexically and semantically speaking. There are, however, some differences highlighted by the comparison and we will turn to those now.

Table 37.1 shows the key semantic domains highlighted from the SoI vs SoE and SoE vs SoI comparisons.

HAPPY is the most key domain from the SoI vs SoE comparison. This contrasts rather sharply with the results from the SoE vs SoI comparison, where the most key domains are FEAR/SHOCK and VIOLENT/ANGRY. This immediately provides us with a semantic contrast which we might relate to Blake's 'Two Contrary States of the Human Soul'.

When using *Wmatrix*'s semantic annotation system, it helps to see what words have been assigned to the semantic categories you are interested in. This can help to

Table 37.1 Key domain results for SoI and SoE

SoI vs SoE				*SoE vs SoI*			
Key domain	*No. SoI (%)*	*No. SoE (%)*	*LL*	*Key domain*	*No. SoE (%)*	*No. SoI (%)*	*LL*
HAPPY	82 (3.36)	30 (1.03)	35.47	FEAR/ SHOCK	21 (0.72)	2 (0.08)	15.03
SPEECH ACTS	27 (1.11)	9 (0.31)	12.99	VIOLENT/ ANGRY	19 (0.65)	2 (0.08)	12.99

understand what the categorisation is telling us about a text (some semantic domains are not as transparent as HAPPY). The words for HAPPY, FEAR/SHOCK and VIOLENT/ANGRY are shown in Table 37.2. *Joy*, *merriment* and *laughter* occur more in SoI than they do in SoE, while SoE seems to be filled with *anger*, *wrath*, *fear* and *terror*.

Moving on to the second most key domain for the SoI vs SoE comparison, SPEECH ACTS, we can see that words to do with communication are more prevalent in SoI than they are in SoE. This could be related to interaction in the poems and provides some evidence towards more spoken communication taking place in SoI when compared with SoE. This, to some extent, ties in with Simpson's (1993) comments, that '*Songs of Innocence* tend on the whole to be *dynamic* – in the sense that active communication takes place' (Simpson 1993: 195). The 'active communication' is, to some extent, manifest in this SPEECH ACTS category shown in Table 37.3.

Turning now to the key words produced by our comparison between *Songs*, Table 37.4 shows that comparing SoI with SoE produced three times more key words than the SoE vs SoI comparison.

A useful first step in any analysis is to eliminate key items that, on initial investigation, do not seem to be interpretively significant. Three items fall into this category: *Lyca*,

Table 37.2 Words assigned to HAPPY, VIOLENT/ANGRY and FEAR/SHOCK domains

HAPPY in SoI		*VIOLENT/ANGRY in SoE*		*FEAR/SHOCK in SoE*	
Word	*Total*	*Word*	*Total*	*Word*	*Total*
joy	16	cruelty	3	fear	6
happy	13	wrath	3	dread	5
smiles	10	cruel	2	fears	5
merry	9	angry	2	terror	2
merrily	7	fiend	2	fearful	2
delight	6	indignant	1	terrors	1
laugh	6	annoy	1		
laughing	5	nipped	1		
laughs	2	wild	1		
rejoice	2	unrest	1		
laughed	1	threat	1		
smile	1	quarrel	1		
relief	1				
cheerful	1				
joys	1				
smiled	1				

Table 37.3 SPEECH ACTS in SoI vs SoE

SoI		*SoE*	
Word	*Total*	*Word*	*Total*
welcome	4	sigh(ing)	2
sigh(s)	4	moan	1
moan(s)	4	calling	1
call(s)(ed)	7	tell	1
tell	2	shriek	1
shouted	1	answer	1
wailing	1	prophesy	1
reply (ied)	2	preach	1
farewell	1		
cries	1		
Total	**27**	**Total**	**9**

Table 37.4 Key word results

SoI vs SoE				*SoE vs SoI*			
Key word	*No. SoI (%)*	*No. SoE (%)*	*LL*	*Key word*	*No. SoE (%)*	*No. SoI (%)*	*LL*
thee	25 (1.03)	5 (0.17)	18.44	what	22 (0.75)	3 (0.12)	13.06
lamb	13 (0.53)	1 (0.03)	14.50	Lyca	9 (0.31)	0 (0.00)	10.91
merry	9 (0.37)	0 (0.00)	14.19				
all	24 (0.98)	8 (0.27)	11.54				
our	15 (0.62)	3 (0.10)	11.06				
merrily	7 (0.29)	0 (0.00)	11.03				

merry and *merrily*. *Lyca* is the second most key word from the SoE vs SoI comparison and is the girl's name featured in 'The Little Girl Lost' and 'The Little Girl Found'. The third and sixth key words from the SoI vs SoE comparison are *merry* and *merrily*, which we have already noticed appear in the top key domain for the SoI vs SoE comparison (HAPPY). Notice, though, that while the key word lists for SoI vs SoE contain words that are included in the HAPPY domain, the key word lists for SoE vs SoI do not contain any key words associated with FEAR/SHOCK, VIOLENT/ANGRY, thus providing a good example of an instance where key words on their own are not enough to capture certain important differences between texts.

We can now consider the top key words from our *Songs* comparisons: *thee* (LL 18.44), *lamb* (LL 14.50) and *what* (LL 13.06). *Thee* (second person singular object pronoun), which is now archaic but was still in use when the poems were written, occurs twenty-five times in SoI and five times in SoE, suggesting that persons, animals or objects are being addressed directly more in SoI than they are in SoE. We can see from some sample concordance lines of *thee* in SoI (see Table 37.5) that direct address is taking place where the persona narrating the poem addresses either an entity within the poem or the implied reader/listener. This relates again to Simpson's comments concerning 'active communication'.

However, looking more closely at the distribution of *thee* shows that it occurs in 'Introduction', 'The Lamb', 'A Cradle Song', 'Night', 'Infant Joy' and 'A Dream'; just six out of the nineteen poems (32 per cent) that make up SoI. So while *thee* indicates that

Table 37.5 Concordances of *thee*

Concordance			*Poem*
Piper , sit	**thee**	down and write In a book	Introduction
Little lamb , who made	**thee**	?	The Lamb
Graze after	**thee**	, and weep	Night
Sweet joy befall	**thee**	!	Infant Joy
Little wanderer , hie	**thee**	home!	A Dream

direct communication takes place, interaction of this type happens in only a minority of the poems.

We can also see from a concordance of *thee* that twelve out of the twenty-five occurrences (48 per cent) of *thee* are in 'The Lamb', thus forming a cluster which focuses our attention on that particular poem. If we look more closely at the poem, the clustering can be broken down further, with eight of the twelve instances of *thee* occurring in the first stanza, forming either the direct object or the indirect object of a series of questions:

The Little Lamb (1st stanza)

Little Lamb, who made **thee**?
Dost thou know who made **thee**?
Gave **thee** life & bid **thee** feed,
By the stream & o'er the mead;
Gave **thee** clothing of delight,
Softest clothing, wooly, bright;
Gave **thee** such a tender voice,
Making all the vales rejoice?
Little Lamb, who made **thee**?
Dost thou know who made **thee**?

(our emphasis)

(The third question, which spans lines 3 to 8, could be analysed as a series of four questions with *who* elided.)

The remaining four instances of *thee*, which occur in the second stanza of the poem, are in response to the questions posed in the first stanza. The first two introduce the answer 'Little lamb I'll tell thee' and the last two form a blessing bestowed on the lamb, 'Little lamb God bless thee!' The poem depicts a scene where (apparently) a child is talking to a lamb. It is structured in two halves, with the first half asking a series of questions and the second half answering the questions. Further analysis of this poem is possible, but we can see that the clustering of *thee* focused our attention on 'The Lamb' and that clustering helped us notice (if we had not already) that *thee* is involved in a question-and-answer structure.

The second highest key word from the SoI vs SoE comparison is *lamb*. While also occurring in 'Introduction', 'Night', 'The Chimney-Sweeper' and 'Spring', it (not surprisingly) relates mostly to the poem of the same name. (*Lambs* also occurs five times in SoI, which, if included in the *lamb*-count, could provide evidence for a recurrent theme throughout the collection – but this would need to be explored more thoroughly). This key word, then, firmly focuses our attention on 'The Lamb'. We will return to this key word shortly.

Turning now to *what*, anybody who is familiar with Blake's *Songs* will probably conjecture that this key word relates to 'The Tyger', as this poem (famously) asks a series of questions (e.g. 'What immortal hand or eye / Could frame thy fearful symmetry?'). This is indeed the case. While *what* is used in other poems, 64 per cent of occurrences are in 'The Tyger'. The top key word, again, seems to focus our attention on a specific poem and a particular device used in that poem. Looking more closely at the questions that are asked in 'The Tyger' (another example, 'And what shoulder and what art / Could twist the sinews of thy heart?') we can see that *what* forms part of a complex subject, 'what shoulder', while the object of the questions consists of a noun phrase post modified by a prepositional phrase ('*the sinews of thy heart?*'), referring to a part of a part (or parts) of the tiger.

Both 'The Tyger' and 'The Lamb' ask a series of questions, but there are some interesting differences. First, the questions in 'The Lamb' have *who* as the subject and *thee* as the object, while in 'The Tyger', *what* + *body part* forms the subject and *thy* + *body part* forms the object. The *who* in 'The Lamb' relates to a human form (God/Christ), while *thee* suggests that the persona narrating sees the Lamb as a whole. However, in 'The Tyger', the narrator does not seem to be sure what made the tiger, and the use of *thy* + *body part* suggests that the speaker sees only individual elements of the animal (a brief discussion of 'The Tyger' pertaining to this point can be found in Short 1996: 73). Lastly, while 'The Lamb' has a question/answer structure, 'The Tyger' only asks questions, but does not offer any answers.

Returning to the key word *lamb*, we can see that this word appears only once in SoE. In fact, it appears on line 20 of 'The Tyger' ('Did He who made the lamb make thee?'). This line is foregrounded in the poem as it asks a *who*-question rather than a *what*-question. It also contains the word *thee* (whereas other lines contain *thy* + *body part*), and thus seems to form a firm link back to 'The Lamb'.

The top key words seem to be directing us to specific poems in *Songs* and to specific elements within those poems that are related. These relations have not gone unnoticed by other critics and 'The Lamb' and 'The Tyger' are often seen as poems working in opposition or as contrasting elements of a connected entity. Bowra sees them as 'symbols for two different states of the human soul' (Bowra 1970: 158).

The final two key words to be considered are *all* and *our* and are used more in SoI than in SoE. Both words appear to encode inclusiveness, which we can illustrate with an investigation of *all*. *All* occurs in twelve out of nineteen poems. There are three instances of *all* being used adverbially for emphasis, while the rest of the time it is used as a (pre) determiner, either referring to the whole (eight times or 38 per cent) or functioning pronominally to refer to everyone (people) (thirteen times or 62 per cent). This contrasts with SoE where, as well as being used significantly less, *all* is used predominately as a (pre)determiner for non-human entities (71 per cent non-human whole, e.g. '*All the night*', vs 29 per cent everyone/people). There is a very general sense, then, that SoI is more inclusive than SoE; SoI includes all people.

Looking more closely at the instances of *all* when it refers to people, we can see that in 'Introduction', 'A Cradle Song', 'The Divine Image' and 'On Another's Sorrow' the reference is unrestricted, sitting within a religious context with some instances forming the object in clauses where the subject (for example, 'Thy maker' in 'A Cradle Song) can be assumed to be Christ or God.

In 'The Echoing Green' and 'The Chimney-Sweeper' *all* refers to a restricted group of people; in the former *all* refers to '*the old folk*' watching the children play; and in the latter the referent is '*thousands of sweepers*'. There is an interesting ambiguity at the end of this poem as the *all* here ('So, if all do their duty, they need not fear harm') could be read as being either restricted or unrestricted and it certainly seems that while the persona narrating more than likely is still referring to the '*thousands of sweepers*', the poet is referring to everyone else and thus commenting on the social situation and the plight of the chimney sweepers at that time.

It should be apparent that in some cases our corpus analysis validates some of the subjective critical responses to *Songs*. Of course, key comparisons can only be a starting point. In order to fully understand the lists produced by a computer tool, we must return to the text. Quantitative analysis guides qualitative analysis, which might guide further quantitative analysis.

4. Blockbuster movie scripts as an object of study

In this section we demonstrate the possibility of constructing and analysing large corpora of dramatic texts to answer questions about genre. Our motivation for studying blockbuster movies comes from existing work on the blockbuster genre within Film Studies. Here we analyse a much larger corpus than the collection of Blake's poems. We also make use of mark-up.

One problem with insights from Film Studies is that they tend to be rather more subjective and rather less detailed than is generally acceptable in stylistics. They also tend to avoid entirely the analysis of film dialogue. Nonetheless, a corpus stylistic approach can be used to validate some of the more subjective comments of film critics, and to provide insights into the linguistic construction of particular genres. To explore this, we constructed a 200,000-word corpus of action/thriller blockbuster film scripts.

The work of the film critics Tasker (1993), Jeffords (2004), Neale (2004) and Langford (2005) contain the following observations:

1. The action blockbuster is defined in part by an imbalance in its representation of gender, biased in favour of the white male hero.
2. The action blockbuster displays clear gendered roles and distinctions between genders.
3. Physical prowess is a trait of the white male hero.
4. The white male hero operates in the margins of society.

However, these are observations made on the basis of qualitative analysis of specific films. In order to explore the validity of the above claims for blockbusters generally, we set out to answer the following research questions:

1. Is there a difference in the amount of male and female speech in the action blockbuster?
2. Are gendered roles reflected in the key topics that male and female characters talk about?
3. Is physical strength and prowess a key semantic domain in action blockbuster screenplays?
4. Does male speech reflect an opposition to authority?

5. A corpus-based case study of blockbuster movie scripts

We took the definition of a blockbuster to refer to 'a film which is extraordinarily successful in financial terms' (Hall 2002: 11) as well as 'those films which need to be this successful in order to have a chance of returning a profit on their equally extraordinary production costs' (Hall 2002: 11). Our corpus comprises the following full film scripts:

1. *Air Force One* (1997)
2. *Alien* (1979)
3. *Armageddon* (1998)
4. *Basic Instinct* (1992)
5. *Bladerunner* (1982)
6. *Collateral Damage* (2002)
7. *Eight Legged Freaks* (2002)
8. *Fantastic Four* (2005)
9. *Ghostbusters* (1984)
10. *Indiana Jones and the Last Crusade* (1989)
11. *Jaws* (1975)
12. *Jurassic Park* (1993)

Practical constraints meant that we were not able to balance our corpus according to year of production. It is also the case that our corpus is relatively small and these issues are obvious caveats to our analysis. Nonetheless, our analytical findings at least provide some measure of objective support for the more subjective claims of Film Studies, which may be further tested against larger corpora.

We began by manually tagging our corpus to enable us to separate out dialogue from screen directions and subtitles. Table 37.6 outlines the mark-up we employed.

We then used Multilingual Corpus Toolkit (available from Scott Piao) to extract the male and female speech into two separate files. We used *WordSmith Tools 4.0* (Scott 2004) to calculate word frequencies and type/token ratios, and *Wmatrix* to calculate key words, key semantic domains and n-grams (for more on n-grams see Greaves and Warren, this volume).

If the Hollywood blockbuster is defined partly by an imbalance in its representation of gender, with a bias in favour of the white male hero, then we might expect to see this reflected in the distribution of speech between male and female characters. An initial count of word frequencies shows this to be the case. In the corpus, there are 64,549 tokens of male speech compared to just 13,898 tokens of female speech. This is a clear

Table 37.6 Mark-up used in the Blockbuster Corpus

Feature	*Marked-up example*
Screen directions	<sdir> INT. MISSION CONTROL – INSIDE THE GLASS-ENCASED ROOM Flip enters the room. Skip writes notes … </sdir>
Character identification and gender	<char id="Temple" gen="M"> I'm going to brief the President. What's going on here, Dan? Why didn't we have warning? </char>
Screen directions embedded in character dialogue	<char id="Temple" gen="M"><sdir> (V.O.) </sdir> Can you go secure? </char>

difference, even without a test for statistical significance. Male speech is clearly dominant in the corpus, which might suggest that male characters have a greater screen presence than female characters and are dominant in that sense. It is, of course, necessary to be careful in our claims. In terms of speech density, there is little difference between male and female speech, as the respective type/token ratios of 45.68 and 43.68 show (standardised type/token ratios were calculated every 1,000 words). It is not necessarily the case, then, that male characters are more linguistically complex characters than females. Nonetheless, in simple quantitative terms, there is evidence in the corpus that there is a bias towards male expression.

Of course, we also need to examine what characters talk *about*. To do this we examined the key words for each character, comparing male and female speech against each other, and against the 501,953 words of spoken demographic data taken from the BNC. Here are some observations from a study of the top twenty over-used key words for which there is 99.99 per cent confidence of statistical significance ($p < 0.0001$; LL critical value = 15.13). These key words are shown in Tables 37.7 and 37.8.

A number of the key words are proper nouns that turn up in one file of the corpus only. Nonetheless, it is perhaps noteworthy that *Ben*, *Johnny*, *Ash* and *Reed* are all names of male characters. No female names turn up as key in either the male or female speech. We can note further aspects of male-oriented discourse in the other key words used by the characters. In Table 37.7, the top key word for male speech when compared against the BNC Spoken Demographic Sampler is the vocative *sir*, addressed, of course, to other male characters. *Guys* too is generally used in the corpus to refer to groups of male characters. It would seem, then, that there is suggestion of a gender-based distinction between the speech of the male and female characters.

We can also note a preponderance of pronouns turning up as key words in both the male and female speech. In the male speech we have plural pronouns (*we*, *us* and *our*) and the first-person object pronoun *me*. These pronouns perhaps suggest a focus on group solidarity, which is often a feature of this genre of films. What particularly stands out in the female speech is the second-person pronoun *you*, since this is key not just in comparison with spoken language as a whole (where it is the most significant key word), but also with the male speech in the corpus (where it is the second most significant key word). There are 649 occurrences of *you* in the female data, and this focus on other

Table 37.7 Positive key words for male speech

Male speech	
Reference corpus: BNC Spoken Demographic Sampler	*Reference corpus: female speech*
sir, we, this, the, us, guys, here, world, kill, me, a_little, uh, of, to, Ben, all_right, hey, our, 're, 'em	the, of, and

Table 37.8 Positive key words for female speech

Female speech	
Reference corpus: BNC Spoken Demographic Sampler	*Reference corpus: male speech*
you, 't, me, kill, all_right, Johnny, 's, us, Ben, my, 're, to, honey, we, are, Jones, out_there, what, sorry, life	I, you, 't, Johnny, don['t], 's, do, Ash, Reed, book, sorry

characters might be described as other-directed facework (cf. self-aggrandisement, perhaps), which appears common of female characters in the corpus. Gender roles are reflected in other key words too. *Honey*, for instance, is a term of endearment only used by female characters. And of the twenty-four instances of *sorry* in the female speech, twenty-two of these are apologies. We might see this as female characters occupying a subservient position wherein they feel called upon to apologise (often for circumstances beyond their control), or alternatively we might see this as evidence that they are characters more attuned to the feelings of others. Either way, this seems to be a clear gender role.

Finally, with regard to key words, it is interesting to note that while *kill* is key in both the male and female speech, only the female speech contains a peripherally related opposite, *life*. This focus on life as well as death might be seen to further reinforce the distinction between the oppositional pair *male* and *female*. Again, this might be seen as effecting a particular gender role for female characters.

There are, of course, other conclusions that we might draw from the list of key words. The proximal deictic terms *this* and *here* in the male speech perhaps reflect a focus on the here-and-now which we might see as a genre feature of blockbuster films. These are fast-moving thrillers as opposed to sedate, reflective art-house films. The fact that the definite article is also key might be a related issue. Definiteness as opposed to indefiniteness may again be a genre feature. We can also note the interpersonal discourse markers (e.g. *hey*) that indicate aspects of characterisation.

We can also draw out some characteristics of male and female speech by examining the key topics that each sex talks about. These were calculated using the key semantic domain function in *Wmatrix* and are outlined in Tables 37.9 and 37.10.

Table 37.9 Positive key domains for male speech

Male speech	
Reference corpus: BNC Spoken Demographic Sampler	*Reference corpus: female speech*
unmatched [= items not recognised by *Wmatrix*; technical terms, some proper nouns, etc.]	in power
dead	numbers
the universe	grammatical bin
warfare, defence and the army; weapons	other proper names
speech acts	objects generally
alive	places
people: male	
location and direction	
in power	
cause and effect/connection	
objects generally	
living creatures: animals, birds, etc.	
geographical terms	
helping	
science and technology in general	
sailing, swimming, etc.	
time: general	
flying and aircraft	
open; finding; showing	
no constraint	

Table 37.10 Positive key domains for female speech

Female speech	
Reference corpus: BNC Spoken Demographic Sampler	*Reference corpus: male speech*
unmatched	pronouns
dead	discourse bin
alive	the media: books
cause and effect/connection	
warfare, defence and the army; weapons	
time: general	
speech acts	
sailing, swimming, etc.	
polite	
personal names	
law and order	
allowed	
mental actions and processes	
living creatures: animals, birds, etc.	
helping	
open; finding; showing	
the media: books	
the universe	
relationship: intimacy and sex	
location and direction	

A number of the key semantic domains listed appear to reflect features of the blockbuster genre as a whole. So we find DEAD and ALIVE and WARFARE, DEFENCE AND THE ARMY: WEAPONS turning up as key in both the male and female speech, and this is no surprise given the typical plots of blockbuster thrillers. What stands out as particularly interesting from a gender standpoint is that PEOPLE: MALE turns up as a key domain in the male speech. An extract from a concordance of words belonging to this semantic category can be seen in Figure 37.1.

Some of these terms are vocatives (*gentlemen*, *Mr*, *Mister*, *fellahs*, *Herr*) while others are nouns referring to other male characters. The concordance demonstrates the predominance of male-oriented discourse, as we noted when we examined the key word *sir* (also part of the PEOPLE: MALE domain). Nonetheless, there also seems to be some evidence of a distinction between male and female speech in those semantic domains that are key for both male and female characters. For example, Figure 37.2 and 37.3 show samples from the concordances of SPEECH ACT.

We can note that male characters use a much greater variety of speech act terms. This perhaps generates a sense of the dominance of male characters in contrast to female characters.

```
. It 's your turn to be afraid .    Gentlemen  , welcome to Air Force One . Pleas
get us home . You are a resilient   man        , Mr. President . You must forgive
ing I 'm gon na do is talk to the   guy        I ripped off . His name is Harry S
threatened mass extinction . The    men        and women of this nation united ,
l make him feel better . Thanks ,   Mr.        Chew . Hey ! You forgot your ... H
ecies is three times as big asthe   male       . Say hello to Consuela . She fill
s is getting away . I think not ,   Herr       Donovan . Not that Jones-the other
let seat . . . . No offense , you   guys       ! Very touchy . All set for the Ha
```

Figure 37.1 Concordance of PEOPLE: MALE (male speech).

and thank you . First I would	ask	you to join me in a moment of s
ission ... alone . That kid 's	name	was Jim Marshall . Most of the
me as if I am a monster , but	answer	me thiswhen your planes bombed
You 're the navigator . Scan .	Contact	traffic control . Keep trying .
t ? The press is going to want	answers	. What are we going to say ? No
In space . All we want is your	advice	in perfecting our drilling arm
ne with you lastnight ? Let me	ask	you something , Ms. Tramell ? A
go offthe hill , do you ? Full	name	, Roxanne Hardy . LastaddressCl
ee you in a minute . I-X-4-P-D	referred	to as a Nexus-6 , The Tyrell Co
dial it in . We might need to	call	you in againto look at some pho
by now ? Common sense does not	apply	tocrazy people . Might as well
ing for the " grandpa " look ?	Accused	by who ? My competitors ? Dange
. Had a little relapse , huh ?	Welcome	back . This is going to be fun
. I want to help you . Do n't	scream	. Okay , okay . But if anything
g up ? It 's not good , Pete .	Tell	him about the Twinkie . I ca n'
sir It is you Junior ! Do n't	call	me that , please . But what are
of three brothers whoswore an	oath	to find the Grailand to guard i
l Dave Axelrod in New York and	tell	him this is from me , and he ow
avicula which we already found	articulating	to the cuboid . Dr. Sattler ! D
peers for too long . Welcome ,	welcome	! Mr. Hammond never lets me pub

Figure 37.2 Concordance of SPEECH ACT (male speech).

, despite strong international	criticism	... Has chosen to join our fight
t . Swell . Yeah . You know the	answer	to that . Do n't worry , you 'll
. Meet me atthe air lock . You	tell	me . I guess the alarm went off
ay ? A.J.-- When you get back ,	ask	them if you can keep the suit It
No . If I moved out now I 'd be	acknowledging	that what happened was real . I
break a lease I 'll know who to	call	. Talk to my accountant . Doctor
hey 're so beautiful . They 're	condemned	, are n't they ? Even those embr

Figure 37.3 Concordance of SPEECH ACT (female speech).

A closer look at some of the key semantic domains in the female speech also reveals gender-related characterisation. POLITE is a key domain, for instance, comprised entirely of thanking expressions, and its absence in the male speech perhaps suggests a gender-related character distinction. In the PERSONAL NAMES category in the female speech, what is striking is that of the 285 instances that comprise the category, 212 are first names. This perhaps reflects a difference in interpersonal relationships expressed by male and female characters. Ervin-Tripp's classic study of sociolinguistic rules of address (1972) suggests that use of first-names indicates social closeness, and it is interesting to note that this seems to be practised by female characters to a statistically significant level but not by male characters. We might hypothesise from this that male characters in blockbusters are emotionally more distant than female characters. Further support for this conceptualisation of male and female characters can be found in the fact that a positive key word in female speech is the endearment term *honey*, whereas such terms are not reflected in the male key words. It also seems noteworthy that RELATIONSHIP: INTIMACY AND SEX is a domain that is key only in the female speech. An extract from the concordance for this domain is presented in Figure 37.4, and what it perhaps suggests is that only female characters in blockbusters are explicitly characterised as intimate and/or sexual beings. Seen in tandem with the findings from the PERSONAL NAMES analysis, this supports the view that females in blockbusters are characterised as strongly emotional whereas males are not.

Finally, we can briefly comment on those key domains revealed when comparing male and female speech against each other. At the top of the list of key domains for female speech compared against male speech we find PRONOUNS, the vast majority of which are personal pronouns. There seems to be some evidence here of female characters

ormation . Swell . Did you ever	sleep with	Ash ? No . What about you . No .
Mama goodbye . Never too old to	kiss	your Mama . We need to know what
yone last night . Yes . I liked	fucking	him . I do n't really feel like
t the pleasure . Didn'tyou ever	fuck	anybody else whileyou were marri
ove to me . You were n't making	love	. I thought you quit . Top drawe
mething 's on withyou . You 're	sleeping with	her , aren'tyou ? My interest is
ng whether I 'm an android or a	lesbian	? I would n't let him . I should
t ? s okay . Maybe you ? re not	gay	after all . What are you talking
ndering when you 'd walk by . "	Sensual	blind chick seeks three-ton , ro
the physical sense . That 's so	romantic	. I beg your pardon ! Just where
, it 's not his shark . Nobody	kisses	hands anymore . I do n't know wh

Figure 37.4 Concordance of RELATIONSHIP: INTIMACY AND SEX (female speech).

tan 's self- proclaimed	dictator	, General Ivan Stravanav
crank watching CNN . No	sir	. Trace confirms the cal
One . They 've retaken	control	of the aircraft . Iraq ,
only twelve telescopes	powerful	enough to see it right n
ytalked about when they	set themselves down	in front of thecampfire
They ? relocked . Glass	won	? t stop them ! Hurry up
own the hall phoned the	manager	. I climbed on the windo
I 'm afraid ... but the	Knight	promised that two " mark
in the ignition , Your	Highness	. You shall have camels
uint ? Serve yourself ,	Chief	. Shark-liver oil ! Best
t 's what ? I found the	command	to restore the original

Figure 37.5 Concordance of IN POWER (male speech).

working harder at interpersonal relationships than their male counterparts. In contrast, the top key domain for male speech compared against female speech is IN POWER. Interestingly, while physical strength and prowess is not explicitly reflected in a key semantic domain (as our research question supposes it might), the concordance extract in Figure 37.5 of IN POWER demonstrates the predominance of power as a theme of male speech. This may be seen as tangentially related to the notion of strength and prowess.

We can now turn to clusters of words, and here we can also observe a number of interesting issues concerning n-grams in male and female speech. The largest clusters in the male speech are 5-grams, seen in Table 37.11.

The first 5-gram is an interrogative that perhaps reflects the element of surprise typical of blockbuster plots. The other 5-grams are all grammatical negatives. These seem to relate to the strong emphasis that blockbusters place on the 'complicating action' in plot terms, that the main protagonists then have to resolve. In the female speech there is just one 5-gram that occurs five times: *I don't want to*. Like the male 5-grams, it is a grammatical negative, but unlike the male examples it expresses a lack of desire to act, which might again be related to a distinction in gender roles. The 4-grams in the female speech are as in Table 37.12.

Table 37.11 5-grams (male speech)

5-gram	*Frequency (5+ only)*
what are you doing here	8
i don t know I	7
i don t know if	6
i don t know where	6
i didn t know you	5
i don t think so	5
i don t have time	5

Table 37.12 4-grams (female speech)

4-gram	*Frequency (5+ only)*
i don t know	14
i m sorry i	10
don t want to	9
what are you doing	9
what do you want	8
why don t you	6
what s the matter	6
i don t want	5

We can note that the most frequent 4-gram utilises the same four initial words as the most frequent male 5-gram, which again we might see as relating to the complicating action of the plot and the difficulties these cause for the characters. With regard to the other 4-grams, again we see a concentration on expressing a lack of desire to act (*I don't want, don't want to*) as well as an apology (*I'm sorry I*) and more interrogatives than we find in the male speech.

Our analysis so far has begun to reveal some potential distinguishing elements of male and female speech in the corpus. From these results we might hypothesise further and say that this gender distinction is a feature of the blockbuster movie as a genre. Nonetheless, our analysis is of a relatively small corpus and one problem concerns its representativeness. In recent years, for example, there has been an increase in blockbuster movies with strong female lead characters (e.g. the *Lara Croft: Tomb Raider* films) and it might be argued that our corpus is skewed because it does not include sufficient numbers of these particular kinds of blockbusters. One possibility, then, would be to compare a sub-set of such films against the other films in our corpus.

Nonetheless, our findings perhaps allow for some tentative answers to the research questions we posed above. We found that there is indeed a difference in the amount of male and female speech in the blockbuster movie, and that male speech clearly dominates (question 1). Gendered roles also appear to be reflected in the key topic that male and female characters talk about, with a greater concentration on intimacy and the mechanics of personal relations in the female speech (question 2). Physical strength and prowess is not a key semantic domain for male speech *per se* (question 3), though this element of the male character might be said to be reflected in the IN POWER domain that is significant in the male speech. With regard to question 4, there does not seem to be any obvious reflection of a male opposition to authority; indeed, the contents of the PEOPLE: MALE domain suggest a clear recognition of hierarchical roles (evident in such vocatives as *sir*). However, further qualitative analysis of the corpus may well reveal more insights with regard to this question. Such analysis would also be likely to reveal further linguistic features of dialogue and screen directions that might constitute defining features of the action/thriller blockbuster genre generally.

We aim to have shown in this chapter how corpora of poetry and drama can be used to validate or invalidate the more subjective analyses of literary critics, and – especially in the case of drama – how a corpus linguistic methodology makes possible the kind of analysis that would not be achievable through manual qualitative analysis. In so doing, we hope to have shown how, for the stylistician, a corpus-based methodology provides a way of achieving the more objective kind of analysis that is the hallmark of the stylistic approach to criticism.

Acknowledgement

We are grateful to Kelly Stanger for her assistance in constructing and tagging the film corpus.

Further reading

Hoey, M., Mahlberg, M., Stubbs, M. and Teubert, W. (eds) (2007) *Text, Discourse and Corpora. Theory and Analysis*. London: Continuum. (In particular Chapter 7 'Corpus Stylistics: Bridging the Gap between Linguistic and Literary Studies' by Michaela Mahlberg discusses some of the issues covered in this chapter.)

O'Halloran, K. A. (2007) 'The Subconscious in James Joyce's "Eveline": A Corpus Stylistic Analysis which Chews on the "Fish Hook"', *Language and Literature* 16(3): 227–44. (This article is an excellent example of corpus stylistics in practice that also deals with some of the theoretical issues surrounding the corpus stylistic methodology.)

References

Bottrall, M. (ed.) (1970) *Songs of Innocence and Experience: A Casebook*. London: Macmillan.

Bowra, C. M. (1970) 'Songs of Innocence and Experience', in M. Bottrall (ed.) *Songs of Innocence and Experience: A Casebook*. London: Macmillan, pp. 136–59.

Ervin-Tripp, S. M. (1972) 'Sociolinguistic Rules of Address', in J. B. Pride and J. Holmes (eds) *Sociolinguistics*. London: Penguin, pp. 225–40.

Hall, S. (2002) 'Tall Revenue Features: The Genealogy of the Modern Blockbuster', in S. Neale (ed.) *Genre and Contemporary Hollywood*. London: British Film Institute, pp. 11–26.

Jeffords, S. (2004) '*Breakdown*: White Masculinity, Class and US Action-adventure Films', in Y. Tasker (ed.) *Action and Adventure Cinema*. London: Routledge, pp. 219–34.

Langford, B. (2005) *Film Genre: Hollywood and Beyond*. Edinburgh: Edinburgh University Press.

Mahlberg, M. (2007) 'A Corpus Stylistic Perspective on Dickens' *Great Expectations*', in M. Lambrou and P. Stockwell (eds) *Contemporary Stylistics*. London: Continuum, pp. 19–31.

Neale, S. (2004) 'Action-adventure as Hollywood Genre', in Y. Tasker (ed.) *Action and Adventure Cinema*. London: Routledge, pp. 71–83.

O'Halloran, K. A. (2007) 'Corpus-assisted Literary Evaluation', *Corpora* 2(1): 33–63.

Rayson, P. (2008) 'Wmatrix: A Web-based Corpus Processing Environment', Computing Department, Lancaster University, available at http://ucrel.lancs.ac.uk/wmatrix/

Rayson, P., Archer, D., Piao, S. and McEnery, T. (2004) 'The UCREL Semantic Analysis System', in *Proceedings of the Workshop on Beyond Named Entity Recognition Semantic Labelling for NLP Tasks, in Association with the 4th International Conference on Language Resources and Evaluation* (LREC 2004). Lisbon: LREC, pp. 7–12.

Scott, M. (2004) *WordSmith Tools 4.0*. Oxford: Oxford University Press.

Semino, E. and Short, M. (2004) *Corpus Stylistics: Speech, Writing and Thought Presentation in a Corpus of English Writing*. London: Routledge.

Short, M. (1996) *Exploring the Language of Poems, Plays and Prose*. London: Longman.

Simpson, M. (1993) 'Blake's *Songs of Innocence and Experience*', in J. Lucas (ed.) *William Blake*. New York: Longman, pp. 189–200.

Tasker, Y. (1993) *Spectacular Bodies: Gender, Genre and the Action Cinema*. London: Routledge.

38

How can corpora be used to explore literary speech representation?

Carolina P. Amador-Moreno

1. Real and fictional speech: similarities and differences

The (re-)creation or (re-)construction of speech in the written text has long been a central issue in literary research (see for example Page 1973; Fowler 1981; Toolan 1992). A number of studies in stylistics (Leech and Short 1981: 159–73; Hughes 1996: 78–89; Simpson 2004: 102–8) have also discussed how fictional conversations differ from real-life conversations. Fictional dialogues often display traces of orality to a greater or lesser extent, but whatever the precise characteristics of this representation of spoken language, verbal interaction in fiction can only be understood and interpreted in relation to the same rules of discourse that govern everyday interaction. As Fowler (1981: 21) points out, fictional dialogues are built upon models of language use which tend to occur in 'non fictional' texts (conversation, meetings, political speeches, news reports, etc.). Although evidently lacking the spontaneity of spoken oral interaction, fictional dialogue is, nonetheless, rooted in ordinary discourse and everyday situations.

However, as indicated by Ives, it is evident that when it comes to fictionalising spoken language, we must concede that there is a degree of incompleteness, given that 'the author is an artist, not a linguist or a sociologist, and his purpose is literary rather than scientific' (Ives 1950: 138). The transcription or reduction of speech to writing (even in the context of courtroom proceedings, parliamentary debates or journalism) always involves a loss (see Toolan 1992: 31): elements of prosody, repetitions, false starts, pause, gesture, voice quality and grammatically complex discourse elements are inevitably lost in transferring speech to writing. In that sense, the authorial mimesis of oral language and the significance of the selection of spoken features that an author makes in order to represent characters' voices is of interest to linguists and stylisticians. How a particular author imagines a speech community into existence is rather telling in terms of the degree of language awareness shown by that author. Also, how a particular character is perceived by the reader is very much subject to the inclusion of certain linguistic features, which often also contribute to creating a literary and linguistic environment that renders a story believable and engaging. 'In skilful hands,' Walpole has argued, 'fictional dialogue can suggest not only the personality, but the sex, age, education, occupation, geographic region, and general social status of the characters' (Walpole 1974: 191).

Although all this can be achieved by the author through descriptive exposition, a more direct way of illustrating it is through dialogues unmediated by the narrative voice (see Short *et al.* 2002: 335). While an analysis of a character's reported speech may be useful, especially if analysed separately from their direct speech, focusing only on the dialogues between the characters assures us that the direct speech represents the author's portrayal of the language of those characters. As Short *et al.* (ibid.) point out, with reported speech, however, the reader depends on the narrator's second-hand and possibly unreliable interpretation of that character's language. Unless, of course, we are dealing with autobiography, in which case it has to be assumed that the narrator's portrayal of the voice of their character is intended to be realistic, something that would add to the reliability of the story and contribute to its presentation as real or authentic. This will be discussed further in the following sections.

Speech representation in literature

Linguistic elements associated with language variation may be especially interesting when it comes to analysing a particular author's use of language. The use of non-standard or regionally marked patterns of cohesion, forms of reference and address, strategies of politeness and discourse markers is as much a characteristic of literary dialogue as conversation (Johnstone 1991: 462). In general, non-standard forms are often found in fictional dialogues and are employed as an indicator of social or regional differences which depict a character (Taavitsainen *et al.* 1999: 13). In Chaucer's *Reeve's Tale*, one of the first English pieces of work to introduce characters speaking a distinctive dialect, the two clerks speak northern English, which contributes to the realist effect sought by the author. The fact that their language is so different from the rest of the tale clearly indicates, as Brook (1969: 201) points out, that the differences are intended. The use of dialect in this case adds effectiveness to the tale.

Considering the role and effectiveness of non-standard language in a text is very much part of what Kirk (1999) refers to as the stylistic approach to the study of dialect. Kirk establishes a distinction between the stylistic and the dialectological approach which has been used in historical studies as a source of evidence of spoken language in the absence of direct spoken data. The dialectological approach, therefore, uses literary data as evidence of the language spoken during a particular period, whereas the stylistic approach focuses on the analysis of language, and its functions within a text.

The use of literary data as a valid source of linguistic evidence is controversial, though, and it has been questioned on the grounds of realism and consistency. However, while it is true that a certain degree of caution is essential when it comes to analysing literary dialect, it is important to bear in mind that, as pointed out by Labov (1972: 109), as long as it is observed and evaluated in relation to the spoken language, the study of literary dialect can be a valuable complement to the evidence of real speech data. The term 'literary dialect' is used here in the sense of 'the representation of non-standard speech literature that is otherwise written in standard English … and aimed at a general readership', as defined by Shorrocks (1996: 386). A more detailed discussion of this and other related concepts is also offered in Ives (1950) and Blake (1981). Comparisons of results drawn from literary sources with real spoken data, in the case of contemporary literature, and with other text types such as emigrant letters (see Montgomery 1995; García-Bermejo and Montgomery 2001), in the case of older texts, can offer interesting insights into the degree of accuracy in the representation of the spoken mode.

One of the main problems that the use of literary dialect data as linguistic evidence can present, however, is that of authenticity. On the part of the author, the realist effect has to be negotiated on the basis of an inevitable attempt to strike the balance between standard and non-standard forms, so that the text is not so full of dialect that it alienates the readers or diverts their attention away from the story. From a stylistic perspective, an author's ability to represent the nuances and complexities of spoken language in an authentic way adds enormous value to their work.

Whether studying this point from a stylistic or a dialectological angle, most researchers working on the representation of dialect in literature are conscious of the fact that consistency is something that is not found in real spoken dialect. No speaker of any particular vernacular, real or fictional, will incorporate every possible feature of that variety into their speech, nor produce speech containing the same features as every other speaker of that variety (see Cohen Minnick 2001). As Tamasi puts it:

> Even if a speaker does use a feature which is associated with a particular dialect, he or she may not use it 100 percent of the time. Therefore, if authors are to portray dialect in literature accurately, they must also incorporate variation in the speech of each individual character. And the reader must keep in mind that when a writer does incorporate linguistic variation into the speech of one character, the writer is actually giving the character complex, realistic human qualities.
>
> (Tamasi 2001: 135)

In her analysis of *Uncle Tom's Cabin*, Burkette (2001) points out that what is considered by some critics as 'inconsistency' might well be a testament to the author's observation of actual speech. Jonsson (2009), adopting a stylistic angle, points out that in the artistic representations of Chicano language use, some predominant features of this vernacular are left out whereas others have been exaggerated in order to create a dramatic effect. Meanwhile, McCafferty (2009), taking a sociolinguistic perspective, draws attention to the fact that this type of inconsistency is precisely what one expects in real spoken language, and it is this kind of variety that makes the speech of fictional characters accurate and realistic. Indeed, variation in an individual's speech is socially contingent: that is, style-shifting correlates with differences in addressee, context, personal goals of the speaker, etc.

2. Using a corpus to compare real and represented speech

Computers have opened new avenues in the field of text analysis (see, for example, Louw 1997; Rochester 2001; Adolphs 2006; and Hoey *et al.* 2007). However, like every other field that the tools of corpus analysis can be applied to, in text analysis, computers are only useful in helping the researcher to achieve a more rigorous study of a particular text. It is then up to the researcher to decide how that data should be interpreted (see Stubbs 2006; Baker 2007: 89). At their address to the IVACS Symposium in Nottingham in 2006, Peter Stockwell and Martin Wynne drew attention to the fact that, despite the pessimism with which it has been received by some, the general field of Corpus Stylistics satisfies the demand for empirical evidence, and allows for transparent and systematic means of interrogating literary critical positions (Stockwell and Wynne 2006).

The use of computers for systematic analysis of fictional dialogue is still in its infancy, and yet, in order to assess literary dialect, for example, we need to determine the features used artistically by an author or a group of authors belonging to the same literary movement and to compare them (if possible) with other contemporary evidence of local speech. With that purpose in mind, recent research has looked at the correspondence between fictional and real spoken data: a special issue of the journal *Language and Literature* dedicated to 'Literary Dialect Analysis with Computer Assistance' contains some interesting papers where the authors' intentions are to demonstrate that the use of computer assistance offers a better means of characterising the language used in texts than by relying only on intuition (see, for example, Burkette 2001; Cohen Minnick 2001).

Some of the studies included in that volume make use of a programme called *LinguaLinks*, one of the software packages that allow the study of language and literature (see Kretzschmar 2001). Other more widely known software suites also used for text analysis are *WordSmith Tools* (Scott 1999; see also Scott this volume), and *TACT* (Lancashire *et al.* 1996). *Perl* and *Python* are also available; however some researchers consider them less user-friendly (see Rochester 2001). *Corpus Presenter*, described in Hickey (2003), consists of twenty-seven programs and, like the packages mentioned above, it allows one to retrieve data from a corpus of one's own. The basic tasks that all these suites perform are very similar: they generate statistics, word lists, frequency charts, concordances, lists of collocations, etc., all of which may be revealing in the context of literary dialect, for example, as will be shown below.

As was suggested above, the use of computerised corpora has facilitated the study of language variation both diachronically (i.e. allowing us to study language development over time) and synchronically (i.e. by exploring language use at a particular point in time). When studying literary dialect, diachronic studies can throw light on the developments of dialectal features by looking at written sources, whereas the synchronic study of different varieties of English allows us to compare written and spoken corpora. Thus, a corpus such as the Helsinki Corpus, which contains around 1.6 million words from the Old English, Middle English and Early Modern English periods, may be used for diachronic study, whereas others, such as the International Corpus of English (ICE), contain both written and spoken data to allow for the synchronic study of different varieties of English (see chapter by Lee, this volume, for extensive coverage of available corpora). In both diachronic and synchronic studies literary dialect can lend itself to two basic types of approaches: intra-textual and inter-textual analyses (see Adolphs 2006). An example of an intra-textual approach would be Culpeper (2002), who compares the speech of six of the characters of *Romeo and Juliet* with all of the other characters in the play. The inter-textual approach, in contrast, is employed in Cohen Minnick's study (2001) of the use that Mark Twain makes of dialect. She compares the features of African American Vernacular English that characterise Jim's speech in *Huckleberry Finn* with those documented by other researchers and in the Linguistic Atlas of the Middle and South Atlantic States (LAMSAS) (see Kretzschmar *et al.* 1993). On a similar topic, Tamasi's (2001) study is led by a different type of inter-textuality: she concentrates on the language of one particular character by looking at that character's speech across different novels. In her study, Tamasi analyses the speech of the character of Huck Finn in *The Adventures of Tom Sawyer* and *The Adventures of Huckleberry Finn* in order to observe how Twain's skill in producing literary dialect develops over time. Such a study, she claims, can reveal the relationship between the development of a character and the development of the representation of that character's speech.

The inter-textual approach is particularly relevant in synchronic studies of literary dialect given that, since the advent of recording devices, we can now compare literary dialogues with real spoken data. The use of a baseline corpus of contemporary spoken language makes comparisons between fictional and real spoken data possible. It enables the identification of how cultural and social contexts are represented (Mahlberg 2007: 221). The Limerick Corpus of Irish English (henceforth LCIE, see Farr *et al.* 2002), for example, may be used as a baseline for Irish Literature (O'Keeffe and Amador-Moreno, 2009). The LCIE, which was recorded between 2001 and 2005, is a one-million-word spoken corpus of Irish English (hereafter IrE) discourse. The transcribed recordings that form the corpus range across age, gender, socio-economic background and geographical location, and they include conversations recorded in a wide variety of mostly informal settings throughout Ireland (excluding Northern Ireland). This makes it an invaluable source for the comparison of real and fictional contemporary IrE. It allows us to analyse, for instance, the distribution and use of the widely known structure *be + after + V-ing* (e.g. *I'm after breaking the pen*) a way of expressing a recently completed action in IrE (O'Keeffe and Amador-Moreno, 2009). By looking at word frequency lists, concordances, etc., generated by the software, it is also possible to compare the use of discourse markers in the LCIE data with their occurrence in contemporary writing (Amador-Moreno, 2010), as will be shown in the next section.

When setting out to study the (re-)creation of a variety of English, of course, one has to consider whether the text(s) one is interested in is already part of a corpus. The test corpus supplied with *Corpus Presenter* contains a small corpus of written IrE which, although consisting mostly of drama, is useful for those researchers interested in stylistic and diachronic analyses of this variety. One could also consider the possibility of building one's own corpus, especially for the study of contemporary Irish writing, in which case copyright issues would also need to be taken into account (see for example Sinclair 2005; McEnery *et al.* 2006: 77–9, see also chapters by Reppen and Nelson, this volume). There are several ways of developing written corpora (Renouf 1987; Wynne 2005). In order to create a corpus, one may sometimes have to scan a written text, edit it manually and turn it into a searchable corpus. However, before embarking on what could be an arduous and time-consuming task, we should consider that a number of internet sites and archives exist nowadays that allow us to have access to spoken and written electronic texts (see Lee, this volume). These are worth considering, as they were conceived with the intention of collecting, cataloguing and preserving electronic literary sources that are made available to the large research and teaching community. Written texts of this type can be obtained from archives such as Project Gutenberg and the Oxford Text Archive. Project Gutenberg contains, at the time of writing, over 28,000 books in electronic format which can be downloaded for free (however, Mahlberg 2007: 224 points out that Project Gutenberg does not follow consistent standards for the digitalisation of its texts). The Oxford Text Archive is also freely accessible and it distributes thousands of texts. Both sites allow users to download texts that can then be saved and run through a computer program like the ones mentioned above.

3. What can a corpus tell us about speech representation in literature?

Quantitative approaches to literary dialect allow for an empirical analysis of the actual language used in a particular text or set of texts. However, a qualitative analysis is also necessary in order to determine the artistic value of the work. In that sense, both types of approaches can be seen as complementary (see Biber *et al.* 1998: 7–8).

One of the first questions the researcher must ask when considering speech representation in literature is whose speech is worth analysing. One option would be to isolate all the dialogues in a novel in order to concentrate on the direct representation of the speaker(s) of interest. In analysing Irish novelist Roddy Doyle's fictionalisation of IrE, Hehir (2005), for example, focuses on the dialogues from the novel *The Snapper* only. Sometimes, however, one may be also interested in the author's voice, especially if we are dealing with autobiographical novels. In that case, one should include not just the dialogues but the whole novel.

Semino and Short (2004) propose a classification of speech representation that is worth taking into consideration in this context, as it allows for a more exhaustive account of the (re-)presentation of speech in writing. Building on the work of Leech and Short (1981), they develop a manual annotation system for speech, writing and thought which is based on the following main categories:

N Narration (e.g. She looked at her compassionately)

NRSA Narrative Report of Speech Acts (e.g. She looked at her compassionately and told her about the death of her friend.)

IS Indirect speech (e.g. She looked at her compassionately and told her that her friend had died. She was shocked.)

FIS Free Indirect Speech (e.g. She looked at her compassionately. Her friend had died!)

DS Direct Speech (e.g. She looked at her compassionately and said 'Maureen has died')

FDS Free Direct Speech (e.g. She looked at her compassionately. 'Maureen has died'. She was shocked)

The application of Leech and Short's model led them to extend and refine some of these categories. The refined categories can then be more easily located once a particular narrative has been tagged following the above classification. This tagging system facilitates the study of spoken features, something that will be revisited in Section 5. Having discussed some of the key issues of fictional speech representation, this chapter will now turn to a case study of two Irish English features, which will illustrate how spoken features in general can be analysed through computer analysis.

4. Case study of corpus-based stylistic analysis

In order to demonstrate some possible uses of corpus-based stylistic analyses, this case study focuses on the Irish novel *The Curious Incident of the Dog in the Nightdress*, where the use of discourse-level features greatly contributes towards the depiction of the characters. The discourse marker *like*, and the Irish English construction *be* + *after* + *V-ing* are chosen here as an illustration of how quantitative data can be used to complement qualitative stylistic analysis in terms of speech representation.

One of the most complete studies of the literary representation of Irish English was carried out in 1980 by Sullivan, who argues that literary forms and their variation 'are not as fictitious as has been suggested and may, when carefully scrutinized, constitute a legitimate source of entry into otherwise inaccessible language situations and linguistic histories' (Sullivan 1980: 195). Indeed, as has been argued here, literary sources are sometimes the only evidence we have in order to determine the language of a particular period, and careful scrutiny of Irish English can now be achieved by means of computer analysis.

Word frequency information is very useful in identifying the main features of a corpus. Table 38.1 shows the top twenty most frequently used words in the LCIE.

As Table 38.1 shows, the word *like* is the fourteenth most frequently used word, something that may not surprise those familiar with this variety of English, which seems to have adopted it as a common discourse marker in recent times. This is certainly something that Dublin best-selling author Paul Howard has observed too and decided to exploit in the *Ross O'Carroll-Kelly* series, a set of eight novels and a play, at the time of writing, where the protagonist, a south-side Dublin rich kid called Ross, narrates his adventures. This set of novels, presented as the oral narrative of Ross, 'as told to Paul Howard', has been praised by the critics for its accurate portrayal of the type of English spoken in some parts of Dublin. That is also the general impression readers are left with after reading the novels. There is, nevertheless, empirical evidence that may help us buttress that claim and this can be achieved by means of computer analysis.

When one compares the frequency list from the LCIE shown in Table 38.1 with that obtained from a small written corpus of 91,008 words such as the novel *The Curious Incident of the Dog in the Nightdress [CIDN]* (O'Carroll-Kelly 2005), one observes that *like* features even higher in the rank of most frequent words (Table 38.2). Notice also that the frequency list in the right column shows the use of what intuition would tell us could be another discourse marker: the word *roysh* (spelt phonetically to indicate the Dublin pronunciation of *right*).

Table 38.1 The top twenty most frequently used words in the Limerick Corpus of Irish English

Word	Frequency	%	Word	Frequency	%
the	36,171	3.84	in	13,401	1.46
I	24,324	2.65	was	10,419	1.14
and	23,709	2.59	is	10,009	1.09
you	23,016	2.51	like	8,667	0.95
to	20,140	2.20	know	8,054	0.88
it	18,245	1.99	he	7,365	0.80
a	17,753	1.94	on	7,281	0.79
that	14,868	1.62	they	7,269	0.79
of	13,948	1.52	have	6,831	0.75
yeah	13,692	1.49	there	6,628	0.72

Source: Data supplied through personal communication with Fiona Farr and Anne O'Keeffe.

Table 38.2 The twelve most frequent words in LCIE and CIDN

N	LCIE	THE CURIOUS INCIDENT…
1	the	and
2	I	the
3	you	I
4	and	to
5	to	like
6	it	I
7	a	of
8	that	I'm
9	of	you
10	yeah	in
11	in	he
12	was	roysh (= right)

Source: The Curious Incident of the Dog in the Nightdress (Dublin: Penguin, 2005), reproduced with permission.

A comparison of the spoken and the written data can provide interesting insights in relation to the fictional use of these two discourse markers in Paul Howard's narrative (Amador-Moreno, 2010).

A detailed analysis of the occurrences of *like* can be carried out by retrieving the concordance lines of this word in the novel. An example of ten concordance lines is provided in Figure 38.1 for illustration.

In all there are 1,961 occurrences of *like*. By carefully scrutinising each concordance line individually it becomes evident that, since what we are interested in is the use of *like* as a discourse marker, certain conventional grammatical uses of *like* (as a preposition, conjunction, suffix, straightforward adverbial or lexical verb), as well as quotatives, have to be excluded from the analysis. A step-by-step analysis of this type would, therefore, involve five different stages: Step 1, devising the criteria for what one wants to include in the study (in order to do this it might be useful to run a pilot search first and look at what type of patterns come up); Step 2, finding all the occurrences of the item one is interested in (i.e. obtaining a concordance of the search item); Step 3, discarding the uses

1penalty in the Leinster Schools Cup final in 1998, and I sort of, **like**, collapse into Sorcha's orms and she's going, 'Don't worry,
2 it and he's, like, ripping the piss on a major scale. He's got, **like**, his orm around her shoulder and he's going, 'You're a very
3 re. My phone beeps and it's, like, a text message. It's from, **like**, Sorcha, the defiant wench. It's like, Wher r u? OMG d bouncrs
4 ar Social Science in Trinity, nipped her a couple of times in, **like** , Reynord's and once in the Ice Bor last summer, we're talking
5 ompany. She goes, 'Fionn wouldn't hurt a fly, Ross,' and I'm **like**, 'Let's not take that chance,' but then totally out of the blue,
6 women's mini-marathon has taken a detour this year. After, **like**, ten minutes of driving around, roysh, I finally pull up outside
7 r, maybe for, like, Greystones, when all of a sudden I get this, **like**, tap on the shoulder, roysh, and I spin around and who is it-
8 t, maybe even more, if there's actually such a thing. I sort of, **like**, cup my hands around my mouth, roysh, and go, 'Come in,
9 f for being so focking weedy. She goes, 'What a pity.' I try to, **like**, change the subject. I'm there, 'How are things going with that
10 eyes, like a mongoose hypnotising a snake. Her eyes are, **like** , filling up with tears and I'd have nipped her there and then,

Figure 38.1 Concordance lines for *like* from CIDN corpus.

that are of no interest for one's study (i.e. cleaning the concordance); and Step 4, analysing the examples one is left with in order to draw our conclusions. This last stage can be subdivided into (a) formal analysis and (b) functional analysis.

In the case study provided, Step 4 involves, first of all, discarding the uses of *like* that are of no interest. Once the grammatical, lexical and quotative tokens are discarded, we can proceed to Step 4a. The total number of lines where *like* is used as a discourse marker is 978, and it occurs in five different main positions:

1 *Preceding (and within) a noun phrase,* e.g. Excuse me? You've got, ***like***, a child?
2 *Preceding (and within) an adjective phrase,* e.g. like I'm a child and he's trying to be, ***like***, patient with me; He just seemed, ***like*** … happy, with his, like, independence.
3 *Preceding (or within) a prepositional phrase,* e.g. I heard that from Wendy, who's, ***like***, in the Institute.
4 *Preceding an adverbial phrase,* e.g. JP is, like, holding her hand and talking to her really, ***like***, seriously.
5 *With verb phrases,* e.g. and the borman just, ***like***, shrugs and focks off down the other end of the …

Step 5 then could involve comparing literary and real spoken data. With regard to function, however, a comparison of the mid-position examples in both corpora shows that the functional behaviour of the discourse marker *like* in the fictional and non-fictional contexts in Irish English is very similar: it generally indicates fuzzy thought; it is used as a hedge, often with a degree of hesitation involved. A close look at both the spoken and the fictional data reveals that mid-position *like* is used when a speaker is searching for an appropriate expression, or an alternative term. It is also very often used with numbers, as a synonym of 'roughly', 'approximately' and it tends to be employed when a speaker/character is trying to emphasise the expression of certain feelings, when exaggerating, or describing unusual actions/surprising events. All of these uses have also sociolinguistic and pragmatic implications which are revealing from both a stylistic point of view and a dialectological perspective.

Other Irish English features such as the *be* + *after* + *V-ing* (e.g. *'She's after changing the code'*) referred to above, can also be subject to corpus analysis. This Irish-influenced construction, which roughly equates to the present perfect aspect in Standard English, is probably the signature construction of Irish English. It has often been used in the portrayal of Irish characters in literature, theatre and cinema, and, although sometimes dismissed as stage Irish and outmoded, it is still widely used in contemporary spoken interactions. By comparing contemporary writing with the LCIE, Amador-Moreno and O'Keeffe (2006) show that this construction is not simply a feature of literary Irish English, but a characteristic element of the English used in Ireland up to the present day. The analysis of the concordance lines obtained in both the fictional and non-fictional contexts indicates that apart from indicating immediacy/recency, the use of this structure marks speaker's perspective, allowing speakers to incorporate their own attitude, as the following examples illustrate:

(1) Your tart is just **after falling** down your lap! [LCIE]
(2) MARY [calling out to her] What is it you're **after whispering** above with himself?

(Synge, *The Tinker's Wedding*)

By looking closely at the patterns of use in the corpus, Amador-Moreno and O'Keeffe's analysis of the *be + after + V-ing construction* also confirms that this structure is frequently found in narrative situations, as pointed out in previous research. However, what all the examples classified as 'narrative device' have in common in the concordance analysis is a dramatic component, whereby the *after* construction presents events as emotionally vivid in the narration.

McCafferty (2005) also examines the use of this structure in eighteenth-century Irish author William Carleton's stories by means of corpus analysis. By comparing Carleton's data with that found in the work of eighteenth- and nineteenth-century Irish writers, McCafferty concludes that the *after*-construction, which has a perfective meaning in present-day Irish English, had a future sense in the eighteenth and nineteenth century. In a more diachronic study, McCafferty's data (2004), drawn from literary representations of Irish English from the late seventeenth century to the present, show that the coexistence of future and perfect uses of this construction coincided with the spread of bilingualism and language shift in Ireland, which facilitated different types of language transfer.

In the context of Irish drama, Hickey (2003: 25) also looks at the occurrence of the *after*-construction and other typically Irish English constructions in order to discuss how a corpus-based analysis of the language of an author's work may well be more indicative of that author's own personal style. Hickey (ibid.) carries out a statistical analysis of two structures across six plays by John Millington Synge where the *be + after + V-ing* construction is analysed alongside the *subordinating and* structure, another Irish-influenced construction where the conjunction *and* is used as a subordinator, thus establishing an asymmetrical relation between the two clauses linked (e.g. Seán rode the bike all the way home *and him holding* two bags of shopping). Hickey's search shows a decrease in the use of these structures from the early plays to the late ones, as illustrated in Table 38.3 and 38.4 (adapted from Hickey 2003: 25).

Synge's decreasing use of these Irish English structures would indicate, according to Hickey, that at the earliest stage of his career this playwright had a special interest in

Table 38.3 Sentences containing *be +after + V-ing*

Be + after + V-ing	*Occurs*	*Total*	*Percentage*
Riders to the Sea (1902)	12	205	5.85%
In the Shadow of the Glen (1902)	11	193	5.70%
The Tinker's Wedding (1904)	13	310	4.19%
The Well of the Saints (1905)	30	641	4.68%
Playboy of the Western World (1907)	29	1109	2.61%
Deirdre of the Sorrows (1910)	7	838	0.84%

Table 38.4 Sentences containing subordinating *and*

Subordinating and + V-ing	*Occurs*	*Total*	*Percentage*
Riders to the Sea (1902)	41	205	20.00%
In the Shadow of the Glen (1902)	69	193	35.75%
The Tinker's Wedding (1904)	70	310	22.58%
The Well of the Saints (1905)	104	641	16.22%
Playboy of the Western World (1907)	98	1109	8.84%
Deirdre of the Sorrows (1910)	81	838	9.67%

representing Irish English. The constructions that he chose to represent the speech of the Irish in his first plays lean towards structures that were heavily influenced by the Irish language. However, the general decrease of these structures 'may have been dictated more by his developing style than by any unconscious insight into the nature of Irish English' (Hickey 2003: 26).

5. What a corpus cannot tell us about representation in literature

One of the limitations of using fictional corpora to study speech representation in general is the question of style. The appearance or absence of a particular feature in the work of an author may be due to their personal style, and this is something that researchers interested in corpus analysis of the kind discussed here need to take into account.

It is important to acknowledge that there may be other limitations in terms of the results obtained with this type of analysis as far as fictional dialogue is concerned. Infrequent uses such as idiomatic expressions or metaphoric language might not be found in fictional representations, for example, and, if they are, they will not appear as frequently used words when running word frequency counts. However, this does not mean that they are not used in real spoken language.

Another limitation has to do with the different spellings of words. Returning to our case study of the representation of Irish English, it is worth taking into account that authors sometimes mark different dialects orthographically in order to render pronunciation. Thus, we often find *just* and *jist*, *sure* and *shure*, *think* and *tink*, *speaking* and *spaking*, *like* and *loike*, etc. Corpus annotation in that sense can help us find those words at a later stage so that all the variant spellings are included in the word count. The addition of tags or labels can certainly be of great benefit. Phonetic annotation in this case would be useful for the purpose expressed above. Stylistic annotation, as discussed in Section 4, would add information about speech (re-) presentation (direct speech, indirect speech, free indirect speech, etc.) so that the features one is looking for can be more easily identified and contextualised. A tagging system based on characters' names of the kind used by Culpeper (2002) can equally be of great benefit in the context of drama in order to identify the speech of each character, and to exclude non-speech material, such as stage directions. As Leech (2005: 20) points out, 'What has been built into the corpus in the form of annotations can also be extracted from the corpus again, and used in various ways.' In that sense, different corpora will require different types of annotation, depending on the kind of analysis the researcher wants to undertake. In a bigger sample than *The Curious Incident of the Dog in the Nightdress*, for example, it would help if one were able to distinguish *like* (verb) from *like* (preposition) without having to search through hundreds or thousands of concordance lines (see Reppen, this volume). If this distinction is already signalled in the corpus by tags, the retrieval can be automatic. Equally, if one is interested in investigating the use of a feature such as cleft sentences, then having this structure labelled from the start will save a lot of painstaking searching.

Keeping a record of the annotation scheme is always recommended. Although different annotation systems are already available (see Leech 2005; McEnery and Xiao 2005), their usefulness depends on the type of analysis one is considering. In any case, good corpus design would help the researcher avoid at least some of the limitations highlighted here (see Reppen, this volume).

Further reading

Adolphs, S. (2006) *Introducing Electronic Text Analysis: A Practical Guide for Language and Literary Studies*. London: Routledge. (This is a good introduction to the topic of written corpora and it provides very useful insights into the analysis of electronic texts in general.)

Culpeper, J. (2002) 'Computers, Language and Characterisation: An Analysis of Six Characters in Romeo and Juliet', in U. Melander-Marttala, C. Östman, M. Kytö (eds) *Conversation in Life and in Literature*. Uppsala: Universitetstryckeriet, pp. 11–30. (This paper analyses *Romeo and Juliet* in terms of keywords. It is a good introduction to corpus analysis in the context of drama. Keyword analysis, as the author suggests in the conclusions, can be applied to other kinds of data, such as particular registers, dialects, media, documents or writings.)

Hori, M. (2004) *Investigating Dickens' Style. A Collocational Analysis*. Basingstoke: Palgrave Macmillan. (This book provides interesting reflections on the study of collocations, and discusses how quantitative and qualitative analyses can complement each other in the context of collocations and style.)

Kretzschmar, W. A., Jr (ed) (2001) *Language and Literature* 10(2), special issue on 'Literary Dialect Analysis with Computer Assistance'. (This special issue contains interesting papers dealing specifically with the study of dialect with computer analysis.)

References

Adolphs, S. (2006) *Introducing Electronic Text Analysis: A Practical Guide for Language and Literary Studies*. London: Routledge.

Amador-Moreno, C. P. (2010) *An Introduction to Irish English*. London: Equinox.

Amador-Moreno, C. P. and O'Keeffe, A. (2006) '*He's After Getting Up a Load of Wind:* A Corpus-based Exploration of *be +after + V-ing* Constructions in Written and Spoken Corpora', paper presented at the BAAL/IRAAL, Cork, September.

Baker, P. (2007) *Using Corpora in Discourse Analysis*, second edition. London: Continuum.

Biber, D., Conrad, S. and Reppen, R. (1998) *Corpus Linguistics: Investigating Language Structure and Use*. Cambridge: Cambridge University Press.

Blake, N. (1981) *Non-Standard Language in English Literature*. London: André Deutsch.

Brook, G. L. (1969) *English Dialects*. 2nd edn. London: Andre Deutsch.

Burkette, A. (2001) 'The Use of Literary Dialect in *Uncle Tom's Cabin*', *Language and Literature* 10(2): 158–70.

Cohen Minnick, L. (2001) 'Jim's Language and the Issue of Race in *Huckleberry Finn*', *Language and Literature* 10(2): 111–28.

Culpeper, J. (2002) 'Computers, Language and Characterisation: An Analysis of Six Characters in *Romeo and Juliet*', in U. Melander-Marttala, C. Östman and M. Kytö (eds) *Conversation in Life and in Literature*. Uppsala: Universitetstryckeriet, pp. 11–30.

Farr, F., Murphy, B. and O'Keeffe, A. (2002) 'The Limerick Corpus of Irish English: Design, Description and Application', *Teanga* 21: 5–29.

Fowler, R. (1981) *Literature as Social Discourse*. London: Batsford.

——(1989) *Linguistics and the Novel*. London: Routledge.

García-Bermejo Giner, M. F. and Montgomery, M. (2001) 'Yorkshire English Two Hundred Years Ago', *Journal of English Linguistics* 29(4): 346–62.

Görlach, M. (1999) *English in the Nineteenth Century: An Introduction*. Cambridge: Cambridge University Press.

Hehir, G. (2005) 'Authentic or Wha?: A Corpus-Based Linguistic Analysis of the Conversational Language of Roddy Doyle's *The Snapper*', unpublished MA dissertation, University of Limerick, Ireland.

Hickey, R. (2003) *Corpus Presenter: Software for Language Analysis with a Manual and A Corpus of Irish English as Sample Data*. Amsterdam: John Benjamins.

Hoey, M., Mahlberg, M., Stubbs, M. and Teubert, W. (eds) (2007) *Text, Discourse and Corpora*. London: Continuum.

Hughes, R. (1996) *English in Speech and Writing: Investigating Language and Literature*. London: Routledge.

Ives, S. (1950) 'A Theory of Literary Dialect', *Tulane Studies in English, New Orleans,* 2: 137–82.

Johnstone, B. (1991) 'Discourse-level Aspects of Dialect in Fiction: A Southern American Example', *Language and Style* 24(4): 461–71.

Jonsson, C. (2009) 'Representing Voice in Chicano Theatre through the Use of Orthography: An Analysis of Three Plays by Cherríe Moraga', in C. P. Amador-Moreno and A. Nunes (eds) *The Representation of the Spoken Mode in Fiction: How Authors Write How People Talk*. New York: Edwin Mellen.

Kallen, J. (1991) 'Sociolinguistic Variation and Methodology: *After* as a Dublin Variable', in J. Cheshire (ed) *English Around the World: Sociolinguistic Perspectives*. Cambridge: Cambridge University Press, pp. 61–74.

Kirk, J. M. (1999) 'Contemporary Irish Writing and a Model of Speech Realism', in I. Taavitsainen, G. Melchers and P. Pahta (eds) *Writing in Nonstandard English*. Amsterdam: John Benjamins, pp. 45–62.

Kretzschmar, William A. (2001) 'Literary Dialect Analysis with Computer Assistance: An Introduction', *Language and Literature*, 10(2): 99–110.

Kretzschmar, W. A., Jr, McDavid, V. G., Lerud, T. K. and Johnson, E. (1993) *Handbook of the Linguistic Atlas of the Middle and South Atlantic States*. Chicago: University of Chicago Press.

Lancashire, I., Bradley, J., McCarty, W., Stairs, M., and Wooldridge, T. R. (1996) *Using TACT with Electronic Texts: A Guide to Text-Analysis Computing Tools, Version 2.1 for MS-DOS and PC DOS*. New York: MLA.

Labov, W. (1972) 'Some Principles of Linguistic Methodology', *Language in Society* 1: 97–120.

Leech, G. (2005) 'Adding Linguistic Annotation', in M. Wynne (ed.) *Developing Linguistic Corpora: A Guide to Good Practice*. Oxford: Oxbow Books, pp. 17–29; available at http://ahds.ac.uk/linguistic-corpora/ (accessed 12 September 2008).

Leech, G. and Short, M. H. (1981) *Style in Fiction*. London: Longman.

LinguaLinks 3.5 Overview and Installation Guide (1999) Dallas: Summer Institute of Linguistics. *LinguaLinks* (software from Summer Institute of Linguistics), available at www.sil.org/lingualinks/ (accessed 12 September 2008).

Louw, B. (1997) 'The Role of Corpora in Critical Literary Appreciation', in A. Wichmann, S. Fligelstone, T. McEnery and G. Knowles (eds) *Teaching and Language Corpora*. London: Longman, pp. 240–51.

McCafferty, K. (2004) 'Innovation in Language Contact: *Be* after *V-ing* as a Future Gram in Irish English, 1670 to the Present', *Diachronica* 21(1): 113–60.

——(2005) 'William Carleton between Irish and English: Using Literary Dialect to Study Language Contact and Change', *Language and Literature* 14(4): 339–62.

——(2009) '"Preserv[ing] Every Thing Irish"? The Hiberno-English Dialect of William Carleton's Peasants', in C. P. Amador-Moreno and A. Nunes (eds) *The Representation of the Spoken Mode in Fiction: How Authors Write How People Talk*. New York: Edwin Mellen.

McEnery, A. and Xiao, R. (2005) 'Character Encoding in Corpus Construction', in M. Wynne (ed.) *Developing Linguistic Corpora: A Guide to Good Practice*. Oxford: Oxbow Books, pp. 47–58; available at http://ahds.ac.uk/linguistic-corpora/ (accessed 12 September 2008).

McEnery, A., Xiao, R. and Tono, Y. (2006) *Corpus-based Language Studies*. London: Routledge.

Mahlberg, M. (2007) 'Corpus Stylistics: Bridging the Gap between Linguistic and Literary Studies', in M. Hoey, M. Mahlberg, M. Stubbs and W. Teubert (eds) *Text, Discourse and Corpora*. London: Continuum.

Montgomery, M. (1995) 'The Linguistic Value of Ulster Emigrant Letters', *Ulster Folklife* 41: 26–41.

O'Carroll-Kelly, R. [P. Howard] (2005) *The Curious Incident of the Dog in the Nightdress*. London: Penguin Books.

O'Keeffe, A. and Amador-Moreno, C. P. (2009) 'The Pragmatics of the *be + after + V-ing* Construction in Irish English', *Intercultural Pragmatics* 6(4): 517–34.

Page, N. (1973) *Speech in the English Novel*. London: Macmillan.

Renouf, A. (1987) 'Corpus Development', in J. M. Sinclair (ed) *Looking Up*. London: HarperCollins, pp. 1–40.

Rochester, E. (2001) 'New Tools for Analyzing Texts', *Language and Literature* 10(2): 187–91.

Scott, M. (1999) *WordSmith Tools*, version 3.0. Oxford: Oxford University Press.

Semino, E. and Short, M. (2004) *Corpus Stylistics. Speech, Writing and Thought Presentation in a Corpus of English Writing*. London and New York: Routledge.

Shorrocks, G. (1996) 'Non-Standard Dialect Literature and Popular Culture', in J. Klemola, M. Kytö and M. Rissanen (eds) *Speech Past and Present: Studies in English Dialectology in Memory of Ossi Ihalainen*. Frankfurt am Main: Peter Lang, pp. 385–411.

Short, M. Semino, E. and Wynne, M. (2002) 'Revisiting the Notion of Faithfulness in Discourse Presentation using a Corpus Approach', *Language and Literature* 11(4): 325–55.

Simpson, P. (2004) *Stylistics*. London: Routledge.

Sinclair, J. (2005) 'Corpus and Text – Basic Principles', in M. Wynne (ed.) *Developing Linguistic Corpora: A Guide to Good Practice*. Oxford: Oxbow Books: pp. 1–16; available at http://ahds.ac.uk/linguistic-corpora/ (accessed 19 July 2008).

Stockwell, P. and Wynne, M. (2006) 'Corpus Stylistics: A Public Inquiry', paper presented at the 3rd International IVACS Conference, University of Nottingham, June.

Stubbs, M. (2006) 'Exploring "Eveline" with Computational Methods', in S. Goodman and K. O'Halloran (eds) *The Art of English: Literary Creativity*. Milton Keynes: Palgrave Macmillan and the Open University, pp. 138–44.

Sullivan, J. P. (1980) 'The Validity of Literary Dialect: Evidence from the Theatrical Portrayal of Hiberno-English Forms', *Language in Society* 9(2): 195–219.

Taavitsainen, I., Melchers, G. and Pahta, P. (eds) (1999) *Writing in Nonstandard English*. Amsterdam: John Benjamins

Tamasi, S. (2001) 'Huck Doesn't Sound Like Himself: Consistency in the Literary Dialect of Mark Twain', *Language and Literature* 10(2): 129–44.

Toolan, M. (1992) 'The Significations of Representing Dialect in Writing', *Language and Literature* 1(1): 29–46.

Walpole, J. R. (1974) 'Eye Dialect in Fictional Dialogue', *College Composition and Communication* 25(2): 191–6.

Wynne, M. (2005) 'Archiving, Distribution and Preservation', in M. Wynne (ed.) *Developing Linguistic Corpora: a Guide to Good Practice*. Oxford: Oxbow Books, pp. 71–8; available at http://ahds.ac.uk/linguistic-corpora/ (accessed 12 September 2008).

Section VIII

Applying corpus linguistics to other areas of research

39

How to use corpus linguistics in sociolinguistics

Gisle Andersen

1. Sociolinguistics and the relevance of corpora

Sociolinguistics is the branch of linguistics that is concerned with linguistic variation and its social significance. Sociolinguists study differences between individual users of language and between language varieties. The discipline encompasses many subtopics which focus on the effect which various social characteristics have on the language of individuals or speaker groups. Sociolinguistic factors include the major demographic categories of age, gender, social class and ethnicity, as well as situational categories like the degree of formality of the speech situation, the social networks of the speaker and so on. Sociolinguistics also focuses on the overall characteristics of language varieties: that is, regional dialects, standard/non-standard varieties of a language, multilingualism, language policy, standardisation etc. Much sociolinguistic research places itself within the variationist paradigm, that is to say, it considers the linguistic variable as the main theoretical construct applicable to the analysis of empirical data (Labov 1966) and sees linguistic variation as potentially indicative of language change. The other main approach can be termed 'interactional sociolinguistics' and uses more qualitative and ethnographical methods in studies of communicative behaviour in real life situations (Hymes 1974; Gumpertz 1982). This approach involves a more dynamic view on the relation between the linguistic and non-linguistic dimensions of communicative events (Duranti and Goodwin 1992) and a shift in focus from dialects to individual speech styles in which complexities of variables are seen to contribute to social meanings (Eckert and Rickford 2001).

The aim of the current chapter is to give an account of how corpora and corpus-linguistic methods can be of help to the researcher who wants to pursue a sociolinguistic research question. Corpus linguistics and sociolinguistics can be seen as two related but historically distinct research traditions. While sociolinguistics is generally considered a specific branch or a paradigm within linguistics, corpus linguistics is not. Rather, corpus linguistics is 'a methodological basis for doing linguistic research' (Leech 1992: 105) and has 'come to embody methodologies for linguistic description in which quantification … is part of the research activity' (Kennedy 1998: 7, see also Tognini Bonelli, this volume). But as a discipline, sociolinguistics crucially depends on authentic language data, and corpus linguistics is one methodological approach which may be used for sociolinguistic purposes. Like other kinds of empirical language data, corpora can be viewed as documentations of the choices made by language users and as surface manifestations of the underlying communicative competence of the speakers whose language the corpus represents (De Beaugrande 1999). Computerised corpora form a well-prepared basis for systematic, descriptive studies of instances of actual speech, for language variation and for how social context constrains communicative practices.

The close connection between corpus linguistics and sociolinguistics can be underlined by the fact that, even in Labov's (1972) pioneering sociolinguistic study in New York City, he used a data collection method which has later been widely applied in corpus linguistics, that of random sampling. His informants were chosen by random sample on the basis of the gender, age, social classes and ethnicities represented in the city, much as a present-day corpus builder would do. Conversely, since the early days of corpus linguistics, there has been an interest in using corpora as a means of exploring linguistic variation, to study for example differences between regional varieties of English. This was the motivation for the compilation of the first-generation written corpora, the Brown and Lancaster–Oslo/Bergen corpora, whose parallel structure and content enabled reliable comparative studies of high-frequency lexical items and grammar. But sociolinguistics first of all requires access to spoken data, and the subsequent development of spoken corpora, like the London–Lund Corpus, the spoken part of the British National Corpus and several other efforts that will be described in this chapter, have made it possible to use ready-made corpora to study variation in speech in a variety of languages.

By now, there are a relatively large and growing number of corpus-based studies with a sociolinguistic focus, using corpora to describe various aspects of socially significant linguistic variation or emerging patterns of discourse (McEnery and Wilson 2001). Variationist sociolinguistics requires access to large amounts of data in order to make reliable generalisations about a language variety, and an increasing number of sociolinguists acknowledge the advantages of applying corpus-linguistic tools and methods as efficient means for organising their language data. There are at least three different ways in which a sociolinguist may apply corpus-linguistic methods as an empirical basis. First, there is the possibility of using one of the many existing corpora as in a sociolinguistic study. This has the obvious advantage that it saves time and other resources. The alternative is to collect one's own data and create a new corpus for a specific sociolinguistic purpose (see chapters on building a corpus by Adolphs and Knight, Nelson and Reppen, this volume). The developer may or may not make it generally available to other users, as publication may or may not be an aim of the corpus-building project. Finally, there is the possibility of using 'corpus-inspired' methods and tools to handle empirical data in a sociolinguistic study, without developing and distributing a fully-fledged corpus. Whether or not to use an existing corpus depends crucially on the overall aims of one's research. The driving force that governs the methodological preferences and choices of the individual researcher should always be the actual research question that one wants to pursue, and the availability of an existing corpus depends on the scope and nature of the language phenomena one wants to explore.

The ambition of many sociolinguists is to get access to the maximally naturally occurring spoken data – spontaneous conversation (although other data types like interviews and word list data are also used; Chambers 1995). This is ideally collected in the environments in which the informants naturally operate. Some sociolinguists use an ethnographical approach, in which the field worker him/herself watches or actively takes part in a social context which is recorded, using participant observation, ethnographic field notes and semi-structured conversations with subjects. Few generally accessible speech corpora (if any) are based on this approach. In variationist sociolinguistic projects, the method of self-recording has begun to be used, in which informants are instructed to record their conversations in everyday contexts in their homes, at work, in school, during leisure activities, etc. This procedure has been established as a standard in modern speech corpus collection, and is applied in such corpora as the British National Corpus and the Spoken Dutch Corpus.

2. Sociolinguistic methods and the use of corpora

So far, the use of corpora has not been the most common way of carrying out socio-linguistic research. In this section it is argued that there are obvious advantages associated with the use of corpus linguistics in sociolinguistics. But there are also pitfalls and problems associated with this approach, and these will also be dealt with here.

Why and how use spoken corpora?

A spoken corpus is a collection of speech data made accessible via a computer, containing at least transcriptions of speech but increasingly also audio and/or video files containing speech (see chapters by Adolphs and Knight and Reppen, this volume). It is usually collected for the purpose of linguistic research or for a related purpose, such as lexico-graphy or natural language processing. The speakers in the corpus have usually been selected via a sampling procedure, and the speech has been listened to carefully and transcribed, often using generally available software for the transcription and annotation of speech, such as *Transcriber*, *Praat* or *ELAN* (cf. Figure 39.1). Corpora containing an orthographic transcription are convenient, given their readability and searchability. Some corpora also include a phonetic or phonemic transcription, depending on the planned use of the corpus. The corpus texts will generally be annotated with linguistic informa-tion which may represent different levels of analysis, such as intonation, morphology, word class, syntactic structure, discourse structure or speech act information, again depending on the overall aims and purpose of the corpus-building initiative. The corpus texts will be annotated with metadata concerning the speakers, the situational context of the speech event, location, recording equipment, etc. The text and the audio and/or video files are made accessible for search, browsing and statistical output via a (usually web-based) user interface.

Given the potentially many-faceted nature of speech data, it is necessary to have access to efficient tools for the handling of data in the compilation stage as well as in the use stage. A flexible tool for transcription and annotation of spoken data is *ELAN*. Based on the same principle as general-purpose media players, the tool can be used for viewing/listening to and easily moving about in video or audio recordings, and it allows the user to inspect the speech waveforms and to play each annotated segment as many times as necessary at a variety of speeds. This is useful for orthographic and phonetic transcription of the speech, for annotation of linguistic information and for the subsequent analysis of the data. Figure 39.1 shows how linguistic information is entered and stored as different annotation layers representing analytical levels like utterance/sentence, word, phoneme, word class, etc. The user can freely add new layers and search through the annotations for particular patterns or characteristic features.

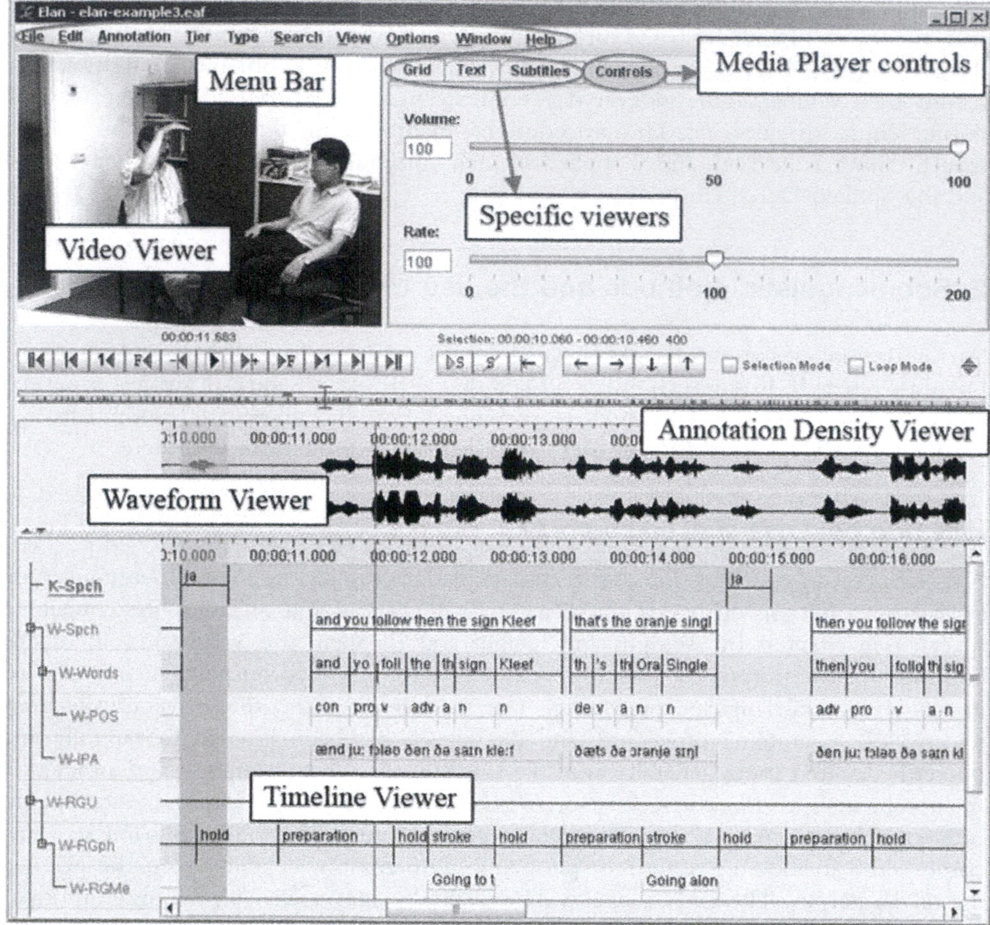

Figure 39.1 Screenshot of *ELANT* (the *Eudico Linguistic Annotator*), by courtesy of Max Planck Institute, Netherlands.

Table 39.1 Types of spoken discourse in Spoken Dutch Corpus

a.	Spontaneous conversations ('face-to-face')
b.	Interviews with teachers of Dutch
c.	Spontaneous telephone dialogues (recorded via a switchboard)
d.	Spontaneous telephone dialogues (recorded on minidisk via a local interface)
e.	Simulated business negotiations
f.	Interviews/discussions/debates (broadcast)
g.	(political) Discussions/debates/meetings (non-broadcast)
h.	Lessons recorded in the classroom
i.	Live (e.g. sports) commentaries (broadcast)
j.	News reports/reportages (broadcast)
k.	News (broadcast)
l.	Commentaries/columns/reviews (broadcast)
m.	Ceremonious speeches/sermons
n.	Lectures/seminars
o.	Read speech

One of the advantages of using one of the large, national corpora, like the British National Corpus (BNC) or the Spoken Dutch Corpus (CGN), is that they have been compiled with a view to representing not only a demographically diverse selection of speakers but also many different speech genres. To exemplify, Table 39.1 gives a survey of the different components distinguished in the CGN.

We note that the spoken corpus contains many genres, including the use of spoken language in formal settings like lectures, sermons and news broadcasts. This typology of spoken data enables the researcher to investigate how language varies contextually across different speech situations and different genres, and to study, for example, differences in intonation patterns between news broadcasts and conversation. An example of a study which has exploited this facility using the CGN is Schelfhout *et al.* (2005), who observe that speakers' use of interjections varies significantly with textual genre as well as with grammatical, functional and prosodic factors of the utterances in which they occur. As can be expected, there is a major difference between public text types like interviews and sports commentaries and private conversation as regards the types of interjections used and the positions they take in speech.

Another advantage of spoken corpora like the BNC and the CGN concerns their size and the possibility of efficiently processing large amounts of naturally occurring spoken data. Deutschmann (2006) describes variation in the use of apology formula – involving lexical items like *excuse*, *afraid*, *pardon*, *regret* and *sorry* – across the various spoken categories of the BNC. The advantage of using this corpus, he says, is that it provides 'unique material for large-scale socio-pragmatic study of spoken British English' (ibid.: 206). The spoken part of the BNC includes 4,700 speakers representing many conversational settings. Deutschmann contrasts this with ethnographic approaches that 'rely on a limited data from single genres or very few respondents' (ibid.: 205).

As mentioned, corpus texts are annotated with metadata about speakers and contexts. These metadata include information about the participants, speech setting, date and time of recording as well as technical information about the recording equipment, editorial comments, etc. This makes it easy to separate language extracts from one speech situation from another, comparing for example a formal conversation with informal chat, or comparing different individual users or user groups. An example of a study which exploits non-linguistic metadata in this way is Andersen (2001), which investigates the use of discourse markers (pragmatic markers) in London English. In this variational study, the language of the Bergen Corpus of London Teenage Language (COLT) is compared with a comparable subset of the BNC. The study shows that the use of *like* as a discourse marker (used with quotative, approximative, metalinguistic and other functions) is primarily a feature of white female speakers in late adolescence, and that social class had no effect on the distribution of this marker (see also chapter by Amador-Moreno, this volume, on the use of *like* in literary speech representation). On the other hand, the use of the form *innit* as an invariant tag (in contexts like *He's a bastard, innit?*) was seen to be spreading via the language of female adolescent speakers with an ethnic minority background and from the lowest socio-economic class. As an exemplification of how sociolinguistic metadata is explored in practice, Figure 39.2 shows the web-based interface to the BNC, where users can restrict their search according to several non-linguistic dimensions.

The first-generation spoken corpora, like the London–Lund Corpus of spoken English (LLC), contain orthographic transcriptions with prosodic annotation, enabling studies of prosody, discourse, grammar and lexis. It should be pointed out that this corpus is narrow

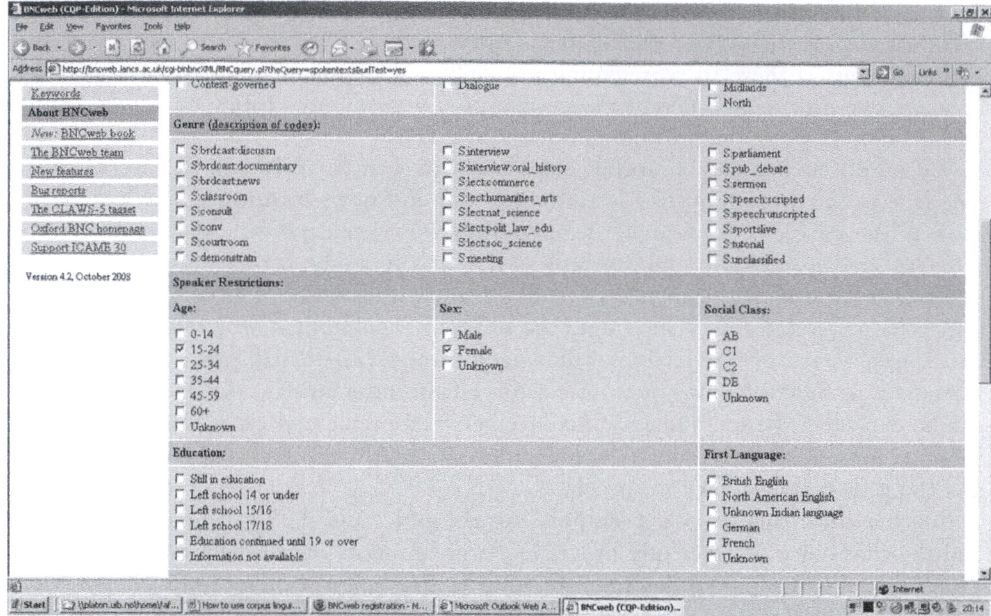

Figure 39.2 The BNC web-user interface.

in terms of selection of speakers and discourse contexts, as it exclusively involves speakers who are highly educated adults working in an academic environment (Greenbaum and Svartvik 1990). A more representative corpus is the spoken component of the BNC, as shown above, which contains ten million words of speech representing a variety of speech styles, including a substantial proportion of conversation in a variety of speaker groups. However, a considerable weakness of both the LLC and the BNC is that the actual speech data, the sound files, are not available to the researcher.

It has become customary to compile multimodal speech corpora, which give users access to the language data in various different formats, including written transcripts, audio recordings or video recordings. For example, audio files are included in the International Corpus of English (ICE), which can be used for cross-varietal sociolinguistic studies of the English spoken in East Africa, Great Britain, Hong Kong, India, New Zealand, the Philippines and Singapore, and in the Spanish Corpus Oral de Lenguaje Adolescente (COLA), which enables comparative studies of the varieties of Spanish used by adolescents in Madrid, Santiago de Chile, Buenos Aires, Guatemala City and Havana. The inclusion of clickable snippets of sound in a spoken corpus has become a much used facility for efficient data retrieval. Some corpus builders have even started to include video files among the resources made accessible to researchers. This applies, for example, to the Norwegian Spoken Corpus (NoTa; cf. Figure 39.3), where spoken data in video format enables the analysis of gestures and facial expressions as part of conversational behaviour.

Another advantage of spoken corpora is that they allow for easy retrieval of spoken data based on searches for words or phrases. If the corpus is lemmatised, this makes it easy to retrieve all possible inflected forms and spelling variants of a word in a single search. This advantage is obviously greater for languages with a richer inflectional system than English, such as Czech, Hungarian or Russian, but even for English it is convenient to

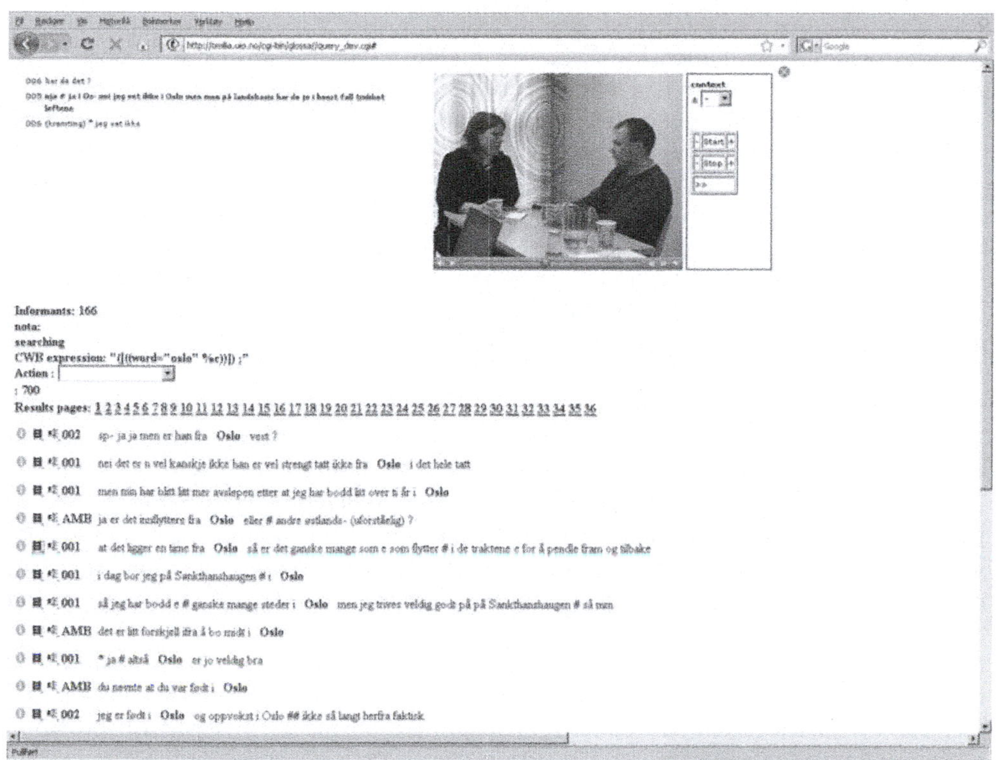

Figure 39.3 Interface of the NoTa speech corpus.

retrieve all forms of e.g. *categorise/categorize* in one go without having to search for the individual finite and non-finite forms of the verb, and thus to analyse frequency distributions based on the lemma rather than on individual word forms. Corpus interfaces are becoming ever more flexible with respect to searchable patterns. Most corpora allow for search with regular expressions and truncated words, which makes it possible to specify exactly what kind of pattern the computer should look for in the analysis of a sociolinguistic variable. For example, Kristoffersen and Simonsen (2008) used the NoTa corpus in a study of the use of retroflex apical variant [ʂ⊠] (and not alveolar [sl]) for the variable /sl/ in words like *rusle* (stroll) and *Oslo*. This to some extent stigmatised pronunciation is generally considered to be on the increase, especially in syllable-medial position. By searching for a limited set of orthographic patterns, *sl* used word-initially and -medially, and *sel* used word-medially and -finally, the authors could easily retrieve relevant forms. The set of searches had to be modified so as not to include tokens which are invariantly pronounced [ʂ⊠] in Eastern Norwegian, orthographically represented as either rsl (as in *varsle*, (alarm, v)) or *rsel*, (as in *hørsel* (hearing, n)). Thereby they established a relevant subset of instances of this variable that were subsequently studied in detail. The corpus-based method reduced the amount of manual work needed for the inspection of this particular variable and simplified the classification of tokens according to their placement in the word and in relation to morphological boundaries.

A major concern in the development of speech corpora is how to treat non-standard and dialectal forms. What do you do with a form like *isn't* in English, which can have a variety of pronunciations depending on the regional background of the speaker?

Essentially, there are two different ways of handling such variation, either producing a dialectal, orthophonic transcription which is as close to the pronunciation as possible, or producing a transcription based on a written standard, but usually allowing for some variation. The latter solution is effectively the one applied in the BNC, where the variable is orthographically realised as one of the written forms *isn't* or *ain't*, or as the non-standard *isnae* (Scottish dialect form), *in't* or *in* (as in the tag *innit*). In other respects, though, the BNC uses standard English spelling (allowing for semi-standardised forms like *gonna* and *wanna*) and not an orthophonic transcription. On the other hand, in the Nordic Dialect Corpus (cf. Section 4), both transcription schemas are used, allowing the user to search for either a normalised form, such as *hvordan* (how) or one of its many different phonetic variants, represented as orthophonic realisations like *koless'n, kossj'n, korr* or the like (Vangsnes 2008).

It is also helpful to the sociolinguistic researcher that the spoken corpus is tagged with syntactic and morphological information, as this allows for disambiguation of homographic words and a wide spectre of other analyses. A researcher who is interested in, for example the pronunciation of *-ing*, which in many dialects alternates between [ɪn] and [ɪŋ], a truncated search may easily retrieve all words with this ending, but a more refined search makes it possible to distinguish between word classes and compare verbal endings with adjectives like *interesting*, nouns like *meeting* and *Epping* and pronouns like *anything*, in order to see if word class or morphological structure has a significant effect on the phonetic realisation of this variable. Similarly, looking at a non-standard grammatical feature like multiple negation, a flexible corpus query language enables the user to easily retrieve relevant patterns. To illustrate, in the spoken part of the BNC, searching for the (admittedly cryptic) pattern *[xx0] do [pni]* retrieves all tokens of the negative particle (*not, n't*) followed by *do* followed by an indefinite pronoun. The search gives the statistics shown in Table 39.2. Coupled with the detailed speaker information in the BNC, the flexible search procedure provides a good starting point for a sociolinguistic study of multiple negation and other morphosyntactic features, including the use of dialect forms like *nowt* and *nuffink* also retrieved by this search. The user does not have to learn the codes for each word class but can select them from a pull-down menu in the web-based interface used to extract these data. To illustrate the flexibility, the

Table 39.2 Search result ([xx0] do [pni]) extracted from the Brigham Young University's web-based interface to the BNC

N'T DO ANYTHING	204
N'T DO NOTHING	31
NOT DO ANYTHING	11
N'T DO SOMETHING	10
N'T DO EVERYTHING	5
N'T DO NONE	4
N'T DO NOWT	4
N'T DO ONE	4
N'T DO NUFFINK	2
NOT DO SOMETHING	2
N'T DO EVERYBODY	1
N'T DO ANYONE	1
N'T DO ANYBODY	1
NOT DO ONE	1
NOT DO EVERYTHING	1

search could easily have been extended to the pattern negative particle + any infinitive verb + indefinite pronoun, in order to also capture tokens of *n't say nothing*, etc., or to negative particle + any verb + indefinite pronoun, to also capture tokens of *n't done nothing*, etc.

But word class tagging only gives access to the syntactic structures at the surface level, making it impossible to distinguish Chomsky's well-known phrases *eager to please* from *easy to please*. Deep-level syntactic structures can be annotated as syntactic trees in databases (corpora) called treebanks. The most well-known examples are the Penn Treebank and ICE-GB, the latter also containing spoken data. Principally, from a sociolinguistic perspective, such parsed corpora may be used to compare degrees of syntactic complexity (e.g. between children and adults) or variability of syntactic structures in different types of discourse or language varieties, but few studies have explored the possibilities of studying sociolinguistic variation based on such resources.

Many researchers restrict their use of corpora to the search of individual words or phrases with the results displayed as a concordance that shows the contexts in which a word or phrase appears, such as a KWIC concordance output. But corpora offer various other means of displaying the data, such as word lists or frequency distributions. A spoken corpus gives swift access to statistical information about linguistic features and distributions across user groups. An example of a study that has utilised statistical output from a corpus is Gabrielatos *et al.*'s (forthcoming) study of the indefinite article forms *a* vs *an*, where they use 'a combination of existing and adapted quantitative/statistical methods used in sociolinguistics and corpus linguistics to analyse the data' (ibid.: 7). Their analysis is based on a comparison of COLT and the Linguistic Innovators Corpus, representing the variety called Multicultural London English. They show that there has been a marked, significant increase and spread of the pattern *a* + vowel, in particular in the speech of young, non-Anglo speakers from Hackney.

Problems and limitations of corpus-linguistic method

Given the previous outline of some of the advantages of the corpus-based approach to sociolinguistics, it must also be acknowledged that there are several problems connected with this approach. The first objection concerns the accessibility of speech data, or lack thereof. In first-generation spoken corpora like the LLC and some second-generation spoken corpora like the BNC, the sound files are unavailable to the general user. This reduces the usability of the corpus drastically, as many potential corpus users need to carry out analyses of real spoken data in order to pursue their research questions. This applies not only to studies in phonetics and phonology, but possibly also to conversation analysis and discourse analysis, where the interpretation of utterances may depend on audible phenomena that are not (fully) represented in the transcripts.

Second, some of the corpora that do have spoken data available are not suitable for detailed phonetic or phonological studies because the sound quality is too poor. This concerns corpora that are collected with pre-digital equipment like a tape recorder, or corpora that are collected in noisy surroundings or conversational settings involving many speakers and a high degree of overlapping speech.

Third, it is a problem for certain types of phonological analysis that there may be few instances of a particular variable in a corpus. Too few tokens per speaker may rule out the possibility of studying individual variation. For such studies, supplementary methods like carefully designed word lists or map tasks may be needed.

Fourth, it may be problematic for corpus users to rely fully on the judgements of the transcriber, especially since transcribers differ with respect to their interpretations of spoken data. Ensuring inter-annotator agreement is a big issue in large corpus creation efforts, and a study such as Raymond *et al.* (2002) has shown that even experienced transcribers have different interpretations, particularly when annotating data at phonetic or prosodic levels. This underlines, of course, the sociolinguist's need for access to the spoken data when using corpora. However, this is a methodological objection that potentially affects many types of empiric linguistic studies, including sociolinguistics.

Fifth, some corpus data are only available as short snippets of sound and not as longer stretches of spoken dialogue. This rules out the possibility of studying the macrostructure of spoken discourse on the basis of such a corpus. For many research purposes, this is a prerequisite, such as studies of the structure and development of narratives in conversation.

Sixth, corpus linguistics relies heavily on the method of searching, and in many cases this is the only way to access the corpus data. Naturally, this is problematic for any type of research which focuses on unmarked structures or phenomena. How do you 'search' for items that are not explicitly represented? Let us assume that a researcher is interested in the use and distribution of relative clauses; how does he/she find the zero-relatives like *the house Jack built*, lacking a relative pronoun? Efficient, large-scale retrieval of unmarked relatives or other structures that lack explicit marking requires a spoken corpus that is fully parsed, but many spoken corpora have not been annotated with this in mind. This shortcoming can, however, be remedied by including a browse facility in an unparsed corpus, and this is becoming more common in corpus interfaces. The drawback, though, is that the extraction of relevant tokens involves time-consuming manual extraction.

Finally, the methods of searching and browsing a corpus are not necessarily the ideal method for doing qualitative analyses. The fact that corpus informants are generally anonymised prevents the researcher from accessing the in-depth background information which would be required for linguistic anthropological studies, although general information about the sex, age, etc., of the speakers is preserved. No corpus is rich enough to supply the valuable personal experience and detailed information that the field worker gets in contact with his/her participants. Corpus linguistics does not replace anthropological field work, but it is a valuable and much appreciated complement to it.

3. Dos and don'ts for the researcher

As will have become evident, the use of corpora in sociolinguistic studies is strongly advocated, despite the limitations listed above. This section contains a few rules of the thumb for corpus-based sociolinguistic research.

Listen to the data

Spoken language should be listened to. As mentioned, modern corpus technology that links transcripts with audio or video data makes it an easy task to consult the multimedia files in addition to the textual output from the corpus. The transcription may not be fully accurate, and in many cases listening to the data solves interpretational ambiguities, such as whether an instance of the word *like* is a discourse marker or represents non-marker usage (Andersen 2001: 211ff.).

Browse and search

Corpus browsing may be equally rewarding as corpus search. Pragmatics and interactional sociolinguistics often concerns phenomena at the discourse level, such as turn-taking, code-switching, the structure of narratives, etc. The transcriber's orthographic rendering of words and phrases depends on how the utterance is interpreted, which again depends on what goes on discourse-globally. Browsing and listening to longer passages of speech is often a prerequisite for analysing both form and function of individual utterances.

Precision and recall

When carrying out quantitative analyses based on corpora, it is essential that the retrieved dataset includes exactly the tokens relevant for the analysis and no irrelevant tokens (precision), and it should not miss out any tokens (recall). A corpus search may well over- or under-generate; if so, a more refined search is needed, or alternatively a combination of searches. If a precise search result cannot be achieved, the lists of retrieved tokens may have to be inspected manually. For example, if studying variation in negative forms of the verb BE in English, a precise token retrieval must include all possible non-standard negative forms of the verb, not just the standard verb forms. This means that the corpus user must have *a priori* knowledge of all the possible variants, which could be gained from consulting the transcription manual or other documentation, or from using a lemmatised search.

Distinguish form from function

The corpus user must make sure to select only the relevant tokens, based on the functional properties of each token. Many words in the language are notoriously multifunctional and (multiply) homographic, such as *well*, which can be an adverb, adjective, noun or discourse marker. Some uses of words are metalinguistic: that is to say, the speaker is speaking about a particular word or phrase, as when one of the COLT speakers utters *We're not allowed to say 'fuck'*. How to treat such tokens – as a case of swearing or not – may vary according to the aims of the research project, and the analyst must make a conscious choice as to whether to disregard or include such tokens in the statistics.

Manual work is needed

Corpus analysis must never be reduced to mere counting and statistics, but manual work, in the sense of qualitative, interpretational analyses, is needed to ensure correctness and accountability. If the analysis of one's spoken data is dependent on syntactic annotation, it is advisable to check the performance of the word class tagger, as spoken language features are notoriously challenging in this respect. This applies in particular to phenomena that involve ongoing structural change affecting the grammatical status of a word or a phrase, such as the grammaticalisation of new complex prepositions like *in view of* (Hoffman 2004).

Comparability of datasets

Corpus-based sociolinguistic studies are usually comparative in nature, involving either the comparison between different corpora or that between different subsets of the same corpus, such as men vs women or young vs older speakers. This begs the question whether the datasets are comparable or not. Have the data been selected in identical ways, and are all other factors controlled for? Comparability requires similar procedures for recruitment of informants and corpus compilation, and this methodological issue should be addressed in comparative studies.

4. Corpus-based sociolinguistics exemplified

The current section gives a brief account of previous and ongoing sociolinguistic research which shows how corpora can be used in studies of language variation at different analytical levels, such as phonetics, syntax and pragmatics.

There is a clear tendency that corpus-linguistic method is becoming an integral part of variationist sociolinguistic method. In several countries we find sociolinguistic projects that utilise well-known corpus-linguistic techniques of making the data accessible via transcriptions that are linked to multimedia files, and implementing web-based search and browse facilities. In the UK, for example, the project Multicultural London English (MLE): The Emergence, Acquisition and Diffusion of a New Variety examines the role of ethnic-minority English in driving forward linguistic innovation at the levels of phonetics, grammar and discourse. The project generates a one-million-word corpus of conversational speech (Kerswill, Cheshire *et al.* 2008). A previous project of the same research group also developed the 1.4 million words Linguistic Innovators Corpus (cf. Cheshire *et al.* 2008; Gabrielatos *et al.*, forthcoming). An example of output from these efforts is an article dealing with change in the pronunciation of diphthongs in the London area (Kerswill, Torgersen and Fox 2008). Here it is shown that inner-city innovations are connected with ethnicity, and that non-Anglo speakers are forerunners of the innovations. Based on the same corpus, Cheshire *et al.* (2008) show that innovative consonant features like DH-stopping (using [f] for /θ/ in words like *bath*) and TH-fronting (using [d] for /ð/ in words like *brother*) are significantly constrained socially; again, it is the non-Anglo speakers who use the more innovative features, which are distinguishable from the traditional Cockney dialect.

The Intonational Variation in English (IViE) Corpus contains speech data and intonation transcriptions from nine urban dialects of British English. The data represent five different speaking styles, including conversation, map task dialogues, retold stories, reading passages and sentences. Fletcher *et al.* (2004) use this corpus in a comparative study of the high-rising terminal (HRT) in four varieties of English. HRT refers to the use of the high-rising intonation contour – generally associated with *yes/no* questions in English – in declarative utterances, which 'correlates with the semantic complexity of the text and therefore the need for checking to see if the audience is understanding what is being said' (Guy and Vonwiller 1984: 25). Previous studies of Australian and New Zealand English have shown that HRT is associated with low-prestige varieties, is socially stigmatised, occurs most often in the telling of narratives and is used predominantly by young adolescent females as part of narratives. Contrary to this, Fletcher *et al.* show that it is the male speakers in IViE who use HRTs the most. As the authors see it, the advantage of using the IViE corpus for this study is that it 'provides sufficient coverage of intonational phenomena across a very large corpus comprising several, very different, varieties of British English' (Fletcher *et al.* 2004: 407).

Wichmann (2004) uses the British component of ICE in a study of the intonation of *please*. The corpus-based approach allows her to investigate a range of linguistic and situational features – and their correlation – such as utterance position, co-occurrence with specific speech act types (requests) and the situational contexts of public and private domains. The study gives a good display of the advantages of using a corpus in a study of intonation, as it shows that typical intonation contours vary according to the speech situation as well as the pragmatic (speech act) function of utterances.

Cheshire and Fox (2009) study *was/were* variation in MLE as part of a more comprehensive morphosyntactic survey, in the 'first sociolinguistic account of morphosyntactic variation and change in the [UK] capital'. They demonstrate an ongoing tendency of dialect levelling, to the effect that *was* is becoming the paradigmatic form used in all positive contexts, while *weren't* is used in all negative contexts, regardless of person or number of the grammatical subject. However, the effect of the levelling was lower in the inner London borough of Hackney, compared to Havering in outer London. Given this, they conclude that 'Inner London does not appear to be the source of the *was/weren't* pattern that is so widespread in other urban centres in the UK' (ibid.: 49).

Another large and ongoing undertaking that focuses on syntax is the development of a multilingual corpus of all the North Germanic languages that are spoken in Denmark, Finland (Swedish), the Faeroe Islands, Iceland, Norway and Sweden. The Nordic Dialect Corpus is compiled primarily to enable studies of dialect syntax within the framework of the ScanDiaSyn project (Bentzen and Vangsnes 2007). The corpus-building effort is part of a systematic study of syntactic variation in this large and disparate region of north-western Europe. The specific research area covers topics such as non-standard lack of subject/verb inversion in Norwegian dialects, adjective incorporation in northern Swedish and central Norwegian dialects, and verb placement in embedded clauses in northern Ostrobothnia in Finland and in northern Norway.

Many corpus-based sociolinguistic studies focus on phenomena at the level of discourse and pragmatics. Stenström *et al.* (2002) is a variationist account where *like* is compared with other quotative constructions used by teenagers, including paralinguistic cues like voice modulation, zero-quotations (usually accompanied by verbal humour and mimicry), and the use of GO and SAY as reporting verbs. Overall, the corpus-based statistics show that the girls in the corpus use more quotations than the boys. There is a considerable female predominance in the use of quotative GO, but no significant difference in the use of SAY, which suggests that it is the adolescent girls who are in the forefront as regards the use of the use of GO as a quotative verb. Moreover, a study by Cheshire *et al.* (2008) provides evidence of yet another structure denoting reported speech, namely the pattern *this is* + subject + quotation, as in *this is me 'I'm from Hackney'*. In their data, this construction is primarily associated with the same group of speakers previously identified as being most phonetically innovative, namely speakers who are members of multi-ethnic friendship groups.

Finally, McCarthy (2002) focuses on the response tokens used in everyday conversation, basing the study on the British CANCODE (Cambridge and Nottingham Corpus of Discourse in English) corpus and the Cambridge–Cornell Corpus of Spoken North American English. While the linguistic behaviour of speakers has been given much attention in the literature, there are far fewer studies focusing on listenership. McCarthy looks at lexical items that serve as response signals, such as *right*, *really?*, *good* and *absolutely!* The comparison of the two varieties shows that '[a]lthough there are differences between the two varieties, they have more in common than what separates them' (ibid.: 69). He points at differences between the two varieties, such as the fact that *lovely*, *brilliant* and *marvellous* are typically British and virtually non-existent as responses in the

American data, while the use of *wow* and *sure* with a response function is more typical of American usage.

5. Possible future developments

As mentioned in Section 2, corpus linguistics has still a way to go in order to allow for the detailed analysis of phonetic features, including the fine-grained properties of speech sounds needed for acoustic phonetic analysis. Owing to the low quality of the sound files (or indeed the absence of such), many spoken corpora cannot be used for the detailed analysis of waveforms and frequency spectrums. This is very likely to change to the better in the near future, given the availability of inexpensive high-quality digital recording equipment, fundable within the budget framework of research projects. Future improvements of technical infrastructures for recording, storage and access, and increased processing capacity are likely to simplify and speed up the process of corpus development, to such an extent that it becomes unrealistic to use *anything but* corpus-linguistic method in dealing with empirical language data, in sociolinguistics and other fields. For one thing, automatic speech recognition (ASR) is becoming a technique that increasingly helps language users throughout the world, and, principally, corpus builders need not be sceptical about using ASR software as a basis for providing a rough transcription which is subjected to subsequent inspection by a human annotator. This requires, however, that the acoustic data have the sufficient sound quality and limited background noise.

Besides, many sociolinguistic studies fail to explore the technical opportunities that are inherent in a corpus, such as the inspection of collocations, n-gram statistics, pos-grams and deep-level parsing. Statistical modelling of speech patterns is a crucial part of NLP and even sociolinguists may benefit from looking at more sophisticated statistical and structural patterns in discourse, in the quest for knowledge about speakers and speaker groups. This information may have a supportive function in relation to other findings based on more traditional variational analysis, or it may be seen as valuable in its own right. For example, a data-driven investigation of the collocation patterns in the speech of, say, adolescents versus adult speakers, may give rise to hitherto undiscovered processes of structural reanalysis, grammaticalisation and lexicalisation. Another possibility for future sociolinguistics is to make use of new types of data that are made readily accessible due to the emergence of new media in the globalised communication society, such as video blogs and other self-recordings, published on the internet.

There is also a need for better standardisation of sociolinguistic and corpus-linguistic methods for annotating and accessing language data. There is a need for harmonisation of annotation schemes, particularly at the levels of discourse, speech acts and interactional structure. This will enable easier cross-corpora comparison, for the benefit of both sociolinguistics and language technology purposes. Important initiatives in this respect are CLARIN, Dublin Core, IMDI and TEI, language resources projects which are well documented on the web. In this respect, it is crucial that sociolinguists and conversation analysts engage actively in the organisation of new, large-scale national and international speech corpus collection projects.

Given the range of studies which have successfully applied corpus-linguistic methods for sociolinguistic purposes, it is beyond doubt that corpus-linguistic methods have a lot to offer to sociolinguistic research. As we have seen, corpora have been used to study linguistic variation between different varieties of a language and between different groups of speakers, by pointing at manifest differences in language use within a corpus or between corpora. Corpus linguistics provides efficient tools and methods for the collection, annotation and study of spoken data. This makes spoken corpora ideal for sociolinguistics.

Further reading

Andersen, G. (2001) *Pragmatic Markers and Sociolinguistic Variation*. Amsterdam: John Benjamins. (This book is a corpus-based study of pragmatic linguistic variation.)

Reppen, Fitzmaurice, R. and Biber, D. (eds) *Using Corpora to Explore Linguistic Variation*. Amsterdam: John Benjamins. (This book explores linguistic variation by addressing a wide range of topics at various levels of linguistic analysis.)

Schneider, K. P. and Barron, A. (2008) *Variational Pragmatics: A Focus on Regional Varieties in Pluricentric Languages*. Amsterdam: John Benjamins. (This book is purposefully designed to establish and explore the field of variational pragmatics and contains several corpus-based studies.)

Tagliamonte, S. (2006) *Analysing Sociolinguistic Variation*. Cambridge: Cambridge University Press. (This book is a comprehensive guide to the formal analysis of sociolinguistic variation.)

References

Andersen, G. (2001) *Pragmatic Markers and Sociolinguistic Variation*. Amsterdam: John Benjamins.

Bentzen, K. and Vangsnes, Ø. A. (eds) (2007) 'Scandinavian Dialect Syntax 2005', special issue of *Nordlyd*, Tromsø: University Library of Tromsø.

Chambers, J. K. (1995) *Sociolinguistic Theory: Linguistic Variation and its Social Significance*. Cambridge: Blackwell.

Cheshire, J. and Fox, S. (2009) 'Was/Were Variation: A Perspective from London', *Language Variation and Change* 21:1–38.

Cheshire, J., Fox, S., Kerswill, P. and Torgersen, E. (2008) 'Ethnicity, Friendship Network and Social Practices as the Motor of Dialect Change: Linguistic Innovation in London', *Sociolinguistica Jahrbuch* 22: 1–23.

De Beaugrande, R. (1999) 'Linguistics, Sociolinguistics, and Corpus Linguistics: Ideal Language versus Real Language', *Journal of Sociolinguistics* 3(1): 128–39.

Deutschmann, M. (2006) 'Social Variation in the Use of Apology Formulae in the British National Corpus', in A. Renouf and A. Kehoe (eds) *The Changing Face of Corpus Linguistics*. Amsterdam: Rodopi, pp. 205–22.

Duranti, A. and Goodwin, C. (1992) *Rethinking Context: Language as an Interactive Phenomenon*. Cambridge: Cambridge University Press.

Eckert, P. and Rickford, J. R. (2001) *Style and Sociolinguistic Variation*. Cambridge: Cambridge University Press.

Fletcher, J., Grabe, E. and Warren, P. (2004) 'Intonational Variation in Four Dialects of English: The High Rising Tune', in S.-A. Jun (ed.) *Prosodic Typology. The Phonology of Intonation and Phrasing*. Oxford: Oxford University Press, pp. 390–410.

Gabrielatos, C., Torgersen, E., Hoffinan, S. and Fox, S. (forthcoming) 'A Corpus-based Sociolinguistic Study of Indefinite Article Forms in London English', *Journal of English Linguistics*.

Greenbaum, S. and Svartvik, J. (1990) 'The London–Lund Corpus of Spoken English', in J. Svartvik (ed.) *The London–Lund Corpus of Spoken English: Description and Research*. Lund: Lund University Press, pp. 11–59.

Gumpertz, J. J. (1982) *Discourse Strategies*. Cambridge: Cambridge University Press.

Guy, G. and Vonwiller, J. (1984) 'The Meaning of an Intonation in Australian English', *Australian Journal of Linguistics* 4: 1–17.

Hoffman, S. (2004) 'Are Low-frequency Complex Prepositions Grammaticalized?', in H. Lindquist and C. Mair (eds) *Corpus Approaches to Grammaticalization in English*. Amsterdam: John Benjamins, pp. 171–210.

Hymes, D. (1974) *Foundations in Sociolinguistics: An Ethnographic Approach*. Philadelphia, PA: University of Pennsylvania Press.

Kennedy, G. (1998) *An Introduction to Corpus Linguistics*. London: Longman.

Kerswill, P., Cheshire, J. Fox, S. and Torgersen, E. (2008) 'Linguistic Innovators: The English of Adolescents in London', final report submitted to the ESRC.

Kerswill, P., Torgersen, E. and Fox, S. (2008) 'Reversing "Drift": Innovation and Diffusion in the London Diphthong System', *Language Variation and Change* 20(3): 451–91.

Kristoffersen, G. and Simonsen, H. G. (2008) 'Osjlo! En undersøkelse av uttalen av sl-sekvenser i NoTa-korpuset', in J. B. Johannessen and K. Hagen (eds) *Språk i Oslo: Ny forskning omkring talespråk*. Oslo: Novus, pp. 96–108.

Labov, W. (1966) *The Social Stratification of English in New York City*. Washington, DC: Center for Applied Linguistics.

——(1972) *Language in the Inner City: Studies in the Black English Vernacular*. Philadelphia, PA: University of Pennsylvania Press.

Leech, G. (1992) 'Corpora and Theories of Linguistic Performance', in J. Svartvik (ed.) *Directions in Corpus Linguistics: Proceedings of Nobel Symposium 82, Stockholm, 4–8 August 1991*. Berlin: Mouton de Gruyter, pp. 105–22.

McCarthy, M. (2002) 'Good Listenership Made Plain: British and American Non-minimal Response Tokens in Everyday Conversation', in R. Reppen, R. Fitzmaurice and D. Biber (eds) *Using Corpora to Explore Linguistic Variation*. Amsterdam: John Benjamins, pp. 73–90.

McEnery, T. and Wilson, A. (2001) *Corpus Linguistics: An Introduction*. Edinburgh: Edinburgh University Press.

Raymond, W. D., Pitt, M., Johnson, K., Hume, E., Makashay, M., Dautricourt, R. and Hilts, C. (2002) *An Analysis of Transcription Consistency in Spontaneous Speech from the Buckeye Corpus*. ICSLP-02, Denver. Columbus: Buckeye Speech Corpus.

Schelfhout, C., Coppen, P.-A., Ostdijk, N. and Van Der Slik, F. (2005) *Interjections in Dutch: A Corpus-based Approach*, available at www.neerlandistiek.nl/publish/articles/000100/article.pdf

Stenström, A.-B., Andersen, G. and Hasund, I. K. (2002) *Trends in Teenage Talk: Corpus Compilation, Analysis, and Findings*. Amsterdam: John Benjamins.

Vangsnes, Ø. (2008) 'Omkring adnominalt åssen/hvordan i Oslo-målet', in J. B. Johannessen and K. Hagen (eds) *Språk i Oslo. Ny forskning omkring talespråk*. Oslo: Novus, pp. 50–62.

Wichmann, A. (2004) 'The Intonation of *Please*-requests: A Corpus-based Study', *Journal of Pragmatics* 36: 1521–49.

40

How to use corpus linguistics in the study of media discourse

Kieran O'Halloran

1. Introduction: corpus linguistics and critical discourse analysis

Using tools of linguistic analysis, the study of how texts, particularly media texts, frame the events or issues they describe is one part of what is known as Critical Discourse Analysis (CDA). This branch of linguistics sheds light on how such framings can constrain appreciation of what is being reported. Before corpus linguistics became mainstream, CDA examined such framings in single texts at a particular point in time, or over a very short period. One of the advantages of the abundance of media texts in electronic form on the world-wide web is the ease with which corpora can be assembled for revealing the following: how media texts might be *repeatedly* framing issues or events which are reported over a significant period of time. This is a real advance for Critical Discourse Analysis. Conveniently, using corpus investigation, critical discourse analysts can now gain insight into the kinds of cultural and ideological meanings being circulated regularly, as well as being potentially reproduced by readers. Increasingly, critical discourse analysts employ corpora in their investigations of media discourse.

This chapter outlines Critical Discourse Analysis (Section 2), and discusses the corpus-based approach to CDA, including further advantages with this approach (Section 3). The substantive section of the chapter contains a case study which demonstrates the value of corpus-based Critical Discourse Analysis in revealing how media texts frame events and issues over a significant period of time (Section 4). Finally, this chapter discusses some ways in which the results of media corpus investigation can be disseminated using relatively recent web-based technologies.

2. Critical Discourse Analysis

CDA investigates how language use reproduces the perspectives, values and ways of talking of the powerful, which may not be in the interests of the less powerful. It thus focuses on the relationship between language, power and *ideology*. Ideologies are representations of aspects of the world which contribute to establishing and maintaining social relations of domination, inequality and exploitation, which CDA views as problematic and in need of addressing. Employing tools of linguistic analysis, critical discourse analysts seek to unpick these problem relations in order to illuminate how language use contributes to the domination and misrepresentation of certain social groups:

> Analysis, description and theory formation play a role especially in as far as they allow better understanding and critique of social inequality, based on gender, ethnicity, class, origin, religion, language, sexual orientation and other criteria that define differences between people. Their ultimate goal is not only scientific, but also social and political, namely *change*. In that case, social discourse analysis takes the form of a *critical* discourse analysis.
>
> (van Dijk 1997: 22–3)

CDA is thus a form of social critique. It encourages reflection on social and cultural processes and their relationship with language use, since it is assumed in CDA that this relationship is 'dialectical' or bi-directional. In other words, reproduction of unequal language use (e.g. 'man and wife' as opposed to 'husband and wife') can help to reproduce unequal cultural processes and vice versa. CDA is a committed form of discourse analysis since analysts are involved in contesting the phenomena they study. Analysts often make their social and political position explicit (usually left-liberal) in revealing and challenging dominance. With such a focus, CDA is drawn to texts where the marginal, and thus relatively powerless, feature, e.g. ethnic immigrants. Through the use of linguistic analysis, CDA 'diagnoses' a text's problems particularly with regard to (mis) representation of the marginal. While one does not need to be a critical discourse analyst to be critical of language and power abuse, a critical discourse analysis would differ from a 'lay' critique by having 'systematic approaches to inherent meanings', relying on 'scientific procedures' and necessarily requiring the 'self-reflection of the researchers themselves' (Fairclough and Wodak 1997: 279). Among the principal architects of CDA are Paul Chilton, Norman Fairclough, Teun van Dijk and Ruth Wodak (see, for example, van Dijk 1991; Wodak *et al.* 1999; Fairclough 2001; Chilton 2004).

3. Corpus-based CDA

Orientation

CDA has not escaped criticism, which has largely been on methodological grounds. Widdowson (2004) accuses CDA of being over-subjective in its analysis of texts because its analysis is directed by political commitment. The charge of subjectivity can be awkward to refute when CD analysts are not part of the target audience of the texts they analyse. This is because the CD analyst may describe aspects of the text which he or she objects to, and go on to produce an interpretation of, when the target audience may not actually generate this interpretation. When there is no kind of empirically based investigation which can shine light on audience-response or the facets of a text that the audience is likely to notice, CDA has been open to the charges of: (i) arbitrariness of analysis; (ii) circularity from analysis to interpretation and back to analysis, since there is nothing to determine which facets of a text to focus on other than what chimes with the political commitment of the analyst.

With a few examples in the 1990s, but with momentum in the first decade of the twenty-first century, CDA is drawing on corpus linguistic modes of investigation. This has helped to improve methodological rigour and, in turn, mitigate attack from critics. For example, use of large reference corpora in CDA, for purposes of comparison with a text(s) under investigation, reveals salient linguistic features in that text. In this way is arbitrariness, and thus analyst subjectivity, reduced since it is the software which reveals salience and not the analyst. Another advantage of corpus-based CDA is that analysts can go beyond single texts and conveniently explore quantitative patterns of ideological meaning in a large number of texts. This can be done either synchronically, i.e. in a set of texts produced on the same day, or diachronically, i.e. looking at linguistic patterns over a period of time. The following are examples of work in corpus-based CDA where media discourse examination features: Stubbs (1996, 2001); Charteris-Black (2004); Adolphs (2006); Baker (2006); O'Keeffe (2006); Mautner (2007); O'Halloran (2007); Baker *et al.* (2008); Koller and Davidson (2008); Hidalgo Tenorio (2009). Studying quantitative patterns can be interesting in itself. But, since CDA is concerned with examining ideological meaning, quantitative analysis needs to be combined with qualitative analysis (Fairclough 2003: 6). The case study in Section 4 will show how quantitative data mined from a corpus can usefully ground qualitative analysis and in so doing help to enhance methodological rigour.

One important inspiration for corpus-based CDA has been the work of the corpus linguist Michael Stubbs (notably Stubbs 1996, 2001), and in particular the way he builds on the work of Raymond Williams' 'cultural keyword' analysis from a corpus-based perspective. Corpus-based CDA has also drawn on another notion of keyword such as that found in Scott (2008). The following section outlines these different notions of 'keyword', notions which are drawn upon in the case study in Section 4.

Keywords

Cultural keywords

For Raymond Williams, the Marxist thinker, 'key' in 'keyword' indicates that a particular concept is salient across a culture. So, for example, 'democracy' and 'revolution' are keywords for Williams. Williams (1983) is a socio-historical, diachronic dictionary of keywords where their semantic development over centuries is traced and interrelationships explored. For this work, Williams used the complete *Oxford English Dictionary* (OED), which runs to several volumes. To help with discriminating different types of keyword, this chapter refers to Williams' notion of keyword as a *cultural keyword* (as, indeed, does Stubbs 1996, 2001).

Corpus-based cultural keywords

Chapters in Stubbs (1996, 2001) also examine cultural keywords. The difference from Williams is that Stubbs' investigation of cultural keywords is done in the main synchronically and is informed by corpus-based methods. 'Standard' is one of the cultural keywords which Williams (1983) investigates using the OED. Stubbs (2001) uses a 200-million-word corpus of contemporary English, which consists mainly of newspaper and magazine media texts, in order to highlight the most common collocates of the word 'standard': 'living', 'high', etc. Collocates are words which commonly accompany other words over short word spans: that is, they form a *collocation* such as 'living standards'. The method is more rigorous than when Williams focuses on contemporary usage since it provides objective quantitative support for the extent to which cultural keywords are being used, and the lexical company they keep. It thus provides a measure of what meanings are being culturally reproduced. We might refer to the cultural keywords Stubbs looks at as *corpus-based cultural keywords*.

Stubbs (1996, 2001) uses corpus-based methods to examine cultural keywords related to the education policy of the UK Conservative Party during the 1980s and 1990s (e.g. correctness, grammar, standards). Here is Stubbs (2001: 158):

> Keywords often inter-collocate, and ideas gain stability when they fit into a frame. Many everyday ideas about language fit very firmly into a frame which contains terms such as:
>
> - standard, standards, accurate, correct, grammar, proper, precise
>
> For linguists, the same terms mean something quite different because they fit into an entirely different lexical field, which contains terms such as:
>
> - dialect, language planning, high prestige language, social variation
>
> These fields are systems of meaning, which use particular vocabulary, take particular things for granted, appeal to different states of knowledge (for example, lay and professional), and therefore allow only particular argumentative moves.

In highlighting how cultural keywords inter-collocate in frames, Stubbs provides a very useful insight.

Corpus-comparative statistical keywords

A large corpus is not only used to provide quantitative support for cultural keywords. It can be used to find a different type of keyword, one which Scott (2008) was designed, in part, to investigate. This type of keyword is defined as words which are statistically more salient in a text or set of texts than in a large reference corpus. 'Keyness' here is established through statistical measures such as log likelihood value (see Dunning 1993; see also chapters by Evison, Scott and Tribble, this volume). Relatively high log likelihoods indicate keywords. In order to distinguish this type of keyword from the ones discussed so far, this chapter uses the expression *corpus-comparative statistical keyword*.

Corpus-comparative statistical keywords can be both lexical and grammatical words. Imagine a comparison of a corpus of several thousand mobile phone text messages in English with a large reference corpus of English consisting of millions of words from a variety of different genres. It is likely that the grammatical word 'da' (a truncation of the definite article) would have relatively high keyness since it is much more likely to feature in text messages than in most other genres. It would then be a corpus-comparative statistical keyword. One important function of the corpus investigation software *WordSmith Tools* (Scott 2008) is revealing these keywords in a text or a corpus in comparison with a much larger reference corpus.

Relationship between corpus-comparative statistical keywords and cultural keywords

Corpus-comparative statistical keywords may or may not coincide with (corpus-based) cultural keywords. This is because the former may be: (i) any lexical word, and thus part of an extremely large set or (ii) any grammatical word. In contrast (corpus-based) cultural keywords are all lexical words from a much smaller set. Although corpus-based cultural keywords have the advantage that collocation patterns are based on quantitative evidence, all the same this is quantitative evidence around cultural keywords which have been pre-established by a human interpreter. This may be uncontroversial as in the case of 'democracy' or 'immigration'. Alternatively, choice of cultural keyword may overly reflect the cultural and political sympathies of the human interpreter. For example, Williams (1983) includes 'peasant' as a cultural keyword. In contrast, an advantage of corpus-comparative statistical keywords is that they are established objectively by software. They are not then intuited by human researchers. Their generation reduces arbitrariness in their identification. However, it must be stressed that though corpus-comparative statistical keywords are generated objectively by software, this objectivity is always *relative* to a particular reference corpus.

Having given an account of different cultural keywords/keywords, this chapter will now supply a case study. This will include a corpus-based critical discourse analysis of a corpus of media texts where these different notions of keywords are important in the analysis and interpretation of ideological meanings that a regular target readership would have been exposed to, and may potentially be reproducing.

4. Case study

Orientation

This case study focuses on a set of texts over a six-week period in the British popular tabloid newspaper *The Sun* on the topic of the European Union (EU) expansion on 1 May 2004. On this date, ten new countries joined the EU, eight of which are located in the east of Europe: Cyprus, Czech Republic, Estonia, Hungary, Latvia, Lithuania, Malta, Poland, Slovakia, Slovenia. It was six weeks prior to 1 May that *The Sun* began producing news texts regularly on the subject of the EU's imminent expansion. In cursory readings of some of the texts, there seemed to be some kind of quasi-campaign being run, a series of predictions being made about imminent immigration from Eastern European countries. On such a reading, there appeared to be a purpose to persuade readers of a set of possibilities (e.g. detrimental effects on social services from huge immigration). But how and where to begin a proper systematic analysis of the texts to establish the kinds of ideological meanings that regular target readers would have been exposed to, and might potentially be reproducing? One could go through the texts and perform a qualitative analysis, but this would run the risk of arbitrariness and thus circularity of interpretation to analysis to interpretation. As will be shown, the advantage of a quantitative corpus-based analysis using software such as *WordSmith Tools* is that we can first establish quantitative patterns of lexis and grammar within which we can ground qualitative interpretation of semantic patterns. This, as will be demonstrated, reduces circularity and arbitrariness of interpretation.

The corpus I investigate consists of all texts in the six weeks prior to 1 May which contain the cultural keywords: '(im)migration', '(im)migrant(s)', 'EU' and 'European'. The corpus consists of seventy-six texts, a total of 26,350 words, and is in chronological order from 20 March to 30 April 2004.

Concordancer collocation analysis and semantic significance

Collocation and frames

The corpus investigation focuses on how Eastern European migrants are realised linguistically. For the first type of quantitative pattern to investigate in the corpus, let me first explore collocation for 'east*' where the asterisk is a wildcard to capture 'east' and 'eastern' ('Europe(an(s))'). There are thirty-seven concordance lines for 'east' (Figure 40.1):

March 12: Ms Hughes reveals 25,000 east Europeans were let into Britain in a
fiasco. Experts predict up to 54,000 East Europeans could head to the UK when
MigrationWatch UK predicts some 40,000 East Europeans will migrate here. Chairman
get OUT of the UK for good - just as East Europeans are queuing to get IN, a
new **rules are dodged or challenged** by East European migrants. The Government
just how easy it is to get a **false** east European passport and exploit the
business plans - many identical - for East Europeans. This gave them the right
crunch point' - days before millions of East Europeans become eligible to live
countries to allow for the arrival of East Europeans. But he will outline the
had been snapped up last night by *poor* East Europeans seeking a better life in
crackdown on migrants, it emerged that East European **vice girls** are set to join
'It's lottery time for girls from the East because they can earn in a night what
54,000 due to *high unemployment* in the East. And there are fears services like
access to jobs for up to seven years. East Europeans who find legitimate work in
,000. Provisional figures show 138,000 eastern Europeans visited in January and
If this trend continues, 1,376,000 eastern Europeans will come to Britain
and unelected institution. 30A 700,000 Eastern Europeans arrived LAST year By NIC
Political Correspondent NEARLY 700,000 eastern Europeans arrived in Britain last
rity stay under a month. Visitors from eastern Europe rose 23 per cent from
masters. The men and women - all from eastern Europe - **were arrested** in dawn
underqualified doctors and nurses from Eastern Europe when their countries join
ber-stamping of **bogus applications** from eastern European countries, but instead of
l keep a tight grip on immigration from Eastern Europe. He is right to recognise
out that many thousands of people from Eastern Europe could be heading here after
head for Britain. With coachloads from Eastern Europe tipped to arrive on Sunday
in a wave of migrants from *impoverished* Eastern Europe. The Sun followed the
een told about a **suspected visa scam** in eastern Europe. Ms Hughes met Prime
ive **criminal scam** has been operating in eastern Europe with the full knowledge and
which nationals of future EU nations in eastern Europe can come to Britain and set
s said the survey did not show how many Eastern Europeans returned home. But the
land, Czech Republic and Hungary. Many eastern Europeans will then be free to
Statistics figures reveal the number of eastern Europeans coming to the UK is
hours before May 1 arrives and most of eastern Europe has the right to live here.
Real culprits DON'T blame the people of Eastern Europe for heading for Britain. The
ve checks to hurry through a backlog of eastern bloc applicants was 'only the tip
er-stamping regime to clear backlogs of eastern European applications in a
Kosice was repeated all through Eastern Europe. Thousands set off to

Figure 40.1 Concordance lines for 'east*' from *The Sun* 26,000-word corpus

The concordancer function of *WordSmith Tools* is useful because it can reveal patterns, and thus a sense of what regular readers would be exposed to (see Tribble, this volume). Collocationally a dominant pattern, with seventeen instances, is numbers of Eastern European migrants who are likely to arrive after 1 May 2004: e.g. 'coachloads', 'many', 'millions'. So we know that regular readers are exposed to the idea of numbers. It is tempting to read more significance than this into the corpus, e.g. the use of numbers signals an alarmist and at worst racist overtones; in other words, *The Sun* is communicating that the UK will be 'swamped' with foreign nationals. However, numbers on their own do not necessarily provide significance. For example, migration is likely to be commonly talked about numerically by government bodies in a neutral sense, and numbers referred to in the concordance lines could be reports of government figures. As such, one should be careful not to over-interpret concordance line data. Having said this, although it is difficult to see from concordance lines the significance of the dominant pattern of numbers and migrants, we can take this as evidence of a *frame* in Stubbs' terms, given the regularity of collocation here. That is, from the evidence above, regular readers of *The Sun* over the six-week period would understand Eastern European migration in association with large numbers.

What kind of migrants are projected to come? One collocation pattern relates to poverty: 'high-unemployment', 'impoverished', 'poor' (in italic in Figure 40.1). But at three instances this can hardly be said to be a major pattern. Second, it is hard to know without more co-text whether these are negative judgements of migrants or perhaps expressions of empathy. Meanings around migrants which are more obviously negative are as follows: 'underqualified doctors and nurses from Eastern Europe'; 'vice-girls'; 'new rules are dodged or challenged by Eastern European migrants'; 'bogus applications from eastern European'; 'The men and women – all from eastern Europe – were arrested'; 'false passports'; 'suspected visa scam'; 'criminal scam' (in bold above).

Ideological reproduction and inferencing

I have indicated that one cannot always show the significance of what is regularly repeated from concordance line data. To fully achieve this, and especially in relation to ideological reproduction, we may need to go beyond looking at collocation in concordance lines and take account of how clauses and indeed sentences relate to one another. In any case, since ideological reproduction through language ultimately requires an inferential contribution, clause/sentence structure may well have a significant effect on the types of inference readers and listeners generate around cultural keywords. The critical discourse analyst Fairclough (1992: 84) gives the following useful example (which includes the word, 'job', identified as a cultural keyword in Stubbs 1996):

> what establishes the coherent link between the two sentences 'She's giving up her job next Wednesday. She's pregnant' is the assumption that women cease to work when they have children. In so far as interpreters take up these positions and automatically make these connections, they are being subjected by and to the text, and this is an important part of the ideological 'work' of texts and discourse in 'interpellating' subjects.

Ideological reproduction would not take place through 'job' or indeed through 'pregnant', but through the coherence inference linking these words, i.e. coherence is set up through text structure. Where corpus-based collocation analysis is useful is in showing what meanings readers are regularly exposed to, and thus the frames they may possess. Where it is often limited is in providing evidence for the kinds of inferences readers are likely to make, as a result of this exposure, in accordance with text structure (which may stretch over sentences and thus not be captured in a single concordance line). In other words, it is limited in showing the *significance* of frames in actual discourse.

In the rest of this case study, I will show the usefulness of corpus investigation in identifying regular text structural patterns – that is, going beyond collocation – which in turn can indicate the kind of ideologically laden inferences that regular target readers could make. To start with, in the next section, I use *WordSmith Tools 5.0* to generate corpus-comparative statistical keywords (henceforth CCSKs). I then examine the extent to which CCSKs repeatedly:

1 co-occur across stretches of text larger than collocational spans in concordance lines;
2 provide text structure.

Then, in the following section, I explore whether CCSKs are potentially providing text structure for a set of semantic patterns which, in turn, can indicate the kinds of ideologically laden inferences readers might make in subsequent reading of related texts in relation to migration.

CCSKs and text structure

CCSKs

Using *WordSmith Tools*, the first procedure is finding the CCSKs of *The Sun* corpus. This is done by comparing *The Sun* corpus with a reference corpus. The reference corpus used is BNC-baby, an approximately four-million-word sample of the British National Corpus, which consists of around one million words each of academic prose, conversation, fiction and newspaper text. This reference corpus is chosen since its genres are mainstream ones and, as a whole, can be taken as a 'snapshot' of mainstream use of English. To ascertain CCSKs, firstly wordlists for both corpora need to be generated; a

Table 40.1 The highest CCSK values for the *Sun* corpus

Keyword	*Frequency*	*% in corpus*	*Reference corpus frequency*	*Keyness*
immigration	135	0.49	40	1,164.79
EU	107	0.39	2	1,051.86
Blair	105	0.38	12	974.53
's	155	0.56	630	781.22
Britain	129	0.47	671	594.45
Hughes	58	0.21	58	420.83
Poland	44	0.16	20	361.40
Blunkett	36	0.13	4	334.56
PM	38	0.14	12	325.59
asylum	36	0.13	15	298.92

wordlist provides word frequencies in a corpus (see chapters by Evison and Scott, this volume). Then, these wordlists are compared by the software to establish keyness values. Table 40.1 shows the ten highest values for 'keyness'. As can be seen, the cultural keyword 'immigration' has high keyness, as does 'EU'. What this means is that 'immigration' and 'EU' occur with greater statistical salience in *The Sun* corpus than in the reference corpus. Since the corpus texts are selected in part from these search words, it is not surprising that they should feature as CCSKs.

CCSKs provide a rough snapshot of salient topics in a corpus. CCSKs with relatively high values indicate the UK politicians being recurrently referred to over this period: Blair (Prime Minister), Blunkett (Home Secretary) and Hughes (Home Office Minister for Citizenship and Immigration) and also other stories connected with immigration, immigration officialdom, etc. but not necessarily connected with Eastern Europeans. (The software treats 's', as in 'Britain's' or 'he's', and 't', as in 'don't', as whole words.)

Keyword dispersion plot

For a word to occur as a CCSK, it does not necessarily need to occur very frequently. For example, 'Trajce' (a town in Poland) has keyness of 30.04; it only occurs three times in *The Sun* corpus but does not occur at all in the reference corpus. Because I am interested in seeing whether repeated semantic patterns in *The Sun* corpus can be identified around CCSKs, keyness is not the only criterion I need to take into account. Another is frequency. However, it must be borne in mind that out of the seventy-six texts, some CCSKs may occur very frequently in just a handful of texts. Because my focus is on identifying regularly recurrent semantic patterns over the whole of the corpus, CCSKs which feature in a concentrated burst are of less relevance to me. I need, then, to find CCSKs which are not only frequent but well dispersed across the six weeks' worth of texts. The dispersion plot facility of *WordSmith Tools* is useful for my purposes. Table 40.2 shows the ten highest dispersion plot values for CCSKs. The dispersion value is a number between 0 and 1, with those CCSKs with a value close to 1 having the greatest dispersion. Organisation is in terms of descending dispersion values. (Plot dispersion uses the first of the three formulae supplied in Oakes 1998: 190–1.)

Interestingly, the grammatical word 'But' (i.e. with a capital 'B') has the third highest dispersion value (0.915); it has keyness (28.93). This is interesting for my focus since, as a

Table 40.2 The highest CCSK dispersion plot values for *The Sun* corpus

Keyword	*Dispersion*	*Keyness*
#	0.948	102.57
said	0.919	52.30
But	0.915	28.93
who	0.914	45.43
's	0.884	781.22
By	0.880	41.31
yesterday	0.879	44.88
Britain	0.871	594.45
has	0.869	56.00
We	0.868	29.62

Note: #, in the first line, refers to numbers.

grammatical word, it signals a contrastive relation across sentences and thus creates text structure. Moreover, 'but' (i.e., with a lower-case 'b') does not have keyness since it has a negative value (-30.53). There are eighty-five instances of 'But' and forty-nine instances of 'but' in *The Sun* corpus (0.31 per cent and 0.18 per cent of the total number of words respectively). However, in BNC-baby there are 6,594 instances of 'But' and 14,619 instances of 'but' (0.16 per cent and 0.36 per cent of the total number of words respectively). The ratio of quantities of 'But'/'but' in *The Sun* corpus is almost the opposite to that of BNC-baby. So, on this comparison, that 'But' has keyness is even more significant. To sum up: in *The Sun* corpus 'But' has significant keyness, frequency and dispersion.

The results for 'But' are interesting especially since, in starting a sentence, 'But' has prominence. This is even more the case if it begins a sentence which initiates a paragraph. And indeed, it is common in *The Sun* for paragraphs to be one sentence in length. So, if 'But' is helping to provide text structure for semantic patterns on a regular basis, in turn the semantic patterns will have prominence. 'But', as a grammatical word, will of course not provide lexical content. So, to ascertain if 'But' is providing structure for semantic patterns (i.e. patterns of meaning which in stretching over clauses go beyond collocation), I need to discern whether there are associations of 'But' with lexical CCSKs. If I can find regular semantic patterns around such associations, then I will have reduced the prospect that I am identifying these arbitrarily. Finding such associations can be done by employing another function of *WordSmith Tools* – keyword links.

Keyword links

The 'keyword links' function of *WordSmith Tools* shows the number of CCSKs which co-occur with a particular CCSK in a designated word span. The highest word span possible is twenty-five words to both the left and the right of a search term. I choose this span so as to capture the maximum possible co-occurrences with 'But'. There are nine CCSK links for 'But' for this span (one which crosses sentence and paragraph boundaries):

Britain, he, home, immigration, Mr, UK, vote, will, yesterday.

The next stage is to search through the entire *Sun* corpus and highlight all instances of 'But', as well as the nine CCSK links to 'But', and then inspect whether regular semantic patterns can be identified around any of these 'But CCSK links' in relation to Eastern European immigration. (The CCSK link span was restricted to -25+25, but this highlighting may go beyond this span.)

Semantic pattern types via 'But'

The five semantic pattern types

In exploring the text fragments with the keyword links, I identified five different semantic pattern types associated with 'But' and the CCSK links. For the semantic patterns identified, the CCSKs which are most repeatedly linked to 'But' are 'will', 'UK', 'Britain', 'immigration' and 'home' (in 'Home Office', the UK government department which deals with immigration). Below, I indicate the five semantic pattern types in the corpus via examples with the CCSKs in italics. In brackets next to each pattern is the number of times each pattern occurred in the corpus.

Semantic Pattern 1 (x 18): for (Eastern European) immigration, there is UK government or official agency incompetence

With this semantic pattern, there is often a reporting of government figures for immigration from new EU countries, the actions of immigration officials, etc. Then 'But' begins a sentence or paragraph which contrasts negatively with the UK government perspective and which sets up negative evaluation, either explicit or implicit, that government, officials, etc., are incompetent, e.g.:

> 26 April The *Home* Office estimates that no more than 13,000 workers *will* come each year.
>
> *But* others put the figure as high as 54,000 due to high unemployment in the East.

Semantic Pattern 2 (x 8): for (Eastern European) immigration, (fear, worry, challenge from) large numbers predicted to arrive in the UK

In this semantic pattern, 'But' is used to provide negative contrast in relation to the UK facing huge (Eastern European) immigration which is a challenge to the government, or a fear/worry for various reasons, e.g.:

> 27 April Stay Strong
>
> THE SUN welcomes Tony Blair's assurance that *he will* keep a tight grip on *immigration* from Eastern Europe.
>
> *He* is right to recognise that people are worried about what *will* happen after May 1.
>
> *But* the PM faces a huge challenge. Thousands are heading for *Britain* in search of a better life.

Semantic Pattern 3 (x 4): for (Eastern European) immigration, there will be strain on social services

With this semantic pattern, there is a projection of numbers of East European 'migrants' arriving in the UK. Then, the semantic pattern via 'But' indicates, through negative contrast, that this will lead to overstretched UK social services, e.g.:

> 26 April THOUSANDS of plane, train and bus seats had been snapped up last night by poor East Europeans seeking a better life in *Britain.*
>
> They are free to come here when ten new countries join the EU this Saturday, May 1.
>
> *But* it is feared that in some areas overstretched *UK* services like schools and hospitals *will* be unable to cope with the influx.

Semantic Pattern (x 4): for (Eastern European) immigration, there will be some illegal (EU) status

Semantic Pattern 4 relates to stories about illegal immigrants in the UK, or predictions that there will be immigrants arriving in the UK from Eastern Europe, who will have illegal EU citizenship (posing as Polish below), e.g.:

> 2 April Lieutenant Miroslaw Szacillo, 46, of the Polish Border Guards, assured *The Sun*: 'Only the most serious criminals with big money can afford to buy false documents in Poland. We make stringent checks on our borders and we are getting more equipment to detect fake documents.'
>
> *But* Poles who do get in and find work in *Britain will* qualify for a range of benefits including free healthcare, child tax credit, child benefit, working tax credit, housing benefit and council tax benefit.

Notice also above that 'But' is used, in negative contrast, in predicting that people claiming to be Polish will be able to claim benefits.

Semantic Pattern 5 (x 2): for (Eastern European) immigration, there will be some criminality

In Semantic Pattern 5, 'But' is used to signal, through negative contrast, the prospect of serious criminality characterising some immigration from Eastern Europe, e.g.:

> 31 March Many new arrivals *will* be good news for *Britain*.
>
> *But* some *will* be up to no good. Gun-happy crime syndicates have already set up vicious vice and drug rackets.
>
> Others want to do our nation harm. The Wall Street Journal says Islamic fanatics are using *immigration* as a 'Trojan horse to expand jihad, or holy war'.

Summing up the corpus-based qualitative analysis

'But' is never used in the corpus to indicate a positive evaluation of migrants as contrasting with a previously stated negative one (e.g. 'some migrants from Eastern Europe may be criminals. But the majority will be good for the economy'). 'But' in the thirty-six semantic patterns signals, either explicitly or implicitly, negative contrast. Thus, the corpus investigation shows there is evidence that 'But' has potentially been 'primed' for regular *Sun* readers to indicate negative evaluative contrast, specifically in relation to predictions around future migration to the UK. However, the priming of 'But' relates also to the grammatical word, 'will', and lexical words such as 'immigration'. The priming is actually, then, lexicogrammatical. (On 'priming' see Hoey 2005). So, regular readers of *The Sun* during the six-week period could well expect 'But' to preface a negative prediction (most likely around 'will') about Eastern European migration to the UK. Conversely, because of these repeated lexicogrammatical associations, regular readers have been positioned into making negative contrast with information on Eastern European immigration in related subsequent texts. In other words, they have been positioned into making negative contrastive inferences from repeated exposure to the five semantic patterns.

Ideological reproduction and the interrelatedness of the semantic patterns

The most common semantic pattern is Semantic Pattern 1 at eighteen instances; the next is Semantic Pattern 2 at eight instances. Individually, Semantic Patterns 3, 4, and 5 are fewer in number than Semantic Patterns 1 and 2. However, they are different in kind to Semantic Patterns 1 and 2 since they are predicted negative consequences of projected Eastern European immigration; taken together, Semantic Patterns 3, 4 and 5 amount to ten instances.

Interestingly, while the patterns are semantically distinct in the texts, they are often in close proximity to each other, linked to each other around the 'But CCSK links'. Consider for example:

> 26 April DON'T blame the **people of Eastern Europe** for heading for *Britain*. (SEMANTIC PATTERN 2).
> The Government has put out the welcome mat. (SEMANTIC PATTERN 1)
> And to **hard-up foreigners** this looks the land of milk and honey.
> *But* **most** *will* end up in unskilled low-paid jobs in the South East.
> How *will* **they** afford to live? And how can schools and hospitals which are already at breaking point find room for **them**? (SEMANTIC PATTERN 3)
>
> (my italics and bold)

Semantic Pattern 1, seemingly so different to Semantic Patterns 2–5, links in the data to other semantic patterns as can be seen in the example above. Because of regular interrelating of semantic patterns around 'But CCSK links', potential has been created for the reader to deduce one or more of the five semantic patterns in subsequent reading of other semantic patterns over the six weeks prior to 1 May. In this way, ideological reproduction would take place. In other words, a discourse is created around new Eastern European migrants where they are not treated with equity.

It is also worth noting that the preponderance of Semantic Pattern 1 (eighteen instances) across the corpus might seem to protect *The Sun* from accusations of bias against immigrants, i.e. it seems to focus much more on government incompetence than on the predicted consequences of migration. However, the interrelatedness of Semantic Pattern 1, along the 'But CCSK links', with other semantic patterns, and the potential for deductions from Semantic Pattern 1 means that in practice it would be disingenuous for *The Sun* to claim that it is always only criticising the government. Such interrelatedness, especially with Semantic Pattern 3, means that seeming expressions of empathy such as 'high unemployment', 'impoverished', 'poor' (see the examples in Figure 40.1) are, in fact, likely to imply migrants will be a drain on social services. Finally, it is also notable that a concordance line for 'Eastern Europe' in the examples in Figure 40.1 cannot show the cohesive pattern of, for example, 'Eastern Europe' to 'hard-up foreigners' to 'most' to 'they' to 'them' in the 26 April fragment above (see my bold). The concordance lines, in turn, are limited in showing the interrelatedness of semantic patterns, and thus the kinds of dynamic meanings regular target readers could be generating.

In the ways I have indicated, ideological reproduction can potentially take place in reading. I have thus shown the value of a corpus-based CDA because it grounds qualitative patterns in quantitative patterns and in so doing can help to reveal patterns of ideological meanings. Furthermore, I have shown the value of grounding interpretation of semantic patterns in corpus-generated data since arbitrariness of identification, and circularity of analysis to interpretation to analysis, has been considerably reduced.

5. Prosumer Critical Discourse Analysis

This chapter began by extolling the advantage of having media texts in electronic form on the world-wide web. With the ever developing world-wide web and the bloom in technological tools which facilitate production and distribution of content, 'media' now means a multitude of things. Not only can it include electronic web versions of print-based media, and internet television and radio, but also 'citizen media'. There are many forms of citizen-produced media (hence the term *prosumer*, producer–consumer) including blogs, vlogs, podcasts, digital storytelling, participatory video. Some forms of citizen-produced media are 'parasitical' on the official media, such as reader electronic comments on a piece of on-line journalism, or contributions to newspaper web discussion forums. The world-wide web has thus facilitated media *prosumption* – citizens can both consume the media and produce it (Tapscott and Williams 2008).

Analysing a media corpus for patterns of ideological meaning can become a form of prosumption if the critical discourse analyst feeds back the results of his or her analysis in a vehicle such as a blog, or even engages with actual readers in a discussion forum in the on-line version of the newspaper investigated. With such contributions, one needs to tread carefully, given copyright issues and the legal restrictions on the purposes for which one can compile web-based corpora (e.g. commercial gain is usually prohibited). Analysts would also need to act quickly in compiling their corpora since the topic under investigation will not necessarily remain a hot one. But, done sensitively and carefully, there is the prospect of a new form of critical discourse engagement: one where target readers can become more aware of the regularity of what they consume and potentially the kinds of ideologically laden inferences they may be making in reading of media texts.

Further reading

Adolphs, S. (2006) *Introducing Electronic Text Analysis*. London: Routledge. (An accessible discussion of the underlying principles and concepts relevant to electronic text analysis; provides an overview of different types of spoken and written corpora.)

Baker, P. (2006) *Using Corpora in Discourse Analysis*. London: Continuum. (A lucid examination and evaluation of a variety of corpus-based concepts and methods including: collocation, keyness, concordances, dispersion plots, as well as building and annotating corpora.)

Bednarek, M. (2006) *Evaluation in Media Discourse: Analysis of a Newspaper Corpus*. London: Continuum. (Presents the first book-length corpus-based account of evaluation, using a corpus of 100 newspaper articles comprising a 70,000 word comparable corpus, drawn from both tabloid and broadsheet media.)

O'Keeffe, A. (2006) *Investigating Media Discourse*. London: Routledge. (Usefully shows how combining corpus linguistic quantitative method with the qualitative methods of discourse analysis and conversation analysis can lead to multiple insights.)

Stubbs, M. (1996) *Text and Corpus Analysis: Computer-assisted Studies of Language and Culture*. Oxford: Blackwell. (A pioneering work in corpus-assisted text analysis; particularly useful for corpus-assisted CDA in showing how software can be used to reveal culturally significant patterns of language use.)

References

Adolphs, S. (2006) *Introducing Electronic Text Analysis*. London: Routledge.

Baker, P. (2006) *Using Corpora in Discourse Analysis*. London: Continuum.

Baker, P., Gabrielatos, C., KhosraviNik, M., Krzyzanowski, M., McEnery, T. and Wodak, R. (2008) 'A Useful Methodological Synergy? Combining Critical Discourse Analysis and Corpus Linguistics to Examine Discourses of Refugees and Asylum Seekers in the UK Press', *Discourse and Society* 19(3): 273–306.

Charteris-Black, J. (2004) *Corpus Approaches to Critical Metaphor Analysis*. Basingstoke: Palgrave Macmillan.

Chilton, P. (2004) *Analysing Political Discourse*. London: Routledge.

Dunning, T. (1993) 'Accurate Methods for the Statistics of Surprise and Coincidence', *Computational Linguistics*. 19: 1 61–74.

Fairclough, N. (1992) *Discourse and Social Change*. Cambridge: Polity.

——(2001) *Language and Power*, second edition. London: Longman.

——(2003) *Analysing Discourse: Textual Analysis for Social Research*. London: Routledge.

Fairclough, N. and Wodak, R. (1997) 'Critical Discourse Analysis', in T. van Dijk (ed.) *Discourse as Social Interaction*. London: Sage, pp. 258–84.

Hidalgo Tenorio, E. (2009) 'The Metaphorical Construction of Ireland', in K. Ahrens (ed.) *Politics, Gender and Conceptual Metaphors*. Houndmills and New York: Palgrave Macmillan, pp. 112–36.

Hoey, M. (2005) *Lexical Priming*. London: Routledge.

Koller, V. and Davidson, P. (2008) 'Social Exclusion as Conceptual and Grammatical Metaphor: A Cross-genre Study of British Policy-making', *Discourse and Society* 19(3): 307–31.

Mautner, G. (2007) 'Mining Large Corpora for Social Information: The Case of "Elderly"', *Language in Society* 36(1): 51–72.

Oakes, M. (1998) *Statistics for Corpus Linguistics*. Edinburgh: Edinburgh University Press.

O'Halloran, K. A (2007) 'Critical Discourse Analysis and the Corpus-informed Interpretation of Metaphor at the Register Level', *Applied Linguistics* 28(1): 1–24.

O'Keeffe, A. (2006) *Investigating Media Discourse*. London: Routledge.

Scott, M. (2008) *WordSmith Tools Version 5.0*. Oxford: Oxford University Press.

Stubbs, M. (1996) *Text and Corpus Analysis: Computer-assisted Studies of Language and Culture*. Oxford: Blackwell.

——(2001) *Words and Phrases: Corpus Studies of Lexical Semantics*. Oxford: Blackwell.

Tapscott, D. and Williams, A. (2008) *Wikinomics: How Mass Collaboration Changes Everything*. London: Atlantic Books.

Van Dijk, T. (1991) *Racism and the Press*. London: Routledge.

——(1997) 'The Story of Discourse', in T. van Dijk, *Discourse as Structure and Process*. London: Sage.

Widdowson, H. G. (2004) *Text, Context, Pretext: Critical Issues in Discourse Analysis*. Oxford: Blackwell.

Williams, R. (1983) *Keywords*, second edition. London: Flamingo.

Wodak, R., de Cillia, R., Reisigl, M. and Liebhart, K. (1999) *The Discursive Construction of National Identity*. Edinburgh: Edinburgh University Press.

41

How to use corpus linguistics in forensic linguistics

Janet Cotterill

1. The notion of the forensic corpus and its potential use in authorship analysis

In an age of computerisation, the use of corpora in many types of forensic linguistic analysis is becoming increasingly commonplace. In fact, there are certain areas such as authorship, where corpus linguistics is seen as the way forward for identification and elimination of candidate authors. This chapter will explore the issues around the use of corpus linguistics in forensic linguistic analysis, including both its potential advantages and also some of the methodological challenges associated with its use.

Within the field of forensic linguistics, the idea of using corpora to analyse legal casework involving texts is a relatively new and cutting-edge concept. As a methodology, it derives from pre-existing work in biblical authorship and Shakespearean authorship, both of which have drawn on corpora of various constitutions. However, as O'Keeffe *et al.* (2007: 20) attest, 'authorship and plagiarism are growing concerns within forensic linguistics, for which corpora can prove a useful instrument of investigation'. It is useful to note the terminology here; corpus linguistics is referred to as an instrument, in a similar way as forensic linguists tend to refer to it as a tool or a resource since no method of analysis, corpus or otherwise, can guarantee the identification or elimination of authors. This issue will be revisited at the end of the chapter.

One of the major difficulties within the forensic field is usually not present in the same way for corpus constructors of more general and widely available texts such as newspaper articles or casual conversation (e.g. the Bank of English, the Brown Corpus or the BNC). As O'Keeffe *et al.* (2007) point out, the construction of corpora and the notion of sampling can be crucial. As they put it, 'any old collection of texts does not make a corpus'. Unfortunately, and frustratingly for the forensic linguist, any old collection of texts is precisely what is provided by either the police or solicitors, who have trawled the home, office and computer of a suspect for any texts which are available. They are unaware of genre/register differences, variations in text size and temporal factors, all of which may influence the potential of texts to be analysed.

There are a range of text types which are commonly found in forensic linguistic casework. These include:

- Threat letters
- Suicide notes
- Blackmail/extortion letters
- Terrorist/bomb threats
- Ransom demands
- E-mails
- Text messages
- Police and witness statements
- Plagiarised texts

Corpora, whether general or specialised, have the potential to be used at any stage of legal proceedings. At the investigative stage, linguists may be brought in to comment on questioned documents at the information gathering stage. Typically, psychologists have taken on this role and linguists are often on the peripheries of this type of work, with psychologists producing profiles which may assist the police in locating a possible offender. Once the trial begins, questions of authorship may be argued for and against in court. Finally, if a case goes to appeal, as is increasingly happening in the UK following the creation of the Criminal Cases Review Commission (CCRC) in 1997, as Olsson (2004: 3) states:

> it is becoming increasingly common for linguists to be called in to assist legal counsel at the appeal stage, either because there may be some dispute about the wording, interpretation or authorship of a statement or confession made to police, or because a new interpretation of a forensic text (such as suicide or ransom note) may have become apparent since the conviction

However, there are a number of constraints which currently restrict the use of corpus linguistics in forensic contexts. Some of these are due to the technology available to the linguist to both collect and analyse the data – this is something which may be resolved in due course as the software evolves; others relate to the text types themselves, which is potentially more of a problematic issue.

All the above listed text types pose a number of challenges for the analyst. The first concerns the length of these texts. In general, all are typically short pieces of writing with very few extending beyond a single page or several pages. In fact, texts such as e-mails and in particular text messages frequently consist of fewer than ten words and as such represent an analytical dilemma for the consultant. Without very much language to work on, it is difficult to establish authorship, in terms of either identification or exclusion of candidate authors.

This kind of work also involves the notion of idiolect and uniqueness of expression, both of which can very effectively involve the use of corpora, as we will see in the case studies discussed below; however, there are additional problems with work of this kind. First, the linguist has to attempt to deal with the thorny issue of genre. Such work in general linguistics which has attempted to define the characteristics of particular genres (for example Biber 1988, 1995; Stubbs 1996) has resulted so far in only partial descriptions of registerial characteristics associated with certain text types. This is perhaps one of the greatest challenges in this type of work.

The first text which comes to light, and which triggers the need for a forensic linguist, is usually a questioned text: that is, a piece of writing (or speech) which comes from an unknown source. In this case, the linguist is asked to do one of two things. They may be asked by the police to consult on the text in terms of its sociolinguistic or idiosyncratic features in an investigative role. If the text is in isolation, without other additional texts, for example a series of threat letters, or if there are no candidate authors, then this is the limit of the linguist's input. Here, corpus linguistics cannot play a very useful role since there is only a single text to be analysed. If, however, there are a number of texts and/or one or more candidate authors, then a more detailed analysis can be carried out.

Police officers and other legal professionals are not usually aware of such issues as genre and timespan and the effect that such variables may have on the nature of the text. Thus, the forensic linguistic is often presented with a set of texts, a 'corpus', which may be very different in their relative genres, dates of production and contexts of writing. Even such variables as mode of production – handwritten texts versus word processed texts, for example – may influence the type of language produced as well as opportunities to edit the text and produce revised versions. During police searches of suspects' computers and personal belongings, such texts as diaries, personal and professional letters, text messages from mobile telephones, e-mails and even greetings cards may be presented to the forensic linguist for comparative analysis with the questioned text. What the police are aiming to do is to connect the questioned text, for example a bomb threat, with the candidate author who is typically in custody. In addition, there are tight time constraints hanging over the analyst since any suspect arrested and cautioned must usually be charged or released within seventy-two hours. Also, the police often present the analyst with texts in a text-by-text fashion, so that the corpus is disjointed and the goalposts are constantly being moved. This is because additional material may emerge from searches carried out later and because the computer technicians require time to undelete files on computers where a guilty suspect may have hurriedly attempted to delete potentially incriminating texts.

A recent case (Cotterill and Grant, in preparation), commonly regarded as the largest and most serious terrorist threat since the September 11th attack in the USA, involved an Al-Qaeda terrorist plot which led to the conviction of eight individuals based predominantly on authorship analysis. A huge international terrorist plot involving major targets in the UK and US had been retrieved, including plans for large-scale explosions, biological and chemical warfare and potentially thousands of victims.

The challenge for the team of forensic linguists was the identification of the author or authors of this text in order to prove a conspiracy charge beyond reasonable doubt. This meant that an analysis of the texts of all eight of the individuals arrested was necessary. The work was carried out in the most extreme circumstances, with only seventy-two hours remaining until the suspects had to be either charged or released. During this time, the team of forensic linguists were bombarded by newly retrieved and discovered texts, often incomplete and in hard copy form, and therefore not lending themselves to corpus analysis as they had not yet been digitised. The whole analysis took over two years and involved many dozens of documents, all of which were eventually presented in digitised form and then became amenable to corpus-assisted analysis.

2. The use of pre-existing linguistic corpora in forensic linguistics

As well as the construction of somewhat opportunistic but bespoke case-specific corpora as in the example discussed above, pre-existing large corpora of English are extremely useful for the forensic linguist in a variety of case types. This may be in an investigative role where the linguist is asked to comment on idiolectal, dialectical or regional features of texts which may aid police officers in identifying and locating a potential perpetrator. It is also possible to use corpora to illustrate common meaning (the difference between a legal meaning and a lay person's 'plain' understanding) of a term in – usually civil cases – of disputed comprehensibility of texts. These include texts such as patient information leaflets included in packs of medication, instructions and warnings. Failure to fully comprehend these types of texts can lead to frustration at best and even injury or death at worst (for a more detailed analysis of this type of forensic casework see Cotterill, in preparation). In examining texts like this, having access to large corpora can be invaluable since it allows the linguist to gauge a sense of the common usage of such terms and hence the common understanding of them, without the need to conduct a large-scale survey which is usually impossible in terms of time and financial resources

One of the first cases involving the use of corpora actually predates the creation of large computerised corpora or even the field of corpus linguistics itself, and was described by Jan Svartvik who investigated the case of Timothy Evans, the lodger of serial killer John Christie. Evans was wrongly convicted of the murder of his young daughter and was hanged in 1950 (Marston 2007). Following Christie's own conviction and execution for the subsequent murder of Evans' wife, Evans was posthumously pardoned. Using a self-constructed mini-corpus, Svartvik demonstrated that certain incriminating sections of statements supposedly produced by Evans and used as a confession at his trial did not match the grammatical style of unchallenged parts of his statements. Had this evidence been available to the jury, the outcome of the trial might have been different.

Thirty years later, Coulthard and his colleagues investigated the re-opened case of Derek Bentley. Bentley, a teenager with learning disabilities, was accused and convicted of the murder of a policeman during a bungled robbery and was hanged. The main evidence against Bentley was a statement which he was alleged to have produced following his arrest. Bentley's claim was that in fact the statement was a composite document comprising not only his own words but those of the police who, he claimed, had contributed incriminating sections to his statement. In Goffman's (1981) terms, Bentley's claim was that one or more corrupt police officer was in fact in part the *author* (or *authors*) of the text, and certainly those parts of it which incriminated him in the crime.

Coulthard (2000) presents Bentley's statement in full, and discusses those features which appear to support Bentley's claim. Intuitively, a number of aspects of the text were identified which seemed to suggest that (a) it was unlikely that Bentley had produced this language and, significantly, (b) the register of the text was more indicative of 'policespeak' than the language of a lay person (Fox 1993). There were unusually specific lexical items such as references to a 'shelter arrangement' on the roof, a 'brickwork entrance' to the door, which are unlikely to have been produced by Bentley, given his low level of verbal competence, and phraseological formulations more indicative of police language than that of a lay person (particularly one of low verbal competence).

The predominant feature which drew attention was the simple word 'then'. In the Bentley case, the word 'then' occurs eleven times in a statement of 582 words. In typical narratives, it may not be remarkable that this word is so common (particularly in relatively 'simple' narratives, for example those produced by children), since an individual describing events may well use 'then' to describe a series of events. The significant factor was the positioning of the word. In most of the instances, 'then' occurred in a medial position between subject and verb, as in the following extracts taken from the statement:

> I **then** caught a bus to Croydon ... Chris **then** jumped over and I followed. Chris **then** climbed a drainpipe to the roof and I followed ... The policeman **then** pushed me down the stairs.

Although linguists and lay people alike are often skilled at spotting these types of unusual features, when presenting evidence to a jury, the burden of proof means that it is necessary for the expert witness linguist to present evidence which is based on more than intuition and experience of language use. In this case, Fox (1993) constructed two small parallel but contrastive corpora, a method which Coulthard terms a 'corpus assisted analysis of register' (Coulthard and Johnson 2007: 178), the term acknowledging the need for human engagement with the text which generally precedes any corpus analysis and which flags up areas of interest to be pursued within corpora. One sub-corpus consisted of witness statements from the Bentley case and others; the other was made up of police officer statements. Coulthard reports the results of a comparative analysis of the word 'then', which he describes as 'startling' (2000: 273); see Table 41.1.

Table 41.1 Comparative analysis of 'then'

Text type	*Frequency of occurrence*
Lay witness statements	1 per 930 words
Police officer statements	1 per 78 words

Comparatively, Bentley's use of the temporal form of 'then', which was calculated at one per fifty-three words, means that his statement is far closer in frequency to the police officer language than that of lay witnesses. To further test his hypothesis, Coulthard used the spoken sub-corpus of the COBUILD Bank of English. The word 'then', both in its clause-initial and clause-medial uses, was found to occur in 1 per 500 words, aligning it more closely with the witness statements than the policespeak. There is also an acknowledgement of this specialised register in the US context (see Philbin 1995). Perhaps even more significantly, in the COBUILD spoken data, the string 'then I' was found to occur ten times more frequently than 'I then', once per 165,000 words versus 1 in 194 words in Bentley's alleged statement. Coulthard concludes that:

> The structure 'I then' does appear to be a feature of policeman's (written) register. More generally, it is in fact the structure Subject (+ Verb) followed by 'then' which is typical of policeman's register – it occurs 26 times in the statements of the ... officers and 7 times in Bentley's own statement.
>
> (Coulthard 2000: 274)

Coulthard goes on to speculate that 'whatever else it was, his [Evans'] statement was not a verbatim record of the dictated monologue' (ibid.). Partly as a result of this evidence, Bentley was posthumously pardoned and his conviction quashed forty-eight years after he was hanged. The Bentley case is a powerful illustration of one of the ways in which forensic linguistics and corpus linguistics can come together to produce compelling evidence. For further discussions of the Bentley case and others, see Coulthard (1992, 1993, 1994, 1997 and 2004).

3. The use of specialised individual corpora to identify or eliminate candidate authors

An interesting case is reported by Eagleson in Gibbons (1994), which involved a 'farewell letter', apparently written by a woman who had left her husband, but who in fact had been murdered by him. The letter was compared with a sample of her previous writings and a similar corpus of those of her husband. Eagleson concluded that the letter had been written by the husband of the missing woman, and when presented with this compelling evidence the husband confessed to having written it himself and to the murder. The features identified by Eagleson in both the disputed letter and the husband's corpus of texts included marked themes, the deletion of prepositions and the misuse of apostrophes, as well as grammatical features such as omissions in the present tense inflections and in the weak past tense ending -ed. Table 41.2 is a summary of Eagleson's analysis: H represents the husband's corpus, F equals the farewell letter of disputed authorship, and W indicates the wife's set of texts.

While the majority of forensic work does not yield such startlingly neat results, Table 41.2 gives an indication of the power of using corpora to analyse texts of this type. Had these personal comparative corpora not existed or not been analysed, it is unlikely that the killer would have confessed since he had denied any involvement in his wife's disappearance until he was presented with the parallel corpora evidence.

It is not only the use of large corpora such as COBUILD or the British National Corpus which enables forensic linguists to contribute to casework. The internet is increasingly being used as a resource for linguistic analysis, although there are certain caveats which need to be applied to its use.

Table 41.2 Summary of comparison of three sets of documents

		H	*F*	*W*
Spelling				
1.1	Errors in individual words	+	+	-
1.2	Capitals with common nouns	+	+	-
1.3	Small letters with proper nouns	+	+	-
1.4	Intrusive apostrophe	+	+	-
Grammatical morphology				
2.1	The verb: present tense	+	+	-
2.2	The verb: past tense	+	+	-
Syntax				
3.1	Sentence structure	+	+	-
3.2	Disrupted structures	+	+	-
Punctuation				
4.1	Comma: with clause was	+	+	-
4.2	Comma: in series	+	+	-
4.3	Asides	+	+	-
4.4	Capitals after full stops	+	+	-

Key: + feature present in sub-corpus of texts.
- feature not present in sub-corpus of texts.
Source: from Eagleson 1994: 373.

4. Using the web as a reference corpus

Caution must be advised in using the internet as a reference corpus both in terms of its construction and its content. Although the web could arguably be seen as the largest corpus in existence, it is also perhaps the most corrupted. There are no controls over what is posted, there are no 'rules' governing its content and certain genres (for example media texts) are somewhat overrepresented. Nevertheless, as a resource for 'the language of the people', it is possible to conduct searches of billions of words in seconds and to gauge some sense of common meanings.

The following case is a striking example of a combination of individual intuition and idiolectal features of language and the use of the internet as a linguistic corpus which spans some thirty years. From 1978 to 1995 Theodore Kaczynski waged a campaign of terror across the US. A disenchanted ex-university professor of mathematics who had become a recluse in a log cabin in Montana sent sixteen letter bombs to a variety of targeted individuals and institutions. His attacks increased in the level of violence used and resulted in three fatalities and twenty-three injuries of varying severity. He was named by the FBI as the Unabomber because of his choice of targets – the **un**iversity and **a**irline **bomber**. In 1995, he contacted *The New York Times* with an ultimatum: he would 'desist from terrorism' but only if either the *Times* or *The Washington Post* agreed to publish a 35,000-word manifesto he had written entitled *Industrial Society and Its Future* (the text of which is available online in numerous locations, including the CourtTV website). Foster (2001) discusses the language and style of the manifesto as a non-linguist. One of the hopes of *The Washington Post* and *The New York Times* who both agreed to publish the manifesto was that someone might recognise the writing style of it. Holt (2000), an expert on Shakespearean authorship, notes that the manifesto contains a number of distinctive features indicative of the writer's idiolectal style. In addition to consistent self-references using the plural form 'we' and/or 'FC' (standing for Freedom Club), the author also capitalises whole words as a means of indicating emphasis. Holt also observed that, although the text displayed 'irregular hyphenation', it was otherwise an error-free text in terms of both spelling and grammar. This was despite the fact that this the author had used an old-fashioned typewriter rather than a word processor with a spelling and grammar checker.

A short time after the manifesto was published, the FBI was contacted by an individual claiming that the document appeared to have been written by his long-estranged brother. In fact, his wife had intuitively recognised stylistic features of the document which rang alarm bells in her mind. The manifesto contained certain unusual expressions such as a self-description of the writer as 'a cool-headed logician'. David Kaczynski, Theodore's brother, discovered a set of letters dating back to the 1970s which appeared to contain 'similar phrasing' to that of the manifesto. This is a clear example of individual recognition of an idiosyncratic and distinctive writing style. Following a search of Kaczynski's property, Kaczynski was arrested and charged with manufacturing and sending the incendiary devices. With the possession of a set of additional documents seized from the property, the FBI's analysis determined that there were multiple similarities between the manifesto and, particularly, a lengthy letter sent to a newspaper on a similar topic.

Following this individual analysis and discovery process, a corpus approach was subsequently adopted. The FBI carried out an analysis of the web, which was significantly smaller in the mid-1990s. Using the web as a reference corpus, they used a set of twelve expressions which had been used in an analysis previously carried out for the defence; see Table 41.3.

Table 41.3 Twelve search items in the Unabomber case web corpus investigation

Single Lexical Items	*Phrases*	*Lemmas*
thereabouts	at any rate	argu*
gotten	more or less	propos*
propaganda	on the other hand	
presumably	in practice	
moreover		
clearly		

When the twelve words and expressions were entered into the search engine, a total of approximately three million hits were returned which contained one or more of them. This is an unsurprising result but was clearly extremely disappointing for the FBI's analyst (confirmed in personal communication with the Special Agent concerned and published by him in Fitzgerald 2004). The query was then refined to include only those documents which contained *all twelve* of the search terms. This produced a remarkable result: only sixty-nine documents on the entire web contained all twelve of these words and phrases. Perhaps more remarkably, each hit consisted of a version of Kaczynski's 35,000-word manifesto. As Coulthard points out in his discussion of the methodology employed in the Unabomber case:

> This was a massive rejection of the defence expert's view of text creation as purely open choice [see Sinclair 1991], as well as a powerful example of the idiolectal habit of co-selection and an illustration of the consequent forensic possibilities that idiolectal co-selection affords for authorship attribution
>
> (Coulthard 2004: 433)

Although the Unabomber case used web searches highly successfully in terms of its resulting conviction, it does illustrate one note of caution regarding the use of the web as a reference corpus. Just as statistics can be represented and misrepresented depending on how they are calculated and used, so the type of search carried out in terms of both search terms and search engines employed can produce very different results, as Tomblin (2004) has also pointed out.

Another example of the use of the internet involves a man who spent twenty-five years in jail for the murder of a woman he claimed never to have met; he was convicted by a confession which he claimed never to have produced. The man claimed that the statement was a composite document consisting of questions asked by a police officer with parallel responses, mostly in the form of positive or negative answers. This dialogue, the man alleged, had then been constructed into a monologic statement. If this was the case, the statement would become inadmissible for the purposes of the court.

Coulthard (2004) employed a corpus-assisted approach in an attempt to explore this claim. Coulthard presents the following pair of sentences which occur in both the (disputed) monologic statement and the (disputed) interview record:

(i) Statement *I asked her if I could carry her bags she said 'Yes'*
Interview *I asked her if I could carry her bags and she said 'yes'*
(ii) Statement *I picked something up like an ornament*
Interview *I picked something up like an ornament*

On this occasion, Coulthard decided to access the internet as a corpus rather than other available corpora such as the Bank of English or the BNC on the grounds that it contained more general language usage than either of the other two.

In and of themselves, the utterances above do not seem at first sight to be remarkable. However, as Coulthard found, neither one occurred at all in an internet search. This, he attributes to Sinclair's (1991) idiom principle, which relies on the notion of pre-constructed chunks, also referred to as linguistic formulae (in Wray's 2006 terms) and as lexical priming by Hoey (2005; Hoey *et al.* 2007), rather than a principle of completely free choice in a slot and filler approach to language use.

The internet search clearly indicates a principle of diminishing returns as the string becomes longer, as is illustrated by the extract from Coulthard's data in Table 41.4 (Coulthard 2004: 441).

Perhaps most striking is the next string, which begins with the most mundane phrase 'I asked' through the equally mundane 'I asked her if I could' until it finally reaches the string in the disputed statement – 'I asked her if I could carry her bags'; see Table 41.5.

Coulthard concludes that clauses such as 'I asked her' seem to display characteristics of pre-formulated chunks of language, but as additional words are added the frequency of occurrence reduces dramatically until it reaches zero. Ultimately, Coulthard takes an optimistic view of data elicited in this way, stating that:

> From evidence like this we can assert that even the sequence as short as 10 running words has a very high chance of being a unique occurrence. Indeed rarity scores like these begin to look like the probability scores that DNA experts proudly present in court.
>
> (Coulthard and Johnson 2007: 198)

Table 41.4 Coulthard's (2004) findings for the string '*I picked something up like an ornment*'

String	*Instances*
I picked	1,060,000
I picked something	780
I picked something up	362
I picked something up like	1
I picked something up like an	0
an ornament	73,700
like an ornament	896
something like an ornament	2

Table 41.5 Coulthard's (2004) findings for the string '*I asked her if I could carry her bags*'

String	*Instances*
I asked	2,170,000
I asked her	284,000
I asked her if	86,000
I asked her if I	10,400
I asked her if I could	7770
I asked if I could carry	7
I asked her if I could carry her	4
I asked her if I could carry her bags	0

Source: Coulthard, R. M. (2004) 'Author Identification, Idiolect, and Linguistic Uniqueness' *Applied Linguistics* 25(4): 441. Reproduced by permission of Oxford University Press.

5. Limitations of corpus linguists in forensic linguistic contexts and future challenges

One of the problems with using corpora in forensic linguistic analysis concerns the presentation of any resulting evidence to a jury of lay people and legal professionals. Lawyers and judges are not usually familiar with the terminology or the methodology associated with corpus linguistics, nor is the jury. Members of a jury are 'lay' in two significant senses: not only are they unaware of the law until instructed on it by the judge in his/her summing up (and as research indicates, even *after* this too) but they are also usually linguistically naïve.

Corpus linguistics represents a particularly tricky area to explain to a group of lay jurors since it involves an explanation not only of the results but also of the methodology. Jurors are paradoxically notoriously bad at assimilating evidence which appears 'scientific' but find it appealing in terms of convincingness. Explanations of concepts such as concordancing, levels of frequency and even the idea of corpora *per se* can be problematic. Many of the 'givens' which linguists take for granted must be explained in minute detail before any results are provided. Thus, the value of using corpora in one's analysis must be weighed carefully against the difficulties which will come inevitably in the courtroom.

Important work remains to be done but is now starting to be explored by scholars using quantitative computational methodologies (Chaski 2001 *inter alia* is a good example of an analyst using such methods). Coulthard and Johnson (2007), and others, advocate the creation of a reference corpus of authentic police and witness statements (among other forensic genres), both to permit

> statistically valid statements in court and to protect [oneself] against the suggestion by hostile cross-examiners that, as any reasonable person will agree, a corpus of general conversation is irrelevant for comparative and normative purposes, because the linguistic behaviour of witnesses and subjects must change when they are making statements under oath
>
> (Coulthard and Johnson 2007: 89)

A number of researchers are attempting to construct specialist corpora of this type, including those consisting of text messages, suicide notes and courtroom interaction. The value of such corpora cannot be overestimated as their use increases and is leading to more and more convictions based on this kind of evidence.

Added to this, perhaps the most pressing issue is the fact that many forensic linguists (at least initially) operate qualitatively and intuitively. This means that the evidence produced may not meet the burden of proof. In the USA, criteria known as the Daubert criteria have been established to prevent the presentation of evidence which is considered 'unreliable' by the courts. Solan and Tiersma (2004) discuss the Daubert criteria, which resulted from a case involving drugs alleged to cause birth defects when given to pregnant women (*Daubert* v. *Dow Merrill Pharmaceuticals, Inc.* (509 U.S. 579 1993)). According to these standards, new, more stringent requirements in determining the admissibility of evidence were implemented:

1 whether the theory offered has been tested;
2 whether it has been subjected to peer review and publication;
3 the known rate of error; and
4 whether the theory is generally accepted in the scientific community.

Within forensic linguistics, as well as corpus linguistics, some of these criteria are difficult if not impossible to meet at present. This is particularly true of the third measure, since both fields have been subject to testing, review, publication and general acceptance within their respective communities.

Corpus linguistics is almost certainly the best placed of all of the tools at the disposal of the forensic linguist to enable linguistic evidence to be admitted in court, since, aside from forensic phonetics work which operates with sound scientific and statistical principles and has a formal accreditation process, corpus linguistics is the most 'scientific' method employed by linguists. Certainly, with the development of large corpora of specialised text corpora of various genres on the horizon, the future for forensic linguistics, particularly in terms of authorship analysis, seems to hang on computerised analysis and the development of robust statistical measures, both of which suggest that corpus linguistics will have an increasingly important role to play in the future in the detection of crime.

Further reading

Coulthard, R. M. (1994) 'On the Use of Corpora in the Analysis of Forensic Texts', *Forensic Linguistics: International Journal of Speech, Language and the Law* 1(1): 27–43. (This article, which appeared in the very first issue of the journal, was and remains seminal to the use of corpus linguistics in forensic linguistics. It explores a number of cases where corpora were employed in order to assist in showing notions of idiolect and register in forensic linguistic casework.)

Fox, G. (1993) 'A Comparison of "Policespeak" and "Normalspeak": A Preliminary Study', in J. Sinclair, M. Hoey and G. Fox (eds) *Techniques of Description: Spoken and Written Discourse*. London: Routledge, pp 183–95. (This important work explores the concept of a police idiolect, crucial to many cases of alleged fabricated confessions and false statements. Employing corpus linguistic methods, Fox discusses conducting comparative analysis of corpora and the potential value of this approach to forensic linguists.)

Solan, L. and Tiersma, P. (2004) 'Author Identification in American Courts', *Applied Linguistics* 25(4): 448–65. (Solan and Tiersma provide a comprehensive outline of the use of corpora in authorship in the US legal context, which is very different to that of the UK. They also provide a discussion of some of the drawbacks of such evidence and the problems of communicating such evidence to jurors.)

Woolls, D. (2003) 'Better Tools for the Trade and How to Use Them', *Forensic Linguistics: International Journal of Speech, Language and Law* 10(1): 102–12. (In this article, Woolls illustrates the use of his computer software *Copycatch* which uses corpora, either self-constructed small-scale and specialised ones or larger, more general pre-existing collections of texts, in cases of plagiarism, disputed authorship of police records and interviews and confessions.)

References

Baker, P. (2007) *Using Corpora in Discourse Analysis*. London: Continuum.

Biber, D. (1988) *Variation across Speech and Writing*. Cambridge: Cambridge University Press.

——(1995) *Dimensions of Register Variation*. Cambridge: Cambridge University Press.

Biber, D., Conrad, S. and Reppen, R. (1998) *Corpus Linguistics: Investigating Language Structure and Use*. Cambridge: Cambridge University Press.

Broeders, A. (1999) 'Some Observations on the Use of Probability Scales in Forensic Identification', *Forensic Linguistics: The International Journal of Speech, Language and the Law* 6(2): 228–41.

Chaski, C. (2001) 'Empirical Evaluations of Language-based Author Identification Techniques', *Forensic Linguistics: The International Journal of Speech, Language and the Law* 8(1): 1–65.

Cotterill, J. (2010, in preparation) 'Keep Taking the Medicine: The Comprehensibility of Patient Information Leaflets'.

Cotterill, J. and Grant, T. (in preparation) 'The Case of Dhiren Barot: Forensic Authorship Analysis and the Prevention of Terrorism'.

Coulthard, R. M. (1992) 'Forensic Discourse Analysis', in R. M. Coulthard (ed.) *Advances in Spoken Discourse Analysis*. London: Routledge, pp. 242–57.

——(1993) 'Beginning the Study of Forensic Texts: Corpus, Concordance, Collocation', in M. P. Hoey (ed.) *Data, Description Discourse*. London: HarperCollins, pp. 86–97.

——(1994) 'On the Use of Corpora in the Analysis of Forensic Texts', *Forensic Linguistics: The International Journal of Speech, Language and the Law* 1(1): 27–43.

——(1996) 'The Official Version: Audience Manipulation in Police Records of Interviews with Suspects', in C. Caldas-Coulthard and R. M. Coulthard (eds) *Texts and Practices: Readings in Critical Discourse Analysis*. London: Routledge, pp. 166–78.

——(1997) 'A Failed Appeal', *Forensic Linguistics: The International Journal of Speech, Language and the Law* 4(2): 287–302.

——(2000) 'Whose Text Is It? On the Linguistic Investigation of Authorship', in S. Sarangi and R. M. Coulthard, *Discourse and Social Life*. London: Longman, pp. 270–89.

——(2004) 'Author Identification, Idiolect, and Linguistic Uniqueness', *Applied Linguistics* 25(4): 431–47.

Coulthard, R. M. and Johnson, A. (2007) *An Introduction to Forensic Linguistics: Language in Evidence*. London: Routledge.

Eagleson, R. (1994) 'Forensic Analysis of Personal Written Texts: A Case Study', in J. Gibbons (ed.) *Language and the Law*. London, Longman, pp. 362–73.

Firth, J. R. (1957) *Papers in Linguistics 1934–1951*. Oxford: Oxford University Press.

Fitzgerald, J. R. (2004) 'Using a Forensic Linguistic Approach to Track the Unabomber', in J. H. Campbell, and D. Denivi (eds) *Profilers*. New York: Prometheus Books, pp. 193–222.

Foster, D. (2001) *Author Unknown: On the Trail of Anonymous*. New York: Holt.

Fox, G. (1993) 'A Comparison of "Policespeak" and "Normalspeak": A Preliminary Study', in J. Sinclair, M. Hoey and G. Fox (eds) *Techniques of Description: Spoken and Written Discourse*. London: Routledge, pp. 183–95.

Gibbons, J. (ed.) (1994) *Language and the Law*. London: Longman.

Goffman, E. (1981) *Forms of Talk*. Philadelphia, PA: University of Pennsylvania Press.

Grant, T. (2007) 'Quantifying Evidence in Forensic Authorship Analysis', *Forensic Linguistics: International Journal of Speech, Language and Law* 14(1): 1–25.

Grant, T. and Baker, K. (2001) 'Identifying Reliable, Valid Markers of Authorship: A Response to Chaski', *Forensic Linguistics: The International Journal of Speech, Language and Law* 8(1): 66–79.

Hoey, M. (2002) 'Textual Colligation: A Special Kind of Lexical Priming', in K. Aijmer and B. Altenberg (eds) *Language and Computers, Advances in Corpus Linguistics. Papers from the 23rd International Conference on English Language Research on Computerized Corpora (ICAME 23)*, Göteborg, 22–26 May, pp 171–94.

——(2005) *Lexical Priming: A New Theory of Words and Language*. London: Routledge.

Hoey, M., Mahlberg, M., Stubbs, M. and Teubert, W. (2007) *Text, Discourse and Corpora: Theory and Analysis*. London: Continuum.

Holt, H. (2000) 'The Bard's Fingerprints', *Lingua Franca*: 29–39.

Howald, B. S. (2008) 'Authorship Attribution under the Rules of Evidence: Empirical Approaches in a Layperson's Legal System', *Forensic Linguistics: The International Journal of Speech, Language and Law* 15 (2): 219–47.

Hunston, S. (2001) 'Colligation, Lexis, Pattern, and Text', in M. Scott and G. Thompson (eds) *Patterns of Text: In Honour of Michael Hoey*. Amsterdam: John Benjamins, pp. 13–34.

Jenkins, C. (2003) 'Stuart Campbell Thought Technology Would Stop the Police Proving that He Murdered His Niece, Danielle Jones. Instead, It Proved His Downfall', *Police Review* (Police Review Publishing Co. Ltd): 28–9.

Johnson, A. (1997) 'Textual Kidnapping – A Case of Plagiarism among Three Student Texts', *Forensic Linguistics: International Journal of Speech, Language and Law* 4(2): 210–25.

Kredens, K. (2001) 'Towards a Corpus-Based Methodology of Forensic Authorship Attribution: A Comparative Study of Two Idiolects', in B. Lewandowska-Tomaszczyk (ed.) *PALC 2001: Practical Applications in Language Corpora*. Frankfurt: Peter Lang, pp. 405–46.

——(2002) 'Idiolect in Forensic Authorship Attribution', in P. Stalmaszczyk (ed.) *Folia Linguistica Anglica*, Vol. 4. Lodz: Lodz University Press.

McMenamin, G. (2001) 'Style Markers in Authorship Studies', *Forensic Linguistics: International Journal of Speech Language and the Law* 8(2): 93–7.

——(2004) 'Disputed Authorship in US Law', *Forensic Linguistics: International Journal of Speech Language and the Law* 11(1): 73–82.

Marston, E. (2007) *John Christie (Crime Archive)*, The National Archives, London.

O'Keeffe, A., McCarthy, M. J. and Carter, R. A. (2007) *From Corpus to Classroom: Language Use and Language Teaching*. Cambridge: Cambridge University Press.

Olsson, J. (2004) *Forensic Linguistics: An Introduction to Language, Crime and the Law*. London: Continuum.

Philbin, P. (1995) *Cop Speak: The Lingo of Law Enforcement and Crime*. London: Wiley.

Risinger, D. and Saks, M. J. (1996) 'Science and Nonscience in the Courts: Daubert Meets Handwriting Identification Expertise', *Iowa Law Review* 82: 21–74.

Sarangi, S. and Coulthard, R. M. (eds) (2000) *Discourse and Social Life*. London: Longman.

Scott, M. (1999) *WordSmith Tools*. Oxford: Oxford University Press.

Shuy, R. W. (2002) *Linguistic Battles in Trademark Disputes*. New York: Palgrave Macmillan.

——(2006) 'From Spam to McDonald's in the Trademark Wars', *Language Log*, 13 October.

Sinclair, J. (1991) *Corpus, Concordance, Collocation*. Oxford: Oxford University Press.

Solan, L. and Tiersma, P. (2004) 'Author Identification in American Courts', *Applied Linguistics* 25(4): 448–65.

——(2005) *Speaking of Crime: The Language of Criminal Justice*. Chicago, IL: University of Chicago Press.

Stubbs, M. (1996) *Text and Corpus Analysis*. Oxford: Blackwell.

Svartvik, J. (1968) *The Evans Statements: A Case for Forensic Linguistics*. Gothenburg: University of Gothenburg Press.

Tiersma, P. and Solan, L. (2002) 'The Linguist on the Witness Stand: Forensic Linguistics in American Courts', *Language* 78: 221–39.

Tomblin, S. D. (2004) 'Author Online: Evaluating the Use of the WWW in Cases of Forensic Authorship Analysis', unpublished MA dissertation, Cardiff University.

——(2009) 'Future Directions in Forensic Authorship Analysis: Evaluating Formulaicity as a Marker of Authorship', unpublished and ongoing PhD thesis, Cardiff University.

Winter, E. (1996) 'The Statistics of Analysing Very Short Texts in a Criminal Context', in H. Kniffka (ed.) *Recent Developments in Forensic Linguistic*. Frankfurt am Main: Peter Lang, pp. 141–79.

Woolls, D. (2003) 'Better Tools for the Trade and How to Use Them', *Forensic Linguistics: International Journal of Speech, Language and Law* 10(1): 102–12.

Woolls, D. and Coulthard, R. M. (1998) 'Tools for the Trade', *Forensic Linguistics: International Journal of Speech, Language and Law* 5(1): 33–57.

Wray, A. (2006) *Formulaic Language and the Lexicon*. Cambridge: Cambridge University Press.

42

How to use corpus linguistics in the study of political discourse

Annelie Ädel

1. What is political discourse?

Political discourse has a long-standing tradition as an object of study across many disciplines, including rhetoric, linguistics and political science. However, this is not to say that it is a well-defined entity. After brief reflection, it quickly becomes apparent that 'political discourse' is a vague term that can be defined rather narrowly or quite broadly. Essentially, our definition of political discourse boils down to how we define 'political'. This stands in contrast to, for example, legal discourse, where 'legal' is a much more restricted concept than 'political'. The reader may wish to look at how 'political' collocates in a large standard corpus, such as the British National Corpus, to learn more about its various meanings.

A narrow definition of 'political discourse' sees it as taking place when 'political actors, in and out of government, communicate about political matters, for political purposes' (Graber 1981: 196). A broader definition of 'political discourse', however, could even include any discourse or part of a discourse which happens to be on a political topic, such as an informal conversation between friends where the topic revolves around an upcoming election or around a politicised issue, such as abortion. An even broader view of what 'political' means can be exemplified by the slogan 'the personal is political' (used in the feminist movement in the 1960s and 1970s). In terms of linguistic research, we can consider for example Ochs and Taylor (1992: 301), who frame a study of family dinner narratives as political discourse, arguing that '[f]amilies are political bodies in that certain members review, judge, formulate codes of conduct, make decisions and impose sanctions that evaluate and impact the actions, conditions, thoughts and feelings of other members'. Some linguists (e.g. Shapiro 1981, cited in Wilson 2003) take the stance that all discourse is essentially political.

We can talk about 'political discourse' in terms of three different definitional scopes. In the narrow scope, *the political genre* is the main criterion; 'political discourse' entails a speech event which takes place in a political context, involving political agents. In the broad scope, *the political topic* becomes the main criterion; 'political discourse' refers to any discourse on a topic which is political. Finally, in the extended scope, *the underlying political issue* is the main criterion; the idea is that power and control are (often or always) enacted through discourse, which makes it possible to consider any discourse in, for example, an educational or institutional setting as 'political'.

In this chapter, a narrow scope will be taken, so the focus will be on the political genre. It would be beyond the scope of this chapter to bring in examples which do not represent 'big politics', even if they may be highly relevant to people's everyday lives. Further, the focus is on linguistic analysis rather than political comment, although O'Halloran (this volume) on critical discourse analysis offers a different perspective. A necessary limitation of the chapter, given space constraints, is the scarce representation of non-English-language studies and corpora.

Genres of political discourse

As political discourse can encompass a range of different speech events, it would perhaps be more appropriate to speak of 'political discourses'. Despite the vagueness of the term, it is still possible to talk about prototypical examples. Many language users, at least in the Western world, would likely cite the political speech or the political debate as prototypical examples of political discourse. Further examples of genres of political discourse are the political manifesto, the political pamphlet, the political press conference, the political editorial, the political media interview, the political poster, the political television advertisement, the political slogan and the political car sticker. One thing that these genres tend to have in common is that political discourse is typically persuasive – that is, its main communicative purpose is to persuade an audience about something.

In this chapter, we will focus on four genres of political discourse: (1) the political speech, (2) parliamentary debates, (3) the governmental press conference and (4) the political news report. These reflect some of the most powerful and visible agents in political discourse: the politicians, the political institution, the government and the political media. They all occur in relatively formal contexts, where talk is 'on the record'.

2. Political discourse and corpora

This section gives an overview of corpora and corpus studies of political discourse from the perspective of the four prototypical genres mentioned above. Further examples of political genres which have been covered in corpus analysis are websites of special interest groups (e.g. Teubert 2002; Koteyko 2007), the media interview of the politician (e.g. Milizia and Spinzi 2008) and the editorial or leader, which expresses the opinion of the editor or publisher of the newspaper on a topical issue (Westin and Geisler 2002; Morley 2004). We will return to these later in the chapter.

Political discourse is frequently represented in corpora, in part because many political genres are not only public but also widely publicised, which makes them more easily accessible than many other types of discourse. It is also the case that, in parliamentary debates in particular, keeping records of the discourse is of importance for legal and democratic reasons.

Political discourse has been represented in standard corpora since the first-generation projects, although in written corpora this primarily takes the form of mediated political discourse; the Brown and the LOB include 'political reportage' and the editorial. The spoken London–Lund Corpus, for its part, also includes political speeches. A more recent example of a standard corpus, the British National Corpus, offers a broader range of both spoken and written political genres: parliamentary speeches, parliamentary debates and public spoken debates. The political discourse represented in the media includes such categories as editorials and letters to the editor. Historical corpora of English in which political discourse is represented also exist; for example, the Lampeter Corpus includes a section of political texts from 1646 to 1730.

Political discourse has also held a strong position in translation corpora, perhaps due primarily to the immense translation activity (often required by law) triggered by multilingual political contexts. The Hansard Corpus, which consists of proceedings from the Canadian Parliament in French and English, can be mentioned as an early example of the translation corpus (see Tognini Bonelli, this volume). Another highly active translation area is the European Union, where laws regulate the production of translations of various political and institutional documents. Such widely accessible documents continue to feed into many corpora.

Although political discourse tends to be fairly well represented in standard corpora, few generally available corpora exist which contain exclusively genres of political discourse. The following sections comment on the corpora available for the four different genres, or the relative ease of ad hoc corpus compilation, and offer examples of studies based on such corpora.

Political speeches

The political speech is typically meticulously prepared, rhetorically elaborate and read from a written manuscript. A corpus of political speeches makes it possible to analyse the idiolect of specific politicians (although note that many politicians use speech writers), for example in terms of rhetorical style or the typical connotations of specific keywords. Many different types of political speeches exist, ranging from live speeches by local politicians to televised presidential inaugural addresses. The political speech can be experienced live by an audience; it can be experienced through radio or television and often the internet; it can be accessed in reading through a transcript; or parts of it can be represented by either direct or indirect reported speech, for example in the news media. All of these representations can be made into corpora of political discourse to be studied in systematic ways.

One corpus resource for political speeches is CORPS (CORpus of tagged Political Speeches), which has been annotated with audience reactions, such as applause or laughter. There are also many online resources for collecting political speeches.

Perhaps not surprisingly, there is a strong tradition in the study of political discourse of focusing on speeches by national leaders. Examples of corpus-based studies include Fairclough's (2000) analysis of the speeches of the British Prime Minister Tony Blair, Charteris-Black's (2002) study of inaugural speeches by various US presidents, and Berber Sardinha's (2008) study of speeches by Brazilian President Lula.

Parliamentary debates

A corpus of parliamentary debates makes it possible to analyse the political discourse of specific political parties or groups. As parliamentary debates are often argumentative, with representatives defending and attacking various political positions, they are of particular interest for the analysis of argumentation strategies.

A corpus resource for parliamentary debates is the Corpus of European Parliament proceedings (EUROPARL), consisting of parallel texts from 1996 to 2006 in the various languages of the EU Parliament. Much more material is available online at official parliamentary or congressional websites. To find material from an English-language context, search for items such as 'British Parliament'; 'Irish Parliament'; 'US Congress'. There are also many resources outside of the English-language context, such as the extensive archives of the EU.

There are several examples of corpus-based analyses of parliamentary debates, for instance Baker (2004) on debates in the UK House of Lords, Bevitori (2006) on debates in the UK House of Commons, and Ilie (2000) on debates in both UK Houses of Parliament. These will be discussed below.

Political press conferences

A corpus of political press conferences makes it possible to analyse language use in government or in the process of governance, as well as the interactions between government and media representatives. These events provide an important channel for an administration's policy-making.

A ready-made corpus resource for press conferences is the Corpus of Spoken Professional American-English (CSPAE; Barlow 2000), half of which contains press conference transcripts from the White House amounting to almost one million words. There are also many official sites for downloading press briefings, for example the official White House website.

An example of corpus-based analysis of this genre is Partington (2003), in which White House press briefings are studied with respect to metaphor, as we will see below.

Mediated political discourse: news reports

A corpus of political news reports makes it possible to analyse political discourse as represented in the media. A great deal of the research carried out on political discourse has been on political news reported in the media, which bears witness to the relative ease of accessibility of media genres and to the special relationship between politics and the media.

It is technically relatively easy to compile one's own database of news reports, for example by using a large searchable database (such as LexisNexis Academic) and searching for specific keywords or phrases (e.g. 'war in Iraq'). This can give access to a great many articles from a range of different newspapers; however, this method tends to produce a great deal of duplicate material, as many papers print only slightly modified versions of articles from large news associations such as the Associated Press. Another potential problem is that it is not always possible to include only news reports and not editorials, for example. It is also important to note that some databases impose extremely restrictive licensing rules. On the other hand, many newspaper sites – in English as well as other languages – make their archives available for the searching and downloading of articles, though copyright laws still prevail.

It is important to know one's corpus and maintain control of what is in it. One way of doing so it to use explicit criteria when collecting one's own material. Garretson and Ädel (2008: 162), for example, drew their articles on the 2004 US election (see Section 4) from eleven high-circulation newspapers in the US. The criteria were as follows: each article had to be at least 400 words long, mention both candidates (Bush and Kerry) and be published within the thirty days before the election. Editorials and letters to the editor were excluded from the corpus manually, as only 'objective' news reports were desired. This procedure resulted in a corpus of 1.74 million words which took only a few days to compile (for more on building a corpus, see chapters by Adolphs and Knight, Biber, Clancy, Koester, Nelson, Reppen and Thompson, this volume).

3. Corpus techniques for exploring political discourse

What can corpus linguistics add to the study of political discourse? The value of the corpus and corpus tools has been discussed at length in the corpus-linguistic literature, and other chapters of this handbook provide a rich coverage of the advantages of taking a corpus-linguistic approach to the study of language use (see, for example, chapters by Evison, Hunston, Scott and Tribble, this volume). Naturally, the general advantages of using corpus-based methods (e.g. the empirical basis and the potential for systematic and semi-automatic analysis) also hold true for the study of political discourse in particular.

Carrying out a corpus-based study can mean different things; as in the case of defining 'political discourse', there are broad and narrow definitions of what a corpus-linguistic study is. Some researchers simply take it to mean that an electronic database of texts was used, whether or not any corpus-linguistic tools, such as the concordancer, were employed. In the majority of cases, however, a researcher using a corpus will also make sure to capitalise on the fact that search tools can be used to automatically locate all instances of a particular word form, or tag in the case of an annotated corpus. Another way in which researchers differ in their approach to the corpus is in how data-driven the analysis is. Most often, the researcher has already decided on the research question before searching the corpus. However, an alternative route the researcher can take is to let the corpus data guide any decisions about what to look for, for example by creating word frequency lists or keyword lists.

This section provides four examples of useful corpus analysis techniques in the context of political discourse: (1) analysing 'how X is talked about', (2) making corpus comparisons, (3) analysing sets of linguistic features marking a particular style, and (4) analysing keywords. There is a certain amount of overlap between the techniques; comparison, in particular, is fundamental and is also part of both (3) and (4), albeit in more complex ways. Furthermore, the techniques by no means represent an exhaustive set, but were selected with an eye towards exemplifying a variety of common techniques useful for analysing political discourse. More detailed information about corpus methods is given in other chapters of this book; Evison, for example, covers the basics of exploring word frequency, concordance lines and keywords.

Analysing 'how X is talked about'

Quantitative and qualitative methods complement each other usefully in corpus studies of political discourse. Researchers often start with the quantitative analysis (looking at frequency and distribution), then proceed in an increasingly qualitative way, looking at concordance lines and finding patterns in the co-text – perhaps also exploring discourse-level phenomena or rhetorical functions. In the process of analysis, there is a great deal of moving back and forth between overall frequencies and more contextualised examples.

The link between the word and the co-text (the concordance lines and broader discourse patterns) bears emphasising: 'While much has been made of single words in political discourse … in most cases it is the context … which carries the political message' (Wilson 2003: 409). Even though the point of departure in corpus analysis is typically a word form, the ultimate interest is in broader topics such as discourse patterns, argumentation patterns, schemas or cultural beliefs. For example, many linguists who study political discourse are interested in 'how X is talked about'.

An early analysis of corpus data with respect to 'how X is talked about' is de Beaugrande (1999), who investigated 'liberal' and related words in corpora from the UK, the US and South Africa. He specifically takes the view that corpus data can be successfully examined for 'expressions which are presumed to undergo ideological contestation' (1999: 259); 'liberal', for example, is said to be used by different groups interested in different aspects of its meaning, e.g. 'for freedom from government regulations and for solidarity of white people with black people' (1999: 273).

A somewhat different approach was used in Ilie (2000) for a pragmatic analysis of political clichés in the British Parliament. What she did was use the term 'cliché' itself as a search term, as in 'We should be careful before uttering a string of good-sounding clichés to solve all the problems', which was then analysed from a pragmatic perspective, examining the words labelled as clichés and the salient argumentation patterns that referred to the clichés under discussion.

Making corpus comparisons

Bringing out what is typical of a particular discourse is really only possible by comparison. Ideally, the analyst should be able to make the comparison to something more than simply his or her own intuitions about other types of discourse. Using representative samples of discourse makes it possible to make more empirically sound and accurate comparisons.

When studying a word, expression or syntactic structure in a specific type of discourse, it is often a good idea to check its frequency and/or use in another type of discourse. Morley (2004), for example, studied generic statements (*X is Y*) in editorials, specifically through searching for present-tense forms of the verb BE. He compared the frequency of present-tense BE in editorials to its frequency in news reports, and found considerably higher numbers in the editorials. Thus, his hypothesis that 'telling the readers what is the case' is a significant function in editorials was strengthened.

In addition to comparing two genres, one can also compare the production of two different speakers in the same genre. A study by Milizia and Spinzi (2008) compared language produced by George W. Bush and Tony Blair in the form of speeches, press conferences and interviews from a specific year (2005). They analysed how the two leaders used multi-word units involving the lemma TERROR differently and found different idiolects at work, 'signalling different cultural and political identity' (2008: 346). For example, Bush preferred the phrase 'war on terror', often co-occurring with 'allies and friends', while Blair preferred 'fight against terrorism', often co-occurring with nouns like 'co-operation', 'solidarity', 'unity' and 'support'. Comparison of the two subcorpora is said to tell us something about the different objectives of the two speakers, for example that 'Bush assumes a more overtly warlike style' (2008: 346).

Yet another option for comparison is to study the discourse of two different groups of speakers with opposing views on a political issue. Especially in the context of a political debate, it may prove useful to create subcorpora for comparison based on the representation of different views, for instance one subcorpus for those speakers who are *for* and one for those who are *against* a specific issue (cf. Baker 2004). This way, the differences in stance can be more easily brought out when analysing how specific topics or populations are talked about.

Analysing sets of linguistic features marking a particular style

Another example of a corpus technique which has been used in studies of political discourse is the analysis of sets of linguistic features that have been shown to be indicative of a particular style – for example, a persuasive or narrative style. This technique has been applied, for example, to diachronic corpora, such that statistically significant variation in these features across sections of the corpus can tell us something about how the genre as a whole has changed over time (see e.g. Biber 1988; Biber, this volume).

One corpus-based study of changes over time in a specific political genre is Westin and Geisler (2002), focusing on editorials in British up-market newspapers from 1900 to 1993. By analysing some forty linguistic features, they demonstrate a development in editorials from less narrative and to more persuasive and argumentative styles throughout the period. Especially during the latter part of the twentieth century, the language of editorials also became less abstract and more informal.

A broad overall increase in informalisation has also been shown in a study of UK party election broadcasts between 1966 and 1997 (Pearce 2005). Twenty-eight linguistic features were selected as indicators of a formal/informal style, including features such as nominalisations, personal pronouns, common adverbs, common lexical verbs, questions and words containing nine or more letters. This trend toward informality was used to support claims made about a general increase in informalisation in public discourse in the twentieth century.

Analysing keywords

Studying keywords is a popular approach to the analysis of political discourse. Keyword analysis is essentially based on the notion that recurrent ways of talking about concepts and ideas reveal something about how we think about the social world. Different researchers mean different things by the term 'keyword', however. A non-technical definition of 'keyword' is any word which is important in a discourse – and, by extension, in the culture in which it is used (for early work on keywords, see Williams 1985). A more technical definition is that a keyword is 'found to be outstanding in its frequency in the text' (Scott 1999; this volume) by comparison to another corpus. Since most concordance programs offer automatic comparison of words across corpora, such data are relatively easily obtained. Note that this technique is more data-driven than the ones mentioned above; that is, the corpus material itself constitutes the starting point of the study.

In this subsection, we will look at two different types of corpus comparisons involving keywords: one example involving a comparison of a specialised corpus with a general corpus and three examples involving comparison of different types of specialised corpora with each other.

An example of how keywords can be studied in a specialised corpus and a general corpus is found in Teubert (2002). The specialised corpus was compiled of text from anti-EU websites in the UK, while the general corpus used was the British National Corpus. First, two word frequency lists were created, one based on the specialised corpus and one based on the general corpus. Next, a keyword list was automatically generated, based on the two word frequency lists. The keyword list highlighted which words were unusually central to the specialised corpus. In other words, the most significant lexical choices in the corpus were revealed, and these say something about what the writers choose to focus on. Among the keywords found in the specialised corpus were 'bureaucratic', 'corrupt', 'prosperity', 'Anglo-Saxon', 'sovereignty' and 'province' – all words which have strong connotations. As Teubert remarks (2002: 11), the anti-EU discourse is quite emotional.

An example of how keywords can be compared across two specialised corpora is found in Fairclough (2000). Here, discourse samples from the same political party but from different time periods – specifically, before and after a major reform – were contrasted. What Fairclough did was to compare keywords from 'New Labour' (the re-named and modernised British Labour Party) material and from earlier Labour material. Some of the keywords of New Labour were 'new', 'business', 'rights', 'values' and 'work'. However, it is only by considering contextualised examples that we can know how these words are used in New versus Old Labour discourse. For example, Fairclough's analysis shows that 'rights' in New Labour tends to collocate with 'responsibilities' or 'duties' (unless used in compounds like 'human/civil rights'), while this pattern is not found in the earlier Labour corpus. There, 'responsibilities' co-occurs instead with mention of public authorities (e.g. 'responsibilities of local councils'). According to Fairclough (2000: 40–1), this illustrates the individualist discourse of New Labour, which is contrasted with the traditional collectivism of 'old' Labour.

4. Examples of topics in corpus-based research on political discourse

In this section, we will look at three different phenomena that have been studied in political discourse using corpora and corpus tools. These are (un)favourable representations, metaphors and reported speech. (Un)favourable representations and metaphor have been widely studied in political discourse even before the advent of the corpus, while reported speech has only recently started to attract researchers' attention.

(Un)favourable representation in political discourse

Researchers interested in studying favourable or unfavourable representations of concepts in political discourse tend to find implicit types more interesting than explicit ones, since these are less obvious and cannot be taken at face value. One long-standing topic of study in political discourse is euphemism. In George Orwell's essay *Politics and the English Language* (1946), political discourse is described as 'largely the defense of the indefensible', by which he was referring to the use of euphemism. Euphemisms – also referred to as 'nukespeak' in work on political discourse (see Wilson 2003: 401) – can be described as 'words with relatively clear definitions but meanings designed to conceal referents' (Gastil 1992: 474). One of Orwell's well-known examples is the term 'pacification', used to refer to a situation in which '[d]efenseless villages are bombarded from the air, the inhabitants driven out into the countryside, the cattle machine-gunned, the huts set on fire with incendiary bullets' (Peterson and Brereton 2008: 324).

Although euphemism is understudied in a corpus context, the analysis of favourable or unfavourable representations of concepts or populations in corpora of political discourse has attracted a great deal of interest. It is an especially active area of research in critical discourse analysis (see O'Halloran, this volume).

An example of a study of lexical differences between oppositional stances is Baker (2004), who studied debates in the UK Parliament's House of Lords on law reform for the age of consent of gay males. His corpus consisted of discourse samples on this specific topic. Guided by the most frequent lexical items used, he focused specifically on how discourses of homosexuality were constructed by the two opposing groups. What he did was to compare the keywords in two subcorpora: one consisting of the speech of the pro-reformers and the other consisting of the speech of the anti-reformers. The qualitative analysis of the keywords uncovered the ways in which the arguments were framed by the debaters (2004: 91). It was found that the pro-reformers used a 'discourse of tolerance', including keywords such as 'convention', 'rights' and 'human'. The anti-reformers, on the other hand, were found to use a complex chain of argumentation involving (1) talking about homosexuality as an act rather than an identity, (2) describing the prototypical act of homosexuality as anal sex, and (3) establishing that 'anal sex is dangerous, criminal and unnatural indulgence' (2004: 103).

To turn to the analysis of the development of (un)favourable representations of concepts over time, Koteyko (2007) studied a diachronic corpus of texts written between 1998 and 2003 by members of the Russian pro-Communist community. Specifically, Koteyko analysed paraphrases (metalinguistic restatements of what has been said) involving English loanwords into Russian such as 'business' and 'businessman' and tracked how these are represented favourably or unfavourably throughout the period. From 1998 to 2002, a negative attitude towards business was found to be prevalent in the form of an association of 'business' with 'stealing' or 'deception of people': '[t]he theme of business as a crime is gradually developed by subsequent texts that enumerate new types of illegal activities of referents of this loanword' (2007: 81). However, starting in the latter half of 2002, a different pattern was found to emerge, with 'business' being used more often in the neutral-to-positive sense, and with the expression 'big businessmen' only (not 'small-scale businessmen') being used pejoratively, paraphrased as 'the oligarchs'.

Metaphor in political discourse

Metaphor has been shown to be highly central to political discourse. One perspective on metaphor is that it 'plays an important rhetorical role in persuasive language because it has the potential to exploit the associative power of language in order to provoke an emotional response on the part of the hearer' (Charteris-Black 2002: 134). This is a traditional rhetorical view. A more cognitive view stresses the idea that in studying patterns of metaphor use, it is possible to examine the ways in which a phenomenon is conceptualised.

It may prove to be a challenge to study metaphor using corpus tools, as searches typically have to be done at the word level. In order to find all examples of the conceptual metaphor SOCIAL ORGANISATIONS ARE PLANTS, for example, it is necessary to first work out a list of possible word forms associated with the metaphor (e.g. 'branch' and 'grow'). Another point to consider is that metaphors are 'not inherent in word forms but arise from the relationship between words and their contexts' (Charteris-Black 2002: 134) – 'path' and 'step', for example, may draw on the domain of journeys, or may equally well be used literally – as in the case of 'steps' referring to the steps of the White House from where the US president sometimes delivers speeches.

A somewhat easier option, from a corpus perspective, is to select a concept (e.g. immigration) and search the corpus for related words to see what metaphors are used in connection to that concept. For example, are refugees described in terms of 'torrents', 'influxes', 'waves' or some other natural disaster which is difficult to control? (See also O'Halloran, this volume.)

Partington (2003) analysed metaphors in a corpus of White House briefings, which were compared to a corpus of political interviews. One of the types of metaphor analysed was the orientational metaphor, which is based on movement in space. It was identified through the unusually high frequency of prepositions and particles in the White House briefings, especially involving 'toward(s)' and 'forward'. The most frequent collocates of these were the various forms of the verb 'move', as shown in the large number of clusters such as 'as we move forward' and 'to move forward with'. Based on the data, two systematic metaphors were found: PROGRESS IS FORWARD MOTION and MOVING FORWARD IS NECESSARY. The fact that these metaphors dominate the briefings shows that the press 'sees immobility as stagnation, as culpable lethargy and so the administration must project itself as being in a state of perpetual motion' (2003: 200). Interestingly, 'move' occurred in the interview material, by contrast, predominantly in reference to moving on to another topic.

Finally, two examples of metaphor studies which incorporate cultural comparison are Musolff (2004) and Charteris-Black (2002). Musolff (2004: 437) investigated the geographical heart metaphor in British and German press coverage of EU politics in the 1990s, pointing out that the human body is a long-standing source of metaphors 'denoting social and political entities in Western culture', with the heart, being such an essential organ, occupying 'a particularly prominent status in political imagery'. While the German sample contained an overwhelming number of positive claims about Germany being 'at/in the heart of Europe', the British sample did not place Britain in this location, but rather placed other geographically peripheral parts of Europe there (such as former Yugoslavia). Furthermore, it was found that the governmental slogan of Britain 'being/ working at the heart of Europe' was recontextualised in the press reports in DISEASE/ILLNESS scenarios (e.g. heart failure) to express scepticism towards integration. The findings are said to reflect 'deep-seated differences in political attitude and perception patterns' (Musolff 2004: 449–50).

Charteris-Black (2002) undertook a cognitive-semantic and corpus-based comparison of metaphor in US inaugural speeches and UK election manifestos, where he identified lexical fields which occurred in only one of the varieties: fire/light and the physical environment in the US corpus, and plants in the UK corpus. The explanations given for these differences are cultural and historical, with the US experience of struggling for independence leading to a positive evaluation of fire metaphors and the UK passion for gardening leading to the positive associations to words like 'nurture' and 'growth'.

It is possible to discern a pattern of increasing reliance on corpus tools in the study of metaphor. While some corpus-based studies of metaphor (e.g. Charteris-Black 2002) start qualitatively and involve reading the corpus texts in looking for potential metaphorical uses, it is becoming increasingly common for studies to start quantitatively, taking a frequency or keyword list as a starting point (e.g. Partington 2003).

Reported speech in political discourse

Human language tends to be full of reproductions of and references to other people's discourse. A great deal of recycling goes on in discourse – not only in the form of explicit references to what has already been said or written, but also in the form of expressions and linguistic structures (with no explicit attribution) which have been used by others. The explicit reference to what other speakers/writers have said/written is a prominent feature of many types of political discourse, such as parliamentary debates and political news reports. Direct quotation is a central tool of argumentation in parliamentary debates, where the official record is often invoked to quote political opponents. Also in governmental press conferences, what has or has not been said is highly topical.

Corpus-based studies of reported speech in political discourse are found in, for example, Bevitori (2006) and Garretson and Ädel (2008). Bevitori (2006) used a corpus of debates on Iraq in the UK House of Commons in 2003 to examine reporting verbs. She started with the types of reporting verbs employed by Members of Parliament and then analysed the context – specifically, the form of evaluative meanings and rhetorical function these verbs carry. Her explicit aim was to 'place the range of reporting verbs in the wider context of the meaning potential of the language by moving from concordance to discourse' (2006: 163). Studying expanded concordance lines and the semantics of the verbs used (e.g. 'acknowledge' or 'suggest'), she examined whether the speaker explicitly aligns with the attributed material or not.

How was the corpus searched? As reporting structures cannot be retrieved automatically from a corpus without any manual analysis, the Bevitori study was restricted to past simple verb forms (with the exception of SAY, which is considerably more frequent than any of the other reporting verbs). A similar method was used by Garretson and Ädel (2008), who first created a list of 'reporting words' (e.g. all forms of the verb lemma STATE, the noun 'statement', and the phrase 'according to') in an attempt to capture as many instances as possible in their data. They then checked all hits and rejected irrelevant examples. In the case of homonymous words like 'state', examples like 'the association *states* that misconceptions continue to affect law' were retained and examples like 'two dozen *states* that allow early voting' were rejected.

Garretson and Ädel's (ibid.) study investigated a corpus of newspaper reports culled from a dozen major US newspapers and relating to the 2004 US presidential election. Some linguists have stressed the difficulty of rendering other people's discourse without the opinions or interpretations of the person doing the reporting becoming part of the message. This led to the question of whether media bias can be reflected in reporting structures. Garretson and Ädel analysed the sources to whom statements in the corpus were attributed in order to find out who got to speak, and whether there was balance between the two sides (Democrats and Republicans) in the election. They also examined how speech was reported in the corpus with respect to the use of direct versus indirect speech, the explicitness of source identification, and the effects that the choice of reporting word can have on the portrayal of a source. Slight evidence was found of an apparent preference for one candidate or the other in certain papers, but overall no statistically significant differences that could be construed as bias were found.

5. Corpus linguistics and political discourse: looking to the future

This final section offers some reflections on possible future developments in corpus analysis of political discourse, considering new genres to study, new types of corpora to compile, and new topics to cover.

New genres to study

It may be that what is considered prototypical political discourse is changing. Political discourse is increasingly channelled through various media: television, radio, newspapers, the internet, e-mail and telephones. This has lead to new (sub-)genres emerging, such as political blogs, special interest group e-mails and message boards, talk radio interviews of politicians, webcasts and political cell-phone messages (introduced in 2008 on a large scale by the Obama campaign in the US). The so-called 'new media' are said to play an increasingly important role in the political process, which makes these important types of discourse to study from a linguistic viewpoint. What is particularly exciting about this development, from the perspective of corpus analysis, is that there is great potential for exploring political discourse on the internet using corpus tools, not least because the material is already accessible in an electronic format.

New types of corpora to compile

It seems reasonable to make two predictions about future types of corpora in the study of political discourse. One prediction is that increasingly specialised corpora will be developed, in particular 'topic-based corpora', each compiled to research a specific topic (such as an armed conflict) or a specific political issue (such as global warming). The second prediction is that we will see the creation of multimodal corpora of political discourse, for example involving text, audio data and image data. This would be of great interest, as persuasive types of discourse can rely heavily on audio or on visual information. The political poster, for example, would be a suitable genre for taking a semiotic approach to both the linguistic and the visual features simultaneously. In order for this type of information to be usefully applied in corpus studies, future textual corpora would need to be annotated for multimodal features – such as images used in a political manifesto, or gestures used in a political speech.

New topics to cover

The study of political discourse would benefit from greater coverage at the pragmatic and discourse level. One thing that would help bring this about is improved general tools for manual or automated annotation of corpus data. With better opportunities for user-defined classification of data, linguistic categories which are difficult or even impossible to search for by means of surface word forms or part-of-speech tagging could be analysed in more systematic ways. Parallel to such developments, there is also a need to develop new ideas for finding 'proxies' for phenomena at the pragmatic or discourse level. For example, in work by Partington (2008), the speech act of teasing (both performing and responding to it) is analysed in political press conferences. As the transcripts were already marked for instances of laughter, and as laughter-talk is frequently associated with teasing, what Partington did was to use the tag [laughter] as a way of identifying instances of teasing (cf. McCarthy and Carter's (2004) study of hyperbole using a similar method).

Finally, one of the major challenges of the corpus-based approach is how to anchor linguistic findings in the social and political world – and how to do so in a systematic and scientific way. Future corpus-based studies of political discourse need to further develop theoretically sound ways of showing – to use a quote from Stubbs (2008: 1) – 'how all the empirical information contributes to solving the great intellectual puzzles of language in society'.

Further reading

Musolff, A. (2004) 'The Heart of the European Body Politic: British and German Perspectives on Europe's Central Organ', *Journal of Multilingual and Multicultural Development* 25(5 and 6): 437–52. (This article is a good example of a corpus-assisted study of metaphor in political discourse.)

Partington, A. (2003) *The Linguistics of Political Argument: The Spin-Doctor and the Wolf-Pack at the White House*. London: Routledge. (This book contains useful chapters on concordance analysis in the context of White House press briefings.)

References

Baker, P. (2004) 'Unnatural Acts: Discourses of Homosexuality within the House of Lords Debates on Gay Male Law Reform', *Journal of Sociolinguistics* 8(1): 88–106.

Barlow, M. (2000) 'Corpus of Spoken Professional American English', Houston, TX: Michael Barlow [producer], Athelstan (www.athel.com) [distributor].

Berber Sardinha, T. (2008) 'Lula e a Metáfora da Conquista [Lula and the Metaphor of "Conquest"]', *Linguagem em (Dis)curso* 8(1): 93–120.

Bevitori, C. (2006) 'Speech Representation in Parliamentary Discourse. Rhetorical Strategies in a Heteroglossic Perspective: A Corpus-based Study', in J. Flowerdew and M. Gotti (eds) *Studies in Specialized Discourse*. Bern: Peter Lang.

Biber, D. (1988) *Variation across Speech and Writing*. Cambridge: Cambridge University Press.

Charteris-Black, J. (2002) 'Why "An Angel Rides in the Whirlwind and Directs the Storm": A Corpus-based Comparative Study of Metaphor in British and American Political Discourse', in K. Aijmer and B. Altenberg (eds) *Advances in Corpus Linguistics*. Amsterdam: Rodopi.

de Beaugrande, R. (1999) 'Discourse Studies and the Ideology of "Liberalism"', *Discourse Studies* 1(3): 259–95.

Fairclough, N. (2000) *New Labour, New Language?* London: Routledge.

Garretson, G. and Ädel, A. (2008) 'Who's Speaking?: Evidentiality in US newspapers during the 2004 Presidential Campaign', in A. Ädel and R. Reppen (eds) *Corpora and Discourse: The Challenges of Different Settings*. Amsterdam: John Benjamins.

Gastil, J. (1992) 'Undemocratic Discourse: A Review of Theory and Research on Political Discourse', *Discourse and Society* 3(4): 469–500.

Graber, D. (1981) 'Political Language', in D. Nimmo and K. Sanders (eds) *Handbook of Political Communication*. Beverly Hills, CA: Sage, pp. 195–224.

Ilie, C. (2000) 'Cliché-based Metadiscursive Argumentation in the Houses of Parliament', *International Journal of Applied Linguistics* 10(1): 65–84.

Koteyko, N. (2007) 'A Diachronic Approach to Meaning: English Loanwords in Russian Opposition Discourse', *Corpora* 2(1): 65–95.

McCarthy, M. J. and Carter, R. A. (2004) '"There's Millions of Them": Hyperbole in Everyday Conversation', *Journal of Pragmatics* 36: 149–84.

Milizia, D. and Spinzi, C. (2008) 'The "Terroridiom" Principle between Spoken and Written Discourse', *International Journal of Corpus Linguistics* 13(3): 322–50.

Morley, J. (2004) 'The Sting in the Tail: Persuasion in English Editorial Discourse', in A. Partington, J. Morley and L. Haarman (eds) *Corpora and Discourse*. Bern: Peter Lang.

Musolff, A. (2004) 'The Heart of the European Body Politic: British and German Perspectives on Europe's Central Organ', *Journal of Multilingual and Multicultural Development* 25(5 and 6): 437–52.

Ochs, E. and Taylor, C. (1992) 'Family Narrative as Political Activity', *Discourse and Society* 3(3): 301–40.

Partington, A. (2003) *The Linguistics of Political Argument: The Spin-Doctor and the Wolf-Pack at the White House*. London: Routledge.

——(2008) 'Teasing at the White House: A Corpus-assisted Study of Face Work in Performing and Responding to Teases', *Text and Talk* 28(6): 771–92.

Pearce, M. (2005) 'Informalization in UK Party Election Broadcasts 1966–97', *Language and Literature* 14 (1): 65–90.

Peterson, J. C. and Brereton, L. H. (eds) (2008) *The Norton Reader: An Anthology of Nonfiction*, twelfth shorter edition. New York: W. W. Norton.

Scott, M. (1999) *WordSmith Tools: Version 3.0.* Oxford: Oxford University Press.

Stubbs, M. (2008) 'Three Concepts of Keywords', revised version of a paper presented to the conference on Keyness in Text at the Certosa di Pontignano, University of Siena, June 2007, available at www.uni-trier.de/fileadmin/fb2/ANG/Linguistik/Stubbs/stubbs-2008-keywords.pdf (accessed 22 March 2009).

Teubert, W. (2002) 'Der britische Anti-Europa-Diskurs und seine Schlüsselwörter', *Sprachreport* 2: 7–12.

Westin, I. and Geisler, C. (2002) 'A Multi-dimensional Study of Diachronic Variation in British Newspaper Editorials', *ICAME Journal* 26: 133–52.

Williams, R. (1985) *A Vocabulary of Culture and Society*. Oxford: Oxford University Press.

Wilson, J. (2003 [2001]) 'Political Discourse', in D. Schiffrin, D. Tannen and H. Hamilton (eds) *The Handbook of Discourse Analysis*. Malden, MA: Blackwell.

43

How to use corpus linguistics in the study of health communication

Sarah Atkins and Kevin Harvey

1. What is healthcare communication and why study it?

Language use is centrally important to the way in which we constitute our experiences of health and illness, as well as ultimately being of clear practical importance to those working in the healthcare professions, who must communicate medical ideas on a regular basis. It is perhaps not surprising then that healthcare communication, in all its various aspects, has become an important research theme in Applied Linguistics. In the following study, we will illustrate how some of the corpus linguistic methodologies you will have encountered so far in this book can be usefully adopted in the field of healthcare communication studies. As a means of practically illustrating the application of these methods, we make a case study of a specific type of healthcare discourse, that of adolescent email language, in particular on the topic of sexual health. This will make use of the one-million-word Adolescent Health Email Corpus (AHEC), a collection of adolescent health emails taken from a UK-based health website, a data-set originally compiled by Harvey (2008). The corpus study here offers us a means of investigating and understanding the language young people use in relation to sexual health issues, which may have important practical implications for healthcare professionals who need to communicate with this age group on a regular basis.

Our experiences of health and illness are not simply based in the biological 'realities' of our bodies, but, crucially, in the language we use to talk about them. If we take the view that language and discourse work to constitute our understanding of ourselves and the world around us, then this is vitally important to the way we make sense of the social experience of health:

> illness cannot be just illness, for the simple reason that human culture is constituted in language … and that health and illness, being things which fundamentally concern humans, and hence need to be 'explained', enter into language and are constituted in language, regardless of whether or not they have some independent reality in nature.
>
> (Fox 1993: 6)

It is certainly true that we are constantly presented with the need to 'explain' illness. In an increasingly medicalised society, discourses surrounding the body saturate the texts we receive on a daily basis, such as in news media and advertising. When we, ourselves, experience illness, we find out about it through the language of healthcare professionals, through conversations with our family and friends, through books and internet media and so on. This central importance of language and discourse in our experience of illness has given rise to a field of study that has become known as 'healthcare communication' over the last three decades. Broadly, this field has incorporated the many diverse aspects and textual genres that impinge on our experiences of what it means to be ill: for example, interactions in hierarchical, institutional medical settings between healthcare practitioners and patients, professional communication between practitioners, patient narratives of experience as well as genres such as government health education material, media representations of health news and advertisements that project particular ideas about health and our bodies.

Research on communication in institutional healthcare settings in particular has contributed significantly to the sociological study of health practitioners and patients (Sarangi 2004: 2). Although, as many commentators point out, the focus of a substantial amount of this research has exclusively been on doctor–patient interaction (Candlin 2000), there exists an increasing body of enquiry into other forms of medical communication which has considered, for example, the verbal routines of a variety of non-physician personnel including nurses (Crawford *et al.* 1998), physiotherapists (Parry 2004), and pharmacists (Pilnick 1999) – as well as exploring written medical discourse in various communicative contexts such as medical note-taking (Hobbs 2003) and case histories (Francis and Kramer-Dahl 2004). Though diverse and wide-ranging, what these studies have in common is their close focus on language in use and the consequent pointing up of the crucial role of language in the practice of medicine and health care (Sarangi 2004: 2).

Methodologically, much of this research has taken a sociolinguistic and discourse analytic perspective, including conversation analysis, text/genre analysis and critical discourse analysis. These perspectives have provided rich points of entry into the description and interrogation of medical practice. Moreover, many healthcare language studies have combined perspectives. There has been, for example, a recent tendency for conversation analysis and interactional sociolinguistic methodologies to be supplemented by a strain of critical discourse analysis, with the research impetus being as much to criticise and change practices in institutional healthcare settings as to describe and understand them (e.g. McHoul and Rapley 2001: xii). However, such studies, as Adolphs *et al.* (2004) observe, are typically qualitative in their approach to analysis, based on relatively small databases and without originating in large collections of data. This has led to a more recent call by a number of researchers in healthcare communication studies to make greater use of more substantial datasets (Skelton and Hobbs 1999a).

2. Key corpus-based studies in healthcare communication

A number of health communication studies have begun to turn to corpus methodologies, although these are few in comparison with other applied linguistic themes, such as lexicographic and lexical studies, grammatical and register variation and genre analysis. Thomas and Wilson (1996), in a comparatively early corpus interrogation of health language, make use of a 1.25-million-word corpus of practitioner–patient exchanges, setting out to demonstrate that computer content analysis can overcome the 'shortcomings of straight quantitative analysis' and has 'the potential to provide results which are in some respects comparable to manual discourse analysis' (1996: 92). Although thoroughly detailing patterns of linguistic use, the question arises whether corpus tools actually contribute anything new to the understanding of healthcare communication here, an understanding that might be otherwise achieved by manual discourse analytic procedures. Indeed, Thomas and Wilson pose this question themselves. Though the use of corpus tools enabled the researchers to quickly and accurately identify significant aspects of the health practitioners' language use, the study gives little emphasis to actual samples of extended stretches of language in use, and how linguistic components actually function in the dialogic context of the practitioner–patient exchanges they were investigating.

More recently, Skelton and colleagues (e.g. Skelton and Hobbs 1999a; Skelton *et al.* 1999, 2002) demonstrate the methodological advantages of integrating quantitative with qualitative approaches. As a starting point, they use frequency counts of words and phrases, complementing such quantitative findings with qualitative assessments of how such phrases operate in context through the use of concordance outputs. The authors contend that it is only through qualitative methods, such as concordance lines with subsequent recourse to extended stretches of text, that general patterns in health language can be explicated. Quantitative methods can identify general patterns, 'but these patterns exist in a complex context that can only partly be described quantitatively' (Skelton 1999b: 111). Skelton and colleagues' research utilises these corpus tools to examine assorted themes in health communication, including metaphor, pronominal usage and linguistic imprecision, demonstrating a range of uses for the corpus approach. Rather than providing a broad linguistic characterisation of the particular communicative practices in question, the authors confine their analyses to investigating specific linguistic phenomena. For this reason, their studies are not concerned with harnessing comparative data, contrasting, for example, their various datasets with general reference corpora.

Such a comparative approach is adopted by Adolphs *et al.* (2004) in their corpus analysis of NHS Direct exchanges between professionals and patient callers. Adolphs *et al.* compare a corpus of health professionals' language with a corpus of general spoken English, identifying a set of keywords that appear with greater frequency in the NHS Direct consultations. As with Skelton and colleagues' research, Adolphs *et al.* (2004) avoid the limitations of decontextualised quantitative analyses. Having isolated a number of linguistic features quantitatively, the researchers examine these key items in their original discourse environment using concordance lines and conversation analysis techniques in order to provide close descriptions of interactional processes. These methodological stages afford the authors a means of understanding the uniqueness of these professional–patient exchanges, enabling them to characterise the nature of NHS Direct consultations where they identify an overarching tendency for professionals to use politeness strategies and the language of convergence in their interactions with callers. As these corpus approaches to health language demonstrate, then, corpus tools are not ends in themselves and cannot provide explanations for the linguistic features observed (McEnery 2005). It is important to supplement quantitative approaches with qualitative support.

3. Building a corpus of adolescent health language

The health email data for the corpus-based case study which we focus on are taken from an online health forum, Teenage Health Freak (www.teenagehealthfreak.org), a UK-based website which provides health information for young people. Operated by two doctors specialising in adolescent health, the Teenage Health Freak website has been running since its launch in 2000. It is designed to be user-friendly, interactive, confidential and evidence-based, employing non-technical, accessible language and colourful graphics, with young people themselves actively being involved in the design and construction of the website.

A central feature of Teenage Health Freak is the 'Ask Dr Ann' facility. This interactive feature of the website allows young people to email their questions in confidence to the online GP persona, 'Dr Ann'. It should be noted that these online requests for advice do not constitute emails in the traditional sense; they are not sent via the contributors' individual, personal email accounts, but communicated anonymously via a universal posting platform on the website. Given the large influx of emails that the site receives, it is not possible for the website doctors to respond to all postings. Our corpus analysis therefore focuses on the adolescent communiqués rather than the professionals' comparatively infrequent returns. Permission was given to collect and analyse emails sent to the Teenage Health Freak website between January 2004 and December 2005. Comprising 62,794 messages (a total of one million words), the corpus contributes a substantial snapshot of the health concerns communicated on a daily basis by the website's teenage contributors.

One of our principal considerations concerning the compilation of the corpus was whether such an amount of data was sufficiently representative: does such a quantity faithfully represent the health communication patterns and concerns of young people who contribute to the website? Although we ideally wanted to collect more data, taken by Sinclair's (1991: 18) pronouncement that a corpus should be as large as possible, we argue that, for the purpose of beginning to identify and describe patterns and commonalities in young people's beliefs about health and illness, one million words is a sufficient amount of data, or at the very least constitutes a substantial starting point. Given its size and focus on a particular communicative setting (the domain of adolescent health advice-seeking), the corpus constitutes a specialised corpus. For a specialised corpus, one million words is by no means a small amount (according to Flowerdew 2004: 19, a corpus is generally considered small if it contains no more than 250,000 words). The methodological advantage of using a specialised corpus is that its smaller size lends itself to a more detailed, qualitative-based examination than is possible with larger, more general corpora, such as the 100-million-word British National Corpus or the Bank of English. The close examination of concordance lines with recourse to the linguistic co-text, for example, provides a rich source of data to complement more quantitative-based studies (Flowerdew 2004). In short, then, our corpus constitutes a suitable linguistic resource for the purposes of beginning to identify and describe patterns and commonalities in young people's beliefs about health and illness.

4. How can a corpus of health language be used to explore patterns?

Identifying themes and lexical items for analysis

In order to initially ascertain the pertinent themes and items to be researched in the AHEC, frequency lists were generated, as well as a keyword comparison being made with the British National Corpus (BNC) using *WordSmith Tools* (Scott 2004). Keywords are an important indicator of both expression and content (Seale *et al.* 2007) and have been used by an increasing number of researchers as a means of identifying key themes characterising health language corpora (Adolphs *et al.* 2004; Harvey *et al.* 2007; Seale *et al.* 2007) (see Scott, this volume, on how keyword significance is calculated). Table 43.1 provides a representative overview of the central health themes that can be seen to emerge in the AHEC through keyword groupings.

Notably, the lexical patterns clustering around the topic of sexual health predominate in the keyword lists, a topic which will be explored in the ensuing study.

Adolescent sexual health and language – background

As well as being a theme flagged up by our keyword analysis of the corpus, the issue of adolescent sexual health has been highlighted as being an urgent contemporary concern (e.g. British Medical Association 2003, 2005; Bradley-Stevenson and Mumford 2007) with the necessity of 'doing something about teenage sexuality and sexual knowledge' pressing on the minds of policymakers (Brown *et al.* 2006: 169). The prevalence of sexually transmitted infections (STIs) among teenagers is high and continues to increase (British Medical Association 2003), including a recent rise in the number of newly acquired cases of HIV/AIDS (Society for Adolescent Medicine 2006). As the Health Protection Agency (2006) report, in the UK people between the ages of sixteen and twenty-four account for approximately 11 per cent of new diagnoses of HIV each year, while the number of young people receiving treatment for the infection has tripled since 1996. Research indicates that, although often aware of the risks involved in taking part in sexual activity, adolescents are liable to have limited and erroneous understandings about reproductive health (Smith *et al.* 2003; Mason 2005). Yet, tellingly, these negative constructions of teenage sexual health are generated by an 'outsider perspective', prompted by what researchers deem to be the issues rather than young people themselves.

Table 43.1 Keyword categorisation of health themes in AHEC

Theme	*Examples of keywords*
Sexual health	Sex, sexual, penis, pregnant, period, orgasm, AIDS, infertile, STD, STI, sperm, contraception, HIV, clitoris, vagina, vulva, PMS, erection, condom, masturbate, gay, abortion, foreplay, intercourse, virgin, unprotected, lesbian, oral, pill, ovulation, herpes, thrush, chlamydia, pregnancy, tampon, testicles, genitalia, viagra, scrotum, labia, glans, ovaries, foreskin, balls, fanny, bisexual, miscarriage
Mental health	Depression, depressed, suicide, suicidal, die, overdose, antidepressants, cut, cuts, cutting, self-harm, scars, prozac, sad, unhappy, self, harm, wrists, stress, stressed, ADHD, paranoid, mental, mad, moods, sad, unhappy, crying, personality, anxiety
Body weight/image	Anorexia, anorexic, weight, size, overweight, fat, obese, underweight, skinny, thin, bulimia, BMI, exercise, diets, kilograms, KG, KGS, bulimia, calories
Drugs/alcohol	Drugs, cannabis, cocaine, heroin, pills, addicted, alcohol, drunk, drinking, poppers, mushrooms, marijuana, crack, ecstasy, addict, stoned, LSD, cigarettes, dope
Serious conditions	Cancer, epilepsy, diabetes, anthrax
Minor conditions	Acne, zits, blackhead, mumps, scabies, dandruff, worms, cystitis
Medication	Medicine, medication, prescribed, antibiotics, tablets, pill, pills

According to Jackson (2005), a different perspective to that provided by much of the literature emerges when young people are asked to formulate their own 'insider perspectives' concerning sexual health, thus indicating whether their sexuality-related concerns 'concur with those in the public and academic world' (Jackson 2005: 85).

Sex is a taboo topic and hence does not comfortably fit into socially acceptable language use (Stewart 2005). Previous research concerning sexual health in adult language has discovered much use of vague terms and euphemistic language. Given the powerful and pervasive influence of sexual taboos, it might be expected that the way in which adolescents communicate sexual concerns would similarly involve circumlocutions, vague language and euphemisms. Yet little is actually known about the precise nature of young people's use of language here. In the context of professional advice-seeking, Ammerman *et al.* (1992) found that young people were much more familiar with non-technical and slang terms rather than common medical lexis in relation to sexual health. Moreover, rather than confine themselves to a limited set of genitourinary-related terms, the adolescents were prone to linguistic variety, employing a range of synonyms. A consequence of this lexical diversity was the increased potential for misunderstanding between professionals and younger patients. Practitioners should therefore not assume, Ammerman *et al.* (1992) suggest, that adolescents understand standard medical vocabulary in discussions of sexual health.

Contrary to Ammerman's study, sociolinguistic research by Harvey *et al.* 2007 revealed that teenagers commonly adopted a medico-technical register in (online) requests for sexual health advice from professionals. The adolescents' messages, moreover, were characterised by non-euphemistic language, with the young people describing themselves, their anatomy and their sexual identities in meticulous and explicit linguistic detail. As Harvey *et al.* (2007) observe, their findings contrast with the degree of vagueness and apparent difficulty in calling experiences to mind that practitioners and researchers have found elsewhere with adolescents. Whether the adolescents would have displayed the same non-euphemistic frankness and meticulous linguistic detail in other communicative contexts, away from the anonymity of online communication, remains yet to be precisely established. Nevertheless, Harvey *et al.*'s (2007) study highlights how valuable language data from the online medium can be for offering access that we might not otherwise have to the communicative strategies adolescents use in talking about sexual health, a medium of communication which will be further investigated here.

Adolescent language and sexual health – corpus analysis

'Sex' and sexually transmitted infections

The AHEC possesses a range of emails dedicated to the subject of sexually transmitted infections (STIs). Table 43.2 lists the total frequencies of all the sexually transmitted infections and related conditions that appear throughout the corpus as a whole.

The table shows that HIV/AIDS makes up 39 per cent of the total number of references to STIs in the AHEC, with mention of other infections being comparatively infrequent. It is interesting to speculate whether the lexical preference for AIDS and HIV is in any way a reaction to or reflection of the recent rise in the number of newly acquired cases of HIV/AIDS among adolescents. Whatever the case, it is certain that practically all young people are aware of HIV/AIDS (Rosenthal and Moore 1994). Thus, given the primacy of HIV and AIDS in the corpus, and its significance to the teenage

Table 43.2 Frequencies of sexually transmitted infections and conditions in the AHEC Corpus

Rank	*Word*	*Frequency*	*%*
1	AIDS	209	25
2	HIV	114	14
3	thrush	106	13
4	crabs	103	12
5	herpes	96	11
6	genital warts	84	10
7	chlamydia	81	10
8	gonorrhoea	19	2
9	syphilis	14	2

population more generally, the remainder of this chapter will focus on the adolescents' knowledge and representation of these two concepts.

Conflation and the metaphorisation of AIDS and HIV

With the advent of AIDS and HIV, it became apparent to everyone that unprotected sex could lead to terrible consequences and sex now carries 'connotations of health risk and death' (Woollett *et al.* 1998: 370). Although it is not possible to ascertain whether the saliency of the terms *HIV* and *AIDS* in the corpus is due to the emotional impact of these two phenomena and their potential lethality, the lexical preference for *HIV* and *AIDS*, the latter in particular, is revealing. Emails about HIV and AIDS (314 in total) cover a range of themes, central among which are questions relating to HIV/AIDS terminology and conceptual definitions of the terms (of which there are seventy-eight occurrences: 24 per cent), concerns regarding transmission and causation (seventy-two: 23 per cent), and questions about symptoms and the likelihood of having HIV/AIDS (sixty: 19 per cent). As Table 43.2 reveals, the lexical item *AIDS* appears nearly twice as regularly (209) as *HIV* (114). Of the 209 occurrences of *AIDS*, seventeen co-occur with *HIV*, which suggests a relationship between the two. The following extended concordances are typical examples (replete with their original spelling, punctuation and capitalisation):

- how does **HIV/AIDS** get passed on
- what happens when a man or women is **hiv** and has **aids**
- how are the drug manufacturers involved in the crisis(**HIV/AIDS**)
- Can you be born with **HIV** or **AIDs** or do have to catch it ?
- I keep reading all peoples advice and knowledge about **HIV** and **AIDS** and it keeps saying infected person. How does someone innitally become infected?
- what is **hiv** or **aids**

In these instances (and in the other twelve messages in which the two terms co-occur), the adolescents clearly, and crucially, distinguish the concepts of HIV and AIDS, conceiving them as separate entities while also being connected in some way (given the oblique (/) or conjuncts ('and', 'or') that co-ordinate them). However, of the remaining 192 occurrences of *AIDS* in the corpus, 192 (92 per cent) appear in isolation: that is, with no mention of HIV, the virus that can cause AIDS (UNESCO 2006). The following examples are typical of the range of contexts in which *AIDS* in isolation is used:

- how do i know if iv got **aids**
- Can you get **AIDS** by being fingered?
- dear dr anne. i am gay and i have given someone a blowjob i think i have **aids** please help
- What does **AIDS** stand for?
- I had sex without using a condom and i am really scared i might be pregnant or might have **aids**
- I received oral sex about 6 months ago, now i am noticing some pimple on my penis, I don't know if it is from masturbating or if it is herpes, could you help me. And also can you get genital warts, or **AIDs** from oral sex.
- i am worried that i have **aids**
- I had unprotected sex with a girl and ejaculated inside her. she has had many sexual partners and im not sure if she had always practiced safe sex. im worried i may have **aids**. is the risk that great?
- i have had sex with my boyfriend for the first time and the condom kept snapping so we decided to not use one what are the chances of me bein pregnant or having **aids**? please answer this im really really wottied

The absence of any reference to HIV and the foregrounding of AIDS indicate a terminological conflation of the two concepts, a misconception that is liable to have profound consequences in terms of how the adolescents conceive of and understand HIV and AIDS. For instance, in a number of the examples, there is the underlying belief that AIDS is a communicable infection, not a syndrome or range of conditions (UNESCO 2006), with its being constructed as, and confused with, a virus or disease, something that can be readily transmitted via sexual activity: 'can you get … AIDS from oral sex', 'can you get AIDS by being fingered?' and so on.

Collapsing the distinction between HIV and AIDS in this way inevitably results in confusion and reinforces 'unrealistic and unfounded fears' (Watney 1989: 184) on the part of the adolescents who may well mistakenly believe themselves to be at risk of AIDS but not HIV. Such extreme worst-case scenarios conceive of AIDS as something that sets in immediately after infection, a unitary phenomenon rather than a collection of different medical conditions – beliefs which obscure, if not efface altogether, the existence of HIV, the virus, which is indeed infectious. Such erroneous conflation of HIV infection with AIDS (by definition, the stage of HIV infection 'when a person's immune system can no longer cope'; Terrence Higgins Trust 2007: 1) repeats some of the early and fundamental misconceptions and negative attitudes about AIDS that were widespread during the 1980s and 1990s (Sikand *et al.* 1996; Helman 2007).

For example, Warwick *et al.*'s (1988) in-depth study into youth beliefs about AIDS revealed that a significant number of young people, as with many adults, were unable to distinguish between HIV infection and AIDS, a finding which they attributed to the media's consistent failure to provide the public with accurate information. This fundamental misunderstanding (identifying AIDS as a transmissible disease) was related to the 'public terror about "catching" AIDS from people in public places or during casual contact' (Grover 1990: 145). Such beliefs (and the emotive linguistic choices encoding them) prevalent during that period are still apparent in the adolescent health emails communicated over twenty years later. For instance, one of the central ways in which adolescents describe becoming infected with HIV or developing AIDS is through use of the lemma CATCH, the second most common verb (thirteen times) used to signify contraction after GET (fifty-two). The use of CATCH as a verb encoding transmission of HIV/AIDS is telling, implying a more active role for subjects:

- can you **catch** aids if havnt had sex?
- how do you prevent **catching** h. i. v
- is the aids virus difficult to **catch**?
- Can you **catch** HIV if you wear a earring that might have been worn by somebody else before?
- out of ten what is the average to **catch** aids when having sex
- how can you **catch** hiv
- if i have sex with someone with aids without protection can i **cath** it
- can you **catch** aids if someone masterbates you
- Can you be born with HIV or AIDs or do have to **catch** it ?
- the other day i had sex without using a condom i am going to take a test but i am also worried i could have **caught** an STI or AIDS or sumthing wot shall i do ?!!!!!
- how do i **catch** HIV?

Biber *et al.* (1999) describe 'catch' as an 'activity verb', a verb denoting actions and events 'that could be associated with choice' (1999: 361). As the above emails illustrate, 'catch' implies specific notions of agency on the part of subjects in the sense that it is within their power to prevent infection, with responsibility framed in terms of both general or universal agency (encoded via the second person: 'Can you catch … ?') or individual control via the first-person singular pronoun: 'Can I catch … ?'. As Johnson and Murray (1985: 152) put it, 'catching' an ailment (as in catching a cold) semantically implies a degree of co-operation: 'We catch things … in ways which are our own fault; we blame ourselves – we should have worn galoshes, and should not have sat in a draught.' This notion of personal agency, of being responsible for becoming infected, communicated through the verbal concept of 'catching', is made further apparent in the adolescents' questions above by their explicitly referring to prevention and avoidance strategies ('how do you prevent catching h. i. v?', 'is the aids virus difficult to catch?'), as well as their seeking clarification as to whether specific activities are liable to result in contracting HIV/AIDS – activities which, by implication, should therefore be avoided: 'can you catch aids if someone masterbates you?', 'if I have sex with someone with aids without protection can i cath it?'. Here, then, both HIV and AIDS, if the requisite care is taken, are constructed as preventable through individual agency. Infection with HIV is not an inevitable outcome as, alarmingly, some young people have perceived it to be (Warwick *et al.* 1988).

However, many commentators and public health bodies stress that neither HIV nor AIDS can be 'caught' (Watney 1989: 184). Indeed, contemporary health promotion literature produced by standard-setting organisations such as UNESCO continually warns against the use of this verb to signify the way that people might become HIV positive, since it only helps to reproduce myths about HIV and AIDS (UNESCO 2006; IFJ 2006). In the health emails above, for example, the various realisations of the lemma CATCH unavoidably and infelicitously conjure notions of the common cold and influenza, as evidence from the British National Corpus (BNC) attests. Consulting the 100-million-word British National Corpus, a corpus representative of both spoken and written English language as a whole, reveals that, as a transitive verb, 'catch' co-occurs with the direct objects 'cold' (113), 'chill' (twenty-one), 'bug' (twenty) and 'colds' (seven). As these collocates indicate, one typical use of the verb 'catch' in general English is to describe the acquiring of relatively minor infections, in the sense of their being widespread and generally innocuous (though 'bug', of course, potentially relates to more serious infections such as MRSA, the so-called 'super bug'; Knifton 2005). With regard to more serious viruses and illnesses, other less euphemistic constructions are used in the BNC to describe the process of becoming infected and the onset of morbidity: for example, HIV is typically 'contracted', 'got', 'acquired', while AIDS is 'got', 'developed', 'contracted'.

Given this association, a corollary of using 'catch' to describe infection with HIV/AIDS is to encode the assumption that the virus can be acquired via casual contact, possessing a transmission efficacy similar to both colds and influenza. As such, talk of 'catching' HIV/AIDS figuratively transforms the virus from something which is, in reality, difficult to transmit and is only communicable via specific routes (Terrence Higgins Trust 2007: 2) to something highly contagious, liable to spread rapidly and extensively. And this underlying metaphor of HIV/AIDS as 'invisible contagion' (Helman 2007: 395) and attacking from without (Weiss 1997) extends to the adolescents' emails about acquiring HIV/AIDS outside of those that explicitly refer to 'catching' the virus. There are, for instance, ten further questions concerning HIV/AIDS transmission that draw on metaphors of contagion:

- my girfreind as already kissed a boy and she wants to kiss me would I get **aids**?
- i want to know if **AIDS** can gotten through kissing?
- Can you get **aids** from dogs?
- does anyone who has **aids** have to be quarantied
- can you get **hiv** from somebody who doesn't have it?
- Hi im 14 (duh) and i have never had sex or used injection drugs (or drugs at all) but from a toothbrush is it possible for me to get **HIV**?
- Dr Ann, I am food for nats and mosquitoes, they absolutly love me, but if they have bitten someone that has **AIDS**, then I am bitten, Can i be at risk of getting **AIDS**? Thanks Ann
- can i get **aids** off my cat?
- i know you said that you cant get **hiv** from kissing. but we were told in sex education that if you are french kissing and swallow the persons spit you can get **hiv**. is this true? please tell me bacause i hav been put off kissing now.

As with the emails evoking notions of 'catching' HIV/AIDS, these adolescents' concerns similarly communicate fear of contagion and pollution. Here, however, ambiguity over transmission is related not just to sexual activity but to a wide and common range of circumstances, with, for instance, even toothbrushes and household pets being potential contaminants and sources of the virus. This perceived infiltration by HIV/AIDS of routine aspects of everyday and domestic life resonates with folk beliefs common in the first years of the AIDS epidemic when the virus was believed to be 'transmitted by virtually any contact with an infected person' (Helman 2007: 395). Such a conception draws on the notion of the 'miasma' theory of disease (Lupton 2006), the folk model of infection which conceives of infected persons as being surrounded as if by a miasma or contagious cloud of poisonous bad air liable to cause disease (Helman 2007: 395). Miasmatic beliefs such as those evident in the foregoing emails, where HIV/AIDS is metaphorised as something highly contagious and invisible, are closely related to what is believed to be the imperceptibility of persons with HIV infection, highlighting the difficulty for some young people of being able to identify who might or be infected (Warwick *et al.* 1988: 117). Although, against the total number of emails relating to HIV and AIDS, there are comparatively few questions from the adolescents about potential 'carriers' of the disease, the small number that are present in the corpus, and reproduced in full below, expose overlapping attitudes towards and attributions about people perceived to be infected with HIV:

- how do you know if a person has **hiv**? can you tell just by looking at them and if they are 16 then will any symptoms be apparent
- is **AIDS** spread by homosexuals
- i have a boyfriend who told me he's been injecting drugs. i heard that drug users can get **hiv/aids** from using needles. is this true? what should i tell my friend? should i tell anyone else?
- have gay men got more chance of getting **HIV**

To have HIV/AIDS here is to possess characteristics or symptoms that are outwardly evident (and therefore discernible simply 'by looking') and to be deemed to belong to certain social categories (to be gay, to be an injecting drug user). One way of making sense of these constructions is to see them as separating those individuals who are assumed to be safe and free of infection (presumably so determined through their clean, asymptomatic appearances) and those whose behaviour constitutes them as a high-risk group. Yet crucially, as Watney (1989: 185) argues, there is no essential relation between HIV and any particular social group or category of people. Risk of HIV infection arises from what people do, what activities they actually participate in, not from what group they belong to or how they are labelled. Consequently, the social distance which these adolescents appear to place between themselves and groups they associate with HIV/AIDS potentially engenders complacency on their part: infection with HIV is seen as something that happens to others, specifically to the perceived 'high-risk' and minority groups first associated with AIDS.

What is HIV/AIDS?

Not all of the adolescents' emails, in the shape of distorting metaphorical transformations and alarmist folk beliefs, display such hysterical responses to HIV and AIDS. The most commonly occurring emails about HIV and AIDS in the adolescent health corpus are fundamental questions concerning definitions and terminology, specifically: 'What is HIV/AIDS?' and 'What does HIV/AIDS stand for?' One way of interpreting these open and elementary types of enquiry is, of course, to regard them as emblematic of knowledge deficits about sexual health. Yet equally, such questions might be considered vital responses to a contemporary and potentially life-threatening condition that, despite being in its third decade, is still commonly misunderstood (Helman 2007). AIDS did not arrive with its own vocabulary and so has been the source of linguistic difficulties from the start (Koestenbaum 1990). As Crystal (1997: 120) observes, the unabbreviated form of AIDS is 'so specialized that it is unknown to most people'. Yet even among health experts the acronym poses problems, having been variously understood as both 'Acquired Immune Deficiency Syndrome' and 'Acquired Immunodeficiency Syndrome', distinctions which although seemingly insignificant nevertheless demonstrate the semantic instability that surrounds the term. Thus if, as Callen (1990: 181) argues, to be AIDS literate involves mastering a specialist language of shorthand, then the questions 'What is AIDS?' and 'What does AIDS stand for?' are very well placed indeed.

5. Conclusions and applications

The results from the corpus analysis have practical relevance for health practitioners and educators concerned with the health of young people. The corpus approach affords an effective means of identifying the 'incremental effect' (Baker 2006: 13) of discursive patterns and commonalities in young people's understanding of sexual health. If educational initiatives are to be successful, then language, as Cameron and Kulick (2003: 154) argue, must not simply be regarded as 'a medium for sex and health education but something that must be discussed explicitly as part of the process', a contestation for which the corpus analysis presented in this chapter provides further support. In particular, it was evident that the adolescents possessed a range of misconceptions about HIV and AIDS, among which perhaps the most alarming was the tendency for some to conflate the two, reinforcing the idea that HIV and AIDS are identical. Such a conflation is liable to obscure awareness of the ways the virus is transmitted, potentially impeding assessments of risk in relation to sexual behaviour. Thus the findings add impetus to the call for evidence-based sex education programmes that provide 'full and factual information' (Independent Advisory Group on Sexual Health and HIV 2007: 12). The corpus analysis further highlighted some of the folk conceptualisations of sexual health adolescents operated with, beliefs that may need to be addressed by educators. Responding to lay beliefs like these is crucial since people are liable to filter official health education messages through popular beliefs about health (Helman 2007), reinterpreting them to suit their own needs (Aggleton and Homans 1987: 25).

Our corpus analysis has highlighted the value of the web-based forum as a means of eliciting the views of a generation who have often been reluctant to consult practitioners and others for sexual health advice (Suzuki and Calzo 2004). Studies of young people's sexuality have been dominated by questionnaire methodologies, often with problem-focused agendas dictated by the researchers. Respondents, pressured into supplying information, may decline to provide answers or substitute random replies for earnest responses (Moore *et al.* 1996: 186). Additionally, respondents may display euphemistic constraint, under-representing their sexual behaviours and attitudes (ibid.). This is, of course, not to suggest that the adolescent health emails interrogated here are entirely free of fabrication or understatement, but the fact that they are non-elicited means the concerns communicated are principally motivated by what young people deem to be personally relevant – a factor which perhaps helps to account for the often frank and meticulous detail of their self-disclosures.

The corpus-based method we have used here is a novel approach for researching sexual health communication, offering a fresh analytical perspective and thus responding to calls for new modes of research into sexual behaviour. Owing to the fact that the right to privacy is, understandably, jealously guarded in this sensitive area (Moore *et al.* 1996: 186), it is not surprising that, despite the increasing amount of survey and epidemiological work on the subject, there is a lack of data concerning how people communicate sexual issues in naturally occurring situations. The adolescent health email corpus therefore constitutes a unique vantage point from which to survey contemporary adolescent sexual health.

Further reading

Baker, P. (2006) *Using Corpora in Discourse Analysis*. London: Continuum. (This text provides invaluable practical help for researchers wishing to build their own corpus and/or conduct their own corpus analysis.)

Brown, B., Crawford, P. and Carter, R. (2006) *Evidence-based Health Communication*. Maidenhead: Open University Press. (This wide-ranging text provides a comprehensive overview of contemporary issues in health communication.)

Gwyn, R. (2002) *Communicating Health and Illness*. London: Sage. (This is an accessible discourse-based survey to health communication.)

References

Adolphs, S., Brown, B., Carter, R., Crawford, P. and Sahota, O. (2004) 'Applied Clinical Linguistics: Corpus Linguistics in Health Care Settings', *Journal of Applied Linguistics* 1: 9–28.

Aggleton, P. and Homans, H. (1987) 'Teaching about AIDS', *Social Science Teacher* 17: 24–8.

Ammerman, S., Perelli, E., Adler, N. and Irwin, C. (1992) 'Do Adolescents Understand What Physicians Say about Sexuality and Health?' *Clinical Pediatrics* 76: 590–5.

Baker, P. (2006) *Using Corpora in Discourse Analysis*. London: Continuum.

Biber, D., Johansson, S., Leech, G., Conrad, S. and Finegan, E. (1999) *Longman Grammar of Spoken and Written English*. London: Longman.

British Medical Association (2003) *Adolescent Health*. London: BMA Publications.

——(2005) *Sexual Health June 2005*, available at www.bma.org.uk/ap.nsf/Content/sexualhealthjune05 (accessed 13 March 2006).

Bradley-Stevenson, C. and Mumford, J. (2007) 'Adolescent Sexual Health', *Paediatric and Child Health* 17: 474–9.

Brown, B., Crawford, P. and Carter, R. (2006) *Evidence-based Health Communication*. Maidenhead: Open University Press.

Callen, M. (1990) 'AIDS: The Linguistic Battlefield', in C. Ricks and L. Michaels (eds) *The State of the Language*, 1990s edition. London: Faber & Faber.

Cameron, D. and Kulick, D. (2003) *Language and Sexuality*. Cambridge: Cambridge University Press.

Candlin, S. (2000) 'New Dynamics in the Nurse–Patient Relationship?' in S. Sarangi and M. Coulthard (eds) *Discourse and Social Life*. London: Longman.

Crawford, P., Brown, B. and Nolan, P. (1998) *Communicating Care: The Language of Nursing*. Gloucester: Stanley Thornes.

Crystal, D. (1997) *The Cambridge Encyclopaedia of the English Language*. Cambridge: Cambridge University Press.

Flowerdew, L. (2004) 'The Argument for Using English Specialized Corpora to Understand Academic and Professional Language', in U. Connor and T. Upton (eds) *Discourse in the Professions: Perspectives from Corpus Linguistics*. Amsterdam: John Benjamins.

Fox, N. (1993) *Postmodernism, Sociology and Health*. Buckingham: Open University Press.

Francis, G. and Kramer-Dahl, A. (2004) 'Grammar in the Construction of Medical Case Histories', in C. Coffin, A. Hewings and K. O' Halloran (eds) *Applying English Grammar: Functional and Corpus Approaches*. London: Arnold.

Grover, J. (1990) 'AIDS: Keywords', in C. Ricks and L. Michaels (eds) *The State of the Language*, 1990s edition. London: Faber & Faber.

Gwyn, R. (2002) *Communicating Health and Illness*. London: Sage.

Hadlow, J. and Pitts, M. (1991) 'The Understanding of Common Health Terms by Doctors, Nurses and Patients', *Social Science and Medicine* 32: 193–6.

Harvey, K. (2008) 'Adolescent Health Communication: A Corpus Linguistics Approach', unpublished thesis, University of Nottingham.

Harvey, K., Brown, B., Crawford, P., Macfarlane, A. and McPherson, A. (2007) 'Am I Normal? Teenagers, Sexual Health and the Internet', *Social Science and Medicine* 65: 771–81.

Health Protection Agency (2006) *A Complex Picture: HIV and Other Sexually Transmitted Infections in the United Kingdom: 2006.* London: Health Protection Agency.

Helman, C. (2007) *Culture, Health and Illness*, fifth edition. London: Hodder Arnold.

Hobbs, P. (2003) 'The Use of Evidentiality in Physician's Progress Notes', *Discourse Studies* 5: 451–78.

IFJ (International Federation of Journalists) (2006) *IFJ Media Guide and Research Report on the Media's Reporting of HIV/AIDS.* Belgium: International Federation of Journalists.

Independent Advisory Group on Sexual Health and HIV (2007) *A Review of the Impact Drugs and Alcohol Have on Young People's Sexual Behaviour.* London: IAG.

Jackson, S. (2005) '"I'm 15 and Desperate for Sex": "Doing" and "Undoing" Desire in Letters to a Teenage Magazine', *Feminism and Psychology* 15: 295–313.

Johnson, D. and Murray, J. (1985) 'Do Doctors Mean What They Say?' in D. Enright (ed.) *Fair of Speech: The Uses of Euphemism.* Oxford: Oxford University Press.

Knifton, C. (2005) 'Social Work and the Rise of the MRSA "Super Bug"', *Practice* 17: 39–42.

Koestenbaum, W. (1990) 'Speaking in the Shadow of AIDS', in C. Ricks and L. Michaels (eds) *The State of the Language*, 1990s edition. London: Faber & Faber.

Lupton, D. (2006) *Medicine as Culture*, second edition. London: Sage.

McEnery, A. (2005) *Swearing in English: Bad Language, Purity and Power from 1856 to the Present.* London: Routledge.

McHoul, A. and Rapley, M. (2001) 'Preface: With a Little Help from Our Friends', in A. McHoul and M. Rapley (eds) *How to Analyse Talk in Institutional Settings.* London: Continuum.

Mason, L. (2005) '"They Haven't a Clue!" A Qualitative Study of the Self-perceptions of 11–14-year-old Clinic Attenders', *Primary Health Care Research and Development* 6: 199–207.

Moore, S., Rosenthal, D. and Mitchell, A. (1996) *Youth, AIDS and Sexually Transmitted Diseases.* London: Routledge.

Parry, R. (2004) 'Communication during Goal-setting in Physiotherapy Treatment Settings', *Clinical Rehabilitation* 18: 668–82.

Pilnick, A. (1999) '"Patient Counselling" by Pharmacists: Advice, Information or Instruction?' *Sociological Quarterly* 40: 613–22.

Rosenthal, D. and Moore, S. (1994) 'Stigma and Ignorance: Young People's Beliefs about STDs', *Venereology* 7: 62–6.

Sarangi, S. (2004) 'Editorial: Towards a Communicative Mentality in Medical and Healthcare Practice', *Communication and Medicine* 1: 1–11.

Scott, M. (2004) *WordSmith Tools, Version 4.0.* Oxford: Oxford University Press.

Seale, C., Boden, S., Williams, S., Lowe, P. and Steinberg, D. (2007) 'Media Constructions of Sleep and Sleep Disorders: A Study of UK National Newspapers', *Social Science and Medicine* 65: 418–30.

Sikand, A., Fisher, M. and Friedman, S. (1996) 'AIDS Knowledge, Concerns, and Behavioural Changes among Inner-city High School Students', *Journal of Adolescent Health* 18: 325–8.

Sinclair, J. (1991) *Corpus, Concordance, Collocation.* Oxford: Oxford University Press.

Skelton, J. and Hobbs, F. (1999a) 'Descriptive Study of Cooperative Language in Primary Care Consultations by Male and Female Doctors', *British Medical Journal* 318: 576–9.

——(1999b) 'Concordancing: Use of Language-based Research in Medical Communication', *Lancet* 353: 108–11.

Skelton, J., Murray, J. and Hobbs, F. (1999) 'Imprecision in Medical Communication: Study of a Doctor Talking to Patients with Serious Illness', *Journal of the Royal Society of Medicine* 92: 620–5.

Skelton, J., Wearn, A. and Hobbs, F. (2002) 'A Concordance-based Study of Metaphoric Expressions used by GPs and Patients in Consultation', *British Journal of General Practice* 52: 114–18.

Smith, D., Roofe, M., Ehiri, J., Campbell-Forester, S., Jolly, C. and Jolly, P. (2003) 'Sociocultural Contexts of Adolescent Sexual Behaviour in Rural Hanover, Jamaica', *Journal of Adolescent Health* 33: 41–8.

Society for Adolescent Medicine (2006) 'HIV Infection and AIDS in Adolescents: An Update of the Position of the Society for Adolescent Medicine', *Journal of Adolescent Health* 38: 88–91.

Stewart, M. (2005) '"I'm Just Going to Wash You Down": Sanitising the Vaginal Examination', *Journal of Advanced Nursing 5*: 587–94.

Suzuki, L. and Calzo, J. (2004) 'The Search for Peer Advice in Cyberspace: An Examination of Online Teen Bulletin Boards about Health and Sexuality', *Applied Developmental Psychology* 25: 685–98.

Terrence Higgins Trust (2007) *Understanding HIV Infection: HIV? AIDS?* fifth edition. London: Terrence Higgins Trust.

Thomas, J. and Wilson, A. (1996) 'Methodologies for Studying a Corpus of Doctor–Patient Interaction', in J. Thomas and M. Short (eds) *Using Corpora for Language Research*. London: Longman.

UNESCO (United Nations Educational, Scientific and Cultural Organisation) (2006) *UNESCO Guidelines on Language and Content in HIV- and AIDS-Related Materials*. Paris: UNESCO.

Warwick, I., Aggleton, P. and Homans, H. (1988) 'Young People's Health Beliefs and AIDS', in P. Aggleton and H. Homans (eds) *Social Aspects of AIDS*. Sussex: Falmer Press.

Watney, S. (1989) 'AIDS, Language and the Third World', in E. Carter and S. Watney (eds) *Taking Liberties: AIDS and Cultural Politics*. London: Serpent's Tail.

Weiss, M. (1997) 'Signifying the Pandemics: Metaphors of AIDS, Cancer, and Heart Disease', *Medical Anthropology Quarterly* 11: 456–76.

Woollett, A., Marshall, H. and Stenner, P. (1998) 'Young Women's Accounts of Sexual Activity and Sexual/Reproductive Health', *Journal of Health Psychology* 3: 369–81.

44

How can corpora be used in teacher education?

Fiona Farr

1. The language teacher education context

Having moved beyond the important but limited use of corpora for language research and the development of reference materials, many in the language teaching profession have been busy investigating, discussing, designing and evaluating ways in which corpus techniques may be used with learners in both direct and mediated ways. All of these very worthy endeavours have placed applied linguists and language teachers in a very privileged position, with an array of corpus-based teaching and reference materials, on-line resources, and an extended repertoire of approaches that can be employed in the classroom. It is possible, and relatively easy, to prepare an English language class exclusively based on findings from corpus research, using corpus-based dictionary, grammar and course-book material, preparing some frequency, keyword or concordance lists in advance, and even getting students to do some exploring using any number of available on-line corpora, or indeed any of those purchased by institutions using more specialised software available to them in computer labs. While such activities and developments have been enhancing language teaching to various degrees, the same cannot be said of the integration and use of corpus linguistics (CL) in language teacher education (LTE).

As a background statement to the present chapter, an internet survey of a random sample of ten general MA programmes in ELT/TESOL/TEFL in both the UK and the US at the time of writing revealed that only three of them make any direct reference to corpus linguistics in their syllabus description literature (there are of course some MA programmes specifically in the area of corpus linguistics but they are not usually integrated education programmes). Although this is far from an empirical finding, it does suggest that teachers may not be exposed to these concepts and techniques during their education and supports the suggestion that 'around the world, in perhaps the overwhelming proportion of teacher education programmes, there is still little systematic account taken of what has been called the "corpus revolution" (Rundell and Stock 1992)' (McCarthy 2008: 563). In fact, it seems that there has been a developing trend for CL to be designated as a specialised area. It is entirely defensible that education programmes do not have the possibility of including all things, but given the argument that the corpus revolution has been said to represent a paradigm shift, triggered by the use of technology in the study of language (McCarthy 2008: 564), this seems to be an illogical omission. On the other hand, there has been some reporting on the inclusion of corpus-based approaches in LTE. This seems to have focused primarily on two areas. First, a number of accounts relay how the examination of classroom discourse and learner corpora has helped in the development and critical evaluation of pedagogic skills among student teachers. These will be explored in further detail in Section 3. Second, CL has been used in the promotion of critical language awareness skills as it provides new dimensions to language description that had not been afforded through the exclusive use of earlier techniques. Published studies and related issues in this area will be elaborated on in Section 4. Both of these discussions will answer the question: how can CL be used to develop pedagogic and linguistic awareness on LTE programmes? But there is a further question which might push the boundaries in terms of what we currently do with CL in the field of LTE, and that is: what can corpus explorations tell us about the ways in which we conduct LTE and how we can develop as a profession of teacher educators? This essentially converts CL into a tool for the professional enhancement not just of student teachers but one which can be utilised by teacher educators to examine, reflect on and improve their practices, as well as providing empirical evidence for those at the initial stages of embarking on such a career. These discussions will be given due attention in this chapter as it is a field which is presently at the very early stages of development.

2. Current models of teacher education and the place of CL

Where are we in terms of how we do teacher education? It is probably safe to say that we are in a cocoon of post-transmissive and post-directive approaches, and we now find ourselves influenced strongly by notions of independent and self-directed learning, and critical and reflective engagement. Certainly, in European and North American contexts, many teacher educators would claim close alliances with these approaches and their theoretical underpinnings. Social constructivism and the work of Vygotsky (1978) have had an important impact. An evolution from retrospective to prospective education has taken place (Kozulin 1998; Kinginger 2002). In this move, the acquisition and reproduction of a body of information does not retain its former elevated status. The focus in current educational theory is on the continuing development of students' cognitions. Consequently, their role becomes much more involved, stemming from two theoretical perspectives (Kozulin 1998: 157): Piaget's thoughts on the need for a stimulating problem-solving context so that innate discovery predispositions are best utilised and Vygotskian views that an independent learner is the culmination of education and not an assumed given at the initial stages of learning (for further discussions see Nyikos and Hashimoto 1997: 506–7; Oxford 1997; Kozulin 1998: Ch. 2). New-found learner roles mean more freedom but also more mediational responsibility for the teacher, who is required to have a greater degree of flexibility and creativity in order to develop appropriate repertoires of approaches and activities to respond to and support the needs of their learners, in the cognitive and social context of each unique teaching event (Halliwell 1993: 67–8). In addition, there has been much discussion of the role of the teacher as reflective practitioner and action researcher (Widdowson 1993; Edge and Richards 1998; Wallace 1998) in attempts to appropriate theory, practice and research, and also to allow for the integration of individual and contextual variables.

Whatever is proposed or changing in general education also carries clear implications for language teacher education, which has the potential to be the core of diffusion for new ideas and practices. In fact, language teacher educators have an additional responsibility because of the double-edged influence of our actions as well as our words. Widdowson (1983: 17–19) provides a useful conceptual distinction between the practices of education and training, which is relevant here. This distinction was later developed by Kinginger (2002: 250) and Freeman (2001: 72, see also Freeman 1982, 1989; Wallace 1991: 3). Widdowson defines training as a process which imparts a set of specific skills, whereas education involves '*developing abilities* as cognitive constructs which allow for the individual's adjustment to changing circumstances' (1983: 18). He subsequently suggests that skills can be taught directly through instruction (training), whereas abilities cannot, and therefore require education. Boote (2001: 66) makes a further useful distinction between 'education' when the intention is to help learners to come to think for themselves in a critical way, and 'indoctrination', which involves inculcating students with unshakable beliefs and stifling their critical thinking. He posits that unethical teaching methods may be at the root of indoctrination, including practices from the not too distant past (and maybe even the present) such as 'lectures with little opportunity for discussion, sanctions for not following prescribed methods or beliefs, and use of personal authority in place of clear reasons' (p.68). The terminological debates are not insignificant as they clearly reflect changing practices in language teaching (from retrospective to prospective) and in teacher education (from training only to training and education) (see also Vaughan, this volume for a discussion of the terms *teacher training* and *teacher education*). We have progressed from knowledge transmission to a more holistic knowledge construction approach (Malderez and Bodóczky 1999: 10; Freeman 2001: 73–4; Hedgcock 2002: 300), as a result of philosophical influences and also empirical insights.

Let us now move to the question of the place of corpus linguistics. There are many easy fits between the integration of CL approaches and current philosophies and practices in LTE. These key, often overlapping, elements are summarised here:

1. Self-directed cognitive development

The idea that individuals take responsibility for their own learning fits perfectly with notions of discovery-based data-driven learning (Johns 1991). Student teachers can explore corpora at their own pace and with their own hypotheses for investigation, and on the journey to discovering some of the answers they may also serendipitously uncover further interesting examples of language use. To this end, corpora can provide data for independent and shared learning tasks, more elaborate project assignments, and indeed, even MA dissertations (Farr 2008).

2. The construction of knowledge

While acknowledging that knowledge transfer may be useful in specific contexts, it is now accepted that noticing, language awareness and inductive investigatory learning (Schmidt 1990; Coniam 1997) are preferred approaches. Corpora are artefacts in this respect as the manipulation of the data through the use of computer software can help to highlight frequent and repeated patterns of language use (Partington 1998; Hunston and Francis 2000; Hunston, this volume) for example, collocations, colligations, semantic prosody and connotations, lexical chunks, etc., which might not otherwise be visible in one-off examples of discourse. In addition, information on frequency and probability of occurrence will add further dimensions to the student teacher's interpretation of language.

3. Mediated and scaffolded acquisition
A clear principle of Vygotsky's approach is that learning is most effective within the Zone of Proximal Development (Kinginger 2002), which requires an individual to be supported, so that they can attain a level of acquisition that could not otherwise have been achieved. This suggests that there are a number of mediated attempts before the ultimate achievement of independence. Again, the pedagogic implementation of CL fits well here. Essentially there are two approaches to the use of CL in any educational context. One, and usually the first, is to prepare, edit and mediate corpus-based materials for use with the student teachers. The second is to allow the student teachers to experience the corpora first hand in an unmediated way directly on the computer. Many use the first approach as a stepping stone to the second (Aston 2000; O'Keeffe and Farr 2003), and this fits perfectly with scaffolded learning. Another advantage here is that it allows for individual learner styles (Oxford 1990), as some students like to engage immediately and directly with the technology while others do not (Farr 2008).

4. The relevance of context
A key aspect of LTE is context-based learning. This is enhanced in two ways through CL. First, the fact that language varies considerably in different contexts, varieties, and genres is, thanks to corpus evidence, now beyond dispute (Biber *et al.* 1999; Reppen *et al.* 2002; Carter and McCarthy 2006). The judicious examination of a range of language varieties exposes student teachers to the influence of context. Second, in terms of pedagogic development, examples of practice from local and relevant situations, for example, classroom data or national varieties of language, are of much greater benefit in the development of students' own pedagogic repertoires (Bax 1997; Gill 1997; Maingay 1997; Trappes-Lomax 2002). In this way CL provides a very suitable framework for the collection, analysis and application of appropriate materials in and for the local teaching context.

3. Pedagogic applications: corpora of classroom language, learner corpora and pedagogic corpora

In this section, three types of corpora will be discussed. The first, and most obviously relevant, is a corpus of classroom language, which can give a much better insider's perspective, and can complement more traditional LTE practices of classroom and peer observations, but without the intrusion and time pressure which comes with these. This type of work began in the 1970s with the publication of Sinclair and Coulthard's (1975) volume, reporting on data collected in the British primary school context and which identified the typical Initiation–Response–Feedback (IRF) classroom interaction pattern formally. More recently research by Walsh (2006, 2011) investigates the EFL context. Walsh, using conversation analysis, develops an elaborate framework which he calls SETT (self evaluating teacher talk) from his corpus (see also Walsh, this volume). This framework, which can be used as a tool in teacher education, identifies various modes of classroom interactions. In more recent work, Walsh has moved to considering the ways in which

CL and CA can be most efficiently merged for the exploitation of this type of discourse (Walsh and O'Keeffe 2007), and this combines well with previous debates on appropriate methodologies for the analysis of classroom discourse (Rampton *et al.* 2002). Also in the EFL classroom, some work has been done on the exploitation of that part of the Limerick Corpus of Irish English (LCIE) for raising pedagogic awareness among student teachers (Farr 2002; O'Keeffe and Farr 2003). In the context of teacher education for teaching French at secondary school, Chambers and O'Riordan (2007) report on ways in which student teachers make use of a number of small purpose-built corpora (approximately 60,000 words) of classroom interactions including recordings of both native and non-native speaker teachers of French in Ireland, France and Belgium. Given the focus of teaching French through French, they exploit the corpora with student teachers to examine those aspects of language use often considered to be further within the realm of native-speaker use, such as appropriate classroom discourse and pragmatic markers, for example, *alors*, and language for classroom management.

There is a second strand to data collected from such educational contexts, which has not normally been married with corpus linguistics, but which arguably should as it has a huge amount to offer teachers in education. Reference is being made here to the type of data used to uncover social and linguistic issues of specific communities, usually in mainstream education. The voices of the pupils and teachers are heard recounting their own experiences or indeed engaging in the classroom context, and these data are used to generate useful discussions in the literature on issues of language, social identity, gender, race, class, ethnicity (see, for example, Leung *et al.* 1997). Such discourse data could usefully be combined with corpus analysis techniques, especially in terms of keyword analysis and concordance patterns, much like the way in which Baker *et al.* (2008) have done in the case of refugees and asylum seekers in the UK press, to allow substantiated rather than anecdotal discussions of such social issues in the classroom.

A lot of work has also been done on the creation of academic language corpora. MICASE (Michigan Corpus of Spoken English) and BASE/BAWE (British Academic Spoken/Written English) are two useful examples as they are large, well-designed corpora, which are freely available (BAS/WE under certain conditions), and allow the user to differentiate context of use, for example lecture versus tutorial, and on the basis of other variables such as type of student, gender and age (see chapters by Coxhead and Lee, this volume). At the time of writing, the University of Limerick and Queen's University, Belfast, have been building a similar corpus, LIBEL CASE (Walsh and O'Keeffe 2007), and the University of Edinburgh has initiated similar activity, with a very specific focus on the interactional habits of Asian students in third-level education (Murphy and Cutting 2009).

While there is merit in a contrastive linguistic examination of corpora, such as that reported on by Xiao *et al.* (2006) comparing passive constructions in English and Chinese, a more direct route to learners' linguistic difficulties is often found in the examination of what are known as learner corpora. It is extremely useful, for syllabus design and lesson preparation, among other things, for student teachers to have access directly to learner language in order to identify errors (usually apparent in frequency and keyword lists), and the frequency with which these errors occur. There is a further bonus to using corpus-based techniques in this respect: not only do obvious semantic and syntactic errors surface, but more and less frequent usages relative to native-speaker norms also surface. This can be very difficult to detect using non-corpus methodologies. The International Corpus of Learner English project, managed by the Université catholique de Louvain in Belgium, was one of the first large-scale endeavours of this type (Granger 2002; see also Gilquin and Granger, this volume). The latest edition of the corpus (Granger *et al.* 2009) contains over 6,000 essays written by students from sixteen different language backgrounds. Since this project, several others have been initiated by the same institution, including LINDSEI (Louvain International Database of Spoken English Interlanguage) and FRIDA (French Interlanguage Database). A large number of publications have come from the analyses of these corpora (see the Centre for English Corpus Linguistics for an extensive listing). However, it could be suggested that the greatest benefit on LTE programmes can be derived from student teachers engaging in action research projects where they actually collect, create and analyse their own learner corpora. Student teachers always gain enormous insights into methodological issues and experience a real sense of achievement from being in the role of teacher as researcher, both of which are excellent experiences for continued professional development for later teacher careers.

Finally in this section, we turn to pedagogic corpora, or corpora which have been specifically designed for language teaching purposes, rather than linguistic analysis *per se*. In relation to such corpora the task for LTE programmes is simply one of making the student teachers aware of which are available and the possibilities for exploitation of corpus resources in the classroom, a topic on which many have published (see Lee, this volume; O'Keeffe *et al.* 2007). Two such resources may be mentioned. The *Compleat Lexical Tutor* is a freely accessible on-line resource with a user-friendly interface and inbuilt corpora in English and French such as the British National Corpus. It also allows users to import their own corpora and analyse them using the Lextutor tools. The SACODEYL (a European Commission-funded project) corpus, which is a corpus of youth language in the form of interviews with teenagers in seven different languages is also a favourite among students. Backbone is a similar corpus, where the interviews, which are available as a multi-modal corpus (audio files, video files and transcriptions), were designed around topics which were identified by teachers as being directly relevant to their language teaching syllabus. The audio-visual clips may be viewed in their entirety and the corpora are also searchable as a whole or by the topics and sub-topics for context specific use, which may be beneficial for LSP instruction. An added benefit is that the transcriptor and annotator software is freely available at the sites to download and use with other databases, including any collected by student teachers. A word search for *teacher* (likely to be of interest to both pupils and teachers in other languages) in the SACODEYL corpus reveals the results shown in Table 44.1 in the format in which they actually appear on the website. Interestingly, language teachers feature high on the list, and the teenagers are reasonably restrained in what they say about their teachers, perhaps because of the interview context in which the data was collected.

And of course, we must remember that the largest corpus of all, albeit uncensored and unedited, is available to our student teachers in the form of the world-wide web. One example of searching software is WebCorp (Renouf *et al.* 2007), which searches through the web for instances of particular words and phrases and is now freely available. As well as providing many examples, this also allows the user to establish the type of language used in web-based communication and information provision of this type (Biber and Kurjian 2007). Recent work has also been done on how to build a corpus using materials and texts from the web (Hundt *et al.* 2007), and this is likely to be a very appealing and manageable task for the present generation of digital native (Prensky 2001) student teachers. Such a resource and appropriate techniques provide a relatively easy route to the creation of LSP and other relevant and interesting materials for student teachers.

4. Corpora and language awareness

However it is labelled, a knowledge and awareness of the way in which a language operates in formal, functional, discoursal and pragmatic ways is inevitably a core component on an LTE programme. In the achievement of this goal, language teacher educators, most notably in the ELT context, are greatly indebted to corpus linguistics in two very significant ways. First, we are in the enviable position of having an array of reference materials available commercially which are completely corpus-based, and this includes two comprehensive grammars based on authentic examples, frequency information and context-differentiated comparative accounts (Biber *et al.* 1999; Carter and McCarthy 2006). Second, much has been written on how to use corpora both in teaching and LTE contexts for raising language awareness (for example, Hunston 1995; Coniam 1997; Chambers 2005; Farr 2008), and any of the commercially or freely available corpora mentioned above and elsewhere in this volume serve these purposes well. Here we discuss two associated issues of language awareness that relate specifically to language varieties in the sense of both context of use and also geographical/national/regional usage.

In terms of context of use, recent research has focused on the language of online, or Computer Mediated Communication (CMC), including blogs, synchronous chat and Virtual Learning Environments (VLE) (Riordan and Murray 2010). Such research is fascinating from the point of view that this variety has not (yet) found its way into pedagogic materials in any systematic way, due primarily to its lack of public availability, but also because it is deemed by many to be ephemeral in nature and therefore not the surest bet for the major publishers of language teaching materials. Furthermore, or possibly consequently, it has not yet been the subject of corpus-based examination. And yet, it is a variety of language use which is likely to be of inherent interest to STs as it is in their repertoire of personal genres, and it is also the subject of curiosity among EFL learners as it is seen to be slightly enigmatic but nonetheless appealing. More importantly, though, it is fascinating as the object of language description as it represents a mélange of the traditional modes of spoken and written language, and also because its orthographic representation is a huge departure from traditional systems, making it a prime example of language creativity, change and evolution, as well as code-switching, and a new and unique mixture of pragmatic conventions. For all of these reasons, it is potentially an extremely rich source to use on LTE programmes for the purposes of developing language awareness skills, and it may encourage STs to collect and create their own examples and interpret them in an emic way drawing on their own experiences and insights, while not forgetting the statistical significance as it is revealed through frequency-based accounts. One of the initial primary motivations behind the creation of the LCIE corpus (Farr *et al.* 2004) was to capture the variety of English spoken in Ireland, which had not been done in any systematic way when the project began. This has proved a very worthwhile investment and has served to investigate and illustrate any aspect of language use that is covered on teacher education programmes at the University of Limerick. Not only is it a significant source of spoken casual conversation, it is localised and therefore more relevant for learners in the Irish-English context in helping them to appreciate language variety issues

Table 44.1 Concordance of *teacher* in the SACODEYL corpus

've been recently thinking about becoming a	***teacher***	but I ' m not sure about that
satisfying. So I was thinking of becoming a	***teacher***	but I don ' t know . it '
about that yet because ... If you became a	***teacher***	what would you teach ? Oh I don '
teach it so much better than our actual	***teacher***	. To kind of take something really complicated
at school. But I think actually my art	***teacher***	had a big influence on me , he taught
that other than when you' re an English	***teacher***	or a literature teacher ? Never ! And so I
in school cos I have a really funny	***teacher***	. Why is she funny ? He He . Why is
where you were really mad at a German	***teacher***	? Today I got really mad at my , actually
got really mad at my, actually my German	***teacher***	because we did this text and it wasn
I really, really hate French and the German	***teacher***	's really nice , so . Yeah it ' s
is Julie and my mother is a gym	***teacher***	in an elementary school , so she teaches kids
you' re an English teacher or a literature	***teacher***	? Never ! And so I don 't know . If
teacher too? Yeah I have a very nice	***teacher***	. She ' s the head of geography and
stuff like that. Maybe you have a nice	***teacher***	too ? Yeah I have a very nice teacher
because I have an English Spanish	***teacher***	so I found it hard to understand when
so. Yeah it ' s important what the	***teacher***	's like isn ' t it ? Yeah . Yeah
kind of worked on it and then the	***teacher***	was like so how ' s that getting

and also in heightening awareness of their own personal language use before entering the world of ELT, where they are most often required to teach to British or American English standards.

5. The discourses of teacher education: using specialised corpora for professional introspection and development

In the final substantive section of this chapter, we return to the important issue raised in the introduction which has the potential to further discussions on ways in which we can extend the potential uses of CL in LTE contexts, beyond those already discussed in this account and elsewhere. The key question here is: what can corpus explorations tell us about the ways in which we conduct LTE and how we can develop as a profession of teacher educators? The basic idea is to add to the techniques and tools used by teacher educators for the purposes of continued professional development. We are all familiar with, and probably engage in, activities such as attending courses and conferences, diary keeping, peer observations, personal development activities, among others. The suggestion here is to record our activities and have them available for our own and others' reflection, critique and ultimate improvement. This can be done through audio-recordings and transcriptions, and the collection of written records used in teacher education contexts, but in the move towards multi-modal corpora (Carter and Adolphs 2008; see Adolphs and Knight this volume) it would probably be even more beneficial if at least some of those records were to exist in visual format also. The present author's research began a number of years ago, at first focusing on the teaching practice (TP) arena of a teacher educator's activities. A number of one-to-one TP feedback sessions involving a total of fourteen student teachers and two tutors were recorded and transcribed. This became the post-observation trainer–trainee interactions (POTTI) corpus, and consists of approximately 80,000 words (Farr 2005a). In order to gain a more holistic perspective on the context, diary entries from the student teachers were collected during the same period, and questionnaires were completed by both parties following each feedback session.

As the intention was always to focus on the interpersonal aspects of the discourse, the examination of this data was primarily pragmatic in nature, drawing on relevant theoretical perspectives from this field and the general fields of discourse and conversation analysis. The big departure from previous work is in the fact that the examination of POTTI was corpus-based and therefore has quantitative as well as qualitative validity. One of the early examinations of the data (Farr 2005b) focused on the corpus as a piece of discourse and identified the following relational strategies used by both parties in the interactions: (1) solidarity strategies, including small talk, personal pronoun reference, independent reference sources, first-name vocatives, shared socio-cultural references; (2) engaged listenership, including overlaps and interruptions (see also Farr 2003, 2007 for more details). Later, using established frameworks for the investigation of similar types of discourse, the POTTI data presented examples of authoritative interventions (including prescriptive, informative and confrontational), and facilitative interventions (including supportive, catalytic and cathartic) (Farr 2005a). Both of these established this type of interaction as being generally within the area of support and advice type discourse used in LTE contexts and also in therapeutic contexts. To lend quantitative weight and identify any more specific linguistic strategies, a bottom-up frequency and keyword analysis was also conducted using *WordSmith Tools* (Scott 2004; see Scott, this volume). These produced statistics on levels of participation on the part of the STs and the tutors (approximately 30:70 per cent), and identified the language which is relatively more significant in POTTI (metadiscourse, cognitive and cathartic words, personal and impersonal referencing techniques, words indicating interactivity, and hedges) (Farr 2007). This also prompted a more detailed analysis on how modality was functioning in pragmatic ways in this context (Farr 2006a). Coupled with an integrated analysis of the accompanying questionnaire data (Farr 2006b) those strategies which were prevalent, effective and ineffective, according to the corpus analysis and the perspectives of the participants, became clear and provide a much better understanding of teaching practice feedback interaction for those engaged in this type of activity (Farr 2011).

So, what added benefit is to be had from this type of corpus collection endeavour? As well as being a rich source for action research by the original teacher-researcher, it has shed light on this context for other members of the LTE community. It can also be used as an awareness-raising tool for the induction of new tutors into the teaching practice context, and for new student teachers who can now get a sneak preview of what feedback will entail before being fully immersed. In other words, it allows for another mode of legitimate peripheral participation (Lave and Wenger 1991). Others have used similar data to complete the action research loop by changing patterns of interaction over a period of time in a successful attempt to increase student teacher participation in feedback conferences (Vásquez and Reppen 2007; see Vaughan, this volume). However, this is just one example of the potential of CL in terms of these types of developmental activities.

This chapter has attempted to illustrate the ways in which corpus linguistics fits appropriately with current models and approaches in teacher education, and how its adaptation into many of the subject contents can aid in the development of student teachers' awareness and understanding of pedagogic issues and practices, as well as their appreciation of formal, discoursal and pragmatic aspects of language used in a variety of context. All of this can be done in exploratory and investigatory ways through both mediated and direct access to corpora, which have the potential to enhance the educational experience and complement other effective, existing approaches. For publishers, corpora are a given; for researchers, corpora are a given; and it is past time for our future teachers to become actively and critically engaged with their use at the first possible opportunity, which, for most, comes during teacher education. McCarthy has recently argued for teachers to become more active user-consumers of such resources and proposes that this can be done through the development of their corpus evaluation skills, and through the 'emergence of the teacher as lobbyist, lobbying academics and publishers and telling those academics and the publishers what it is they want and need of this new technology' (2008: 565). For this to happen most efficiently, teacher educators also need to take an active and responsible role in affording corpus integration the required space in initial and in-service programmes, not as a segregated specialisation, but as a thread woven through many components of the course content and delivery.

Further reading

Hunston, S. (1995) 'Grammar in Teacher Education: The Role of a Corpus', *Language Awareness* 4(1): 15–31. (This details the potential role that corpus linguistics can have in the grammar component of a teacher education programme, particularly in identifying grammatical patterning.)

McCarthy, M. (2008) 'Accessing and Interpreting Corpus Information in the Teacher Education Context', *Language Teaching* 41(4): 563–74. (This raises issues in relation to the lack of inclusion of corpus-based approaches and materials in teacher education and outlines the ways in which they could and should be included to give future teachers more critical adaptation skills and influential lobbying power with researchers and publishers of corpus-based teaching materials.)

O'Keeffe, A. and Farr, F. (2003) 'Using Language Corpora in Language Teacher Education: Pedagogic, Linguistic and Cultural Insights', *TESOL Quarterly* 37(3): 389–418. (This outlines a number of ways in which localised and specialised corpora in particular can be included to enhance the ways in which teacher education is conducted.)

Vásquez, C. and Reppen, R. (2007) 'Transforming Practice: Changing Patterns of Participation in Post-observation Meetings', *Language Awareness* 16(3): 153–72. (This illustrates how the collection of a corpus of teaching practice feedback meetings was used to identify what was considered to be an unsatisfactory participation balance between student teachers and tutors, the remedial action taken by the tutors, and the resulting improvement in the second part of the teaching practice cycle.)

References

Aston, G. (2000) 'Corpora and Language Teaching', in L. Burnard and T. McEnery (eds) *Rethinking Language Pedagogy from a Corpus Perspective. Papers from the Third International Conference on Teaching and Language Corpora.* Frankfurt: Peter Lang, pp. 1–18.

Baker, P., Gabrielatos, C., Khosravinik, M., Krzyzanowski, M., McEnery, T. and Wodak, R. (2008) 'A Useful Methodological Synergy? Combining Critical Discourse Analysis and Corpus Linguistics to Examine Discourses of Refugees and Asylum Seekers in the UK Press', *Discourse and Society* 19(3): 273–305.

Bax, S. (1997) 'Roles for a Teacher Educator in Context-sensitive Teacher Education', *English Language Teaching Journal* 51(3): 232–41.

Biber, D. and Kurjian, J. (2007) 'Towards a Taxonomy of Web Registers and Text Types: a Multi-Dimensional Analysis', in M. Hundt, N. Nesselhauf and C. Biewer (eds) *Corpus Linguistics and the Web.* Amsterdam: Rodopi, pp. 109–32.

Biber, D., Johansson, S., Leech, G., Conrad, S. and Finegan, E. (1999) *Longman Grammar of Spoken and Written English.* London: Longman.

Boote, D. N. (2001) 'An "Indoctrination Dilemma" in Teacher Education?' *Journal of Educational Thought* 35(1): 61–82.

Carter, R. and Adolphs, S. (2008) 'Linking the Verbal and Visual: New Directions for Corpus Linguistics', in 'Language, People, Numbers', special issue of *Language and Computers* 64: 275–91.

Carter, R. and McCarthy, M. J. (2006) *Cambridge Grammar of English.* Cambridge: Cambridge University Press.

Chambers, A. (2005) 'Integrating Corpus Consultation in Language Studies', *Language Learning and Technology* 9(2): 111–25.

Chambers, A. and O'Riordan, S. (2007) 'Learning to Teach through French from a Corpus of Classroom Discourse: Giving Corrective Feedback', in J. E. Conacher and H. Kelly-Holmes (eds) *New Learning Environments for Language Learning.* Frankfurt: Peter Lang, pp. 87–101.

Coniam, D. (1997) 'A Practical Introduction to Corpora in a Teacher Training Language Awareness Programme', *Language Awareness* 6(4): 199–207.

Edge, J. and Richards, K. (1998) 'Why *Best Practice* is Not Good Enough', *TESOL Quarterly* 32(3): 569–76.

Farr, F. (2002) 'Classroom Interrogations – How Productive?' *Teacher Trainer* 16(1): 19–23.

——(2003) 'Engaged Listenership in Spoken Academic Discourse: The Case of Student–Tutor Meetings', *Journal of English for Academic Purposes* 2(1): 67–85.

——(2005a) 'Reflecting on Reflections: The Spoken Word as a Professional Development Tool in Language Teacher Education', in R. Hughes (ed.) *Spoken English, Applied Linguistics and TESOL: Challenges for Theory and Practice.* Hampshire: Palgrave Macmillan, pp. 182–215.

——(2005b) 'Relational Strategies in the Discourse of Professional Performance Review in an Irish Academic Environment: the Case of Language Teacher Education', in K. Schneider and A. Barron (eds) *Variational Pragmatics: The Case of English in Ireland.* Berlin: Mouton de Gruyter, pp. 203–34.

——(2006a) 'Modality in Context: Spoken Language, Variety and the Classroom', in A. Gallagher and M. Ó. Laoire (eds) *Language Education in Ireland: Current Practice and Future Needs.* Dublin: IRAAL, pp. 165–84.

——(2006b) 'Strengthening Interpretative Research through the Use of Complementary Data Sources in Corpus-Based Spoken Discourse Analysis', paper presented at the Third IVACS International Conference, University of Nottingham, 23–24 June.

——(2007) 'Spoken Language as an Aid to Reflective Practice in Language Teacher Education: Using a Specialised Corpus to Establish a Generic Fingerprint', in M.-C. Campoy and M.-J. Luzón (eds) *Spoken Corpora in Applied Linguistic.* Bern: Peter Lang, pp. 235–58.

——(2008) 'Evaluating the Use of Corpus-Based Instruction in a Language Teacher Education Context: Perspectives from the Users', *Language Awareness* 17(1): 25–43.

Farr, F. (2011) *The Discourse of Teaching Practice Feedback: An investigation of spoken and written modes.* New York: Routledge.

Farr, F., Murphy, B. and O'Keeffe, A. (2004) 'The Limerick Corpus of Irish English: Design, Description and Application', in F. Farr, and A. O'Keeffe (eds) 'Corpora, Varieties and the Language Classroom', special edition of *Teanga 21.* Dublin: IRAAL, pp. 5–29.

Freeman, D. (1982) 'Observing Teachers: Three Approaches to In-Service Training and Development', *TESOL Quarterly* 16(1): 21–8.

——(1989) 'Teacher Training, Development, and Decision Making: A Model of Teaching and Related Strategies for Language Teacher Education', *TESOL Quarterly* 23(1): 27–45.

——(2001) 'Second Language Teacher Education', in R. Carter, and D. Nunan (eds) *The Cambridge Guide to Teaching English to Speakers of Other Languages.* Cambridge: Cambridge University Press, pp. 72–9.

Gill, S. (1997) 'Local Problems, Local Solutions', in I. McGrath (ed.) *Learning to Train: Perspectives on the Development of Language Teacher Trainers.* Hemel Hampstead: Prentice Hall, pp. 215–24.

Granger, S. (2002) 'A Bird's-eye View of Learner Corpus Research', in S. Granger, J. Hung, and S. Petch-Tyson (eds) *Computer Learner Corpora, Second Language Acquisition and Foreign Language Teaching.* Amsterdam: John Benjamins, pp. 3–33.

Granger, S., Dagneaux, E., Meunier, F. and Paquot, M. (2009) *The International Corpus of Learner English. Handbook and CD-ROM. Version 2.* Louvain-la-Neuve: Presses Universitaires de Louvain.

Halliwell, S. (1993) 'Teacher Creativity and Teacher Education', in D. Bridges, and T. Kerry (eds) *Developing Teachers Professionally. Reflections for Initial and In-service Trainers*. London: Routledge, pp. 67–79.

Hedgcock, J. S. (2002) 'Toward a Socioliterate Approach to Second Language Teacher Education', *Modern Language Journal* 86(3): 299–317.

Hundt, M., Nesselhauf, N. and Biewer, C. (2007) 'Corpus Linguistics and the Web', in M. Hundt, N. Nesselhauf and C. Biewer (eds) *Corpus Linguistics and the Web*. Amsterdam: Rodopi, pp. 1–6.

Hunston, S. (1995) 'Grammar in Teacher Education: The Role of a Corpus', *Language Awareness* 4(1): 15–31.

Hunston, S. and Francis, G. (2000) *Pattern Grammar: A Corpus-driven Approach to the Lexical Grammar of English*. Amsterdam: John Benjamins.

Johns, T. (1991) 'Should You Be Persuaded – Two Samples of Data-driven Learning Materials', *English Language Research Journal* 4: 1–16.

Kinginger, C. (1997) 'A Discourse Approach to the Study of Language Educators' Coherence Systems', *Modern Language Journal* 81(1): 6–14.

——(2002) 'Defining the Zone of Proximal Development in US Foreign Language Education', *Applied Linguistics* 23(2): 240–61.

Kozulin, A. (1998) *Psychological Tools. A Sociocultural Approach to Education*. Cambridge, MA: Harvard University Press.

Lave, J. and Wenger, E. (1991) *Situated Learning. Legitimate Peripheral Participation*. Cambridge: Cambridge University Press.

Leung, C., Harris, R. and Rampton, B. (1997) 'The Idealised Native Speaker, Reified Ethnicities, and Classroom Realities', *TESOL Quarterly* 31(3): 543–60.

McCarthy, M. (2008) 'Accessing and Interpreting Corpus Information in the Teacher Education Context', *Language Teaching* 41(4): 563–74.

Maingay, P. (1997) 'Raising Awareness of Awareness', in I. McGrath (ed.) *Learning to Train: Perspectives on the Development of Language Teacher Trainers*. Hemel Hempstead: Prentice Hall, pp. 117–26.

Malderez, A. and Bodóczky, C. (1999) *Mentor Courses. A Resource Book for Trainer-Trainers*. Cambridge: Cambridge University Press.

Murphy, B. and Cutting, J. (2009) 'EDASE (Edinburgh Academic Spoken English) Corpus', paper presented at IVACS Symposium, University of Edinburgh, 22 January.

Nyikos, M. and Hashimoto, R. (1997) 'Constructivist Theory Applied to Collaborative Learning in Teacher Education: In Search of ZPD', *Modern Language Journal* 81(4): 506–17.

O'Keeffe, A. and Farr, F. (2003) 'Using Language Corpora in Language Teacher Education: Pedagogic, Linguistic and Cultural Insights', *TESOL Quarterly* 37(3): 389–418.

O'Keeffe, A., McCarthy, M. and Carter, R. (2007) *From Corpus to Classroom: Language Use and Language Teaching*. Cambridge: Cambridge University Press.

Oxford, R. (1990) *Language Learning Strategies: What Every Teacher Should Know*. New York: Newbury House.

——(1997) 'Constructivism: Shape-Shifting, Substance, and Teacher Education Applications', *Journal of Education* 72(1): 35–66.

Partington, A. (1998) *Patterns and Meaning: Using Corpora for English Language Research and Teaching*. Amsterdam: John Benjamins.

Prensky, M. (2001) 'Digital Natives, Digital Immigrants Part 2: Do They Really Think Differently?' *On the Horizon* 9(6): 1–6.

Rampton, B., Roberts, C., Leung, C. and Harris, R. (2002) 'Methodology in the Analysis of Classroom Discourse', *Applied Linguistics* 23(3): 373–92.

Renouf, A., Kehoe, A. and Banerjee, J. (2007) 'WebCorp: An Integrated System for Web Text Search', in M. Hundt, N. Nesselhauf and C. Biewer (eds) *Corpus Linguistics and the Web*. Amsterdam: Rodopi, pp. 47–68.

Reppen, R., Fitzmaurice, S. M. and Biber, D. (eds) (2002) *Using Corpora to Explore Linguistic Variation*. Amsterdam: John Benjamins.

Riordan, E. and Murray, L. (2010) 'A Corpus-based Analysis of Online Synchronous and Asynchronous Modes of Communication within Language Teacher Education', *Classroom Discourse* 1(2): 181–98.

Rundell, M. and Stock, P. (1992) 'The Corpus Revolution', *English Today* 30: 9–14.

Schmidt, R. W. (1990) 'The Role of Consciousness in Second Language Learning', *Applied Linguistics* 11(2): 129–58.

Scott, M. (2004) *WordSmith Tools 4*. Oxford: Oxford University Press.

Sinclair, J. M. and Coulthard, R. M. (1975) *Towards an Analysis of Discourse. The English Used by Teachers and Pupils*. Oxford: Oxford University Press.

Trappes-Lomax, H. (2002) 'Language in Language Teacher Education: A Discourse Perspective', in H. Trappes-Lomax and G. Ferguson (eds) *Language in Language Teacher Education*. Amsterdam: John Benjamins, pp. 1–21.

Vásquez, C. and Reppen, R. (2007) 'Transforming Practice: Changing Patterns of Participation in Post-Observation Meetings', *Language Awareness* 16(3): 153–72.

Vygotsky, L. S. (1978) *Mind in Society. The Development of Higher Psychological Processes*. Cambridge MA: Harvard University Press.

Wallace, M. (1991) *Training Foreign Language Teachers*. Cambridge: Cambridge University Press.

——(1998) *Action Research for Language Teachers*. Cambridge: Cambridge University Press.

Walsh, S. (2006) *Investigating Classroom Discourse*. London and New York: Routledge.

——(2011) *Exploring Classroom Discourse: Language in Action*. London and New York: Routledge.

Walsh, S. and O'Keeffe, A. (2007) 'Applying CA to a Modes Analysis of Third-Level Spoken Academic Discourse', in H. Bowles and P. Seedhouse (eds) *Conversation Analysis in Languages for Specific Purposes*. Berlin: Peter Lang, pp. 101–39.

Widdowson, H. G. (1983) *Learning Purpose and Language Use*. Oxford: Oxford University Press.

——(1993) 'Innovation in Teacher Development', *Annual Review of Applied Linguistics* 13: 260–75.

Xiao, R., McEnery, T. and Qian, Y. (2006) 'Passive Constructions in English and Chinese: A Corpus-Based Contrastive Study', *Languages in Contrast* 6(1): 109–49.

45

How can corpora be used in language testing?

Fiona Barker

1. What is language testing?

This chapter considers how corpora can be used in the field of language testing. Referred to as Language Testing and Assessment (LTA), this field is concerned with measuring the language proficiency of individuals in a variety of contexts and for a range of purposes, assessing language knowledge, performance or application. The general aim of language testing is to measure a latent trait in order to make inferences about an individual's language ability. Language tests allow us to observe behaviours which can be evaluated by attaching test scores which provide evidence for an individual's ability in a specific skill or their overall language competence. For an introduction to LTA and its terminology see ALTE Members (1998), McNamara (2000) and Hughes (2003).

One useful way of thinking about testing language proficiency is to explore the essential principles, or test qualities, that underlie good assessment. There are various elaborations of such principles in the LTA literature, following Bachman's 'essential measurement qualities' of Validity and Reliability (Bachman 1990: 24–6) and the addition of Impact and Practicality (Cambridge ESOL 2008). Validity means that a test measures what it sets out to measure, so that a test score reflects an underlying ability accurately (there are many types of Validity, see Weir 2005). Reliability means that a test's results are accurate, consistent and dependable. Impact is the effect, preferably positive, which a test has on test takers and other stakeholders, including society. A test score needs to be meaningful to those who base decisions on it and for purposes such as admission to university or access to professional training. The fourth principle, Practicality, means that a test is practicable in terms of the resources needed to write, deliver and mark the test. In order for language proficiency to be assessed successfully, the purpose of testing must be clearly defined and the approach taken must be 'fit for purpose'. Key considerations of designing and administering tests that will be explored further below include: establishing the purpose for a test; deciding what to test and how to test this; and working out how to score and report a result. We shall explore these areas of language testing before suggesting how corpora relate to these different stages in the lifecycle of a test (Saville 2003).

Establishing the purpose of a language test may arise from the need to assess students' current level of general language proficiency for placement purposes into a suitable language learning class, or their suitability to enter a particular course or to study abroad. A test can also be used to measure students' progress through or achievement at the end of a language learning course, or to give them a widely recognised qualification that allows access to educational, professional or other opportunities. Market forces also drive the provision of new tests, as do governments, education ministries, companies and professional bodies that require tests for specific groups, e.g. school leavers, or for specific purposes, e.g. the accreditation of overseas medical staff. Alongside a well-defined test purpose, we need to understand the historical and social context of any language test. In the USA, for example, the psychometric tradition (viewing language proficiency as a psychological trait that can be measured along a single dimension; see ALTE Members 1998: 158, 168) and 'objective' test formats such as multiple-choice questions are better suited to testing discrete aspects of language, for example specific grammatical points, whereas the testing tradition in Western Europe, in the UK in particular, has maintained its interface with pedagogy and its focus on task-based testing. This legacy is reflected in the history of the oldest English language exam in existence, Cambridge ESOL's Certificate of Proficiency in English, which celebrates its centenary in 2013 (see Weir 2003 for its development; see Spolsky 1995 for the US tradition and its influence on the TOEFL, the Test of English as a Foreign Language).

The next consideration is deciding what to test, i.e. the abstract construct that is to be realised in an assessment instrument. This construct incorporates the tester's view of how to approach the assessment of language proficiency, for example by testing individual skills which are commonly grouped into receptive (reading and listening), productive (writing and speaking) and enabling skills (including grammatical, vocabulary and pragmatic knowledge). Sometimes two skills are assessed together by means of an integrative task where, for example, a test taker has to combine spoken and written input with their own ideas to produce a written response (see McNamara 2000: 14). All language testers need to establish and explain their own approach to assessing language, for example in their publicity and support materials.

The test construct informs the specification of how each skill is operationalised in specific task formats and how each skill should be scored or rated. The test designer needs to work out how to test the construct, i.e. what task types to use to get the test taker to recognise, produce or manipulate the required linguistic phenomenon (for example, the most appropriate word to fill a gap). Part of this process involves identifying the functions and facets of the skill that are to be tested which are normally stated in test specifications documentation available to test writers; a simpler version may also be available for test takers, teachers and other stakeholders. For example, when testing reading at an elementary level, level A2 on the Common European Framework of Reference (CEFR, Council of Europe 2001), Cambridge ESOL tests 'a range of reading skills with a variety of texts, ranging from very short notices to longer continuous texts' with assessment focusing on the 'ability to understand the meaning of written English at word, phrase, sentence, paragraph and whole text level' (UCLES 2008: 2). The tasks used to assess language proficiency at any level should match the cognitive and psychological ability of the test taker as well as their linguistic knowledge; these are some of the test taker characteristics that influence how an individual performs on any test and which form part of a socio-cognitive framework for test development (see Weir 2005). There are various task formats, some used for one skill or level, others being used for many skills and across levels. Common task types for assessing receptive skills (reading and listening) include gapfill, multiple matching and multiple-choice questions. A gapfill (or cloze) task contains a prose passage or set of sentences with gaps where the correct word or phrase needs to be inserted (open cloze) or selected (multiple-choice cloze). Multiple-matching involves matching paragraphs, sentences or words with the correct picture, definition, etc., or re-arranging them in the most logical order. Multiple-choice questions include a question and a set of answers, one or more of which are correct. Tasks that test productive skills tend to include a rubric (the instructions the test taker reads or hears) and there may also be some written or visual input (the prompt), for example a letter or a diagram. There are also word, phrase or sentence formation tasks and error identification or correction tasks that may be used for either receptive or productive skills.

A final aspect of task design concerns the authenticity of the format and content, which relates to the real-worldness of the activity given to the test taker. In the Western European tradition, the testing of writing and speaking is as realistic as possible, with test takers interacting with each other and examiners in speaking tests, and writing tasks requiring them to undertake life-like communicative activities, so that they can demonstrate aspects of their Communicative Language Ability (Bachman 1990: 84; also see Purpura 2008). Inferences based on test scores are made by test users (teachers, employers, etc.), so it is essential that language testers ensure that what is being tested is relevant and appropriate to what is required by these users; i.e. that a language test actually assesses what test takers need to be able to demonstrate for a specific purpose or situation.

Corpora, as generalist or specialist collections of texts, clearly have a role to play in helping language testers to decide on the constructs that they intend to test, by providing evidence of what is involved in expert, or native-like, texts of various types. In relation to test design, corpora have a role in helping language testers to write more realistic tasks, by basing them on or by taking inspiration from real-life texts. Additionally, evidence from corpora, particularly collocational or colligational information, is extremely useful in informing, ratifying or refuting test designers' intuitions about what should or should not be tested in a specific area, for example lexico-grammatical knowledge.

The final consideration in test design is working out how to rate or score a test. This includes deciding whether to mark according to a description of what a satisfactory performance is on a particular task (criterion referenced), or comparing an individual's response to those of other test takers (norm referenced), or to use a combination of both approaches. This decision is linked to how the test results will be used, whether to measure what a learner can already do in a specific or general area, or whether to suggest the next steps to be taken in learning a particular language (see McNamara 2000: 62–6). Corpora also have a role in this process, as evidence of what both learners and proficient users of a language or particular variety *can do* leads to the use of such data to describe typical performances at various levels. The Association of Language Testers in Europe (ALTE) has developed a set of 'Can-do' statements aligned to the CEFR which illustrate general ability at each of the six CEFR levels and typical ability in three skill areas of Social and Tourist, Work, and Study, such as 'CAN write letters on any subject and full notes of meetings or seminars with good expression and accuracy' (C2 level writing overall general ability; see ALTE Members 2008).

Beyond establishing the purpose of a language test, deciding on the construct and the means of testing and rating this, there are wider societal aspects of language testing, such as the moral and ethical dimension which includes maintaining fairness and equality of access for all test takers (see McNamara 2000: 67–77). Clearly language testing and assessment involve many inter-related aspects and take place in a variety of contexts, for various purposes, involving both experts and non-experts who may have to design or administer tests or make decisions based on test results. There are formal, external, potentially life-changing assessments of language proficiency (high stakes tests) that contrast with lower stakes tests which are important in a localised context but have fewer life-changing implications for the test taker and are therefore less well-researched and reported in the LTA literature.

Language testing occurs in a range of local, regional, national and international contexts, and language tests should take into account both the social context and the cognitive make-up of test takers and have various degrees of impact on them. Within this complex picture, where do, and should, corpora fit? It is clear from this volume that Corpus Linguistics (CL) has contributed to a range of pure and applied fields of study for many years. Corpora of various types are currently used for theoretical and applied research in various fields associated with LTA, including developing teaching materials and in publishing. They also have both practical and theoretical uses in large-scale language testing carried out by awarding institutions as well as in smaller-scale, more localised learning and teaching contexts (see Taylor and Barker 2008 for an overview). The following sections outline the development and current use of corpora in language testing and look to the future of corpus-informed language testing.

2. The development of corpus use in language testing

One of the first direct involvements of corpora in the field of language testing occurred with the development of electronic collections of learner data by examination boards, publishers and academic institutions. In the UK, the Cambridge Learner Corpus (hereafter CLC) was set up by the EFL Division of the University of Cambridge Local Examinations Syndicate (UCLES EFL) and Cambridge University Press in the early 1990s as an archive of general English examination scripts together with accompanying demographic and score data (see the CLC website for information and corpus-informed publications). The CLC was designed as a unique collection of learner writing at various proficiency levels; it has expanded to include other domains and proficiency levels of English beyond the initial three levels of general English exams at its inception (the First Certificate in English, Certificate in Advanced English and Certificate of Proficiency in English). This corpus is used for exam validation and related research, as described below.

Another key learner corpus instigated around this time is the International Corpus of Learner English (ICLE), developed at the Centre for English Corpus Linguistics (CECL) in Belgium (Granger *et al.* 2009). The CECL team have continued to develop a suite of comparative native and learner corpora to support their Contrastive Interlanguage Analysis approach (Granger 1996; also see Gilquin and Granger, this volume). ICLE consists of argumentative essays and literature papers collected by research teams worldwide; contributors are required to provide writing from advanced students defined as 'university students of English in their 3rd or 4th year of study' with any 'doubtful cases' being checked by the corpus developers (a detailed bibliography is available online, see Centre for English Corpus Linguistics 2008). Establishing the nature of language proficiency at different levels is vital for language testers seeking to design tests that either aim to assess candidates at a particular proficiency level or report results across part of or the whole proficiency scale. Language testers therefore need to use corpus data to identify the linguistic exponents of a particular proficiency level which can only be done reliably if a learner's level is correctly identified and recorded in a corpus.

Other corpora have been developed specifically to inform tests of English or other languages. For reasons including data protection and commercial sensitivity, some of these corpora are only accessible outside the contributing institutions under certain conditions, including through funded research awards (see IELTS or TOEFL websites). An International English Language Testing System funded study using exam scripts is reported in Kennedy and Thorp (2007). This research highlights key features of L2 writing performance at different levels of proficiency which led to a reformulation of the band descriptors used to assess IELTS writing. A domain-specific corpus that informs language test development is the TOEFL 2000 Spoken and Written Academic Language Corpus (T2K-SWAL) built by Educational Testing Services (ETS; Biber *et al.* 2004). This contains spoken and written texts that typify American academic discourses and it has been used to design receptive components of the TOEFL 2000 exam and also to enhance research into US academic registers. Biber *et al.* (2004) identified representative patterns of language use in each register, followed by the development of a suite of tools to compare reading and listening tasks from the TOEFL 2000 test with the corpus data. Other corpora of academic English include MICASE for American English and BASE and BAWE for British English (see their websites).

It is clear that language testers both started to develop and find ways of using learner and native corpora in the 1990s. However, there was little discussion of corpora in the LTA literature until Alderson (1996) outlined various applications of corpora in language testing including writing test items and scoring tests. A decade later, Alderson investigated native speaker judgements of frequency for languages without large corpora; the results indicate a surprising lack of agreement between the expert raters that suggests that corpora are indeed the best way to obtain reliable word frequency measures (Alderson 2007: 407). The benefits of reference or domain-specific native corpora for language testing are now established, and for a number of years language testers have been taking into account native *and* learner evidence, in the same way that publishers, authors and teachers had been doing since the 1980s.

In the lengthy and complex process of designing and administering language tests, corpora can be used in various ways. On a practical level, native corpora provide evidence that test writers use alongside their intuitions and experience to decide whether a particular structure or phrase is sufficiently common in a particular language variety for inclusion in a test (either as input material or as an item to be tested). For example, Cambridge ESOL has used native reference corpora such as the British National Corpus (BNC; see website) to inform the test writing process for a number of years (see Saville 2003). Barker (2004) describes how native and learner evidence informs the development of word and structure lists used by test writers to produce question papers for specific levels. Learner corpora allow comparisons of task performance over time or between proficiency levels and analysing learner errors can suggest what could be tested to distinguish between particular levels. Hargreaves (2000) describes how native reference corpora were used alongside a corpus of candidates' scripts to identify collocations to feed into a new task type within an advanced general English test. On a more theoretical level, corpora are used to develop rating scales and linguistic descriptions of proficiency levels of learner writing and speech (see Hawkey and Barker 2004; Hendriks 2008).

This review suggests that the use of corpora in language testing is fairly recent compared to their use in related fields such as lexicography or language teaching (see chapters by Coxhead, Flowerdew, Jones and Durrant, and Walter, this volume). Nevertheless, language testers develop specialist corpora of learner output and test materials, and use both native and learner corpora to inform the development and validation of their examinations in the ways outlined above. Essentially, corpus data reveal what people actually do with language in real life, learning and testing contexts. Corpora therefore can be used to inform our understanding of learner and expert discourse in various domains, as well as suggesting suitable aspects of language to test or to avoid and, additionally, to show what differentiates learners of different proficiency levels from each other and from an expert user of the language. We will now consider in more depth the ways in which learner corpora can be used to inform language testing and assessment.

3. How can we use a learner corpus to inform language testing?

This section describes some examples of the use of learner corpora in LTA. Learner corpora tend to be designed for a specific purpose from the outset, enhancing their applicability in certain areas, for example the study of academic discourse, while limiting their generalisability beyond their specific focus, meaning that they would be inappropriate for lexicographic work requiring a large general language sample. We therefore start with some recent learner corpus developments which could have direct applications for LTA, before turning to specific ways in which language testers use learner corpora.

The Varieties of English for Specific Purposes Database (VESPA), initiated in 2008, contains written ESP texts from various L1 groups spanning academic disciplines, text types and writer expertise (see Centre for English Corpus Linguistics website). Contributors are encouraged to undertake collaborative research, one of the strengths of multinational and inter-disciplinary corpus-building enterprises, although the contributor guidelines stress that only academic research will be permissible, which could be viewed as a missed opportunity for improving the formal assessment of language for specific purposes. Another CECL resource under development is the LONGDALE Project (Longitudinal Database of Learner English) which will include written and spoken longitudinal data collected by European, Asian and American researchers (see Centre for English Corpus Linguistics website). Alongside learners' production, demographic details and task information are being collected and, importantly for ascertaining learner levels, all students are required to take two language tests whenever they contribute to the corpus in order to obtain an objective measure of their proficiency level (see Centre for English Corpus Linguistics website). This approach is similar to that being taken in collection of new corpora for the English Profile Programme (see Alexopoulou 2008). It is not yet clear whether any commercial research will be permissible using this resource, but academic research will surely lead to improvements in our understanding of SLA and teaching practices.

Learner corpora of other languages under development include a spoken corpus of L2 Italian, the Lexicon of Spoken Italian by Foreigners (LIPS), which was developed in Siena (Barni and Gallina 2009). This corpus contains 1,500 speaking tests from the Certificate of Italian as a Foreign Language (CILS) and researchers have used this corpus to investigate lexical acquisition and development, and to develop word lists for comparing vocabulary size and range with native data (Gallina 2008). The LIPS corpus has various planned applications in publishing, teaching and assessment: it will inform a dictionary for L2 Italian; it will be used to develop curricula and teaching materials, to inform the selection of input texts for future versions of the CILS, and to explore the learners' proficiency in writing and speaking. Future research could compare the same learners' spoken data with written data, something also being planned for English Profile and the LONGDALE Project. In a comparative study, Mendikoetxea (2006) reports on the WOSLAC project that uses two written learner corpora: WriCLE (L1 Spanish–L2 English) and CEDEL2 (L1 English–L2 Spanish) to investigate the properties which influence word order in the interlanguage of L2 learners of these languages. This has clear applications for learning, teaching and assessing such structures.

There are many ways in which learner corpora can inform various stages in the life-cycle of a language test: we shall concentrate on their applications in defining user needs and test purpose; in test design; and in task rating. In relation to user needs and test purpose, learner corpora show us what learners of a language *can do* at certain levels of proficiency, which can inform what is tested at a particular proficiency level, whether overall or at task or item level (see ALTE Members 2008). This adds a qualitative dimension to the language tester's traditionally quantitative approach to analysing test data, and informs the writing of test materials and how they are rated (see Cambridge ESOL 2008). Hawkey and Barker (2004) used learner corpus data and CL analysis techniques to support tabula rasa manual analysis in the development of a Common Scale for assessing writing across a wide range of proficiency levels and types of English. Another exam board, the Testing and Certification Division of the University of Michigan English Language Institute (ELI-UM) in the USA, used a corpus of test-taker writing and speech to inform changes to their scoring criteria for the Examination for the Certificate of Competency in English (ECCE), a B2-level general English exam. The test takers' output was analysed and the criterion-referenced rating scales revised to include five levels on four criteria (content and development; organisation and connection of ideas; linguistic range and control; and communicative effect), to better reflect the linguistic features of learners' output (see ELI-UM Testing and Certification Division website).

In relation to test design, learner corpora can reveal much about the influence of demographic variables, test mode (paper-based or computer-based) and learning environment on the learners' output. Both learner and native corpora form part of an interdisciplinary research programme, English Profile, whose primary aim is to develop Reference Level Descriptors (RLDs) for English, a project registered with the Council of Europe (see the English Profile website). English Profile uses the thirty-million-word CLC as its starting point and is developing both written and spoken corpora to complement this resource (see Alexopoulou 2008). Data collection involves international teams submitting sets of learner data, written responses, spoken data, background information plus self-, teacher and external assessments of proficiency level, from various educational contexts with the aim of balancing the existing range of mother tongues, text types and proficiency levels in the CLC, as well as exploring hypotheses about specific features that seem to be criterial for identifying a specific proficiency level or L1 influence. See the English Profile website for a summary of English Profile activities, including the tagging and parsing of the CLC and analysis of learner errors and discourse and sentence level features at different proficiency levels and by L1.

Learner corpora also help language testers to more accurately describe various linguistic domains. Horner and Strutt (2004) analysed business English vocabulary using a word list derived from a learner corpus; they applied four categories to the list, then asked native and non-native informants to apply these to a subset of 600 words. While both groups had difficulty in applying the categories consistently when asked to identify core and non-core vocabulary, the study identified ways of classifying vocabulary using meaning-based categories (Horner and Strutt 2004: 8).

Learner corpora are used by test writers to explore the collocational patterning of learners' written or spoken production at various levels, which can be used to show what patterns are common/less frequent at certain levels, guiding the inclusion of these in tests, or additionally what are the most frequent errors or misuse of specific collocational pairings, therefore suggesting suitable distractors for multiple choice options. Learner corpora are also used to support or refute item writers' intuitions about what learners can be expected to know at a certain level, based on evidence of what they can already produce. Furthermore, analysing learners' most frequent errors (by first language or proficiency level) will suggest to the language tester what could be tested to distinguish between candidates at a particular level and could also inform teaching materials and practices (see Section IV in this volume on using a corpus for language pedagogy and methodology).

In relation to task rating, various researchers are exploring ways of automatically scoring or evaluating writing and speaking, which links to research to detect errors in learners' output. In the USA, ETS started using corpora and various CL and Natural Language Processing (NLP) techniques to develop automated systems for assessing writing in the late 1990s (see Burstein *et al.* 2004). Tetreault and Chodorow (2008) present a system for error detection in non-native essays, focusing on preposition errors; they also evaluate other systems that use non-English corpora. In another study, Deane and Gurevich (2008) describe the use of a corpus of both native and non-native speakers responding to the same TOEFL writing test prompt, in order to identify similarities and differences between the phrasing and content of both groups' responses. This type of research has implications for the automatic rating of writing and for systems which provide formative feedback for learners. Exam boards are starting to offer online evaluations of learners' written production whereby learners, or their teachers, upload written text and receive back personalised feedback. This process can contribute to corpus development if the evaluation system captures data usage permissions and background information alongside learners' language samples.

Language testers vary in their view and use of automatic rating software and it is worth noting that impact and practicality often drive their use. Generally speaking, the use of technology to rate learner output is not done to the exclusion of human involvement in the assessment process as no software can rate a learner's production in the exact same way a human can, i.e. according to the successful completion of a communicative task. Computer software can only rate what it is trained to recognise, such as specific measurable linguistic features (vocabulary, collocations, word stress, etc.), usually by comparing a learner's text with a standardised dataset that includes examples of performance at given levels. While it does not tire or err on the side of caution, rating software can be tricked into giving a high rating that would not be given by a human rater. Technology certainly has a role to play in rating language performance and providing evaluative feedback, but as an accompaniment to human raters, rather than as a replacement for them. An example of a package for classroom-based assessment is the CALPER GOLD (graphic online diagnostic) software, which enables teachers to enter their students' data directly into an online tool so that they can analyse emergent structures over time, with graphical displays rather than statistical tables, thus informing teaching practices and guiding students' assessment (McCarthy 2008: 571).

Having explored how learner corpora are being developed and used to inform LTA, we shall now consider how native speaker corpora are being used in the same field before looking to the future of this alliance between fields and methodologies. We should bear in mind, however, that many of the applications of learner corpora outlined above also apply to the use of native corpora so we will only outline specific additional uses of native corpora below.

4. How can we use a native speaker corpus to inform language testing?

In relation to user needs and test purpose, native corpora are of particular relevance to testing language for specific purposes; they are needed to support the recent growth in language tests for areas beyond the established academic and business domains (for example, financial and legal domains). For academic English, a key resource is MICASE, a spoken corpus of American university speech (native and non-native) (Simpson *et al.* 2002; see MICASE website for related studies). The ELI-UM Testing and Certification Division has used this corpus to develop and validate various examinations; for example, word frequencies have informed new listening test items for a high-level test, the Examination for the Certificate of Proficiency in English (ECPE). The analysis of candidates' responses to a listening test revealed that listening items 'containing MICASE phraseology' successfully discriminated between high- and low-scoring test takers (see MICASE website). Furthermore, the test specifications used by test writers have been updated to include an indication of the range of different speech events a word occurs in as well as their frequency. Future work will compile academic frequency word lists, concentrating on lexical bundles, and core and specialised vocabulary, as Horner and Strutt (2004) attempted to do for the business domain. The ELI-UM Testing and Certification Division intend to use MICASE to obtain information about realistic speech rates and other aspects of spoken English in the academic US setting, presumably to better inform their test writers. In the UK, Brooks (2001) developed a checklist to identify communicative functions used in academic IELTS speaking tests; the resulting checklist is used to validate speaking tasks for various domains.

In test design, native corpora are used by language testers to ensure that all parts of a test are valid and reliable. Native corpora either provide authentic texts to be used 'as is' or simplified, or model texts that test writers can base their own texts on. Hughes (2008) investigates the impact that the editing of authentic texts has on the language within thirteen First Certificate in English (FCE) reading passages, comparing original with edited versions and additionally comparing the lexis from the FCE reading texts with native corpus frequencies. Hughes (2008) established that these reading tasks are fair to test takers in that they provide evidence for their ability to decode English by using phraseologies they would normally expect to meet in everyday language, lending further support to the use of corpora to ensure that a test's content is directly relevant to the world beyond the testing situation. Crossley *et al.* (2007) analysed eighty-four simplified and twenty-one authentic reading passages from beginner-level English textbooks, grammar books and basic-level readers, in order to describe the linguistic structures of both types of reading passages and to assess the implications for language learning. The results indicate that the simplified texts differed from authentic texts in a number of ways but there were no significant differences in the abstractness and ambiguity between the two groups of texts (Crossley *et al.* 2007: 1, 27). This research will be of use, therefore, to those involved in writing, or selecting, prose passages for use in examinations.

With regard to establishing text readability, researchers at the University of Memphis have developed Coh-Metrix, an online tool that assesses a text's coherence and cohesion on over 600 measures, linking approaches from computational and psycho-linguistics (see Coh-Metrix website). This tool is increasingly used for L2 testing applications such as measuring L2 lexical proficiency, distinguishing between high- and low-proficiency essays (Crossley *et al.* 2008), and developing reading competency profiles based on reading passages in the SAT Reasoning Test, a US college entry test (VanderVeen *et al.* 2007).

Most test writers would know of, and some would frequently use, native reference corpora, corpus-informed reference works, and some would now also turn to the web for evidence (see Lee, this volume). Alongside the use of native corpora for large-scale language assessment, there is growing recognition in their use in language teaching. Shortall (2007), for example, investigates whether frequency data derived from the Bank of English (see website) provides a more realistic representation of the present perfect tense than current textbooks. What he says in relation to writing and using textbooks also applies to assessing language proficiency: 'textbook language would more truly reflect the cross-structural hybrids commonly found in authentic language … there is clearly a role for both pedagogic necessity and frequency of occurrence in natural language in the devising of learner materials' (Shortall 2007: 178–9). This mirrors how language testers triangulate corpus and other research methodologies to inform test validation procedures (Hawkey and Barker 2004).

A final use of CL techniques within LTA that relies on both native and learner corpora is the identification of malpractice in language tests, for example the growing use of plagiarism detection software in higher education and other contexts (also see Cotterill, this volume). Having summarised key aspects of using corpora for language testing, we now look to the future in the final section.

5. Looking to the future of corpus-informed language testing

The use of corpora in LTA has been established over the past twenty years and surely has a promising future as new corpora are developed and innovative ways of using these resources are found. The application of corpora and related analytical techniques seems poised to grow further, used alongside the expertise of the teams of professionals who develop, administer and mark language tests. Why does this seem to be the case?

The growing popularity of computer-based tests of language proficiency, whether for general language or for other domains such as business, legal or aviation language, will enable domain-specific corpora to be developed more easily than has been possible before, partly thanks to the automated collection of test takers' demographic and other information, their language sample and their scores. Similarly, improvements in the digital recording and storing of soundfiles will make the collection of spoken corpora more straightforward, thus increasing their availability for language testers. Alongside newer types of corpora, including the web as corpus, multi-modal corpora and corpora of new language varieties, there will remain a place for regular collections of native and learner writing and speech in LTA. Increasingly, corpus development will involve individuals and teachers uploading work directly to web portals and getting back a personalised evaluation.

The field of corpus-informed language testing is growing rapidly, aided by theoretical, technological and methodological advances in the fields of language testing and assessment and corpus linguistics. More work clearly remains to be done in this area, and this will benefit from the increasing number of corpus resources being built and shared worldwide between the corpus linguistics and language testing and assessment communities.

Further reading

ALTE Members (1998) *Multilingual Glossary of Language Testing Terms* (*Studies in Language Testing* vol. 6). Cambridge: UCLES and Cambridge University Press. (This multilingual glossary provides full definitions of technical terms in LTA in ten European languages, allowing readers to explore the LTA literature through their own language.)

Centre for English Corpus Linguistics (2008) *Learner Corpus Bibliography*, available at http://cecl.fltr.ucl.ac.be/learner%20corpus%20bibliography.html (accessed 23 December 2008). (This bibliography of works relating to learner corpora is relevant for those interested in using or developing learner corpora, particularly in relation to pedagogical uses and contrastive analysis.)

Taylor, L. and Barker, F. (2008) 'Using Corpora for Language Assessment', in E. Shohamy and N. H. Hornberger (eds) *Encyclopedia of Language and Education*, second edition, vol. 7, *Language Testing and Assessment*. New York: Springer, pp. 241–54. (This chapter summarises the development and use of corpora in language testing, focusing on high-stakes uses. It provides a summary of the development of computerised corpora since the 1960s and links to the LTA literature.)

References

Alderson, J. C. (1996) 'Do Corpora Have a Role in Language Assessment?' in J. A. Thomas and M. H. Short (eds) *Using Corpora for Language Research*. London: Longman, pp. 248–59.

——(2007) 'Judging the Frequency of English Words', *Applied Linguistics* 28(3): 383–409.

Alexopoulou, T. (2008) 'Building New Corpora for English Profile', *Research Notes* 33: 15–19, Cambridge: UCLES.

ALTE Members (1998) *Multilingual Glossary of Language Testing Terms* (*Studies in Language Testing* vol. 6). Cambridge: UCLES/Cambridge University Press.

——(2008) *The Can-do Statements*, available at www.alte.org/cando/index.php (accessed 28 April 2009).

Bachman, L. F. (1990) *Fundamental Considerations in Language Testing*. Oxford: Oxford University Press.

Barker, F. (2004) 'Corpora and Language Assessment: Trends and Prospects', *Research Notes* 26: 2–4, Cambridge: UCLES.

Barni, M. and Gallina, F. (2009) 'Il corpus LIPS (Lessico dell'italiano parlato da stranieri): problemi di trattamento delle forme e di lemmatizzazione', in *Atti del Convegno 'Corpora di italiano L2:tecnologie, metodi, spunti teorici'*, Pavia, November, Perugia: Guerra Edizioni, pp. 139–51.

Biber, D., Conrad, S., Reppen, R., Byrd, P., Helt, M., Clark, V. Cortes, V., Csomay, E. and Urzua, A. (2004) *Representing Language Use in the University: Analysis of the TOEFL 2000 Spoken and Written Academic Language Corpus* (Report Number: RM-04–03, Supplemental Report Number: TOEFL-MS-25). Princeton, NJ: Educational Testing Service.

Brooks, L. (2001) 'Converting an Observation Checklist for Use with the IELTS Speaking Test,' *Research Notes* 11: 20–1, Cambridge: UCLES.

Burstein, J., Chodorow, M. and Leacock, C. (2004) 'Automated Essay Evaluation: The Criterion Online Writing Evaluation Service', *AI Magazine* 25(3): 27–36.

Cambridge ESOL (2008) *Research: At the Heart of What We Do*, available at www.cambridgeesol.org/what-we-do/research/index.html (accessed 21 December 2008).

Centre for English Corpus Linguistics (2008) *Learner Corpus Bibliography*, available at http://cecl.fltr.ucl.ac.be/learner%20corpus%20bibliography.html (accessed 23 December 2008).

Council of Europe (2001) *Common European Framework of Reference for Languages: Learning, Teaching, Assessment.* Cambridge: Cambridge University Press.

Crossley, S. A., Louwerse, M., McCarthy, P. M. and McNamara, D. S. (2007) 'A Linguistic Analysis of Simplified and Authentic Texts', *Modern Language Journal* 91: 15–30.

Crossley, S. A., Miller, N. C., McCarthy, P. M. and McNamara, D. S. (2008) 'Distinguishing between Low and High Proficiency Essays Using Cognitively-inspired Computational Indices', paper presented at the 38th Annual Meeting of the Society for Computers in Psychology, Chicago, November.

Deane, P. and Gurevich, O. (2008) *Applying Content Similarity Metrics to Corpus Data: Differences between Native and Non-native Speaker Responses to a TOEFL Integrated Writing Prompt* (Report Number: RR-08-51). Princeton, NJ: Educational Testing Service.

Gallina, F. (2008) 'The LIPS Corpus (Lexicon of Spoken Italian by Foreigners)', paper presented at the international seminar New Trends in Corpus Linguistics for Language Teaching and Translation Studies. In Honour of John Sinclair, Granada, September.

Granger, S. (1996) 'From CA to CIA and Back: An Integrated Approach to Computerized Bilingual and Learner Corpora', in K. Aijmer, B. Altenberg and M. Johansson (eds) *Languages in Contrast. Papers from a Symposium on Text-based Cross-linguistic Studies, Lund 4–5 March 1994* (*Lund Studies in English* 88). Lund: Lund University Press.

Granger, S., Dagneaux, E., Meunier, F. and Paquot, M. (2009) *The International Corpus of Learner English. Handbook and CD-ROM. Version 2.* Louvain-la-Neuve: Presses Universitaires de Louvain.

Hargreaves, P. (2000) 'How Important is Collocation in Testing the Learner's Language Proficiency?' in M. Lewis (ed.) *Teaching Collocation – Further Developments in the Lexical Approach.* Hove: Language Teaching Publications, pp. 205–23.

Hawkey, R. and Barker, F. (2004) 'Developing a Common Scale for the Assessment of Writing', *Assessing Writing* 9: 122–59.

Hendriks, H. (2008) 'Presenting the English Profile Programme: In Search of Criterial Features', *Research Notes* 33: 7–10, Cambridge: UCLES.

Horner, D. and Strutt, P. (2004) 'Analysing Domain-specific Lexical Categories: Evidence from the BEC Written Corpus', *Research Notes* 15: 6–8, Cambridge: UCLES.

Hughes, A. (2003) *Testing for Language Teachers*, second edition. Cambridge: Cambridge University Press.

Hughes, G. (2008) 'Text Organisation Features in an FCE Reading Gapped Sentence Task', *Research Notes* 31: 26–31, Cambridge: UCLES.

Kennedy, C. and Thorp, D. (2007) 'A Corpus-based Investigation of Linguistic Responses to an IELTS Academic Writing Task', in L. Taylor and P. Falvey (eds) *IELTS Collected Papers: Research in Speaking and Writing Assessment* (*Studies in Language Testing* vol. 19). Cambridge: UCLES and Cambridge University Press, pp. 316–77.

McCarthy, M. (2008) 'Assessing and Interpreting Corpus Information in the Teacher Education Context', *Language Teaching* 41(4): 563–74.

McNamara, T. (2000) *Language Testing.* Oxford: Oxford University Press.

Mendikoetxea, A. (2006) 'Exploring Word Order in Learner Corpora: The Woslac Project', unpublished presentation to Corpus Research Group, 20 November, Lancaster, available at http://eprints.lancs.ac.uk/285/ (accessed 23 December 2008).

Purpura, J. (2008) 'Assessing Communicative Language Ability: Models and Components', in N. Hornberger and E. Shohamy (eds) *Encyclopedia of Language and Education*, second edition, vol. 7, *Language Testing and Assessment.* New York: Springer, pp. 53–68.

Saville, N. (2003) 'The Process of Test Development and Revision within UCLES EFL', in C. J. Weir and M. Milanovic (eds) *Continuity and Innovation: Revising the Cambridge Proficiency in English Examination 1913:2002* (*Studies in Language Testing* vol. 15). Cambridge: UCLES and Cambridge University Press, pp. 57–120.

Shortall, T. (2007) 'The L2 Syllabus: Corpus or Contrivance?' *Corpora* 2(2): 157–85.

Simpson, R. C., Briggs, S. L., Ovens, J. and Swales, J. M. (2002) *The Michigan Corpus of Academic Spoken English*. Ann Arbor, MI: The Regents of the University of Michigan.

Spolsky, B. (1995) *Measured Words: The Development of Objective Language Testing*. Oxford: Oxford University Press.

Taylor, L. and Barker, F. (2008) 'Using Corpora for Language Assessment', in E. Shohamy and N. H. Hornberger (eds) *Encyclopedia of Language and Education*, second edition, vol. 7, *Language Testing and Assessment*. New York: Springer, pp. 241–54.

Tetreault, J. and Chodorow, M. (2008) 'Native Judgments of Non-native Usage: Experiments in Preposition Error Detection', paper presented at COLING Workshop on Human Judgments in Computational Linguistics, Manchester, UK, August.

UCLES (2008) *KET Handbook for Teachers*, available at www.cambridgeesol.org/assets/pdf/resources/teacher/ket_handbook.pdf (accessed 21 December 2008).

VanderVeen, A., Huff, K., Gierl, M., McNamara, D. S., Louwerse, M. and Graesser, A. C. (2007) 'Developing and Validating Instructionally Relevant Reading Competency Profiles Measured by the Critical Reading Section of the SAT Reasoning Test', in D. S. McNamara (ed.) *Reading Comprehension Strategies: Theories, Interventions, and Technologies*. Mahwah, NJ: Lawrence Erlbaum, pp. 137–72.

Weir, C. J. (2003) *Continuity and Innovation: Revising the Cambridge Proficiency in English Examination 1913:2002* (*Studies in Language Testing* vol. 15). Cambridge: UCLES and Cambridge University Press.

——(2005) *Language Testing and Validation: An Evidence-Based Approach*. Houndmills: Palgrave Macmillan.

Index

Lightning Source UK Ltd.
Milton Keynes UK
UKOW07f0742030816

279750UK00016B/191/P

9 780415 622639